W9-CTA-430

University Casebook Series

November, 1988

ACCOUNTING AND THE LAW, Fourth Edition (1978), with Problems Pamphlet (Successor to Dohr, Phillips, Thompson & Warren)

George C. Thompson, Professor, Columbia University Graduate School of Business.
Robert Whitman, Professor of Law, University of Connecticut.
Ellis L. Phillips, Jr., Member of the New York Bar.
William C. Warren, Professor of Law Emeritus, Columbia University.

ACCOUNTING FOR LAWYERS, MATERIALS ON (1980)

David R. Herwitz, Professor of Law, Harvard University.

ADMINISTRATIVE LAW, Eighth Edition (1987), with 1983 Problems Supplement (Supplement edited in association with Paul R. Verkuil, Dean and Professor of Law, Tulane University)

Walter Gellhorn, University Professor Emeritus, Columbia University.
Clark Byse, Professor of Law, Harvard University.
Peter L. Strauss, Professor of Law, Columbia University.
Todd D. Rakoff, Professor of Law, Harvard University.
Roy A. Schotland, Professor of Law, Georgetown University.

ADMIRALTY, Third Edition (1987), with Statute and Rule Supplement

Jo Desha Lucas, Professor of Law, University of Chicago.

ADVOCACY, see also Lawyering Process

AGENCY, see also Enterprise Organization

AGENCY—PARTNERSHIPS, Fourth Edition (1987)

Abridgement from Conard, Knauss & Siegel's Enterprise Organization, Fourth Edition.

AGENCY AND PARTNERSHIPS (1987)

Melvin A. Eisenberg, Professor of Law, University of California, Berkeley.

ANTITRUST: FREE ENTERPRISE AND ECONOMIC ORGANIZATION, Sixth Edition (1983), with 1983 Problems in Antitrust Supplement and 1988 Case Supplement

Louis B. Schwartz, Professor of Law, University of Pennsylvania.
John J. Flynn, Professor of Law, University of Utah.
Harry First, Professor of Law, New York University.

BANKRUPTCY (1985)

Robert L. Jordan, Professor of Law, University of California, Los Angeles.
William D. Warren, Professor of Law, University of California, Los Angeles.

BANKRUPTCY AND DEBTOR-CREDITOR LAW, Second Edition (1988)

Theodore Eisenberg, Professor of Law, Cornell University.

BUSINESS ORGANIZATION, see also Enterprise Organization

BUSINESS PLANNING, Temporary Second Edition (1984)

David R. Herwitz, Professor of Law, Harvard University.

BUSINESS TORTS (1972)

Milton Handler, Professor of Law Emeritus, Columbia University.

CHILDREN IN THE LEGAL SYSTEM (1983) with 1988 Supplement

Walter Wadlington, Professor of Law, University of Virginia.
Charles H. Whitebread, Professor of Law, University of Southern California.
Samuel Davis, Professor of Law, University of Georgia.

CIVIL PROCEDURE, see Procedure

CIVIL RIGHTS ACTIONS (1988), with 1988 Supplement

Peter W. Low, Professor of Law, University of Virginia.
John C. Jeffries, Jr., Professor of Law, University of Virginia.

CLINIC, see also Lawyering Process

COMMERCIAL AND DEBTOR-CREDITOR LAW: SELECTED STATUTES, 1988 EDITION

COMMERCIAL LAW, Second Edition (1987)

Robert L. Jordan, Professor of Law, University of California, Los Angeles.
William D. Warren, Professor of Law, University of California, Los Angeles.

COMMERCIAL LAW, Fourth Edition (1985)

E. Allan Farnsworth, Professor of Law, Columbia University.
John Honnold, Professor of Law, University of Pennsylvania.

COMMERCIAL PAPER, Third Edition (1984)

E. Allan Farnsworth, Professor of Law, Columbia University.

COMMERCIAL PAPER, Second Edition (1987) (Reprinted from COMMERCIAL LAW, Second Edition (1987))

Robert L. Jordan, Professor of Law, University of California, Los Angeles.
William D. Warren, Professor of Law, University of California, Los Angeles.

COMMERCIAL PAPER AND BANK DEPOSITS AND COLLECTIONS (1967), with Statutory Supplement

William D. Hawkland, Professor of Law, University of Illinois.

COMMERCIAL TRANSACTIONS—Principles and Policies (1982)

Alan Schwartz, Professor of Law, University of Southern California.
Robert E. Scott, Professor of Law, University of Virginia.

COMPARATIVE LAW, Fifth Edition (1988)

Rudolf B. Schlesinger, Professor of Law, Hastings College of Law.
Hans W. Baade, Professor of Law, University of Texas.
Mirjan P. Damaska, Professor of Law, Yale Law School.
Peter E. Herzog, Professor of Law, Syracuse University.

COMPETITIVE PROCESS, LEGAL REGULATION OF THE, Third Edition (1986), with 1987 Selected Statutes Supplement

Edmund W. Kitch, Professor of Law, University of Virginia.
Harvey S. Perlman, Dean of the Law School, University of Nebraska.

CONFLICT OF LAWS, Eighth Edition (1984), with 1987 Case Supplement

Willis L. M. Reese, Professor of Law, Columbia University.
Maurice Rosenberg, Professor of Law, Columbia University.

CONSTITUTIONAL LAW, Seventh Edition (1985), with 1988 Supplement

Edward L. Barrett, Jr., Professor of Law, University of California, Davis.
William Cohen, Professor of Law, Stanford University.

CONSTITUTIONAL LAW, CIVIL LIBERTY AND INDIVIDUAL RIGHTS, Second Edition (1982), with 1987 Supplement

William Cohen, Professor of Law, Stanford University.
John Kaplan, Professor of Law, Stanford University.

CONSTITUTIONAL LAW, Eleventh Edition (1985), with 1988 Supplement (Supplement edited in association with Frederick F. Schauer, Professor of Law, University of Michigan)

Gerald Gunther, Professor of Law, Stanford University.

CONSTITUTIONAL LAW, INDIVIDUAL RIGHTS IN, Fourth Edition (1986), (Reprinted from CONSTITUTIONAL LAW, Eleventh Edition), with 1988 Supplement (Supplement edited in association with Frederick F. Schauer, Professor of Law, University of Michigan)

Gerald Gunther, Professor of Law, Stanford University.

CONSUMER TRANSACTIONS (1983), with Selected Statutes and Regulations Supplement and 1987 Case Supplement

Michael M. Greenfield, Professor of Law, Washington University.

CONTRACT LAW AND ITS APPLICATION, Fourth Edition (1988)

Arthur Rosett, Professor of Law, University of California, Los Angeles.

CONTRACT LAW, STUDIES IN, Third Edition (1984)

Edward J. Murphy, Professor of Law, University of Notre Dame.
Richard E. Speidel, Professor of Law, Northwestern University.

CONTRACTS, Fifth Edition (1987)

John P. Dawson, Professor of Law Emeritus, Harvard University.
William Burnett Harvey, Professor of Law and Political Science, Boston University.
Stanley D. Henderson, Professor of Law, University of Virginia.

CONTRACTS, Fourth Edition (1988)

E. Allan Farnsworth, Professor of Law, Columbia University.
William F. Young, Professor of Law, Columbia University.

CONTRACTS, Selections on (statutory materials) (1988)

CONTRACTS, Second Edition (1978), with Statutory and Administrative Law Supplement (1978)

Ian R. Macneil, Professor of Law, Cornell University.

COPYRIGHT, PATENTS AND TRADEMARKS, see also Competitive Process; see also Selected Statutes and International Agreements

COPYRIGHT, PATENT, TRADEMARK AND RELATED STATE DOCTRINES, Second Edition (1981), with 1988 Case Supplement, 1987 Selected Statutes Supplement and 1981 Problem Supplement

Paul Goldstein, Professor of Law, Stanford University.

UNIVERSITY CASEBOOK SERIES—Continued

COPYRIGHT, Unfair Competition, and Other Topics Bearing on the Protection of Literary, Musical, and Artistic Works, Fourth Edition (1985), with 1985 Statutory Supplement

Ralph S. Brown, Jr., Professor of Law, Yale University.
Robert C. Denicola, Professor of Law, University of Nebraska.

CORPORATE ACQUISITIONS, The Law and Finance of (1986), with 1988 Supplement

Ronald J. Gilson, Professor of Law, Stanford University.

CORPORATE FINANCE, Third Edition (1987)

Victor Brudney, Professor of Law, Harvard University.
Marvin A. Chirelstein, Professor of Law, Columbia University.

CORPORATE READJUSTMENTS AND REORGANIZATIONS (1976)

Walter J. Blum, Professor of Law, University of Chicago.
Stanley A. Kaplan, Professor of Law, University of Chicago.

CORPORATION LAW, BASIC, Third Edition (1989), with Documentary Supplement

Detlev F. Vagts, Professor of Law, Harvard University.

CORPORATIONS, see also Enterprise Organization

CORPORATIONS, Sixth Edition—Concise (1988), with Statutory Supplement (1988)

William L. Cary, late Professor of Law, Columbia University.
Melvin Aron Eisenberg, Professor of Law, University of California, Berkeley.

CORPORATIONS, Sixth Edition—Unabridged (1988), with Statutory Supplement (1988)

William L. Cary, late Professor of Law, Columbia University.
Melvin Aron Eisenberg, Professor of Law, University of California, Berkeley.

CORPORATIONS AND BUSINESS ASSOCIATIONS—STATUTES, RULES AND FORMS (1988)

CORPORATIONS COURSE GAME PLAN (1975)

David R. Herwitz, Professor of Law, Harvard University.

CORRECTIONS, SEE SENTENCING

CREDITORS' RIGHTS, see also Debtor-Creditor Law

CRIMINAL JUSTICE ADMINISTRATION, Third Edition (1986), with 1988 Case Supplement

Frank W. Miller, Professor of Law, Washington University.
Robert O. Dawson, Professor of Law, University of Texas.
George E. Dix, Professor of Law, University of Texas.
Raymond I. Parnas, Professor of Law, University of California, Davis.

CRIMINAL LAW, Fourth Edition (1987)

Fred E. Inbau, Professor of Law Emeritus, Northwestern University.
Andre A. Moenssens, Professor of Law, University of Richmond.
James R. Thompson, Professor of Law Emeritus, Northwestern University.

CRIMINAL LAW AND APPROACHES TO THE STUDY OF LAW (1986)

John M. Brumbaugh, Professor of Law, University of Maryland.

CRIMINAL PROCESS, Fourth Edition (1987), with 1987 Supplement

Lloyd L. Weinreb, Professor of Law, Harvard University.

DAMAGES, Second Edition (1952)

Charles T. McCormick, late Professor of Law, University of Texas.
William F. Fritz, late Professor of Law, University of Texas.

DEBTOR-CREDITOR LAW (1984) with 1986 Supplement

Theodore Eisenberg, Professor of Law, Cornell University.

DECEDENTS' ESTATES AND TRUSTS, Sixth Edition (1982)

John Ritchie, Emeritus Dean and Wigmore Professor of Law, Northwestern University.
Neill H. Alford, Jr., Professor of Law, University of Virginia.
Richard W. Effland, Professor of Law, Arizona State University.

DOMESTIC RELATIONS, see also Family Law

DOMESTIC RELATIONS, Successor Edition (1984) with 1987 Supplement

Walter Wadlington, Professor of Law, University of Virginia.

ELECTRONIC MASS MEDIA, Second Edition (1979)

William K. Jones, Professor of Law, Columbia University.

EMPLOYMENT DISCRIMINATION, Second Edition (1987)

Joel W. Friedman, Professor of Law, Tulane University.
George M. Strickler, Professor of Law, Tulane University.

EMPLOYMENT LAW (1987), with 1987 Statutory Supplement

Mark A. Rothstein, Professor of Law, University of Houston.
Andria S. Knapp, Adjunct Professor of Law, University of California, Hastings College of Law.
Lance M. Liebman, Professor of Law, Harvard University.

ENERGY LAW (1983) with 1986 Case Supplement

Donald N. Zillman, Professor of Law, University of Utah.
Laurence Lattman, Dean of Mines and Engineering, University of Utah.

ENTERPRISE ORGANIZATION, Fourth Edition (1987), with 1987 Corporation and Partnership Statutes, Rules and Forms Supplement

Alfred F. Conard, Professor of Law, University of Michigan.
Robert L. Knauss, Dean of the Law School, University of Houston.
Stanley Siegel, Professor of Law, University of California, Los Angeles.

ENVIRONMENTAL POLICY LAW 1985 Edition, with 1985 Problems Supplement (Supplement in association with Ronald H. Rosenberg, Professor of Law, College of William and Mary)

Thomas J. Schoenbaum, Professor of Law, University of Georgia.

EQUITY, see also Remedies

EQUITY, RESTITUTION AND DAMAGES, Second Edition (1974)

Robert Childres, late Professor of Law, Northwestern University.
William F. Johnson, Jr., Professor of Law, New York University.

ESTATE PLANNING, Second Edition (1982), with 1985 Case, Text and Documentary Supplement

David Westfall, Professor of Law, Harvard University.

UNIVERSITY CASEBOOK SERIES—Continued

ENTERPRISE ORGANIZATION, Fourth Edition (1987), with 1987 Corporation and Partnership Statutes, Rules and Forms Supplement

Alfred F. Conard, Professor of Law, University of Michigan.
Robert L. Knauss, Dean of the Law School, University of Houston.
Stanley Siegel, Professor of Law, University of California, Los Angeles.

ENVIRONMENTAL POLICY LAW 1985 Edition, with 1985 Problems Supplement (Supplement in association with Ronald H. Rosenberg, Professor of Law, College of William and Mary)

Thomas J. Schoenbaum, Professor of Law, University of Georgia.

EQUITY, see also Remedies

EQUITY, RESTITUTION AND DAMAGES, Second Edition (1974)

Robert Childres, late Professor of Law, Northwestern University.
William F. Johnson, Jr., Professor of Law, New York University.

ESTATE PLANNING, Second Edition (1982), with 1985 Case, Text and Documentary Supplement

David Westfall, Professor of Law, Harvard University.

ETHICS, see Legal Profession, Professional Responsibility, and Social Responsibilities

ETHICS AND PROFESSIONAL RESPONSIBILITY (1981) (Reprinted from THE LAWYERING PROCESS)

Gary Bellow, Professor of Law, Harvard University.
Bea Moulton, Legal Services Corporation.

EVIDENCE, Sixth Edition (1988 Reprint)

John Kaplan, Professor of Law, Stanford University.
Jon R. Waltz, Professor of Law, Northwestern University.

EVIDENCE, Eighth Edition (1988), with Rules, Statute and Case Supplement (1988)

Jack B. Weinstein, Chief Judge, United States District Court.
John H. Mansfield, Professor of Law, Harvard University.
Norman Abrams, Professor of Law, University of California, Los Angeles.
Margaret Berger, Professor of Law, Brooklyn Law School.

FAMILY LAW, see also Domestic Relations

FAMILY LAW Second Edition (1985), with 1988 Supplement

Judith C. Areen, Professor of Law, Georgetown University.

FAMILY LAW AND CHILDREN IN THE LEGAL SYSTEM, STATUTORY MATERIALS (1981)

Walter Wadlington, Professor of Law, University of Virginia.

FEDERAL COURTS, Eighth Edition (1988)

Charles T. McCormick, late Professor of Law, University of Texas.
James H. Chadbourn, late Professor of Law, Harvard University.
Charles Alan Wright, Professor of Law, University of Texas, Austin.

FEDERAL COURTS AND THE FEDERAL SYSTEM, Hart and Wechsler's Third Edition (1988), with the Judicial Code and Rules of Procedure in the Federal Courts (1988)

Paul M. Bator, Professor of Law, University of Chicago.
Daniel J. Meltzer, Professor of Law, Harvard University.
Paul J. Mishkin, Professor of Law, University of California, Berkeley.
David L. Shapiro, Professor of Law, Harvard University.

FEDERAL COURTS AND THE LAW OF FEDERAL-STATE RELATIONS (1987), with 1988 Supplement

Peter W. Low, Professor of Law, University of Virginia.
John C. Jeffries, Jr., Professor of Law, University of Virginia.

FEDERAL PUBLIC LAND AND RESOURCES LAW, Second Edition (1987), with 1984 Statutory Supplement

George C. Coggins, Professor of Law, University of Kansas.
Charles F. Wilkinson, Professor of Law, University of Oregon.

FEDERAL RULES OF CIVIL PROCEDURE and Selected Other Procedural Provisions, 1988 Edition

FEDERAL TAXATION, see Taxation

FOOD AND DRUG LAW (1980), with Statutory Supplement

Richard A. Merrill, Dean of the School of Law, University of Virginia.
Peter Barton Hutt, Esq.

FUTURE INTERESTS (1958)

Philip Mechem, late Professor of Law Emeritus, University of Pennsylvania.

FUTURE INTERESTS (1970)

Howard R. Williams, Professor of Law, Stanford University.

FUTURE INTERESTS AND ESTATE PLANNING (1961), with 1962 Supplement

W. Barton Leach, late Professor of Law, Harvard University.
James K. Logan, formerly Dean of the Law School, University of Kansas.

GOVERNMENT CONTRACTS, FEDERAL, Successor Edition (1985)

John W. Whelan, Professor of Law, Hastings College of the Law.

GOVERNMENT REGULATION: FREE ENTERPRISE AND ECONOMIC ORGANIZATION, Sixth Edition (1985)

Louis B. Schwartz, Professor of Law, Hastings College of the Law.
John J. Flynn, Professor of Law, University of Utah.
Harry First, Professor of Law, New York University.

HEALTH CARE LAW AND POLICY (1988)

Clark C. Havighurst, Professor of Law, Duke University.

HINCKLEY JOHN W., TRIAL OF: A Case Study of the Insanity Defense (1986)

Peter W. Low, Professor of Law, University of Virginia.
John C. Jeffries, Jr., Professor of Law, University of Virginia.
Richard C. Bonnie, Professor of Law, University of Virginia.

INJUNCTIONS, Second Edition (1984)

Owen M. Fiss, Professor of Law, Yale University.
Doug Rendleman, Professor of Law, College of William and Mary.

INSTITUTIONAL INVESTORS, (1978)

David L. Ratner, Professor of Law, Cornell University.

INSURANCE, Second Edition (1985)

William F. Young, Professor of Law, Columbia University.
Eric M. Holmes, Professor of Law, University of Georgia.

INTERNATIONAL LAW, see also Transnational Legal Problems, Transnational Business Problems, and United Nations Law

INTERNATIONAL LAW IN CONTEMPORARY PERSPECTIVE (1981), with Essay Supplement

Myres S. McDougal, Professor of Law, Yale University.
W. Michael Reisman, Professor of Law, Yale University.

INTERNATIONAL LEGAL SYSTEM, Third Edition (1988), with Documentary Supplement

Joseph Modeste Sweeney, Professor of Law, University of California, Hastings.
Covey T. Oliver, Professor of Law, University of Pennsylvania.
Noyes E. Leech, Professor of Law Emeritus, University of Pennsylvania.

INTRODUCTION TO LAW, see also Legal Method, On Law in Courts, and Dynamics of American Law

INTRODUCTION TO THE STUDY OF LAW (1970)

E. Wayne Thode, late Professor of Law, University of Utah.
Leon Lebowitz, Professor of Law, University of Texas.
Lester J. Mazor, Professor of Law, University of Utah.

JUDICIAL CODE and Rules of Procedure in the Federal Courts, Students' Edition, 1988 Revision

Daniel J. Meltzer, Professor of Law, Harvard University.
David L. Shapiro, Professor of Law, Harvard University.

JURISPRUDENCE (Temporary Edition Hardbound) (1949)

Lon L. Fuller, late Professor of Law, Harvard University.

JUVENILE, see also Children

JUVENILE JUSTICE PROCESS, Third Edition (1985)

Frank W. Miller, Professor of Law, Washington University.
Robert O. Dawson, Professor of Law, University of Texas.
George E. Dix, Professor of Law, University of Texas.
Raymond I. Parnas, Professor of Law, University of California, Davis.

LABOR LAW, Tenth Edition (1986), with 1986 Statutory Supplement

Archibald Cox, Professor of Law, Harvard University.
Derek C. Bok, President, Harvard University.
Robert A. Gorman, Professor of Law, University of Pennsylvania.

LABOR LAW, Second Edition (1982), with Statutory Supplement

Clyde W. Summers, Professor of Law, University of Pennsylvania.
Harry H. Wellington, Dean of the Law School, Yale University.
Alan Hyde, Professor of Law, Rutgers University.

LAND FINANCING, Third Edition (1985)

The late Norman Penney, Professor of Law, Cornell University.
Richard F. Broude, Member of the California Bar.
Roger Cunningham, Professor of Law, University of Michigan.

LAW AND MEDICINE (1980)

Walter Wadlington, Professor of Law and Professor of Legal Medicine, University of Virginia.
Jon R. Waltz, Professor of Law, Northwestern University.
Roger B. Dworkin, Professor of Law, Indiana University, and Professor of Biomedical History, University of Washington.

LAW, LANGUAGE AND ETHICS (1972)

William R. Bishin, Professor of Law, University of Southern California.
Christopher D. Stone, Professor of Law, University of Southern California.

LAW, SCIENCE AND MEDICINE (1984), with 1989 Supplement

Judith C. Areen, Professor of Law, Georgetown University.
Patricia A. King, Professor of Law, Georgetown University.
Steven P. Goldberg, Professor of Law, Georgetown University.
Alexander M. Capron, Professor of Law, University of Southern California.

LAWYERING PROCESS (1978), with Civil Problem Supplement and Criminal Problem Supplement

Gary Bellow, Professor of Law, Harvard University.
Bea Moulton, Professor of Law, Arizona State University.

LEGAL METHOD (1980)

Harry W. Jones, Professor of Law Emeritus, Columbia University.
John M. Kernochan, Professor of Law, Columbia University.
Arthur W. Murphy, Professor of Law, Columbia University.

LEGAL METHODS (1969)

Robert N. Covington, Professor of Law, Vanderbilt University.
E. Blythe Stason, late Professor of Law, Vanderbilt University.
John W. Wade, Professor of Law, Vanderbilt University.
Elliott E. Cheatham, late Professor of Law, Vanderbilt University.
Theodore A. Smedley, Professor of Law, Vanderbilt University.

LEGAL PROFESSION, THE, Responsibility and Regulation, Second Edition (1988)

Geoffrey C. Hazard, Jr., Professor of Law, Yale University.
Deborah L. Rhode, Professor of Law, Stanford University.

LEGISLATION, Fourth Edition (1982) (by Fordham)

Horace E. Read, late Vice President, Dalhousie University.
John W. MacDonald, Professor of Law Emeritus, Cornell Law School.
Jefferson B. Fordham, Professor of Law, University of Utah.
William J. Pierce, Professor of Law, University of Michigan.

LEGISLATIVE AND ADMINISTRATIVE PROCESSES, Second Edition (1981)

Hans A. Linde, Judge, Supreme Court of Oregon.
George Bunn, Professor of Law, University of Wisconsin.
Fredericka Paff, Professor of Law, University of Wisconsin.
W. Lawrence Church, Professor of Law, University of Wisconsin.

LOCAL GOVERNMENT LAW, Second Revised Edition (1986)

Jefferson B. Fordham, Professor of Law, University of Utah.

MASS MEDIA LAW, Third Edition (1987)

Marc A. Franklin, Professor of Law, Stanford University.

MENTAL HEALTH PROCESS, Second Edition (1976), with 1981 Supplement

Frank W. Miller, Professor of Law, Washington University.
Robert O. Dawson, Professor of Law, University of Texas.
George E. Dix, Professor of Law, University of Texas.
Raymond I. Parnas, Professor of Law, University of California, Davis.

MUNICIPAL CORPORATIONS, see Local Government Law

NEGOTIABLE INSTRUMENTS, see Commercial Paper

NEGOTIATION (1981) (Reprinted from THE LAWYERING PROCESS)

Gary Bellow, Professor of Law, Harvard Law School.
Bea Moulton, Legal Services Corporation.

NEW YORK PRACTICE, Fourth Edition (1978)

Herbert Peterfreund, Professor of Law, New York University.
Joseph M. McLaughlin, Dean of the Law School, Fordham University.

OIL AND GAS, Fifth Edition (1987)

Howard R. Williams, Professor of Law, Stanford University.
Richard C. Maxwell, Professor of Law, University of California, Los Angeles.
Charles J. Meyers, Dean of the Law School, Stanford University.
Stephen F. Williams, Judge of the United States Court of Appeals.

ON LAW IN COURTS (1965)

Paul J. Mishkin, Professor of Law, University of California, Berkeley.
Clarence Morris, Professor of Law Emeritus, University of Pennsylvania.

PATENTS AND ANTITRUST (Pamphlet) (1983)

Milton Handler, Professor of Law Emeritus, Columbia University.
Harlan M. Blake, Professor of Law, Columbia University.
Robert Pitofsky, Professor of Law, Georgetown University.
Harvey J. Goldschmid, Professor of Law, Columbia University.

PLEADING AND PROCEDURE, see Procedure, Civil

POLICE FUNCTION, Fourth Edition (1986), with 1988 Case Supplement

Reprint of Chapters 1–10 of Miller, Dawson, Dix and Parnas's CRIMINAL JUSTICE ADMINISTRATION, Third Edition.

PREPARING AND PRESENTING THE CASE (1981) (Reprinted from THE LAWYERING PROCESS)

Gary Bellow, Professor of Law, Harvard Law School.
Bea Moulton, Legal Services Corporation.

PROCEDURE (1988), with Procedure Supplement (1988)

Robert M. Cover, late Professor of Law, Yale Law School.
Owen M. Fiss, Professor of Law, Yale Law School.
Judith Resnik, Professor of Law, University of Southern California Law Center.

PROCEDURE—CIVIL PROCEDURE, Second Edition (1974), with 1979 Supplement

The late James H. Chadbourn, Professor of Law, Harvard University.
A. Leo Levin, Professor of Law, University of Pennsylvania.
Philip Shuchman, Professor of Law, Cornell University.

PROCEDURE—CIVIL PROCEDURE, Fifth Edition (1984), with 1988 Supplement

Richard H. Field, late Professor of Law, Harvard University.
Benjamin Kaplan, Professor of Law Emeritus, Harvard University.
Kevin M. Clermont, Professor of Law, Cornell University.

PROCEDURE—CIVIL PROCEDURE, Fourth Edition (1985), with 1988 Supplement

Maurice Rosenberg, Professor of Law, Columbia University.
Hans Smit, Professor of Law, Columbia University.
Harold L. Korn, Professor of Law, Columbia University.

PROCEDURE—PLEADING AND PROCEDURE: State and Federal, Fifth Edition (1983), with 1988 Supplement

David W. Louisell, late Professor of Law, University of California, Berkeley.
Geoffrey C. Hazard, Jr., Professor of Law, Yale University.
Colin C. Tait, Professor of Law, University of Connecticut.

PROCEDURE—FEDERAL RULES OF CIVIL PROCEDURE, 1988 Edition

PRODUCTS LIABILITY (1980)

Marshall S. Shapo, Professor of Law, Northwestern University.

PRODUCTS LIABILITY AND SAFETY (1980), with 1985 Case and Documentary Supplement

W. Page Keeton, Professor of Law, University of Texas.
David G. Owen, Professor of Law, University of South Carolina.
John E. Montgomery, Professor of Law, University of South Carolina.

PROFESSIONAL RESPONSIBILITY, Fourth Edition (1987), with 1988 Selected National Standards Supplement

Thomas D. Morgan, Dean of the Law School, Emory University.
Ronald D. Rotunda, Professor of Law, University of Illinois.

PROPERTY, Fifth Edition (1984)

John E. Cribbet, Professor of Law, University of Illinois.
Corwin W. Johnson, Professor of Law, University of Texas.

PROPERTY—PERSONAL (1953)

S. Kenneth Skolfield, late Professor of Law Emeritus, Boston University.

PROPERTY—PERSONAL, Third Edition (1954)

Everett Fraser, late Dean of the Law School Emeritus, University of Minnesota.
Third Edition by Charles W. Taintor, late Professor of Law, University of Pittsburgh.

PROPERTY—INTRODUCTION, TO REAL PROPERTY, Third Edition (1954)

Everett Fraser, late Dean of the Law School Emeritus, University of Minnesota.

PROPERTY—REAL AND PERSONAL, Combined Edition (1954)

Everett Fraser, late Dean of the Law School Emeritus, University of Minnesota.
Third Edition of Personal Property by Charles W. Taintor, late Professor of Law, University of Pittsburgh.

PROPERTY—FUNDAMENTALS OF MODERN REAL PROPERTY, Second Edition (1982), with 1985 Supplement

Edward H. Rabin, Professor of Law, University of California, Davis.

PROPERTY—PROBLEMS IN REAL PROPERTY (Pamphlet) (1969)

Edward H. Rabin, Professor of Law, University of California, Davis.

PROPERTY, REAL (1984), with 1988 Supplement

Paul Goldstein, Professor of Law, Stanford University.

PROSECUTION AND ADJUDICATION, Third Edition (1986), with 1988 Case Supplement

Reprint of Chapters 11–26 of Miller, Dawson, Dix and Parnas's CRIMINAL JUSTICE ADMINISTRATION, Third Edition.

PSYCHIATRY AND LAW, see Mental Health, see also Hinckley, Trial of

PUBLIC REGULATION OF DANGEROUS PRODUCTS (paperback) (1980)

Marshall S. Shapo, Professor of Law, Northwestern University.

PUBLIC UTILITY LAW, see Free Enterprise, also Regulated Industries

REAL ESTATE PLANNING, Second Edition (1980), with 1980 Problems, Statutes and New Materials Supplement

Norton L. Steuben, Professor of Law, University of Colorado.

REAL ESTATE TRANSACTIONS, Revised Second Edition (1988), with Statute, Form and Problem Supplement (1988)

Paul Goldstein, Professor of Law, Stanford University.

RECEIVERSHIP AND CORPORATE REORGANIZATION, see Creditors' Rights

REGULATED INDUSTRIES, Second Edition, (1976)

William K. Jones, Professor of Law, Columbia University.

REMEDIES, Second Edition (1987)

Edward D. Re, Chief Judge, U. S. Court of International Trade.

RESTITUTION, Second Edition (1966)

John W. Wade, Professor of Law, Vanderbilt University.

SALES, Second Edition (1986)

Marion W. Benfield, Jr., Professor of Law, University of Illinois.
William D. Hawkland, Chancellor, Louisiana State Law Center.

SALES AND SALES FINANCING, Fifth Edition (1984)

John Honnold, Professor of Law, University of Pennsylvania.

SALES LAW AND THE CONTRACTING PROCESS (1982)

Reprint of Chapters 1–10 of Schwartz and Scott's Commercial Transactions.

SECURED TRANSACTIONS IN PERSONAL PROPERTY, Second Edition (1987) (Reprinted from COMMERCIAL LAW, Second Edition (1987))

Robert L. Jordan, Professor of Law, University of California, Los Angeles.
William D. Warren, Professor of Law, University of California, Los Angeles.

SECURITIES REGULATION, Sixth Edition (1987), with 1988 Selected Statutes, Rules and Forms Supplement and 1988 Cases and Releases Supplement

Richard W. Jennings, Professor of Law, University of California, Berkeley.
Harold Marsh, Jr., Member of California Bar.

SECURITIES REGULATION, Second Edition (1988), with Statute, Rule and Form Supplement (1988)

Larry D. Soderquist, Professor of Law, Vanderbilt University.

SECURITY INTERESTS IN PERSONAL PROPERTY, Second Edition (1987)

Douglas G. Baird, Professor of Law, University of Chicago.
Thomas H. Jackson, Professor of Law, Stanford University.

SECURITY INTERESTS IN PERSONAL PROPERTY (1985) (Reprinted from Sales and Sales Financing, Fifth Edition)

John Honnold, Professor of Law, University of Pennsylvania.

SENTENCING AND THE CORRECTIONAL PROCESS, Second Edition (1976)

Frank W. Miller, Professor of Law, Washington University.
Robert O. Dawson, Professor of Law, University of Texas.
George E. Dix, Professor of Law, University of Texas.
Raymond I. Parnas, Professor of Law, University of California, Davis.

SOCIAL RESPONSIBILITIES OF LAWYERS, Case Studies (1988)

Philip B. Heymann, Professor of Law, Harvard University.
Lance Liebman, Professor of Law, Harvard University.

SOCIAL SCIENCE IN LAW, Cases and Materials (1985)

John Monahan, Professor of Law, University of Virginia.
Laurens Walker, Professor of Law, University of Virginia.

TAX, POLICY ANALYSIS OF THE FEDERAL INCOME (1976)

William A. Klein, Professor of Law, University of California, Los Angeles.

TAXATION, FEDERAL INCOME, Second Edition (1988)

Michael J. Graetz, Professor of Law, Yale University.

TAXATION, FEDERAL INCOME, Sixth Edition (1987)

James J. Freeland, Professor of Law, University of Florida.
Stephen A. Lind, Professor of Law, University of Florida and University of California, Hastings.
Richard B. Stephens, Professor of Law Emeritus, University of Florida.

TAXATION, FEDERAL INCOME, Successor Edition (1986), with 1988 Legislative Supplement

Stanley S. Surrey, late Professor of Law, Harvard University.
Paul R. McDaniel, Professor of Law, Boston College.
Hugh J. Ault, Professor of Law, Boston College.
Stanley A. Koppelman, Professor of Law, Boston University.

TAXATION, FEDERAL INCOME, VOLUME II, Taxation of Partnerships and Corporations, Second Edition (1980), with 1988 Legislative Supplement

Stanley S. Surrey, late Professor of Law, Harvard University.
William C. Warren, Professor of Law Emeritus, Columbia University.
Paul R. McDaniel, Professor of Law, Boston College.
Hugh J. Ault, Professor of Law, Boston College.

TAXATION, FEDERAL WEALTH TRANSFER, Successor Edition (1987)

Stanley S. Surrey, late Professor of Law, Harvard University.
Paul R. McDaniel, Professor of Law, Boston College.
Harry L. Gutman, Professor of Law, University of Pennsylvania.

TAXATION, FUNDAMENTALS OF CORPORATE, Second Edition (1987)

Stephen A. Lind, Professor of Law, University of Florida and University of California, Hastings.
Stephen Schwarz, Professor of Law, University of California, Hastings.
Daniel J. Lathrope, Professor of Law, University of California, Hastings.
Joshua Rosenberg, Professor of Law, University of San Francisco.

TAXATION, FUNDAMENTALS OF PARTNERSHIP, Second Edition (1988)

Stephen A. Lind, Professor of Law, University of Florida and University of California, Hastings.
Stephen Schwarz, Professor of Law, University of California, Hastings.
Daniel J. Lathrope, Professor of Law, University of California, Hastings.
Joshua Rosenberg, Professor of Law, University of San Francisco.

TAXATION, PROBLEMS IN THE FEDERAL INCOME TAXATION OF PARTNERSHIPS AND CORPORATIONS, Second Edition (1986)

Norton L. Steuben, Professor of Law, University of Colorado.
William J. Turnier, Professor of Law, University of North Carolina.

TAXATION, PROBLEMS IN THE FUNDAMENTALS OF FEDERAL INCOME, Second Edition (1985)

Norton L. Steuben, Professor of Law, University of Colorado.
William J. Turnier, Professor of Law, University of North Carolina.

TAXES AND FINANCE—STATE AND LOCAL (1974)

Oliver Oldman, Professor of Law, Harvard University.
Ferdinand P. Schoettle, Professor of Law, University of Minnesota.

TORT LAW AND ALTERNATIVES, Fourth Edition (1987)

Marc A. Franklin, Professor of Law, Stanford University.
Robert L. Rabin, Professor of Law, Stanford University.

TORTS, Eighth Edition (1988)

William L. Prosser, late Professor of Law, University of California, Hastings.
John W. Wade, Professor of Law, Vanderbilt University.
Victor E. Schwartz, Adjunct Professor of Law, Georgetown University.

TORTS, Third Edition (1976)

Harry Shulman, late Dean of the Law School, Yale University.
Fleming James, Jr., Professor of Law Emeritus, Yale University.
Oscar S. Gray, Professor of Law, University of Maryland.

TRADE REGULATION, Second Edition (1983), with 1987 Supplement

Milton Handler, Professor of Law Emeritus, Columbia University.
Harlan M. Blake, Professor of Law, Columbia University.
Robert Pitofsky, Professor of Law, Georgetown University.
Harvey J. Goldschmid, Professor of Law, Columbia University.

TRADE REGULATION, see Antitrust

TRANSNATIONAL BUSINESS PROBLEMS (1986)

Detlev F. Vagts, Professor of Law, Harvard University.

TRANSNATIONAL LEGAL PROBLEMS, Third Edition (1986) with Documentary Supplement

Henry J. Steiner, Professor of Law, Harvard University.
Detlev F. Vagts, Professor of Law, Harvard University.

TRIAL, see also Evidence, Making the Record, Lawyering Process and Preparing and Presenting the Case

UNIVERSITY CASEBOOK SERIES—Continued

TRIAL ADVOCACY (1968)

A. Leo Levin, Professor of Law, University of Pennsylvania.
Harold Cramer, of the Pennsylvania Bar.
Maurice Rosenberg, Professor of Law, Columbia University, Consultant.

TRUSTS, Fifth Edition (1978)

George G. Bogert, late Professor of Law Emeritus, University of Chicago.
Dallin H. Oaks, President, Brigham Young University.

TRUSTS AND SUCCESSION (Palmer's), Fourth Edition (1983)

Richard V. Wellman, Professor of Law, University of Georgia.
Lawrence W. Waggoner, Professor of Law, University of Michigan.
Olin L. Browder, Jr., Professor of Law, University of Michigan.

UNFAIR COMPETITION, see Competitive Process and Business Torts

UNITED NATIONS LAW, Second Edition (1967), with Documentary Supplement (1968)

Louis B. Sohn, Professor of Law, Harvard University.

WATER RESOURCE MANAGEMENT, Third Edition (1988)

Charles J. Meyers, Esq., Denver, Colorado, formerly Dean, Stanford University Law School.
A. Dan Tarlock, Professor of Law, II Chicago-Kent College of Law.
James N. Corbridge, Jr., Chancellor, University of Colorado at Boulder, and Professor of Law, University of Colorado School of Law.
David H. Getches, Professor of Law, University of Colorado School of Law.

WILLS AND ADMINISTRATION, Fifth Edition (1961)

Philip Mechem, late Professor of Law, University of Pennsylvania.
Thomas E. Atkinson, late Professor of Law, New York University.

WORLD LAW, see United Nations Law

University Casebook Series

CASES AND MATERIALS
ON
CRIMINAL LAW
AND
PROCEDURE

By

ROLLIN M. PERKINS

Connell Professor of Law Emeritus, UCLA
Professor Emeritus, University of California
Hastings College of the Law

and

RONALD N. BOYCE

Professor of Law, The University of Utah

SIXTH EDITION

Mineola, New York
The Foundation Press, Inc.
1984

Printed in the United States of America

Library of Congress Cataloging in Publication Data

Perkins, Rollin Morris, 1889–
Cases and materials on criminal law and procedure.

(University casebook series)
Includes bibliographical references and indexes.
1. Criminal law—United States—Cases. 2. Criminal procedure—United States—Cases. I. Boyce, Ronald N. II. Title. III. Series.
KF9218.P42 1984 345.73 84–4031
347.305

ISBN 0–88277–168–X

Perkins & Boyce Cs.Cr.L. & P. 6th Ed. UCB
3rd Reprint—1988

PREFACE TO THE SIXTH EDITION

One of the favorite sayings of Dean Roscoe Pound was: "The law must be stable but it cannot stand still." So far as the criminal law is concerned, there may be questions as to its stability, but there is no doubt that it has not been standing still. Recently most states have adopted new criminal codes. And to a considerable extent the new codes are worded differently than the old. A change of wording does not necessarily mean a change in the result, but the question is presented every step of the way. Has the result been changed and if so to what extent? This edition of the casebook includes more than 50 new cases. This is many more new cases than would ordinarily be expected in the sixth edition of a casebook, but it was required here. Some of the new cases involve new situations, such as the case involving the credit card ripoff. Some, involve situations in which criminal liability is now imposed where none was recognized before, as in the field now designated as "theft." Some demonstrate situations in which the actual result is the same as it was before.

Every lawyer needs to be familiar with the substantive criminal law and to have some acquaintance with the general problems of criminal procedure. Without this he cannot claim to be "learned in the law" and is not adequately prepared to counsel clients desiring to be law-abiding. Hence this book is intended to give the student an opportunity to become well grounded on the criminal law of today, which is made up of the common law of crimes, as modified by statutes that have been rather widely adopted, and to have an introduction to the procedural side of the field. One who intends to engage in the practice of criminal cases needs an advanced course in criminal procedure which cannot be taken to advantage in the first year of law study.

The urge for improvement in the criminal law has been widespread and insistent. The most exhaustive effort ever taken to meet this need resulted in the drafting of the Model Penal Code[1] by the American Law Institute. It was this Code that triggered the movement which resulted in the new criminal codes mentioned above. And while the Code has not been adopted, as such, it has exercised substantial influence in the redrafting. The usual procedure of a legislative committee charged with this task was to start with a consideration of each section by an examination of the corresponding section of the Model Penal Code. If what is found there was satisfactory to the committee, it was adopted, although frequently with some changes in the wording. If what was found in the Code

[1] The Proposed Official Draft of the Model Penal Code was adopted by the American Law Institute at its annual meeting in May, 1962. The quotations herein are from that draft and are with the express permission of the Institute.

did not appeal to the committee, some entirely different statement was drafted.

Since every additional change in the criminal law will at least involve a consideration of the Code, the law student needs to be aware of its existence and to have some familiarity with it. But care must be taken to be sure he does not confuse it with existing law. It should be emphasized that while the Restatements of the Law, also prepared by the American Law Institute, purport to represent existing law, the Model Penal Code was drafted primarily for the purpose of suggesting change. Hence it represents existing law only to the extent that the changes it suggests have been adopted.

Some years ago a university president complained that all of his professors of political science wanted to teach law and all of his professors of law wanted to teach political science. He made it quite clear that he did not expect those in either field to ignore the other; his objection was that each seemed inclined to ignore his own. In recent years a comparable situation has come into prominence. Some in charge of the course on criminal law have become so interested in criminology that it seems not important to them to give the students any real familiarity with the existing law of crimes. This is not something entirely new in the law-school world but seems to have assumed unusual proportions at the present time. Needless to say, the teacher of criminal law cannot ignore criminology, but the first-year classroom is not the place for extensive inter-disciplinary collaboration between the behavioral sciences and the administration of justice. In the words of Dean Pound, first in the legal profession to emphasize the importance of non-legal disciplines, the law teacher must teach "the actual law by which courts decide."[2] However, a seminar on criminology would seem to have a strong claim for a place in the law-school curriculum.[3]

It is expected that the student will supplement his study of the cases with a careful examination of the treatment of the same field in the text.[4] The two books have been keyed together chapter by chapter and section by section, except that the casebook gives an introduction to criminal procedure which is beyond the scope of the text.

For the most part citations in cases are of no help to a first-year law student and serve only to distract his attention. Hence such citations have been omitted unless there was some special reason for inclusion. Furthermore the purpose of a casebook seems not to make it important to use ellipsis marks where only citations have been omitted, and they are employed only to indicate omission of some part of the opinion proper. Frequently the parts omitted dealt with matters other than the point for which the case was included. At other

[2] Pound, The Need for a Sociological Jurisprudence, 19 Green Bag 607, 612 (1907).

[3] See Glueck, On the Conduct of a Seminar in the Administration of Criminal Justice, 16 J.Legal Ed. 71 (1963).

[4] Perkins & Boyce, Criminal Law, Third Edition (1982).

times space limitations required omission of part of the opinion dealing with that point.

Where official footnotes are included, the official number is used. And if parts of the opinion are omitted the result is that the first number under a case may be other than 1, and the following footnotes may not be in normal sequence. If the official footnotes are indicated by letters, the same letters are used in these pages. An appropriate indication is given whenever there might be doubt as to whether or not a footnote is official.

ROLLIN M. PERKINS
RONALD N. BOYCE

March, 1984

*

PREFACE TO THE FIRST EDITION

THE LAW school course known as criminal law and procedure, or simply as criminal law, has had a wide range of treatment and experimentation. At one extreme has been the plan by which each case is "squeezed dry" before the following case is presented. This involves not only an exhaustive consideration of the actual holding of the case and any dictum found in the opinion but also of numerous problems developed by analogy from either. In its most extreme form this plan starts with the first case in the book and proceeds case by case, with no deviation of method until the end of the school year. This permits consideration of only a small fraction of the field but the explanation offered is that the important consideration is not the extent of coverage but only the method of study. Outside reading is not emphasized. In fact there have been times when outside reading has been frowned upon as something comparable to the use of a "pony" in a Latin class. The study of a course by this method is an intellectual experience but the sacrifices are too great, at least for criminal law. The student ends the course with no appreciation of the field as a whole and the calls upon his time outside the classroom have been entirely inadequate.

At the other extreme is the plan which undertakes to cover the entire field of criminal law and procedure, prorating the time to each topic according to its relative importance. This may be suited to a class of students who do not intend to become lawyers, and who seek merely an introduction to the field as a background for other purposes, but with the time limitations of the present schedule it has no place in the law-school program.

Between these two extremes are many possibilities. What seems to be the best adopts much from each. This plan contemplates digging deeply and exhaustively here and there while other parts of the field are covered much more generally,—to a large extent by assignments for outside reading. This has the advantage of both depth and breadth. Substantially the entire field is covered but the student also acquires that appreciation of the subject which comes only with intensive and thorough study.

No doubt every major course in the curriculum has run this gamut but criminal law has had even wider experimentation. At one extreme is the approach which assumes that the existing law is entirely adequate and satisfactory. The plan is to teach the common law, with reference to changes made by some of the more widely adopted statutes, but with no effort to question the desirability of existing rules. At the other extreme is the attitude that the existing law of crimes and punishments is so entirely bad that attempting to grasp it is not worth while. Hence the cases in the book are used as mere pegs on which to hang general discussions of criminology. While there have been deviations in the practice of some instructors the general history of the teaching of criminal law appears to be this: The starting point was the first of the two extremes which held sway for many years. Before World War I there was a trend away from that extreme which gradually moved to solid ground between the two. Then the swing of the pendulum carried further until there was a tendency to reach the second extreme. Now, quite fortunately, there is a trend back toward the middle position. Rules which have come down to us as a result of historical accident, and which tend to hinder rather than to promote the general scheme of social discipline, should not be presented as the "perfection of reason." On the other hand the teacher should not forget that the first need of the lawyer is to know what the law is. And with a field as vast and as complicated as criminal law and procedure it will tax the skill of the instructor and the ability of the student to give the latter even a fair grasp of the law as it now exists. The student will not close his mind to the need for changes in the law if the teacher makes any reasonable effort to keep it open. On the other hand, great care must be taken to avoid an emphasis which will result in confusion. A class made up of beginning law students must not be conducted as if it were a lawyer's seminar. The teacher must make a studious effort to avoid placing such stress upon his notions of what the law should be that these ideas will be recalled by the student at a later time in the form of misconceptions of existing law. And so far as criminology is concerned the greatest contribution to be made in the criminal law classroom is for the teacher to raise questions which he persistently refuses to foreclose by any categorical answers. In the classroom, as elsewhere in life, he who is the jack of all trades is master of none. And he who undertakes to teach knowledge in general, rather than some very small fragment thereof, actually succeeds in teaching nothing.

A casebook is a "study tool" as well as "teaching device". And in a course on criminal law and procedure, offered to first-year students, it is important for the "study tool" to change as the work progresses. A determined effort has been made to fill that need in these pages. At the start the same subject is presented both in cases and in text form (in the appendix). The need at this point is to get something of an introduction to the field rather rapidly. After this introduction the plan is changed. Some subjects are presented only by cases and others only in text form (for outside reading). Still later another change is made. Both text and cases are used to present the same subject,—but not the same parts of the subject. Some of the simpler problems are disposed of by text statements while certain of the more difficult problems are left entirely to the cases. Thus in the section on Intoxication the older problems are presented in text form while the cases deal with the newer problems arising out of the automobile cases. And in the section on Prevention of Crime the use of deadly force for this purpose, which is the difficult part of the subject, is left to the cases after a simple text statement of the other matters.

. . .

It is impossible to give due acknowledgment to all the contributions to these pages. Many of them have come, through the years, from ordinary conversations with teachers, lawyers, judges, peace officers, probation officers, prison officials, criminologists and others. Two specific references, however, are in order. Grateful acknowledgment is due to my wife who painstakingly read the manuscript in three different drafts. Without this generous help the work could not have been completed. And during most of the time when the manuscript was being prepared my office was directly across the hall from that of the greatest legal scholar of our time. As those doors were never closed there was hardly a day during that period when I was not in his office or he in mine. I may have failed to take full advantage thereof but I certainly had the opportunity to get Dean Roscoe Pound's ideas on a multitude of problems of criminal law and procedure, as well as his ideas on classroom presentation and casebook construction. These have made outstanding contributions to this volume.

ROLLIN M. PERKINS

Los Angeles
June 20, 1952

*

SUMMARY OF CONTENTS

*

TABLE OF CONTENTS

PART 2. PROCEDURE AND ENFORCEMENT

CHAPTER 12. PROCEEDINGS PRELIMINARY TO TRIAL—Continued

*

TABLE OF CASES

The principal cases are in italic type. Roman type indicates cases cited or discussed in the text and footnotes. References are to Pages.

*

CASES AND MATERIALS
ON
CRIMINAL LAW
AND
PROCEDURE

*

Part 1

THE SUBSTANTIVE CRIMINAL LAW

Chapter 1

DEFINITION AND CLASSIFICATION

SECTION 1. DEFINITION

A crime is any social harm defined and made punishable by law.

The definition suggested by Blackstone is as follows: "A crime or misdemeanour is an act committed or omitted, in violation of a public law either forbidding or commanding it." [1] Although definitions of crime have tended to follow the Blackstone pattern, with variations as to the exact wording, the emphasis is faulty. Suppose, for example, **D** stabbed **X** unlawfully, inflicting a serious injury that resulted in **X**'s death six weeks thereafter. Under the theory of the common law of crimes, unchanged by statute, **D** should be punished for the unlawful killing of **X,** but **X**'s death was the result of **D**'s act rather than the act itself, which was thrusting the knife.[2] If, quite by accident, a surgeon should have come upon **X** so soon after the wounding as to be able to save his life this would not in any way change **D**'s act. The knife thrust by **D** would be unaltered by this fortuitous occurrence although the difference in the consequences would be tremendous. And although **D**'s act would be the same in either case his crime would be entirely different because under the first assumption he is to be punished for an unlawful killing whereas under the second, there would be no killing and the punishment would be for unlawful wounding. In other words it is more accurate to define crime in terms of the social harm caused rather than the act committed.[3]

1. 4 Bl.Comm. * 5.

2. "The word 'act' is used throughout the Restatement of this Subject to denote an external manifestation of the actor's will and does not include any of its results even the most direct, immediate and intended." Restatement, Second, Torts § 2 (1965).

3. For this reason reason Bishop defined crime in terms of the "wrong" done. "A crime is any wrong which the government deems injurious to the public at large, and punishes through a judicial proceeding in its own name." 1 Bishop, New Criminal Law § 32 (8th ed. 1892).

To repeat: A crime is any social harm defined and made punishable by law.[4]

Criminologists and sociologists have sometimes given the concept of crime a broader definition.[5] Whatever benefit that may have for such purposes, from the standpoint of the law a crime is not such until it is recognized as a crime by law.[6] Although some civil remedies may involve sanctions similar to those normally imposed by criminal courts, i.e., fines, loss of rights, the degree of sanction[7] imposed by the criminal law is usually much more severe and the opprobrium associated with the criminal sanction is, except for minor offenses, usually more extreme.[8]

PALMER v. CITY OF EUCLID, OHIO

Supreme Court of the United States, 1971.
402 U.S. 544, 91 S.Ct. 1563.

PER CURIAM. Appellant Palmer was convicted by a jury of violating the City of Euclid's "suspicious person ordinance," that is, of being

"Any person who wanders about the streets or other public ways or who is found abroad at late or unusual hours in the night without any visible or lawful business and who does not give satisfactory account of himself."

He was fined $50 and sentenced to 30 days in jail. The County Court of Appeals affirmed the judgment and appeal to the Supreme Court of Ohio was dismissed "for the reason that no substantial constitutional question exists herein." We noted probable jurisdiction.

We reverse the judgment against Palmer because the ordinance is so vague and lacking in ascertainable standards of guilt that, as applied to Palmer, it failed to give "a person of ordinary intelligence fair notice that his contemplated conduct is forbidden . . . ." United States v. Harriss, 347 U.S. 612, 617, 74 S.Ct. 808, 812, 98 L.Ed. 989 (1954).

The elements of the crime defined by the ordinance apparently are (1) wandering about the streets or being abroad at late or unusual

4. There were witnesses to a murder who were well acquainted with the killer. But since he was one of identical twins and no witness could be sure which of the twins committed the crime, there could be no conviction. People v. Lopez, 72 Ill.App.3d 713, 28 Ill.Dec. 906, 391 N.E.2d 105 (1979).

5. Bottomley, Criminology in Focus 1–38 (1979).

6. "No relevant statutory provision makes punishable as a crime a person's disobedience of an order closing a body of water . . . In the absence of such an express penal provision, the statute cannot be a basis for criminal prosecution. . . . " People v. Boyd, 642 P.2d 1, 3 (Colo.1982).

7. A civil contempt may result in confinement to coerce a person to take some action. Matter of Thornton, 560 F.Supp. 183 (S.D.N.Y.1983). The purpose is not a punitive sanction, but to obtain compliance with a court order.

8. Hart, The Aims of the Criminal Law, 23 Law and Contemp.Prob. 401, 404–406 (1958).

hours; (2) being at the time without visible or lawful business; * and (3) failing to give a satisfactory explanation for his presence on the streets. Palmer, in his car, was seen late at night in a parking lot. A female left his car and entered by the front door an adjoining apartment house. Palmer then pulled onto the street, parked with his lights on and used a two-way radio. He was not armed. He said he had just let off a friend. He was then arrested. At the station he gave three different addresses for himself and said he did not know his friend's name or where she was going when she left his car. Palmer could reasonably be charged with knowing that he was on the streets at a late or unusual hour and that denying knowledge of his friend's identity and claiming multiple addresses amounted to an unsatisfactory explanation under the ordinance. But in our view the ordinance gave insufficient notice to the average person that discharging a friend at an apartment house and then talking on a car telephone while parked on the street was enough to show him to be "without visible or lawful business." Insofar as this record reveals, everything petitioner did was quite visible and there is no suggestion whatsoever that what he did was unlawful under the local, state, or federal law. If his conduct nevertheless satisfied the being-without-visible-or-lawful-business element of the ordinance, as the state courts must have held, it is quite unreasonable in our view to charge him with notice that such would be the construction of the ordinance. "The underlying principle is that no man shall be held criminally responsible for conduct which he could not reasonably understand to be proscribed." United States v. Harriss, supra; at 617, 74 S.Ct. at 812; Bouie v. Columbia, 378 U.S. 347, 84 S.Ct. 1697, 12 L.Ed.2d 894 (1964); Wright v. Georgia, 373 U.S. 284, 83 S.Ct. 1240, 10 L.Ed.2d 349 (1963).

The judgment of the Ohio court is reversed.[a]

It is so ordered.

* The ordinance seemingly requires a "business" purpose to be on the streets. But it seems irrational to construe the ordinance as permitting only visible and lawful commercial activities on the streets, thus in effect converting the ordinance into a curfew with exceptions for lawful commercial conduct. Neither the lower court nor the State suggests that the ordinance should be construed in this manner or that anyone would expect that it would be so construed.

a. [Added by the Compiler.] An ordinance made it an offense for "three or more persons to assemble . . . on any of the sidewalks . . . and conduct themselves in a manner annoying to persons passing by. . . ." This was held to be unconstitutional *on its face.* Among other reasons it was said to be void for vagueness because it provided no standard by which it could be determined what conduct constitutes an annoyance. Coates v. City of Cincinnati, 402 U.S. 611, 91 S.Ct. 1686, 29 L.Ed.2d 214 (1971).

The statute prohibiting the mailing of "firearms capable of being concealed on the person" is not void for vagueness, and a conviction based upon the mailing of a 22-inch long sawed-off shotgun is affirmed. The statute "intelligibly forbids a definite course of conduct: the mailing of concealable firearms. While doubts as to the applicability of the language in marginal fact situations may be conceived, we think that the statute gave respondent adequate warning that her mailing of a sawed-off shotgun of some 22 inches in length was a criminal offense. Even as to more doubtful cases than that of the respondent, we have said that 'the law is full of instances where a man's fate depends on his estimating

MR. JUSTICE HARLAN concurs in the result.

MR. JUSTICE STEWART, with whom MR. JUSTICE DOUGLAS joins, concurring.

While I agree with the Court that Euclid's "suspicious person" ordinance is unconstitutional as applied to the appellant, I would go further and hold that the ordinance is unconstitutionally vague on its face.[b]

rightly, that is, as the jury subsequently estimates it, some matter of degree.' Nash v. United States, 229 U.S. 373, 377, 33 S.Ct. 780, 781, 57 L.Ed. 1232 (1913)." United States v. Powell, 423 U.S. 87, 93, 96 S.Ct. 316, 320 (1975).

"A criminal statute must be sufficiently definite to give notice of the required conduct to one who would avoid its penalties, and to guide the judge in its application and the lawyer in defending one charged with its violation, But, . . . no more than a reasonable degree of certainty can be demanded. Nor is it unfair to require that one who deliberately goes perilously close to an area of proscribed conduct shall take the risk that he may cross the line." State v. Marley, 54 Hawaii 450, 460, 509 P.2d 1095, 1103 (1973).

A state statute prohibiting the obstruction of vehicular or pedestrian traffic by a person having the intent of causing public inconvenience or annoyance, or recklessly creating a risk thereof, is not on its face overbroad or vague. The court emphasized that an obstruction which inconveniences or annoys is a physical condition which is apparent to all "men of common intelligence." Arbeitman v. District Court of Vermont, 522 F.2d 1031 (2d Cir.1975).

"And the Court has recognized that a scienter requirement may mitigate a law's vagueness, especially with respect to the adequacy of notice to the complainant that his conduct is proscribed." Village of Hoffman Estates v. Flipside, Hoffman Estates, 455 U.S. 489, 102 S.Ct. 1186, 1193 (1982).

"A statute is too vague when it fails to give fair notice of what it prohibits. It is overbroad when its language, given its normal meaning, is so broad that the sanctions may apply to conduct which the state is not entitled to regulate." State ex rel. Purcell v. Superior Court, 111 Ariz. 582, 584, 535 P.2d 1299, 1301 (1975). State v. Blocker, 291 Or. 255, 630 P.2d 824 (1980).

"It is settled that a statute so vague and indefinite, in form and as interpreted, as to permit within the scope of its language the punishment of incidents fairly within the protection of the guarantee of free speech is void. . . . A feature of a statute limiting freedom of expression to give fair notice of what acts will be punished and such a statute's inclusion of prohibitions against expressions protected by principles of the First Amendment, violates an accused's rights under procedural due process and freedom of speech or press. Winters v. New York, 333 U.S. 507, 509–510, 68 S.Ct. 665, 667–668 (1948).

b. Accord, State v. Grahovac, 52 Hawaii 527, 556, 480 P.2d 148 (1971).

By Act of Congress (the "Ten Major Crimes Act") it is provided that an Indian who commits any one of the ten listed crimes in Indian Country shall be subject to the exclusive jurisdiction of the United States courts. One of the listed crimes is incest, and Acunia was convicted of incest in the federal court on proof that he, being an Indian, had sexual intercourse with his daughter in Indian Country. This conviction was reversed because while Congress had, directly or indirectly, defined each of the other nine listed crimes, it had not provided any definition of incest. And there can be no valid conviction of an undefined offense. Acunia v. United States, 404 F.2d 140 (9th Cir. 1968).

". . . a statute is sufficiently certain if it employs words of long usage or with a common law meaning." Upholding a statute punishing conspiracy to " 'pervert or obstruct justice or the due administration of the laws.' " State v. Nielsen, 19 Utah 2d 66, 426 P.2d 13, 16 (1967).

The Supreme Court upheld the constitutionality of Article 133 U.C.M.J., 10 U.S.C. 933, "conduct unbecoming an officer and gentleman" and Article 134 U.C.M.J., 10 U.S.C. 934 "disorders and neglects to the prejudice of good order and discipline." "Each of these articles has been construed by the United States Court of Military Appeals or by other

A policeman has a duty to investigate suspicious circumstances, and the circumstance of a person wandering the streets late at night without apparent lawful business may often present the occasion for police inquiry. But in my view government does not have constitutional power to make that circumstance, without more, a criminal offense.

SECTION 2. CLASSIFICATION

The common law divided crime into three major groups: (1) treason, (2) felony and (3) misdemeanor. To remove the uncertainty which had developed in the ancient law, the Statute of Treasons enacted in 1350[1] specified exactly what should constitute this offense including, among certain other wrongs, a manifested intent to kill the king, queen or prince, levying war against the king, adhering to his enemies, giving them aid and comfort. The original determinant of felony was forfeiture of lands and goods, although three influences tended to obscure this fact: (1) under the English common law all felonies carried also the death penalty except mayhem for which mutilation was substituted,[2] (2) misdemeanors were never punished capitally and (3) early statutes creating new felonies regularly imposed and emphasized the penalty of death. Because of these facts there has been a tendency to say that under the common-law plan all offenses punished by death were felonies whereas those punished only by some milder penalty were misdemeanors. This is very nearly accurate but it is well to bear in mind that the actual determinant was forfeiture.[3]

What has been said shows the common-law classification to be unsound because one category was determined by the nature of the wrong perpetrated and the other two by the penalty provided. In fact, since treason was punished by forfeiture of lands and goods (and by death) it was strictly speaking a felony, although it was convenient to deal with it as a separate category for procedural reasons. Statutes in this country commonly divide offenses into two classes: (1) felony and (2) misdemeanor. The determinant is usually the penalty imposed although the exact nature of the penalty employed for this purpose is not uniform and nowhere has any resemblance to the

military authorities in such a manner as to at least partially narrow its otherwise broad scope. . . . The effect of these constructions . . . by the Court of Military Appeals and by other military authorities has been twofold: It has narrowed the very broad reach of the literal language of the articles, and at the same time has supplied considerable specificity by way of examples of the conduct which they cover. . . . But even though sizable areas of uncertainty as to the coverage of the articles may remain after their official interpretation by authoritative military sources, further content may be supplied even in these areas by less formalized custom and usage." Parker v. Levy, 417 U.S. 733, 752, 754, 94 S.Ct. 2547, 2559–2560 (1974).

1. 25 Edw. 111, c. 2.

2. Whipping was substituted for death as the penalty for petit larceny, but this was a change from the common law resulting from an early statute. Statute of Westminster, 1, c. 15 (1275).

3. In the words of Blackstone, "the true criterion of felony is forfeiture". 4 Bl.Comm. * 97.

common law [4] in this regard except that a capital offense is a felony. Very few felonies are capital today and the other type of penalty used to distinguish felony from misdemeanor usually follows one of two patterns. It is based upon either: (1) the type of institution in which the offender may be incarcerated (such as the state prison), or (2) the length of term which may be imposed (as, for example, a term exceeding one year).

The United States Code divides offenses into (1) felonies, (2) misdemeanors and (3) petty offenses. A petty offense is one the penalty for which does not exceed imprisonment for six months, or a fine of $500, or both. 18 U.S.C.A. § 1.

Some state codes have included a classification under which still a different category is included, not called a "crime". Thus the California Penal Code, as amended in 1969, gives the following: Section 16. Crimes and public offenses include: 1 Felonies; 2 Misdemeanors; and 3 Infractions. It is expressly provided (in § 19c) that an infraction is not punishable by imprisonment, and that one charged with an infraction is not entitled to a jury trial, nor to assigned counsel if indigent.

For certain purposes quite a different classification may be employed. For a consideration of the specific offenses, for example, it is common to have categories dependent upon the particular type of social harm involved, such as (1) offenses against the person, (2) offenses against property, (3) offenses against habitation and occupancy, and so forth, as indicated in the following chapter.

One very important classification scheme divides offenses into (1) capital crimes and (2) noncapital crimes. Under modern statutes a capital crime is one which *may* by punished by death; the customary provision being that one convicted of such an offense "shall be punished by death or by imprisonment for life." Another special dichotomy in crime classification is based upon the concept of infamy, and divides the field into (1) infamous crimes and (2) noninfamous crimes.

GREGG v. GEORGIA

Supreme Court of the United States, 1976.
428 U.S. 153, 96 S.Ct. 2909, 2971.

MR. JUSTICE STEWART, MR. JUSTICE POWELL, and MR. JUSTICE STEVENS announced the judgment of the Court and filed an opinion delivered by MR. JUSTICE STEWART.

4. "The common law of England has been by statute adopted as a rule of decision in this state, § 8–17, W.S.1957; and statutes are to be construed in harmony with existing law and their meaning determined in the light of the common law." Goldsmith v. Cheney, 468 P.2d 813, 816 (Wyo.1970).

"The English common law, so far as it is reasonable in itself, suitable to the condition and business of our people, and consistent with the letter and spirit of our federal and state constitutions and statutes, has been and is followed by our courts, and may be said to constitute a part of the common law of Ohio." Bloom v. Richards, 2 Ohio St. 387, 390 (1853); State v. McElhinney, 88 Ohio App. 431, 433, 100 N.E.2d 273, 275 (1950).

The issue in this case is whether the imposition of the sentence of death for the crime of murder under the law of Georgia violates the Eighth and Fourteenth Amendments. . . .

Before considering the issues presented it is necessary to understand the Georgia statutory scheme for the imposition of the death penalty. The Georgia statute, as amended after our decision in Furman v. Georgia, 408 U.S. 238, 92 S.Ct. 2726, 33 L.Ed.2d 346 (1972), retains the death penalty for six categories of crime: murder, kidnapping for ransom or where the victim is harmed, armed robbery, rape, treason, and aircraft hijacking. Ga.Code Ann. §§ 26–1101, 26–1311, 26–1902, 26–2001, 26–2201, 26–3301 (1972). The capital defendant's guilt or innocence is determined in the traditional manner, either by a trial judge or a jury, in the first stage of a bifurcated trial.

If trial is by jury, the trial judge is required to charge lesser included offenses when they are supported by any view of the evidence. After a verdict, finding, or plea of guilty to a capital crime, a presentence hearing is conducted before whomever made the determination of guilt. The sentencing procedures are essentially the same in both bench and jury trials. At the hearing,

"the judge [or jury] shall hear additional evidence in extenuation mitigation, and aggravation of punishment, including the record of any prior criminal convictions and pleas of guilty or pleas of nolo contendere of the defendant, or the absence of any prior conviction and pleas: Provided, however, that only such evidence in aggravation as the State has made known to the defendant prior to his trial shall be admissible. The judge [or jury] shall also hear argument by defendant or his counsel and the prosecuting attorney . . . regarding the punishment to be imposed."

The defendant is accorded substantial latitude as to the types of evidence that he may introduce. Evidence considered during the guilt stage may be considered during the sentencing stage without being resubmitted.

In the assessment of the appropriate sentence to be imposed the judge is also required to consider or to include in his instructions to the jury "any mitigating circumstances or aggravating circumstances otherwise authorized by law and any of [10] statutory aggravating circumstances which may be supported by the evidence . . . ." The scope of the nonstatutory aggravating or mitigating circumstances is not delineated in the statute. Before a convicted defendant may be sentenced to death, however, except in cases of treason or aircraft hijacking, the jury, or the trial judge in cases tried without a jury, must find beyond a reasonable doubt one of the 10 aggravating circumstances specified in the statute. The sentence of death may be imposed only if the jury (or judge) finds one of the statutory aggravating circumstances and then elects to impose that sentence. If the verdict is death the jury or judge must specify the aggravating circumstance(s) found. In jury cases, the trial judge is bound by the jury's recommended sentence.

In addition to the conventional appellate process available in all criminal cases, provision is made for special expedited direct review by the Supreme Court of Georgia of the appropriateness of imposing the sentence of death in the particular case. The court is directed to consider "the punishment as well as any errors enumerated by way of appeal," and to determine:

"(1) Whether the sentence of death was imposed under the influence of passion, prejudice, or any other arbitrary factor, and

"(2) Whether, in cases other than treason or aircraft hijacking, the evidence supports the jury's or judge's finding of a statutory aggravating circumstance as enumerated in section 27.2534.1(b), and

"(3) Whether the sentence of death is excessive or disproportionate to the penalty imposed in similar cases, considering both the crime and the defendant."

If the court affirms a death sentence, it is required to include in its decision reference to similar cases that it has taken into consideration.

A transcript and complete record of the trial, as well as a separate report by the trial judge, are transmitted to the court for its use in reviewing the sentence. The report is in the form of a six and one-half page questionnaire, designed to elicit information about the defendant, the crime, and the circumstances of the trial. It requires the trial judge to characterize the trial in several ways designed to test for arbitrariness and disproportionality of sentence. Included in the report are responses to detailed questions concerning the quality of the defendant's representation, whether race played a role in the trial, and, whether, in the trial court's judgment, there was any doubt about the defendant's guilt or the appropriateness of the sentence. A copy of the report is served upon defense counsel. Under its special review authority, the court may either affirm the death sentence or remand the case for resentencing. In cases in which the death sentence is affirmed there remains the possibility of executive clemency.

We address initially the basic contention that the punishment of death for the crime of murder is, under all circumstances, "cruel and unusual" in violation of the Eighth and Fourteenth Amendments of the Constitution. In Part IV of this opinion, we will consider the sentence of death imposed under the Georgia statutes at issue in this case.

The Court on a number of occasions has both assumed and asserted the constitutionality of capital punishment. In several cases that assumption provided a necessary foundation for the decision, as the Court was asked to decide whether a particular method of carrying out a capital sentence would be allowed to stand under the Eighth

Amendment. But until Furman v. Georgia, 408 U.S. 238, 92 S.Ct. 2726, 33 L.Ed.2d 346 (1972), the Court never confronted squarely the fundamental claim that the punishment of death always, regardless of the enormity of the offense or the procedure followed in imposing the sentence, is cruel and unusual punishment in violation of the Constitution. Although this issue was presented and addressed in *Furman,* it was not resolved by the Court. Four Justices would have held that capital punishment is not unconstitutional *per se;* two Justices would have reached the opposite conclusion; and three Justices, while agreeing that the statutes then before the Court were invalid as applied, left open the question whether such punishment may ever be imposed. We now hold that the punishment of death does not invariably violate the Constitution. . . .

But, while we have an obligation to insure that constitutional bounds are not overreached, we may not act as judges as we might as legislators.

"Courts are not representative bodies. They are not designed to be a good reflex of a democratic society. Their judgment is best informed, and therefore most dependable, within narrow limits. Their essential quality is detachment, founded on independence. History teaches that the independence of the judiciary is jeopardized when courts become embroiled in the passions of the day and assume primary responsibility in choosing between competing political, economic and social pressures."

Therefore, in assessing a punishment selected by a democratically elected legislature against the constitutional measure, we presume its validity. We may not require the legislature to select the least severe penalty possible so long as the penalty selected is not cruelly inhumane or disproportionate to the crime involved. And a heavy burden rests on those who would attack the judgment of the representatives of the people.

The deference we owe to the decisions of the state legislatures under our federal system, is enhanced where the specification of punishments is concerned, for "these are peculiarly questions of legislative policy." Caution is necessary lest this Court become, "under the aegis of the Cruel and Unusual Punishment Clause, the ultimate arbiter of the standards of criminal responsibility . . . throughout the country." A decision that a given punishment is impermissible under the Eighth Amendment cannot be reversed short of a constitutional amendment. The ability of the people to express their preference through the normal democratic processes, as well as through ballot referenda, is shut off. Revisions cannot be made in the light of further experience. . . .

The death penalty is said to serve two principal social purposes: retribution and deterrence of capital crimes by prospective offenders.

In part, capital punishment is an expression of society's moral outrage at particularly offensive conduct. This function may be unappealing to many, but it is essential in an ordered society that asks its citizens to rely on legal processes rather than self-help to vindicate their wrongs.

"The instinct for retribution is part of the nature of man, and channeling that instinct in the administration of criminal justice serves an important purpose in promoting the stability of a society governed by law. When people begin to believe that organized society is unwilling or unable to impose upon criminal offenders the punishment they 'deserve,' then there are sown the seeds of anarchy—of self-help, vigilante justice, and lynch law."

"Retribution is no longer the dominant objective of the criminal law," but neither is it a forbidden objective nor one inconsistent with our respect for the dignity of men. Indeed, the decision that capital punishment may be the appropriate sanction in extreme cases is an expression of the community's belief that certain crimes are themselves so grievous an affront to humanity that the only adequate response may be the penalty of death.

Statistical attempts to evaluate the worth of the death penalty as a deterrent to crimes by potential offenders have occasioned a great deal of debate. The results simply have been inconclusive. . . .

The value of capital punishment as a deterrent of crime is a complex factual issue the resolution of which properly rests with the legislatures, which can evaluate the results of statistical studies in terms of their own local conditions and with a flexibility of approach that is not available to the courts. Indeed, many of the post-*Furman* statutes reflect just such a responsible effort to define those crimes and those criminals for which capital punishment is most probably an effective deterrent.

In sum, we cannot say that the judgment of the Georgia legislature that capital punishment may be necessary in some cases is clearly wrong. Considerations of federalism, as well as respect for the ability of a legislature to evaluate, in terms of its particular state the moral consensus concerning the death penalty and its social utility as a sanction, require us to conclude, in the absence of more convincing evidence, that the infliction of death as a punishment for murder is not without justification and thus is not unconstitutionally severe. . . .

We hold that the death penalty is not a form of punishment that may never be imposed, regardless of the circumstances of the offense, regardless of the character of the offender, and regardless of the procedure followed in reaching the decision to impose it. . . .

We now turn to consideration of the constitutionality of Georgia's capital-sentencing procedures. In the wake of *Furman*, Georgia amended its capital punishment statute, but chose not to narrow the scope of its murder provisions. Thus, now as before *Furman*, in Georgia "[a] person commits murder when he unlawfully and with

malice aforethought, either express or implied, causes the death of another human being." Ga.Code Ann., § 26–1101(a) (1972). All persons convicted of murder "shall be punished by death or by imprisonment for life." § 26–1101(c) (1972).

Georgia did act, however, to narrow the class of murderers subject to capital punishment by specifying 10 statutory aggravating circumstances, one of which must be found by the jury to exist beyond a reasonable doubt before a death sentence can ever be imposed. In addition, the jury is authorized to consider any other appropriate aggravating or mitigating circumstances. The jury is not required to find any mitigating circumstances in order to make a recommendation of mercy that is binding on the trial court, but it must find a *statutory* aggravating circumstance before recommending a sentence of death.

These procedures require the jury to consider the circumstances of the crime and the criminal before it recommends sentence. No longer can a Georgia jury do as *Furman's* jury did: reach a finding of the defendant's guilt and then, without guidance or direction, decide whether he should live or die. Instead, the jury's attention is directed to the specific circumstances of the crime: Was it committed in the course of another capital felony? Was it committed for money? Was it committed upon a peace officer or judicial officer? Was it committed in a particularly heinous way or in a manner that endangered the lives of many persons? In addition, the jury's attention is focused on the characteristics of the person who committed the crime: Does he have a record of prior convictions for capital offenses? Are there any special facts about this defendant that mitigate against imposing capital punishment (e.g., his youth, the extent of his cooperation with the police, his emotional state at the time of the crime). As a result, while some jury discretion still exists, "the discretion to be exercised is controlled by clear and objective standards so as to produce non-discriminatory application."

As an important additional safeguard against arbitrariness and caprice, the Georgia statutory scheme provides for automatic appeal of all death sentences to the State's supreme court. That court is required by statute to review each sentence of death and determine whether it was imposed under the influence of passion or prejudice, whether the evidence supports the jury's finding of a statutory aggravating circumstance, and whether the sentence is disproportionate compared to those sentences imposed in similar cases.

In short, Georgia's new sentencing procedures require as a prerequisite to the imposition of the death penalty, specific jury findings as to the circumstances of the crime or the character of the defendant. Moreover to guard further against a situation comparable to that presented in *Furman,* the Supreme Court of Georgia compares each death sentence with the sentences imposed on similarly situated defendants to ensure that the sentence of death in a particular case is not disproportionate. On their face these procedures seem to satisfy the concerns of *Furman.* No longer should there be "no meaningful basis for distinguishing the few cases in which [the death penalty] is imposed from the many cases in which it is not." . . .

The basic concern of *Furman* centered on those defendants who were being condemned to death capriciously and arbitrarily. Under the procedures before the Court in that case, sentencing authorities were not directed to give attention to the nature or circumstances of the crime committed or to the character or record of the defendant. Left unguided, juries imposed the death sentence in a way that could only be called freakish. The new Georgia sentencing procedures, by contrast, focus the jury's attention on the particularized nature of the crime and the particularized characteristics of the individual defendant. While the jury is permitted to consider any aggravating or mitigating circumstances, it must find and identify at least one statutory aggravating factor before it may impose a penalty of death. In this way the jury's discretion is channeled. No longer can a jury wantonly and freakishly impose the death sentence; it is always circumscribed by the legislative guidelines. In addition, the review function of the Supreme Court of Georgia affords additional assurance that the concerns that prompted our decision in *Furman* are not present to any significant degree in the Georgia procedure applied here.

For the reasons expressed in this opinion, we hold that the statutory system under which Gregg was sentenced to death does not violate the Constitution. Accordingly, the judgment of the Georgia Supreme Court is affirmed.

It is so ordered.[1]

1. Under comparable statutory provisions, death sentences for murder in Florida and Texas were also affirmed. Proffitt v. Florida, 428 U.S. 242, 96 S.Ct. 2960 (1976); Jurek v. Texas, 428 U.S. 262, 96 S.Ct. 2950 (1976). But the statutes of Louisiana and North Carolina, which provided mandatory death sentence for first-degree murder were held to be unconstitutional. Roberts v. Louisiana, 428 U.S. 325, 96 S.Ct. 3001 (1976); Woodson v. North Carolina, 428 U.S. 280, 96 S.Ct. 2978 (1976). In both of these cases Burger, C.J., and Blackmun, Rehnquist and White, JJ., dissented.

In a later case the court reversed the death sentence on the ground that the Georgia statute had been unconstitutionally applied. The jury had imposed the death sentence on a finding that the murder "was outrageously or wantonly vile, horrible and inhuman." This was a statutory cause for the imposition of the death sentence, but it was pointed out that in earlier cases the Georgia court had held that this comprehended only the kind of mental state that led the killer to torture or commit aggravated battery before killing the victim. In this case there was nothing of that nature to support the jury's finding since the victims had been killed instantly. It was a case of "standardless sentencing discretion." Godfrey v. Georgia, 446 U.S. 420, 100 S.Ct. 1759 (1980).

In another case the defendant had been convicted of rape and sentenced to death on a finding of two of the circumstances for imposing such a sentence. This sentence was reversed but there was no opinion of the Court. The opinions filed seemed to indicate that the Court will hold that capital punishment is always, regardless of circumstances, a disproportionate penalty for rape. Justice Powell pointed out that not so much was involved and indicated the hope that the Court might uphold the death penalty for rape if the jury found that it was an outrageous rape resulting in serious and lasting harm to the victim. Coker v.

[BURGER, C.J., and BLACKMUN, REHNQUIST and WHITE, JJ., concurred in the judgment, affirming the sentence of death, but did not concur in the opinion above. Three joined in an opinion by White, J., and Blackmun filed a statement saying that he concurred in the judgment for reasons given in his dissent to *Furman.*]

MR. JUSTICE BRENNAN, dissenting.

The Cruel and Unusual Punishments Clause "must draw its meaning from the evolving standards of decency that mark the progress of a maturing society." . . .

This Court inescapably has the duty, as the ultimate arbiter of the meaning of our Constitution, to say whether, when individuals condemned to death stand before our Bar, "moral concepts" require us to hold that the law has progressed to the point where we should declare that the punishment of death, like punishments on the rack, the screw and the wheel, is no longer morally tolerable in our civilized society. My opinion in Furman v. Georgia concluded that our civilization and the law had progressed to this point and that therefore the punishment of death, for whatever crime and under all circumstances, is "cruel and unusual" in violation of the Eighth and Fourteenth Amendments of the Constitution. I shall not again canvass the reasons that led to that conclusion. I emphasize only that foremost among the "moral concepts" recognized in our cases and inherent in the Clause is the primary moral principle that the State, even as it punishes, must treat its citizens in a manner consistent with

Georgia, 433 U.S. 584, 97 S.Ct. 2861 (1977).

The Florida capital-punishment statute established a three-level review system. After a defendant is found guilty of a capital offense an evidentiary hearing is held. The jury then decides whether the sentence should be death or life imprisonment. The jury's verdict is advisory only, and the actual sentence is imposed by the trial judge after he conducts his own review of the evidence. McCray was tried for murder and found guilty. After the evidentiary hearing the jury recommended a life sentence. The trial judge rejected this recommendation and imposed the death sentence. He found three aggravating circumstances: (1) the defendant was a convicted felon, (2) the murder was "especially heinous, atrocious and cruel" (the victim had been beaten before she died) and (3) the murder was during the commission of rape. The Florida Supreme Court affirmed the trial judge's decision to override the jury's recommendation. McCrae (Sic) v. State, 395 So.2d 1145 (Fla.1981). Petition for a writ of certiorari was denied. McCray v. Florida, 454 U.S. 1041, 102 S.Ct. 583 (1981). But see Upshaw v. State, 350 So.2d 1358 (Miss.1977).

The Court has held it to be unconstitutional to impose a mandatory death sentence for the murder of a policeman. The Court or jury must still be permitted to weigh the justification for the death penalty in the particular case. Roberts v. Louisiana, 431 U.S. 633, 97 S.Ct. 1993 (1977).

The sentencer must be permitted to consider any relevant mitigating factor or mitigating evidence. Lockett v. Ohio, 438 U.S. 586, 98 S.Ct. 2954 (1978); Eddings v. Oklahoma, 455 U.S 104, 102 S.Ct. 869 (1982).

It would be cruel and unusual punishment, in violation of the Eighth Amendment, to impose the death penalty upon one who aids and abets a felony in the course of which others commit murder, but who did not himself kill, attempt to kill, or intend that killing take place, or that lethal force be employed. Enmund v. Florida, 458 U.S. 782, 102 S.Ct. 3368 (1982).

their intrinsic worth as human beings—a punishment must not be so severe as to be degrading to human dignity. . . .

MR. JUSTICE MARSHALL, dissenting.

In Furman v. Georgia, 408 U.S. 238, 314, 92 S.Ct. 2726, 2764, 33 L.Ed.2d 346 (1972), I set forth at some length my views on the basic issue presented to the Court in these cases. The death penalty, I concluded, is a cruel and unusual punishment prohibited by the Eighth and Fourteenth Amendments. That continues to be my view.

I have no intention of retracing the "long and tedious journey," id., at 370, 92 S.Ct, at 2793, that led to my conclusion in *Furman*. . . .

The death penalty, unnecessary to promote the goal of deterrence or to further any legitimate notion of retribution, is an excessive penalty forbidden by the Eighth and Fourteenth Amendments. I respectfully dissent from the Court's judgment upholding the sentences of death imposed upon the petitioners in these cases.

UNITED STATES v. MORELAND

Supreme Court of the United States, 1922.
258 U.S. 433, 42 S.Ct. 368.

MR. JUSTICE MCKENNA delivered the opinion of the Court.

The question in the case is what procedure, in the prosecution and conviction for crime, the Fifth Amendment of the Constitution of the United States makes dependent upon the character of punishment assigned to the crime.

The amendment provides that—

"No person shall be held to answer for a capital, or otherwise infamous crime, unless on a presentment or indictment of a grand jury, except in cases arising in the land or naval forces, or in the militia, when in actual service in time of war or public danger. . . ."

The respondent, Moreland, was proceeded against in the juvenile court of the District of Columbia by information, not by presentment or indictment by a grand jury, for the crime of willfully neglecting or refusing to provide for the support and maintenance of his minor children. The statute prescribes the punishment to a be "a fine of not more than $500 or by imprisonment in the workhouse of the District of Columbia at hard labor for not more than twelve months or by both such fine and imprisonment." 34 Stat. 86.

He was tried by a jury and found guilty, and, after certain proceedings with which we have no concern, he was sentenced to the workhouse at hard labor for six months.

The Court of Appeals reversed the judgment and remanded the case to the juvenile court, with directions to dismiss the complaint. The court considered that it was constrained to decide that the judgment was in violation of the Fifth Amendment, and, therefore, to reverse it on the authority of Wong Wing v. United States, 163 U.S. 228, 16 S.Ct. 977, 41 L.Ed. 140.

The United States resists both the authority and extent of that case by the citation of others, which, it asserts, modify or overrule it. A review of it, therefore, is of initial importance.

Certain statutes of the United States made it unlawful under certain circumstances for a Chinese laborer to be in the United States, and provided for his deportation by certain officers, among others, a commissioner of a United States court. And one of them (Act of 1892 [Comp.St. § 4318]) provided that, if a Chinese person or one of that descent was "convicted and adjudged to be not lawfully entitled to be or remain in the United States," he should "be imprisoned at hard labor for a period not exceeding one year, and thereafter removed from the United States."

Wong Wing, a Chinese person (there were others arrested, but for the purpose of convenience of reference we treat the case as being against him only), was arrested and taken before a commissioner of the Circuit Court for the Eastern District of Michigan and adjudged to be unlawfully within the United States and not entitled to remain therein. It was also adjudged that he be imprisoned at hard labor at and in the Detroit House of Correction for the period of 60 days.

The court, considering the statutes, said they operated on two classes—one which came into the country with its consent; the other which came in without consent and in disregard of law—and that Congress had the constitutional power to deport both classes and to commit the enforcement of the law to executive officers.

This power of arrest by the executive officers and the power of deportation were sustained; but the punishment provided for by the act, and which was pronounced against Wong Wing, that is, imprisonment at hard labor, was decided to be a violation of the Fifth Amendment; he not having been proceeded against by presentment or indictment by a grand jury.

The court noted the argument and the cases cited and sustained the power of exclusion, but said that when Congress went further, and inflicted punishment at hard labor, it "must provide for a judicial trial to establish the guilt of the accused." And this because such punishment was infamous and prohibited by the Fifth Amendment; the conditions prescribed by the amendment not having been observed. The necessity of their observance was decided, because, to repeat, imprisonment at hard labor was an infamous punishment. . . .

The ultimate contention of the United States is that the provision of the Act of March 23, 1906, for punishment by fine or imprisonment are severable, and that, therefore, it was error in the Court of Appeals in holding the act unconstitutional, and in directing the dismissal of the case, instead of sending it back for further proceedings.

The contention is untenable. It is what sentence can be imposed under the law, not what was imposed, that is the material consideration. When an accused is in danger of an infamous punishment, if convicted, he has a right to insist that he be not put upon trial, except on the accusation of a grand jury. Ex parte Wilson and Mackin v. United States, supra.

Judgment affirmed.[1]

MR. JUSTICE CLARKE took no part in the consideration and decision of this case.

MR. JUSTICE BRANDEIS, with whom concurs MR. CHIEF JUSTICE TAFT and MR. JUSTICE HOLMES, dissenting. . . .

It is not the provision for hard labor, but the imprisonment in a penitentiary, which now renders a crime infamous. Commitment to a penitentiary, with or without hard labor, connotes infamy, because it is proof of the conviction of a crime of such a nature that infamy was a prescribed consequence. Confinement in a penitentiary is the modern substitute for the death penalty and for the other forms of corporal punishment which, at the time of the adoption of the Fifth Amendment, were still administered in America for most of the crimes deemed serious. It was then believed that even capital punishment should be inflicted under conditions involving public disgrace. Largely for this reason hangings were public, as in earlier days men had been drawn and quartered. If the life of an offender was spared, it was then thought that some other punishment involving disgrace must be applied to render his loss of reputation permanent. When in 1786 Pennsylvania, shrinking from the physical cruelties inflicted under sentence of the courts, took the first step in reform by substituting imprisonment for death as the penalty for some of the lesser felonies, the exposure to infamy was still deemed an essential of punishment. The measure then enacted provided specifically that the imprisonment should be attended by "continuous hard labor publicly and disgracefully imposed." Hard labor as thus prescribed and practiced was merely an instrument of disgrace. The statutory direction was carried out by employing the convicts in gang labor along the public roads, chained by fetters with bomb shells attached and iron collars, with shaved heads, and wearing a distinctive infamous dress. The demoralizing influence both upon the community and the convict of these public manifestations of disgrace was soon realized, and led, shortly after the adoption of our Constitution, to their discontinuance in Pennsylvania and to the establishment in Philadelphia of America's first penitentiary.

1. The statute making a sentence to an infamous punishment a ground for divorce means the sentence actually imposed and not the potential sentence. Hull v. Donze, 164 La. 199, 113 So. 816 (1927).

Hard labor was not considered an essential element of the penitentiary punishment; and experience proved that it was in fact an alleviation. The most severe punishment inflicted was solitary confinement without labor. Hard labor regularly pursued and productively employed had for two centuries been applied as a corrective measure in the effort to deal with social delinquents. Then the belief spread that it might be effectively employed also in the reformation of criminals—a class of persons theretofore generally considered incorrigible. And when reform and rehabilitation of those convicted of serious crimes became a chief aim of the penal system, the dignity of labor was proclaimed and the practices of the workhouse were adopted and developed in the penitentiary. Thus hard labor, which, in inficting punishment for serious crimes, had first been introduced as a medium of disgrace, became the means of restoring and giving self-respect. . . .

Imprisonment in a penitentiary where the convict is (or used to be) "subject to solitary imprisonment, to have his hair cropped, to be clothed in conspicuous prison dress, subjected to hard labor without pay, to hard fare, coarse and meager food, and to severe discipline" is a punishment deemed infamous; but commitment to a "house of correction, under that and the various names of workhouse or bridewell," although some of the incidents of the confinement are identical, "has not the same character of infamy attached to it." There is thus no basis for the contention that sentence to hard labor as an incident of confinement necessarily renders a punishment infamous, or that commitment to a workhouse at hard labor can be made only upon indictment by a grand jury. . . .[2]

MELTON v. OLESON

Supreme Court of Montana, 1974.
165 Mont. 424, 530 P.2d 466.

JOHN C. HARRISON, JUSTICE.

Defendants appeal from a judgment of the district court, Flathead County, ordering plaintiff's registration as a voter, voiding plaintiff's removal as a college trustee, and awarding plaintiff $4,500 attorney fees.

Plaintiff is Perry S. Melton, a voter residing in Flathead County, Montana, and a trustee of Flathead Valley Community College. Defendants are the Flathead county attorney, the county clerk and re-

2. An infamous crime is one punishable in a penitentiary. Mackin v. United States, 117 U.S. 348, 6 S.Ct. 777 (1886). That requires a sentence in excess of one year under federal law.

Criminal contempts are not infamous crimes requiring indictment even if punished by imprisonment for more than one year. Green v. United States, 356 U.S. 165, 78 S.Ct. 632 (1958).

"An offense which may be punished by imprisonment for a term exceeding one year or at hard labor shall be prosecuted by indictment. . . ." Rule 7(a), 18 U.S.C.A. (1979), Federal Rules of Criminal Procedure.

corder and the board of trustees of the college. The county attorney was subsequently dismissed as a party defendant.

The material facts are undisputed. In 1933, in the United States district court in Montana, Melton plead guilty to three violations of federal liquor laws. Counts one and two of the indictment involved the sale of liquor to Indians; count three involved concealing liquor with intent to defraud the federal government of taxes due thereon.

Melton was sentenced to 40 days in jail on counts one and two and fined $500 on count three. The fine was suspended and Melton was placed on probation for five years. After 40 years it is impossible to explain these sentences. The 40 day sentence was 20 days less than the minimum sentence set by statute. The penalty for the sale of liquor to any Indian was, at the time of the crime, a minimum sentence of 60 days in jail or a $100 fine, or both, with a maximum of not more than 2 years imprisonment and a fine of not more than $300 for each offense. We can find no authorization in the federal law, at the time, authorizing probation for a period of 5 years, some 3 years over the maximum sentence.

Forty years later the Flathead county attorney's office filed a certified copy of the 1933 conviction with the county clerk and recorder. It was accompanied by an opinion that Melton had thus been convicted of a felony. The clerk and recorder thereupon struck Melton's name from the voting rolls.

The county attorney's office then advised the board of trustees of Flathead Valley Community College that Melton was no longer a registered voter and that his position as college trustee should therefore be declared vacant. The board subsequently so declared.

In the meantime Melton had filed suit in the district court of Flathead County seeking restoration of his voting rights and to prevent his removal as college trustee. This action became entangled in a procedural morass that defies description. In our view these procedural complexities are not germane to our decision and may be disregarded except as hereafter discussed in connection with attorney fees.

The end result of the district court proceedings was a judgment, (1) ordering the clerk and recorder to register Melton as a voter, (2) declaring null and void the action of the college board of trustees declaring Melton's seat vacant, and (3) ordering Flathead County to pay Melton's $4,500 attorney fees. All defendants appeal from this judgment.

The controlling issues on appeal can be condensed to three:

(1) Was Melton convicted of a felony within the meaning of Montana's voter qualification laws? . . .

The first issue is the principal substantive issue in this case. Melton's voting rights and his eligibility as college trustee turn on this issue. The difficulty arises because of contrary definitions of a felony under federal and state law.

At all material times, federal law has defined a felony as "Any offense punishable by death or imprisonment for a term exceeding one year . . . ." See 18 U.S.C.A., Sec. 1 and its predecessors. Under federal law the possible punishment that may be imposed determines whether a given crime is a felony or a misdemeanor without regard to the sentence actually imposed. Ex parte Margrave, 275 F. 200.

At the time of Melton's conviction, the crime of selling liquor to Indians was punishable by a maximum imprisonment of two years and a fine of not more than $300 for each offense. Act of March 15, 1864, Ch. 33, 13 Stat. 29. The minimum sentence could have been a sentence of 60 days in jail or a fine of $100 or both. 29 Stat. 506. This offense is clearly a felony by federal definition despite the 40 day sentence actually imposed on Melton for both violations.

A different definition of a felony is prescribed by Montana law. At the time of Melton's conviction Montana's statute, Section 10723, R.C.M.1921, declared:

"A felony is a crime which is punishable with death or by imprisonment in the state prison. Every other crime is a misdemeanor."

The same statute further provided:

"When a crime, punishable by imprisonment in the state prison, is also punishable by fine or imprisonment in a county jail, in the discretion of the court or jury, it is a misdemeanor for all purposes after a judgment imposing a punishment other than imprisonment in the state prison." [1]

Thus in Montana, the sentence actually imposed after conviction determines whether the defendant has been convicted of a felony. This same definition and classification of crimes has been preserved in Montana's new Criminal Code of 1973. Section 94–2–101(15) and (31), R.C.M.1947.

1. Under such a provision the offense is regarded as a felony for all purposes until judgment. The judge can make it a misdemeanor by a misdemeanor sentence, but if no judgment is pronounced it remains a felony. People v. Banks, 53 Cal.2d 370, 1 Cal.Rptr. 669, 348 P.2d 102 (1959). The court may grant probation to a defendant and declare the offense a misdemeanor and it is a conviction for a misdemeanor. Cal.Penal Code § 17.

A "wobbler" is an offense punishable as either a felony or a misdemeanor. People v. Municipal Court of City and County of San Francisco, 88 Cal.App.3d 206, 151 Cal.Rptr. 861 (1979).

Unless a misdemeanor sentence is entered against a defendant found guilty of forgery of a narcotics prescription, the offense stands provisionally as a felony, but if probation is granted without pronouncement of sentence, the probationer retains his ordinary civil rights. In re Trummer, 60 Cal.2d 658, 36 Cal.Rptr. 281, 388 P.2d 177 (1964).

Whether a federal offense is a felony or a misdemeanor depends upon the potential penalty rather than that actually imposed. In re Johnson, 3 Cal.3d 404, 90 Cal.Rptr. 569, 475 P.2d 841 (1970).

We recognize that Montana's statutory definition of a felony relates only to crimes under state law and does not apply to crimes classified by federal statutes. Nonetheless a fundamental difference of approach is apparent in this state's classification of crimes and the difference of approach between felonies and misdemeanors.

The crux of the problem here is whether state or federal law determines the definition of a felony mandating cancellation of voter registration. At the time of cancellation of Melton's voter registration state law, section 23–3014, R.C.M.1947, provided in material part:

"(1) The registrar [county clerk and recorder] shall cancel any [voter] registration card:

". . . (e) If a certified copy of a final judgment of conviction of any elector of a felony is filed . . . ."

(Bracketed words added.)

In construing section 23–3014, R.C.M.1947, is Montana bound by the federal felony definition at odds with our own law? In 1932 this Court so held in construing a state statute relating to forfeiture of a public office. State ex rel. Anderson v. Fousek, 91 Mont. 448, 455, 8 P.2d 791.

In *Fousek* a city police lieutenant was convicted in federal court of conspiracy to violate federal liquor laws and sentenced to pay a fine of $100. The crime involved carried a maximum punishment of a $10,000 fine and two years imprisonment. This Court held:

". . . The character of an offense, i.e., whether a felony or a misdemeanor, must be determined by the laws of the jurisdiction where the crime was committed."

As federal law classified the offense as a felony because the maximum punishment exceeded one year, the police lieutenant's position was declared vacant because of "His conviction of a felony" within the meaning of section 511, R.C.M.1921.

Several weaknesses are apparent in this holding and the statutory construction supporting it. It is the responsibility of the Montana legislature to establish qualifications for holding public office (as in *Fousek*) and voting qualifications (as in the instant case). On what basis are we to imply that they delegated this responsibility to another legislative body, be it Congress or the legislature of another state, absent explicit statutory language to that effect? Yet that would be the result of the holding in *Fousek*—that Montana is bound by foreign classifications of crimes.

Glaring injustices would result in many cases. For example, by federal definition the following federal offenses are felonies: Using profanity in a "ham" radio transmission, 18 U.S.C.A. § 1464; purchasing a field jacket from a member of the Armed Forces, 18 U.S.C.A. § 1024; attempting to mail a letter using a stamp which has already been cancelled if committed by a postal employee, 18 U.S.

C.A. § 1720. Did our Montana legislature intend to deny its citizens the right to vote for offenses like these?

In the instant case none of the three violations of which Melton was convicted would constitute a felony under our statutory definition and classification of crime. The more recent and persuasive authorities from our sister states hold that persons violating federal liquor laws are not disqualified from voting or holding public office where, as here, the offenses would not be felonies under state law.

We hold that in construing state statutes relating to voter disqualification, a Montana voter cannot be denied the right to vote because of conviction of an offense in federal court that would not be a felony by Montana statutory definition. We expressly overrule the holding in *Fousek* that "The character of an offense, i.e., whether a felony or a misdemeanor, must be determined by the laws of the jurisdiction where the crime was committed."

Therefore, Melton was not disqualified from voting rights; and his position as college trustee was not vacant. . . .

In summary, we hold that: Melton was not convicted of a felony within the meaning of Montana's voter disqualification law; Melton is entitled to be registered as a voter and elector of Flathead County, Montana; the award of attorney fees against Flathead County is vacated and set aside; and, costs are awarded to plaintiff in the district court and upon appeal.

We remand the case to the district court of Flathead County for entry of judgment accordingly.

CASTLES, DALY, and HASWELL, JJ., concur.

JAMES T. HARRISON, CHIEF JUSTICE (concurring in part and dissenting in part):

I concur in the holding that Melton is now entitled to be registered as a voter and elector, and the vacating and setting aside of the attorney fee award.

I dissent to the holding that Melton was not convicted of a felony, and the overruling of State ex rel. Anderson v. Fousek, 91 Mont. 448, 455, 8 P.2d 791.

OTSUKA v. HITE

Supreme Court of California, In Bank, 1966.
64 Cal.2d 596, 51 Cal.Rptr. 284, 414 P.2d 412.

MOSK, JUSTICE. Plaintiffs appeal from a judgment which upholds a refusal of defendant, Los Angeles County Registrar of Voters, to register plaintiffs as voters.

This case presents the difficult question whether bona fide conscientious objectors who pleaded guilty more than 20 years ago to a violation of the federal Selective Service Act can constitutionally be treated as persons convicted of an "infamous crime" and hence rendered ineligible to vote by article II, section 1, of the California Constitution.[1] After reviewing the history and purpose of this ground of voter disqualification we have concluded that to preserve its constitutionality it must be limited to conviction of crimes involving moral corruption and dishonesty, thereby branding their perpetrator as a threat to the integrity of the elective process. Plaintiffs' crime was not "infamous" as thus construed, and hence the judgment must be reversed.

The facts are not in dispute. During World War II plaintiff Otsuka, a Quaker, was classified 1A–O, i.e., a conscientious objector subject to noncombatant service in the armed forces of the United States. By reason of his religious training and belief, however, he felt he could not perform military service of any kind and should have been classified 4E, i.e, a conscientious objector subject to civilian work of national importance. He informed his draft board of his decision and refused to report for induction, surrendering himself instead at the office of the New York District Attorney. Upon his plea of guilty he was convicted of a violation of the Selective Service and Training Act of 1940 (former 50 U.S.C.App. § 311), and was sentenced by the federal district court to three years in the penitentiary. He served his term of imprisonment and was duly released.

Plaintiff Abbott's conscientious objection to military participation in any form was recognized by his draft board, and he was classified 4E. He complied with an order to report to a civilian work camp, but subsequently left the camp when it appeared to him that such activity was "an integral part of the war effort." Like Otsuka, Abbott pleaded guilty in federal court to a violation of the Selective Service Act; he was sentenced to two years in the penitentiary, served his term, and was duly released.

Now, more than 20 years later, the Los Angeles County Registrar of Voters has refused to register either plaintiff as a voter because of his wartime conviction of violating the Selective Service Act. It is conceded that in all other respects each plaintiff is a qualified elector

1. Article II, section 1, provided in relevant part: "Every native citizen of the United States of America . . . and every naturalized citizen thereof . . . of the age of 21 years, who shall have been a resident of the State one year next preceding the day of the election, and of the county . . . 90 days, and in the election precinct 54 days, shall be entitled to vote at all elections . . . ; provided, further, no alien ineligible to citizenship, no idiot, no insane person, no person convicted of any infamous crime, no person hereafter convicted of the embezzlement or misappropriation of public money, and no person who shall not be able to read the Constitution in the English language and write his or her name, shall ever exercise the privileges of an elector in this State . . . ."

At the general election in November, 1974, the original provision of the California constitution with reference to disfranchisement of convicted felons was deleted and provision was made for the temporary "disqualification" of electors while they are imprisoned or on parole for conviction of felony. Hence this problem cannot arise again in California although it might in some other state. In any event *Otsuka* is still important for the light it throws upon the concept of infamous crime.

under California law. Plaintiffs joined in this suit to compel registration (Elec.Code, § 350), and the matter was submitted on the pleadings together with a stipulation as to certain testimony plaintiffs would have given if called as witnesses. The trial court made findings in accord with the above statement of facts; in particular, the court found that in violating the federal statute each plaintiff "acted pursuant to his personal conscientious opposition to participation in war in any form," and that such violation was "the sole reason" for defendant's refusal to register either plaintiff as a voter. The court concluded as a matter of law, however, that under article II, section 1, of the California Constitution such convictions rendered plaintiffs ineligible to be voters, and entered judgment upholding defendant's refusal to register them. . . .

Plaintiffs contend that the disqualification of article II, section 1, is too broad in time, as it declares that no person convicted of the relevant crimes "shall ever" exercise the right to vote in this state. To presume, plaintiffs argue, that a man who commits a crime and is punished therefor remains forever morally corrupt is to concede him no possibility of rehabilitation, a view totally at odds with modern penological theory and legislation. This would be an appealing argument but for the fact that the Legislature has expressly provided for restoration of the right to vote to persons previously convicted of crime in California, either by court order after completion of probation (Pen.Code § 1203.4) or, if a prison term was served, by executive pardon after completion of rehabilitation proceedings (Pen.Code, §§ 4852.01–4852.17). Plaintiffs were convicted in federal courts of a crime against the United States, and a similar though not identical method of regaining their right to vote was open to them under federal administrative procedure. (28 C.F.R., §§ 1.1–1.9 [application for pardon, investigation as to applicant's rehabilitation, and recommendation to Executive].) The use of statutory or administrative processes of this kind should be encouraged, for it provides an orderly, objective determination of the often difficult question whether a former convict has become rehabilitated to the point that he may safely be restored all the rights and privileges of citizenship.

Plaintiffs apparently have not applied for such a pardon and restoration of voting rights, although they have long been eligible to do so. The point is not discussed in the briefs. It could be argued that this is in effect a failure to exhaust administrative remedies which renders the present action premature. On the other hand, this procedural deficiency should not bar plaintiffs from challenging the constitutionality of the underlying classification: i.e., if in the first place it was unconstitutional to deprive them of their right to vote on the ground here in issue, it should be immaterial that they did not thereafter apply for restoration of that right by act of executive clemency.

We turn, then, to the more serious problem of the scope of the classification adopted by article II, section 1. Defendant contends that "infamous crime" should be construed to mean *any* felony; and that when it is so construed, the section does not discriminate because it "treats all persons convicted of felonies alike." But it is settled that "the fact that a State is dealing with a distinct class and treats the members of that class equally does not end the judicial inquiry. 'The courts must reach and determine the question whether the classifications drawn in a statute are reasonable in light of its purpose . . . .'" The unreasonableness of a classification disfranchising all former felons, regardless of their crime, is readily demonstrable: it raises the spectre of citizens automatically deprived of their right to vote upon conviction, for example, of seduction under promise of marriage (Pen.Code, § 268), failure to provide family support (Pen.Code, § 270), wife-beating (Pen.Code, § 273d), or second-offense indecent exposure (Pen.Code, § 311); worse yet, since conspiracy to commit a misdemeanor is itself a felony (Pen.Code, § 182, subd. 1), disfranchisement would automatically follow from conviction of conspiracy to operate a motor vehicle without a muffler (Veh.Code, § 27150) or to violate any other of the myriads of lesser misdemeanor statutes on the books. No reasonable relation is apparent between this result and the purpose of protecting the integrity of the elective process. . . . "All our history gives confirmation to the view that liberty of conscience has a moral and social value which makes it worthy of preservation at the hands of the state. So deep in its significance and vital, indeed, is it to the integrity of man's moral and spiritual nature that nothing short of the self-preservation of the state should warrant its violation; and it may well be questioned whether the state which preserves its life by a settled policy of violation of the conscience of the individual will not in fact ultimately lose it by the process.' Stone, The Conscientious Objector, 21 Col.Univ.Q. 253, 269 (1919)."

In view of the foregoing, it cannot reasonably be said that plaintiffs' violation of the Selective Service Act branded them as morally corrupt and dishonest men convicted of an "infamous crime" as that phrase is used in article II, section 1, of the California Constitution.

The judgment is reversed.

PETERS, TOBRINER and PEEK, JJ., concur.

[Three justices dissented on the ground that "neither the registrars of voters nor the courts ought to be expected to attempt a determination of whether a convicted felon should be permitted to vote, until after he has first exhausted the administrative remedies made available under federal and state procedures."]

Note. The actual holding in *Otsuka* is only that a violation of the federal Selective Service Act by a conscientious objector, although a felony, was not an "infamous Crime" as that term is used in Article II, Section 1 of the California Constitution. But there was a clear statement to the effect that other felonies, not involving moral corruption and dishonesty, are also included. Unfortunately no guidelines were provided and the enforcement resulted in utter confusion. A felony, the conviction of which would bar the convict as a voter in one county, would not bar him in another. And such discrepancies were numerous and widespread. This caused attention to be focused on another section of the California Constitution, Article XX, Section 11, which provided for loss of suffrage by persons convicted of certain named offenses "or other high crimes." The California Court felt obliged to hold that this included all felonies, but held that to enforce this as to all felons who had completed their sentences and paroles would violate the federal Constitution. This holding was reversed by the Supreme Court in *Richardson.*[2] The Court said: "We therefore hold that the Supreme Court of California erred in holding that California may no longer, consistent with the Equal Protection Clause of the Fourteenth Amendment, exclude from the franchise convicted felons who have completed their sentences and paroles." [3] The case was sent back to the California Court for further action under this holding, but it was pointed out that in the meantime the California Constitution had been amended whereby the "Legislature is simply directed by new section 4 of Article II to provide for the temporary "disqualification" of electors while they are mentally incompetent, imprisoned or on parole for the conviction of a felony.[4] Hence the problem had become moot. A case such as *Otsuka* cannot again arise in California, but it might arise under the constitution of some other state.

MODEL PENAL CODE*

Section 1.04 Classes of Crimes; Violations.

(1) An offense defined by this Code or by any other statute of this State, for which a sentence of [death or of] [1] imprisonment is authorized, constitutes a crime. Crimes are classified as felonies, misdemeanors or petty misdemeanors.

(2) A crime is a felony if it is so designated in this Code or if persons convicted thereof may be sentenced [to death or] to imprisonment for a term which, apart from an extended term, is in excess of one year.[2]

2. Richardson v. Ramirez, 418 U.S. 24, 94 S.Ct. 2655 (1974).

3. Id. at p. 56, 94 S.Ct. 2671.

4. Ramirez v. Brown, 12 Cal.3d 912, 117 Cal.Rptr. 562, 528 P.2d 378, 379 (1974). Art. 154 Cal.Const.

* Prepared by the American Law Institute. All references to the Model Penal Code herein, unless otherwise indicated, are to the Proposed Official Draft, 1962. Such quotations have been expressly authorized by the American Law Institute.

1. Since a few jurisdictions do not have capital punishment all references to the death sentence are bracketed in the Code.

2. A felony punished by death is a separate category. Aside from this, felonies are divided into three degrees. For a felony of the first degree the maximum penalty is life imprisonment; for a felony of the second degree the maximum is ten years; and for a felony of the third degree the maximum is five years.

(3) A crime is a misdemeanor if it is so designated in this Code or in a statute other than this Code enacted subsequent thereto.

(4) A crime is a petty misdemeanor if it is so designated in this Code or in a statute other than this Code enacted subsequent thereto or if it is defined by a statute other than this Code which now provides that persons convicted thereof may be sentenced to imprisonment for a term of which the maximum is less than one year.

(5) An offense defined by this Code or by any other statute of this State constitutes a violation if it is so designated in this Code or in the law defining the offense or if no other sentence than a fine, or fine and forfeiture or other civil penalty is authorized upon conviction or if it is defined by a statute other than this Code which now provides that the offense shall not constitute a crime. A violation does not constitute a crime and conviction of a violation shall not give rise to any disability or legal disadvantage based on conviction of a criminal offense.

(6) Any offense declared by law to constitute a crime, without specification of the grade thereof or of the sentence authorized upon conviction, is a misdemeanor.

(7) An offense defined by any statute of this State other than this Code shall be classified as provided in this Section and the sentence that may be imposed upon conviction thereof shall hereafter be governed by this Code.

Section 6.08 Sentence of Imprisonment for Misdemeanors and Petty Misdemeanors; Ordinary Terms.

A person who has been convicted of a misdemeanor or a petty misdemeanor may be sentenced to imprisonment for a definite term which shall be fixed by the Court and shall not exceed one year in the case of a misdemeanor or thirty days in the case of a petty misdemeanor.

Chapter 2

OFFENSES AGAINST THE PERSON

SECTION 1. HOMICIDE

DOWNEY v. PEOPLE

Supreme Court of Colorado, en Banc, 1950.
121 Colo. 307, 215 P.2d 892.

MOORE, JUSTICE. David Albert Downey, the defendant in the lower court and to whom we hereinafter refer as defendant, or by name, was charged by information filed in the district court of El Paso county on July 28, 1947, with having "feloniously, wilfully and of his malice aforethought" killed and murdered one Lolly Lila Downey. Defendant entered a plea of not guilty and the cause came on for trial October 7, 1947. The jury returned a verdict of guilty of murder in the first degree and fixed the penalty at "life imprisonment at hard labor in the State Penitentiary." Motion for new trial was thereafter filed, argued, and denied, and appropriate judgment was entered by the court. Defendant brings the cause here by writ of error, and relies for reversal upon alleged errors of the lower court in the conduct of the trial as follows: . . .

3rd. The court erred in overruling defendant's motion for a directed verdict upon the ground that the corpus delicti had not been established. . . .

Between one and two o'clock in the afternoon of July 18, 1947, a Dr. Wilson was driving on the Rampart Range road when he observed the defendant being assisted into a car by a Mr. Hubbard from Texas. Dr. Wilson stopped his automobile and noticed blood on the left side of defendant's shirt. He testified that defendant stated, "I am not hurt—that is my wife's blood. . . . She may be dead." Dr. Wilson and Mr. Hubbard were unable to find Mrs. Downey and returned to defendant's automobile and he thereupon assisted them in locating the body. According to Dr. Wilson the body was not disarranged. It was placed out very carefully. Mrs. Downey was dead but the body was warm. Defendant complained of injuries received from a fall, police authorities were notified, and defendant was taken to a hospital in Colorado Springs where he remained until Saturday, July 19, when he was lodged in the county jail. Dr. Wilson testified that while at the hospital defendant asked him, "if her tongue was out" and when the doctor asked the reason for the question defendant stated, "She seemed to be strangling and I tried to remove her tongue." The terrain where the body was found was rugged, being a mass of rocks and boulders. It was not, however, a dangerous area as to being precipitous. The body was lying at the foot of a ledge of rock about three feet in height, on the suface of which there was a considerable amount of blood. About thirty-four feet up the hill from the point where the body was found there was some evidence that a scuffle had occurred. An autopsy was performed which disclosed superficial scratches and bruises. There was a two inch wound in the back of the head which penetrated the scalp but did no further damage and was not the cause of death, which, as testified by the experts performing the autopsy, was asphyxia due to strangulation. . . .

Second: *Was the corpus delicti sufficiently established by the evidence?*

At the close of all the evidence the defendant moved for a directed verdict of not guilty "for the reason that the corpus delicti has not been established without recourse to the alleged confession of the defendant." The motion was overruled and error is assigned on the ruling.

In Bruner v. People, 113 Colo. 194, 156 P.2d 111, 117, we said: "It is well settled in this jurisdiction that the corpus delicti consists of two components: death as a result and the criminal agency of another as the means, and it is equally settled that the corpus delicti may be established by either direct or circumstantial evidence. . . . "[1]

1. Whether the *uncorroborated confession of the accused* in a criminal case is alone sufficient to support a conviction is a question which for more than a hundred years was left unsettled in English law. . . .

"The proposed rule appeared in two variations: by the one, the corroborative evidence might be of *any sort* whatever; by the other, it must specifically relate to the '*corpus delicti* ', i.e. the fact of injury. The latter form tended to prevail; but in neither form did the rule obtain a general footing. So far as it can be supposed to obtain at all today in the English and Irish courts, it is apparently restricted to the case of homicide: . . .

"The conflicting state of the English rulings left the Courts and the Legisltures of the United States to choose which rule might commend itself. Except in a few jurisdictions, they seem to have preferred, wherever the question has come up for decision, to adopt the fixed rule that corroboration was necessary,—chiefly moved, in all probability, by Professor Greenleaf's suggestion that 'this opinion certainly best accords with the humanity of the criminal code and with the great degree of caution applied in receiving and weighing the evidence of confessions in other cases.'

"In a few jurisdictions, the rule is properly not limited to evidence concerning the 'corpus delicti'; i.e. the corroborating facts may be of *any sort whatever*, provided only that they tend to produce a confidence in the truth of the confession: . . .

"The meaning of the phrase '*corpus delicti* ' has been the subject of much loose judicial comment, and an apparent sanction has often been given to an unjustifiably broad meaning. It is clear that an analysis of every crime, with reference to this element of it, reveals three component parts, *first*, the *occurrence* of the specific kind of injury or loss (as, in homicide, a person deceased; in arson, a house burnt; in larceny, property missing); *secondly*, somebody's criminality (in contrast, e.g. to accident) as the source of the loss,—these two together involving the commission of a crime by *somebody;* and *thirdly*, the accused's *identity* as the doer of this crime.

"(1) Now, the term 'corpus delicti' seems in its orthodox sense to signify merely the first of these elements, name-

The Bruner case is authority for the rule prevailing in this jurisdiction that circumstantial evidence is sufficient to establish the corpus delicti in a homicide case if it is such as to prove the essentials thereof to a reasonable certainty.

In Lowe v. People, 76 Colo. 603, 234 P. 169, 173, we stated:

"Proof that one charged committed a felonious homicide involves three elements; First, the death; Second, the criminal agency of another as the cause; Third, the identity of the accused as that other. The first two constitute what is known in law as the corpus delicti . . . Each of these elements must be established by the prosecution to the satisfaction of the jury beyond a reasonable doubt. The court, however, is not the judge of the weight of the evidence. When sufficient evidence has been produced to justify a submission to the jury and support a verdict of guilty, should such a verdict be returned thereon, the requirements of the law have been met. This rule applies to each of the elements of the corpus delicti as it does to the proof of the identity of the accused as the perpetrator; no more no less."

"That proof may be made by any legal evidence, the same as proof of other facts."

It is true that a conviction of crime cannot be upheld where it is based upon the uncorroborated confession of the person accused. There must be evidence of the corpus delicti apart from the statements contained in the confession. In the case at bar there is ample evidence, apart from the confession, from which the jury might properly find that the wife of defendant was dead, and that her death was brought about by "the criminal agency of another as the means." Defendant was the sole companion of his wife at the time of her death. There was blood on his shirt, which he stated was that of his wife. He directed those first upon the scene to the place where her body was found. The body was still warm. The position of the body, the fact that her clothing was not disarranged, the fact that pressure had been applied to both of her wrists and her throat, the general topography of the terrain where she was found, were all inconsistent with the theory of accidental death. The ragged scalp wound in the back of the head of deceased corroborated the statement of defendant that he struck her a blow with a "rock about the size of two

ly, the *fact of the specific loss or injury sustained:* . . .

"(2) But by most judges the term is made to include the second element also, i.e., *somebody's criminality:* . . .

"This broader form makes the rule much more difficult for the jury to apply amid a complex mass of evidence, and tends to reduce the rule to a juggling-formula.

"(3) A third view, indeed, too absurd to be argued with, has occasionally been advanced, at least by counsel, namely, that the 'corpus delicti' includes the third element also, i.e., *the accused's identity* or agency as the criminal. By this view, the term 'corpus delicti' would be synonymous with the whole of the charge, and the rule would require that the whole be evidenced in all three elements independently of the confession, which would be absurd." VII Wigmore on Evidence, §§ 2070–2072 (3d ed. 1940). Reprinted by permission of the publisher, Little, Brown and Company.

teacups." The defendant directed an inquiry to Dr. Wilson as to whether deceased's tongue was out when he first observed the body, and this unusual question was wholly the thought of defendant. The doctors who performed the autopsy testified that the cause of death was strangulation produced by pressure applied to the throat. Competent evidence tending to establish these facts was sufficient to establish the corpus delicti of the crime of murder, and the trial court did not commit error in overruling defendant's motion for a directed verdict on the ground that the corpus delicti had not been sufficiently proven. . . .

The defendant was capably represented at the trial, and here, by counsel of ability and experience, and we are persuaded that he was afforded a fair trial in accordance with established rules of law. The assignments upon which he relies for reversal are overruled, and accordingly the judgment is affirmed.

HICKS v. SHERIFF, CLARK COUNTY

Supreme Court of Nevada, 1970.
86 Nev. 67, 464 P.2d 462.

BATJER, JUSTICE: Appellant was charged with the murder of Glenn E. Christiernsson. After an extensive preliminary examination the charge was dismissed because the state had failed to prove the corpus delicti and had also failed to prove that Christiernsson's death was caused by the criminal agency of the appellant.

Thereafter, the state filed a petition in the district court for leave to file an information against the appellant under NRS 173.035(2),[1] attaching to the petition the transcript of the testimony taken at the preliminary examination. Also attached to the petition was an affidavit of a Ronald Elton King, who had been a cellmate of the appellant in the Clark County jail. The affidavit of King alleged that the appellant, while in jail, had admitted to him, the killing of Christiernsson. There was also attached to the petition an affidavit of a deputy district attorney which recited that the appellant had been discharged after preliminary examination, but alleged that the testimony adduced was sufficient compliance with NRS 173.035(2), and that it contained sufficient facts to justify the issuance of an information against the appellant.

1. NRS 173.035(2): "If, however, upon the preliminary examination the accused has been discharged, or the affidavit or complaint upon which the examination has been held has not been delivered to the clerk of the proper court, the district attorney may, upon affidavit of any person who has knowledge of the commission of an offense, and who is a competent witness to testify in the case, setting forth the offense and the name of the person or persons charged with the commission thereof, upon being furnished with the names of the witnesses for the prosecution, by leave of the court first had, file an information, and process shall forthwith issue thereon. The affidavit mentioned herein need not be filed in cases where the defendant has waived a preliminary examination, or upon such preliminary examination has been bound over to appear at the court having jurisdiction."

The district court granted leave to file the information; the appellant was rearrested and then applied for a writ of habeas corpus which was denied by the district court.

This appeal is taken from the order denying the writ of habeas corpus. We reverse the order of the district court. . . .

The only question before us is whether the facts laid before the district court, prior to the filing of the information, established a corpus delicti and probable cause to believe that the appellant committed the crime as charged.

The record of the preliminary examination is absolutely devoid of proof of the corpus delicti to support the filing of an information charging the crime of murder. The appellant was properly discharged by the justice of the peace on the evidence presented at that hearing.

Except in the affidavit of King, we find no testimony or other evidence about the cause of death of Christiernsson. All that we find relating to his death is testimony that his body was found on December 6, 1967, in the desert; that it was identified by a military service identification tag and a thumb print, and that the body was partially clothed. There is absolutely no evidence before either the justice's court or the district court that a criminal agency of the appellant or anyone else was responsible for the alleged victim's death.

The affidavit of the appellant's fellow prisoner to the effect that the appellant admitted to him that he had murdered the victim, does not supply the proof necessary to show that death was caused by criminal means. Only after the corpus delicti has been proved by lawful evidence may confessions and admissions be considered in establishing probable cause to show that the accused was the criminal agency causing the death. Azbill v. State, 84 Nev. 345, 440 P.2d 1014 (1968). In re Kelly, 28 Nev. 491, 83 P. 223 (1905). In Kelly, supra, this court said: ". . . It is not requisite, however, that the crime charged be conclusively established by evidence independent of the confession or admission. It is sufficient if there be other competent evidence tending to establish the fact of the commission of the crime." Here there is absolutely no evidence independent of the appellant's purported admission.

The testimony at the preliminary examination establishing that the deceased and the appellant were seen together shortly before the deceased's disappearance on or about October 9, 1967, as well as testimony concerning the appellant's behavior prior to arrest, and the fact that he was driving Christiernsson's car at the time of his arrest would only have been material to show probable cause that the appellant was guilty of the crime of murder if the corpus delicti of that crime had been established.

In Azbill v. State, supra, we held: "If in considering all the evidence admissible upon the element of corpus delicti, it cannot be said there was sufficient evidence to make it appear the death resulted from another's criminal agency the state has failed in its burden and the person charged may not be held to stand trial on that charge."

At the very least there must be established, independent of any confession or admission by the accused, the fact of death and that it resulted from the criminal agency of another and not from natural causes, accident or suicide. Sefton v. State, 72 Nev. 106, 295 P.2d 385 (1956).

In his affidavit, King swore that the appellant told him that he beat Christiernsson to death and then stabbed him to make sure he was dead. If King is telling the truth there surely must have been some evidence on the body of the decedent showing bruises, contusions, abrasions, wounds or fractures.

Neither the justice of the peace, the district court judge, who ordered the information to be filed pursuant to NRS 173.035(2), the district court judge who denied habeas corpus, nor this court "may speculate that a criminal agency caused the death. There must be sufficient proof of the hypothesis of death by criminal means." Azbill v. State, supra.

The evidence before the district court is insufficient to show probable cause of the corpus delicti of the crime of murder. Accordingly we reverse the order of the district court, and order that appellant be freed from custody under the information charging murder unless within a reasonable time the state elects to bring a new charge against him for that crime.[1]

COLLINS, C.J., and ZENOFF, MOWBRAY and THOMPSON, JJ. concur.

1. Contrast the case where in a murder prosecution thirty bone fragments of a human skull were found in the desert with three bullet holes. The pathologist could not definitely state the cause of death. A shoe similar to that worn by the deceased was found nearby. The alleged victim had also disappeared. The court held, "Although the pathologist testified he could not definitely state whether the actual cause of death resulted from the bullet wounds or whether the bullet holes were placed in the body [skull] after death, the evidence presented to the grand jury was more susceptible of belief that death was caused by a criminal agency." Sheriff, Clark County v. Larsgaard, 96 Nev. 486, 611 P.2d 625, 627 (1980).

In a prosecution for manslaughter where there was no independent proof that D rather than decedent was driving the automobile at the time of the fatal crash, D would not be found guilty on his own extra-judicial confession as there is a failure to prove the corpus delicti independent of the confession. Allen v. State, 314 So.2d 154 (Fla.App.1975). Proof of the corpus delicti, for the preliminary purpose of permitting the jury to consider D's extra-judicial confession does not require identity of the one who caused the actus reus, but if the decedent caused his own death there was no homicide.

WARMKE v. COMMONWEALTH

Court of Appeals of Kentucky, 1944.
297 Ky. 649, 180 S.W.2d 872.

FULTON, CHIEF JUSTICE. This appeal is from a manslaughter sentence of nine years imposed on the appellant in connection with the death of her infant child. The sole ground urged for reversal was that the corpus delicti was not sufficiently shown.

The appellant resided in Utica, a village in Davies County. Some weeks prior to July 8, 1943 she went to Louisville and there gave birth to an illegitimate child. On July 8, 1943, she traveled to Cloverport, in Breckenridge County, by bus arriving about 8 o'clock p.m. It was raining very hard and she went into a drug store for shelter. A.T. Couch, an employee of the store, loaned her a coat in which to wrap her baby. She went out leaving her suitcase in the store. She called Couch by telephone about 10:30, requesting him to come to the store so that she might get her suitcase. When she met Couch at the store she did not have the baby but returned the borrowed coat. Early the next morning she went to the home of a kinswoman, Mrs. Pate. The town marshal, having learned that the baby was missing, went to Mrs. Pate's home and questioned the appellant. She told him that after she left the drug store she started to cross a railroad trestle near the town in an effort to get to the home of a friend and that while she was crossing a train approached and she crawled over on the edge of the ties and accidentally dropped the baby. The town marshal and a highway patrolman then took the appellant to the trestle and she pointed out where the baby had been dropped. There was a creek under the trestle at this point. It was flooded and the current was swift. A baby's cap was found on the bank of the creek and the appellant exclaimed, "There is my little baby's cap". The baby's body was never found.

When the officers returned to town with the appellant she told them after some questioning, that she purposely threw the baby into the creek because she was unable to face the humiliation of going home with an illegitimate child.

On the trial she repudiated the confession she had made to the officers and testified that she dropped the baby accidentally, in the manner she first told the officers. She testified that she was scared and excited and didn't remember saying she dropped the baby purposely. She said that after she dropped the baby she wandered around all night barefooted and in a dazed condition and that in the morning she put on her shoes and stockings and went to Mrs. Pate's. She gave as a reason for stopping off at Cloverport that it was her father's home town and that she desired to talk to a friend, Mrs. Atwill, and obtain advice. She did not see Mrs. Atwill but says that she was looking for her house when she dropped the baby and that thereafter she remembered nothing until early morning.

It is axiomatic that the corpus delicti must be shown.[1] This term means the body of the offense, the substance of the crime. Proof of the corpus delicti in homicide cases involves two principal facts, namely, that the person is dead and that he died as a result of the injury alleged to have been received. In short, there must be proof of a death and proof that such death was caused by the criminal agency of the accused.

But the law does not subscribe to the rigid formula that the body must be found or seen after death. The death may be established by circumstantial evidence. 26 Amer.Juris. 376. As said in 13 R.C.L. 737, the death may be shown "by proof of criminal violence adequate to produce death and which accounts for the disappearance of the body. In short, the body must be found or there must be proof of death which the law deems to be equivalent to direct evidence that it was found."

We think there was sufficient proof of the death of the baby in the case before us. It was dropped, either purposely or accidentally, by the appellant from the railroad trestle into the flooded creek below and was never found. It seems beyond the bounds of possibility that the baby survived this ordeal and was never thereafter heard of. At least, we think the evidence was ample to justify the jury's finding that death ensued.

It is argued for the appellant, however, that the corpus delicti must be established by evidence other than the confession of the accused out of court and that there was no other evidence here. The soundness of the legal proposition thus advanced may be admitted. There must be proof of the component elements of the corpus delicti, a death and the criminal agency of the accused, by proof in addition to the confession of the accused made out of court. But, as indicated above, the appellant testified that the baby was dropped into the

1. In Commonwealth v. Burns, 409 Pa. 619, 187 A.2d 552 (1963), **D** was convicted of first-degree murder although the body of the alleged victim was never found. Circumstantial evidence was held to be sufficient proof of the corpus delicti to entitle the jury to consider **D**'s extrajudicial confession. In answer to **D**'s objection that the judge had admitted **D**'s confession into evidence before the corpus delicti had been established by independent evidence, it was said: "The order of proof is a matter within the realm of his judicial discretion." And the conviction was affirmed.

D was charged with the unlawful killing of Ronnie Baca. Proof that **D** unlawfully killed a boy, with no proof that the deceased was Ronnie Baca, will not support a conviction of manslaughter because the corpus delicti has not been established. State v. Vallo, 81 N.M. 148, 464 P.2d 567 (1970).

A confession from a mentally unstable defendant is an insufficient basis upon which to establish a conviction for murder where the only evidence of death was that the alleged victim failed to return to work one day. Lemons v. State, 49 Md. App. 467, 433 A.2d 1179 (1981).

"Once substantial evidence of the corpus delicti is introduced, a defendant's confession is admissible, if together they provide a basis for a finding of both the corpus delicti and the defendant's guilt beyond a reasonable doubt." Smith v. State, 659 P.2d 330, 333 (Okl.Cr.App. 1983).

creek. Thus there was proof of the death independent of the appellant's confession made out of court.

The remaining question is whether there was proof, in addition to the appellant's confession made out of court, of her criminal agency in causing the death. Her agency in causing the death was admitted from the witness stand. Was there evidence, independent of her confession out of court, that this agency was criminal? We think there was an abundance of such evidence. Such independent evidence may be circumstantial as well as direct.

Circumstances pointing clearly to the fact that the appellant purposely dropped the baby from the trestle may be thus summarized. She had an impelling motive, concealment of the birth of the illegitimate child. Her reason for going to Cloverport instead of her home is rather vague and unsatisfactory. This reason was that she decided to consult her friend, Mrs. Atwill, yet she never did so. She eventually wound up at Mrs. Pate's and not at Mrs. Atwill's. But most illuminating of all is her failure to notify any one that she had dropped the baby from the trestle, if it was dropped accidentally. She accounts for this by saying she was in a dazed condition, nevertheless she called Mr. Couch by telephone to come to the drug store so that she might get her suitcase. She returned the coat to him. She had borrowed this coat to wrap the baby in. It is singular that she would have accidentally dropped the baby without dropping the coat. It is even more singular that she never notified Mrs. Pate, her kinswoman, the next morning of the loss of the baby. These circumstances and the justifiable inferences to be drawn from them, amply warranted the jury in finding that the dropping of the baby from the trestle was purposely, and not accidentally, done by the appellant.

Affirmed.[2]

STATE v. PYLE

Supreme Court of Kansas, 1975.
216 Kan. 423, 532 P.2d 1309.

FOTH, COMMISSIONER:

Appellant Michael Duane ("Mike") Pyle was convicted by a jury of the first degree murder of his grandmother, Mrs. Golda ("Goldie") Millar, and of arson for the burning of her house.

Mrs. Millar was last seen by her customary associates on April 5, 1971. Her ranch home in Kiowa county, between Haviland and Belvidere, burned to the ground in the early morning hours of April 8, 1971. No one has seen or heard from her since, and no trace of her body has ever been found.

2. "A defendant who testifies is just as competent to establish *corpus delicti* as any other witness." People v. Small, 7 Cal.App.3d 347, 354, 86 Cal.Rptr. 478, 482 (1970).

The absence of a body gives rise to two of appellant's contentions on appeal, namely that the state failed to prove . . . the corpus delicti . . . of the alleged murder. . . .

Background

Goldie Millar was 78 when she disappeared. She owned a 3100 acre ranch near Belvidere, worth more than $340,000. She had two daughters, Mrs. Lois Allen of Hampton, Virginia, and Mrs. Billie Kratzer of Colorado Springs, Colorado. Mrs. Kratzer was the mother by a former marriage of the appellant Michael Pyle.

Mike had been a troubled child, presenting discipline problems punctuated by aggressive assaults on younger boys, including his brother. The result was a referral at the age of twelve to The Menninger Foundation of Topeka for a psychiatric evaluation, followed shortly by five years at a military academy. Attempts at higher education were failures, and in 1964 or 1965 he went to live with his grandmother Goldie on her ranch. Relations between them were harmonious for several years; in 1967 Goldie made a will in which she left the bulk of her estate to Mike, including the ranch. In 1968 Mike married Linda Clarkson, and he and his wife went to live on the ranch. It appears that some hostility soon developed between Goldie and the new bride.

In 1969 relations between Mike and his grandmother also began to deteriorate. That summer he beat her, cutting her lip and bruising her arms. In July of that year Goldie withdrew her will from the probate court where it had been deposited, took it to her lawyer's office, and there revoked it by tearing off her signature. As it later developed, Mike was unaware of the revocation and in April, 1971, still thought he was her primary beneficiary.

In August, 1969, Mike administered yet another beating to her, and later that month she was forced to call the sheriff to quell a violent argument between herself and Mike and Linda. At that time the sheriff suggested that the young people should leave the ranch. Mike agreed, but told the sheriff as he left, "This is my ranch and I am going to have it, one way or the other."

In 1969 Mike sought to enlist the aid of his aunt, Lois Allen, to have Goldie declared incompetent so that he could gain control of the ranch. He already had a power of attorney. Her response was to call her mother, Goldie, and urge that she revoke the power of attorney. Goldie said she would.

Over the fall and winter of 1969–70 matters became progressively worse. On one occasion Mike removed some tools and other property from the ranch, and Goldie wanted to prosecute him for theft. The sheriff and county attorney mediated the dispute. On another occasion, Mike attempted to remove a water pump from the ranch. Goldie called the undersheriff, who came out and persuaded him to reinstall it.

In the spring of 1970 Goldie suffered a slight stroke. Mrs. Allen came from Virginia to be with her mother, and discovered that Mike's power of attorney was still outstanding. She took Goldie to a lawyer where a formal revocation was prepared and Goldie executed it. Mrs. Allen had told Mike she would have no part of his plan to have Goldie committed.

In 1970 Mike sued Goldie on a note.

That October Goldie entered into negotiations with Alfred Barby, of Meade, to sell him the ranch. They agreed on a price of $110 an acre for a little more than 3100 acres and had contract papers prepared, but at the last minute she backed out. Instead, in November she leased the land for two-and-a-half years at $4 per acre per year. When she approached Barby again in December, 1970, the proposition was less attractive to him because of the outstanding lease.

That is the way matters stood when the parties entered the fateful days of April, 1971. Goldie was on the ranch, wishing to sell. Mike and his wife, Linda, were living in Pratt, some thirty-odd miles away, but Mike still came to the ranch on occasion and still got some mail at Belvidere. Relations between Goldie and Mike were strained.

The First Week of April 1971

Thursday, April 1: Goldie went into Belvidere and picked up her mail. Belvidere is a town of some twenty persons, about two to three miles south and east of the ranch. There she visited with, among others, Geneva Braden, the postmistress, and Ellen Davis, keeper of the general store and gas station. She seemed fine to them. Both were longtime friends who saw Goldie at least every few days and sometimes every day. Neither has seen her since, although Geneva Braden talked to her on the telephone the next Monday.

Friday, April 2: Luther Lemon was on the ranch taking care of cattle for his employer, Stanley Dannebohm, who leased the 3100 acres of pasture. He saw Goldie standing in the yard talking to Dannebohm and his son, and later stopped and visited with her. He observed nothing unusual about her. He never saw her again.

Saturday, April 3: Dannebohm was at the ranch again. Goldie called him into the house and attempted to sell him the 3100 acres he was renting from her. At her asking figure of $123 per acre the price was too much for him to handle, and he told her so. He never saw or heard from her again.

That same evening Alfred Barby, who had almost bought the ranch before, was passing through Haviland and called Goldie to talk to her about it once more. They again agreed on a price of $110 per acre. Goldie wanted him to come to the ranch that night and give her $5,000 earnest money, but he demurred. It was late, they had no contract, she was just recovering from the flu, and he didn't want to tangle with her dog, who had "got a hold of" him a time or two before. He would call here within two weeks.

Sunday, April 4: This appears to have been a day of solitude for Goldie. No one reports seeing or talking to her.

Monday, April 5: Bill Hogan, Kiowa county sheriff, telephoned Goldie about 5:53 p.m. He had a Pratt county warrant for Mike's arrest on bad check charges. He hadn't seen Mike for some time, and wondered if he was living at the ranch. Goldie told him Mike lived in Pratt, but she was expecting him that evening and would tell him to see the sheriff about the warrant.

Around 7:00 to 7:30 p.m. Mrs. Harley Septer telephoned Goldie to see about some materials Goldie was to furnish to fence off some cultivated land on the ranch. Mr. Septer was to do the fencing next day for Harlin Yost, who rented the cultivated land. Goldie told Mrs. Septer the material would be in the yard, and that if she wasn't in the yard when her husband arrived the next day he should not come in the house because she had a bad headache.

Around the same time Geneva Braden, the Belvidere postmistress, also called. Mike had telephoned her from Haviland to see about picking up his mail, and Mrs. Braden wondered if Goldie would like him to get hers while he was there. Goldie said yes, she would appreciate that very much.

Those two calls, from Mrs. Septer and Mrs. Braden in the evening of Monday, April 5, represent the last contact with Goldie by anyone other than Mike. The balance of the tale must therefore focus on his activities.

Around 8:00 or 8:30 that Monday evening Mike appeared at the Belvidere post office and picked up his and Goldie's mail from Geneva Braden. Around 8:45 he burst into sheriff Hogan's house visibly upset. He ignored Mrs. Hogan—an unusual thing for him to do—and demanded to talk to the sheriff. Mike said that his grandmother had been drunk for three weeks and was vomiting blood. He had been having to go to the ranch twice a day to take care of the dog because she was in no condition to do so. When the sheriff asked him about the bad check warrant, Mike said he had plenty of money to take care of it, but didn't want Goldie to know how much he had. He and sheriff Hogan agreed he would go to the Pratt county sheriff's office the next morning and take care of it, rather than submit to arrest in Kiowa county. Mike never kept that appointment.

Tuesday, April 6: Harley Septer went to the ranch looking for the fencing material Goldie had said would be laid out in the yard. He found no material, and saw no one around the place, so he left.

Around 9:00 to 10:00 that morning Mike, with his wife Linda, appeared at Linda's sister's house in Sawyer, some twenty miles east of the ranch. Linda asked if she could spend the day, and when the sister said yes, Mike left Linda and went on. Linda explained to her sister that Mike had been informed of a fire at his grandmother's and was going down to check; he didn't want Linda or their dog along down at the ranch. In mid-afternoon Mike called Linda and reported, as Linda told her sister, that there hadn't been a fire at the ranch that day, after all.

Wednesday, April 7: Mike and Linda went to a farm sale in the morning. Around 11:00, Mike picked up his mail from Mrs. Braden. She asked about Goldie's flu of the previous week, and Mike replied that she "gets her flu in pint bottles."

In the early afternoon Mike called his stepfather, Bill Kratzer, in Colorado Springs, charging the call to Goldie's number. Mike said he had some business to discuss, and they agreed he would go to Colorado the next day.

Around 4:00 to 5:00 that afternoon Mike and Linda were in the Belvidere general store. While there, he told Ellen Davis that his grandmother was on "a helluva binge." She was unconscious, he said, and he was going to Colorado the next day to see his mother to see what could be done. Mrs. Davis saw him dial Goldie's number on the store's phone, but he got no response. He had also mentioned Goldie's drinking to Mrs. Davis a couple of days before—the first time he had ever talked about her like that.

Thursday, April 8: At 5:15 a.m., a truck driver reported to a Greensburg policeman that there was a fire somewhere south of Haviland. Pratt police were alerted by the dispatcher but were unable to locate the fire. The Haviland city marshal was called at 5:20, and he drove south until he located first a glow, then a pasture fire, and finally the ranch house burned to the ground. The ranch is some ten to twelve miles south of Haviland. He arrived at 5:55 a.m., and was soon joined by firemen he had summoned on the way, and other police officers.

Ten minutes later Mike called his mother in Colorado Springs from Lamar, Colorado. It was 5:05 a.m., Mountain time. He wanted to announce that he would be there in a few hours. When his mother asked how Goldie was, Mike told her it was not a business trip, that his grandmother was very sick, and that "this time she isn't going to make [it] if you don't come and take her to the hospital."

Twenty to thirty minutes later around 5:30, Mrs. Kratzer had another call, this time from Ellen Davis of Belvidere. Mrs. Davis broke the news that Goldie's house had burned down, and that neither Goldie nor her dog could be found. Mrs. Kratzer had given the dog to her mother, and knew he was her constant companion.

Yet a third call came to the Kratzer house at 8:00 a.m. This was from a ham radio operator, saying that Mike had called him on his truck radio and asked him to relay a message that he would arrive in about fifteen minutes. At 8:15, Mountain time, Mike arrived as promised. He then learned from his stepfather, ostensibly for the first time, that his grandmother's house had burned.

In the meantime, however, more than two hours earlier, Mike had made the telephone call that was eventually to lead to his undoing. Mrs. Mildred Elving operated the apartment house where Mike and Linda lived in Pratt. At 7:00 a.m. Central time (6:00 Mountain time) her phone rang and it was Mike. He asked her to go down to their apartment and get Linda—it was an emergency. Mrs. Elving did, and Linda came to the phone. She became hysterical while listening, and after she hung up reported "That was Mike, and he said that his grandmother burned up in a fire."

The Aftermath

Mike's first reaction to the news of his grandmother's probable death was silence, so his stepfather invited him into the house. There the first thing he did was to call the electric company serving the ranch and arrange for a hot wire at the transformer so the yard light would be on twenty-four hours a day. Then, about 10:30, he and his mother got in his truck and headed for the ranch. En route his mother wondered out loud how the fire could have started. Mike suggested first that Goldie hung her clothes around the hot water heater, and second, that she kept gasoline around for dry cleaning. The conversation turned to the state of Goldie's affairs, and Mike reassured his mother that they were all in order. He added: "Don't forget, I don't want it to cause hard feelings—But—the will is made out to me. Your sister and you get one thousand dollars apiece, and I think Carla and Bill [Mike's sister and brother] get something, but it's all mine."

They arrived at the ranch around 5:30 p.m., to find numerous police officers at the scene. At that time Mike told a K.B.I. agent that he had been at the ranch shortly after midnight to check on his grandmother. She was very drunk when he left her to go to Colorado; he only learned of the fire when he got to his mother's house at Colorado Springs. He speculated first that the fire was caused by the furnace, which had been acting up, and later thought the cause might have been pack rats chewing through the electrical wiring. He delivered to the officers the keys to Goldie's car, which was still in the garage.

An intensive and extensive search was conducted for Goldie Millar or her body, extending over a period of several weeks. The ashes at the house were sifted and resifted: the ranch was combed by men on foot, in trucks and on horseback; missing persons bulletins were circulated. Skin divers and scuba divers searched the ponds and airplanes surveyed the landscape.

The ashes of the house produced nothing in the way of human remains. Expert testimony was that a normal house fire is not hot enough to burn a human body without leaving a trace. The ashes did yield the badly charred remains of Goldie's dog, a German shepherd named Brandie. He was described as having been very devoted to and protective of her. No stranger could approach unless Goldie told Brandie to stay back. (This was the same dog that had "got hold of" Alfred Barby in the past.) Brandie's head was charred but largely intact. Later medical examination revealed a .22 caliber shell casing lodged in one eye socket. The cartridge had exploded from heat, and bore no marking from a firing pin. A .22 pistol was found in the ruins in the basement.

The officers' investigation as well as the search for Goldie continued. On April 29, K.B.I. agent Dewey interviewed Mike again, and heard him recount again his midnight visit to the ranch and his trip to Colorado. He again told of Goldie's heavy drinking, this time adding that "the house was full of Old Charter whisky bottles." He again asserted that the first he learned of the fire was in Colorado Springs at 9:00 Central time, when his stepfather told him of Ellen Davis's call.

Continued investigation began to turn up weaknesses in Mike's story. Contrary to his tales about her three week binge, all the witnesses who saw Goldie during the first week of April—and they were many—testified that she seemed normal, cheerful, and totally sober. They detected no evidence that she had been drinking. A sifting of the house ashes turned up no molten glass globules of the dark brown color characteristic of Old Charter bottles; expert testimony indicated that they would be there if such bottles had been in the house. Most critical of all, the investigators turned up Mike's telephone call to Linda, telling of the fire and his grandmother's death some two hours before he was supposed to have learned of it.

Armed with this information the officers again confronted Mike and secured a series of statements, to be discussed later, implicating him in the death of Goldie and in setting the fire. The result was a charge of first degree murder and aggravated arson, and the present conviction of first degree murder and simple arson. This appeal followed.

I. THE CORPUS DELICTI

The foregoing, rather lengthy exposition of the state's evidence is made necessary primarily by the claim on appeal that the state failed to prove the corpus delicti. While we have no reported murder case in this state in which no portion of the victim's body was found, we have recognized that "It is well-established that any material facts, including the corpus delicti itself, may be proved by direct testimony or by indirect or circumstantial evidence, or a combination of both." To the same effect, we have observed that "No exclusive mode of proof of the *corpus delicti* is prescribed by the law."

As to what must be proved we have said, "In homicide cases the *corpus delicti* is the body or substance of the crime which consists of the killing of the deceased by some criminal agency and is established by proof of two facts, that one person was killed and that another person killed him."

Even though we have not previously had occasion to consider a homicide case in which the proof of the corpus delicti was purely circumstantial, the foregoing principles clearly establish that such proof is sufficient. Many other jurisdictions have so held in murder cases where no body was found. The applicable rules are aptly stated and amply supported by citations of authority in People v. Bolinski, 260 Cal.App.2d 705, 714–15, 67 Cal.Rptr. 347, 353:

"The corpus delicti of murder consists of two elements: the death of the alleged victim and the existence of some criminal agency as the cause, either or both of which may be proved circumstantially or inferentially. [Citations omitted.] The elements must be established independently of admissions or confessions of the defendant . . . but as a basis for introduction of the defendant's confession or admission, the prosecution is not required to establish corpus delicti by proof as clear and convincing as is necessary to establish guilt; a slight or prima facie showing is sufficient. [Citations omitted.] Once corpus delicti is shown by independent evidence, the degree of the crime not being a part of the corpus delicti, the circumstances of the murder and its degree may be shown by extrajudicial statements of the accused. [Citations omitted.] It is for the trial court to determine whether a prima facie showing has been made. [Citations omitted.]

"Production of the body of the missing person or of evidence of the means used to produce death are not essential to the establishment of corpus delicti or to sustain a murder conviction. [Citations omitted.]"

In this case there was ample evidence, independent of Mike's admissions, from which first the court and later the jury might infer that Goldie was dead, and that she had been the victim of foul play. Such evidence included: the fact that she was never heard from after April 5 by her friends and customary associates; the strained relations between Mike and Goldie; the carefully constructed alibi consisting of his fabricated charges of drunkenness and the all-night trip to Colorado; the false-alarm fire of two days before; Mike's avowed intention to get the ranch "one way or the other;" and ultimately his premature display of knowledge of the fire and her death. Some of this evidence served a dual purpose; it not only showed that Goldie was dead by criminal means, but pointed the finger of guilt at Mike. The fact that it bore also on who was guilty does not detract from the efficacy of this evidence in establishing the corpus delicti. . . .

[Mike confessed on six different occasions and at one time agreed to show the officers where Goldie's body was hidden, but changed his mind after talking with his wife.]

The defense moved for an acquittal on the ground that the corpus delicti was not proved. The motion was properly overruled.

The judgment is affirmed.[1]

Approved by the Court.

KEELER v. SUPERIOR COURT OF AMADOR COUNTY

Supreme Court of California, In Bank, 1970.
2 Cal.3d 619, 87 Cal.Rptr. 481, 470 P.2d 617.

MOSK, JUSTICE. In this proceeding for writ of prohibition we are called upon to decide whether an unborn but viable fetus is a "human being" within the meaning of the California statute defining murder (Pen.Code, § 187). We conclude that the Legislature did not intend such a meaning, and that for us to construe the statute to the contrary and apply it to this petitioner would exceed our judicial power and deny petitioner due process of law.

The evidence received at the preliminary examination may be summarized as follows: Petitioner and Teresa Keeler obtained an interlocutory decree of divorce on September 27, 1968. They had been married for 16 years. Unknown to petitioner, Mrs. Keeler was then pregnant by one Ernest Vogt, whom she had met earlier that summer. She subsequently began living with Vogt in Stockton, but concealed the fact from petitioner. Petitioner was given custody of their two daughters, aged 12 and 13 years, and under the decree Mrs. Keeler had the right to take the girls on alternate weekends.

On February 23, 1969, Mrs. Keeler was driving on a narrow mountain road in Amador County after delivering the girls to their home. She met petitioner driving in the opposite direction; he blocked the road with his car, and she pulled over to the side. He walked to her vehicle and began speaking to her. He seemed calm, and she rolled down her window to hear him. He said, "I hear you're pregnant. If you are you had better stay away from the girls and from here."

1. Defendant's extrajudicial admissions of essential facts are of the same character as confessions and require corroboration. This is true even if in the form of an "exculpatory statement." But in such a case it is sufficient if there is evidence *aliunde* which tends to establish the trustworthiness of the admission and to establish every element of the *corpus delicti.* Opper v. United States, 348 U.S. 84, 75 S.Ct. 158 (1954).

"Once prima facie proof of the corpus delicti is made, the extrajudicial statements, admissions and confessions of a defendant may be considered in determining whether all the elements of a crime have been established." People v. Duncan, 51 Cal.2d 523, 528, 334 P.2d 858, 861 (1959).

"The corpus delicti rule is satisfied 'by the introduction of evidence which creates a reasonable inference that death could have been caused by a criminal agency . . . even in the presence of an equally plausible noncriminal explanation of the event.'" People v. Towler, 31 Cal.3d 105, 181 Cal.Rptr. 391, 641 P.2d 1253 (1982).

D's admissions at the time of the arrest, and at the place where evidence of the crime then being perpetrated was found, were part of the *res gestae* and admissible for that reason. State v. La Rue, 67 N.M. 149, 353 P.2d 367 (1960). The charge was operating a game of chance.

She did not reply, and he opened the car door; as she later testified, "He assisted me out of the car. . . . [I]t wasn't roughly at this time." Petitioner then looked at her abdomen and became "extremely upset." He said, "You sure are. I'm going to stomp it out of you." He pushed her against the car, shoved his knee into her abdomen, and struck her in the face with several blows. She fainted, and when she regained consciousness petitioner had departed.

Mrs. Keeler drove back to Stockton, and the police and medical assistance were summoned. She had suffered substantial facial injuries, as well as extensive bruising of the abdominal wall. A Caesarian section was performed and the fetus was examined *in utero*. Its head was found to be severely fractured, and it was delivered stillborn. The pathologist gave as his opinion that the cause of death was skull fracture with consequent cerebral hemorrhaging, that death would have been immediate, and that the injury could have been the result of force applied to the mother's abdomen. There was no air in the fetus' lungs, and the umbilical cord was intact.

Upon delivery the fetus weighed five pounds and was 18 inches in length. Both Mrs. Keeler and her obstetrician testified that fetal movements had been observed prior to February 23, 1969. The evidence was in conflict as to the estimated age of the fetus;[1] the expert testimony on the point, however, concluded "with reasonable medical certainty" that the fetus had developed to the stage of viability, i.e., that in the event of premature birth on the date in question it would have had a 75 percent to 96 percent chance of survival.

An information was filed charging petitioner, in Count I, with committing the crime of murder (Pen.Code, § 187) in that he did "unlawfully kill a human being, to wit Baby Girl VOGT, with malice aforethought." In Count II petitioner was charged with wilful infliction of traumatic injury upon his wife (Pen.Code, § 273d), and in Count III, with assault on Mrs. Keeler by means of force likely to produce great bodily injury (Pen.Code, § 245). His motion to set aside the information for lack of probable cause (Pen.Code, § 995) was denied, and he now seeks a writ of prohibition; as will appear, only the murder count is actually in issue. Pending our disposition of the matter, petitioner is free on bail.

I

Penal Code section 187 provides: "Murder is the unlawful killing of a human being, with malice aforethought." The dispositive ques-

1. Mrs. Keeler testified, in effect, that she had no sexual intercourse with Vogt prior to August 1968, which would have made the fetus some 28 weeks old. She stated that the pregnancy had reached the end of the seventh month and the projected delivery date was April 25, 1969. The obstetrician, however, first estimated she was at least 31½ weeks pregnant, then raised the figure to 35 weeks in the light of the autopsy report of the size and weight of the fetus. Finally, on similar evidence an attending pediatrician estimated the gestation period to have been between 34½ and 36 weeks. The average full-term pregnancy is 40 weeks.

tion is whether the fetus which petitioner is accused of killing was, on February 23, 1969, a "human being" within the meaning of this statute. If it was not, petitioner cannot be charged with its "murder" and prohibition will lie.

Section 187 was enacted as part of the Penal Code of 1872. Inasmuch as the provision has not been amended since that date, we must determine the intent of the Legislature at the time of its enactment. But section 187 was, in turn, taken verbatim from the first California statute defining murder, part of the Crimes and Punishments Act of 1850. (Stats.1850, ch. 99, § 19, p. 231.)[2] Penal Code section 5 (also enacted in 1872) declares: "The provisions of this Code, so far as they are substantially the same as existing statutes, must be construed as continuations thereof, and not as new enactments." We begin, accordingly, by inquiring into the intent of the Legislature in 1850 when it first defined murder as the unlawful and malicious killing of a "human being."

It will be presumed, of course, that in enacting a statute the Legislature was familiar with the relevant rules of the common law, and, when it couches its enactment in common law language, that its intent was to continue those rules in statutory form. (Baker v. Baker (1859) 13 Cal. 87, 95–96; Morris v. Oney (1963) 217 Cal.App.2d 864, 870, 32 Cal.Rptr. 88.) This is particularly appropriate in considering the work of the first session of our Legislature: its precedents were necessarily drawn from the common law, as modified in certain respects by the Constitution and by legislation of our sister states.

We therefore undertake a brief review of the origins and development of the common law of abortional homicide. (For a more detailed treatment, see Means, The Law of New York concerning Abortion and the Status of the Foetus, 1664–1968: A Case of Cessation of Constitutionality (1968) 14 N.Y.L.F. 411 [hereinafter cited as Means]; Stern, Abortion: Reform and the Law (1968) 59 J.Crim.L., C. & P.S. 84; Quay, Justifiable Abortion—Medical and Legal Foundations II (1961) 49 Geo.L.J. 395.) From that inquiry it appears that by the year 1850—the date with which we are concerned—an infant could not be the subject of homicide at common law *unless it had been born alive.* Perhaps the most influential statement of the "born alive" rule is that of Coke, in mid-17th century: "If a woman be quick with childe, and by a potion or otherwise killeth it in her wombe, or if a man beat her, whereby the childe dyeth in her body, and she is delivered of a dead childe, this is a great misprision [i.e., misdemeanor], and no murder; but if the childe be born alive and dyeth of the potion, battery, or other cause, this is murder; for in law it is accounted a reasonable

2. "Murder is the unlawful killing of a human being, with malice aforethought, either express or implied. The unlawful killing may be effected by any of the various means by which death may be occasioned." The revisers of 1872 did no more than transpose the "express or implied malice" language of this provision to the following section (§ 188), and delete the second sentence as surplusage. (Code Commissioners' Note, Pen.Code of Cal. (1st ed. 1872), p. 80.)

creature, *in rerum natura,* when it is born alive." (3 Coke, Institutes *58 (1648).) In short, "By Coke's time, the common law regarded abortion as murder only if the foetus is (1) quickened, (2) born alive, (3) lives for a brief interval, and (4) then dies." (Means, at p. 420.) Whatever intrinsic defects there may have been in Coke's work (see 3 Stephen, A History of the Criminal Law of England (1883) pp. 52–60), the common law accepted his views as authoritative. In the 18th century, for example, Coke's requirement that an infant be born alive in order to be the subject of homicide was reiterated and expanded by both Blackstone and Hale. . . .

We conclude that in declaring murder to be the unlawful and malicious killing of a "human being" the Legislature of 1850 intended that term to have the settled common law meaning of a person who had been born alive, and did not intend the act of feticide—as distinguished from abortion—to be an offense under the laws of California. . . .

Properly understood, the often cited case of People v. Chavez (1947) 77 Cal.App.2d 621, 176 P.2d 92, does not derogate from this rule. There the defendant was charged with the murder of her newborn child, and convicted of manslaughter. She testified that the baby dropped from her womb into the toilet bowl; that she picked it up two or three minutes later, and cut but did not tie the umbilical cord; that the baby was limp and made no cry; and that after 15 minutes she wrapped it in a newspaper and concealed it, where it was found dead the next day. The autopsy surgeon testified that the baby was a full-term, nine-month child, weighing six and one-half pounds and appearing normal in every respect; that the body had very little blood in it, indicating the child had bled to death through the untied umbilical cord; that such a process would have taken about an hour; and that in his opinion "the child was born alive, based on conditions he found and the fact that the lungs contained air and the blood was extravasated or pushed back into the tissues, indicating heart action." (Id. at p. 624, 176 P.2d at p. 93.)

On appeal, the defendant emphasized that a doctor called by the defense had suggested other tests which the autopsy surgeon could have performed to determine the matter of live birth; on this basis, it was contended that the question of whether the infant was born alive "rests entirely on pure speculation." (Id. at p. 624, 176 P.2d 92.) The Court of Appeal found only an insignificant conflict in that regard (id. at p. 627, 176 P.2d 92), and focused its attention instead on testimony of the autopsy surgeon admitting the possibility that the evidence of heart and lung action could have resulted from the child's breathing "after presentation of the head but before the birth was completed" (id. at p. 624, 176 P.2d at p. 93).

The court cited the mid-19th century English infanticide cases mentioned hereinabove, and noted that the decisions had not reached uniformity on whether breathing, heart action, severance of the umbilical cord, or some combination of these or other factors established the status of "human being" for purposes of the law of homicide. (Id. at pp. 624–625, 176 P.2d 92.) The court then adverted to the state of modern medical knowledge, discussed the phenomenon of viability, and held that "a viable child *in the process of being born* is a human being within the meaning of the homicide statutes, whether or not the process has been fully completed. It should at least be considered a human being where it is a living baby and where in the natural course of events *a birth which is already started* would naturally be successfully completed." (Italics added.) (Id. at p. 626, 176 P.2d at p. 94.) Since the testimony of the autopsy surgeon left no doubt in that case that a live birth had at least begun, the court found "the evidence is sufficient here to support the implied finding of the jury that this child *was born alive and became a human being within the meaning of the homicide statutes.*" (Italics added.) (Id. at p. 627, 176 P.2d at p. 95.)[19]

Chavez thus stands for the proposition—to which we adhere—that a viable fetus "in the process of being born" is a human being within the meaning of the homicide statutes. But it stands for no more; in particular it does not hold that a fetus, however viable, which is *not* "in the process of being born" is nevertheless a "human being in the law of homicide. On the contrary, the opinion is replete with references to the common law requirement that the child be "born alive," however that term is defined, and must accordingly be deemed to reaffirm that requirement as part of the law of California.[20] . . . And the text writers of the same period are no less unanimous on the point. (Perkins on Criminal Law, supra, pp. 29–30; Clark & Marshall, Crimes (6th ed. 1958) § 10.00, pp. 534–536; 1 Wharton, Criminal Law and Procedure (Anderson ed. 1957) § 189; 2 Burdick, Law of Crime (1946) § 445; 40 Am.Jur.2d, Homicide, §§ 9, 434; 40 C.J.S. Homicide § 2b.)

We conclude that the judicial enlargement of section 187 now urged upon us by the People would not have been foreseeable to this petitioner, and hence that its adoption at this time would deny him due process of law.

19. Penal Code section 192, which the defendant in *Chavez* was convicted of violating, defines manslaughter as "the unlawful killing of a human being without malice."

20. In People v. Belous (1969) 71 Cal. 2d 954, 968, 80 Cal.Rptr. 354, 458 P.2d 194, a majority of this court recognized "there are major and decisive areas where the embryo and fetus are not treated as equivalent to the born child. . . . The intentional destruction of the born child is murder or manslaughter. The intentional destruction of the embryo or fetus is never treated as murder, and only rarely as manslaughter but rather as the lesser offense of abortion." While the case was decided after the occurrence of the acts with which petitioner is charged, it nonetheless indicates that *Chavez* did not change California law on this point. Indeed, in footnote 13 we proceeded to distinguish *Chavez* as a case holding that "for purposes of the manslaughter and murder statutes, human life may exist where childbirth has commenced but has not been fully completed." (Accord, Perkins on Criminal Law (2d ed. 1969), p. 30.) In the case at bar, of course, the record is devoid of evidence that "childbirth" had commenced at the time of the acts charged.

Corpus-Delicti case

Let a peremptory writ of prohibition issue restraining respondent court from taking any further proceedings on Count I of the information, charging petitioner with the crime of murder.[a]

a. [Added by the Compiler.] Even if a malicious attack on a pregnant woman caused an eight-month-old fetus to be born dead, this does not constitute murder. State v. Gyles, 313 So.2d 799 (La. 1975).

Fetuses which are the victims of a criminal blow or wound upon their mother, and are subsequently born alive, and thereafter die by reason of a chain of circumstances precipitated by such blow or wound, may be victims of murder. State v. Anderson, 135 N.J.Super. 423, 343 A.2d 505 (1975).

Some statutes provide that the unlawful killing of an unborn fetus may be deemed manslaughter. See State v. Shaw, 219 So.2d 49 (Fla.1969). The Florida statute reads: "The wilful killing of an unborn quick child, by an injury to the mother of such child which would be murder if it resulted in the death of such mother, shall be deemed manslaughter." F.S.A. § 782.09. See also the differently-worded statute in State v. Barnett, 249 Or. 226, 437 P.2d 821 (1968) and Goodman v. State, 573 P.2d 400 (Wyo.1977).

"It has always been difficult to procure conviction in cases like these. The necessary evidence is hard to obtain. In England there is a statute making it a crime to conceal the birth of an infant, and reference to the English cases will show that most of the convictions obtained are of concealment and not of murder." Morgan v. State, 148 Tenn. 417, 421, 256 S.W. 433, 434 (1923).

Aftermath, Cal.Pen.Code § 187. "Murder is the unlawful killing of a human being, *or a fetus*, with malice aforethought. . . ." The words in italics were added by amendment in 1970, "triggered" by *Keeler*. Legal abortions are excluded from the current California statute.

The California statute defining murder of a fetus is not unconstitutionally vague. People v. Apodaca, 76 Cal.App. 3d 479, 142 Cal.Rptr. 830 (1977).

In accepting the "brain-death" theory of death it was held that removal of artificial life-support system from homicide victim after all electrical activity in the brain had ceased was not an independent, intervening cause of death so as to relieve defendant of criminal responsibility. In other words, the victim was dead although his heartbeat could have been continued for some time by artificial means. People v. Saldana, 47 Cal.App.3d 954, 121 Cal.Rptr. 243 (1975).

"Because of increased interest in organ transplants, it was felt by some that a different definition of death was necessary. As a result, the National Conference of Commissioners on Uniform State Laws proposed the Uniform Brain Death Act that stated, 'for legal and medical purposes an individual who has sustained irreversible cessation of all functioning of the brain including the brain stem is dead.' The uniform law provides that a determination of brain death must be made 'in accordance with reasonable medical standards.'" State v. Fierro, 124 Ariz. 182, 603 P.2d 74, 77–78 (1979). "Brain death" is sufficient to establish death in a case of criminal homicide. Commonwealth v. Golston, 373 Mass. 249, 366 N.E.2d 744 (1977). Now we have a Uniform Determination of Death Act. "An individual who has sustained either (1) irreversible cessation of circulatory and respiratory functions, or (2) irreversible cessation of all functions of the entire brain, including the brain stem, is dead." This was accepted as a statement of the common law in In re Welfare of Bowman, 94 Wn.2d 407, 617 P.2d 731 (1980).

"In the absence of statute, the term 'person', 'human being', 'another' (in the context 'person') do not include an unborn fetus for the purposes of the crime of homicide." State v. Larsen, 578 P.2d 1280, 1282 (Utah 1978).

Death occurring to a child because an assault on the mother before death of the child is sufficient to sustain a murder conviction where the child was born alive, had spontaneous respiration and heart rate, and survived 12 hours before dying from a condition caused by premature birth due to the assault. Ranger v. State, 249 Ga. 315, 290 S.E.2d 63 (1982).

At common law the death of the victim had to occur within a year and a day after receiving injury by the defendant in order for a homicide prosecution against the defendant to be sustained. In many jurisdictions there has been a trend away from the common-law rule. People v. Stevenson, 416 Mich. 383, 331 N.W.2d 143 (1982).

McCOMB, PETERS, and TOBRINER, JJ., and PEEK, J. pro tem.,* concur.

BURKE, Acting Chief Justice (dissenting). . . .

SULLIVAN, J., concurs.

PATTERSON v. NEW YORK

Supreme Court of the United States, 1977.

432 U.S. 197, 97 S.Ct. 2319.

MR. JUSTICE WHITE delivered the opinion of the Court.

The question here is the constitutionality under the Fourteenth Amendment's Due Process Clause of burdening the defendant in a New York State murder trial with proving the affirmative defense of extreme emotional disturbance as defined by New York law.

After a brief and unstable marriage, the appellant, Gordon Patterson, became estranged from his wife, Roberta. Roberta resumed an association with John Northrup, a neighbor to whom she had been engaged prior to her marriage to appellant. On December 27, 1970, Patterson borrowed a rifle from an acquaintance and went to the residence of his father-in-law. There, he observed his wife through a window in a state of semiundress in the presence of John Northrup. He entered the house and killed Northrup by shooting him twice in the head.

Patterson was charged with second-degee murder. In New York there are two elements of this crime: (1) "intent to cause the death of another person"; and (2) "caus[ing] the death of such person or of a third person." N.Y. Penal Law § 125.25 (McKinney 1975). Malice aforethought is not an element of the crime. In addition, the State permits a person accused of murder to raise an affirmative defense that he "acted under the influence of extreme emotional disturbance for which there was a reasonable explanation or excuse."

New York also recognizes the crime of manslaughter. A person is guilty of manslaughter if he intentionally kills another person "under circumstances which do not constitute murder because he acts under the influence of extreme emotional disturbance." Appellant confessed before trial to killing Northrup, but at trial he raised the defense of extreme emotional disturbance.

The jury was instructed as to the elements of the crime of murder. Focusing on the element of intent, the trial court charged,

* Retired Associate Justice of the Supreme Court sitting under assignment by the Acting Chairman of the Judicial Council.

"Before you, considering all of the evidence, can convict this defendant or any one of murder, you must believe and decide that the People have established beyond a reasonable doubt that he intended, in firing the gun, to kill either the victim himself or some other human being. . . . Always remember that you must not expect or require the defendant to prove to your satisfaction that his acts were done without the intent to kill. Whatever proof he may have attempted, however far he may have gone in an effort to convince you of his innocence or guiltlessness, he is not obliged, he is not obligated to prove anything. It is always the People's burden to prove his guilt, and to prove that he intended to kill in this instance beyond a reasonable doubt." . . .

The jury was further instructed, consistently with New York law, that the defendant had the burden of proving his affirmative defense by a preponderance of the evidence. The jury was told that if it found beyond a reasonable doubt that appellant had intentionally killed Northrup but that appellant had demonstrated by a preponderance of the evidence that he had acted under the influence of extreme emotional disturbance, it must find appellant guilty of manslaughter instead of murder.

The jury found appellant guilty of murder. . . . While appeal to the New York Court of Appeals was pending, this Court decided Mullaney v. Wilbur, 421 U.S. 684, 95 S.Ct. 1881, 44 L.Ed.2d 508 (1975), in which the Court declared Maine's murder statute unconstitutional. Under the Maine statute, a person accused of murder could rebut the statutory presumption that he committed the offense with "malice aforethought" by proving that he acted in the heat of passion on sudden provocation. The Court held that this scheme improperly shifted the burden of persuasion from the prosecutor to the defendant and was therefore a violation of due process. In the Court of Appeals appellant urged that New York's murder statute is functionally equivalent to the one struck down in Mullaney and that therefore his conviction should be reversed.

The Court of Appeals rejected appellant's argument, holding that the New York murder statute is consistent with due process. . . .

In determining whether New York's allocation to the defendant of proving the mitigating circumstances of severe emotional disturbance is consistent with due process, it is therefore relevant to note that this defense is a considerably expanded version of the common law defense of heat of passion on sudden provocation and that at common law the burden of proving the latter, as well as other affirmative defenses—indeed, "all . . . circumstances of justification, excuse or alleviation"—rested on the defendant. 4 W. Blackstone, Commentaries *201; M. Foster, Crown Law 255 (1762); Mullaney v. Wilbur, supra, 421 U.S., at 693–694, 95 S.Ct., at 1886–1887. This was the rule when the Fifth Amendment was adopted, and it was the American rule when the Fourteenth Amendment was ratified.

In 1895 the common law view was abandoned with respect to the insanity defense in federal prosecutions. This ruling had wide impact on the practice in the federal courts with respect to the burden of proving various affirmative defenses, and the prosecution in a majority of jurisdictions in this country sooner or later came to shoulder the burden of proving the sanity of the accused and of disproving the facts constituting other affirmative defenses, including provocation. . . .

[In Leland v. Oregon, 343 U.S. 790, 72 S.Ct. 1002 (1958), the Supreme Court upheld the constitutionality of requiring a defendant to prove his insanity beyond a reasonable doubt.]

In 1970, the court declared that the Due Process Clause "protects the accused against conviction except upon proof beyond a reasonable doubt of every fact necessary to constitute the crime with which he is charged." . . . [T]he Court further announced that under the Maine law of homicide, the burden could not constitutionally be placed on the defendant of proving by a preponderance of the evidence that the killing had occurred in the heat of passion on sudden provocation. . . .

Subsequently, the Court confirmed that it remained constitutional to burden the defendant with proving his insanity defense when it dismissed, as not raising a substantial federal question, a case to which the appellant specifically challenged the continuing validity of Leland v. Oregon. . . .

We cannot conclude that Patterson's conviction under the New York law deprived him of due process of law. The crime of murder is defined by the statute, which represents a recent revision of the State criminal code, as causing the death of another person with intent to do so. The death, the intent to kill, and causation are the facts that the State is required to prove beyond reasonable doubt if a person is convicted of murder. No further facts are either presumed or inferred in order to constitute the crime. The statute does provide an affirmative defense—that the defendant acted under the influence of extreme emotional disturbance for which there was a reasonable explanation—which, if proved by a preponderance of the evidence, would reduce the crime to manslaughter, an offense defined in a separate section of the statute. It is plain enough that if the intentional killing is shown, the State intends to deal with the defendant as a murderer unless he demonstrates the mitigating circumstances.

Here, the jury was instructed in accordance with the statute, and the guilty verdict confirms that the State successfully carried its burden of proving the facts of the crime beyond reasonable doubt. Nothing in the evidence, including any evidence that might have been offered with respect to Patterson's mental state at the time of the crime, raised a reasonable doubt about his guilt as a murderer; and clearly the evidence failed to convince the jury that Patterson's affirmative defense had been made out.

In convicting Patterson under its murder statute, New York did no more than Leland and Rivera permitted it to do without violating the Due Process Clause. Under those cases, once the facts constituting a crime are established beyond reasonable doubt, based on all the evidence including the evidence of the defendant's mental state, the State may refuse to sustain the affirmative defense of insanity unless demonstrated by a preponderance of the evidence.

The New York law on extreme emotional disturbance follows this pattern. . . . Here, in revising its criminal code, New York provided the affirmative defense of extreme emotional disturbance, a substantially expanded version of the older heat of passion concept; but it was willing to do so only if the facts making out the defense were established by the defendant with sufficient certainty. The State was itself unwilling to undertake to establish the absence of those facts beyond reasonable doubt, perhaps fearing that proof would be too difficult and that too many persons deserving treatment as murderers would escape that punishment if the evidence need merely raise a reasonable doubt about the defendant's emotional state. It has been said that the new criminal code of New York contains some 25 affirmative defenses which exculpate or mitigate but which must be established by the defendant to be operative.[1] The Due Process Clause, as we see it, does not put New York to the choice of abandoning those defenses or undertaking to disprove their existence in order to convict for a crime which otherwise is within its constitutional powers to sanction by substantial punishment.

The requirement of proof beyond reasonable doubt in a criminal case is "bottomed on a fundamental value determination of our society that it is far worse to convict an innocent man than to let a guilty man go free." The social cost of placing the burden on the prosecution to prove guilt beyond a reasonable doubt is thus an increased risk that the guilty will go free. While it is clear that our society has

1. The State of New York is not alone in this result:

"Since the Model Penal Code was completed in 1962, some 22 states have codified and reformed their criminal laws. At least 12 of these jurisdictions have used the concept of an 'affirmative defense' and have defined that phrase to require that the defendant prove the existence of an 'affirmative defense' by a preponderance of the evidence. Additionally, at least six proposed state codes and each of the four successive versions of a revised federal code use the same procedural device. Finally, many jurisdictions that do not generally employ this concept of 'affirmative defense' nevertheless shift the burden of proof to the defendant on particular issues." . . .

willingly chosen to bear a substantial burden in order to protect the innocent, it is equally clear that the risk it must bear is not without limits; and Justice Harlan's aphorism provides little guidance for determining what those limits are. . . .

It is said that the common law rule permits a State to punish one as a murderer when it is as likely as not that he acted in the heat of passion or under severe emotional distress and when, if he did, he is guilty only of manslaughter. But this has always been the case in those jurisdictions adhering to the traditional rule. It is also very likely true that fewer convictions for murder would occur if New York were required to negative the affirmative defense at issue here. But in each instance of a murder conviction under the present law, New York will have proved beyond reasonable doubt that the defendant has intentionally killed another person, an act which it is not disputed the State may constitutionally criminalize and punish. If the State nevertheless chooses to recognize a factor that mitigates the degree of criminality or punishment, we think the State may assure itself that the fact has been established with reasonable certainty. To recognize at all a mitigating circumstance does not require the State to prove its nonexistence in each case in which the fact is put in issue, if in its judgment this would be too cumbersome, too expensive, and too inaccurate.[2]

We thus decline to adopt as a constitutional imperative, operative country-wide, that a State must disprove beyond reasonable doubt every fact constituting any and all affirmative defenses related to the culpability of an accused. Traditionally, due process has required that only the most basic procedural safeguards be observed; more subtle balancing of society's interests against those of the accused have been left to the legislative branch. We therefore will not disturb the balance struck in previous cases holding that the Due Process Clause requires the prosecution to prove beyond reasonable doubt all of the elements included in the definition of the offense of which the defendant is charged. Proof of the nonexistence of all affirmative defenses has never been constitutionally required; and we perceive no reason to fashion such a rule in this case and apply it to the statutory defense at issue here.

2. The drafters of the Model Penal Code would, as a matter of policy, place the burden of proving the nonexistence of most affirmative defenses, including the defense involved in this case, on the prosecution once the defendant has come forward with some evidence that the defense is present. The drafters recognize the need for flexibility, however, and would, in "some exceptional situations," place the burden of persuasion on the accused. "Characteristically these are situations where the defense does not obtain at all under existing law and the Code seeks to introduce a mitigation. Resistance to the mitigation, based upon the prosecution's difficulty in obtaining evidence, ought to be lowered if the burden of persuasion is imposed on the defendant. Where that difficulty appears genuine and there is something to be said against allowing the defense at all, we consider it defensible to shift the burden in this way." ALI, Model Penal Code § 1.13, Comment, p. 113 (Tentative Draft No. 4, 1955).

This view may seem to permit state legislatures to reallocate burdens of proof by labeling as affirmative defenses at least some elements of the crimes now defined in their statutes. But there are obviously constitutional limits beyond which the States may not go in this regard. "[I]t is not within the province of a legislature to declare an individual guilty or presumptively guilty of a crime." . . . The legislature cannot "validly command that the finding of an indictment, or mere proof of the identity of the accused, should create a presumption of the existence of all the facts essential to guilt." . . .

It is urged that Mullaney v. Wilbur necessarily invalidates Patterson's conviction. In Mullaney the charge was murder, which the Maine statute defined as the unlawful killing of a human being "with malice aforethought either express or implied." The trial court instructed the jury that the words "malice aforethought" were most important "because malice aforethought is an essential and indispensable element of the crime of murder." Malice, as the statute indicated and as the court instructed, could be implied and was to be implied from "any deliberate, cruel act committed by one person against another suddenly or without a considerable provocation," in which event an intentional killing was murder unless by a preponderance of the evidence it was shown that the act was committed "in the heat of passion upon sudden provocation." The instructions emphasized that "malice aforethought and heat of passion on sudden provocation are two inconsistent things"; thus, by proving the latter the defendant would negate the former." . . .

Mullaney's holding, it is argued, is that the State may not permit the blameworthiness of an act or the severity of punishment authorized for its commission to depend on the presence or absence of an identified fact without assuming the burden of proving the presence or absence of that fact, as the case may be, beyond reasonable doubt. In our view, the Mullaney holding should not be so broadly read. . . .

Mullaney surely held that a State must prove every ingredient of an offense beyond a reasonable doubt, and that it may not shift the burden of proof to the defendant by presuming that ingredient upon proof of the other elements of the offense. This is true even though the State's practice, as in Maine, had been traditionally to the contrary. Such shifting of the burden of persuasion with respect to a fact which the State deems so important that it must be either proved or presumed is impermissible under the Due Process Clause.

It was unnecessary to go further in Mullaney. The Maine Supreme Court made it clear that malice aforethought, which was mentioned in the statutory definition of the crime, was not equivalent to premeditation and that the presumption of malice traditionally arising in intentional homicide cases carried no factual meaning insofar as premeditation was concerned. Even so, a killing became murder in

Maine when it resulted from a deliberate, cruel act committed by one person against another, "suddenly, and without any, or without considerable, provocation." Premeditation was not within the definition of murder; but malice, in the sense of the absence of provocation, was part of the definition of that crime. Yet malice, i.e., lack of provocation, was presumed and could be rebutted by the defendant only by proving a preponderance of the evidence that he acted with heat of passion upon sudden provocation. In Mullaney we held that however traditional this mode of proceeding might have been, it is contrary to the Due Process Clause as construed in Winship.

As we have explained, nothing was presumed or implied against Patterson; and his conviction is not invalid under any of our prior cases. The judgment of the New York Court of Appeals is affirmed.[3]

ERRINGTON and OTHERS' CASE

Newcastle Assizes, 1838.
2 Lewin C.C. 217, 168 Eng.Rep. 1133.

. . .

The case against the prisoners was a very serious one. It appeared, that the deceased, being in liquor, had gone at night into a glass-house, and laid himself down upon a chest: and that while he was there asleep the prisoners covered and surrounded him with straw, and threw a shovel of hot cinders upon his belly; the consequence of which was, that the straw ignited, and he was burnt to death.

3. In a murder trial, proof of defendant's commission of the homicide by evidence not tending to show any justification, excuse or mitigation, places upon him the burden of establishing the existence of any such factor if he can. State v. Burris, 80 Idaho 395, 331 P.2d 265 (1958).

The people do not have to disprove self-defense where there are no facts that raise the issue. People v. Martin, 61 Mich.App. 102, 232 N.W.2d 191 (1975).

Where under Montana's deliberate homicide law the jury was instructed that "the law presumes that a person intends the ordinary consequences of his lawful acts", it was held the instruction denied the defendant due process by shifting the burden of proof on the issue of purpose or knowledge. "Because David Sandstrom's jury may have interpreted the judge's instruction as constituting either a burden-shifting presumption . . . or a conclusive presumption . . . and because either interpretation would have deprived defendant of his right to the due process of law, we hold the instruction given in this case unconstitutional." Sandstrom v. Montana, 442 U.S. 510, 524, 99 S.Ct. 2450 (1979).

Instruction that "when there are no circumstances to prevent or rebut the presumption, the law presumes that a reasonable person intends all the natural, probable and usual consequences of his deliberate acts" did not violate due process. Pigee v. Israel, 670 F.2d 690 (7th Cir.1982).

Instruction that "design to effect death . . . may be inferred from the fact of killing unless the circumstances raise a reasonable doubt whether such a design existed" is merely a permissible inference and is not improper. Thibodeau v. State, 298 N.W.2d 818 (S.D.1980). Accord Mancuso v. Harris, 677 F.2d 206 (2d Cir.1982). See also Mason v. Balkcom, 669 F.2d 222 (5th Cir.1982).

The felony murder does not create an unconstitutional presumption of malice aforethought. People v. Sims, 136 Cal. App.3d 942, 186 Cal.Rptr. 793 (1982).

There was no evidence in the case of express malice; but the conduct of the prisoners indicated an entire recklessness of consequences, hardly consistent with anything short of design.

PATTESON, J., cited from the text books the law applicable to the case, and pointed the attention of the jury to the distinctions which characterise murder and manslaughter. He then adverted to the fact of there being no evidence of express malice; but told them, that if they believed the prisoners really intended to do any serious injury to the deceased, although not to kill him, it was murder; but if they believed their intention to have been only to frighten him in sport, it was manslaughter.

The jury took a merciful view of the case, and returned a verdict of manslaughter only.

COMMONWEALTH v. McLAUGHLIN

Supreme Court of Pennsylvania, 1928.
293 Pa. 218, 142 A. 213.

Opinion by MR. JUSTICE SCHAFFER, May 7, 1928.

Defendant, a young man, twenty years of age at the time of the occurrence we are to deal with, appeals from his conviction and sentence for murder of the second degree, contending that the evidence produced against him did not establish this crime.

With two companions he was driving his father's automobile about half past ten o'clock at night along Northampton Street in Wilkes-Barre Township in the County of Luzerne. His progress was down grade and was at the rate of twenty or twenty-five miles an hour. The highway was well lighted. Frank Ravitt and his wife were walking in the cartway of the street ahead of and in the same direction as the automobile, their presence within the street limits and not on the sidewalk being due to the pavement's bad condition. They were at the right-hand side of the center of the cartway, the wife in or near the street car track, the husband on her right. He was pushing a baby coach in which was their infant child. Defendant so drove his automobile that it struck the group in the cartway, killing the husband and the baby and seriously injuring the wife. The impact was with such force as to knock the bodies of the man and woman a distance of from twenty-five to fifty feet and the child out of the coach and over onto the pavement. There was a dispute in the testimony as to whether the lights on the automobile were lit and as to whether defendant sounded his horn as he approached the stricken people; whether he was intoxicated was likewise a controverted fact.

One of the Commonwealth's most material witnesses, Lawrence Brosinski, the only person except defendant and the two others who were in the car with him who actually saw the tragedy, testified that if defendant "had swung his machine toward the side instead of the middle of the road he would never have struck these people." Defendant's story in amplification of this was that he blew his horn and noticed the two persons walking in the center of the road, that he had ample room to pass them to the right, that when he blew his horn "they seemed to be going to the left, and all of a sudden they veered to the right, and as they did I applied my brakes, but it was too late. I had already struck them—he [the husband] seemed to dart to the right quicker than I could get the machine stopped." In this recital he was corroborated by the two young men who were in the car with him. The automobile ran some distance, perhaps 200 feet beyond the point of the collision. Defendant and his companions ascribed this to the circumstance that in his excitement he took his foot off the brake. It appeared in the prosecution's case by the testimony of more than one witness that the brakes were applied, as they heard their screeching before the crash. Immediately after the automobile stopped, defendant ran back, picked up the woman and aided in placing her and the husband in automobiles, one of them in his own, to convey them to the hospital. Upon this evidence the jury found defendant guilty of murder of the second degree and the question to be decided is whether that finding can be sustained.

Murder, as defined by the common law, consists of the unlawful killing of a human being with malice aforethought, express or implied: Com. v. Harman, 4 Pa. 269, 271. Malice is a legal term which comprehends not only a particular ill will, but every case where there is wickedness of disposition, hardness of heart, cruelty, recklessness of consequences, or a mind regardless of social duty: Com. v. Drum, 58 Pa. 9, 15. In this State the legislature has divided the common law crime of murder into two degrees. The statute defines murder of the first degree, and then provides that "all other kinds of murder shall be deemed murder of the second degree": Act of March 31, 1860, P.L. 332, section 74. Thus murder of the second degree is common law murder, but the killing is not accompanied by the distinguishing features of murder of the first degree. The crime includes every element which enters into murder of the first degree except the intention to kill. "Premeditation is essential as in other cases of murder". It is apparent, therefore, that malice is a necessary element of the crime of murder of the second degree, and it was with this in view that we recently said "it is rarely that the facts in a motor vehicle accident will sustain a charge of murder. The element of malice is usually missing. There must be a consciousness of peril or probable peril to human life imputed to the operator of a car before he can be held for murder". In the present case one of the things which seems to have been given much weight by the court below in its opinion sustaining the conviction was defendant's failure to see the people on the road in time to avoid striking them. This negatives any specific intent to injure them. Unless he intended to strike them, which we think it manifest from the evidence he did not, or was recklessly disregardful of their safety, which the testimony does not establish, he could not legally be convicted of murder. Malice may be inferred from the wanton and reckless conduct of one who kills another from wicked disregard of the consequences of his acts, but here defend-  ant's actions after the collision negative the idea of wickedness of disposition or hardness of heart. He endeavored as best he knew how to care for those he had injured. Moreover, it cannot be implied from the circumstances of the accident that defendant was driving his car with wanton disregard of the rights and safety of others upon the highway. The mere fact that he was intoxicated (conceding this to have been proved), without more being shown, would not sustain the conviction. Consequently, we are of the opinion that it could not properly be found, upon the evidence presented, that defendant either purposely, intentionally, recklessly, or wantonly drove his car upon the deceased, and therefore that he should not have been convicted of murder.

If defendant was guilty of any crime, it was that of involuntary manslaughter, which consists in "the killing of another without malice and unintentionally, but in doing some unlawful act not amounting to a felony nor naturally tending to cause death or great bodily harm, or in negligently doing some act lawful in itself, or by the negligent omission to perform a legal duty".

Defendant may still be tried on the indictment charging involuntary manslaughter, notwithstanding that the district attorney entered a nolle prosequi on the indictment. A nolle prosequi is a voluntary withdrawal by the prosecuting attorney of present proceedings on a particular bill. At common law it might at any time be retracted, and was not a bar to a subsequent prosecution on another indictment, but it might be so far cancelled as to permit a revival of the proceedings on the original bill. Whatever the rule may be elsewhere, such action in this jurisdiction is not a bar to a subsequent indictment for the same offense, or may be so far cancelled as to permit a revival of proceedings on the original bill.

The first assignment of error is sustained and the judgment of sentence is reversed without prejudice to the Commonwealth's right to proceed against defendant for the crime of involuntary manslaughter.[1]

Dissenting Opinion by MR. JUSTICE SIMPSON:

The majority opinion states that defendant, while driving his father's automobile struck three persons who were travelling in front of him and going in the same direction he was, killing two of them

1. D and another were engaged in an automobile race on a state highway at a speed of from 100 to 120 miles an hour. While traveling almost abreast they overtook the deceased who was riding a motorcycle and both cars struck him while he was crossing a bridge, killing him instantly and knocking the motorcycle 300 feet or more from the point of collision. A conviction of murder was affirmed. Clemon v. State, 218 Ga. 755, 130 S.E.2d 745 (1963).

The general murder statutes are not preempted by vehicular manslaughter and death from vehicle collision could be prosecuted as second degree murder. People v. Watson, 30 Cal.3d 290, 179 Cal. Rptr. 43, 637 P.2d 279 (1981).

and greatly injuring the third; that the car then ran some 200 feet further, after which he returned and helped convey two of the three to the hospital, and from this concludes that "defendant's actions after the collision negative the idea of wickedness of disposition or hardness of heart." With all due respect, the jury and trial judge who saw the witnesses when they testified, and the colleagues of the latter who obtained from him a clear picture of their conduct on the witness stand, were far better able to draw the true inferences, than the judges of this court who must rely upon what appears in cold type only. At least as possible an inference from the facts above stated is that the defendant, while running the 200 feet beyond the place of the accident, concluded he would be better off if he came back than if he fled further, and hence the fact of his return did not negative the conclusion, which the jury drew from all the evidence, that defendant's "wanton and reckless conduct . . . [*at the time of the accident* shows his] wicked disregard of the consequences of his acts," and this, if found to be true, as it was, the majority agree would be sufficient to sustain the verdict and sentence. For this reason I dissent.

The chief justice concurred in this dissent.

BANKS v. STATE

Court of Criminal Appeals of Texas, 1919.
85 Tex.Cr.R. 165, 211 S.W. 217.

LATTIMORE, JUDGE. In this case appellant was convicted in the District Court of Polk County of the offense of murder and his punishment fixed at death.

On his appeal but one question is presented and but one question was contained in the motion for new trial, namely, that the evidence does not show appellant guilty of that character of homicide which should be punished by the extreme penalty of death.

It appears from the record that on the night of the homicide, and while at his post of duty on a moving railroad train one Hawkins, a . . . brakeman was shot and killed by some member of a party . . . who were walking along a dirt road near to the railroad track. No reason is assigned for such shooting and it does not appear that appellant or any member of the party was acquainted with any of the parties on the train and that any specific malice could be directed toward the deceased, but under our law the same is not necessary.

One who deliberately uses a deadly weapon in such reckless manner as to evince a heart regarless [sic] of social duty and fatally bent on mischief, as is shown by firing into a moving railroad train upon which human beings necessarily are, cannot shield himself from the consequences of his acts by disclaiming malice. Malice may be toward a group of persons as well as toward an individual. It may exist without former grudges or antecedent menaces. The intentional doing of any wrongful act in such manner and under such circumstances as that the death of a human being may result therefrom is malice. In the instant case the appellant admits his presence and participation in the shooting which resulted in the death of the deceased. . . .

An examination of this statement shows a deliberate unprovoked shooting into a moving train—an act which could reasonably result in the destruction of human life. No excuse or justification is pleaded or shown in the evidence for the act. It is true that appellant says that he shot each time that his companion shot, but that he fired into the ground, which gives rise to the contention here that the State having introduced this declaration is bound by it; but the rule applicable is that the State is only bound when there is no other evidence upon which the jury may base their rejection of any part of such statement. In this case the proof shows that two pistols were used, and appellant so states in his statement above, and also he therein says that the pistol he used was a 38-calibre and the one used by his companion was a 45-calibre. It was conclusively shown by the other evidence that the bullet which killed deceased at the front end of the moving train, and also the one which entered the caboose at the rear of the same train were 38-calibre bullets. This evidence negatives the fact that the fatal shot was fired by appellant's companion and fully justified the jury in concluding that the portion of appellant's statement in which he says that he fired into the ground, was untrue, and also fully sustained the conclusion of the jury that his were the shots which took the life of deceased. Nor can we see that the jury was not justified in assessing the extreme penalty of the law. That man who can coolly shoot into a moving train, or automobile, or other vehicle in which are persons guiltless of any wrongdoing toward him or provocation for such attack, is, if possible, worse than the man who endures insult or broods over a wrong, real or fancied, and then waylays and kills his personal enemy. The shame of the world recently has been the unwarranted killing of persons who were noncombatants and who were doing nothing and were not capable of inflicting injury upon their slayers. Of kindred spirit is he who can shoot in the darkness into houses, crowds or trains and recklessly send into eternity those whom he does not know and against whom he has no sort of reason for directing his malevolence.

The only contention here being that the evidence does not support the verdict, with which we are unable to agree, and there being no errors shown in the charge of the court, or otherwise, we direct that the judgment of the lower court be affirmed.

The judgment of the lower court is affirmed.[1]

Affirmed.

1. Cf. State v. Capps, 134 N.C. 622, 46 S.E. 730 (1904).

STATE v. HOKENSON

Supreme Court of Idaho, 1974.
96 Idaho 283, 527 P.2d 487.

DONALDSON, JUSTICE.

Appellant Fred W. Hokenson, armed with a homemade bomb and a knife, entered Dean's Drug Center, Lewiston, on the evening of January 13, 1972 with the intent to commit robbery. The resulting course of events ended with the death of Officer Ross D. Flavel. In June, 1972, trial was held in the Second Judicial District Court for Nez Perce County and a jury found the appellant guilty of murder in the first degree. Judgment of conviction was entered and sentence of life imprisonment was imposed. This appeal is from that judgment.

On the evening of January 13, 1972, Kent Dean, owner and manager of Dean's Drug Center, Lewiston, received a call from an individual (later identified as appellant Fred W. Hokenson) asking him to return to the store and fill a prescription which was urgently needed. Upon agreeing to do so, Mr. Dean, accompanied by his wife and two small sons, returned to the store arriving shortly after 7:00 p.m. After a short wait, appellant Fred W. Hokenson entered the rear of the Drug Center wearing a gas mask and carrying a sack close to his shoulder in his right hand. He stated, "Nobody moves, nobody gets hurt."

Kent Dean immediately raced over to the appellant and grabbed him in a bear hug. The two men struggled, rolled against the counter, and Dean obtained a headlock on Hokenson. Hokenson then stated that he had a bomb. Mr. Dean asked his wife to call the police and to get his gun. While she was doing so, the two men fell to the ground and the appellant again mentioned the bomb. Dean managed to grasp the sack the appellant was holding and to slide it approximately ten feet away. Upon coming to rest, cylindrical rods could be seen protruding from the sack's top.

While both men were still on the floor, Dean heard the appellant say, "Okay, I have a knife and this is it." Dean felt the knife at the back of his neck but changed his position and managed to wrestle it away.

Mrs. Dean called the police and returned to the rear of the store. She was holding a gun on the appellant and Mr. Dean was still grasping Hokenson in a headlock when the police arrived. Officer Ross D. Flavel entered the store through the rear door and upon learning the facts started handcuffing Hokenson. After securing appellant's left wrist, he told Mrs. Dean that another officer, Tom Saleen, was at the front of the store. Mrs. Dean promptly let him in and the two officers along with Mr. Dean completed the task of handcuffing Hokenson.

Officer Flavel then left the store and backed the patrol car to the rear door. Upon his return Mrs. Dean mentioned the bomb. Officer Flavel approached the device, picked it up and identified it as being a bomb. Some conflict then exists in the testimony concerning the following events. Officer Saleen testified that Officer Flavel began pulling wires out of the device and that Hokenson stated that it would make no difference since they only had thirty seconds to live.[1] The Deans testified that Officer Flavel merely had his hands on the sack at the time of Hokenson's statement and subsequent explosion. Nonetheless, the device did explode killing Officer Flavel and injuring Officer Tom Saleen and Kent Dean.

The following morning two handwritten notes were found near the rear of the store. One established drugs as being the object of the robbery and the other contained a threat against Dean's family. . . .

Appellant pleaded not guilty to murder under I.C. § 18–603 applicable at the time.[2] It reads as follows:

"18–603. *Murder.* —(1) Except as provided in section 18–604(1)(b) of this code, criminal homicide constitutes murder when:

(a) it is committed purposely or knowingly; or

(b) it is committed recklessly under circumstances manifesting extreme indifference to the value of human life. Such recklessness and indifference are presumed if the actor is engaged or is an accomplice in the commission of, or an attempt to commit, or flight after committing or attempting to commit robbery, rape, or deviate sexual intercourse by force or threat of force, arson, burglary, kidnaping or felonious escape.

(2) Murder is a felony of the first degree, but a person convicted of murder may be sentenced to death, as provided in section 18–607 of this code." . . .

Asserted error in denying appellant's motion for acquittal, or in the alternative, the verdict is contrary to the evidence.

Appellant argues that since he was under arrest and in custody at the time of the explosion, the attempted crime had been fully terminated and therefore he was not liable for the death under I.C. § 18–603.

Idaho Code § 18–603 provides that a criminal homicide is murder if it is committed recklessly under circumstances manifesting extreme indifference to the value of human life. This recklessness and indifference is presumed if the actor is engaged in the commission of, attempt to commit, or flight after committing or attempting to commit robbery. The state argues that the evidence presented showed beyond a reasonable doubt that the homicide was committed reckless-

1. The remains of the device were sent for F.B.I. analysis and no evidence of a timing device was found.

2. Former I.C. § 18–603 (S.L.1971, Ch. 143, Sec. 1, p. 676) was repealed effective April 1, 1972.

ly under circumstances manifesting extreme disregard to human life. As such, the state argues their case was established without the aid of the felony-murder presumption. We agree.

The statute requires no showing that the homicide took place during the attempted robbery. The appellant's act of carrying an active bomb into the store, knowing it to be extremely dangerous as shown by his handling, manifests extreme indifference to the value of human life. This act, coupled with the ensuing explosion and death, suffices without the presumption to establish murder under I.C. § 18–603(1)(b).

Further, this Court cannot accept the appellant's contention that he should escape liability under the felony-murder rationale. The record shows that the appellant entered the store armed with a homemade bomb and a knife with the intent to commit robbery. His handling of the bomb illustrated his full cognizance of its characteristics. The fact he was met by resistance on the part of his intended victim, and in fact placed under arrest, does not release him from the final consequence of his act.

In the case of People v. Welch, 8 Cal.3d 106, 104 Cal.Rptr. 217, 501 P.2d 225 (1972) the California Supreme Court stated:

". . . homicide is committed in perpetration of the felony if the killing and the felony are parts of one continuous transaction . . . . The person killed need not be the object of the felony." 104 Cal.Rptr. at 225, 501 P.2d at 233.

In Commonwealth v. Banks, 454 Pa. 401, 311 A.2d 576, 578 (1973) the court stated that liability would be imposed where the conduct causing the death was done in furtherance of the design to commit the felony.

The explosion causing the death of Officer Flavel clearly falls within the above two definitions. A person is criminally liable for the natural and probable consequences of his unlawful acts as well as unlawful forces set in motion during the commission of an unlawful act. The appellant voluntarily set in motion an instrumentality which carried a very real probability of causing great bodily harm. Death ensued, and the fact appellant was under arrest does not erase criminal liability. . . .

Judgment affirmed.

SHEPARD, C.J., and MCQUADE, MCFADDEN and BAKES, JJ., concur.[3]

3. Where the death of a child was due to starvation; a murder conviction of the mother was upheld under a statute defining murder as "evidencing a depraved indifference to human life". State v. Nicholson, 585 P.2d 60 (Utah 1978).

D shot V after she refused to let him use her car. D had attempted to persuade V by placing a loaded gun to her head. A conviction was upheld on a theory of killing involving a high degree of life endangering risk. The court stated:

"As we have attempted to explain, however, the continuum of death-causing behavior for which society imposes sanctions is practically limitless with

PEOPLE v. PHILLIPS

Supreme Court of California, In Bank, 1966.
64 Cal.2d 574, 51 Cal.Rptr. 225, 414 P.2d 353.

[The evidence indicated that D, a doctor of chiropractic, committed the felony of grand theft by repeatedly assuring the parents of a minor cancer patient scheduled to undergo surgery, that D could cure the patient without surgery and that this caused the parents to remove the patient from the hospital without surgery with the result that her life was shortened.]

TOBRINER, JUSTICE. Defendant, a doctor of chiropractic, appeals from a judgment of the Superior Court of Los Angeles County convicting him of second degree murder in connection with the death from cancer of one of his patients. We reverse solely on the ground that the trial court erred in giving a felony murder instruction. . . .

Defendant challenges the propriety of the trial court's instructions to the jury. The court gave the following tripartite instruction on murder in the second degree: . . .

"(3) If the killing is done in the perpetration or attempt to perpetrate a felony such as Grand Theft. If a death occurs in the perpetration of a course of conduct amounting to Grand Theft, which course of conduct is a proximate cause of the unlawful killing of a human being, such course of conduct constitutes murder in the second degree, even though the death was not intended."

The third part of this instruction rests upon the felony murder rule and reflects the prosecution's theory that defendant's conduct amounted to grand theft by false pretenses in violation of Penal Code section 484.

We shall point out why we have [agreed with] defendant's contention that . . . (2) the felony murder instruction given here was erroneous in that such a charge can properly be grounded *only* upon a felony "inherently dangerous to life," and grand theft is not such a crime; (3) the erroneous instruction caused defendant prejudice because it removed from the jury the issue of malice, and (4) the prosecution cannot successfully argue that even though the instruction erroneously permitted the jury to convict without finding malice, no

the gradations of more culpable conduct imperceptibly shading into conduct for the less culpable. Our high court has drawn this line placing in the more culpable category not only those deliberate life-endangering acts which are done with a subjective awareness of the risk involved, but also life-endangering conduct which is 'only' done with the awareness the conduct is contrary to the laws of society. Although behavior in the latter category may not be as morally heinous as the former, the difference in culpability does not require the latter crime to be legally shifted into manslaughter slots."

People v. Love, 111 Cal.App.3d 98, 168 Cal.Rptr. 407, 412 (1980).

prejudice resulted because the jury necessarily found facts which established malice as a matter of law. . . .

Despite defendant's contention that the Penal Code does not expressly set forth any provision for second degree felony murder and that, therefore, we should not follow any such doctrine here, the concept lies imbedded in our law. We have stated in People v. Williams (1965) 63 Cal.2d 452, 47 Cal.Rptr. 7, 406 P.2d 647, that the cases hold that the perpetration of some felonies, exclusive of those enumerated in Penal Code section 189, may provide the basis for a murder conviction under the felony murder rule. (See also People v. Ford (1964) 60 Cal.2d 772, 795, 36 Cal.Rptr. 620, 388 P.2d 892).

We have held, however, that only such felonies as are in themselves "inherently dangerous to human life" can support the application of the felony murder rule. We have ruled that in assessing such peril to human life inherent in any given felony "we look to the elements of the felony in the abstract, not the particular 'facts' of the case." (People v. Williams, supra, 63 Cal.2d 452, 458, fn. 5, 47 Cal. Rptr. 7, 10, 460 P.2d 647, 650.)

We have thus recognized that the felony murder doctrine expresses a highly artificial concept that deserves no extension beyond its required application.[5] Indeed the rule itself has been abandoned by the courts of England, where it had its inception. It has been subjected to severe and sweeping criticism. No case to our knowledge in any jurisdiction has held that because death results from a course of conduct involving a felonious perpetration of a fraud, the felony murder doctrine can be invoked.

Admitting that grand theft is not inherently dangerous to life, the prosecution asks us to encompass the entire course of defendant's conduct so that we may incorporate such elements as would make his crime inherently dangerous. In so framing the definition of a given felony for the purpose of assessing its inherent peril to life the prosecution would abandon the statutory definition of the felony as such and substitute the factual elements of defendant's actual conduct. In the present case the Attorney General would characterize that conduct as "grand theft medical fraud," and this newly created "felony," he urges, clearly involves danger to human life and supports an application of the felony murder rule.

5. As we stated in People v. Washington (1965) 62 Cal.2d 777, 783, 44 Cal.Rptr. 442, 446, 402 P.2d 130, 134 "The felony-murder rule has been criticized on the grounds that in almost all cases in which it is applied it is unnecessary and that it erodes the relation between criminal liability and moral culpability. (See e.g., Model Penal Code) (Tent.Draft No. 9, May 8, 1959) § 201.2, comment 4 at pp. 37–39; Report of the Royal Commission on Capital Punishment, Cmd. No. 8932, at pp. 34–43, 45 (1949–1953); 3 Stephen, History of the Criminal Law of England 57–58, 74–75 (1883); Packer, The Case for Revision of the Penal Code, 13 Stan. L.Rev. 252, 259; Morris, The Felon's Responsibility for the Lethal Acts of Others, 105 U.Pa.L.Rev. 50; 66 Yale L.J. 427.) Although it is the law in this state (Pen.Code, § 189), it should not be extended beyond any rational function that it is designed to serve. . . . " (Fn. omitted.)

To fragmentize the "course of conduct" of defendant so that the felony murder rule applies if any segment of that conduct may be considered dangerous to life would widen the rule beyond calculation. It would then apply not only to the commission of specific felonies, which are themselves dangerous to life, but to the perpetration of *any* felony during which defendant may have acted in such a manner as to endanger life.

The proposed approach would entail the rejection of our holding in *Williams.* That case limited the felony murder doctrine to such felonies as were themselves inherently dangerous to life.[a] That decision eschews the prosecution's present sweeping concept because, once the Legislature's own definition is discarded, the number or nature of the contextual elements which could be incorporated into an expanded felony terminology would be limitless. We have been, and remain, unwilling to embark on such an uncharted sea of felony murder.

The felony murder instruction should not, then, have been given; its rendition, further, worked prejudice upon defendant. It withdrew from the jury the issue of malice, permitting a conviction upon the bare showing that Linda's death proximately resulted from conduct of defendant amounting to grand theft. The instruction as rendered did not require the jury to find either express malice or the implied malice which is manifested in an "intent with conscious disregard for life to commit acts likely to kill." . . .

The judgment is reversed.

TRAYNOR, C.J., and PETERS and PEEK, JJ., concur.

a. [Added by the Compiler.] Phillips was tried again, this time without reference to felony-murder, and was once more convicted of second-degree murder. This conviction was affirmed in People v. Phillips, 270 Cal.App.2d 381, 75 Cal.Rptr. 720 (1969).

The furnishing, selling or administering narcotics to a minor is a dangerous felony, hence death resulting therefrom is murder in the second degree. People v. Poindexter, 51 Cal.2d 142, 330 P.2d 763 (1958).

Possession of a concealable firearm by one who has been convicted of a felony is not an inherently dangerous felony. People v. Satchell, 6 Cal.3d 28, 98 Cal. Rptr. 33, 489 P.2d 1361 (1971).

The wilful and malicious burning of another's automobile is a felony inherently dangerous to human life and if it results in death, however unintentionally, the homicide is second-degree murder. People v. Nichols, 3 Cal.3d 150, 89 Cal.Rptr. 721, 474 P.2d 673 (1970).

"We have held that escape from the scene of the underlying felony is part of the *res gestae* of a crime so that a murder committed to facilitate the flight can be felony murder." People v. McCrary, 190 Colo. 538, 549 P.2d 1320, 1331 (1976).

The felony-murder rule in Maine is limited to cases in which the felony was committed or attempted in a manner which presents a serious threat to human life or is likely to cause serious bodily harm. State v. Wallace, 333 A.2d 72 (Me. 1975).

"In summary, in a felony murder charge, involving a collateral lesser-degree felony, that felony must be inherently dangerous or committed under circumstances that are inherently dangerous. In cases where the collateral felony is a first-degree felony the *res gestae* test shall be used." State v. Harrison, 90 N.M. 439, 564 P.2d 1321, 1324 (1977).

BURKE, JUSTICE (dissenting).

I dissent. The majority opinion reverses the judgment of conviction of second degree murder "solely on the ground that the trial court erred in giving a felony murder instruction." Under section 4½, article VI, of the California Constitution "No judgment shall be set aside . . . on the ground of misdirection of the jury . . . unless, after an examination of the entire cause, including the evidence, the court shall be of the opinion that the error complained of has resulted in a miscarriage of justice." I submit that here a miscarriage of justice did not result from any error in giving the instruction in view of the overwhelming evidence that defendant, motivated by mercenary greed, acted in conscious disregard for the life of 8-year-old Linda Epping when he induced her parents to cancel the scheduled cancer operation and place her under his care, thereby shortening her life. . . .

I would affirm the judgment of conviction under the mandate of section 4½, article VI, of the California Constitution.

MCCOMB and SCHAUER, JJ., concur.

REYNOLDS v. STATE

Court of Criminal Appeals of Oklahoma, 1980.
617 P.2d 1357.

CORNISH, PRESIDING JUDGE: Larry Charles Reynolds was charged with the crime of Murder in the First Degree in the District Court, Comanche County, Case No. CRF–76–725. He was convicted of Manslaughter in the First Degree and sentenced to twenty (20) years' imprisonment. On appeal, he has challenged the jury instructions and further complains that the State was allowed to impeach its own witnesses.

The following facts are undisputed. The appellant and his estranged wife, Sandra Reynolds, were at a party at Robinson's Landing, Lake Lawtonka, on September 5, 1976. Mrs. Reynolds came to the party with another man, and the appellant was accompanied by another woman, Ms. Lake. During the evening, the appellant engaged in drunken horseplay and fired a pistol into the air. The third time he fired the pistol his wife was struck and killed. Following the shooting, the appellant and Ms. Lake left the party in the car in which Mrs. Reynolds' body had been placed on the back seat. While driving they were stopped for a traffic violation by a Comanche County Deputy Sheriff, who saw the decedent lying in the back seat with blood on her chest.

The State attempted to prove that the homicide was premeditated. The prosecutor introduced evidence of an argument between the appellant and the decedent the night before the shooting. The State's witness Marcia Colyer testified that during the evening in question the appellant stated that if he could not have his wife, then no one could.

Although the appellant admitted holding the gun at the time his wife was shot, he introduced evidence to show that the shooting was accidental. The appellant testified that at the time of the fatal shot he had intended to fire the pistol into the air again, but his hand was grabbed by Dale Brooks and the gun discharged, striking Mrs. Reynolds. The testimony of Dale Brooks substantially corroborated that of the appellant. However, the State introduced evidence that the appellant's hand was grabbed after the shot was fired, rather than before. Other evidence by the defense indicated a compatible relationship between the appellant and his wife, both before the incident and on the evening of the homicide.

At the conclusion of the evidence, the trial court instructed the jury as to murder in the first degree, manslaughter in the first degree, and justifiable homicide. The refusal of the trial judge to present to the jury the appellant's requested instruction on manslaughter in the second degree, 21 O.S.1971, § 716, is the first alleged error for consideration. The appellant contends the evidence shows the homicide was either intentional or accidental, and that since the jury could have determined that the homicide was an accident involving culpable negligence, they should have been instructed on manslaughter in the second degree.

In Miller v. State, Okl.Cr., 523 P.2d 1118 (1974), we stated that if a person is culpably negligent while engaged in the commission of a misdemeanor, the misdemeanor-manslaughter doctrine, set forth in ¶ 1 of 21 O.S.1971, § 711, becomes operative and effectively precludes the possibility of a finding of manslaughter in the second degree. In *Miller,* the misdemeanor committed by the defendant causing the homicide was pointing a gun, 21 O.S.1971, § 1279. In this case, the appellant was engaged in the misdemeanor of reckless conduct under the Oklahoma Firearms Act, 21 O.S.1971, § 1289.11.

When a person is handling a deadly weapon, the law requires that person to use a higher degree of care than if using an instrument ordinarily harmless. The evidence overwhelmingly demonstrates conduct in violation of the statute by "creating a situation of unreasonable risk and probability of death or great bodily harm to another, and demonstrating a conscious disregard for the safety of another person." Title 21 O.S.1971, § 1289.11.

Such a situation must be determined by considering the totality of the surrounding circumstances. The appellant was recklessly carrying and firing his pistol in proximity to a group of people with whom he had been consuming intoxicating beverages. As admitted by the appellant, this conduct was the proximate cause of the decedent's death. In previous cases construing the statute prohibiting reckless conduct with a firearm, the circumstances considered have included the deliberate pointing of a firearm at unarmed people. However, the pointing of a firearm at a person is not a necessary element of reckless conduct with a firearm.

Because the evidence, even when construed most favorably to the appellant, shows at least an accidental homicide during the commission of a misdemeanor, it was not error for the trial court to refuse to instruct the jury as to manslaughter in the second degree. Affirmed.[1]

STATE v. FARRIS

Supreme Court of New Mexico, 1980.
95 N.M. 96, 619 P.2d 541.

FEDERICI, JUSTICE. Defendant was convicted of first degree murder and sentenced to life imprisonment. He appeals, alleging a voluntary manslaughter instruction should have been given to the jury.

Defendant shot his wife on the morning of April 9, 1979 in the family home. Defendant had separated from his wife some time prior to the shooting. The testimony was that they had been married for about 20 years, and that during this time they had separated several times, always because of alleged "boyfriends" of the wife. There was evidence that during the final separation period, his wife's boyfriend and the boyfriend's brother had threatened defendant twice, and he bought a gun to protect himself. Defendant suffered from a nervous condition during this period. On the morning of the shooting, he arranged to meet with his wife, and went over to talk with her. A quarrel ensued, and she poked him in the chest and told him to leave her boyfriend alone, that the boyfriend could come into the house any time he wanted. Defendant relates that he does not remember what ensued; he "lost his head," and shot her.

The elements of voluntary manslaughter are stated in N.M. U.J.I. Crim. 2.20, N.M.S.A.1978. If a defendant was sufficiently provoked by conduct which aroused anger, rage, fear, sudden resentment, terror or some other extreme emotion, and the provocation was such that an ordinary person of average disposition would have lost self control and not yet cooled, the defendant is guilty of manslaughter rather than murder.

In State v. Benavidez, 94 N.M. 419, 616 P.2d 419 (1980), we looked to several factors which might contribute to such provocation. They included prior bad acts of the victim directed at the defendant and members of defendant's family, prior threats of killing both defendant and a member of his family and a motion towards defendant at

1. Defendants pushed a piece of stone off a bridge onto the front of an approaching train striking a guard on the train and killing him. A manslaughter conviction based on the unlawful doing of a wrongful act was upheld. "It makes it plain (a) that an accused is guilty of manslaughter if it is proved that he intentionally did an act which was unlawful and dangerous and that that act inadvertently caused death." DPP v. Newburg, [1976] 2 All E.R. (H.L.) 365, 367, L. Salmon.

the time of the killing which could have been an attempt to strike defendant or move for a weapon. Of these circumstances, those most important are those within the res gestae of the killing. For there must be evidence of a sudden quarrel or heat of passion at the time of the commission of the crime. We have also stated that "words alone, however scurrilous or insulting, will not furnish the adequate provocation required for this purpose. (Citation omitted.)" State v. Nevares, 36 N.M. 41, 44–45, 7 P.2d 933, 935 (1932). See State v. Castro, 92 N.M. 585, 592 P.2d 185 (Ct.App.1979), cert. denied, 92 N.M. 621, 593 P.2d 62 (1979).

Defendant's attempts to distinguish *Nevares* and *Castro* by claiming that the insulting words spoken there were sufficiently prior to the killing to have allowed the defendants to cool. Defendant claims that this was the true basis for finding lack of provocation at the time of the killing. Defendant's reliance is misplaced. We find no evidence in those cases that words alone can ever be sufficient provocation.

In the case before us, there may well have been circumstances in the marital relationship which provoked defendant. But at the time of the killing, the only evidence of provocation consists of defendant's wife talking to him and poking him in the chest. We do not think the mere addition of poking in the chest to "words alone" is sufficient to show provocation at the time of the killing. Absent this essential element, a conviction of manslaughter could not be sustained. Smith v. State, supra. Therefore, it would not have been proper to give the jury a voluntary manslaughter instruction in this case.

The trial court is affirmed.

IT IS SO ORDERED.

EASLEY, SENIOR JUSTICE, and PAYNE, J., concur.[1]

1. It was held to be reversible error to give an instruction telling the jury in substance that an intentional killing without justification or excuse is murder and that a killing under great provocation can not be held to be manslaughter unless the slayer's mind was so disturbed that he was not really aware of what he was doing. A killing in the sudden heat of passion engendered by great provocation is manslaughter, "not because the law supposes that this passion made him unconscious of what he was about to do, and stripped the act of killing of an intent to commit it, but because it presumes that passion disturbed the sway of reason, and made him regardless of her admonitions". It is an "indulgence which the law accords to human infirmity suddenly provoked into passion". State v. Hill, 20 N.C. 629 (1839)

A killing by one lawfully exercising his privilege of self-defense is no crime at all and must not be confused with an unlawful killing in a sudden heat of passion engendered by great provocation. State v. Ramey, 273 N.C. 325, 160 S.E.2d 56 (1968).

Where there was evidence which the jury might find to be sufficient provocation to reduce the killing to voluntary manslaughter, it was reversible error for the judge to instruct that in his opinion there was no evidence of a legally sufficient cause of provocation. Commonwealth v. McNeill, 462 Pa. 438, 341 A.2d 463 (1975).

STATE v. GRUGIN

Supreme Court of Missouri, Division Two, 1898.
147 Mo. 39, 47 S.W. 1058.

SHERWOOD, J. The appeal in this instance is taken by defendant from the judgment of the trial court, which, based on the verdict of the jury, adjudged and sentenced him to the penitentiary for the term of fifteen years as punishment for the crime of murder in the second degree.

The indictment was for murder in the first degree. . . .

[Under Missouri procedure this case had been submitted to the supreme court of the state for answers to certain interrogatories.]

2. The second interrogatory is next for consideration. It embodies and comprehends the question whether *words* constitute a sufficient or reasonable provocation in law? Of course the books abound in utterance of the platitude that words however opprobrious constitute no provocation in law. Speaking as the organ of this court I have often uttered this platitude myself, but the statement is subject to many qualifications. The general good sense of mankind has in some instances so far qualified the rigor of what is termed the ancient rule that a statute has been passed in Texas which reduces a homicide to manslaughter where insulting words are used to or concerning a female relative, the killing is reduced to manslaughter where it occurs as soon as the parties meet after the knowledge of the insult.

In Alabama, a statute provides that opprobrious words shall in some circumstances justify an assault and battery. And in that State, without any statutory provision on the subject, it has been determined that *"insult by mere words,"* when the defendant acts on them and he has not provoked them, may be weighed by the jury with other evidence in determining whether the killing was murder in the first or second degree.

After speaking of Morley's Case, Hale says: "Many, who were of opinion, that bare words of slighting, disdain, or contumely would not of themselves make such a provocation as to lessen the crime into manslaughter, yet were of this opinion, that if A. gives indecent language to B., and B. thereupon strikes A., but not mortally; and then A. strikes B. again, and then B. kills A. that this is but manslaughter. For the second stroke made a new provocation, and so it was but a sudden falling out; and though B. gave the first stroke, and after a blow received from A., B. gives him a mortal stroke, this is but manslaughter, according to the proverb, the second blow makes the affray. And this was the opinion of myself and some others." [1 Hale, P.C. 456.]

Now in the case Hale supposes, it is as he says the second stroke that made a *"new provocation,"* but the second stroke was given by

A. Then what made the *old* provocation? Evidently, the "*indecent words*" of A. which, given by A. to B., prompted the latter to give the *first* stroke. So in Morley's Case, it was agreed that "if upon ill words both of the parties suddenly fight, and one kill the other, this is but manslaughter; for it is a combat betwixt two upon a sudden heat, which is the legal description of manslaughter." [6 How.St.Tr. 771.] In that instance, also, it must be noted that "ill words" were the provocation that made the hot blood which resulted only in manslaughter: To test this matter further, suppose no "ill words" used, what then the crime? Evidently *murder.*

It is said in the books that though an *insufficient* assault or demonstration do not import coming violence, still it and *insulting words combined,* may so excite the passions as to reduce the killing to manslaughter.

If the inchoate assault be *naught* as provocation, and the approbrious [sic] words be *naught* as provocation, I am unable to see how the addition of these *two ciphers* can make a *unit.* "The moment, however, the person is touched with apparent insolence, then the provocation is one which, ordinarily speaking, reduces the offense to manslaughter." And it is held that such "*apparent insolence*" may be manifested in a variety of ways, as for instance, by a contemptuous jostling on the street, by tweaking the nose, by filliping on the forehead, or by spitting in the face. In most of these instances and illustrations there is no *physical pain or injury inflicted,* the "sudden *heat*" springs from the *indignity* the *insult* offered, and from nothing else. This being true the law should not be so unreasonable as to deny to an *insult* offered *in words* the same force and effect which all men recognize that it has as a matter *of fact.* If it "so excite the passions of the mass of men as to enthrall their reason, the law should hold it adequate cause" for the reduction of the grade of the offense, resulting from the use of the insulting words. No sound distinction can, it seems, be taken in principle between insult offered by acts and that offered by foul and opprobrious words.

I will now refer to some adjudications where insulting words have been held a sufficient basis for a charge or an instruction on the offense of manslaughter. Where the prisoner was indicted for the willful murder of his wife, Blackburn, J., in summing up, said: "As a general rule of law, no provocation of words will reduce the crime murder to that of manslaughter, but under special circumstances there may be such a provocation of words as will have that effect; for instance if a husband suddenly hearing from his wife that she had committed adultery, and he, having no idea of such a thing before, were thereupon to kill his wife, it might be manslaughter. Now, in this case, words spoken by the deceased just previous to the blows inflicted by the prisoner were these: 'Aye; but I'll take no more for thee, for I will have no more children of thee. I have done it once, and I'll do it again.' Now, what you will have to consider is, would these words, which were spoken just previous to the blows, amount to such a provocation as would in an ordinary man, not in a man of violent or passionate disposition, provoke him in such a way as to justify him in striking her as the prisoner did?" [Reg. v. Rothwell, 12 Cox C.C. 145.] In that case (tried in 1871) the husband seized a pair of tongs, close at hand, and struck his wife three violent blows on the head from which she died within a week, and the verdict was for manslaughter.

In Reg. v. Smith, tried in 1866, a woman had left her husband and gone off and lived in adultery with one Langley. He having died, she returned to her home, and her husband forgave her, but she did not prize this forgiveness, because on the next night after her return she violently abused him, taunting him with her preference for Langley and declaring had he not died, she had not returned. Whilst this was going on, she was so violent as to have to be held by two other women who were present; her husband sat by her on the seat trying to pacify her. Finally she broke from the women who were holding her and repeating with much foul language her preference for Langley, spat towards her husband, whereupon he, who was then standing up within a yard of her, gave her a blow in the neck with a sharp pointed pocket knife, which caused her immediate death. And the jury were in substance charged: An assault, too slight in itself to be sufficient provocation to reduce murder to manslaughter, may become sufficient for that purpose, when coupled with words of *great insult.* [4 F. & F. 1066.] A verdict of guilty of manslaughter was returned. . . .

So it will be seen that there *are* circumstances where *words do amount to a provocation in law,* i.e., a reasonable provocation to be submitted to the determination of the jury, and if found by them to exist, then the crime is lowered to the grade of manslaughter. If there ever was a case to which this principle should be applied, it would seem it should be applied to the case at bar. A father is informed that his young daughter just budding into womanhood has been ravished by his son-in-law, while under the supposed protection of his roof. Arriving where the son-in-law is, and making inquiry of him why he had done the foul deed, the father receives the answer, "*I'll do as I damn please about it.*" This insolent and defiant reply amounted to an affirmation of Hadley's guilt! So long as human nature remains as God made it, such audacious and atrocious avowals will be met as met by defendant. It should be held, therefore, that the words in question should have been left to the jury to say whether, in the circumstances detailed in evidence, they constituted a reasonable provocation, and if so found, that then defendant was guilty of no higher offense than manslaughter in the fourth degree. . . .

The judgment should be reversed and the cause remanded. Burgess, J., concurs *in toto;* Gantt, P.J., does not concur as to that portion of paragraph 2 in reference to words being regarded as a reasonable provocation by either court or jury.[1]

PEOPLE v. BORCHERS

Supreme Court of California, In Bank, 1958.
50 Cal.2d 321, 325 P.2d 97.

SCHAUER, JUSTICE. The People appeal "from an Order of the Superior Court . . . modifying the verdict in the above entitled cause by reducing the punishment imposed." (Pen.Code, § 1238(6).) Defendant does not appeal. A jury found defendant guilty of murder of the second degree and found that he was sane at the time of the commission of the offense. The trial judge denied defendant's motion for a new trial on the issue of sanity and ordered that "Defendant's motion for new trial on the case in chief is ruled upon as follows: In lieu of granting a new trial, the verdict of second degree Murder is reduced to Voluntary Manslaughter." The People argue that the evidence was sufficient to justify the implied finding of malice aforethought, that the evidence did not show that defendant was guilty of voluntary manslaughter, and that the trial court erred in reducing the class of crime found by the jury. We have concluded that no ground for reversal is shown.

Defendant, a Pasadena insurance broker, aged 45, met deceased, referred to throughout the testimony as "Dotty," aged 29, at a zoo on May 13, 1956. With Dotty was Tony, an illegitimate child of four whom Dotty had cared for since 16 days after his birth. Defendant was attracted by the "warmth," "kindness," and "sweetness" with which Dotty spoke to the child. Defendant spoke to the boy and thus

1. "The rule in this State is, as it was at common law, that the law regards no mere epithet or language, however violent or offensive, as sufficient provocation for taking life. Williams v. State, 3 Heisk. 376, 392;" Wharton on Homicide (3d Ed.) sec. 173.

"Courts have often had under consideration, in connection with the existence of adequate cause, the use of the vile epithet used by deceased just before he was killed, 'son of a bitch,' and quite without exception have held these words not to constitute adequate cause of provocation." Freddo v. State, 127 Tenn. 376, 155 S.W. 170 (1912).

"We agree with the great weight of authority that words alone are not adequate provocation to justify reducing an intentional killing to manslaughter." State v. Doss, 116 Ariz. 156, 568 P.2d 1054, 1060 (1977).

"In order for a homicide to be reduced from second degree murder to voluntary manslaughter on the theory that a defendant acted under the influence of sudden passion, the heat of passion suddenly aroused by provocation must be of such nature as the law would deem adequate to temporarily displace malice. Mere words however abusive are not sufficient provocation to reduce second-degree murder to manslaughter. Legal provocation must be under circumstances amounting to an assault or threatened assault." State v. Montague, 298 N.C. 752, 259 S.E.2d 899, 903 (1979).

D, who intentionally killed his infant son, was not entitled to an instruction on voluntary manslaughter based upon heat of passion resulting from a quarrel with his wife. "The weight of authority is against allowing transferrence of one's passion from the object of the passion to a related bystander." State v. Gutierrez, 88 N.M. 448, 541 P.2d 628 (1975).

became acquainted with Dotty. They had dinner together that night and thereafter, according to defendant's testimony, "went together steadily from then on" until he killed her on October 9, 1956. From May 13 until October 9 "excepting the days that I was away on a business trip to Mexico and one other day . . . there was not a day that went by but what Tony and Dotty and I saw each other". . . .

[Although defendant was married (divorce proceedings had been started) he and Dotty became "engaged" nine days after they first met. He provided an apartment for her and Tony, and took her on a trip to Las Vegas. There they recited a "common-law marriage ceremony". After they returned to Pasadena he learned that Marvin Prestidge and another man were "hanging around" Dotty and using her automobile. As these men had criminal records, defendant employed Fagg, a private detective, to investigate. Fagg reported that Prestidge had a police record as a pimp, that he was having sexual relations with Dotty, and that she was taking money from defendant and giving it to Prestidge. Defendant believed she was acting because of fear of Prestidge although Fagg assured him that fear was not the reason.

On October 5, 1956, while returning from a trip to San Diego, she said she wished she were dead and tried to jump from the moving car. A few nights later, while they were riding, she repeatedly suggested suicide. She took a pistol from the glove compartment, saying she was going to shoot him, but permitted him to take the weapon. She said he should kill her, Tony and himself. Then she turned to him and said: "Go ahead and shoot. What is the matter—are you chicken?" And as defendant told it, "he heard the explosion of the gun as he shot Dotty in the back of the head."]

Section 1181, paragraph 6 of the Penal Code provides that the trial court may grant a new trial "When the verdict is contrary to law or evidence, but if the evidence shows the defendant to be not guilty of the degree of the crime of which he was convicted, but guilty of a lesser degree thereof, or of a lesser crime included therein, the court may modify the verdict, finding or judgment accordingly without granting or ordering a new trial . . . "

The trial court in ruling on the question of reducing the class of the crime stated that in its opinion there was "a duty fixed on the trial court to independently weigh and consider the testimony and all of the ramifications of it and determine in his own mind if he is satisfied that the evidence beyond a reasonable doubt shows guilt of second degree murder. Tested in that light and tested further in the light of the evidence of the psychiatrists on the mental condition of this defendant, I am not satisfied that the evidence is sufficient to sustain the finding of malice to make this second degree murder; hence, the Court in lieu of granting a new trial will reduce the degree to that of voluntary manslaughter."

In passing on a motion for new trial it is not only the power but also the duty of the trial court to consider the weight of the evidence. The power and duty of the trial court in considering the question of the reduction of the class or degree of the crime are the same.

In a criminal trial the burden is upon the prosecution to prove beyond any reasonable doubt every essential element of the crime of which a defendant is to be convicted. Here, from the evidence viewed as a whole, the trial judge was amply justified in concluding that defendant did not possess the state of mind known as "malice aforethought" which is an essential ingredient of murder. (Pen. Code, § 187.) "Such malice may be express or implied. It is express when there is manifested a deliberate intention unlawfully to take away the life of a fellow-creature. It is implied, when no considerable provocation appears, or when the circumstances attending the killing show an abandoned and malignant heart." (Pen.Code, § 188.)

Voluntary manslaughter is "the unlawful killing of a human being, without malice . . . upon a sudden quarrel or heat of passion." (Pen.Code, § 192.)

From the evidence viewed as a whole the trial judge could well have concluded that defendant was roused to a heat of "passion" by a series of events over a considerable period of time: Dotty's admitted infidelity, her statements that she wished she were dead, her attempt to jump from the car on the trip to San Diego, her repeated urging that defendant shoot her, Tony, and himself on the night of the homicide, and her taunt, "are you chicken." As defendant argues persuasively, "passion" need not mean "rage" or "anger". According to dictionary definition, "passion" may be any "violent, intense, highwrought, or enthusiastic emotion." (Webster's New International Dictionary, 2d ed.) As stated in People v. Logan (1917), 175 Cal. 45, 49, 164 P. 1121, "the fundamental of the inquiry (in determining whether a homicide is voluntary manslaughter) is whether or not the defendant's reason was, at the time of his act, so disturbed or obscured by some passion—not necessarily fear and never, of course, the passion for revenge—to such an extent as would render ordinary men of average disposition liable to act rashly or without due deliberation and reflection, and from this passion rather than from judgment." It may fairly be concluded that the evidence on the issue of not guilty supports a finding that defendant killed in wild desperation induced by Dotty's long continued provocatory conduct. . . .

The trial judge here is to be commended for his diligent alertness to the power and duty, reposed *only in trial courts,* to reappraise the weight of the evidence on motion for new trial. He very properly showed no hesitance in reducing the class of the homicide in the light of his determination, supported by a reasonable view of the evidence, that there was no sufficient showing of malice aforethought. Such unhesitant exercise of this power by the trial judge, when he is satisfied that the action is indicated by the evidence, not only makes for justice in the individual case but tends also to lighten the burden of reviewing courts and to expedite the finality of judgments.

For the reasons above stated the order appealed from is affirmed.[1]

GIBSON, C.J., and SHENK, CARTER, TRAYNOR, SPENCE and McCOMB, JJ., concur.

STATE v. HARDIE

Supreme Court of Iowa, 1878.
47 Iowa 647.

ROTHROCK, CH. J. I. It appears from the evidence that the defendant was a boarder in the family of one Gantz, who is his brother-in-law. On the day of the homicide defendant was engaged in varnishing furniture. Mrs. Sutfen, a neighbor, called at the house, and after some friendly conversation she went into the kitchen. When she came back defendant picked up a tack hammer and struck on the door. She said, "My God, I thought it was a revolver." A short time afterwards she went into the yard to get a kitten. Defendant said he would frighten her with the revolver as she came in. He took a revolver from a stand drawer and went out of the room, and was in the kitchen when the revolver was discharged. He immediately came in and said to Mrs. Gantz, his sister, "My God, Hannah, come and see what I have done." His sister went out and found Mrs. Sutfen lying on the sidewalk at the side of the house, with a gunshot wound in the head, and in a dying condition. A physician was immediately called and made an examination of the deceased, took the revolver from the defendant, and informed him that nothing could be done for the deceased, whereupon the defendant became violent, said the shot was

1. Heat of passion includes "an emotional state characterized by anger, rage, hatred, furious resentment or terror." State v. Lott, 207 Kan. 602, 485 P.2d 1314, 1317 (1971).

The statutory enumeration of non-malicious criminal homicides is not exclusive, and factors other than sudden quarrel or heat of passion may render a person incapable of harboring malice. People v. Mosher, 1 Cal.3d 379, 82 Cal.Rptr. 379, 461 P.2d 659 (1969).

It has been pointed out, very properly, that in cases of voluntary homicide there may be recognized mitigation other than the "rule of provocation" because there is an intermediate zone which falls short of justification or excuse without going to the other extreme of malice aforethought. Allison v. State, 74 Ark. 444, 86 S.W. 409 (1905). By way of illustration the Court said: "The mere fact that a man believes that he is in great and immediate danger of life or great bodily harm does not of itself justify him in taking life. There must be some reasonable grounds for such belief, or the law will not excuse him for taking the life of another. But if the slayer acts from an honest belief that it is necessary to protect himself, and not from malice or revenge, even though he formed such conclusion hastily and without due care, and when the facts did not justify it, still under such a case, although such a belief on his part will not justify him, it may go in mitigation of the crime, and reduce the homicide from murder to manslaughter."

Provocation based on evidence that the victim had at one time stolen defendant's television set, introduced defendant's son to heroin, assaulted defendant in the past, threatened defendant and his son and was arguing with defendant and made some motion towards defendant was sufficient for manslaughter. State v. Benavidez, 94 N.M. 706, 616 P.2d 419 (1980).

accidental, and exclaimed several times that he would kill himself. It became necessary to secure him, which was done by tying him with ropes.

The revolver had been in the house for about five years. It was found by Gantz in the road. There was one load in it when found. Some six months after it was found Gantz tried to shoot the load from it and it would not go off. He tried to punch the load out, but could not move it. He then laid it away, thinking it was harmless. The defendant was about the house and knew the condition of the revolver. Upon one occasion Gantz said he would try to kill a cat with the revolver. Defendant being present said he would not be afraid to allow it to be snapped at him all day. The revolver remained in the same condition that it was when found, no other load having been put into it, and it was considered by the family as well as defendant as entirely harmless.

The foregoing is the substance of all the evidence.

The State did not claim that the defendant was guilty of murder, but that he was guilty of manslaughter because of criminal carelessness. The defendant insisted that there was no such carelessness as to render the act criminal, and that it was homicide by misadventure, and therefore excusable.

The court instructed the jury as follows: "5. And on the charge of manslaughter, I instruct you that if the defendant used a dangerous and deadly weapon, in a careless and reckless manner, by reason of which instrument so used he killed the deceased, then he is guilty of manslaughter, although no harm was in fact intended."

Other instructions of like import were given, and the question of criminal carelessness was submitted to the jury, as follows: "8th. And in this case I submit to you to find the facts of recklessness and carelessness under the evidence, and if you find that the death of the party was occasioned through recklessness and carelessness of the defendant then you should convict him, and if not you should acquit. And by this I do not mean that defendant is to be held to the highest degree of care and prudence in handling a dangerous and deadly weapon, but only such care as a reasonably prudent man should and ought to use under like circumstances, and if he did not use such care he should be convicted, otherwise he should be acquitted."

There can be no doubt that the instructions given by the court embody the correct rule as to criminal carelessness in the use of a deadly weapon. Counsel for defendant insist that the instructions of the court do not go far enough, and upon the trial asked that the court give to the jury the following instruction:

"3. Although the deceased came to her death from the discharge of a pistol in the hands of the defendant, yet if the defendant had good reason to believe, and did believe, that the pistol which caused her death was not in any manner dangerous, but was entirely harmless, and if he did nothing more than a man of ordinary prudence and caution might have done under like circumstances, then the jury should find him not criminally liable and should acquit."

This instruction and others of like import were refused by the court, and we think the ruling was correct. That the revolver was in fact a deadly weapon is conclusively shown by the terrible tragedy consequent upon defendant's act in firing it off. If it had been in fact unloaded no homicide would have resulted, but the defendant would have been justly censurable for a most reckless and imprudent act in frightening a woman by pretending that it was loaded, and that he was about to discharge it at her. No jury would be warranted in finding that men of ordinary prudence so conduct themselves. On the contrary, such conduct is grossly reckless and reprehensible, and without palliation or excuse. Human life is not to be sported with by the use of firearms, even though the person using them may have good reason to believe that the weapon used is not loaded, or that being loaded it will do no injury. When persons engage in such reckless sport they should be held liable for the consequences of their acts.

II. It is argued that the evidence does not show the defendant guilty of criminal carelessness, because it does not appear that the defendant pointed the pistol at the deceased, or how it happened to be discharged. The fact that defendant took the weapon from the drawer with the avowed purpose of frightening the deceased, and while in his hands it was discharged with fatal effect, together with his admission that he did the act, fully warranted the jury in finding that he purposely pointed the pistol and discharged it at the deceased.

Affirmed.[1]

1. Evidence that the defendant took a loaded revolver from his belt area, with his finger on the trigger and pointed it in the direction of the deceased a short distance away and the weapon discharged justified a conviction for manslaughter in the second degree. ". . . there was ample evidence demonstrating defendant's subjective awareness and conscious disregard of the risk." People v. Licitra, 47 N.Y.2d 554, 419 N.Y.S.2d 461, 393 N.E.2d 456, 459 (1979).

Two friends had a revolver. There was one cartridge in the chamber, so placed that they thought it would not fire until the trigger had been pulled about five times. One playfully put the weapon against the side of the other and pulled the trigger three times. The third pull resulted in a fatal shot. A conviction of second-degree murder was affirmed. Commonwealth v. Malone, 354 Pa. 180, 47 A.2d 445 (1946).

PEOPLE v. RODRIGUEZ

District Court of Appeal, Second District, Division 3, California, 1961.
186 Cal.App.2d 433, 8 Cal.Rptr. 863.

VALÉE, JUSTICE. By information defendant was accused of manslaughter in that on November 8, 1959 she did wilfully, unlawfully, feloniously, and without malice kill Carlos Quinones. In a nonjury trial she was found guilty of involuntary manslaughter. A new trial was denied. She appeals from the judgment and the order denying a new trial.

In November 1959 defendant was living with her four children in a single-family residence at 130 South Clarence Street, Los Angeles. The oldest child was 6 years of age. Carlos Quinones was the youngest, either 2 or 3 years of age.

Olive Faison lived across the street from defendant. About 10:45 p.m. on November 8, 1959 Miss Faison heard some children calling, "Mommy, mommy." For about 15 or 20 minutes she did not "pay too much attention." She noticed the cries became more shrill. She went to the front window and saw smoke coming from defendant's house. She "ran across the street and commenced to knock the door in and started pulling the children out." There was a screen door on the outside and a wooden door inside the screen door. The screen door was padlocked on the outside. The other door was open. She broke the screen door and with the help of neighbors pulled three of the children out of the house. She tried to get into the house through the front door but could not because of the flames. A neighbor entered through the back door but could not go far because of the flames. Miss Faison took the three children to her apartment and shortly thereafter returned to the scene of the fire. . . .

Maria Lucero, defendant's sister, went to defendant's home about 12 p.m. on November 8, 1959. She went looking for defendant. She found her about 2 or 2:30 a.m. in the same block as "Johnny's Place." Defendant was nervous and frightened, said she knew about the fire and that she went over to tell Johnny Powers about it. Defendant had not been drinking.

Carlos Quinones died from "thermal burns, second and third degree involving 50 to 60 per cent of the body surface." Defendant did not testify. . . .

"Manslaughter is the unlawful killing of a human being without malice. It is of three kinds: . . . 2. Involuntary—in the commission of an unlawful act, not amounting to felony; or in the commission of a lawful act which might produce death, in an unlawful manner, or without due caution and circumspection . . . ." Pen.Code, § 192. "In every crime or public offense there must exist a union, or joint operation of act and intent, or criminal negligence." Pen.Code, § 20. Section 20 of the Penal Code makes the union of act and wrongful intent or criminal negligence an invariable element of every crime unless it is excluded expressly or by necessary implication. Section 26 of the Penal Code lists, among the persons incapable of committing crimes, "[p]ersons who committed the act or made the omission charged through misfortune or by accident, when it appears that there was no evil design, intention, or culpable negligence." Thus the question is: Was there any evidence of criminal intent or criminal negligence? . . .

It appears from the record that guilt was predicated on the alleged "commission of a lawful act which might produce death, in an unlawful manner, or without due caution and circumspection." Pen. Code, § 192.

In People v. Penny, 44 Cal.2d 861, 285 P.2d 926, the defendant was convicted of involuntary manslaughter. While engaged in the practice of "face rejuvenation" she applied a formula containing phenol to the skin. Death was caused by phenol poisoning. The trial court charged the jury that ordinary negligence was sufficient to constitute lack of "due caution and circumspection" under Penal Code, § 192. The court said (44 Cal.2d at page 869, 285 P.2d at page 931): "It has been held that without 'due caution and circumspection' is the equivalent of 'criminal negligence.' "[1] After reviewing numerous California authorities, the court continued (44 Cal.2d at page 876, 285 P.2d at page 935):

"So far as the latest cases are concerned, it appears that mere negligence is sufficient to constitute a lack of due caution and circumspection under the manslaughter statute. Pen.Code, § 192, subd. 2. This does not appear to be a correct rule. Something more, in our opinion, is needed to constitute the criminal negligence required for a conviction of manslaughter." . . .

"We hold, therefore, that the general rule just quoted, sets forth the standard to be used in California for negligent homicide, Pen.Code § 192, subd. 2, in other than vehicle cases. Defendant here was charged with a violation of section 192, subdivision 2, of the Penal Code."

It is generally held that an act is criminally negligent when a man of ordinary prudence would foresee that the act would cause a high degree of risk of death or great bodily harm. The risk of death or great bodily harm must be great. Whether the conduct of defendant was wanton or reckless so as to warrant conviction of manslaughter must be determined from the conduct itself and not from the resultant harm. Criminal liability cannot be predicated on every careless act merely because its carelessness results in injury to another. The act must be one which has knowable and apparent potentialities for

1. "To constitute involuntary manslaughter, the homicide must have resulted from the defendant's failure to exercise due caution and circumspection, which has been held to be the equivalent of 'criminal negligence' or 'culpable negligence' ". State v. Sorenson, 104 Ariz. 503, 507, 455 P.2d 981, 985 (1969).

resulting in death. Mere inattention or mistake in judgment resulting even in death of another is not criminal unless the quality of the act makes it so. The fundamental requirement fixing criminal responsibility is knowledge, actual or imputed, that the act of the accused tended to endanger life.

In a case of involuntary manslaughter the criminal negligence of the accused must be the proximate cause of the death. . . .

It clearly appears from the definition of criminal negligence stated in People v. Penny, supra 44 Cal.2d 861, 285 P.2d 926, that knowledge, actual or imputed, that the act of the slayer tended to endanger life and that the fatal consequences of the negligent act could reasonably have been foreseen are necessary for negligence to be criminal at all. Must a parent never leave a young child alone in the house on risk of being adjudged guilty of manslaughter if some unforeseeable occurrence causes the death of the child? The only reasonable view of the evidence is that the death of Carlos was the result of misadventure and not the natural and probable result of a criminally negligent act. There was no evidence from which it can be inferred that defendant realized her conduct would in all probability produce death. There was no evidence as to the cause of the fire, as to how or where it started. There was no evidence connecting defendant in any way with the fire. There was no evidence that defendant could reasonably have foreseen there was a probability that fire would ignite in the house and that Carlos would be burned to death. The most that can be said is that defendant may have been negligent; but mere negligence is not sufficient to authorize a conviction of involuntary manslaughter. . . .

The judgment and order denying a new trial are reversed.[2]

SHINN, P.J., concurs.

FORD, J., did not participate.

STATE v. BIER

Supreme Court of Montana, 1979.
181 Mont. 27, 591 P.2d 1115.

SHEA, JUSTICE. Defendant appeals from a conviction of negligent homicide, section 95–4–104, R.C.M.1947, now section 45–5–104 MCA, following a jury trial in the Cascade County District Court.

The facts show that in the early morning of June 25, 1977, Deputy Sheriff Donovan responded to a call concerning a possible suicide at the Red Wheel Trailer Court in Great Falls. He arrived at about 1:30 a.m. and noticed defendant Richard Bier wave and holler at him to hurry. Donovan entered the trailer and saw defendant's wife, Shar-

2. In a case in which the mother locked the children in the house and went to join her paramour in his apartment it was held that the jury could find culpable negligence. Delay v. Brainard, 182 Neb. 509, 156 N.W.2d 14 (1968).

on Bier, on the floor in the doorway between the bedroom and hall of the trailer. She was bleeding from a neck wound. Defendant told Donovan that his wife shot herself. A .357 Magnum revolver lay on the bed in the bedroom. Moments later, an ambulance arrived. Temporary aid was administered and Sharon Bier was transported to the hospital accompanied by the defendant. Deputy Donovan stayed behind. He washed his hands in the trailer's bathroom and noticed blood in the basin and on a cabinet. He photographed the interior of the trailer, identified and took custody of the gun, bullets and spent casing, and saw that the two minor children present were cared for before proceeding to the hospital.

When Deputy Donovan arrived at the hospital, he placed each of Mrs. Bier's hands in plastic bags and taped them shut to preserve any evidence of gun powder. He then located defendant for questioning. After being read his rights, defendant related the events leading up to the shooting.

Defendant stated he and his wife had been at the stock car races all evening and consumed a total of three six-packs of beer. Mrs. Bier, normally a mild social drinker, finished two six-packs. When the couple returned home, an argument ensued. Intent on leaving and avoiding further quarrel, defendant went into the bedroom to ready his departure. Mrs. Bier stood in the bedroom doorway, apparently to block his exit. Defendant reached into the closet, pulled a gun from its holster, cocked it and cast it on the bed stating words to the effect that to stop him she'd have to shoot him. Defendant turned away and his wife picked up the gun, held it with both thumbs on the trigger and pointed it at her head. Defendant shouted "that damn thing's loaded" and either grabbed or slapped at the gun to avert its aim. It discharged and Mrs. Bier collapsed on the floor.

Pursuant to police procedure, Deputy Donovan took hand swabs of defendant and his wife for analysis of possible gun powder residue by the proper authorities. The test results showed no appreciable level of residue from which to conclude either Mr. or Mrs. Bier was holding the gun when it discharged. Defendant had washed his hands while his wife was being administered medical aid at the trailer. Mrs. Bier never regained consciousness and died six days after the shooting.

About a month after the incident, defendant was questioned at the Cascade County Sheriff's Office. He essentially recounted the statement previously given except that he thought maybe he'd grabbed rather than slapped at the gun when it discharged, and that perhaps this had caused the gun to fire.

On October 17, defendant was charged with negligent homicide and on October 19, he entered a plea of not guilty.

The State's case consisted of Deputy Donovan, two expert witnesses from Washington, D.C., and the ambulance attendant who answered the emergency call at the Bier residence. One of the experts testified to the slight force necessary to discharge a cocked .357 Magnum revolver and that the handgun fired at a distance of one foot produced a powder dispersal pattern of four to five inches in diameter. Exhibits revealed a four-inch dispersal pattern on Mrs. Bier's neck. The other expert witness reported the results of the hand swab analysis conducted in Washington, D.C. He could not determine who held the gun when it fired.

Defendant testified on his own behalf. He was a career Air Force Sergeant and the father of three minor children by Mrs. Bier. He stated on direct examination, "I don't know if I made her hands squeeze the trigger or if she squeezed the trigger, or how it happened." On cross-examination he admitted that he was aware of his wife's intoxicated condition and should have realized the danger involved.

During defendant's testimony, defense counsel attempted to show through defendant's testimony and diagrams that the angle of the bullet's path was such as to preclude any possibility that defendant held the gun when it discharged. The County Attorney objected to this line of questioning on the ground that evidence relating to the bullet's angle was a technical subject requiring the testimony of an expert. Following an intense exchange between court and counsel, the court ruled that all evidence relating to bullet's angle would be excluded as a technical subject admissible only through expert testimony.

Defendant raises five issues for our review:

(1) Whether the facts presented preclude a finding of negligent homicide as a matter of law.

(2) Whether the District Court abused its discretion by denying defendant's motion for a jury view of the mobile home in which the shooting occurred. . . .

Defendant contends the State failed to prove the required mental state and causation elements for a prima facie case of negligent homicide. Concerning the mental element, defendant argues that his conduct did not evidence a conscious disregard for his wife's life. Negligent homicide is defined by statute as follows:

> "(1) Criminal homicide constitutes negligent homicide when it is committed negligently.
>
> "(2) A person convicted of negligent homicide shall be imprisoned in the state prison for any term not to exceed ten (10) years." Section 95–4–104, R.C.M.1947, now section 45–5–104 MCA.

Negligence is defined as follows:

> ". . . [A] person acts negligently with respect to a result or to a circumstance described by a statute defining an offense when he consciously disregards a risk that the result will occur or that the circumstance exists *or if he disregards a risk of which he should be aware* that the result will occur or that the circumstance exists.

The risk must be of such a nature and degree that to disregard it involves *a gross deviation* from the standard of conduct that a reasonable person would be observe in the actor's situation. Gross deviation means a deviation that is *considerably greater than lack of ordinary care.* Relevant terms such as 'negligent' and 'with negligence' have the same meaning." (Emphasis added.) Section 94–2–101(31), R.C.M.1947, now section 45–2–101(31) MCA.

In *State v. Kirkaldie* (1978), Mont., 587 P.2d 1298, 1304, 35 St.Rep. 1532, 1538, this Court explained that "[u]nlike deliberate homicide, which requires that the offense be committed purposely or knowingly, negligent homicide does not require such purpose or knowledge. Negligent homicide only requires a gross deviation from a reasonable standard of care." A gross deviation under the statutory definition is analogous to gross negligence in the law of torts. Although somewhat nebulous in concept, gross negligence is generally considered to fall short of a reckless disregard for consequences and is said to differ from ordinary negligence only in degree, not in kind. See, Prosser, Law of Torts, 183–84 (4th Ed.1971). Here, defendant's conduct in pulling out, cocking and throwing a loaded gun within reach of his intoxicated wife clearly qualifies as a gross deviation giving rise to criminal culpability.

Defendant also contends he should not be held responsible to have foreseen his wife's alleged suicide attempt. Generally, where a crime is based on some form of negligence the State must show not only that defendant's negligent conduct was the "cause in fact" of the victim's death, but also that the victim was foreseeably endangered, in a manner which was foreseeable and to a degree of harm which was foreseeable. Clearly, the risk created by defendant's conduct under the circumstances (that in a highly intoxicated state his wife would shoot either the defendant or herself), was a foreseeable risk. Indeed, he challenged her to use the gun. Affirmed.[1]

PEOPLE v. WATKINS

Supreme Court of Colorado, En Banc, 1978.
196 Colo. 377, 586 P.2d 43.

PRINGLE, JUSTICE. Defendant Henry Lee Watkins was convicted of second-degree murder of Walter McDonald and of first-degree assault upon David Buckner. He contends that the trial court's refusal to give instructions to the jury relating to lesser included offenses

1. For the statutory offense known as "automobile homicide"—causing a fatal traffic accident by driving carelessly while under the influence of liquor or drug, see State v. Twitchell, 8 Utah 2d 314, 333 P.2d 1075 (1959).

Vehicular homicide caused by drunken driving is a violation of the motor vehicle negligent homicide statute and not the general manslaughter statute. Lopez v. State, 586 P.2d 157 (Wyo.1978).

under the circumstances of this case was error. We agree and reverse.

A rather full recital of the evidence in this case is necessary to put the legal issues in perspective. Eddie Watkins and the deceased, Walter McDonald, argued over access to the pool table at New Joe's Bar where they were drinking. Eddie and Walter apparently resolved the dispute between them, but the argument flared again between Walter and a friend of Eddie's. This latter dispute was left unresolved.

Walter McDonald and his brother Byron then went to another bar where they met David Buckner. Evidently there was some discussion that they should return to New Joe's and "settle the score." They did, in fact, return to New Joe's but walked past the defendant and Eddie and into the bar. The defendant testified, however, that one of them pointed out his brother Eddie and said, "That's our man." Later the two McDonald brothers, Buckner and Eddie went outside to play craps.

During the dice game the shooting occurred. The defendant testified that he saw David Buckner pull a knife on his brother when Eddie bent down to throw the dice and that Walter McDonald had yelled to Buckner, "Cut that nigger's throat." When the defendant tried to warn his brother, Buckner turned toward him with the knife. The defendant fired his gun at Buckner. The defendant testified that Walter McDonald had started toward him with a gun and that he had shot him in self-defense.

An open knife was later found in the bar but no other evidence was presented to support the defendant's testimony. The trial judge instructed the jury on first and second-degree murder but refused the defendant's request that the jury be instructed on criminally negligent homicide. The trial court based its refusal on the grounds that there was *no evidence* that Walter McDonald's death was negligently rather than intentionally caused. The jury was also instructed on the affirmative defense of self-defense.

I

Error which requires reversal stems from the trial court's refusal to give defendant's tendered instruction on criminally negligent homicide. We held in Read v. People, 119 Colo. 506, 205 P.2d 233 (1949), and reiterated in People v. Miller, 187 Colo. 239, 529 P.2d 648 (1974), that "when there is any evidence, however improbable, unreasonable or slight, which tends to reduce the homicide to [a lesser grade], the defendant is entitled to an instruction thereon upon the hypothesis that the same is true, and that it is for the jury, under proper instructions, and not the trial judge, to weigh and consider the evidence and determine therefrom what grade of crime, if any, was committed; and that the court's refusal to instruct thereon is reversible error."

During the trial, the defendant testified that he believed, in good faith, that his brother Eddie's, and then his own, life was threatened. Such a belief, even if unreasonable, presents a case for criminally negligent homicide. Section 18–3–105, C.R.S.1973.

The People cite People v. Shannon, 189 Colo. 287, 539 P.2d 480 (1975), and People v. Rivera, 186 Colo. 24, 525 P.2d 431 (1974), to buttress their position that there was no "rational basis" to justify a criminally negligent homicide instruction. In *Shannon,* the victims suffered grievous gunshot wounds at the hands of the defendant and there was absolutely no evidence given to support a lesser charge of third-degree assault. In *Rivera,* we specifically held that the defendant is entitled to have the court instruct the jury on the defense theory of the case as revealed by the evidence. The mere fact that the evidence in this case was supplied by the defendant who took the stand in his own defense does not preclude it from the jury's consideration.

As in People v. Miller, supra, we quote with approval from Crawford v. People, 12 Colo. 290, 20 P. 769 (1888):

> "We do not say that . . . the jury would have found differently had they been properly instructed. What we do say is that there was not an entire absence of evidence tending to establish the crime of manslaughter, and that defendant was entitled to an instruction with reference thereto. It is obviously impossible for us to hold that the error thus committed was without prejudice."

There is no doubt that the defendant shot Walter McDonald and David Buckner. However, while a jury might not believe that a reasonable man would be in fear of his life under the circumstances of this case, they might in fact believe that the defendant held a good faith belief, though an unreasonable one, that he feared for his life. Such a belief by the jury would entitle him to a verdict of criminally negligent homicide rather than second-degree murder under the legislative definitions which appear in our statutes.

II

We recently decided that where a jury determined that the defendant committed the assault in the good faith but unreasonable belief that his actions were justified, the sentence imposed can be no greater than that which could be imposed upon a defendant under the criminally negligent homicide statute. Since, in this case, there was evidence to support a jury instruction based on the defendant's good faith but unreasonable fear of serious harm, and since the assault charge and the homicide arose out of the same incident, on remand, the trial judge should provide such an instruction as to the assault charge to the jury and, if the defendant is again found guilty of first-degree assault, sentence the defendant in accordance with *Bramlett.*

III

We find the defendant's argument that there was insufficient evidence to support the jury's finding that the defendant caused "serious bodily injury" as required for first-degree assault, Section 18–3–202, C.R.S.1973 (1977 Supp.), to be without merit. The evidence presented at trial indicated that Buckner had been shot and wounded by the defendant. It is within the province of the jury to determine the degree of the injury and we find that there was sufficient evidence for them to determine in this case that the injury was serious.

The judgment is reversed and the cause remanded to the district court for a new trial.

HARRIS v. STATE

Court of Appeals of Georgia, 1937.
55 Ga.App. 189, 189 S.E. 680.

MacIntyre, J. W.J. Harris was convicted of voluntary manslaughter, and his punishment was fixed by the verdict at not less than ten nor more than fifteen years. His motion for a new trial was overruled, and he excepted.

1. Taking the view of the evidence which is most unfavorable to the accused, which we do in passing on a motion for new trial, it in effect shows that the defendant, who was somewhat drawn with rheumatism, was smaller in size than the deceased; that, after an argument about a certain jug which had been left with the defendant at his place of business by the deceased, the defendant not only called the deceased a liar, but also a God damn liar; that the deceased, an able-bodied, strong, and robust man, thereupon struck the defendant two hard blows with his fists, and that the defendant killed the deceased by shooting him three times, once in the thigh, once in the stomach above the navel, and once in the shoulder. A witness testified: "The first shot hit him in the leg. I know, 'cause I seen him give. He just kept right on going down. The second shot missed him. I seen it dig dirt up by him. Harris [the defendant] was shooting somewhere 'bout his legs along about here" (indicating). On the other hand, the effect of the defendant's statement and one of his witness's testimony was that the deceased, after hitting the defendant twice with his fists, hit him a third time over the head with the stick, which knocked him down, and that the deceased thereupon picked up his small goat-cart, or wagon, and was trying to advance on the defendant with that weapon when the defendant shot him. The wagon, or goat-cart, and stick were introduced in evidence by the defendant, without objection. We think the jury were authorized to render a verdict of voluntary manslaughter. . . .

3. The defendant assigns error on the failure of the court to charge the law on involuntary manslaughter. This assignment is

based on the evidence of two witnesses, one of whom testified as follows: "Mr. Harris [the defendant] was not shooting up in the body. He was shooting down in his legs, shooting at his feet, yes." The other testified, "Mr. Harris was shooting somewhere about his legs along here" (indicating). The defendant contends that this evidence shows conclusively "that Harris in shooting Pittman down in his legs, at his feet, somewhere about his legs along here (indicating), was the act of a man trying to keep Pittman from unmercifully beating him, and disproves clearly that Harris had any intention at the time to kill Pittman." We can not agree to this contention of the defendant. "Where one voluntarily fires a loaded pistol at another, without excuse and not under circumstances of justification, and kills the person at whom he shot, the law will hold the slayer responsible for the consequences of his act. It conclusively presumes malice on the part of the slayer; and the grade of the homicide, so committed, will not be reduced to involuntary manslaughter, even if the intent of the slayer, under such circumstances, was to wound or cripple the deceased, and not to kill." . . .[1]

STATE v. SETY

Court of Appeals of Arizona, Division 1, Department A, 1979.
121 Ariz. 354, 590 P.2d 470.

SCHROEDER, JUDGE. In the morning hours of March 19, 1976, Donald Cue died as the result of injuries inflicted by the appellant, David Sety, during a bizarre series of confrontations at an isolated campground. Appellant was tried on an open charge of murder. During trial the court granted a directed verdict of acquittal as to first degree murder, and the jury convicted the appellant of second degree murder. On post trial motions, the trial court reduced the charge to voluntary manslaughter and sentenced Sety to serve not less than nine nor more than ten years in the Arizona State Prison.

1. "We think, however, that an instruction should have been given whereunder Vires could have been found guilty of voluntary manslaughter if the jury believe that the shooting was the result of reckless, wanton and felonious disregard of the safety of human life. Also there should have been an instruction authorizing the jury to find Vires guilty of involuntary manslaughter if he was found to be guilty of the reckless use of firearms, though the shooting was not done wantonly and feloniously." Vires v. Commonwealth, 308 Ky. 707, 215 S.W.2d 837 (1948).

Involuntary manslaughter is distinguished from voluntary manslaughter by lack of an intent to kill. State v. Childers, 217 Kan. 410, 536 P.2d 1349 (1975).

An assailant who commits an unlawful assault and battery on another without malice, resulting in death, is guilty of manslaughter although the death was not intended and the assault was not of a character likely to result fatally. State v. Black, 360 Mo. 261, 227 S.W.2d 1006 (1950).

To sustain a charge of involuntary manslaughter the state must prove an unintentional killing and that D was at the time of the killing either engaged in the commission of a misdemeanor or committing a lawful act in a wanton manner. State v. Betts, 214 Kan. 271, 519 P.2d 655 (1974).

Appellant Sety appeals from the judgment and sentence, and the State appeals from the trial court's reduction of the conviction from second degree murder to voluntary manslaughter. We affirm the conviction and modify the sentence.

SUFFICIENCY OF THE EVIDENCE SUPPORTING VOLUNTARY MANSLAUGHTER AND SECOND DEGREE MURDER

Sety initially contends that the court should have directed a verdict of acquittal with respect to all charges. In its appeal the State urges that the trial court abused its discretion when, following the trial, it reduced the conviction from second degree murder to voluntary manslaughter. Resolution of both issues turns upon the unusual facts developed at trial.

On the day in question, the appellant was camping alone in an area below Bartlett Lake Dam in Maricopa County, Arizona. Sety testified that at approximately 6:00 a.m., the obviously intoxicated victim, Mr. Cue, awakened him and engaged him in a rambling discussion, primarily about weapons. Cue admired the appellant's hunting knife, asked Sety to sharpen Cue's own knife and then boasted of having killed eight people with that knife. Sety testified that he was shaken by this talk and that he crawled into his camper to get a pistol. Sety stated that as he emerged from the camper Cue was pointing a gun directly at his head and laughing in a threatening manner.

Cue continued to talk about weapons, pulled a number of them from his car, and then began firing a large caliber rifle across the river. Thereafter, Cue loaded his weapon, repeatedly pointed it at Sety and joked about how afraid Sety was of him. Finally, Sety grabbed his own pistol and told Cue to "freeze." The armed Cue continued to approach, prompting Sety to fire two warning shots and to take Cue's rifle from him. Sety testified that Cue then reached into his jacket as if to take a gun from his belt. The appellant fired, striking Cue in the side, told Cue he was making a citizen's arrest and ordered him to begin walking toward the dam keeper's house. The two men then left the site near the camper, referred to at trial as site A, and proceeded toward the house. The physical evidence and Sety's testimony up to that point are not in dispute. The State does not contend that Sety was guilty of any culpable conduct prior to the time that the men left site A.

The two men then headed in the direction of the dam keeper's house, with Sety constantly prodding the resistant Cue. According to Sety's testimony, when Cue attempted to flee back toward the arsenal of weapons at site A, Sety fired first one or more warning shots and then two shots which struck Cue in the back. The victim fell on his back and lay motionless, apparently dead. As Sety approached him, however, Cue grabbed him and pulled him to the ground. Sety stated that he choked the victim into unconsciousness, went back to the camper to reload his pistol and then returned to where Cue was lying, designated during trial as site B. Sety then cut off part of the victim's clothing explaining at various times that he did so in order to make it harder for Cue to flee, to search for weapons or to determine the extent of the victim's wounds. Physical evidence found at site B, including the outer shirt worn by Cue, shell casings and evidence of a struggle corroborated Sety's version of the events.

At this point, however, the physical evidence and Sety's version of the incident diverge somewhat. Sety testified that as he again began prodding Cue in the direction of the dam keeper's house, Cue knocked the rifle from Sety's grasp and ran. Sety fired several pistol shots from what he claimed was a distance of roughly 75 feet. Cue fell and, by Sety's account, pretended to be dead. Sety testified, however, that as he looked more closely Cue reached up suddenly to grab him. As he jerked away, Sety claimed that his gun discharged striking Cue in the head. Certain at last that Cue was dead Sety continued to the dam keeper's house and reported the homicide to the Sheriff's Department.

Thus, according to Sety, the wounds which he inflicted upon Cue after they left site B were all either in self defense or in justified furtherance of a citizen's arrest. He argues that, based upon his testimony, he should have been acquitted of all charges.

The physical evidence, however, does not fully support Sety's version of what transpired after Cue and Sety left site B. Although Sety testified that Cue had bolted from scene B and had been shot at a distance of approximately 75 feet, Cue's undershirt, which he was wearing at the time the final shots were fired, showed evidence of powder burns indicating shots fired at a very close range. Shell casings were found fairly close to the corpse rather than at the greater distance indicated by Sety's testimony. The State also presented evidence of the trajectory of the bullets which could be interpreted as rebutting Sety's claim that he fired these shots from a distance at the fleeing Cue. The State's evidence suggests that Sety fired at least two final shots, in addition to the shot which struck Cue in the head, at very close range, and not, as he asserted, while Cue was in flight. The State thus presented evidence from which the jury could have concluded that the victim was shot repeatedly in circumstances which no longer justified deadly force. This evidence contradicted Sety's proffered defenses. We conclude that the evidence presented was sufficient to find criminal culpability.

Having rejected the appellant's argument that he was entitled to a judgment of acquittal of all charges we now consider the State's contention that the trial court erred in reducing the conviction to voluntary manslaughter from second degree murder.

The presence of malice distinguishes murder from manslaughter under the statutes in effect at the time of this incident. A.R.S. § 13–451(A) provided that "murder is the unlawful killing of a human being with malice aforethought." A.R.S. § 13–455 defined manslaughter as "the unlawful killing of a human being without malice." Malice has been defined as the absence of justification, excuse or mitigation. The trial court properly reduced the conviction to manslaughter only if the evidence was not sufficient to show an absence of justification, excuse or mitigation.

The State's principal argument in its appeal is that Sety's use of a deadly weapon supplies the element of malice. This is, however, only a presumption and may be rebutted by evidence of mitigation, justification or excuse sufficient to raise a reasonable doubt as to the existence of malice. We find it difficult to conceive of a case in which this presumption is rebutted by stronger evidence of mitigation. In its briefs and at trial the State has conceded that Sety's initial use of force was fully justified and not culpable. There is no doubt that the provocation and terror which precipitated this killing were instigated by the intrusion of the seemingly crazed Cue into the pre-dawn solitude of the appellant's campground. In our view, this is a classic illustration of manslaughter resulting from mitigating circumstances.

> . . . As a matter of juridical science, any circumstance of substantial mitigation should be sufficient to reduce to manslaughter a killing that would otherwise be murder. Suppose, for example, the defendant thought he was in imminent danger of death and must kill to save himself from being murdered, and that he did kill for that reason. Suppose, also, there was no actual danger to his life at the moment, and the facts fell a little short of reasonable grounds for a belief in such danger. His homicide is not excused; but if the circumstances came rather close to such as would constitute an excuse his guilt is of manslaughter rather than murder, . . . Perkins, Criminal Law (1st ed. 1957), at 40. (footnote omitted).

The real factual issue presented in this case was whether the amount of force used by Sety was excessive under the circumstances. We believe that there was sufficient evidence for the jury to reject Sety's defenses and to convict him of manslaughter, but that the evidence did not support a murder conviction. At most, appellant was guilty of excessive retaliation constituting manslaughter rather than murder.

Accordingly, we conclude that the trial court's reduction of the conviction from second degree murder to voluntary manslaughter was mandated by the evidence. Conviction affirmed, sentenced modified.[1]

1. The "rule of provocation" has not been changed in some of the new codes. For example:

"The provocation is not sufficient, however, if an ordinary person would have cooled off before acting." State v. Reynolds, 98 N.M. 527, 650 P.2d 811, 813 (1982).

Skip

COMMONWEALTH v. DRUM

Supreme Court of Pennsylvania, 1868.
58 Pa. 9.

William Drum was charged in the Court of Quarter Sessions of Westmoreland County for the murder of David Mohigan. A true bill having been found by the grand jury of that court, it was certified into the Court of Oyer and Terminer of the same county. . . .

JUSTICE AGNEW charged the jury as follows: . . .

A life has been taken. The unfortunate David Mohigan has fallen into an untimely grave; struck down by the hand of violence; and it is for you to determine whose was that hand, and what its guilt. The prisoner is in the morning of life; as yet so fresh and fair. As you sat and gazed into his youthful face, you have thought, no doubt, most anxiously thought, is his that hand? Can he, indeed, be a murderer? This, gentlemen, is the solemn question you must determine upon the law and the evidence.

At the common law murder is described to be, when a person of sound memory and discretion unlawfully kills any reasonable creature in being and under the peace of the Commonwealth, with malice aforethought, express or implied. The distinguishing criterion of murder is malice aforethought. But it is not malice in its ordinary understanding alone, a particular ill-will, a spite or a grudge. Malice is a legal term, implying much more. It comprehends not only a particular ill-will, but every case where there is wickedness of disposition, hardness of heart, cruelty, recklessness of consequences, and a mind regardless of social duty, although a particular person may not be intended to be injured. Murder, therefore, at common law embraces cases where no intent to kill existed, but where the state or frame of mind termed malice, in its legal sense, prevailed.

In Pennsylvania, the legislature, considering that there is a manifest difference in the degree of guilt, where a deliberate intention to kill exists, and where none appears, distinguished murder into two grades—murder of the first and murder of the second degree; and provided that the jury before whom any person indicted for murder should be tried, shall, if they find him guilty thereof, ascertain in their verdict whether it be murder of the first or murder of the second degree. By the Act of 31st March 1860, "all murder which shall be perpetrated by means of poison,[a] or by lying in wait, or by any other kind of wilful, deliberate and premeditated killing, or which shall be committed in the perpetration of, or attempt to perpetrate

a. Some statutes have added by means of torture. This does not require an intent to kill, but it does require a wilful, deliberate and premeditated intent to inflict extreme and prolonged pain. People v. Steger, 16 Cal.3d 539, 128 Cal.Rptr. 161, 546 P.2d 665 (1976).

California provides that it is murder in the first degree if perpetrated by means of a "destructive device or explosive, knowing use of ammunition designed primarily to penetrate metal or armor. . . ." West's Ann.Cal.Pen.Code § 189 (1982).

any arson, rape, robbery or burglary, shall be deemed murder of the first degree; and all other kinds of murder shall be deemed murder of the second degree." [1]

In this case we have to deal only with that kind of murder in the first degree described as "wilful, deliberate, and premeditated." Many cases have been decided under this clause, in all of which it has been held that the *intention* to kill is the essence of the offence. Therefore, if an intention to kill exists, it is wilful; if this intention be accompanied by such circumstances as evidence a mind fully conscious of its own purpose and design, it is deliberate; and if sufficient time be afforded to enable the mind fully to frame the design to kill, and to select the instrument, or to frame the plan to carry this design into execution, it is premeditated. The law fixes upon no length of time as necessary to form the intention to kill, but leaves the existence of a fully formed intent as a fact to be determined by the jury, from all the facts and circumstances in the evidence. . . . [2]

The proof of the intention to kill, and of the disposition of mind constituting murder in the first degree, under the Act of Assembly, lies on the Commonwealth. But this proof need not be express or positive. It may be inferred from the circumstances. If, from all the facts attending the killing, the jury can fully, reasonably, and satisfactorily infer the existence of the intention to kill, and the malice of heart with which it was done, they will be warranted in so doing. He who uses upon the body of another, at some vital part, with a manifest intention to use it upon him, a deadly weapon, as an axe, a gun, a knife or a pistol, must, in the absence of qualifying facts, be pre-

1. This is essentially the same as the first statute which divided murder into degrees, enacted in Pennsylvania in 1794. It was adopted, sometimes with minor variations, in over two-thirds of the states.

2. "No specific period of time is required but if the time is sufficient to fully and clearly conceive the design to kill and purposely and deliberately execute it, the requirements of the statute are satisfied." State v. Pierce, 4 N.J. 252, 267–8, 72 A.2d 305, 313 (1950).

" 'When a design to kill another person is once formed, the haste with which it is put into execution in no way affects or modifies the degree of guilt incurred.' " State v. Gregory, 66 Nev. 423, 427, 212 P.2d 701, 703–4 (1949).

"To prove deliberate premeditation the Commonwealth must show that a defendant's resolution to kill was a result of reflection which 'is not so much a matter of time as logical sequence. First the deliberation and premeditation, then the resolution to kill, and lastly the killing in pursuance of the resolution; and all this may occur in a few seconds.' " Commonwealth v. Soares, 377 Mass. 461, 387 N.E.2d 499, 506 (1979).

A wilful, deliberate and premeditated killing requires "not a general malice, but a special malice that aims at the life of a person." Keenan v. Commonwealth, 44 Pa. 55, 57 (1862).

A killing by "lying in wait" is a killing resulting from ambush for the purpose of killing. State v. Olds, 19 Or. 397, 24 P. 394 (1890). In other words it is a particular kind of wilful, deliberate and premeditated killing. Accord: State v. Gause, 227 N.C. 26, 40 S.E.2d 463 (1946); Commonwealth v. Mondollo, 247 Pa. 526, 93 A. 612 (1915); Burgess v. Commonwealth, 4 Va. 483 (1825). But the California court held that murder by "lying in wait" does not require a deliberate and premeditated plan to kill, but may be perpetrated by killing from ambush as a result of the intentional inflicting of bodily injury under circumstances likely to cause death. People v. Mason, 54 Cal.2d 164, 4 Cal.Rptr. 841, 351 P.2d 1025 (1960).

sumed to know that his blow is likely to kill; and, knowing this, must be presumed to intend the death which is the probable and ordinary consequence of such an act. He who so uses a deadly weapon without a sufficient cause of provocation, must be presumed to do it wickedly, or from a bad heart. Therefore, he who takes the life of another with a deadly weapon, and with a manifest design thus to use it upon him, with sufficient time to deliberate, and fully to form the conscious purpose of killing, and without any sufficient reason or cause of extenuation, is guilty of murder in the first degree.

All murder not of the first degree, is necessarily of the second degree, and includes all unlawful killing under circumstances of depravity of heart, and a disposition of mind regardless of social duty; but where no intention to kill exists or can be reasonaby and fully inferred. Therefore, in all cases of murder, if no intention to kill can be inferred or collected from the circumstances, the verdict must be murder in the second degree.

Manslaughter is defined to be the unlawful killing of another without malice expressed or implied; which may be voluntarily in a sudden heat, or involuntarily, but in the commission of an unlawful act. . . .

You will now take the case and render such a verdict as the evidence warrants; one which will do justice to the Commonwealth and to the prisoner.

PEOPLE v. CORNETT

Supreme Court of California, In Bank, 1948.
33 Cal.2d 33, 198 P.2d 877.

TRAYNOR, J. Defendant was charged with the murder of Fred Weaver Cole, the stepfather, of his divorced wife. A jury found him guilty of murder in the first degree and made no recommendation as to penalty. The trial court denied his motion for a new trial and sentenced him to death. This is an automatic appeal from the judgment imposing the death penalty. (Pen.Code, § 1239(b).) . . .

The trial court also erred in giving the following instruction: "There must be an intent to kill, but there need be, however, no appreciable space of time between the forming of the intent to kill and the overt act—they may be as instantaneous as successive thoughts of the mind. A man may do a thing wilfully, deliberately and intentionally from a moment's reflection as well as after pondering over the subject for a month or a year. He can premeditate, that is, think before doing the act, the moment he conceives the purpose, as well as if the act was the result of long preconcert or preparation." As held in People v. Bender, 27 Cal.2d 164, 182, 163 P.2d 8, and People v. Valentine, 28 Cal.2d 121, 134, 169 P.2d 1, such a combination of instructions is wholly erroneous. "Of course the instruction that there need be 'no appreciable space of time between the intention to kill and the act of killing . . . .' is abstractly a correct statement of the law. It will be properly understood (at least upon *deliberation*) by those learned in the law as referring only to the interval between the fully formulated intent and its execution, *and as necessarily presupposing that true deliberation and premeditation characterized the process of, and preceded ultimate, formulation of such intent* . . . But holding that such declaration is a correct statement of the abstract principle of law is not a holding that the same declaration made to a jury without explanation is not error. Particularly is it misleading when read in the context in which it was used. It excludes from the required showing any deliberation and premeditation between the intent and the act of killing and since other portions of the instructions eliminate any necessity for deliberation or premeditation in forming the intent ('He can premeditate . . . the moment he conceives the purpose . . . .,' etc.), we find that the court has wholly deleted the only difference, in this type of case, between first and second degree murder." To say that the defendant "can premeditate . . . . the moment he conceives the purpose" precludes the meaning of careful thought and the weighing of considerations embodied in the ordinary dictionary meaning of "deliberation" and "premeditation."

The trial court, however, gave other instructions relating to the meaning of "deliberation and premeditation" essential for murder in the first degree: "The law does not undertake to measure in units of time the length of the period during which the thought must be pondered before it can ripen into an intent to kill which is truly deliberate and premeditated. The time will vary with different individuals and under varying circumstances. The true test is not the duration of time, but rather the extent of the reflection. A cold, calculated judgment and decision may be arrived at in a short period of time, but a mere unconsidered and rash impulse, even though it includes an intent to kill, is not such deliberation and premeditation as will fix an unlawful killing as murder of the first degree. To constitute a deliberate and premeditated killing, the slayer must weigh and consider the question of killing and the reasons for and against such a choice and, having in mind the consequences, decide to and commit the unlawful act causing death." Although the foregoing instruction states the proper meaning of the deliberation and premeditation required to establish the offense of murder in the first degree, it did not cure the error, but instead created a serious conflict in the instructions. Where it is impossible to determine which of inconsistent instructions were followed by the jury, conflicting instructions have been held to constitute reversible error. It cannot reasonably be said that the jury, even though given the proper instruction, was not misled by the further instruction that "a man may do a thing . . . deliberately and intentionally from a moment's reflection. . . .[a] He can pre-

a. West's Ann.Cal.Pen.Code, § 189 (1981) provides: "To prove the killing was 'deliberate and premeditated' it shall not be necessary to prove the defendant

meditate, that is, think before doing the act, the moment he conceives the purpose. . . . " The jury could find defendant guilty of murder in the first degree only by finding that the murder was the result of deliberation and premeditation, since the killing did not take place during the commission of the felonies enumerated in section 189 of the Penal Code. The evidence is without conflict that defendant fired at the decedent after whirling around from a position in which he was looking behind a bed or screen. The jury could have found defendant guilty of murder in the first degree on the basis of either of the following findings: (1) Following the correct instruction it may have found that the defendant had formed an intent to kill after carefully weighing and considering the question of killing, or that the killing may have even been deliberated before his arrival at the home of the decedent; (2) it may have found that defendant entered the upstairs room without previously considering the question of shooting the decedent but that he conceived the thought "upon a moment's reflection" as he whirled around. In view of the evidence it is impossible to determine, therefore, whether or not the jury reached its verdict on the basis of the correct instructions. Clearly the evidence under proper instructions would have supported a verdict of murder in the first degree; it is also clear, however, that it is reasonably probable that the jury, if it was properly and unambiguously instructed, could find defendant guilty of murder of lesser degree, since it could have concluded that he shot the decedent as the result of a sudden impulse engendered by an argument that had taken place between the two men, or by defendant's fear of his own life caused by the tense relationship between them at that time. . . .

After a consideration of the entire record it is clear that the giving of this erroneous instruction, particularly when considered with the other erroneous instructions, has resulted in a miscarriage of justice.

The judgment and the order denying the motion for new trial are reversed.[1]

GIBSON, C.J., CARTER, J., SCHAUER, J., and SPENCE, J., concurred.

maturely and meaningfully reflected upon the gravity of his or her act."

1. For guilt of first-degree murder under the willful, deliberate and premeditated clause of the statute there must have been time for reflection—for a "second look"—between the formation of homicidal intent and the fatal act. People v. Hoffmeister, 394 Mich. 155, 229 N.W.2d 305 (1975).

To establish a wilful, deliberate and premeditated murder "the state must prove (a) premeditation, which is the conception of the design to kill, (b) deliberation, which is a reconsideration of the design to kill, a weighing of the pros and cons with respect to it, and (c) wilfulness, which means an intentional execution of the plan to kill which had been conceived and deliberated upon; . . . " State v. Anderson, 35 N.J. 472, 173 A.2d 377, 379 (1961).

"Premeditation and deliberation may be established by proof of a motive for the killing combined with a showing of planning activity or of an exacting method of execution." People v. Haskett, 30 Cal.3d 841, 180 Cal.Rptr. 640, 640 P.2d 776, 781 (1982).

In People v. Anderson, 70 Cal.2d 15, 73 Cal.Rptr. 550, 447 P.2d 942 (1968), the court said "the legislative classification of murder into two degrees would be meaningless if 'deliberation' and 'premed-

PEOPLE v. WILSON

Supreme Court of California, In Bank, 1969.
1 Cal.3d 431, 82 Cal.Rptr. 494, 462 P.2d 22.

[After Wilson's wife had left him and taken a separate apartment he broke into that apartment one night, shot and killed his wife and Washington, and shot and wounded Stoglin. He testified that the men had taunted and threatened him and that he had gone to the apartment with no intention of harming anyone but "just to scare them". Witnesses had testified that he was a friendly person never known to engage in arguments or fights. He was found guilty of first-degree murder of his wife, second-degree murder of Washington and assault with a deadly weapon upon Champion, who also had been in the apartment at the time.

In an earlier case (*Ireland*, cited infra) the court was dealing with homicide resulting from an assault with a deadly weapon. As such an assault is a statutory felony the trial judge had instructed the jury that if **D** caused the death of the deceased while assaulting him with a deadly weapon he was guilty of second-degree murder. In reversing the resulting conviction the court held that the felony-murder rule applies only when **D** is perpetrating or attempting an independent felony—one that is not an ingredient of the homicide itself. It was said the jury might convict of second-degree murder in such a case if they found malice aforethought from the nature and circumstances of the assault, but not on the basis of felony-murder.]

MOSK, JUSTICE . . . .

The following instructions among others were given to the jury relevant to a verdict of first degree murder:

"All murder which is perpetrated by any kind of willful, deliberate and premeditated killing, or which is committed in the perpetration or attempt to perpetrate burglary, is murder of the first degree, and all other kinds of murder are of the second degree."

itation' were construed as requiring no more reflection than may be involved in the mere formation of a specific intent to kill".

Adequate time for premeditation does not necessarily establish its existence. Where the evidence is as consistent with a killing in a senseless frenzy as it is with premeditation, the prosecution has not satisfied its burden of proof for guilt of first-degree murder and the conviction is reduced to murder in the second degree. Hemphill v. United States, 402 F.2d 187 (D.C.Cir.1968).

Montana's statutory scheme punishes deliberate homicide which requires that the killing be committed purposely or knowingly. State v. Powers, ___ Mont. ___, 645 P.2d 1357 (1982). See also Model Penal Code 210(1)(a).

"The achievement of a mental state contemplated in a statute such as ours can immediately precede the act of killing. Hence what is really meant by the language 'willful, deliberate and premeditated' in W.Va.Code 61-2-1 (1923) is that the killing be intentional." State v. Schrader, ___ W.Va. ___, 302 S.E.2d 70, 75 (1982). (Note, this takes us back to the original theory of *Drum* and gives no meaning to deliberate and premeditated.)

"The unlawful killing of a human being, whether intentional, unintentional or accidental, which is committed in the perpetration or attempt to perpetrate burglary, the commission of which crime itself must be proved beyond a reasonable doubt, is murder of the first degree."

"Every person who enters any house, room, apartment, tenement, or other building, with intent to unlawfully steal, take and carry away the personal property of another of any value or to commit any felony is guilty of burglary. The essence of a burglary is entering a place such as I have mentioned with such specific intent; and the crime is complete as soon as the entry is made, regardless of whether the intent thereafter is carried out." . . .

"Assault with a deadly weapon is a felony."

The clear purport of these instructions as applied to the present case is that if defendant entered his wife's apartment or any room thereof with an intent to commit an assault with a deadly weapon, he was guilty of burglary; and if in the course of such burglary he killed his wife and/or Washington, such killing was first degree murder, whether it was intentional, negligent, or accidental.

. . . The first degree conviction for the killing of Mrs. Wilson must, therefore, have been based either on a finding that (1) defendant developed the necessary premeditation in the few seconds between the killing of Washington in the living room and the killing of Mrs. Wilson in the bathroom, or that (2) he entered the bathroom with an intent to commit an assault with a deadly weapon and thereby committed a burglary, in the course of which he killed his wife and thus committed first degree felony murder. Because the instructions permit this latter course of reasoning by the jury, we must reverse defendant's conviction.

In People v. Ireland (1969) supra, 70 Cal.2d 522, 539, 575–576, 75 Cal.Rptr. 188, 198, 450 P.2d 580, 590, this court expressly declined to reach the question of the validity of first degree felony-murder instructions identical to those given in the case at hand. . . .

We have heretofore emphasized "that the felony-murder doctrine expresses a highly artificial concept that deserves no extension beyond its required application."

"The purpose of the felony-murder rule is to deter felons from killing negligently or accidentally by holding them strictly responsible for killings they commit." [a] Where a person enters a building with

a. [Compiler's note.] The Utah statute reads:

"Criminal homicide constitutes murder in the first degree if the actor intentionally or knowingly causes the death of another [when] . . . (d) The homicide was committed while the actor was engaged in the commission of, or an attempt to commit, or flight after committing or attempting to commit, aggravated robbery, robbery, rape, forcible sodomy, or aggravated sexual assault, aggravated arson, arson, aggravated burglary, burglary, aggravated kidnapping or kidnapping." This requires an intent to kill. State v. Wood, 648 P.2d 71, 75 (Utah 1982).

an intent to assault his victim with a deadly weapon, he is not deterred by the felony-murder rule. That doctrine can serve its purpose only when applied to a felony independent of the homicide. In *Ireland,* we reasoned that a man assaulting another with a deadly weapon could not be deterred by the second degree felony-murder rule, since the assault was an integral part of the homicide. Here, the only distinction is that the assault and homicide occurred inside a dwelling so that the underlying felony is burglary based on an intention to assault with a deadly weapon, rather than simply assault with a deadly weapon.

We do not suggest that no relevant differences exist between crimes committed inside and outside dwellings. We have often recognized that persons within dwellings are in greater peril from intruders bent on stealing or engaging in other felonious conduct. Persons within dwellings are more likely to resist and less likely to be able to avoid the consequences of crimes committed inside their homes. However, this rationale does not jusitfy application of the felony-murder rule to the case at bar. Where the intended felony of the burglar is an assault with a deadly weapon, the likelihood of homicide from the lethal weapon is not significantly increased by the site of the assault. Furthermore, the burglary statute in this state includes within its definition numerous structures other than dwellings as to which there can be no conceivable basis for distinguishing between an assault with a deadly weapon outdoors and a burglary in which the felonious intent is solely to assault with a deadly weapon.[3]

In *Ireland,* we rejected the bootstrap reasoning involved in taking an element of a homicide and using it as the underlying felony in a second degree felony-murder instruction. We conclude that the same bootstrapping is involved in instructing a jury that the intent to assault makes the entry burglary and that the burglary raises the homicide resulting from the assault to first degree murder without proof of malice aforethought and premeditation. To hold otherwise, we would have to declare that because burglary is not technically a lesser offense included within a charge of murder, burglary constitutes an independent felony which can support a felony-murder instruction. However, in *Ireland* itself we did not assert that assault with a deadly weapon was a lesser included offense in murder; we asserted only that it was "included in fact" in the charge of murder, in that the elements of the assault were necessary elements in the homicide. In the same sense, a burglary based on intent to assault with a deadly weapon is included in fact within a charge of murder, and cannot support a felony-murder instruction.

3. Included are any "shop, warehouse, store, mill, barn, stable, outhouse or other building, tent, vessel, railroad car, trailer coach . . ., vehicle . . ., aircraft . . ., mine or any underground portion thereof . . . ." (Pen.Code, § 459.)

We recognize that *Ireland* dealt with a court-made rule while this case involves first degree felony murder, which is statutory.[4] However, the statutory source of the rule does not compel us to apply it in disregard of logic and reason. Indeed, a literal interpretation of section 189 would have limited the felony-murder doctrine to the role of converting all "murder" committed in the course of the perpetration of the named felonies to first degree murder. Instead, we have more broadly interpreted the word "murder" to mean "homicide" or "killings," so that the elements of the crime of murder need not be proved under the felony-murder doctrine.

Furthermore, other jurisdictions which have adopted the so-called merger doctrine[5] have done so in the face of similar statutes codifying the felony-murder rule. For example, in New York the statute provided that the killing of a person without design to effect death was first degree murder if committed by one engaged in the perpetration of *any felony*. Nevertheless, the New York courts have interpreted that language to include only felonies independent of the homicide, which do not merge therein. In *Ireland*, we adopted the reasoning underlying the merger doctrine.

Holding as we do that an instruction on first degree felony murder is improper when the underlying felony is burglary based upon an intention to assault the victim of the homicide with a deadly weapon, it is necessary to overrule, insofar as inconsistent herewith, two decisions which previously approved an identical instruction. (People v. Hamilton (1961) supra, 55 Cal.2d 881, 901, 13 Cal.Rptr. 649, 362 P.2d 473; and People v. Talbot (1966) supra, 64 Cal.2d 691, 703, 51 Cal.Rptr. 417, 414 P.2d 633.) A reading of *Ireland* contrasted with the text in *Hamilton* makes this result inevitable.[6] This court in *Hamilton* conceded that the merger doctrine followed in New York would require an independent felony to support a felony-murder instruction and that burglary based on an intent to assault the victim of the homicide was generally not such a felony, but it simply hesitated to adopt that line of authority. In *Ireland*, we overruled language in *Hamilton* and *Talbot* which rejected the New York merger doctrine, and we approve the rule in cases originating in New York and other jurisdictions. We therefore adhere to the more recent *Ireland* rationale.

The judgment convicting defendant of first and second degree murder is reversed; it is affirmed insofar as it convicts him of assault with a deadly weapon.

4. Penal Code section 189 provides that "All murder . . . which is committed in the perpetration or attempt to perpetrate . . . burglary . . . is murder of the first degree . . . ."

5. "Merger" refers to the concept that only felonies independent of the homicide can support a felony-murder instruction; felonies that are an integral part of the homicide are *merged* in the homicide.

6. *Talbot* relied entirely on language in *Hamilton* on this point and, therefore, we need only be concerned with *Hamilton*.

TRAYNOR, C.J., and PETERS, TOBRINER, BURKE and SULLIVAN, JJ., concur.[b]

MCCOMB, JUSTICE (dissenting).

I dissent. I would affirm the judgment in its entirety. (See Cal. Const., art. VI, § 13.)

CONRAD v. STATE

Supreme Court of Ohio, 1906.
75 Ohio St. 52, 78 N.E. 957.

DAVIS, J. It was charged in the indictment that the plaintiff in error broke into a dwelling-house at night with intent to take and carry away personal property which was in the dwelling; and that while in the perpetration of such burglary, he, the plaintiff in error, shot and killed one Daniel E. Davis. . . .

In substance, the argument in this case is that the perpetration of the burglary was complete when the house was entered, or at least while the burglars were within the house, and that as they carried nothing away in their flight the crime of burglary was complete when they left the house. The body of Officer Davis was found twenty-five or thirty feet from the house and on another lot. Therefore, it is argued, the killing was not in the perpetration of a burglary.

We will pause here to emphasize a distinction which will be apparent to any one on reflection. It is the distinction between the definition of a burglary and a statement of the circumstances which may

b. [Compiler's note.] The merger doctrine was rejected in the case of a killing occurring during a robbery. People v. Burton, 6 Cal.3d 375, 99 Cal.Rptr. 1, 491 P.2d 793 (1971). The merger doctrine is inapplicable to felony-murder during the commission of child abuse. State v. O'Blasney, 297 N.W.2d 797 (S.D.1980).

The merger doctrine was rejected in a burglary felony murder case. ". . . the established rule . . . requires that one must honor the terms of the statute as the best evidence of the intention of the legislature and cannot properly undertake to arrive at an interpretation of this statute in accord with our ideas of 'logic and reason'." State v. Reams, 292 Or. 1, 636 P.2d 913 (1981).

In a prosecution for first-degree murder based upon the claim that the killing was in the perpetration of robbery, the defendant asked for an instruction on second-degree murder. The refusal to give such an instruction was held to be proper. The court said that second-degree murder is not a lesser-included offense of robbery-murder, but it was emphasized that there was no evidence to support a claim of second-degree murder. State v. Lee, 13 Wash.App. 900, 538 P.2d 538 (1975).

Illegally furnishing heroin is a felony dangerous to human life and if death results it is second-degree murder under the felony-murder rule. People v. Taylor, 11 Cal.App.3d 57, 89 Cal.Rptr. 697 (1970).

Homicide caused by driving a car on the highway while under the influence of a narcotic drug is second-degree murder. Such driving is a felony inherently dangerous to human life, is complete as soon as such driving starts, and hence is not a necessary element of a resulting homicide, which is murder in the second degree. People v. Calzada, 13 Cal.App.3d 603, 91 Cal.Rptr. 912 (1970).

The Georgia legislature intended felony-murder to apply to all felonies, not just dangerous or forcible felonies. Baker v. State, 236 Ga. 754, 225 S.E.2d 269 (1976).

have occurred "in the perpetration" of a burglary. The former is invariable. The latter varies with each case. The definition of a burglary is the breaking into a house in the night season, with intent to commit a felony; and if a house be so entered it is a burglary whether the felony be executed or not, and regardless of the kind of felony intended, or the manner of its execution, or the manner in which the felony may be frustrated, or the value of the property taken, or any other circumstance which is not intrinsic. On the other hand, while the circumstances which differentiate the crime may be a small part of the transaction, and must always be the same, the things which occur "in the perpetration" of a crime change with every case, and may be numerous.

For example, when a burglary has been planned, in order to carry it out, or, in other words, to perpetrate it, the burglar must go to the building, he must break and enter it; he may effect his purpose or attempt it, and he must come away; for the very nature of the transaction implies that the burglar will not remain in the building. An infinite variety of things may happen in carrying out the crime. The perpetrator may kill a man while going to or trying to enter the building, he may kill a man after he has broken and entered the house, and he may kill a man while trying to escape, either in the house or outside of it. Can any sound reason be suggested why the killing in any one of these instances might be in the perpetration of or attempt to perpetrate a burglary, and not so in the others? The crime of murder in the first degree as defined by the statute (Section 6808, Revised Statutes) certainly can not by any reasonable construction be confined to the moment of breaking and entering the house, the crucial point of the definition of burglary; and it should be noted here again that it is not burglary which we are to define in this case, but murder in the first degree.

Let us suppose a case. Two confederates intending to break and enter a dwelling for a felonious purpose are met by the owner at the door or window which they are forcing and they kill him. Would anybody question that such a killing was in the perpetration, or attempt to perpetrate, a burglary? Surely not. Then let us go further back in the order of time. Suppose that while these confederates are watching the house and waiting for the opportune time, they see the owner of the dwelling come out with a lantern and go across the road to his barn, and they there set upon him and inflict injuries from which he dies, but they take no money or property. They afterwards go across the road towards the house, and, getting inside the yard, are frightened by somebody approaching and hurry away. Would that be murder in an attempt to commit a burglary? It was argued that it was not; but the Supreme Court of Pennsylvania held that it was. Commonwealth v. Eagan, 190 Pa. 10, 42 A. 374.

Suppose another case. The confederates so far succeed as to break and enter the building. A technical burglary has been completed; but afterwards and while yet in the building they shoot and kill somebody. Is that a killing "in the perpetration" of a burglary within the meaning of the statute defining murder in the first degree? It was vigorously contended in the Court of Appeals of New York and also in the Supreme Court of Indiana, that such a killing is not murder in the first degree, but a killing after the crime of burglary had been completed. Both courts hold that the crime in such case is murder in the first degree, notwithstanding that the killing and the breaking and entering are not coincident. Dolan v. People, 64 N.Y. 485; Bissot v. State, 53 Ind. 408.

Now, if the taking of life before reaching the building, and also after breaking and entering the building and before leaving it, is a taking of life in the perpetration, or attempt to perpetrate, a burglary, at what point after the breaking and entering is the line of distinction to be drawn? At what point can it be drawn, short of the absolute completion or abandonment of the whole enterprise? It seems to us that logically there can be no such intermediate point; and we know of no case which holds otherwise. The case of Lamb v. People, 96 Ill. 73, cited by counsel for plaintiff in error is not pertinent here. There the burglars got away with the plunder. They were in undisturbed possession of the goods. Lamb left the party and some time thereafter the others were detected in unloading the goods at a pawnbroker's. Then the shooting occurred.

Take another case. Three men entered a pawnshop, locked the door behind them, beat the proprietor into insensibility, took from the safe certain articles of value and escaped through back windows. They were pursued by a constable who chased them for the distance of four blocks and across two streets. They then turned and fired at the constable and a pistol ball missing him struck a tree and glanced off, killing a boy. The men were indicted for murder while engaged in committing a robbery. A conviction of murder in the first degree resulted as to one of the defendants; and the Supreme Court, in State v. Brown, 7 Or. 186 said:

"The defendant admits that he committed a robbery in the pawnshop of O'Shea, but insists that the crime was completed when he and his co-defendants forcibly seized the property described in the indictment, and, being completed, he denies that the killing of Joseph was done in the commission of the robbery. We do not assent to the correctness of this conclusion. . . . When a person takes with force and violence the goods of another from his person or presence and against his will, he has committed robbery . . . but it does not necessarily complete the crime. It constitutes robbery so far as to render the perpetrator liable to conviction for it; but the *act of robbery itself may be prolonged beyond the time when that liability is fixed.* When Brown and his co-defendants took the property by force . . . they committed the crime of robbery so far as to render themselves liable to punishment for it, but the robbery in contemplation of law was not completed until the taking and carrying away was ended. . . . And while anything remains to be done by the robbers to secure complete control over the property taken, the robbery is incomplete. The act of taking and carrying away in the case of Brown and his co-defendants commenced when the seizure was made in the pawnshop of O'Shea, and continued until they had *unmolested dominion* over the property which they had taken. When they first acquired that control the robbery was ended and not before" (pp. 208, 209). . . .

Thus it appears that in all these cases which we have reviewed, cases of killing before, during and after the technical perfection of the collateral crime, the courts practically concur in the view expressed by the Court of Appeals of New York, that, "If, while there engaged in securing his plunder, or *in any of the acts immediately connected with his crime,* he kills any one resisting him, he is guilty of murder under the statute" (Dolan v. People, supra); and by the Supreme Court of Indiana as follows: "In our opinion when the homicide is committed within the *res gestae* [1] of the felony charged, it is committed in the perpetration of, or attempt to perpetrate, the felony, within the meaning of the statute" (Bissot v. State, supra). For the reasons which we have endeavored to make clear, we believe that this construction of the statute is not only reasonable, consistent, conservative and just, but that it exactly conforms to the legislative intent as expressed. . . .

The judgment of the circuit court is

Affirmed.

SHAUCK, C.J., SUMMERS and SPEAR, JJ., concur.[2]

(PRICE and CREW, JJ., dissented.)

1. "The res gestae embraces not only the actual facts of the transaction and the circumstances surrounding it, but the matters immediately antecedent to and having a direct causal connection with it, as well as acts immediately following it and so closely connected with it as to form in reality a part of the occurrence." State v. Fouquette, 67 Nev. 505, 221 P.2d 404, 417 (1950).

Accord, People v. Salas, 7 Cal.3d 812, 103 Cal.Rptr. 431, 500 P.2d 7 (1972).

"The turpitude involved in the robbery takes the place of intent to kill or premeditated malice, and the purpose to kill is conclusively presumed from the criminal intention required for robbery." State v. Bradley, 210 Neb. 882, 317 N.W.2d 99 (1982).

2. Contra: After the burglar has left the building empty-handed he is no longer in the perpetration or attempted perpetration of burglary and hence a killing by him 25 or 30 feet from the house and on another lot, in his effort to resist arrest was not first-degree murder under the felony-murder rule. It might have been first-degree murder but the conviction is reversed because of an improper instruction on the felony-murder rule. People v. Huter, 184 N.Y. 237, 77 N.E. 6 (1906).

Under the circumstances of this case the jury might find that killing a trooper 45 minutes after the robbery and 37.75 miles from the situs, was a killing during immediate flight after the offense. People v. Donovan, 385 N.Y.S.2d 385 (App. Div.1976).

Evidence that the victim, who had observed burglars leave his home after attempting to enter, followed them and encountered them two or three blocks away, within a matter of minutes, and was killed is sufficient to establish a killing during an attempted burglary. State

MODEL PENAL CODE
Article 210. Criminal Homicide

Section 210.0 Definitions.

In Articles 210–213, unless a different meaning plainly is required:

(1) "human being" means a person who has been born and is alive;

(2) "bodily injury" means physical pain, illness or any impairment of physical condition;

(3) "serious bodily injury" means bodily injury which creates a substantial risk of death or which causes serious, permanent disfigurement, or protracted loss or impairment of the function of any bodily member or organ;

(4) "deadly weapon" means any firearm, or other weapon, device, instrument, material or substance, whether animate or inanimate, which in the manner it is used or is intended to be used is known to be capable of producing death or serious bodily injury.

Section 210.1 Criminal Homicide.

(1) A person is guilty of criminal homicide if he purposely, knowingly, recklessly [1] or negligently [2] causes the death of another human being.

v. Hearron, 228 Kan. 693, 619 P.2d 1157 (1980).

In affirming a conviction under a statute providing a special punishment for robbery if, "in the course of the commission of the robbery" the robber intentionally inflicts great bodily injury upon the victim, it was said (People v. Carroll, 1 Cal.3d 581, 584, 83 Cal.Rptr. 176, 178, 463 P.2d 400, 402, 1970):

"Question: *Did the trial court properly find that defendant, with the intent to do so, inflicted great bodily injury upon Gulsvig's person during commission of the robbery of Gulsvig?*

"*Yes.* It should be noted, to begin with, that the taking of Gulsvig's wallet constituted a robbery even though defendant discarded it as soon as he discovered it was empty. It may reasonably be inferred that at the time defendant demanded and received the wallet it was his intention to deprive the owner of it permanently. (People v. Hall, 253 Cal.App. 2d 1051, 1054 [2], 61 Cal.Rptr. 676.)

Defendant contends, however, that after he discovered there was no money in Gulsvig's wallet and threw it on the wash basin, the robbery of Gulsvig was completed, and that any offense thereafter committed was separate and distinct and did not occur in the commission of his robbery of Gulsvig. . . .

"The fact that defendant was not engaged in the asportation of any loot at the time he shot Gulsvig is immaterial. He became angry after discovering no money in the wallet and having the rest room door slammed in his face. His purpose in running into the bar appears to have been to exact his revenge from Gulsvig. Under the circumstances, the robbery and shooting of Gulsvig constituted one indivisible transaction, with the shooting flowing directly from the taking of the wallet.

"In addition, it is settled that the crime of robbery is not confined to the act of taking property from victims. The nature of the crime is such that a robber's escape with his loot is just as important to the execution of the crime as obtaining possession of the loot in the first place. Thus, the crime of robbery is not complete until the robber has won his way to a place of temporary safety."

In a case of immediate pursuit, with shots being exchanged between the police and the fleeing robbers, a fatal traffic accident 3.2 miles from, and 8 minutes after, a robbery was held to be within the perpetration thereof. People v. Ulsh, 211 Cal.App.2d 258, 27 Cal.Rptr. 408 (1962).

1. "Recklessly" is defined elsewhere in the Code to mean that the actor consciously disregards a substantial and unjustifiable risk amounting to a "gross

(2) Criminal homicide is murder, manslaughter or negligent homicide.

Section 210.2 Murder.

(1) Except as provided in Section 210.3(1)(b), criminal homicide constitutes murder when:

(a) it is committed purposely or knowingly; or

(b) it is committed recklessly under circumstances manifesting extreme indifference to the value of human life. Such recklessness and indifference are presumed if the actor is engaged or is an accomplice in the commission of, or an attempt to commit, or flight after committing or attempting to commit robbery, rape or deviate sexual intercourse by force or threat of force, arson, burglary, kidnapping or felonious escape.

(2) Murder is a felony of the first degree [but a person convicted of murder may be sentenced to death, as provided in Section 210.6].

Section 210.3 Manslaughter.

(1) Criminal homicide constitutes manslaughter when:

(a) it is committed recklessly; or

(b) a homicide which would otherwise be murder is committed under the influence of extreme mental or emotional disturbance for which there is reasonable explanation or excuse. The reasonableness of such explanation or excuse shall be determined from the viewpoint of a person in the actor's situation under the circumstances as he believes them to be.

(2) Manslaughter is a felony of the second degree.

Section 210.4 Negligent Homicide.

(1) Criminal homicide constitutes negligent homicide when it is committed negligently.

(2) Negligent homicide is a felony of the third degree.

Section 210.5 Causing or Aiding Suicide.

(1) Causing Suicide as Criminal Homicide. A person may be convicted of criminal homicide for causing another to commit suicide only if he purposely causes such suicide by force, duress or deception.

(2) Aiding or Soliciting Suicide as an Independent Offense. A person who purposely aids or solicits another to commit suicide is guilty of a felony of the second degree if his conduct causes such suicide or an attempted suicide, and otherwise of a misdemeanor.

(Since a few states do not have capital punishment, provisions for such a penalty in the Code are bracketed, since they would not be needed in such states. A sentence for a felony of the first degree would mean that the maximum would be life imprisonment.)

deviation" from due care. Section 2.02(2)(c).

2. "Negligently" is defined elsewhere in the Code in terms equivalent to "inadvertent criminal negligence". Section 2.02(2)(d).

Section 210.6 Sentence of Death for Murder; Further Proceedings to Determine Sentence.

(1) Death Sentence Excluded. When a defendant is found guilty of murder, the Court shall impose sentence for a felony of the first degree if it is satisfied that:

(a) none of the aggravating circumstances enumerated in Subsection (3) of this Section was established by the evidence at the trial or will be established if further proceedings are initiated under Subsection (2) of this Section; or

(b) substantial mitigating circumstances, established by the evidence at the trial, call for leniency; or

(c) the defendant, with the consent of the prosecuting attorney and the approval of the Court, pleaded guilty to murder as a felony of the first degree; or

(d) the defendant was under 18 years of age at the time of the commission of the crime; or

(e) the defendant's physical or mental condition calls for leniency; or

(f) although the evidence suffices to sustain the verdict, it does not foreclose all doubts respecting the defendant's guilt.

. . .

(If the penalty may be death the Code provides that this shall be determined in a separate proceeding after guilt has been established. The sentence may not be death unless (a) there is found one of the aggravating circumstances enumerated in subsection (3) *and* (b) *no* "mitigating circumstances sufficient to call for leniency".)

(3) Aggravating Circumstances.

(a) The murder was committed by a convict under sentence of imprisonment.

(b) The defendant was previously convicted of another murder or of a felony involving the use or threat of violence to the person.

(c) At the time the murder was committed the defendant also commited another murder.

(d) The defendant knowingly created a great risk of death to many persons.

(e) The murder was committed while the defendant was engaged or was an accomplice in the commission of, or an attempt to commit, or flight after committing or attempting to commit robbery, rape or deviate sexual intercourse by force or threat of force, arson, burglary or kidnapping.

(f) The murder was committed for the purpose of avoiding or preventing a lawful arrest or effecting an escape from lawful custody.

(g) The murder was commited for pecuniary gain.

(h) The murder was especially heinous, atrocious or cruel, manifesting exceptional depravity.

(4) Mitigating Circumstances.

(a) The defendant has no significant history of prior criminal activity.

(b) The murder was committed while the defendant was under the influence of extreme mental or emotional disturbance.

(c) The victim was a participant in the defendant's homicidal conduct or consented to the homicidal act.

(d) The murder was committed under circumstances which the defendant believed to provide a moral justification or extenuation for his conduct.

(e) The defendant was an accomplice in a murder committed by another person and his participation in the homicidal act was relatively minor.

(f) The defendant acted under duress or under the domination of another person.

(g) At the time of the murder, the capacity of the defendant to appreciate the criminality [wrongfulness] of his conduct or to conform his conduct to the requirements of law was impaired as a result of mental disease or defect or intoxication.

(h) The youth of the defendant at the time of the crime.[3]

SECTION 2. ASSAULT AND BATTERY[a]

STATE v. JIMERSON

Court of Appeals of Washington, Division 3, Panel Three, 1980.
27 Wn.App. 415, 618 P.2d 1027.

MUNSON, JUDGE. Raymond Arthur Jimerson, Jr., appeals his conviction on two counts of second-degree assault. We reverse for failure to give an instruction on simple assault.

On December 22, 1978, Jimerson was driving his car and was accompanied by several friends. The car spun out on ice and snow near two off-duty policemen walking to a Christmas party. The policemen went over to the car to suggest that Jimerson drive more carefully. Jimerson and party responded by hurling epithets; Jimerson started to get out of the car, apparently prepared to fight. What then ensued is in question, but it appears the policemen identified themselves and forced Jimerson back into the car by pushing or possibly by grabbing his hair. Jimerson then drove away in one direction while the police proceeded in another. However, Jimerson turned around and accelerated rapidly toward the policemen on the other side of the

3. Copyright: 1962 by the American Law Institute. Reprinted with the permission of the American Law Institute.

a. "An assault is a necessary element of battery, and it is impossible to commit battery without assaulting the victim. The assault, to adopt the statutory language, is 'necessarily included therein' ". (Quoting from an earlier decision.) Gomez v. Superior Court, 50 Cal.2d 640, 648, 328 P.2d 976, 981 (1958).

"An assault is an unlawful attempt, coupled with a present ability, to commit a violent injury on the person of another, or in other words it is an attempt to commit a battery." People v. Rocha, 3 Cal. 3d 893, 92 Cal.Rptr. 172, 176, 479 P.2d 372, 376 (1971).

Under statutes providing different penalties for battery and for assault it was held that where the victim suffered no physical contact, directly or indirectly, there was no battery and the charge was reduced from assault and battery to a simple assault. Reese v. State, 3 Tenn. Cr.App. 97, 457 S.W.2d 877 (1970).

street. The two officers tried to evade the car by climbing an embankment. One of them pulled his service revolver and fired at the oncoming car, putting a hole in a door; no occupant was injured. The car swerved toward the officers, but missed them. Jimerson then drove away and went home. Both he and his wife later called the police to report this incident; an investigation resulted in Jimerson's arrest and eventual conviction.

Jimerson testified that he had no intention of running down the officers, but merely intended to drive by, splashing them with slush. A jury nevertheless found him guilty of second-degree assault. He asserts two grounds of appeal.

Jimerson first argues that he should have been allowed a jury instruction as to the lesser included offense of simple assault. Jimerson was charged with assault in the first degree under RCW 9A.36.010,[1] and an instruction was given as to the lesser included offense of assault in the second degree pursuant to RCW 9A.36.020.[2] Jimerson's proposed instruction on simple assault was denied because the court believed there was insufficient evidence.

In State v. Workman, 90 Wash.2d 443, 447–48, 584 P.2d 382 (1978), the court held:

> Under the Washington rule, a defendant is entitled to an instruction on a lesser included offense if two conditions are met. First, each of the elements of the lesser offense must be a necessary element of the offense charged. . . . Second, the evidence . . . must support an inference that the lesser crime was committed.

(Citations omitted.)

Neither the present nor the former criminal codes defined the word "assault." We presume this is because it has been firmly es-

1. RCW 9A.36.010:

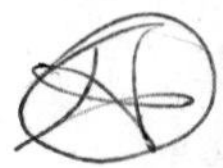

"(1) Every person, who with intent to kill a human being, or to commit a felony upon the person or property of the one assaulted, or of another, shall be guilty of assault in the first degree when he:

"(a) Shall assault another with a firearm or any deadly weapon or by any force or means likely to produce death; or

"(b) Shall administer to or cause to be taken by another, poison or any other destructive or noxious thing so as to endanger the life of another person.

"(2) Assault in the first degree is a class A felony."

2. RCW 9A.36.020:

"(1) Every person who, under circumstances not amounting to assault in the first degree shall be guilty of assault in the second degree when he:

"(a) With intent to injure, shall unlawfully administer to or cause to be taken by another, poison or any other destructive or noxious thing, or any drug or medicine the use of which is dangerous to life or health; or

"(b) Shall knowingly inflict grievous bodily harm upon another with or without a weapon; or

"(c) Shall knowingly assault another with a weapon or other instrument or thing likely to produce bodily harm; or

"(d) Shall knowingly assault another with intent to commit a felony.

"(2) Assault in the second degree is a class B felony."

tablished in this state that an assault is an attempt, with unlawful force, to inflict bodily injury upon another, accompanied with apparent present ability to give effect to the attempt if not prevented. Thus, simple assault as defined by the legislature [3] concerns an assault which involves neither the intent nor the result denoted in the definition of assault in the first, second or third degree.[4] The first condition of lesser included offenses has been met. State v. Johnson, 184 Wash. 493, 496, 52 P.2d 317 (1935).

As to the second element, whether the evidence supports the inference that the lesser crime was committed, the facts determine whether a lesser-included-offense instruction should be given. State v. Johnson, supra at 496, 52 P.2d 317, quoting from State v. Reynolds, 94 Wash. 270, 276, 162 P. 358 (1917), states:

"In law, assault in the third degree [under the previous criminal code assault in the third degree was defined in the same manner as is simple assault now] is included within a charge of assault in the second degree, but where a defendant is charged with assault in the second degree, the question whether he is guilty of assault in the third degree should not be submitted to the jury unless the facts of the particular case are such that they will sustain a conviction of assault in the third degree."

In *Johnson*, there is no statement of facts and so it is impossible for this court to determine how the assault was committed. However, in State v. Emerson, 19 Wash.2d 700, 144 P.2d 262 (1943), the evidence supported an allegation that an assault had been committed with a knife. There, the court held that the defendant was guilty of assault in the second degree or not guilty of any degree of assault. Similarly, in State v. Snider, 70 Wash.2d 326, 422 P.2d 816 (1967), on the charge of robbery, Snider had pleaded guilty to grand larceny resulting from his taking a wristwatch off the victim's arm after an affray had ceased. Snider also testified that a codefendant, Olson, had been engaged in the fight and had some money and a wallet in his hands. The court there held that as to Olson there was no error in failing to give a lesser-included-offense instruction because he was either guilty of the robbery or nothing. Here, the state argues that a simple as-

3. RCW 9A.36.040 states:

"(1) Every person who shall commit an assault or an assault and battery not amounting to assault in either the first, second, or third degree shall be guilty of simple assault.

"(2) Simple assault is a gross misdemeanor."

4. RCW 9A.36.030 states:

"(1) Every person who, under circumstances not amounting to assault in either the first or second degree, shall be guilty of assault in the third degree when he:

"(a) With intent to prevent or resist the execution of any lawful process or mandate of any court officer or the lawful apprehension or detention of himself or another person shall assault another; or

"(b) With criminal negligence, shall cause physical injury to another person by means of a weapon or other instrument or thing likely to produce bodily harm.

"(2) Assault in the third degree is a class C felony."

assault is not to be carried out by the car but rather the car is to be used to put some other nondeadly force into motion which amounts to an assault, such as slush or water from a mud puddle, then the car could be used to commit a simple assault. Here, Jimerson testified his intention was not to hit the officers with his car, but only to spray them with slush from the icy and wet road. He also testified that he drove the car up the bank and then swerved away as a reflex action upon seeing one of the officers draw his gun. The trial court apparently weighed this testimony and found it wanting.[5]

Jimerson is entitled to a jury instruction on a lesser included offense if any evidence was produced which would justify a reasonable person in concluding that the lesser included offense had been committed. The credibility of Jimerson's testimony was for the jury to decide. We find the instruction on the lesser included offense of simple assault should have been given and the failure to do so was prejudicial error. . . .

Reversed and remanded for new trial.[6]

McInturff, Acting C.J., and Roe, J., concur.

5. The court in chambers stated:

"I examined that question and concluded that it would be improper for me to give instructions as to simple assault, not being supported by the evidence, that is, the only evidence one could find of simple assault was disputed and denied by the defendant. The police officers did not allege that the door opening incident constituted any part of the assault, and other than that, I couldn't find any evidence that I could warrant the giving of that Instruction to the jury.

"As you say, the defendant has indicated that his intent was to splash these parties. I didn't hear any evidence that it was possible to splash the parties by way of their location and by way of road conditions. In addition, the evidence was that the automobile went up on whatever we call it, the knoll or embankment or whatever word you are prepared to accept.

". . .

". . . And it just didn't in any way cause me to believe a charge of simple assault for the actions alleged would apply. As a consequence, I denied that."

6. "It has long been established, both in tort and criminal law, that 'the least touching' may constitute a battery. In other words, *force* against the person is enough, it need not be violent or severe, it need not cause bodily harm or even pain, and it need not leave any mark." People v. Rocha, 3 Cal.3d 893, 92 Cal. Rptr. 172, 479 P.2d 372, footnote 12 (1971).

A kick is a battery if unlawful, even if the kick was with a bare foot against the booted leg of the other. People v. Martinez, 3 Cal.App.2d 886, 83 Cal.Rptr. 914 (1970).

It is a battery to spit in another's face, Regina v. Cotesworth, 6 Mod. 172, 87 Eng.Rep. 928 (1705), or to cut the clothes he is wearing. Regina v. Day, 1 Cox C.C. 207 (1845). It is also a battery for a man to kiss a woman against her will, or to lay hands on her for this purpose. Moreland v. State, 125 Ark. 24, 188 S.W. 1 (1916). But it is not an assault (battery) for a man to kiss an intimate friend when he has good reason to believe this will be agreeable to her. Weaver v. State, 66 Tex.Cr.R. 366, 146 S.W. 927 (1912).

Squeezing and pinching prosecutrix while she was standing in line at a restaurant constituted "simple battery" in violation of Georgia Code § 26–1304(b) which provides that simple battery is committed when one intentionally causes physical harm to another. As she was "firmly grabbed" and "squeezed" some pain may be presumed to have resulted. Mize v. State, 135 Ga.App. 561, 218 S.E.2d 450 (1975).

Throwing an egg and striking at Congressman with it constitutes an assault on a member of Congress under 18 U.S.C.A. § 351(e). United States v. Guerrero, 667 F.2d 862 (10th Cir.1981).

GOVERNMENT OF VIRGIN ISLANDS v. STULL

District Court, Virgin Islands, D. St. Thomas and St. John, 1968.
280 F.Supp. 460.

MEMORANDUM OPINION

WALTER A. GORDON, DISTRICT JUDGE.

This is an appeal from a judgment of the Municipal Court of the Virgin Islands convicting the appellant, Ray Stull, of a violation of 14 VIC 299, simple assault and battery. The judgment of the court was entered on November 3, 1967, sentencing Stull to a suspended fine of $50.00. From that judgment and sentence he has appealed. For the reasons outlined in this opinion, the judgment of conviction is vacated and the case is remanded to the Municipal Court with instructions to enter a verdict of not guilty.

FACTS

Appellant is part owner and manager of Trader Dan's which in the words of his counsel is "a waterfront saloon and poolroom which cannot be expected to attract clientele always likely to maintain the highest degree of order." The record indicates that Stull considered the complaining witness, Matthew, to be a minor trouble maker and that on recent previous occasion had told Matthew to leave the establishment and not come back. It appears, however, that due to the intercession of a police officer, the complaining witness did not leave and was in fact allowed to return. On the night of August 10, when the alleged assault occurred, it appears that Stull heard a disturbance in the upstairs poolroom portion of the bar and upon entering saw the complaining witness standing at the bar arguing with another patron. Stull told him to leave and when Matthew objected, Stull, in his words, "grabbed him by the arm and led him to the door." Stull's characterization of the event is corroborated by the upstairs bartender, Ronald Lucas, who also testified that Matthew was involved in a loud argument with one of the pool players.

While there may be a question of creditability in the testimony of Stull and his employee, Lucas, this characterization of the event appears to have been accepted by the Municipal Court. This is especially true in light of that court's reduction of the charge from aggravated to simple assault based on the court's disbelief of the complaining witness's testimony that Stull had kicked him. The trial judge stated, "From the testimony . . . I can't find beyond a reasonable doubt that this complaining witness was kicked by the defendant. I do, however, find that there was simple assault and I do find that the techniques used by the defendant were unnecessary under the circumstances. . . ."

OPINION

The Municipal Court apparently recognized, as this court does, that the owner of a bar or other public or semi-public place has the right to eject unwanted or disorderly persons from the premises. Indeed, the law is rather clear on this point:

"The owner, occupant, or person in charge of any public or semi-public place of business may request the departure of a person who does not rightfully belong there or who by his conduct has forfeited his right to be there, and may treat him as a trespasser, using reasonable force to eject him from the premises." 1 Wharton's Crim.Law, Sec. 356. . . .

Under the circumstances of the present case, the Court cannot see how appellant could have used any lesser degree of force in removing Matthew from the premises, an act which he had the right to do. Matthew, in Stull's view, was causing a disturbance. He was told to leave. He objected. Whereupon Stull took him by the arm and led him out. It was not incumbent upon Stull to argue or plead with Matthew. His license to remain on the premises had been terminated, and reasonably so, as the court views the facts. His failure to leave when requested to do so authorized Stull to exercise a reasonable degree of force. Had Stull kicked Matthew, as Matthew alleged, this would be a different case, but the taking of Matthew by the arm and pushing, pulling, or leading him to the door was, in the Court's opinion, entirely reasonable and in fact the minimal amount of force employable under the circumstances.

The judgment of conviction is vacated with instructions to enter a verdict of not guilty.

UNITED STATES v. JACOBS

United States Court of Appeals, Seventh Circuit, 1980.
632 F.2d 695.

DUMBAULD, SENIOR DISTRICT JUDGE.*

The jury found appellant Isaac Jacobs guilty, under Count I of the indictment, of assault resulting in serious bodily injury in violation of 18 U.S.C. § 113(f).[1] He was acquitted of assault with a dangerous weapon, with intent to commit bodily harm, an offense charged in Count II of the indictment as a violation of 18 U.S.C. § 113(c).[2] De-

* The Honorable Edward Dumbauld, United States District Judge from the Western District of Pennsylvania, sitting by designation.

1. "Whoever, within the special maritime and territorial jurisdiction of the United States, is guilty of an assault, shall be punished as follows: . . . (f) Assault resulting in serious bodily injury, by fine of not more than $10,000 or imprisonment for not more than ten years, or both."

2. "Whoever, within the special maritime and territorial jurisdiction of the United States, is guilty of an assault, shall be punished as follows: . . . (c) Assault with a dangerous weapon, with intent to do bodily harm, and without just

fendant and his victim were both Indians, and the offense took place "within the Indian country." [3]

The evidence disclosed that because of a family quarrel defendant planned to evict the victim Earl Bodoh and his family from their home on the disputed premises. He blocked the driveway with his car while the Bodohs were away. But when they returned, Earl Bodoh drove around the obstacle, and proceeded to enter the house. As he reached for the door with his left hand he could feel an unusual condition, and upon looking at his arm saw that he had been shot. Not until then did he see defendant with his gun about eight or ten feet away. He did not see defendant until after he was shot and was not aware that defendant had aimed the gun at him, although other witnesses testified to that fact. Earl Bodoh, after seeing defendant, hurried into the house fearing further gunfire. Defendant followed him in and struck him and others with the gun. Defendant insisted that the gun was discharged accidently.

Defendant now constructs an ingenious argument designed to show that because the victim Bodoh did not see his assailant before being shot there can be no violation of § 113(f). That provision must be construed, according to defendant, as requiring the assault to occur before the "serious bodily injury" is inflicted, because it makes punishable only an "assault *resulting* in serious bodily injury." This causal relationship requires that the assault take place before the bodily injury is produced as an effect. The Government, on the other hand, contends that the "apprehension" contemplated by the standard definition of simple assault [4] suffices if it occurs *after* the bodily harm is inflicted. (Brief, p. 12).

On this point defendant has the better of the argument. While clearly Bodoh's fear of a second shot while standing in the line of fire after seeing defendant with his gun pointed towards Bodoh would constitute an assault, it would be a subsequent assault and would not constitute the assault "resulting in serious bodily injury" for which

cause or excuse, by fine of nor more than $1,000 or imprisonment for not more than five years, or both.

3. Accordingly, both 18 U.S.C. §§ 113(c) and 113(f) were made applicable by 18 U.S.C. § 1153, which provides:

> "Any Indian who commits against the person or property of another Indian or other person any of the following offenses, namely . . . assault with a dangerous weapon, assault resulting in serious bodily injury . . . within the Indian country, shall be subject to the same laws and penalties as all other persons committing any of the above offenses, within the exclusive jurisdiction of the United States."

4. "Any act of such a nature as to excite an apprehension of a battery may constitute an assault." Prosser, Handbook of the Law of Torts (3d ed. 1964) 38; Restatement, Torts 2d, § 21. The instruction given, taken from Devitt and Blackmar, Federal Jury Practice and Instructions (3rd ed. 1977) § 42.04 states that "any intentional display of force such as would give the victim reason to fear or expect immediate bodily harm, constitutes an assault." App.Ex. H–1. The testimony of other witnesses shows that defendant's action "would give" the victim reason to fear harm *if he had seen it* or if an objective rather than subjective standard is applicable. Is an assault upon a blind or deaf person legally impossible when the victim is unaware of the impending danger?

defendant was convicted, for such injury had already been received before the subsequent simple assault occurred. In response to the Government's contention the words used by the venerable Virginia jurist George Wythe in argument against his illustrious pupil Thomas Jefferson are pertinent: "it would not be less preposterous than that an effect should be prior to its cause, or than that a thing should act before it exists." [5]

But this does not exonerate the defendant. Another established rule is that when an actual battery is committed it includes an assault.[6] In the case at bar the actual battery was clearly proved,[7] and such proof will support a conviction for the included offense of assault.

Finally, it should be noted that defendant's attempt to invalidate his conviction under Count I of the indictment by reason of his acquittal under Count II is unprofitable. Even if defendant's refined course of reasoning succeeded in demonstrating logical inconsistency in the implications derivable from the separate determinations reached by the jury, it would avail him nothing. For it is a settled rule that inconsistent or compromise verdicts are permissible and legitimate.

But Judge Warren states very persuasively in denying defendant's motion for new trial that the verdict in the case at bar is not inconsistent.

> The jury in this case, based upon the evidence presented, could well have found that defendant Isaac Jacobs intended to commit an assault by placing the Bodohs in fear through a display of force, but that Mr. Jacobs did not intend to do the bodily injury that resulted. The evidence clearly supports such a factual finding. Such a factual determination would make Jacobs guilty of violating section 113(f) but not guilty of section 113(c), because the specific intent to do bodily harm was absent.

For the foregoing reasons, the judgment of the District Court is affirmed.[8]

5. Dumbauld, Thomas Jefferson and the Law, 118 (1978).

6. Prosser disagrees. "It is not accurate to say that 'every battery includes an assault'". Handbook (3d ed. 1964) 41.

7. Battery may be inflicted by means of a gun, just as well as by fists, a club, knife, bow and arrow, or any other "substance put in motion" by an aggressor. 563 F.2d at 323.

8. "An assault and battery may be committed with a motor vehicle by striking a person, or a vehicle in which he is riding, either intentionally or by driving so negligently as to constitute a reckless disregard of human life and safety. . . .

"Of course, mere negligence would not impute an intent. If negligence be relied on, then it must amount to reckless, willful, and wanton disregard of the rights of others, in which state of case the intent is imputed to the accused." Woodward v. State, 164 Miss. 468, 144 So. 895 (1932).

Cf. State v. Hamburg, 34 Del. 62, 143 A. 47 (1928). An inexperienced driver, who drove his car on the sidewalk and hit two persons while he was attempting to dodge a child who suddenly ran into the street, was held not guilty of assault and battery. People v. Waxman, 232 App. Div. 90, 249 N.Y.S. 180 (1931).

UNITED STATES v. BELL

United States Court of Appeals, Seventh Circuit, 1974.
505 F.2d 539.

Before FAIRCHILD, SPRECHER and TONE, CIRCUIT JUDGES.

TONE, CIRCUIT JUDGE.

The defendant Tommie Bell was convicted in a bench trial of assault with intent to commit rape at a place within the special territorial jurisdiction of the United States, in violation of 18 U.S.C. § 113(a). On appeal he raises only one question, *viz.*, whether it is necessary to the offense of assault that the victim have a reasonable apprehension of bodily harm. We answer this question in the negative and affirm the conviction.

It is conceded that while defendant was a patient in the detoxification ward for alcoholic and drug addiction patients in the Veterans Administration Hospital, Downey, Illinois, he attempted to rape a female geriatric patient. It is also undisputed that the victim was suffering from a mental disease which made her unable to comprehend what was going on. Defendant's only asserted defense in the trial court and here is that, because the victim was incapable of forming a reasonable apprehension of bodily harm, there was no assault.

Defendant's contention is squarely contradicted by this court's statement in United States v. Rizzo, 409 F.2d 400, 403 (7th Cir.1969), cert. denied, 396 U.S. 911, 90 S.Ct. 226, 24 L.Ed.2d 187 (1969). There, in sustaining a jury instruction defining assault (taken from W. Mathes and E. Devitt, Federal Jury Practice and Instructions § 43.07 (1965)), the court recognized that there are two concepts of assault in criminal law, the first being an attempt to commit a battery and the second an act putting another in reasonable apprehension of bodily harm. While the second concept was applicable in that case, the court, said with respect to the first:

"There may be an attempt to commit a battery, and hence an assault, under circumstances where the intended victim is unaware of danger. Apprehension on the part of the victim is not an essential element of that type of assault." (Footnotes omitted.)

We adhere to that statement of the law. When a federal criminal statute uses a common law term without defining it, the term is given

In a prosecution for murder it is error to instruct the jury that if they find that **D** committed a battery upon the deceased but also find that this did not contribute to the death, they should find **D** not guilty. This removed from the jury a consideration of guilt of battery as a lesser included offense. Cook v. State, 134 Ga.App. 357, 214 S.E.2d 423 (1975).

A defendant charged with aggravated assault, under a statute defining the offense as the use of force likely to produce serious bodily injury, may be convicted on proof of reckless conduct. State in Interest of McElhaney, 579 P.2d 328 (Utah 1978).

"We see no reason in logic or in law why a person who recklessly applies physical force to the person of another should be outside the criminal law of assault." Reg. v. Venna, [1975] 3 All E.R. 788, 794 (C.A.).

its common law meaning. A criminal assault at common law was originally an attempt to commit a battery. 1 W. Hawkins, Pleas of the Crown c. 62, § 1 (6th ed. 1788) states:

"It seems that an assault is an attempt or offer, with force and violence, to do a corporal hurt to another. . . . [E]very battery includes an assault. . . . "

See also 3 S. Greenleaf, Evidence § 59 (16th ed. Harriman 1899); R. Perkins, Criminal Law 114 et seq. (2d ed. 1969). This is the definition given the term in the federal cases. The second concept of assault referred to in *Rizzo,* an act putting another in reasonable apprehension of bodily harm, originated in the law of torts. R. Perkins, id. at 114. Most jurisdictions recognize both concepts of criminal assault.

The notion that a reasonable apprehension on the part of the victim is an essential element of criminal assault probably originated with Bishop, who confused the two concepts in a single definition of the offense and included the element of creating a reasonable apprehension of immediate physical injury in that definition. 2 J. Bishop, Criminal Law § 23 (9th ed. 1923). . . . *

Since an attempted battery is an assault, it is irrelevant that the victim is incapable of forming a reasonable apprehension. Occasions for so holding seem rarely to have been presented. Alderson, B., in The Queen v. Camplin, 1 Cox C.C. 220, 221 (1845), reports that there was such a case in his experience. Regina v. March, 1 Car. & K. 496 (1844), was a conviction for assault against a newborn infant. There are many statements to the effect that an attempt upon an unconscious or otherwise insensitive victim is an assault. . . .

Defendant's attempt to rape an insensitive victim was an assault under 18 U.S.C. § 113(a). His conviction is affirmed.

Affirmed.[1]

Certiorari denied, 95 S.Ct. 1357 (1975).

* By statute in Illinois assault is defined as the reasonable-apprehension offense (Ill.Rev.Stat., Ch. 38, § 12–1 (1973)) and the attempted-battery offense is covered by the general attempt section (id. § 8–4). A similar approach is adopted in the proposed bill to revise the Federal Criminal Code. See Revised Committee Print of Amended S. 1, 93d Cong., 2d Sess. §§ 1001, 1613, 1614 (Oct. 15, 1974). In the statutes of other states assault is defined as an attempted battery, but most state statutes, like the federal, do not define the term assault. See Comments to § 201.10, ALI, Model Penal Code, Tentative Draft No. 9, p. 83 (1959). Appendix H to the Comments lists and classifies the state statutes. Id. at 141. ALI, Proposed Official Draft of the Model Penal Code (1962), p. 134, with some refinements not relevant here, recognizes both the attempted-battery and reasonable-apprehension types of assault as offenses.

1. [Added by the Compiler.] An apprehension of immediate bodily harm is required under the Kansas statute of aggravated assault. State v. Warbritton, 215 Kan. 534, 527 P.2d 1050 (1974).

Under Arizona law an attempt to commit a physical injury is not a necessary element of assault. Hence one may be guilty of assault with a deadly weapon by pointing a gun at another even if he did not intend to cause bodily harm. State v. Gary, 112 Ariz. 470, 543 P.2d 782 (1975), cert. denied 425 U.S. 916, 96 S.Ct. 1517.

For a discussion of the two theories of assault see State v. Frazier, 81 Wash.2d 628, 503 P.2d 1073 (1972).

STATE v. CAPWELL

Court of Appeals of Oregon, 1981.
52 Or.App. 43, 627 P.2d 905.

GILLETTE, PRESIDING JUDGE. This is a criminal case in which defendant seeks reversal of his conviction for Assault in The Fourth Degree. ORS 163.160. Defendant contends that the trial court erred in denying his motion for acquittal on the basis of insufficient evidence. We agree and reverse his conviction.[1]

ORS 163.160 provides, in pertinent part, that a person commits the crime of Assault in the Fourth Degree if he "intentionally, knowingly or recklessly causes physical injury to another. . . . " "Physical injury" is defined as "impairment of physical condition or substantial pain." ORS 161.015(6). Defendant claims that there is no evidence that the alleged victim suffered any impairment of his physical condition or substantial pain.

At approximately 3 a.m. on June 1, 1980, the victim's wife noticed a man, later identified as the defendant, standing in front of their house and carrying a gas can. She awakened her husband, Tenderella, who is an Oregon State Police officer. After dressing he picked up his nightstick and went outside to investigate the matter. He told the defendant to stop where he was. The defendant, who appeared startled, swung the gas can at Tenderella but did not hit him. Tenderella identified himself as a police officer and began to question the defendant about his activities. At that point, he noticed a bulge underneath the defendant's coat and attempted to pat him down for weapons. The defendant pulled back and swung the gas can at Tenderella again, this time hitting him in the arm. Tenderella testi-

May a criminal assault be committed by pointing an unloaded firearm at another within shooting distance but not within striking distance (as a club)?

It was held "yes" under a statute defining assault as a wilful and unlawful attempt or offer, with force or violence, to do a corporal hurt to another. State v. Wiley, 52 S.D. 110, 216 N.W. 866 (1927).

It was held "no" under a statute defining assault as an unlawful attempt, coupled with present ability, to commit violent injury. Klein v. State, 9 Ind.App. 365, 36 N.E. 763 (1894).

Without basing the decision on the wording of the statute it was held that while such a menace is sufficient for a civil action it does not constitute a criminal assault. Chapman v. State, 78 Ala. 463 (1885). A contrary view was expressed in State v. Deso, 110 Vt. 1, 1 A.2d 710 (1938).

D thrust his hand against **X**, said "stick 'em up", and began to go through **X's** pockets until **X** noticed that **D** did not have a gun and pushed him away. This was held to be an assault with intent to rob. People v. Rockwood, 358 Ill. 422, 193 N.E. 449 (1934).

Exposing a child to the weather was held not to constitute an assault where the child was rescued before suffering any injury. Regina v. Renshaw, 2 Cox C.C. 285 (1847).

1. Defendant also claims that the trial court erred in conditioning his probation on the requirement that he "obey all rules and regulations imposed upon him by . . . [the] Marion County Department of Community Corrections." Because of our disposition of defendant's first assignment of error, we need not reach this issue.

fied that he felt pain, a stinging sensation, when the defendant hit him.

Tenderella told the defendant that he was under arrest. The defendant attempted to leave and Tenderella tried "to put him down" by hitting him around the knee area with his nightstick. The defendant reacted by swinging the gas can and kicking out at Tenderella. At one point the defendant kicked him in the arm, knocking the nightstick out of his hand. The victim testified that this "hurt." He could not recall, however, whether the defendant was wearing soft or hard shoes.[2]

The officer did not know exactly how many times he was hit with the gas can. He stated that it was a "couple of times" and that each time he stopped the blow with his arm. He reported no sensation other than it "hurt" and was painful. There is no indication of bruising or any other injury to the victim. He stated that he did not seek medical treatment after the scuffle and did not miss any work.

The question to be answered in determining the sufficiency of the evidence in this case is

> ". . . whether, after viewing the evidence in the light most favorable to the prosecution, any rational trier of fact could have found the essential elements of the crime beyond a reasonable doubt."

There is no evidence that the victim suffered any impairment of his physical condition as a result of defendant's blows. The question is whether there is sufficient evidence to allow the jury to find, beyond a reasonable doubt, guilt according to the alternative statutory requirement, *viz.*, that the victim suffered substantial pain. We conclude that there is not.

"Substantial" is defined as

> "(1) That is or exists as a substance; having a real existence, subsisting by itself; (2) of ample or considerable amount, quantity or dimensions, (3) having substance, not imaginary, unreal or apparent only; true, solid real." Oxford English Dictionary, Compact Edition (1971).

Substantial pain means considerable pain. In this case, the victim testified that he had pain and that it hurt when the defendant struck him. There is no other evidence of the degree of the pain or that it was anything more than a fleeting sensation.[3] The state was re-

2. These facts are presented in a light most favorable to the state. The defendant claimed that Officer Tenderella hit him first and that he, the defendant, was acting in self-defense.

3. The legislative history reveals that criminal assault, in whatever degree, requires the infliction of actual physical injury. Petty batteries not producing injury do not constitute criminal assault. See Criminal Law Revision Commission, Proposed Criminal Code, Final Draft, 123, Commentary to § 94 and 219 Commentary to § 223. The term "physical injury" recognizes that the cause of such an injury is some form of external violence that produces a harmful effect upon the body. See Criminal Law Revision Commission, Proposed Criminal Code, Final Draft, 3, Commentary to § 3.

quired to prove that the defendant's blows caused either physical impairment or substantial pain to the victim. We conclude that there was insufficient evidence to support such a finding in this case.

Having stated that the evidence is insufficient to convict defendant of the offense of Assault in the Fourth Degree, the question remains: what disposition must be made of this case?

Assault in the Fourth Degree is a Class A misdemeanor. ORS 163.160. ORS 161.405 provides, in pertinent part:

> "(1) A person is guilty of an attempt to commit a crime when he intentionally engages in conduct which constitutes a substantial step toward commission of the crime.
>
> "(2) An attempt is a:
>
> ". . .
>
> "(e) Class B misdemeanor if the offense attempted is a Class A misdemeanor.
>
> ". . ."

The Oregon Constitution, Amend. Art. VII, § 3 directs:

> ". . . if, in any respect, the judgment appealed from should be changed, and the [appellate court] shall be of the opinion that it can determine what judgment should have been entered in the court below, it shall direct such judgment to be entered . . . ."

In the present case, the trier of fact necessarily found that defendant had taken a "substantial step" toward commission of the assault offense. Entry of a judgment for Attempted Assault in the Fourth Degree is appropriate.[4]

Reversed and remanded for entry of a new judgment and for resentencing.

MODEL PENAL CODE

Article 211. Assault; Reckless Endangering; Threats

Section 211.0 Definitions.

In this Article, the definitions given in Section 210.0 apply unless a different meaning plainly is required.

Section 211.1 Assault.

(1) Simple Assault. A person is guilty of assault if he:

(a) attempts to cause or purposely, knowingly or recklessly causes bodily injury to another; or

4. ORS 163.160 provides that Assault in the Fourth Degree may be committed "intentionally, knowingly *or recklessly*." However, our disposition of this case is permissible because the trial court, in instructing the jury, instructed the jury that they must find that the defendant acted intentionally. No mention was made of recklessness.

(b) negligently causes bodily injury to another with a deadly weapon; or

(c) attempts by physical menace to put another in fear of imminent serious bodily injury.

Simple assault is a misdemeanor unless committed in a fight or scuffle entered into by mutual consent, in which case it is a petty misdemeanor.

(2) Aggravated Assault. A person is guilty of aggravated assault if he:

(a) attempts to cause serious bodily injury to another, or causes such injury purposely, knowingly or recklessly under circumstances manifesting extreme indifference to the value of human life: or

(b) attempts to cause or purposely or knowingly causes bodily injury to another with a deadly weapon.

Aggravated assault under paragraph (a) is a felony of the second degree; aggravated assault under paragraph (b) is a felony of the third degree.

Section 211.2 Recklessly Endangering Another Person.

A person commits a misdemeanor if he recklessly engages in conduct which places or may place another person in danger of death or serious bodily injury. Recklessness and danger shall be presumed where a person knowingly points a firearm at or in the direction of another, whether or not the actor believed the firearm to be loaded.

Section 211.3 Terroristic Threats.

A person is guilty of a felony of the third degree if he threatens to commit any crime of violence with purpose to terrorize another or to cause evacuation of a building, place of assembly, or facility of public transportation, or otherwise to cause serious public inconvenience, or in reckless disregard of the risk of causing such terror or inconvenience.[1]

SECTION 3. OTHER OFFENSES AGAINST THE PERSON

(A) ABDUCTION

The social interest in the personal security of the individual member of the community goes far beyond the effort to safeguard his life and to protect him against an ordinary attack. Viewed in the most primitive light, the state must undertake to deal with various other types of personal harm in order to have any adequate check upon violent acts of private retaliation. It must do so, furthermore, if the organized group is to continue to strive for an ever higher level of cultural development, and "a more abundant" life, intellectually and morally, as well as physically.

There was no such crime as abduction known to the English common law, but a statute, passed a few years before Columbus discovered America, created a felony which is the forerunner of all the present statutes on abduction. This early statute was designed primarily to protect young heiresses from designing fortune hunters, although its wording was not so limited. It provided in substance that if any person should take any woman ("maid, widow or wife") against her will, unlawfully, and such woman had substance in the form of lands or goods or was the heir apparent of her ancestor, such person should be guilty of felony. It was stated in an introduction to the statute that a woman, so taken, was often thereafter married to or defiled by the misdoer, or to or by another with his consent, but this was not made an element of the original crime itself. This element, however, has been included in many of the modern statutes. Some jurisdictions also have statutes making it a crime for any person to take or entice any unmarried female under a certain age for the purpose of prostitution (or for the purpose of sexual intercourse, concubinage or prostitution). This general field, often involving two or more statutes which may be in different parts of the code, has come to be referred to as *abduction*.

Some statutes prohibit the unlawful taking (perhaps adding enticing or detaining) of a girl under a specified age from her parent or guardian for the purpose of depriving the parent or guardian of his lawful custody; and some make a similar provision with reference to such taking of "any child," and hence extend the protection to boys as well as girls. Such a statute goes beyond the scope of "abduction" as it is ordinarily understood and carries over into the field of kidnaping. The word "abduction," meaning literally a taking or drawing away, was employed by Blackstone in his definition of kidnaping, and "child stealing" is frequently included as a special form of that offense.

(B) ABORTION AND CONTRACEPTIVISM

(i) ABORTION

Abortion literally means miscarriage. It was a misdemeanor at common law to cause the miscarriage of a woman after the foetus had quickened unless necessary or reasonably believed to be necessary to save her life, and the word "abortion" came to be applied to this offense. Most of the statutes in this country have no requirement that the foetus must have quickened, and do not make actual miscarriage essential to guilt. Many do not even require that the woman be actually pregnant at the time, belief in such pregnancy being sufficient. Such an offense is frequently, and more properly, called "attempt to procure an abortion," and consists of the administration of a drug, use of an instrument, or employment of other means with intent to cause a miscarriage not necessary, or reasonably supposed to be necessary, to save the life of the woman.

Some states have made it a statutory offense for a woman to solicit medicine, drugs or substances and use the same herself, or submit to any operation or treatment, with intent to procure her miscarriage unless necessary to preserve her life. And in at least a dozen states the crime of manslaughter has been extended, by statute, to include certain types of foeticide.

Any medicine or means for producing a miscarriage is known as an abortifacient and statutes punishing the unauthorized sale thereof are not uncommon.

Therapeutic abortion is, literally, a miscarriage induced for medical reasons. It has been generally understood to refer to one for the purpose of saving the mother's life since justifiable abortion was commonly thus restricted in this country, England and Canada. The present trend is in the direction of a substantial relaxation of this strict position. The leading suggestions have been to authorize abortion not only when it seems reasonably necessary to save the life of the mother, but also where it is important to preserve (1) her health, including (2) mental health, and where it is necessary to prevent (3) gravely defective offspring or (4) offspring resulting from rape or incest. Several states have enacted statutes to authorize abortion for all or most of these purposes.

The most recent suggestion has been to leave the matter of abortion entirely to the discretion of the woman and her doctor, and some of the enactments go almost that far.

This was how the law stood up to 1973, when the Supreme Court made a drastic change in the law of abortion.[1] The Court held that during the first trimester of pregnancy the abortion decision must be left entirely to the decision of the woman and her physician without interference by the state. After the first stage the state may, if it chooses, reasonably regulate abortion procedure to preserve and protect maternal health. Subsequent to viability the state may regulate an abortion to protect the life of the fetus and may even proscribe abortion except where necessary for the preservation of the life or health of the mother.

H___ L___ v. MATHESON

Supreme Court of Utah, 1979.
604 P.2d 907.

MAUGHAN, JUSTICE: Plaintiff, seeking declaratory and injunctive relief, initiated this action for the purpose of having Section 76–7–304(2) declared unconstitutional and to enjoin the enforcement there-

1. Roe v. Wade, 410 U.S. 113, 93 S.Ct. 705 (1973); Doe v. Bolton, 410 U.S. 179, 93 S.Ct. 739 (1973).

of. The trial court found the provision constitutionally valid, and plaintiff appeals therefrom. The judgment is affirmed. All statutory references are to the 1953 Utah Code Annotated, as amended.

Plaintiff, a fifteen year old girl, alleged she was pregnant with an unwanted child. She asserted she was in her first trimester of pregnancy. She claimed she did not wish to inform her parents of her condition, and she believed it to be in her best interests not to impart such information to her parents. She averred, she was determined to secure an abortion after consultation with her counselor.

Plaintiff consulted her physician. He advised her, under Section 76–7–304(2), he could not and would not perform the abortion, without first notifying her parents.

Section 76–7–304, provides:

> To enable the physician to exercise his best medical judgment, he shall:
>
> (1) Consider all factors relevant to the well-being of the woman upon whom the abortion is to be performed including, but not limited to,
>
> (a) Her physical, emotional and psychological health and safety,
>
> (b) Her age,
>
> (c) Her familial situation.
>
> (2) Notify, if possible, the parents or guardian of the woman upon whom the abortion is to be performed, if she is a minor or the husband of the woman, if she is married.

This provision is part of the criminal code, as provided in Section 76–7–314(3). Such may be punishable by imprisonment for a term not exceeding one year, as provided in Section 76–3–204(1); together with a fine not exceeding $1,000, pursuant to Section 76–3–301(3).

Plaintiff proceeded in a class action, asserting the statute constituted an invasion of privacy of each member of the class, whom she represented. Specifically, she claimed the right of privacy encompassed the right to have an abortion, particularly in the first trimester of pregnancy, free from regulation or interference by the State of Utah. She urged the statute unconstitutionally infringed the right of privacy and thus violated the Fourteenth Amendment of the Constitution of the United States. She further asserted the statute was an overly-broad regulation, which interfered with her right to consult freely with her treating physician, and to secure treatment, where appropriate, in the effectuation of an abortion without any compelling State interest in such regulation.

In its order denying a temporary restraining order, the trial court found plaintiff had made no special showing of detriment which might result if her parents were notified except for plaintiff's allegations she did not wish to inform her parents, and believed it was in her best interests to withhold this information. The trial court further found the identity of the parents was known or could be easily ascertained by the consulting physician. The trial court concluded, while a State may not regulate or interfere with the decision of an adult woman, and that of her physician, to terminate an unwanted pregnancy during the first trimester, there was no binding decision, which precluded a State from enacting a legislative provision requiring a physician to notify the parents of a minor prior to performing an abortion.

The trial court entered a judgment, dismissing plaintiff's action. The trial court found plaintiff was unmarried, fifteen years of age, resided at home, was a dependent of her parents, and was in the first trimester of her pregnancy at the time her complaint was filed. The Court further ruled plaintiff was an appropriate representative to represent the class she purported to represent. The trial court interpreted Section 76–7–304(2) as requiring the treating physician to notify, if it be physically possible, viz., if he knows or can determine the identity of the parents of a minor, and he is physically able to notify them, that he do so prior to the performance of an abortion upon a minor. The trial court ruled, as thus interpreted, the statute was valid and did not unconstitutionally restrict the right of privacy of a minor to secure an abortion, or to enter into a doctor-patient relationship.

On appeal, plaintiff contends Section 76–7–304(2), as interpreted by the trial court, violates the Fourteenth Amendment of the Constitution of the United States. She urges, in the first trimester, the State cannot interfere at all with the fundamental interest of the pregnant woman in making an abortion decision in consultation with her physician. In the alternative, plaintiff contends this overly-broad regulation of the exercise of constitutionally protected rights can be so construed as to be valid. Specifically, plaintiff urges the term "if possible" be interpreted as conferring on the physician and patient the discretion to determine if medically, socially, psychologically, and physically it would be appropriate to notify the minor's parents.

In Roe v. Wade [1] the Court ruled the right of privacy, found in the Fourteenth Amendment's concept of personal liberty and restrictions upon state action, is broad enough to encompass a woman's decision as to whether to terminate her pregnancy. This right of personal privacy, including the abortion decision is not unqualified and must

1. 410 U.S. 113, 153, 93 S.Ct. 705, 35 L.Ed.2d 147.

be considered against state interests in regulation. However, a regulation limiting a fundamental right may be justified only by a compelling state interest. Furthermore, such legislative enactments must be narrowly drawn to express only the legitimate state interests at stake.

The Court ruled in Roe v. Wade,[2] with respect to the stage prior to approximately the end of the first trimester, "[T]he attending physician, in consultation with his patient, is free to determine, without regulation by the State, that, in his medical judgment, the patient's pregnancy should be terminated. If that decision is reached, the judgment may be effectuated by an abortion free of interference by the State."

It further held the State may place increasing restrictions on abortion as the period of pregnancy lengthens, so long as those restrictions are tailored to the recognized state interests. The Court stated:

> . . . The decision vindicates the right of the physician to administer medical treatment according to his professional judgment up to the points where important state interests provide compelling justifications for intervention. Up to those points, the abortion decision in all its aspects is inherently, and primarily, a medical decision, and basic responsibility for it must rest with the physician. If an individual practitioner abuses the privilege of exercising proper medical judgment, the usual remedies, judicial and intra-professional are available.[3]

In the companion case of Doe v. Bolton [4] the Court ruled the abortion determination, so far as the physician is concerned, is made in the exercise of his best clinical judgment in the light of all the attendant circumstances. The physician may range farther afield wherever his medical judgment, properly and professionally exercised, so dictates and directs him. His "medical judgment may be exercised in the light of all factors physical, emotional, psychological, familial, and the woman's age—relevant to the well-being of the patient. All these factors relate to health. This allows the attending physician the room he needs to make his best medical judgment. And it is room that operates for the benefit, not the disadvantage, of the pregnant woman."

The aforecited factors, which the physician may consider in making his best medical judgment were incorporated in subsection (1) of Section 76–7–304, the challenged statute. The notification provision of subsection (2) is substantially and logically related to the factors in subsection (1), for it is the parent of the minor, who would frequently possess additional information, which might prove invaluable to the physician in exercising his "best medical judgment." The notification provision merely gives the parents the option to respond and to consult with the physician and child. The statute does not confer a veto-

2. 410 U.S. 163, 93 S.Ct. 732.

3. 410 U.S. 165–166, 93 S.Ct. 733.

4. 410 U.S. 179, 191–192, 93 S.Ct. 739, 35 L.Ed.2d 201 (1972).

power on anyone to overrule the determination of the doctor and his patient.[5]

Neither the *Roe* nor the *Doe* decision considered the issue of a pregnant minor seeking an abortion. In Planned Parenthood of Central Missouri v. Danforth [6] the Court ruled the State may not impose a blanket provision, requiring the consent of a parent or person in *loco parentis* as a condition for abortion of an unmarried minor during the first twelve weeks of her pregnancy. The Court explained the State does not have the constitutional authority to give a third party an absolute, and possibly arbitrary veto over the decision of the physician and his patient, to terminate the patient's pregnancy, regardless of the reason for withholding the consent.

The Court stated:

> Constitutional rights do not mature and come into being magically only when one attains the state-defined age of majority. Minors, as well as adults, are protected by the Constitution and possess constitutional rights. [Citations] The Court indeed, however, long has recognized that the State has somewhat broader authority to regulate the activities of children than of adults. [Citations] It remains, then, to examine whether there is any significant state interests in conditioning an abortion on the consent of a parent or person in *loco parentis* that is not present in the case of an adult.

It was urged before the court the State had a substantial interest in safeguarding the family unit and parental authority. The court responded it could not conclude conferring a veto power on the parent would strengthen the family unit or enhance parental authority and control where the minor and nonconsenting parent were so fundamentally in conflict, and the existence of the pregnancy already had fractured the family structure.

> Any independent interest the parent may have in the termination of the minor daughter's pregnancy is no more weighty than the right of privacy of the competent minor mature enough to have become pregnant.

The Court did qualify its holding by stating it had not suggested every minor, regardless of age or maturity, might give effective consent for termination of her pregnancy. The fault of the challenged Missouri statute was it imposed a special consent provision, exercisable by a person other than the woman and her physician, as a prerequisite to a minor's termination of her pregnancy; and did so without a sufficient justification for the restriction, thus violating the strictures of *Roe* and *Doe*. . . .

5. The issue of parental consent for a surgical procedure on a minor child has not been presented to the court and will not be discussed.

6. 428 U.S. 52, 74–75, 96 S.Ct. 2831, 49 L.Ed.2d 788 (1976).

Under *Danforth,* the issue then is whether the statute serves "any significant state interest" that is not present in the case of an adult, which would justify as a condition precedent to the obtaining of an abortion by a minor, the notification of her parents. First and foremost, the statute does not per se impose any restriction on the minor as to her decision to terminate her pregnancy. Second, as mentioned ante, the parent is in a position to provide valuable information concerning the factors which the physician may consider in exercising his best clinical judgment. Third, the State has a special interest in encouraging (but does not require), an unmarried pregnant minor to seek the advice of her parents in making the important decision as to whether or not to bear a child. . . .

The Legislature in enacting Section 76–7–304(2) has strictly limited parental involvement in the minor's abortion decision. The provision does not confer on the parent an absolute and arbitrary veto, which was found impermissible in *Danforth.* There is no basis to conclude this provision unduly burdens the constitutional right of the minor woman, in consultation with her physician, to choose to terminate her pregnancy; thus, it is constitutional.

Plaintiff further urges the term "if possible" in subsection (2) of Section 76–7–304 be construed as conferring on the consulting physician discretion to determine if medically, socially, psychologically, and physically, it would be appropriate to notify the minor's parents.

There is no ambiguity in the term "if possible" within the context of subsection (2); and, therefore, there is no basis to construe the term beyond its literal, plain meaning.[7] The trial court's interpretation is consistent with the clearly expressed legislative intent, viz., the consulting physician must notify the parents, if under the circumstances, in the exercise of reasonable diligence, he can ascertain their identity and location and it is feasible or practicable to give them notification.[8] Furthermore, within the context of what is reasonable under the circumstances, the time element is an important factor, for there must be sufficient expedition to provide an effective opportunity for an abortion.[a]

CROCKETT, C.J., and WILKINS, HALL and STEWART, JJ., concur.

7. ". . . there is nothing to construe where there is no ambiguity in the statute." State v. Archuletta, Utah, 526 P.2d 911, 912 (1974).

8. See 20 Words and Phrases, 1979 Supplement, p. 8, "If Possible."

a. Affirmed, H.L. v. Matheson, 450 U.S. 398, 101 S.Ct. 1164 (1981). See also Bellotti v. Baird, 443 U.S. 622, 99 S.Ct. 3035 (1979), holding that a state's interest in protecting immature minors will sustain a requirement of a consent for abortion by parent or parent substitute like a judicial body.

A local ordinance requiring that an abortion subsequent to the first trimester be performed in a hospital is unconstitutional since abortions are safely performed under less demanding circumstances during part of the second trimester. A 24 hour waiting period is unconstitutional as is a parental consent requirement where no judicial substitute is provided. City of Akron v. Akron

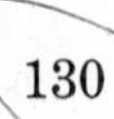

(ii) Contraceptivism

Contraceptivism is unlawful trafficking in contraceptives. It is not a common-law offense, and has not received widespread adoption as a statutory crime although it is to be found in a few of the codes.

(iii) Indecent Advertising

Statutes punishing "indecent advertising" often include advertising the sale of contraceptives and abortifacients.

(iv) Federal Offenses

Contraceptives and abortifacients have been grouped with a number of other things such as obscene books and pictures and declared "non-mailable" by Act of Congress. Knowingly to deposit any such article for mailing or to take from the mails for the purpose of disposition is a federal felony. It is also a federal felony to deposit such an article with a common carrier for interstate transportation or to import it into the United States from a foreign country.

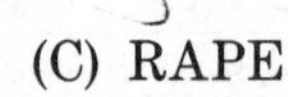

(C) RAPE

Rape, at common law, is unlawful carnal knowledge of a woman without her consent. Any sexual penetration, however slight, is sufficient to complete the crime if the other elements are present.

"By force and against her will" is the phrase often used in the definitions, but as unlawful carnal knowledge of a woman who is insensibly drunk at the time is held to be rape unless she had consented in advance, it is obvious that no more is required than that the deed be done without her consent. Sexual intercourse by a man with his lawful wife is not unlawful and hence is not rape even if she does not consent.[1] But while a husband cannot rape [2] his wife he can be guilty

Center, ___ U.S. ___, 103 S.Ct. 2481 (1983).

Virginia law requiring a second trimester abortion be performed in a hospital, and defining hospital to included licensed outpatient clinics, is constitutional and criminal conviction for violation is proper. Simopoulos v. Virginia, ___ U.S. ___, 103 S.Ct. 2532 (1983).

1. "Rape is an act of sexual intercourse committed by a man with a woman not his wife without her consent and when the woman's resistance has been overcome by force or fear." State v. Clark, 218 Kan. 726–728, 544 P.2d 1372, 1375 (1976).

If D believed, reasonably and in good faith, that the woman consented to go to his apartment and have sexual intercourse with him, he was not guilty of rape. And the erroneous refusal to give the mistake-of-fact instruction was reversible error. People v. Mayberry, 15 Cal.3d 143, 125 Cal.Rptr. 745, 542 P.2d 1337 (1975).

While holding that it was error for the judge to refuse to instruct, in a rape case, that the charge of rape is easily made and difficult to defend against, the court held that the refusal to so charge was harmless error in the case at bench, and that for the future such an instruction will be considered inappropriate and is disapproved. People v. Rincon-Pineda. 14 Cal.3d 864, 123 Cal.Rptr. 119, 538 P.2d 247 (1975).

2. Some states have modified the traditional rule by statute either abrogat-

of the crime of rape committed upon her. That is, if **A** should aid **B** in having sexual intercourse with **A**'s wife without her consent, both **A** and **B** would be guilty of rape.

Statutory rape. It is commonly provided by statute that unlawful carnal knowledge is a crime committed upon a girl under a certain age (called the age of consent) even if she consents. To distinguish between this and the other type of rape, the first is often called "statutory rape" or "carnal knowledge of a child" and the other "common-law rape." [3]

The so-called "age of consent" varies in the different jurisdictions. An early English statute fixed the age at twelve. Modern statutes usually provide a substantially higher age,—not infrequently eighteen.

DINKENS v. STATE

Supreme Court of Nevada, 1976.
92 Nev. 74, 546 P.2d 228.

ZENOFF, JUSTICE. Early in the evening of August 10, 1973, a young teenage girl was walking home from a youth recreation center in Las Vegas where she had spent the previous two or three hours. At that time, she was considering whether to visit a classmate friend who worked at a concession stand at a public park several miles distant. Observing a small boy riding as a passenger in an approaching pickup truck, she thought the situation afforded her the opportunity to obtain safe transportation to the park and decided to make the visit. Delmar Dinkens, driver of the vehicle, observed the girl, noted her outstretched thumb, pulled the truck to the side of the road and offered her a ride. She accepted.

Once in the vehicle the trio drove to a motel where Dinkens ordered the boy out of the truck and told him to wait for his father. Out of earshot of the girl, Dinkens informed the boy that he was going to "get that girl." Alone with the girl, Dinkens drove in the general direction of her stated destination, Paradise Park. Engaging her in a conversation, he learned that she was nearly fourteen years old. Dinkens mentioned to the girl that he had difficulty hearing her and suggested that she sit closer to him to remedy that problem. Becoming inwardly apprehensive, she refused. Thereafter, it soon became apparent that Dinkens was not heading towards the park and

ing the limitation on rape by a spouse, or by modifying it to cover situations where the parties are separated or living apart. Comment, Spousal Exemption to Rape, 65 Marq.L.Rev. 120 (1981).

3. Michael M. v. Superior Court, 450 U.S. 464, 101 S.Ct. 1200 (1981).

Although the new statute, covering the same misconduct, does not use the word "rape" that appeared in the repealed statute, there was no defect in the verdict finding defendant guilty of "statutory rape", since the record shows there could have been no uncertainty in the minds of the court, the prosecutor or the defendant, of the crime of which he was convicted. Carver v. Martin, 664 F.2d 932 (4th Cir.1981).

the girl reached for the door handle in an attempt to escape. Dinkens grabbed her and pulled her to him. She cried, "Please don't kill me", to which he replied, "I'm just going to play with you for a little while."

Dinkens parked his vehicle off the road and commenced to fondle his victim. Abruptly, she was ordered to disrobe and was forced to assume a prone position on the seat of the car. Dinkens thereupon engaged her in the act of sexual intercourse. Various attempts to penetrate her rectum in a similar manner proved futile. During the course of the assault, Dinkens demanded that the girl give him "a little head" and he thrust his penis towards her mouth. The girl resisted and, distracted by an approaching car, he temporarily abandoned that endeavor. After the car passed, Dinkens directed his vehicle to a more remote area where he engaged the victim once again in the act of sexual intercourse. Afterwards he apologized, told the girl to dress and ultimately released her in the vicinity of the park which had been her destination from the outset.

At Paradise Park she found that her friend had departed but was able to obtain a ride home from the mother of another girl. Frightened and nervous, she did not reveal her encounter with the strange man to her father but confided in her older sister. After her mother returned home from Indiana nine days later, the incident was reported to her and subsequently to the police. The arrest and prosecution of Dinkens followed.

For no explained or understandable reason the district attorney charged Dinkens with forcible rape, not statutory rape. NRS 200.365. The first, of course, requires a showing of forcible entry but a charge of statutory rape would have obviated any concern over the claim of Dinkens that the young girl consented to his sex acts. Dinkens was also charged in two counts with the infamous crime against nature and attempt to commit said crime for his efforts to engage in anal intercourse and to place his penis in the girl's mouth.

A jury verdict of not guilty was returned on the charge of anal intercourse and verdicts of guilty were returned on the charges of rape and attempted oral copulation. Thereafter, Dinkens was sentenced to serve two concurrent 20-year terms in the Nevada State Prison.

1. The principal issue raised by Dinkens on review is that the girl consented in the absence of fear of force or violence to the acts he committed upon her. His argument focuses on the evidence presented at trial as it relates to the element of force. He claims that the evidence is insufficient to support a conviction for forcible rape.

"Forcible rape" is defined in NRS 200.363 as "carnal knowledge of a female against her will." The statute does not require a showing that the defendant employed force to achieve his objective but only that the act was committed against the will of the victim. Physical force is not a necessary ingredient in the commission of the crime of rape. The crucial question is not whether the victim was "physically forced" to engage in sexual intercourse but whether the act was committed without her consent. There is no consent where the victim is induced to submit to the sexual act through fear of death or serious bodily injury.

Under the circumstances shown in this case it is apparent that the girl submitted because of fear. The requirement of force and fear are of a different and less degree for a child than a person of more mature years.

Here, the girl related that a few months prior to her encounter with Dinkens, a uniformed officer had told her that if she was approached by a person driving a red car she should submit to any demands he made of her. If she refused, she would be killed. That admonition was recalled when the girl realized that Dinkens was not driving towards her intended destination and was responsible for the plea for her life emitted at the instant Dinkens grabbed her and pulled her to him foiling her attempt to escape.

The young victim testified that she was forced to assume a lying position and was forced to maintain that position until the sexual act was completed. The fact that the record suggests that Dinkens employed no violence or express threats to obtain the girl's submission does not preclude a finding of forcible rape. The fact that force was exerted (albeit no injury resulted therefrom) in combination with the girl's age and the fact that she expressed fear for her life at the instant Dinkens touched her sufficiently support the finding of the jury that the sexual act was committed "against her will." NRS 200.363. A rape victim is not required to do more than her age, strength, surrounding facts and all attending circumstances make it reasonable for her to do in order to manifest her opposition.

2. After engaging his victim in the act of sexual intercourse, appellant thrust his penis to within inches of her mouth and demanded that she give him "a little head." The girl resisted and covered her mouth with her hand but Dinkens persisted in this endeavor until informed of an approaching car. Based on these facts, it is argued, a conviction for attempted infamous crime against nature cannot stand. We are not persuaded. The jury was presented with sufficient evidence to support a finding that Dinkens committed each element necessary to constitute an attempted infamous crime against nature.

3. The claim that the state must show that the victim acted as an objectively reasonable woman in submitting to appellant's sexual assault is not convincing. So long as the evidence establishes that the victim was induced to submit to the sexual acts by actual fear, whether a "reasonable" woman under such circumstnaces would have experienced the same fear is not a determination that courts and juries have to make. Hence, appellant's request that the jury be instructed that submission by the prosecutrix to appellant's sexual assault must have been induced by a "reasonable" fear was properly refused.

4. We have already denied the contention that NRS 201.190, proscribing the infamous crime against nature, is unconstitutionally vague. Appellant's claim that fellatio does not constitute a crime against nature is similarly rejected.

Nor do we deem the circumstances of this case appropriate to merit a discussion of whether NRS 201.190 constitutionally applies to married couples or consenting adults. Here, appellant attempted to perpetrate the prohibited act on a non-spouse child who did not willingly consent. Thus applied, there is little doubt as to the constitutionality of the statute.

We have reviewed other assignments of error and find them to be without merit.[a]

Affirmed.

(D) FALSE IMPRISONMENT

False imprisonment is the unlawful confinement of a person and is an indictable misdemeanor at common law. One may be *imprisoned* not only in the public jail or a private house or in the stocks but even by being detained against his will on the public street. An *imprisonment* may be accomplished by physical barriers or physical force, or it may be by threat of force or assertion of authority which results in submission. One is not imprisoned merely because he is prevented from going in one certain direction, or in several directions, so long as there is an obvious way open for his departure. On the other hand imprisonment is not necessarily stationary. One may be locked in a moving ship or car or may be *imprisoned* by being forcibly taken from one place to another.[1]

Imprisonment is not *false* if it is lawful, as where an officer makes a lawful arrest or a parent in a proper manner confines a little child. On the other hand an arrest made under circumstances in

a. "This court has consistently held that the slightest penetration of the sexual organ is sufficient, if established beyond a reasonable doubt, to constitute the necessary element of penetration in a prosecution. . . ." State v. Tatum, 206 Neb. 625, 294 N.W.2d 354 (1980). Vaginal penetration is not necessary, any penetration of the female genitalia by the penis is sufficient. People v. Karsai, 131 Cal.App.3d 224, 182 Cal.Rptr. 406 (1982).

Several states have changed the statutory framework of what used to be rape and now refer to the offense in terms of sexual conduct. See People v. Sommerville, 100 Mich.App. 470, 299 N.W.2d 387 (1980).

California's "statutory rape" law does not violate the equal protection clause although it is only sex with a female under the age of 18 that is punished. Michael M. v. Superior Court, 450 U.S. 464, 101 S.Ct. 1200 (1981).

The California Penal Code, § 264.1 establishes a separate crime of rape in concert. People v. Best, 143 Cal.App.3d 232, 191 Cal.Rptr. 614 (1983).

The "rape shield statute," which excludes evidence of the victim's prior sexual conduct (with certain exceptions), applies equally to evidence offered to show that the victim was a virgin. State v. Gavigan, 111 Wis.2d 150, 330 N.W.2d 571 (1983).

1. Forcing one to change seats in a car and to remain in the car is false imprisonment. People v. Zilbauer, 44 Cal. 2d 43, 279 P.2d 534 (1955). But locking a person *out of* a particular room is not. Martin v. Lincoln Park West Corp., 219 F.2d 622 (7th Cir.1955).

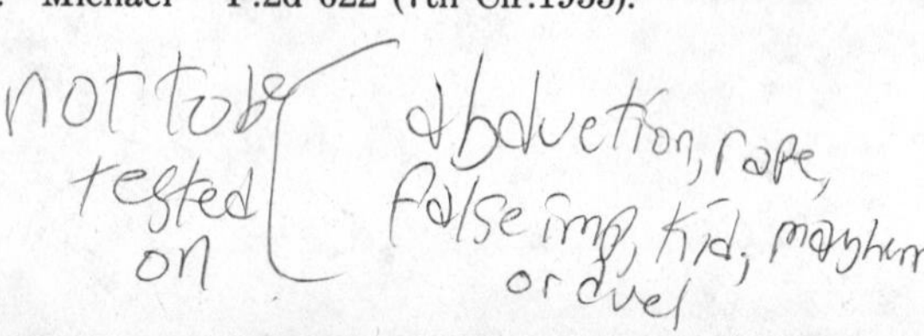

which there is no lawful authority to take the prisoner into custody constitutes false imprisonment.

Some of the modern statutes expressly provide for the punishment of false imprisonment; others do not include this crime as such, although the aggravated features may be included in some other offense such as abduction or kidnaping.

(E) KIDNAPING

Kidnaping is aggravated false imprisonment.

(i) Simple Kidnaping

There is some disagreement among the different jurisdictions as to the exact ingredients needed to place this type of misconduct in the category of the graver crime. At common law kidnaping was defined as the forcible abduction or stealing away of a man, woman or child from his own country and sending him into another. In other words it was false imprisonment aggravated by conveying the victim out of the country. This would be kidnaping anywhere today but the statutes go beyond this, the most common addition being false imprisonment with intent to cause the victim to be imprisoned secretly within the state.[1] Some enactments go even further, such as including within the offense the forcible or fraudulent taking of a person from his place of residence without authority of law.[2]

(ii) Kidnaping for Ransom

Kidnaping was a misdemeanor at common law, punished by fine, imprisonment and pillory. Under modern statutes it is a felony, and the special form of the offense known as "kidnaping for ransom" is regarded as one of the gravest of crimes, not infrequently made a capital offense. A wrongdoer is guilty of kidnaping for ransom if he participates in any of the three elements of the offense,—(1) unlawful seizure, (2) secret confinement, or (3) extortion of ransom.[3] This includes one who acts as a go-between to collect the ransom for the actual abductors.

1. One type of statute includes imprisonment with intent, (1) to send the victim out of the state, or (2) to confine him secretly within the state. Vandiver v. State, 97 Okl.Cr. 217, 261 P.2d 617 (1953).

2. Where hitchhikers consented to be driven to their homes, but instead, over their objections and under threats of death, were driven to a far distant and remote place where one was raped; they were kidnaped. Matter of Appeal in Maricopa Cty. J.A. No. J–72472S., 25 Ariz.App. 377, 543 P.2d 806 (1975).

3. ". . . to be found guilty of first-degree kidnapping a defendant must be shown either to have secretly confined or imprisoned another, *or* to have held another person to service in any way with the intent to extort or obtain money or reward for his release or disposition." State v. Quinlivan, 81 Wn.2d 124, 499 P.2d 1268 (1972).

(iii) CHILD STEALING

The "child-stealing" statutes commonly provide a penalty for anyone who shall lead, take, entice or detain a child under a specified age with intent to keep or conceal it from its parent, guardian, or other person having lawful care or control thereof. Great variation is found in the age used for this purpose, such as any child under the age of 12, 14 or 16,—or any minor child. Recently Congress enacted legislation to assist in locating one parent who has stolen a child from the custody of another parent.[1]

(iv) CONSENT

There has been no kidnaping if the person who was confined or transported freely consented thereto, without being under any legal, physical or mental disability at the time, or being subjected to any coercion, threats or fraud. A child under the age specified in a child-stealing statute is incapable of giving a legally-recognized consent.

(v) THE FEDERAL KIDNAPING ACT (THE LINDBERGH LAW)

It is a federal felony to take a kidnaped person from one state to another if the captive was "held for ransom or reward or otherwise," and the punishment may be for any term of years or for life.

(F) MAYHEM

Mayhem, according to the English common law, is maliciously depriving another of the use of such of his members as may render him less able, in fighting, either to defend himself or to annoy his adversary. To cut off a hand or a finger or to put out an eye or knock out a front tooth were all mayhems at common law, if done maliciously, because they rendered the victim less efficient as a fighting man (for the king's army). But to cut off an ear or to slit the nose was not mayhem because it merely disfigured the person. This distinction whereby the penalty for maiming was much more severe than for disfiguring (a mere battery), may have seemed quite appropriate in very ancient times but was not viewed with approval in the seventeenth century when malefactors intentionally slit the nose of a member of Parliament. A statute in 1670, prompted by the facts of that atrocity, provided the death penalty for maliciously intentional disfigurement,—and since such an injury should not be punished more severely than that of the other type the same penalty was provided for mayhem if intentionally perpetrated. This statutory offense, known as mayhem, did not displace the common-law crime of that name but was in addition to it. Thus the definition in terms of English law of the time was required to be in some such form as this: Mayhem is

1. Parental Kidnapping Prevention Act of 1980, 18 U.S.C.A. § 1073, note.

maliciously maiming or maliciously and intentionally disfiguring another,—with the explanation that the penalty for maiming was more severe if it was intentional as well as malicious than if malicious but not actually intentional (such as a wrongful act done in wanton and wilful disregard of the likelihood of maiming but without a specific intent to maim).

This distinction between the two types of injury, traceable to historical accident, has not met with general approval here. Our statutes commonly include both but whereas some follow the common law otherwise and say only "maliciously," others adopt the addition of the English statute and require the injury to be inflicted maliciously and intentionally. Hence mayhem under American statutes is maliciously maiming or disfiguring another, except that in a number of states a specific intent to maim or disfigure is required.

(G) DUELING

Dueling is fighting by previous agreement with deadly weapons. It is usually under a so-called "code of honor" which establishes rules for the conduct of the fight as well as for the preliminary arrangements.

The social interest in the life and security of the individual member of the community is too great to permit the settlement of private disputes and grudges by deadly combat. Hence the law does not permit persons to consent to such an encounter, and no justification or excuse can be established by the fact that such consent was given. Furthermore, since the combat is deliberately arranged the law does not even take notice of whatever provocation there may have been, and which might have been recognized as a mitigating circumstance had the conflict flared up in the heat of passion on the spur of the moment. Because of these facts, one who kills another in a duel is guilty of murder. And since the duel probably would not have been fought if no persons had been found willing to serve as seconds, the seconds are held to have aided and abetted in the killing and hence are also guilty of the murder. This applies to the second for the deceased as well as to the second for the victor. If the duel does not result in death, the participants are guilty of an attempt to commit murder at common law (and usually of some aggravated assault under modern statutes,—such as assault with intent to murder, or assault with a deadly weapon).

The duel is itself a common-law misdemeanor; and parties may be guilty of a misdemeanor even if the duel does not actually take place. One is guilty who challenges another to fight a duel, whether the challenge is accepted or not. One is guilty who is knowingly the bearer of such a challenge, whether it is accepted or not. One is guilty who intentionally provokes such a challenge. In this case, while guilt does not depend upon the actual fighting of the duel, it is necessary that the intentional provocation actually result in the issuance of a challenge.

Dueling does not present a present-day problem and has been omitted from many of the new penal codes. Some states have a form of statute prohibiting challenges to fight.[1]

1. Wilmeth v. State, 96 Nev. 403, 610 P.2d 735 (1980).

Chapter 3

OFFENSES AGAINST THE HABITATION

SECTION 1. BURGLARY

WOODS v. STATE

Supreme Court of Mississippi, Division A, 1939.
186 Miss. 463, 191 So. 283.

GRIFFITH, J., delivered the opinion of the court.

Appellant was indicted and convicted under the charge of the burglary of a dwelling house. The undisputed proof showed that the house in question, although intended for a dwelling house, had been only recently erected and had not yet been occupied as a dwelling. It was vacant.

Appellant relies on Haynes v. State, 180 Miss. 291, 177 So. 360, wherein the court held that a house from which the occupants had permanently removed on the day before the night of the burglary was not a dwelling at the time of the commission of the alleged crime; and that proof of the burglary of such a house would not sustain the conviction under an indictment charging the burglary of a dwelling. Appellant submits that if a house from which the occupants have permanently removed is not a dwelling house within the statutes on burglary, then, upon the same reasoning, a house into which no dwellers have ever yet moved is not a dwelling house; and in this contention appellant is clearly correct. . . .

Reversed and remanded.[1]

1. The room of a transient guest at an inn should be laid as the dwelling house of the innkeeper, not of the guest, whether the innkeeper lives in the inn or elsewhere. Rogers v. People, 86 N.Y. 360 (1881). Cf. Russell v. State, 36 Ala.App. 19, 52 So.2d 230 (1951), certiorari denied 255 Ala. 581, 52 So.2d 237.

"However, a dwelling house has been defined as a place where a man lives with his family. Thus, it is possible for a mobile home to be a dwelling house." (citations omitted.) People v. Winhoven, 65 Mich.App. 522, 526, 237 N.W.2d 540, 542 (1976).

Although the dweller had not lived in the building for a year and a half, during which time it had been used for storage, as he still regarded it as his home it had not lost its character as a "dwelling." Hamilton v. State, 354 So.2d 27 (Ala.App. 1977).

A dwelling is occupied where owner slept in a bedroom on weekends and holidays and spent days working on the interior of the home. People v. McClain, 105 Mich.App. 323, 306 N.W.2d 497 (1981).

A tack shed may be an occupied structure. State v. Sunday, ___ Mont. ___, 609 P.2d 1188 (1980).

STATE v. NEFF

Supreme Court of Appeals of West Virginia, 1940.
122 W.Va. 549, 11 S.E.2d 171.

HATCHER, JUDGE. The two Neffs were charged with burglariously breaking and entering in the night time a chicken house, an outhouse adjoining the dwelling house of J.A. Trent and belonging to him, and stealing from the chicken house his chickens valued at $30.00. The Neffs were found guilty of burglary and sentenced to the penitentiary.

The evidence is incomplete as to the size of the alleged chicken house and its proximity to the Trent dwelling. The former is described as a "small house", having a floor space of four and a half by five feet; but neither its height, nor evidence from which the height might be estimated, is shown. It had a hinged door fastened by a chain drawn through holes bored in the door and "the building face", respectively. The dwelling "sets back about" seventy-five feet from a public road; the chicken house is "out across" the road somewhere, but its distance from the road or the dwelling is not shown.

At common law burglary was "an offense against the habitation not against the property." But burglary could be committed on uninhabited structures, provided they were "parcel of" and within the same common fence as the mansion-house, though not contiguous to it. The Virginia Assembly, Acts 1847–8, Ch. IV, Sec. 13, modified the common law by restricting the burglary of a building other than the dwelling house to "an outhouse adjoining thereto and occupied therewith." That restriction remained in the Virginia statute until this state was formed and then we adopted it. West Virginia Acts, 1882, Ch. 148, Sec. 11, substituted the alternative "or" for the connective "and", so that the phrase read "outhouse adjoining thereto (the dwelling-house) or occupied therewith." There has been no further change.

All the words in the phrase are plain and well understood. No reason appears for not holding that they are used in their ordinary sense. We held in State v. Crites, 110 W.Va. 36, 156 S.E. 847, that the word "outhouse" was so used, and, in effect, that it meant a building constructed at least large enough for an adult to enter erect and to turn around comfortably within. The State, failing to show the height of the structure in question, did not prove it to be a house at all. But if we should concede that because the Trents called it a house, it should be taken as such, the State has still failed to make a case because the so-called house, being across the public road one hundred feet or more from the dwelling house, can not, under any

[Compilers' addition.]

In a prosecution for the statutory offense of aggravated burglary, it was reversible error to fail to instruct on the essential element that some person was likely to have been present in the burglarized dwelling. Glenn v. Dallman, 686 F.2d 418 (6th Cir. 1982).

fair construction, be said to adjoin it. Since the statute limits the burglary of an outhouse not occupied in connection with the dwelling house, to one "adjoining" it, such contiguity must be proven. We are not advised of any decision on a statute like ours. But the statute, as amended in 1882, differs from the common law more in words than substance. And under the common law an outhouse across a public road from its owner's dwelling house is held to be not parcel thereof and not the subject of burglary.

The judgment is reversed, the verdict set aside and a new trial awarded defendants.[1]

Reversed and remanded.

DAVIS v. COMMONWEALTH

Supreme Court of Appeals of Virginia, 1922.
132 Va. 521, 110 S.E. 356.

KELLY, P., delivered the opinion of the court.

The defendant, Annie Davis, under indictment for burglary was convicted and sentenced to confinement in the penitentiary for a term of five years.

The indictment charged that in the nighttime she broke and entered the dwelling house of one E.P. Fowlkes, and "feloniously and burglariously" stole and carried away therefrom the sum of $412.50 belonging to one Dolly Wingfield.

1. "2. The section of the statute upon which the foregoing indictment is framed is as follows: 'Every person who shall be convicted of breaking and entering: *First,* any building within the curtilage of a dwelling house, but not forming a part thereof; or, *second,* any shop, store, booth, tent, warehouse or other building, or any boat or vessel, or any railroad car in which there shall be at the time some human being, or any goods, wares, merchandise, or other valuable thing kept or deposited, with intent to steal or commit any felony therein, shall, on conviction, be adjudged guilty of burglary in the second degree.' R.S.1889, sec. 3526. . . .

"If the indictment be based on the second clause of the section, then it is bad because the rule as to matters *ejusdem generis* applies—that good rule of construction which requires that 'where a particular class . . . is spoken of, and general words follow, the class first mentioned is to be taken as the most comprehensive, and the general words treated as referring to matters *ejusdem generis* with such class.' Broom, Leg. Max. (6 Ed.) * 625.

"Here the term 'chicken house building' is not of the same kind of class as those previously mentioned and therefore can not fall within the definition of the term 'other buildings.' State v. Bryant, 90 Mo. 534, 2 S.W. 836, and cases cited. See, also, State ex rel. v. Seibert, 123 Mo. loc. cit. 424, 438, 27 S.W. 626." State v. Schuchman, 133 Mo. 111, 34 S.W. 842 (1896). Cf. State v. Thompson, 38 Wash. 2d 774, 232 P.2d 87 (1951).

A gasoline tank sunk in the ground is a "storehouse" within the meaning of the statute. Moss v. Commonwealth, 271 Ky. 283, 111 S.W.2d 628 (1937). As to a "dwelling" or a "store building" on wheels see Luce v. State, 128 Tex.Cr.R. 287, 81 S.W.2d 93 (1935); People v. Burley, 26 Cal.App.2d 213, 79 P.2d 148 (1938); State v. Ebel, 92 Mont. 413, 15 P.2d 233 (1932).

The case is before us for review, and the sole assignment of error is that the court refused to set aside the verdict as being contrary to the law and the evidence.

It is insisted that the evidence failed to show that the alleged theft was committed in a house owned by E.P. Fowlkes, and also failed to show that the defendant was the thief. As to this contention we express no opinion, because the judgment will have to be reversed and a new trial awarded upon another ground, namely, that there was no "breaking" within the meaning of the familiar definition of burglary.

The evidence tends to show that, as contended by the Commonwealth, the theft was committed in a house owned by Fowlkes, and in a room therein occupied and controlled by Dolly Wingfield, the owner of the stolen money. The testimony of Fowlkes and Dolly Wingfield conclusively shows that the defendant was and long had been their intimate associate and friend, and that with their consent and encouragement she carried a key to the house, was "just the same as at home there," was "over there day and night, and anything she wanted there she came and got it." She was not in any sense a servant or employee of the owners, nor a care keeper or custodian of the property. Her relationship was that of a companion and friend, her right to enter the premises up to the time of the alleged theft being as free and unlimited as that of Dolly Wingfield herself. She came and went at will; she ate and slept there whenever she pleased; and, in short, as expressed by Fowlkes she was "treated the same as homefolks."

Breaking, as an element of the crime of burglary, may be either actual or constructive. There is a constructive breaking when an entrance has been obtained by threat of violence, by fraud, or by conspiracy. The entrance to the premises in the instant case was not obtained by either of these means, and cannot be classed as a constructive breaking.

Actual breaking involves the application of some force, slight though it may be, whereby the entrance is effected. Merely pushing open a door, turning the key, lifting the latch, or resort to other slight physical force is sufficient to constitute this element of the crime.[1] See the authorities cited, supra. But a breaking, either actual or constructive, to support a conviction of burglary, must have resulted in an entrance contrary to the will of the occupier of the house.

. . .

1. "However, the breaking necessary to constitute the crime of burglary may be by any act of physical force, however slight, by which obstructions to entering are forcibly removed, and the opening of a closed door in order to enter a building may constitute a breaking." Luker v. State, 552 P.2d 715, 718 (Okl.Cr.1976).

"It is not necessary that splinters fly to have a breaking. Opening a closed door, effecting an entrance thereby, is a breaking". United States v. Evans, 415 F.2d 340, 342 (5th Cir. 1969).

One who arrived at the scene of burglary after the building had been broken and entered, and thereafter assisted the burglar in carrying out his intended larceny therein, could not be convicted of burglary since it had been committed before his arrival. People v. Davenport, 122 Mich.App. 159, 332 N.W.2d 443 (1983).

But in the instant case the right of the defendant to enter the premises as freely and unrestrictedly as either Fowlkes or Dolly Wingfield is undisputed, and it follows that she did not "break" and enter the house, and therefore cannot be convicted of the alleged burglary.

The following language of Judge Moncure, who delivered the opinion of the court in Clarke's Case, supra, may well be applied here:

"We have seen no case, and think there has been none, in which the entry was by the voluntary act and consent of the owner or occupier of the house, which has been held to be burglary. And were we to affirm the judgment in this case, we would establish a doctrine of constructive burglary which would not only be new, but contrary to the well known definition of that offense. While the legislature might make such a change, we think it would be judicial legislation in us to do so. If the question, upon principle, were more doubtful than it is, we would be inclined *in favorem vitae,* not to apply the doctrine of constructive burglary to this new case. The offense of burglary may be punished with death."

It is only fair and proper to say that the point upon which we are reversing the judgment does not seem to have been raised in the lower court. The point is one, however, which goes to the substance of the Commonwealth's case, and the failure to raise it at an earlier stage does not deprive the accused of the right to take advantage of it here.

Reversed.[2]

PEOPLE v. GAUZE

Supreme Court of California, In Bank, 1975.
15 Cal.3d 709, 125 Cal.Rptr. 773, 542 P.2d 1365.

MOSK, JUSTICE.

Can a person burglarize his own home? That is the quandry which emerges in the case of James Matthew Gauze, who appeals from a judgment of conviction of assault with a deadly weapon (Pen. Code, § 245, subd. (a)) and burglary (Pen.Code, § 459).

Defendant shared an apartment with Richard Miller and a third person and thus had the right to enter the premises at all times. While visiting a friend one afternoon, defendant and Miller engaged in a furious quarrel. Defendant directed Miller to "Get your gun because I am going to get mine." While Miller went to their mutual home, defendant borrowed a shotgun from a neighbor. He returned to his apartment, walked into the living room, pointed the gun at Miller and fired, hitting him in the side and arm. Defendant was convict-

2. Under Arizona statute that defines burglary as entry to commit a felony "and nothing more", defendant's entry into a dwelling, where defendant had lived on occasion, to commit a felony is burglary. State v. Van Dyke, 127 Ariz. 335, 621 P.2d 22 (1980).

ed of assault with a deadly weapon and burglary; the latter charge was predicated on his entry into his own apartment with the intent to commit the assault.

Common law burglary was generally defined as "the breaking and entering of the dwelling *of another* in the nighttime with intent to commit a felony." (Italics added.) (Perkins on Criminal Law (2d ed. 1969) p. 192.) The present burglary statute, Penal Code section 459, provides in relevant part that "Every person who enters *any* house, room, apartment . . . with intent to commit grand or petit larceny or any felony is guilty of burglary." (Italics added.)

Facially the statute is susceptible of two rational interpretations. On the one hand, it could be argued that the Legislature deliberately revoked the common law rule that burglary requires entry into the building of another.[1] On the other hand, the Legislature may have impliedly incorporated the common law requirement by failing to enumerate one's own home as a possible object of burglary. (Comment, Burglary: Punishment Without Justification, 1970 Ill.L.Rev. 391, 397.) No cases directly on point have been found.[2] Therefore, in determining which statutory interpretation should be adopted, it is necessary to examine the purposes underlying common law burglary and how they may have been affected by the enactment of the Penal Code.

Common law burglary was essentially an offense "against habitation and occupancy." (Perkins, op. cit. supra, p. 192.) By proscribing felonious nighttime entry into a dwelling house, the common law clearly sought to protect the right to peacefully enjoy one's own home free of invasion. In the law of burglary, in short, a person's home was truly his castle. (2 Blackstone, Commentaries (Jones ed. 1916) § 258, p. 2430.) It was clear under common law that one could not be convicted of burglary for entering his *own* home with felonious intent. This rule applied not only to sole owners of homes, but also to joint occupants. (Clarke v. Commonwealth (1874) 66 Va. 908; Perkins, op. cit. supra, p. 206.) The important factor was occupancy, rather than ownership.

California codified the law of burglary in 1850. (Stats.1850, ch. 99, § 58, p. 235.) That statute and subsequent revisions and amendments preserved the spirit of the common law, while making two major changes. First, the statute greatly expanded the type of buildings protected by burglary sanctions. Not only is a person's home his castle under the statute, but so, inter alia, are his shop, tent, airplane, and outhouse. (See fn. 1, ante.) This evolution, combined with

1. The term "building" is used throughout this opinion for literary convenience; section 459 actually encompasses entry into a variety of structures, not all of them buildings.

2. Several early cases involving pleading problems appear to have assumed one cannot be charged with burglarizing his own premises. See, e.g., People v. Price (1904) 143 Cal. 351, 353, 77 P. 73; People v. LaMarr (1942) 51 Cal.App.2d 24, 28, 124 P.2d 77; People v. Redman (1919) 39 Cal.App. 566, 568, 179 P. 725.

elimination of the requirement that the crime be committed at night, signifies that the law is no longer limited to safeguarding occupancy rights. However, by carefully delineating the type of structures encompassed under section 459, the Legislature has preserved the concept that burglary law is designed to protect a possessory right in property, rather than broadly to preserve any place from all crime.

The second major change effected by codification of the burglary law was the elimination of the requirement of a "breaking": under the statute, every person who *enters* with felonious intent is a burglar. This means, at a minimum, that it no longer matters whether a person entering a house with larcenous or felonious intent does so through a closed door, an open door or a window. The entry with the requisite intent constitutes the burglary.

The elimination of the breaking requirement was further interpreted in People v. Barry (1892) 94 Cal. 481, 29 P. 1026, to mean that trespassory entry was no longer a necessary element of burglary. In *Barry,* this court held a person could be convicted of burglary of a store even though he entered during regular business hours.[a] A long line of cases has followed the *Barry* holding.

Barry and its progeny should not be read, however, to hold that a defendant's right to enter the premises is irrelevant. Indeed, the court in *Barry,* by negative implication, substantiated the importance of determining the right of an accused to enter premises. When the defendant thief in *Barry* argued he had a right to be in the store, the court could have replied that his right to enter the store was immaterial. Instead the court declared, "To this reasoning, we can only say a party who enters with the intention to commit a felony enters without an invitation. He is not one of the public invited, nor is he entitled, to enter. Such a party could be refused admission at the threshold, or ejected from the premises after the entry was accomplished." (Id., 94 Cal. at p. 483, 29 P. at p. 1027.) Thus, the underlying principle of the *Barry* case is that a person has an implied invitation to

a. [Inserted by the Compiler.] Accord, State v. Baker, 183 Neb. 499, 161 N.W.2d 864 (1968); United States v. Kearney, 162 U.S.App.D.C. 110, ___, 498 F.2d 61, 65 (1974).

Where the public is invited to enter the entry cannot be trespassory and hence cannot constitute burglary. Macias v. People, 161 Colo. 233, 421 P.2d 116 (1966). Accord, State v. Starkweather, 89 Mont. 381, 297 P. 497 (1931); People v. Peery, 180 Colo. 161, 503 P.2d 350 (1972).

When entry was limited as to place, time or purpose, (statutory) burglary may be committed if the entry is outside the limitation. State v. Pappan, 193 Neb. 80, 225 N.W.2d 416 (1975). See also State v. Hartfield, 290 Or. 583, 624 P.2d 588 (1981).

Having been caught shoplifting, D was served with a written notice prohibiting him from entering the store again at any time without written consent of a corporate officer of the store. Some months later, without such consent and with intent to steal, he entered the store while it was open for business. His conviction of second-degree burglary was affirmed. The notice given under these circumstances was valid. And since he was expressly prohibited to enter, he was not one of the general public who was entitled to enter whenever the store was open for business. State v. Ocean, 24 Or. App. 289, 546 P.2d 150 (1976).

enter a store during business hours for legal purposes only. The cases have preserved the common law principle that in order for burglary to occur, "The entry must be *without consent.* If the possessor actually invites the defendant, or actively assists in the entrance, e.g., by opening a door, there is no burglary." (1 Witkin, Cal.Crimes (1963) Crimes Against Property, § 457, p. 420.) (Italics in original.)

Thus, section 459, while substantially changing common law burglary, has retained two important aspects of that crime. A burglary remains an entry which invades a possessory right in a building. And it still must be committed by a person who has no right to be in the building.

Applying the foregoing reasoning, we conclude that defendant cannot be guilty of burglarizing his own home. His entry into the apartment, even for a felonious purpose, invaded no possessory right of habitation; only the entry of an intruder could have done so. More importantly defendant had an absolute right to enter the apartment. This right, unlike that of the store thief in *Barry,* did not derive from an implied invitation to the public to enter for legal purposes. It was a personal right that could not be conditioned on the consent of defendant's roommates. Defendant could not be "refused admission at the threshold" of his apartment, or be "ejected from the premises after the entry was accomplished." (People v. Barry (1892) supra, 94 Cal. 481, 483, 29 P. 1026, 1027.) He could not, accordingly, commit a burglary in his own home.

. . .

To hold otherwise could lead to potentially absurd results. If a person can be convicted for burglarizing his own home, he could violate section 459 by calmly entering his house with intent to forge a check. A narcotics addict could be convicted of burglary for walking into his home with intent to administer a dose of heroin to himself. Since a burglary is committed upon entry, both could be convicted even if they changed their minds and did not commit the intended crimes.

In positing such hypotheticals, we indulge in no idle academic exercise. The differing consequences are significant, for the punishment for burglary is severe. First degree burglary is punishable by imprisonment for five years to life,[6] while a second degree burglar is subject to imprisonment in the county jail for a one-year maximum or in state prison for one to fifteen years. (Pen.Code, § 461.) In contrast, the punishment for assault with a deadly weapon, the underlying crime committed in this case, is less severe: imprisonment in state prison for six months to life or in county jail for a maximum of one year, or a fine. (Pen.Code, § 245, subd. (a).)[7]

6. First degree burglary, the crime charged in the present case, includes nighttime burglaries of dwellings and armed burglaries. (Pen.Code, § 460.)

7. The penalties for both burglary and assault with a deadly weapon are substantially increased when a firearm is

For the foregoing reasons, we conclude defendant cannot be guilty of burglarizing his own home, and the judgment of conviction for burglary must therefore be reversed. . . .

The judgment is reversed on count I (burglary) and affirmed on count II (assault with a deadly weapon).

WRIGHT, C.J., and MCCOMB, TOBRINER, SULLIVAN, CLARK and RICHARDSON, JJ., concur.[a]

STOWELL v. PEOPLE [1]

Supreme Court of Colorado, en Banc, 1939.
104 Colo. 255, 90 P.2d 520.

BURKE, JUSTICE. . . . Defendant was a freight conductor employed by the Rock Island railway. As such he was furnished with a "switch key" which he used in his work. It opened all switches and all depot and freight room doors on his division. There were no regulations governing its use. By means of it he entered the company's freight warehouse at Genoa and had taken therefrom two parcels of the value of $10, when he was arrested. The question here presented was raised by an instruction tendered and refused and by motion for a directed verdict at the close of all the evidence.

Had the switch key not been furnished defendant by the company, nor any authority given him under the terms of his employment to enter the building at the time and place in question, the evidence would have supported a conviction of burglary under the statute. For present purposes we assume, without deciding, that it would also have supported a conviction under this information. From the record it appears that defendant had a right to enter this warehouse at the time and in the manner he did, provided his intent in so doing was lawful. Hence this offense, if burglary, is raised to that grade solely by his unlawful intent. But intent alone is not always sufficient for that purpose. There is "no burglary, if the person entering has a right so to do, although he may intend to commit, and may actually commit, a felony, and although he may enter in such a way that there would be a breaking if he had no right to enter." Considering the history of the crime of burglary, and its evolution, this rule appears reasonable and necessary. The common law crime was an offense

used in commission of the crime. (Pen. Code, § 12022.5.)

[Added by Compilers.]

R was convicted of first-degree burglary under a statute speaking in terms, inter alia, of burglary by one armed with a burglar's tool. R had effected entry by breaking the glass of a window with a beer bottle. It was held that a beer bottle is not a burglar's tool within the meaning of the statute. This provision was aimed at the professional burglar, and picking up the first thing available to break a window does not indicate a professional. Conviction was reduced to second-degree burglary. State v. Reid, 36 Or.App. 417, 585 P.2d 411 (1978).

a. Since each spouse had a legal right to be on the premises so long as the marriage existed entry onto the premises could not be a burglary. Vazquez v. State, 350 So.2d 1094 (Fla.App.1977).

1. Cited with approval. People v. Woods, 182 Colo. 3, 510 P.2d 435 (1973).

against habitation. Its purpose was to give security to the home when it was presumably least protected. Essential elements thereof were an actual *breaking,* in the *night time,* with intent to commit a *felony.* It has been extended by statute in most states to entry in any way, into any kind of building, at any time, for any unlawful purpose. Under the rule of strict construction of statutes in derogation of the common law courts must necessarily be careful not to extend such acts beyond the clear intent of the Legislature. For instance, among the buildings enumerated in our statute are "schoolhouses". Hence, but for the rule above stated, a school teacher, using the key furnished her by the district to re-open the schoolhouse door immediately after locking it in the evening, for the purpose of taking (but not finding) a pencil belonging to one of her pupils, could be sent to the penitentiary. . . .

The judgment is accordingly reversed.[2]

PEOPLE V. DUPREE

Supreme Court of Michigan, 1893.
98 Mich. 26, 56 N.W. 1046.

GRANT, J. The respondent was convicted of burglary under section 9132, How.St. The evidence on the part of the people tended to show that the owner of the dwelling house occupied the front room for a shoe shop, and the rear and overhead part as a dwelling. The shop was upon the ground floor, and had two windows, each about four feet from the ground. These windows had double sash; were without pulley weights; were fastened when raised, and bolted when down, by stops operated by springs. When the windows were closed, the springs threw the bolts into the slots in the cases, so that the window could not be raised without drawing the bolt. One of these windows was opened during the night of October 8th, and three pairs of shoes were stolen. The owner closed the shades on the night of the 6th, and did not notice that the window was raised even an eighth of an inch. On the morning of the 9th, on opening his shop, he found the window raised about 1½ feet. The respondent called at the house on October 6th, between noon and 2 P.M., and asked for dinner. He asked permission to step into the shoe shop for the purpose of changing his pantaloons. This request was granted. The window was not broken. If the bolt was in the slot, the window could have been raised from the inside only. On Monday following the burglary, respondent had in his possession, and offered for sale, a pair of shoes alleged to have been taken upon the night of October 8th. On the following Wednesday, he sold a pair of shoes which were identified as one of the three pairs stolen on October 8th. The complaining witness testified that he believed that the window was unfastened and

2. Permission to enter when the dweller is present is not permission to enter when he is absent. And entry when he is absent is trespassory. State v. McKinney, 535 P.2d 1392 (Or.App. 1975).

raised on October 6th from the inside, and something placed under the sash so as to keep the bolt from entering the slot. The owner left the shop about the time it was necessary to light the lamps to see, and did not return to it till the next morning. No testimony was introduced on the part of the respondent. His counsel moved the court to discharge the respondent for the reason that the crime was not established against him. This the court refused.

It is contended on behalf of the respondent (1) that no breaking or entering in the nighttime was established; (2) that this shop was not a part of the dwelling house; (3) that if the window was partially raised on October 6th, and was further raised on the night of the 8th, the crime was not established. We think the motion was properly overruled, and the case properly submitted to the jury. . . .

3. The theory of the prosecution was that the respondent, when in the shop, either on the 6th or 7th of October, (the court, in its charge, referred to the date as Friday, October 7th,) raised the window just enough to prevent the bolt from entering the slot, and there was evidence to sustain it. It is insisted that even if this was so, and the respondent raised the window on the following night, it did not establish the crime of burglary. We cannot agree with this contention. It is said in Dennis v. People, 27 Mich. 151: "If an entry is effected by raising a trapdoor which is kept down merely by its own weight, or by raising a window kept in its place only by pulley weight, instead of its own, or by descending an open chimney, it is admitted to be enough to support the charge of breaking; and I am unable to see any substantial distinction between such cases and one where an entry is effected through a hanging window over a shop door, and which is only designed for light above, and for ventilation, and is down, and kept down by its own wieght, and so firmly as to be opened only by the use of some force, and so situated as to make a ladder, or something of the kind, necessary to reach it for the purpose of passing through it." We think the doctrine there enunciated covers the present case. If there had been no bolt, and respondent had raised the window and entered in the nighttime, under all the authorities, he would have been guilty of burglary. Upon what reason can it be said that his removal of the bolt, or his raising the window a fraction of an inch, in the daytime, changes the character of his offense? If the owner had failed to see that the bolts were in place, or if something had been accidentally placed upon the window sill, which was of slight thickness, but sufficient to prevent the bolts from entering the slots, the raising of the window would have been sufficient breaking to support the charge. How can the act be relieved of criminality by secretly fixing the window in the daytime so that the bolt or lock will not be effective, and thus render the perpetration of the crime more easy and certain? There is no reason in such a rule. In Lyons v. People, the door was left unlocked, and the court was requested to instruct the jury that, in order to constitute the crime, it must appear that the door was secured in the ordinary way. The

supreme court, in determining the question, said: "We are not aware of any authority which goes to the extent of these instructions. To hold that the carelessness of the owner in securing and guarding his property shall be a justification to the burglar or thief would leave communities very much to the mercy of this class of felons. It would in effect be a premium offered for their depredations, by the removal of the apprehension of punishment. Whether property is guarded or not, it is larceny in the thief who steals it. When a door is closed, it is burglary for any one, with a felonious intent, to open it, and enter the house, in the nighttime, without the owner's consent; and it makes no difference how many bolts and bars might have been used to secure it, but which were neglected." The language of the court was perhaps too broad, in stating that if the window was raised any distance, but was not sufficient to permit the defendant to enter, and he raised it further, it would be breaking, in the meaning of the law;[1] but the entire evidence was to the effect that it was raised so little as not to attract the notice of the occupant. We therefore think that the jury could not have been misled by the language. . . .

Conviction affirmed. The other justices concurred.[2]

NICHOLLS v. STATE

Supreme Court of Wisconsin, 1887.

68 Wis. 416, 32 N.W. 543.

CASSODAY, J. There is undisputed testimony on the part of the state to the effect that Saturday, July 25, 1885, the plaintiff in error was stopping at a hotel in Black River Falls, having his name registered as W.H. Eldredge, and a room assigned him opposite thereto. He had then been there about three days. In the afternoon of the day named he had a box or chest taken from the depot to his room, weighing about 150 pounds. No evidence was given as to what was in it. About three o'clock in the afternoon of the same day he arranged with the local express agent for the sending of a box to Chica-

1. Accord: People v. White, 153 Mich. 617, 117 N.W. 161 (1908); State v. Rosencrans, 24 Wash.2d 775, 167 P.2d 170 (1946). Contra: Rose v. Commonwealth, 40 S.W. 245, 19 Ky.L.Rep. 272 (1897); Commonwealth v. Strupney, 105 Mass. 588 (1870).

If a door is partly open, but insufficient for entrance, the further opening of the door constitutes a breaking. Jones v. State, 537 P.2d 431 (Okl.Cr.1975).

2. In a prosecution for burglary it was error to instruct that entry through an open window constitutes a "breaking". People v. Williams, 29 A.D.2d 780, 287 N.Y.S.2d 797 (1968).

In Stehl v. State, 283 Ala. 22, 214 So.2d 299 (1968), it was held reversible error to refuse to charge, in a trial for burglary, that **D** "would not be guilty, even though he were in the house, if he entered through an open door or window without further opening such door or window."

Opening a door constitutes a breaking although another door was open through which entry could have been effected. State v. Campbell, 190 Neb. 394, 208 N.W.2d 670 (1973).

go, then at the hotel, and represented by him as weighing about 225 pounds. By his prearrangement, the box was brought to the depot just in time for the 7:50 P.M. Chicago train, and was shipped in the express car thereon by the local agent, as directed. Soon after the starting of the train, there seems to have been a suspicion as to the contents of the box. This suspicion was increased as telegrams were received at different stations from Black River Falls respecting the box. Finally, being convinced by such dispatches that there was a man in the box, the train-men telegraphed forward to Elroy to secure the presence of an officer on the approach of the train to make the arrest. On reaching Elroy, in the night, this box in the express car was opened, and the plaintiff in error was found therein, with a revolver, billy, razor, knife, rope, gimlet, and a bottle of chloroform. There was also evidence tending to show that there were packages of money in the custody of the express agent on the car; that such agent had an assistant as far as Elroy; that from there to Chicago such car was usually in charge of only one man; that after the arrest, and when asked his object in being thus shipped in the box, the prisoner voluntarily admitted, in effect, that he had considered his chances carefully; that he went into the thing as a matter of speculation; that he needed money, and needed it quickly; that he expected to get fully $50,000; that had he passed out of Elroy he would have got off with the money; that, in a case of that kind, if a human life stood in his way, it did not amount to a snap of the finger. . . .

2. The question recurs whether the proofs show that there was a breaking in fact, within the meaning of the statute. Certainly not in the sense of picking a lock, or opening it with a key, or lifting a latch, or severing or mutilating the door, or doing violence to any portion of the car. On the contrary, the box was placed in the express car with the knowledge, and even by the assistance, of those in charge of the car. But it was not a passenger car, and the plaintiff in error was in no sense a passenger. The railroad company was a common carrier of passengers as well as freight. But the express company was exclusively a common carrier of freight, that is to say, goods, wares and merchandise. As such carrier, it may have at times transported animals, birds, etc., but it may be safely assumed that it never knowingly undertook to transport men in packages or boxes for special delivery. True, the plaintiff in error contracted with the local express agent for the carriage and delivery of such box, but neither he nor any one connected with the express car or the train had any knowledge or expectation of a man being concealed within it. On the contrary, they each and all had the right to assume that the box contained nothing but inanimate substance,—goods, wares, or merchandise of some description. The plaintiff in error knew that he had no right to enter the express car at all without the consent of those in charge. The evidence was sufficient to justify the conclusion that he unlawfully gained an entrance without the knowledge or consent of

those in charge of the car, by false pretenses, fraud, gross imposition, and circumvention, with intent to commit the crime of robbery or larceny, and, in doing so, if necessary, the crime of murder. This would seem to have been sufficient to constitute a constructive breaking at common law, as defined by Blackstone, thus: "To come down a chimney is held a burglarious entry; for that is as much closed as the nature of things will permit. So, also, to knock at the door, and, upon opening it, to rush in with a felonious intent; or, under pretense of taking lodgings, to fall upon the landlord and rob him; or to procure a constable to gain admittance in order to search for traitors, and then to bind the constable and rob the house. All these entries have been adjudged burglarious, though there was no actual breaking, for the law will not suffer itself to be trifled with by such evasions, especially under the cloak of legal process. And so, if a servant opens and enters his master's chamber door with a felonious design; or if any other person, lodging in the same house or in a public inn, opens and enters another's door with such evil intent, it is burglary. Nay, if the servant conspires with a robber and lets him into the house by night, this is burglary in both; for the servant is doing an unlawful act, and the opportunity afforded him of doing it with greater ease rather aggravates than extenuates the guilt." 4 Bl.Comm. 226, 227.

So it has frequently been held in this country that, "to obtain admission to a dwelling-house at night, with the intent to commit a felony, by means of artifice or fraud or upon a pretense of business or social intercourse, is a constructive breaking, and will sustain an indictment charging a burglary by breaking and entering." The same was held in Ohio under a statute against "forcible" breaking and entering. But it is claimed that in this state the common-law doctrine of constructive breaking has no application to a case of this kind, and in fact is superseded by statute, except in so far as it is re-affirmed. Thus: *"Any unlawful entry of* a dwelling-house or other building with intent to commit a felony, shall *be deemed* a breaking and entering of such dwelling-house or other building, within the meaning of the last four sections." Sec. 4411, R.S. This section merely establishes a rule of evidence whereby the scope of constructive breaking is enlarged so as to take in *"any* unlawful entry of a dwelling-house or other building with intent to commit a felony." It in no way narrows the scope of constructive breaking, as understood at common law, but merely enlarges it in the particulars named. In all other respects such constructive breaking signifies the same as at common law. It necessarily follows that as the word "break," used in sec. 4410, had obtained a fixed and definite meaning at common law when applied to a dwelling-house proper or other buildings within the curtilage, the legislature must be presumed to have used it in the same sense when therein applied to other statutory breakings. That is to say, they must be deemed to have used the word as understood at common law in relation to the same or a like subject matter. We must hold the evidence sufficient to support the charge of breaking. . . .

By the Court. The judgment of the circuit court is affirmed.[1]

DANIELS v. STATE

Supreme Court of Georgia, 1886.
78 Ga. 98.

HALL, JUSTICE. 1. The indictment charges the defendant with breaking and entering the depot building of the Western and Atlantic Railroad Company, where valuable goods were contained, with intent to steal, etc. The proof showed that the outer door was left open, but that after getting into the building, which had numerous apartments, the doors to each of these, in which the postage stamps belonging to the company were deposited, were broken and entered and they were stolen and carried away by the defendant. It is now insisted that neither the charge in the indictment nor the facts in proof made out the offence of burglary against the defendant; that in order to fix legal guilt upon him, it should have been alleged and proved that he effected his entrance by breaking the door through which he got into the house, and not by showing that, after entering it, he broke either of the doors of the departments in it, where the valuables in question were found. Such, however, is not our apprehension of the law. It is well-settled, by a number of cases, that where a party is indicted for breaking and entering an out-house within the curtilage or protection of a mansion or dwelling, the burglary should be laid as having been done in the dwelling-house. If this be true as to an out-house within the protection of the mansion or dwelling-house, *a fortiori* would it be so as to an apartment in the house, a party's place of business in which his goods, wares, etc., were stored or contained, and which was broken and entered with an intent to commit a larceny upon the articles of value therein contained. This indictment does not allege in terms that the depot was the place of business of the railroad company, but no specific objection was taken to it on this account, and had there been one, we are not prepared to hold that it was tenable, as the offence, though not charged in the terms and language of the code, is so plainly set forth that its nature could be easily understood

1. One who enters a store while it is open for business, secretes himself therein and is apprehended after closing hours under circumstances which indicate an intent to steal, can be convicted of storehouse breaking Code Article 27, § 32. His failure to leave when the store closed for business made his original entrance an illegal breaking and entering *ab initio.* Brooks v. State, 25 Md.App. 194, 333 A.2d 352 (1975).

N.B. Many cases have held that there is no doctrine of trespass *ab initio* in the criminal law.

The Montana statute reads: "A person commits the offense of burglary if he knowingly enters or remains unlawfully in an occupied structure with the purpose to commit a felony therein." Mont.Crim. Code of 1973, Sec. 94–6–204. Under this statute remaining in a store after closing hours constituted a trespass. State v. Watkins, 163 Mont. 491, 518 P.2d 259 (1974).

by the jury. It is always best, however, to avoid cavil or dispute, to conform to the very words of the statute on which the accusation is based. On this point, there was no error in the instruction given by the court. . . .

Judgment affirmed.[1]

UNITED STATES v. PHILLIPS

United States Court of Appeals, Eighth Circuit, 1979.
609 F.2d 1271.

STEPHENSON, CIRCUIT JUDGE. Defendant-appellants, Phillips and Eaves, appeal from their convictions by a jury of (1) entering a bank with intent to commit larceny, 18 U.S.C. § 2113(a) (paragraph 2); . . . Appellants contend that the government failed to show an "entry" as required by 18 U.S.C. § 2113(a); . . .

On August 11, 1978, appellants, with two other persons, robbed the National City Bank, Sheraton-Ritz facility, in Minneapolis, Minnesota, of $8,754.00. Phillips and Eaves drove up to a drive-in teller window at the bank and manipulated the drive-up teller mechanism. A co-conspirator, working as a teller at the bank, sent out the money. Phillips reached in and took the money out, and both appellants drove off. Another co-conspirator then walked up to the drive-up teller window and placed in the mechanism a fake bomb device and a demand note. Shortly after he walked away, the teller/co-conspirator announced that she had been robbed. The theory was that if the co-conspirator who passed the note and fake bomb device was caught, since he would not have the money, he would escape prosecution.

Section 2113(a) (paragraph 2) of Title 18 provides that "[w]hoever enters or attempts to enter any bank . . . or any building used in whole or in part as a bank . . . with intent to commit in such bank, . . . or building, or part thereof . . . any larceny" shall be fined or imprisoned. It is appellants' contention that, primarily because of the physical structure and location of the drive-up teller mechanism, there was no entry for purposes of the statute. The trial court instructed the jury as follows:

> If you find—now, remember you start with a "blank"; I can't find anything for you, and I don't intend to—but if you come to the point where the evidence convinces you beyond a reasonable doubt that these defendants, or persons acting with them (and I've read you the principal statute and the aiding and abetting statute) came across bank property, property owned or leased by the bank, and manipulated the mechanism therefor the purpose of committing the crime of taking money of the bank, then you may find that to be covered by the statute which prohibits entering a bank.

1. Although the English common law required a "breaking into" the building, a prohibited entry followed by a breaking out is sufficient under the Kentucky statute. Lawson v. Commonwealth, 160 Ky. 180, 169 S.W. 587 (1914).

> So if they went up on that property knowingly and willfully knowing that they were going to do it for the purpose of committing this crime of bank larceny and they manipulated this machinery provided by the bank in furtherance of that, if you find that beyond a reasonable doubt, then that would be prohibited by the statute in terms of the place at which they did it, you see, because the statute says, "Whoever enters any bank or any building used in whole or in part as a bank." If you find they went up onto that leased property and manipulated that machinery, that's enough for finding the necessary entry under the law, you see.

Appellants argue that all they did was drive into a driveway next to the bank; it is their argument that the trial court failed to make a distinction between entry into a building or part thereof, which the statute requires, and entry onto the property, which they allege is not covered by the statute.

In United States v. Lankford, 573 F.2d 1051 (8th Cir.1978), our court was faced with a similar question involving the same statute and a night depository of a bank. The depository mechanism was located on the outside wall of a bank building in a recessed entryway leading to the main entrance to the bank. When deposits were placed in the depository, they would fall down a chute inside the wall into a safe. Our court stated:

> [2] The words of the statute reading "such bank, . . . or building, or part thereof, so used" reflect that Congress by appropriate language intended to make it a crime to enter any party of a bank building with intent to steal. The depository chute at the National Bank of Washington is located inside the outer wall of the bank, and the safe which receives the night deposits is located inside the inner wall of the bank. We hold under these circumstances that an attempt to enter the night depository is an attempt to enter the bank within the meaning of the statute.

Id. at 1053. In this case, the drive-up window is similar to the night depository discussed in *Lankford.* The receptacle is attached to the outside wall of the hotel building with a conveyer belt which runs under the floor to the office area in the hotel that the bank leases from the Sheraton-Ritz. The bank also leases the driveway up to the window, the receptacles, and the conveyer belt, which carries to the office inside the building the tubes in which the customers place their slips and money. We hold that "entry" was proved sufficiently to satisfy 18 U.S.C. § 2113(a).

Appellants also contend that Counts I (18 U.S.C. § 2113(a)) and II (18 U.S.C. § 2113(b)) are multiplicitous.

Affirmed.[1]

1. A defendant who pushed in a window to a shop and whose finger extended into the shop committed a sufficient entry to constitute burglary. Rex v. Davis, 168 Eng.Rep. 917, Crown Case R'vd. 1823.

The putting of a hand through the window would constitute an entry. People

WALKER v. STATE

Supreme Court of Alabama, 1879.
63 Ala. 49.

BRICKELL, C.J. The statute (Code of 1876, § 4343) provides, that "any person, who, either in the night or day time, with intent to steal, or to commit a felony, breaks into and enters a dwelling-house, or any building, structure or inclosure within the curtilage of a dwelling-house, though not forming a part thereof, or into any shop, store, warehouse, or other building, structure or inclosure in which any goods, merchandise, or other valuable thing is kept for use, sale, or deposit, *provided* such structure, other than a shop, store, warehouse or building, is specially constructed or made to keep such goods, merchandise or other valuable thing, is guilty of burglary," &c.

The defendant was indicted for breaking into and entering "a corncrib of Noadiah Woodruff and Robert R. Peeples, a building in which corn, a thing of value, was at the time kept for use, sale, or deposit, with intent to steal," &c. He was convicted; and the case is now presented on exceptions taken to instructions given, and the refusal of instructions requested, as to what facts will constitute a breaking into and entry, material constituents of the offense charged in the indictment. The facts, on which the instructions were founded, are: that in the crib was a quantity of shelled corn, piled on the floor; in April, or May, 1878, the crib had been broken into, and corn taken therefrom, without the consent of the owners, who had the crib watched; and thereafter the defendant was caught under it, and, on coming out, voluntarily confessed that, about three weeks before, he had taken a large auger, and, going under the crib, had bored a hole through the floor, from which the corn, being shelled, ran into a sack he held under it; that he then got about three pecks of corn, and with a cob closed the hole. On these facts, the City Court was of opinion, and so instructed the jury, that there was such a breaking and entry of the crib, as would constitute the offense, and refused instructions requested asserting the converse of the proposition. . . .

The boring the hole through the floor of the crib, was a sufficient breaking; but with it there must have been an entry. Proof of a breaking, though it may be with an intent to steal, or the intent to commit a felony, is proof of one only of the facts making up the offense, and is as insufficient as proof of an entry through an open door, without breaking. If the hand, or any part of the body, is intruded within the house, the entry is complete. The entry may also

v. Lamica, 274 Cal.App.2d 640, 79 Cal. Rptr. 491 (1969).

"Here it is undisputed that defendant invaded the space between the outer storm window and the inner window. We hold under the circumstances there was sufficient evidence of entry to the house to support the aggravated burglary conviction under Count 13." State v. Crease, 230 Kan. 541, 638 P.2d 939, 940 (1982).

be completed by the intrusion of a tool, or instrument, within the house, though no part of the body be introduced. Thus, if A. breaks the house of B. in the night time, with intent to steal goods, and breaks the window, and puts his hand, or puts in a hook, or other engine, to reach out goods; or puts a pistol in at the window, with an intent to kill, though his hand be not within the window, this is burglary."—1 Hale, 555. When no part of the body is introduced—when the only entry is of a tool, or instrument, introduced by the force and agency of the party accused, the inquiry is, whether the tool or instrument was employed solely for the purpose of *breaking,* and thereby effecting an *entry;* or whether it was employed not only to *break and enter,* but also to aid in the consummation of the criminal intent, and its capacity to aid in such consummation. Until there is a *breaking* and *entry,* the offense is not consummated. The offense rests largely in intention; and though there may be sufficient evidence of an attempt to commit it, which, of itself, is a crime, the attempt may be abandoned—of it there may be repentance, before the consummation of the offense intended. The *breaking* may be at one time, and the *entry* at another. The *breaking* may be complete, and yet an *entry* never effected. From whatever cause an *entry* is not effected, burglary has not been committed. When one instrument is employed to *break,* and is without capacity to aid otherwise than by opening a way of *entry,* and another instrument must be used, or the instrument used in the breaking must be used in some other way or manner to consummate the criminal intent, the intrusion of the instrument is not, of itself, an *entry.* But when, as in this case, the instrument is employed not only to *break,* but to effect the only *entry* contemplated, and necessary to the consummation of the criminal intent; when it is intruded within the house, *breaking* it, effecting an *entry,* enabling the person introducing it to consummate his intent, the offense is complete. The instrument was employed, not only for the purpose of *breaking* the house, but to effect the larceny intended. When it was intruded into the crib, the burglar acquired dominion over the corn intended to be stolen. Such dominion did not require any other act on his part. When the auger was withdrawn from the aperture made with it, the corn ran into the sack he used in its asportation. There was a *breaking* and *entry,* enabling him to effect his criminal intent, without the use of any other means, and this satisfies the requirements of the law.

Let the judgment be affirmed.[1]

1. Boring a hole through the door, near the bolt, is not an entry in the law of burglary even if the point of the bit penetrates into the interior of the building. The King v. Hughes, 1 Leach 406, 168 Eng.Rep. 305 (1785).

Pounding a small hole in the wall without being able to commit larceny or any felony is not burglary. The instrument must be inserted not merely for the purpose of breaking, but for the purpose of committing the contemplated felony. People v. Davis, 3 Ill.App.3d 738, 279 N.E.2d 179 (1972).

Although it is otherwise as to the intrusion of an instrument, the "entry by part of the body is sufficient to support a burglary" even if "done for purposes oth-

GRAY v. STATE

Supreme Court of Wisconsin, 1943.
243 Wis. 57, 9 N.W.2d 68.

MARTIN, J. The dwelling of Edmund Feldner, located on Highway 38, about three fourths of a mile west of the village of Rosendale in the town of Fond du Lac, Fond du Lac county, Wisconsin, was burglarized on the night of June 19, 1941. Mr. Feldner and members of his family retired at about 8:30 p.m. When he retired his overalls and two suits of clothing were hanging on a hook in his bedroom. His winter overcoat was in a room next to his bedroom. When Mr. Feldner arose at 5:30 a.m. the following morning he noticed that his overalls, his two suits, and overcoat were missing and that some of the rooms of his residence had been ransacked. He found his overalls and the vest and coat of one suit lying outside. One suit, the overcoat, and trousers of the other suit were missing.

At about 1 a.m., on June 20, 1941, George Habeck, a truck driver, left the city of Fond du Lac for Ripon and Berlin via Highway 38. When he reached a point on said highway about three fourths of a mile west of Rosendale, in the immediate vicinity of the Feldner residence he saw three Negroes, whom he later identified as the defendants, with their car parked alongside the road. Defendants followed Habeck to Ripon. At Ripon they inquired of Habeck as to the direction to Fond du Lac. He gave them the proper direction, whereupon defendants left but did not go in the direction which had been given them. The facts here related took place between 1 and 2:30 a.m. on June 20th. . . .

To the information charging burglary of a dwelling in the nighttime with intent to commit larceny, defendants entered a plea of not guilty. The jury found defendants guilty in the manner and form as charged in the information. Defendants contend that the evidence did not establish beyond a reasonable doubt that the Feldner dwelling was burglarized in the nighttime. Sec. 352.32, Stats., defines the term "nighttime" as follows:

"The term 'nighttime,' when used in any statute, ordinance, indictment or information shall be construed to mean the time between one hour after the setting of the sun on one day and one hour before the rising of the same on the following day; and the time of sunset and sunrise shall be ascertained according to the mean solar time of the ninetieth meridian west from Greenwich, commonly known as central time, as given in any published almanac."

Sunset on the evening of June 19th was at 7:39 p.m., and sunrise on the morning of June 20th was at 4:23 a.m. Thus, nighttime, within the meaning of the statute, on the night in question, was from 8:39

er than the direct commission of the intended offense." People v. Palmer, 83 Ill.App.3d 732, 39 Ill.Dec. 262, 404 N.E.2d 853, 856 (1980).

p.m., June 19th, to 3:23 a.m., June 20th. Defendants argue that since Feldner testified that he retired about 8:30 p.m. on June 19th, and that he arose at about 5:30 a.m. the following morning, his dwelling may have been burglarized either in the daytime or in the nighttime, and that therefore the state failed to establish that the crime had been committed in the nighttime as alleged in the information. It is definitely established that the crime was committed sometime between 8:30 p.m., June 19th, and 5:30 a.m., June 20th. The witness Habeck testified that he left the city of Fond du Lac at about 1 a.m. on June 20th. Rosendale is about eleven miles west of the city of Fond du Lac. According to Habeck's testimony, he would, with normal driving, have arrived at the place where he saw the three defendants and their parked car in the immediate vicinity of the Feldner residence at about 1:30 a.m. The circumstance of defendants having been seen in the immediate vicinity of the burglarized residence at the time fixed by Habeck, well warranted the jury in concluding that the burglary had been committed in the nighttime. See Simon v. State, 125 Wis. 439, 103 N.W. 1100; Winsky v. State, 126 Wis. 99, 102, 105 N.W. 480. In the latter case, referring to State v. Bancroft, 10 N.H. 105, it is said:

"There was no direct proof that the burglary was committed in the nighttime, other than the fact that the property was in the house after dark and was missing the next morning when the witness arose; and the court said that this evidence 'led very strongly to the conclusion that it was taken in the course of the night, although the precise hour when the witness called it dark did not appear, and the time when she arose in the morning was not stated. At whatever time in the morning the loss was discovered, the jury might well weigh the probability whether the article would have been taken from the house in the daytime, in connection with the other evidence. It was sufficient that, upon the whole case, they had no reasonable doubt that the act was done in the nighttime.' Sufficient appears from the evidence in the case before us to warrant the jury in finding that the entry was made in the nighttime. Simon v. State, supra." . . .

By the Court—Judgment affirmed.[1]

1. Where the uncontradicted evidence showed that if D committed the burglary he did so at night it was proper to instruct the jury that they must either find the defendant not guilty or guilty of the offense charged. There was no need to instruct the jury in regard to the lesser included offense of burglary in the daytime. People v. White, 218 Cal.App.2d 267, 32 Cal.Rptr. 322 (1963).

But where there was conflicting evidence as to the time it was error not to submit this issue to the jury. State v. Miller, 104 Ariz. 335, 452 P.2d 509 (1969).

Nighttime under the Iowa statutes is the same as at common law, "a period between sunset and sunrise during which there is not enough daylight to discern a man's face." State v. Billings, 242 N.W.2d 726 (Iowa 1976).

A TV store was broken into and a color TV set stolen. This set had been on display in the store window, with a black and white set on top. B's palm-print had been found on the black and white set. As B had not had access to this set before the burglary, this evidence proved that B had moved one set to get the oth-

GOLDMAN v. ANDERSON

United States Court of Appeals, Sixth Circuit, 1980.
625 F.2d 135.

BOYCE F. MARTIN, JR., CIRCUIT JUDGE. Petitioner is an inmate subject to the jurisdiction of the Michigan Department of Corrections. His incarceration is the result of a 1976 Michigan conviction of breaking and entering a real estate office with intent to commit larceny therein contrary to MCLA 750.110; MSA 28.305. Upon conviction in Detroit Recorder's Court by a jury, he was sentenced to a term of five to ten years in prison. Petitioner appeals to this Court from a judgment entered November 19, 1979 by the Honorable James P. Churchill in the United States District Court for the Eastern District of Michigan which dismissed his petition for habeas corpus on the basis of Wainwright v. Sykes.

During the trial, a police officer testified that she responded at 5:00 a.m. to a call that a breaking and entering of a real estate office was in progress. When she arrived at the reported address, she saw the petitioner leaving the premises. He ran, but was later apprehended by a private citizen and returned to the scene. The officer further testified that petitioner had white plaster dust on his clothes. Another officer found a hole in the wall of the real estate office which was adjacent to a bar, and found a sledgehammer, crowbar, screwdriver, and flashlight near the hole. Nothing had been stolen from either establishment, perhaps because of the arrival of the police.

Petitioner testified that he was never in the building but that he had been arrested for running *by* the building near the time of the break-in; he denied ever having run from the police. . . .

Petitioner argues that (a) the evidence was insufficient to establish his intent to larcenize the real estate office, hence, his conviction was a denial of due process . . . .

Petitioner bases his argument regarding the sufficiency of the evidence upon the thesis that the evidence clearly showed intent to larcenize the adjacent bar and not the real estate office. Hence, he argues, evidence of intent to larcenize the real estate office had not been established and petitioner could not be convicted of MCLA 750.110. While petitioner's argument raises an interesting problem in conceptualization and may point out some ambiguity in the statute, we are constrained to note that "the relevant question is whether,

er, and this was sufficient to support his conviction of burglary, although the missing set was not found. State v. Bright, 64 Haw. 226, 638 P.2d 330 (1981).

A burglary conviction may be sustained on a theory of entry with intent to steal even though on entry the defendant took nothing and left. A trespassory entry coupled with circumstances corroborating an intent to steal is enough. State v. Brooks, 631 P.2d 878 (Utah 1981).

after viewing the evidence in the light most favorable to the prosecution, *any* rational trier of fact could have found the essential elements of the crime beyond a reasonable doubt." (emphasis in the original) Jackson v. Virginia, supra at 319, 99 S.Ct at 2789. In determining whether this standard has been met, the habeas court may properly take cognizance of state evidentiary law. Thus, in Moore v. Duckworth, 443 U.S. 713, 99 S.Ct. 3088, 61 L.Ed.2d 865 (1979), where the question was whether the state had met its burden of proof of sanity beyond a reasonable doubt, the United States Supreme Court held that it was proper for the federal habeas court to take cognizance of state evidentiary law to the effect that lay rather than expert testimony was sufficient to prove the element of sanity.

As in every case where intent is material, larcenous intent may be inferred from the surrounding circumstances. "Because such mischief is a normal incident to a breaking and entering, and because of the difficulty of proving the actor's state of mind, circumstantial evidence has been found sufficient to sustain the conclusion that the defendant entertained the requisite [larcenous] intent." People v. Palmer, 42 Mich.App. 549, 551–552, 202 N.W.2d 536 (1972). See also People v. Jablonski, 70 Mich.App. 218, 223, 245 N.W.2d 571 (1976).

Under Michigan law, intent to commit larceny may be inferred from the totality of circumstances disclosed by the testimony.[1] Such intent may be inferred from the nature, time, or place of the defendant's acts before and during the breaking and entering.

Here, the testimony reveals that a real estate office was broken into at approximately 5:00 a.m. on Sunday, July 25, 1976. The real estate agency was an ongoing business, not open for business at the time, and the owner had given no one permission to enter that morning. A witness saw the petitioner inside the real estate office. Later, an officer apprehended him after he fled the building. A forced entry had been made into the real estate office. Further, the police discovered a crow bar, a screwdriver, a flashlight, and a sledgehammer inside the office as well as a hole in the wall separating the office from an adjacent bar.

Appellant argues that whoever broke into the real estate office did so for the purpose of breaking a hole in the party wall so that entry could be gained into the bar next door, and that an intent to break through the party wall leading to the bar was incompatible

1. To convict under the habitual criminal act, prior convictions of burglary in another jurisdiction may be shown if the misdeed would have constituted burglary if committed here. But the mere proof of a burglary conviction in Oklahoma, without more, is not sufficient because an intent to commit any misdemeanor is sufficient for the burglarious intent there while in California petty larceny is the only misdemeanor included in such category. People v. Stanphill, 166 Cal.App. 2d 467, 333 P.2d 270 (1958).

In affirming a conviction of burglary it was held that the circumstances of **D**'s arrest just past midnight as he was furtively coming out of a building, in which offices had been ransacked, was enough to support the presumption that he had entered to commit larceny even though he said otherwise. Boyle v. State, 86 Nev. 30, 464 P.2d 493 (1970).

with an intent to commit larceny in the real estate office. But nothing precluded petitioner from having both the intent to commit larceny within the office and in the bar next door. Based on the hour, the nature of the business involved, the burglar tools used, and the unexplained presence of petitioner inside the building, the jury could well have inferred that petitioner intended to steal anything of value within either the real estate office or the bar. To this extent, we agree with the district court that there was sufficient evidence in the record to leave the jury verdict undisturbed. . . .

Accordingly, the petition for a writ of habeas corpus is denied.[2]

2. Where the charge of burglary was based upon an alleged intent to commit rape, proof of the breaking and entering without proof of an intent to commit rape will not support a conviction. Smith v. State, 239 So.2d 284 (Fla.App.1970).

An indictment for burglary may lay the offense with several intents, as with intent to steal and intent to murder or rape. Such an indictment is not duplicitous. It is sufficient for the state to prove one of the alleged intents. If there is evidence of more than one intent the judge may submit the case to the jury on alternative theories. State v. Boyd, 287 N.C. 131, 214 S.E.2d 14 (1975).

When burglary is involved the information, instruction and verdict should state what felony was intended. Champlain v. State, 53 Wis.2d 751, 193 N.W.2d 868 (1972).

Some jurisdictions are not so strict. "Nor is it required that jurors decide what felony a burglar intended at the time of his entry . . . ." People v. Heideman, 58 Cal.App.3d 321, 333, 130 Cal.Rptr. 349, 356 (1976).

D's illicit nighttime breaking and entering into the dwelling of another warrants the inference that he was there to steal something. State v. Johnson, 116 R.I. 449, 358 A.2d 370 (1976).

The statutory presumption that a person who unlawfully breaks and enters shall be deemed to have done so with intent to commit grand or petit larceny or felony therein in the absence of an explanation, is not violative of due process. Tucker v. State, 92 Nev. 486, 553 P.2d 951 (1976).

D, on trial for burglary, admitted that he broke and entered the home of another but claimed it cannot be burglary because his only intent was to steal certain drugs which were illegally kept there. The fact that his only intent was to steal contraband was held not a defense and his conviction was affirmed. State v. Taylor, 25 Ariz.App. 477, 544 P.2d 714 (1976).

W broke into a building, not to commit any offense therein, but merely to gain access to another place wherein he intended to commit larceny. Hence the information for burglary had been amended by striking out the word "therein." The claim that the information as amended did not state an offense was rejected on the ground that if the entry was an integral part of a plan to commit larceny in the immediate vicinity of the place entered, it was not necessary that the intent be to commit it "therein." People v. Wright, 206 Cal.App.2d 184, 23 Cal.Rptr. 734 (1962). The court mentioned that some definition of burglary contained the word "therein" but that there is no such requirement in common-law burglary. It should be added that unfortunately some of the new penal codes do include this word.

S broke into a building with intent to commit the felony of lascivious acts with a child. It was no defense to a charge of burglary that his intent was to commit the offense on the roof rather than in the building. People v. Shields, 70 Cal.App. 2d 628, 161 P.2d 475 (1945).

Where the entrance was through an open outside door, a breaking into an inside room in furtherance of a design to commit a felony in the house was sufficient even if the felony was to be committed in another room. Rolland v. Commonwealth, 85 Pa. 66 (1877).

STATE v. MANN

Court of Appeals of Arizona, Division 2, 1981.
129 Ariz. 24, 628 P.2d 61.

OPINION

HOWARD, JUDGE. Is the Salvation Army collection box a "structure" within the meaning of A.R.S. Sec. 13–1506(A) and Sec. 13–1501(8)? We hold that it is and affirm appellants' conviction of burglary, third-degree.

Appellants were caught by the police while they were removing used clothing from a Salvation Army collection box. The box in question was located on a corner of the intersection of Ft. Lowell Road and Dodge Boulevard in Tucson. It was approximately six feet high and four feet deep by four feet wide, made of tin metal. About four feet from the bottom of one side it had an unlockable chute-like door for depositing items. The items in the box were regularly collected about every 36 hours. The Salvation Army removed the articles through a locked trap door located near the bottom of another side. Mary Lou Mann removed the clothing by reaching into the unlocked chute.

A.R.S. Sec. 13–1506 provides in part:

> "A. A person commits burglary in the third degree by entering or remaining unlawfully in a non-residential structure . . . with the intent to commit any theft . . . therein."

The word structure is defined in A.R.S. Sec. 13–1501(8):

> " 'Structure' means any building, object, vehicle, railroad car or place with sides and a floor, separately securable from any other structure attached to it and used for lodging, business, transportation, recreation or storage."

Appellants contend that the trial court erred when it instructed the jury that the Salvation Army collection box was a nonresidential structure as a matter of law. They claim that this was a question of fact for the jury. We do not agree. The box had sides and a floor and it was used for storage. There were no facts in dispute and its nature was a question of law for the court. The trial court did not err in its instruction.

Appellants next contend the trial court erred in refusing to give their Instruction No. 14 which stated that abandoned property cannot be the subject of a theft. Appellants' contention that the clothing inside the Salvation Army collection box was abandoned, however, is without merit. The property was not abandoned but was donated to the Salvation Army and in its possession.

Appellants also argue that the trial court erred in the giving of an aiding and abetting instruction to the jury. We note, first of all, that no objection was ever made at trial to the giving of this instruction.

In any event, if there were any error, it was harmless beyond a reasonable doubt since appellants were caught "red-handed" and when they took the witness stand at trial, they admitted they took the clothing from the box in order to sell it at a swap meet.

Affirmed.

UNITED STATES v. BRANDENBURG

United States Court of Appeals, Third Circuit, 1944.
144 F.2d 656.

[In North Carolina Pitts broke into a storehouse and attempted to blow open a safe with dynamite. This constituted the statutory offense of burglary by explosives. To avoid prosecution he left the state, and because of information he had received in prison, went to New Jersey to have his appearance altered and his fingerprints removed by Dr. Brandenburg, explaining why it was important. This was accomplished by reducing the area of a large scar and removing most of the fingerprints. It resulted in a conviction of misprision of felony [1]—the felony charged being a violation of the Federal Fugitive Felon Act [2] by Pitts.]

[Numbered footnotes by the court.]

1. Section 146 of the Criminal Code, R.S. § 5390, 18 U.S.C.A. § 251, creating the federal offense of misprision of felony, provides:

"Whoever, having knowledge of the actual commission of the crime of murder or other felony cognizable by the courts of the United States, conceals and does not as soon as may be disclose and make known the same to some one of the judges or other persons in civil or military authority under the United States, shall be fined not more than $500, or imprisoned not more than three years, or both."

2. The Act of May 18, 1934, c. 302, 48 Stat. 782, 18 U.S.C.A. § 408e, commonly know as the Fugitive Felon Act, provides:

"It shall be unlawful for any person to move or travel in interstate or foreign commerce from any State . . . with intent either (1) to avoid prosecution for murder, kidnaping, burglary, robbery, mayhem, rape, assault with a dangerous weapon, or extortion accompanied by threats of violence, or attempt to commit any of the foregoing, under the laws of the place from which he flees, or (2) to avoid giving testimony in any criminal proceedings in such place in which the commission of a felony is charged. Any person who violates the provision of this section shall, upon conviction thereof, be punished by a fine of not more than $5,000 or by imprisonment for not longer than five years, or by both such fine and imprisonment. Violations of this section may be prosecuted only in the Federal judicial district in which the original crime was alleged to have been committed."

Section 335 of the Criminal Code, 18 U.S.C.A. § 541 provides: "All offenses which may be punished by death or imprisonment for a term exceeding one year shall be deemed felonies. . . . "

The indictment in the case at bar charges that the defendant, Brandenburg, ". . . well knew that . . . Pitts, on . . . May 16, 1941 . . . had unlawfully . . . travelled . . . in interstate commerce from the State of North Carolina . . . to and into the District of New Jersey, with intent to avoid prosecution by the . . . State of North Carolina for two certain burglaries committed by . . . Pitts . . . in . . . the State of North Carolina [and] did wilfully and unlawfully and feloniously conceal the commission of the aforesaid offense against the United States, and did not as soon as he might have, disclose and make known the same to any of the Judges or any other person in Civil authority of the United States, ..."

[Added by the Compiler.]

BIGGS, CIRCUIT JUDGE. . . .

The purpose of the Fugitive Felon Act was stated by Congressman Sumners, Chairman of the Committee on the Judiciary of the House of Representatives, quoting the comments of the Attorney General of the United States on the bill as follows: "One of the most difficult problems which local law-enforcement agencies have to deal with today is the ease with which criminals are able to flee from the State to avoid prosecution . . . . The above bill is considered the most satisfactory solution of this problem, which the States have never been able to solve effectively. This bill will not prevent the States from obtaining extradition of roving criminals, but the complicated process of extradition has proved to be very inefficient. The ability of Federal officers to follow a criminal from one State to any other State or States, as provided in the above bill, should furnish the desired relief from this class of law evaders. . . . " Report No. 1458 of the House Committee on the Judiciary, to accompany S. 2253, May 3, 1934, 73rd Congress, 2nd Session. The same report shows that the word "burglary" and the other specific offenses named in the Act were substituted for the words "a felony" used in the original bill. The general purpose of the Act was to assist in the enforcement of state laws. Compare Jerome v. United States, 318 U.S. 101, 63 S.Ct. 483, 87 L.Ed. 640.

The appellee takes the position, citing Benson v. McMahon, 127 U.S. 457, 464, 8 S.Ct. 1240, 32 L.Ed. 234, that Congress could not have had the common law offenses in mind when it named specific crimes in the Fugitive Felon Act. The appellant contends to the contrary. This court stated in United States v. Patton, 3 Cir., 120 F.2d 73, 75, "It is . . . well settled that when a federal statute uses a term known to the common law to designate a common law offense and does not define that term, courts called upon to construe it should apply the common law meaning," . . .

Cogent arguments can be made in support of both contentions. We shall discuss some of them. The congressional report from which we have quoted shows that the aim of the Act was to impose penalties on a "class of law evaders," viz., "roving criminals" who would be subject to extradition. But seven States do not denominate the offense of burglary as "burglary." [6] New Jersey is an example. If an offender broke into the dwelling house of another in New Jersey

The Fugitive Felon Act has since been amended to omit any reference to crimes by name. 18 U.S.C.A. § 1073. The relevant words are "a crime, or an attempt to commit a crime, punishable by death or which is a felony under the laws of the place from which the fugitive flees, or which, in the case of New Jersey, is a high misdemeanor under the laws of said State, . . ."

6. See:

	Burglary
Florida Stats.Ann.	Sec. 810.01
Massachusetts Ann.Laws ch. 266, Sec. 14 New Hampshire Rev.Laws 1942	c. 453, Sec. 1
Page's Ohio Gen. Code	Vol. 10, Sec. 12441
New Jersey Stats.Ann.	Title 2:115–1
Vermont Pub.Laws 1933	Sec. 8436
Wisconsin Stats. 1943	Sec. 343.09

in the nighttime with the intent to commit a felony therein and thereby committed "burglary" as that offense is defined at the common law, he would not be guilty of a crime designated as "burglary" under the law of New Jersey but would be guilty of a "high misdemeanor." If the phrase "under the laws of the place from which he flees" is deemed to modify the word "burglary" instead of the word "prosecution," an offender, who had committed in New Jersey (or in any of the other six States indicated in footnote 6) acts which would constitute common law burglary, would not be within the purview of the Fugitive Felon Act upon fleeing the State, even though he entered that "class of law evaders" which the congressional report refers to as "roving criminals" subject to extradition. A criminal, therefore, would escape the penalty of the Act simply because he had committed his offense in a State which did not make use of the word "burglary" in its statute. We think that such a result was not intended by Congress. . . .

It is our duty to reconcile the provisions of the Act and to hold the Statute constitutional if its provisions can be construed so as to afford an adequate and certain definition of the crime which it purports to create. We think these ends may be accomplished as follows. We conclude that it was the manifest intention of Congress to cause the Act to have universal application throughout the States since this is the purpose expressed in the congressional report. Restricting ourselves solely to the crime of "burglary" named in the Fugitive Felon Act, we say that there is no State in which acts constituting burglary as defined at common law would not be within the purview of an applicable criminal statute. In other words there is no State in which the offense of breaking into the dwelling house of another in the nighttime with the intent to commit a felony therein would not be a crime cognizable under an appropriate state statute. Each State has created numerous statutory offenses which include such crimes as breaking into a dwelling house, a warehouse, a shop, an office, a freight car, or even a boat with the intent to commit a felony therein. These are variously denominated as burglaries, felonies, or high misdemeanors, and in our opinion were not intended by Congress to fall within the crime of "burglary" named in the Fugitive Felon Act. If we boil the Act down and leave in it only those words which create and define the crime, it will read, "It shall be unlawful for any person to move in interstate commerce with intent to avoid prosecution for burglary under the law of the State from which he flees." The statute thus simplified without rearranging any of its component parts, makes good sense, meets the test which we have imposed and provides that if a person who has committed acts which would constitute the crime of burglary at common law flees from a State to avoid prosecution under the law of that State, he has violated the Fugitive Felon Act. The crime which it creates is defined with sufficient certainty to meet the requirements of the Fifth Amendment. Our conclusion is that the qualifying clause must be deemed to modify the word "prosecution" and that the crime of "burglary" referred to in the Act is burglary as defined at common law.

It is obvious that Pitts fled from North Carolina to escape prosecution for the crimes which he had committed. Section 4232 of the North Carolina Code (Consolidated Statutes of 1939) provides that: "There shall be two degrees in the crime of burglary as defined at the common law. If the crime be committed in a dwelling-house, or in a room used as a sleeping apartment in any building, and any person is in the actual occupation of any part of said dwelling-house or sleeping apartment at the time of the commission of such crime, it shall be burglary in the first degree. If such crime be committed in a dwelling house or sleeping apartment not actually occupied by any one at the time of the commission of the crime, or if it be committed in any house within the curtilage of a dwelling-house or in any building not a dwelling-house, but in which is a room used as a sleeping apartment and not actually occupied as such at the time of the commission of the crime, it shall be burglary in the second degree."

We conclude that Pitts did not commit burglary in either the first or the second degree as defined by Section 4232 of the North Carolina Code. While evidence was offered to show that the store of C.A. Lowe & Sons contained a room in which there was a cot occasionally occupied at night by a member of the firm serving as a guard, it is clear that this cannot be considered to be a sleeping apartment within the terms of the statute. The room was unoccupied on the night of the crime. The Supreme Court of North Carolina has held that the sleeping apartment referred to in the statute must be one in which a person regularly sleeps. State v. Foster, 129 N.C. 704, 40 S.E. 209. The offense which Pitts committed bears little resemblance to the crime of burglary as defined at common law.

What was the crime which Pitts committed? Section 4237(a) of the North Carolina Code (Consolidated Statutes of 1939) provides as follows: "Burglary with explosives.—Any person who, with intent to commit crime, breaks and enters, either by day or by night, any building, whether inhabited or not, and opens or attempts to open any vault, safe, or other secure place by use of nitro-glycerine, dynamite, gunpowder, or by any other explosive, or acetylene torch, shall be deemed guilty of burglary with explosives." It is upon this statute that the United States rests this phase of its case. Was Pitts guilty of burglary with explosives? From his own testimony it is clear that he broke into the warehouse bringing explosives with him with the intent of using them to blow open the safe. By removing the dial on the safe Pitts committed an affirmative act sufficient to demonstrate his intent within the meaning of the statute. There was sufficient evidence from which a jury could have found that Pitts was guilty of burglary with explosives committed in North Carolina. This was his crime.

The crime of "burglary with explosives" was unknown to the common law. It follows that when Pitts fled from North Carolina to avoid prosecution for "burglary with explosives" he did not commit an offense within the purview of the Fugitive Felon Act. From this we must conclude that Brandenburg did not commit the crime of misprision of felony within the purview of Section 146 of the Criminal Code.

The judgment of conviction is reversed.[a]

MODEL PENAL CODE

Article 221. Burglary and Other Criminal Intrusion

Section 221.0 Definitions.

In this Article, unless a different meaning plainly is required:

(1) "occupied structure" means any structure, vehicle or place adapted for overnight accommodation of persons, or for carrying on business therein, whether or not a person is actually present.

(2) "night" means the period between thirty minutes past sunset and thirty minutes before sunrise.

Section 221.1 Burglary.

(1) Burglary Defined. A person is guilty of burglary if he enters a building or occupied structure, or separately secured or occupied portion thereof, with purpose to commit a crime therein, unless the premises are at the time open to the public or the actor is licensed or privileged to enter. It is an affirmative defense to prosecution for burglary that the building or structure was abandoned.

(2) Grading. Burglary is a felony of the second degree if it is perpetrated in the dwelling of another at night, or if, in the course of committing the offense, the actor:

(a) purposely, knowingly or recklessly inflicts or attempts to inflict bodily injury on anyone; or

a. In holding that "robbery" in the Hobbs Act, proscribing the interference of interstate commerce by robbery, means common-law robbery, the court said:

"To the same effect see United States v. Turley, 1957, 352 U.S. 407, 77 S.Ct. 397, 1 L.Ed.2d 430. It was there said (352 U.S. at page 411, 77 S.Ct. at page 399):

" 'We recognize that where a federal criminal statute uses a common-law term of established meaning without defining it, the general practice is to give that term its common-law meaning.' " United States v. Nedley, 255 F.2d 350, 357 (3d Cir.1958).

Although it was not necessary for the decision of the case at bench, the court said: "However, for the guidance of the trial courts, it seems advisable to say that we think the word 'burglary' in sections 106 and 107 (dealing with murder and degrees of murder) means burglary at common law." State v. Burrell, 120 N.J.L. 277, 282, 199 A. 18, 22 (1938).

"Storehouse breaking" (i.e., statutory burglary) is not included as one of the crimes under the felony-murder clause of the first-degree murder statute. Jeter v. State, 9 Md.App. 575, 267 A.2d 319 (1970).

A burglar who steals unloaded guns thereby arms himself with deadly weapons for purposes of prosecution for aggravated burglary. State v. Luna, 99 N.M. 76, 653 P.2d 1222 (App.1982).

(b) is armed with explosives or a deadly weapon. Otherwise, burglary is a felony of the third degree. An act shall be deemed "in the course of committing" an offense if it occurs in an attempt to commit the offense or in flight after the attempt or commission.

(3) Multiple Convictions. A person may not be convicted both for burglary and for the offense which it was his purpose to commit after the burglarious entry or for an attempt to commit that offense, unless the additional offense constitutes a felony of the first or second degree.

Section 221.2. Criminal Trespass.

(1) Buildings and Occupied Structures. A person commits an offense if, knowing that he is not licensed or privileged to do so, he enters or surreptitiously remains in any building or occupied structure, or separately secured or occupied portion thereof. An offense under this Subsection is a misdemeanor if it is committed in a dwelling at night. Otherwise it is a petty misdemeanor.

(2) Defiant Trespasser. A person commits an offense if, knowing that he is not licensed or privileged to do so, he enters or remains in any place as to which notice against trespass is given by:

(a) actual communication to the actor; or

(b) posting in a manner prescribed by law or reasonably likely to come to the attention of intruders; or

(c) fencing or other enclosure manifestly designed to exclude intruders.

An offense under this Subsection constitutes a petty misdemeanor if the offender defies an order to leave personally communicated to him by the owner of the premises or other authorized person. Otherwise it is a violation.

(3) Defenses. It is an affirmative defense to prosecution under this Section that:

(a) a building or occupied structure involved in an offense under Subsection (1) was abandoned; or

(b) the premises were at the time open to members of the public and the actor complied with all lawful conditions imposed on access to or remaining in the premises; or

(c) the actor reasonably believed that the owner of the premises, or other person empowered to license access thereto, would have licensed him to enter or remain.[1]

SECTION 2. ARSON

Common-law arson is the malicious burning of the dwelling house of another.

This crime is usually the result of a deliberate intent and this may anciently have been assumed to be requisite. It has been rather common, for example, to give the definition in this form: Arson is the

wilful (or voluntary) and malicious burning of the dwelling house of another. The addition of either word, however, lost all meaning when it became established that an intent to burn might be implied by law when it did not exist in fact. Thus, if without justification, excuse or mitigation, one sets a fire which obviously creates an unreasonable fire hazard for another's dwelling, which is actually burned thereby, the result is common-law arson even if this was not an intended consequence but there was hope that it would not happen. The ancient explanation that an intent to burn is implied under such circumstances is quite outmoded. The true explanation is that the law does not require the burning to be intentional but only that it be malicious, and that such a burning of the dwelling house of another *is malicious.*

Common-law arson was a felony and in point of gravity ranked only a little less than the crime of murder. It was very distinctly not regarded as a mere violation of property rights. The harm done to the habitation was the primary consideration. Every man's house was his "castle" no matter how humble it might be, and the essence of this crime was the violation of the "castle." Hence one might be guilty of arson for burning a building which he himself *owned,* if someone else was the actual dweller therein; but he could not commit this offense (at common law) by burning his own habitation, if he did not also burn the habitation of another, even if another held the title and hence would suffer the financial loss. The terror caused by seeing one's abode in flames, and the grave risk to human life, were also taken into consideration. This was not only a capital crime at common law, but in the reign of Edward the First the execution was by burning.

Arson had four requisites at common law:

1. There must be some actual burning (but the requirement does not include a destruction of the building or of any substantial part of the building).

2. The burning must be malicious.

3. The object burned must be a dwelling house [1] (but as in burglary any out-house "within the curtilage," was regarded as "parcel of the dwelling house").

4. The house burned must be the habitation of another.

An actual burning of some part of the house is essential but it is not necessary that the building should be destroyed. A blackening by smoke or blistering of the paint by heat is not enough. On the other hand, if any of fiber of the wood is actually consumed by fire, this is a *burning* even if it does not actually burst into flame.[2]

1. A structure "unoccupied for several months, in a dilapidated condition, not habitable without renovation, and boarded up to prevent ingress and egress" does not constitute a "dwelling" as that word is used in the arson statute. People v. Reed, 13 Mich.App. 75, 163 N.W.2d 704 (1968).

2. Accord, State v. Nielson, 25 Utah 2d 11, 474 P.2d 725 (1970).

A negligent burning of the dwelling of another does not constitute arson. The burning must be malicious. An intentional burning of such a building will be malicious unless there is some justification, excuse or mitigation for the deed. In fact, as mentioned above, an obvious fire hazard may be created under circumstances which will amount to a malicious burning if fire does result, even without an actual intent to cause the particular harm which ensues. One, for example, who set fire to his own dwelling to defraud the insurer was held guilty of arson for the burning of his neighbor's house because he had wantonly and wilfully exposed the other building to this hazard, even though he hoped the fire would not spread to the other building.

Although it is not common-law arson for one to burn his own dwelling if no other is burned by this fire, it is a common-law misdemeanor if the burning is intentional and the house is situated in a city or town, or is beyond those limits but so near to other houses as to create a danger to them. Some statutes on arson have eliminated the requirement that the building be the dwelling "of another," thereby including under this offense the wilful burning of one's own dwelling (for the purpose of collecting insurance or otherwise).[3] Other enactments have expressly prohibited this very type of burning—sometimes without using the label "arson." Burning personal property to defraud the insurer has also been made a statutory crime.

It has also been common for statutes to provide a penalty (under the name of arson or otherwise) for the malicious burning of buildings other than dwellings, such as stores, shops, warehouses and so forth. The term "statutory arson" is employed to designate the entire area of statutory proscription which is analogous to, but not included in common-law arson.

MODEL PENAL CODE
OFFENSES AGAINST PROPERTY

Article 220. Arson, Criminal Mischief and other Property Destruction
Section 220.1 Arson and Related Offenses.

(1) Arson. A person is guilty of arson, a felony of the second degree, if he starts a fire or causes an explosion with the purpose of:

(a) destroying a building or occupied structure of another; or

(b) destroying or damaging any property, whether his own or another's, to collect insurance for such loss. It shall be an affirmative defense to prosecution under this paragraph that the actor's conduct did not recklessly endanger any building or occupied structure of another or place any other person in danger of death or bodily injury.

3. An arson statute which makes it a felony intentionally to set fire to any building or other structure, so drawn as to include the intentional burning of one's own property for a proper purpose, is unconstitutional. State v. Dennis, 80 N.M. 262, 454 P.2d 276 (1969).

Although the wilful and malicious burning of another's automobile is a felony, and is in the chapter on "arson", it is not "arson" within the special clause of the first degree murder statute. People v. Nichols, 3 Cal.3d 150, 89 Cal.Rptr. 721, 474 P.2d 673 (1970).

(2) Reckless Burning or Exploding. A person commits a felony of the third degree if he purposely starts a fire or causes an explosion, whether on his own property or another's, and thereby recklessly:

(a) places another person in danger of death or bodily injury; or

(b) places a building or occupied structure of another in danger of damage or destruction.

(3) Failure to Control or Report Dangerous Fire. A person who knows that a fire is endangering life or a substantial amount of property of another and fails to take reasonable measures to put out or control the fire, when he can do so without substantial risk to himself, or to give a prompt fire alarm, commits a misdemeanor if:

(a) he knows that he is under an official, contractual, or other legal duty to prevent or combat the fire; or

(b) the fire was started, albeit lawfully, by him or with his assent, or on property in his custody or control.

(4) Definitions. "Occupied structure" means any structure, vehicle, or place adapted for overnight accommodation of persons or for carrying on busines therein, whether or not a person is actually present. Property is that of another, for the purposes of this section, if anyone other than the actor has a possessory or proprietary interest therein. If a building or structure is divided into separately occupied units, any unit not occupied by the actor is an occupied structure of another.

Section 220.2 Causing or Risking Catastrophe.

(1) Causing Catastrophe. A person who causes a catastrophe by explosion, fire, flood, avalanche, collapse of building, release of poison gas, radioactive material or other harmful or destructive force or substance, or by any other means of causing potentially widespread injury or damage, commits a felony of the second degree if he does so purposely or knowingly, or a felony of the third degree if he does so recklessly.

(2) Risking Catastrophe. A person is guilty of a misdemeanor if he recklessly creates a risk of catastrophe in the employment of fire, explosives or other dangerous means listed in Subsection (1).

(3) Failure to Prevent Catastrophe. A person who knowingly or recklessly fails to take reasonable measures to prevent or mitigate a catastrophe commits a misdemeanor if:

(a) he knows that he is under an official, contractual or other legal duty to take such measures; or

(b) he did or assented to the act causing or threatening the catastrophe.

Section 220.3 Criminal Mischief.

(1) Offense Defined. A person is guilty of criminal mischief if he:

(a) damages tangible property of another purposely, recklessly, or by negligence in the employment of fire, explosives, or other dangerous means listed in Section 220.2(1); or

(b) purposely or recklessly tampers with tangible property of another so as to endanger person or property; or

(c) purposely or recklessly causes another to suffer pecuniary loss by deception or threat.

(2) Grading. Criminal mischief is a felony of the third degree if the actor purposely causes pecuniary loss in excess of $5,000, or a substantial interruption or impairment of public communication, transportation, supply of water, gas or power, or other public service. It is a misdemeanor if the actor purposely causes pecuniary loss in excess of $100, or a petty misdemeanor if he purposely or recklessly causes pecuniary loss in excess of $25. Otherwise criminal mischief is a violation.[1]

Chapter 4

OFFENSES AGAINST PROPERTY

SECTION 1. LARCENY[1]

(A) PERSONAL PROPERTY

Larceny was one of the common-law felonies, punishable anciently by total forfeiture—the loss of life and lands and goods. Had it not been for this drastic penalty the courts would probably have recognized, as a possible subject of larceny, any property capable of being taken into possession and removed to another place. As it was, many such things were held not to be the subject of larceny. This applied to animals of a "base nature". Thus it was larceny to steal a horse, cow, pig or chicken, but not to steal a cat, monkey or fox. Many instruments or documents were excluded. The paper or parchment was no longer the subject of larceny, as such, because it was deemed to have been completely merged in the legal instrument or document written upon it. The latter, in turn, was deemed to be merged in whatever was represented by it. As real estate was not the subject of larceny, so neither was a deed to land. A contract represented an intangible right which could not be stolen and hence the wrongful taking of the written evidence of a contract was not larceny. Even negotiable notes and bills were held to be outside the larceny field. A pawn ticket, on the other hand, was the subject of larceny because it represented a specific chattel which could be stolen. Natural gas was the subject of larceny because it can be taken and carried away although not so easily handled as many other things. Electric current, by the prevailing view, was not, on the theory that it is not a substance but comparable to water power which may be used but not "taken and carried away".

These arbitrary exclusions from the scope of larceny have been almost entirely eliminated today, to a considerable extent as a result of legislation.[2]

1. There being no statutory definition of larceny in Michigan, all the elements of common-law larceny are required. People v. Anderson, 7 Mich.App. 513, 152 N.W.2d 40 (1967).

2. The wrongful use of another's machinery to spin 20,000 pounds of raw wool into yarn does not constitute larceny. People v. Ashworth, 220 App.Div.

PEOPLE v. CARIDIS

Court of Appeals of California, First Appellate District, 1915.
29 Cal.App. 166, 154 P. 1061.

LENNON, P.J. The defendant in this case was, by an information filed in the superior court of the city and county of San Francisco, charged with the crime of grand larceny, alleged to have been committed as follows:

"The said Antonio Caridis on the 29th day of July, A.D.1914, at the said City and County of San Francisco, State of California, did then and there willfully, unlawfully and feloniously steal, take and carry away one lottery ticket of the Original Nacional Company, No. 16235, that theretofore and on the 27th day of July, 1914, the said ticket was, after a drawing held by said Original Nacional Company, and its officers, representatives and agents, declared by said Original Nacional Company and its officers, representatives and agents, to be one of the winning tickets of the said Original Nacional Company, and its officers, representatives and agents, after said drawing aforesaid, did become liable for and did promise to pay to the holder of said ticket the sum of twelve hundred and fifty ($1250.00) dollars in gold coin of the United States of America and did then and there promise to pay to the holder of said ticket the sum of twelve hundred and fifty ($1250.00) dollars in gold coin of the United States of America;

"That thereafter, and on the 30th day of July, 1914, the said Antonio Caridis did present said ticket to said Original Nacional Company and to its officers, representatives and agents, and did receive from said Original Nacional Company, and its officers, representatives and agents, the sum of twelve hundred and fifty ($1250) dollars in gold coin of the United States of America therefor;

"That at all of said times the said lottery ticket was the personal property of Jim Papas and was of the value of twelve hundred and fifty ($1250.00) dollars in gold coin of the United States of America."

A demurrer to the information was allowed upon the ground that the facts stated did not constitute a public offense, in the particular that it affirmatively appeared that the subject matter of the alleged

498, 222 N.Y.S. 24 (1927). The court said:

"Personal property has been variously defined. That which may be the subject of larceny is well comprehended in the following statement (36 Corpus Juris, 737): It 'should have corporeal existence, that is, be something the physical presence, quantity, or quality of which is detectable or measurable by the senses or by some mechanical contrivance; for a naked right existing merely in contemplation of law, although it may be very valuable to the person who is entitled to exercise it, is not a subject of larceny.' "

Intellectual property is not property that could justify a larceny prosecution at common law, nor within statutory coverage, and therefore cannot be the subject of theft. Commonwealth v. Yourawski, 384 Mass. 386, 425 N.E.2d 298 (1981).

larceny had no legitimate value. The action was thereupon dismissed and the people have appealed from the order allowing the demurrer.

The ruling of the court below was correct. It is essential to the commission of the crime of larceny that the property alleged to have been stolen have some value—intrinsic or relative—which, where grand larceny is charged and the property was not taken from the person of another, must exceed the sum of fifty dollars.

Evidently the information in the present case was framed to fit the requirements of section 492 of the Penal Code, which fixes the value in cases of the larceny of written instruments by providing that "If the thing stolen consists of any evidence of debt, or other written instrument, the amount of money due thereupon, or secured to be paid thereby and remaining unsatisfied, or which in any contingency might be collected thereon or the value of the property the title to which is shown thereby, or the sum which might be recovered in the absence thereof, is the value of the thing stolen." Clearly this section contemplates and controls the value to be placed only upon written instruments which create some legal right and constitute a subsisting and an enforceable evidence of a debt.

The lottery ticket which was the subject matter of the larceny charged in the present case had no relative value save, as affirmatively alleged in the information, as the evidence of a debt due from an enterprise which was denounced by law and which apparently existed and was conducted by its promoters in defiance of the law. (Pen. Code, sec. 319 et seq.) It is a well-settled principle that an obligation which exists in defiance of a law which denounces it has, in the eye of the law, neither validity nor value. An instance of the application of this principle is to be found in the analogous case of Culp v. State, 1 Port. (Ala.) 33, 26 Am.Dec. 357, where the court held that an indictment charging the larceny of several "bills of credit of the United States Bank," which were alleged to be of the aggregate value of $310, could not be sustained because each of the bills was for a sum less than the bank was authorized by its charter to issue, and consequently could not, in contemplation of law, be the subject matter of a larceny.

The fact as alleged in the information, that the drawing had taken place prior to the alleged larceny of the ticket, and that the defendant ultimately collected thereon the sum of $1,250 from the lottery company, added nothing to the validity or value of the ticket. Being a void and valueless obligation in the eye of the law from its very inception, it could not be transformed into a legitimate and valuable thing by a voluntary payment, which in itself was a contravention of the law. Moreover, the sufficiency of the information must be determined by the facts as they existed at the time of the alleged taking, and not by anything that may have occurred subsequently.

Considered as a mere piece of paper, the lottery ticket in question possessed perhaps some slight intrinsic value, which, however small, would have sufficed to make the wrongful taking of it petit larceny, and if that had been the charge preferred against the defendant, it doubtless would have stood the test of demurrer.

The order appealed from is affirmed.[1]

PEOPLE ex rel. KOONS v. ELLING, Sheriff

Supreme Court, Special Term, Ontario County, New York, 1948.
190 Misc. 998, 77 N.Y.S.2d 103.

CRIBB, JUSTICE. The relator, Walter Koons, by this habeas corpus proceeding, seeks his release from the sentence of imprisonment under which he is confined in the Ontario County jail. . . .

It is conceded that the money with the larceny of which relator was charged was removed by him and his confederates from slot machines, commonly referred to as "one armed bandits", located in a room of the Moose Club, by the drilling of a small hole in the machine, through which, by means of an inserted wire, the mechanism was tripped allowing moneys inside to drop down into an exposed receptacle in the same manner as if the machine had been operated in the usual way and had paid out in some amount. The information charged the relator with committing the crime of petit larceny against the property of the named club; the relator plead guilty to the charge. However, if the moneys could not be the subject of larceny, and, as he contends, he therefore committed no crime, his plea of guilty was a nullity. A plea of guilty may not be substituted for the crime itself. Relator maintains that his plea of guilty was a nullity because the moneys were taken from unlawful slot machines in which, as well as in their contents, no person had or could have any title or possessory rights, and that therefore there was no larceny from the "true owner" as contemplated by section 1290 of the Penal Law. The question is therefore presented as to whether money in an unlawful slot machine may be the subject of larceny. Counsel have cited no cases, and the independent search of this Court has discovered none, determinative of the question.

In this case relator was not convicted of stealing the slot machines, which concededly were gambling devices and unlawful under the provisions of section 982 of the Penal Law but rather of stealing moneys contained in them. He was convicted of petit larceny. It is the opinion of this Court that the reasoning adopted by the Court in People v. Otis, 235 N.Y. 421, 139 N.E. 562, is equally applicable in the instant case. In that case the defendant having been indicted for stealing a quantity of whiskey, was convicted of petit larceny. The whiskey was unlawfully possessed under the provisions of the National Prohibition Act, 27 U.S.C.A. § 1 et seq. The question presented was whether the conviction could be sustained under such circum-

1. A dog may be the subject of larceny and receiving stolen property. State v. Hernandez, 121 Ariz. 544, 592 P.2d 378 (App.1979).

stances. The Court said: "The possessor not being able to make any legal use of it, it is said the liquor itself has no value. This is, however, to make the value of a chattel to its possessor the test as to whether it is the subject of larceny. Such is not the rule. It is enough if the object taken has inherent value. No one can doubt that whiskey has such value. It may be sold by the government and the proceeds covered into the treasury. It may be sold by druggists. That it is held illegally is immaterial." [1] Although the statute, 27 U.S.C.A. § 39, under discussion in that case specifically provided that "no property rights shall exist" in liquor illegally possessed, the Court held that such liquor could be the subject of larceny, and after referring to the statutory provisions for the issuance of search warrants, the seizure and final disposition by the courts of liquor so illegally possessed, and the prohibitory provision as to property rights in such liquor, the Court further said: "Property rights in such liquor are not forever ended. They pass to the government." . . .

An order may be issued dismissing the writ of habeas corpus heretofore granted in this proceeding and remanding relator to the custody of the sheriff of Ontario County to serve the remainder of his sentence in accordance with the provisions of law applicable thereto.[2]

BELL v. STATE

Supreme Court of Tennessee, 1874.
63 Tenn. 426.

DEADERICK, J., delivered the opinion of the Court.

The plaintiff in error was convicted at the November Term, 1874, of the Criminal Court of Montgomery County, of petit larceny, for stealing as charged, cabbage and sweet potatoes, the goods and chattels of G.B. White, the prosecutor, and sentenced to the penitentiary for one year.

It is insisted that the charge of the Judge was erroneous in its definition of the offence charged.

In the beginning of his charge the Judge gives a full and accurate definition of the offence, and correctly instructs the jury as to the difference between grand and petit larceny, and the punishment annexed to each.

1. Accord, People v. Odenwald, 104 Cal.App. 203, 285 P. 406 (1930), overruling People v. Spencer, 54 Cal.App. 54, 201 P. 130 (1921), which had held such liquor was not the subject of larceny, because the statute provided that "no property right shall exist in any such liquor".

One who larcenously takes the stolen object from a thief may be convicted of larceny despite the criminality of the possession of the latter. Commonwealth v. Rourke, 64 Mass. 397 (1852).

2. Theft under 18 U.S.C.A. § 641 is established by the taking of any "thing of value;" and the selling of information from a government computer is prohibited by the statute. United States v. Lambert, 446 F.Supp. 890 (D.C.Conn.1978), affirmed United States v. Girard, 601 F.2d 69 (2d Cir.1979).

It is true, in a subsequent part of his instructions, as introductory to the definition of "personal property," he says: "The jury will observe that larceny is the felonious taking away of personal property." He then proceeds to state to the jury when vegetables, etc., growing in or upon the ground, may become "personal property," and the subject of larceny, and uses this language: "If defendant went at night into the garden of another, intending to steal, and dug a lot of sweet potatoes, laying them on the ground, or cut a lot of cabbage, severing them from the earth, and afterwards picked up the vegetables, put them in a bag, and carried them off, that would be larceny."

This latter part of the charge is not strictly accurate, according to the rule of the common law. In 3 Greenleaf on Ev., § 163, it is said: "If the severance and asportation were one continued act of the prisoner, it is only a trespass; but if the severance were the act of another person, or if, after the severance by the prisoner, any interval of time elapsed, after which he returned and took the article away, the severance and asportation being two distinct acts, it is larceny," citing 1 E. Hale P.C., 510; 2 East P.C., 587. . . .

The principle is, that when the severance and asportation constitute one continuous act, then it is a trespass only, but if the severance is a distinct act, and not immediately connected with or followed by the asportation it is a larceny.

To dig potatoes, whereby they are cast upon the surface of the earth, and then immediately to pick them up, and put them in a bag, and carry them away, would be one continuous act, although the picking up, necessarily, was after the digging, and after they had lain upon the ground. The act would be continuous, without cessation, until the asportation, as well as the severance, was completed, and thus a trespass only. And so, also, of cutting a "lot of cabbages," "severing them from the earth," the "severing" necessarily preceded the taking away, yet, when the taking away immediately follows, it is a "continuous act," and is trespass only.

It is argued by the Attorney-General, that the taking of vegetables severed from the ground, and the carrying of stolen goods into another county, seem to stand upon the same footing, although it is conceded that the authorities hold, as to the first mentioned, that the possession is not in the owner as personalty, and in the latter, that the legal possession still remains in him.

The trespasser holds the severed property, as personalty, but he cannot be convicted of a larceny, for he did not obtain that possession feloniously. No felony was committed in the taking and carrying away from the owner, but a trespass only.

In the case of an original felonious taking and carrying away, every moment's continuance of the trespass and felony amounts to a new caption and asportation, (2 Arch.Cr.Pr. & Pl., 343, note 1,) and the offence is considered as committed in every county or jurisdiction into which the thief carries the goods. Ibid. It is difficult to see any difference in the moral guilt of one who takes and carries away immediately upon the severance from the freehold and one who severs at one time and takes away at another, but the Legislature has not altered the distinction made by the common law, and it is still in force in Tennessee.[1]

The judgment of the Criminal Court will be reversed.[2]

THE QUEEN v. TOWNLEY

Court for Crown Cases Reserved, 1871.
L.R. 1 C.C. 315, 12 Cox C.C. 59.

BOVILL, C.J. The prisoner in this case has been convicted of felony in stealing rabbits, and the question is, whether he has been properly convicted. The facts are, that the rabbits, 126 in number, were taken and killed upon land the property of the Crown. The rabbits were then, together with 400 yards of net, placed in a ditch on the same land on which they had been taken; some of them being in bags, and some in bundles strapped together by the legs. They were placed there by the poachers, who in so placing them had no intention to abandon the wrongful possession which they had acquired by taking them, but placed them in the ditch as a place of deposit till they could conveniently remove them. Here they were found by the keepers at about eight in the morning. At about a quarter to eleven the prisoner arrived, went straight to the place where the rabbits were concealed, and began to remove them.

Now, the first question is as to the nature of the property in these rabbits. In animals ferae naturae there is no absolute property. There is only a special or qualified right of property—a right ratione soli to take and kill them. When killed upon the soil they become the absolute property of the owner of the soil. This was decided in the case of rabbits by the House of Lords in Blade v. Higgs.[1] And the same principle was applied in the case of grouse in Lord Lonsdale v. Rigg.[2] In this case therefore the rabbits, being started and killed on land belonging to the Crown, might, if there were no other circumstance in the case, become the property of the Crown. But before there can be a conviction for larceny for taking anything not capable in its original state of being the subject of larceny, as for instance,

1. The legislature made the change later. Williams v. State, 186 Tenn. 252, 257, 209 S.W.2d 29, 31 (1948).

Copper wire taken from poles was realty not personalty and could not be the subject of larceny. Parker v. State, 352 So.2d 1386 (Ala.App.1977).

2. Since the *statutory* offense of "theft" includes the taking of anything of value the fact that what was taken was severed from the realty is unimportant. State v. Mills, 214 La. 979, 39 So.2d 439 (1949). Some courts reached a similar result in regard to larceny without the aid of statute. Ex parte Willke, 34 Tex. 155 (1870); Stephens v. Commonwealth, 304 Ky. 38, 199 S.W.2d 719 (1947). The wrongful severance of a part of the realty and its appropriation is expressly made larceny in some of the statutes. More frequently it is punished as some other offense, such as malicious mischief and trespass.

1. [Footnotes by the Court.] 11 H.L.C. 621; 34 L.J.(C.P.) 286.

2. 1 H. & N. 923; 26 L.J.(Ex.) 196.

things fixed to the soil, it is necessary that the act of taking away should not be one continuous act with the act of severance or other act by which the thing becomes a chattel, and so is brought within the law of larceny. This doctrine has been applied to stripping lead from the roof of a church, and in other cases of things affixed to the soil. And the present case must be governed by the same principle. It is not stated in the case whether or not the prisoner was one of the poachers who killed the rabbits. But my Brother Blackburn says that such must be taken to be the fact. Under all the circumstances of the case I think a jury ought to have found that the whole transaction was a continuous one; and the conviction must be quashed. . . .

(MARTIN, B., BRAMWELL, B., BYLES, J., and BLACKBURN, J., were of the same opinion, and the conviction was quashed.)

(B) "OF ANOTHER"

1. IN GENERAL

STATE v. COHEN

Supreme Court of Minnesota, 1935.
196 Minn. 39, 263 N.W. 922.

(The defendant, having had her fur coat repaired by a furrier, regained control of it by the pretense of trying it on, after which she concealed it and refused either to return it or to pay for the work done. She appealed from a conviction of the crime of grand larceny in the second degree.)

HOLT, JUSTICE. . . . The verdict is not contrary to law. A person may be guilty of larceny of his own property if taken from the possession of one who has a lien thereon under which possession may lawfully be retained until the lien is discharged. Sections 8507 and 8508, 2 Mason Minn.St.1927, gave a possessory lien to Mellon, and the way defendant procured the coat to see how it looked on her person does not, as a matter of law, bring her within the protection of 2 Mason Minn.St.1927, § 10372. On the contrary, the jury had warrant for finding that defendant's scheme of trying on the coat and disappearing with it was with the felonious intent of depriving Mellon of his lien and his right of possession until the lien was discharged. An owner of personal property may be found guilty of larceny thereof when he wrongfully takes it from a pledgee or from one whom he has given possession for the purpose of having it cared for or repaired under statutes such as ours giving a lien therefor and the right to retain possession until the lien is paid. State v. Hubbard, 126 Kan.

129, 266 P. 939, annotated in 58 A.L.R. 327, 330, 331, where the authorities are cited and this conclusion therefrom is stated:

"If personal property in the possession of one other than the general owner by virtue of some special right or title is taken from him by the general owner, such taking is larceny if it is done with the felonious intent of depriving such person of his rights, or of charging him with the value of the property." . . .

Defendant complains of the ruling excluding evidence of an expert that the material and labor which Mellon expended in making the agreed alterations and repairs on the coat did not enhance its value. We think the ruling right. Defendant was permitted to testify as to her opinion of Mellon's work; that it ruined the coat instead of enhancing its value; that she thought he had substituted inferior fur for that which was in the coat when delivered to him; and that she took possession because she was afraid the value of the coat would be utterly destroyed. All this properly went to disprove felonious intent. But we think the amount of Mellon's lien was not an issue that could be litigated in this case. It was not between the proper parties. The quantum of proof is not the same in this criminal case as it would be in an action between Mellon and defendant either to establish or defeat a lien. We take it that in this prosecution the only value in issue was the value of the coat which defendant feloniously took and concealed.[1] Mellon was entitled to the possession of the entire coat until his lien was determined in a lawful manner. And defendant was not entitled to have the amount of Mellon's possessory lien determined in this criminal case. It was conceded that possession of the coat had been given by her to Mellon in order that he might alter and repair it at an agreed price.

Other assignments of error are made. They had been examined, but we do not consider them of sufficient merit to note in this opinion.

The conviction is affirmed.[2]

1. If the thief gave consideration for, or had a legal interest in, the stolen property, the amount of such consideration or value shall be deducted from the total value of the property. W.S.A. 943.20.

2. It was held not to be larceny for a wife to appropriate money belonging to 30 people, one of whom was her husband. Rex v. Willis, 1 Moody 375, 168 Eng.Rep. 1309 (1833). It was held otherwise under a statute authorizing a married woman to acquire, hold and transfer property as freely as if she were single. Fugate v. Commonwealth, 308 Ky. 815, 215 S.W.2d 1004 (1948).

One partner does not commit larceny by wrongfully appropriating partnership property since each partner has an individual interest therein. State v. Elsbury, 63 Nev. 463, 175 P.2d 430 (1946).

"Proof of a greater right to possession than the thief is always sufficient proof of 'ownership' ". State v. Lemon, 203 Kan. 464, 454 P.2d 718 (1969).

It is no defense to a charge of robbery or larceny that the victim is not the true owner of the property because larceny can be committed against one who is himself a thief. People v. Moore, 4 Cal.App. 3d 668, 84 Cal.Rptr. 771 (1970).

2. Distinction Between Custody and Possession

There was no common-law crime known as "embezzlement", which is a statutory crime enacted to fill certain gaps that appeared during the development of the crime of larceny. These gaps (there were others) grew out of the holding that no appropriation by one having lawful possession could constitute the felony of larceny. One of the refinements of this development was the distinction between custody and possession, because the rule came to be that if the one having control of the property had custody only, and not possession, his conversion of the property could result in larceny. And because the statutory offense was intended to fill "gaps" in the law of larceny it was held there was no overlapping. The result was a mutually-exclusive area, and in this area a holding that the appropriation constituted embezzlement was a holding that it did not constitute larceny, and vice versa.

PEOPLE v. WALKER

Colorado Court of Appeals, Div. II, 1980.
44 Colo.App. 249, 615 P.2d 57.

Enoch, Chief Judge. Defendant was convicted by a jury of theft in violation of § 18–4–401(4), C.R.S.1973 (1978 Repl. Vol. 8). He contends that the trial court erred in failing to grant a judgment of acquittal and improperly refused to give certain jury instructions. We affirm.

These facts are undisputed: A team of six Denver police officers, including one who was posing as a drunk, were positioned near the intersection of 15th and Welton Streets in downtown Denver around 10 p. m. on September 22, 1977. The policeman pretending to be drunk was lying face down in the entryway to a "hock" shop and carried a wallet containing marked bills. He testified that someone approached him, that he was asked, "What's the matter, brother?" but that he remained silent. He said his wallet was taken.

Others on the police team testified that defendant was apprehended less than a block away. The marked money—two one-hundred-dollar bills and two twenty-dollar bills—was found in his pocket.

Defendant testified on his own behalf that he first approached the decoy officer in the belief that he was injured, but that he saw no signs of violence and noted that the body of the prone officer was stiff. Defendant concluded that he had encountered a dead man. He then admitted taking the money from a wallet on the officer's person.

Defendant contends first that the evidence does not sufficiently establish that he had the specific intent required to support a conviction of theft. The argument in support of this contention is not clear; however, from the record we interpret it to be that defendant could not have had the specific intent, as required by the statute, to permanently deprive another of a thing of value because he took the money from what he thought to be a dead body. Thus, he did not intend to "deprive another." We disagree.

Even if defendant in good faith believed that he was taking money from a dead man's wallet, he was not entitled to possession of that property. From the moment of death, the heirs or devisees become the rightful possessors of property until the estate of the deceased has passed through probate or administration. See § 15–11–101 et seq., and § 15–12–101 et seq., C.R.S.1973. Therefore, it makes no difference whether the money was taken from a living person or a dead body. Affirmed.

THE KING v. BAZELEY

Court for Crown Cases Reserved, 1799.
2 Leach 835, 168 Eng.Rep. 517.

At the Old Bailey in February Session 1799, Joseph Bazeley was tried before John Silvester, Esq. Common Serjeant of the city of London, for feloniously stealing on the 18th January preceding, a Bank-note of the value of one hundred pounds, the property of Peter Esdaile, Sir Benjamin Hammett, William Esdaile, and John Hammett.

The following facts appeared in evidence. The prisoner, Joseph Bazeley, was the principal teller at the house of Messrs. Esdaile's and Hammett's bankers, in Lombard-street, at the salary of £100 a year, and his duty was to receive and pay money, notes, and bills, at the counter. The manner of conducting the business of this banking-house is as follows: There are four tellers, each of whom has a separate money-book, a separate money-drawer, and a separate bag. The prisoner being the chief teller, the total of the receipts and payments of all the other money-books were every evening copied into his, and the total balance or rest, as it is technically called, struck in his book, and the balances of the other money-books paid, by the other tellers, over to him. When any monies, whether in cash or notes, are brought by customers to the counter to be paid in, the teller who receives it counts it over, then enters the Bank-notes or drafts, and afterwards the cash, under the customer's name, in his book; and then, after casting up the total, it is entered in the customer's book. The money is then put into the teller's bag, and the Bank-notes or other papers, if any, put into a box which stands on a desk behind the counter, directly before another clerk, who is called the cash book-keeper, who makes an entry of it in the received cash-book in the name of the person who has paid it in, and which he finds written by the receiving teller on the back of the bill or note so placed in the drawer. The prisoner was treasurer to an association called "The Ding Dong Mining Company"; and in the course of the year had many bills drawn on him by the Company, and many bills drawn on other persons remitted to him by the Company. In the month of January 1799, the prisoner had accepted bills on account of the Company, to the amount of £112, 4s. 1d. and had in his possession a bill of £166, 7s. 3d. belonging to the Company, but which was not due until the 9th February. One of the bills, amounting to £100, which the prisoner had accepted, became due on 18th January. Mr. William Gilbert, a grocer, in the surry-road, Black-friars, kept his cash at the banking-house of the prosecutors, and on the 18th January 1799, he sent his servant, George Cock, to pay in £137. This sum consisted of £122 in Bank-notes, and the rest in cash. One of these Bank-notes was the note which the prisoner was indicted for stealing. The prisoner received this money from George Cock, and after entering the £137 in Mr. Gilbert's Bank-book, entered the £15 cash in his own money-book, and put over the £22 in Bank-notes into the drawer behind him, keeping back the £100 Bank-note, which he put into his pocket, and afterwards paid to a banker's clerk the same day at a clearing-house in Lombard-street, in discharge of the £100 bill which he had accepted on account of the Ding Dong Mining Company. To make the sum in Mr. Gilbert's Bank-book, and the sum in the book of the banking-house agree, it appeared that a unit had been added to the entry of £37 to the credit of Mr. Gilbert, in the book of the banking-house, but it did not appear by any direct proof that this alteration had been made by the prisoner; it appeared however that he had made a confession, but the confession having been obtained under a promise of favour it was not given in evidence.

Const and Jackson, the prisoner's Counsel, submitted to the Court, that to constitute a larceny, it was necessary in point of law that the property should be taken from the possession of the prosecutor, but that it was clear from the evidence in this case, that the Bank-note charged to have been stolen, never was either in the actual or the constructive possession of Esdaile and Hammett, and that even if it had been in their possession, yet that from the manner in which it had been secreted by the prisoner, it amounted only to a breach of trust.

The Court left the facts of the case to the consideration of the Jury, and on their finding the prisoner Guilty, the case was reserved for the opinion of the Twelve Judges on a question, whether under the circumstances above stated, the taking of the Bank-note was in law a felonious taking, or only a fraudulent breach of trust.

The case was accordingly argued before nine of the Judges (Lord Kenyon, L. C. J.; C. J. Eyre, C. B. Macdonald, Mr. Baron Hotham, Mr. B. Perryn, Mr. Baron Thompson, Mr. J. Grose, Mr. J. Lawrence, Mr. J. Rooke) in the Exchequer Chamber, on Saturday, 27th April 1799, by Const for the prisoner, and by Fielding for the Crown. . . .

The Judges, it is said, were of opinion, upon the authority of Rex v. Waite, that this Bank-note never was in the legal custody or possession of the prosecutors, Messrs. Esdailes and Hammett; but no opinion was ever publicly delivered [a]; and the prisoner was included in the Secretary of State's letter as a proper object for a pardon.

(In consequence of this case the statute 39 Geo. III, c. 85 was passed, entitled: "An Act to protect Masters and others against Embezzlement, by their Clerks or Servants." The scope of embezzlement has been greatly enlarged by subsequent enactments—both in England and in this country.)

REX v. SULLENS

Court for Crown Cases Reserved, 1826.
1 Moody 129, 168 Eng.Rep. 1212.

The prisoner was tried before Alexander C. B., at the Spring Assizes for the county of Essex, in the year 1826, on an indictment at common law: the first count of which charged the prisoner with stealing at Doddinghurst, on the 25th September, 1825, one promissory note, value £5, the property of Thomas Nevill and George Nevill, his master; the second count with stealing silver coin, the property of Thomas Nevill and George Nevill.

It appeared in evidence that Thomas Nevill, the prisoner's master, gave him a £5 country note, to get change, on the said 25th of September; that he got change, all in silver, and on his obtaining the change he said it was for his master, and that his master sent him. The prisoner never returned.

The jury found the prisoner not guilty on the first count, but guilty on the second count.

The question reserved for the consideration of the Judges was, whether the conviction was proper, or whether the indictment should not have been on the statute 39 Geo. III. c. 85, for embezzlement?

In Easter Term, 1826, the Judges met and considered this case, and held that the conviction was wrong, because as the masters never had possession of the change, except by the hands of the prisoner, he

a. On consultation among the Judges, some doubt was at first entertained but at last all assembled agreed that it was not felony, inasmuch as the note was never in the possession of the bankers, distinct from the possession of the prisoner: though it would have been otherwise if the prisoner had deposited it in the drawer, and had afterwards taken it. (Vide Chipchase's case, ante, p. 699.) And they thought that this was not to be differed from the cases of Rex v. Waite, ante, p. 28, and Rex v. Bull, ante, p. 841, which turned on this consideration, that the thing was not taken by the prisoner out of the possession of the owner: and here it was delivered into the possession of the prisoner. That although to many purposes the note was in the actual possession of the masters, yet it was also in the actual possession of the servant, and that possession not to be impeached; for it was a lawful one. Eyre, C. J. also observed that the cases ran into one another very much, and were hardly to be distinguished: That in the case of Rex v. Spears, ante, p. 825, the corn was in the possession of the master under the care of the servant: and Lord Kenyon said that he relied much on the Act of Parliament respecting the Bank not going further than to protect the Bank. 2 East, C.L. 574.

was only amenable under the statute 39 Geo. III. c. 85. (Rex v. Headge, Russ & Ry. C. C. R. 160; Rex. v. Walsh, ib. 215.)

COMMONWEALTH v. RYAN

Supreme Judicial Court of Massachusetts, 1892.
155 Mass. 523, 30 N.E. 364.

HOLMES, J. This is a complaint for embezzlement of money. The case for the government is as follows. The defendant was employed by one Sullivan to sell liquor for him in his store. Sullivan sent two detectives to the store, with marked money of Sullivan's, to make a feigned purchase from the defendant. One detective did so. The defendant dropped the money into the money drawer of a cash register, which happened to be open in connection with another sale made and registered by the defendant, but he did not register this sale, as was customary, and afterward—it would seem within a minute or two—he took the money from the drawer. The question presented is whether it appears, as matter of law, that the defendant was not guilty of embezzlement, but was guilty of larceny, if of anything. The defendant asked rulings to that effect on two grounds: first, that after the money was put into the drawer it was in Sullivan's possession, and therefore the removal of it was a trespass and larceny; . . .

We must take it as settled that it is not larceny for a servant to convert property delivered to him by a third person for his master, provided he does so before the goods have reached their destination, or something more has happened to reduce him to a mere custodian; while, on the other hand, if the property is delivered to the servant by his master, the conversion is larceny.

This distinction is not very satisfactory, but it is due to historical accidents in the development of the criminal law, coupled, perhaps with an unwillingness on the part of the judges to enlarge the limits of a capital offence. . . .

. . . It was settled by St. 21 Hen. VIII. c. 7, that the conversion of goods delivered to a servant by his master was felony, and this statute has been thought to be only declaratory of the common law in later times, since the distinction between the possession of a bailee and the custody of a servant has been developed more fully, on the ground that the custody of the servant is the possession of the master. . . . But probably when the act was passed it confirmed the above mentioned doubt as to the master's possession where the servant was intrusted with property at a distance from his master's house in cases outside the statute, that is, when the chattels were delivered by a third person. In Dyer, 5a, 5b, it was said that it was not within the statute if an apprentice ran off with the money received from a third person for his master's goods at a fair, because he had it not by the delivery of his master. This, very likely, was correct, because the statute only dealt with delivery by the master; but the case was taken before long as authority for the broader proposition that the act is not a felony, and the reason was invented to account for it that the servant has possession, because the money is delivered to him. 1 Hale, P.C. 667, 668. This phrase about delivery seems to have been used first in an attempt to distinguish between servants and bailees; Y.B. 13 Edw. IV. 10, pl. 5; Moore, 248; but as used here it is a perverted remnant of the old and now exploded notion that a servant away from his master's house always has possession. The old case of the servant converting a horse with which his master had intrusted him to go to market was stated and explained in the same way, on the ground that the horse was delivered to the servant. Crompton, Just. 35b, pl. 7. See The King v. Bass, 1 Leach, (4th ed.) 251. Yet the emptiness of the explanation was shown by the fact that it still was held felony when the master delivered property for service in his own house. Kelyng 35. The last step was for the principle thus qualified and explained to be applied to a delivery by a third person to a servant in his master's shop, although it is possible at least that the case would have been decided differently in the time of the Year Books; Y.B. 2 Edw. IV. 15, pl. 7; Fitzh.Nat.Brev. 91 E; and although it is questionable whether on sound theory the possession is not as much in the master as if he had delivered the property himself. . . .

The last mentioned decisions made it necessary to consider with care what more was necessary, and what was sufficient, to reduce the servant to the position of a mere custodian. An obvious case was when the property was finally deposited in the place of deposit provided by the master, and subject to his control, although there was some nice discussion as to what constituted such a place. . . . But it is plain that the mere physical presence of the money there for a moment is not conclusive while the servant is on the spot and has not lost his power over it; as, for instance, if the servant drops it, and instantly picks it up again. Such cases are among the few in which the actual intent of the party is legally important; for, apart from other considerations, the character in which he exercises his control depends entirely upon himself. . . .

It follows from what we have said, that the defendant's first position cannot be maintained, and that the judge was right in charging the jury that, if the defendant before he placed the money in the drawer intended to appropriate it, and with that intent simply put it in the drawer for his own convenience in keeping it for himself, that would not make his appropriation of it just afterwards larceny. The distinction may be arbitrary, but, as it does not affect the defendant otherwise than by giving him an opportunity, whichever offence he was convicted of, to contend that he should have been convicted of the other, we have the less uneasiness in applying it. . . .

Exceptions overruled.[1]

MORGAN v. COMMONWEALTH

Court of Appeals of Kentucky, 1932.
242 Ky. 713, 47 S.W.2d 543.

DIETZMAN, C. J. Appellant was convicted of the offense of grand larceny, sentenced to serve two years in the penitentiary, and appeals.

The undisputed facts in this case are these: The Western Union Telegraph Company has for a number of years maintained a local office in Irvine, Ky. In February, 1930, the appellant was put in full charge of this office. It is not clear how many employees were under him, but at least it is shown that there were a porter and a young lady employee who worked under his direction. The office was equipped with a safe. At the time appellant was put in charge of the office, the combination on this safe was reset and he was given a copy of it. Another copy of the combination was sealed in an envelope and sent to the main office of the company in Nashville, where it was placed among the archives not to be opened unless the appellant severed his connection with the company and it became necessary to ascertain what the combination was in order to get into the safe. Thus although the company could, by opening this sealed envelope, apprise itself of what the combination was, yet so long as appellant continued in its employ it remained in actual ignorance of the combination to the safe and the appellant was the only one who had actual access to the safe. Inside of the safe was a small portable steel vault or box, the keys to which were intrusted to appellant. In this steel vault or box appellant placed at night the funds which came into the office during the day, and in the morning took them out either for use as change, for deposit in bank, or to be forwarded to the company. On the morning of July 5, 1930, the safe was discovered open. Its handle and dial were broken off, and the steel vault or box which had in it approximately $90 of the funds of the company was missing. It was later discovered empty in a field near by appellant's boarding house. We shall assume for the purpose of the decision of this case, and without detailing the facts at length, that the commonwealth's

1. "The distinction between larceny by fraud and embezzlement is sometimes very close. Whether larceny is committed by fraud or whether the taker is guilty of embezzlement is determined with reference to the time when the fraudulent intent to convert the property to the taker's own use arises. If the criminal intent exists at the time of the taking of the property, it is 'larceny' but if the intent does not arise until after the defendant received possession, then it is 'embezzlement' ". Lovick v. State, 646 P.2d 1296, 1297–98 (Okl.Cr.App.1982).

Where defendant never had control over money taken although he was in charge of the store. Money was in a drop box handled exclusively by the store manager. The offense is larceny not embezzlement. State v. Stahl, 93 N.M. 62, 596 P.2d 275 (1979).

proof made out a case to go to the jury that the abstraction of the steel vault from the safe and the conversion of the funds that it contained were done by the appellant. Appellant was indicted, as stated, for the offense of grand larceny, and he insists on this appeal that his motion for a peremptory instruction should have been sustained because the proof shows that if any offense was committed it was that of embezzlement and not larceny.

The main distinction between embezzlement and larceny in cases like the instant one turns on the distinction between custody and possession. We quote from the case of Warmoth v. Commonwealth, 81 Ky. 135:

"A distinction exists where a servant has merely the custody and where he has the possession of the goods. In the former case the felonious appropriation of the goods is larceny; in the latter it is not larceny, but embezzlement. . . ."

In 20 C.J. 410, it is said: "Embezzlement differs from larceny in that it is the wrongful appropriation or conversion of property where the original taking was lawful, or with the consent of the owner, while in larceny the taking involves a trespass, and the felonious intent must exist at the time of such taking. Thus, a bailee who obtains possession of property without fraudulent intent is not guilty of larceny where he subsequently converts it. So long as he has lawful possession he cannot commit a trespass with respect to the property. But where a person enters into a contract of bailment and obtains possession of the property with felonious intent, existing at the time, to appropriate or apply the property to his own use, he is guilty of a trespass and larceny, and not embezzlement, and if one enters into a contract of bailment fraudulently, but without felonious intent, and afterward converts the property, his offense is larceny and not embezzlement. . . . Since, therefore, larceny at common law involves the element of an original wrongful taking or trespass, it cannot apply to the stealing or wrongful conversion of property by an agent or bailee, or by a servant having the possession, as distinguished from the mere custody, or by anyone else intrusted with the possession of the property; and to remedy this defect and prevent an evasion of justice in such cases, statutes of embezzlement were passed."

Under the peculiar facts of this case, we are constrained to the view that at the time the appellant converted the funds here involved (as we have assumed the evidence so establishes) he had the possession as distinguished from the custody of such funds. They were in the safe, the combination of which was known actually only by him. It was intended, in the absence of some untoward circumstance, that at least until he forwarded these funds to the company they should be in his possession. They came into his possession as the servant of the Western Union. He was in full charge of the office. It was he who locked the safe at night and it was only he who could open it in the morning. Although the company had the right to demand the funds of him at any time, and although the company could potentially enter the safe by opening the sealed envelope and apprising itself of the combination, yet it was not intended by the company that it should interfere with appellant's control and possession of the contents of this safe and the funds of the company unless and until some condition which had not occurred in this case at the time of the conversion had come to pass. It is quite manifest that the possession of these funds at the time they were converted was in the appellant and that it had not yet become that of the Western Union. This being true, the conversion amounted to an embezzlement and not larceny. Warmoth v. Commonwealth, supra. The two offenses are not degrees of one another. They are distinct offenses. Hence appellant could not be convicted of the offense of larceny when it was shown that what he did constituted embezzlement and not larceny. It follows that appellant's motion for a peremptory instruction should have been sustained. Judgment reversed, with instructions to grant the appellant a new trial in conformity with this opinion.

Whole court sitting.[1]

UNITED STATES v. BOWSER

United States Circuit Court of Appeals, Ninth Circuit, 1976.
532 F.2d 1318.

OPINION

Before BROWNING and DUNIWAY, CIRCUIT JUDGES, and CHRISTENSEN,* DISTRICT JUDGE.

CHRISTENSEN, DISTRICT JUDGE.

The larceny from the bank may have been a fake as far as the appellant and a coconspirator teller were concerned; it was very real as to the bank from which more than $5,000 of its money was taken and carried away without its consent by a third conspirator according to the proofs of the government. This distinction leads to our rejection of the primary contention on this appeal: that there was fatal variance between the allegations of the indictment based on a theory of larceny and the proof which established no more than that appellant was associated with the teller in the commission of embezzlement.

A three count indictment jointly charged Sharon Held, Robert P. Farrelly and appellant Curtis Bowser with the offenses of entering a bank with intent to commit a felony, to-wit: bank larceny, in violation

1. The manager of a service station who wrongfully appropriated the cash "bank" of the station was guilty of embezzlement. Reynolds v. People, 172 Colo. 137, 471 P.2d 417 (1970).

* Honorable A. Sherman Christensen, Senior United States District Judge for the District of Utah, sitting by designation.

of 18 U.S.C.A. § 2113(a),[1] bank larceny in violation of 18 U.S.C. § 2113(b),[2] and conspiracy to commit bank larceny in violation of 18 U.S.C. § 371.[3] Upon arraignment each defendant entered a plea of not guilty. Thereafter, Farrelly and Held withdrew such pleas and entered pleas of guilty to count three of the indictment, the other counts being dismissed as to them. Appellant stood trial before a jury and was convicted and sentenced on all three counts.

The evidence adduced by the government, in the light of appellant's testimony and the other evidence he presented as to his claimed alibi, was ample to prove that he, Held and Farrelly conspired to take money from the Crocker Bank, 1 Montgomery Street, San Francisco, California, through feigned intimidation of Held as teller of the bank; that pursuant to their plan appellant waited outside in a getaway car and Farrelly entered the bank and handed Held a note demanding money under threat of bodily harm; [4] that Held delivered the sum of $5,158.37 of the bank's funds to Farrelly, who placed the money into a dark attache case he had carried with him into the bank; that Farrelly then joined appellant in the getaway car, and that Held waited moments after Farrelly left her window, then told a superior in the bank that she had been robbed and produced the note.

Appellant claims here, as he maintained below, that he was charged under the wrong statutes; that the basis of the indictment should have been embezzlement by an employee of an insured bank in violation of 18 U.S.C. § 656,[5] and for this reason his conviction must be reversed.

There would be a certain poetic justice in rejecting this contention out of hand by taking the conspirators at their word that this was, indeed, a trespassory taking under threat of violence, as documented by the note handed to the teller. But we have looked deeper to assure ourselves that the substance of the circumstances as well as their form warranted the charges as laid.

1. Whoever enters . . . any bank . . . with intent to commit in such bank . . . any felony affecting such bank . . . and in violation of any statute of the United States, or any larceny—

Shall be fined not more than $5,000 or imprisoned not more than twenty years, or both.

2. Whoever takes and carries away, with intent to steal or purloin, any property or money . . . exceeding $100 belonging to, or in the care, custody, control, management, or possession of any bank . . . shall be fined not more than $5,000 or imprisoned not more than ten years, or both. . . .

3. If two or more persons conspire either to commit any offense against the United States, or to defraud the United States, or any agency thereof in any manner or for any purpose, and one or more of such persons do any act to effect the object of the conspiracy, each shall be fined not more than $10,000 or imprisoned not more than five years, or both.

4. "This is a robbery, give me large bills only. I am not alone, cooperate or I will shoot."

5. Whoever, being an . . . employee of . . . any . . . national bank or insured bank . . . embezzles, abstracts, purloins or willfully misapplies any of the moneys . . . of such bank . . . shall be fined not more than $5,000 or imprisoned not more than five years, or both . . . .

As we view it, it is much less realistic to think that appellant and Farrelly aided and abetted Held in embezzlement than that Held's cooperative compliance made it easier for them to accomplish larceny. It may be conceded that up to a point Held was lawfully in possession of the funds as a trusted employee of the bank. But in turning over the bank's money to one obviously entitled to neither its benefits nor its possession, Held was not representing the bank but was acting adversely to it by aiding in accomplishing a trespassory taking and carrying away of bank property.

Perhaps from as early as *The Carrier's Case* in 1473,[6] most common law courts would have thought the circumstances sufficient to establish the offense of larceny. We need not be troubled by the idea of feigned or sham crimes which have been of concern in other contexts [7] since, as we observed at the beginning, the offense of larceny was real and unconsented to as far as the bank was concerned. To establish that the gist of the present case is bank larceny pure and simple, resort need not be had to any expansion of the statute in question by reference to legislative history or general purpose.[8] The authorities primarily relied upon by appellant, LeMasters v. United States, 378 F.2d 262 (9th Cir.1967), and Bennett v. United States, 399 F.2d 740 (9th Cir.1968), demonstrate the significant distinctions.

In *LeMasters* the defendant was charged with bank larceny in claimed violation of § 2113(b) and with related offenses, as in the present case. However, in that case the facts in no way suggested a trespassory taking.[9] In *Bennett* a similar conclusion was reached because the bank intended to part with its funds and there was no taking or carrying away with intent to steal or purloin.[10]

6. Y. B. Pasch., 13 Edw. 4, f. 9, pl. 5 (1473), 64 Selden Soc'y 30 (1945), see Fletcher, The Metamorphosis of Larceny, 89 Harv.L.Rev. 469, 481 (1976).

7. Fletcher, The Metamorphosis of Larceny, supra, note 6, at 491–96.

8. Cf. United States v. Turley, 352 U.S. 407, 77 S.Ct. 397, 1 L.Ed.2d 430 (1957), which deals with the Dyer Act. The rationale of *Turley* which interpreted the word "stolen" so as not to limit it to situations which at common law would be considered larceny was considered in reference to the statute here in question and rejected in LeMasters v. United States, 378 F.2d 262 (9th Cir. 1967).

9. In *LeMasters,* ". . . the appellant succeeded in persuading a teller, acting as such, at the bank that he was Tournour, that he had lost his savings account pass book, that the bank should issue him a new pass book, of course in the name of Tournour." 378 F.2d at 263. Tournour had not given the appellant any authority to withdraw any money, but appellant succeeded in obtaining the money by signing Tournour's name to a withdrawal slip and thus duping the bank. There was no federal law against obtaining money under false pretenses. A judgment of conviction was reversed by this court because a trespassory taking had not been shown.

10. The defendant as an intermediary in procuring a loan, obtained a check from a borrower for $8,000 which he presented to the bank in which he was an officer for a cashier's check made out to himself. Then he deposited the check to his own account and wrongfully converted the proceeds. This court held that he was not guilty of bank larceny, although the money was obtained unlawfully either through employees of the bank or by acts of the defendant constituting the taking of property by false pretenses.

United States v. Brown, 455 F.2d 1201 (9th Cir.), cert. denied, 406 U.S. 960, 92 S.Ct. 2069, 32 L.Ed.2d 347 (1972), is more in point. Wells Fargo Bank in Oakland, California, had been robbed of approximately $6500. Mrs. Hoff, the victimized teller, reported the incident and furnished a description of the robber to the FBI. After further investigation and questioning, Mrs. Hoff admitted her involvement in the crime, contending that she was forced to take part. She was indicted, but the charges against her were dismissed in exchange for her testimony against the codefendants who were convicted of bank larceny. At the trial and on appeal, among other things, the latter contended that the evidence did not support the crime of larceny; they argued that because of Mrs. Hoff's position as a trusted employee of the bank, the most they were guilty of was embezzlement. This court held that "[r]egardless of Mrs. Hoff's status, the evidence establishes the requisite intent coupled with a trespassory taking sufficient to constitute larceny." Id. at 1204.

The appellant here attempts to draw some significant distinctions by pointing out that in *Brown* the teller cooperated with the robbers out of fear of exposure of her indiscretions to her husband if she did not participate while Sharon Held in this case admitted that she was a willing participant. Subjective motivations of a conspirator cannot carry such decisive consequences in the present context. Whether through fear, blackmail, intimidation, persuasion, love, avarice, hunger, or complex combinations of other forces to which the human mind may be subjected, the fact remains that in both cases there was a trespassory taking as against the bank whose consent could not be constructed out of the adverse conduct of the teller, however, motivated. There was no variance between allegations and proof in this case any more than in *Brown*. . . .

Affirmed.[1]

(C) TAKING

THOMPSON v. STATE

Supreme Court of Alabama, 1891.
94 Ala. 535, 10 So. 520.

Indictment for larceny from the person. The opinion states the material facts. Charge No. 1, asked and refused, was in these words: "The jury must believe, beyond a reasonable doubt, that the defendant got the money into his hand, or actual possession of it, before they can convict him of larceny."

1. The federal bank robbery statute, 18 U.S.C. § 2113(b), which imposes a criminal sanction on anyone who "takes and carries away" bank property with intent to steal, applies to common law larcenies as well as obtaining by false pretenses if there is a "carrying away." Bell v. United States, ___ U.S. ___, 103 S.Ct. 2398 (1983).

WALKER, J. The witness for the State testified that he held out his open hand with two silver dollars therein, showing the money to the defendant; that the defendant struck witness' hand, and the money was either knocked out of his hand or was taken by the defendant, he could not tell positively which. It was after twelve o'clock at night, and the witness did not see the money, either in defendant's possession or on the ground. The court charged the jury: "If the jury find from the evidence that the defendant, with a felonious intent, grabbed for the money, but did not get it, but only knocked it from the owner's hand with a felonious intent, this would be a sufficient carrying away of the money, although defendant never got possession at any time of said money." This charge was erroneous. To constitute larceny, there must be a felonious taking and carrying away of personal property. There must be such a caption that the accused acquires dominion over the property, followed by such an asportation or carrying away as to supersede the possession of the owner for an appreciable period of time. Though the owner's possession is disturbed, yet the offense is not complete if the accused fails to acquire such dominion over the property as to enable him to take actual custody or control. It is not enough that the money was knocked out of the owner's hand, if it fell to the ground and the defendant never got possession of it. The defendant was not guilty of larceny, if he did not get the money under his control. If the attempt merely caused the money to fall from the owner's hand to the ground, and the defendant ran off without getting it, the larceny was not consummated, as the dominion of the trespasser was not complete. Charge No. 1 was a proper statement of the law as applicable to the evidence above referred to, and it should have been given.

Reversed and remanded.

CUMMINS v. COMMONWEALTH

Kentucky Court of Appeals, 1883.
5 Ky.L.Rep. 200.

The appellant, Cummins, according to the evidence, told Sweet he wished to sell him a sow and pigs, and after agreement on the price, went to where a sow and pigs were lying down on the commons and pointed them out as his, and Sweet paid him $7 in money for them and then drove them off. The sow and pigs belonged to John Flauher, who lived near by.

The appellant seems to have been out of money and resorted to this means of obtaining some to supply his wants, and then proceeded to the fair.

Having been convicted of the offense of larceny or hog stealing under the statute, the appellant has appealed, and his counsel contend that his offense was not larceny because there was no asportation *by him*, but it was obtaining money by false pretenses if anything.

He was not indicted for obtaining the $7 for the sow and pigs, but for stealing the sow and pigs. Whether his acts constituted both offenses of larceny of the hogs and obtaining money by false pretenses, for which he might be punished, need not be determined, as there has been no attempt to try him twice for the same acts.

The owner of the sow and pigs never parted with the possession or the property in them. The asportation was by the hand or physical act of Sweet, but the act of felonious taking was that of the appellant committed through Sweet, who was his instrument in committing the trespass upon the property of Flauher.

East, Hale and Hawkins, who are approved by Archbold, say that if the taking be by the hand of another, it is the same as if by the hand of the thief himself. For instance, if the thief procure a child within the age of discretion, or an idiot, to steal goods for him, such taking must be charged to him. . . .

The judgment is therefore affirmed.[1]

(D) NECESSITY OF TRESPASS

1. Cases of Fraud

Another gap that appeared during the development of the law of larceny was due to the rule that no larceny could be recognized in a transaction in which the wrongdoer acquired title to the property in question. This led to the enactment of an English statute, old enough to be common law in this country, which created the offense of obtaining property by false pretenses—often abbreviated to "false pretenses". This offense and larceny were also interpreted to be mutually exclusive.[1]

THE KING v. PEAR

Court for Crown Cases Reserved, 1779.
1 Leach 212, 168 Eng.Rep. 208.

The prisoner was indicted for stealing a black horse, the property of Samuel Finch. It appeared in evidence that Samuel Finch was a Livery-Stable-keeper in the Borough; and that the prisoner, on the 2d

1. Accord: Smith v. State, 11 Ga.App. 197, 74 S.E. 1093 (1912); State v. Hunt, 45 Iowa 673 (1877); State v. Patton, 364 Mo. 1044, 271 S.W.2d 560 (1954).

Contra: State v. Laborde, 202 La. 59, 11 So.2d 404 (1942). The court said: "Since the defendant at no time had the actual or constructive possession of the animal, the act of the purchaser in carrying it away for his own account cannot be said in legal contemplation to have been the act of the seller. The facts of the case repel any idea of implied agency, because Jeansonne unquestionably acted as a bona fide purchaser for himself."

1. "The subtle distinction which the statute was intended to remedy was this: that if a person, by fraud, induced another to part with the possession only of goods and converted them to his own use, this was larceny; while if he induced another by fraud to part with the property in [i.e., ownership of] the goods as well as the possession, this was not larceny." The Queen v. Killam, L.R. 1 C.C. 261 (1870).

of July 1779, hired the horse of him to go to Sutton, in the county of Surry, and back again, saying on being asked where he lived, that he lodged at No. 25 in King-street, and should return about eight o'clock the same evening. He did not return; and it was proved that he had sold the horse on the very day he had hired it, to one William Hollist, in Smithfield Market; and that he had no lodging at the place to which he had given the prosecutor directions.

The learned Judge said: There had been different opinions on the law of this class of cases; . . . that in the present case the horse was hired to take a journey into Surry, and the prisoner sold him the same day, without taking any such journey; that there were also other circumstances which imported that at the time of the hiring the prisoner had it in intention to sell the horse, as his saying that he lodged at a place where in fact he was not known. He therefore left it with the Jury to consider, Whether the prisoner meant at the time of the hiring to take such journey, but was afterwards tempted to sell the horse? for if so he must be acquitted; but that if they were of opinion that at the time of the hiring the journey was a mere pretence to get the horse into his possession, and he had no intention to take such journey but intended to sell the horse, they would find that fact specially for the opinion of the Judges.

The Jury found that the facts above stated were true; and also that the prisoner had hired the horse with a fraudulent view and intention of selling it immediately.

The question was referred to the Judges, Whether the delivery of the horse by the prosecutor to the prisoner, had so far changed the possession of the property, as to render the subsequent conversion of it a mere breach of trust, or whether the conversion was felonious? (see the case of Sharpless and Another, ante, page 92, case 52).

The Judges differed greatly in opinion on this case; and delivered their opinions *seriatim* upon it at Lord Chief Justice De Gray's house on 4th February 1780 and on the 22nd of the same month Mr. Baron Perryn delivered their opinion on it. The majority of them thought, That the question, as to the original intention of the prisoner in hiring the horse, had been properly left to the jury; and as they had found, that his view in so doing was fraudulent, the parting with the property had not changed the nature of the possession, but that it remained unaltered in the prosecutor at the time of the conversion; and that the prisoner was therefore guilty of felony.[1]

1. The majority held that this was "such a taking as would have made the prisoner liable to an action of trespass at the suit of the owner, . . . " 2 East P.C. 688.

In this jurisdiction the crime of larceny remains as it was at common law. Hence it requires that the taking of the property be by trespass. If the taking was fraudulent it was by trespass and the subsequent appropriation was larceny. Farlow v. State, 9 Md.App. 515, 265 A.2d 578 (1970).

THE QUEEN v. PRINCE

Court for Crown Cases Reserved, 1868.
L.R. 1 C.C. 150.

(Mrs. Allen forged her husband's signature and thereby obtained money equal to his entire deposit in the bank. She then left Allen and ran away with Prince. She gave some of this money to Prince who was convicted of knowingly receiving money stolen from the bank.)

BOVILL, C. J. I am of opinion that this conviction cannot be sustained. The distinction between larceny and false pretences is material. In larceny the taking must be against the will of the owner. That is of the essence of the offence. The cases cited by Mr. Collins on behalf of the prisoner are clear and distinct upon this point, shewing that the obtaining of property from its owner, or his servant absolutely authorized to deal with it, by false pretences will not amount to larceny. The cases cited on the other side are cases where the servant had only a limited authority from his master. Here, however, it seems to me that the bank clerk had a general authority to part with both the property in and possession of his master's money on receiving what he believed to be a genuine order, and that as he did so part with both the property in and possession of the note in question the offence committed by Mrs. Allen falls within the cases which make it a false pretence, and not a larceny, and therefore the prisoner cannot be convicted of knowingly receiving a stolen note.

CHANNEL, B. I am of the same opinion. . . .

BYLES, J. I am of the same opinion. I would merely say that I ground my judgment purely on authority.

BLACKBURN, J. I also am of the same opinion. I must say I cannot but lament that the law now stands as it does. The distinction drawn between larceny and false pretences, one being made a felony and the other a misdemeanour—and yet the same punishment attached to each—seems to me, I must confess, unmeaning and mischievous. The distinction arose in former times, and I take it that it was then held in favour of life that in larceny the taking must be against the will of the owner, larceny then being a capital offence. However, as the law now stands, if the owner intended the property to pass, though he would not so have intended had he known the real facts, that is sufficient to prevent the offence of obtaining another's property from amounting to larceny; and where the servant has an authority co-equal with his master's, and parts with his master's property, such property cannot be said to be stolen, inasmuch as the servant intends to part with the property in it. If, however, the servant's authority is limited, then he can only part with the possession, and not with the property; if he is tricked out of the possession, the offence so committed will be larceny. In Reg. v. Longstreeth [1], the carrier's servant had no authority to part with the goods, except to the right consignee. His authority was not generally to act in his master's business, but limited in that way. The offence was in that case held to be larceny on that ground, and this distinguishes it from the pawnbroker's case [2], which the same judges, or at any rate some of them, had shortly before decided. There the servant, from whom the goods were obtained, had a general authority to act for his master, and the person who obtained the goods was held not to be guilty of larceny. So, in the present case, the cashier holds the money of the bank with a general authority from the bank to deal with it. He has authority to part with it on receiving what he believes to be a genuine order. Of the genuineness he is the judge; and if under a mistake he parts with money, he none the less intends to part with the property in it, and thus the offence is not, according to the cases, larceny, but an obtaining by false pretences. The distinction is inscrutable to my mind, but it exists in the cases. There is no statute enabling a count for larceny to be joined with one for false pretences; and as the prisoner was indicted for the felony, the conviction must be quashed.

LUSH, J. I also agree that the conviction must be quashed. . . . [a]

WILKINSON v. STATE

Supreme Court of Mississippi, 1952.
215 Miss. 327, 60 So.2d 786.

[Three head of cattle belonging to Leonard had strayed and were picked up by Ferguson who was holding them for the owner, without knowing who the owner was. Some of Whittington's cattle had strayed and he went to Ferguson's farm to see the strays being held there. He ascertained that the strays were not his, but his hired hand, Wilkinson, persuaded him to claim them which he did. Ferguson delivered the cattle to Whittington and Wilkinson, believing that they belonged to Whittington. Whittington sold the cattle and gave part of the purchase money to Wilkinson.]

ETHRIDGE, JUSTICE. Appellant, Fred Wilkinson, was indicted and convicted at the January 1952 term of the Circuit Court of Franklin County of grand larceny, consisting of the theft of three head of cat-

1. [Numbered footnotes by the Court.] 1 Mood.C.C. 137.

2. Reg. v. Jackson, 1 Mood.C.C. 119.

a. See Anderson v. State, 33 Ala.App. 531, 36 So.2d 242 (1948).

It was held to be larceny if the title did not actually pass although the intention had been to pass both title and possession. English v. State, 80 Fla. 70, 85 So. 150 (1920). Contra: Rex v. Adams, Russ. & Ry. 225, 168 Eng.Rep. 773 (1812); Rex v. Atkinson, 2 East P.C. 673 (1799).

A check payable to **D**(1) was sent by mistake to **D**(2), a different person but having the same name. **D**(2), knowing it was not intended for him, indorsed his name on the back and cashed it. This was held not to be larceny but a different crime—false pretenses. Hinman v. State, 179 Miss. 503, 176 So. 264 (1937).

tle. He argues here that the conviction was against the great weight of the evidence, was based upon the uncorroborated testimony of an accomplice, and that he was indicted and convicted under the wrong statute. . . .

Secondly, the indictment was properly found under the grand larceny statute, Sec. 2240. The general rule is set forth in 32 Am.Jur., Larceny, Sec. 33: "Although there is some authority to the contrary, the better rule is that one who falsely personates another and in such assumed character receives property intended for such other person is guilty of larceny if he does so with the requisite felonious intent, provided the transaction does not involve the passing of title to the property from the owner to him. Although express statutes to this effect exist in some jurisdictions, it is larceny at common law for a person to pretend that he is the owner or person entitled to personal property in order to obtain possession thereof with the felonious intent of converting it to his own use and depriving the owner of it. Subject to this rule, one who fraudulently claims an estray from the person taking it up or lost property from the finder may be convicted of larceny."

The distinction, a rather fine one, between the crimes of obtaining property by false pretenses and that of larceny through obtaining possession by fraud seems to rest in the intention with which the owner parts with possession. Thus if the possession is obtained by fraud and the owner intends to part with his title as well as his possession, the crime is that of obtaining property by false pretenses, provided the means by which it is acquired comply therewith. But if the possession is fraudulently obtained with a present intent on the part of the person obtaining it to convert the property to his own use, and the owner intends to part with his possession merely and not with the title, the offense is larceny. . . .

At common law, for a person to pretend that he was the owner of the property in order to get possession of it with the felonious intent of converting it to his own use constituted larceny. Accordingly convictions of larceny have been sustained where a person has fraudulently claimed an estray from the person taking it up, and where a person has claimed to be the owner of lost property from the finder. . . .

The foregoing authorities support the conviction under the general grand larceny statute, Sec. 2240. The distinction rests upon the intention with which the owner or possessor parts with possession. Here the possessor of the estrays, Ferguson, obviously had no intent to part with any title to the estrays. Like Sims in the Atterberry case, Ferguson thought he was transferring simply the possession back to the true owner. This accords with the principle that if possession is fraudulently obtained, with present intent on the part of the person obtaining it, to convert the property to his own use, and the owner or possessor intends to part with his possession merely and not with the title, the offense is larceny. The crime for which appellant was convicted constitutes grand larceny both at common law and under Code Sec. 2240. . . .

McGEHEE, C. J., and LEE, KYLE and ARRINGTON, JJ., concur.[1]

REGINA v. HANDS

Court for Crown Cases Reserved, 1887.
16 Cox C.C. 188, 56 L.T. 370.

LORD COLERIDGE, C. J. In this case a person was indicted for committing a larceny from what is known as an "automatic box," which was so constructed that, if you put a penny into it and pushed a knob in accordance with the directions on the box, a cigarette was ejected on to a bracket and presented to the giver of the penny. Under these circumstances there is no doubt that the prisoners put in the box a piece of metal which was of no value, but which produced the same effect as the placing a penny in the box produced. A cigarette was ejected which the prisoners appropriated; and in a case of that class it appears to me there clearly was larceny. The means by which the cigarette was made to come out of the box were fraudulent, and the cigarette so made to come out was appropriated. . . .

2. LOST PROPERTY

REGINA v. THURBORN

Court for Crown Cases Reserved, 1848.
1 Den. 387, 169 Eng.Rep. 293.

The prisoner was tried before PARKE, B., at the Summer Assizes for Huntingdon, 1848, for stealing a bank note.

He found the note, which had been accidentally dropped on the high road. There was no name or mark on it, indicating who was the

1. "Although the crimes of larceny by trick and obtaining property under false pretenses are very similar, there is a distinction which the statutes and case law clearly draw between the two crimes.

The distinction turns on the intent of the victim in parting with the property. . . .

The absence of an intent on the part of the cashiers to knowingly and voluntarily transfer possession or title to any money in excess of that received places the defendant's conduct within the ambit of larceny rather than the ambit of obtaining property under false pretenses." People v. Long, 93 Mich.App. 579, 286 N.W.2d 909, 910–911 (1980). The Michigan Supreme Court reversed on the application of the facts to the law observing:

"The creation of the offense of false pretenses by statute had its historical origins in the lawmaker's need to fill a void in the common law which existed by virtue of the fact that common-law larceny did not extend to punish the party who, without taking and carrying away, had obtained both possession and title to another's property. Against this historical background, our Legislature early chose to recognize the offense. The conduct charged against defendant falls within the legislatively recognized category; thus marked, it is distinct from larceny." People v. Long, 409 Mich. 346, 294 N.W.2d 197, 200 (Mich.1980).

owner, nor were there any circumstances attending the finding which would enable him to discover to whom the note belonged when he picked it up; nor had he any reason to believe that the owner knew where to find it again. The prisoner meant to appropriate it to his own use, when he picked it up. The day after, and before he had disposed of it, he was informed that the prosecutor was the owner, and had dropped it accidentally; he then changed it, and appropriated the money taken to his own use. The jury found that he had reason to believe, and did believe it to be the prosecutor's property, before he thus changed the note.

The learned Baron directed a verdict of guilty, intimating that he should reserve the case for further consideration. Upon conferring with Maule J., the learned Baron was of opinion that the original taking was not felonious, and that in the subsequent disposal of it, there was no taking, and he therefore declined to pass sentence, and ordered the prisoner to be discharged, on entering into his own recognizance to appear when called upon.

On the 30th of April, A.D. 1849, the following judgment was read by Parke B.

A case was reserved by Parke B. at the last Huntingdon Assizes. It was not argued by counsel, but the Judges who attended the sitting of the Court after Michaelmas Term, 1848, namely, the L. C. Baron, Patteson J., Rolfe B., Cresswell J., Williams J., Coltman J., and Parke B., gave it much consideration on account of its importance, and the frequency of the occurrence of cases in some degree similar, in the administration of the criminal law, and the somewhat obscure state of the authorities upon it. [The learned Baron here stated the case.] . . .

The result of these authorities is, that the rule of law on this subject seems to be, that if a man find goods that have been actually lost, or are reasonably supposed by him to have been lost, and appropriates them, with intent to take the entire dominion over them, really believing when he takes them, that the owner cannot be found, it is not larceny. But if he takes them with the like intent, though lost, or reasonably supposed to be lost, but reasonably believing that the owner can be found, it is larceny.

In applying this rule, as indeed in the application of all fixed rules, questions of some nicety may arise, but it will generally be ascertained whether the person accused had reasonable belief that the owner could be found, by evidence of his previous acquaintance with the ownership of the particular chattel, the place where it is found, or the nature of the marks upon it. In some cases it would be apparent, in others appear only after examination.

It would probably be presumed that the taker would examine the chattel as an honest man ought to do, at the time of taking it, and if he did not restore it to the owner, the jury might conclude that he took it, when he took complete possession of it, *animo furandi.* The mere taking it up to look at it, would not be a taking possession of the chattel.

To apply these rules to the present case; the first taking did not amount to larceny, because the note was really lost, and there was no mark on it or other circumstance to indicate then who was the owner, or that he might be found, nor any evidence to rebut the presumption that would arise from the finding of the note as proved, that he believed the owner could not be found, and therefore the original taking was not felonious; and if the prisoner had changed the note or otherwise disposed of it, before notice of the title of the real owner, he clearly would not have been punishable; but after the prisoner was in possession of the note, the owner became known to him, and he then appropriated it, *amino furandi,* and the point to be decided is whether that was a felony.

Upon this question we have felt considerable doubt.

If he had taken the chattel innocently, and afterwards appropriated it without knowledge of the ownership, it would not have been larceny, nor would it, we think, if he had done so, knowing who was the owner, for he had the lawful possession in both cases, and the conversion would not have been a trespass in either. But here the original taking was not innocent in one sense, and the question is, does that make a difference? We think not, it was dispunishable as we have already decided, and though the possession was accompanied by a dishonest intent, it was still a lawful possession and good against all but the real owner, and the subsequent conversion was not therefore a trespass in this case more than the others, and consequently no larceny.

We therefore think that the conviction was wrong.[1]

BROOKS v. STATE

Supreme Court of Ohio, 1878.
35 Ohio St. 46.

(Charles B. Newton lost a $200 roll of bank bills. Notice of the loss was published in a newspaper. Nearly a month later George Brooks found the money in the street. There is no evidence that he had seen the published notice or knew of Newton's loss, but he was with other workmen at the time and took pains not to let them know of his find. He appropriated the money shortly thereafter. He was convicted of larceny.)

1. One who appropriated a coat he found on a bench is not guilty of larceny if the original taking was with intent to restore it to the owner. Milburne's Case, 1 Lewin 251, 168 Eng.Rep. 1030 (1829).

"Under the common law, the person last in possession of property retains constructive possession until he abandons it, gives it to another person, or until another person otherwise acquires actual possession." United States v. Sellers, 670 F.2d 853, 854 (9th Cir. 1982).

WHITE, J. We find no ground in the record for reversing the judgment.

The first instruction asked was properly refused. It was not necessary to the conviction of the accused that he should, at the time of taking possession of the property, have known, or have had reason to believe he knew, the *particular person* who owned it, or have had the means of identifying him *instanter*. The charge asked was liable to this construction, and there was no error in its refusal.

The second instruction asked was substantially given in the general charge.

Larceny may be committed of property that is casually lost as well as of that which is not. The title to the property, and its constructive possession, still remains in the owner; and the finder, if he takes possession of it for his own use, and not for the benefit of the owner, would be guilty of trespass, unless the circumstances were such as to show that it had been abandoned by the owner.

The question is, under what circumstances does such property become the subject of larceny by the finder?

In Baker v. The State, 29 Ohio St. 184, the rule stated by Baron Parke, in Thurborn's case, was adopted. It was there laid down, that "when a person finds goods that have actually been lost, and takes possession with intent to appropriate them to his own use, really believing, at the time, or having good ground to believe, that the owner can be found, it is larceny."

It must not be understood from the rule, as thus stated, that the finder is bound to use diligence or to take pains in making search for the owner.[1] His belief, or grounds of belief, in regard to finding the owner, is not to be determined by the degree of diligence that he might be able to use to accomplish that purpose, but by the circumstances apparent to him at the time of finding the property. If the property has not been abandoned by the owner, it is the subject of larceny by the finder, when, at the time he finds it, he has reasonable ground to believe, from the nature of the property, or the circumstances under which it is found, that if he does not conceal but deals honestly with it, the owner will appear or be ascertained. But before the finder can be guilty of larceny, the intent to steal the property must have existed at the time he took it into his possession. . . .[2]

Judgment affirmed.

1. Some of the statutes require diligence on the part of the finder if the circumstances of the finding suggest a means of inquiry. See West's Ann.Cal. Pen.Code § 485 (1970).

2. Regina v. Shea, 7 Cox C.C. 147 (1856).

"For a person to be guilty of the common law offense of misappropriation of lost property, two elements must coexist at the time the finder discovers the lost property. The finder must intend to convert the property absolutely to his own use. Secondly, the circumstances surrounding the finding must afford some reasonable clues for determining the identity of the rightful owner." State v. Campbell, 536 P.2d 105, 110 (Alaska, 1975).

OKEY, J. I do not think the plaintiff was properly convicted. A scavenger, while in the performance of his duties in cleaning the streets, picked up from the mud and water in the gutter, a roll of money, consisting of bank bills of the denominations of five, ten, and twenty dollars, and amounting, in the aggregate, to two hundred dollars. It had lain there several weeks, and the owner had ceased to make search for it. The evidence fails to show that the plaintiff had any information of a loss previous to the finding, and in his testimony he denied such notice. There was no mark on the money to indicate the owner, nor was there any thing in the attending circumstances pointing to one owner more than another. He put the money in his pocket, without calling the attention of his fellow-workmen to the discovery, and afterward, on the same day, commenced applying it to his own use.

No doubt the plaintiff was morally bound to take steps to find the owner. An honest man would not thus appropriate money, before he had made the finding public, and endeavored to find the owner. But in violating the moral obligation, I do not think the plaintiff incurred criminal liability. . . .

GILMORE, C. J., concurs in the dissenting opinion.

STATE v. KAUFMAN

Supreme Court of North Dakota, 1981.
310 N.W.2d 709.

PAULSON, JUSTICE. Frank Kaufman was convicted in the Stutsman County Court of Increased Jurisdiction of theft of property lost, mislaid, or delivered by mistake, under § 12.1–23–04 of the North Dakota Century Code, and was sentenced to serve six months in the Stutsman County jail with $2^1/_2$ months suspended, pay a $100 fine and $79.75 in restitution. Kaufman appeals his conviction and sentence. We affirm.

In November and December, 1980, the Jamestown West End Hide and Fur Company, a junk dealership, purchased several large rolls of scrap copper wire from Otter Tail Power Company. This wire was stored in the hide and fur company's open yard. In early December, 1980, Mr. Archie Oster, a partner in the company, noticed that several rolls of wire were missing. In checking with the manager of Porter Brothers, another junk dealership in the area, Oster learned that a similar roll of wire had been purchased by Porter Brothers on December 4, 1980, from Frank Kaufman. At trial, Oster identified the wire that Porter Brothers had purchased from Kaufman as the same wire which had been missing from the hide and fur company's yard.

Jack Miller, Deputy Sheriff of Stutsman County, testified that he had contacted Kaufman during his investigation of the theft and that Kaufman had stated that he found the wire "out by Windsor". The trial judge found Kaufman guilty of theft of property "lost, mislaid, or delivered by mistake", § 12.1–23–04, N.D.C.C., and sentenced him to six months in the Stutsman County jail, with 2½ months suspended, and that he pay a $100 fine and $79.75 in restitution. Kaufman appeals his conviction and sentence.

Three issues are presented on appeal:

1. Is property which is stolen and later abandoned by the thief "lost" for the purpose of § 12.1–23–04, N.D.C.C., which makes appropriation of "lost" property unlawful?
2. Was the evidence sufficient to support the conviction? . . .

I

Kaufman's first contention is that the copper wire was stolen from the hide and fur company's yard, and, therefore, was not "lost" and could not be the basis of a prosecution under § 12.1–23–04, N.D. C.C., which provides:

> "*12.1–23–04. Theft of property lost, mislaid, or delivered by mistake.*—A person is guilty of theft if he:
>
> "1. Retains or disposes of property of another when he knows it has been lost or mislaid; or
>
> "2. Retains or disposes of property of another when he knows it has been delivered under a mistake as to the identity of the recipient or as to the nature or amount of the property,
>
> and with intent to deprive the owner of it, he fails to take readily available and reasonable measures to restore the property to a person entitled to have it."

Although this court has never previously been presented with this issue, courts in other jurisdictions have indicated that property which is stolen and abandoned by the thief is indeed "lost" to the original owner. For example, in Automobile Insurance Co. of Hartford v. Kirby, 25 Ala.App. 245, 144 So. 123 (1932), that Court stated that "when property is stolen and is afterwards abandoned by the thief at a place unknown to the owner, such property is lost within the meaning of our statute". Id. 144 So. at 124.

Although Title 12.1, N.D.C.C., does not provide a definition of "lost", this court has previously discussed the term. In State v. Brewster, 72 N.D. 409, 7 N.W.2d 742 (1943), the court, in discussing a predecessor to § 12.1–23–04, N.D.C.C., noted that "The term 'lost' is concerned with *the involuntary change of location or inability to find*". *Brewster,* supra 7 N.W.2d at 744 (emphasis added). Applying this definition to the evidence in the instant case, it is clear that the location of the hide and fur company's wire had been changed and it could not be found by the company at the time that Kaufman found it. We therefore conclude that the stolen wire was "lost" when Kaufman found it.

Support is lent to this conclusion by the anomalous result which would follow from the interpretation of the statute urged by Kaufman. Kaufman would have this court hold that stolen property abandoned by the thief is not lost and, therefore, cannot be the basis for prosecution under § 12.1–23–04, N.D.C.C. If this interpretation were adopted, a person who found property, believing it to be lost or mislaid, and who thereafter sold it or otherwise deprived the owner of possession might escape prosecution merely because, unbeknownst to him, the property had previously been stolen from the true owner.

Such a result would be contrary to the purpose of Chapter 12.1–23, N.D.C.C. Section 12.1–23–04 was adopted verbatim from § 1734 of the Final Report of the National Commission on Reform of Federal Criminal Laws. This court has previously indicated that the Commission's Working Papers may be considered when construing provisions of North Dakota's Criminal Code. The Comment to § 1734 indicates that the intent behind such section is to make the appropriation of found or discovered property constitute theft:

> "The point, of course, is that the actor is just as culpable if he intends to appropriate property he knows to belong to another whether he takes it, finds it, or discovers it as it is being mistakenly delivered to him. And it is just as clear that the extent of his criminal liability should not turn on technical differences between whether the money was lost, mislaid, or simply placed somewhere for safekeeping. This, in any event, is the premise of the proposal to make appropriation of found or discovered property theft just like any other kind of theft." [Working Papers of the National Commission on Reform of Federal Criminal Laws, Vol. II, p. 939 (1970)].

A result which would relieve a person from criminal liability simply because of the occurrence of a fortuitous act such as an unknown prior theft of the property would defeat the purpose of the statute.

We hold that property which is stolen and later abandoned by the thief is "lost" for the purposes of § 12.1–23–04, N.D.C.C., making appropriation of lost property unlawful.

II

Kaufman also contends that the evidence at trial was insufficient to support a verdict of guilty of the crime charged. Specifically, he contends that the State failed to prove that the copper wire which he sold to Porter Brothers was the "property of another", and that the State failed to prove that he knew the property was lost or mislaid.

We have consistently held that a verdict based upon circumstantial evidence is accorded the same presumption of correctness as other verdicts and will not be disturbed on appeal unless the verdict is unwarranted. The role of the Supreme Court on appeal is to merely review the record to determine if there is competent evidence which allowed the factfinder to draw an inference reasonably tending to prove guilt and fairly warranting a conviction. . . .

Affirmed.[1]

3. Delivery by Mistake

COOPER v. COMMONWEALTH

Court of Appeals of Kentucky, 1901.
110 Ky. 123, 60 S.W. 938.

Opinion of the Court by JUDGE O'REAR. Reversing.

Appellants, Grant Cooper, Fred Cooper, Thomas Harris and Sandy Waggener, were convicted in the Union Circuit Court of the crime of grand larceny, under the following state of facts: The four named had been shucking corn, and were paid $6 for their services. In order to divide the money equally among themselves, they went to the Bank of Uniontown to have $2 of the money changed into smaller denominations. Appellant, Sandy Waggener, went into the bank and to the cashier's counter, handed him the $2 and asked for the change. The cashier handed him two half dollars and a roll of small-sized coin wrapped in paper saying, "There are twenty nickels." Waggener, without unwrapping the coins, and not knowing what was in the paper, except from the statement of the cashier, rejoined his companions; and the four together went a distance of some four squares, to a more secluded spot, to divide their money. On opening the package they discovered it contained twenty 5-dollar gold coins, instead of nickels. Waggener remarked, "Boys, banks don't correct mistakes," and the money was divided among the four and appropriated by them. Upon this evidence the court gave the jury the following instruction: "If you believe from the evidence, to the exclusion of a reasonable doubt, that in this county, and prior to the finding of the indictment herein, the defendants, Grant Cooper, Fred Cooper and Thos. Harris and Sandy Waggener, sought to have some money changed at the Bank of Uniontown in order to get twenty nickels, or some small change, and that Chas. Kelleners, the assistant cashier of said bank, in making said change delivered by mistake to the defendants twenty five-dollar gold pieces, wrapped in a paper, believing at the time that he was giving them twenty nickels, and that the defendants, sharing in that belief, shortly thereafter opened said paper, and found therein twenty five-dollar gold pieces, and failed to return said gold pieces to said bank—now, if you further believe from the evidence, to the exclusion of a reasonable doubt, that when said defendants unwrapped said paper, and found therein, and in their possession, the said five-dollar gold pieces, they knew that same had been delivered to them by said Kelleners through mistake, and knew or

1. See Harris v. State, 207 Miss. 241, 42 So.2d 183 (1949); Long v. State, 33 Ala.App. 334, 33 So.2d 382 (1949).

had the means of ascertaining that the bank was the owner of said gold pieces, but thereupon nevertheless feloniously converted the same to their own use, intending to premanently [sic] deprive the owner thereof, you will find them guilty as charged; and in your verdict you will fix their punishment at confinement in the penitentiary for not less than one nor more than five years." Appellants objected to the foregoing, and asked the court to give the jury these instructions: "(a) The court instructs the jury that, to find the defendants guilty of larceny, they must believe that at the time they received the money from Chas. Kelleners they must have then had the purpose and intent to convert the excess which they received over and above what was justly due them as change to their own use and benefit, and to deprive the bank of its money feloniously; that, unless the felonious intent was proven at the time of receiving the money, the law is for the defendants, and the jury will so find. (b) The court instructs the jury that the felonious intent must exist at the time of receiving the money, and that no felonious intent, subsequent or wrongful conversion, will amount to a felony"—which were rejected by the court.

It was held in Elliott v. Com., 12 Bush 176, that where the possession of the goods was obtained by the accused for a particular purpose, with the intent then, however, on the part of the accused, to convert them to his own use, which he subsequently did, it would constitute larceny. In Snapp v. Com., 82 Ky. 173, we held that, where money came into the hands of the accused lawfully, his subsequent felonious conversion would not be larceny. In the last-named case the court said it devolved upon the Commonwealth to show an unlawful taking of this money from the city (the owner) by the accused with a felonious intent, and that "the money had been received without fraud and as a matter of right, and in such a case, although he may have the *animus furandi* afterwards, and convert it to his own use, he was not guilty of larceny." In Smith v. Com., 96 Ky. 85, 87, 27 S.W. 852, this court announced, "The general and common-law rule is that when property comes lawfully into the possession of a person, either as agent, bailee, part owner, or otherwise, a subsequent appropriation of it is not larceny, unless the intent to appropriate it existed in the mind of the taker at the time it came into his hands." Whart.Cr.Law, section 958, says, "To constitute larceny in receiving an overpayment, the defendant must know at the time of the overpayment, and must intend to steal." The authorities seem to be agreed that, to constitute the crime of larceny, there must be a simultaneous combination of an unlawful taking, an asportation, and a felonious intent.

We conclude that the instructions asked by appellants should have been given to the jury, and that the idea expressed in the first instruction given—that if appellants received the money under a mutual mistake, and after discovering it feloniously converted it—should not have been given. Judgment reversed and cause remanded for a new trial, and for proceedings consistent herewith.[1]

COMMONWEALTH v. HAYS

Supreme Judicial Court of Massachusetts, 1859.
80 Mass. (14 Gray) 62.

Indictment on St.1857, c. 233, which declares that "if any person, to whom any money, goods or other property, which may be the subject of larceny, shall have been delivered, shall embezzle, or fraudulently convert to his own use, or shall secrete, with intent to embezzle or fraudulently convert to his own use, such money, goods, or property, or any part thereof, he shall be deemed, by so doing, to have committed the crime of simple larceny". The indictment contained two counts, one for embezzlement, and one for simple larceny.

At the trial in the court of common pleas in Middlesex, at October term 1858, before Aiken, J., Amos Stone, called as a witness by the Commonwealth, testified as follows: "I am treasurer of the Charlestown Five Cent Savings Bank. On the 17th day of October 1857, the defendant came into the bank, and asked to draw his deposit, and presented his deposit book. I took his book, balanced it, and handed it back to him. It was for one hundred and thirty dollars, in one item. I then counted out to him two hundred and thirty dollars, and said, 'There are two hundred and thirty dollars.' The defendant took the money to the end of the counter, and counted it, and then left the room. Soon after the defendant had left, I discovered that I had paid him one hundred dollars too much. After the close of bank hours I went in search of the defendant, and told him that I had paid him one hundred dollars too much, and asked him to adjust the matter. The defendant asked me how I knew it. He asked me if I could read. I said 'Yes.' He then showed me his book, and said, 'What does that say?' I took it, and read in it one hundred and thirty dollars. The defendant then said, 'That is what I got.' He exhibited two fifties, two tens, and a ten dollar gold piece, and said, 'That is what I got.' I then said to him, 'Do you say that is all and precisely what I gave you?' He replied, 'That is what I got.' I then said to him, 'I can prove that you got two hundred and thirty dollars.' He replied, 'That

1. The purchaser of a supposedly empty trunk converted a coat and vest which he found therein. This was held to be larceny. Robinson v. State, 11 Tex. App. 403 (1882). The court said: "The owner, or rather his clerk, whilst selling and delivering the trunk never intended to convey and did not convey either the title or possession of its contents; for he was wholly ignorant of its contents. So was defendant, when he purchased and became possessed of the trunk. The goods, so far as these parties were concerned, were lost, because they neither knew anything of their existence or their whereabouts. When defendant opened, examined and came across them in the trunk, they were in every sense lost goods which he found; as much so as if he had come across them upon the public highway or any other place where the owner had dropped, mislaid, left them by mistake, or lost them." Accord: Merry v. Green, 7 Mees. and W. 623, 151 Eng. Rep. 916 (1841).

is what I want; if you can prove it, you will get it; otherwise you wont.' I intended to pay the defendant the sum of two hundred and thirty dollars and did so pay him. I then supposed that the book called for two hundred and thirty dollars. Books are kept at the bank containing an account with depositors, wherein all sums deposited are credited to them, and all sums paid out are charged to them."

The defendant asked the court to instruct the jury that the above facts did not establish such a delivery or embezzlement as subjected the defendant to a prosecution under the St. of 1857, c. 233, and did not constitute the crime of larceny.

The court refused so to instruct the jury; and instructed them "that if the sum of two hundred and thirty dollars was so delivered to the defendant, as testified, and one hundred dollars, parcel of the same, was so delivered by mistake of the treasurer, as testified, and the defendant knew that it was so delivered by mistake, and knew he was not entitled to it, and afterwards the money so delivered by mistake was demanded of him by the treasurer, and the defendant, having such knowledge, did fraudulently, and with a felonious intent to deprive the bank of the money, convert the same to his own use, he would be liable under this indictment." The jury returned a verdict of guilty, and the defendant alleged exceptions.

BIGELOW, J. The statute under which this indictment is found is certainly expressed in very general terms, which leave room for doubt as to its true construction. But interpreting its language according to the subject matter to which it relates, and in the light of the existing state of the law, which the statute was intended to alter and enlarge, we think its true meaning can be readily ascertained.

The statutes relating to embezzlement, both in this country and in England, had their origin in a design to supply a defect which was found to exist in the criminal law. By reason of nice and subtle distinctions, which the courts of law had recognized and sanctioned, it was difficult to reach and punish the fraudulent taking and appropriation of money and chattels by persons exercising certain trades and occupations, by virtue of which they held a relation of confidence or trust towards their employers or principals, and thereby became possessed of their property. In such cases the moral guilt was the same as if the offender had been guilty of an actual felonious taking; but in many cases he could not be convicted of larceny, because the property which had been fraudulently converted was lawfully in his possession by virtue of his employment, and there was not that technical taking or asportation which is essential to the proof of the crime of larceny. The King v. Bazeley, 2 Leach, (4th ed.) 835. 2 East P.C. 568.

The statutes relating to embezzlement were intended to embrace this class of offences; and it may be said generally that they do not apply to cases where the element of a breach of trust or confidence in the fraudueInt conversion of money or chattels is not shown to exist.

This is the distinguishing feature of the provisions in the Rev.Sts. c. 126, §§ 27–30, creating and punishing the crime of embezzlement, which carefully enumerate the classes of persons that may be subject to the penalties therein provided. Those provisions have been strictly construed, and the operation of the statute has been carefully confined to persons having in their possession, by virtue of their occupation or employment, the money or property of another, which has been fraudulently converted in violation of a trust reposed in them. Commonwealth v. Williams, 3 Gray 461. In the last named case it was held, that a person was not guilty of embezzlement, under Rev. Sts. c. 126, § 30 who had converted to his own use money which had been delivered to him by another for safe keeping.

The St. of 1857, c. 233, was probably enacted to supply the defect which was shown to exist in the criminal law by this decision, and was intended to embrace cases where property had been designedly delivered to a person as a bailee or keeper, and had been fraudulently converted by him. But in this class of cases there exists the element of a trust or confidence reposed in a person by reason of the delivery of property to him, which he voluntarily takes for safe keeping, and which trust or confidence he has violated by the wrongful conversion of the property. Beyond this the statute was not intended to go. Where money paid or property delivered through mistake has been misappropriated or converted by the party receiving it, there is no breach of a trust or violation of a confidence intentionally reposed by one party and voluntarily assumed by the other. The moral turpitude is therefore not so great as in those cases usually comprehended within the offence of embezzlement, and we cannot think that the legislature intended to place them on the same footing. We are therefore of opinion that the facts proved in this case did not bring it within the statute, and that the defendant was wrongly convicted.

Exceptions sustained.[1]

4. APPROPRIATION BY WIFE OR HUSBAND

At common law neither spouse could commit larceny of the other's property. The marital relation was held to be such that possession of either was possession by both and hence neither could take possession from the other. That premise no longer prevails, but the rule is sometimes continued today on the theory that it is socially desirable to have such family matters settled in some manner other than by resort to the criminal court. It has been abrogated by the Married Women's Acts as interpreted in some of the states. There is no accord in the very few states in which the problem is directly controlled by statute. "Where the property involved is that of the offender's spouse, no prosecution for theft may be maintained unless the parties

1. It was held to be larceny for the holder of a check for $36.00 to appropriate over $4,000.00 which was handed to him by the bank teller who misread the check. Sapp v. State, 157 Fla. 605, 26 So. 2d 646 (1946).

were not living together as man and wife and were living in separate abodes at the time of the alleged theft." [2] "It is no defense that the theft was from the actor's spouse, except that misappropriation of household and personal effects or other property normally accessible to both spouses is theft only if it involves the property of the other spouse and only if it occurs after the parties have ceased living together." [3]

5. APPROPRIATION BY BAILEE [4]

REX v. BANKS

Court for Crown Cases Reserved, 1821.

Russ. & Ry. 441, 168 Eng.Rep. 887.

The prisoner was tried and convicted before Mr. Justice Baylay, at the Lancaster Lent assizes, in the year 1821, for horse-stealing.

It appeared that the prisoner borrowed a horse, under pretence of carrying a child to a neighbouring surgeon. Whether he carried the child thither did not appear; but the day following, after the purpose for which he borrowed the horse was over, he took the horse in a different direction and sold it.

The prisoner did not offer the horse for sale, but was applied to sell it, so that it was possible he might have had no felonious intention till that application was made.

The jury thought the prisoner had no felonious intention when he took the horse; but as it was borrowed for a special purpose, and that purpose was over when the prisoner took the horse to the place where he sold it, the learned judge thought it right upon the authority of 2 East, P.C. 690, 694, and 2 Russ. 1089, 1090 [a], to submit to the consideration of the judges, whether the subsequent disposing of the horse, when the purpose for which it was borrowed was no longer in view, did not in law include in it a felonious taking?

2. E.g. Smith-Hurd, Ill.Ann.Stat. ch. 38, § 16–4 (1977).

3. E.g. Ky.Rev.Stat. 514.020(2) (1981).

4. A bailee who intends to appropriate the chattel at the time he first receives it from the bailor is guilty of larceny. Cunningham v. District Court, 432 P.2d 992 (Okl.Cr.1967).

a. In 2 Russ. 1089, it is said that, "In the case of a delivery of a horse upon hire or loan, if such delivery were obtained *bona fide*, no subsequent wrongful conversion pending the contract will amount to felony; and so of other goods. But when the purpose of the hiring, or loan, for which the delivery was made, has been ended, felony may be committed by a conversion of the goods."

In Easter term, 1821, the judges met and considered this case. They were of opinion that the doctrine laid down on this subject in 2 East, P.C. 690 & 694, and 2 Russell, 1089 & 1090 was not correct. They held that if the prisoner had not a felonious intention when he originally took the horse, his subsequent withholding and disposing of it did not constitute a new felonious taking, or make him guilty of felony; consequently the conviction could not be supported.[1]

The Breaking Bulk Doctrine

In 1473 one who had bargained to take certain bales to Southampton wrongfully took them to another place where he broke open the bales and appropriated the contents. Whether or not this was larceny was debated in the Star Chamber. A motion to transfer the case to the common-law court was rejected because "the complainant was a merchant stranger, whose case ought to be judged by the law of nature in Chancery, and without the delay of a trial by jury". Hence it was disposed of in the Exchequer Chamber where most of the judges held that it was larceny, but for different reasons.[1] The reason offered by one was that the carrier had possession of the bales but not the contents so that he committed trespass by removing the contents from the bales. This was later adopted as the holding of the case and resulted in this anomalous rule: If a bailee having lawful possession of a bale wrongfully appropriates it, bale and all, it is not larceny; but if he wrongfully breaks it open and appropriates part or all [2] of the contents this is larceny. In the course of time the doctrine of "breaking bale" seems to have changed to one of "breaking bulk", which was even more peculiar. Under this notion if property such as wheat was delivered in bulk to the bailee's own vehicle it was not larceny if the bailee converted it all, but was larceny if he separated a portion from the mass and converted only that portion.[3] The whole doctrine has been largely, if not entirely, wiped out by legislation.

1. [Note by Compiler.] This case repudiates the theory of the trial court in Tunnard's Case, 1 Leach 214 note, 168 Eng.Rep. 209 note (1729).

If possession of the property was acquired innocently, but later there was a change of mind resulting in appropriation, there was no larceny because there was no trespass. Farlow v. State, 9 Md. App. 515, 265 A.2d 578 (1970).

1. Carrier's Case, Year Book, 13 Ed. IV, 9, pl. 5 (1473).

2. A bailee who wrongfully opens up a bag and takes all of the contents is just as much guilty of larceny as if he had taken only a part. Rex v. Brazier, Russ. and Ry. 337, 168 Eng.Rep. 833 (1817).

Armored car employee who opened money bags could be convicted of "stealing" under 18 U.S.C.A. § 2113(a) on a theory of breaking the bulk. United States v. Mafnas, 701 F.2d 83 (9th Cir.1983).

3. Commonwealth v. Brown, 4 Mass 580 (1808); Nichols v. People, 17 N.Y. 114 (1858); Rex v. Howell, 7 Car. and P. 325, 173 Eng.Rep. 145 (1836); Rex v. Pratley, 5 Car. and P. 533, 172 Eng.Rep. 1086 (1833). Contra: Rex v. Madox, Russ. and Ry. 92, 168 Eng.Rep. 700 (1805).

6. Continuing Trespass

REGINA v. RILEY

Court of Criminal Appeal, 1853.

6 Cox C.C. 88, Dearsly 149, 169 Eng.Rep. 674.

At the General Quarter Sessions of the Peace for the county of Durham, held at the city of Durham (before Rowland Burdon, Esq., Chairman), on the 18th of October, in the year of our Lord 1852, the prisoner was indicted for having, on the 5th day of October, 1852, stolen a lamb, the property of John Burnside. The prisoner pleaded Not Guilty. On the trial it was proved that on Friday, the 1st day of October, in the year of our Lord 1852, John Burnside, the prosecutor, put ten white-faced lambs into a field in the occupation of John Clarke, situated near to the town of Darlington. On Monday, the 4th day of October, the prisoner went with a flock of twenty-nine black-faced lambs to John Clarke, and asked if he might put them into Clarke's field for a night's keep, and upon Clarke agreeing to allow him to do so for one penny per head, the prisoner put his twenty-nine lambs into the same field with the prosecutor's lambs. At half-past seven o'clock in the morning of Tuesday, the 5th of October, the prosecutor went to Clarke's field, and in counting his lambs he missed one, and the prisoner's lambs were gone from the field also. Between eight and nine o'clock in the morning of the same day, the prisoner came to the farm of John Calvert, at Middleton St. George, six miles east from Darlington, and asked him to buy twenty-nine lambs. Calvert agreed to do so, and to give 8*s.* a-piece for them. Calvert then proceeded to count the lambs, and informed the prisoner that there were thirty instead of twenty-nine in the flock, and pointed out to him a white-faced lamb; upon which the prisoner said, "If you object to take thirty, I will draw one." Calvert however bought the whole, and paid the prisoner 12*l.* for them. One of the lambs sold to Calvert was identified by the prosecutor as his property, and as the lamb missed by him from Clarke's field. It was a half-bred white-faced lamb, marked with the letter "T.," and similar to the other nine of the prosecutor's lambs. The twenty-nine lambs belonging to the prisoner were black-faced lambs. On the 5th October, in the afternoon, the prisoner stated to two of the witnesses that he never had put his lambs into Clarke's field, and had sold them on the previous afternoon, for 11*l.* 12*s.*, to a person on the Barnard Castle-road, which road leads west from Darlington.

There was evidence in the case to show that the prisoner must have taken the lambs from Clarke's field early in the morning, which was thick and rainy.

It was argued by the counsel for the prisoner, in his address to the jury, that the facts showed that the original taking from Clarke's field was by mistake; and if the jury were of that opinion, then, as the original taking was not done *animo furandi*, the subsequent appropriation would not make it a larceny, and the prisoner must be acquitted. The chairman, in summing up, told the jury that though they might be of opinion that the prisoner did not know that the lamb was in his flock, until it was pointed out to him by Calvert, he should rule that, in point of law, the taking occurred when it was so pointed out to the prisoner and sold by him to Calvert, and not at the time of leaving the field. The jury returned the following verdict: The jury say that at the time of leaving the field the prisoner did not know that the lamb was in his flock, and that he was guilty of felony at the time it was pointed out to him.

The prisoner was then sentenced to six months' hard labour in the house of correction at Durham; and being unable to find bail, was thereupon committed to prison until the opinion of this court could be taken upon the question, whether Charles Riley was properly convicted of larceny. . . .

POLLOCK, C. B. We are all of opinion that the conviction is right. The case is distinguishable from those cited. R. v. Thristle decides only that if a man once gets into rightful possession, he cannot, by a subsequent fraudulent appropriation, convert it into a felony. So in R. v. Thurborn, in the elaborate judgment delivered by my brother Parke on behalf of the court of which I was a member, the same rule is laid down. It is there said that the mere taking up of a lost chattel to look at it, would not be a taking possession of it; and no doubt that may be done without violating any social duty. A man may take up a lost chattel and carry it home, with the proper object of endeavouring to find the owner; and then afterwards, if he yields to the temptation of appropriating it to his own use, he is not guilty of felony. In Leigh's Case, also, the original taking was rightful, but here the original taking was wrongful. I am not desirous of calling in aid the technicality of a continuing trespass; and I think this case may be decided upon the ground either that there was no taking at all by the prisoner in the first instance, or a wrongful taking, and, in either case, as soon as he appropriates the property, the evidence of felony is complete.

PARKE, B. I think that this case may be disposed of on a short ground. The original taking was not lawful, but a trespass, upon which an action in that form might have been founded; but it was not felony, because there was no intention to appropriate. There was, however, a continuing trespass up to the time of appropriation, and at that time, therefore, the felony was committed. Where goods are carried from one county to another, they may be laid as taken in the second county, and the difference between this and Leigh's Case, as well as the others cited, is that the original taking was no trespass.

It was by the implied licence of the owner, and the same thing as if he had been entrusted by the prosecutor with the possession of the goods.

WILLIAMS, TALFOURD, and CROMPTON, JJ., concurred.

Conviction affirmed.[1]

STATE v. COOMBS

Supreme Judicial Court of Maine, 1868.
55 Me. 477.

DICKERSON, J. Exceptions. The prisoner was indicted for the larceny of a horse, sleigh and buffalo robes. The jury were instructed that, if the prisoner obtained possession of the team by falsely and fraudulently pretending that he wanted it to drive to a certain place, and to be gone a specified time, when in fact he did not intend to go to such place, but to a more distant one, and to be absent a longer time, without intending at the time to steal the property, the team was not lawfully in his possession, and that a subsequent conversion of it to his own use, with a felonious intent while thus using it, would be larceny.

It is well settled that where one comes lawfully into possession of the goods of another, with his consent, a subsequent felonious conversion of them to his own use, without the owner's consent, does not constitute larceny, because the felonious intent is wanting at the time of the taking.

But how is it when the taking is fraudulent or tortious, and the property is subsequently converted to the use of the taker with a felonious intent? Suppose one takes his neighbor's horse from the stable, without consent, to ride him to a neighboring town, with the intention to return him, but subsequently sells him and converts the money to his own use, without his neighbor's consent, is he a mere trespasser, or is he guilty of larceny? In other words, must the felonious intent exist at the time of the original taking, when that is fraudulent or tortious, to constitute larceny?

When property is thus obtained, the taking or trespass is continuous. The wrongdoer holds it all the while without right, and against the right and without the consent of the owner. If at this point no other element is added, there is no larceny. But, if to such taking there be subsequently superadded a felonious intent, that is, an intent to deprive the owner of his property permanently without color of

1. One who took another's bull from the range, thinking it was his own, and sold it under such claim, was not guilty of larceny even if the owner had laid claim to the bull before the sale was made. Wilson v. State, 96 Ark. 148, 131 S.W. 336 (1910).

right, or excuse, and to make it the property of the taker without the owner's consent, the crime of larceny is complete. . . . [1]

Exceptions overruled.

Judgment for the State.

(E) CARRYING AWAY

PEOPLE v. KHOURY

Appellate Department, Superior Court, Los Angeles County, 1980.
108 Cal.App.3d Supp. 1, 166 Cal.Rptr. 705.

FAINER, JUDGE. Defendant appeals his conviction, by jury trial, for violation of Penal Code section 487, subdivision 1 (grand theft). The pertinent facts of this case were that defendant, after being observed for several hours pushing a shopping cart around a Fed Mart Store, was seen pushing a cart, with a large cardboard chandelier box on it, up to a check stand in the store. An alert cashier at the check stand, noticing that the box was loosely taped, stated that he would have to open and check the contents of the box before he would allow defendant to pay the price marked and remove the box from the store. Defendant then walked back through the check stand and into the store, leaving the box with the cashier. Defendant was arrested by store security after the box was opened, disclosing in excess of $900.00 worth of store items, consisting of batteries, tools, and chain saws, but no chandelier.

Defendant contends that these facts were insufficient evidence to convict him of grand theft. More specifically, defendant contends that the evidence was insufficient to show an asportation or carrying away of the personal property of the Fed Mart Store and therefore was, at most, an attempt to commit grand theft.

Our function on appeal in this case is to determine first the applicable law of theft by larceny, which is the theft for which defendant was specifically charged, and then to examine the record to ascertain whether there was substantial evidence of the disputed element of the crime to support the judgment of conviction.

The crime of larceny is the stealing or taking of the property of another. (Pen.Code, § 484.) "The completed crime of larceny—as distinguished from attempted larceny—requires *asportation* or carrying away, in addition to the taking."

> "The element of asportation is not satisfied unless it is shown that 'the goods were severed from the possession or custody of the owner, and in the possession of the thief, though it be but for a moment.' "

1. Accord: Commonwealth v. White, 11 Cush. 483 (Mass.1853).

The other element of theft by larceny is the specific intent in the mind of the perpetrator ". . . to deprive the owner permanently of his property . . . ."

The sufficiency of the evidence to support a finding of intent is not a claim of error on this appeal but is important in reviewing the jury's determination of the existence of the element of asportation or carrying away, a question of fact. The jury was instructed that "[I]n order to constitute a carrying away, the property need not be . . . actually removed from the premises of the owner. Any removal of the property from the place where it was kept or placed by the owner, done with the specific intent to deprive the owner permanently of his property . . . , whereby the perpetrator obtains possession and control of the property for any period of time, is sufficient to constitute the element of carrying away."

The cases make a distinction between fact patterns in which the defendant takes possession of the owner's property and moves it with the intent to carry it away, so that it is not attached to any other property of the owner and those cases in which a thief is frustrated in his attempt to carry the property away. All of the cases cited above make it clear that the property does not have to be actually removed from the premises of the owner. The jury was properly instructed as to the necessary elements of the crime of theft by larceny. They were not told that there could be no taking or carrying away or asportation unless defendant was able to get the chandelier box containing other store property past the cashier. This was a factor to be considered by the jury, as the trier of fact, in determining whether there was or was not an asportation.

The defendant was seen pushing a shopping cart carrying a carton or container for packaging a chandelier; the chandelier had been removed from the carton and the items already described, of a value of $900, were in the carton. The carton was taped. It was the recent taping of the carton that prompted the cashier not to permit the defendant to go through the check stand until the contents of the carton were checked. The defendant, on being informed of this, walked back into the store, leaving the carton behind. These facts, and the reasonable inferences which can be drawn therefrom support the jury's finding of asportation by substantial evidence.

The intent to permanently deprive the store of its merchandise was clear. The defendant in this appeal does not even attempt to negate the element of intent by proof of innocent though careless mistake.

The judgment of conviction is affirmed.

IBANEZ, P. J., concurs.[a]

a. Accord: State v. Eagle, 611 P.2d 1211 (Utah 1980); State v. Grant, 135 Vt. 222, 373 A.2d 847 (1977). See People v. Bradovich, 305 Mich. 329, 9 N.W.2d 560 (1943); Adams v. Common-

BIGELOW, JUDGE. I respectfully dissent.

In my opinion, as a matter of law, the facts fail to show sufficient asportation of the items to constitute a completed theft. The defendant is only guilty of *attempted* grand theft in violation of Penal Code sections 664, 484, and 487, subdivision (1).

In People v. Thompson (1958) 158 Cal.App.2d 320, 322 P.2d 489, the defendant entered a Thrifty Drug Store, concealed several records under his coat and went through the check stand without paying for the records. He was arrested 10 feet beyond the check stand, but before he left the store.

The physical layout of the store in our case at bench was similar to that of the store in the *Thompson* case, supra. In each case there was a check stand where the items selected for purchase are to be paid for by the customer. The *Thompson* case, supra, at page 323, 322 P.2d at page 490, stated, "The carrying of the records through the check stand constituted an asportation of the goods, as the act effectively removed them from the store's possession and control, even if only for a moment.

In this case, an alert clerk at the check stand prevented defendant from removing the items from the store's possession and control, even for a moment. All the other facts of placing the items in a box, taping it, etc., are proof of his intent to permanently deprive the owner-store of its property without paying the proper marked prices for them. Defendant's attempted theft was frustrated and he did not asportate the goods past the check stand.

I would modify the verdict and judgment to provide that the defendant is guilty of the offense of attempted grand theft (Pen.Code, §§ 664, 484, 487, subd. 1), affirm the judgment as modified and remand the matter to the trial court for resentencing of the defendant.

wealth, 153 Ky. 88, 154 S.W. 381 (1913); Rex v. Coslet, 1 Leach C.C. 236 (1782).

As to the killing of animals as sufficient asportation see McKenzie v. State, 111 Miss. 780, 72 So. 198 (1916); State v. Alexander, 74 N.C. 232 (1876). Contra: Lundy v. State, 60 Ga. 143 (1878). In the Georgia case the evidence was that defendants had shot and killed a cow but were frightened away when they had the animal half skinned. The court said that in the skinning process the men must have moved the carcass about somewhat which was enough taking and carrying away to constitute larceny.

D may be convicted of the larceny of a cow although the only asportation was after he had killed the animal. He had been found dragging the carcass away. State v. Tryfonas, 26 Utah 2d 140, 486 P.2d 389 (1971).

Electric debiting and crediting, the means by which funds in defendant's scheme moved from one bank to another, constituted transportation of funds within the meaning of the statute proscribing transportation of funds obtained by fraud. United States v. Gilboe, 684 F.2d 235 (2d Cir.1982).

(F) WITH INTENT TO STEAL

PEOPLE v. BROWN

Supreme Court of California, 1894.
105 Cal. 66, 38 P. 518.

GAROUTTE, J. The appellant was convicted of the crime of burglary, alleged by the information to have been committed in entering a certain house with intent to commit grand larceny. The entry is conceded, and also it is conceded that appellant took therefrom a certain bicycle, the property of the party named in the information, and of such a value as to constitute grand larceny. The appellant is a boy of 17 years of age, and, for a few days immediately prior to the taking of the bicycle, was staying at the place from which the machine was taken, working for his board. He took the stand as a witness, and testified: "I took the wheel to get even with the boy, and, of course, I didn't intend to keep it. I just wanted to get even with him. The boy was throwing oranges at me in the evening, and he would not stop when I told him to, and it made me mad, and I left Yount's house Saturday morning. I thought I would go back and take the boy's wheel. He had a wheel, the one I had the fuss with. Instead of getting hold of his, I got Frank's, but I intended to take it back Sunday night; but, before I got back, they caught me. I took it down by the grove, and put it on the ground, and covered it with brush, and crawled in, and Frank came and hauled off the brush, and said: 'What are you doing here?' Then I told him . . . I covered myself up in the brush so that they could not find me until evening, until I could take it back. I did not want them to find me. I expected to remain there during the day, and not go back until evening." Upon the foregoing state of facts, the court gave the jury the following instruction: "I think it is not necessary to say very much to you in this case. I may say, generally, that I think counsel for the defense here stated to you in his argument very fairly the principles of law governing this case, except in one particular. In defining to you the crime of grand larceny, he says it is essential that the taking of it must be felonious. That is true; the taking with the intent to deprive the owner of it; but he adds the conclusion that you must find that the taker intended to deprive him of it permanently. I do not think that is the law. I think in this case, for example, if the defendant took this bicycle, we will say for the purpose of riding twenty-five miles, for the purpose of enabling him to get away, and then left it for another to get it, and intended to do nothing else except to help himself away for a certain distance, it would be larceny, just as much as though he intended to take it all the while. A man may take a horse, for instance, not with the intent to convert it wholly and permanently to his own use, but to ride it to a certain distance, for a certain purpose he may have, and then leave it. He converts it to that extent to his own use and purpose feloniously." This instruction is erroneous, and demands a reversal of the judgment. If the boy's story be true, he is not guilty of larceny in taking the machine; yet, under the instruction of the court, the words from his own mouth convicted him. The court told the jury that larceny may be committed, even though it was only the intent of the party taking the property to deprive the owner of it temporarily. We think the authorities form an unbroken line to the effect that the felonious intent must be to deprive the owner of the property permanently. The illustration contained in the instruction as to the man taking the horse is too broad in its terms as stating a correct principle of law. Under the circumstances depicted by the illustration, the man might, and again he might not, be guilty of larceny. It would be a pure question of fact for the jury, and dependent for its true solution upon all the circumstances surrounding the transaction. But the test of law to be applied to these circumstances for the purpose of determining the ultimate fact as to the man's guilt or innocence is, did he intend to permanently deprive the owner of his property? If he did not intend so to do, there is no felonious intent, and his acts constitute but a trespass. While the felonious intent of the party taking need not necessarily be an intention to convert the property to his own use, still it must in all cases be an intent to wholly and permanently deprive the owner thereof. . . . For the foregoing reasons, it is ordered that the judgment and order be reversed, and the cause remanded for a new trial.[1]

We concur: MCFARLAND, J.; HARRISON, J.; VAN FLEET, J.; FITZGERALD, J.; DE HAVEN, J.

STATE v. SAVAGE

Court of General Sessions for Sussex County, Delaware, 1936.
37 Del. 509, 186 A. 738.

LAYTON, C. J., sitting. The indictment was for larceny. The evidence on the part of the State was that the defendant took from the unattended automobile of the prosecuting witness a metal can and three gallons of gasoline contained therein; that after taking the property he drove away and at a place about one mile distant he poured the gasoline into the tank of his car and threw the can into a nearby branch, and that he made no effort to inform the owner of his act, or to restore the property or pay for it.

1. *Brown* was cited and quoted with approval in People v. Kunkin, 9 Cal.3d 245, 107 Cal.Rptr. 184, 507 P.2d 1392 (1973).

An intent to deprive permanently is an essential ingredient of grand theft (meaning larceny in this case). State v. Ross, 107 Ariz. 240, 485 P.2d 810 (1971).

"Larceny, as defined in the common law, generally consists of taking and carrying away the personal property of another with the intent to deprive the owner of his property permanently, and to convert the property to the use of someone other than the owner." United States v. Waronek, 582 F.2d 1158, 1161 (7th Cir.1978).

The defendant was allowed to testify that while driving his automobile he ran out of gasoline and seeing the car of the prosecuting witness nearby, went to it and there found the can and gasoline; that he then and there poured the gasoline in his own car and drove off; that he left the can near the branch instructing a companion to return the can to the prosecuting witness and to inform him that he would return a like amount of gasoline. This was denied by the companion.

LAYTON, C. J., charged the jury, in part, as follows:

Larceny has been defined to be the taking and carrying away of the personal property of another with felonious intent to convert it to his own use without the owner's consent.

It is incumbent upon the State to prove to the satisfaction of the jury beyond a reasonable doubt every material element of the crime charged. So, the State must prove that the taking of the property occurred in Sussex County; that the property was of some value; that the person alleged to be the owner had a general or special property in the goods taken; that the defendant took and carried away the property, or some part of it, against the consent of the owner; and that the taker at the time of the taking had the felonious intent to convert the property to his own use.

The word "felonious," as applied to an act, simply means wrongful, in that there was no color of right or excuse for the act.

The issue in this case is within a narrow compass. The defendant admits the taking in Sussex County. There is no denial that the property was of some value. It is not pretended that the taking was with the consent of the owner. That the person named in the indictment as the owner had such a special property in the goods as would support the indictment was sufficiently proved.

The defendant does deny that he took the property with felonious intent to convert it to his own use. He contends that he took it for a temporary purpose, then and there intending to restore that property which was capable of being restored in specie, and a like quantity of gasoline.

It is not every taking of the property of another without his knowledge or consent that amounts to larceny. To constitute the crime the intent must be wholly to deprive the owner of the property. The general rule may be said to be that a taking of property for a temporary purpose with the bona fide intention to return the property to the owner does not amount to larceny, however liable the taker may be in a civil action of trespass. So, a borrowing of property, even though it be wrongful as being without the owner's knowledge or consent, with the intention of returning the property to its owner, is not larceny.

The property here is of two kinds, the can which could be restored, and the gasoline which admittedly was consumed, but exactly the same thing in quantity and quality could be restored, and, on principle, it would seem that if the defendant took the gasoline intending then and there to return a like quantity, the taking would not amount to larceny. It would be a different matter, perhaps, if the property taken were of some particular kind or quality which the owner reasonably might desire to be returned in specie.

It must be kept in mind, however, another principle, that if the defendant, at the time he took the property, had no intention of restoring it to the owner, but took it with the intention of converting it to his own use, the fact that he later repented, and desired or attempted to restore the goods would not purge him of guilt. The taking in such circumstances would be larceny.

You must find the intent with which the defendant took the property from all the facts and circumstances. You, of course, may and should, consider the testimony of the defendant, and, like all other testimony, you should give to it that degree of credit which you think it ought to have. You may also consider the manner and place of the taking, the conduct of the defendant thereafter, and his effort or attempt, if any, to restore the property or to account to the owner for it.

If you shall find from the evidence that the defendant took the property for a temporary purpose, and with the intention, then and there, to restore the can to the owner, and to account to the owner for the gasoline taken, or if you shall entertain a reasonable doubt of the felonious intent with which the defendant is charged, your verdict should be not guilty.[1]

On the other hand, if you shall find beyond a reasonable doubt that the defendant took the goods and chattels with no intention of making restoration, but with the intention of converting the property to his own use, your verdict should be guilty.

1. Compare Mason v. State, 32 Ark. 238 (1877). One who obtained $110,000.00 from a bank by wrongfully having an assistant cashier "juggle" the books and accounts over a period of months cannot defend on the theory that he intended sometime to repay the money. People v. Colton, 92 Cal.App.2d 704, 207 P.2d 890 (1949). One who obtained goods on credit by falsely and fraudulently representing that he had $12,000.00 cash and owed nothing, when he had only $4,500.00 and owed $10,000.00, is guilty of false pretenses even if he intended to pay for the goods. People v. Wieger, 100 Cal. 352, 34 P. 826 (1893).

Where a defendant has an intent to return the property taken a conviction for larceny would be improper, but where the defendant admits throwing away some of the property taken, a larceny conviction is proper as to the items discarded. United States v. Griffen, 9 U.S. C.M.A. 215, 25 C.M.R. 477 (1958).

REGINA v. HALL

Court for Crown Cases Reserved, 1849.
3 Cox C.C. 245, 1 Den. 382, 169 Eng.Rep. 291.

The following case was reserved by the Recorder of Hull:

John Hall was tried at the last Epiphany Quarter Sessions for the borough of Hull on an indictment charging him with stealing fat and tallow, the property of John Atkin.

John Atkin, the prosecutor, is a tallow-chandler, and the prisoner at the time of the alleged offence was a servant in his employment. On the morning of the 6th of December last, the prosecutor, in consequence of something that had occurred to excite his suspicions, marked a quantity of butcher's fat, which was deposited in a room immediately above the candle-room in his warehouse. In the latter room was a pair of scales used in weighing the fat, which the prosecutor bought for the purposes of his trade. At noon, the foreman and the prisoner left the warehouse to go to dinner, when the former locked the doors and carried the keys to the prosecutor. At that time there was no fat in the scales. In about ten minutes, the prisoner came back and asked for the keys, which the prosecutor let him have. The prosecutor watched him into the warehouse, and saw that he took nothing in with him. In a short time he returned the keys, to the prosecutor, and went away. The prosecutor then went into the candle-room, and found that all the fat which he had marked had been removed from the upper room, and after having been put into a bag, had been placed in the scales in the candle-room. The prosecutor then went into the street, and waited until a man of the name of Wilson came up, who was shortly followed by the prisoner. The latter, on being asked where the fat came from that was in the scales, said it belonged to a butcher of the name of Robinson; and Wilson, in the prisoner's presence, stated that he had come to weigh the fat which he had brought from Mr. Robinson's. The prosecutor told Wilson that he would not pay him for the fat until he had seen Mr. Robinson, and left the warehouse for that purpose. Wilson immediately ran away, and the prisoner, after offering, to the prosecutor's wife if he was forgiven, to tell all, ran away too, and was not apprehended until some time afterwards, at some distance from Hull.

I told the jury that if they were satisfied that the prisoner removed the fat from the upper room to the candle-room, and placed it in the scales with the intention of selling it to the prosecutor as fat belonging to Mr. Robinson, and with the intention of appropriating the proceeds to his own use, the offence amounted to larceny.

The jury found the prisoner guilty.

Dearsley for the prisoner. There was no larceny in this case. The offence was an attempt to commit a statutable misdemeanor, and only punishable as such. The case of R. v. Holloway, supra, p. 241, decides it. There was an asportation; but no intention to dispose of the property, for it was part of the very scheme that the owner should not be deprived of his property in the fat. There must to constitute larceny, be a taking, with intention of gain, and of depriving the owner of the property for ever. The last ingredient is wanting here:

ALDERSON, B. If a man takes my bank note from me, and then brings it to me to change, does he not commit a larceny?

Dearsley. A bank note is a thing unknown to the common law, and therefore the case put could not be larceny at common law.

LORD DENMAN, C. J. The taking is admitted. The question is whether there was an intention to deprive the owner entirely of his property; how could he deprive the owner of it more effectually than by selling it? to whom he sells it cannot matter. The case put of the bank note would be an ingenious larceny, but no case can be more extreme than this.

PARKE, B. In this case there is the intent to deprive the owner of the dominion over his property, for it is put into the hands of an intended vendor, who is to offer it for sale to the owner, and if the owner will not buy it, to take it away again. The case is distinguishable from that of R. v. Holloway by the existence of this intent, and, further, by the additional impudence of the fraud.

ALDERSON, B. I think that he who takes property from another intends wholly to deprive him of it, if he intend that he shall get it back again under a contract by which he pays the full value for it.

COLERIDGE, J., and COLTMAN, J., concurred.

Conviction affirmed.[1]

REGINA v. HOLLOWAY

Court for Crown Cases Reserved, 1849.
3 Cox C.C. 241, 2 Car. and K. 942, 175 Eng.Rep. 395.

The prisoner, William Holloway, was indicted at the General Quarter Sessions, holden in and for the borough of Liverpool, on December 4th, 1848, for stealing within the jurisdiction of the court 120 skins of leather, the property of Thomas Barton and another.

Thomas Barton and another were tanners, and the prisoner was one of many workmen employed by them at their tannery, in Liverpool, to dress skins of leather. Skins when dressed were delivered to the foreman, and every workman was paid in proportion to, and on account of the work done by himself. The skins of leather were afterwards stored in a warehouse adjoining to the workshop. The pris-

1. D issued short weight slips to his employer's customers for meat scraps he received. He gave the scraps to his employer and received money as reimbursement for the full weight. D's conviction for embezzlement from his employer was reversed. State v. Taylor, 14 Utah 2d 107, 378 P.2d 352 (1963).

oner, by opening a window and removing an iron bar, got access clandestinely to the warehouse, and carried away the skins of leather mentioned in the indictment, and which had been dressed by other workmen. The prisoner did not remove these skins from the tannery; but they were seen and recognized the following day at the porch or place where he usually worked in the workshop. It was proved to be a common practice at the tannery for one workman to lend work, that is to say, skins of leather dressed by him, to another workman, and for the borrower in such case to deliver the work to the foreman, and get paid for it on his own account, and as if it were his own work.

A question of fact arose as to the intention of the prisoner in taking the skins from the warehouse. The jury found that the prisoner did not intend to remove the skins from the tannery and dispose of them elsewhere, but that his intention in taking them was to deliver them to the foreman and to get paid for them as if they were his own work; and in this way he intended the skins to be restored to the possession of his masters.

The jury under direction of the court found the prisoner guilty, and a point of law raised on behalf of the prisoner was reserved, and is now submitted for the consideration of the justices of either Bench and barons of the Exchequer.

"The question is, whether on the finding of the jury, the prisoner ought to have been convicted of larceny?

"Judgment was postponed, and the prisoner was liberated on bail taken for his appearance at the next or some subsequent Court of Quarter Sessions to receive judgment, or some final order of the court." . . .

PARKE, B. I am of the same opinion. We are bound by the authorities to say that this is not larceny. There is no clear definition of larceny applicable to every case; but the definitions that have been given, as explained by subsequent decisions, are sufficient for this case. The definition in East's Pleas of the Crown is on the whole the best; but it requires explanation, for what is the meaning of the phrase "wrongful and fraudulent?" It probably means "without claim of right." All the cases, however, show that, if the intent was not at the moment of taking to usurp the entire dominion over the property, and make it the taker's own, there was no larceny. If, therefore, a man takes the horse of another with intent to ride it to a distance, and not return it, but quit possession of it, he is not guilty of larceny. So in R. v. Webb, in which the intent was to get a higher reward for work from the owner of the property. If the intent must be to usurp the entire dominion over the property, and to deprive the owner wholly of it, I think that that essential part of the offence is not found in this case.

ALDERSON, B. I cannot distinguish this case from R. v. Webb.

COLERIDGE, J., concurred.

COLTMAN, J. We must not look so much to definitions, which it is impossible *a priori* so to frame that they shall include every case, as to the cases in which the ingredients that are necessary to constitute the offence are stated. If we look at the cases which have been decided, we shall find that in this case one necessary ingredient, the intent to deprive entirely and permanently, is wanting.[1]

Conviction reversed.

STATE v. LANGIS

Supreme Court of Oregon, Department 1, 1968.
251 Or. 130, 444 P.2d 959.

DENECKE, JUSTICE. The defendant was convicted of larceny of a motor vehicle. He appeals, contending that the court improperly instructed the jury.

The defendant and one Richard Carrier were traveling from Vancouver, B.C., to San Francisco and had gone as far as Eugene by bus and hitchhiking. The car was taken in Eugene. The State Police stopped the car south of Eugene and north of Roseburg, Oregon. Roseburg is the next principal city south of Eugene on the interstate freeway. They are 70 miles apart. Carrier testified that he actually took the car in Eugene and was driving at the time of apprehension. (This testimony was verified by the officer.) Carrier testified that he intended to leave the car in Roseburg in "perfect condition."

In order to prove larceny there must be proof that the defendant had ". . . the intent to deprive such other of such property permanently . . . ." ORS 164.310.

At the prosecution's request the trial court instructed the jury as follows:

"You are further instructed that if you find that the defendant took the automobile with the intent to appropriate it to his own use and with intent to abandon later the automobile in such circumstances as would render its recovery by the owner difficult or unlikely, then you may find that the taking was with the intent to permanently deprive the owner of the property."

The defendant excepted to the instruction upon the ground that there was no evidence of an intent to abandon in circumstances that would render recovery by the owner difficult or unlikely, and even if there were, such intent does not amount to an intent to deprive the owner of the property permanently.

There was evidence from which the jury could have found that the defendant intended to abandon the vehicle under circumstances that would render recovery difficult or unlikely. The defendant's witness,

1. Cf. Fort v. State, 82 Ala. 50, 2 So. 477 (1886).

Carrier, said they were going to abandon the car in Roseburg. However, in view of the evidence that their destination was San Francisco, about 500 miles to the south, the jury reasonably could have believed that defendant intended to abandon it in San Francisco.

The substance of the instruction is also correct. Intent to deprive the owner of the property permanently can be inferred from abandonment under certain circumstances:

". . . An intent to take the property of another by trespass, use it for a temporary purpose and then abandon it, *may* be an intent to steal. An intent of the latter type is not an intent to steal if the intended abandonment is under such circumstances that the property will in all probability be restored to the owner; but it is an intent to steal if the intended abandonment will create a considerable risk of permanent loss to the owner. To take a horse from the owner's pasture on a farm, ride it a mile or two, and then turn it loose does not create any considerable risk of permanent loss to the owner; but such risk is created if a traveler, caught in an unexpected rain, takes an umbrella in one city and abandons it in another city some miles away. . . . ." Perkins, Criminal Law, 225 (1957).

The crux of the instruction is the phrase that the circumstances of the abandonment make recovery "difficult or unlikely." "Unlikely" accurately describe [sic] the concept that the circumstances of the abandonment are such that there is considerable risk that the owner will suffer a permanent deprivation of his property. "Difficult" is not as accurate in describing this concept and we do not encourage its use. Nevertheless, we conclude that its use in this context was not error. It is true that there is some degree of difficulty in recovering any car that has been abandoned any appreciable distance from the location of the owner; however, we find that the jury could reasonably have understood that "difficult" means so arduous that the chances were substantial that the owner would be permanently deprived of his property.[1]

Affirmed.

1. An intended robbery resulted in D's taking nothing but the gun, after disarming the victim. As the gun was intended to be left where it was unlikely the owner would recover it, this was sufficient for the *animus furandi* and hence was robbery. State v. Smith, 268 N.C. 167, 150 S.E.2d 194 (1966).

Larceny was committed by one who took a shotgun by trespass, intending to return it, but later turned it over to a casual acquaintance, whose name and address he did not know, who later disappeared with the gun. People v. James, 130 Cal.App.3d 520, 181 Cal.Rptr. 818 (1982). He deliberately exposed the gun to an unreasonable risk of permanent loss, after having taken it by trespass.

One who wrongfully took and carried away another's property to pawn it, though he said it was his intent to redeem and return the property, was properly convicted of larceny because he was unemployed and had no reasonable expectation of being able to carry out that intent. Putinski v. State, 223 Md. 1, 161 A.2d 117, 82 A.L.R.2d 859 (1960).

"The correct rule is that the taking of property under a contractual claim of right, in good faith, however ill-advised, is not larceny." State v. Abbey, 13 Ariz. App. 55, 474 P.2d 62 (1970).

(G) GRAND LARCENY

Larceny was a capital crime under the common law of England but an early statute divided the offense into two grades—grand larceny if the value of the stolen property exceeded twelve pence, and petit (or petty) larceny if it did not. Both were felonies under this statute, but whipping was substituted for death as the penalty for petit larceny. This statute is old enough to be common law in this country but under modern statutes petit larceny is usually a misdemeanor. At one time the dividing line between the two was generally $10. Recently the commonest determinative value has been $50 and under some statutes it is much higher.[1]

STATE v. DELMARTER

Supreme Court of Washington, 1980.
94 Wn.2d 634, 618 P.2d 99.

DOLLIVER, JUSTICE. Defendant, Rodney Guy Delmarter, was charged with simple assault and attempted theft in the first degree of property in Warren's Drug Store. None of the witnesses who testified at trial saw defendant enter the store, nor noticed him until he was near the prescription counter at the back of the store.

Defendant testified that he went to the drugstore to purchase some cough syrup, placed his change on the pharmacy counter, and some of it rolled off the counter to the floor inside the pharmacy area. Defendant stated he then went behind the counter, which is off limits to customers, to pick up his change. He further testified that he was looking for the pharmacist at that time. Entry to the pharmacy area is through a swinging door and a step up about 8 inches onto the raised floor.

The pharmacist testified that he first observed defendant in the area near the prescription counter walking around among the shelves and magazine racks, and that he saw defendant weaving and looking behind the counter to see if anybody was there. Later, he found defendant inside the pharmacy area crouched down on the floor in front of but facing away from a camouflaged cash drawer. The pharmacist also testified that, shortly before the incident, a clerk had obtained change from the cash drawer; that it was used to make change many times a day; and that the requests for change were sometimes shouted by clerks at the other end of the store. When the pharmacist confronted defendant, a struggle ensued which resulted in the assault conviction. Defendant broke away and fled from the store with his two companions.

Testimony at trial established that a camouflaged cash drawer, which appeared to be nothing more than a shelf containing medica-

1. Grand larceny includes petit larceny as a necessarily included offense. Theriault v. United States, 434 F.2d 212 (5th Cir. 1970).

tions, was situated behind the prescription counter approximately 17 feet from the swinging door used to enter the pharmacy area and that employees using the cash drawer could be seen from various parts of the store. Approximately $1,800 in cash was in the drawer at the time of this incident along with certain controlled substances. The drugs concealed in the cash drawer were valued at approximately $100 acquisition cost while the retail value of all the drugs in the store was around $15,000.

Defendant was convicted of simple assault and attempted theft in the first degree. After the jury returned its verdict, defendant moved for a new trial and, in the alternative, asked the court to reduce the conviction to attempted theft in the third degree to conform with the evidence. Both motions were denied.

Defendant appealed only the conviction of attempted theft in the first degree. The Court of Appeals affirmed. We granted defendant's petition for review in which defendant seeks a remand of the case with instructions to reduce the grade of the conviction to attempted theft in the third degree.

Defendant was convicted of attempted theft in the first degree under RCW 9A.28.020(1), which provides:

> A person is guilty of an attempt to commit crime if, *with intent to commit a specific crime,* he does any act which is a substantial step toward the commission of that crime.

(Italics ours.) Theft is defined in RCW 9A.56.020 as follows:

> (1) "Theft" means:
>
> (a) To wrongfully obtain or exert unauthorized control over the property or services of another or the value thereof, with intent to deprive him of such property or services; . . .

RCW 9A.56.030 establishes the elements of theft in the first degree:

> (1) A person is guilty of theft in the first degree if he commits theft of:
>
> (a) Property or services which exceed(s) one thousand five hundred dollars in value; . . .

While defendant concedes there is sufficient evidence to convict him of attempted theft, he asserts the evidence is insufficient to prove he had the specific intent to take property valued in excess of $1,500.

Initially, defendant contends that to be convicted of attempted first-degree theft, the state must prove he knew the property he attempted to steal had a value in excess of $1,500.[1] Defendant confuses knowledge with intent. RCW 9A.56.020–.030(1)(a) does not in-

1. In a grand larceny case market value at the time of the theft is the applicable test. Pickles v. State, 313 So.2d 715 (Fla.1975), State v. Clark, 13 Wash. App. 782, 537 P.2d 820 (1973).

"The general test for determining the market value of stolen property is the price a willing buyer would pay a willing seller either at the time and the place the property was stolen or at any time dur-

clude as an element of the crime that defendant must have knowledge of the value of the property. Defendant cites no case authority for his position other than State v. Leach, 36 Wash.2d 641, 219 P.2d 972 (1950), which concerns intent, not knowledge, and is not in point.

The crucial question is whether there is sufficient evidence that defendant intended to steal from the camouflaged cash drawer. Defendant claims that since there is no evidence he knew of the existence of the cash drawer there is insufficient evidence to convict.

The rule applied in this state by an appellate court in determining the sufficiency of the evidence in a criminal case has been altered recently by the United States Supreme Court in Jackson v. Virginia, 443 U.S. 307, 99 S.Ct. 2781, 61 L.Ed.2d 560 (1979). Prior to *Jackson,* it was necessary for the court,

> to be satisfied that there [was] 'substantial evidence' to support either the state's case, or the particular element in question. When that quantum of evidence has been presented, there is *some proof* of the element or crime in question and the motion in arrest of judgment must be denied.

State v. Randecker, 79 Wash.2d 512, 518, 487 P.2d 1295 (1971). The standard of review enunciated in *Jackson,* however, now requires us to determine:

> whether, after viewing the evidence in the light most favorable to the prosecution, *any* rational trier of fact could have found the essential elements of the crime *beyond a reasonable doubt.*

Jackson v. Virginia, supra, 443 U.S. at 319, 99 S.Ct. at 2789. We have recently applied the *Jackson* test in analyzing the sufficiency of the evidence in a criminal case.

ing the receipt or concealment of the property." United States v. Perry, 638 F.2d 862, 865 (5th Cir. 1981).

Experimental pills were being distributed without charge and hence had no market price or market value. They were stolen to be sold illegally. Held, underworld value may be used in determining the value for the purpose of larceny. People v. Colasanti, 35 N.Y.2d 434, 363 N.Y.S.2d 577, 322 N.E.2d 269 (1974).

Two suits of clothes which had been stolen were shown to have been old stock which had been on the shelves of the store three and a half years. For purposes of grand larceny it was held that "the proof must show the fair, cash market value at the time and place of the theft". People v. Fognini, 374 Ill. 161, 165, 28 N.E.2d 95, 97 (1940).

A federal statute making the embezzlement or theft of government property a felony if the value is over $100.00, and otherwise a misdemeanor provides: "The word 'value' means face, par, or market value, or cost price, either wholesale or retail, whichever is greater." 18 U.S.C.A. § 641.

"If property is stolen from a retail merchant the market value is the retail sales price. If property is stolen from a wholesale merchant the market value is the wholesale price." United States v. Robinson, 687 F.2d 359, 360 (11th Cir. 1982).

"A person who is present and participating with others in the taking of property in the commission of larceny is chargeable with the entire value of the goods taken, even though such person may not have personally taken away each and every one of the items subject to the larceny." State v. Riley, ___ W.Va. ___, 282 S.E.2d 623, 624 (1981).

Upon reviewing the evidence in the light most favorable to the State, we conclude that any rational trier of fact could have found the essential elements of attempted theft in the first degree. In determining the sufficiency of the evidence, circumstantial evidence is not to be considered any less reliable than direct evidence. Furthermore, the specific criminal intent of the accused may be inferred from the conduct where it is plainly indicated as a matter of logical probability.

The following evidence and inferences to be drawn therefrom support our holding that any rational trier of fact could have found the essential elements of the crime beyond a reasonable doubt:

(1) The defendant was in a restricted access area without authorization; (2) the restricted character of the area was obvious, indicating a lack of the possibility of mistake; (3) the defendant was crouching in front of the cash drawer well inside the pharmacy, indicating knowledge of the existence of the drawer; (4) the cash drawer is some 17 feet inside the pharmacy area, indicating a lack of unintentional or mistaken entry into the area; (5) the cash drawer is 9 feet past the cash register, indicating that the defendant's actions were directed at the acquisition of the contents of the drawer; (6) patrons of Warren's Drug could, by observing the actions of store employees, learn of the existence and function of the drawer; and (7) immediately prior to the incident, store employees had obtained money from the cash drawer.

The Court of Appeals is affirmed.

ROSELLINI, STAFFORD, WRIGHT and BRACHTENBACH, JJ., concur.

WILLIAMS, JUSTICE (dissenting).

Although the majority opinion correctly states the applicable test for analyzing a challenge to the sufficiency of the evidence, I believe the majority has misapplied the test and reached the wrong result. I would remand the case with instructions to reduce the conviction to attempted theft in the third degree.

In my view, our task is to determine whether, after viewing the evidence in the light most favorable to the State, any rational trier of fact could have found the elements of attempted first-degree theft.

Applying this doctrine, there is no question, and indeed the defendant concedes, that a rational trier of fact could have found beyond a reasonable doubt the elements of attempted theft in the third degree. The statute provides, in pertinent part:

> (1) A person is guilty of theft in the third degree if he commits theft of property or services which does not exceed two hundred and fifty dollars in value.

RCW 9A.56.050(1).

There was substantial evidence in the record to establish the elements of attempted third-degree theft. *See* Majority Opinion, at 101. A reasonable trier of fact could find beyond a reasonable doubt that all the elements of attempted third-degree theft were present, from the following evidence: (1) defendant was in a restricted access area without authorization; (2) the restricted character of the area was obvious to customers; (3) the defendant was crouching down well inside the restricted area of the pharmacy; and (4) there was property of value within easy reach of defendant.

The entire record evidence fails, however, to rise to the level required for a rational trier of fact to find the elements of attempted *first-degree* theft beyond a reasonable doubt. The record contains *no* evidence establishing which property defendant intended to take. There is no evidence that he had seen a store employer use the drawer, either immediately before the incident in question or at any time. The suggestion that defendant knew of the location of the camouflaged cash drawer is speculation at best. The existence of an intent to wrongfully obtain the contents of the drawer may be plausible but more likely is an inference that defendant intended to take controlled substances from shelves adjoining the hidden cash drawer. The pharmacist testified that such drugs were in clear view on nearby shelves. In my opinion, no reasonable trier of fact, on the evidence adduced in this case, could find beyond a reasonable doubt that defendant intended to commit theft of the contents of the cash drawer.

Accordingly, I am compelled to dissent.

UTTER, C. J., and HOROWITZ and HICKS, JJ., concur.[2]

SECTION 2. ROBBERY

PEOPLE v. BUTLER

Supreme Court of California, In Bank, 1967.
65 Cal.2d 569, 55 Cal.Rptr. 511, 421 P.2d 703.

[**B** shot and killed **A** (and also wounded **L**). **B** testified that **A** owed him money and that **A** admitted owing it but kept postponing the payment. He testified that he threatened **A** in order to compel **A** to pay what he owed, and that the gun went off when **A** grabbed for it.]

2. It is larceny to steal the clothing from a buried corpse. Haynes Case, 12 Co.Rep. 113, 77 Eng.Rep. 1389 (1614).

A series of acts may be aggregated to establish the level of theft involved in a single criminal impulse. In appropriate circumstances, the question of whether aggregation is proper is to be left to the jury as a question of fact. State v. Amsden, 300 N.W.2d 882 (Iowa 1981).

D was apprehended in an alley near three partially stripped cars. **D**'s fingerprints were found on the steering wheel of one of the cars and on car-parts located on the ground. He was charged with grand theft-auto and found guilty. The trial judge entered judgment of guilty of the statutory offense of "tampering" with a vehicle. This was upheld on the ground that "tampering" with a vehicle is necessarily included as a lesser offense of the charge of theft of the vehicle. People v. Anderson, 15 Cal.3d 806, 126 Cal.Rptr. 235, 543 P.2d 603 (1975).

Where **D**, charged with larceny of a car, testified that he moved the car in question to tow another car, he was entitled to an instruction on the lesser-included offense of operating a motor vehicle without consent. State v. Walker, 218 N.W.2d 915 (Iowa 1974).

TRAYNOR, CHIEF JUSTICE. Defendant was charged by information with the murder of Joseph H. Anderson and with assault with intent to murder William Russell Locklear. A jury convicted defendant of first degree felony murder and of assault with a deadly weapon; it fixed the penalty for the murder at death. This appeal is automatic. (Pen.Code, § 1239, subd. (b).)

We have determined that error in the guilt phase of the trial deprived defendant of his primary defense to the charge of first degree felony murder. The judgment of conviction of murder must therefore be reversed. . . .

No evidence of premeditation or deliberation was adduced by the prosecution. The court instructed the jury that since these elements were not present, it could find first degree murder only if defendant committed the killing in the perpetration of a robbery.

Defendant testified that he did not intend to rob Anderson when he went to the house, but intended only to recover money owed to him. Over his objection, the prosecutor argued to the jury, "If you think a man owes you a hundred dollars, or fifty dollars, or five dollars, or a dollar, and you go over with a gun to try to get his money, it's robbery." And, "If you go into a man's home and merely because he's supposed to owe you some money, you take money from him at gunpoint, you have robbed him." Again objecting to further argument by the prosecutor that a robbery was committed even if defendant believed Anderson owed him money, defendant suggested that a necessary element of theft, the intent to steal, was requisite to robbery, but was overruled by the court.

Defendant's objection was well taken. "Robbery is a felonious taking of personal property in the possession of another, from his person or immediate presence, and against his will, accomplished by means of force or fear." (Pen.Code, § 211.) An essential element of robbery is the felonious intent or *animus furandi* that accompanies the taking. Since robbery is but larceny aggravated by the use of force or fear to accomplish the taking of property from the person or presence of the possessor, the felonious intent requisite to robbery is the same intent common to those offenses that, like larceny, are grouped in the Penal Code designation of "theft." [1] The taking of property is not theft in the absence of an intent to steal, and a specific intent to steal, i.e., an intent to deprive an owner permanently of his property, is an essential element of robbery.

1. "Every person who shall feloniously steal, take, carry, lead, or drive away the personal property of another, or who shall fraudulently appropriate property which has been entrusted to him, or who shall knowingly and designedly, by any false or fraudulent representation or pretense, defraud any other person of money, labor or real or personal property, or who causes or procures others to report falsely of his wealth or mercantile character and by thus imposing upon any person, obtains credit and thereby fraudulently gets or obtains possession of money, or property or obtains the labor or service of another, is guilty of theft. . . . " (Pen.Code, § 484.)

Although an intent to steal may ordinarily be inferred when one person takes the property of another, particularly if he takes it by force, proof of the existence of a state of mind incompatible with an intent to steal precludes a finding of either theft or robbery. It has long been the rule in this state and generally throughout the country that a bona fide belief, even though mistakenly held, that one has a right or claim to the property negates felonious intent. A belief that the property taken belongs to the taker, or that he had a right to retake goods sold is sufficient to preclude felonious intent. Felonious intent exists only if the actor intends to take the property of another without believing in good faith that he has a right or claim to it.[2]

Defendant testified that in going to Anderson's home "my sole intention was to try to get my money; and that was all." The jury was properly instructed that if the intent to take the money from Anderson did not arise until after Anderson had been fatally wounded, the killing could not be murder in the perpetration of robbery. Since the jury returned a verdict of first degree murder it believed defendant intended to take money from Anderson by force before the shooting occurred. Accordingly, defendant's only defense to robbery-murder was the existence of an honest belief that he was entitled to the money. The trial court's approval of the prosecutor's argument that no such defense exists removed completely from the consideration of the jury a material issue raised by credible, substantial evidence. It precluded any finding that an intent to steal was absent. Defendant has a constitutional right to have every significant issue determined by a jury. The denial of that right was a miscarriage of justice within the meaning of article VI, section 13 * of the California Constitution and requires reversal.

The judgment of conviction of murder is reversed. In all other respects the judgment is affirmed.[a]

PETERS, TOBRINER, BURKE and PEEK, JJ., concur.

2. Defendant concedes, as he must, that although the offense could not constitute robbery absent an intent to steal, an unprovoked assault accompanying an attempt to collect a debt may be a crime other than robbery. Among the range of offenses that might have been committed are: assault (Pen.Code, § 240), assault with a deadly weapon (Pen.Code, § 245), assault with intent to commit murder (Pen.Code, § 217).

* Amendment adopted Nov. 8, 1966. [By the Compiler.]

a. Commonwealth v. White, 5 Mass. App. 483, 363 N.E.2d 1365 (1977). Accord: Richardson v. United States, 131 U.S.App.D.C. 168, 403 F.2d 574 (1968); People v. Gallegos, 130 Colo. 232, 274 P.2d 608 (1954); State v. Hollyway, 41 Iowa 200 (1875), approved although distinguished in State v. Kobylasz, 242 Iowa 1161, 1168, 47 N.W.2d 167, 171 (1951); Barton v. State, 88 Tex.Cr. 368, 227 S.W. 317, 13 A.L.R. 147 (1921).

One is not guilty of larceny when he openly and avowedly takes the property of another, without consent, in settlement of or to secure a bona fide debt claimed to be due him by the other. Hylton v. Phillips, 270 Or. 766, 529 P.2d 906 (1974).

If the defendant, in good faith, believed he was entitled to the money he was demanding, he could not be guilty of robbery as there was no felonious intent. People v. Karasek, 63 Mich.App. 706, 234 N.W.2d 761 (1975).

McComb, Justice. In my opinion there was no prejudicial error. Therefore, under the provisions of article VI, section 13, of the California Constitution, I would affirm the judgment in its entirety.

Mosk, Justice. I dissent.

Penal Code section 211 defines robbery as "the felonious taking of personal property in the possession of another, from his person or immediate presence, and against his will, accomplished by means of force or fear." This code section was enacted in 1872 and has remained unchanged since that date.

It is significant that the section requires the taking be from the *possession* of another, and makes no reference whatever to *ownership* of the property.

The question here, then, is whether the defendant may assert *ipse dixit* his belief that he was entitled to an unpaid debt taken from another by force or fear as a defense to a charge of robbery, and by extrapolation as a defense to a charge of murder committed in the course of a robbery. While there is some authority suggesting this query be answered in the affirmative (People v. Devine (1892) 95 Cal. 227, 30 P. 378; People v. Vice (1863) 21 Cal. 344; People v. Stone (1860) 16 Cal. 369), there has been no explicit holding of this court on the issue.

Thus, the question is ultimately one of basic public policy, which unequivocally dictates that the proper forum for resolving debt dis-

Contra: People v. Uselding, 107 Ill. App.2d 305, 247 N.E.2d 35 (1969).

An intent to collect a debt is no defense to robbery. State v. Ortiz, 124 N.J. Super. 189, 305 A.2d 800 (1973); Crawford v. State, 509 S.W.2d 582 (Tex.Cr. App.1974); Commonwealth v. Sleighter, 495 Pa. 262, 433 A.2d 469 (1981).

Rule that robbery cannot be based on the taking of property to satisfy a debt does not apply where the debt is unliquidated. State v. Bonser, 128 Ariz. 95, 623 P.2d 1251 (App.1981).

It is no defense to robbery that the defendant used force to collect a debt which he honestly believed was owed to him. State v. Russell, 217 Kan. 481, 536 P.2d 1392 (1975).

N.B. The court seems to feel that any other rule would authorize the use of force in the collection of a debt.

At gunpoint D obtained a refund of $25.15 for a pair of shoes that did not fit. This constituted robbery. Williams v. State, 317 So.2d 425 (Miss.1975). The Court mentioned that the shoes had been worn and "scuffed" before they were returned. Even so, four judges filed a vigorous dissent.

Forcible retaking of gambling losses constitutes robbery. People v. Coates, 64 A.D.2d 1, 407 N.Y.S.2d 866 (1978).

D telephoned **X**, manager of a store, telling **X** that bombs were located in the store and would be detonated unless a sum of money was deposited at a designated place. **X** deposited the money at that place. **D** was arrested when he took possession of the money and started to leave. **D**'s conviction of robbery was reversed on the ground that the facts showed extortion and theft—but not robbery. People v. Moore, 184 Colo. 110, 518 P.2d 944 (1974).

Defendant cannot be convicted of both robbery and assault if the force relied upon for the charge of assault is the force which was used to perpetrate the robbery. "Where an act constituting a crime also constitutes an element of another crime, a defendant is placed in double jeopardy if he is charged with both crimes." State v. Bresolin, 13 Wash.App. 386, 394, 534 P.2d 1394, 1400 (1975).

putes is a court of law, pursuant to legal process—not the street, at the business end of a lethal weapon. . . .

I would rely upon the specific provisions of Penal Code section 211, which raise no issue of ownership of property forcibly taken, but only its possession. Here, possession of the money was in the deceased, and when it was taken from him by means of force, the crime of robbery was committed.

STATE v. SKAGGS

Court of Appeals of Oregon, 1979.
42 Or.App. 763, 601 P.2d 862.

JOSEPH, PRESIDING JUDGE. Defendant was convicted in a jury trial of theft in the first degree, assault in the second degree, robbery in the third degree and unauthorized use of a vehicle. He appeals, assigning as error (1) denial of his motion for a directed verdict of acquittal for robbery, (2) entering of a separate conviction for robbery, and (3) entering of a separate conviction for unauthorized use of a vehicle.[1]

Late in the evening of October 25, 1976, defendant and another person were accosted by a Clackamas County deputy sheriff while they were apparently in the act of stealing a vehicle. The officer engaged in a scuffle with the other person over possession of the officer's service revolver. During the struggle defendant stabbed the officer twice and then grabbed him by the hair, held an object to his throat and said, "Let go of the gun or I'll cut it," or "I'll slit it." After being struck a third time, the officer lost control of the revolver. The two assailants made their escape from the scene in the officer's patrol car, taking the gun with them.

On the first assignment of error defendant argues that there was insufficient evidence to show intent to commit theft of the revolver, which was the theft element in the robbery charge, because the evidence suggested that defendant's original and continuing intent was to steal a car. He asserts that his actions were intended only to disarm the officer and to escape and that the intent to disarm excluded intent to commit theft of the gun.

The crime of robbery does not require an actual taking of property, but only intent to commit theft, for "repression of violence is the principal reason for being guilty of robbery." Commentary, Oregon Criminal Code of 1971, 190 (1975 ed.). The requisite intent under the

1. Defendant was charged under two indictments. The first was for theft in the first degree. The second contained counts of attempted murder, assault in the second degree, robbery in the first degree and unauthorized use of a vehicle. The cases were consolidated for trial. The trial court merged the convictions for robbery, assault and unauthorized use in sentencing defendant on the assault charge.

robbery statute [2] is derived from the theft statute [3] and the definitions of theft.[4] Intent to commit theft is present where there is intent to dispose of property "under such circumstances as to render it unlikely that an owner will recover such property." ORS 164.005(2)(b).

As stated in State v. Gibson, 36 Or.App. 111, 115, 583 P.2d 584, *rev. den.* 285 Or. 319 (1978),

> "[T]he issue is not whether we believe defendant guilty beyond a reasonable doubt, but whether the evidence was sufficient for the trier of fact so to find."

In State v. Mack, 31 Or.App. 59, 569 P.2d 624 (1977), we held that for purposes of determining commission of theft, intent permanently to deprive the owner of possession of property could be inferred from the circumstances surrounding the act.

From the circumstances of the episode, an inference could reasonably have been drawn by the jury that the deputy sheriff was unlikely to recover his revolver after the violent attempt to disarm him and the escape. The revolver was not left behind at the scene of the incident, and a witness testified that he saw the gun later that evening when defendant and a co-defendant were trying to operate the jammed mechanism. Next morning the witness brought the gun to the police and assisted in the arrest of defendant. The question was properly submitted to the jury.

Affirmed in part.[a]

2. ORS 164.395 provides in pertinent part:

> "(1) A person commits the crime of robbery in the third degree if in the course of committing or attempting to commit theft he uses or threatens the immediate use of physical force upon another person with the intent of:
>
> "(a) Preventing or overcoming resistance to his taking of the property or to his retention thereof immediately after the taking; or . . . ."

3. ORS 164.015 provides in pertinent part:

> "A person commits theft when, with intent to deprive another of property or to appropriate property to himself or to a third person, he:
>
> "(1) Takes, appropriates, obtains or withholds such property from an owner thereof; or . . . ."

4. ORS 164.005(2):

> " 'Deprive another of property' or 'deprive' means to:
>
> "(a) Withhold property of another or cause property of another to be withheld from him permanently or for so extended a period or under such circumstances that the major portion of its economic value or benefit is lost to him; or
>
> "(b) dispose of the property in such manner or under such circumstances as to render it unlikely that an owner will recover such property."

a. D, who stole three bottles of wine and one of soft drink from a store and threw two of the bottles at the pursuing storekeeper, was properly convicted of third-degree robbery. The statute expressly covers the use of force, or threatened force, to overcome resistance to the retention of property immediately after the taking. State v. Rios, 24 Or.App. 393, 545 P.2d 609 (1976).

Purse-snatching, per se, is larceny from the person rather than robbery. It is not an inherently dangerous felony. People v. Morales, 49 Cal.App.3d 134, 122 Cal.Rptr. 157 (1975).

Simple snatching of a purse from the fingertips of an unsuspecting possessor did not constitute the use of such force as to warrant a robbery conviction. Peo-

SECTION 3. EMBEZZLEMENT

There is no common-law crime known as embezzlement. If an employee received, for his employer, property which was delivered to him by a third party, and appropriated this property before it had come into the possession of his employer, this was held not to constitute larceny; and the first statute on embezzlement was enacted to provide a punishment for this kind of misconduct.

Additional statutes, under the name of embezzlement, were enacted to provide a penalty for the wrongful appropriation of property by such persons as brokers, bankers, attorneys, agents and trustees, who may have title to, as well as possession of, what has been entrusted to them.

This still left an important "gap" due to the rule that the appropriation by an ordinary bailee was not larceny if he had had no wrongful intent at the time he took possession of the property bailed to him. By statute this also was punished as embezzlement.

As the statutes on embezzlement were enacted to fill "gaps" which had appeared in the development of the law of larceny, the two offenses were held to be mutually exclusive. The same evidence which would prove guilt of one would disprove guilt of the other.[1]

ple v. Patton, 76 Ill.2d 45, 27 Ill.Dec. 766, 389 N.E.2d 1174 (1979).

Robbery does not require that defendant's violence or intimidation be for the very purpose of taking the victim's property. It is sufficient if he takes advantage of a situation which he created for some other purpose. Thus defendant is guilty of robbery if he took advantage of the fear he created in order to obtain the victim's property, even if his primary purpose had been to commit rape. State v. Iaukea, 56 Haw. 343, 537 P.2d 724 (1975).

Because robbery is aggravated larceny, larceny is a lesser included offense in a robbery charge. State v. Wingate, 87 N.M. 397, 534 P.2d 776 (1975).

Asportation is an essential element of the crime of robbery. United States v. Rivera, 521 F.2d 125 (2d Cir.1975).

The evidence indicated that J smashed a window of the car in which Ms. C was sitting alone in a parking lot. Fearing for her safety, C hastily left the car on the far side and fled, leaving her purse on the front seat. When she returned shortly thereafter, her purse was gone, and J was just driving away. It was held error to dismiss a count charging J with robbery. The court held that "a taking constitutes robbery even if the taking is fully completed without the victim's knowledge, if such knowledge is prevented by the use of force or fear." Sheriff v. Jefferson, ___ Nev. ___, 649 P.2d 1365 (1982).

Although the money was taken from the body of the victim three hours after he was killed, the court held that "where the act of force and the taking of the property are so connected as to form a continuous chain of events so that the prior force makes it possible for the defendant to take the property from the victim's body without resistance, that is sufficient for a conviction of the crime of robbery under K.S.A. 21–3426." State v. Myers, 230 Kan. 697, 640 P.2d 1245, 1250 (1982).

"The statutory elements of robbery, RCA 9A.56.190, presuppose that intent to deprive the victim of property is a necessary element." State v. Corwin, 32 Wash.App. 493, 649 P.2d 119, 122 (1982).

1. "There is a difference between the crimes of embezzlement and stealing. The crimes are inconsistent. Embezzlement presupposes lawful possession and theft does not." United States v. Trevino, 491 F.2d 74, 75 (5th Cir.1974).

"The elements necessary to establish embezzlement are a trust relation, possession or control of property by virtue of the trust relation, and a fraudulent appropriation of the property to a use or

For this reason it is more effective to deal with them together than separately, and for the most part they were included in the cases on larceny.

STATE v. STAHL

Court of Appeals of New Mexico, 1979.
93 N.M. 62, 596 P.2d 275.

OPINION

WOOD, CHIEF JUDGE. Defendant was convicted of embezzling over $100. To have embezzled the money, defendant must have been entrusted with the money. Section 30–16–8, N.M.S.A.1978. Defendant contends there is no evidence that he was entrusted with over $100. We agree.

Defendant was a clerk at a store. The store had two cash registers and a drop-box. There was a slit in the counter; money pushed through this slit went into the drop-box. The drop-box was locked with two padlocks, the keys to which were retained by the manager. When money accumulated in the registers, portions of the accumulation were placed in the drop-box through the slit in the counter.

About 7:30 p.m. on the night in question, the manager removed the money from the drop-box. About 11:00 p.m. the clerk on duty closed down one of the registers, placing the money from that register into the drop-box. When defendant went on duty at midnight, the one register being used contained $50 to $75. Defendant's shift was from midnight to 8:00 a.m. At 3:00 a.m., defendant was absent from the store. The drop-box had been pried open and its money removed. There is evidence that defendant took a total of $612 from the drop-box and the register being used.

purpose not in the due and lawful execution of the trust." State v. Gomez, 27 Ariz.App. 248, 553 P.2d 1233, 1237 (1976).

In this jurisdiction the crime of larceny remains as it was at common law. Hence it requires that the taking of the property be by trespass. If the taking was fraudulent it was by trespass and the subsequent appropriation is larceny. But if the original taking was without trespass the subsequent wrongful appropriation is embezzlement and not larceny. Farlow v. State, 9 Md.App. 515, 265 A.2d 578 (1970).

Property involuntarily entrusted may be embezzled. Property which should have been sent to the bank was inadvertently sent to defendant, who converted it with knowledge of the situation. A conviction of embezzlement was affirmed. People v. Newman, 49 Cal.App. 3d 426, 122 Cal.Rptr. 455 (1975).

Where one, in good faith, believes he is authorized to appropriate property which he is accused of embezzling, the fraudulent intent which is a necessary element of that crime is lacking. People v. Stewart, 16 Cal.3d 133, 127 Cal.Rptr. 117, 544 P.2d 1317 (1976).

Since the statute in this state provides that part ownership is no defense to larceny, it is held that it is also no defense to embezzlement. Babcock v. State, 91 Nev. 312, 535 P.2d 786 (1975).

If **D** altered a $22 check to make it read $2200 he could be convicted of embezzlement of the $22 check despite his guilt of forgery. State v. Vanderlinden, 21 Ariz.App. 358, 519 P.2d 211 (1974).

Defendant was the only clerk on duty when the money was taken; he was "in charge of the whole store" and "responsible for the entire store." The register being used, and its contents, were for defendant's use in performing his duties. Defendant does not claim that he was not entrusted with the money in this register and does not contend that the money he took from this register was not embezzlement. However, there is no proof that the money taken from the register was over $100, and no proof that the amount of money in the register, plus money from sales after defendant went on duty, ever amounted to $100.

The State asserts that defendant was also entrusted with money which defendant took from the register and placed in the drop-box. We need not answer this contention because there is no evidence that defendant placed any money into the drop-box.

To reach a monetary amount over $100, the money taken from the drop-box must be included. Under the evidence, the money in the drop-box was put there by another clerk, and before defendant was on duty. Defendant did not have the keys to the drop-box, he had no permission or authority to get any money out of the box, he had no permission to have possession of the money in the drop-box, or "use it for change or anything . . . ." The only one supposed to take money from the drop-box was the manager. These facts are not disputed.

The trial court denied defendant's motion for a directed verdict on the charge of embezzlement over $100. Because defendant was in charge of the store, the trial court was of the view that defendant had been entrusted with "everything there on the premises" including the drop-box. We disagree; defendant had not been entrusted with the contents of the drop-box.

"Entrust" means to commit or surrender to another with a certain confidence regarding his care, use or disposal of that which has been committed or surrendered. The money in the drop-box would not have been entrusted to defendant unless the money came into defendant's possession by reason of his employment.

2 Wharton's Criminal Law and Procedure, § 468 (1957) states:

> A clerk taking money or goods from his employer's safe, till or shelves is guilty of larceny unless he is authorized to dispose of such money or goods at his discretion. An employee who feloniously appropriates to his own use property of his master or employer to which he has access only by reason of a mere physical propinquity as an incident of the employment, and not by reason of any charge, care, or oversight of the property entrusted to him, may be guilty of larceny by such act the same as any stranger.

Although defendant was in charge of the entire store, the undisputed facts show that the money in the drop-box was not committed or surrendered to defendant's care, use or disposal; that money was to be handled exclusively by the manager. Defendant was excluded from having anything to do with that money. Defendant's offense, as to the money in the drop-box, was larceny, not embezzlement, because he had not been entrusted with that money.

Because of an absence of evidence showing that defendant was entrusted with over $100 of the money he took, his embezzlement conviction is reversed.

IT IS SO ORDERED.[1]

LOPEZ and WALTERS, JJ., concur.

UNITED STATES v. FAULKNER

United States Court of Appeals, Ninth Circuit, 1981.
638 F.2d 129.

Before SKOPIL, ALARCON and BOOCHEVER, CIRCUIT JUDGES.

SKOPIL, CIRCUIT JUDGE:

INTRODUCTION

Faulkner appeals his conviction of violation of 18 U.S.C. § 659, which prohibits embezzlement or theft from an interstate shipment. He contends that the evidence was insufficient to establish his guilt, because he never physically removed goods from the truck, and never sold the goods. We affirm.

FACTS

Faulkner was a truck driver for North American Van Lines. He picked up 105 refrigerators in San Diego, which he was to transport to Hartford, Connecticut. Faulkner stopped in Las Vegas, Nevada. He called Richard Urbauer, the owner of an appliance store, and offered to sell the refrigerators. Urbauer informed the police.

Faulkner and Urbauer discussed the sale of the refrigerators. Faulkner left the store and returned with his truck. He broke the truck's seals, entered the rear, and opened two cartons to show Urbauer the refrigerators. Urbauer examined the two refrigerators while Faulkner rearranged the boxes in the truck.

Faulkner and Urbauer went back to the store and tried to consummate a deal They were unable to reach an agreement. Faulkner started to leave the store and was arrested.

Faulkner was convicted by a jury of embezzlement or theft from an interstate shipment, in violation of 18 U.S.C. § 659. He appeals.

1. Whether a bailee who converts property bailed to him is guilty of larceny or embezzlement depends upon the time of his intent. "If the criminal intent exists at the time of the taking of the property, it is 'larceny,' but if the intent does not arise until after the defendant receives possession, then it is 'embezzlement.'" Lovick v. State, 646 P.2d 1296, 1297–98 (Okl.Cr.App.1982).

ISSUE

Faulkner contends that the evidence was insufficient to support his conviction.

DISCUSSION

I. Standard of Review.

This court must uphold the verdict if the evidence, considered in the light most favorable to the government as prevailing party, would permit a rational conclusion by the jury that the accused was guilty beyond a reasonable doubt.

18 U.S.C. § 659 provides, in pertinent part: "Whoever embezzles, steals, or unlawfully takes, carries away, or conceals, or by fraud or deception obtains from any . . . motor-truck . . . with intent to convert to his own use any goods . . . which are a part of . . . an interstate or foreign shipment" shall be guilty of an offense.

In enacting section 659 Congress sought to protect the channels of interstate commerce from interference. The statute must be construed broadly to accomplish this purpose. It is not limited in its application to the strictly defined offense of common law larceny.

The stealing or unlawful taking contemplated by the statute consists of taking over possession and control with intent to convert to the use of the taker. The statute does not require physical removal of the goods, nor even asportation in the common law larceny sense.

The felonious intent required by the statute consists of the intent to appropriate or convert the property of the owner. An intent to return the property does not exculpate the defendant.

We hold that there was sufficient evidence establishing the requisite act and intent. Faulkner exercised dominion and control over the refrigerators by leaving his assigned route to go to Urbauer's store and negotiate a sale. There was competent evidence that Faulkner broke the truck's seals, opened the cartons and moved the goods to exhibit them to Urbauer, in furtherance of his attempt to sell them. The jury could therefore find that Faulkner had assumed possession and control of the goods. These facts also permitted the jury to conclude that Faulkner intended to convert the goods to his own use. It was not necessary that Faulkner remove the goods from the truck, nor complete the sale.

CONCLUSION

The evidence was sufficient to support Faulkner's conviction of violating section 659. The judgment appealed from is AFFIRMED.

SECTION 4. FALSE PRETENSES

In addition to those "gaps" in the criminal law which were due to the rule that there is no larceny without trespass de bonis (which have been largely, though not entirely, closed by statutes on embezzlement), a very important hiatus resulted from the holding that no larceny was committed by a transaction in which the wrongdoer obtained the title or ownership of the property in question.

One who cheated another in a sale or trade was guilty of a misdemeanor known as a common-law cheat if he made use of some false token, as it was called, such as a false weight or false measure; but guilty of no crime at all under the English common law if the deceit was merely by spoken words, no matter how wilful and extreme the deceit might be. This called forth the English statute which made it an offense to obtain the property of another by false pretenses. This statute, enacted in 1757, was generally accepted in the Colonies and is a part of our common law.

The result again is two offenses that are mutually exclusive, the familiar statement being that if the wrongdoer, by his fraud, obtained possession only, his appropriation of the property was larceny by trick; whereas if he obtained both title and possession the crime was false pretenses.[1]

PEOPLE v. ASHLEY

Supreme Court of California, In Bank, 1954.
42 Cal.2d 246, 267 P.2d 271.

TRAYNOR, JUSTICE. Defendant was convicted of four counts of grand theft under section 484 of the Penal Code. He "appeals from the verdicts and judgments as to each count," and from the order denying his motion for a new trial. . . .

1. "In 'larceny' owner of the property has no intention to part with title therein *to the person taking it* although he may intend to part with possession, while in 'false pretenses' owner intends to part with both his possession and title but such are obtained from him by fraud." Neel v. State, 454 P.2d 241, 242 (Wyo. 1969).

False pretenses declared criminal under modern statutes are not limited to representations made by words. Acts or conduct may constitute a false pretense within the meaning of such statutes. State v. Winters, 2 Conn.Cir. 508, 202 A.2d 908 (1963).

"It is true that appellant made no spoken representation to the bank, but false pretense may be made by acts, symbols or even by concealment." Neece v. State, 210 So.2d 657, 661 (Miss.1968).

It was proper to instruct the jury that they might consider nondisclosure of an important fact as a false pretense. People v. Vida, 2 Mich.App. 409, 140 N.W.2d 559 (1966).

The false pretense can be the failure to speak when it was necessary to do so. If **D** sold a new automobile without revealing the fact that it was mortgaged, he was deliberately acting a falsehood, and such conduct is as objectionable as a spoken falsehood. People v. Etzler, 292 Mich. 489, 290 N.W. 879 (1940).

Although the crimes of larceny by trick and device and obtaining property by false pretenses are much alike, they are aimed at different criminal acquisitive techniques. Larceny by trick and device is the appropriation of property, the possession of which was fraudulently acquired; obtaining property by false pretenses is the fraudulent or deceitful acquisition of both title and possession. In this state these two offenses, with other larcenous crimes, have been consolidated into the single crime of theft, Pen.Code, § 484, but their elements have not been changed thereby. The purpose of the consolidation was to remove the technicalities that existed in the pleading and proof of these crimes at common law. Indictments and informations charging the crime of "theft" can now simply allege an "unlawful taking." Pen.Code, §§ 951, 952. Juries need no longer be concerned with the technical differences between the several types of theft, and can return a general verdict of guilty if they find that an "unlawful taking" has been proved. The elements of the several types of theft included within section 484 have not been changed, however, and a judgment of conviction of theft, based on a general verdict of guilty, can be sustained only if the evidence discloses the elements of one of the consolidated offenses. In the present case, it is clear from the record that each of the prosecuting witnesses intended to pass both title and possession, and that the type of theft, if any, in each case, was that of obtaining property by false pretenses. Defendant was not prejudiced by the instruction to the jury relating to larceny by trick and device. Indeed, he requested instructions relating to both larceny by trick and device and obtaining property by false pretenses. Moreover, his defense was not based on distinctions between title and possession, but rather he contends that there was no unlawful taking of any sort.

To support a conviction of theft for obtaining property by false pretenses, it must be shown that the defendant made a false pretense or representation with intent to defraud the owner of his property, and that the owner was in fact defrauded. It is unnecessary to prove that the defendant benefitted personally from the fraudulent acquisition. The false pretense or representation must have materially influenced the owner to part with his property, but the false pretense need not be the sole inducing cause. If the conviction rests primarily on the testimony of a single witness that the false pretense was made, the making of the pretense must be corroborated. Pen.Code, § 1110.

The crime of obtaining property by false pretenses was unknown in the early common law, see Young v. The King, 3 T.R. 98, 102 [1789], and our statute, like those of most American states, is directly traceable to 30 Geo. II, ch. 24, section 1 (22 Statutes-at-Large 114 [1757]). In an early Crown Case Reserved, Rex v. Goodhall, Russ. & Ry. 461 (1821), the defendant obtained a quantity of meat from a merchant by promising to pay at a future day. The jury found that the promise was made without intention to perform. The judges concluded, however, that the defendant's conviction was erroneous because the pretense "was merely a promise of future conduct, and common prudence and caution would have prevented any injury arising from it." Russ. & Ry. at 463. The correctness of this decision is questionable in light of the reasoning in an earlier decision of the King's Bench, Young v. The King, supra—not mentioned in Rex v. Goodhall. By stating that the "promise of future conduct" was such that "common prudence and caution" could prevent any injury arising therefrom, the new offense was confused with the old common law "cheat." The decision also seems contrary to the plain meaning of the statute, and was so interpreted by two English writers on the law of crimes. Archbold, Pleading and Evidence in Criminal Cases 183 [3rd ed., 1828]; Roscoe, Digest of the Law of Evidence in Criminal Cases 418 [2d Amer. ed., 1840]. The opinion in Rex v. Goodhall, supra, was completely misinterpreted in the case of Commonwealth v. Drew, 1837, 19 Pick. 179, at page 185, 36 Mass. 179, at page 185, in which the Supreme Judicial Court of Massachusetts declared by way of dictum, that under the statute "naked lies" could not be regarded as "false pretences." On the basis of these two questionable decisions, Wharton formulated the following generalization: " . . . the false pretense to be within the statute, must relate to a state of things averred to be at the time existing, and not to a state of things thereafter to exist." Wharton, American Criminal Law 542 [1st ed., 1846]. This generalization has been followed in the majority of American cases, almost all of which can be traced to reliance on Wharton or the two cases mentioned above. . . .

In California, the precedents are conflicting. Early decisions of the district courts of appeal follow the general rule as originally formulated by Wharton, . . . but more recently it has been held, and the holdings were approved by this court in People v. Jones, 36 Cal.2d 373, 377, 224 P.2d 353 that a promise made without intention to perform is a misrepresentation of a state of mind, and thus a misrepresentation of existing fact, and is a false pretense within the meaning of section 484 of the Penal Code. . . . These decisions, like those following the majority rule, were made with little explanation of the reasons for the rule. The Court of Appeals for the District of Columbia has, however, advanced the following reasons in defense of the majority rule: "It is of course true that then, [at the time of the early English cases cited by Wharton, supra] as now, the intention to commit certain crimes was ascertained by looking backward from the act and finding that the accused intended to do what he did do. However, where, as here, the act complained of—namely, failure to repay money or use it as specified at the time of borrowing—is as consonant with ordinary commercial default as with crimial conduct, the danger of applying this technique to prove the crime is quite apparent. Business affairs would be materially incumbered by the ever present threat that a debtor might be subjected to criminal penalties if the prosecutor and jury were of the view that at the time of borrowing he was mentally a cheat. The risk of prosecuting one who is guilty of nothing more than a failure or inability to pay his debts is a very real consideration. . . .

"If we were to accept the government's position the way would be open for every victim of a bad bargain to resort to criminal proceedings to even the score with a judgment proof adversary. No doubt in the development of our criminal law the zeal with which the innocent are protected has provided a measure of shelter for the guilty. However, we do not think it wise to increase the possibility of conviction by broadening the accepted theory of the weight to be attached to the mental attitude of the accused." Chaplin v. United States, 81 U.S. App.D.C. 80, 157 F.2d 697, 698–699, 168 A.L.R. 828; but see the dissenting opinion of Edgerton, J., 157 F.2d at pages 699–701. We do not find this reasoning persuasive. In this state, and in the majority of American states as well as in England, false promises can provide the foundation of a civil action for deceit. Civ.Code, §§ 1572, subd. 4, 1710, subd. 4; see 125 A.L.R. 881–882. In such actions something more than nonperformance is required to prove the defendant's intent not to perform his promise. Nor is proof of nonperformance alone sufficient in criminal prosecutions based on false promises. . . . In such prosecutions the People must, as in all criminal prosecutions, prove their case beyond a reasonable doubt. Any danger, through the instigation of criminal proceedings by disgruntled creditors, to those who have blamelessly encountered "commercial defaults" must, therefore, be predicated upon the idea that trial juries are incapable of weighing the evidence and understanding the instruction that they must be convinced of the defendant's fraudulent intent beyond a reasonable doubt, or that appellate courts will be derelict in discharging their duty to ascertain that there is sufficient evidence to support a conviction.

The problem of proving intent when the false pretense is a false promise is no more difficult than when the false pretense is a misrepresentation of existing fact, and the intent not to perform a promise is regularly proved in civil actions for deceit. Specific intent is also an essential element of many crimes. Moreover, in cases of obtaining property by false pretenses, it must be proved that any misrepresentations of fact alleged by the People were made knowingly and with intent to deceive. If such misrepresentations are made innocently or inadvertently, they can no more form the basis for a prosecution for obtaining property by false pretenses than can an innocent breach of contract. Whether the pretense is a false promise or a misrepresentation of fact, the defendant's intent must be proved in both instances by something more than mere proof of nonperformance or actual falsity. Cf. U.S. v. Ballard, 322 U.S. 78, 64 S.Ct. 882, 88 L.Ed. 1148, and the defendant is entitled to have the jury instructed to that effect. "[T]he accepted theory of the weight to be attached to the mental attitude of the accused" is, therefore, not "broadened," but remains substantially the same. Cf. Chaplin v. United States, supra, 157 F.2d 697, 699. . . .

The purported appeals from the verdicts are dismissed as nonappealable. The judgment and the order denying the motion for a new trial are affirmed.[a]

GIBSON, C.J., and SHENK, EDMONDS and SPENCE, JJ., concur.

SCHAUER, JUSTICE. I concur in the judgment solely on the ground that the evidence establishes, with ample corroboration, the making by the defendant of false representations as to existing facts. On that evidence the convictions should be sustained pursuant to long accepted theories of law.

It is unnecessary on the record to make of this rather simple case a vehicle for the revolutionary holding, contrary to the weight of authority in this state and elsewhere, that a promise to pay or perform at a future date, if unfulfilled, can become the basis for a criminal prosecution on the theory that it was a promise made without a present intention to perform it and that, therefore, whatever of value was received for the promise was property procured by a false representation. Accordingly, I dissent from all that portion of the opinion which discusses and pronounces upon the theories which in my view are extraneous to the proper disposition of any issue actually before us. . . .

CARTER, J., concurs.[1]

Rehearing denied; CARTER and SCHAUER, JJ., dissenting.

a. California Penal Code sec. 476a makes it an offense to issue a check with intent to defraud, without sufficient funds or credit with the bank. D issued a check without sufficient funds. He told the payee that his account was insufficient but promised to make the necessary deposit, which he did not do. It was held that a false promise is not sufficient for conviction under this statute. People v. Poyet, 6 Cal.3d 530, 99 Cal.Rptr. 758, 492 P.2d 1150 (1972).

1. In a prosecution for cheating an intention not to meet a future obligation is a question of fact and a misrepresentation of a present state of mind as to such intention is a false statement as to an existing fact. State v. McMahon, 49 R.I. 107, 140 A. 359 (1928). "Promises, if made without intent to perform, have long been regarded as frauds" in prosecutions for conspiracy to violate the federal statute prohibiting the use of the mails to defraud. United States v. Rowe, 56 F.2d 747, 749 (2d Cir.1932).

A conviction for interstate transportation of money taken by fraud could be upheld where the defendant represented that he was "going" to do something or "would do" something if he knew the statements regarding his state of mind were false at the time they were made. United States v. O'Boyle, 680 F.2d 34 (6th Cir.1982).

A Maryland statute makes it a misdemeanor to obtain services of another with intent to defraud, on a promise of payment of wages, and to fail to pay such wages. Noted in 53 Harv.L.Rev. 893 (1940). Cf. Pollock v. Williams, 322 U.S. 4, 64 S.Ct. 792, 88 L.Ed. 1095 (1944).

A misstatement of law will not support a conviction of false pretenses. State v. Edwards, 178 Minn. 446, 227 N.W. 495 (1929).

STATE v. DUNCAN

Supreme Court of Montana, 1979.
181 Mont. 382, 593 P.2d 1026.

SHEEHY, JUSTICE. Defendant Norman Duncan appeals from his conviction following a nonjury trial in the District Court, Gallatin County, of deceptive practices and the sale of unregistered securities.

Defendant was president of Smart Pak, Inc., of Montana, which produced and marketed a dry granulated charcoal lighter (Smart Start) and a combination package of Smart Start and charcoal briquettes (Smart Pak). Smart Pak, Inc., was one of five corporations set up by defendant in different states to produce and market these products. The parent corporation was Survival Heat Products, Inc., of Idaho Falls.

In the fall of 1975 and spring of 1976, defendant discovered that automated packaging machines could not properly seal the special "child-proof" paper used to package his products. Thereafter, he and other company employees began selling "package sealer agreements" in Gallatin County. The buyers of these contracts paid from $500 to $5000 to become package sealers for Smart Pak. The company supplied them with manual sealing machines and rolls of package paper depending on the amount paid by the sealer. After the sealers sealed the bags on three sides, they sold all properly sealed bags back to the company for 5¢ per bag.

The operation worked smoothly for a short time, but then, due to a series of mix-ups, the sealers did not receive their quota of bags to be sealed. These mix-ups, as asserted by defendant, included a paper shortage and errors in printing the bags.

In March 1976 Smart Pak came under investigation by both the Federal Securities Exchange Commission and the State Auditor's Office in which securities sold in Montana are to be registered. At that point, the focus of these investigations concerned only whether the package sealer agreements were in fact investment contracts which defendant had failed to register.

Although neither agency told defendant to cease operations beyond ceasing to advertise and sell the questioned package sealer agreements, defendant did in fact close down his entire operation and refused to accept or pay for any sealed bags from the sealers or to send any more bags to be sealed. The reason defendant gave for his action was that the adverse publicity concerning the investigations had dried up the sales of these products.

In June 1976 defendant filed a receivership petition for Smart Pak. The sealers were thus left holding the "bags." After the initial few months, they did not receive payment for their work or recoupment of their investment.

On July 9, 1976, the State filed an information against defendant. The information consisted of four counts: Count I charged deceptive practices in violation of section 94–6–307, R.C.M.1947, now section 45–6–317 MCA; Count II charged fraudulent securities practices in violation of section 15–2005(1), R.C.M.1947, now section 30–10–301 MCA; Count III charged failure to register securities violation of section 15–2007, R.C.M.1947, now section 30–10–202 MCA; and Count IV charged issuing a bad check in violation of section 94–6–309(1), R.C.M.1947, now section 45–6–316 MCA. Defendant filed a motion to dismiss the information. On February 22, 1977, the court dismissed Count IV and defendant pleaded "not guilty" to the remaining three counts. On that same day, defendant signed a written waiver of his right to trial by jury.

The case then came on for a hearing, on February 23, 1977, to the court sitting without a jury. On April 4, 1977, the District Court, in open court, found defendant guilty of Counts I and III. The court dismissed Count II. On May 6, 1977, the court entered written findings of fact and imposed sentence of five years imprisonment on Count I and three years imprisonment on Count III, the sentences to run concurrently. Defendant, thereafter, brings this appeal.

Additional facts are discussed as they become pertinent.

The issues presented for our consideration are:

1. Whether the evidence is sufficient to sustain defendant's conviction of deceptive practices? . . .

Defendant was convicted of violating section 94–6–307, R.C.M.1947, now section 45–6–317 MCA. This Court has not construed this statute since its enactment in 1973. Defendant would have us apply the same elements to this statute as we found in its predecessor, "Obtaining money, property or services by false pretenses", section 94–1805, R.C.M.1947. Under the former statute, we held it was necessary to prove four elements for a conviction:

> " . . . (1) The making by the accused to the person injured, of one or more representations of past events or existing facts; (2) that such injured party believed such representations to be true and, relying thereon, parted with money or property, which was received by the accused; (3) that such representations were false; and (4) were made knowingly and designedly, with the intent to defraud such other person." State v. Bratton (1919), 56 Mont. 563, 566, 186 P. 327, 328.

The new statute clearly modifies the elements of proof necessary for conviction and for that reason the cases cited by defendant are inapplicable. Breaking the new statute down into its elements, we determine the State need prove only that:

(1) the defendant acted "purposely or knowingly" in

(2) making or directing another to make a false or deceptive statement

(3) addressed to the public or any person

(4) for the purpose of promoting or procuring the sale of property or services.

Gone are any requirements that the statements relate to past events or existing facts or that the injured party relied thereon in parting with money or property. In addition, "[s]ection 94–6–307 is designed to cover a greater variety of deceptive practices than were formerly proscribed by Montana law." Commission Comment, section 94–6–307, R.C.M.1947. The legislative intent to expand the spectrum of criminal activities in the area of false pretenses previously punishable under Montana law is obvious. It is against these guidelines that we measure defendant's actions.

Initially we note that no real challenge is made by defendant to elements 1, 3, and 4 listed above. Defendant concedes he deliberately sought people to enter into these contracts at specified costs (elements 1 and 4) and that in so doing he caused to be broadcast and published various advertisements asking people to contact him or his employees (element 3). The only question concerns whether his statements to potential sealers were false or deceptive.

The State in its information alleged that defendant or defendant's employees acting at his direction repeatedly made five false statements with the purpose to induce persons to enter into the package sealer contracts at a cost of between $500 and $5000. Proof beyond a reasonable doubt of any one of these five false statements is sufficient to sustain defendant's conviction.

The State alleged that in the package sealer contract itself defendant promised that 5 percent of each sealer's deposit was "to be held in trust for the purpose of guaranteeing repayment of deposit made by Package Sealer at the execution of this Agreement." The contract further stated that the trust fund was to be established at a specified bank in Bozeman.

The evidence presented at trial showed, however, that defendant made only nominal deposits to an escrow, not trust, account until the day before his meeting on March 30, 1976, with State and federal officials concerning possible securities registration violations. At that time, he suddenly deposited $15,000 to this account on advice of counsel. Thereafter, defendant withdrew virtually the entire amount between April 26 and May 6, 1976. Clearly, defendant had no intention of honoring his contractual promise regarding the 5 percent trust reserve.

The other allegations by the State were also supported by sufficient evidence. For example defendant told or implied by means of a prominent wall chart to those persons entering contracts that only 55 such contracts would be sold in the Bozeman area. In fact, 82 contracts were sold in Bozeman and approximately 275 were sold throughout Montana.

Defendant guaranteed each sealer a set quota of bags and a regular income depending on the amount of deposit. Yet as early as January 1976 many sealers were receiving less than their guaranteed quota of bags. Later the corporation office refused to accept or pay for sealed bags from the sealers. Indeed, as defendant himself testified, he needed monthly income of approximately $360,000 to buy the unsealed bags from the supplier and to pay his sealers for sealing them, without taking into account any other expenses or profits. When this figure is compared to the actual monthly income from sales of the products of $2,700, one is compelled to conclude that defendant knew his contractual promises would fail at the time they were made.

As a final example, defendant repeatedly represented that he had secured large contracts for the purchase of his products with Safeway Stores and the Coleman Company, among others. In fact, Safeway had agreed to only a trial contract and the Coleman Company formally demanded that defendant cease misrepresenting the existence of *any* contracts between them.

In sum defendant sold $417,000 worth of package sealer contracts on behalf of his company which had capital stock of only $3,100 and total income from product sales of only $13,500 over five months. The financial obligation under these contracts exceeded $500,000 per month. The inescapable conclusion is that defendant deliberately made false statements to induce others to enter these contracts. His conviction on this count is affirmed.

The judgment of the District Court convicting defendant of deceptive practices and of selling unregistered securities is affirmed.[1]

HASWELL, C. J., and HARRISON, J., concur.

1. Accord: Chaplin v. United States, 81 U.S.App.D.C. 80, 157 F.2d 697 (1946); Commonwealth v. Althause, 207 Mass. 32, 93 N.E. 202 (1910); State v. Allison, 186 S.W. 958 (Mo.App.1916); People v. Karp, 298 N.Y. 213, 81 N.E.2d 817 (1948).

In reversing a conviction of false pretenses based upon promissory fraud the court said: "We recognize there is authority for the view contended for by appellee that misrepresentation of intention is a misrepresentation of an existing fact. We are not persuaded by that argument and hold with the majority opinion that such is not the correct construction. Many cases could be cited. . . ." Bonney v. United States, 254 F.2d 392, 394 (9th Cir.1958).

To obtain payment for a lease in advance is not larceny even if there is no intention of turning over possession of the premises to the lessee because it is merely a false promise. People v. Noblett, 244 N.Y. 355, 155 N.E. 670 (1927).

A selection from the whole truth so partial and fragmentary as to give a misleading impression may be ground for criminal liability despite the literal truth of every statement made. Rex v. Kylsant, 48 T.L.R. 62 (1931).

The Model Penal Code takes the position that a false promise (made without the intention of performance) should be sufficient for conviction but adds that "a majority of the American states adhere to a rule of nonliability in false pretense prosecutions". Tentative Draft No. 2, § 206.2(2), and comment 7 (1954).

A false promise is not sufficient for guilt of false pretenses. Dean v. State, 258 Ark. 32, 522 S.W.2d 421 (1975).

It "cannot amount to a statutory false pretense." Id. at 423.

A false pretense conviction may not be had in Michigan upon a misrepresentation of the present intent to do a future act. People v. Cage, 410 Mich. 401, 301 N.W.2d 819 (1981).

DALY, JUSTICE, concurring in part and dissenting in part:

I concur in the majority decision on Issue Nos. 1, 3, 4, 5, and 6. I further concur in the adoption of the broadened flexible definition of "investment contract" as that term is used in the Securities Act of Montana.

It is to the majority's application to defendant of this newly broadened definition, not before adopted in Montana, that I respectfully dissent.

ALLEN v. STATE

Court of Appeals of Ohio, Lucas County, 1926.
21 Ohio App. 403, 153 N.E. 218.

RICHARDS, J. The plaintiff in error was convicted of obtaining $400 in money by false pretenses. . . .

On Application for Rehearing

RICHARDS, J. The judgment finding the plaintiff in error guilty of obtaining money under false pretenses was affirmed on February 23, 1926. The money which he was convicted of obtaining under false pretenses was in his possession as agent of the owner. It is now urged that the trial court erred in charging the jury as follows:

"It is not a matter of concern as to whether she paid him the money out of her own pocket, or whether it was money which he had collected and held for her as her agent."

As the statute provides for punishing whoever "obtains" anything of value by false and fraudulent pretenses, it is insisted that the conviction could not be had for obtaining money of which the accused already had the possession, and, no doubt, as a general proposition, that is true; but the rule can have no application where the delivery of the money is not necessary in order to obtain dominion over it. If the defendant had possession of the money as agent, and obtained the title to it by false and fraudulent pretenses, that would be sufficient obtaining of the property within the meaning of the statute. The principal [sic] was directly decided in Commonwealth v. Schwartz, 92 Ky. 510, 18 S.W. 775, 36 Am.St.Rep. 609. I quote the third proposition of the syllabus:

"Where one who is in possession of money belonging to another obtains the title by false pretenses, he is guilty of the statutory offense of obtaining money by false pretenses. In such a case it is not

Accord, Kellogg v. State, 551 P.2d 301 (Okl.Cr.1976).

The Kansas "statute does not equate a false promise with a false pretense." State v. Hamilton, 6 Kan.App.2d 646, 631 P.2d 1255 (1981).

necessary to constitute the offense that the possession should have been obtained by false pretenses."

In that case a banker had the money in his possession, which he had collected for the owner, and he thereafter obtained the title to it by false and fraudulent pretenses. He was held to be rightly convicted; the court deciding that the general rule requiring that both the property and the title should be obtained by false pretenses only applies where it takes delivery of the possession to complete the transfer of the title.

Rehearing denied.[1]

WILLIAMS and YOUNG, JJ., concur.

BARKER v. STATE

Supreme Court of Wyoming, 1979.
599 P.2d 1349.

ROSE, JUSTICE. This appeal by appellant-Kenneth L. Barker from a conviction of obtaining property by false pretenses under § 6–3–106, W.S.1977[1], presents only one issue which we need resolve, namely:

> Was § 6–3–106, W.S.1977 (the false-pretenses statute, fn. 1, supra), repealed by § 6–3–110, W.S.1977[2] (the insufficient-funds-check law), insofar as the use of a check with insufficient funds is concerned, thereby precluding a conviction under § 6–3–106?

We will hold that it was not, and affirm the trial court.

1. One who obtained title to property by false pretenses, but did not have possession and never succeeded in getting possession away from the other, was not guilty of false pretenses. Commonwealth v. Randle, 119 Pa.Super. 217, 180 A. 720 (1935).

1. Section 6–3–106, W.S.1977, provides, in relevant part:

> "If any person or persons shall knowingly and designedly, by false pretense or pretenses, obtain from any other person or persons any choses in action, money, goods, wares, chattels, effects, or other valuable thing whatever, with intent to cheat or defraud any such person or persons of the same, every person so offending shall be deemed a cheat, and upon conviction, where the value of such chose in action, money, goods, wares, chattels, effects or other valuable thing shall be twenty-five dollars ($25.00) or more, shall be imprisoned in the penitentiary for a period not more than ten (10) years. . . . "

2. Section 6–3–110, W.S.1977, provides, in relevant part:

> "(a) Whoever, with intent to defraud by obtaining money, merchandise, property, credit, or other thing of value, although no express representation is made in reference thereto, or who, in the payment of any obligation, shall make, draw, utter or deliver any check, draft or order for the payment of money in the sum of fifty dollars ($50.00) or upwards upon any bank, depository, person, firm or corporation, knowing at the time of such making, drawing, uttering or delivering that the maker or drawer has not sufficient funds in such bank, depository, person, firm or corporation for the payment of such check, draft or order in full upon its presentation, shall be guilty of a misdemeanor and upon conviction thereof shall be fined not more than one thousand dollars ($1,000.00) or imprisoned in the county jail for not more than one (1) year or both. . . . "

We parse the aforementioned statutes as follows:

The *insufficient-funds* statute—§ 6–3–110 (later statute) provides:

(1) Whoever writes an insufficient-funds check with intent to defraud *by obtaining property* or

(2) whoever writes an insufficient-funds check with intent to defraud *in the payment of any obligation*

is guilty of a crime.

The *false-pretenses* statute—§ 6–3–106 (earlier statute) says:

Whoever by *false pretenses obtains property* . . . is guilty of a crime.

The essential facts are that Barker opened a checking account with the First Wyoming Bank of Rawlins on April 25, 1978. At the same time, he had the bank prepare a "customer's draft" directing a Montana bank to transfer by wire $30,000.00 to the Rawlins Bank, while representing that he had sufficient funds in the Montana bank to cover the draft. In point of fact, appellant had no current account with the Montana Bank. The following day, Barker returned to the First Wyoming Bank of Rawlins and cashed a $500.00 check against his new checking account. The Rawlins bank cashed Barker's check without ascertaining whether or not the Montana bank had wired the money as he had requested. The Montana bank returned the "customer's draft" unpaid, and the check drawn against the new Rawlins account was without funds.

Appellant seems to concede that the State has proved all of the elements of the crime of obtaining property by false pretenses (§ 6–3–106, supra). Driver v. State, Wyo., 589 P.2d 391, 393 (1979), reh. den. It is, however, his contention that § 6–3–110, supra, was the statute that was violated and that § 6–3–110 repeals § 6–3–106, supra, by implication; therefore he was not subject to trial and conviction under § 6–3–106.

Appellant observes that the false-pretenses statute (§ 6–3–106, supra) was enacted earlier than the insufficient-funds statute (§ 6–3–110, supra), and since the violation of the earlier statute is a felony if the value of the property wrongfully obtained is $25.00 or greater, and since both statutes prohibit the same, identical act, he, therefore, is entitled to be charged with and tried for violation of § 6–3–110, the later insufficient-funds statute (violation of which is a misdemeanor) instead of the more stringent statute making it a crime to obtain property under false pretenses.

The State responded by urging that §§ 6–3–106 and 6–3–110 are calculated to govern different categories of criminal conduct and, therefore, require proof of distinct and different material or essential elements. They do not, it is therefore contended, conflict in the factual setting of this case and no repeal by implication is required.

Our inquiry leads us to the conclusions that obtaining property is never a necessary element of violating the insufficient-funds statute, while the obtaining of property is always a necessary element of the false-pretenses enactment. The insufficient-funds statute prohibits two types of conduct: (1) The mere issuance of a bad check with *intent to defraud by obtaining property* is a violation of the statute, and we do not read in a requirement that property must actually be obtained. (2) Giving a bad check in payment of an obligation is also a violation of the statute, in which case the crime may be committed even though property is not obtained as a result of writing the bad check.[3]

There is authority from other jurisdictions to the effect that, if an insufficient-funds statute does not require as an element for its violation the actual obtaining of property, a prosecution for a more serious theft offense is proper where an insufficient-funds check is issued and property is obtained. State v. Roderick, 85 Idaho 80, 375 P.2d 1005, 1007 (1962); Christiansen v. State, Tex.Cr.App., 575 S.W.2d 42, 44 (1979); State v. Covington, 59 N.J. 536, 284 A.2d 532, 533 (1971); and State v. Culver, 103 Ariz. 505, 446 P.2d 234, 236 (1968).

The State also urges that where the deceit extends beyond the mere passing of an insufficient-funds check, an insufficient-funds statute should not serve to provide protection against a greater theft offense. Authority for this proposition is found in State v. Hodge, 266 Minn. 193, 123 N.W.2d 323 (1963). In that case the Supreme Court of Minnesota stated that the mere passing of an insufficient-funds check would not suffice for prosecution of the felony of swindling—as opposed to prosecution for the gross misdemeanor of issuing checks with knowledge of insufficient funds to back them. However, the court found that additional misrepresentations—defendant's use of his wife's maiden name, a driver's license in that name, the wearing of post office insignia—sufficed to support a felony conviction. Additional authority for this point is found in the discussion in People v. LaRose, 87 Mich.App. 298, 274 N.W.2d 45, 47 (1978), reh. den., of People v. Vida, 2 Mich.App. 409, 140 N.W.2d 559 (1966), aff'd 381 Mich. 595, 166 N.W.2d 465 (1969).

We also find instructive the following thoughts on legislative intent from the Supreme Court of Iowa on the difference between the then-existing misdemeanor bad-check statute and the felony of cheating by false pretenses:

> " . . . It may have been thought that the drawing of checks upon depleted bank accounts was a sin so nearly universal, and which carried so many gradations of moral turpitude, that, even though fraudulent, a seven-year term in the penitentiary was too severe a punishment therefor . . . Section 13047 [the bad-

3. See, Bailey v. State, Wyo., 408 P.2d 244 (1965), in which defendant was convicted of writing a bad check to settle an account for a series of meals previously received.

check statute] seems to cover completely those cases of false pretense *wherein the pretense consists in presenting a check* upon a bank where knowingly sufficient funds are not on deposit . . . ." [Emphasis supplied] State v. Marshall, 202 Iowa 954, 211 N.W. 252, 253 (1926).

In our case, it is clear that the appellant's deceitful scheme extended beyond the mere writing of a bad check and a simple express or implied assurance that the check was good.

The combination of these two arguments for affirmance persuades us to affirm this conviction, with the holding that the crime of obtaining property by false pretenses has been and can be committed, notwithstanding the fact that the property was obtained by writing a bad check where, as in this case, (1) the accused actually obtains property by writing a bad check, and (2) the false representation is more than a simple express or implied statement that the check is good, and (3) all of the other elements of the crime of obtaining property by false pretenses are met.

Affirmed.

BELL v. UNITED STATES

Supreme Court of the United States, 1983.
___ U.S. ___, 103 S.Ct. 2398.

JUSTICE POWELL delivered the opinion of the Court.

The issue presented is whether 18 U.S.C. § 2113(b), a provision of the Federal Bank Robbery Act, proscribes the crime of obtaining money under false pretenses.

I

On October 13, 1978, a Cincinnati man wrote a check for $10,000 drawn on a Cincinnati bank. He endorsed the check for deposit to his account at Dade Federal Savings & Loan of Miami and mailed the check to an agent there. The agent never received the check. On October 17, petitioner Nelson Bell opened an account at a Dade Federal branch and deposited $50—the minimum amount necessary for new accounts. He used his own name, but gave a false address, birth date, and social security number. Later that day, at another branch, he deposited the Cincinnati man's $10,000 check into this new account. The endorsement had been altered to show Bell's account number. Dade Federal accepted the deposit, but put a 20-day hold on the funds. On November 7, as soon as the hold had expired, Bell returned to the branch at which he had opened the account. The total balance, with accrued interest, was then slightly over $10,080. Bell closed the account and was paid the total balance in cash.

Bell was apprehended and charged with violating 18 U.S.C. § 2113(b). The statute provides, in relevant part:

> "Whoever takes and carries away, with intent to steal or purloin, any property or money or any other thing of value exceeding $100 belonging to, or in the care, custody, control, management, or possession of any bank, credit union, or any savings and loan association, shall be fined not more than $5,000 or imprisoned not more than ten years, or both . . . ."

Bell was convicted after a jury trial . . . .

We now affirm.

II

In the 13th century, larceny was limited to trespassory taking: a thief committed larceny only if he feloniously "took and carried away" another's personal property *from his possession.* The goal was more to prevent breaches of the peace than losses of property, and violence was more likely when property was taken from the owner's actual possession.

As the common law developed, protection of property also became an important goal. The definition of larceny accordingly was expanded by judicial interpretation to include cases where the owner merely was deemed to be in possession. Thus when a bailee of packaged goods broke open the packages and misappropriated the contents, he committed larceny. The Carrier's Case, Y.B.Pasch. 13 Edw. IV, f. 9, pl. 5 (Star Ch. and Exch. Ch. 1473), reprinted in 64 Selden Society 30 (1945). The bailor was deemed to be in possession of the contents of the packages, at least by the time of the misappropriation. Similarly, a thief committed "larceny by trick" when he obtained custody of a horse by telling the owner that he intended to use it for one purpose when he in fact intended to sell it and to keep the proceeds. King v. Pear, 1 Leach 212, 168 Eng.Rep. 208 (Cr.Cas.Res.1779). The judges accepted the fiction that the owner retained possession of the horse until it was sold, on the theory that the thief had custody only for a limited purpose.

By the late 18th century, courts were less willing to expand common-law definitions. Thus when a bank clerk retained money given to him by a customer rather than depositing it in the bank, he was not guilty of larceny, for the bank had not been in possession of the money. King v. Bazeley, 2 Leach 835, 168 Eng.Rep. 517 (Cr.Cas.Res. 1799). Statutory crimes such as embezzlement and obtaining property by false pretenses therefore were created to fill this gap.

The theoretical distinction between false pretenses and larceny by trick may be stated simply. If a thief, through his trickery, acquired *title* to the property from the owner, he has obtained property by false pretenses; but if he merely acquired *possession* from the owner, he has committed larceny by trick. In this case the parties agree that Bell is guilty of obtaining money by false pretenses. When the teller at Dade Federal handed him $10,080 in cash Bell acquired title to the money. The only dispute is whether 18 U.S.C. § 2113(b) proscribes the crime of false pretenses, or whether the statute is instead limited to common-law larceny.

III

A

Bell's argument in favor of the narrower reading of § 2113(b) relies principally on the statute's use of the traditional common-law language "takes and carries away." He cites the rule of statutory construction that when a federal criminal statute uses a common-law term without defining it, Congress is presumed to intend the common-law meaning. In § 2113(b), however, Congress has not adopted the elements of larceny in common-law terms. The language "takes and carries away" is but one part of the statute and represents only one element of common-law larceny. Other language in § 2113(b), such as "with intent to steal or purloin," has no established meaning at common law. See *Turley,* supra, at 411–412, 77 S.Ct., at 399–400. Moreover, "taking and carrying away," although not a necessary element of the crime, is entirely consistent with false pretenses.

Two other aspects of § 2113(b) show an intention to go beyond the common-law definition of larceny. First, common-law larceny was limited to thefts of tangible personal property. This limitation excluded, for example, the theft of a written instrument embodying a chose in action. Section 2113(b) is thus broader than common-law larceny, for it covers "any property or money or any other thing of value exceeding $100." Second, and of particular relevance to the distinction at issue here, common-law larceny required a theft from the possession of the owner. When the definition was expanded, it still applied only when the owner was deemed to be in possession. Section 2113(b), however, goes well beyond even this expanded definition. It applies when the property "belong[s] to," or is "in the care, custody, control, management, or possession of," a covered institution.

In sum, the statutory language does not suggest that it covers only common-law larceny. Although § 2113(b) does not apply to a case of false pretenses in which there is not a taking and carrying away, it proscribes Bell's conduct here. The evidence is clear that he "t[ook] and carrie[d] away, with intent to steal or purloin, [over $10,000 that was] in the care, custody, control, management, or possession of" Dade Federal Savings & Loan.

B

The legislative history of § 2113(b) also suggests that Congress intended the statute to reach Bell's conduct. As originally enacted in

1934, the Federal Bank Robbery Act, ch. 304, 48 Stat. 783, governed only robbery—a crime requiring a forcible taking. Congress apparently was concerned with " 'gangsters who operate habitually from one State to another in robbing banks.' "

By 1937 the concern was broader, for the limited nature of the original Act " 'ha[d] led to some incongruous results.' " It was possible for a thief to steal a large amount from a bank " 'without displaying any force or violence and without putting any one in fear,' " and he would not violate any federal law. Congress amended the Act to fill this gap, adding language now found at § 2113(a) and (b). Although the term "larceny" appears in the legislative reports, the congressional purpose plainly was to protect banks from those who wished to steal banks' assets—even if they used no force in doing so.

The congressional goal of protecting bank assets is entirely independent of the traditional distinction on which Bell relies. To the extent that a bank needs protection against larceny by trick, it also needs protection from false pretenses. We cannot believe that Congress wished to limit the scope of the amended Act's coverage, and thus limit its remedial purpose, on the basis of an arcane and artificial distinction more suited to the social conditions of 18th century England than the needs of 20th century America. Such an interpretation would signal a return to the "incongruous results" that the 1937 amendment was designed to eliminate.

IV

We conclude that 18 U.S.C. § 2113(b) is not limited to common-law larceny. Although § 2113(b) may not cover the full range of theft offenses, it covers Bell's conduct here. His conviction therefore was proper, and the judgment of the Court of Appeals accordingly is

Affirmed.

STATE v. MOSES

Court of Appeals of Arizona, Division 1, Department B, 1979.
123 Ariz. 296, 599 P.2d 252.

OPINION

SCHROEDER, PRESIDING JUDGE. Appellant, Willie Joe Moses, was convicted after a jury trial of obtaining money by a confidence game in violation of former A.R.S. § 13–312, and of obtaining money by means of a scheme or artifice to defraud in violation of former A.R.S. § 13–320.01.[1] He appeals only from his conviction under the latter section and the sentence imposed on that conviction of not less than five nor more than ten years.

1. With some modifications, these statutes have been enacted in the present Criminal Code as A.R.S. § 13–2310.

Appellant's conviction under A.R.S. § 13–320.01 was based upon his participation in a scam known as the "Jamaican Switch." The appellant approached the victim and, in an assumed foreign accent, asked directions to a boarding house. The appellant's accomplice, Patricia Hard, then approached appellant and offered to show him to a boarding house. Appellant then showed the victim that he had a large amount of cash and stated that he did not trust the woman. He prevailed upon the victim to hold the cash for him, and to indicate his good faith by placing the victim's own money in the same handkerchief with that of the appellant. The handkerchief was then deposited in the trunk of the victim's automobile. Unknown to the victim, however, the appellant switched the handkerchiefs. When the victim later opened the handkerchief, he found only folded paper. He was unable to relocate either the appellant or Hard.

The sole issue raised in this appeal is whether the state must prove that the victim intended to transfer title of the property to the appellant in order to support a conviction under § 13–320.01. The appellant argues that this essential element is missing because the victim merely intended to part with his money temporarily as a display of good faith.

A.R.S. § 13–320.01 provides as follows:

> Any person who, pursuant to a scheme or artifice to defraud, knowingly and intentionally obtains or attempts to obtain money, property or any other thing of value by means of false or fraudulent pretenses, representations or promises is guilty of a felony punishable by imprisonment in the state prison for not more than twenty years, by a fine not to exceed twenty thousand dollars, or both.

Appellant argues that this provision is a codification of the common law crime of false pretenses, and that even though the statute itself makes no reference to any requirement of intent to transfer title or ownership, that element is nevertheless embodied in it. Appellant relies upon cases in other jurisdictions holding that proof of an intent to pass to the victim only temporary possession of the property is not sufficient to sustain a conviction under the statutes of those states. That view is succinctly stated in Perkins on Criminal Law, ch. 4 § 4(C)(1) 2nd ed. 1969, p. 306:

> . . . [T]he generally accepted view is that the crime of false pretenses has not been committed unless the wrongdoer, by his fraudulent scheme, has obtained the title or ownership—or whatever property interest the victim had in the chattel if it was less than title.

Appellant's entire argument is premised on the assumption that in enacting A.R.S. § 13–320.01 the legislature intended to codify a common law crime of false pretenses. We disagree. The State correctly recognizes that the section was derived from the Federal Mail Fraud

Statute, 18 U.S.C. §§ 1341–1343. It was not enacted until 1976 and encompasses a very broad range of fraudulent activities.

We hold that the State offered sufficient evidence to support the appellant's conviction of fraudulently obtaining money pursuant to a scheme or artifice, in violation of former A.R.S. § 13–320.01.

Affirmed.

OGG, C.J., concurring.

JACOBSON, J., concurs in the result.

SECTION 5. THEFT

The technical distinctions between larceny, embezzlement and false pretenses serve no useful purpose in the criminal law but are useless handicaps from the standpoint of the administration of criminal justice. One solution has been to combine all three in one section of the code, under some such name as "larceny" or "theft". Some of the new penal codes include these three offenses under the name of "theft" but with definitions that include much that had not been included before. A more sweeping provision, adopted in a few states, provides that the offense of theft shall include the offenses previously known as larceny, embezzlement, false pretenses, extortion, blackmail and receiving stolen property, and is also worded so as to provide punishment for conduct not previously punishable.

STATE v. McCARTNEY

Supreme Court of Montana, 1978.
179 Mont. 49, 585 P.2d 1321.

HASWELL, CHIEF JUSTICE. Defendant appeals from his conviction by the District Court, Fergus County, after a nonjury trial before Judge LeRoy L. McKinnon. Defendant was charged with one count of felony theft and one count of felony forgery. The trial court found defendant guilty of both crimes and sentenced him to five years in the state penitentiary, with four years suspended. On appeal, defendant contends that the state failed to prove the elements of felony theft and forgery, that the evidence was insufficient to sustain the judgment of conviction, and that he was tried by the District Court without properly having waived his right to trial by jury.

The facts, essentially undisputed, are as follows:

In April 1970, defendant and James T. Johnson entered into a cattle sharing agreement which provided that defendant was to receive 60 percent and Johnson 40 percent of the yearly calf production from cows owned by Johnson which were to be pastured on land leased by defendant. The calves were to be branded in the spring with Johnson's 3-Lazy T brand and the 60-40 split was to be made when the calves were sold in the fall.

The agreement ended in 1974 and the remaining calves were apparently sold at that time. Defendant thereafter sold his ranch. In 1975, a cow was found on property owned by the Ayers Hutterite colony, which bordered the land defendant had leased. The cow carried Johnson's brand. The president of the Ayers colony, John Stahl, believing the stray belonged to defendant, approached defendant about purchasing the cow. Defendant agreed to sell, and made out a bill of sale on November 26, 1976. Defendant signed Johnson's name as "seller" and his own name as "witness" on the bill of sale. Defendant also drew a Lazy T in the middle of a 3, as the brand of the cow to be sold, on the bill of sale. That brand was similar to Johnson's 3-Lazy T brand. The Ayers colony promised defendant some beef as consideration for the sale.

On March 1, 1977, Stahl checked with the brand office in Lewistown about the Lazy T in the middle of a 3 brand. He had noticed the cow's brand did not match that brand as drawn by defendant on the bill of sale. Stahl was told the brand on the bill of sale was not Johnson's brand and he then called defendant who told him to "put on the other brand." Stahl assumed defendant meant Johnson's 3-Lazy T brand.

On March 2, 1977, Stahl sold the cow at the Central Montana Livestock Market for $241. The brand office thereafter contacted Johnson, and upon learning he had not sold the cow, began an investigation of the transaction. Defendant was charged and arrested for theft and forgery, both felonies, as a result of that investigation.

Defendant first contends he had neither actual nor constructive possession of the cow prior to its sale and did not deliver the cow to anyone and therefore cannot be guilty of theft. Under the old criminal code provisions and cases interpreting them, the State had to prove a defendant took possession of another's property and carried it away to secure a larceny conviction. Defendant cites cases to that effect and Am.Jur.2d comments concerning the classic elements of larceny. The classic taking and carrying away, however, has not been continued in the criminal codes under which defendant was convicted.

Section 94–6–302, R.C.M.1947, provides in pertinent part:

> "*Theft.* (1) A person commits the offense of theft when he purposely or knowingly obtains or exerts unauthorized control over property of the owner and:
>
> "(a) has the purpose of depriving the owner of the property;
>
> "(b) purposely or knowingly uses, conceals, or abandons the property in such manner as to deprive the owner of the property . . ."

Section 94–2–101(32), R.C.M.1947, defines "obtain" as:

> "(a) in relation to property, to bring about a transfer of interest or possession whether to the offender or to another."

Section 94–2–101(33), R.C.M.1947, provides:

> " 'Obtains or exerts control' includes but is not limited to the taking, carrying away, or sale, conveyance, transfer of title to, interest in, or possession of property."

The Commission comment to section 94–6–302, provides in part:

> "After extended and exhaustive study and consideration by the commission, matching various combinations of the subsections to cover every type of conduct proscribed by the old law, and extending such matching to conduct covered by statutes in other states, it is believed this section will cover any conceivable form of theft.
>
> ". . .
>
> ". . . the method by which unauthorized control is obtained or exerted is immaterial in subsection (1) . . . "

It is clear that these statutes encompass more than the actual taking and asportation of another's property. This state has adopted its code provisions from Illinois. The precursor of section 94–6–302, is Chapter 38, § 16–1 of the Illinois Criminal Code. In discussing the scope of "theft" under this statute, the Illinois Court stated in People v. Nunn (1965), 63 Ill.App.2d 465, 212 N.E.2d 342, 344:

> "Section 16–1(a)(1) is not limited to the theft of property in which only the actor who initiates the wrongful asportation is guilty of the offense. A person who 'knowingly obtains or exerts unauthorized control over property of the owner' is the statutory description of a thief, provided only that his act is accompanied by the requisite mental state. As expressly pointed out in section 15–8, the phrase 'obtains or exerts control' over property includes, but is not limited to, the taking or carrying away of the property. It also includes (though still not exclusively) the bringing about of a transfer of possession of the property."

In People v. Petitjean (1972), 7 Ill.App.3d 231, 287 N.E.2d 137, the court held the theft statute included the wrongful sale or conveyance of property and was not limited to theft of property in which only the actor who institutes the wrongful asportation is guilty of the offense.

In the present case, the State proved that defendant brought about a transfer of title and possession of James E. Johnson's cow to one other than the owner through a wrongful sale which resulted in depriving James E. Johnson of his property. If the requisite mental state is proven along with this, no more is required under section 94–6–302.

Defendant's next contention is that the State did not prove he acted knowingly or purposely with respect to obtaining or exerting unauthorized control over Johnson's cow. He contends in essence the District Court was required to accept his testimony which was plausible, and therefore the testimony negated any finding by the District Court that he had the requisite mental state. There was however, sufficient circumstantial evidence for the trial court to conclude otherwise.

Defendant testified that in the spring of 1970 or 1971, he branded a calf with the 3-Lazy T brand believing the calf was from one of Johnson's cows. Two weeks later he saw that calf following one of his own cows. Realizing he had been mistaken as to the calf's origin, defendant branded it again, this time with one of his own brands. When Stahl called him about the stray in 1976, defendant thought it was the twice-branded cow. He further testified he signed Johnson's name as "seller" on the bill of sale because he thought the 3-Lazy T would "show up better" than his own brand when the cow was examined. He wanted the seller's name to conform to the most legible brand. Defendant also asserts that when he told Stahl to "put the other brand" on the bill of sale, he meant his own brand, not Johnson's. The entire episode, according to defendant, was a mistake compounded by misunderstanding.

On the other hand, the circumstantial evidence negating this misunderstanding, includes: defendant's failure to ask Stahl whether the stray had two brands when he was told of the cow's discovery; defendant's failure to mention the twice-branded cow story when Stahl called him about the brand discrepancy; defendant's drawing of a brand similar to Johnson's rather than his own on the bill of sale; defendant's signing of Johnson's name on the "seller" line and his own name on the "witness" line on the bill of sale; and defendant's failure to apprise Johnson of the situation at any time before or after the sale. We note moreover, that defendant had experience as a brand inspector and knew that the brand drawn on the bill of sale must be that of the animal's seller as listed on the bill of sale.

Clearly, under these circumstances, the determination of intent was to be made by the trial court as the trier of fact. As we stated in State v. Farnes (1976), 171 Mont. 368, 558 P.2d 472, 475, 33 St.Rep. 1270.

> "The element of felonious intent in every contested criminal case must necessarily be determined from facts and circumstances of the particular case—this for the reason that criminal intent, being a state of mind, is rarely susceptible of direct or positive proof and therefore must usually be inferred from the facts testified to by witnesses and the circumstances as developed by the evidence . . ."

Here, the District Court resolved the question of intent against defendant.

The Judgment is affirmed.[1]

1. Theft by receiving is properly charged under the general theft statute. State v. Taylor, 570 P.2d 697 (Utah 1977). For another broad consolidation statute punishing several forms of unauthorized control over the property of another, see State v. Bourbeau, 250 N.W.2d 259 (N.D.1977). The specific theory of theft need not be alleged in the indictment. Williams v. State, 648 P.2d 603 (Alaska App.1982).

STATE v. SAYLOR

Supreme Court of Kansas, 1980.
228 Kan. 498, 618 P.2d 1166.

PRAGER, JUSTICE. This is a direct appeal from a conviction of theft by deception (K.S.A.1979 Supp. 21–3701[*b*]). The Court of Appeals in a published opinion, State v. Saylor, 4 Kan.App.2d 563, 608 P.2d 421 (1980), reversed and remanded with directions to grant the defendant a new trial on the lesser included offense of attempt to commit theft by deception. We granted review on petition of the State.

The facts in the case are well summarized in the opinion of the Court of Appeals. On September 27, 1978, in the city of Lawrence, a K-Mart store security officer observed the defendant, Glenn Lee Saylor, as he made numerous trips through the store placing items in his shopping cart. He would go to the hardware department with items in the cart, but would leave that department with an empty cart. The security officer observed the defendant move about in one particular area, but was unable to see exactly what he was doing. She saw him take a bottle of glue to the area, use it, and then return it to a counter. The defendant then made a minor purchase and left the store. The security officer notified her supervisor. On investigation, she found in the hardware department a cardboard box which should have been located in the toy department and which ordinarily would contain a $13.97 plastic pig toy chest. The cover of the box had recently been resealed with glue. The security officer did not move or otherwise touch the box. When the defendant returned to the store later that evening, the security officer and the police were on hand. The defendant went to the hardware department where he placed the box in a shopping cart. He proceeded to the checkout counter and paid for two items—a quart of oil and a plastic pig toy chest priced at $13.97. The checkout cashier did not suspect there was anything wrong. The defendant was arrested outside the store in the parking lot. There the box was opened and found to contain several chainsaws, metal rules, cigarettes, heavy duty staple guns, and record albums, with a total value in excess of $500. The defendant was arrested for theft. He was charged with and convicted of theft by deception under K.S.A. 1979 Supp. 21–3701(*b*).

The defendant appealed raising several points of alleged error. The Court of Appeals reversed the conviction, finding error in the trial court's failure to instruct the jury on *attempted* theft by deception. Noting this court's decision in State v. Finch, 223 Kan. 398, 573 P.2d 1048 (1978), the Court of Appeals held that, since there had been no actual reliance by or actual deception of the corporate victim, K-Mart, the defendant could only be guilty of attempted theft by deception. The Court of Appeals reversed the conviction and directed a new trial on attempted theft by deception.

On petition for review, the State of Kansas urges this court to reconsider the elements of theft by deception as enumerated by *Finch,* claiming that by interpreting 21–3701(*b*) to require reliance by or actual deception of the owner, the court added to the offense of theft an element not contained in the statutory definition. Alternatively, the State argues that the present case is distinguishable from *Finch,* claiming that there was actual deception in this case, at least in part, since the checkout cashier was totally unaware of defendant's larcenous intent and no one within the employment of K-Mart had more than a suspicion of defendant's scheme at the time defendant purchased the merchandise and left the store with the box. The State finally argues that, under the consolidated theft statute, a conviction of theft should be sustained, even though the burden of proof is not met as to the offense specified in the indictment or information, if the evidence supports conviction of theft under any other subsection of K.S.A. 1979 Supp. 21–3701.

We have reconsidered the rule announced in State v. Finch, and have concluded that it is a correct statement of the law. The syllabus in *Finch* states the rule which is consistent with prior decisions of this court and with the rule generally accepted throughout the United States:

> "In order to convict a defendant of theft by deception under K.S.A. 21–3701(*b*) the state must prove that the defendant with the required intent obtained control over another's property *by means* of a false statement or representation. To do so the state must prove that the victim was actually deceived and relied in whole or in part upon the false representation."

The rationale of the rule and the reasons why it was adopted by this court are discussed in depth in that opinion. We have concluded, however, that, under its particular facts, the present case is distinguishable from *Finch,* in that the K-Mart checkout cashier, who permitted the defendant to leave the store premises with the box, was completely unaware of the true contents hidden in the box and relied upon the deception practiced by the defendant at that time.

The State argues that the defendant could have properly been charged under section (*a*) of K.S.A. 1979 Supp. 21–3701, since the evidence established that the defendant, with intent to deprive the owner permanently of the possession, use, or ownership of the owner's property, exerted unauthorized control over the property by concealing the articles in the cardboard box. We agree with the State. It is clear to us that where a customer in a self-service store conceals on his person, or in a box or receptacle, property of the store and has the requisite specific criminal intent, that customer has committed a theft under subsection (*a*) of K.S.A. 1979 Supp. 21–3701. The specific criminal intent is difficult to prove, however, unless the customer actually fails to make proper payment for the property at the cashier's desk and leaves the store with the same remaining concealed. In this case, the defendant was not specifically charged under subsection (*a*) of K.S.A. 1979 Supp. 21–3701. The State did not seek to amend the information to include that subsection, nor was an appropriate instruction on that subsection given to the jury. The State thus relied only on proving theft by *deception* under subsection (*b*). The conviction of the defendant must stand or fall on the sufficiency of the evidence to show that the defendant, with the required specific intent, obtained control over the property by deception. We have concluded that the evidence was sufficient and that an instruction on attempted theft was not required.

In concluding that the evidence established a completed theft by deception, the trial court pointed out that the security employees of K-Mart had only a suspicion that the defendant was planning to steal articles of merchandise from the store. The actual merchandise taken was not determined until the box was opened following the defendant's arrest in the parking lot. We think it also important to note that the act of deception and false representation did not actually occur until the defendant deceived the cashier into believing that the box contained a plastic pig toy chest of a value of $13.97.

The rule of *Finch* simply requires the State to prove that the victim was actually deceived and relied wholly or *in part* upon the false representation made by the defendant. We note that this same result was reached under similar factual circumstances in Lambert v. State, 55 Ala.App. 242, 314 So.2d 318, cert. denied 294 Ala. 763, 314 So.2d 322 (1975). In *Lambert,* it was held that *reliance* upon a misrepresentation was proved in a prosecution for false pretense, although the evidence showed that numerous persons in the store knew of defendant's scheme to change price tags on merchandise, where the checkout girl to whom defendant took the falsely priced merchandise relied upon the false representation as to those prices and parted with the merchandise, having no knowledge of the defendant's scheme. Since the undisputed evidence in this case showed the cashier at the checkout counter at K-Mart relied upon the false representation made by the defendant as to the contents of the box and permitted defendant to take control of the box and its contents outside the confines of the store, we hold that the trial court did not err in concluding that there was the required reliance and thus an instruction on the lesser offense of attempted theft by deception was not required.

We now address the contention of the State that, under the consolidated statute, K.S.A. 1979 Supp. 21–3701, a conviction of theft may be upheld even though the burden of proof is not sustained as to the particular subsection specified in the information, if the evidence supports the conviction of theft under any one of the other subsections. We agree with the State that the primary purpose of the consolidated theft statute was to eliminate the complexities of pleading and proving the vague historical distinctions in the various types of theft.

See comment, Judicial Council, 21–3701 (1968). Professor Paul E. Wilson, in his article, Thou Shalt Not Steal: Ruminations on the New Kansas Theft Law, 20 Kan.L.Rev. 385 (1972), makes the following observation:

> "[C]onsolidation should eliminate the procedural difficulties that sometimes result from the fact that boundaries between the traditional theft crimes are obscure and the defendant who is charged with one crime cannot be convicted by proving another. An inexperienced—or even an experienced—prosecutor may have difficulty in determining whether a given set of facts indicates larceny, false pretense, or embezzlement. And even though the right charge is selected, a conviction based on borderline facts is more likely to be challenged on appeal. The objective, then, has been to define the crime broadly enough to include all vaguely separated theft offenses, so that evidence of appropriation by any of the forbidden methods will support the charge." p. 393.

Likewise, the Model Penal Code, § 223.1 (Proposed Off. Draft, May 4, 1962), provides:

> "(1) *Consolidation of Theft Offenses.* Conduct denominated theft in this Article constitutes a single offense embracing the separate offenses heretofore known as larceny, embezzlement, false pretense, extortion, blackmail, fraudulent conversion, receiving stolen property, and the like. An accusation of theft may be supported by evidence that it was committed in any manner that would be theft under this Article, notwithstanding the specification of a different manner in the indictment or information, subject only to the power of the Court to ensure fair trial by granting a continuance or other appropriate relief where the conduct of the defense would be prejudiced by lack of fair notice or by surprise."

Under the former Kansas code as it existed prior to the adoption of the present code, effective July 1, 1970, the crime of false pretenses was covered by K.S.A. 21–551 and 21–552 (Corrick 1964). The legislature recognized the difficulties of proof in this area by enacting K.S.A. 21–553 (Corrick 1964):

> "21–553. Conviction of larceny under 21–551, 21–552. If upon the trial of any person indicted for any offense prohibited in the last two sections, it should be proved that he obtained the money or other thing in question in such manner as to amount in law to a larceny, he shall not by reason thereof be entitled to an acquittal, but he shall be convicted and punished as if the offense had been proved as charged."

In Talbot v. Wulf, 122 Kan. 1, 5, 251 P. 438 (1926), this court stated that G.S. 21–553 was designed to prevent a failure of justice on account of a variance between pleading and proof dependent on the distinction between the crime of larceny and the crime of obtaining property by false pretense.

It is obvious to us that one of the purposes of the enactment of the consolidated theft statute, K.S.A. 21–3701, was to avoid the pitfalls of pleading where a defendant might escape a conviction for one type of theft by proof that he had committed another type of theft. There is now only the single crime of theft which is complete when a man takes property not his own with the intent to take it and deprive the owner thereof. A defendant may be convicted of theft upon proof of facts establishing either embezzlement, larceny, receiving stolen property, or obtaining property by false pretense. It has long been the law of Kansas that an accusatory pleading in a criminal action may, in order to meet the exigencies of proof, charge the commission of the same offense in different ways. In such a situation, a conviction can be upheld only on one count, the function of the added counts in the pleading being to anticipate and obviate fatal variance between allegations and proof. Thus, it has been held proper to charge by several counts of an information the same offense committed in different ways or by different means to the extent necessary to provide for every possible contingency in the evidence.

Where there is a question in the mind of the prosecutor as to what the evidence will disclose at trial, the correct procedure is to charge the defendant in the alternative under those subsections to K.S.A. 1979 Supp. 21–3701 which may possibly be established by the evidence. This may properly be done under Kansas law by charging several counts in the information to provide for every possible contingency in the evidence. By so doing, the jury may properly be instructed on the elements necessary to establish the crime of theft under any of the subsections charged and the defendant will have no basis to complain that he has been prejudiced in his defense.

It should also be noted that, under K.S.A. 1979 Supp. 22–3201(4), a trial court may permit a complaint or information to be amended at any time before verdict or finding if no additional crime is charged and if substantial rights of the defendant are not prejudiced. Following that statute, we have a number of decisions which hold that it is proper for the State to amend the information during trial by adding words which change the method by which the particular crime was committed in the particular case. For example in State v. Lamb, 215 Kan. 795, 798, 530 P.2d 20 (1974), the State was permitted to amend a charge of kidnapping by adding the words "or deception" to the allegation "by means of force," since there was evidence presented in the case that the kidnapping was accomplished both through force and deception. In State v. Bell, 224 Kan. 105, 106, 577 P.2d 1186 (1978), the State was permitted to amend certain counts in the information, charging kidnapping, to add the words "by force and deception" to make the information conform to the evidence presented. See also State v. Rives, 220 Kan. 141, 144–45, 551 P.2d 788 (1976) (where the information was amended to charge that the defendant took the purloined property "from the presence of" a named individual rather than "from the person of" the same individual); State v. Ferguson,

221 Kan. 103, 105, 558 P.2d 1092 (1976) (where the State was permitted to amend the *date* of the violation originally charged in the information). In this case, as mentioned above, the State did not seek to amend the charge of theft contained in the information to include an allegation of theft under subsection (*a*) of K.S.A. 1979 Supp. 21–3701 and the jury was not instructed on that charge. Thus, the jury could not properly consider the question of defendant's guilt or innocence of the crime of theft under subsection (*a*).

In closing, it should be noted that we have considered the other point of complained error raised in defendant's brief that the district court erred in allowing the State to introduce certain rebuttal testimony. We find this point to be without merit.

For the reasons set forth above, we hold that the judgment of the district court upholding the conviction of the defendant for theft by deception (K.S.A. 1979 Supp. 21–3701[*b*]) is affirmed. It is further ordered that the judgment of the Court of Appeals is reversed for the reasons set forth in the opinion.

UNITED STATES v. WILSON

United States Court of Appeals, Eighth Circuit, 1980.
636 F.2d 225.

LAY, CHIEF JUDGE. James T. Wilson was found guilty by a jury of conversion of government property in violation of 18 U.S.C. § 641. Specifically, Wilson is charged with using a government secretary to type documents for a private business venture.[1] The district court found that Wilson lacked the requisite criminal intent to steal or convert government property and granted a motion for judgment of acquittal. The United States has appealed. We affirm the judgment of acquittal.

Wilson was employed in the Kansas City Regional Office of the Department of Health, Education and Welfare (HEW), where he held the position of assistant regional director in charge of the Office of Planning & Evaluation (P & E). From 1975 until April, 1978, Irma Mullane was his secretary. In July, 1977, a reorganization of HEW was ordered. The regional Planning & Evaluation Offices were abolished effective September 30, 1977. Wilson remained on the payroll after September 30, but the P & E staff was gone and P & E had no further duties. In February 1978, Wilson was appointed director of the Kansas City Office of Service Delivery Assessment (SDA). This office was similar to P & E in that it evaluated the effectiveness of HEW programs, but where P & E was directed by regional officials, the various SDA offices received their work orders from a central

1. We have recognized that misuse of federal funds and equipment and the time of federal employees may be grounds for criminal convictions. See, e.g., United States v. Pintar, 630 F.2d 1270 (8th Cir.1980); United States v. May, 625 F.2d 186, 190–92 (1980); United States v. Anderson, 579 F.2d 455 (8th Cir.), cert. denied, 439 U.S. 980, 99 S.Ct. 567, 58 L.Ed.2d 651 (1978).

office in Washington, D.C. which coordinated the efforts of the regional SDAs.

In the summer and fall of 1977 Wilson began exploring the possibility of starting a business known as "The Woodworks". This business was to make working space, advice and equipment available to people working on woodworking projects. Wilson's initial task was to prepare a 176 page "business plan" discussing the prospects for a business of this nature. He concedes that his secretary, Irma Mullane, typed most of this plan and did other typing for The Woodworks during the period between the abolition of P & E and the first duties of SDA. Mullane testified that Wilson first asked her to do this work in the late summer of 1977, and that from then until her retirement in April 1978 she "worked on it pretty constant", and that "many weeks it was almost 100 percent."

After Mullane's retirement, Wilson asked secretaries Charla Phipps and Barbara Proenza to do typing for his business. Phipps apparently spent several weeks preparing a lease for business property and Proenza typed approximately 18 letters over a period of several months. These secretaries agreed the work was voluntary and did not interfere with their official duties.

An undercover investigation by a Kansas City newspaper reporter revealed Wilson's use of secretaries for his business and Wilson was charged in a six count indictment.[2] The district court dismissed Counts One and Four prior to trial. The jury convicted Wilson of Count Five (renumbered as Count Three) for conversion of Mullane's services and acquitted him on all other counts.

Evidence of Intent.

A conviction under 18 U.S.C. § 641 requires proof of "criminal intent to steal or knowingly convert, that is, *wrongfully* to deprive another of possession of property." Our inquiry here is whether the evidence showed that Wilson possessed the requisite criminal intent during the period named in the indictment, October 1977 through March 1978.

Wilson does not dispute Mullane's testimony that she performed this work beginning in the late summer of 1977. Wilson testified, however, that he told Mullane to do this work only when she had no official work and that she was not to allow this work to interfere with government work. No one contradicted this testimony. Further,

2. Count One alleged mail fraud. The alleged scheme involved diversion of government supplies, equipment and secretarial time; the mailing was a letter from Wilson discussing the lease. Count Two charged Wilson with wire fraud based upon the same scheme and the transmission of Charla Phipps' "Time & Attendance Report." Count Three alleged false statements (18 U.S.C. §§ 1001–02) based on issuance of a Time & Attendance Report for Irma Mullane misrepresenting her work; Count Four also alleged false statements by Wilson during the initial investigation by HEW regional officials. Count Five alleged conversion of Irma Mullane's services between October 1, 1977 and March 31, 1978, and Count Six charged Wilson with conversion of a government three-ring binder.

Wilson insisted that when Mullane did this typing, he and Mullane had little or no government work to do because of a period of inactivity caused by the transition from P & E to SDA.

The order to abolish P & E came out in July 1977, effective September 30, 1977. From July to October the P & E employees finished their projects and all but Wilson and Mullane left the P & E payroll. Thomas Budd, a P & E employee, said the reorganization caused P & E work to come to a standstill. After September 30, Wilson said he had no more P & E duties and had not been named to the SDA staff. Wilson's first contact with SDA occurred in January of 1978 when he attended an SDA organizational meeting in Washington, D.C. Although an agenda for SDA work projects was distributed at this meeting, Wilson was not yet an SDA employee. After he attended the meeting he decided he would be interested in working with SDA and expressed this desire to Thomas Higgins, the principal regional official in Kansas City. Wilson did not receive his official appointment until February 7, 1980. He insists he had no SDA duties until March or April of 1978.[3]

Wilson acknowledged that he was told at the SDA meeting in January that he could work on regional office projects, and claimed he did some small projects for Higgins during this period. Higgins, who began his job in September 1977, agreed that Wilson did some reports to help Higgins learn about his job. Higgins also agreed that the P & E office was "on hold" until SDA projects got underway, and that there was a lag in work assignments until SDA began. Libby Halperin, the former head of SDA, agreed the transition caused a lag in work, but said that she believed Wilson had work from the regional office.

The United States claims that Wilson's intent is shown by his failure to report his inactivity and by testimony that he avoided opportunities to take on other work. However, Wilson claimed he told Higgins when he had nothing to do and that he made his lack of work known to Halperin. Higgins and Halperin denied that Wilson ever told them he was not busy but were not specific about the time period.[4] There was some testimony about failures to seek out or accept work, but it apparently referred to periods later than the months when Mullane did her typing. James Bergfalk, formerly Higgins' assistant, testified that Wilson declined to participate in some regional projects and that Wilson never told him about a lack of work. The

3. The major project Mullane worked on was the business plan. It is not clear when she finished this, although Wilson implied it was finished in December when he began to pursue other aspects of the proposal. If this is correct, the bulk of Mullane's work came before Wilson had even gone to his first meeting with SDA.

4. In fact, Higgins implied that he knew Wilson had nothing to do during at least part of this period. He stated that "once they [SDA] started doing assessments, I don't recall them ever saying they had nothing to do. There was a period of time prior to the [SDA] operation getting its first assessment when obviously they didn't have that much to do."

record would indicate, however, that Bergfalk had to be referring to periods later than the period of this count since he did not begin his job until just before Mullane retired. Similarly, Milton Fick, a former SDA employee, claimed that files could have been worked on and that Wilson could have volunteered for other work that was pending in other regions or in the Kansas City region. However, Fick did not start working with SDA until January 1978, and his testimony refers to periods of inactivity in late spring and summer of 1978 and in July-August of 1979. Thus, there is no clear testimony identifying work that Wilson declined to do during the period in question.[5]

Finally, there was no testimony that Wilson ordered Mullane to conceal her efforts, or that Wilson concealed this work at the time it was being performed. There is also no indication he reported his activities or the activities of his secretary during this period to anyone although later that spring Wilson informed Higgins that he was working on a private business project.

This court recently observed that "[t]he touchstone of conversion is the exercise of such control over property that serious interference with the rights of the owner result . . . ." In order to constitute a violation of section 641 the government must prove the defendant's criminal intent beyond a reasonable doubt; that is, that the defendant knowingly and purposely exercised control over the property in such a manner that a serious interference with the rights of the government would result. As our discussion indicates, the agency reorganization left Wilson and his secretary with little or no assigned work during the period named in this count. Further, there is no convincing evidence that Wilson avoided work or concealed the use of his secretary for private work. Under these unique circumstances, although there may have been a breach of fiduciary duty by Wilson, we find insufficient evidence to allow a jury to find beyond a reasonable doubt that the defendant possessed criminal intent to convert or steal government property.

. . .

This case is a troublesome one. It would appear the defendant may have misused his position and violated his obligation to render loyal service to his employer, the United States Government. Nevertheless, under the circumstances presented here, the conduct was not criminal. The Government failed to present evidence sufficient for the jury to find intent to convert beyond a reasonable doubt and, therefore, we agree with the trial court that the prosecution failed to prove the requisite criminal intent.

The judgment for acquittal is affirmed.

5. There is repeated testimony that Wilson completed the work assigned to him and that he did excellent work. The closest anyone came to claiming interference with work was Fick's testimony that the files suffered. Both Phipps and Proenza testified that they were told to do the work only if they had no government work to do, and that the work never interfered with government projects.

UNITED STATES v. GIRARD

United States Court of Appeals, Second Circuit, 1979.
601 F.2d 69.

Before OAKES, GURFEIN, and VAN GRAAFEILAND, CIRCUIT JUDGES.

VAN GRAAFEILAND, CIRCUIT JUDGE:

Appellants have appealed from judgments convicting them of the unauthorized sale of government property (18 U.S.C. § 641) and of conspiring to accomplish the sale (18 U.S.C. § 371) . . . .

In May 1977, appellant Lambert was an agent of the Drug Enforcement Administration, and Girard was a former agent. During that month, Girard and one James Bond began to discuss a proposed illegal venture that involved smuggling a plane-load of marijuana from Mexico into the United States. Girard told Bond that for $500 per name he could, through an inside source secure reports from the DEA files that would show whether any participant in the proposed operation was a government informant. Unfortunately for Mr. Girard, Bond himself became an informant and disclosed his conversations with Girard to the DEA. Thereafter, dealings between Bond and Girard were conducted under the watchful eye of the DEA. Bond asked Girard to secure reports on four men whose names were furnished him by DEA agents. DEA records are kept in computerized files, and the DEA hoped to identify the inside source by monitoring access to the four names in the computer bank. In this manner, the DEA learned that Girard's informant was Lambert, who obtained the reports through a computer terminal located in his office. The convictions on Counts One and Two are based on the sale of this information.

Section 641, so far as pertinent, provides that whoever without authority sells any "record . . . or thing of value" of the United States or who "receives . . . the same with intent to convert it to his use or gain, knowing it to have been embezzled, stolen, purloined or converted", shall be guilty of a crime. Appellants contend that the statute covers only tangible property or documents and therefore is not violated by the sale of information. This contention was rejected by District Judge Daly in a well-reasoned opinion reported at 446 F.Supp. 890. We agree with the District Judge's decision and can do little more than harrow the ground he has already plowed.

Like the District Judge, we are impressed by Congress' repeated use of the phrase "thing of value" in section 641 and its predecessors. These words are found in so many criminal statutes throughout the United States that they have in a sense become words of art. The word "thing" notwithstanding, the phrase is generally construed to cover intangibles as well as tangibles. For example, amusement is held to be a thing of value under gambling statutes. Sexual intercourse, or the promise of sexual intercourse, is a thing of value under a bribery statute. So also are a promise to reinstate an employee, and an agreement not to run in a primary election. The testimony of a witness is a thing of value under 18 U.S.C. § 876, which prohibits threats made through the mails with the intent to extort money or any other "thing of value."

Although the content of a writing is an intangible, it is nonetheless a thing of value. The existence of a property in the contents of unpublished writings was judicially recognized long before the advent of copyright laws. This property was "not distinguishable from any other personal property" and was "protected by the same process, and [had] the benefit of all the remedies accorded to other property so far as applicable." Although we are not concerned here with the laws of copyright, we are satisfied, nonetheless, that the Government has a property interest in certain of its private records which it may protect by statute as a thing of value. It has done this by the enactment of section 641. Section 641 is not simply a statutory codification of the common law of larceny. Indeed, theft is not a requisite element of the proscribed statutory offense, which is based upon unauthorized sale or conversion. If, as the Court said in *Morissette*, supra, conversion is the "misuse or abuse of property" or its use "in an unauthorized manner", the defendants herein could properly be found to have converted DEA's computerized records.

The District Judge also rejected appellants' constitutional challenge to section 641 based upon alleged vagueness and overbreadth, and again we agree with his ruling. Appellants, at the time of the crime a current and a former employee of the DEA, must have known that the sale of DEA confidential law enforcement records was prohibited. The DEA's own rules and regulations forbidding such disclosure may be considered as both a delimitation and a clarification of the conduct proscribed by the statute. . . .

The evidence was amply sufficient to support the judgments of conviction on all counts. Appellants' claims of procedural error are without merit. The judgments appealed from are affirmed.

PEOPLE v. HOME INSURANCE CO.

Supreme Court of Colorado, En Banc, 1979.
197 Colo. 260, 591 P.2d 1036.

LEE, JUSTICE. The People appeal from the dismissal of theft and theft-related charges by the trial court at the close of the prosecution's case. The charges arose from the surreptitious procurement by agents of the insurance company defendants of confidential medical information concerning two patients of a Denver hospital. The trial court granted the dismissal because the medical information obtained was not a "thing of value" as defined in the pertinent statute and therefore was not subject to theft. We affirm.

The defendants hired an injury claims investigative service to obtain medical information reports on two claimants. Through the use of the telephone, an investigator for the service obtained a verbatim reading of the medical reports which he later transcribed and sent to the defendants. The actual medical records themselves never left the hospital file room; rather, only the medical information contained in the records was thus acquired.

The theft statute, section 18–4–401(1)(a), C.R.S.1973 (1978 Repl. Vol. 8), reads in pertinent part:

> "A person commits theft when he knowingly obtains or exercises control over anything of value of another without authorization, or by threat or deception, and:
>
> "(a) Intends to deprive the other person permanently of the use or benefit of the thing of value . . . ."

Crucial to our determination of this case is the definition of "thing of value" contained in section 18–1–901(3)(r), C.R.S.1973 (1978 Repl.Vol. 8):

> "'Thing of value' includes real property, tangible and intangible personal property, contract rights, choses in action, services, and any rights or use or enjoyment connected therewith."

The People argue that the confidentiality inherent in one's personal medical information is a "thing of value" within the meaning of the theft statute inasmuch as the confidentiality is intangible personal property. We do not agree with this expansive interpretation of the theft statute.

In determining the meaning of criminal statutes, we are guided by the principle that such statutes must be strictly construed in favor of the accused and they cannot be extended either by implication or construction.

As far as we have been able to determine, and no cases have been cited by the People to the contrary, confidentiality has never been considered as intangible personal property. Rather, the term intangible personal property has been held to be property which is merely representative of value, such as certificates of stock, bonds, promissory notes, patents, copyrights, tradebrands and franchises. We, therefore, would have to expand unduly the traditional concept of intangible property if we were to accept the People's contention.

Furthermore, the General Assembly has specifically addressed the violation of analogous privacy interests in the criminal code. Thus, it has authorized criminal sanctions for the theft of trade secrets, section 18–4–408, C.R.S.1973 (1978 Repl.Vol. 8),[1] unauthorized wiretapping of telephone or telegraph communication, section 18–9–303,

1. Although traditionally there has been a civil remedy for appropriation of trade secrets, see Trade Secret Litigation: Injunctions and Other Equitable Remedies, 48 U.Colo.L.Rev. 189 (1977), the legislature considered the increasing encroachment on this type of confidentiality as warranting criminal penalties.

C.R.S.1973 (1978 Repl.Vol. 8); eavesdropping, section 18–9–304, C.R.S.1973 (1978 Repl.Vol. 8); and unauthorized reading, learning or disclosure of telephone, telegraph or mail messages, section 18–9–306, C.R.S.1973 (1978 Repl.Vol. 8). The foregoing amply demonstrates that the General Assembly has the legislative competence, if inclined to do so, to make illegal the invasion of privacy or confidentiality. The legislature, however, has not chosen to apply criminal sanctions to the invasion of the confidentiality of medical information. We will not now do so by an unwarranted interpretation of the meaning of intangible personal property as it is used in the statutory definition of "thing of value."

In the civil context the legislature has considered the importance of confidentiality of medical information. Section 25–1–802, C.R.S. 1973 (1978 Supp.) concerns confidentiality of patient records in the custody of health care facilities. Section 27–10–120, C.R.S.1973, provides that all information obtained in the course of providing services to the mentally ill in state institutions shall be confidential and privileged. Section 25–1–312, C.R.S.1973, makes records of alcoholics compiled at treatment facilities confidential and privileged. Section 24–72–204(3), C.R.S.1973, provides that public records containing medical and psychological data shall not be available for public inspection except in certain prescribed circumstances. The legislature, therefore, has taken specific steps to protect the confidentiality of medical information by creating statutory duties, the breach of which could serve as the basis for a civil remedy. However, the legislature has not imposed criminal penalties for violations of the confidentiality or privilege.

Finally, the acceptance of the People's contention that invasion of the confidentiality of one's medical records constitutes theft would have far-reaching ramifications. Conceivably, a person who committed one of the four recognized torts for the invasion of privacy[2] could be tried for theft. Also, the breach of one of the recognized privileges (e.g., husband-wife, attorney-client, clergyman-penitent, doctor-patient, accountant-client and psychologist-client, *see* section 13–90–107, C.R.S.1973) might possibly be construed as theft. In our view, such an expansion of criminal liability could not have been intended by the legislature when it adopted the theft statute. Although we agree with the trial court that the defendants' conduct was "reprehensible and outrageous," that conduct simply was not made criminal under the theft statute. Proof of moral turpitude is not alone sufficient to authorize a criminal conviction.

Because of our disposition, it is unnecessary to address the issue of how to calculate the monetary worth of the medical information or

2. According to W. Prosser, Torts § 117 (4th ed. 1971), the common law tort of invasion of privacy contains four distinct kinds of invasion of four different interests: (1) intrusion upon physical solitude; (2) public disclosure of private facts; (3) false light in the public eye; and (4) appropriation of name or likeness.

the issue of whether the evidence established the element of permanent deprivation.

The judgment is affirmed.

CARRIGAN, J., does not participate.

SECTION 6. RECEIVING (OR CONCEALING) STOLEN PROPERTY

Under the common law and early statutes of England one who received stolen property, knowing it was stolen, was punishable although not always under the same theory. Under one of these statutes he was guilty of a separate substantive offense known as receiving stolen property, and most of the penal codes in this country have taken that position.[1] Some of the statutes extend the coverage to include one who "aids in concealing" such property.

In the early English cases the "receiver" was guilty of a misdemeanor except that under one of the statutes he was declared to be guilty as accessory after the fact to the larceny by which the goods had originally been taken. This, of course, made him a felon. Under most of the modern American statutes the offense is either a felony or a misdemeanor depending upon the value of the property stolen—or sometimes upon the kind of property.[2]

SECTION 7. MALICIOUS MISCHIEF

Malicious mischief, sometimes called malicious trespass, is the malicious destruction of, or damage to, the property of another, whether real or personal. It is a misdemeanor at common law but an occasional statute has provided that it may be a felony depending upon either the nature of the property or the value thereof.

SECTION 8. FORGERY AND UTTERING A FORGED INSTRUMENT

Forgery is the fraudulent making of a false writing having apparent legal significance. It may be accomplished by starting with blank paper or a blank form and doing all the writing which results in the

1. A thief cannot be guilty of receiving stolen property from himself. State v. Dechand, 13 Or.App. 530, 511 P.2d 430 (1973).

Under a statute which provides for the punishment of "receiving, retaining or disposing of stolen property" the thief who sells the property he has stolen can be convicted of both the larceny and the disposing of stolen property. State v. Tapia, 89 N.M. 221, 549 P.2d 636 (1976).

2. "We think there can be no doubt that the federal offense of receiving stolen property defined by § 2315 incorporates the common law exception for possession with the purpose of restoring stolen property to the owner. And the exception applies when the purpose of restoring the property is accompanied by an expectation of a reward, provided the reward has been announced or is believed to have been announced. . . ." Godwin v. United States, 687 F.2d 585, 588 (2d Cir.1982).

false instrument; or by starting with a genuine writing and fraudulently altering it so as to make it false.

Uttering a forged instrument is knowingly offering, as genuine, one known to be false. The offer itself completes the uttering even if promptly rejected.

Both forgery and uttering were misdemeanors at common law but are almost universally felonies under modern statutes.

UNITED STATES v. McGOVERN

United States Court of Appeals, Third Circuit, 1981.
661 F.2d 27.

OPINION OF THE COURT

ALDISERT, CIRCUIT JUDGE. The question for decision is whether the appellants' conduct constituted a violation of paragraph four of 18 U.S.C. § 2314:

> Whoever, with unlawful or fraudulent intent, transports in interstate or foreign commerce any traveler's checks bearing a forged countersignature . . . shall be fined . . . or imprisoned . . . or both.

Convicted in a bench trial, McGovern and Scull argue in this appeal that the government failed to prove the predicate of the federal statutory offense: common law forgery. Appellants contend that the existence of authority to sign another's name to an instrument defeats a forgery charge, and that here appellant McGovern, purchaser of the traveler's checks, authorized appellant Scull to sign McGovern's name to the checks. We will affirm essentially for the reasons set forth by Chief Judge Weber.

I.

In the modern idiom, the appellants' fascinating plan could be dubbed "CITISCAM," because the participants devised a novel method of defrauding Citibank Corporation and certain businesses. The motive for the operation was the existence of an $1,800 debt McGovern owed an increasingly impatient Scull. The scheme was obvious: McGovern would buy $2,400 (for good measure) in traveler's checks from a bank; Scull would sign McGovern's name to the checks and cash them and McGovern would claim to the bank that he had lost the checks, knowing that according to highly advertised traveler's check policy the issuer would promptly "refund" his "lost" checks. If the scheme was successful, either the businesses or the issuer of the checks would bear the loss.

Citibank, one of the planned victims under the scheme, issued the checks to McGovern through a Niagara Falls, New York, bank. The purchase agreement that McGovern signed stated:

> The purchaser agrees to sign each check in the upper left corner at the time of purchase with the same signature used in signing this agreement; and to countersign each check in the lower left corner when cashed, in the presence of the person cashing it.

Not attuned to the consequences of crossing state lines, McGovern then proceeded to Erie, Pennsylvania, thereby vesting the federal authorities with jurisdiction over the conspirators' activities. There, tutored by McGovern, Scull practiced imitating McGovern's signature, and then, armed with his co-conspirator's driver's license as identification, Scull entered two Erie banks and a GTE store where he cashed the checks and collected $2,400. Playing out the scenario, McGovern then reported to the New York police that his checks had been stolen from his automobile while in Buffalo; one day later he reported the loss to Citibank and, not surprisingly, Citibank issued McGovern $2,400 in replacement checks.

II.

As explained in detail by Chief Judge Weber, forgery in § 2314 means what the term meant under common law in 1823. Common law forgery has three elements: (a) The false making or material alteration (b) with intent to defraud (c) of a writing which, if genuine, might be of legal efficacy.

McGovern and Scull contend that under the facts, the first element cannot be established. They rely on the common law precept that authority to sign another's name to a written instrument negates a charge of forgery regardless of fraud or falsehood in the transaction. Whatever validity this argument may have in other contexts, we do not believe that those cases control a traveler's check transaction.

The purchaser's agreement to sign each traveler's check at the time of purchase and to counter-sign the checks only in the presence of the person cashing them, in our view, invalidates his attempt to authorize another to sign his name. As the fifth circuit observed in Berry v. United States, 271 F.2d 775, 777 (5th Cir.1959), cert. denied, 362 U.S. 903, 80 S.Ct. 612, 4 L.Ed.2d 555 (1960), traveler's checks are unique. Unlike other negotiable instruments, they are cashed not on the credit of the negotiator, but on the credit of the issuer together with the conformity of the negotiator's signature with that on the face of the instrument. These instruments are negotiated freely because of the assured credit of the check issuer and relative ease of determining signature validity. The traveler's check contract clearly denies the purchaser the right to authorize another to sign for him and the reason seems clear: a representative signature complicates the negotiation process and thereby dilutes the advantage of ready acceptance. Without authority to delegate the check-cashing power to another, a purported delegation is of no effect under the law of agency. Thus, the decisions holding that authority to sign another's name negates a charge of "false making" are *a fortiori* inapplicable to this case.

Moreover, under the facts presented here, the businesses cashing the checks were deliberately deceived into believing that the person signing the checks was the purchaser. They, as much as Citibank, were defrauded in the transaction because Scull was impersonating McGovern. This case, therefore, differs from cases in which the person accepting the instrument was informed of the purported authorization. If the authorization was valid, there would be no forgery and no defrauding of the cashing person. Of course, a person who cashes a traveler's check in those circumstances is on notice that the issuer of the check may refuse to honor the instrument because of an invalid signature. But the knowledge of the cashing person that the person signing is acting in a representative capacity negates a charge of forgery. When the person signing the traveler's checks is an imposter, however, his unauthorized signature on a traveler's check, when accompanied by an intent to defraud, constitutes common law forgery.

McGovern, the purchaser of the traveler's checks, knew the effect his actions would have on Citibank and on the business cashing them—indeed, appellants conceded that this was the sole purpose of having Scull sign the checks. Scull was an imposter and possessed no authority to sign the checks because McGovern could not grant him this authority. When coupled with the appellants' intent to defraud, the unauthorized signature on the otherwise legally sufficient instruments constituted common law forgery. The elements of the offense having been established we conclude that the convictions must stand.

III.

Accordingly, for the foregoing reasons and as more elaborately set forth by the district court, the judgment of the district court will be affirmed.[1]

SECTION 9. COUNTERFEITING

Counterfeiting is the unlawful making of false money in the similitude of the genuine. As a federal crime it belongs in a different category—offenses affecting sovereignty or the administration of governmental functions (Chapter 5, Section 3). But since counterfeiting is for the purpose of defrauding others, both counterfeiting and

1. 18 U.S.C.A. § 2314 prohibiting interstate transportation of a forged security did not require proof of forgery before the item is taken across state lines. McElroy v. United States, 445 U.S. 642, 102 S.Ct. 1332 (1982).

knowingly uttering counterfeit money are offenses against property and punishable as felonies under many of the state statutes.

SECTION 10. EXTORTION

Common-law extortion is the corrupt collection of an unlawful fee by an officer under color of his office. At common law, and for the most part under statutes, it is a misdemeanor.

Statutory extortion, commonly called blackmail, is either (1) the unlawful extraction of money or other value by means of a threat not sufficient for robbery, or (2) a communication for the purpose of such extraction. It is usually a felony.

MODEL PENAL CODE

Article 223. Theft and Related Offenses[1]

Section 223.0 Definitions.

In this Article, unless a different meaning plainly is required:

(1) "deprive" means: (a) to withhold property of another permanently or for so extended a period as to appropriate a major portion of its economic value, or with intent to restore only upon payment of reward or other compensation; or (b) to dispose of the property so as to make it unlikely that the owner will recover it.

(2) "financial institution" means . . .

(3) "government" means . . .

(4) "movable property" means property the location of which can be changed, including things growing on, affixed to, or found in land, and documents although the rights represented thereby have no physical location. "Immovable property" is all other property.

(5) "obtain" means: (a) in relation to property, to bring about a transfer or purported transfer of a legal interest in the property, whether to the obtainer or another; or (b) in relation to labor or service, to secure performance thereof.

(6) "property" means anything of value, including real estate, tangible and intangible personal property, contract rights, choses-in-action and other interests in or claims to wealth, admission or transportation tickets, captured or domestic animals, food and drink, electric or other power.

(7) "property of another" includes property in which any person other than the actor has an interest which the actor is not privileged to infringe, regardless of the fact that the actor also has an interest in the

1. The Oklahoma statute on theft (21 O.S.Supp.1974, § 1733) read as follows:

"Theft is any of the following acts done with intent to deprive the owner permanently of the possession, use or benefit of his property.

"1. Obtaining or exerting unauthorized control over property;

"2. Obtaining by deception control over property;

"3. Obtaining by threat control over property; or

"4. Obtaining control over stolen property knowing the property to have been stolen . . . ."

This was held "in its entirety, to be unconstitutional" (void for vagueness). Rowell v. Smith, 534 P.2d 689 (Okl.Cr. 1975).

property and regardless of the fact that the other person might be precluded from civil recovery because the property was used in an unlawful transaction or was subject to forfeiture as contraband. Property in possession of the actor shall not be deemed property of another who has only a security interest therein, even if legal title is in the creditor pursuant to a conditional sales contract or other security agreement.

Section 223.1 Consolidation of Theft Offenses; Grading; Provisions Applicable to Theft Generally.

(1) Consolidation of Theft Offenses. Conduct denominated theft in this Article constitutes a single offense. An accusation of theft may be supported by evidence that it was committed in any manner that would be theft under this Article, notwithstanding the specification of a different manner in the indictment or information, subject only to the power of the Court to ensure fair trial by granting a continuance or other appropriate relief where the conduct of the defense would be prejudiced by lack of fair notice or by surprise.

(2) Grading of Theft Offenses.

(a) Theft constitutes a felony of the third degree if the amount involved exceeds $500, or if the property stolen is a firearm, automobile, airplane, motor cycle, motor boat or other motor-propelled vehicle, or in the case of theft by receiving stolen property, if the receiver is in the business of buying or selling stolen property.

(b) Theft not within the preceding paragraph constitutes a misdemeanor, except that if the property was not taken from the person or by threat, or in breach of a fiduciary obligation, and the actor proves by a preponderance of the evidence that the amount involved was less than $50, the offense constitutes a petty misdemeanor.

(c) The amount involved in a theft shall be deemed to be the highest value, by any reasonable standard, of the property or services which the actor stole or attempted to steal. Amounts involved in thefts committed pursuant to one scheme or course of conduct, whether from the same person or several persons, may be aggregated in determining the grade of the offense.

(3) Claim of Right. It is an affirmative defense to prosecution for theft that the actor:

(a) was unaware that the property or service was that of another; or

(b) acted under an honest claim of right to the property or service involved or that he had a right to acquire or dispose of it as he did; or

(c) took property exposed for sale, intending to purchase and pay for it promptly, or reasonably believing that the owner, if present, would have consented.

(4) Theft from Spouse. It is no defense that theft was from the actor's spouse, except that misappropriation of household and personal effects, or other property normally accessible to both spouses, is theft only if it occurs after the parties have ceased living together.

Section 223.2 Theft by Unlawful Taking or Disposition.

(1) Movable Property. A person is guilty of theft if he unlawfully takes, or exercises unlawful control over, movable property of another with purpose to deprive him thereof.

(2) Immovable Property. A person is guilty of theft if he unlawfully transfers immovable property of another or any interest therein with purpose to benefit himself or another not entitled thereto.

Section 223.3 Theft by Deception.

A person is guilty of theft if he purposely obtains property of another by deception. A person deceives if he purposely:

(1) creates or reinforces a false impression, including false impressions as to law, value, intention or other state of mind; but deception as to a person's intention to perform a promise shall not be inferred from the fact alone that he did not subsequently perform the promise; or

(2) prevents another from acquiring information which would affect his judgment of a transaction; or

(3) fails to correct a false impression which the deceiver previously created or reinforced, or which the deceiver knows to be influencing another to whom he stands in a fiduciary or confidential relationship; or

(4) fails to disclose a known lien, adverse claim or other legal impediment to the enjoyment of property which he transfers or encumbers in consideration for the property obtained, whether such impediment is or is not valid, or is or is not a matter of official record.

The term "deceive" does not, however, include falsity as to matters having no pecuniary significance, or puffing by statements unlikely to deceive ordinary persons in the group addressed.

Section 223.4 Theft by Extortion.

A person is guilty of theft if he purposely obtains property of another by threatening to:

(1) inflict bodily injury on anyone or commit any other criminal offense; or

(2) accuse anyone of a criminal offense; or

(3) expose any secret tending to subject any person to hatred, contempt or ridicule, or to impair his credit or business repute; or

(4) take or withhold action as an official, or cause an official to take or withhold action; or

(5) bring about or continue a strike, boycott or other collective unofficial action, if the property is not demanded or received for the benefit of the group in whose interest the actor purports to act; or

(6) testify or provide information or withhold testimony or information with respect to another's legal claim or defense; or

(7) inflict any other harm which would not benefit the actor.

It is an affirmative defense to prosecution based on paragraphs (2), (3) or (4) that the property obtained by threat of accusation, exposure, lawsuit or other invocation of official action was honestly claimed as restitution or indemnification for harm done in the circumstances to which such accusation, exposure, lawsuit or other official action relates, or as compensation for property or lawful services.

Section 223.5 Theft of Property Lost, Mislaid, or Delivered by Mistake.

A person who comes into control of property of another that he knows to have been lost, mislaid, or delivered under a mistake as to the nature or amount of the property or the identity of the recipient is guilty of theft if, with purpose to deprive the owner thereof, he fails to take reasonable measures to restore the property to a person entitled to have it.

Section 223.6 Receiving Stolen Property.

(1) Receiving. A person is guilty of theft if he purposely receives, retains, or disposes of movable property of another knowing that it has been stolen, or believing that it has probably been stolen, unless the property is received, retained, or disposed with purpose to restore it to the owner. "Receiving" means acquiring possession, control or title, or lending on the security of the property.

(2) Presumption of Knowledge. The requisite knowledge or belief is presumed in the case of a dealer who:

(a) is found in possession or control of property stolen from two or more persons on separate occasions; or

(b) has received stolen property in another transaction within the year preceding the transaction charged; or

(c) being a dealer in property of the sort received, acquires it for a consideration which he knows is far below its reasonable value.

"Dealer" means a person in the business of buying or selling goods, or a pawnbroker.

Section 223.7 Theft of Services.

(1) A person is guilty of theft if he purposely obtains services which he knows are available only for compensation, by deception or threat, or by false token or other means to avoid payment for the service. "Services" includes labor, professional service, transportation, telephone or other public service, accommodation in hotels, restaurants or elsewhere, admission to exhibitions, use of vehicles or other movable property. Where compensation for service is ordinarily paid immediately upon the rendering of such service, as in the case of hotels and restaurants, refusal to pay or absconding without payment or offer to pay gives rise to a presumption that the service was obtained by deception as to intention to pay.

(2) A person commits theft if, having control over the disposition of services of others, to which he is not entitled, he knowingly diverts such services to his own benefit or to the benefit of another not entitled thereto.

Section 223.8 Theft by Failure to Make Required Disposition of Funds Received.

A person who purposely obtains property upon agreement, or subject to a known legal obligation, to make specified payment or other disposition, whether from such property or its proceeds or from his own property to be reserved in equivalent amount, is guilty of theft if he deals with the property obtained as his own and fails to make the required payment or disposition. The foregoing applies notwithstanding that it may be impossible to identify particular property as belonging to the victim at the time of the actor's failure to make the required payment or disposition. An officer or employee of the government or of a financial institution is presumed: (i) to know any legal obligation relevant to his criminal liability under this Section, and (ii) to have dealt with the property as his own if he fails to pay or account upon lawful demand, or if an audit reveals a shortage or falsification of accounts.

Section 223.9 Unauthorized Use of Automobiles and Other Vehicles.

A person commits a misdemeanor if he operates another's automobile, airplane, motorcycle, motorboat, or other motor-propelled vehicle without consent of the owner. It is an affirmative defense to prosecution under this Section that the actor reasonably believed that the owner would have consented to the operation had he known of it[2].

Chapter 5

OTHER OFFENSES

SECTION 1. OFFENSES AGAINST MORALITY AND DECENCY

The whole field of substantive criminal law constitutes a rather stern moral code. It is not exhaustive in this respect but represents the points at which conduct is deemed so offensive to the moral judgment of the community as to call for punishment. This frequently leads to the question: Why are certain crimes spoken of as offenses against morality?

There is reason to believe that at a very early day the Church preempted jurisdiction over certain types of misconduct. It is known that the starting point of benefit of clergy was the Church's refusal to permit members of the clergy to be tried for crime in lay courts. The time came when benefit of clergy could be claimed only after guilt had been established, by verdict or plea, but this was after a very substantial change in the relative power of Church and State. Much earlier the Church had said to the common-law judges, in effect: "If a charge of misconduct is brought against a clergyman, that is none of your business. That is our business; send him to us and we shall handle the matter." And for generations this is exactly what happened.

In like manner it is more than probable that at the peak of its power the Church made it known to the common-law judges that jurisdiction over certain types of misconduct belonged exclusively to the ecclesiastical court. In any event the Church did take jurisdiction over those offenses and the common-law judges did not do so for many years—not in fact until they had been made punishable by acts of Parliament. Prior to that time they were no doubt referred to as "offenses only against morality".

(A) ADULTERY, FORNICATION AND ILLICIT COHABITATION

Adultery is punished as a crime under many of the modern statutes, some of which provide that both parties to the illicit intercourse are guilty of this offense if either is married to a third person.

Fornication—illicit intercourse which is not adultery—is punished in a few states.

Illicit cohabitation is living together in a relation of either adultery or fornication. At one time this was an offense under many of the statutes.

None of the three was a common-law crime except that if illicit cohabitation was so open and notorious as to create a public scandal it was punishable.

(B) BIGAMY

Bigamy is contracting a second marriage during the existence of a prior marital relation or the marrying of more than one spouse at the same time. It was not a common-law crime but is punished under modern statutes.

(C) INCEST

In its broadest scope, incest is either marriage, or sexual intercourse without marriage, between persons related within the degrees in which marriage is prohibited by law. Originally it was only an ecclesiastical offense but has very generally been made a crime by statute.

(D) SEDUCTION

Although a statutory crime in some states, seduction was not punished by the common law. The statutes are not uniform, but in general seduction may be said to be illicit sexual intercourse obtained by a man with a woman whom he has induced to surrender her chastity by a promise of marriage, or in some states either by such a promise or some other seductive art.

(E) SODOMY

Sodomy is a generic term which includes both "bestiality" and "buggery".

Bestiality is carnal copulation with a beast.

Buggery is copulation per anum—sometimes enlarged by statute to include the case where the act is in the mouth.

Sodomy was not a crime according to the common law of England, being left to the jurisdiction of the ecclesiastical courts. It was made a felony there by early statutes generally assumed to be part of the American common law. Sodomy is usually included in the penal code although some of the statutes refer to it only as the "crime against nature".

(F) PROSTITUTION, OBSCENITY AND INDECENCY

Prostitution is the common lewdness of a woman for gain. It was only an ecclesiastical offense in itself but the keeping of a bawdy house, or house of prostitution, was a common-law nuisance.

Pandering is the paid procurement of a female as an inmate of a house of prostitution. The procurer is often referred to as a "pimp".

The Mann Act, or white slave traffic law, is a federal statute which provides a penalty for the interstate transportation of a female for prostitution or other immoral purpose. Congress has also prohibited the transportation of minors for prostitution or prohibited sexual conduct.[1]

Obscenity is that which is offensive to chastity. It is material which deals with sex in a manner appealing to prurient interest.

Indecency is often used with the same meaning, but may also include anything which is outrageously disgusting. These were not the names of common-law crimes, but were words used in describing or identifying certain deeds which were.

An obscene libel is a writing, book or picture of such an obscene nature as to shock the public sense of decency. It is a misdemeanor at common law to publish such a libel.

Indecent exposure of the person in public is a common-law nuisance, as is also the public utterance of obscene or profane language in such a manner as to annoy the public.

The Model Penal Code suggests something of a return to the original position. It does not penalize nonviolent, uncommercialized sexual sins—fornication, adultery, sodomy or other consensual illicit sexual activity not involving imposition upon children, mental incompetents, wards or other dependents. The position taken is that such matters are best left to religious, educational or other social influences. It does penalize open lewdness, by which others are likely to be affronted or alarmed (Section 251.1), professional prostitution (Section 251.2), and commercialized obscenity (Section 251.4). Also forbidden under penalty are bigamy and polygamy (Section 230.1), incest (Section 230.2) and unjustified abortion (Section 230.3).[2] What is said above gives the traditional definition of prostitution, but modern criminal law has been forced to recognize the male prostitute, particularly in regard to homosexual and other deviate sexual relations. This suggests the following definition:

Prostitution is commercialized sex, including deviate sex.

The California court held that the public nuisance statutes may properly regulate the exhibition of obscene material to consenting adults.[3] It was mentioned that the Supreme Court had categorically disapproved the theory "that obscene, pornographic films acquire constitutional immunity from state regulation simply because they

1. 18 U.S.C.A. § 2423 (1978).

2. For presentations of the Code's position on these matters see the Model Penal Code, Tent. Draft No. 4 pp. 204–238; Tent. Draft No. 6 pp. 5–95; Tent. Draft No. 9 pp. 146–162. And for a scholarly discussion see Schwartz, Morals Offenses and the Model Penal Code, 63 Colum.L.Rev. 669 (1963).

3. People ex rel. Busch v. Projection Room Theater, 17 Cal.3d 42, 130 Cal. Rptr. 328, 550 P.2d 600 (1976).

are exhibited for consenting adults only."[4] However, a nuisance ordinance directed at controlling obscene material may be so broadly drawn as to constitute an invalid prior restraint.[5]

SECTION 2. OFFENSES AGAINST THE PUBLIC PEACE

(A) BREACH OF THE PEACE

Misconduct which disturbs the peace and tranquillity of the community may have a special name, such as affray. If not, it is called "breach of the peace", "disturbing the peace" or "public disturbance".

(B) FIGHTING

There is no common-law crime known as "fighting" but a fight (other than a friendly contest of strength or skill) usually constitutes a crime. It may be only an assault and battery—by one, if the other is not exceeding his privilege of self-defense—otherwise by both.

An *affray* is a mutual fight in a public place to the terror or alarm of the public. It is a common-law misdemeanor. Prize-fighting was not punishable at common law unless held in a public place. In some states it is prohibited, in some it is an offense unless licensed by public authority.

(C) UNLAWFUL ASSEMBLY, ROUT AND RIOT

Each of these was a misdemeanor at common law.

An *unlawful assembly* is a meeting of three or more persons with intent to—

(a) commit a crime by force or violence, or

(b) execute a common design, lawful or unlawful, in a manner likely to cause courageous persons to apprehend a breach of the peace.

A *rout* is the movement of unlawful assemblers on the way to carry out their common design.

A *riot* is a tumultuous disturbance by unlawful assemblers in the execution of their plan.[1]

Three or more persons who happen to be together for some other purpose could suddenly engage in a riot. On the other hand they

4. Paris Adult Theater I v. Slaton, 413 U.S. 49, 57, 93 S.Ct. 2628, 2635 (1973).

5. Vance v. Universal Amusement Co., Inc., 445 U.S. 308, 100 S.Ct. 1156 (1980).

1. Illegal conduct is not protected merely because it is in part carried out by language. When clear and present danger of riot appears, the power of the state to prevent or punish is clear. People v. Davis, 68 Cal.2d 481, 67 Cal.Rptr. 547, 439 P.2d 651 (1968).

might gather at one place to make plans, go to another place and there accomplish their purpose. If so, they have committed three offenses at common law. Under some statutes a riot may be a felony, and under some no more than two persons are required for any of these three offenses. Rout has frequently been omitted from the codes.

(D) DISTURBANCE OF PUBLIC ASSEMBLY

Any unauthorized disturbance of a public assembly is a misdemeanor at common law, except that it would be excused if quite unintentional.

(E) DISORDERLY HOUSE

Any house in which disorderly persons are permitted to congregate, and to disturb the tranquillity of the neighborhood by fighting, quarreling, swearing or other type of disorder, is a disorderly house; and the keeping thereof is a misdemeanor at common law.

(F) FORCIBLE ENTRY AND DETAINER

A mere trespass upon the land of another is not a crime, but if an entry is accomplished by force or intimidation; or if such methods are employed for detention after peaceable entry, there is a crime according to English law known as forcible entry and detainer. Whether it was punishable by the English common law or not it was made a crime by English statutes old enough to be common law in this country.

Any unlawful act of forcible entry or detainer will involve some other crime, such as an assault. For this reason it is omitted from some penal codes.

(G) LIBEL

Libel is the malicious publication of durable defamation. A common explanation is that the malicious publication of defamation is slander if oral and libel if written. This gives the idea in a general way but libel may be committed without writing, as by hanging a man in effigy. In law "publication" means to make known, and showing the defamatory matter is sufficient. Any intentional publication of defamation is malicious in the absence of some justification or excuse.

Most of the libel cases in modern times have been tort cases and there is substantial support for the view that this is an area properly left to control by civil sanctions. It is not included in the Model Penal Code.

(H) CARRYING WEAPONS

Because of its tendency to stir up breaches of the peace, "terrifying the good people of the land" by *riding or going armed* with dangerous or unusual weapons" was a common-law misdemeanor. Apparently the wearing of a sword in the customary manner by a person "of quality" was not deemed alarming, for this was not an offense; but the position of one of lower degree was less fortunate.

Unlike the theory of the ancient law which regarded the display of arms in a manner calculated to cause alarm as the harm to be prevented, the modern basic statute has been directed against the carrying of *concealed* weapons. Some of the provisions do not go beyond this but some do—such as the clause forbidding the carrying of a pistol or revolver "whether concealed or otherwise" in a vehicle, without a license therefor.

(I) VAGRANCY

The Statute of Labourers, enacted in 1349, provided for the imprisonment of an able-bodied male under sixty, without means of support, who refused to work. It was preventive rather than punitive because incarceration could be avoided by giving assurance that work would be undertaken, supported by a bond with acceptable surety. The primary purpose was to require the man without means to work for a living rather than to gain subsistence by begging, but this was not all. If the man without means found it difficult to satisfy all his desires by begging he might be tempted to try other methods even more antisocial in their nature, hence the enforcement of this statute may well have had a tendency to prevent crime.

Modern vagrancy statutes include proscriptions against living in idleness without visible means of support; roaming, wandering or loitering; begging; being a common prostitute, drunkard, beggar or gambler; and sleeping outdoors or in a non-residential building without permission. Many of the provisions of the vagrancy statutes have been held to be unconstitutional either because of vagueness or because of imposing a punishment for what is not properly punishable.

The Model Penal Code (Sec. 250.6) would omit the provisions of the present vagrancy statutes and substitute a section on "loitering or prowling". It would authorize the arrest of one loitering or prowling in a place, time or manner unusual for law-abiding individuals and under circumstances that warrant alarm for the safety of persons or property. This would constitute what the Code calls a "violation", meaning that it would be punishable only by fine, not by a jail sentence. It is not entirely certain that it could withstand a constitutional attack.

SECTION 3. OFFENSES AFFECTING SOVEREIGNTY OR THE ADMINISTRATION OF GOVERNMENTAL FUNCTIONS

(A) TREASON

Treason against the United States is defined by the Constitution and consists only "in levying war against them, or in adhering to their enemies, giving them aid and comfort". Breach of allegiance is the essence of treason and hence this offense cannot be committed by a non-resident foreigner.

(B) PERJURY AND SUBORNATION

The common law had two similar offenses, both misdemeanors. Perjury is a false oath in a judicial proceeding in regard to a material matter. A false oath is a wilful and corrupt sworn statement without sincere belief in its truthfulness. False swearing is what would be perjury except that it is not in a judicial proceeding but in some other proceeding or matter in which an oath is required by law. Many of the statutes combine the two under the name of perjury, which is now usually a felony. An affirmation is now generally recognized as the legal equivalent of an oath. And constructive perjury does not require either oath or affirmation, being a signature attached "under the penalties of perjury".

Subornation of perjury is the procurement of perjury by another.

(C) BRIBERY

Bribery is the corrupt conveyance or receipt of a private price for official action. It was a common-law misdemeanor and is frequently a felony under modern statutes. There has been a tendency for legislation to extend the offense beyond the original field of official bribery. Such enactments may provide a penalty for quasi-official bribery (such as bribery of employees of public institutions), commercial bribery (as where a wholesaler bribes an agent of a retailer), or bribery in sports.

(D) MISCONDUCT IN OFFICE (OFFICIAL MISCONDUCT)

Misconduct in office is corrupt misbehavior by an officer in the exercise of the duties of his office or while acting under color of his office.

Common-law extortion is the corrupt collection of an unlawful fee by an officer under color of his office. (Statutory extortion is what is popularly known as blackmail.)[1]

1. The Hobbs Antiracketeering Act, 18 U.S.C.A. § 1951 (1970) makes it a federal crime to obstruct commerce by extortion and reaches actions done under

If the illegal act of the officer, done corruptly to the harm of another and under color of his office, takes some form other than extortion the offense is known as oppression. If the illegal and corrupt act of the officer takes the form of a fraud or breach of trust affecting the public it is known as fraud by an officer or breach of trust by an officer. If it takes the form of wilful forbearance to perform a duty of his office it is called neglect of official duty.

(E) EMBRACERY

Embracery is an attempt, by corrupt and wrongful means, to influence a juror in regard to a verdict to be found.

(F) COUNTERFEITING

Counterfeiting is the unlawful making of false money in the similitude of the genuine.

(G) OBSTRUCTION OF JUSTICE

Any wilful act of corruption, intimidation or force which tends to distort or impede the administration of law, either civil or criminal, is an offense usually known as obstruction of justice, unless it has been given a special name, such as bribery or embracery. One of the common forms of this offense involves an interference with a public officer in the discharge of his official duty.

(H) ESCAPE AND KINDRED OFFENSES

Escape is unauthorized departure of a prisoner from legal custody without the use of force. If the escape is by use of force the offense is *prison breach,* or breach of prison. These two common-law offenses are frequently combined under the name of "escape" in modern statutes.[1]

If the officer in charge of a prisoner permits him to escape the officer is guilty of the offense of *permitting escape,* which is usually punishable more severely if intentional than if merely negligent.

Rescue is forcibly freeing a prisoner from lawful custody.

Violation of parole is commonly made an offense by statute.

(I) MISPRISION OF FELONY

Misprision of felony is concealment and (or) nondisclosure of the known felony of another. In ancient times when the Hue and Cry was at the peak point of its importance, the private person, who was required to join in the chase in the effort to track down the felon,

color of official right. United States v. Rabbitt, 583 F.2d 1014 (8th Cir.1978).

1. D's claim that he had been improperly convicted of attempted burglary is no defense to the charge of attempted escape. Self-help is not an acceptable method of challenging the legality of a conviction. United States v. Haley, 417 F.2d 625 (4th Cir.1969).

may have had a duty to report any known felony in order that the Hue and Cry might be started. It is said that in 1314 those present when *murder* was committed, and did not report it, were fined.[1] If there was ever a duty to report every known felony it tended to disappear at a very early day and years ago. Judge Stephen referred to the "practically obsolete offense of misprision." [2] However, it is not entirely obsolete in England, and one who failed to disclose knowledge of the theft of 100 pistols, 4 submachine guns and 1960 rounds of ammunition was convicted of misprision of felony.[3] But it seems that the use of this offense in England is limited to crimes of an "aggravated complexion." [4]

In this country, misprision of felony in the form of mere non-disclosure of a known felony, is rare indeed. The federal Code of Crimes has a section entitled "misprision of felony." [5] It is not violated, however, by mere nondisclosure of a known felony. Something in the way of concealment is required.[6] It was held that the section does not violate the privilege against self-incrimination because it requires concealment in addition to nondisclosure.[7] Most of the states do not recognize misprision of felony in any form, and it is not included in the Model Penal Code.

(J) COMPOUNDING CRIME

Following the lead of an English statute in the 1500s it has been common to authorize the compromise of certain crimes, usually with the court's consent as a requirement. It is an offense known as compounding crime to accept anything of value under an agreement not to prosecute a known offender for any offense unless the compromise is authorized by law.[1]

1. Year Books of Edward II, 24 Seldon Society 152–53.

2. 2 Stephen History of the Criminal Law of England 238 (1883).

3. Sykes v. Director of Public Prosecutions, [1961] 3 All.Eng.L.Rep. 33.

4. Williams, Criminal Law, 423 (2d ed. 1961).

5. 18 U.S.C. sec. 4 (1973).

6. Neal v. United States, 102 F.2d 643, 649 (8th Cir.1939).

Misprision of felony under 18 U.S.C. § 4, requires some act of concealment. Mere failure to report a known felony is not sufficient. United States v. Johnson, 546 F.2d 1225 (5th Cir.1977).

7. United States v. Daddano, 432 F.2d 1119 (7th Cir.1970).

Misprision of felony under the federal statute requires more than mere nondisclosure of a known federal felony. And even if this element is found **D** could not be convicted of misprision if his disclosure of the felony might tend to cause him to be charged with complicity therein. United States v. King, 402 F.2d 694 (9th Cir.1968).

The statute relating to harboring and concealing a person from arrest proscribes acts calculated to obstruct efforts of authorities to effect the arrest of a fugitive, but it does not impose a duty on one who is aware of the whereabouts of a fugitive to reveal this information on pain of criminal prosecution. United States v. Foy, 416 F.2d 940 (7th Cir.1969).

1. Statutes sometimes require that certain persons report evidence that may indicate crime, such as requiring medical personnel to report wounds apparently resulting from violence, or requiring certain persons such as social workers or teachers to report evidence of child-abuse. See a Note, Compounding Crimes, 27 Hastings L.J. 175, 181–187 (1975).

(K) MAINTENANCE, CHAMPERTY AND BARRATRY

In the early days in England, when the administration of the law was in a very insecure position, one form of "racket" was an officious intermeddling in a lawsuit in which the meddler had no interest, by assisting one of the parties with means to prosecute or to defend the suit. There is reason to believe that the mere fact that one of the barons or other person of great power was connected with the case (in which he had no proper interest) exerted a very unwholesome influence upon the outcome of the suit. And this practice became so intolerable that it was made a crime under the name of "*maintenance.*" No doubt the meddler charged a price for his improper assistance in any case, but if this price was a share of the matter in suit in case of success the offense was called "*champerty.*" An habitual offender in this field was guilty of still another offense, known as "*barratry,*" or "common barratry." Guilt of either maintenance or champerty could be established by proof of a single act, but a series of such acts—three or more—was necessary for conviction of barratry.

The conditions which gave rise to these offenses disappeared long ago and they have become entirely obsolete.[1] Confusion has resulted, however, because in a particular jurisdiction one or more of these words may be found as the name of a crime, though not with the original signification. At present it is not unlawful for one, who has no interest of his own in the litigation, to give help by money or otherwise to either the plaintiff or the defendant, present or prospective, if the suit or the defense for which it is given is just or is reasonably believed to be so, and there is no impropriety in the manner in which, or the motive with which, the assistance is given. As it is improper to stir up litigation known to be unfounded or unjust, any wilful misconduct of this nature may be made punishable by statute, perhaps under the name of "maintenance," and the practice of doing so (three or more instances) may constitute an offense called "barratry" which is actually more often included in the modern codes.

Misconduct under the name of "champerty" (or sometimes "maintenance") is much more likely to be encountered today as a defense to a civil action than as a criminal offense. Statutes prohibiting "stirring up quarrels and suits" are not uncommon, the following (former Iowa Code Ann. § 740.6) being an example:

"If any judge, justice of the peace, clerk of any court, sheriff, coroner, constable, attorney, or counselor at law, encourage, excite or stir up any action, quarrel or controversy between two or more persons, with intent to injure such persons, he shall be fined not exceed-

1. The common-law doctrines of champerty and maintenance were never adopted in California. The statute forbidding fee-splitting applies only to the attorney and not to the layman. Cain v. Burns, 131 Cal.App.2d 439, 280 P.2d 888 (1955).

ing five hundred dollars, and shall be answerable to the party injured in treble damages."

(L) CONTEMPT

Misconduct adversely affecting the administration of a governmental function may take the form of improper interference with the work of the legislative body or of the court. In England either house of Parliament could commit for contempt of itself, and in this country the power to commit for contempt extends to the Senate and House of Representatives of the United States and to the corresponding bodies of the respective states. Such contempt includes any insult to the legislative body in the form of disrespectful or disorderly conduct in its presence and also any wilful obstruction of the performance of a legislative function. Such misconduct, it is to be noted, is not indictable but is punished by the legislative body itself. Contempt of Congress, or its committees, has been made a misdemeanor by statute and hence such misbehavior may now be dealt with the same as any other offense of corresponding grade.

Under the common law of England courts had the inherent power to punish for contempt and this has been accepted as a part of our common law at least so far as courts of record are concerned. Contempt of court has been classified in two different ways: (a) depending upon the purpose of the proceeding, into (1) civil contempt and (2) criminal contempt, and (b) depending upon the factor of proximity or remoteness, into (1) direct contempt and (2) constructive (indirect or consequential) contempt. Civil contempt is misconduct in the form of disobedience to an order or direction of the court by one party to a judicial proceeding to the prejudice of the other litigant. The harm is to the injured litigant rather than to the public and the "penalty" imposed, being purely coercive in purpose, can be avoided by compliance with the court's order. Thus a person who had wrongfully taken a child from its lawful guardian and disobeyed the order of the judge to bring the child into court or disclose its whereabouts was ordered committed to jail until she should obey the court's order.

A criminal contempt[1] on the other hand is misconduct which is disrespectful to the court, calculated to bring the court into disrepute,

1. It had been held repeatedly that a "criminal contempt", though resembling a crime, was not a crime and hence the proceedings for the punishment thereof were not subject to the requirements of a criminal trial. For example, it was held that the contemner was not entitled to a jury trial. United States v. Barnett, 376 U.S. 681, 84 S.Ct. 984, 12 L.Ed.2d 23 (1964). Overruling all such holdings it has now been held that a "criminal contempt" is a crime and hence if the punishment is to be more than imprisonment for six months a jury trial may be demanded. Bloom v. Illinois, 391 U.S. 194, 88 S.Ct. 1477 (1968). ("Any misdemeanor, the penalty for which does not exceed imprisonment for a period of six months or a fine of not more than $500, or both, is a petty offense." 18 U.S.C. § 1(3) (1968).)

During **M**'s trial in a state court, **M** acted as his own counsel and on eleven different occasions he vilified the judge in extreme fashion. After the conclusion of the trial the judge sentenced **M** to one-to-two years on each of eleven counts, or

or of a nature which tends to obstruct the administration of justice, and the purpose of convicting for such contempt is vindication of the public interest by punishment of contemptuous conduct. The same misdeed may constitute both a civil contempt and a criminal contempt and in one such case the judgment was that the contemnor be imprisoned for one day (punishment for his criminal contempt) and that after the expiration of the first day he remain in prison until he complied with the order of the court (coercive and avoidable by prompt compliance).

A direct contempt is one committed in the presence of the court, or of a judge at chambers, or so near thereto as to interrupt or hinder judicial proceedings. Illustrations include an assault on the marshal in open court or a vindictive and uncalled for remark to the court. A constructive, or indirect contempt is an act done, not in the presence of the court or a judge acting judicially, but at a distance under circumstances that reasonably tend to degrade the court or the judge as a judicial officer, or to obstruct, prevent, or embarrass the administration of justice by the court or judge. It may be committed in many ways, such for example, as by violating the judge's instructions to jurors not to separate or make contact with outsiders during trial, or by published criticism of the judicial proceedings of a nature tending to "scandalize the court" to use the familiar phrase. Insofar as a constructive contempt is in the form of a wilful violation of an order of the court, or other direct obstruction of the judicial proceedings, no difficulty is encountered; but so great and so important is the public interest in a public trial that out-of-court discussions and publications in regard to such a proceeding are protected by constitutional privilege even if they tend to cast discredit upon the court or the judge unless carried to such an extreme as to create a "clear and present danger" to the administration of justice.

(M) OTHER OFFENSES

If space permitted, numerous other offenses might be considered in this connection. An important governmental function of a democracy is the holding of elections to fill public offices and to determine certain public questions; hence penalties are provided for unlawful registration as a voter, illegal voting, and various other election offenses. Another such function is the raising of public funds; wherefore penalties are provided for failure to file a required income tax return and various other taxation offenses. Most of the states have undertaken to regulate the manufacture and sale of intoxicating li-

a total of 11 to 22 years. The conviction was vacated and remanded on the ground that the contempt trial should have been before a separate judge. The Court said that the judge "could, with propriety, have instantly acted, holding petitioner in contempt, . . . ". But since he waited until the trial was over the contempt proceeding should have been before another judge. Mayberry v. Pennsylvania, 400 U.S. 455, 91 S.Ct. 499 (1971).

Spitting on the judge in open court constitutes direct contempt of court. Knox v. Municipal Court, 185 N.W.2d 705 (Iowa 1971).

quor, and the results are certain liquor offenses. To this list might be added countless offenses connected with the regulations of trades, occupations, monopolies, banking and finance, the sale of securities and other matters of a similar nature. Only one sample will be used from this list.

Fraudulent banking. This phrase, which might be applied to other misdeeds in the banking field, is usually used only to refer to the following offense. In many states it is made a crime for an officer of a bank to accept a deposit when his bank is insolvent, to his knowledge. A few of the jurisdictions have made a more severe requirement, making it an offense for the officer of a bank, which is in fact insolvent, to accept a deposit when he knows *or has reason to believe* that it is insolvent. Although the distinction between these two types of legislation was overlooked in one case, the proper interpretation is this: Under the first type the banker who accepts a deposit while his bank is insolvent is excused from guilt if he believes in good faith that his bank is solvent, even if he is at fault in not being aware of the insolvency. Under the second type, the banker is not excused unless the insolvency has occurred under such unusual circumstances that he not only does not know of this fact, but is free from criminal negligence in not knowing. Some of the banking laws do not include any such provision, on the ground that whether a bank is or is not insolvent at a certain critical moment in a depression may be difficult to ascertain, and thus the threat of such a penalty may force the closing of banks which it would be in the public interest to have kept open. Many jurisdictions punish the making of false reports by business or other financial institutions in order to insure proper regulation of banking practices.

Chapter 6

IMPUTABILITY

SECTION 1. THE NECESSITY OF AN ACT

4 Blackstone, Commentaries on the Laws of England, 78–79. Let us next see what is a *compassing* or *imagining* of the death of the king &c. These are synonymous terms, the word *compass* signifying the purpose or design of the mind or will, and not, as in common speech, the carrying such design to effect. . . . But, as this compassing or imagining is an act of the mind, it cannot possibly fall under any judicial cognizance, unless it be demonstrated by some open or *overt* act. . . . There is no question, also, but that taking any measures to render such treasonable purposes effectual, as assembling and consulting on the means to kill the king, is a sufficient overt act of high treason.[1]

STATE v. QUICK

Supreme Court of South Carolina, 1942.
199 S.C. 256, 19 S.E.2d 101.

FISHBURNE, JUSTICE. The defendant was convicted of the unlawful manufacture of intoxicating liquor under Section 1829, Code 1932, and amendments thereto. The main question in the case, as we see it, is whether the lower Court erred in refusing to direct a verdict of acquittal, a motion therefor having been made at the close of the evidence offered by the State. . . .

We think there can be no doubt but that the evidence overwhelmingly tends to show an intention on the part of the appellant to manufacture liquor; certainly such inference may reasonably be drawn. But intent alone, not coupled with some overt act toward putting the intent into effect, is not cognizable by the Courts. The law does not concern itself with mere guilty intention, unconnected with any overt act. State v. Kelly, 114 S.C. 336, 103 S.E. 511; 14 Am.Jur., Sec. 25, Page 786. . . .

In our opinion the defendant is entitled to a new trial in any event. But because of the error in overruling his motion for a directed ver-

1. 18 U.S.C.A. § 871 (1976) punishes knowingly and willfully making a threat against the President. It requires proof of a true threat but it need not be communicated to the President. United States v. Frederickson, 601 F.2d 1358 (8th Cir.1979).

dict the judgment is reversed, with direction to enter a verdict of not guilty.

BONHAM, C.J., BAKER and STUKES, JJ., and WM. H. GRIMBALL, A.A.J., concur.

STATE v. RIDER

Supreme Court of Missouri, 1886.
90 Mo. 54, 1 S.W. 825.

HENRY, C.J. At the September term, 1885, of the Saline criminal court the defendant was indicted for murder for killing one R.P. Tallent, and was tried at the November term of said court, 1885, and convicted of murder in the first degree. From that judgment he has appealed to this court.

The evidence for the state proved that he killed the deceased, and of that fact there is no question. It also tended to prove that he armed himself with a gun, and sought the deceased with the intent to kill him. The evidence tended to prove that the relations between the defendant and his wife were not of the most agreeable character, and that the deceased was criminally intimate with her, and on the day of the homicide had taken her off in a skiff to Brunswick. That defendant went in search of his wife to the residence of the deceased, armed with a shot gun, and met the latter near his residence. What then occurred no one witnessed, except the parties engaged, but defendant testified as follows: "Well, me and Mr. Merrill went to this path that was leading toward the river. When we come to that path Mr. Merrill stopped, and I went on in the direction of Mr. Tallent's house, to see if I could learn anything about where my wife was, and I discovered no sign of her there, and I started back north on this path, going down on the slough bank; after going down some distance from the bank I meets Mr. Tallent; I spoke to Mr. Tallent and asked him if he knew where my wife was, and he made this remark: 'I have taken her where you won't find her;' and he says, 'God damn you, we will settle this right here.' He started at me with his axe in a striking position, and I bid Mr. Tallent to stop; then he advanced a few feet, and I fired. I fired one time." The axe of deceased, found on the ground, had a shot in the handle near the end farthest from the blade, and on the same side as the blade, and this evidence had a tendency to corroborate the testimony of the accused, showing that the axe was pointing in the direction from which the shot came, and was held in an upright position.

The court, for the state, instructed the jury as follows:

"The court instructs the jury, that if they believe from the evidence that prior to the killing of the deceased, the defendant prepared and armed himself with a gun, and went in search of, and sought out, deceased, with the intention of killing him, or shooting him, or doing him some great bodily harm, and that he did find, overtake, or intercept, deceased, and did shoot and kill deceased while he was returning from the river to his home, then it makes no difference who commenced the assault, and the jury shall not acquit the defendant; and the jury are further instructed that in such case they shall disregard any and all testimony tending to show that the character or reputation of deceased for turbulency, violence, peace and quiet was bad, and they shall further disregard any and all evidence of threats made by deceased against the defendant."

The mere intent to commit a crime is not a crime. An attempt to perpetrate it is necessary to constitute guilt in law. One may arm himself with the purpose of seeking and killing an adversary, and may seek and find him, yet, if guilty of no overt act, commits no crime. It has been repeatedly held in this and nearly every state in the Union, that one against whom threats have been made by another is not justifiable in assaulting him unless the threatener makes some attempt to execute his threats. A threat to kill but indicates an intent or purpose to kill; and the unexpressed purpose or intent certainly affords no better excuse for an assault by the person against whom it exists than such an intent accompanied with a threat to accomplish it. The above instruction authorized the jury to convict the defendant even though he had abandoned the purpose to kill the deceased when he met him, and was assaulted by deceased and had to kill him to save his own life. . . .

For the errors above noted the judgment is reversed and cause remanded. All concur.[1]

SECTION 2. WHAT CONSTITUTES AN ACT

STATE v. TAFT

Supreme Court of Appeals of West Virginia, 1958.
143 W.Va. 365, 102 S.E.2d 152.

GIVEN, JUDGE. . . . The indictment in the instant case is in two counts. The first count charges defendant with having driven an automobile while "under the influence of intoxicating liquor". . . . On the verdict of the jury, the judgment was that defendant serve six months in the county jail, the sentence to run consecutively to the sentence mentioned in case No. 10907. . . .

After the jury had considered of a verdict for some time, the foreman requested the trial court to answer the question, "Is there a legal definition for what constitutes driving a car?" Whereupon, over objection of defendant, the court instructed the jury "that the term 'driving' has been defined and construed as requiring that a vehicle be in motion in order for the offense to be committed". Defendant then offered, in writing, an instruction which would have told the ju-

1. Rider was tried again under proper instructions and again convicted. This conviction was affirmed. State v. Rider, 95 Mo. 474, 8 S.W. 723 (1888).

ry "that if they believe from the evidence that defendant got in his parked car for the purpose of waiting for someone else, and that the brakes of his car accidentally released and the car drifted some two to three feet into the rear end of a car parked in front of said Taft car, and that the movement of said car was accidental, and not the act and intent of the defendant, then you are authorized to find and determine that the defendant was not then and there driving his said car, and if you so find that the defendant was not then and there driving his said car, you may find the defendant not guilty."

The statute on which the indictment is based makes it a criminal offense for a person "to drive any vehicle on any highway of this state" while "under the influence of intoxicating liquor"; or "under the influence of any narcotic drug". The question posed by the action of the court, as related to the instructions mentioned above, is whether the mere motion of the vehicle constituted "driving" of the vehicle, within the meaning of the statute. We think that it does not.

Though movement of a vehicle is an essential element of the statutory requirement, the mere movement of a vehicle does not necessarily, in every circumstance, constitute a "driving" of the vehicle. To "drive" a vehicle necessarily implies a driver or operator and an affirmative or positive action on the part of the driver. A mere movement of the vehicle might occur without any affirmative act by a driver, or, in fact by any person. If a vehicle is moved by some power beyond the control of the driver, or by accident, it is not such an affirmative or positive action on the part of the driver as will constitute a driving of a vehicle within the meaning of the statute. This being true, the instruction telling the jury that the vehicle must "be in motion in order for an offense to be committed" necessarily, in view of the evidence before the jury, had the effect of telling them that any accidental movement of the vehicle was sufficient to constitute a driving of the vehicle within the meaning of the statute, and constituted prejudicial error. What is said in this respect also indicates prejudicial error in the refusal to give to the jury the instruction offered by defendant, quoted above, after the giving of the instruction first mentioned. . . .

For the reasons indicated, the judgment of the circuit court is reversed, the verdict of the jury set aside, and defendant is awarded a new trial.[1]

Reversed; verdict set aside; new trial awarded.

1. The statute makes it an offense to be in "actual physical control of a motor vehicle while under the influence of intoxicating liquor." One may be in "actual physical control" of a motor vehicle without actually driving it. Hughes v. State, 535 P.2d 1023 (Okl.Cr.1975).

A person who is asleep and whose vehicle is off the road and not running is not in actual physical control of the vehicle. State v. Bugger, 25 Utah 2d 404, 483 P.2d 442 (1971).

Defendant was in actual physical control of a vehicle where he was asleep behind the steering wheel of a vehicle stuck in a borrow pit. State v. Taylor ___ Mont. ___, 661 P.2d 33 (1983).

PEOPLE v. DECINA

Court of Appeals of New York, 1956.
2 N.Y.2d 133, 157 N.Y.S.2d 558, 138 N.E.2d 799.

[Defendant was convicted of the statutory offense known as "criminal negligence in the operation of a vehicle resulting in death". He appealed, insisting that the court erred (1) in overruling his demurrer to the indictment and (2) in the admission of incompetent testimony. The Appellate Division held that the demurrer was properly overruled but reversed and granted a new trial on the second ground. From this determination both parties appealed.]

FROESSEL, JUDGE. . . . We turn first to the subject of defendant's cross appeal, namely, that his demurrer should have been sustained, since the *indictment* here does not charge a crime. The indictment states essentially that defendant, *knowing* "that he was subject to epileptic attacks or other disorder rendering him likely to lose consciousness for a considerable period of time", was culpably negligent "in that he *consciously* undertook to and *did operate* his Buick sedan on a public highway" (emphasis supplied) and "while so doing" suffered such an attack which caused said automobile "to travel at a fast and reckless rate of speed, jumping the curb and driving over the sidewalk" causing the death of 4 persons. In our opinion, this clearly states a violation of section 1053–a of the Penal Law. The statute does not require that a defendant must deliberately intend to kill a human being, for that would be murder. Nor does the statute require that he knowingly and consciously follow the precise path that leads to death and destruction. It is sufficient, we have said, when his conduct manifests a "disregard of the consequences which may ensue from the act, and indifference to the rights of others. No clearer definition, applicable to the hundreds of varying circumstances that may arise, can be given. Under a given state of facts, whether negligence is culpable is a question of judgment." People v. Angelo, 246 N.Y. 451, 457, 159 N.E. 394, 396.

Assuming the truth of the indictment, as we must on a demurrer, this defendant knew he was subject to epileptic attacks and seizures that might strike *at any time.* He also knew that a moving motor vehicle uncontrolled on a public highway is a highly dangerous instrumentality capable of unrestrained destruction. With this *knowledge,* and without anyone accompanying him, he deliberately took a chance by making a conscious choice of a course of action, in disregard of the consequences which he knew might follow from his conscious act, and which in this case did ensue. How can we say as a matter of law that this did not amount to culpable negligence within the meaning of section 1053–a?

To hold otherwise would be to say that a man may freely indulge himself in liquor in the same hope that it will not affect his driving, and if it later develops that ensuing intoxication causes dangerous and reckless driving resulting in death, his unconsciousness or involuntariness at that time would relieve him from prosecution under the statute. His awareness of a condition which he knows may produce such consequences as here, and his disregard of the consequences, renders him liable for culpable negligence, as the courts below have properly held. To have a sudden sleeping spell, an unexpected heart or other disabling attack, without any prior knowledge or warning thereof, is an altogether different situation, and there is simply no basis for comparing such cases with the flagrant disregard manifested here. . . .

Accordingly, the Appellate Division properly sustained the lower court's order overruling the demurrer, as well as its denial of the motion in arrest of judgment on the same ground. . . .

[The court agreed with the Appellate Division that reversible error had been committed in the admission of evidence.]

Accordingly, the order of the Appellate Division should be affirmed.[1]

DESMOND, JUDGE (concurring in part and dissenting in part).

I agree that the judgment of conviction cannot stand but I think the indictment should be dismissed because it alleges no crime. Defendant's demurrer should have been sustained. . . .

Just what is the court holding here? No less than this: that a driver whose brief blackout lets his car run amuck and kill another has killed that other by reckless driving. But any such "recklessness" consists necessarily not of the erratic behavior of the automobile while its driver is unconscious, but of his driving at all when he knew he was subject to such attacks. Thus, it must be that such a black-out-prone driver is guilty of reckless driving. Vehicle and Traffic Law, Consol.Laws, c. 71, § 58, whenever and as soon as he steps into the driver's seat of a vehicle. Every time he drives, accident or no accident, he is subject to criminal prosecution for reckless driving

1. D was convicted under a federal statute which declared that "whoever, without authority, shall have in his possession" any die in the likeness of a die designed for making genuine coin of the United States should be punished. D claimed that the statute was invalid because it would cover unwitting possession. The conviction was affirmed on the ground that the statute must be construed to mean "a willing and conscious possession". Baender v. Barnett, 255 U.S. 224, 41 S.Ct. 271, 65 L.Ed. 597 (1921).

D, who had been awakened with great difficulty from a very deep sleep, almost at once killed the one who had awakened him, a complete stranger. A conviction of manslaughter was reversed because the trial judge had excluded evidence offered to prove that D had been a sleepwalker from infancy, that frequently when aroused from sleep he seemed frightened and attempted violence as if resisting an assault, and for some minutes seemed unconscious of what he did or what went on around him. Fain v. Commonwealth, 78 Ky. 183 (1879).

A person ordered from his home by police cannot be convicted of public intoxication. People v. Martin, 31 Ala.App. 334, 17 So.2d 427 (1944), but see O'Sullivan v. Fisher [1954] So.Aust.L.R. 33.

It violates the Eighth Amendment to punish a defendant for being addicted to the use of narcotics. Robinson v. California, 370 U.S. 660, 82 S.Ct. 1417 (1962).

or to revocation of his operator's license, Vehicle and Traffic Law, § 71, subd. 3. And how many of this State's 5,000,000 licensed operators are subject to such penalties for merely driving the cars they are licensed to drive? No one knows how many citizens or how many or what kind of physical conditions will be gathered in under this practically limitless coverage of section 1053–a of the Penal Law and section 58 and subdivision 3 of section 71 of the Vehicle and Traffic Law. It is no answer that prosecutors and juries will be reasonable or compassionate. A criminal statute whose reach is so unpredictable violates constitutional rights, as we shall now show. . . .

CONWAY, CH. J., DYE and BURKE JJ., concur with FROESSEL, J.; DESMOND, J., concurs in part and dissents in part in an opinion in which FULD and VAN VOORHIS, JJ., concur.

Order affirmed.

MODEL PENAL CODE

Article 2. General Principles of Liability

Section 2.01 Requirement of Voluntary Act; (Omission as Basis of Liability;) Possession as an Act.

(1) A person is not guilty of an offense unless his liability is based on conduct which includes a voluntary act or the omission to perform an act of which he is physically capable.

(2) The following are not voluntary acts within the meaning of this Section:

(a) a reflex or convulsion;

(b) a bodily movement during unconsciousness or sleep;

(c) conduct during hypnosis or resulting from hypnotic suggestion;

(d) a bodily movement that otherwise is not a product of the effort or determination of the actor, either conscious or habitual.

. . .

(4) Possession is an act, within the meaning of this Section, if the possessor knowingly procured or received the thing possessed or was aware of his control thereof for a sufficient period to have been able to terminate his possession.[1]

SECTION 3. ATTEMPT AND KINDRED PROBLEMS

(A) ATTEMPT

(i) In General

MOFFETT v. STATE

Supreme Court of Nevada, 1980.
96 Nev. 822, 618 P.2d 1223.

Per Curiam. Although appellant makes several assignments of error, we recognize only one as meriting discussion, namely, whether there is sufficient evidence to support the attempted murder conviction.

In the early morning hours of August 29, 1978, the victim, Linda Exner, was asleep alone in her apartment. She was awakened by appellant, Deanna Moffett, who had begun to tie her up. Deanna was accompanied by Bobby McPherson, age 14, who held a knife to the throat of the victim. Appellant then threatened Linda and untied her hands to enable Linda to write in her own handwriting, her "suicide note" appellant had written earlier. The note provided:

> Dear Ed, you might think I'm happy seeing you like this, but I'm not. I know that I will never really have you and I can't bear that. You're always looking at other girls when I'm with you, and when you don't spend the night with me, I know you are making love to someone else so I'm ending it. I love you, Linda.

Thereafter, Moffett instructed the victim to write the above message and told her that afterwards she would give her some pills to make her sleep for 48 hours.

The victim wrote approximately one line of the letter before she escaped following a struggle. The appellant and her accomplice then fled and returned to the residence of Ed McPherson where they were apprehended. Upon their arrival at Linda's apartment, the police found the following incriminating evidence: a bottle of wine, a switchblade knife, a flashlight, a bottle of pills, another knife, a short length of hemp rope, and the note.

Dr. Green, a board certified pathologist and toxicologist, testified that the pills found at the victim's apartment were sleeping pills. He stated that a high dosage was dangerous and would be fatal absent immediate and adequate medical intervention. He further testified that if alcohol was ingested in conjunction with the pills, the effect would be even more extreme.

Found guilty of both attempted murder and burglary, felonies, appellant appeals.

To prove an attempt to commit a crime, the prosecution must establish (1) the intent to commit the crime; (2) performance of some act towards its commission; and (3) failure to consummate its commission. Appellant alleges that there was insufficient evidence presented to establish the performance of some act, beyond mere preparation, toward the commission of murder. We disagree.

The preparation for a crime consists in "devising or arranging the means or measures necessary for the commission of the offense; the attempt is the direct movement towards the commission after the preparations are made." In interpreting NRS 208.070,[1] we stated in Darnell v. State, 92 Nev. at 682, 558 P.2d at 625, that a "direct but ineffectual act toward the commission of the crime" is the required *actus reus* for an attempted crime. The act need not be, as appellant herein asserts, actual commencement of the potentially death producing action.

Here, appellant's own testimony showed, *inter alia,* that she obtained the keys to the victim's apartment without the victim's or Ed McPherson's knowledge or consent; that she made a list of the instruments she was taking to Linda's apartment; and the night before she went to Linda's apartment she wrote the note she wanted Linda to write to Ed. After entering Linda's apartment, the appellant tied the victim's hands, woke the victim up, and started to dictate to the victim the note that appellant had previously written. Appellant further testified that she had planned the incident about two days in advance of her going to the victim's apartment. She acquired the necessary materials prior to entering the victim's apartment, then pursuant to her plan, entered the victim's apartment and exercised sufficient control over the victim to begin to effectuate her plan. Had it not been for Linda's fortuitous escape, appellant would have effectuated her purpose.

We will "not destroy the practical and common sense administration of the law with subtleties as to what constitutes preparation and [acts] done toward the commission of a crime." Appellant clearly took sufficient steps beyond mere preparation, to support the attempted murder conviction.

Other assignments of error are either not supported by persuasive authority or are without merit and we need not consider them.

Accordingly, we affirm both judgments of conviction.[a]

1. NRS 208.070 provides in part: "An act done with intent to commit a crime, and tending but failing to accomplish it, is an attempt to commit that crime . . . ."

a. ". . . an attempt to commit a misdemeanor is a misdemeanor, whether the offence is created by statute or was an offence at common law." Rex v. Roderick, 7 Car. and P. 795 (1837).

(ii) PERPETRATING ACT

WILSON v. STATE

Supreme Court of Mississippi, 1904.

85 Miss. 687, 38 So. 46.

CALHOON, J., delivered the opinion of the court.

Wilson was convicted of an attempt to commit forgery, the court below properly charging the jury that it could not convict of the crime itself. The instrument of which attempt to commit forgery is predicated is a draft for "two and 50–100 dollars," as written out in the body of it, having in the upper right-hand corner the figures $2.50–100," as is customary in checks, drafts, and notes, and having plainly printed and stamped on the face of the instrument the words "Ten Dollars or Less." Wilson, with a pen, put the figure "1" before the figure "2" in the upper right-hand corner, making these immaterial figures appear "$12.50" instead of "$2.50," and undertook to negotiate it as $12.50. This was not forgery, because it was an immaterial part of the paper, and because it could not possibly have injured anybody. In order to constitute the crime, there must be not only the intent to commit it, but also an act of alteration done to a material part, so that injury might result. . . . These authorities might be numerously added to, but it is enough to say now that they sustain what we have said, and establish also that an instrument void on its face is not the subject of forgery, and that, in order to be so subject, it must have been capable of working injury if it had been genuine, and that the marginal numbers and figures are not part of the instrument, and their alteration is not forgery.

This being true, can the conviction of an attempt to commit forgery be sustained in the case before us? We think not. No purpose appears to change anything on the paper except the figures in the margin, and this could not have done any hurt. Our statute (Code 1892, § 1106) confines the crime of forgery to instances where "any person may be affected, bound, or in any way injured in his person or property." This is not such a case, and sec. 974 forbids convicting of an attempt "when it shall appear that the crime intended or the offense attempted was perpetrated." In this record the innocuous prefix of the figure "1" on the margin was fully accomplished, and no other effort appears, and, if genuine, could have done no harm; and so the appellant is guiltless, in law, of the crime of which he was convicted.

Reversed and remanded.

PEOPLE v. PALUCH

Appellate Court of Illinois, 1966.
78 Ill.App.2d 356, 222 N.E.2d 508.

DAVIS, JUSTICE. The defendant, Michael Paluch, was charged, in the Circuit Court of the 18th Judicial Circuit, DuPage County, with attempting to practice barbering without a certificate of registration as a barber in violation of Ill.Rev.Stat.1965, ch. 16¾, par. 14.92(b)(1). The case was tried before the court without a jury and the defendant was found guilty as charged and a fine in the sum of $25 was imposed. The defendant contends that the evidence was not sufficient to sustain the judgment.

On November 5, 1965, Ernie Pinkston, an agent of the barber's union, went to a barber shop located in Glen Ellyn. It was 9:00 A.M. and the shop was not yet open. He then saw the defendant unlock the rear door and enter the shop. Shortly thereafter, he went to the front door and asked the defendant if the shop was open. The defendant unlocked the door, admitted Pinkston, walked over to the barber chair, put on his smock and offered the chair to Pinkston. The defendant had his own barber tools—clipping shears, razors and combs.

Pinkston then showed the defendant his business card and asked to see his license. The defendant twice motioned to a particular license which, in fact, was not his. No one else was in the shop at the time. When later asked if he worked at the shop, the defendant answered "yes" and admitted that he had no license.

Both the defendant and the State refer to the Criminal Code of 1961, Ill.Rev.Stat.1965, ch. 38, par. 8–4(a) with reference to the elements necessary to establish the offense of an "attempt," which provides:

"A person commits an attempt when, with intent to commit a specific offense, he does any act which constitutes a substantial step toward the commission of that offense."

Two elements must be present to constitute an attempt: (1) an intent to commit a specific offense, and (2) an act which is a substantial step towards its commission. The defendant contends that all that can be shown by the record in this case is a mere preparation to do something, but that no act constituting a substantial step toward barbering was committed.

As pointed out in the Committee Comments to par. 8–4 of the Criminal Code of 1961 (Smith-Hurd Ann.St. ch. 38 sec. 8–4, p. 357), the determination of when the preparation to commit an offense ceases and the preparation of the offense begins, is a troublesome problem. The distinction between the preparation and the attempt is largely a matter of degree, and whether certain given conduct constitutes an actual attempt is a question unique to each particular case.

In order to constitute an attempt, it is not requisite that the act of the defendant is necessarily the last deed immediately preceding that which would render the substantive crime complete. In Commonwealth v. Peaslee, 177 Mass. 267, 59 N.E. 55 (1901), Mr. Justice Holmes, as Chief Justice of the Supreme Judicial Court of Massachusetts, discussed the considerations necessary in determining whether there were sufficient acts to constitute an attempt to commit an offense under circumstances where further acts were required to perpetrate the offense. He there noted that the acts may then be nothing more than preparation to commit an offense which is not punishable, but also stated that given preparations may constitute an attempt, the determining factor being a matter of degree. As illustrative of this comment, his opinion at page 56 states:

"If the preparation comes very near to the accomplishment of the act, the intent to complete it renders the crime so probable that the act will be a misdemeanor, although there is still a locus poenitentiae, in the need of a further exertion of the will to complete the crime. As was observed in a recent case, the degree of proximity held sufficient may vary with circumstances, including, among other things, the apprehension which the particular crime is calculated to excite."

The crux of the determination of whether the acts are sufficient to constitute an attempt really is whether, when given the specific intent to commit an offense, the acts taken in furtherance thereof are such that there is a dangerous proximity to success in carrying out the intent. In Hyde v. United States, 225 U.S. 347, 32 S.Ct. 793, 56 L.Ed. 1114 (1911), Mr. Justice Holmes, in his dissenting opinion, at pages 387 and 388, 32 S.Ct. at page 810, adequately delineates the distinction between the mere preparation to commit an offense and an attempt to perpetrate the offense, in these words:

"But combination, intention, and overt act may all be present without amounting to a criminal attempt,—as if all that were done should be an agreement to murder a man 50 miles away, and the purchase of a pistol for the purpose. There must be dangerous proximity to success. But when that exists the overt act is the essence of the offense."

The language of par. 8–4 of the Criminal Code, stating that there must be a substantial step toward the commission of the offense indicates that it is not necessary for an "attempt" that the last proximate act to the completion of the offense be done. In addition, the Illinois Supreme Court has likewise considered this problem. In People v. Woods, supra, 24 Ill.2d at page 158, 180 N.E.2d at page 478, it stated:

"Mere preparation to commit a crime, of course, does not constitute an attempt to commit it. We feel however that an attempt does exist where a person, with intent to commit a specific offense, performs acts which constitute substantial steps toward the commission of that offense."

The defendant, who conceded that he worked at the barber shop, was the only person there. He had a key and unlocked the shop. He had barber tools. He had a fraudulent license which was posted near the barber chair. He admitted Pinkston to the shop, put on his smock—as it was referred to by the witness—and motioned him to the chair. At this point the defendant was precluded from barbering without a certification of registration, only by the fact that the witness showed the defendant his business card and did not get into the chair. These facts are sufficient to establish the defendant's attempt to violate the statute, as charged.

The defendant argues that barber tools need not be used exclusively for barbering, and that there is nothing to establish that he had a specific intent to practice barbering. In view of the foregoing facts, we find it unbelievable that the defendant had any intent other than to barber and to use the barbering tools, chair and shop for that purpose.

The acts of the defendant were not of such serious character and consequence that he could be expected to feel genuinely apprehensive about what he was doing. The degree of proximity to the actual commission of a crime necessary for there to be an attempt is, in part, determined by the apprehension which the particular crime is calculated to excite. The greater the apprehension, the greater the likelihood that a would be offender will not follow through with his intended plans. Inasmuch as the offense involved was only a misdemeanor and the penalty inconsequential, there was no cause for serious apprehension on the part of the defendant in connection with the commission of this particular offense, and it was inconceivable that at this late moment he would repent and alter his course of conduct out of fear or concern. He had then taken substantial steps toward the commission of the act of barbering without a certificate of registration. His intention and overt acts resulted in conduct in the very close proximity to the commission of the offense and constituted an attempt.

We believe that the trial court was warranted in finding, on the facts here recited, that the defendant had taken substantial steps to commit the act of barbering. Its findings and conclusions are not against the manifest weight of the evidence,—an opposite conclusion is not clearly evident. Under such circumstances, a reviewing court will not disturb a finding of fact made by the trial court. Consequently, the judgment of the lower court is affirmed.

Judgment affirmed.[1]

SEIDENFELD, J., concurs.

1. Putting poison on the under side of a moustache cup and leaving it where the owner was expected to drink from it and be killed, is an attempt to commit murder. Commonwealth v. Kennedy, 170 Mass. 18, 48 N.E. 770 (1897).

"The majority of jurisdictions considering the issue have also held that solicitation is not an attempt." State v. Otto, 102 Ida. 250, 629 P.2d 646 (1981).

The fact that the crime was committed does not prevent conviction of an attempt

MORAN, PRESIDING JUSTICE (dissenting). I agree with the majority opinion up to the point where it holds that the defendant was guilty of certain acts which constituted a substantial step toward the commission of the offense charged. It is this facet of the case alone with which I disagree.

While it is true that the distinction between the preparation and the substantial step toward the commission of an act, is one of degree, and must be determined by the circumstances of each case; nevertheless, I believe the facts in the case at bar are insufficient to establish the act which constitutes a substantial step toward the commission of the offense.

The majority opinion relies upon, among others, People v. Woods, 24 Ill.2d 154, 158, 180 N.E.2d 475 (1962); however, in that case the defendant commenced toward performance of the act by giving the complaining witness a sedative, although not taken by her, nevertheless it was directed toward her. There was, in addition, the fact that the defendant had received a fee for services to be rendered; the fact that instruments needed to perform the operation were in a pan on the stove; and the fact that the complaining witness stated she was ready and began to remove her clothing.

In the case at bar, while there is no doubt that the necessary intent was present, still there is no evidence that the defendant took a "first step" toward commission of the intended crime against Pinkston, the complaining witness. Pinkston, the only one present other than the defendant at the time of the alleged "act", testified that the defendant unlocked the barbershop door, walked back to the barber chair and put on his smock. He further testified that he, Pinkston, walked over and set his brief case down and the defendant "offered me to get into the chair; at that, I handed him my business card." Thereafter, Pinkston looked around to see where his license was but did not see it. In addition, the defendant had his own barber tools present.

This is the only evidence offered to establish the act which together with the intent is a necessary element to constitute the offense of

to commit it. Failure to consummate the crime of burglary is not an essential element of attempted burglary. State v. Gallegos, 193 Neb. 651, 228 N.W.2d 615 (1975).

In an attempted abortion case the defendant claimed because there were still things to be done to the woman after she left defendant's office no attempt occurred. The court said, "the emphasis should be on 'what the defendant has already done toward committing the crime not on what remains to be done.' " State v. Lewis, ___ Ind. ___, 429 N.E.2d 1110, 1116–7 (1981).

It was error to prosecute and convict the defendant for assault with intent to ravish where the proof was conclusive that the sexual encounter was more than that; i.e. that the sexual act was completed. Young v. State, 317 So.2d 402 (Miss. 1975).

N.B. This was under a statute which expressly enjoins courts from convicting of assault with intent to rape when rape was committed. Since he could not be convicted in the first trial he was not in jeopardy.

an "attempt." I would concede that if Pinkston had sat in the barber chair, as offered, and an over-garment placed upon him, then it could be said that a substantial step toward the commission of the offense charged had taken place—even though not one hair was clipped from his head. However, this is not the evidence. The best that can be said of the evidence adduced in this case toward the charge of attempting to practice barbering without a certificate of registration as a barber, is that the defendant started preparing himself but never got to the point of preparing the person against whom the attempt was to have been made. Therefore, I must, and do, dissent from my learned colleagues.

PEOPLE v. RIZZO

Court of Appeals of New York, 1927.
246 N.Y. 334, 158 N.E. 888.

CRANE, J. The police of the city of New York did excellent work in this case by preventing the commission of a serious crime. It is a great satisfaction to realize that we have such wide-awake guardians of our peace. Whether or not the steps which the defendant had taken up to the time of his arrest amounted to the commission of a crime, as defined by our law, is, however, another matter. He has been convicted of an attempt to commit the crime of robbery in the first degree and sentenced to State's prison. There is no doubt that he had the intention to commit robbery if he got the chance. An examination, however, of the facts is necessary to determine whether his acts were in preparation to commit the crime if the opportunity offered, or constituted a crime in itself, known to our law as an attempt to commit robbery in the first degree. Charles Rizzo, the defendant, appellant, with three others, Anthony J. Dorio, Thomas Milo and John Thomasello, on January 14th planned to rob one Charles Rao of a payroll valued at about $1,200 which he was to carry from the bank for the United Lathing Company. These defendants, two of whom had firearms, started out in an automobile, looking for Rao or the man who had the payroll on that day. Rizzo claimed to be able to identify the man and was to point him out to the others who were to do the actual holding up. The four rode about in their car looking for Rao. They went to the bank from which he was supposed to get the money and to various buildings being constructed by the United Lathing Company. At last they came to One Hundred Eightieth street and Morris Park avenue. By this time they were watched and followed by two police officers. As Rizzo jumped out of the car and ran into the building all four were arrested. The defendant was taken out of from the building in which he was hiding. Neither Rao nor a man named Previti, who was also supposed to carry a payroll, were at the place at the time of the arrest. The defendants had not found or seen the man they intended to rob; no person with a payroll was at any of the places where they had stopped and no one had been pointed out or identified by Rizzo. The four men intended to rob the payroll man, whoever he was; they were looking for him, but they had not seen or discovered him up to the time they were arrested.

Does this constitute the crime of an attempt to commit robbery in the first degree? The Penal Law, section 2, prescribes, "An act, done with intent to commit a crime, and tending but failing to effect its commission, is 'an attempt to commit that crime.' " The word *"tending"* is very indefinite. It is perfectly evident that there will arise differences of opinion as to whether an act in a given case is one *tending* to commit a crime. "Tending" means to exert activity in a particular direction. Any act in preparation to commit a crime may be said to have a tendency towards its accomplishment. The procuring of the automobile, searching the streets looking for the desired victim, were in reality acts tending toward the commission of the proposed crime. The law, however, has recognized that many acts in the way of preparation are too remote to constitute the crime of attempt. The line has been drawn between those acts which are remote and those which are proximate and near to the consummation. The law must be practical, and, therefore, considers those acts only as tending to the commission of the crime which are so near to its accomplishment that in all reasonable probability the crime itself would have been committed but for timely interference. The cases which have been before the courts express this idea in different language, but the idea remains the same. The act or acts must come or advance very near to the accomplishment of the intended crime. In People v. Mills, 178 N.Y. 274, 284, 70 N.E. 786, it was said: "Felonious intent alone is not enough, but there must be an overt act shown in order to establish even an attempt. An overt act is one done to carry out the intention, and it must be such as would naturally effect that result, unless prevented by some extraneous cause." In Hyde v. U. S., 225 U.S. 347, 32 S.Ct. 793, 56 L.Ed. 1114, it was stated that the act amounts to an attempt when it is so near to the result that the danger of success is very great. "There must be dangerous proximity to success." Halsbury in his "Laws of England" (Vol. IX, p. 259) says: "An act, in order to be a criminal attempt, must be immediately, and not remotely, connected with and directly tending to the commission of an offence." Commonwealth v. Peaslee, 177 Mass. 267, 59 N.E. 55, refers to the acts constituting an attempt as coming *very near* to the accomplishment of the crime.

The method of committing or attempting crime varies in each case so that the difficulty, if any, is not with this rule of law regarding an attempt, which is well understood, but with its application to the facts. As I have said before, minds differ over proximity and the nearness of the approach.

How shall we apply this rule of immediate nearness to this case? The defendants were looking for the payroll man to rob him of his money. This is the charge in the indictment. Robbery is defined in section 2120 of the Penal Law as "the unlawful taking of personal property, from the person or in the presence of another against his will, by means of force, or violence, or fear of injury, immediate or future, to his person;" and it is made robbery in the first degree by section 2124 when committed by a person aided by accomplices actually present. To constitute the crime of robbery the money must have been taken from Rao by means of force or violence, or through fear. The crime of attempt to commit robbery was committed if these defendants did an act tending to the commission of this robbery. Did the acts above described come dangerously near to the taking of Rao's property? Did the acts come so near the commission of robbery that there was reasonable likelihood of its accomplishment but for the interference? Rao was not found; the defendants were still looking for him; no attempt to rob him could be made, at least until he came in sight; he was not in the building at One Hundred and Eightieth street and Morris Park avenue. There was no man there with the payroll for the United Lathing Company whom these defendants could rob. Apparently no money had been drawn from the bank for the payroll by anybody at the time of the arrest. In a word, these defendants had planned to commit a crime and were looking around the city for an opportunity to commit it, but the opportunity fortunately never came. Men would not be guilty of an attempt at burglary if they had planned to break into a building and were arrested while they were hunting about the streets for the building not knowing where it was. Neither would a man be guilty of an attempt to commit murder if he armed himself and started out to find the person whom he had planned to kill but could not find him. So here these defendants were not guilty of an attempt to commit robbery in the first degree when they had not found or reached the presence of the person they intended to rob.

For these reasons, the judgment of conviction of this defendant, appellant, must be reversed and a new trial granted. . . .[1]

1. Two men planned to rob a payroll clerk of his payroll. They went to the bank where he was to receive the payroll and stationed themselves to waylay him, but were arrested just before the clerk arrived. This was held to be an attempt to rob. People v. Gormley, 222 App.Div. 256, 225 N.Y.S. 653 (1927).

Two men planned to rob a third. They made inquiries about him, procured masks, and hired a taxi to hunt for him. This was held to be preparation only. Groves v. State, 116 Ga. 516, 42 S.E. 755 (1902).

Two men planned to rob the persons in a saloon. They procured arms and masks. They went to the saloon, pushed open the door and started to enter, but withdrew hastily when they saw a large crowd inside. This was held to be an attempt to rob. People v. Moran, 18 Cal. App. 209, 122 P. 969 (1912).

D planned to kill his wife with the aid of an accomplice. The "accomplice," who pretended to agree but had no intention of doing so, was to gain access to the house as a pretended buyer so that **D** could get in and kill her. After the accomplice had been sent in, **D** was arrested in a car in front of the house, with a rifle in the rear of the car. A conviction of attempted murder was affirmed. People v. Parrish, 87 Cal.App.2d 853, 197 P.2d 804 (1948).

Defendant, who obtained keys to the victim's apartment, made a list of instruments she was taking to the apartment, wrote a suicide note for the victim, and entered the victim's apartment and tied her hands, could be convicted of attempt

(iii) IMPOSSIBILITY

STATE v. MITCHELL

Supreme Court of Missouri, Division Two, 1902.
170 Mo. 633, 71 S.W. 175.

GANTT, J. Defendant was tried upon an information filed by the prosecuting attorney of Clinton county at the May term, 1901, and convicted of an attempt to murder John O. Warren. His punishment was assessed at five years in the penitentiary. . . .

I. The first insistence is that the first count in the information is so defective that it will not sustain the sentence. Whether the objection is well taken or not, depends upon what constitutes the offense and what is essential to be proven. The statute provides that "every person who shall attempt to commit an offense prohibited by law, and in such an attempt shall do any act towards the commission of such offense, but shall fail in the perpetration thereof, or be intercepted or prevented from executing the same," etc., shall be punished as therein provided. Murder is an offense prohibited. When the defendant armed himself with a loaded revolver and went to the window of the room in which he believed John O. Warren was sleeping, from his knowledge acquired by visiting his family, and fired his pistol at the place where he thought Warren was lying, he was attempting to assassinate and murder him. The fact that Warren was not there as he believed him to be, did not make it any the less an attempt to murder. Our statute on this subject is substantially like that of Massachusetts, construed in Com. v. McDonald, 5 Cush. 365, and Com. v. Sherman, 105 Mass. 169, in which it was held "that neither allegation nor proof was necessary, that there was any property, capable of being stolen, in the pocket or upon the person of the one against whom the attempt to commit larceny was made." . . .[1]

So in this case the intent evidenced by the firing into the bedroom with a deadly weapon accompanied by a present capacity in defendant

to commit murder. The attempt to kill need not be the actual commencement of the potentially death-producing action. Moffett v. State, 96 Nev. 822, 618 P.2d 1223 (1980).

In what seems to have been a plan to swindle a depositor, he was persuaded to withdraw $400.00 from the bank. A former victim of the swindler recognized him while the check was being drawn and the depositor did not withdraw the money. A conviction of attempted larceny by trick was reversed. Commonwealth v. Kelley, 162 Pa.Super. 526, 58 A.2d 375 (1948).

1. Accord: People v. Moran, 123 N.Y. 254, 25 N.E. 412 (1890).

An English case held, contra, that larceny cannot be attempted by reaching into an empty pocket. Regina v. Collins, 9 Cox C.C. 497 (1864). This case was later overruled. See Regina v. Ring, 17 Cox C.C. 491 (1892).

to murder Warren if he were in the room, and the failure to do so only because Warren haply retired upstairs instead of in the bed into which defendant fired, made out a perfect case of an attempt within the meaning of the statute, and the information is sufficient. The evidence conclusively supported the information. It discloses a deliberate and dastardly attempt at assassination, which was only averted by the intended victim's going upstairs to bed that night. . . .

We find no error in the record, and affirm the judgment. All concur.

PEOPLE v. ROJAS

Supreme Court of California, In Bank, 1961.
55 Cal.2d 252, 10 Cal.Rptr. 465, 358 P.2d 921.

[Hall, who had stolen $4,500 worth of electrical conduit, was arrested while in possession of the stolen property and taken to the police station. He said he had an arrangement with one of the defendants to sell him any and all electrical materials obtained. From the police station Hall made three phone calls, monitored by the police, which resulted in a plan by which Hall left a truck, containing the conduit, at a place designated by the defendants. Later one of the defendants came and drove away the truck to a lot near his place of business. He was arrested next morning when he began to unload the truck.]

SCHAUER, JUSTICE. In a trial by the court, after proper waiver of jury, defendants Rojas and Hidalgo were found guilty of a charge of receiving stolen property. Defendants' motions for new trial were denied. Rojas was granted probation without imposition of sentence and Hidalgo was sentenced to state prison. They appeal, respectively, from the order granting probation, the judgment, and the orders denying the motions for new trial.

Defendants urge that they were guilty of no crime (or, at most, of an attempt to receive stolen property) because when they received the property it had been recovered by the police and was no longer in a stolen condition. The attorney general argues that because the thief stole the property pursuant to prearrangement with defendants he took it as their agent, and the crime of receiving stolen property was complete when the thief began its asportation toward defendants and before the police intercepted him and recovered the property. We have concluded that defendants are guilty of attempting to receive stolen goods; that other matters of which they complain do not require a new trial; and that the appeal should be disposed of by modifying the finding that defendants are guilty as charged to a determination that they are guilty of attempting to receive stolen property, and by reversing with directions to the trial court to enter such judgments or probation orders as it deems appropriate based upon the modified finding. . . .

The offense with which defendants were charged and of which they were convicted was receiving "property which has been *stolen . . . , knowing the same to be so stolen.*" Pen.Code, § 496, subd. 1; italics added. Defendants, relying particularly upon People v. Jaffe (1906), 185 N.Y. 497, 501 [78 N.E. 169, 9 L.R.A.,N.S., 263, 266], urge that they neither received stolen goods nor criminally attempted to do so because the conduit, when defendants received it, was not in a stolen condition but had been recovered by the police. In the Jaffe case the stolen property was recovered by the owner while it was en route to the would-be receiver and, by arrangement with the police, was delivered to such receiver as a decoy, not as property in a stolen condition. The New York Court of Appeals held that there was no attempt to receive stolen goods "because neither [defendant] nor anyone else in the world could know that the property was stolen property inasmuch as it was not in fact stolen property. . . . If all which an accused person intends to do would if done constitute no crime it cannot be a crime to attempt to do with the same purpose a part of the thing intended."

Defendants also cite People v. Zimmerman (1909), 11 Cal.App. 115, 118, 104 P. 590, which contains the following dictum concerning a state of facts like that in the Jaffe case: "The circumstances of the transaction . . . did not constitute an offense, as the goods were taken to the defendant's house with the consent and at the request of the owner."

As pointed out by the District Court of Appeal in Faustina v. Superior Court (1959), 174 Cal.App.2d 830, 833 [1], 345 P.2d 543, "The rule of the Jaffe case has been the subject of much criticism and discussion." . . .

In the case at bench the criminality of the attempt is not destroyed by the fact that the goods, having been recovered by the commendably alert and efficient action of the Los Angeles police, had, unknown to defendants, lost their "stolen" status, any more than the criminality of the attempt in the case of In re Magidson (1917), 32 Cal.App. 566, 568, 163 P. 689, was destroyed by impossibility caused by the fact that the police had recovered the goods and taken them from the place where the would-be receiver went to get them. In our opinion the consequences of intent and acts such as those of defendants here should be more serious than pleased amazement that because of the timeliness of the police the projected criminality was not merely detected but also wiped out. . . .

The orders denying defendants' motions for new trial are affirmed. The trial court's finding that defendants are guilty as charged is modified to find them guilty of the offense of attempting to receive stolen property. The judgment and probation order are reversed and the cause is remanded to the trial court for further proceedings not inconsistent with the views hereinabove expressed, and with directions to enter such lawful judgment or order against each defendant, based on the modified finding, as the court deems appropriate.[1]

GIBSON, C.J., and TRAYNOR, MCCOMB, PETERS, WHITE and DOOLING, JJ., concur.

BOOTH v. STATE

Court of Criminal Appeals of Oklahoma, 1964.
398 P.2d 863.

[Having stolen a coat, the thief telephoned to Booth saying he had it and would let Booth have it for $20.00. It was arranged that Booth would meet the thief at the latter's house at 11:00 A.M. to effect the transfer. In the meantime the thief was arrested and confessed. The police recovered the coat and called in the owner who identified it. It was then returned to the thief to carry out the original plan which was done, after which Booth was arrested. From a conviction of attempting to receive stolen property an appeal was taken.]

NIX, JUDGE. . . . In People v. Finkelstein, 21 Misc.2d 723, 197 N.Y.S.2d 31 (1960) the court said:

"A defendant may not be convicted for receiving stolen property if property is no longer in category of stolen property when he receives it."

The law seems to be clear on this point, leaving the only question to be decided as whether or not the defendant could be convicted of an attempt to receive stolen property in such cases. It is the defendant's contention that if he could not be convicted of the substantive charge, because the coat had lost its character as stolen property; neither could he be convicted of an attempt because the coat was not in the category of stolen property at the time he received it.

The briefs filed in the case, and extensive research has revealed that two states have passed squarely on the question—New York and California. It is definitely one of first impression in Oklahoma.

1. One who receives what he believes to be stolen property may be convicted of an attempt to receive stolen property even if the property was not in fact stolen. State v. Carner, Ariz.App., 541 P.2d 947 (1975); People v. Moss, 55 Cal.App.3d 179, 127 Cal.Rptr. 454 (1976); People v. Darr, 193 Colo. 445, 568 P.2d 32 (1977).

Where property stolen by burglars was recovered by police, who had an undercover agent sell it to D, D could not properly be convicted of receiving stolen property, because it had lost its character of stolen property. But D could be convicted of an attempt to receive stolen property if he believed it was stolen. State v. Niehuser, 21 Or.App. 33, 533 P.2d 834 (1975).

"Does stolen property lose its identity as stolen property when it is recovered by law enforcement officers? We conclude that it does." State v. Sterling, 230 Kan. 790, 640 P.2d 1264 (1982).

The New York Court, in passing upon the question, laid down the following rule in the case of People v. Jaffe, 185 N.Y. 497, 78 N.E. 169, 6 L.R.A.,N.S., 263, on the following facts:

"A clerk stole goods from his employer under an agreement to sell them to accused, but before delivery of the goods the theft was discovered and the goods were recovered. Later the employer redelivered the goods to the clerk to sell to accused, who purchased them for about one-half of their value, believing them to have been stolen.

"Held, that the goods had lost their character as stolen goods at the time defendant purchased them, and that his criminal intent was insufficient to sustain a conviction for an attempt to receive stolen property, knowing it to have been stolen."

The Jaffe case, supra, was handed down in 1906, and has prevailed as the law in New York state 58 years without modification—being affirmed in People v. Finklestein [sic] supra; . . . and finally in the case of People v. Rollino (1962), 37 Misc.2d 14, 233 N.Y.S.2d 580.

The State of California has passed upon the question several times and up until 1959, they followed the rule laid down in the Jaffe case, supra.

In 1959, in the case of People v. Camodeca, 52 Cal.2d 142, 338 P.2d 903, the California Court abandoned the Jaffe rationale that a person accepting goods which he believes to have been stolen, but which was not in fact stolen goods, is not guilty of an attempt to receive stolen goods, and imposed a liability for the attempt, overruling its previous holding to the contrary in the above cited cases. The Camodeca case, supra, was affirmed in People v. Rojas, 55 Cal.2d 252, 10 Cal.Rptr. 465, 358 P.2d 921, 85 A.L.R.2d 252, 1961.

Though the instant case, insofar as it pertains to the specific crime of attempting to receive stolen property is one of first impression in Oklahoma. This Court held in the Nemecek v. State, 72 Okl.Cr. 195, 114 P.2d 492, 135 A.L.R. 1149, involving attempting to receive money by false pretenses:

"An accused cannot be convicted of an attempt to commit a crime unless he could have been convicted of the crime itself if his attempt had been successful. Where the act, if accomplished, would not constitute the crime intended, there is no indictable attempt."

In the Nemecek case, supra, the Court quotes with approval, In re Schurman, 40 Kan. 533, 20 P. 277; wherein the Kansas Court said:

"With reference to attempt, it has also been said that 'if all which the accused person intended would, had it been done, constitute no substantive crime, it cannot be a crime, under the name "attempt," to do, with the same purpose, a part of this thing.' "

The two paramount cases of latest date; Rojas of Calif.1961, supra, and Rollino of New York 1962, supra; present two rationales directly contrary to each other relative to an attempt to receive stolen property after it had been recovered by the police. . . .

The authorities in the various states and the text-writers are in general agreement that where there is a "legal impossibility" of completing the substantive crime, the accused cannot be successfully charged with an attempt, whereas in those cases in which the "factual impossibility" situation is involved, the accused may be convicted of an attempt. Detailed discussion of the subject is unnecessary to make it clear that it is frequently most difficult to compartmentalize a particular set of facts as coming within one of the categories rather than the other. . . . Your writer is of the opinion that the confusion that exists as a result of the two diverse rationales laid down in the Rollino case (NY) supra, and the Rojas case (Calif) supra, was brought about by the failure to recognize the distinction between a factual and a legal impossibility to accomplish the crime. In the Camodeca case (Calif) supra, the facts revealed a prevention of the crime because of a factual situation as stated on page 906, 338 P.2d:

"In the present case there was not a legal but only a factual impossibility of consummating the intended offense . . . ."

In the Rojas case, supra, wherein was adopted the departure from the Jaffe case, by saying:

"The situation here is materially like those considered in People v. Camodeca."

The Rojas case was definitely not materially the same. In the Rojas case the facts reveal a legal and not factual impossibility.

In the case at bar the stolen coat had been recovered by the police for the owner and consequently had, according to the well-established law in this country, lost its character as stolen property. Therefore, a legal impossibility precluded defendant from being prosecuted for the crime of Knowingly Receiving Stolen Property. . . . Sayre, 41 Harvard Law Review 821, 853–54 (1928) states the rationale in this manner:

"It seems clear that cases (where none of the intended consequences is in fact criminal) cannot constitute criminal attempts. If none of the consequences which the defendant sought to achieve constitute a crime, surely his unsuccessful efforts to achieve his object cannot constitute a criminal attempt. The partial fulfillment of an object not criminal cannot itself be criminal. If the whole is not criminal, the part cannot be."

The defendant in the instant case leaves little doubt as to his moral guilt. The evidence, as related by the self-admitted and perpetual law violator indicates defendant fully intended to do the act with which he was charged. However, it is fundamental to our law that a man is not punished merely because he has a criminal mind. It must be shown that he has, with that criminal mind, done an act which is forbidden by the criminal law.

Adhering to this principle, the following example would further illustrate the point.

A fine horse is offered to A at a ridiculously low price by B, who is a known horse thief. A, believing the horse to be stolen buys the same without inquiry. In fact, the horse had been raised from a colt by B and was not stolen. It would be bordering on absurdity to suggest that A's frame of mind, if proven, would support a conviction of an attempt. It would be a "legal impossibility" . . . .

In view of our statutory law, and the decisions herein related, it is our duty to Reverse this case, with orders to Dismiss, and it is so ordered. However, there are other avenues open to the County Attorney which should be explored.[1]

JOHNSON, P.J., and BUSSEY, J., concur.

[Rehearing denied Feb. 17, 1965.]

UNITED STATES v. OVIEDO

United States Court of Appeals, Fifth Circuit, 1976.
525 F.2d 881.

Before GODBOLD, DYER and MORGAN, CIRCUIT JUDGES.

DYER, CIRCUIT JUDGE.

Oviedo appeals from a judgment of conviction for the attempted distribution of heroin, in violation of 21 U.S.C.A. § 846.[1] Oviedo contends that under the facts of this case, he is not guilty of any criminal offense. We agree and reverse.

Oviedo was contacted by an undercover agent, who desired to purchase narcotics. Arrangements were made for the sale of one pound of heroin. The agent met Oviedo at the appointed time and place. Oviedo transferred the substance to the agent, and asked for his money in return. However, the agent informed Oviedo that he would first have to test the substance. A field test was performed with a positive result. Oviedo was placed under arrest.

Subsequent to the arrest, a search warrant was issued for Oviedo's residence. When the search was executed, two pounds of a similar substance was found hidden in a television set. Up to this point, the case appeared unexceptional.

A chemical analysis was performed upon the substances seized, revealing that the substances were not in fact heroin, but rather procaine hydrochloride, an uncontrolled substance.[2] Since any attempt

1. "In sum, to be convicted of attempt the defendant's objective actions, taken as a whole, must strongly corroborate the required culpability." United States v. Innella, 690 F.2d 834 (11th Cir.1982).

1. 21 U.S.C.A. § 846 (1981) provides:

Any person who attempts or conspired to commit any offense defined in this subchapter is punishable by imprisonment or fine or both which may not exceed the maximum punishment prescribed for the offense, the commission of which was the object of the attempt or conspiracy.

2. Although not an opium derivative, procaine hydrochloride will give a positive reaction to the Marquis Reagent Field Test.

to prosecute for distribution of heroin would have been futile, the defendant was charged with an attempt to distribute heroin.

At trial, Oviedo took the stand and stated that he knew the substance was not heroin, and that he, upon suggestion of his cohorts, was merely attempting to "rip off" the agent. It was, in his view, an easy way to pocket a few thousand dollars.

The court instructed the jury that they could find Oviedo guilty of attempted distribution if he delivered the substance thinking it to be heroin.[3] The jury rejected Oviedo's claimed knowledge of the true nature of the substance, and returned a verdict of guilty. Although Oviedo argues on appeal that there was insufficient evidence to establish that he thought the substance was heroin, this contention is without merit.[4] We thus take as fact Oviedo's belief that the substance was heroin.

The facts before us are therefore simple—Oviedo sold a substance he thought to be heroin, which in reality was an uncontrolled substance. The legal question before us is likewise simple—are these combined acts and intent cognizable as a criminal attempt under 21 U.S.C.A. § 846. The answer, however, is not so simple.

Oviedo and the government both agree the resolution of this case rests in an analysis of the doctrines of legal and factual impossibility as defenses to a criminal attempt. Legal impossibility occurs when the actions which the defendant performs or sets in motion, even if fully carried out as he desires, would not constitute a crime. U. S. v. Conway, 5 Cir.1975, 507 F.2d 1047. Factual impossibility occurs when the objective of the defendant is proscribed by the criminal law but a circumstance unknown to the actor prevents him from bringing about that objective. Id. at 1050. The traditional analysis recognizes legal impossibility as a valid defense, but refuses to so recognize factual impossibility. U. S. v. Berrigan, 3 Cir.1973, 482 F.2d 171.

These definitions are not particularly helpful here, for they do nothing more than provide a different focus for the analysis. In one sense, the impossibility involved here might be deemed legal, for those *acts* which Oviedo set in motion, the transfer of the substance in his possession, were not a crime. In another sense, the impossibility is factual, for the *objective* of Oviedo, the sale of heroin, was pro-

3. The court charged the jury on this issue:

In other words, if you find beyond a reasonable doubt that Mr. Oviedo did knowingly and unlawfully and intentionally attempt to distribute what you have found beyond a reasonable doubt . . . he believed to be one pound of heroin . . . it would be no defense that the substance involved was not actually heroin. On the other hand, if you do not find beyond a reasonable doubt that the Defendant believed the substance involved to be heroin, even though you might find all of the other elements of the offense present beyond a reasonable doubt, then it would be your duty to acquit the Defendant.

4. The fact that the procaine was secreted inside a television set, together with the discussions between Oviedo and the undercover agent, lead to the reasonable inference that Oviedo thought the substance to be heroin, and support the jury's conclusion.

scribed by law, and failed only because of a circumstance unknown to Oviedo.[5]

Although this issue has been the subject of numerous legal commentaries,[6] federal cases reaching this question are few, and no consensus can be found.[7] United States v. Berrigan, 3 Cir.1973, 482 F.2d 171; United States v. Heng Awkak Roman, S.D.N.Y.1973, 356 F.Supp. 434, aff'd 2 Cir.1973, 484 F.2d 1271; Rosado v. Martinez, D.P.R., 1974, 369 F.Supp. 477; United States v. Hair, D.C.1973, 356 F.Supp. 339; see also United States v. Marin, 2 Cir.1975, 513 F.2d 974.

In *Roman,* the defendants were transporting a suitcase containing heroin. Through the aid of an informer and unknown to the defendants, the contents of the suitcase were replaced with soap powder. The defendants were arrested when they attempted to sell the contents of the suitcase, and were subsequently charged with *attempted* possession with intent to distribute. The court rejected defendants' contention that they could not be charged with attempted possession, since it was impossible for them to possess heroin. Recognizing the difficulty in distinguishing between legal and factual impossibility, the court never so categorized the case. Nevertheless, the court concluded that since the objective of the defendants was criminal, impossibility would not be recognized as a defense.

The defendants in *Berrigan* were charged with attempting to violate 18 U.S.C.A. § 1791, prohibiting the smuggling of objects into or out of a federal correctional institution. Since the evidence estab-

5. At least one writer has recognized that legal impossibility is logically indistinguishable from factual impossibility. See Hall, Criminal Attempt—A Study of Foundations of Criminal Liability, 49 Yale L.J. 789, 836 (1940).

6. See articles listed in United States v. Berrigan, 3 Cir.1973, 482 F.2d 171, 187, fn. 29.

7. State court cases are similarly divergent. State courts have labelled the following situations as involving legal impossibility, and concluded that there could be no attempt: (1) A person who accepts goods which he believes to be stolen, but which are not in fact stolen, is not guilty of attempting to receive stolen goods. People v. Jaffe, 1906, 185 N.Y. 497, 78 N.E. 169. (2) A person who offers a bribe to one whom he believes to be a juror, but who was not a juror, is not guilty of attempting to bribe a juror. State v. Taylor, 1939, 345 Mo. 325, 133 S.W.2d 336. (3) A hunter who shoots a stuffed deer, believing it to be alive, is not guilty of attempting to shoot a deer out of season. State v. Guffey, Mo.App. 1953, 262 S.W.2d 152.

In other apparently analogous situations, courts have concluded that the impossibility is factual, and therefore no defense to a charge of attempt: (1) A person who fires a gun at a bed, thinking it to be occupied by a man, is guilty of attempted murder, even though the bed is empty. State v. Mitchell, 1902, 170 Mo. 633, 71 S.W. 175. (2) A person who possesses a substance thinking it is narcotics, is guilty of attempted possession, notwithstanding that the substance is in fact talcum powder. People v. Siu, 1954, 126 Cal.App.2d 41, 271 P.2d 575. (3) A person who introduces instruments into a woman for the purpose of producing an abortion is guilty of attempting an abortion, even though the woman is not pregnant. People v. Cummings, 1956, 141 Cal.App.2d 193, 296 P.3d 610.

Other impossibility cases are collected in Annot., 37 A.L.R.3d 375. We list these cases not to offer support to our conclusions, but rather to illustrate the inconsistency of approach which plagues this area of legal theory.

lished that the warden had knowledge of the smuggling plan, and since lack of knowledge was a necessary element of the offense, the defendants could not be found guilty of violating the statute. The court held that such knowledge by the warden would also preclude conviction for the attempt, since "attempting to do that which is not a crime is not attempting to commit a crime." *Berrigan,* at 190.

The *Berrigan* court rested its determination on a strict view of legal impossibility. According to the court, such impossibility exists when there is an intention to perform a physical act, the intended physical act is performed, but the consequence resulting from the intended act does not amount to a crime. In this analysis, the intent to perform a physical act is to be distinguished from the motive, desire or expectation to violate the law.[8]

The application of the principles underlying these cases leads to no clearer result than the application of our previous definitions of legal and factual impossibility. Applying *Roman,* we would not concern ourselves with any theoretical distinction between legal and factual impossibility, but would affirm the conviction, since the objective of Oviedo was criminal. Applying *Berrigan,* we would look solely to the physical act which Oviedo "intended", the transfer of the procaine in his possession, and we would conclude that since the transfer of procaine is not criminal, no offense is stated. The choice is between punishing criminal intent without regard to objective acts, and punishing objective acts, regarding intent as immaterial.

In our view, both *Roman* and *Berrigan* miss the mark, but in opposite directions. A strict application of the *Berrigan* approach would eliminate any distinction between factual and legal impossibility, and such impossibility would *always* be a valid defense, since the "intended" physical acts are never criminal.[9] The *Roman* approach turns the attempt statute into a new substantive criminal statute where the critical element to be proved is *mens rea simpliciter.* It would allow us to punish one's thoughts, desires, or motives, through indirect evidence, without reference to any objective fact. See *Berrigan,* supra at 189, fn. 39. The danger is evident.

We reject the notion of *Roman,* adopted by the district court, that the conviction in the present case can be sustained since there is sufficient proof of intent, not because of any doubt as to the sufficiency of the evidence in that regard, but because of the inherent dangers such a precedent would pose in the future.

8. This distinction is easily illustrated. If A takes a book which he thinks belongs to B, his desire or expectation is criminal. However, if the book turns out to belong to A, A does not have the requisite intent to be guilty of a criminal attempt, for his intent is to take the book, and it is not criminal to take one's own book. See *Berrigan,* supra, at 188, fn. 35.

9. If the "intended" physical acts were criminal, the defendant would be guilty of the completed crime, rather than the attempt.

When the question before the court is whether certain conduct constitutes mere preparation which is not punishable, or an attempt which is, the possibility of error is mitigated by the requirement that the objective acts of the defendant evidence commitment to the criminal venture and corroborate the *mens rea.* United States v. Mandujano, 5 Cir.1974, 499 F.2d 370. To the extent this requirement is preserved it prevents the conviction of persons engaged in innocent acts on the basis of a *mens rea* proved through speculative inferences, unreliable forms of testimony, and past criminal conduct.

Courts could have approached the preparation—attempt determination in another fashion, eliminating any notion of particular objective facts, and simply could have asked whether the evidence at hand was sufficient to prove the necessary intent. But this approach has been rejected for precisely the reasons set out above, for conviction upon proof of mere intent provides too great a possibility of speculation and abuse.

In urging us to follow *Roman,* which found determinative the criminal intent of the defendants, the government at least implicitly argues that we should reject any requirement demanding the same objective evidentiary facts required in the preparation—attempt determination. We refuse to follow that suggestion.

When the defendant sells a substance which is actually heroin, it is reasonable to infer that he knew the physical nature of the substance, and to place on him the burden of dispelling that inference. United States v. Moser, 7 Cir.1975, 509 F.2d 1089, 1092; United States v. Joly, 2 Cir.1974, 493 F.2d 672, 676.[10] However, if we convict the defendant of attempting to sell heroin for the sale of a non-narcotic substance, we eliminate an objective element that has major evidentiary significance and we increase the risk of mistaken conclusions that the defendant believed the goods were narcotics.[11]

Thus, we demand that in order for a defendant to be guilty of a criminal attempt, the objective acts performed, without any reliance on the accompanying *mens rea,* mark the defendant's conduct as criminal in nature. The acts should be unique rather than so com-

10. A similar inference obtains when possession is established, but the defendant contends that he did not know of the presence of the controlled substance. See, e.g., U. S. v. Squella-Avendano, 5 Cir.1973, 478 F.2d 433, 438; U. S. v. Dixon, 9 Cir.1972, 460 F.2d 309; U. S. v. Hood, 9 Cir.1974, 493 F.2d 677, 681.

11. Enker, Impossibility in Criminal Attempts—Legality and the Legal Process, 53 Minn.L.R. 665, 680 (1969).

Mens rea is within one's control but, as already seen, it is not subject to direct proof. More importantly perhaps, it is not subject to direct refutation either. It is the subject of inference and speculation. The act requirement with its relative fixedness, its greater visibility and difficulty of fabrication, serves to provide additional security and predictability by limiting the scope of the criminal law to those who have engaged in conduct that is itself objectively forbidden and objectively verifiable. Security from officially imposed harm comes not only from the knowledge that one's thoughts are pure but that one's acts are similarly pure. So long as a citizen does not engage in forbidden conduct, he has little need to worry about possible erroneous official conclusions about his guilty mind.

Id. at 688.

monplace that they are engaged in by persons not in violation of the law.

Here we have only two objective facts. First, Oviedo told the agent that the substance he was selling was heroin, and second, portions of the substance were concealed in a television set. If another objective fact were present, if the substance were heroin, we would have a strong objective basis for the determination of criminal intent and conduct consistent and supportative of that intent. The test set out above would be met, and, absent a delivery, the criminal attempt would be established. But when this objective basis for the determination of intent is removed, when the substance is not heroin, the conduct becomes ambivalent, and we are left with a sufficiency-of-the-evidence determination of intent rejected in the preparation—attempt dichotomy. We cannot conclude that the objective acts of Oviedo apart from any indirect evidence of intent mark his conduct as criminal in nature. Rather, those acts are consistent with a noncriminal enterprise. Therefore, we will not allow the jury's determination of Oviedo's intent to form the sole basis of a criminal offense. . . .

Reversed.[12]

PREDDY v. COMMONWEALTH

Supreme Court of Appeals of Virginia, 1946.
184 Va. 765, 36 S.E.2d 549.

[From a judgment of conviction of the crime of attempted rape, the elderly defendant appealed. He had offered evidence tending to show impotency, and claimed that error had been committed by an instruction which told the jury that impotence is not a defense to the crime of attempted rape. Reliance was placed upon a case which had held that since (under Virginia law) a boy under 14 years of age is

12. [Added by Compilers.] To clarify *Oviedo* the court held in another case that where D's intent to sell cocaine was not disputed (he admitted it), he may be convicted of an intent to sell cocaine although it was actually a simulated substance. United States v. Hough, 561 F.2d 594 (5th Cir.1977).

"We are convinced that Congress intended to eliminate the defense of impossibility when it enacted [21 U.S.C. § 846] . . . When Congress enacted section 846 the doctrine of impossibility had become enmeshed in unworkable distinctions and was no longer widely accepted as part of the meaning of 'attempt' at common law." United States v. Everett, 700 F.2d 900, 904 (3d Cir.1983).

The enactment of KSA 21–3301(2) eliminated both legal and factual impossibility as a defense to an attempt charge. State v. Logan, 232 Kan. 646, 656 P.2d 777 (1983).

Under the New York Revised Penal Code it is not a defense to a charge of attempted murder that the victim was already dead when the attempt was made. If it cannot be shown beyond a reasonable doubt that the victim was alive at the time, there can be no conviction of murder, but the defendant can be convicted of attempted murder if he thought the victim was alive when he shot him. People v. Dlugash, 395 N.Y.S.2d 419, 41 N.Y.2d 725, 363 N.E.2d 1155 (1977).

To subject one who delivers a substance falsely represented to be an illegal drug to a harsher penalty than is provided for the actual delivery of the real thing, is a violation of due process. People v. Wagner, 89 Ill.2d 308, 60 Ill.Dec. 470, 433 N.E.2d 267 (1982).

incapable of committing rape he is "also incapable in law of an attempt to commit it".]

CAMPBELL, CHIEF JUSTICE. . . . The question whether or not an adult who claims to be impotent is incapable of committing the crime of attempt to rape is one of first impression. . . .

In Wharton's Criminal Law, 12th Ed., sec. 223, it is said: "If there be juridical incapacity for the consummated offense (e.g., infancy) there can be no conviction of the attempt; and therefore a boy under fourteen (14) cannot, according to the prevalent opinion, be convicted of an attempt to commit rape as a principal in the first degree. It is otherwise, where the incapacity is merely nervous or physical. A man may fail in consummating a rape for some nervous or physical incapacity intervening between attempt and execution. But this failure would be no defense to the indictment for an attempt. At the same time there must be apparent capacity."

In the case at bar, we are dealing with the question of alleged physical incapacity. Neither at common law nor by statute is an adult clothed with the presumption that he is incapable of committing the crime of rape, or an attempt to rape.

"According to the decided weight of authority, both in England and in this country, an apparent possibility to commit the crime is enough." Clark and Marshall, Crimes, sec. 123.

In Wharton's Criminal Law, 10th Ed., section 552, it is said: "Impotency is a sufficient defense for the consummated offence, though not for an assault with intent." See Wharton & St.Med.Jur., sec. 20.

In an illuminating article in 78 Penn.Law Review, p. 971, it is stated: "When a defendant, with rape in mind, and with the expectation of accomplishing penetration, seizes his female victim in the customary manner in order to achieve his purpose and finds penetration impossible, because of impotency the authorities agree that he is guilty of a real criminal attempt to rape, and his impotency has no bearing on the case except possibly negativing the specific intention to accomplish penetration." . . .

We are of opinion that there is no error in the judgment of the circuit court and that it must be affirmed.[1]

Affirmed.

1. In a charge of assault with intent to rape, evidence of the impotency of **D** is admissible on the issue of intent. In this case, however, the conviction was affirmed because there was no evidence of inability to have sexual penetration, or if so, that **D** was actually aware of it. Waters v. State, 2 Md.App. 216, 234 A.2d 147, 23 A.L.R.3d 1339 (1967).

For an exhaustive annotation on attempt to commit rape or assault with intent to rape where impotency is claimed as a defense, see 23 A.L.R.3d 1351 (1969).

One too drunk to accomplish sexual penetration may be guilty of an assault with intent to commit rape. United States v. Contreras, 422 F.2d 828 (9th Cir.1970).

"Legal impossibility occurs when the actions which the defendant performs, or sets in motion, even if fully carried out as he desires, would not constitute a

BROWNING, JUSTICE (dissenting). I do not think that the Commonwealth has proven the case against the defendant beyond a reasonable doubt and this, notwithstanding the verdict of the jury. I think that the testimony of Dr. Mason, who is a distinguished physician, if there were nothing more, casts grave doubt upon the guilt of the accused. Of this, of course, he should have the benefit.

(iv) INTENT

STATE v. HOUSE

Court of Appeals of Oregon, In Banc, 1978.
37 Or.App. 131, 586 P.2d 388.

RICHARDSON, JUDGE. The court sustained defendant's demurrer to a criminal complaint. The state appeals pursuant to ORS 138.060(1).

Defendant was charged with violating ORS 164.045, by complaint, as follows:

> "The said defendant, on or about June 12, 1977, in Multnomah County, State of Oregon, did unlawfully and knowingly attempt to commit theft of Two (2) pharmaceutical items, Two (2) containers of soap, One (1) container of wax and Five (5) foodstuff items, of the total value of less than Two Hundred Dollars, the property of Fred Meyer, Inc."

Defendant's demurrer stated:

> ". . . that [the complaint] fails to state a crime of Attempt. Specifically, the complaint alleges that the defendant knowingly attempted to commit theft where the statute requires the defendant to intentionally engage in conduct. . . ."

The state contends that the use of the word "attempt" charges defendant with the necessary mental state. We agree.

In light of the present criminal procedure code the accusatory instrument has lost much of its historical significance as a means of notifying defendant of the crime charged. The liberal discovery provisions of ORS 135.805 to 135.873 augment the defendant's ability to prepare a defense. As a result, the trend in Oregon has been to require less specificity in the accusatory instrument. The complaint is merely a formal method of initiating the criminal process and of identifying the crime charged. If the complaint, read in conjunction with the statutory definition of the terms used, informs the defendant of the elements of the offense with which he is charged it is sufficient.

In State v. Jim/White, 13 Or.App. 201, 508 P.2d 462, rev. den. (1973), we reviewed a challenge to an accusatory instrument which

crime. Thus an indictment for attempted rape can be defeated by showing that the woman the defendant attempted to ravish was his wife." United States v. Conway, 507 F.2d 1047, 1050 (5th Cir.1975).

alleged "theft" without a separate allegation of criminal intent. We stated:

> ". . . [T]hat the word 'theft' when used in an indictment is a term of art. (Citation omitted.) By the use of the word 'theft' the indictment is alleging that a certain act (the appropriation of property) was done with a certain intent (the intent to substantially interfere with the property rights of the owner). . . . [T]he statute in question here fully defines the meaning of the word 'theft' and the defendants need look no further to discover what act and crime is being charged. Where the words used in the indictment necessarily imply other words those words need not be used in the indictment. (Citation omitted.) Where the words used in the indictment are sufficiently defined in the statute the definitions need not be included in the indictment. (Citation omitted.)" 13 Or.App. at 220–21, 508 P.2d at 471.

The rationale of *Jim/White* is applicable to this case. "Attempt" is a statutory word of art. ORS 161.405(1) provides a person is guilty of an attempt to commit a crime ". . . when he intentionally engages in conduct which constitutes a substantial step toward commission of the crime." By the allegation, "attempt to commit theft," the complaint, under the *Jim/White* analysis, is read to state "defendant intentionally engaged in conduct which constituted a substantial step toward commission [attempt] of the crime of intentionally depriving another of the specified property [theft]." The state is not required to repeat statutory definitions of the terms used in the accusatory instrument. Those definitions are incorporated by the use of the terms. Inclusion of the word "knowingly" in the complaint is surplusage and does not affect the sufficiency of the complaint. The demurrer should have been overruled.

Reversed and remanded for trial.[1]

1. An attempt to run down a pedestrian with a car will support conviction of an assault with intent to kill. Figeroa v. State, 244 Ark. 457, 425 S.W.2d 516 (1968).

Since an assault (under the California statute) requires an attempt to commit a battery, a conviction of assault with a deadly weapon cannot be supported by proof of the use of a weapon merely to frighten. People v. Marceaux, 3 Cal. App.3d 613, 83 Cal.Rptr. 798 (1970).

". . . the trial court erred in instructing the jury that it need not find a specific intent to kill in order to convict of attempted murder." People v. Collie, 30 Cal.3d. 43, 177 Cal.Rptr. 458, 634 P.2d 534, 535 (1981).

Implied malice will not support conviction for assault with intent to commit murder. People v. Johnson, 30 Cal.3d 444, 179 Cal.Rptr. 209, 637 P.2d 676 (1981).

In upholding a conviction of burglary under an indictment charging that the dwelling had been broken into "with intent to commit larceny", the court said (referring to State v. Van Gilder, 140 Kan. 66, 33 P.2d 936 (1934)): "In the opinion we cited State v. Woodruff, 208 Iowa 236, 225 N.W. 254. Numerous cases are cited in a well considered opinion in the Iowa case holding the clear weight of authority to be that an unexplained breaking and entering of a dwelling house in the nighttime is in itself sufficient to sustain a verdict that the breaking and entering was done with the intent to commit *larceny* rather than some other felony. The Iowa case contains quotations from some of the many cases so holding, which need not be repeated here. The fundamental theory

(B) AGGRAVATED ASSAULT

STATE v. WILSON

Supreme Court of Oregon, 1959.
218 Or. 575, 346 P.2d 115.

O'CONNELL, JUSTICE. The defendant appeals from a judgment of the circuit court for Multnomah county entered on a verdict pronouncing him guilty of the crime of attempted assault with a dangerous weapon under Count I of the indictment, . . .

[The evidence showed that defendant had confronted and threatened his estranged wife in her place of employment, after which he procured a loaded shotgun from his car just outside to carry out his threat. He was unable to reach his wife the second time, however, because she was then safely behind locked doors.]

The crime of assault with a dangerous weapon is defined in ORS 163.250 as follows:

"Any person, who is armed with a dangerous weapon and assaults another with such weapon, shall be punished upon conviction by imprisonment in the penitentiary for not more than 10 years, or by imprisonment in the county jail not less than one month nor more than one year, or by a fine of not less than $100 nor more than $1,000."

There is no statute dealing specifically with an attempt to commit assault with a dangerous weapon. The state relies upon the general attempt statute, ORS 161.090, which reads in part as follows:

"Any person who attempts to commit a crime, and in the attempt does any act towards the commission of the crime but fails or is prevented or intercepted in the perpetration thereof, shall be punished upon conviction, when no other provision is made by law for the punishment of such attempt, as follows: . . ."

The defendant attacks Count I of the indictment on the ground that it does not state a crime under the laws of this state. Defendant

upon which the inference of intent to commit larceny is based, absent evidence of other intent or an explanation for the breaking and entering, is that the usual object or purpose of burglarizing a dwelling house at night is theft." State v. Gatewood, 169 Kan. 679, 684, 221 P.2d 392, 396–7 (1950). Accord: State v. Walker, 109 W.Va. 351, 154 S.E. 866 (1930).

Although it has been held that an intent to commit larceny may be inferred from an unexplained and unauthorized breaking and entering of another's dwelling at night, such an inference is not supported by an unauthorized entry, under a statute which does not require a breaking. State v. Rood, 11 Ariz.App. 102, 462 P.2d 399 (1969).

D was convicted of an assault with intent to commit mayhem on evidence that she threw red pepper at X, apparently intended for his face. There was no evidence tending to show that she thought red pepper would produce blindness. The conviction was reversed. Dahlberg v. People, 225 Ill. 485, 80 N.E. 310 (1907).

One charged with rape may be convicted of assault with intent to commit rape even though the testimony, if believed by the jury, shows the commission of the greater offense. People v. Alcala, 63 Mich.App. 120, 234 N.W.2d 172 (1975).

argues that there is no such crime as an attempted assault with a dangerous weapon. In stating his grounds for objecting to the introduction of evidence in proof of the first count counsel for defendant said ". . . it is the contention of the defendant that there is no such thing as an attempted assault; it is no more than an attempt to inflict an injury or battery, . . . If then, there is such a crime as attempted assault, the one so attempting must have intent to commit an assault. Does he then intend to commit a battery?" To answer this rhetorical question defendant relies upon the following language in Wilson v. State, 1874, 53 Ga. 205, 206:

". . . Plainly and in terms, they say they find him guilty of attempt to make an assault. The question is, can any judgment be entered upon such a verdict? Is it a legal verdict? Is there any such crime? . . . As an assault is itself an attempt to commit a crime, an attempt to make an assault can only be an attempt to attempt to do it, or to state the matter still more definitely, it is to do any act towards doing an act towards the commission of the offense. This is simply absurd. . . ."

The charge that an attempt to attempt to do an act is beyond understanding, seems at first blush to be justified. It could be interpreted to be the equivalent of a statement that one is guilty of a crime if he proceeds to act in such a way that, if not interrupted, his conduct would result in the commission of an act which if not interrupted would result in a substantive crime.

The bulk of the Oregon cases defining criminal assault, however, do so in terms of attempted battery and limit the crime to acts which are intended to cause corporal injury under circumstances in which the actor has the present ability to carry out his intent. Typical of such definitions is that found in Smallman v. Gladden, 1956, 206 Or. 262, 272, 291 P.2d 749, 754, where the court said:

". . . An assault is an intentional attempt by one person by force or violence to do an injury to the person of another, coupled with present ability to carry the intention into effect. . . ."

Under the latter definition, apprehension of injury on the part of the victim need not be shown to make out the crime. Further, it seems clear that an act done with the intention to place one in apprehension of injury only and not to inflict corporal injury would not constitute the crime of assault in this state. And too, according to the definition, an act done with the intention to inflict corporal injury, but where the actor did not have the present ability to inflict corporal injury would not be a criminal assault . . . We are of the opinion that criminal assault, even as defined by this court, should be regarded as a distinct crime rather than as an uncompleted battery.

If we should regard assault as an attempted battery, is it reasonable to recognize the crime of attempted assault? It has been categorically asserted that there can be no attempt to commit a crime which is itself merely an attempt. 1 Wharton, Criminal Law & Procedure

(Anderson ed.). Upon the basis of this premise it is said that there can be no such offense as an attempted assault. 1 Wharton, op. cit. supra, § 72 at 154, states that "as an assault is an attempt to commit a battery there can be no attempt to commit an assault." The same idea is found in Clark & Marshall, Crimes (6th ed.) § 4.07, p. 218, where it is said:

"Since a simple assault is nothing more than attempt to commit a battery, and aggravated assaults are nothing more than attempts to commit murder, rape, or robbery, an attempt to commit an assault, whether simple or aggravated is not a crime."

. . . The mere fact that assault is viewed as preceding a battery should not preclude us from drawing a line on one side of which we require the present ability to inflict corporal injury, denominating this an assault, and on the other side conduct which falls short of a present ability, yet so advanced toward the assault that it is more than mere preparation and which we denominate an attempt. . . . The acts of the defendant after obtaining the gun from his automobile may not have been sufficient to establish that he had the present ability to inflict corporal injury upon his wife who was behind a locked door, but he had proceeded far beyond the stage of preparation and it is reasonable to treat his conduct as an attempt within the meaning of ORS 161.090. It is the function of the law of criminal attempt to permit the courts to adjust the penalty in cases where the conduct falls short of a completed crime. 40 Yale L.J. 53, 74, 75. Our legislature has provided that assault with a dangerous weapon is a crime. ORS 161.090 permits the courts of this state to treat conduct which is short of statutory crimes as a crime, and we regard an attempt to commit an assault as within the intendment of this statute. . . .

The judgment of the lower court is affirmed.[1]

McAllister, C.J., dissents.

1. In California there is no such crime as an attempt to assault. In re M., 9 Cal. 3d 517, 108 Cal.Rptr. 89, 510 P.2d 33 (1973). There is no such crime as attempted felonious assault. People v. Banks, 51 Mich.App. 685, 216 N.W.2d 461 (1974).

Although an attempt to do an act placing another in apprehension of receiving an immediate battery would be an attempt to assault, there is no such offense as an attempt to assault with intent to murder. People v. Etchison, 123 Mich. App. 448, 333 N.W.2d 309 (1983). There is no offense of attempted assault and battery. Joplin v. State, 663 P.2d 746 (Okl.Cr.1983).

D was convicted of an attempt to commit conspiracy to commit first-degree murder. This conviction was reversed on the ground that there is no such crime as an attempt to commit conspiracy. It was held that D could have been convicted of solicitation to commit murder. Hutchinson v. State, 315 So.2d 546 (Fla.App. 1975).

A conviction of attempted assault was reversed for lack of evidence. The court assumed that there was such an offense, but did not expressly pass upon the point. State v. Merseal, 167 Mont. 412, 538 P.2d 1366 (1975).

It was error to instruct the jury on the theory of attempted reckless murder. There is no crime of attempt to act recklessly. State v. Smith, 21 Or.App. 270, 534 P.2d 1180 (1975): . . . "one cannot attempt to act recklessly."

Id. at 1184.

(C) SOLICITATION

STATE v. BLECHMAN

New Jersey Supreme Court, 1946.
135 N.J.L. 99, 50 A.2d 152.

HEHER, J. . . . Although we have but a meager description of the content of the indictment, it would seem, as said, that it accuses plaintiff in error merely of counseling another to set fire to the dwelling house; and it is urged at the outset that such is not an offense denounced by the cited statute unless the wrongful act thus counseled is done, and the injured property is actually burned. We do not so read the statute. It plainly classifies as a high misdemeanor the counseling or solicitation of another to set fire to or burn any insured building, ship or vessel, or goods, wares, merchandise or other chattels, with intent to prejudice or defraud the insurer; and in this regard the statute is primarily declaratory of the common law.

At common law, it is a misdemeanor for one to counsel, incite or solicit another to commit either a felony or a misdemeanor, certainly so if the misdemeanor is of an aggravated character, even though the solicitation is of no effect, and the crime counseled is not in fact committed. The gist of the offense is the solicitation. It is not requisite that some act should be laid to have been done in pursuance of the incitement. While the bare intention to commit evil is not indictable, without an act done, the solicitation, itself, is an act done toward the execution of the evil intent and therefore indictable. An act done with a criminal intent is punishable by indictment. It was said by an eminent common law judge (Lawrence, J., in Rex v. Higgins, infra) that under the common law all offenses of a public nature, *i.e.*, "all such acts or attempts as tend to the prejudice of the community," are indictable; and it goes without saying that an attempt to incite another to commit arson or a kindred offense is prejudicial to the community and public in its nature. . . . In the case of State v. Brand, 76 N.J.L. 267, 69 A. 1092, affirmed 77 N.J.L. 486, 72 A. 131, this court construed the statute as denouncing two separate and distinct offenses, *i.e.*, the willful or malicious setting fire to or burning of insured property, with intent to prejudice the underwriter, and aiding, counseling, procuring or consenting to the setting fire to or burning of such property; but our court of last resort found it unnecessary to consider the question, for there the indictment used the statutory terms in the conjunctive and thus charged that the merchandise was in fact burned.

The solicitation constitutes a substantive crime in itself,[1] and not an abortive attempt to perpetrate the crime solicited. It falls short of

1. "The solicitation itself is a distinct offense, and is punishable irrespective of the reaction of the person solicited; i.e. the solicitor is guilty even though that person immediately rejects the request or proposal." Hutchins v. Municipal Court

an attempt, in the legal sense, to commit the offense solicited.[2] An attempt to commit a crime consists of a direct ineffectual overt act toward the consummation of the crime, done with an intent to commit the crime. Neither intention alone nor acts in mere preparation will suffice. There must be an overt act directly moving toward the commission of the designed offense—such as will apparently result, in the usual and natural course of events, if not hindered by extraneous causes, in the commission of the crime itself.

Of course, at common law one who counsels, incites or solicits another to commit a felony, is indictable as a principal or an accessory before the fact, if the designed felony is accomplished, depending upon his presence and participation or absence at the time of its commission.

Plaintiff in error sets great store upon the case of Wimpling v. State, 171 Md. 362, 189 A. 248. But it is not in point. The statute there under review was substantially different; it defined the offense of "arson" in terms that clearly signified an actual burning of the property as an indispensible [sic] ingredient of the crime.

We think that, apart from the statutory recognition of a subsisting common law offense, the prime, if not the exclusive, purpose of the legislative act in question was the classification as a high misdemeanor of what would otherwise be a misdemeanor. . . .

Let the judgment be affirmed.[3]

(D) ABANDONMENT

STEWART v. STATE

Supreme Court of Nevada, 1969.
85 Nev. 388, 455 P.2d 914.

MOWBRAY, JUSTICE. A jury found Ernest Stewart guilty of attempted robbery. He has appealed to this court, seeking a reversal, on the sole ground that the evidence received during his trial was insufficient to support the jury's verdict.

of Los Angeles, 61 Cal.App.3d 77, 88, 132 Cal.Rptr. 158, 165 (1976).

2. "Therefore in conformity with the weight of authority, we hold that merely soliciting one to commit a crime does not constitute an attempt." State v. Davis, 319 Mo. 1222, 1229, 6 S.W.2d 609, 612 (1928).

3. Orally addressing a crowd and urging them to kill and rob and commit other acts of violence, is an offense. State v. Schleifer, 99 Conn. 432, 121 A. 805 (1923).

One who asks a woman to have sexual intercourse with him is not guilty of solicitation for prostitution under the Iowa statute. State v. Oge, 227 Iowa 1094, 290 N.W. 1 (1940).

Montana's solicitation statute defining solicitation as "when, with intent that an offense be committed, he commands, encourages or requests another to commit that offense" is not unconstitutionally vague. "The common law has been affirmatively changed in some jurisdictions by statutes which provide that it is no defense to a charge of solicitation that the solicitee is unaware of the criminal nature of the conduct solicited or of the defendant's purpose." State v. Bush, ___ Mont. ___, 636 P.2d 849, 852 (1981).

Marvin Luedtke, who was the victim of the crime, and two police officers appeared for the State. Their testimony stands uncontroverted. It shows that the appellant, Stewart, approached Luedtke, a service station operator, and after brandishing a loaded .32 caliber automatic pistol, said, "I want all of your money." When Luedtke told him that the money was kept in a cash box located near the fuel pumps in front of the station, Stewart demanded the contents of Luedtke's wallet, which Luedtke promptly produced. It was at this juncture that the two police officers drove into the station. One of the officers actually saw the pistol in Stewart's hand. When Stewart saw the officers, he directed Luedtke to bring him two cans of oil and to act as though he, Stewart, were purchasing the oil. Luedtke gave him the oil. Stewart took one can, put his pistol in Luedtke's desk drawer, and attempted to leave the station. He was immediately apprehended by the officers.

Stewart argues that the attempted robbery was not proved because the evidence shows that he had abandoned his intent to commit the crime when he put down the pistol and left the station. We do not agree. The attempted robbery of Luedtke was completed when Stewart produced his pistol and demanded the money. The fact that Luedtke was apprehended on the spot does not lessen his guilt. As the court said in People v. Robinson, 180 Cal.App.2d 745, 4 Cal.Rptr. 679, 682 (1960), ". . . once an intent to commit a crime has been formed and overt acts toward the commission of that crime have been committed by a defendant he is then guilty of an attempt, whether he abandoned that attempt because of the approach of other persons or because of a change in his intentions due to a stricken conscience."

Affirmed.[1]

COLLINS, ZENOFF, BATJER and THOMPSON, JJ., concur.

STATE v. PETERSON

Supreme Court of Minnesota, 1942.
213 Minn. 56, 4 N.W.2d 826.

PETERSON, JUSTICE. Defendant was convicted of arson in the second degree, and appeals.

1. "Since abandonment is not a defense to the commission of the crime of criminal attempt under Nebraska law, ..." State v. Manchester, 213 Neb. 670, 331 N.W.2d 776, 781 (1983).

"We are persuaded by the trend of modern authority and hold that voluntary abandonment is an affirmative defense to a prosecution for criminal attempt. . . . Abandonment is not 'voluntary' when the defendant fails to complete the attempted crime because of unanticipated difficulties, unexpected resistance, or circumstances which increase the probability of detention or apprehension." People v. Kimball, 109 Mich.App. 273, 311 N.W.2d 343, 349 (1981).

"By the specific terms of the statute, § 18–2–101(3), C.R.S.1973, abandonment is an affirmative defense to an attempt crime." People v. Johnson, 41 Colo.App. 220, 585 P.2d 306, 308 (1978).

The indictment charges her with burning her dwelling house on October 30, 1940. The house was at Lake Minnetonka in Hennepin county.

The state claimed, and its evidence was to the effect, that she did not personally set the fire, but caused it to be set by an accomplice, one August Anderson. There was no dispute as to Anderson's having set the fire. Defendant stoutly maintained that she did not have anything to do with the burning of her house and that she not only directed Anderson not to go to the house on the occasion when the fire was set, but that she tried to persuade him before he set the fire to leave the premises to which he had gone contrary to her directions. . . .

Numerous errors are assigned to the effect . . . and (4) that, assuming the truth of the state's evidence that Anderson and defendant were accomplices, defendant is not liable because she withdrew before the fire was set. Since it is decisive, only the last point need be discussed.

It is important to bear in mind that defendant is not charged with the crime of conspiracy.[1] A conspiracy to commit arson is a misdemeanor. Mason St.1927, §§ 10055, 10056. Arson is a felony. Id. §§ 10309–10310; Id. 1940 Supp. § 10311. A conspiracy to commit a crime is a separate offense from the crime which is the object of the conspiracy.

One who has procured, counseled, or commanded another to commit a crime may withdraw before the act is done and avoid criminal responsibility by communicating the fact of his withdrawal to the party who is to commit the crime. . . .

By her efforts through Carlson to induce Anderson to leave the premises before he set the fire and to go immediately to her in the hospital where she was then confined, the defendant in the instant case took the most effective measures within her power to arrest the execution of the plan, if there was one, to burn the house. Anderson must have known that if she wanted him to comply with her request to leave the premises before he set the fire she did not want him to burn the house. She not only withdrew in ample time from any plan to burn the house, but made that fact known to Anderson in an unmistakable manner. By withdrawing, defendant avoided criminal responsibility. Anderson was solely criminally responsible for the fire which he set. The facts being undisputed on this point, the verdict cannot stand.

Reversed.[2]

1. "In the Bridgewater Case [unreported], referred to at the bar, and in which I was counsel, nothing was done in fact; yet a gentleman was convicted because he had entered into an unlawful combination from which almost on the spot he withdrew altogether. No one was harmed, but the public offence was complete." Per Lord Coleridge in Mogul S.S. Co. v. McGregor, Gow & Co., 21 Q.B.D. 544, 549 (1888).

2. The effect of this judgment was that the case was remanded for a new trial. State v. Peterson, 214 Minn. 204, 7 N.W.2d 408 (1943).

MR. JUSTICE STONE, absent because of illness, took no part in the consideration or decision of this case.

MODEL PENAL CODE

Article 5. Inchoate Crimes

Section 5.01 Criminal Attempt.

(1) Definition of Attempt. A person is guilty of an attempt to commit a crime if, acting with the kind of culpability otherwise required for commission of the crime, he:

(a) purposely engages in conduct which would constitute the crime if the attendant circumstances were as he believes them to be; or

(b) when causing a particular result is an element of the crime, does or omits to do anything with the purpose of causing or with the belief that it will cause such result without further conduct on his part; or

(c) purposely does or omits to do anything which, under the circumstances as he believes them to be, is an act or omission constituting a substantial step in a course of conduct planned to culminate in his commission of the crime.

(2) Conduct Which May Be Held Substantial Step Under Subsection (1)(c). Conduct shall not be held to constitute a substantial step under Subsection (1)(c) of this Section unless it is strongly corroborative of the actor's criminal purpose. Without negativing the sufficiency of other conduct, the following, if strongly corroborative of the actor's criminal purpose, shall not be held insufficient as a matter of law:

(a) lying in wait, searching for or following the contemplated victim of the crime;

(b) enticing or seeking to entice the contemplated victim of the crime to go to the place contemplated for its commission;

(c) reconnoitering the place contemplated for the commission of the crime;

(d) unlawful entry of a structure, vehicle or enclosure in which it is contemplated that the crime will be committed;

(e) possession of materials to be employed in the commission of the crime, which are specially designed for such unlawful use or which can serve no lawful purpose of the actor under the circumstances;

(f) possession, collection or fabrication of materials to be employed in the commission of the crime, at or near the place contemplated for its commission, where such possession, collection or fabrication serves no lawful purpose of the actor under the circumstances;

(g) soliciting an innocent agent to engage in conduct constituting an element of the crime.

(3) Conduct Designed to Aid Another in Commission of a Crime. A person who engages in conduct designed to aid another to commit a crime which would establish his complicity under Section 2.06 if the crime were commit-

ted by such other person, is guilty of an attempt to commit the crime, although the crime is not committed or attempted by such other person.

(4) Renunciation of Criminal Purpose. When the actor's conduct would otherwise constitute an attempt under Subsection (1)(b) or (1)(c) of this Section, it is an affirmative defense that he abandoned his effort to commit the crime or otherwise prevented its commission, under circumstances manifesting a complete and voluntary renunciation of his criminal purpose. The establishment of such defense does not, however, affect the liability of an accomplice who did not join in such abandonment or prevention.

Within the meaning of this Article, renunciation of criminal purpose is not voluntary if it is motivated, in whole or in part, by circumstances, not present or apparent at the inception of the actor's course of conduct, which increase the probability of detection or apprehension or which make more difficult the accomplishment of the criminal purpose. Renunciation is not complete if it is motivated by a decision to postpone the criminal conduct until a more advantageous time or to transfer the criminal effort to another but similar objective or victim.

Section 5.02 Criminal Solicitation.

(1) Definition of Solicitation. A person is guilty of solicitation to commit a crime if with the purpose of promoting or facilitating its commission he commands, encourages or requests another person to engage in specific conduct which would constitute such crime or an attempt to commit such crime or which would establish his complicity in its commission or attempted commission.

(2) Uncommunicated Solicitation. It is immaterial under Subsection (1) of this Section that the actor fails to communicate with the person he solicits to commit a crime if his conduct was designed to effect such communication.

(3) Renunciation of Criminal Purpose. It is an affirmative defense that the actor, after soliciting another person to commit a crime, persuaded him not to do so or otherwise prevented the commission of the crime, under circumstances manifesting a complete and voluntary renunciation of his criminal purpose.

Section 5.04 Incapacity, Irresponsibility or Immunity of Party to Solicitation or Conspiracy.

(1) Except as provided in Subsection (2) of this Section, it is immaterial to the liability of a person who solicits or conspires with another to commit a crime that:

(a) he or the person whom he solicits or with whom he conspires does not occupy a particular position or have a particular characteristic which is an element of such crime, if he believes that one of them does; or

(b) the person whom he solicits or with whom he conspires is irresponsible or has an immunity to prosecution or conviction for the commission of the crime.

(2) It is a defense to a charge of solicitation or conspiracy to commit a crime that if the criminal object were achieved, the actor would not be guilty of a crime under the law defining the offense or as an accomplice under Section 2.06(5) or 2.06(6)(a) or (b).

Section 5.05 Grading of Criminal Attempt, Solicitation and Conspiracy; Mitigation in Cases of Lesser Danger; Multiple Convictions Barred.

(1) Grading. Except as otherwise provided in this Section, attempt, solicitation and conspiracy are crimes of the same grade and degree as the most serious offense which is attempted or solicited or is an object of the conspiracy. An attempt, solicitation or conspiracy to commit a [capital crime or a] felony of the first degree is a felony of the second degree.

(2) Mitigation. If the particular conduct charged to constitute a criminal attempt, solicitation or conspiracy is so inherently unlikely to result or culminate in the commission of a crime that neither such conduct nor the actor presents a public danger warranting the grading of such offense under this Section, the Court shall exercise its power under Section 6.12 [1] to enter judgment and impose sentence for a crime of lower grade or degree or, in extreme cases, may dismiss the prosecution.

(3) Multiple Convictions. A person may not be convicted of more than one offense defined by this Article for conduct designed to commit or to culminate in the commission of the same crime.[2]

SECTION 4. NEGATIVE ACTS

BIDDLE v. COMMONWEALTH

Supreme Court of Appeals of Virginia, 1965.
206 Va. 14, 141 S.E.2d 710.

I'ANSON, JUSTICE. Defendant, Shirley Mae Biddle, having waived a jury trial, was tried by the court on an indictment charging her with the murder of her three-month-old baby girl and found guilty of murder in the first degree. After receiving a report from the probation officer, the trial court fixed her punishment and sentenced her to the State penitentiary for a period of twenty years. We granted her a writ of error.

Defendant contends that the trial court erred . . . and (2) in holding that the evidence was sufficient to sustain a conviction of first degree murder. . . .

The defendant says that the evidence is sufficient to sustain a conviction of manslaughter but it fails to support her conviction of murder in the first degree, because the death of the baby resulted from negligence and not from a malicious omission of duty.

1. Section 6.12 provides: "If, when a person, having been convicted of a felony, the Court having regard to the nature and circumstances of the crime and to the history and character of the defendant, is of the view that it would be unduly harsh to sentence the offender in accordance with the Code, the Court may enter judgment of conviction for a lesser degree of felony or for a misdemeanor and impose sentence accordingly."

2. Copyright: 1962 by the American Law Institute. Reprinted with the permission of the American Law Institute.

When the detectives visited defendant's home on the night of January 22, 1964, Henley observed the deceased baby's body in an extreme condition of malnutrition, and when he unpinned her diaper he found blood spots on it and on her private parts from diaper rash. He observed another infant lying on newspapers in a bassinet, with a leather jacket over her, and her diapers were wet and dirty and there was a rash on her buttocks. In the kitchen, the detectives saw a large, open can of Pet milk, with a saucer covering the top, and food on the stove which appeared to have been there for several days.

Medical testimony shows that when the baby was born on October 18, 1963, she "seemed to be perfectly healthy." There was also evidence that the baby weighed 5 pounds 8 ounces at birth.

Testimony of the medical examiner reveals that he made a postmortem examination of the baby's body two days after her death; that she weighed 4 pounds 5½ ounces; that the intestinal tract and stomach were entirely empty, and that the body was dehydrated. It was his opinion that the child had not been fed for several days.

The defendant . . . testified that she fed the baby every day but she was small and sometimes would not drink all the milk she gave her; that she fed her three times on the day she died; that she ate very little pablum and fruit; that she never cried because she was hungry; that she loved the baby and did not treat her any differently from the rest of her children; that she had the means to buy food for the children and had milk and other baby food on hand at all times; that she knew the baby had lost weight but had not taken her to a doctor; that her husband had accused her of having the baby by her stepfather and her other children by other men, and she stayed upset most of the time over his untrue accusations.

Defendant's mother said that the baby had been in her home during the day she died and that she had fed her a small amount of fruit and pablum twice on that day, but that she did not appear to be very well.

Section 18.1–21, Code of 1950, as amended, 1960 Repl.Vol., 1964 Cum.Supp., distinguishes the degrees of murder, but it does not define murder itself. . . .

Murder at common law is a homicide committed with malice aforethought, either express or implied.

The precise question presented here seems never to have been decided by this Court. The general rule, supported by numerous authorities in England and the United States, is that if death is the direct consequence of the malicious omission of the performance of a duty, such as of a mother to feed her child, this is a case of murder; but if the omission is not wilful, and arose out of neglect only, it is manslaughter. . . .

Thus, from the authorities heretofore quoted, whether the defendant was guilty of manslaughter or murder depends upon the nature and character of the act or acts which resulted in the child's death.

Here the defendant was harassed by her husband's accusations that none of her children was his, and the baby's feedings appeared to depend upon how she and her husband got along. When the relationship between them was pleasant she fed the baby, but when it was not she neglected her. She had milk in the house to feed the baby the night it died, but it is apparent from the medical examiner's testimony that she had not fed her for several days. The conditions found when the detectives first went to the apartment and the statements contained in the second signed paper writing made by the defendant to Henley at police headquarters show that she neglected the baby and was careless and indifferent in the performance of her duties not only to the baby, but to other members of her family as well. But, from a consideration of all the facts and circumstances of the case, the Commonwealth has not proved beyond a reasonable doubt that defendant wilfully or maliciously withheld food and liquids from the baby. Hence the conviction of first degree murder is not supported by the evidence, and for this reason the judgment is reversed and the case is remanded for a new trial.

Defendant's court-appointed counsel is allowed a fee of $200, plus expenses, for representing her on the appeal in this Court.

Reversed and remanded.[1]

REGINA v. HOGAN

Court of Criminal Appeal, 1851.
5 Cox C.C. 255.

[An indictment charged Mary Hogan with unlawfully abandoning her bastard child of tender age without having provided means for its support and with the unlawful intent of burdening the parish with its care.]

POLLOCK, C.B. We are all of opinion that this indictment cannot be sustained. No doubt, to neglect a child so as to injure its health is an offence in the person whose duty it is to take care of it; but here there is no allegation of any injury to the child, nor that the mother had the means of supporting it. As to the supposed injury to the parish, we are not disposed to go beyond the authorities, and there is no authority for saying that any person is indictable who occasions loss to a parish by throwing upon it the maintenance of a child as casual poor. It is quite consistent with every allegation in this indict-

1. "The question thus posed to the jury was whether defendant's omission to provide food for his child was 'aggravated, culpable, gross, or reckless' neglect 'incompatible with a proper regard for human life' (involuntary manslaughter) or involved such a high degree of probability that it would result in death that it constituted 'a wanton disregard for human life' making it second degree murder." People v. Burden, 72 Cal.App. 3d 603, 140 Cal.Rptr. 282, 289 (1977).

ment, that the mother, being unable to maintain the child left it for a moment, so that it might fall into the hands of those who could, and were bound to, take care of it.

PARKE, B. I am entirely of the same opinion. Irrespectively of the intention to burthen the parish, it is quite clear that the mere act of deserting a child unable to take care of itself is not an indictable offence, unless it be followed by some injury to the health of the child. Then, as to the intention to burthen the parish, the indictment is defective, because there is no averment that the mother had any means of supplying it with nourishment; and if she was unable to carry it to its place of settlement, as might well be, it would be quite consistent with her duty to leave it to be maintained by the parish as casual poor; and any allegation in the indictment is consistent with such a state of facts.

PATTESON, J. Mr. Phinn puts the case upon the abandonment of the child; but what can that signify to the parish? If the mother had not the means of supporting it, the parish must have maintained it as casual poor for the time, whether it was abandoned or not.[1]

WIGHTMAN, J., and MARTIN, B., concurred. . . .

Conviction quashed.

REGINA v. DOWNES

Court of Criminal Appeal, 1875.
13 Cox C.C. 111.

Case reserved for the opinion of this Court by BLACKBURN, J.

1. The prisoner was indicted at the Center Criminal Court for the manslaughter of Charles Downes.

2. It appeared on the trial before me by the evidence that Charles Downes was an infant who, at the time of his death, was a little more than two years old. The child had been ill, and wasting away for eight or nine months, before its death. The prisoner, who resided at Woolwich, was the father of the deceased, and had during the whole of this time the custody of the child.

3. The prisoner was one of a sect who call themselves "The Peculiar People."

4. During the whole period of the child's illness he did not procure any skilled advice as to the treatment of the child, but left it to the charge of women who belonged to his sect, and called in at intervals George Hurry, an engine driver, who prayed over the child, and anointed it with oil.

5. The reason of this course of conduct was explained by George Hurry, who was called as a witness.

1. A mother, unable to support her two-year-old son, left it on Bourbon Street where she knew it would soon be in the hands of the authorities. This did not constitute cruelty to a juvenile. State v. Barr, 354 So.2d 1344 (La.1978).

6. He stated that the Peculiar People never call in medical advice or give medicines in case of sickness. They had religious objections to doing so. They called in the elders of the church who prayed over the sick person, anointing him with oil in the name of the Lord. This he said they did in literal compliance with the directions in the 14th and 15th verses of the fifth chapter of the Epistle of St. James, and in hope that the cure would follow.

7. This course was pursued with regard to the deceased infant during its illness. The prisoner consulted the witness Hurry as to what was the matter with the child, and as to what should be given to it. They thought it was suffering from teething; and he advised the parents to give it port wine, eggs, arrowroot, and other articles of diet which he thought suitable for a child suffering from such a complaint, all of which were supplied accordingly. There was no evidence that this treatment was mischievous, and though this was probably not logically consistent with the doctrines of his sect as described by him, I saw no reason to doubt that it was all done in perfect sincerity.

8. He was asked by the counsel for the prosecution whether if one of their sect met with an accident, such as a broken bone, their principles would prevent their calling in a surgeon to set it, and he answered that he thought they probably would call in a surgeon in such a case, but it had never yet arisen. He was asked whether they trusted to nature in cases of childbirth. He said they did not call in midwives, which would be against their principles, but that several sisters of their persuasion were as skilful as any midwives, and that they assisted the woman in labour.

9. He was further asked whether he had not himself on the trial of Hurry before Mr. Justice Byles promised that in future medical advice should be called in when necessary. He explained that in that case the disease was infectious, and that he understood the judge to say that the law forbade them to endanger the lives of others; and as it was one of their principles to obey the law, he had given a pledge that they would call in medical advice where the disease was infectious, which pledge they had kept. . . .

COLERIDGE, C.J. I think that this conviction should be affirmed. For my own part, but for the statute 31 & 32 Vict. c. 122, s. 37, I should have much doubt about this case, and should have desired it to be further argued and considered. Perhaps it is enough to say that the opinions of Willes, J., and Pigott, B., are deserving of grave consideration. The statute 31 & 32 Vict. c. 122, s. 37, however, is a strong argument in favour of the conviction. By that enactment it is made an offence punishable summarily if any parent wilfully neglects to provide (*inter alia*) medical aid for his child being in his custody under the age of fourteen years, whereby the health of such child shall have been or shall be likely to be seriously injured. That enactment I understand to mean that if any parent intentionally, *i.e.*, with the knowledge that medical aid is to be obtained, and with a deliberate intention abstains from providing it, he is guilty of an offence. Under that enactment upon these facts the prisoner would clearly have been guilty of the offence created by it. If the death of a person results from the culpable omission of a breach of duty created by the law, the death so caused is the subject of manslaughter. In this case there was a duty imposed by the statute on the prisoner to provide medical aid for his infant child, and there was the deliberate intention not to obey the law—whether proceeding from a good or bad motive is not material. The necessary ingredient to constitute the crime of manslaughter existed, therefore, in this case, and for that reason this conviction ought to be affirmed.

BRAMWELL, B. I am of the same opinion. The 31 & 32 Vict. c. 122, s. 37, has imposed a positive and absolute duty on parents, whatever their conscientious or superstitious opinions may be, to provide medical aid for their infant children in their custody. The facts show that the prisoner thought it was irreligious to call in medical aid, but that is no excuse for not obeying the law.

MELLOR, J. I am of the same opinion. The 31 & 32 Vict. c. 122, s. 37, does not seem to have been called to the attention of Pigott, B., in Reg. v. Hines, or by brother Blackburn upon the trial of the present case. Otherwise it may be that Pigott, B., would have summed up differently to the jury.

GROVE, J., and POLLOCK, B., concurred.

Conviction affirmed.[1]

JONES v. UNITED STATES

United States Court of Appeals, District of Columbia Circuit, 1962.
113 U.S.App.D.C. 352, 308 F.2d 307.

[Shirley Green was the mother of the two children mentioned. Because she was not married and was living with her parents at the time, she arranged to have appellant take Robert from the hospital to appellant's home and agreed to pay appellant $72 a month for his care. There was a dispute in the evidence as to whether these payments were continued beyond five months. When Anthony was born, and was ready to leave the hospital, he also was taken to appellant's home. There seems to have been no specific monetary agreement

1. Cf. Regina v. Wagstaffe, 10 Cox C.C. 530 (1868); People v. Pierson, 176 N.Y. 201, 68 N.E.2d 243 (1903).

A woman, entrusted with her grandchild, who became so intoxicated that she allowed it to be suffocated although its screams could be heard throughout the neighborhood, is guilty of manslaughter. Cornell v. State, 159 Fla. 687, 32 So.2d 610 (1947). A guard at a railroad crossing, who did not see an approaching train because he was looking the other way and hence did not operate the safety devices, with the result that a motorist was killed, is guilty of manslaughter. State v. Benton, 38 Del. 1, 187 A. 609 (1936). Compare Regina v. Smith, 11 Cox C.C. 210 (1869) with Rex v. Pittwood, 19 Times Law Rep. 37 (1902) and State v. Harrison, 107 N.J.L. 213, 152 A. 867 (1930).

covering his support, but he remained at appellant's home. Shirley also lived there for at least three weeks, there was a dispute in the evidence as to where she was living later.]

WRIGHT, CIRCUIT JUDGE. Appellant, together with one Shirley Green, was tried on a three-count indictment charging them jointly with (1) abusing and maltreating Robert Lee Green, (2) abusing and maltreating Anthony Lee Green, and (3) involuntary manslaughter through failure to perform their legal duty of care for Anthony Lee Green, which failure resulted in his death. At the close of evidence, after trial to a jury, the first two counts were dismissed as to both defendants. On the third count, appellant was convicted of involuntary manslaughter. Shirley Green was found not guilty. . . .

Appellant also takes exception to the failure of the trial court to charge that the jury must find beyond a reasonable doubt, as an element of the crime, that appellant was under a legal duty to supply food and necessities to Anthony Lee. Appellant's attorney did not object to the failure to give this instruction, but urges here the application of Rule 52(b).

The problem of establishing the duty to take action which would preserve the life of another has not often arisen in the case law of this country. The most commonly cited statement of the rule is found in People v. Beardsley, 150 Mich. 206, 113 N.W. 1128, 1129, 13 L.R.A.,N.S., 1020:

"The law recognizes that under some circumstances the omission of a duty owed by one individual to another, where such omission results in the death of the one to whom the duty is owing, will make the other chargeable with manslaughter. . . . This rule of law is always based upon the proposition that the duty neglected must be a legal duty, and not a mere moral obligation. It must be a duty imposed by law or by contract, and the omission to perform the duty must be the immediate and direct cause of death. . . ."

There are at least four situations in which the failure to act may constitute breach of a legal duty. One can be held criminally liable: first, where a statute imposes a duty to care for another; second, where one stands in a certain status relationship to another; third, where one has assumed a contractual duty to care for another; and fourth, where one has voluntarily assumed the care of another and so secluded the helpless person as to prevent others from rendering aid.

It is the contention of the Government that either the third or the fourth ground is applicable here. However, it is obvious that in any of the four situations, there are critical issues of fact which must be passed on by the jury—specifically in this case, whether appellant had entered into a contract with the mother for the care of Anthony Lee or, alternatively, whether she assumed the care of the child and secluded him from the care of his mother, his natural protector. On both of these issues, the evidence is in direct conflict, appellant insisting that the mother was actually living with appellant and Anthony

Lee, and hence should have been taking care of the child herself, while Shirley Green testified she was living with her parents and was paying appellant to care for both children.

In spite of this conflict, the instructions given in the case failed even to suggest the necessity for finding a legal duty of care. The only reference to duty in the instructions was the reading of the indictment which charged, inter alia, that the defendants "failed to perform their legal duty." A finding of legal duty is the critical element of the crime charged and failure to instruct the jury concerning it was plain error. . . .

Reversed and remanded.[a]

THE QUEEN v. WHITE

Court for Crown Cases Reserved, 1871.
L.R. 1 C.C. 311.

Case stated by the Chairman of the Hants Quarter Sessions.

Indictment under 24 & 25 Vict. c. 100, s. 27 [1] for unlawfully and wilfully abandoning and exposing a child under the age of two years, whereby the life of the child was endangered.

At the trial at Winchester, it appeared from the evidence that Emily White (the wife of William White), who was not included in the indictment, was the mother of the child, which was about nine months old at the time mentioned in the indictment. On the 19th of October, 1870, she had an interview with her husband, from whom she had been living apart since the 11th of August of the same year, and asked him if he intended to give her money or victuals; he passed by her without answering, and went into his house; this was about 7 P.M. His mother, the prisoner Maria White, shut the wicket of the garden, and forbade his wife from coming in; the wife then went to the door of the house, laid the child down close to the door, and called out, "Bill, here's your child, I can't keep it—I am gone." She left, and was seen no more that night. Shortly after William White came out of the house, stepped over the child, and went away. About 8:30

a. A conviction of murder ws affirmed in a case in which the jury could have found that an unmarried mother placed her infant child in the attic and left it there unattended until it died. Commonwealth v. Hall, 322 Mass. 523, 78 N.E.2d 644 (1948).

If lives were lost by drowning, when a ship was lost at sea, because the life preservers were unsafe and unsuitable, and the crew untrained and undisciplined, the master is guilty of manslaughter. United States v. Van Schaick, 134 F. 592 (2d Cir.1904).

"It would be an unwarranted extension of the spousal duty of care to impose criminal liability for failure to summon medical aid for a competent adult spouse who has made a rational decision to eschew medical assistance." People v. Robbins, 83 A.D.2d 271, 443 N.Y.S.2d 1016, 1018 (1981).

1. 24 & 25 Vict. c. 100, s. 27, enacts that,

"Whosoever shall unlawfully abandon or expose any child, being under the age of two years, whereby the life of such child shall be endangered, . . . shall be guilty of a misdemeanour." . . .

P.M. two witnesses found the child lying in the road outside the wicket of the garden, which was a few yards from the house-door; it was dressed in short clothes, with nothing on its head; they remained at the spot till about 10 P.M., when William White came home. They told him that his child was lying in the road; his answer was, "It must bide there for what he knew, and then the mother ought to be taken up for the murder of it." Another witness, Maria Thorn (the mother of his wife), deposed also to the fact that about the same time, in answer to her observation that he ought to take the child in, he said, "He should not touch it—those that put it there must come and take it." She then went into the house. About 11 P.M., one of the two witnesses went for a police constable, and returned with him to the place about 1 A.M., when the child was found lying on its face in the road, with its clothes blown over its waist, and cold and stiff. The constable took charge of it, and by his care it was restored to animation. At 4:30 A.M. the constable went to the house, and asked William White if he knew where his child was; he said, "No." On being asked if he knew it was in the road, he answered, "Yes." It appeared that, during the time which elapsed between William White leaving his house, about 7 P.M., and his return, about 10 P.M., he had been to the police constable stationed at Beaulieu, and told him that there had been a disturbance between him and his wife, and wished him to come up and settle it, but he did not say anything about the child.

The prisoner's counsel objected that upon these facts there was no evidence of abandonment or exposure, under the Act, by William White.

He also objected that there was no evidence against John White and Maria White.

The Court were of opinion that there was no evidence against the two last-named prisoners, but overruled the objection as to William White, as to whom the case was left to the jury, who found him guilty.

The question for the Court was, whether the prisoner, William White, was properly convicted upon the facts as above stated.

April 29. No counsel appeared.

Cur. adv. vult.

May 6. BOVILL, C.J. We have considered this case, and we are of opinion that the conviction was right, and ought to be affirmed. The prisoner was indicted, under 24 & 25 Vict. c. 100, s. 27, for unlawfully abandoning and exposing a child, under the age of two years, whereby its life was endangered. On the facts stated in the case the objection was taken that there was no evidence of abandonment or exposure. Now, the prisoner was the father of the child, and as such was entitled to the custody and control of it, and was not only morally but legally bound to provide for it. Then it appears that when the child was lying at the door he saw it, stepped over it, and left it there. Afterwards, when the child was in the road, he knew it was there. I am clearly of opinion that there was evidence here upon which the jury might and ought to convict the prisoner. Instead of protecting and providing for the child, as it was his duty to do, he allowed it to remain lying, first at his door, and afterwards in the road, insufficiently clothed, and at a time of year when the result was likely to be the child's death. I think, therefore, he was guilty both of abandonment and exposure.[a]

MARTIN, B. I am of the same opinion, though I have entertained some doubt upon the question. The statute makes it an offence unlawfully to abandon or expose a child, and, construing these words according to their natural meaning, I thought at first that they could only apply to persons who had had the actual custody and possession of the child. But as the prisoner here was the father of the child, entitled to its custody and legally bound to its protection, I do not differ from the rest of the Court.

BRAMWELL, B. I am of the same opinion. If the person who had had the actual custody of the child, and who left it at its father's door, had been a stranger with whom it had been left at nurse, there could, I think, have been no doubt about the case; and I do not think the fact that it was the mother makes any difference.

BLACKBURN, J. I am of the same opinion. The question turns upon the meaning of the words "abandon or expose" in the statute. The Court before whom the prisoner was tried were right in directing the acquittal of the two other persons accused, because there was no legal duty upon them to protect the child, but only a duty of imperfect obligation. But the father's case is different; for upon him there is a strict legal duty to protect the child. And when the child is left in a position of danger of which he knows, and from which he has full power to remove it, and he neglects his duty of protection, and lets the child remain in danger, I think this is an exposure and abandonment by him. If the child had died, the facts were such that a jury might have convicted him of murder, though they might have taken a more merciful view, and found him guilty only of manslaughter; and as the child, though its life was endangered, did not die, the case is within the section.

CHANNELL, B. My Brother Byles, who was a member of the Court when the case was first before the Court, concurs in the judgment; and, having had an opportunity of considering the case this morning, I am of the same opinion.

Conviction affirmed.

a. [Added by the Compiler.] Although the beating of the child was inflicted by another, the mother who did not seek aid could be convicted of abuse to such minor child. State v. Fabritz, 276 Md. 416, 348 A.2d 275 (1975).

REX v. RUSSELL

Supreme Court of Victoria, 1932.
[1933] Vict.L.R. 59.

(Russell was charged with murder in three counts (1) for the murder of his wife, (2) for the murder of his son Harold, and (3) for the murder of his son Eric. Harold was three and a half years old and Eric one and one-half. There was evidence which seems to have led the jury to believe that the wife drowned herself and the children while defendant stood by without either encouraging her or trying to stop her. And in reply to a question the judge charged the jury that under such facts the defendant would be guilty of manslaughter. Defendant was convicted of manslaughter on all three counts and applies for leave to appeal.)

MANN, J. It was with some doubt as to the principles of law applicable to the case that I answered the question propounded by the jury, and I therefore postponed judgment and intimated my intention of reserving a case for the Full Court. This became unnecessary when the prisoner decided to appeal against the verdict. The appeal attacks the verdict on all three counts, while a case reserved would have dealt with the second and third counts only.

The question of the jury was: "Assuming that the woman took the children into the water without the assistance of putting them in the water by the man, but that he stood by, conniving to the act, what is the position from the standpoint of the law?" [1] This question, heard with knowledge of the course of the trial, including the addresses of counsel and my own charge to the jury, was clearly directed, as I thought and still think, to the second and third counts only, which charged the accused with murder of his two children.

Upon the further consideration given to the matter upon this appeal, I am of opinion that the proper answer for me to have given to the question was that in the case supposed the accused would be guilty of murder.

But apart altogether from the question of murder or manslaughter, it is important that a decision as to the criminal liability of the accused in given circumstances should be referred to the right legal principles. I rested my answer to the jury in effect upon the principles of such cases as R. v. Instan,[e] R. v. Gibbins and Proctor [f] and R. v. Bubb.[g] These cases may be regarded as defining the legal sanctions which the law attaches to the moral duty of a parent to protect his children of tender years from physical harm. If applicable to the

1. N.B. When the jury asked the question quoted above the judge asked: "Are you supposing a case where he is offering no encouragement or persuasion to her to do it, but simply standing by and watching the wife drown the children? Is that the Case?" The Foreman: "That is the position."

e. [1893] 1 Q.B. 450.

f. [1918] 13 Cr.App.R. 134.

g. [1850] 4 Cox C.C. 455.

present case, those authorities would point to the accused's being guilty of what I may call an independent crime of murder. The outstanding difference between the facts of such cases as I have cited and the facts of the present case is the interposition in the latter of a criminal act of a third person which is the immediate cause of death; and the difficulty in such a case is in saying, in the absence of express authority, that the inaction of the accused has caused the death of the children, within the meaning of the criminal law.

I think the more correct view in the present case is that the prisoner on the facts supposed, while perhaps guilty of an independent crime, was certainly guilty as participator in the murder committed by his wife. The moral duty of the accused to save his children, the control which by law he has over his wife, and his moral duty to exercise that control, do not in this view cease to be elements in his crime. On the contrary, it is these elements which as a matter of law give to the acquiescence of the father in the acts of the mother committed in his presence the quality of participation. The control which the law recognizes as exercisable by a husband over his wife is well illustrated in the doctrine that the mere presence of the husband at the commission by his wife of a felony, other than murder, is generally enough to exempt the wife altogether from criminal liability. The physical presence and the "connivance" of a parent in the position of the accused has in law, in my opinion, a criminal significance not attaching to the presence and connivance of the mere "passerby" referred to in some of the cases.

It follows that the case put by me to the jury by way of contrast, though based upon a sound theoretical distinction, was not applicable to the special facts. The facts necessary to constitute aiding and abetting were too narrowly conceived, since no legal distinction can be made between tacit and oral concurrence, and a correct direction would be that not only was the accused morally bound to take active steps to save his children from destruction, but by his deliberate abstention from so doing, and by giving the encouragement and authority of his presence and approval to his wife's act, he became an aider and abetter and liable as a principal offender in the second degree. . . .

With regard to the first count, my brother Cussen's view is that the verdict shows a belief in the mind of the jury that in answering the question submitted to me I was also directing them as to the law applicable to the first count; and he thinks that with regard to this count also the prisoner was criminally liable as aiding and abetting in the suicide of his wife. I do not take this view of the matter. I can find no reason, having regard to the various hypotheses put forward at the trial, for saying with certainty that the jury thought the wife committed suicide at all. I think that, the verdict upon the first count being one which was legally open to the jury upon the evidence and no misdirection being established with regard to it, it is unnecessary and unwise to enter upon what seems to me a speculative enquiry as to the process, or perhaps the different processes, of thought by which the jury arrived at that verdict.

I think the appeal fails as to all three counts. . . .

The opinions of CUSSEN, A.C.J., and MCARTHUR, J., are omitted. (MCARTHUR, J., thought the conviction on the first count should be quashed.)

Application refused.[2]

MORELAND v. STATE

Supreme Court of Georgia, 1927.
164 Ga. 467, 139 S.E. 77.

(The owner of a car and his chauffeur were jointly indicted for murder, based upon a fatal accident. The owner alone was tried (the chauffeur not having been apprehended) and was convicted of involuntary manslaughter in the commission of an unlawful act.)

HILL, J. . . . The Penal Code of 1910, § 67, provides that "Involuntary manslaughter shall consist in the killing of a human being without any intention to do so, but in the commission of an unlawful act, or a lawful act, which probably might produce such a consequence, in an unlawful manner: provided, that where such involuntary killing shall happen in the commission of an unlawful act which, in its consequences, naturally tends to destroy the life of a human being, or is committed in the prosecution of a riotous intent, or of a crime punishable by death or confinement in the penitentiary, the offense shall be deemed and adjudged to be murder." . . . Under the above definition of what constitutes involuntary manslaughter in the commission of an unlawful act, there can be no question that that offense was committed by whomever was responsible for the operation of the automobile in question at the time of the unfortunate homicide. Whoever was responsible, it can not be questioned under the facts as stated by the Court of Appeals that the automobile of Moreland was being operated in violation of the law of this State. It was being run at a rate of fifty miles per hour, when the law says that it could be run upon the public highway at a rate not exceeding thirty miles per hour. It was in violation of the law which prevents one vehicle passing another on the wrong side of the road. It was violating the law in running at a rate of speed in violation of a penal statute which provides that on a sharp curve an automobile shall not exceed the speed of ten miles per hour. And the sole question to be decided is, is Moreland, the owner of the automobile, liable for the acts of his chauffeur done in his presence. He was present, and

2. See Regina v. Popen, 60 CCC 2d 232 (Ont.Ct.App.1981).

A mother who was present when her child was assaulted and failed to take reasonable steps to prevent the assault, may be found guilty of aiding and abetting the assault. State v. Walden, 306 N.C. 466, 293 S.E.2d 780 (1982).

there is nothing to indicate that he remonstrated with the chauffeur, or attempted to prevent him from running at the high rate of speed of fifty miles per hour, around a curve, while it was raining. Under these circumstances we are of the opinion that the owner of the car was in control thereof, and that he should have seen to it that his chauffeur did not operate the car in such a manner contrary to law as might produce such a consequence in an unlawful manner as that which happened on this fateful occasion. It must be held, therefore, that the owner of the car must have known, and did know, that it was being operated contrary to law, and that he consented and agreed to the running of the car at such a high rate of speed; and that being true, he is responsible for what happened in consequence of such violation of the law. It would be the owner's duty, when he saw that the law was being violated and that his machine was being operated in such a way as to be dangerous to the life and property of others on the highway, to curb and restrain one in his employment and under his control, and prevent him from violating the law with his own property. The owner of the automobile was bound to know that it was very dangerous for his chauffeur to run and operate the car at fifty miles per hour during a rainstorm along a public highway and at a dangerous curve. He was bound to know that a car operated at such a place and in such a manner was liable to come in collision and injure occupants of other automobiles upon the highway; and that being so, he was equally guilty with his employee in causing the homicide in question, although he may have had no intention of injuring or killing the woman in question. It is not insisted that the operator of the car, or the owner, wilfully intended to kill the party named in the indictment. As already stated, it is a question of intentional neglect not to curb the operator of the car when he was violating the highway law of the State. Nor is it a question here that the owner and operator of the car entered into a conspiracy to kill the party so killed, or any one else. The question of conspiracy is not involved.

So we reach the conclusion that the question propounded by the Court of Appeals must be answered in the affirmative.

All the Justices concur.

BECK, P.J., and GILBERT, J., concurred specially.

COMMONWEALTH v. PUTCH

County Court, Allegheny County, Pennsylvania, 1932.
18 Pa.D. & C. 680.

MUSMANNO, J., October 22, 1932. When the owner of an automobile knows that his car, in which he is riding, has struck a dog, even though he is not driving, and he makes no effort to have the car stopped to give aid to the suffering beast, he is guilty of the offense charged under the Act of March 29, 1869, P.L. 22, which provides:

"Any person who shall . . . wantonly or cruelly ill-treat . . . or otherwise abuse any animal . . . and every person who shall encourage, aid or assist therein, . . . " shall be subject to fine or imprisonment.

Such a person certainly wantonly and cruelly abuses an animal in a common-sense and humane interpretation of the act. Ill-treatment and abuse does not need to be active; it may be passive. It does not need to be the commission of an act; it may be the omission to do what the circumstances require.

In the case at bar the evidence shows that on May 2, 1932, in the early evening, the defendant, Samuel F. Putch, in his own car driven by an employe, was proceeding eastward along California Avenue between Whitmer Street and Benton Avenue, traveling on the right-hand side of the street between car track and curb, when a large collie dog belonging to J.W. Connolly, of No. 3911 California Avenue, came upon the street in full view of the driver of the automobile and some distance ahead. The wheel or some other part of the right front of the car struck the dog on its left flank, knocking it to the ground, and in its effort to escape or being thrown about by reason of the force of the collision, it fell upon the street and the car proceeding ran over its tail. Two witnesses, one upon a lawn abutting the scene of the accident and just across the sidewalk from the car and the other upon an adjoining lawn, hearing the cries, endeavored with call and gesture to halt the car of the defendant, but without avail. It passed on, leaving the dog lying at the curb, nor did the defendant or his driver offer any assistance or call to evidence any interest in their victim. The dog was carried into the house by the owner, where it lay about for several days, when it was taken to a veterinary, who pronounced its injuries such that it should be put out of its misery, and, under instructions from the owner, he ended its life humanely.

The evidence shows that the injured animal cried out so loudly as to be heard within one of the neighboring houses; that after striking the dog the driver slowed up his car, hesitated, turned to one side and went on; and that at least two neighbors, one opposite the car and but a few feet distant across the sidewalk, called and gestured in an effort to halt the car, and all this on the side of the car on which defendant sat in the front seat.

We do not know as a positive fact whether the defendant heard and saw what transpired at the time the poor beast was injured, but common experience would establish that he could not avoid knowing what had taken place.

We cannot find the defendant guilty, however, because the information is defective. It charges that on May 2, 1932, the defendant, "after having struck a female collie dog with a certain automobile on a public highway in the said City of Pittsburgh, to wit, California avenue near residence number 3911, did then and there wilfully and unlawfully fail and neglect to stop and render assistance, said dog being the property of a certain W.J. Connolly and the said defendant was operating the said machine on a public highway in the said city in a reckless and careless manner and at an excessive rate of speed."

The evidence clearly shows that it was not the defendant who was driving the car, and the Commonwealth admits this. With the record in the shape that it is, the summary conviction rendered by the alderman must be reversed and the defendant discharged.

VAN BUSKIRK v. STATE

Court of Criminal Appeals of Oklahoma, 1980.
611 P.2d 271.

CORNISH, PRESIDING JUDGE. On July 9, 1977, during an argument between the appellant and her boyfriend, Robert Rose, the pair stopped in a low place between two hills on the road from Allen to Ada, Oklahoma. Rose was ordered to get out of the car, and he was thereafter struck by the appellant's vehicle. The appellant then drove away, leaving Rose in the roadway. Subsequently, Rose was struck by another car moving at a high speed. The appellant was charged with Murder in the Second Degree in Pontotoc County District Court. She was convicted of Manslaughter, Second Degree, and sentenced to two (2) years' imprisonment.

I

The first question for determination is whether the trial court erred in instructing the jury on Manslaughter in the Second Degree. The appellant's position is that the manslaughter in the second degree statute, 21 O.S.1971, § 716, was impliedly repealed when the negligent homicide statute, 47 O.S.1971, § 11–903, was passed. The appellant's assertion is correct to the extent that motor vehicles are involved. Atchley v. State, Okl.Cr., 473 P.2d 286 (1970). However, the negligent homicide statute applies only when death is caused "by the driving of any vehicle in reckless disregard of the safety of others." Section 11–903(a). A review of the facts indicates that § 11–903(a) is not applicable here.

According to the appellant's testimony, she was driving when Rose slapped her, knocking her eyeglasses off her face. She stopped the car, ordered Rose to get out and searched for her glasses. Rose left the passenger's side of the car and started to walk in front of the vehicle around to the driver's side. The appellant said that as she leaned over to look for her eyeglasses she accidentally pressed the gas pedal. The result was that the car lurched forward, lifting Rose onto the hood. Rose pounded on the windshield, cursing, and the appellant then hit the brake pedal, throwing Rose to the ground. The appellant testified that Rose was starting to get up as she put the vehicle in reverse, swerved around him and drove away.

A passing motorist saw Rose lying in the roadway. He stopped his car and attempted to signal to a rapidly approaching car. The motorist said that Rose was "sort of moaning." The motorist's efforts to stop the approaching car were to no avail. The automobile struck Rose and dragged him a short distance down the highway. Having ascertained that Rose was dead, he pulled the body from the road.

Under these facts, we do not believe that Rose was the victim of negligent homicide. The crime was committed, not when the appellant struck Rose, but when she abandoned him in a position of peril. At that time she could reasonably have anticipated that another vehicle might strike Rose. The foreseeability of such a consequence—where the victim lay helpless in a lane of traffic, in a low place between two hills—is apparent. It places the appellant squarely within the scope of 21 O.S.1971, § 716:

> "Every killing of one human being by the act, procurement *or culpable negligence* of another, which, under the provisions of this chapter, is not murder, nor manslaughter in the first degree, nor excusable nor justifiable homicide, is manslaughter in the second degree." (Emphasis added)

Thus, the trial court correctly instructed the jury on Manslaughter in the Second Degree.

II

In the fourth, fifth, and sixth assignments of error the appellant complains that the trial court failed to give instructions on proximate cause, justifiable homicide and/or self-defense, and circumstantial evidence. The record indicates that at the time of the trial the appellant neither objected to the instructions given by the trial court nor requested that any particular instruction be given. In such a situation, this Court will generally limit itself to an examination of the instructions which were given, to see whether they fairly covered the issues raised during the trial. We have carefully examined the trial court's instructions and find that they adequately cover the subject matter of inquiry.

III

The next alleged error also relates to the jury instructions. The fourth instruction defines murder in the second degree, but the ninth instruction informs the jury that the trial judge made a judicial determination that the facts of the case would not support a conviction for murder in the second degree, and that they should not consider that charge. The appellant argues that the combination of instructions must have prejudiced the jury against her. Although we are uncertain why the trial court chose to proceed in this manner, we fail to see how the appellant suffered any prejudice thereby. The appellant raises no more than speculation as to the effect of the instructions. Where, as here, the appellant has been deprived of no fundamental right, this Court will not search the books for authorities to support the mere assertion that the trial court has erred.

IV

The remaining allegations of error relate to the sufficiency of the evidence. The appellant argues that her demurrer to the evidence should have been sustained, that the trial court erred in failing to direct a verdict in her favor, and that the verdict is contrary to the evidence. When an appellant challenges the sufficiency of the evidence presented at the trial, the function of this Court is to determine whether the State presented a prima facie case. If so, then all questions of fact were properly submitted to the jury. In the case before us, the State did present a prima facie case, and these assignments of error are without merit. The judgment and sentence is AFFIRMED.

BRETT and BUSSEY, JJ., concur.

MODEL PENAL CODE

Section 2.01 (Requirement of Voluntary Act;) Omission as Basis of Liability; (Possession as an Act.)

. . .

(3) Liability for the commission of an offense may not be based on an omission unaccompanied by action unless:

(a) the omission is expressly made sufficient by the law defining the offense; or

(b) a duty to perform the omitted act is otherwise imposed by law.[1]

. . .

1. Copyright: 1962 by the American Law Institute. Reprinted with the permission of the American Law Institute.

SECTION 5. CONSPIRACY [1]

A conspiracy is a combination for an unlawful purpose but the purpose may be unlawful even if it would not be punishable if perpetrated by one alone. The classic illustration of a punishable conspiracy to do a non-criminal act is the combination to defraud another without the use of a false token. Such a fraud is punishable today, even if perpetrated by one alone, but before the English statute on false pretenses it was punishable for two or more to combine to perpetrate such a fraud. And more recently a combination of three persons whereby they lent small sums of money to poor people and charged them exorbitant rates of interest was held to be a punishable conspiracy although usury was not a crime.[a]

The rule of the common law that the purpose of an agreement may be sufficiently "unlawful" to make the combination a conspiracy, even if what is agreed upon is not in itself punishable as a crime, has been abandoned by many of the new codes. Under them a conspiracy is a combination for the commission of a crime. For the most part, harms deemed sufficiently "unlawful" to make the combination therefor a conspiracy, have since been made punishable as crimes, if they were not so at common law, and the original rule is no longer necessary.

1. Conspiracy is a separate offense, distinct from the substantive crime which was the object of the conspiracy, and there may be a valid conviction of both the substantive offense and the conspiracy to commit it. Wright v. United States, 519 F.2d 13 (7th Cir.1975).

Defining conspiracy as "co-operating" to aid in doing an unlawful act, was sufficient. Goddard v. People, 172 Colo. 498, 474 P.2d 210 (1970).

a. Commonwealth v. Donoghue, 250 Ky. 343, 63 S.W.2d 3 (1933).

The term "unlawful" in relation to conspiracy, includes situations where the purpose of a group plan or the proposed means of accomplishing that plan, "even if not criminal, involve 'an evil intent to oppress and injure the public' (or, perhaps, third persons) by activity, which is 'illegal, void and against public policy' ". Commonwealth v. Bessette, 351 Mass. 148, 154, 217 N.E.2d 893 (1966).

A conspiracy may be between two or more officers or employees of a corporation, or two or more corporations acting through an officer or employee representing each corporation, or between a person and a corporation acting through a separate person. See United States v. Santa Rita Store Co., 16 N.M. 3, 113 P. 620 (1911). Welling, Intra-Corporate Plurality in Criminal Conspiracy Law, 33 Hast.L.J. 1155, 1174–1199 (1982).

The common-law theory, that husband and wife are one, made it impossible for them to be guilty of conspiracy if no third person was involved. Dawson v. United States, 10 F.2d 106 (9th Cir.1926); People v. Miller, 82 Cal. 107, 22 P. 934 (1889). But the tendency is to abandon this theory and hold that they can be guilty of conspiracy even without the cooperation of anyone else. For example, Dawson and Miller have both been overruled. United States v. Dege, 364 U.S. 51, 80 S.Ct. 1589, 4 L.Ed.2d 1563 (1960); People v. Pierce, 61 Cal.2d 879, 40 Cal. Rptr. 845, 395 P.2d 893 (1964).

UNITED STATES v. FIGUEREDO

United States District Court, M.D. Florida, Tampa Division, 1972.
350 F.Supp. 1031, rev'd 490 F.2d 799.

MEMORANDUM OPINION

KRENTZMAN, DISTRICT JUDGE.

Eight named defendants are charged in an indictment with conducting an illegal gambling operation in violation of 18 U.S.C. § 1955, and with conspiracy to violate § 1955. Several motions to dismiss the indictment have been filed, and a hearing was held on said motions September 6, 1972. Based upon a consideration of these motions and the grounds urged in support thereof, the following memorandum opinion and order is entered.

Section 1955 was enacted as a part of the Organized Crime Control Act of 1970. This statute prohibits the operation of any "illegal gambling business." An illegal gambling business is statutorily defined as one which: 1) is a violation of state law; 2) involves five or more persons; and 3) has been in substantially continuous operation for over thirty days or has a gross revenue of $2,000 in any single day. Thus, an element of proof in the government's case is that "five or more persons" be shown to have been involved in the gambling business. This requirement was inserted in the statute in order to make the crime federally cognizable. Only gambling businesses of a substantial size are proscribed. . . .

II. Wharton's Rule

Defendants contend that they cannot be prosecuted for conspiracy to violate § 1955. The Supreme Court has consistently recognized the rule that the commission of a substantive offense and a conspiracy to commit it are separate and distinct offenses. Defendants urge that an important exception to this doctrine is the rule of law commonly known as Wharton's Rule. This Rule states:

"An agreement by two persons to commit a particular crime cannot be prosecuted as a conspiracy when the crime is of such a nature as to necessarily require the participation of two persons for its commission." Anderson, 1 Wharton's Criminal Law & Procedure, § 89, p. 191 (1957).

The theory behind the Rule is that where certain crimes, such as adultery, require the concerted action of two persons, these persons cannot be charged with a conspiracy to commit the offense. "[T]he conspiracy is merged into the substantive offense, or at least is such an integral part of it that the two cannot be considered separate offenses." 11 A.L.R. 196 (1921). This rule of criminal law has long been recognized in federal courts.

Wharton's Rule has generally been applied to crimes such as abortion, adultery, bribery, incest, and dueling. In each case, the crime cannot be effectuated without the concerted activity of two people. To charge the two persons with both the substantive crime and with a conspiracy to commit the crime would be grossly improper, for the substantive offense cannot logically be committed without a conspiracy. Thus conspiracy is an inherent element of the substantive offense and should not be made an additional crime.

Conspiracies are made punishable because of the increased danger involved in group offense. A conspiracy is a separate crime because it is felt that when two or more persons combine to accomplish a criminal purpose, the added element of combination is sufficiently evil to be punished separately.

Conspiracy is a crime with common law roots and with an unpopular background. See Sayre, Criminal Conspiracy, 35 Harv.L.Rev. 393. Justice Jackson once commented upon the concept of conspiracy as a separate crime:

"[T]he looseness and pliability of the doctrine present inherent dangers which should be in the background of judicial thought wherever it is sought to extend the doctrine to meet the exigencies of a particular case."

Krulewitch v. United States, 336 U.S. 440, 449, 69 S.Ct. 716, 721, 93 L.Ed. 367 (1949) (Jackson, J., concurring).

The Supreme Court has indicated that it will view with disfavor attempts to broaden the scope of conspiracy prosecutions. When seen in this context, Wharton's Rule presents itself as a logical limitation on the use of conspiracy charges by prosecutors.

In the instant case the èlderly and respectible Rule runs up against a modern penal statute directed toward organized crime activities of a sufficiently large size to come within the ambit of federal jurisdiction. Consideration of the problem by federal courts in two circuits have resulted in different holdings.

In United States v. Greenberg, 334 F.Supp. 1092 (N.D.Ohio 1971), the Court applied Wharton's Rule and held that thirteen defendants therein could not be charged with a conspiracy to violate § 1955. That Court stated:

". . . Congress has made the offense federally cognizable only when there are five or more participants. One of the bases of federal intervention is a concert of action between the parties. In other words, the offense is one involving the element of *concursis necessarius.* That is, it is absolutely necessary that there be a plurality of parties and it is necessary that there be concerted action among them. It therefore appears that a charge of conspiring to commit the offense should not be maintainable." Id. at 1095.

The Second Circuit, however, disagreed with the *Greenberg* result. In United States v. Becker, 461 F.2d 230 (2 Cir.1972), that Court held that Wharton's Rule had no application where more than five persons were charged with violating § 1955. Since § 1955 requires only five persons to be involved in the gambling operation, the Court held that charging more than five persons brought the case outside of the application of the Rule. Citing a recent case in that circuit,[2] the Court stated that:

"[A]s long as the conspiratorial concert of action and the substantive offense underlying it are not coterminous and fewer participants are required for the commission of the substantive offense than are named as joining in a conspiracy to commit it, there is no infirmity in the conspiracy indictment." Id. at 234. . . .

. . . Resolution of the problem requires, among other things, a careful analysis of Wharton's Rule and the various exceptions which have been applied to it. Wharton's Rule has a valid place in modern criminal law. Even though the Rule was designed in relation to common law crimes necessarily involving two persons, 1955 is a statute logically connected to such crimes. One man alone cannot violate § 1955; indeed, any number of persons less than five cannot violate the statute. At least five persons must be involved in the gambling business. Thus, each would be guilty if, and only if, at least four others were also involved. Concerted action is of the essence in this crime.

There are four generally recognized exceptions to the application of Wharton's Rule. See Anderson, 1 Wharton's Criminal Law & Procedure § 89, pp. 191–94. The Rule does not apply when the offense could be committed by one of the conspirators alone. This exception has no application with regard to § 1955, as five persons *must* be involved.

It could be argued that under § 1955, only one person could be charged with the crime. This does not, however, affect the application of the Rule. In any of the crimes coming within the Rule, only one of the participants could conceivably be charged. For instance, only one duelor might be charged, but this does not affect the fact that at least one other person necessarily committed the crime with the one charged. In the instant case, if only one defendant were charged in the indictment, at least four others would have to be shown to have necessarily committed the crime, or else the statute was not in fact violated.

The Rule has been rejected when concerted action was not logically necessary, even though as a practical matter the offense could not be committed without cooperation. . . .

The exception which has the most relevance to the instant case is the "third person" exception to the Rule. Under this exception, the

2. United States v. Benter, 457 F.2d 1174, 1178 (2 Cir.1972).

Rule is limited to cases where the essential participants are the only conspirators. When those whose cooperation is necessary for the commission of the substantive crime conspire with another person to commit the offense, all are guilty of conspiracy. For example, when a third person conspires with a man and a woman for the commission of adultery by the latter two, all three are guilty of conspiracy. State v. Clemenson, 123 Iowa 524, 99 N.W. 139 (1904).

The third person rule has no application in the instant case. The argument cannot be made that the three "extra" defendants (there are a total of eight defendants charged) are "third persons." They, too, could be found guilty of the substantive charge, unlike the adultery "matchmaker" in the *Clemenson* case. In that case, the commission of adultery was compounded by the additional element of a combination between the adulterors and the third person. In the instant case, the added element of the alleged agreement between all eight defendants amounts to nothing that was not already present in the alleged commission of the crime. Thus, the exception is not applicable.

The *Becker* case, which held that Wharton's Rule is not applicable to § 1955 charges when more than five defendants are charged, ultimately rested on a mistaken use of the third party exception. In support of its holding, *Becker* cited United States v. Benter, 457 F.2d 1174, 1178 (2 Cir.1972). That case involved a conspiracy to commit bribery as a government employee. The Court held that Wharton's Rule did not apply because "here the agreement involved more participants than were necessary for the commission of the substantive offense." Id. at 1178.

In support of that statement, the *Benter* Court cited United States v. Smolin, 182 F.2d 782, 786 (2 Cir.1950). In the *Smolin* case, three persons were charged in a conspiracy to sell and receive stolen goods. The third person was a "go-between," and thus not a necessary participant in the substantive offense. The Court stated:

"While the crime of receiving and possessing stolen goods necessarily involves the cooperation of the thief and the buyer, it does not necessarily involve the cooperation of the buyer and a go between. . . ." Id.

The line of cases upon which the *Becker* Court relied were thus examples of the third party exception. The language which the prior courts employed was misleading and painted too broad an exception over Wharton's Rule. See also Baker v. United States, 393 F.2d 604, 610 (9 Cir.1968). These statements, taken out of context, imply that the mere number charged in the indictment takes on a talismanic quality which obviates the application of the Rule. It is not, however, the mere number charged, but rather the nature of the "extra" defendants, which determines the result in the individual case. As Justice Holmes once commented: "To rest upon a formula is a slumber that, prolonged, means death." Holmes, Collected Legal Papers, p. 306. . . .

The objection to charging a conspiracy to violate § 1955 is not one of multiplicity. Multiplicity is the charging of one offense in several counts. Multiplicity may be remedied by election of counsel or by instructions given by the Court. Where Wharton's Rule is applicable, however, conspiracy simply cannot be charged; the conspiracy count must be dismissed. Accordingly, an order will be entered dismissing Count I of the indictment against the eight defendants. . . .[a]

GEBARDI v. UNITED STATES

Supreme Court of the United States, 1932.
287 U.S. 112, 77 L.Ed. 206, 53 S.Ct. 35.

MR. JUSTICE STONE delivered the opinion of the Court.

This case is here on certiorari, 286 U.S. 539, 52 S.Ct. 648, 76 L.Ed. 1278, to review a judgment of conviction for conspiracy to violate the Mann Act (36 Stat. 825; 18 U.S.C. § 397 et seq.). Petitioners, a man and a woman, not then husband and wife, were indicted in the District Court for Northern Illinois, for conspiring together, and with others not named, to transport the woman from one state to another for the purpose of engaging in sexual intercourse with the man. At the trial without a jury there was evidence from which the court could have found that the petitioners had engaged in illicit sexual relations in the course of each of the journeys alleged; that the man purchased the railway tickets for both petitioners for at least one journey, and that in each instance the woman, in advance of the purchase of the tickets, consented to go on the journey and did go on it voluntarily for the specified immoral purpose. There was no evidence supporting the allegation that any other person had conspired. The trial court overruled motions for a finding for the defendants,

a. [Added by the Compiler.] The court quotes the Supreme Court to the effect that Wharton's Rule "has current vitality only as a judicial presumption, to be applied in the absence of legislative intent to the contrary. Iannelli v. United States, 420 U.S. 770, 782, 95 S.Ct. 1284, 1292 (1975)." It then says the structure and history of the drug abuse act (21 U.S.C. § 3841(a)(1) et seq.) indicate an intent not to be limited by Wharton's Rule. But it admits that more than the seller and the buyer were involved in this case so that Wharton's Rule itself would not bar a conviction for conspiracy in addition to conviction of the target offense. United States v. Bommarito, 524 F.2d 140 (2d Cir.1975).

"The widely recognized rule of construction known as Wharton's Rule states that when a substantive offense necessarily requires the participation of two persons, and where no more than two persons are alleged to have been involved in the agreement to commit the offense, the charge of conspiracy will not lie . . . . If a third person does participate so as to enlarge the scope of the agreement, however, all three may be charged with conspiracy." State v. Langworthy, 92 Wn.2d 148, 594 P.2d 908, 910 (1979).

Extortion and conspiracy to commit extortion are not effected by Wharton's Rule. "In practice, Wharton's Rule generally operates as a judicial presumption to proscribe a conspiracy charge in the absence of legislative intent to the contrary." People v. Carter, 415 Mich. 558, 330 N.W.2d 314, 321 (1983).

and in arrest of judgment, and gave judgment of conviction, which the Court of Appeals for the Seventh Circuit affirmed 57 F.2d 617, on the authority of United States v. Holte, 236 U.S. 140, 35 S.Ct. 271, 59 L.Ed. 504. . . .

Section 2 of the Mann Act (18 U.S.C. § 398), violation of which is charged by the indictment here as the object of the conspiracy, imposes the penalty upon "Any person who shall knowingly transport or cause to be transported, or aid or assist in obtaining transportation for, or in transporting in interstate or foreign commerce . . . any woman or girl for the purpose of prostitution or debauchery or for any other immoral purpose . . ." Transportation of a woman or girl whether with or without her consent, or causing or aiding it, or furthering it in any of the specified ways, are the acts punished, when done with a purpose which is immoral within the meaning of the law.

The Act does not punish the woman for transporting herself; it contemplates two persons—one to transport and the woman or girl to be transported. For the woman to fall within the ban of the statute she must, at the least, "aid or assist" someone else in transporting or in procuring transportation for herself. But such aid and assistance must, as in the case supposed in United States v. Holte,* supra 236 U.S. 145, 35 S.Ct. 271, 59 L.Ed. 504, be more active than mere agreement on her part to the transportation and its immoral purpose. For the statute is drawn to include those cases in which the woman consents to her own transportation. Yet it does not specifically impose any penalty upon her, although it deals in detail with the person by whom she is transported. In applying this criminal statute we cannot infer that the mere acquiescence of the woman transported was intended to be condemned by the general language punishing those who aid and assist the transporter, any more than it has been inferred that the purchaser of liquor was to be regarded as an abettor of the illegal sale. The penalties of the statute are too clearly directed against the acts of the transporter as distinguished from the consent of the subject of the transportation. So it was intimated in United States v. Holte, supra, and this conclusion is not disputed by the Government here, which contends only that the conspiracy charge will lie though the woman could not commit the substantive offense.

We come thus to the main question in the case, whether, admitting that the woman, by consenting, has not violated the Mann Act, she may be convicted of a conspiracy with the man to violate it. Section 37 of the Criminal Code (18 U.S.C., § 88), punishes a conspiracy by two or more persons "to commit any offense against the United States." The offense which she is charged with conspiring to commit

* *Holte* held that an indictment charging the man and woman with a conspiracy to have her transported across state lines for the purpose of prostitution was not demurrable because she would be guilty of conspiracy if the plan called for her to do much more than merely acquiesce in the transportation.

is that perpetrated by the man, for it is not questioned that in transporting her he contravened § 2 of the Mann Act. Hence we must decide whether her concurrence, which was not criminal before the Mann Act, nor punished by it, may, without more, support a conviction under the conspiracy section, enacted many years before.

As we said in the Holte Case (p. 144 of 236 U.S., 35 S.Ct. 271, 272), an agreement to commit an offense may be criminal, though its purpose is to do what some of the conspirators may be free to do alone. Incapacity of one to commit the substantive offense does not necessarily imply that he may with impunity conspire with others who are able to commit it. For it is the collective planning of criminal conduct at which the statute aims.[1] The plan is itself a wrong which, if any act be done to effect its object, the state has elected to treat as criminal, Clune v. United States, 159 U.S. 590, 595, 16 S.Ct. 125, 40 L.Ed. 269. And one may plan that others shall do what he cannot do himself.

But in this case we are concerned with something more than an agreement between two persons for one of them to commit an offense which the other cannot commit. There is the added element that the offense planned, the criminal object of the conspiracy, involves the agreement of the woman to her transportation by the man, which is the very conspiracy charged.

Congress set out in the Mann Act to deal with cases which frequently, if not normally, involve consent and agreement on the part of the woman to the forbidden transportation. In every case in which she is not intimidated or forced into the transportation, the statute necessarily contemplates her acquiescence. Yet this acquiescence, though an incident of a type of transportation specifically dealt with by the statute, was not made a crime under the Mann Act itself. Of this class of cases we say that the substantive offense contemplated by the statute itself involves the same combination or community of purpose of two persons only which is prosecuted here as conspiracy. If this were the only case covered by the Act, it would be within those decisions which hold, consistently with the theory upon which conspiracies are punished, that where it is impossible under any circumstances to commit the substantive offense without coöperative action, the preliminary agreement between the same parties to commit the offense is not an indictable conspiracy either at common law, or under the federal statute. But criminal transportation under the Mann Act may be effected without the woman's consent, as in cases of intimidation or force (with which we are not now concerned). We assume therefore, for present purposes, as was suggested in the Holte case, supra, 145 of 236 U.S., 35 S.Ct. 271, 272, that the decisions last mentioned do not in all strictness apply. We do not rest

1. "The government's ability to deter and punish those who increase the likelihood of crime by concerted action has long been established." United States v. Spock, 416 F.2d 165, 171 (1st Cir.1969).

our decision upon the theory of those cases, nor upon the related one that the attempt is to prosecute as conspiracy acts identical with the substantive offense. United States v. Dietrich, 126 F. 664. We place it rather upon the ground that we perceive in the failure of the Mann Act to condemn the woman's participation in those transportations which are effected with her mere consent, evidence of an affirmative legislative policy to leave her acquiescence unpunished. We think it a necessary implication of that policy that when the Mann Act and the conspiracy statute came to be construed together, as they necessarily would be, the same participation which the former contemplates as an inseparable incident of all cases in which the woman is a voluntary agent at all, but does not punish, was not automatically to be made punishable under the latter. It would contravene that policy to hold that the very passage of the Mann Act effected a withdrawal by the conspiracy statute of that immunity which the Mann Act itself confers.

It is not to be supposed that the consent of an unmarried person to adultery with a married person, where the latter alone is guilty of the substantive offense, would render the former an abettor or a conspirator, compare In re Cooper, 162 Cal. 81, 85, 121 P. 318, or that the acquiescence of a woman under the age of consent would make her a co-conspirator with the man to commit statutory rape upon herself. The principle, determinative of this case, is the same.

On the evidence before us the woman petitioner has not violated the Mann Act and, we hold, is not guilty of a conspiracy to do so. As there is no proof that the man conspired with anyone else to bring about the transportation, the convictions of both petitioners must be

Reversed.[2]

MR. JUSTICE CARDOZO concurs in the result.

2. Accord: Regina v. Murphy & Bieneck, 60 CCC 2d 1 (Albt.1981).

The status of prostitution under state law has no bearing on the legality of an agreement under the Mann Act. A conspiracy conviction was upheld for transporting a prostitute to Nevada where prostitution is not illegal. United States v. Pelton, 578 F.2d 701, 712 (8th Cir. 1978).

At one time the California law did not make it an offense for one serving a sentence of life imprisonment to escape from prison, although it did make it an offense for one serving less than a life sentence to escape. At that time **C**, serving a life sentence and **P**, serving a term less than life, agreed to escape from prison with whatever force was required. In this escape **P** killed a guard. **C** was convicted of first-degree murder, and the conviction was affirmed although there was no evidence that he had ever touched the deceased. People v. Creeks, 170 Cal. 368, 149 P. 821 (1915).

"Under Minn.St. 609.175, subd. 2, defendant was properly convicted of conspiracy to commit a crime even though the person with whom he conspired feigned agreement and at no time intended to go through with the plan." (Syllabus by the Court). State v. St. Christopher, 305 Minn. 226, 232 N.W.2d 798, 799 (1975).

N.B. This is under a statute which expressly provides for "unilateral" conspiracy. See Model Penal Code § 5.04.

UNITED STATES v. FALCONE

United States Circuit Court of Appeals, Second Circuit, 1940.
109 F.2d 579.

L. HAND, CIRCUIT JUDGE. . . . In the light of all this, it is apparent that the first question is whether the seller of goods, in themselves innocent, becomes a conspirator with—or, what is in substance the same thing, an abettor of—the buyer because he knows that the buyer means to use the goods to commit a crime. That came up a number of times in circuit courts of appeal while the Eighteenth Amendment was in force, and the answer was not entirely uniform. The first case we have found is Pattis v. United States, 9 Cir., 17 F.2d 562, where, although the accused appears to have been in fact more closely connected with the buyer's crime than merely as a seller, the court affirmed a charge to the jury that he was guilty if he merely had notice of the future destination of the goods. That appears to be the settled doctrine in that circuit. The same is true of the Seventh Circuit. And of the Sixth. The Fifth has, however, held otherwise, though by a divided court, Young v. United States, 5 Cir., 48 F.2d 26. In that case the judges differed because of their interpretation of Edenfield v. United States, 273 U.S. 660, 47 S.Ct. 345, 71 L.Ed. 827, which, on the authority of United States v. Katz, 271 U.S. 354, 46 S.Ct. 513, 70 L.Ed. 986, reversed a conviction upon a count for conspiracy to manufacture liquor without a license. The indictment also contained a count for conspiracy to manufacture liquor contrary to the National Prohibition Law, 41 Stat. 305, and the conviction on this the court did not disturb; the question was whether in doing so it had held that the mere sale of materials for making a still, and of sugar and meal to make liquor, was enough to convict. The opinion below (Edenfield v. United States, 5 Cir., 8 F.2d 614) indicated that there had been nothing more to hold the seller, but when the same court in Young v. United States, supra (5 Cir., 48 F.2d 26), came to consider the effect of the reversal, the majority said that there had in fact been much more; i.e., that the accused had taken part in setting up the stills, and in selling the liquor after it was made. We do not think, therefore, that Edenfield v. United States, supra, 273 U.S. 660, 47 S.Ct. 345, 71 L.Ed. 827, should be regarded as passing upon the point. We are ourselves committed to the view of the Fifth Circuit. United States v. Peoni, 2 Cir., 100 F.2d 401. In that case we tried to trace down the doctrine as to abetting and conspiracy, as it exists in our criminal law, and concluded that the seller's knowledge was not alone enough. Civilly, a man's liability extends to any injuries which he should have apprehended to be likely to follow from his acts. If they do, he must excuse his conduct by showing that the interest which he was promoting outweighed the dangers which its protection imposed upon others; but in civil cases there has been a loss, and the only question is whether the law shall transfer it from the sufferer to another. There are indeed instances of criminal liability of the same kind, where the law imposes punishment merely because the accused did not forbear to do that from which the wrong was likely to follow; but in prosecutions for conspiracy or abetting, his attitude towards the forbidden undertaking must be more positive. It is not enough that he does not forego a normally lawful activity, of the fruits of which he knows that others will make an unlawful use; he must in some sense promote their venture himself, make it his own, have a stake in its outcome. The distinction is especially important today when so many prosecutors seek to sweep within the drag-net of conspiracy all those who have been associated in any degree whatever with the main offenders. That there are opportunities of great oppression in such a doctrine is very plain, and it is only by circumscribing the scope of such all comprehensive indictments that they can be avoided. We may agree that morally the defendants at bar should have refused to sell to illicit distillers; but, both morally and legally, to do so was toto coelo different from joining with them in running the stills.

For these reasons the prosecution did not make out a case against either of the Falcones, Alberico, or John Nole; and this is especially true of Salvatore Falcone. As to Nicholas Nole the question is closer, for when he began to do business as the "Acme Yeast Company", he hid behind the name of a cousin, whom he caused to swear falsely that the affiant was to do the business. Yet it seems to us that this was as likely to have come from a belief that it was a crime to sell the yeast and the cans to distillers as from being in fact any further involved in their business. It showed a desire to escape detection and that was evidence of a consciousness of guilt, but the consciousness may have as well arisen from a mistake of law as from a purpose to do what the law in fact forbade. We think therefore that even as to him no case was made out. . . .

The convictions of Salvatore and Joseph Falcone, of Alberico and of Nicholas and John Nole are reversed. . . .[1]

(Affirmed 311 U.S. 205, 61 S.Ct. 204, 85 L.Ed. 128.)

1. If the commodities involved in the sale are not articles of free commerce such as sugar and cans, but restricted commodities such as narcotic drugs which can be sold only by compliance with order forms and registration and are incapable of further legal use without compliance with rigid regulations, the seller's knowledge of the buyer's extensive illegal use of the drugs over an extended period of time may be sufficient to establish a conspiracy. Direct Sales Co. v. United States, 319 U.S. 703, 63 S.Ct. 1265, 87 L.Ed. 1674 (1943).

C sold a gun to D under such circumstances that it was criminally negligent for him to do so because of the likelihood that D would use it to kill X, which D did. D was convicted of first-degree murder and C was convicted of involuntary manslaughter. People v. Howk, 56 Cal.2d 687, 16 Cal.Rptr. 370, 365 P.2d 426 (1961).

"One who sells a gun to another knowing that he is buying it to commit a murder, would hardly escape conviction as an accessory to the murder by showing that he received full price for the gun." Backun v. United States, 112 F.2d 635, 637 (4th Cir.1940).

One may commit treason by selling critical materials with knowledge that they are to be used to help the enemy wage war against the seller's government. His claim that his intent was not to aid the enemy but only to make money

PINKERTON v. UNITED STATES

Supreme Court of the United States, 1946.
328 U.S. 640, 66 S.Ct. 1180.

MR. JUSTICE DOUGLAS delivered the opinion of the Court.

Walter and Daniel Pinkerton are brothers who live a short distance from each other on Daniel's farm. They were indicted for violations of the Internal Revenue Code. The indictment contained ten substantive counts and one conspiracy count. The jury found Walter guilty on nine of the substantive counts and on the conspiracy count. It found Daniel guilty on six of the substantive counts and on the conspiracy count. Walter was fined $500 and sentenced generally on the substantive counts to imprisonment for thirty months. On the conspiracy count he was given a two year sentence to run concurrently with the other sentence. Daniel was fined $1,000 and sentenced generally on the substantive counts to imprisonment for thirty months. On the conspiracy count he was fined $500 and given a two year sentence to run concurrently with the other sentence. The judgments of conviction were affirmed by the Circuit Court of Appeals. 151 F.2d 499. The case is here on a petition for a writ of certiorari which we granted, 66 S.Ct. 702, because one of the questions presented involved a conflict between the decision below and United States v. Sall, 116 F.2d 745, decided by the Circuit Court of Appeals for the Third Circuit.

A single conspiracy was charged and proved. Some of the overt acts charged in the conspiracy count were the same acts charged in the substantive counts. Each of the substantive offenses found was committed pursuant to the conspiracy. . . .

It is contended that there was insufficient evidence to implicate Daniel in the conspiracy. But we think there was enough evidence for submission of the issue to the jury.

There is, however, no evidence to show that Daniel participated directly in the commission of the substantive offenses on which his conviction has been sustained, although there was evidence to show that these substantive offenses were in fact committed by Walter in furtherance of the unlawful agreement or conspiracy existing between the brothers. The question was submitted to the jury on the theory that each petitioner could be found guilty of the substantive offenses, if it was found at the time those offenses were committed

is rejected. Carlisle v. United States, 83 U.S. 147, 21 L.Ed. 426 (1872); Sprott v. United States, 87 U.S. 459, 22 L.Ed. 371 (1874).

"Mengal's mere giving of blood with the knowledge that it would be used for the unlawful purpose would be enough to convict him as an aider and abettor." United States v. Eberhardt, 417 F.2d 1009, 1013 (4th Cir.1969). This blood, with the addition of a large amount of animal blood was poured over documents in the Selective Service Files.

petitioners were parties to an unlawful conspiracy and the substantive offenses charged were in fact committed in furtherance of it.

Daniel relies on United States v. Sall, supra. That case held that participation in the conspiracy was not itself enough to sustain a conviction for the substantive offense even though it was committed in furtherance of the conspiracy. The court held that, in addition to evidence that the offense was in fact committed in furtherance of the conspiracy, evidence of direct participation in the commission of the substantive offense or other evidence from which participation might fairly be inferred was necessary.*

We take a different view. We have here a continuous conspiracy. There is here no evidence of the affirmative action on the part of Daniel which is necessary to establish his withdrawal from it. Hyde v. United States, 225 U.S. 347, 369, 32 S.Ct. 793, 803, 56 L.Ed. 1114, Ann.Cas.1914A, 614. As stated in that case, "Having joined in an unlawful scheme, having constituted agents for its performance, scheme and agency to be continuous until full fruition be secured, until he does some act to disavow or defeat the purpose he is in no situation to claim the delay of the law. As the offense has not been terminated or accomplished, he is still offending. And we think, consciously offending,—offending as certainly, as we have said, as at the first moment of his confederation, and consciously through every moment of its existence." And so long as the partnership in crime continues, the partners act for each other in carrying it forward. It is settled that "an overt act of one partner may be the act of all without any new agreement specifically directed to that act." United States v. Kissel, 218 U.S. 601, 608, 31 S.Ct. 124, 126, 54 L.Ed. 1168. Motive or intent may be proved by the acts or declarations of some of the conspirators in furtherance of the common objective. A scheme to use the mails to defraud, which is joined in by more than one person, is a conspiracy. Yet all members are responsible, though only one did the mailing. The governing principle is the same when the substantive offense is committed by one of the conspirators in further-

* [Added by the Compiler.]

In Massachusetts the rule, that the act of one conspirator in carrying out the common purpose is the act of all, applies only when two or more are jointly engaged in the commission of the crime which is the object of the conspiracy. Commonwealth v. Stasiun, 349 Mass. 38, 206 N.E.2d 672 (1965).

"*Pinkerton,* however, rests upon the general principle of conspiracy law that each conspirator is responsible for the acts of the others pursuant to and in furtherance of the conspiracy. . . ." United States v. Roselli, 432 F.2d 879, 894 (9th Cir.1970).

One who joins a conspiracy which has already been in operation, knowing of its unlawful purpose, may be held responsible for acts done in furtherance of the conspiracy both prior to and subsequent to his joining. This sweeping statement, however, seems only to refer to guilt of the conspiracy itself. It does not appear that anyone was held guilty of any substantive offense on a basis of ratification. United States v. Bridgeman, 173 U.S. App.D.C. 150, 523 F.2d 1099 (1975).

A conspirator is bound by acts done in furtherance of the conspiracy whether or not he performed or was aware of them. United States v. Brasco, 516 F.2d 816 (2d Cir.1975). See Perkins, The Act of One Conspirator, 26 Hast.L.J. 337 (1974).

ance of the unlawful project. The criminal intent to do the act is established by the formation of the conspiracy. Each conspirator instigated the commission of the crime. The unlawful agreement contemplated precisely what was done. It was formed for the purpose. The act done was in execution of the enterprise. The rule which holds responsible one who counsels, procures, or commands another to commit a crime is founded on the same principle. That principle is recognized in the law of conspiracy when the overt act of one partner in crime is attributable to all. An overt act is an essential ingredient of the crime of conspiracy under § 37 of the Criminal Code, 18 U.S.C. § 88, 18 U.S.C.A. § 88. If that can be supplied by the act of one conspirator, we fail to see why the same or other acts in furtherance of the conspiracy are likewise not attributable to the others for the purpose of holding them responsible for the substantive offense.

A different case would arise if the substantive offense committed by one of the conspirators was not in fact done in furtherance of the conspiracy, did not fall within the scope of the unlawful project, or was merely a part of the ramifications of the plan which could not be reasonably foreseen as a necessary or natural consequence of the unlawful agreement. But as we read this record, that is not this case.

Affirmed.**

MR. JUSTICE JACKSON took no part in the consideration or decision of this case.

MR. JUSTICE RUTLEDGE, dissenting in part. . . .

** The statements of one conspirator made during the conspiracy and in furtherance thereof are admissible against his co-conspirator as an exception to the hearsay rule. People v. Brawley, 1 Cal. 3d 277, 82 Cal.Rptr. 161, 461 P.2d 361 (1969); United States v. McGann, 431 F.2d 1104, 1108 (5th Cir.1970).

Although the admissions and declarations of one conspirator, made at the police station after arrest, are not admissible against his co-conspirator because the conspiracy is then at an end, the statement of one *to the other* at the time of arrest: "So they got you too," is admissible as part of the *res gestae*. State v. Watson, 182 Neb. 692, 157 N.W.2d 156 (1968).

"It is settled that in federal conspiracy trials the hearsay exception that allows evidence of out-of-court statements of one conspirator to be admitted against his fellow conspirators applies only if the statement was made in the course of and in furtherance of the conspiracy, and not during a subsequent period when the conspirators were engaged in nothing more than concealment of the criminal enterprise." This, however, is a federal rule of evidence and not a constitutional limitation. Hence the Georgia rule which permits a conspirator's out-of-court statement during the concealment phase of the conspiracy, and while in prison, to be used against the co-conspirator, is valid. Dutton v. Evans, 400 U.S. 74, 81, 91 S.Ct. 210, 215–16, 27 L.Ed.2d 213 (1970).

Where an employee conspired with an outsider to steal from the employer, which was done, the employee could be convicted of embezzlement, the outsider convicted of larceny, and both convicted of conspiracy to commit larceny. State v. Palumbo, 137 N.J.Super. 13, 347 A.2d 535 (1975).

UNITED STATES v. ROSADO-FERNANDEZ

United States Court of Appeals, Fifth Circuit, 1980.
614 F.2d 50.

AINSWORTH, CIRCUIT JUDGE: Appellants Jose Eligio Borges and Angel Oscar Rosado-Fernandez, along with two other defendants, were convicted of conspiracy to possess with intent to distribute cocaine, 21 U.S.C. § 846, and possession with intent to distribute cocaine, 21 U.S.C. § 841(a)(1), 18 U.S.C. § 2. Rosado was also convicted of use of a communication facility during the course of and in the commission of a felony, in violation of 21 U.S.C. §§ 841(a)(1), 846, 843(b). On appeal, Borges contends that there is insufficient evidence to convict him of the conspiracy charge, and also contends that he cannot be found guilty of the possession charge since he never had actual possession of the cocaine in question. Rosado contends that the Government failed to prove that the cocaine involved in the attempted drug transaction was "L" cocaine rather than purportedly legal "D" cocaine. The contentions of both appellants are meritless and we affirm.

On January 3, 1979, Agent John Lawler of the Drug Enforcement Agency (DEA), acting in an undercover capacity as a New York cocaine buyer, went to the residence of appellant Borges. Lawler informed Borges that he wanted to buy three kilos of cocaine. Borges quoted a price, and stated that delivery could be arranged. During the conversation Borges was sifting a white powder on his kitchen table. He stated the cocaine would be better than that on the table. Borges then made a phone call in Spanish and told Lawler to return later that evening. When Lawler returned the parties agreed to meet still later at a nearby restaurant. Borges indicated he would bring his supplier to the restaurant.

Later that evening, Borges came to the restaurant accompanied by appellant Rosado, and Rosado's stepfather. Borges introduced Rosado to Lawler, and Lawler stated he was interested in purchasing three kilos of cocaine. Rosado stated it would be no problem as he had 40 kilos in the area. Borges was present during this entire conversation. Rosado then made a phone call and told Lawler the cocaine would be delivered to an apartment. Rosado and Lawler discussed delivery and agreed that they would be the only ones present during the actual transaction. Borges concurred in this arrangement. No actual delivery took place that evening.

The next day Lawler and Rosado had a series of telephone conversations, which were recorded and played for the jury. During the conversations, Rosado apologized for the delay and stated the price would be $46,000 per kilo. Lawler and Rosado later met at the home of the third codefendant Nelson Garcia. A quantity of white powder was produced, and Lawler tested it. The test indicated that the powder was cocaine. Shortly thereafter arrests were made. While Garcia and Rosado were being arrested, the fourth codefendant Zayas took the cocaine and dumped it into the swimming pool. Agent Lawler dove in the pool and recovered samples of the water and the cocaine, as well as a sample from the table inside. All samples were found to contain cocaine.

Borges does not deny that he introduced Agent Lawler to codefendant Rosado, but he contends that he had no part of the final drug transaction involving Rosado and codefendant Garcia. He argues that the Rosado-Garcia drug transaction is a separate conspiracy, as the purchase arranged by him was to involve Rosado and a drug source other than Garcia. The fact that Rosado eventually obtained the cocaine from a source not originally contemplated by Borges, however, is not sufficient to exonerate Borges.

To be convicted of conspiracy, a defendant must have knowledge of the conspiracy, and must intend to join or associate himself with the objectives of the conspiracy. Knowledge, actual participation and criminal intent must be proved by the Government. Participation, however, need not be proved by direct evidence; a common purpose and plan may be inferred from a pattern of circumstantial evidence. The essential elements of a criminal conspiracy are an agreement among the conspirators to commit an offense attended by an overt act by one of them in furtherance of the agreement. However, under the provisions of the drug conspiracy statute involved here, it is not necessary that an overt act be alleged or proved.

The facts at trial established a conspiracy between Borges and Rosado to sell cocaine to Lawler. They agreed to commit an offense against the United States. Borges was the organizer of the venture. He set up the meeting, and was present during the negotiations for the sale of the cocaine. The conspirators need not know each other nor be privy to the details of each enterprise comprising the conspiracy as long as the evidence is sufficient to show that each defendant possessed full knowledge of the conspiracy's general purpose and scope. Borges knew that Lawler wanted to buy cocaine. Borges knew that Rosado would obtain the cocaine for Lawler from one of Rosado's several sources. Under these circumstances the conspiracy was proved.

Borges next contends that he cannot be convicted of possession since the evidence shows he never had physical control of the cocaine involved in the transaction. It is undisputed, however, that Rosado had possession of the drug. A party to a continuing conspiracy may be responsible for a substantive offense committed by a coconspirator in furtherance of the conspiracy even though that party does not participate in the substantive offense or have any knowledge of it. As we stated recently in United States v. Michel, 588 F.2d 986, 999 (5th Cir.1979):

> Once the conspiracy and a particular defendant's knowing participation in it has been established beyond a reasonable doubt, the

defendant is deemed guilty of substantive acts committed in furtherance of the conspiracy by any of his criminal partners. This principle has been repeatedly applied by this circuit in cases involving drug conspiracies and substantive drug violations.

Affirmed.[1]

UNITED STATES v. FOX

United States Circuit Court of Appeals, Third Circuit, 1942.
130 F.2d 56.

GOODRICH, CIRCUIT JUDGE. The appellant William Fox, was indicted with two other persons, J. Warren Davis and Morgan S. Kaufman, charged with conspiracy to obstruct justice and to defraud the United States. The indictment contained the usual residuary clause charging conspiracy of the named conspirators "with divers other persons whose names are to the Grand Jurors unknown, ..." The appellant entered a guilty plea and became a witness for the United States at the trial. The first jury, being unable to agree, was discharged without a verdict. Subsequently, a second trial was had which again resulted in a disagreement and this jury was likewise discharged without a verdict. The appellant was a witness for the government in the second trial also. Sometime thereafter a nolle prosequi was entered upon the application of the government as to the defendants, Davis and Kaufman. The appellant both before and subsequent to the nolle prosequi moved for leave to withdraw his plea of guilty. He also moved, subsequently to the nolle prosequi for a vacation or modification of the sentence which had been imposed prior to entry of judgment of the nolle prosequi. The District Judge refused both requests and his action is assigned as error upon this appeal.

The case for the appellant in this court rests on two grounds. One concerns the doctrines of the law relating to conspiracy to the facts of his case. The other is whether the trial judge went beyond his discretion in refusing the appellant permission to withdraw his guilty plea.

The law of conspiracy has been nearly as proliferative as that of larceny in its development of technical doctrine. The question in this case is limited, however, to the growth of one branch. By definition conspiracy is a group offense; therefore, two or more people must participate to create the crime. Then it is held that where an indict-

1. "From this we conclude that, in addition to the mere act of aiding, there is an intent requirement necessary to convict, but that such intent is implicit in the act of aiding with *knowledge of the perpetrator's guilty state of mind.*" People v. Green, 130 Cal.App.3d 1, 181 Cal. Rptr. 507, 511 (1982).

"Once the existence of a conspiracy is established, evidence establishing beyond a reasonable doubt a connection of a defendant with the conspiracy, even though the *connection is slight,* is sufficient to convict him with knowing participation in the conspiracy. Thus, the word 'slight' properly modifies 'connection' and not 'evidence.'" United States v. Dunn, 564 F.2d 348, 357 (9th Cir.1977).

ment for conspiracy names only two, an acquittal or reversal as to one is an acquittal or reversal as to the other. This is no doubt the law announced by the majority of the decisions including the federal courts, although as the New York court says the "contrary view is arguable". This result, however, is not to be expanded into a general "all or none" rule. The conviction of some alleged conspirators does not fall because others named are acquitted, even though the conviction of the others is logically required for the finding of guilty of those held. Nor is the conviction of one alleged conspirator vitiated because of the possible later acquittal of co-defendants not yet tried or even apprehended. Furthermore, one may be convicted and punished for a conspiracy even though his fellow conspirators may be immune from prosecution because of the immunity attaching to representatives of foreign governments, the Fifth Circuit declaring that "The rule that the acquittal of all save one of alleged conspirators results in the acquittal of all applies to acquittals on the merits".

The appellant does not contend that his alleged fellow conspirators were acquitted, but does argue that the nolle prosequi puts an end to charges made by this indictment and so should be treated as having the same effect as an acquittal. This point will be taken up later. . . .

We think that to treat a convicted conspirator whose fellow conspirator's case has ended by a nolle prosequi like the case where one is convicted and the other is acquitted goes too far. The analogy overlooks the difference between an acquittal and a nolle prosequi. The courts seem to have treated the acquittal in this connection as though the jury had expressly found that the defendant did not participate in the conspiracy charged. Therefore, the defendant who is convicted stands in the situation of having been found to conspire by himself, a manifest impossibility by the definition of conspiracy. One may criticize that rule as being founded upon a false premise, for a not guilty verdict is not necessarily a declaration of innocence by the jury, but simply an indication of lack of proof of guilt beyond reasonable doubt. Be that as it may, the acquittal of the alleged conspirator does free the accused from further prosecution for the offense charged. The nolle prosequi does not. As in the case of disagreement of a jury, "The prisoner has not been convicted or acquitted, and may again be put upon his defence." It is not a bar to a second indictment covering the same matter, although it does terminate the proceedings in which the nolle prosequi occurs. It is a very considerable step which has to be taken to apply the rule as to acquittal to the termination of proceedings by a nolle prosequi. We are not called upon to take it either by reason or by authority. . . .

The Judgment of the District Court is affirmed.[1]

(Certiorari denied 317 U.S. 666, 63 S.Ct. 74, 87 L.Ed. 535.)

1. Where A and B were separately tried on a conspiracy charge and A acquitted B could still be tried and convicted. DPP v. Shannon, [1975] A.C. 717.

ALONZI v. PEOPLE

Supreme Court of Colorado, En Banc, 1979.
198 Colo. 160, 597 P.2d 560.

ROVIRA, JUSTICE.

Jack Alonzi (petitioner) was convicted by a jury of felony theft and conspiracy. . . .

The evidence submitted by the People at trial showed that the petitioner was contacted on September 15, 1975, by an undercover agent of the Colorado Bureau of Investigation (CBI), who indicated an interest in buying stolen cars. The two individuals talked with each other repeatedly over the next four days. The CBI agent recorded sixteen telephone conversations on a cassette tape recorder. In these conversations, the petitioner indicated that he could obtain two stolen Lincoln Continentals for the agent to purchase, although the petitioner noted that he did not steal the vehicles. On September 20, 1975, the agent and the petitioner met, at the direction of the latter, in a motel parking lot where a third party delivered the two automobiles. The petitioner accepted payment from the agent and was then arrested. . . .

We next address the petitioner's contention that his conduct in this case does not constitute theft. The People argue that the petitioner is legally accountable for theft because of the complicity statute, section 18–1–603, C.R.S.1973, which states:

> "18–1–603. Complicity. A person is legally accountable as principal for the behavior of another constituting a criminal offense if, with the intent to promote or facilitate the commission of the offense, he aids, abets, or advises the other person in planning or committing the offense."

Accord: Commonwealth v. Byrd, 490 Pa. 544, 417 A.2d 173 (1980). Where both A and B were tried together and convicted but A's conviction is set aside on appeal B's conviction was upheld. Queen v. Darby, 56 Aust.L.J.Rpts. 688 (Aust.H.C. 1982).

Contra, State v. Jackson, 7 S.C. 283 (1876).

No overt act was required by common law for conviction of conspiracy. As to the effect of statutes requiring such an act, see Hyde v. United States, 225 U.S. 347, 32 S.Ct. 793, 56 L.Ed. 1114 (1912).

Where an overt act is required by statute for conviction of conspiracy the required act need not be sufficient to constitute an attempt. People v. George, 74 Cal.App. 440, 241 P. 97 (1925).

No overt act is required for conviction of conspiracy to violate the Controlled Substances Act. United States v. Dreyer, 533 F.2d 112 (3d Cir.1976).

Where two of three persons charged with conspiracy may have been guilty it was error to instruct the jury to convict all three or none. State v. Carroll, 51 N.J. 102, 237 A.2d 878 (1968).

Where there is no evidence of any other guilty party and the conviction of one of two charged with conspiracy must be reversed, the conviction of the other must be reversed also. Petty v. People, 167 Colo. 240, 447 P.2d 217 (1968).

Where there were only three alleged conspirators, and two had been tried and found not guilty, the state was estopped from trying the third. People v. Superior Court, In and For Cty. of San Bernadino, 44 Cal.App.3d 494, 118 Cal.Rptr. 702 (1975).

This statute was amended in 1971 to remove the word "encourages" from its language. The petitioner concedes that, viewing the evidence in the light most favorable to the prosecution, his conviction would have to be affirmed under the prior complicity statute because his conduct did constitute encouragement. However, the petitioner argues that the amendment of the provision to remove the word "encourages" indicates the legislature's intent to treat the mere encouragement of an offense differently than the commission of the substantive offense itself. The People contend that the legislature removed the word simply because "encourages" is implicit in "abets."

Under the plain language of the statute, one who abets the commission of a criminal offense is legally accountable for the violation of the substantive offense. The evidence at trial clearly supported the conclusion that the petitioner encouraged the substantive offense of theft in this case. Thus, the resolution of this issue turns on whether or not the definition of "abets" encompasses "encourages." We hold that it does.

Words in a statute should be given their familiar and generally accepted meanings. "Encourage" is included in the accepted definition of "abet." Black's Law Dictionary 17 (4th ed. 1951); Webster's Third New International Dictionary 3 (1961). In addition, although this court has not previously defined the word, other courts have expressly included "encourage" within the definition of "abet."

The plain meaning of "abet" includes "encourage." If the language of a statute is plain, it will not be subjected to a strained interpretation. As such, the petitioner's conduct in this case falls within the complicity statute and his conviction for felony theft must stand.

As noted above, the petitioner's other contentions were correctly resolved by the court of appeals. Accordingly, the judgment is affirmed.

ERICKSON and CARRIGAN, JJ., dissent.

MODEL PENAL CODE

Section 5.03 Criminal Conspiracy.

(1) Definition of Conspiracy. A person is guilty of conspiracy with another person or persons to commit a crime if with the purpose of promoting or facilitating its commission he:

(a) agrees with such other person or persons that they or one or more of them will engage in conduct which constitutes such crime or an attempt or solicitation to commit such crime; or

(b) agrees to aid such other person or persons in the planning or commission of such crime or of an attempt or solicitation to commit such crime.

(2) Scope of Conspiratorial Relationship. If a person guilty of conspiracy, as defined by Subsection (1) of this Section, knows that a person with whom he conspires to commit a crime has conspired with another person or persons to commit the same crime, he is guilty of conspiring with such other

person or persons, whether or not he knows their identity, to commit such crime.

(3) Conspiracy With Multiple Criminal Objectives. If a person conspires to commit a number of crimes, he is guilty of only one conspiracy so long as such multiple crimes are the object of the same agreement or continuous conspiratorial relationship.

(4) Joinder and Venue in Conspiracy Prosecutions.

(a) Subject to the provisions of paragraph (b) of this Subsection, two or more persons charged with criminal conspiracy may be prosecuted jointly if:

(i) they are charged with conspiring with one another; or

(ii) the conspiracies alleged, whether they have the same or different parties, are so related that they constitute different aspects of a scheme of organized criminal conduct.

(b) In any joint prosecution under paragraph (a) of this Subsection:

(i) no defendant shall be charged with a conspiracy in any county [parish or district] other than one in which he entered into such conspiracy or in which an overt act pursuant to such conspiracy was done by him or by a person with whom he conspired; and

(ii) neither the liability of any defendant nor the admissibility against him of evidence of acts or declarations of another shall be enlarged by such joinder; and

(iii) the Court shall order a severance or take a special verdict as to any defendant who so requests, if it deems it necessary or appropriate to promote the fair determination of his guilt or innocence, and shall take any other proper measures to protect the fairness of the trial.

(5) Overt Act. No person may be convicted of conspiracy to commit a crime, other than a felony of the first or second degree, unless an overt act in pursuance of such conspiracy is alleged and proved to have been done by him or by a person with whom he conspired.

(6) Renunciation of Criminal Purpose. It is an affirmative defense that the actor, after conspiring to commit a crime, thwarted the success of the conspiracy, under circumstances manifesting a complete and voluntary renunciation of his criminal purpose.

(7) Duration of Conspiracy. For purposes of Section 1.06(4):

(a) conspiracy is a continuing course of conduct which terminates when the crime or crimes which are its object are committed or the agreement that they be committed is abandoned by the defendant and by those with whom he conspired; and

(b) such abandonment is presumed if neither the defendant nor anyone with whom he conspired does any overt act in pursuance of the conspiracy during the applicable period of limitation; and

(c) if an individual abandons the agreement, the conspiracy is terminated as to him only if and when he advises those with whom he conspired of his abandonment or he informs the law enforcement authorities of the existence of the conspiracy and of his participation therein.

Section 5.05 Grading of Criminal Attempt, Solicitation and Conspiracy; Mitigation in Cases of Lesser Danger; Multiple Convictions Barred.

(1) Grading. Except as otherwise provided in this Section, attempt, solicitation and conspiracy are crimes of the same grade and degree as the most serious offense which is attempted or solicited or is an object of the conspiracy. An attempt, solicitation or conspiracy to commit a [capital crime or a] felony of the first degree is a felony of the second degree.

(2) Mitigation. If the particular conduct charged to constitute a criminal attempt, solicitation or conspiracy is so inherently unlikely to result or culminate in the commission of a crime that neither such conduct nor the actor presents a public danger warranting the grading of such offense under this Section, the Court shall exercise its power under Section 6.12 to enter judgment and impose sentence for a crime of lower grade or degree or, in extreme cases, may dismiss the prosecution.

(3) Multiple Convictions. A person may not be convicted of more than one offense defined by this Article for conduct designed to commit or to culminate in the commission of the same crime.[1]

[Section 5.04 Incapacity, Irresponsibility or Immunity of Party to Solicitation or Conspiracy, was quoted at the end of Section 3.]

SECTION 6. AGENCY

REX v. HUGGINS

King's Bench, 1730.
2 Ld.Raym. 1574, 92 Eng.Rep. 518.

(An indictment charged the warden of a prison, and his deputy, with the murder of a prisoner, by keeping him in an unwholesome place, and so forth, until he died. The jury returned a special verdict. The LORD CHIEF JUSTICE—RAYMOND—delivered the opinion of the justices.)

In this case two questions have been made. 1. What crime the facts found upon Barnes in the special verdict will amount to? 2. Whether the prisoner at the Bar is found guilty of the same offence with Barnes?

1. As to the first question, it is very plain that the facts found upon Barnes do amount to murder in him. Murder may be committed without any stroke. The law has not confined the offence to any particular circumstances or manner of killing; but there are as many ways to commit murder, as there are to destroy a man, provided the act be done with malice, either express or implied. Hale P.C. 46. 3 Inst. 52. Murder is, where a person kills another of malice, so he dies

1. Copyright: 1962 by the American Law Institute. Reprinted with the permission of the American Law Institute.

within a year and a day. Hale P.C. 43. And malice may be either expressed or implied. In this case the jury have found the malice express: for the facts charged on Barnes are laid in the indictment to be ex malitia sua praecogitata, to wit, that he having the custody of Arne assaulted him, and carried him to this unwholesome room, and confined him there by force against his will, and without his consent, and without proper support, ex malitia sua praecogitata; by means of which he languished and died. And the jury have found that Barnes did all these facts, modo et forma prout in indictamento praedicto specificatur. . . .

The Judges are all unanimously of opinion, that the facts found in this special verdict do not amount to murder in the prisoner at the Bar; but as this special verdict is found, they are of opinion, that he is not guilty. Though he was warden, yet it being found, that there was a deputy; he is not, as warden, guilty of the facts committed under the authority of his deputy. He shall answer as superior for his deputy civilly,[1] but not criminally. It has been settled, that though a sheriff must answer for the offences of his gaoler civilly, that is, he is subject in an action, to make satisfaction to the party injured; yet he is not to answer criminally for the offences of his under-officer. He only is criminally punishable, who immediately does the act, or permits it to be done.[2] Hale's P.C. 114. So that if an act be done by an under-officer, unless it is done by the command or direction, or with the consent of the principal, the principal is not criminally punishable for it. In this case the fact was done by Barnes; and it no where appears in the special verdict, that the prisoner at the Bar ever commanded, or directed, or consented to this duress of imprisonment, which was the cause of Arne's death. 1. No command or direction is found. And 2. It is not found, that Huggins knew of it. That which made the duress in this case was, 1. Barnes's carrying, and putting, and confining Arne in this room by force and against his consent. 2. The situation and condition of this room. Now it is not found that Huggins knew these several circumstances, which made the duress. 1. It is not found, that he knew any thing of Barnes's carrying Arne thither. 2. Nor that he was there without his consent, or without proper support. 3. As to the room, it is found by the verdict, 1. That the room was built of brick and mortar. 2. That the walls were valde humidae. 3. That the room was situate on the common sewer of the prison, and near the place where the filth of the prison and excrement of the prisoners were usually laid, ratione quorum the room was very unwholesome, and the life of any man kept there was in great danger But all that is found with respect to the prisoner's knowledge is, that for fifteen

1. But see Oppenheimer v. Los Angeles, 104 Cal.App.2d 545, 232 P.2d 26 (1951).

2. "The civil doctrine of respondeat superior was not conceived, nor is it to be applied, to include the responsibility of a master to the state for the independent acts of the servant." Lovelace v. State, 191 Miss. 62, 2 So.2d 796 (1941).

days before Arne's death he knew that the room was then lately built, recenter, that the walls were made of brick and mortar, and were then damp. But it is not found, nor does it appear, that he knew, they were dangerous to a man's life, or that there was a want of necessary support. Nor is it found, that he directed, or consented, that Arne should be kept or continued there. . . .

Upon the whole, there is no authority against the Court's giving judgment of acquittal, upon a verdict that is not sufficient to convict; and therefore this verdict, not finding facts sufficient to make the prisoner guilty of murder, he must be adjudged not guilty. And he was discharged.

REGINA v. HOLBROOK

Queen's Bench Division, 1877.
13 Cox C.C. 650.

This was a criminal information for libel, tried at Winchester before Lindley, J., and a special jury, a verdict of guilty having been found against the defendants, who are the proprietors and publishers of the *Portsmouth Times and Naval Gazette.*

The information had been granted at the instance of Mr. John Howard, the clerk of the peace for the borough of Portsmouth, who in effect, had been charged by an article in that newspaper with having packed a grand jury at the borough quarter sessions, for the purpose of improperly dealing with an indictment for personation at a municipal election.

The defendants, who pleaded Not Guilty only, were proved to be the publishers of the paper and to be actively engaged in the management. It appeared, however, that they employed a competent editor to superintend that part of the paper in which the libel appeared, and he had general authority to publish whatever he thought proper. The defendants then tendered evidence to show their exemption from liability under the 7th section of Lord Campbell's Act (6 & 7 Vict. c. 96). This evidence the learned judge refused to admit, and he directed the jury that the defendants were not in a position to avail themselves of that section. . . .

COCKBURN, C.J. I am of opinion that this rule must be made absolute. The facts, as I understand them, show that the defendants are the three joint proprietors of this newspaper; but it appears that, when not absent from Portsmouth, the duties of conducting the paper are divided between four persons, viz., the three defendants and an editor appointed by them to manage the literary department. The defendants undertake respectively the commercial, the advertising, and the publishing duties. At the time of the publication of this libel one of the defendants was absent in Somerset on account of his health, and he clearly was not cognisant of the publication. The others were present, and discharging their ordinary duties; but, as the editor had full discretion to publish whatever he thought proper in that department which issued the libellous publication without consulting them, all the defendants must be taken, for the purpose of this rule, to have known nothing of the insertion of the article complained of. The question is whether the defendants, or either of them, are criminally responsible. It is an undoubted principle of law that a man is responsible criminally only for his own acts, or those authorised expressly by him through his appointed agent. It is not to be implied or inferred from the fact that the defendants gave their editor a general authority to manage the paper as he thought proper, that they authorised him to do what was unlawful in the conduct of his ordinary business. Although this is the rule of law, there seems to have been introduced an exception with respect to libel. Lord Tenterden, at Nisi Prius in 1829, following a previous direction of Lord Kenyon, and a statement of the law in Hawkins' Pleas of the Crown, laid down that a proprietor of a newspaper was criminally responsible for a libel, although he took no part in the publication of the newspaper, nor of the libel in question. He further proceeded to justify this ruling, and expatiated upon the danger to the public which its modification might cause. It is not necessary to say how far we dissent from that doctrine; it was considered an anomaly by high authority at the time, and I cannot doubt that the 7th section of Lord Campbell's Act was passed to put an end to it. It has been suggested that the object of this legislation was only to get rid of the presumption from particular evidence created by previous statute, or to apply to a case where the libel has been inserted by some one who had no authority to interfere at all with the publication. The answer to both these suggestions is that the section was unnecessary for the accomplishment of either of these objects; and I can come to no other conclusion than that it was intended by these words to reverse this anomaly, and to render libel subject to the general law. If then, as I think, this provision was designed to protect the proprietor of a newspaper from criminal responsibility for the act of another person, committed through no fault of his and without his authority, does not the case here come within its application? As to the defendant who was absent, he clearly is protected unless the prosecution can show that his general authority to the editor expressly included power to publish libels. As to the other two defendants, the section provides protection from liability for a publication made without a publisher's authority, consent, or knowledge, if he has exercised due care and caution: it would then be a question for the jury looking at all the circumstances, whether those defendants can show themselves entitled to that protection. If the jury should be in the defendants' favour on these points they can neither of them be criminally liable. I say nothing about their position civilly, but it seems to me that the section can have no application at all if it does not apply to this case. It is not for us to say whether it is expedient or desirable that proprietors of newspapers should be freed from liability under such circumstances; and I do not consider that question. Simply this section is, in my opinion, applicable to the facts upon which this rule has been granted; I think it must be made absolute, and the case must go back for a new trial.

MELLOR, J. I regret much that I am unable to concur with the Lord Chief Justice and my brother Lush in their view of this matter. I dissent with the greatest diffidence, but I cannot think that the Legislature intended to apply sect. 7 of this Act to persons situated as these defendants are. They do not in the ordinary way live at any distance from the publishing office, they do not keep away from the general management of the paper, and the whole business is conducted for their profit and by their authority. The editor might by inadvertence have published this libel, but the want of care would then deprive the publication of the protection given in the Act. I think, too, that the absent partner is in the same position as the other two; they all gave their editor a general authority to do what he liked; they vested their discretion in him, they put themselves in his hands, and they must be taken to have authorized whatever he has done. The 7th section requires not only the absence of authority, consent, and knowledge, but also the presence of care and caution. . . .

Rule absolute for a new trial.[a]

MODEL PENAL CODE

Section 2.06 Liability for Conduct of Another; Complicity.

(1) A person is guilty of an offense if it is committed by his own conduct or by the conduct of another person for which he is legally accountable, or both.[1]

SECTION 7. INCORPORATION

"A corporation is not indictable, but the particular members are." This statement of Chief Justice Holt [2] represents the original position of the common law which held firm for many years. It was repeated in substance by Blackstone [3] and in judicial opinion in this country.[4] Now, however, it represents little more than an echo from a bygone day. The change from this position originated in the area where the proceeding is criminal in form but civil in substance,—the so-called "civil offense." And the first step was unavoidable. To insure proper maintenance of roads and bridges a statutory fine was provided for those who, having the duty to make needed repairs thereof, failed to do so. If a corporation had such a duty, which it neglected to per-

a. One cannot commit a crime by ratifying what is already done. The rule that subsequent ratification is equivalent to prior authorization cannot be applied to criminal cases. Cook v. Commonwealth, 141 Ky. 439, 132 S.W. 1032 (1911).

1. Copyright: 1962 by the American Law Institute. Reprinted with the permission of the American Law Institute.

2. Anonymous, 12 Mod. 559, 88 Eng. Rep. 1518 (K.B. 1701).

3. 1 Bl.Comm. * 476.

4. State v. Great Works Milling & Manufacturing Co., 20 Me. 41 (1841).

form, no sound reason against its conviction was available. And it was but a short step from recognition of corporate guilt of a civil offense based on nonfeasance to such guilt based on misfeasance. Since such an offense does not have the normal mens rea requirement for criminal guilt, and conviction may be supported on the basis of *respondeat superior,* the possibility of convicting a corporation of a civil offense became firmly established.[5] For years it seemed that the change from the original position would stop at this point and that a corporation would be held incapable of committing a true crime on the ground that the corporation could not have mens rea. "[C]orporations are not properly indictable for crimes involving a criminal state of mind, . . ." said a writer[6] as late as 1914. And ten years later another writer pointed out that the numerous statements in regard to convicting a corporation were chiefly *dicta* except in the civil offense field.[7] Gradually, however, the change moved forward into the area of true crime. On the one hand it was urged that the punishment,—a fine imposed on the corporation, falls upon those who are entirely free from fault as well as upon others who are blameworthy, and hence is unjust.[8] Others urged that nothing less would suffice to keep corporate activities in proper hands.[9] No one seriously urged that it would withhold the hand of the law from the guilty individuals because conviction of the corporation would be no bar to a prosecution of those persons who actually caused the harm.

If a truck driver has a fatal traffic accident, as a result of his criminal negligence in driving the vehicle, he is guilty of manslaughter. This will not of itself be sufficient to taint his employer with criminal guilt, but the employer might have sent out the driver with such instructions as to speed, or with a vehicle known to him to be so unsafe, that the employer also acted with criminal negligence. If so, the employer also is guilty of manslaughter if he is an individual. Would a corporate employer be guilty of manslaughter in such a case? The New Jersey court said yes.[10] The New York court said no.[11] In the latter case, however, it was recognized that a corporation can be guilty of a true crime and the reversal of this conviction was based entirely upon the definition of the particular offense. The court pointed out that manslaughter requires homicide and that homicide is defined by its statute (as at common law) as the killing of one human being "by another." This was held, quite properly, to mean the killing by another human being. The court then concluded that a

5. Overland Cotton Mill Co. v. People, 32 Colo. 263, 75 P. 924 (1904).

6. Canfield, Corporate Responsibility for Crime, 14 Col.L.Rev. 469, 480 (1914).

7. Francis, Criminal Responsibility of the Corporation, 18 Ill.L.Rev. 305 (1924). "Punishment falls on the individual members alone. Such being the case, the punishment is awkward, unscientific, and uncertain." Id. at 322.

8. See the articles in notes 6 and 7.

9. Edgerton, Corporate Criminal Responsibility, 36 Yale L.Jour. 827 (1927).

10. State v. Lehigh Valley R. Co., 90 N.J.L. 372, 103 A. 685 (1917).

11. People v. Rochester Railway & Light Co., 195 N.Y. 102, 88 N.E. 22 (1909).

corporation cannot be guilty of manslaughter, overlooking entirely that the corporation can do nothing except by aid of human beings. There could never be a case in which a corporation has killed a human being who was not killed by a human being. Under certain circumstances the act of the employee is imputed to the employer. The difficult problem is to determine whose criminal negligence (or knowledge or intent and so forth) shall be held to be the criminal negligence of the corporation as distinguished from that of an agent of the corporation.[12] Recently, a few courts have held corporations to be subject to homicide prosecutions. The conclusion has been supported by a statutory definition defining homicide in terms of a killing by a "person" and including corporations within the definition of the term person.[13]

UNITED STATES v. GEORGE F. FISH, INC.

United States Circuit Court of Appeals, Second Circuit, 1946.
154 F.2d 798.

CLARK, CIRCUIT JUDGE. An information filed in the District Court charged the defendants George F. Fish, Inc., a wholesale dealer in fruits and vegetables, and Michael Simon, its salesman, with "unlawfully, wilfully and knowingly" evading the provisions of Revised Maximum Price Regulation No. 426, issued under the authority of § 2, Emergency Price Control Act of 1942, 50 U.S.C.A.Appendix, § 902. After a jury verdict of guilt, the court entered judgment of a fine against the corporate defendant, and imprisonment against the individual defendant. 50 U.S.C.A.Appendix, §§ 904, 925(b). Defendants appeal from the conviction, urging the invalidity of the regulation, the failure of the information to allege a crime, the insufficiency of the evidence to support the verdict, and the nonliability of the corporate defendant to criminal prosecution for the acts charged. . . .

The corporate defendant makes a separate contention that the guilt of its salesman is not to be attributed to it. But the Supreme Court has long ago determined that the corporation may be held criminally liable for the acts of an agent within the scope of his employment, and the state and lower federal courts have been consistent in their application of that doctrine. . . .

No distinctions are made in these cases between officers and agents, or between persons holding positions involving varying degrees of responsibility. And this seems the only practical conclusion in any case, but particularly here where the sales proscribed by the Act will almost invariably be performed by subordinate salesmen,

12. "In all cases where a corporation is convicted of an offense for the commission of which a natural person would be punishable with imprisonment, as for a felony, such corporation is punishable by a fine of not more than five thousand dollars." N.Y.Pen.Laws 1932.

13. See State v. Ford Motor Co., 47 L.W. 2515 (Ind.Super.1979). See, Corporate Criminal Liability for Employee-Endangering Activities, 18 Colum.J.L. & Soc.Probs. 39 (1983).

rather than by corporate chiefs, and where the corporate hierarchy does not contemplate separate layers of official dignity, each with separate degrees of responsibility. The purpose of the Act is a deterrent one; and to deny the possibility of corporate responsibility for the acts of minor employees is to immunize the offender who really benefits, and open wide the door for evasion. Here Simon acted knowingly and deliberately and hence "wilfully" within the meaning of the Act, and his wilful act is also that of the corporation. . . .

Judgment affirmed.

(Certiorari denied 328 U.S. 869, 66 S.Ct. 1377, 90 L.Ed. 1639.)

PEOPLE v. CANADIAN FUR TRAPPERS CORP.

Court of Appeals of New York, 1928.
248 N.Y. 159, 161 N.E. 455.

CRANE, J. The defendant, a corporation, has been found guilty of grand larceny, second degree, and fined $5,000. The argument presented here is that a corporation cannot commit the crime of larceny as it is impossible for a corporation as such to have intent to steal or misappropriate property.

We think this question has been fairly well settled to the contrary. . . .

It has long been the law that a corporation may be liable criminally for the acts of its agents in doing things prohibited by statute. . . .

This is the law for corporations whose servants violate positive prohibitions or commands of statutes regarding corporate acts. Such offenses do not necessarily embody the element of intent to commit a crime. The corporation would be guilty of the violation in many instances irrespective of intent or knowledge.

When it comes, however, to such crimes as larceny, there enters as a necessary element the intent accompanying the act. There must be the intent to steal, to misappropriate, to apply the property of another to the use of the corporation to constitute the crime. The mere knowledge and intent of the agent of [or] the servant to steal would not be sufficient in and of itself to make the corporation guilty. While a corporation may be guilty of larceny, may be guilty of the intent to steal, the evidence must go further than in the cases involving solely the violation of prohibitive statutes. The intent must be the intent of the corporation and not merely that of the agent. How this intent may be proved or in what cases it becomes evident depends entirely upon the circumstances of each case. Probably no general rule applicable to all situations could be stated. It has been said that the same evidence which in a civil case would be sufficient to prove a specific or malicious intention upon the part of a corporation defendant would be sufficient to show a like intention upon the part of a corporation charged criminally with the doing of an act prohibited by law (U.S. v. Kelso Co., 86 F. 304), and Judge Hough in U.S. v. New York Herald Co., 159 F. 296, said: "To fasten this species of knowledge upon a corporation requires no other or different kind of legal inference than has long been used to justify punitive damages in cases of tort against an incorporated defendant." See, also, People v. Star Co., 135 App.Div. 517, 120 N.Y.S. 498, where the malicious intent of the agents in writing a libel was attributable to the corporation. See, also, Grant Bros. Construction Co. v. U.S., 13 Ariz. 388, 114 P. 955, and State v. Salisbury Ice & Fuel Co., 166 N.C. 366, 81 S.E. 737, involving false pretenses. Also Standard Oil Co. v. State, 117 Tenn. 618, 100 S.W. 705, where the intent of the officers became the intent of the corporation. Sufficient to say that in this case the law was correctly laid down to the jury by the trial judge when he said: "The defendant is liable in a prosecution for larceny only for acts which it authorizes through action of its officers or which is done with the acquiescence of its officers, and unless the jury find beyond a reasonable doubt such authority or acquiescence, there must be an acquittal." This in my judgment was a correct statement of the law for this case. . . .

In this case the able assistant district attorney, Mr. Marcy, recognized the rule and attempted to bring his evidence within it. He sought to prove that one of the officers of the corporation had given instructions to do the acts constituting larceny and he also sought to prove that there had been such a long-continued user of felonious practices as to prove knowledge or intent upon the part of the corporation. In his attempt to substantiate these elements of the crime, he was largely frustrated by the rulings of the trial judge.

At this point it may be well to state the facts in order to elucidate our meaning. The defendant was a domestic corporation known as Canadian Fur Trappers Corporation, carrying on the business of selling fur coats on the installment plan in Buffalo, N.Y., under the name of "Fields." Four brothers, named Dornfeldt, constituted the corporation and were its only officers. It advertised attractive sales during the summer of 1926. The prosecuting witness, Mrs. Ella Stanley, bought a coat at one of these sales for $295, paying a deposit of $25, the coat to be delivered to her upon payment of the balance. There was no time fixed in which the balance was to be paid. The evidence fairly shows that the defendant agreed to keep the coat in storage or on deposit for Mrs. Stanley until the balance was paid. Later in the fall when she paid the balance the coat was gone. It had been disposed of and there was evidence which would justify the jury in believing that some one in the defendant's employ had resold the coat. The defendant's employees and officers attempted to deliver to Mrs. Stanley another coat which they said was the one she had selected. In this they were evidently mistaken, if not willfully falsifying, as the coat was of a different size and make. The evidence is quite conclusive upon this point. There is also evidence to show that the coat which this defendant through its employees attempted to deliver to

Mrs. Stanley as the one purchased had been theretofore sold to Vera M. Owen. Whatever became of Mrs. Stanley's coat no one apparently knows. The fact is she did not receive it when she paid the balance of her money, and the coat which was offered to her was not the one she had selected. The evidence sustains this conclusion. Of course upon these facts alone, these two transactions, the defendant could not be found guilty of larceny as defined by our penal law. It is at this point the People, therefore, attempted to prove that the officers of the corporation had instructed the employees to resell the coats held on deposit and that this was the method of doing business. When a coat was purchased and the deposit paid, instead of keeping the coat for the purchaser, as the defendant promised to do, until the balance was paid, the course of business was to resell the coat many times and deliver it to whomever first paid the full purchase price. Such facts, if proved, would no doubt establish larceny by the corporation. The difficulty arises over the failure of this proof. . . .

This leaves the charge against the defendant resting upon the sale to Mrs. Stanley and the evidence of the resale or attempted resale later of Mrs. Owen's coat to Mrs. Stanley. The defendant's officers and employees denied that they had resold Mrs. Stanley's coat or that such was their method of doing business.

Under the law as correctly charged in this case by the trial judge, the defendant corporation was criminally liable only for such felonious acts as it had authorized through the Dornfeldts, the officers of the corporation, or for such acts as through a course of business must have been known to the corporation and its officers, and thus authorized by them. The People failed to prove that the officers or any one acting as manager of the Buffalo store, in the place and stead of the officers had authorized a resale of the complainant's coat; and further, that if the complainant's coat was resold, the resale of purchased coats was a continuous and established practice in the defendant's establishment. . . .

There are other rulings which we think were not quite correct, but it is unnecessary to refer to them, as in view of what is here said the judgment of the Appellate Division and that of the County Court should be reversed and a new trial ordered.

CARDOZO, C.J., POUND, ANDREWS, LEHMAN, KELLOGG and O'BRIEN, JJ., concur.

Judgments reversed, etc.[1]

1. A corporation is not guilty of the crime of extortion unless the act was authorized, requested, commanded, performed or recklessly tolerated by the board of directors or a high managerial agent acting on its behalf. State v. Adjustment Department Credit Bureau, 94 Idaho 156, 483 P.2d 687 (1971).

The president of a corporation is not criminally liable for the acts of his subordinate unless they are authorized or consented to by him. State v. Carmean, 126 Iowa 291, 102 N.W. 97 (1905). But the president of a corporation can be convicted, on proof by circumstantial evidence, that he aided and abetted his subordi-

MODEL PENAL CODE

Section 2.07 Liability of Corporations, Unincorporated Associations and Persons Acting, or Under a Duty to Act, in Their Behalf.

(1) A corporation may be convicted of the commission of an offense if:

(a) the offense is a violation or the offense is defined by a statute other than the Code in which a legislative purpose to impose liability on corporations plainly appears and the conduct is performed by an agent of the corporation acting in behalf of the corporation within the scope of his office or employment, except that if the law defining the offense designates the agents for whose conduct the corporation is accountable or the circumstances under which it is accountable, such provisions shall apply; or

(b) the offense consists of an omission to discharge a specific duty of affirmative performance imposed on corporations by law; or

(c) the commission of the offense was authorized, requested, commanded, performed or recklessly tolerated by the board of directors or by a high managerial agent acting in behalf of the corporation within the scope of his office or employment.

(2) When absolute liability is imposed for the commission of an offense, a legislative purpose to impose liability on a corporation shall be assumed, unless the contrary plainly appears.

(3) An unincorporated association may be convicted of the commission of an offense if:

(a) the offense is defined by a statute other than the Code which expressly provides for the liability of such an association and the conduct is performed by an agent of the association acting in behalf of the association within the scope of his office or employment, except that if the law defining the offense designates the agents for whose conduct the association is accountable or the circumstances under which it is accountable, such provisions shall apply; or

(b) the offense consists of an omission to discharge a specific duty of affirmative performance imposed on associations by law.

(4) As used in this Section:

(a) "corporation" does not include an entity organized as or by a governmental agency for the execution of a governmental program;

(b) "agent" means any director, officer, servant, employee or other person authorized to act in behalf of the corporation or association and, in the case of an unincorporated association, a member of such association;

(c) "high managerial agent" means an officer of a corporation or an unincorporated association, or, in the case of a partnership, a partner, or any other agent of a corporation or association having duties of such responsibility that his conduct may fairly be assumed to represent the policy of the corporation or association.

(5) In any prosecution of a corporation or an unincorporated association for the commission of an offense included within the terms of Subsection (1)

nates in their criminal activities. Nye & Nissen v. United States, 336 U.S. 613, 69 S.Ct. 766, 93 L.Ed. 919 (1949).

(a) or Subsection (3)(a) of this Section, other than an offense for which absolute liability has been imposed, it shall be a defense if the defendant proves by a preponderance of evidence that the high managerial agent having supervisory responsibility over the subject matter of the offense employed due diligence to prevent its commission. This paragraph shall not apply if it is plainly inconsistent with the legislative purpose in defining the particular offense.

(6)(a) A person is legally accountable for any conduct he performs or causes to be performed in the name of the corporation or an unincorporated association or in its behalf to the same extent as if it were performed in his own name or behalf.

(b) Whenever a duty to act is imposed by law upon a corporation or an unincorporated association, any agent of the corporation or association having primary responsibility for the discharge of the duty is legally accountable for a reckless omission to perform the required act to the same extent as if the duty were imposed by law directly upon himself.

(c) When a person is convicted of an offense by reason of his legal accountability for the conduct of a corporation or an unincorporated association, he is subject to the sentence authorized by law when a natural person is convicted of an offense of the grade and the degree involved.[a]

SECTION 8. PARTIES TO CRIME

The common law applied the label "accessory" to certain parties guilty of crime. This was in felony cases only. There was no accessory to treason or to misdemeanor. This has reference only to the label and not to the question of guilt. With one exception the party who would be called *accessory* in a felony case is a guilty *principal* in case of either treason or misdemeanor.[1] The lone exception is this: one who would be an accessory *after* the fact in a felony case is not regarded as a guilty party if the offense is a misdemeanor. He is a principal if it is treason.

In felony cases the ancient common law used the word principal to apply only to the perpetrator of the crime. Any other guilty party was an accessory. And based upon the elements of time and place, accessories were classified as (1) accessory before the fact, (2) accessory at the fact, and (3) accessory after the fact.[2] One who was not himself the perpetrator of the felony, but who counseled or commanded it, or encouraged or assisted the perpetrator in any way with guilty knowledge, was an accessory before the fact if not present at the perpetration and an accessory at the fact if present at that time. After the felony had been committed one, not himself the perpetrator[3] but having knowledge of the felony, who gave aid to the perpe-

1. State v. Scott, 80 Conn. 317, 323, 68 A. 258, 260 (1907).

2. Ibid.

3. "One who is a principal cannot be an accessory after the fact." People v. Chadwick, 7 Utah 134, 138, 25 P. 737, 738 (1891). One who would have been an accessory before the fact at common law probably may be accessory after the fact also, even if declared to be a principal by

trator in order to hinder his apprehension, trial, conviction or punishment, was an accessory after the fact.[4]

At a relatively early day a change was made in one of the labels used. The guilty party who anciently was called accessory at the fact came to be known as a principal in the second degree.[5] Hence the modern common law, in felony cases, recognizes two kinds of guilty parties and two varieties of each. Principals are either in the first degree or the second degree, and accessories are either before the fact or after the fact. The closest resemblance is between the principal in the second degree and the accessory before the fact. Exactly the same kind of guilty counsel, command, encouragement or aid which will make one a principal in the second degree, if present at the moment of perpetration, will make him an accessory before the fact if he is absent,[6]—except that factually more opportunities are available if he is present. This came to be the determining factor at this point of the classification scheme. One so situated as to be in a position to give actual assistance to the perpetrator, at the very moment of perpetration, is held to be present constructively if not actually.[7] Hence if one so situated is a guilty party he is a principal in the second degree even if his guilt consisted in counsel or encouragement given at a previous time. The typical case of a guilty party who is constructively present (and hence a principal in the second degree rather than an accessory before the fact) is the lookout who is posted on the outside of a building while another enters to commit a felony inside.[8] The most extreme example involved the hold-up of a stagecoach. One of the conspirators stationed himself on a mountain top, thirty or forty miles from the intended ambush and signaled the approach of the vehicle by smoke from a controlled fire. Because so situated as to be of assistance at the moment he was held to be a principal in the second degree.[9]

The law of accessories developed at a time when all felonies (except petit larceny) were punishable by death, and when statutes had made felonies out of a multitude of misdeeds not sufficiently grave to

statute. Cf. Aaronson v. United States, 175 F.2d 41 (4th Cir.1949). In order to avoid an absurd result in the interpretation of statutes dealing with the testimony of an accomplice, the California court felt it was necessary to say that a murderer can be accessory after the fact to his own murder. People v. Wallin, 32 Cal.2d 803, 197 P.2d 734 (1948). This is quite out of line with the body of the case law.

4. One who attempts to frustrate the prosecution of a murderer, by telling those present at the time of the crime not to tell what they know, is accessory after the fact. Fields v. State, 213 Ark. 899, 214 S.W.2d 230 (1948).

5. 1 Hale P.C. * 437.

6. Id. at p. 435.

7. 4 Bl.Comm. * 34. See Skidmore v. State, 80 Neb. 698, 700, 115 N.W. 288, 289 (1908).

"One who watches at a distance to prevent surprise while others commit a crime is deemed in law to be a principal and punishable as such." State v. Neil, 203 Kan. 473, 454 P.2d 136, 138 (1969).

One state provides for an "accessory during the fact". It is discussed in Martinez v. People, 166 Colo. 524, 444 P.2d 641 (1968).

8. Clark v. Commonwealth, 269 Ky. 833, 108 S.W.2d 1036 (1937).

9. State v. Hamilton, 13 Nev. 386 (1878).

merit such a penalty. It was one of several devices employed to reduce the number of capital convictions. These handicaps upon prosecution have been removed for the most part by modern statutes and hence will be stated very briefly. Chiefly they were: (1) Jurisdiction. A principal was triable at the situs of the crime,[10] but an accessory who incited the perpetration of a felony in another jurisdiction was triable only where his act of accessoryship occurred.[11] (2) Pleading. One charged as a principal could not be convicted if the evidence established accessorial guilt,[12] and one charged as accessory could not be convicted on proof showing him to be a principal.[13] (3) Trial. The accessory could not be forced to trial before the trial of the principal.[14] Hence if the principal was never apprehended, or died before conviction, or was acquitted, there was no possibility of convicting the accessory.[15] (4) Degree of guilt. An accessory could not be recognized as guilty of a higher crime than the principal.[16]

The fact that there was no need for such rules (other than to reduce the number of capital convictions) is shown by the fact that no corresponding rules applied to principals in different degrees. (1) Jurisdiction. Since the principal in the second degree is always present at the perpetration, constructively if not actually, his abetment (in legal theory) is always at the same place as the perpetration by the principal in the first degree. Hence the court having jurisdiction over the case of one principal will also have jurisdiction over that of the other.[17] (2) Pleading. It is not necessary for the indictment or information to disclose whether the defendant is a principal in one degree or the other.[18] (3) Trial. The principal in the second degree may be tried and convicted prior to the trial of the principal in the first degree,[19] or even after his acquittal.[20] (4) Degree of guilt. The principal in the second degree may be convicted of a higher degree of guilt

10. State v. Hall, 114 N.C. 909, 19 S.E. 602 (1894).

11. 1 Hale P.C. * 623.

By decisions of this Nation's courts . . . it has been held, consistent with the common law rule, that absent a statute which provides otherwise an accessory before the fact may be tried where the accessorial act took place and only there." Goldsmith v. Cheney, 468 P.2d 813, 816 (Wyo.1970).

12. Smith v. State, 37 Ark. 274 (1881); Skidmore v. State, 80 Neb. 698, 115 N.W. 288 (1908).

13. Regina v. Brown, 14 Cox C.C. 144 (1878).

14. 1 Hale P.C. * 623; 2 Pollock and Maitland, History of English Law 509 (2d ed.1899).

15. 1 Hale P.C. * 625. Commonwealth v. Phillips, 16 Mass. 423, 425 (1820).

16. 4 Bl.Comm. * 36; Tomlin v. State, 155 Tex.Cr.R. 207, 233 S.W.2d 303 (1950).

17. State v. Hamilton, 13 Nev. 386 (1878).

18. 1 Hale P.C. * 437–8; Adkins v. State, 187 Ga. 519, 1 S.E.2d 420 (1939).

19. 1 Hale P.C. * 437; Regina v. Griffeth, 1 Pl. 97, 75 Eng.Rep. 152 (1553).

20. Regina v. Wallis, 1 Salk. 334, 91 Eng.Rep. 294 (1703); Rooney v. United States, 203 F. 928 (9th Cir.1913); People v. Newberry, 20 Cal. 439 (1862); State v. Lee, 91 Iowa 499, 60 N.W. 119 (1894); State v. Phillips, 24 Mo. 475 (1857). And see People v. Blackwood, 35 Cal.App.2d 728, 733, 96 P.2d 982 (1939). Contra: State v. Haines, 51 La.Ann. 731, 25 So. 372 (1899). The trend of the modern statutes is in the direction of permitting an accessory to be convicted after the acquittal of the principal. The guilt of the principal must be shown in order to convict the accessory but the previous ac-

than the principal in the first degree. The former may be convicted of murder, for example, although the latter has been convicted of manslaughter,[21] since an abettor may counsel with malice aforethought what the other perpetrates in the sudden heat of passion.[22] In other words, the designation of a principal as of one degree or the other is merely a factual description without legal significance.[23] The accessory before the fact to a felony is often the "man higher up" who is more of a social menace than the underlings he employs. There is no sound reason why he should not be called a "principal," and treated as such for all purposes, just as he would be if the crime were treason or misdemeanor. The law in most jurisdictions is now to this effect.

With reference to the accessory after the fact the problem is somewhat different. Although anciently his punishment was the same as that of the principal,[24] provisions for a milder penalty made their appearance at a very early day.[25] The present law is to retain the label "accessory after fact" in some jurisdictions whereas in others the offense is labeled an "obstruction of justice or governmental operation," [26] the trend is to remove procedural obstacles [27] from the prosecution and conviction of such a party, provide a milder punishment than that established for the principal, and exclude from this type of guilt those who are intimately related to the principal.

Differences are to be found in the enactments and in their interpretation. And to what extent, if any, the present law of a particular state falls short of the trends mentioned, in regard to one type of accessory or the other, can be determined only by a study of its statutes and decisions.

In outline form the character of the party (1) and the name applied (2) may be indicated as follows:

A. (1) The actual perpetrator of the crime:

(2) Felony—principal in the first degree. Treason—principal. Misdemeanor—principal.

quittal of the principal is not *res judicata* of the principal's innocence as between the commonwealth and the accused. Commonwealth v. Long, 246 Ky. 809, 56 S.W.2d 524 (1933).

The fact that no principal was ever identified and convicted did not preclude defendant's conviction for aiding and abetting where the prosecution proved the substantive offense had been committed by someone. United States v. Campa, 679 F.2d 1006 (1st Cir.1982).

21. 1 Hale P.C. * 438; Bruce v. State, 99 Ga. 50, 25 S.E. 760 (1896); State v. McAllister, 366 So.2d 1340 (La.1978).

22. 1 East P.C. 350 (1803).

23. "[T]he distinction between principals in the first and second degrees is a distinction without a difference." State v. Whitt, 113 N.C. 716, 720, 18 S.E. 715, 719 (1893). Quoting from Wharton on Criminal Law.

24. 4 Bl.Comm. * 39.

25. A number of the early statutes denied benefit of clergy to the principal and to the accessory before, without extending such denial to the accessory after. Ibid.

26. See § 242.3 and .4 Model Penal Code (1962).

27. People v. Williams, 117 Mich.App. 505, 324 N.W.2d 70 (1982).

B. (1) One not the actual perpetrator who, with mens rea, counsels or commands the other to commit the crime, or gives him any encouragement or assistance in doing so, and is present actually or constructively at the moment of perpetration: [28]

(2) Felony—principal in the second degree. Treason—principal. Misdemeanor—principal.

C. (1) Same, except not present either actually or constructively at the moment of perpetration:

(2) Felony—accessory before the fact, at common law, with the statutory trend in the direction of applying the label "principal". Treason—principal. Misdemeanor—principal.

D. (1) One not the perpetrator who, with knowledge of the crime, gives aid or comfort to the perpetrator in the effort to hinder his apprehension, trial, conviction or punishment:

(2) Felony—accessory after the fact. Treason—principal. Misdemeanor—not a guilty party without additional facts.

The word "accomplice" is a broader word than either "principal" or "accessory". There is some authority for using the word accomplice to include all principals and all accessories to a particular crime. The preferred usage, however, is to include all principals and all accessories before the fact, but to exclude accessories after the fact,[29] except that one accessory after the fact might be the accomplice of another accessory after the fact to the same felony.

Under statute, one who at common law would have been either a principal in the first degree, a principal in the second degree or an accessory before the fact, is a principal; and an accessory under the statute is one who would have been an accessory after the fact at common law.[30]

28. The mere fact that a bystander does not interfere in the effort to prevent a murder being committed in his presence does not make him a guilty party to the murder. Connaughty v. State, 1 Wis. 159 (1853). It is otherwise if the bystander owes a duty to protect the victim of the attack. Mobley v. State, 227 Ind. 335, 85 N.E.2d 489 (1949).

G, who knew before the building was entered that his cohorts intended to commit rape, and who wandered through the building looking for things to steal while the rape was being perpetrated, was guilty of aiding and abetting the rape. People v. Gray, 121 Mich.App. 788, 329 N.W.2d 493 (1983).

29. See Levering v. Commonwealth, 132 Ky. 666, 677, 679, 117 S.W. 253, 257 (1909); People v. Sweeney, 213 N.Y. 37, 46, 106 N.E. 913, 917 (1914); People v. Chadwick, 7 Utah 134, 25 P. 737 (1891).

30. Wilson v. State, 552 P.2d 1404 (Okl.Cr.1976).

PEOPLE v. AH GEE

District Court of Appeal, Third Appellate District, California, 1918.
37 Cal.App. 1, 174 P. 371.

HART, J. Defendant and two others, Toy Lee and Foo Kee, were jointly charged, in an information filed by the district attorney of San Joaquin County, with the murder of one Lee Wun, in the city of Stockton, on March 21, 1917. Separate trials of the defendants were had and Ah Gee was convicted of the crime of murder of the first degree and was sentenced to imprisonment in the state prison for the term of his natural life. The appeal is from the judgment and from an order denying defendant's motion for a new trial.

The record discloses that Lee Wun met his death during a tong war. He and the three defendants above named were engaged in the shooting and Foo Kee testified that he was fired upon by one Lim Buck Hee.

There is but one point urged for a reversal and it is this: That the prosecution presented its case upon two distinct and inconsistent theories, to wit: 1. That the defendant aided, abetted, and assisted Toy Lee in the murder of Lee Wun and 2. That Ah Gee himself actually killed and murdered said Lee Wun. In support of this proposition, appellant calls attention to the testimony of the witnesses, C.W. Potter and A.F. Peterson, who testified to having been eyewitnesses to the homicide and who gave testimony for the people. . . .

According to the testimony of Potter, so the argument goes, the defendant, having fired two unavailing shots at the deceased and then ran [sic] away or disappeared from the scene of the homicide, merely aided, abetted, and assisted Toy Lee in the commission of the crime, while, on the other hand, according to the testimony of Peterson, the defendant actually fired the shot which produced the death of Lee Wun. Hence, so the argument proceeds, there were presented by the people two inconsistent theories of the part taken by the defendant in the commission of the crime, and this, it is claimed, is fatal to the result reached by the jury.

The position of the defendant, as above set forth, is not well taken.

Under the common law, a principal in the commission of a crime was of two degrees, viz.: 1. One who was the actual actor or absolute perpetrator of the crime, who was a principal in the first degree; 2. One who was present, actually or constructively, aiding and abetting the fact to be done, who was a principal in the same [sic] degree. (4 Cooley's Blackstone, 4th ed., p. 34.) One who, being absent at the time of the crime committed, procured, counseled, or commanded another to commit the crime, was an accessory before the fact, and under the common law it was necessary to prosecute, try, and punish him as such accessory and not as a principal. (Id., p. 37). The distinction between a principal in the second degree and an accessory before the fact, it will be observed, was founded upon the presence or nonpresence at the commission of the crime of the party aiding and abetting the actual perpetrator of the act which constituted the final consummation of the crime in its commission. . . .

Thus, undoubtedly, our legislature viewed the proposition and, therefore, by express mandate, has abrogated the mere formal distinction (and it was no more than this) existing at common law between principals in the commission of crimes and accessories before the fact, or those participating in their commission without actually perpetrating the acts which, with the intent, constitute the crime. Therefore, whatever may be the law in other jurisdictions, the rule in this state, as laid down by the legislature, is that "all persons concerned in the commission of a crime, whether it be felony or misdemeanor, *and whether they directly commit the act constituting the offense, or aid and abet in its commission, or, not being present, have advised and encouraged its commission,* . . . are principals in any crime so committed." (Pen.Code, sec. 31.) Again, the rule, as promulgated by the legislature, is that "the distinction between an accessory before the fact and a principal, and between principals in the first and second degree, in cases of felony, is abrogated; and all persons concerned in the commission of a felony, *whether they directly commit the act constituting the offense, or aid and abet in its commission, though not present,* shall hereafter be *prosecuted, tried* and punished as principals, and no other facts need be alleged in any indictment or information against such an accessory than are required in an indictment or information against his principal." (Pen.Code, sec. 971.). . . .

Under our code sections, above quoted herein, an accessory is not only to be charged in the accusatory pleading as a principal, but is also to be *tried* as a principal; hence it is immaterial what the proof shows was the nature of the part that the accused took in the commission of the crime—that is, it is not a matter of material importance whether he is shown to have been the actual perpetrator of the criminal act or only aided and abetted in its commission. In either case, he is a principal, and it can make no difference in the proof of the charge what particular act he did or part he took in the execution of the criminal act that made him one.

In the present case, the defendant, jointly with two others, is charged in the information with the murder of Lee Wun. There is but one count in the information and that is the usual or common one by which murder, as defined by the law, is charged. There is no attempt at describing how or in what manner the act was committed or any allegation that the defendant was merely an aider and abettor of the crime, an allegation which is not required under our law. The prosecution was entitled to prove the charge by any testimony which would reveal the defendant's connection therewith. It happened that, while one of the witnesses presented by the people to support the charge testified that he saw the defendant fire a shot into the body of Lee Wun, another witness, likewise presented, testified that the accused fired a couple of shots at the deceased, which apparently failed of their mark, and then disappeared from the scene of the shooting. Even according to the common law, the defendant would be a principal under the testimony of the witness Potter. But the testimony of both witnesses was material, relevant, and competent, and, therefore, clearly admissible in any event as tending to prove the ultimate fact in issue, viz.: That the defendant killed and murdered Lee Wun. Indeed, the objection to the testimony on the ground that it tended to establish two different theories upon which the defendant might have been a participant in the commission of the crime does not go to the proposition that said testimony does not show, or tend to show, the guilt of the accused of the crime charged but to the proposition that he was a party to the commission of the crime in two different ways. As we view the situation, the proposition is no different in principle from a case where one witness for the people had testified that the deceased had been killed by a blow with a club in the hands of and wielded by the defendant, while another witness for the people had testified that the death of the deceased had been produced by the defendant by means of a knife, the particular manner in which death was produced not being alleged in the indictment.

But, as stated, the people had the right to make the proof as it was made and leave to the judgment of the jury the question whether upon the whole the evidence was of sufficient probative force to warrant the conviction in their minds that, beyond a reasonable doubt, the defendant, whatever might have been the nature or extent of the part he might have taken in the commission of the act, was guilty as charged. . . .

The judgment and the order are affirmed.[1]

CHIPMAN, P.J., and BURNETT, J., concurred.

1. One who comes under the complicity statute is equivalent to a principal. People v. Saiz, 42 Colo.App. 469, 600 P.2d 97 (1979). One may be convicted of voluntary manslaughter as an accessory before the fact although the perpetrator has been convicted of murder in the first degree. Moore v. Lowe, Sheriff, 116 W.Va. 165, 180 S.E. 1 (1935), certiorari denied 296 U.S. 574, 56 S.Ct. 130, 80 L.Ed. 406. Cf. State v. McVay, 47 R.I. 292, 132 A. 436 (1926).

"In order to sustain the conviction of a defendant who had been charged as an aider or abettor, it is necessary that there be evidence showing an offense to have been committed by a principal and that the principal was aided and abetted by the accused, although it is not necessary that the principal be convicted or even that the identity of the principal be established." Hendrix v. United States, 327 F.2d 971, 975 (5th Cir.1964).

The principal need not be identified. United States v. Campa, 679 F.2d 1006 (1st Cir.1982).

Although the proof established that **D**, who was charged with robbery, aided and abetted another to commit the robbery, there was no fatal variance and the conviction of robbery was proper. McWilliams v. State, 87 Nev. 302, 486 P.2d 481 (1971).

A petition to have the cause heard in the supreme court, after judgment in the district court of appeal, was denied by the supreme court on June 14, 1918.

PEOPLE v. KEEFER

Supreme Court of California, Department One, 1884.
65 Cal. 232, 3 P. 818.

McKINSTRY, J. Counsel for defendant asked the court to charge the jury:

"If you believe from the evidence that the defendant James Keefer was not present when the Chinaman *Lee Yuen* was killed by *Chapman,* and did not aid and abet in the killing, and that defendant, at the time or prior to the killing, had not conspired with *Chapman* to commit the act, and that he had not advised and encouraged *Chapman* therein, and that the killing was not done in pursuance of any conspiracy between this defendant and *Chapman* to rob said Chinaman, and that this defendant only assisted in throwing the dead body of the Chinaman into the creek, then you are instructed that, under the indictment, you must find the defendant not guilty."

It is to be regretted that the foregoing instruction was not given to the jury. Of course, if defendant had done no act which made him responsible for the murder, the mere fact that he aided in concealing the dead body would render him liable only as accessory after the fact—an offense of which he could not be found guilty under an indictment for murder.[1] However incredible the testimony of defendant he was undoubtedly entitled to an instruction based upon the hypothesis that his testimony was entirely true.

Assuming the testimony of defendant to be true, there was evidence tending to show that no robbery was committed or attempted. In robbery, as in larceny, it must appear that the goods were taken

To convict **D** as an aider and abettor in the commission of a crime it is necessary to prove that the crime was committed by a principal and that **D** aided and abetted the principal in the perpetration. If this is proved beyond a reasonable doubt it is not material that the principal was acquitted in a separate trial. The miscarriage of justice in the other trial does not require a miscarriage in this. State v. Spillman, 105 Ariz. 523, 468 P.2d 376 (1970).

"Neither fairness nor justice argue for allowing these aiders and abettors to escape responsibility for their criminal activity merely because their respective principals have escaped punishment." United States v. Standefer, 610 F.2d 1076, 1090 (3d Cir.1979).

1. Proof that **D** destroyed other counterfeit bills after one had been passed might be sufficient to convict her as accessory after the fact to the uttering but she was not charged as accessory. Roberts v. United States, 416 F.2d 1216 (5th Cir.1969).

Evidence which established that the defendant had knowledge of the perpetrator's criminal purpose and entered a store and stood unarmed observing the action in robbing the store was sufficient to support a conviction that the defendant aided and abetted the robbery. People v. Sims, 136 Cal.App.3d 942, 186 Cal. Rptr. 793 (1982).

Although defendant took no part in a drug exchange where he set up the transaction and quoted a price he could properly be convicted as an aider and abettor. United States v. Winston, 687 F.2d 832 (6th Cir.1982).

animo furandi; and there was evidence tending to prove that his property was not taken from deceased *lucri causa,* or with intent to deprive him of it permanently. So also there was evidence tending to prove that defendant was not personally present at the killing, and that the killing was not done in pursuance of any agreement or understanding to which defendant was a party, but that it was done by Chapman without the knowledge, assent, or connivance of the defendant.

The testimony of defendant was to the effect that he did not advise or encourage Chapman to follow and *tie* the deceased. But even if we could be supposed to be justified in deciding the *fact,* in holding that his conduct conclusively proved—notwithstanding his testimony to the contrary—that he did encourage Chapman in his purpose to follow and tie the deceased, such encouragement would not of itself, make him accessory to the killing. An accessory before the fact to a robbery (or any other of the felonies mentioned in section 198 of the Penal Code), although not present when the felony is perpetrated or attempted, is guilty of a murder committed in the perpetration or attempt to perpetrate the felony. This is by reason of the statute, and because the law super-adds the intent to kill to the original felonious intent. One who has only advised or encouraged a misdemeanor, however, is not *necessarily* responsible for a murder committed by his co-conspirator, not in furtherance, but independent of the common design.

In the case at bar, if defendant simply encouraged the *tying* of the deceased—a misdemeanor which did not and probably could not cause death or any serious injury—as the killing by Chapman was neither necessarily nor probably involved in the battery or false imprisonment, nor incidental to it, but was an independent and malicious act with which defendant had no connection, the jury were not authorized to find defendant guilty of the murder, or of manslaughter. If the deceased had been strangled by the cords with which he had been carelessly or recklessly bound by Chapman, or had died in consequence of exposure to the elements while tied, defendant might have been held liable. But, if the testimony of defendant was true—and as we have said, he was entitled to an instruction based upon the assumption that the facts were as he stated them to be—the killing of deceased was an independent act of Chapman, neither aided, advised, nor encouraged by him, and not involved in nor incidental to any act by him aided, advised, or encouraged. The court erred in refusing the instruction. . . .

Judgment and order reversed and cause remanded for a new trial.

ROSS, J., concurring. As there was testimony tending to show that defendant was not personally present at the killing, and that the killing was not done in pursuance of any agreement or undertaking to which defendant was a party, I agree that the court below erred in refusing to give the instruction first set out in the opinion of MR.

JUSTICE MCKINSTRY, and therefore concur in the judgment. I also agree with what is said in the opinion upon the last point discussed.

MCKEE, J., concurred in the opinion of MR. JUSTICE ROSS.[2]

STATE v. WILLIAMS

Supreme Court of North Carolina, 1948.
229 N.C. 348, 49 S.E.2d 617.

The defendants were indicted for being accessories after the fact to the felony of the murder of Thompson Hooker by Bud Hicks. The indictment contained the specific allegation that the aid rendered to the principal offender, Bud Hicks, by the defendants consisted in transporting him from the scene of his crime for the purpose of enabling him to escape apprehension and punishment.

Testimony was presented at the trial by both the prosecution and the defense. This evidence is stated below in the light most favorable to the State.

On the afternoon of Sunday, June 6, 1948, Bud Hicks deliberately shot and wounded Thompson Hooker without provocation while the latter was standing before his doorstep at 404 Ramseur Street in Sanford. Immediately after the shooting, Hicks fled from Sanford to a rural section of Lee County in an automobile owned by himself and driven by the defendant, Prentiss Watson. Hicks and Watson were accompanied on this flight by the defendants, Annie Williams and Elizabeth Badgett. Peace officers found Hicks and his companions at the home of Annie Williams in a country neighborhood in Lee County at a later hour of the afternoon. Hicks, Watson, and Annie Williams thereupon sought unsuccessfully to dissuade the officers from arresting Hicks by falsely representing that Hicks had not been in Sanford any time that day. After all these events had transpired, namely, on Monday, June 7, 1948, Thompson Hooker died in consequence of his gun-shot wound.

Elizabeth Badgett was acquitted, but the jury found Annie Williams and Prentiss Watson guilty as charged in the bill of indictment. Judgment was pronounced against both of these parties. Watson accepted his sentence, and Annie Williams appealed to this Court, assigning as error the denial of her motion for judgment of nonsuit made when the State rested its case and renewed when all the evidence was concluded.

ERVIN, JUSTICE. When the State prosecutes one upon the charge of being an accessory after the fact to the felony of murder, it assumes the burden of proving the three essential elements of the offense, namely: (1) That the principal felon had actually committed the

2. If an officer is disarmed, and killed with his own weapon, one who had assisted in the disarming is not guilty of murder if he did not know, or have reason to know, that shooting was intended. Lee v. State, 152 Tex.Cr.R. 401, 214 S.W.2d 619 (1948).

felony of murder; (2) that the accused knew that such felony had been committed by the principal felon; and (3) that the accused received, relieved, comforted, or assisted the principal felon in some way in order to help him escape, or to hinder his arrest, trial, or punishment. . . .

In the nature of things, one cannot become an accessory after the fact to a felony until such felony has become an accomplished fact. Consequently, it is well established in law that "one cannot be convicted as an accessory after the fact unless the felony be complete, and until such felony has been consummated, any aid or assistance rendered to a party in order to enable him to escape the consequences of his crime will not make the person affording the assistance an accessory after the fact." . . .

Thus, it is held that a person cannot be convicted as an accessory after the fact to a murder because he aided the murderer to escape, when the aid was rendered after the mortal wound was given, but before death ensued, as a murder is not complete until the death results. . . .

Such is the instant case. The evidence disclosed that the assistance, which was alleged to have been rendered by the appellant, Annie Williams, with intent to enable the principal felon, Bud Hicks, to escape, was given after Thompson Hooker had been mortally wounded, but before he died. Hence, the testimony showed that the felony of murder was not an accomplished fact when the assistance was given, and the Court erred in denying the appellant's motion for judgment of involuntary nonsuit. G.S. § 15–173.

The statute provides for punishment for any person becoming an accessory after the fact to any felony, "whether the same be a felony at common law or by virtue of any statute made, or to be made." G.S. § 14–7. Since no such charge is laid in the present indictment, we refrain from expressing any opinion as to whether the evidence made out a case for the jury against the appellant as an accessory after the fact to the statutory felony of a secret assault under G.S. § 14–31 or the statutory felony of an assault with intent to kill under G.S. § 14–32. But it is noted that there are at least two interesting decisions in other States in which similar problems are considered. . . .

For the reasons stated, the judgment pronounced against the appellant, Annie Williams, in the court below is

Reversed.[1]

1. Aid to the felon in the form of supplying him with a false alibi is sufficient to make the aider guilty of the felony as accessory after the fact. People v. Duty, 269 Cal.App.2d 97, 74 Cal.Rptr. 606 (1969).

D, having seen the murder committed, concealed the murder weapon and gave the officers false evidence as to the killing, intending to throw suspicion away from the killer. **D**'s conviction of being "an accessory after the fact to murder" was affirmed. Self v. People, 167 Colo. 292, 448 P.2d 619 (1968. Rehearing denied Jan. 13, 1969).

STATE v. TRUESDELL

Court of Criminal Appeals of Oklahoma, 1980.
620 P.2d 427.

BUSSEY, JUDGE. The State has appealed to this Court from a ruling of the District Court in Nowata County, dismissing Case No. CRF–79–41. In that case Zola V. Truesdell was charged with being an accessory to the crime of Shooting With the Intent to Kill after her ex-husband was shot ten times by their twelve-year-old son. There was a preliminary hearing and she was ordered to be held for trial, but at a subsequent motion hearing a district judge ruled that a juvenile cannot commit a felony and that therefore there was no crime to which Ms. Truesdell could have been an accessory. . . .

In Oklahoma, all parties to a crime are either principals or accessories after the fact. The elements of the crime of accessory after the fact are that the predicate felony be completed, that the offender have knowledge that the person she's aiding (the principal) committed the crime, and that the accessory conceal or aid the principal. Title 21 O.S.1971, § 173. This Court has held that an accessory is not connected with the offender after the original offense has been committed. Thus, the crime of accessory after the fact is a separate and distinct crime, standing on its own particular elements. And because accessory after the fact is a separate and distinct crime, a conviction of the principal is not a condition precedent to the conviction of an accessory after the fact.

Accordingly, the fact that the principal, the Truesdell child, was not charged with the assault has no bearing on whether Ms. Truesdell has committed the crime of accessory after the fact. The fact that the principal is a minor goes to his legal status, not his factual status, and it is immaterial as to the guilt or innocence of the defendant on the charge of accessory after the fact. A conviction of accessory after the fact depends on whether there is sufficient evidence presented to show that there was a principal who was guilty of the crime charged, regardless of whether or not the principal was ever charged with the criminal offense. Britto v. People, supra. Thus it was error for the District Court to dismiss the case.

CORNISH, P.J., and BRETT, J., concur in results.

BRETT, JUDGE: concurring in results.

I concur that the trial court order be reversed and this matter be remanded for further proceedings. It is clear that the trial court sus-

"It was incumbent upon the Government to prove three essential elements to establish the offense charged (accessory after the fact to bank robbery). It was required to prove first, that Jay Rux committed the bank robbery; second, that appellant had actual knowledge of Jay's participation in the robbery; and third, that with such knowledge appellant in some way assisted Jay in order to hinder or prevent his apprehension, trial or punishment." United States v. Rux, 412 F.2d 331 (9th Cir.1969).

tained defendant's motion to quash the information. That order has been properly appealed under the provisions of 22 O.S.1971, § 1053. Clearly Laws 1977, c. 42, § 1, 21 O.S.Supp.1977, § 652, now, 21 O.S. Supp.1979, § 652, defines the offense of Shooting With Intent to Kill. 21 O.S.1971, § 173, defines the offense of being an Accessory. The Juvenile Code in Title 10, is a procedural statute describing treatment of a juvenile who commits an offense that would be a felony if committed by an adult.

Therefore, insofar as the reason given for sustaining defendant's motion ("the Court finds that the commission by a juvenile of a felony cannot be the predicate act for accessory to commit said felony as set out in the instant information") was in error, I agree that this matter be REVERSED and REMANDED for further proceedings.[1]

THE KING v. RICHARDSON

Old Bailey, 1785.
1 Leach 387, 168 Eng.Rep. 296.

At the Old Bailey in June Session 1785, Daniel Richardson and Samuel Greenow were indicted before Mr. Justice Buller for a highway robbery on John Billings.

It appeared in evidence, that the two prisoners accosted the prosecutor as he was walking along the street, by asking him, in a peremptory manner, what money he had in his pocket? that upon his replying that he had only two-pence half-penny, one of the prisoners immediately said to the other, "if he really has no more do not take that," and turned as if with an intention to go away; but the other prisoner, stopped the prosecutor, and robbed him of the two-pence half-penny, which was all the money he had about him. But the prosecutor could not ascertain which of them it was that had used this expression, nor which of them had taken the half-pence from his pocket.

THE COURT. The point of law goes to the acquittal of both the prisoners; for if two men assault another with intent to rob him, and one of them, before any demand of money, or offer to take it be made, repent of what he is doing, and desist from the prosecution of

1. A person not a state official may be guilty of the crime of embezzling public funds if he aids and abets an official in this act. People v. Hess, 104 Cal.App. 2d 642, 234 P.2d 65 (1951).

Although only a minor can be guilty of the offense of being a minor in possession of alcoholic liquor, one not a minor may be guilty of aiding and abetting a minor in the commission of that offense. State v. Norman, 193 Neb. 719, 229 N.W.2d 55 (1975).

Former § 262 of the California Penal Code precluded conviction of rape by one under 16 at the time of the act "unless his physical ability to accomplish penetration is proved as an independent fact, and beyond a reasonable doubt." This meant that it be proved "independently of the testimony of the rape victim. . . ." This might be established by physical evidence of seminal fluid and sperm in a victim who had not had sexual intercourse with anyone other than the defendant. In re Tony C., 21 Cal.3d 888, 148 Cal. Rptr. 366, 582 P.2d 957 (1978).

such intent, he cannot be involved in the guilt of his companion who afterwards takes the money; for he changed his evil intention before the act, which completes the offence, was committed. That prisoner therefore, whichever of the two it was who thus desisted, cannot be guilty of the present charge; and the prosecutor cannot ascertain who it was that took the property. One of them is certainly guilty, but which of them personally does not appear. It is like the Ipswich case, where five men were indicted for murder; and it appeared, on a special verdict, that it was murder in one, but not in the other four; but it did not appear which of the five had given the blow which caused the death, and the Court thereupon said, that as the man could not be clearly and positively ascertained, all of them must be discharged.

The two prisoners were accordingly acquitted.[1]

MODEL PENAL CODE

Section 2.06 Liability for Conduct of Another; Complicity.

(1) A person is guilty of an offense if it is committed by his own conduct or by the conduct of another person for which he is legally accountable, or both.

(2) A person is legally accountable for the conduct of another person when:

(a) acting with the kind of culpability that is sufficient for the commission of the offense, he causes an innocent or irresponsible person to engage in such conduct; or

(b) he is made accountable for the conduct of such other person by the Code or by the law defining the offense; or

(c) he is an accomplice of such other person in the commission of the offense.

(3) A person is an accomplice of another person in the commission of an offense if:

(a) with the purpose of promoting or facilitating the commission of the offense, he

(i) solicits such other person to commit it; or

(ii) aids or agrees or attempts to aid such other person in planning or committing it; or

(iii) having a legal duty to prevent the commission of the offense, fails to make proper effort so to do; or

(b) his conduct is expressly declared by law to establish his complicity.

(4) When causing a particular result is an element of an offense, an accomplice in the conduct causing such result is an accomplice in the commis-

1. If two conspire to commit robbery, and the victim is killed in the prosecution of the common design, both are guilty of murder even if the slayer had assured the other that there would be no killing. Miller v. State, 25 Wis. 384 (1870).

A counseled **D** to murder **X.** **D** killed **Y,** mistaking him for **X.** **A** was held to be an accessory to the murder of **Y.** State v. Kennedy, 85 S.C. 146, 67 S.E. 152 (1909).

sion of that offense, if he acts with the kind of culpability, if any, with respect to that result that is sufficient for the commission of the offense.

(5) A person who is legally incapable of committing a particular offense himself may be guilty thereof if it is committed by the conduct of another person for which he is legally accountable, unless such liability is inconsistent with the purpose of the provision establishing his incapacity.

(6) Unless otherwise provided by the Code or by the law defining the offense, a person is not an accomplice in an offense committed by another person if:

(a) he is a victim of that offense; or

(b) the offense is so defined that his conduct is inevitably incident to its commission; or

(c) he terminates his complicity prior to the commission of the offense and

(i) wholly deprives it of effectiveness in the commission of the offense; or

(ii) gives timely warning to the law enforcement authorities or otherwise makes proper effort to prevent the commission of the offense.

(7) An accomplice may be convicted on proof of the commission of the offense and of his complicity therein, though the person claimed to have committed the offense has not been prosecuted or convicted or has been convicted of a different offense or degree of offense or has an immunity to prosecution or conviction or has been acquitted.

Section 242.3 Hindering Apprehension or Prosecution.

A person commits an offense if, with purpose to hinder the apprehension, prosecution, conviction or punishment of another for crime, he:

(1) harbors or conceals the other; or

(2) provides or aids in providing a weapon, transportation, disguise or other means of avoiding apprehension or effecting escape; or

(3) conceals or destroys evidence of the crime, or tampers with a witness, informant, document or other source of information, regardless of its admissibility in evidence; or

(4) warns the other of impending discovery or apprehension, except that this paragraph does not apply to a warning given in connection with an effort to bring another into compliance with law; or

(5) volunteers false information to a law enforcement officer.

The offense is a felony of the third degree if the conduct which the actor knows has been charged or is liable to be charged against the person aided would constitute a felony of the first or second degree. Otherwise it is a misdemeanor.

Section 242.4 Aiding Consummation of Crime.

A person commits an offense if he purposely aids another to accomplish an unlawful object of a crime, as by safeguarding the proceeds thereof or converting the proceeds into negotiable funds. The offense is a felony of the third degree if the principal offense was a felony of the first or second degree. Otherwise it is a misdemeanor.

Section 242.5 Compounding.

A person commits a misdemeanor if he accepts or agrees to accept any pecuniary benefit in consideration of refraining from reporting to law enforcement authorities the commission or suspected commission of any offense or information relating to an offense. It is an affirmative defense to prosecution under this Section that the pecuniary benefit did not exceed an amount which the actor believed to be due as restitution or indemnification for harm caused by the offense.[1]

SECTION 9. CAUSATION

"Starting with a human act, we must next find a causal relation between the act and the harmful result; for in our law—and, it is believed, in any civilized law—liability cannot be imputed to a man unless it is in some degree a result of his act." Beale, The Proximate Consequences of An Act, 33 Harv.L.Rev. 633, 637 (1920).

"As the law of evidence excludes much that is evidential, the law of causation excludes much that is consequential." Edgerton, Legal Cause, 72 U. of Pa.Law Rev. 343, 344 (1924).

"John Stuart Mill, in his work on logic 9th Eng.Ed. 378–383 says, in substance, that the cause of an event is the sum of all the antecedents, and that we have no right to single out one antecedent and call that the cause. . . . The question is not what philosophers or logicians will say is the cause. The question is what the courts will regard as the cause." Jeremiah Smith, Legal Cause in Actions of Tort, 25 Harv.Law Rev. 103, 104 (1911).

"It would seem too clear for argument that considerations of fairness or justice have a bearing." McLaughlin, Proximate Cause, 39 Harv.Law Rev. 149, 155 (1925).

"It has been said that an act which in no way contributed to the result in question cannot be a cause of it; but this, of course, does not mean that an event which *might* have happened in the same way though the defendant's act or omission had not occurred, is not a result of it. The question is not what would have happened, but what did happen." Beale, The Proximate Consequences of An Act, 33 Harv.Law Rev 633, 638 (1920).

"Here is the key to the juridical treatment of the problems of causation. We pick out the cause which in our judgment ought to be treated as the dominant one with reference, not merely to the event itself, but to the jural consequences that ought to attach to the event." Cardozo, The Parodoxes of Legal Science, 83 (1928).

The line of demarkation between causes which will be recognized as "proximate" and those disregarded as "remote" "is really a flexible line." I Street, Foundations of Legal Liability, 111 (1906).

"There are no cases where it can be truthfully said that legal cause exists where cause in fact does not though it may happen by reason of relaxation of proof that liability will be imposed in cases where cause in fact is not by the ordinary rules of proof shown to exist." Carpenter, Workable Rules for Determining Proximate Cause, 20 Cal.Law Rev. 396, 407 (1932).

"A primary requisite to either criminal or civil liability is that the act of the defendant be the cause in fact of the injury. This requirement is embodied in the familiar *causa sine qua non* rule, generally called the 'but for' rule. This test generally is satisfactory when applied in negative form, and it is a basic principle that a defendant is not liable unless the injury would not have resulted but for his wrongful act. But as an affirmative test the 'but for' rule provides no infallible standard and does not constitute a fair test of liability in the absence of further qualifications. . . .

"The modern authorities, while agreed that the 'but for' test is inadequate differ materially in their concepts of proximate causation. The theories conveniently may be placed into two groups. One group seeks the necessary connection between the result and the act; the other, between the result and the actor's mind." Focht, Proximate Cause In the Law of Homicide—With Special Reference To California Cases, 12 So.Cal.L.Rev. 19, 20–21 (1938).

"There are three, and only three, tests of proximateness, namely, intention, probability and the non-intervention of an independent cause.

"Any intended consequence of an act is proximate. It would plainly be absurd that a person should be allowed to act with an intention to produce a certain consequence, and then when that very consequence in fact follows his act, to escape liability for it on the plea that it was not proximate.

"Probability . . . is a name for some one's opinion or guess as to whether a consequence will result. . . .

"The person whose opinion is taken is a reasonable and prudent man in the situation of the actor. . . .

"The third test of proximateness is the non-intervention of an independent cause between the original cause and the consequence in question. . . . Therefore it will be convenient to call it an isolating cause." Terry, Proximate Consequences in the Law of Torts, 28 Harv.L.Rev. 10, 17–20 (1914).[1]

1. "A cause must be the efficient, commonly called the proximate, cause or it is not a cause at all in law". State v. Osmus, 73 Wyo. 183, 276 P.2d 469, 474 (1954).

If **D** intentionally pointed a loaded and cocked gun at deceased who was killed by a discharge thereof, **D** is the legally-recognized cause of the death even if the discharge resulted when the other grabbed for the gun. State v. Madden, 104 Ariz. 111, 449 P.2d 39 (1969).

STATE v. HALLETT

Supreme Court of Utah, 1980.
619 P.2d 335.

CROCKETT, CHIEF JUSTICE: Defendant Kelly K. Hallett appeals his conviction of negligent homicide, in that he caused the death of Betty Jean Carley.

On the evening of September 24, 1977, a number of young people gathered at the defendant's home in Kearns. During the evening, some of them engaged in drinking alcoholic beverages. At about 10:30 p.m., they left the home, apparently bent on revelry and mischief. When they got to the intersection of 5215 South and 4620 West, defendant and the codefendant Richard Felsch (not a party to this appeal) bent over a stop sign, which faced northbound traffic on 4620 West, until it was in a position parallel to the ground. The group then proceeded north from the intersection, uprooted another stop sign and placed it in the backyard of a Mr. Arlund Pope, one of the state's witnesses. Traveling further on, defendant and his friends bent a bus stop sign over in a similar manner.

The following morning, Sunday, September 25, 1977, at approximately 9:00 a.m., one Krista Limacher was driving east on 5215 South with her husband and children, en route to church. As she reached the intersection of 4620 West, the deceased, Betty Jean Carley, drove to the intersection from the south. The stop sign was not visible, since the defendant had bent it over, and Ms. Carley continued into the intersection. The result was that Mrs. Limacher's vehicle struck the deceased's car broadside causing her massive injuries which resulted in her death in the hospital a few hours later.

Defendant was charged with manslaughter on the ground that his unlawful act was the cause of the death of Ms. Carley. Upon a trial to the court, he was found guilty of the lesser offense of negligent homicide, a class A misdemeanor. . . .

Defendant next argues that the pulling down of a stop sign does not show the requisite intent to constitute negligent homicide. It is recognized that one should not be so convicted unless he acts with some degree of culpable intent.[7] Our statute provides that a person is guilty of negligent homicide if he causes the death of another:

> (4) With criminal negligence or is criminally negligent with respect to circumstances surrounding his conduct or the result of his

7. U.C.A.1953, Sec. 76-2-101 provides:

> Requirements of criminal conduct and criminal responsibility.—No person is guilty of an offense unless his conduct is prohibited by law and:
>
> (1) He acts intentionally, knowingly, recklessly or with criminal negligence with respect to each element of the offense as the definition of the offense requires; or
>
> (2) His acts constitute an offense involving strict liability.

conduct when he ought to be aware of a substantial and unjustifiable risk that the circumstances exist or the result will occur. The risk must be of such a nature and degree that the failure to perceive it constitutes a gross deviation from the standard of care that an ordinary person would exercise in all the circumstances as viewed from the actor's standpoint.[8]

As to the issue of the defendant's intent: The inquiry is whether from the evidence and the reasonable inferences to be drawn therefrom, the trial court could believe beyond a reasonable doubt that the defendant's conduct met the elements of that statute. In his analysis of the evidence, the trial court was justified in viewing the situation thus: The defendant could not fail to know that stop signs are placed at particular intersections where they are deemed to be necessary because of special hazards; and that without the stop sign, the hazards which caused it to be placed there would exist; and that he should have foreseen that its removal would result in setting a trap fraught with danger and possible fatal consequences to others.

From what has been delineated above, the trial judge expressly found that the defendant should have foreseen that his removal of the stop sign created a substantial risk of injury or death to others; and that his doing so constituted a gross deviation from the standard of care that an ordinary person would exercise in all the circumstances.

Defendant makes a separate argument that the evidence does not support the conclusion that his acts were the proximate cause of Ms. Carley's death. He starts with a uniformly recognized definition: that proximate cause is the cause which through its natural and foreseeable consequence, unbroken by any sufficient intervening cause, produces the injury which would not have occurred but for that cause. His urgence here is that there was evidence that as the deceased approached from the south, she was exceeding the speed limit of 25 mph; and that this was the subsequent intervening and proximate cause of her own death. This is based upon the fact that a motorist, who was also coming from the south, testified that he was going 25 mph and that Ms. Carley passed him some distance to the south as she approached the intersection.

In regard to that contention, there are three observations to be made: The first is that the evidence just referred to would not necessarily compel the trial court to believe that the deceased was exceeding 25 mph as she got close to and entered the intersection, nor did the trial court make any such finding. Second, even if it be assumed that she was so exceeding the speed limit, the reasonable and proper assumption is that if the stop sign had been there, she would have heeded it and there would have been no collision.

8. See U.C.A.1953, Sec. 76–2–103.

The foregoing provides sufficient justification for the trial court's rejection of the defendant's contentions. But there is yet a third proposition to be considered. It is also held that where a party by his wrongful conduct creates a condition of peril, his action can properly be found to be the proximate cause of a resulting injury, even though later events which combined to cause the injury may also be classified as negligent, so long as the later act is something which can reasonably be expected to follow in the natural sequence of events. Moreover, when reasonable minds might differ as to whether it was the creation of the dangerous condition (defendant's conduct) which was the proximate cause, or whether it was some subsequent act (such as Ms. Carley's driving), the question is for the trier of the fact to determine.

Reflecting upon what has been said above, we are not persuaded to disagree with the view taken by the trial court: that whether the defendant's act of removing the stop sign was done in merely callous and thoughtless disregard of the safety of others, or with malicious intent, the result, which he should have foreseen, was the same: that it created a situation of peril; and that nothing that transpired thereafter should afford him relief from responsibility for the tragic consequences that did occur.

Affirmed. No costs awarded.

MAUGHAN, WILKINS and STEWART, JJ., concur.

HALL, JUSTICE (dissenting).

I respectfully dissent.

The offense of negligent homicide is consummated where "the actor, acting with criminal negligence, causes the death of another." [1] The language of the statute punctuates the necessity of a substantial causal relationship between the act of defendant and the death of the victim, which relationship constitutes a necessary element of the offense. To this end, criminal law adopts the notion of proximate cause—the defendant's conduct must proximately result in the victim's injury. As in other areas of the law, a defendant's criminal liability is cut off where the injury in question arose from the operation of an unforeseeable, independent intervening force. Under such circumstances, the defendant's conduct becomes a remote cause, which gives rise to no legal responsibility. This holds true even where the defendant, by negligent action, creates a condition which is subsequently acted upon by another unforeseeable, independent and distinct agency to produce the injury, even though the injury would not have occurred except for defendant's act. It is, moreover, noteworthy that proximate causation, like any other element of a crime, must be proven beyond a reasonable doubt. Where, on appeal, it appears from the evidence (viewed in a light most favorable to the state) that reasonable minds must have entertained a reasonable doubt regard-

1. U.C.A., 1953, 76–5–206.

ing the causal relationship in question, reversal and dismissal are in order.

The evidence produced at trial does not discount beyond a reasonable doubt the possibility that the actions of the decedent on the morning of September 25, 1977, constituted an independent, unforeseeable intervening cause. In this regard, it is to be noted that the evidence produced at trial clearly established that the accident occurred in broad daylight and that the stop sign in question had not been removed from the intersection, but merely bent over into a position where it was still marginally visible. Moreover, the word "Stop" was clearly printed in large block letters on the pavement leading into the intersection. Even if we were to assume, however, that defendant's action in bending the stop sign over erased all indication that vehicles proceeding north on 4620 West were obliged to yield right-of-way, such would render the location of the accident an unmarked intersection. The law requires due care in approaching such intersections, with such reasonable precautions as may be necessary under the circumstances.

Evidence also appearing in the record indicates that decedent was moving at an imprudent speed when she entered the intersection. Although the exact rate of speed is disputed, it is unchallenged that she had, less than a block behind, passed a truck which, itself, was doing the legal speed limit. All parties testified that she made no attempt to slow or brake upon entering the intersection. Under such circumstances, reasonable minds must entertain a reasonable doubt that the defendant's conduct was the sole efficient legal cause of her death.

I would reverse the trial court and dismiss the charge of negligent homicide.[a]

GAY v. STATE

Supreme Court of Tennessee, 1891.
90 Tenn. 645, 18 S.W. 260.

LEA, J. The plaintiff in error was indicted and convicted of a nuisance in keeping and maintaining a hog-pen in a filthy condition. There were several witnesses who proved it was a nuisance. There were several who proved that the pen was kept remarkably clean, and was no nuisance; and several proved that, if there was a nuisance, it was caused by a number of hog-pens in the neighborhood.

His Honor, among other things, charged the jury: "If the jury find that the smell created by the defendant's pen was not sufficient within itself to constitute a nuisance, yet it contributed with other

a. Although **D** admitted he shot the deceased, claiming the shot was fired in self-defense, a conviction of manslaughter must be reversed because the jury were not instructed that the state was required to show that deceased came to his death as the proximate result of **D**'s shot. State v. Ramey, 273 N.C. 325, 160 S.E.2d 56 (1968).

pens in the neighborhood to forming a nuisance, the defendant would be guilty."

This was error. The defendant can only be held liable for the consequences which his act produced. The nuisance complained of must be the natural and direct cause [result] of his own act.[1]

PEOPLE v. LEWIS

Supreme Court of California, Department Two, 1899.
124 Cal. 551, 57 P. 470.

TEMPLE, J. The defendant was convicted of manslaughter and appeals from the judgment and from an order refusing a new trial. It is his second appeal. The main facts are stated in the decision of the former appeal, People v. Lewis, 117 Cal. 186, 48 P. 1088, 59 Am.St. Rep. 167. . . .

Defendant and deceased were brothers-in-law, and not altogether friendly, although they were on speaking and visiting terms. On the morning of the homicide the deceased visited the residence of the defendant, was received in a friendly manner, but after a while an altercation arose, as a result of which defendant shot deceased in the abdomen, inflicting a wound that was necessarily mortal. Farrell fell to the ground, stunned for an instant, but soon got up and went into the house, saying: "Shoot me again; I shall die anyway." His strength soon failed him and he was put to bed. Soon afterwards, about how long does not appear, but within a very few minutes, when no other person was present except a lad about nine years of age, nephew of the deceased and son of the defendant, the deceased procured a knife and cut his throat, inflicting a ghastly wound, from the effect of which, according to the medical evidence, he must necessarily have died in five minutes. The wound inflicted by the defendant severed the mesenteric artery, and medical witnesses testified that under the circumstances it was necessarily mortal, and death would ensue within one hour from the effects of the wound alone. Indeed, the evidence was that usually the effect of such a wound would be to cause death in less time than that, but possibly the omentum may have filled the wound, and thus, by preventing the flow of the blood from the body, have stayed its certain effect for a short period. Internal hemorrhage was still occurring, and, with other effects of the gunshot wound, produced intense pain. The medical witnesses thought that death was accelerated by the knife wound. Perhaps some of them considered it the immediate cause of death.

1. What seems to be the oldest case involving an annoyance of this nature was a civil case in which it was held that an action on the case would lie for erecting a "hogstye" so near the plaintiff's house that the air thereof was corrupted. William Alfred's Case, 9 Co.Rep. 57b, 77 Eng.Rep. 816 (K.B.1611). The court was not impressed with the argument that "one ought not to have so delicate a nose, that he cannot bear the smell of hogs." (Id. at 58a).

Now, it is contended that this is a case where one languishing from a mortal wound is killed by an intervening cause, and, therefore, deceased was not killed by Lewis. To constitute manslaughter, the defendant must have killed some one, and if, though mortally wounded by the defendant, Farrell actually died from an independent intervening cause, Lewis, at the most, could only be guilty of a felonious attempt. He was as effectually prevented from killing as he would have been if some obstacle had turned aside the bullet from its course and left Farrell unwounded. And they contend that the intervening act was the cause of death, if it shortened the life of Farrell for any period whatever.

The attorney general does not controvert the general proposition here contended for, but argues that the wound inflicted by the defendant was the direct cause of the throat cutting, and, therefore, defendant is criminally responsible for the death. He illustrates his position by supposing a case of one dangerously wounded and whose wounds had been bandaged by a surgeon. He says, suppose through the fever and pain consequent upon the wound the patient becomes frenzied and tears away the bandage and thus accelerates his own death. Would not the defendant be responsible for a homicide? Undoubtedly he would be, for in the case supposed the deceased died from the wound, aggravated, it is true, by the restlessness of the deceased, but still the wound inflicted by the defendant produced death. Whether such is the case here is the question.

The attorney general seems to admit a fact which I do not concede, that the gunshot wound was not, when Farrell died, then itself directly contributory to the death. I think the jury were warranted in finding that it was. But if the deceased did die from the effect of the knife wound alone, no doubt the defendant would be responsible, if it was made to appear, and the jury could have found from the evidence, that the knife wound was caused by the wound inflicted by the defendant in the natural course of events. If the relation was causal, and the wounded condition of the deceased was not merely the occasion upon which another cause intervened, not produced by the first wound or related to it in other than a casual way, then defendant is guilty of a homicide. But, if the wounded condition only afforded an opportunity for another unconnected person to kill, defendant would not be guilty of a homicide, even though he had inflicted a mortal wound. In such case, I think, it would be true that the defendant was thus prevented from killing.

The case, considered under this view, is further complicated from the fact that it is impossible to determine whether deceased was induced to cut his throat through pain produced by the wound. May it not have been from remorse, or from a desire to shield his brother-in-law? In either case the causal relation between the knife wound and the gunshot wound would seem to be the same. In either case, if defendant had not shot the deceased, the knife wound would not have been inflicted.

Suppose one assaults and wounds another intending to take life, but the wound, though painful, is not even dangerous, and the wounded man knows that it is not mortal, and yet takes his own life to escape pain, would it not be suicide only? Yet, the wound inflicted by the assailant would have the same relation to death which the original wound in this case has to the knife wound. The wound induced the suicide, but the wound was not, in the usual course of things, the cause of the suicide. . . .

This case differs from that in this, that here the intervening cause, which it is alleged hastened death, was not medical treatment, designed to be helpful, and which the deceased was compelled to procure because of the wound, but was an act intended to produce death, and did not result from the first wound in the natural course of events. But we have reached the conclusion by a course of argument unnecessarily prolix, except from a desire to fully consider the earnest and able argument of the defendant, that the test is—or at least one test—whether, when the death occurred, the wound inflicted by the defendant, did contribute to the event. If it did, although other independent causes also contributed, the causal relation between the unlawful acts of the defendant and the death has been made out. Here, when the throat was cut, Farrell was not merely languishing from a mortal wound. He was actually dying—and after the throat was cut he continued to languish from both wounds. Drop by drop the life current went out from both wounds, and at the very instant of death the gunshot wound was contributing to the event. If the throat cutting had been by a third person, unconnected with the defendant, he might be guilty; for although a man cannot be killed twice, two persons, acting independently, may contribute to his death and each be guilty of a homicide. A person dying is still in life, and may be killed, but if he is dying from a wound given by another both may properly be said to have contributed to his death. . . .

The court refused to instruct the jury as follows: "If you believe from the evidence that it is impossible to tell whether Will Farrell died from the wound in the throat, or the wound in the abdomen, you are bound to acquit." The instruction was properly refused. It assumed that death must have resulted wholly from one wound or the other, and ignored the proposition that both might have contributed—as the jury could have found from the evidence.

The other points are relatively trivial. I have examined them and cannot see how injury could have resulted, supposing the rulings to have been erroneous.

The judgment is affirmed.[1]

McFARLAND, J., and HENSHAW, J., concurred.

Hearing in Bank denied.

1. **D** inflicted a knife wound on **X** after which **D**'s son shot **X**. It was held that if the knife wound contributed to the death of **X**, **D** may be convicted of mur-

EX PARTE HEIGHO

Supreme Court of Idaho, 1910.
18 Idaho 566, 110 P. 1029.

AILSHIE, J. Petitioner was held by the probate judge of Washington county to answer the charge of manslaughter, and has applied to this court for his discharge on the ground that the facts of the case do not disclose the commission of a public offense. The evidence produced at the preliminary examination has been attached to the petition. This court cannot weigh the evidence on habeas corpus, but, if it wholly fails to disclose a public offense for which a prisoner may be held on preliminary examination, then the petitioner would be entitled to his discharge. In re Knudtson, 10 Idaho 676, 79 P. 641.

The facts disclosed by the evidence are in substance as follows: On the 4th day of August, 1910, at Weiser, Washington county, the petitioner, Edgar M. Heigho, hearing that one J. W. Barton had made remarks derogatory to petitioner's character, called one of his employes, Frank Miller, and requested him to accompany petitioner to the residence of Barton. Heigho and Miller went to Barton's residence about 7 o'clock in the evening, ascended the front porch, and Heigho rang the doorbell. Mrs. Sylvia Riegleman, the mother-in-law of Barton, was living at the Barton residence, and was in a bedroom at the front of the house, and immediately off from and adjoining the reception room or hallway, at the time the doorbell rang. Barton responded to the call, and, as he passed through the front room and was about to open the front door, Mrs. Riegleman, who was then near him, exclaimed, "Oh, he has a gun." Barton stepped out at the door and found Heigho standing on the front porch with a gun, commonly called a revolver or pistol, hanging in a holster or scabbard which was strapped about his body. Miller stood by the side of Heigho. Heigho asked Barton some questions as to the statements Barton had been making about him, and, upon Barton asserting that he had not told anything that was not true or not common talk in the town, Heigho struck him in the face with his fist, and Barton stag-

der even if there was no preconcert between D and his son, and the knife wound was not necessarily fatal. Henderson v. State, 11 Ala.App. 37, 65 So. 721 (1913).

One who inflicted a mortal wound by a shot fired in privileged self defense, and later fired another shot after all danger to himself had obviously come to an end is guilty of murder if the second shot contributed to the death. People v. Brown, 62 Cal.App. 96, 216 P. 411 (1923).

Where the conduct of two or more persons contributes concurrently as proximate causes of a death, the conduct of each of said persons is a proximate cause of the death regardless of the extent to which each contributes to the death. A cause is concurrent if it was operative at the moment of death and acted with another cause to produce the death.

Where a group of persons, including defendant, beat the victim in a brawl, the defendant is responsible for the injuries caused to the victim. State v. Thomas, 210 Neb. 298, 314 N.W.2d 15 (1981).

gered back, and fell into the wire netting on the screen door. Barton did not rise for a few seconds, and in the meanwhile his wife came and assisted him to arise. Heigho and Miller backed off the porch and stood in front of the doorway. Barton advanced on Heigho and struck him a couple of blows, whereupon they clinched, and the wife interfered and separated them, and ordered Heigho and Miller off the premises. Mrs. Riegleman was at this time at the door crying, and had been heard to say a time or two, "He will kill you," or "He has a gun." Barton and wife immediately mounted the porch where Mrs. Riegleman was on her knees, resting against or over the banister, apparently unable to rise. She remarked to Barton that she was dying, and again repeated something about "him having a gun." She began spitting a bloody froth and rattling in the chest. A physician was called, and was unable to give her any relief, and she died inside of about 30 minutes from the time of the appearance of Heigho on the front porch. The physician who attended her made a post mortem examination, and testified that she had an aneurism of the ascending aorta, and this had ruptured into the superior vena cava and caused her death. He said that excitement was one of three principal causes that will produce such a result. Heigho was thereafter arrested on the charge of manslaughter in causing the death of Mrs. Riegleman by terror and fright while he was engaged in the commission of an unlawful act not amounting to felony.

We are now asked to determine whether under the statute of this state a person can be held for manslaughter where death was caused by fright, fear, or nervous shock, and where the prisoner made no assault or demonstration against the deceased, and neither offered nor threatened any physical force or violence toward the person of the deceased. In the early history of the common law a homicide to be criminal must have resulted from corporal injury. Fright, fear, nervous shock, or producing mental disturbance, it was said, could never be the basis of a prosecution for homicide. East in his Pleas of the Crown, c. 5, § 13, says: "Working upon the fancy of another or treating him harshly or unkindly, by which he dies of grief or fear, is not such a killing as the law takes notice of." An examination of the ancient English authorities fully corroborates and establishes this to have been the early English rule. 1 Hale P.C. 425–29; Steph.Dig.Cr. Law, art. 221. This rule appears, however, to have been gradually modified and greatly relaxed in modern times by most of the English courts. So in later years we find the court holding a prisoner for manslaughter where his conduct toward his wife caused her death from shock to her nervous system. Reg. v. Murton, 3 F. & F. 492. And in Reg. v. Dugal, 4 Quebec, 492, the Canadian court held the prisoner guilty of manslaughter where with violent words and menaces he had brandished a table knife over his father, and the latter became greatly agitated and weakened from the fright, and died in 20 minutes thereafter of syncope. . . .

As to whether a death caused from fright, grief, or terror, or other mental or nervous shock, can be made the basis for a criminal prosecution, has been touched upon but lightly by the text-writers, and none have ventured to enunciate a modern rule on the subject. Such comments and observations as the text-writers have made are valuable as indicating the personal views of the writers touching this matter. Sir James Stephen in his note to article 221 of his Digest of Criminal Law, commenting on the old rule, says: "Suppose a man were intentionally killed by being kept awake till the nervous irritation of sleeplessness killed him; might not this be murder? Suppose a man kills a sick man, intentionally, by making a loud noise which wakes him when sleep gives him a chance of life, or suppose, knowing that a man has aneurism of the heart, his heir rushes into his room and roars in his ear, 'Your wife is dead,' intending to kill and killing him, why are not these acts murder? They are no more 'secret things belonging to God' than the operation of arsenic. As to the fear that by admitting that such acts are murder people might be rendered liable to prosecution for breaking the hearts of their fathers or wives by bad conduct, the answer is that such an event could never be proved. A long course of conduct gradually 'breaking a man's heart' could never be the 'direct or immediate' cause of death. If it was, and it was intended to have that effect, why should it not be murder?" The author of the text in 21 Am. & Eng.Ency. of Law (2d Ed.) p. 98, speaking of the reason for the old rule and the modern trend of authority, says: "A hint of the reason for this exclusion may be gathered from Lord Hale's assertion that 'secret things belong to God,' upon which Sir James Stephen comments that he suspects the fear of encouraging prosecutions for witchcraft was the real reason. In default of a better explanation it would seem, therefore, that the rule has no firmer foundation than the ignorance and superstition of the time in which it was formulated. Hence the courts have in some later cases shown a tendency to break away from the old rule where substantial justice required it. It will be observed, however, that in all these cases the death has been caused by shock of terror produced by an assault, so that the question in many of its aspects may still be regarded as unsettled. Yet on principle there is no reason why a death from nervous irritation or shock should not be as criminal as any other. It certainly entails greater difficulty in the matter of proof, but this is purely a question of fact, and, if the prosecution is able to establish its case by evidence satisfactory to a jury, there seems to be no sufficient reason why the law should forbid a conviction." Clark & Marshall on the Law of Crimes (2d Ed.) p. 314, says: "It is no doubt very true that the law cannot undertake to punish as for homicide when it is claimed that the death was caused solely by grief or terror, for the death could not be traced to such causes with any degree of certainty. Working upon the feelings and fears of another, however, may be the direct cause of physical or corporeal injury resulting in death, and in such a case the person causing the injury may be as clearly responsible for the death as if he had used a knife." The statute of this state (section 6565, Rev.Codes) defines manslaughter as follows: "Manslaughter is the unlawful killing of a human being without malice. It is of two kinds: (1) Voluntary—upon a sudden quarrel or heat of passion; (2) involuntary—in the commission of an unlawful act, not amounting to felony, or in the commission of a lawful act which might produce death, in an unlawful manner, or without due caution and circumspection." Manslaughter has perhaps in the variety of its circumstances no equal in the catalogue of crimes. An unlawful killing, though unintentional and involuntary, if accomplished by one while engaged in the commission of an unlawful act, is defined by the statute as manslaughter, and this statute does not circumscribe the means or agency causing the death. The law clearly covers and includes any and all means and mediums by or through which a death is caused by one engaged in an unlawful act. The statute has the effect of raising the grade of the offense in which the party is engaged to the rank of manslaughter where it results in the death of a human being.

With such aid as we get from the foregoing authorities and the independent consideration we have been able to give the matter, we reach the conclusion that it would be unsafe, unreasonable, and often unjust for a court to hold as a matter of law that under no state of facts should a prosecution for manslaughter be sustained where death was caused by fright, fear or terror alone, even though no hostile demonstration or overt act was directed at the person of the deceased. Many examples might be called to mind where it would be possible for the death of a person to be accomplished through fright, nervous shock, or terror as effectually as the same could be done with a knife or gun. If the proof in such a case be clear and undoubted, there can be no good reason for denying a conviction. If A. in a spirit of recklessness shoot through B.'s house in which a sick wife or child is confined, and the shock and excitement to the patient cause death, the mere fact that he did not shoot at or hit any one and that he did not intend to shoot any one should not excuse him. It should be enough that he was at the time doing an unlawful act or was acting "without due caution and circumspection." It would seem that in some instances force or violence may be applied to the mind or nervous system as effectually as to the body (1 Russel on Crimes, p. 489). Indeed, it is a well-recognized fact, especially among physicians and metaphysicians, that the application of corporal force or violence often intensifies mentally and nervously the physical effects that flow from the use and application of such force or violence.[1]

1. Defendant's negligently-parked car on a hillside crashed into a house in which deceased was sleeping. He had high blood pressure and a heart condition and it was claimed his death from heart failure ten days later was due to fright induced by the crash, and defendant was sued by deceased's widow. His motion for summary judgment was denied on the ground that direct physical impact is not essential to a recovery for death from fright. Colla v. Mandella, 1 Wis.2d 594, 85 N.W.2d 345, 64 A.L.R.2d 45

We express no opinion whatever and refrain from any comment on the evidence in this case. That is a matter to be passed on by a jury. They should determine from all the facts and circumstances whether the accused was the direct and actual cause of the death of the deceased. As was said by Justice Denman in the Towers Case, it would be "laying down a dangerous precedent for the future" for us to hold as a conclusion of law that manslaughter could not be committed by fright, terror, or nervous shock. The fair and deliberate judgment of a jury of 12 men can generally be relied upon as an ample safeguard for the protection of one who should in fact be acquitted. The dangers of unwarranted prosecutions for such causes are no greater or more imminent than from any other cause, while, on the other hand, the proofs will generally be more difficult. The difficulty of making proofs, however, should never be considered as an argument against the application of a rule of law.

The writ is quashed, and the prisoner is remanded to the custody of the sheriff of Washington county.[2]

SULLIVAN, C.J., concurs.

PEOPLE v. STAMP

Court of Appeal of California, Second District, Division 3, 1970.
2 Cal.App.3d 203, 82 Cal.Rptr. 598.

COBEY, ASSOCIATE JUSTICE. These are appeals by Jonathan Earl Stamp, Michael John Koory and Billy Dean Lehman, following jury verdicts of guilty of robbery and murder, both in the first degree. Each man was given a life sentence on the murder charge together with the time prescribed by law on the robbery count.

Defendants appeal their conviction of the murder of Carl Honeyman who, suffering from a heart disease, died between 15 and 20 minutes after Koory and Stamp held up his business, the General Amusement Company, on October 26, 1965, at 10:45 a.m. Lehman, the driver of the getaway car, was apprehended a few minutes after the robbery; several weeks later Stamp was arrested in Ohio and Koory in Nebraska.

(1957). Accord, Savard v. Cody Chevrolet, 126 Vt. 405, 234 A.2d 656 (1967).

2. **D** placed his hand, or hands, around **X**'s throat and choked him. Within seconds **D** released his grip whereupon **X** slumped to the ground. **X** died two months and seventeen days later without having recovered consciousness for any substantial period, if at all. A doctor testified that **X** had had high blood pressure and expressed the opinion that death was caused by cerebral hemorrhage, resulting from excitement. There had been no autopsy but the death certificate gave pneumonia as the primary cause of death with cerebral hemorrhage as a secondary cause. A conviction of manslaughter was reversed on the ground that it cannot be said with any degree of certainty that **X** died as a result of any criminal agency. Fine v. State, 193 Tenn. 422, 246 S.W.2d 70 (1952).

D unlawfully struck **B** who had a child in her arms at the time, the infant became frightened and went into convulsions and thereafter died. **D**'s guilt on manslaughter was held to be a jury question. Verdict: Not guilty. R. v. Towers, 12 Cox C.C. 530 (1874).

Broadly stated, the grounds of this appeal are: (1) insufficiency of the evidence on the causation of Honeyman's death; (2) inapplicability of the felony-murder rule to this case; . . . .

On this appeal appellants primarily rely upon their position that the felony-murder doctrine should not have been applied in this case due to the unforeseeability of Honeyman's death.

THE FACTS

Defendants Koory and Stamp, armed with a gun and a blackjack, entered the rear of the building housing the offices of General Amusement Company, ordered the employees they found there to go to the front of the premises, where the two secretaries were working. Stamp, the one with the gun, then went into the office of Carl Honeyman, the owner and manager. Thereupon Honeyman, looking very frightened and pale, emerged from the office in a "kind of hurry." He was apparently propelled by Stamp who had hold of him by an elbow.

The robbery victims were required to lie down on the floor while the robbers took the money and fled out the back door. As the robbers, who had been on the premises 10 to 15 minutes, were leaving, they told the victims to remain on the floor for five minutes so that no one would "get hurt."

Honeyman, who had been lying next to the counter, had to use it to steady himself in getting up off the floor. Still pale, he was short of breath, sucking air, and pounding and rubbing his chest. As he walked down the hall, in an unsteady manner, still breathing hard and rubbing his chest, he said he was having trouble "keeping the pounding down inside" and that his heart was "pumping too fast for him." A few minutes later, although still looking very upset, shaking, wiping his forehead and rubbing his chest, he was able to walk in a steady manner into an employee's office. When the police arrived, almost immediately thereafter, he told them he was not feeling very well and that he had a pain in his chest. About two minutes later, which was 15 to 20 minutes after the robbery had occurred, he collapsed on the floor. At 11:25 he was pronounced dead on arrival at the hospital. The coroner's report listed the immediate cause of death as heart attack.

The employees noted that during the hours before the robbery Honeyman had appeared to be in normal health and good spirits. The victim was an obese, sixty-year-old man, with a history of heart disease, who was under a great deal of pressure due to the intensely competitive nature of his business. Additionally, he did not take good care of his heart.

Three doctors, including the autopsy surgeon, Honeyman's physician, and a professor of cardiology from U.C.L.A., testified that although Honeyman had an advanced case of atherosclerosis, a progressive and ultimately fatal disease, there must have been some immediate upset to his system which precipitated the attack. It was their conclusion in response to a hypothetical question that but for the robbery there would have been no fatal seizure at that time. The fright induced by the robbery was too much of a shock to Honeyman's system. There was opposing expert testimony to the effect that it could not be said with reasonable medical certainty that fright could ever be fatal.

SUFFICIENCY OF THE EVIDENCE RE CAUSATION

Appellants' contention that the evidence was insufficient to prove that the robbery factually caused Honeyman's death is without merit. The test on review is whether there is substantial evidence to uphold the judgment of the trial court, and in so deciding this court must assume in the case of a jury trial the existence of every fact in favor of the verdict which the jury could reasonably have deduced from the evidence. A review of the facts as outlined above shows that there was substantial evidence of the robbery itself, that appellants were the robbers, and that but for the robbery the victim would not have experienced the fright which brought on the fatal heart attack.[2]

APPLICATION OF THE FELONY-MURDER RULE

Appellants' contention that the felony-murder rule is inapplicable to the facts of this case is also without merit. Under the felony-murder rule of section 189 of the Penal Code, a killing committed in either the perpetration of or an attempt to perpetrate robbery is murder of the first degree. This is true whether the killing is wilfull, deliberate and premeditated, or merely accidental or unintentional, and whether or not the killing is planned as a part of the commission of the robbery. People v. Washington, 62 Cal.2d 777, 783, 44 Cal. Rptr. 442, 402 P.2d 130, merely limits the rule to situations where the killing was committed by the felon or his accomplice acting in furtherance of their common design. (See People v. Gilbert, 63 Cal.2d 690, 705, 47 Cal.Rptr. 909, 408 P.2d 365.)

2. Appellants' position that the medical evidence was insufficient to prove the causal link between the robbery and the death because the physicians testifying to the result did so solely in response to a hypothetical question which was erroneous and misleading, and because the doctors answered in terms of "medical probability rather than actual certainty" is not well taken. A conviction on the basis of expert medical testimony, couched in terms of "reasonable medical certainty" rather than of "beyond a reasonable doubt" is valid (People v. Phillips, 64 Cal. 2d 574, 579, fn. 2, 51 Cal.Rptr. 225, 414 P.2d 353, 357) and a hypothetical question need not state all the evidence in a case so long as it does not omit essential facts and issues. This did not occur here. (See McCullough v. Langer, 23 Cal.App.2d 510, 521, 73 P.2d 649, hear. den.) Furthermore, an appellate court will not overrule a trial court on the matter of the sufficiency of the qualifications of expert witnesses in the absence of a manifest abuse of such discretion. (People v. Phillips, 64 Cal.2d at 578–579, fn. 1, 51 Cal.Rptr. 225, 414 P.2d 353.) An examination of the record shows that there was no such abuse by the trial court in permitting the prosecution's expert medical witnesses to testify as to the cause of the heart attack.

The doctrine presumes malice aforethought on the basis of the commission of a felony inherently dangerous to human life.[3] This rule is a rule of substantive law in California and not merely an evidentiary shortcut to finding malice as it withdraws from the jury the requirement that they find either express malice or the implied malice which is manifested in an intent to kill. Under this rule no intentional act is necessary other than the attempt to or the actual commission of the robbery itself. When a robber enters a place with a deadly weapon with the intent to commit robbery, malice is shown by the nature of the crime.

There is no requirement that the killing occur, "while committing" or "while engaged in" the felony, or that the killing be "a part of" the felony, other than that the few acts be a part of one continuous transaction. (People v. Chavez, 37 Cal.2d 656, 670, 234 P.2d 632.) Thus the homicide need not have been committed "to perpetrate" the felony. There need be no technical inquiry as to whether there has been a completion or abandonment of or desistence from the robbery before the homicide itself was completed.

The doctrine is not limited to those deaths which are foreseeable. Rather a felon is held strictly liable for *all* killings committed by him or his accomplices in the course of the felony. (People v. Talbot, 64 Cal.2d 691, 704, 51 Cal.Rptr. 417, 414 P.2d 633.) As long as the homicide is the direct causal result of the robbery the felony-murder rule applies whether or not the death was a natural or probable consequence of the robbery. So long as a victim's predisposing physical condition, regardless of its cause, is not the *only* substantial factor bringing about his death, that condition, and the robber's ignorance of it, in no way destroys the robber's criminal responsibility for the death. So long as life is shortened as a result of the felonious act, it does not matter that the victim might have died soon anyway. In this respect, the robber takes his victim as he finds him. . . .

The judgment is affirmed.[a]

SCHWEITZER and ALLPORT, JJ., concur.

3. In view of the fact that the Legislature has not seen fit to change the language of Penal Code section 189 since the decisions holding that the requisite malice aforethought is to be implied from the commission of those felonies inherently dangerous to human life, it must be presumed that these cases accurately state the law. (People v. Hallner, 43 Cal. 2d 715, 720, 277 P.2d 393.)

a. [Added by the Compiler.] **F** struck **G** on the jaw once with his fist. Under other circumstances the moderate blow might well have been forgotten, but **G** was a hemophiliac and a slight laceration resulted on the inside of the mouth. At the time and place there was no medical skill competent to stop the bleeding and **G** died ten days later as a result of the uninterrupted hemorrhage. A conviction of manslaughter was affirmed although **F** did not know **G** was a hemophiliac and had no reason to expect serious consequences from the relatively mild battery. State v. Frazier, 339 Mo. 966, 98 S.W.2d 707 (1936).

Defendant struck V several blows to the head. V died from a pulmonary embolism resulting from a leg vein thrombosis due to immobility as a result of the blows. A murder conviction was affirmed. State v. Hall, 129 Ariz. 589, 633 P.2d 398 (1981).

STATE v. SAUTER

Supreme Court of Arizona, In Banc, 1978.
120 Ariz. 222, 585 P.2d 242.

STRUCKMEYER, VICE CHIEF JUSTICE.

Appellant, Richard Robert Sauter, was convicted after trial by jury of voluntary manslaughter, and appeals. Jurisdiction is pursuant to Rule 47(e)(5), Rules of the Supreme Court. Judgment affirmed.

The record in the court below established that appellant, while intoxicated and during the course of an altercation, stabbed Matt Charles Lines. Lines was taken to the emergency room of a hospital in Phoenix, Arizona, where he was attended by a general surgeon. The surgeon opened the abdominal cavity and repaired lacerations to both the anterior and posterior stomach walls, the main stomach artery, the superior pancreatic artery and pancreatic tissue. The surgeon also palpitated the abdominal aorta, but did not observe bleeding in the area. After the surgery, Lines continued to lose large amounts of blood. An autopsy revealed that he died from the loss of blood, principally through a one-inch, unrepaired laceration in the abdominal aorta.

Appellant's position is that he was guilty of assault rather than homicide because of the intervening malpractice of the surgeon who did not discover the laceration in Lines' aorta, and he urges that error occurred when the trial court refused to allow evidence of the surgeon's failure to discover the wound to Lines' aorta. We, however, do not think so.

In State v. Myers, 59 Ariz. 200, 125 P.2d 441 (1942), we quoted with approval from State v. Baruth, 47 Wash. 283, 91 P. 977, to the effect that where one unlawfully inflicts a wound upon another calculated to endanger his life, it is no defense to a charge of murder to show that the wounded person might have recovered if the wound had been more skillfully treated. We said in State v. Ulin, 113 Ariz. 141, 143, 548 P.2d 19 (1976), that medical malpractice will break the chain of causation and become the proximate cause of death only if it constitutes the sole cause of death. We think these cases correctly summarize the law relative to intervening acts arising out of medical treatment in the United States. See 100 A.L.R.2d 769, anno. "Homicide; liability where death immediately results from treatment or mistreatment of injury inflicted by defendant." See also the cases cited supporting the basic rule, commencing at page 783 and running through page 784. For example, in People v. Stamps, 8 Ill.App.3d 896, 291 N.E.2d 274, 279 (1972), the court held:

> "* * * it is the generally recognized principle that where a person inflicts upon another a wound which is dangerous, that is, calculated to endanger or destroy life, it is no defense to a charge of homicide that the alleged victim's death was contributed to by,

or immediately resulted from, unskillful or improper treatment of the wound or injury by attending physicians or surgeons."

See also People v. Stewart, 40 N.Y.2d 692, 389 N.Y.S.2d 804, 358 N.E. 2d 487, 491 (1976), where the court said:

> "Neither does 'direct' mean 'unaided' for the defendant will be held liable for the death although other factors, entering after the injury, have contributed to the fatal result. Thus if 'felonious assault is operative as a cause of death, the causal co-operation of erroneous surgical or medical treatment does not relieve the assailant from liability for homicide'."

Only if the death is attributable to the medical malpractice and not induced at all by the original wound does the intervention of the medical malpractice constitute a defense. Such is not the case here.

Judgment affirmed.[1]

BELK v. PEOPLE

Supreme Court of Illinois, 1888.
125 Ill. 584, 17 N.E. 744.

MR. JUSTICE SHOPE delivered the opinion of the Court.

The plaintiffs in error, John Belk, John Hill and George Williams, with George Belk, were jointly indicted, in the Jo Daviess circuit court, for the murder of Ann Reed, the indictment charging in the

1. If a gun-shot wound inflicted by **D** on a pregnant woman caused a miscarriage, and the miscarriage caused septic peritonitis which in turn resulted in death, **D** has caused the death even if the medical treatment received by the woman in the hospital was not of the best. People v. Kane, 213 N.Y. 260, 107 N.E. 655 (1915).

If pneumonia was the *sole* cause of the death of a wounded man, he who inflicted the wound did not cause the death. Quinn v. State, 106 Miss. 844, 64 So. 738 (1914).

H and **S** had an argument which resulted in a fight. During the fight **H** knocked **S** down and in a fit of rage jumped on his face and kicked him in the head. **S** was taken to the hospital in semi-comatose condition. He was violent and in shock. After receiving a blood transfusion **S** had tubes inserted into his nasal passages and trachea in order to maintain the normal breathing process. It was necessary to restrain his violence by fastening leather handcuffs on him. When it became desirable to change the bed clothes, the restraints were removed and were not put back because he was no longer violent. Early the following morning **S** had a convulsion and immediately thereafter pulled out the tubes with his own hands. He died an hour later of asphyxiation.

Being tried for the murder of **S**, **H** claimed that **S** had killed himself by pulling out the tubes which were necessary for his breathing because of his injured condition. It was not clear whether the pulling out of the tubes was a reflex action, or was a conscious deliberate act. Under either possibility it was held that **H** was the proximate cause of **S**'s death and he was convicted of manslaughter. United States v. Hamilton, 182 F.Supp. 548 (D.D.C.1960).

Even if physicians were negligent in believing the victim was dead before they performed a nephrectomy and even if such negligence was a contributing factor to the victim's death, the physicians' negligence does not break the chain of causation and death is still attributable to the victim being shot by the defendant. Cranmore v. State, 85 Wis.2d 722, 271 N.W.2d 402 (1978).

Removal of life support systems where the original need was due to the wrong-

various counts, in varying forms, that the murder was committed by the defendants, by willfully, recklessly, negligently, wrongfully and feloniously driving a team of horses hitched to a wagon, upon and against a wagon in which the deceased was riding, thereby causing the horses attached to the wagon in which she was so riding, to run away, thereby throwing said Ann Reed upon the ground, whereby she received wounds and injuries from which she died the following day. A trial resulted in an acquittal of said George Belk, and a verdict of guilty of manslaughter as to plaintiffs in error, and fixing their punishment at confinement in the penitentiary at one year each. Motions for new trial and in arrest were severally overruled, and sentence pronounced by the court upon the verdict. . . .

Some question is made whether the collision was the proximate cause of the team running away, and of the injury and death of Mrs. Reed; but it is enough to say, the evidence was sufficient upon which to base the finding of the jury in that respect. The question was submitted under proper instructions, and there is no ground for disturbing the verdict for that reason. There was direct causal connection between the collision and the death of the deceased. Between the acts of omission or commission of the defendants, by which it is alleged the collision occurred, and the injury of the deceased, there was not an interposition of a human will acting independently of the defendants, or any extraordinary natural phenomena, to break the causal connection.[1] It may be fairly said that what followed the colliding of the defendants' team with the wagon in which the deceased was riding, was the natural and probable effect of the collision, and the collision was in consequence of the manner in which the team of the defendants was controlled. It can make no difference whether the driver of the team after which the deceased was riding, was guilty of negligence in not controlling or failing to control his team after the collision. It may be that persons standing by, or the driver, might, by the exercise of diligence and care, have checked the horses, and thereby prevented the final catastrophe; but because they did not do so, and were derelict in moral or even legal duty in that regard, will not release defendants from the responsibility of their wrongful act or omission of their legal duty. If the driver, instead of being negligent, as is claimed in controlling his team, had done some act contributing to the running away of his horses, or driven upon a bank, whereby the carriage had been overturned and the deceased thrown out, or the like, it might justly be said that it was the act of

ful conduct of the defendant renders the defendant liable for homicide even if the doctors failed to follow acceptable procedures in terminating a life support system. R v. Malcherek [1981] All E.R. 422 (Ct.App.)

1. From the evidence the jury might have found that **D**'s reckless conduct left the victim in the street where she was run over and killed by a second car. Even so **D**'s reckless conduct was the cause of the death. The second car did not constitute a supervening cause but was an intermediate cause reasonably foreseeable by **D**. People v. Parra, 35 Ill. App.3d 240, 340 N.E.2d 636 (1975). See also People v. Kibbe, 35 N.Y.2d 407, 362 N.Y.S.2d 848, 321 N.E.2d 773 (1974).

the driver, and not of the defendants, to which the death of the deceased was legally attributable. Wharton on Crim.Law, 341, et seq.; Roscoe on Crim.Ev. 700, et seq. . . .

(For other reasons the judgment was reversed.)

LETNER v. STATE

Supreme Court of Tennessee, 1927.

156 Tenn. 68, 299 S.W. 1049.

MR. JUSTICE MCKINNEY delivered the opinion of the Court.

Plaintiff in error, referred to herein as the defendant, was indicted for murder of Alfred Johnson. The jury found him guilty of involuntary manslaughter and fixed his punishment at two years in the penitentiary.

Alfred Johnson, nineteen years of age, his older brother, Walter Johnson, and Jesse Letner, seventeen years of age, half brother of the defendant, were crossing Emory River in a boat from the west to the east side, at a point known as "Devil's Race Track," this being a dangerous place, of unknown depth, where the water circles and eddies continuously. When in the middle of the river some man on the high bluff above the west bank shot into the water about six feet east of the boat, which caused the water to splash up. A second shot was fired, which hit the water nearer the boat; thereupon Walter Johnson, who was steering the boat, jumped out of same into the river, resulting in its being capsized, and Alfred and Walter were drowned.

The only question of fact is were either of these shots fired by defendant? He did not testify, and offered no evidence in his behalf. . . .

(4) It is also assigned for error that the court improperly charged the jury as follows:

"If you should believe from the evidence, and that beyond a reasonable doubt, that this defendant saw the deceased and other boys in a canoe or boat, and shot into the river near them without any purpose of hitting the deceased, but to play a prank on the deceased, and if the deceased became frightened and jumped into the river and was drowned, then in that event, the defendant would be guilty of involuntary manslaughter."

This was a correct statement of the law, but was inaccurate so far as the facts of this case are concerned. The uncontroverted testimony shows that deceased did not jump out of the boat, but that his brother, Walter, jumped out and, in doing so, capsized the boat and precipitated the deceased into the water. No criticism, however, is made with respect to this feature of the charge.

The act of the defendant, whether he was shooting to kill or only to frighten these boys, was an unlawful one, and comes within the universal rule that every person will be held to contemplate and be responsible for the natural consequences of his own act; but he will not be held criminally responsible for a homicide unless his act can be said to be the cause of death.

(5) When a person unintentionally or accidentally kills another, while engaged in an unlawful act, the authorities all hold that he is guilty of some degree of homicide.

In this case if defendant had accidentally struck the deceased, causing his death, or had capsized the boat and deceased had drowned, unquestionably he would have been guilty of some grade of homicide. . . .

From the foregoing it appears that the defendant is liable even where his act was not the immediate cause of the death, if he was connected with the intervening cause, or if the act or intervention was the natural result of his act.

(7) In other words, the defendant cannot escape the consequences of his wrongful act by relying upon a supervening cause when such cause naturally resulted from his wrongful act.

By firing the gun the defendant caused Walter Johnson to take to the water, resulting in the overturn of the boat and the drowning of Alfred. . . .

The judgment should also provide that the defendant undergo confinement in the penitentiary (in this case) not less than one nor more than two years. As thus modified, the judgment of the trial court will be affirmed.[1]

STATE v. LEOPOLD

Supreme Court of Errors of Connecticut, 1929.

110 Conn. 55, 147 A. 118.

BANKS, J. In the early morning of February 5, 1928, an explosion followed by a fire occurred in a building on Baldwin street in Waterbury, and two boys, the sons of a tenant of the building, were burned to death. The fee of the property was in the name of the wife of the accused, and a portion of the building was used for the storage of

1. D made improper advances to a girl in a moving automobile. To avoid him she jumped from the car and was killed by the fall. A conviction of murder was reversed because the judge's charge to the jury permitted conviction of murder without requiring a finding (a) that deceased's fear of a felonious assault was a reasonable one, or (b) that her act in jumping was an act of a reasonably prudent person under the circumstances, or (c) that her act in jumping was one which in its consequences naturally tended to destroy the life of a human being. Patterson v. State, 181 Ga. 698, 184 S.E. 309 (1936). Cf. State v. Myers, 7 N.J. 465, 81 A.2d 710 (1951); State v. Selby, 183 N.J.Super. 273, 443 A.2d 1076 (1981).

furniture by the Waterbury Furniture Company, a corporation of which the accused was a majority stockholder. The accused, jointly with one Shellnitz, was indicted upon a charge of murder in the first degree, and of having caused the death of the two boys by willfully burning the building. The charge against the accused was that he employed Weiss to set fire to the building, for the purpose of collecting insurance upon the building and the furniture stored in it. Weiss was burned to death in the fire. . . .

Error is predicated upon the refusal of the court to charge as requested, upon the charge as given, and upon numerous rulings upon evidence. The accused claimed that the two boys who were burned to death were awake after the fire, and were on their way out of the building, and would not have met their death if they had continued on their way, but that of their own will they remained in the building, or were sent back into a room of the building by their father to recover some money or other property there deposited, and requested the court to charge that, if they had a reasonable opportunity to escape from the burning building, and would have escaped but for their own conduct, or the act of their father in directing them to return, the accused could not be found guilty of causing their death. The court did not so charge, but told the jury that the negligence of the victims of a crime did not diminish or nullify the crime, and that, even if they found the claim as to the conduct of these boys to be true, the accused would not thereby be excused. This was a correct statement of the law. . . . Every person is held to be responsible for the natural consequences of his acts, and if he commits a felonious act and death follows, it does not alter its nature or diminish its criminality to prove that other causes co-operated to produce that result. The act of the accused need not be the immediate cause of the death; he is responsible, though the direct cause is an act of the deceased, if such act, not being itself an independent and efficient cause, results naturally from, and is reasonably due to, the unlawful act of the accused. If the death of these boys resulted in a natural sequence from the setting of the building on fire, even though their conduct contributed to, or was the immediate cause of it, the accused would be responsible, and the effort of a person to save property of value which is liable to destruction by fire is such a natural and ordinary course of conduct that it cannot be said to break the sequence of cause and effect. . . .

A careful examination of the entire record fails to disclose any error prejudicial to the accused, and makes it clear that he had a fair trial.

There is no error.

All the Judges concur.[1]

1. **D** maliciously set fire to a store building and a fireman lost his life while fighting the fire. A conviction of first degree murder was affirmed. State v. Glover, 330 Mo. 709, 50 S.W.2d 1049 (1932).

COMMONWEALTH v. MOYER

Supreme Court of Pennsylvania, 1947.
357 Pa. 181, 53 A.2d 736.

Opinion by MR. CHIEF JUSTICE MAXEY, June 30, 1947.

Charles Frederick Moyer and William Paul Byron were jointly tried for the murder of Harvey Zerbe, which occurred during the perpetration of a robbery. The jury convicted them of murder in the first degree and imposed the death penalty. . . .

The second assignment of error is based on the excerpt from the charge of the court in which the jury was instructed that: "All of the participants in an attempted robbery are guilty of murder in the first degree if someone is killed in the course of the perpetration of the first-named crime. That is the law of the Commonwealth of Pennsylvania." The appellants challenge that statement and say that the issue in this case is whether or not the decedent met his death by a wound inflicted by the defendant Moyer or by the garage owner Shank.

This assignment of error poses the question whether or not these defendants can legally be convicted of murder if the bullet which killed Zerbe came from the revolver fired by the latter's employer in an attempt by him to frustrate the attempted robbery. We have no doubt that even under these facts, which facts the Commonwealth does not concede, the complained of conviction was proper.

A man or men engaged in the commission of such a felony as robbery can be convicted of murder in the first degree if the bullet which causes death was fired not by the felon but by the intended victim in repelling the aggressions of the felon or felons. This is a question which apparently has never before arisen in this Commonwealth and has arisen elsewhere only rarely. Our Act of June 24, 1939, P.L. 872, section 701, 18 P.S. 4701, reads as follows: "All murder which shall be . . . committed in the perpetration of, or attempting to perpetrate any arson, rape, robbery, burglary, or kidnapping, shall be murder in the first degree." This section is, with the addition of the word "kidnapping" and with a negligible change in phraseology, a re-enactment of the corresponding provision of the Criminal Code of March 31, 1860, P.L. 382, and of later Acts and of the Act of 1794. . . .

. . . For any individual forcibly to defend himself or his family or his property from criminal aggression is a primal human instinct.[3] It is the right and duty of both individuals and nations to meet criminal aggression with effective countermeasures. Every robber or burglar knows when he attempts to commit his crime that he is inviting dangerous resistance. Any robber or burglar who carries deadly

3. "Such homicide as is committed for the prevention of any forcible and atrocious crime is justifiable by the law of nature; and also by the law of England." 4 Blackstone, section 181. [Court's footnote.]

weapons (as most of them do and as these robbers did) thereby reveals that he expects to meet and overcome forcible opposition. What this court said in Commonwealth v. LeGrand, 336 Pa. 511, 518, 9 A.2d 896, about burglars, applies equally to robbers: "Every burglar is a potential assassin and when his felonious purpose encounters human opposition his *intent to steal* becomes an *intent to kill* and any weapon he finds at hand becomes a weapon of murder." Every robber or burglar knows that a likely later act in the chain of events he inaugurates will be the use of deadly force against him on the part of the selected victim. For whatever results follow from that natural and legal use of retaliating force, the felon must be held responsible. For Earl Shank, the proprietor of a gas station in Ridley Township, Delaware County, which at 11 P.M. on July 13, 1946, was being attacked by armed robbers, to return the fire of these robbers with a pistol which he had at hand was as proper and as inevitable as it was for the American forces at Pearl Harbor on the morning of December 7, 1941, to return the fire of the Japanese invaders. The Japanese felonious invasion of the Hawaiian Islands on that date was in law and morals the proximate cause of all the resultant fatalities. The Moyer-Byron felonious invasion of the Shank gas station on July 13, 1946, was likewise the proximate cause of the resultant fatality.

If *in fact* one of the bullets fired by Earl Shank in self-defense killed Harvey Zerbe, the responsibility for that killing rests on Moyer and his co-conspirator Byron, who had armed themselves with deadly weapons for the purpose of carrying out their plan to rob Shank and whose murderous attack made Shank's firing at them in self-defense essential to the protection of himself and his employees and his property. If, for example, a father sees his child being kidnapped and opens fire, as any normal father would be expected to do if he had a gun available, and if the bullet which he fires at the kidnapper inadvertently kills the child, the death of the child is properly attributable to the malicious act of the kidnapper. The principle which sustains this conclusion is expressed by Bishop on Criminal Law, 9th Ed., Vol. 2, section 637, page 480, as follows: "It is a rule both of reason and law that whenever one's will contributes to impel a physical force, whether another's, his own, or a combined force proceeding from whatever different sources, he is responsible for the result, the same as if his own unaided hand had produced it. The contribution, however, must be of such magnitude, and so near the result, that sustaining to it the relation of contributory cause to effect, the law takes it within its cognizance."

Stephen's History of the Criminal Law of England, Vol. 3, page 21, says that at common law "murder was homicide with malice aforethought and that the latter consisted of any of the following states of mind: 1. . . . 2. . . . 3. . . . 4. An intent to commit any felony whatever." Blackstone, Book IV, pages 192–193, says: "When an involuntary killing happens in consequence of an unlawful act it would be either murder or manslaughter according to the nature of the act which occasioned it, but in consequences naturally tending to bloodshed it will be murder."

In Keaton v. State, 41 Tex.Cr.R. 621, 57 S.W. 1125, the Court of Criminal Appeals of Texas held that where the defendant and others went to rob a train, and, after stopping it, forced the fireman to the door of the express car, after being warned that some one would probably commence shooting at them from the rear of the car, and persons resisting the attempted robbery, and *intending to kill the robbers, shot and killed the fireman,* the defendant was held guilty of murder. . . .

In Johnson v. Alabama, 142 Ala. 70, 38 So. 182, 2 L.R.A.,N.S., 897, it was held by the Supreme Court of Alabama that one who, by interfering in aid of his insane parent, whom officers are attempting to arrest, frees his hands, and enables him to kill one of the officers, is guilty of murder. "The person who unlawfully sets the means of death in motion . . . is the guilty cause of the death at the time and place at which his unlawful act produces its fatal result; . . . ": Gray, J. in Com. v. Macloon, 101 Mass. 1, 100 Am.Dec. 89. . . .

This same principle is illustrated in the so-called "Squib Case" of Scott v. Shepherd, 2 William Blackstone's Rep. 892. In that case, there was instituted an action of trespass for tossing a lighted squib against the infant plaintiff and striking him on the face and so burning one of his eyes that he lost the sight of it. The facts were that on the 28th of October 1770, defendant threw a lighted squib made of gunpowder from the street into the market house. A large concourse of people were assembled there. One Willis to prevent injury to himself and to the goods of one Yates, grasped the lighted squib and threw it across the market house where it fell upon one Ryal. The latter, to save his own goods from being injured, took up the lighted squib and threw it to another part of the market house and struck the plaintiff in the face, putting out one of his eyes. In that case, Justice Gould said, ". . . the defendant may be considered in the same view as if he himself had personally thrown the squib in the plaintiff's face. The terror impressed upon Willis and Ryal excited self-defense, and deprived them of the power of recollection. What they did therefore was the inevitable consequence of the defendant's unlawful act." Chief Justice Degrey said, "The throwing the squib was an act unlawful and tending to affright the bystanders. So far, mischief was originally intended; not any particular mischief, but mischief indiscriminate and wanton. Whatever mischief therefore follows, he is the author of it;—*Egrediturpersonam,*[1] as the phrase is in criminal cases. And though criminal cases are no rule for civil ones, yet in trespass I think there is an analogy. Every one who does an unlawful act is considered as the doer of all that follows;

1. [By the Compiler.] This is written as one word in the state report and two words in the Atlantic Reporter. The former is obviously a misprint.

if done with a deliberate intent, the consequence may amount to murder. . . ." The court held that an action of trespass was maintainable against the defendant Shepherd whose unlawful act started the squib on its journey through two other hands to the eyes of the plaintiff. . . .

The judgments are affirmed and the record is remitted so that the sentences may be executed.[2]

PEOPLE v. WASHINGTON

Supreme Court of California, In Bank, 1965.
62 Cal.2d 777, 44 Cal.Rptr. 442, 402 P.2d 130.

TRAYNOR, CHIEF JUSTICE. Defendant appeals from a judgment of conviction entered upon jury verdicts finding him guilty of first degree robbery (Pen.Code, §§ 211, 211a) and first degree murder and fixing the murder penalty at life imprisonment. (Pen.Code, §§ 187, 189, 190, 190.1.) He was convicted of murder for participating in a robbery in which his accomplice was killed by the victim of the robbery.

Shortly before 10 p.m., October 2, 1962, Johnnie Carpenter prepared to close his gasoline station. He was in his office computing the receipts and disbursements of the day while an attendant in an adjacent storage room deposited money in a vault. Upon hearing someone yell "robbery," Carpenter opened his desk and took out a revolver. A few moments later, James Ball entered the office and pointed a revolver directly at Carpenter, who fired immediately, mortally wounding Ball. Carpenter then hurried to the door and saw an unarmed man he later identified as defendant running from the vault with a moneybag in his right hand. He shouted "Stop." When his warning was not heeded, he fired and hit defendant who fell wounded in front of the station.

The Attorney General, relying on People v. Harrison, 176 Cal. App.2d 330, 1 Cal.Rptr. 414, contends that defendant was properly convicted of first degree murder. In that case defendants initiated a gun battle with an employee in an attempt to rob a cleaning business. In the cross fire, the employee accidentally killed the owner of the

2. In an attempted robbery the robber shot at the victim who returned the fire. In the ensuing gun battle a third person was killed. "Whether the fatal act was done by the defendant, an accomplice, another victim, or a bystander is, under the facts here, not controlling. . . . The felony-murder conviction is affirmed." State v. Moore, 580 S.W.2d 747, 752–53 (Mo.1979).

D unlawfully attacked L and during an exchange of shots a bystander was killed. A conviction was reversed because the judge's instruction permitted conviction of D even if the fatal shot was fired by L. State v. Oxendine, 187 N.C. 658, 122 S.E. 568 (1924).

In the course of an armed robbery, a fleeing co-felon was killed either by the robbery victim or a police officer. The court held the co-felon could not be convicted under the felony murder doctrine. The court stated ". . . that the tort liability concept of proximate cause has no proper place in prosecutions for criminal homicide." Campbell v. State, 293 Md. 438, 444 A.2d 1034, 1041 (1982).

business. The court affirmed the judgment convicting defendants of first degree murder, invoking Commonwealth v. Alameida, 362 Pa. 596, 68 A.2d 595, 12 A.L.R.2d 183, and People v. Podolski, 332 Mich. 508, 52 N.W.2d 201, which held that robbers who provoked gunfire were guilty of first degree murder even though the lethal bullet was fired by a policeman.

Defendant would distinguish the Harrison, Almeida, and Podolski cases on the ground that in each instance the person killed was an innocent victim, not one of the felons. He suggests that we limit the rule of the Harrison case just as the Supreme Courts of Pennsylvania and Michigan have limited the Almeida and Podolski cases by holding that surviving felons are not guilty of murder when their accomplices are killed by persons resisting the felony. (Commonwealth v. Redline, 391 Pa. 486, 137 A.2d 472; [1] People v. Austin, 370 Mich. 12, 120 N.W.2d 766; see also People v. Wood, 8 N.Y.2d 48, 201 N.Y.S.2d 328, 167 N.E.2d 736.) A distinction based on the person killed, however, would make the defendant's criminal liability turn upon the marksmanship of victims and policemen. A rule of law cannot reasonably be based on such a fortuitous circumstance. The basic issue therefore is whether a robber can be convicted of murder for the killing of any person by another who is resisting the robbery.

"Murder is the unlawful killing of a human being, with malice aforethought." (Pen.Code, § 187.) Except when the common-law-felony-murder doctrine is applicable, an essential element of murder is an intent to kill or an intent with conscious disregard for life to commit acts likely to kill. The felony-murder doctrine ascribes malice aforethought to the felon who kills in the perpetration of an inherently dangerous felony. That doctrine is incorporated in section 189 of the Penal Code, which provides in part: "All murder . . . committed in the perpetration or attempt to perpetrate . . . robbery . . . is murder of the first degree." Thus, even though section 189 speaks only of degrees of "murder," inadvertent or accidental

1. In Commonwealth v. Redline, 391 Pa. 486, 137 A.2d 472 (1958), **D** was convicted of first-degree murder for the death of his co-felon who was killed by a police officer while the two were attempting to flee from the scene of their armed robbery. This conviction was reversed on the ground that the killing of the robber by the officer was justifiable homicide, whereas the accidental killing of the innocent victim in Almeida was only excusable homicide. The court admitted the distinction was rather slim. "However, the factual difference, so noted, admits of a recognizable distinction with respect to a felon's responsibility for an incidental killing (which another has committed), depending upon whether the killing was justifiable or excusable, and such distinction serves the useful purpose of thwarting further extension of the rule enunciated in Commonwealth v. Almeida . . . ."

The Pennsylvania court later recognized the absurdity of trying to use the distinction between justifiable and excusable homicide in the determination of proximate cause and took the position that a robber cannot be held to have caused a death occurring during the perpetration of a robbery if the fatal shot was fired by the victim or some other in defending against the robbery. Commonwealth ex rel. Smith v. Myers, 438 Pa. 218, 261 A.2d 550 (1970). Chief Justice Bell filed a vigorous dissent.

killings are first degree murders when committed by felons in the perpetration of robbery.

When a killing is not committed by a robber or by his accomplice but by his victim, malice aforethought is not attributable to the robber, for the killing is not committed by him in the perpetration or attempt to perpetrate robbery. It is not enough that the killing was a risk reasonably to be foreseen and that the robbery might therefore be regarded as a proximate cause of the killing. Section 189 requires that the felon or his accomplice commit the killing, for if he does not, the killing is not committed to perpetrate the felony. Indeed, in the present case the killing was committed to thwart a felony. To include such killings within section 189 would expand the meaning of the words "murder . . . which is committed in the perpetration . . . [of] robbery . . . " beyond common understanding.

The purpose of the felony-murder rule is to deter felons from killing negligently or accidentally by holding them strictly responsible for killings they commit. This purpose is not served by punishing them for killings committed by their victims. . . .

A defendant need not do the killing himself, however, to be guilty of murder. He may be vicariously responsible under the rules defining principals and criminal conspiracies. All persons aiding and abetting the commission of a robbery are guilty of first degree murder when one of them kills while acting in furtherance of the common design.[2] Moreover, when the defendant intends to kill or intentionally commit acts that are likely to kill with a conscious disregard for life, he is guilty of murder even though he uses another person to accomplish his objective.

Defendants who initiate gun battles may also be found guilty of murder if their victims resist and kill.[3] Under such circumstances, "the defendant for a base, anti-social motive and with wanton disregard for human life, does an act that involves a high degree of probability that it will result in death", and it is unnecessary to imply malice by invoking the felony-murder doctrine. To invoke the felony-murder doctrine to imply malice in such a case is unnecessary and overlooks the principles of criminal liability that should govern the responsibility of one person for a killing committed by another.

2. If one of two, who are engaged in the perpetration of robbery, kills a police officer, the other cannot avoid application of the felony-murder rule on the theory of an agreement not to injure anyone. People v. Bowen, 12 Mich.App. 438, 162 N.W.2d 911 (1968). However, see People v. Aaron, infra p. 439.

[Added by the Compiler.]

3. "However, depending upon the circumstances, a gun battle can be initiated by acts of provocation falling short of firing the first shot." Taylor v. Superior Court, 3 Cal.3d 578, 91 Cal.Rptr. 275, 477 P.2d 131 (1970). In this case one of the robbers not only pointed a gun but said: "Don't move or I'll blow your head off. . . . Don't move or we'll have an execution right here". And it was said in an extremely menacing manner.

Where an innocent person shot at a robber and killed the robber's "shield" by mistake a conviction of first degree murder was upheld. Pizano v. Superior Court of Tulare County, 21 Cal.3d 128, 145 Cal.Rptr. 524, 577 P.2d 659 (1978).

To invoke the felony-murder doctrine when the killing is not committed by the defendant or by his accomplice could lead to absurd results. Thus, two men rob a grocery store and flee in opposite directions. The owner of the store follows one of the robbers and kills him. Neither robber may have fired a shot. Neither robber may have been armed with a deadly weapon. If the felony-murder doctrine applied, however, the surviving robber could be convicted of first degree murder, even though he was captured by a policeman and placed under arrest at the time his accomplice was killed.

The felony-murder rule has been criticized on the grounds that in almost all cases in which it is applied it is unnecessary and that it erodes the relation between criminal liability and moral culpability. . . . Although it is the law in this state (Pen.Code, § 189), it should not be extended beyond any rational function that it is designed to serve. Accordingly, for a defendant to be guilty of murder under the felony-murder rule the act of killing must be committed by the defendant or by his accomplice acting in furtherance of their common design. . . .[4]

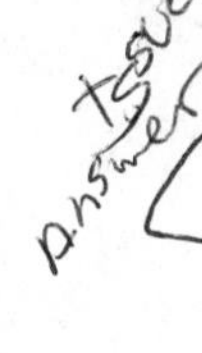

The judgment is affirmed as to defendant's conviction of first degree robbery and reversed as to his conviction of first degree murder.

PETERS, TOBRINER, PEEK and WHITE, JJ., concur.

BURKE, JUSTICE (dissenting).

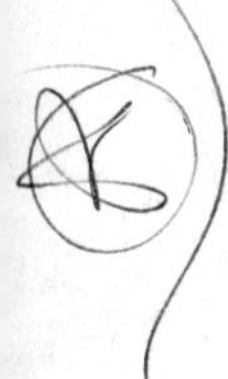

I dissent. The unfortunate effect of the decision of the majority in this case is to advise felons:

"Henceforth in committing certain crimes, including robbery, rape and burglary, you are free to arm yourselves with a gun and brandish it in the faces of your victims without fear of a murder conviction unless you or your accomplice pulls the trigger. If the menacing effect of your gun causes a victim or policeman to fire and kill an innocent person or a cofelon, you are absolved of responsibility for such killing unless you shoot first."

Obviously this advance judicial absolution removes one of the most meaningful deterrents to the commission of armed felonies.

4. Shortly after a burglary was committed by A and B, officers approached B while A was not shown to be present. In the effort to avoid arrest, B shot at an officer who returned the fire and killed B. A was charged with the murder of B (together with other offenses). The judge instructed the jury on the felony-murder rule and on the vicarious liability of one for the crime of his co-conspirator. It seems to have been assumed that the killing could be held to be within the perpetration of the recently-committed burglary; but it was held that A could not properly be held guilty of the murder of B. Felony-murder would not apply because the fatal shot was not fired by one of the conspirators but by the police. And A cannot be held guilty of the murder of B on the basis of vicarious liability for the crime of a co-conspirator because B could not be guilty of the murder of himself. Since B was not guilty of murder, neither was A. People v. Antick, 15 Cal.3d 79, 123 Cal.Rptr. 475, 539 P.2d 43 (1975).

Compare, In re Tyrone B., 58 Cal.App. 3d 884, 130 Cal.Rptr. 245 (1976).

In the present case defendant's accomplice was killed when the robbery victim fired after the accomplice had pointed a revolver at him. In People v. Harrison (1959) 176 Cal.App.2d 330, 1 Cal.Rptr. 414 (hearing in Supreme Court denied without a dissenting vote), the rationale of which the majority now disapprove, the robbery victim was himself accidentally killed by a shot fired by his employee after defendant robbers had opened fire, and the robbers were held guilty of murder for the killing. The majority now attempt to distinguish Harrison on the ground that there the robbers "initiated" the gun battle; in the present case the victim fired the first shot. As will appear, any such purported distinction is an invitation to further armed crimes of violence. There is no room in the law for sporting considerations and distinctions as to who fired first when dealing with killings which are caused by the actions of felons in deliberately arming themselves to commit any of the heinous crimes listed in Penal Code section 189. If a victim—or someone defending the victim—seizes an opportunity to shoot first when confronted by robbers with a deadly weapon (real or simulated), any "gun battle" *is* initiated by the armed robbers. In such a situation application of the felony-murder rule of section 189 of the Penal Code supports, if not compels, the conclusion that the surviving robbers committed murder even if the lethal bullet did not come from one of their guns, and whether it is an innocent person or an accomplice who dies. . . .

McComb, J., concurs.

PEOPLE v. AARON

Supreme Court of Michigan, 1980.
409 Mich. 672, 299 N.W.2d 304.

Fitzgerald, Justice. The existence and scope of the felony-murder doctrine have perplexed generations of law students, commentators and jurists in the United States and England, and have split our own Court of Appeals. In these cases, we must decide whether Michigan has a felony murder rule which allows the element of malice required for murder to be satisfied by the intent to commit the underlying felony or whether malice must be otherwise found by the trier of fact. We must also determine what is the *mens rea* required to support a conviction under Michigan's first-degree murder statute. . . .

Felony murder has never been a static, well-defined rule at common law, but throughout its history has been characterized by judicial reinterpretation to limit the harshness of the application of the rule. Historians and commentators have concluded that the rule is of questionable origin and that the reasons for the rule no longer exist, making it an anachronistic remnant, "a historic survivor for which there is no logical or practical basis for existence in modern law." . . .

Thus, we conclude that Michigan has not codified the common-law felony-murder rule. The use of the term "murder" in the first-degree statute requires that a murder must first be established before the statute is applied to elevate the degree.

The prosecution argues that even if Michigan does not have a statutory codification of the felony-murder rule, the common-law definition of murder included a homicide in the course of a felony. Thus, the argument continues, once a homicide in the course of a felony is proven, under the common-law felony-murder rule a murder has been established and the first-degree murder statute then becomes applicable. This Court has ruled that the term murder as used in the first-degree murder statute includes all types of murder at common law. Hence, we must determine whether Michigan in fact has a common-law felony-murder rule.

Our research has uncovered no Michigan cases, nor do the parties refer us to any, which have expressly considered whether Michigan has or should continue to have a common-law felony-murder doctrine. . . .

However, our finding that Michigan has never specifically adopted the doctrine which defines malice to include the intent to commit the underlying felony is not the end of our inquiry. In Michigan, the general rule is that the common law prevails except as abrogated by the Constitution, the Legislature or this Court.

This Court has not been faced previously with a decision as to whether it should abolish the felony-murder doctrine. Thus, the common-law doctrine remains the law in Michigan. Moreover, the assumption by appellate decisions that the doctrine exists, combined with the fact that Michigan trial courts have applied the doctrine in numerous cases resulting in convictions of first-degree felony-murder, requires us to address the common-law felony-murder issue. The cases before us today squarely present us with the opportunity to review the doctrine and to consider its continued existence in Michigan. Although there are no Michigan cases which specifically abrogate the felony-murder rule, there exists a number of decisions of this Court which have significantly restricted the doctrine in Michigan and which lead us to conclude that the rule should be abolished. . . .

Our review of Michigan case law persuades us that we should abolish the rule which defines malice as the intent to commit the underlying felony. Abrogation of the felony-murder rule is not a drastic move in light of the significant restrictions this Court has already imposed. Further, it is a logical extension of our decisions as discussed above. . . .

Accordingly, we hold today that malice is the intention to kill, the intention to do great bodily harm, or the wanton and willful disregard of the likelihood that the natural tendency of defendant's behavior is to cause death or great bodily harm. We further hold that malice is an essential element of any murder, as that term is judicially defined, whether the murder occurs in the course of a felony or otherwise. The facts and circumstances involved in the perpetration of a felony may evidence an intent to kill, an intent to cause great bodily harm, or a wanton and willful disregard of the likelihood that the natural tendency of defendant's behavior is to cause death or great bodily harm; however, the conclusion must be left to the jury to infer from all the evidence. Otherwise, "juries might be required to find the fact of malice where they were satisfied from the whole evidence it did not exist." . . .

Whatever reasons can be gleaned from the dubious origin of the felony-murder rule to explain its existence, those reasons no longer exist today. Indeed, most states, including our own, have recognized the harshness and inequity of the rule as is evidenced by the numerous restrictions placed on it. The felony-murder doctrine is unnecessary and in many cases unjust in that it violates the basic premise of individual moral culpability upon which our criminal law is based.

We conclude that Michigan has no statutory felony-murder rule which allows the mental element of murder to be satisfied by proof of the intention to commit the underlying felony. Today we exercise our role in the development of the common law by abrogating the common-law felony-murder rule. We hold that in order to convict a defendant of murder, as that term is defined by Michigan case law, it must be shown that he acted with intent to kill or to inflict great bodily harm or with a wanton and willful disregard of the likelihood that the natural tendency of his behavior is to cause death or great bodily harm. We further hold that the issue of malice must always be submitted to the jury.

The first-degree murder statute will continue to operate in that all *murder* committed in the perpetration or attempted perpetration of the enumerated felonies will be elevated to first-degree murder.

This decision shall apply to all trials in progress and those occurring after the date of this opinion.

In *Aaron*, the judgment of conviction of second-degree murder is reversed and this case is remanded to the trial court for a new trial. In *Thompson* and in *Wright*, the decisions of the Court of Appeals are affirmed and both cases are remanded to the trial court for new trial.

COLEMAN, C.J., and MOODY, LEVIN and KAVANAGH, JJ., concur.

RYAN, JUSTICE (concurring in part, dissenting in part).

I concur in the results reached by Justice Fitzgerald in these cases but write separately to express my disagreement with the reasoning employed in his opinion. . . .

STATE v. PETERSEN

Court of Appeals of Oregon, 1974.
17 Or.App. 478, 522 P.2d 912. Reversed in part 270 Or. 166, 526 P.2d 1008.

Before SCHWAB, C.J., and FORT and TANZER, JJ.

TANZER, JUDGE. . . .

The indictment alleges that defendant "recklessly cause[d] the death of another human being . . . ." This allegation follows the language of the manslaughter statute, and is therefore sufficient to state a crime and is valid against a demurrer. Where the statutory allegations are followed by particular allegations, as in *Andrews,* the indictment is not insufficient simply because the particulars standing alone do not constitute a crime. The particulars are in the nature of surplusage. State v. Andrews, Or.App., 98 Adv.Sh. 698, 517 P.2d 1062 (1974).

Defendant contends that the particulars alleged in the indictment negate the statutory allegation of the crime because although he was alleged to be a participant in the automobile race, he was not alleged to be a driver of either of the vehicles directly involved in the collision. Where the particulars contradict the statutory allegations, we should look to whether the allegation of a crime is negated.

The issue of the criminal responsibility of one racing driver for the death of a person actually killed by another racer appears to be a matter of first impression in Oregon, but it has been the subject of appellate decisions in other jurisdictions. At least as early as 1846, it was held that where two individuals were racing their vehicles (in that case, horsedrawn carts) along a public road, and one of them ran into and killed a third person during the course of the race, both racers were guilty of manslaughter. Regina v. Swindall, 2 Car & K 230, 175 Eng Reprint 95 (1846). Each participant engages mutually in reckless conduct which causes death. Regardless of which vehicle strikes the victim, the recklessness of both causes the death. That principle has been adhered to by most courts which have addressed the issue. . . .

We adopt the general rule and hold that one who recklessly participates in an automobile race may be criminally responsible for a death resulting therefrom, even though his vehicle is not the direct instrument of death. . . .

Having concluded that the state adequately alleged the crime of manslaughter, the next question is whether the trial court correctly denied defendant's motion for judgment of acquittal on the manslaughter charge. Consideration of this question requires an examination of the evidence presented at trial to determine whether it was sufficient to enable the fact-finder to find that defendant was reckless and that the death resulted from his recklessness.

On the evening of February 19, 1973, defendant and one Mike Barlow encountered Daniel Warren (the decedent for whose death defendant was indicted) and Richard Wille at a service station, and Mr. Wille expressed an interest in racing his Chevrolet Nova against defendant's pickup truck. An acceleration race was attempted near the service station, but the participants decided to move to a different area because of the number of cars on that street. Wille led the way to a point on Southeast 148th Street between Powell Boulevard and Division Street and, heading north on 148th toward Division Street, they engaged in an "acceleration standoff."[1] Then, the vehicles turned around and headed south on 148th. The vehicles stopped for a moment some 100 feet south of Division Street, there was a short conversation and then both vehicles took off rapidly in the direction of Powell. The Chevrolet Nova, occupied by driver Richard Wille and passenger Daniel Warren, was in the right lane. The pickup truck, occupied by defendant, who was driving, and Mike Barlow, was in the inside lane. The distance from Division Street to Powell Boulevard on 148th Street is approximately four-tenths of a mile. Defendant's pickup was in the lead from the start and continued in the lead as the vehicles reached speeds estimated at 60–80 miles per hour. The posted speed limit was 35 miles per hour. At some point prior to coming to the intersection with Powell Boulevard, defendant began to decelerate his pickup and brought his vehicle to a stop in the left turn lane at the intersection of 148th and Powell. As defendant came to a stop, Wille passed defendant and proceeded without any apparent diminution in speed through a stop sign into the intersection where his car was struck by a truck which was travelling west on Powell. Both Wille and his passenger, Warren, were killed.

Following the collision, defendant remained in the left turn lane for a short time and then turned left onto Powell. He left the vicinity of the accident without rendering assistance or informing anyone of his identity.

The testimony indicates that there was no agreed-upon finish line to the race. Defendant's passenger, Barlow, stated that his understanding was that the race would finish when "we figured it was a safe distance for getting up to the speed and closing down and stopping in time." James Stewart, who worked at the service station where the plans were laid for the race, testified on the practices of street racers. He stated that the distance to be raced in a street race is somewhat indistinct, depending on "the distance you have before you have to stop." . . .

The next issue to be considered with regard to this assignment of error is the sufficiency of the evidence of causation: Whether defendant's reckless conduct caused the death of Daniel Warren. Analysis of this issue involves a two-step approach: First, was defendant's

1. The witness did not define the term "acceleration standoff" beyond stating that it is not a race.

conduct a cause in fact of the death? Second, if so, was it also a legal cause of the death in the contemplation of statutes imposing criminal liability? LaFave and Scott, Criminal Law 248, § 35 (1972).

The test for causation in fact can be stated as follows: Was the defendant's conduct a substantial factor in bringing about the forbidden result? LaFave and Scott, supra, at 250; Perkins on Criminal Law 695–696, § 9 (1969). In this case, had defendant not engaged in the unlawful race with Richard Wille, the accident would never have occurred. Defendant helped create the dangerous situation, and was a part of it. His conduct was a substantial factor in bringing about the decedent's death.

Was defendant's conduct the legal cause of the death? Defendant's argument centers on a discussion of tort concepts such as proximate cause, intervening cause, and foreseeability of harm, but tort concepts are of limited utility in criminal prosecutions since they spring from different policy considerations. LaFave and Scott, supra, at 251–252; Perkins, supra, at 693. Basically, criminal culpability exists where the result is within the area of risk which the rules of caution violated by the defendant are intended to minimize.

In this case, the decedent was clearly within the class endangered by the conduct of street-racing, i.e., motorists, pedestrians, etc., and the collision was the sort of injurious event which the prohibitions against street-racing are supposed to prevent. ORS 483.122(1).[3] Therefore, there is a clear legal causative connection between the defendant's acts and the death.

Defendant suggests that Wille's act of accelerating his auto past defendant's pickup truck and into the intersection was an intervening cause, and that defendant was thereby relieved of responsibility, i.e., that Wille's act superseded defendant's conduct as the cause of death. However, in order to be a superseding cause, the intervening cause must be independent, that is, it must not be a consequence of defendant's antecedent conduct. Perkins on Criminal Law, supra, at 722–725. In the case at bar, Wille's conduct was within the risk of the race, particularly since no finish line had been agreed upon.

Defendant suggests that a distinction should be drawn between cases where the decedent was not a participant in the race and cases where he was a participant, and that, since the evidence showed that the decedent was a passenger in one of the racing automobiles, defendant could not be criminally liable for the death. This is also the position taken by the dissent. However, there is no indication that such an exception was intended by the legislature. The words of the statutes are inclusive. They specify no exception. One is guilty of manslaughter if he "recklessly . . . causes the death of another human being." ORS 163.005, 163.125(1)(a). Had the legislature in-

3. ORS 483.122(1) provides:

"No race or contest for speed shall be held upon any road, street or highway in this state."

tended that liability not attach if the victim were a participant in the events leading to the death, it could have easily so provided. It did so regarding felony murder, ORS 163.115(1)(c), and was capable of specifying a similar exception to manslaughter if it had intended to create one. In the absence of such a provision, this court ought not to amend the statute under the rubric of "policy."

Moreover, logic does not compel the carving out of such an exception. The gravamen of the offense charged in the indictment is recklessness, i.e., the conscious disregard of a substantial and unjustifiable risk that a death would occur, and a death resulting therefrom. That a participant's passenger was killed rather than an innocent third party was an immaterial matter of chance. Such tort concepts as contributory negligence and assumption of the risk are not defenses against responsibility for criminal conduct. State v. Mellenberger, 163 Or. 233, 95 P.2d 709, 128 A.L.R. 1506 (1939); see generally Perkins on Criminal Law 969–973 (2d ed. 1970). The defendant's conduct is equally reckless, equally causative and equally anti-social regardless of which person is killed in a collision of participants and non-participants or whether a car happens to hit a utility post or a pedestrian. He remains criminally liable or not regardless of how the civil law may allocate responsibility for money damages.

The dissent, to over-simplify, argues that policy requires that assumption of risk negates the element of causation. In support of that proposition it cites examples such as skydivers and race-track drivers who mutually engage in dangerous activities. We need not decide this case upon extreme examples because these facts are easily distinguishable. The activity at bar presents a substantial risk to the nonparticipating public. As noted, the chance death of a participant does not diminish the danger of the act to others. The examples cited by the dissent incur only a negligible risk to the public and speculation regarding legislative intent toward coverage of such acts has no application to the facts of this case.

There was sufficient evidence to justify the trier of fact in concluding that defendant was guilty of manslaughter. Defendant's motion for judgment of acquittal on Count I was properly denied. . . .[a]

Affirmed.

SCHWAB, CHIEF JUDGE (dissenting).

I would reverse the manslaughter conviction. . . .

a. [Added by the Compiler.] Three men engaged in target practice under circumstances of extreme negligence. Using a rifle that was sighted for 900 yards and would probably be fatal at a mile, they fired across three highways and intervening territory, with no precautions. One shot killed a boy who was playing in his garden. There was no evidence as to which one fired the fatal shot. All three were convicted of manslaughter. The court took the position, in substance, that as they had joined in a criminally-negligent enterprise, each shot was, in legal effect, the shot of all. Regina v. Salmon, 14 Cox C.C. (1880).

N.B. Had careful shooting at the target been safe, and only the fatal shot fired with criminal negligence, it would not have imputed to the others.

REGINA v. BENGE AND ANOTHER

Maidstone Crown Court, Kent Summer Assizes, 1865.
4 F. & F. 504, 176 Eng.Rep. 665.

[Benge and Gallimore were indicted for manslaughter, but it was admitted that there was no case against Gallimore and the case proceeded only against Benge. He was foreman of a crew employed to repair rails on a certain portion of the track. He had a book telling exactly when trains were due but looked at the wrong date and as a result ordered certain rails removed from a bridge shortly before a train was due. As was usual he sent one of the crew with a flag to signal if any train should approach while the rails were not in place. This man was to go at least 1000 yards in the direction from which a train would come, but he went only 540 yards. The flag signal could be seen by the engineer at a distance of 500 yards or more but he was inattentive and did not see it until abreast of the flagman. He did all he could to stop the train but it was then too late and a wreck resulted in which many lives were lost. There was evidence showing that the train could easily have been stopped within 1000 yards at any speed.]

PIGOTT, B., said, that assuming culpable negligence on the part of the prisoner which materially contributed to the accident, it would not be material that others also by their negligence contributed to cause it. Therefore he must leave it to the jury whether there was negligence of the prisoner which had been the substantial cause of the accident. In summing up the case to the jury, he said, their verdict must depend upon whether the death was mainly caused by the culpable negligence of the prisoner. Was the accident caused by the taking up of the rails at a time when an express train was about to arrive, was that the act of the prisoner, and was it owing to culpable negligence on his part? . . . Now, here the primary cause was certainly the taking up of the rails at a time when the train was about to arrive, and when it would be impossible to replace them in time to avoid the accident. And this the prisoner admitted was owing to his own mistake. Was that mistake culpable negligence, and did it mainly or substantially cause the accident? Then as to its being the main cause of the accident, it is true that the company had provided other precautions to avoid any impending catastrophe, and that these were not observed upon this particular occasion; but was it not owing to the prisoner's culpable negligence that the accident was impending, and if so, did his negligence the less cause it, because if other persons had not been negligent it might possibly have been avoided?[1]

Verdict—Guilty.

1. D shot X who was taken to a hospital promptly and in time to have been saved by proper surgical treatment. But he died from hemorrhage because the surgeon neglected for more than ten hours to control the bleeding. A convic-

REGINA v. MICHAEL

Court for Crown Cases Reserved, 1840.
2 Moody 120, 169 Eng.Rep. 48.

The prisoner Catherine Michael was tried before MR. BARON ALDERSON of the Central Criminal Court in April 1840 (MR. JUSTICE LITTLEDALE being present), for the wilful murder of George Michael, an infant of the age of nine months, by administering poison.

The indictment alleged that the prisoner contriving and intending to kill and murder George Michael on the 31st of March, in the third year of the reign of her present Majesty, upon the said George Michael feloniously, &c. did make an assault; and that the prisoner a large quantity, to wit half an ounce weight of a certain deadly poison called laudanum, feloniously, &c. did give and administer unto said George Michael, with intent that he should take and swallow the same down into his body (she then and there well knowing the said laudanum to be a deadly poison), and the said laudanum so given and administered unto him by the said Catherine Michael as aforesaid, the said George Michael did take and swallow down into his body, by reason and by means of which said taking and swallowing down the said laudanum into his body as aforesaid, the said George Michael became and was mortally sick and distempered in his body, of which said mortal sickness and distemper the said George Michael from &c. till &c. did languish &c. and died; and concluding in the usual form as in cases of murder.

It appeared in evidence that the prisoner on the 27th day of March last, delivered to one Sarah Stephens, with whom the child was at nurse, a quantity of laudanum about an ounce, telling the said Sarah Stephens that it was proper medicine for the child to take, and directing her to administer to the child every night a teaspoonful thereof. That such a quantity as a teaspoonful was quite sufficient to kill a child; and that the prisoner's intention, as shewn by the finding of the jury in so delivering the laudanum and giving such directions as aforesaid, was to kill the child.

tion of manslaughter was affirmed on the ground that the surgeon's gross neglect was not superseding. "The factual situation is in legal effect the same, whether the victim bleeds to death because surgical attention is not available, or because, although available, it is delayed by reason of the surgeon's gross neglect or incompetence." People v. McGee, 31 Cal.2d 229, 243, 187 P.2d 706, 715 (1947).

"The fact that a third person might have, but did not, rescue the victims cannot lessen defendant's responsibility for the consequences of his acts." People v. Nichols, 3 Cal.3d 150, 89 Cal.Rptr. 721, 725, 474 P.2d 673, 677 (1970).

If death would not have resulted had it not been for the gross negligence of the attendant physician, the one who caused the original injury cannot be said to have caused the death. Gross negligence is abnormal human conduct which is not foreseeable, and is superseding. People v. Calvaresi, 188 Colo. 277, 534 P.2d 316 (1975).

That Sarah Stephens took home with her the laudanum, and thinking the child did not require medicine had no intention of administering it. She however not intending to give it at all, left it on the mantelpiece of her room, which was in a different house from where the prisoner resided, she, the prisoner, then being a wet nurse to a lady; and some days afterwards, that is, on the 31st of March, a little boy of the said Sarah Stephens, of the age of five years, during the accidental absence of Sarah Stephens, who had gone from home for some hours, removed the laudanum from its place and administered to the prisoner's child a much larger dose of it than a teaspoonful, and the child died in consequence.

The jury were directed that if the prisoner delivered to Sarah Stephens the laudanum, with intent that she should administer it to the child and thereby produce its death, the quantity so directed to be administered being sufficient to cause death; and that if the (prisoner's original intention still continuing) the laudanum was afterwards administered by an unconscious agent, the death of the child under such circumstances was murder on the part of the prisoner.

They were directed that if the teaspoonful of laudanum was sufficient to produce death, the administration by the little boy of a much larger quantity would make no difference.

The jury found the prisoner guilty. The judgment was respited, that the opinion of the Judges might be taken, whether the facts above stated constituted an administering of the poison by the prisoner to the deceased child.

This case was considered by all the Judges (except GURNEY, B. and MAULE, J.) in Easter Term, 1840, and they were unanimously of opinion that the conviction was right.

BUSH v. COMMONWEALTH

Court of Appeals of Kentucky, 1880.

78 Ky. 268.

JUDGE HINES delivered the opinion of the court.

For the purpose of testing the correctness of the instructions, we will assume that every deduction that the jury were authorized from the evidence to make, is a fact established by the evidence.

The jury might have found, 1st, that the girl was accidentally shot by appellant in an attempt to shoot, in necessary self-defense, her father; 2d, that the accused had the pistol in his hand for defense from an anticipated assault, and that the shot producing the wound was unintentional, both as to the firing of the pistol and as to the person wounded; 3d, that the killing was deliberate murder. The finding was guilty of murder, and a sentence of death by hanging. . . .

It is proper, in this connection, to state that the evidence was such as to justify the jury in finding that the wound inflicted by the shot was neither necessarily nor probably mortal, and that the death ensued, not from the wound, but from scarlet fever, negligently communicated by the attending physician.

As said in Commonwealth v. Hackett (2 Allen 136, 141), the rule of the common law would seem to be, that if the wound was a dangerous wound, that is, calculated to endanger or destroy life, and death ensued therefrom, it is sufficient proof of murder or manslaughter; and that the person who inflicted it is responsible, though it may appear that the deceased might have recovered if he had taken proper care of himself, or submitted to a surgical operation, or that unskillful or improper treatment aggravated the wound and contributed to the death, or that death was immediately caused by a surgical operation rendered necessary by the condition of the wound. The principle on which this rule is founded is, that every one is held to contemplate and to be responsible for the natural consequences of his own acts. But if the wound is not dangerous in itself, and death results from improper treatment, or from disease subsequently contracted, not superinduced by or resulting from the wound, the accused is not guilty. When the disease is a consequence of the wound, although the proximate cause of the death, the person inflicting the wound is guilty, because the death can be traced as a result naturally flowing from the wound and coming in the natural order of things; but when there is a supervening cause, not naturally intervening by reason of the wound and not produced by any necessity created by the wound, the death is by the visitation of Providence and not from the act of the party inflicting the wound. In the case under consideration, the fever was not the natural consequence of the wound, nor was it produced by any necessity created by the infliction of the wound. It did not render it necessary to have the wound treated by a physician just recovering from the scarlet fever, even if it be conceded that medical treatment was necessary at all. If the death was not connected with the wound in the regular chain of causes and consequences, there ought not to be any responsibility. If a new and wholly independent instrumentality interposed and produced death, it cannot be said that the wound was the natural or proximate cause of the death. This view of the law was not so presented to the jury as to give the appellant its full benefit. It should have been clearly and definitely presented to the jury that if they believed from the evidence that death would not have resulted from the wound but for the intervention of the disease, they should not find the accused guilty of murder or manslaughter, but that they might find him guilty of wilfully and maliciously shooting and wounding under section 2, article 6, chapter 29,

General Statutes; or of shooting and wounding in sudden affray, or in sudden heat and passion, without malice, under section 1, article 17, chapter 29, General Statutes. . . .

We deem it unnecessary to pass in detail upon each of the instructions granted and refused, as the intimation here given will be a sufficient guide in a retrial of the cause.

Judgment reversed, and cause remanded, with directions for further proceedings consistent with this opinion.[1]

MODEL PENAL CODE[a]

Section 2.03 Causal Relationship Between Conduct and Result; Divergence Between Result Designed or Contemplated and Actual Result or Between Probable and Actual Result.

(1) Conduct is the cause of a result when:

(a) it is an antecedent but for which the result in question would not have occurred; and

(b) the relationship between the conduct and result satisfies any additional causal requirements imposed by the Code or by the law defining the offense.

(2) When purposely or knowingly causing a particular result is an element of an offense, the element is not established if the actual result is not within the purpose or the contemplation of the actor unless:

(a) the actual result differs from that designed or contemplated, as the case may be, only in the respect that a different person or different property is injured or affected or that the injury or harm designed or contemplated would have been more serious or more extensive than that caused; or

(b) the actual result involves the same kind of injury or harm as that designed or contemplated and is not too remote or accidental in its occurrence to have a [just] bearing on the actor's liability or on the gravity of his offense.

(3) When recklessly or negligently causing a particular result is an element of an offense, the element is not established if the actual result is not within the risk of which the actor is aware or, in the case of negligence, of which he should be aware unless:

(a) the actual result differs from the probable result only in the respect that a different person or different property is injured or affected or that the probable injury or harm would have been more serious or more extensive than that caused; or

1. Bush was tried again and convicted. This conviction was reversed by the Supreme Court of the United States on other grounds. Bush v. Kentucky, 107 U.S. 110, 1 S.Ct. 625, 27 L.Ed. 354 (1882).

a. See Causation in the Model Penal Code, 78 Col.L.Rev. 1249 (1978).

(b) the actual result involves the same kind of injury or harm as the probable result and is not too remote or accidental in its occurrence to have a [just] bearing on the actor's liability or on the gravity of his offense.

(4) When causing a particular result is a material element of an offense for which absolute liability is imposed by law, the element is not established unless the actual result is a probable consequence of the actor's conduct.[2]

Chapter 7

RESPONSIBILITY: IN GENERAL

SECTION 1. MENS REA

Responsibility means answerability or accountability. It is used in the criminal law in the sense of "criminal responsibility" and hence means answerability to the criminal law. No one is answerable to the criminal law for consequences not legally imputable to him. The present problem does not arise except in connection with consequences attributable to the one accused within the rules of imputability. On the other hand, consequences properly imputable to a certain person may be very harmful and yet not under such circumstances as to require him to answer criminally for what he has done. Whether they do or do not require him so to answer presents the problem of "responsibility."

Crime is frequently said to require both act and intent. As so used the word "intent" has quite a different meaning than "intention." An effort to avoid this variant use of the word has led to this suggestion: For guilt of crime there must be the union or joint operation of act and intent, or criminal negligence. This is not an improvement. It implies the use of "intent" in the strict sense of "intention," and with this limitation the mere addition of "criminal negligence" is inadequate to give full scope to the mental element involved in crime. Either form of expression, however, emphasizes the existence of the mental element. Leaving aside for the moment (1) the so-called "civil offenses" which are beyond the periphery of true crime, (2) the possibility of change by statute, and (3) difficulties of interpretation in certain situations, we find blameworthiness essential to criminal guilt.

The phrase "criminal intent" often has been used to express this requirement of blameworthiness. At other times "general criminal intent" has been employed to emphasize that the mental element so designated is not limited to actual intention.[1] Hence it is necessary to draw a very sharp line between actual intent (in the strict sense) and the various states of mind included within the very loose label of "general criminal intent."

1. "Criminal intent" in its narrow and proper sense is "nothing more than the intentional doing of 'that which the law declares to be a crime,' . . ." People v. Zerillo, 36 Cal.2d 222, 232, 223 P.2d 223, 230 (1950). "It is the criminal mind and purpose going with the act which distinguishes a criminal trespass from a mere civil injury." State v. Smith, 135 Mont. 18, 334 P.2d 1099, 1102 (1959).

The requirement of blameworthiness frequently has been couched in law Latin: "*Actus non facit reum, nisi mens sit rea.*" And it has been common to pick two words from this sentence and substitute "*mens rea*" for "guilty mind" or "mind at fault." Hence *mens rea* is essential to criminal guilt (with the qualifications mentioned above as to blameworthiness, which will receive attention under the head of "strict liability" and will be assumed here without further repetition).

Stated in other words, every crime is made up of two constituent parts: (1) the physical part and (2) the mental part. These may be described quite adequately as "the physical part of the crime" and "the mental part of the crime." Shorter labels are needed, however, for discussion purposes. The terms "guilty deed" and "guilty mind" are not entirely satisfactory because the former may be thought to be sufficient for punishment, whereas the union of both parts is required for conviction of crime. Hence it may be well to substitute Latin phrases which have the same meaning. These phrases are *actus reus* and *mens rea.*

If we can prove the existence of the physical part of the crime charged, and that this happening is attributable to the defendant within the legal rules of imputability, we have established his *actus reus.* And if we can prove that in doing what he did the defendant's state of mind was one which satisfies the requirements of the mental element of the crime charged we have established his *mens rea.* Neither one alone is sufficient for conviction; it is the combination of the two which constitutes criminal guilt.

The general mens rea. The mental element of crime is sometimes regarded as a state of mind common to all offenses, and sufficient for some, although an additional mental element may be required for others. Stated as a formula: "State-of-mind-X is common to all crimes and is sufficient for conviction unless the particular offense requires some additional mental element such as state-of-mind-Y or state-of-mind-Z."

Such a formula may have some value if care is taken to limit its application rather narrowly. A person may be so young that nothing can exist in his mind which will meet the juridical requirement of *mens rea*; hence it may be said that for *mens rea* the mind of the person must not be too young. Again, for *mens rea* the mental faculties must not be too greatly disturbed by mental disease; and under many circumstances a sane mind must not be too greatly diverted by a misunderstanding of the relevant facts or constrained by certain types of compulsion. Without going further into detail it is sufficient to point out the need of excluding every mental pattern which contains any factor sufficient in law to exculpate one who has done the particular deed in question. If every such factor is excluded and there is present an intent to do the deed which constitutes the *actus reus* of a certain offense, the result may be said to be the "general *mens rea.*" It is necessary to add, however, that for certain crimes it is possible to substitute some other mental factor (such as criminal negligence) for the actual intent to do the *actus reus.*

In brief, while *mens rea* has certain factors which remain constant, these have to do with the general outlines of the mental pattern rather than with the minute details. For *mens rea:* (1) on the negative side there must not be found any factor which is sufficient for exculpation; (2) on the positive side there must be found an intent to do the deed which constitutes the *actus reus* of the offense charged (or some other mental element recognized as a substitute as, for example, criminal negligence in prosecutions for certain crimes). This is the so-called "general *mens rea*" or "general criminal intent" which is common to all true crime. It is indispensable, and is sufficient for guilt of some offenses although some additional mental element is required for others.

The *actus reus* may be the same in two crimes as in murder and manslaughter. For the most part, however, it differs from crime to crime. In burglary the *actus reus* is the nocturnal breaking into the dwelling house of another; in murder it is homicide; in battery it is the unlawful application of force to the person of another. The other constituent part also differs from crime to crime. In common-law burglary the *mens rea* is the intent to commit a felony; in murder it is malice aforethought; in battery no more is needed than the so-called "general criminal intent" which in a particular case may be criminal negligence. Hence in considering whether or not the actual *mens rea* has been established in a particular case, it is necessary to direct attention, not only to the state of mind with which the defendant acted, but also to the particular offense with which he is charged.

STATE v. CHICAGO, MILWAUKEE & ST. PAUL RAILWAY CO.

Supreme Court of Iowa, 1903.
122 Iowa 22, 96 N.W. 904.

The defendant's line of road crosses that of the Northwestern Railroad Company at Slater on the level. On the 14th day of February, 1902, the defendant, through its engineer, pulled its freight train over said crossing without stopping, as required by section 2073 of the Code, and in this action recovery of the penalty as therein provided was claimed. Trial to jury resulted in verdict and judgment for the state. The defendant appeals.—Reversed.

LADD, J. The defendant admitted the failure of its train to stop within 800 feet and more than 200 feet from the crossing, and interposed the defense that the engineer in charge did all he could to stop it, but that, owing to the brakes not working in the usual manner, the momentum of the train carried it over the crossing. The court submitted the case to the jury on the theory that the burden of proof was on the defendant, in order to exonerate itself from liability, to show by a preponderance of evidence that the failure to stop was not due to any negligence on the part of its employes in operating the train, or of the company in not having proper appliances, or in keeping those had in proper condition, and that the company might be liable even though the engineer was not. Possibly that should have been the law, but it was not so written by the legislature. The statute in question reads: "All trains run upon any railroad in this state which intersects or crosses any other railroad on the same level shall be brought to a full stop at a distance of not less than two hundred and not more than eight hundred feet from the point of intersection or crossing, before such intersection or crossing is passed, except as otherwise provided in this chapter. Any engineer violating the provisions of this section shall forfeit one hundred dollars for each offense, to be recovered in an action in the name of the state for the benefit of the school fund, and the corporation on whose road the offense is committed shall forfeit the sum of two hundred dollars for each offense to be recovered in like manner." Section 2073, Code. The latter part of the statute is purely penal in character, with the evident object of punishing the offender, rather than afford [sic] a remedy for the wrongful act. In this respect it differs radically from provisions awarding damages flowing from certain acts, such as the setting out of fire. Its meaning, then, cannot be extended beyond the terms employed. But one offense is denounced by it, and that is the omission of the engineer to stop the train as required. The first sentence commands what shall be done—defines a duty; the first clause of the second sentence imposes a penalty on any engineer for "each offense" of omitting such duty; the second clause of the second sentence adds a penalty against the corporation "on whose road such offense is committed." To what do these last words refer? Manifestly, to the offense of which the engineer is guilty. No other is mentioned in the section. The statute cannot be fairly read otherwise. The thought seems to have been that, as the engineer controls the train, the fault in failing to stop as required is primarily his, and secondarily that of the company for which he acts. There is no ground for holding that the company may be liable independent of any fault of the engineer. The forfeiture of the corporation is made to depend upon his guilt of the offense defined, and upon that only.

II. As the statute is purely penal in character, it ought not to be construed as fixing an absolute liability. A failure to stop may sometimes occur, notwithstanding the utmost efforts of the engineer. In such event this omission cannot be regarded as unlawful. The law never designs the infliction of punishment where there is no wrong. The necessity of intent of purpose is always to be implied in such statutes. An actual and conscious infraction of duty is contemplated. The maxim, "*Actus non facit reum nisi meus* [sic] *sit rea,*" obtains in all penal statutes unless excluded by their language. See Regina v. Tolson, 23 Q.B.Div. 168, where it was said, "Crime is not committed where the mind of the person committing the act is innocent."

See, also, Sutherland on Statutory Construction, section 354 et seq. No doubt many statutes impose a penalty regardless of the intention of those who violate them, but these ordinarily relate to matters which may be known definitely in advance. In such cases commission of the offense is due to neglect or inadvertence. But even then it can hardly be supposed the offender would be held if the act were committed when in a state of somnambulism or insanity. As it is to be assumed in the exercise of the proper care that the engineer has control of his train at all times, proof of the mere failure to stop makes out a *prima facie* case. But this was open to explanation, and if, from that given, it was made to appear that he made proper preparation, and intended to stop, and put forth every reasonable effort to do so, he should be exonerated. . . .

Reversed.[1]

STATE v. PEERY

Supreme Court of Minnesota, 1947.
224 Minn. 346, 28 N.W.2d 851.

THOMAS GALLAGHER, JUSTICE. Two appeals involving a conviction for indecent exposure, one from an order of the municipal court of St. Paul vacating its prior order granting defendant a new trial, and the other from a subsequent order denying defendant's motion for a new trial on the ground of newly discovered evidence. . . .

The evidence presented at the trial indicates that defendant, 23 years of age, a veteran of four major campaigns of the United States army in the South Pacific and at the time in question a seminar student at Concordia College awaiting the opening of the fall term at the University of Minnesota, occupied a corner ground-floor room in the Men's Dormitory at Concordia. The room has two windows, one opening to the west and the other to the north. About 15 to 20 feet from the west window, a cement sidewalk passes through the college grounds. It is used by the public generally and particularly by employees going to and coming from their work at the Brown & Bigelow plant nearby.

The state's witnesses here, several young ladies employed by Brown & Bigelow, testified in substance that on several occasions in passing by the Men's Dormitory on their way from work about 5 p.m. they had observed defendant unclothed, standing in front of or near

1. Where a statute outside of the Criminal Code provides for imprisonment and the legislature has not shown an intent to dispense with a culpable mental state, the prosecution must at least establish criminal negligence to convict. McNutt v. State, 56 Or.App. 545, 642 P.2d 692 (1982).

A requisite state of mind of "knowingly" would be implied from a statute punishing criminal trespass even though not expressly designated in the statute. Bollier v. People, 635 P.2d 543 (Colo.1981). Accord, for crime of assault on a police officer. People v. Hart, 658 P.2d 857 (Colo.1983).

the north window of his room, and that he later walked across and stood in the same condition near the west window; that on one such occasion they had observed him raise the west window shade and stand near this window exposed to view, entirely unclothed. There is no evidence that defendant had signaled or called to these witnesses or otherwise endeavored to direct their attention to himself.

In his defense, defendant testified that he returned to his room in the dormitory about 5 p.m. each evening; that it was his custom then to change his work clothing, take a shower in the basement of the dormitory, return to his room, and dress for his evening meal and classes. He denied that he had intentionally exposed himself. He admitted that on some occasions he may have neglected to draw the shades, but testified that he was not conscious of passers-by on the days in question; that he was careful as to his conduct at all times because of his high regard for his classmates who occupied neighboring dormitories. He stated that on at least one of the dates testified to by the state's witnesses he had not worked or changed his clothing at the time such witnesses had testified that they had passed his quarters and observed him.

Dr. Hugo W. Thompson, professor of Religion and Philosophy at Macalester College in St. Paul, testified that he was in charge of the industrial seminar at Concordia College attended by defendant; that the classes therein were held at night; that the students, including defendant, taking such course had been carefully selected from other colleges and were required, as part of the seminar, to be employed during the daytime; that defendant had always conducted himself as a gentleman, and the records of the project so indicated; that he (Dr. Thompson) had often used the walk in front of the Men's Dormitory at about the same time of day the state's witnesses passed defendant's quarters; that on such occasions he had often looked toward the Men's Dormitory, including defendant's room, but at no time had he witnessed any such incidents as testified to by the state's witnesses; that the walk is on college property and not a public street; that west of the walk is a thick hedge; that it is 40 feet from the west wall of the building to said walk; that defendant's room could be seen from his office across the way, but at no time had he seen any conduct on the part of defendant such as testified to by the state's witnesses. A portion of the settled case which the trial court certified as true and correct stated:

"There was no testimony by any of the witnesses either for the Prosecution or the Defense that defendant had waved or signaled to any of the girl witnesses for the Prosecution who claimed to have seen any of the exposures, or that he had in any way attempted to attract their attention or that he had called to or whistled at them or made any sound or done anything else calculated to attract their attention or the attention of anyone; other than the facts hereinbefore specifically recited.

"There was no testimony by any of the witnesses that defendant had committed any lewd or indecent acts other than the claimed exposures." . . .

1. The principle is well established that under either the ordinance or the statute, before the offense of indecent exposure can be established, the evidence must be sufficient to sustain a finding that the misconduct complained of was committed with the deliberate intent of being indecent or lewd. Ordinary acts or conduct involving exposure of the person as the result of carelessness or thoughtlessness do not in themselves establish the offense of indecent exposure. This would seem to be particularly true where the acts complained of take place within the privacy of a lodging removed from public places and where observation thereof is to some extent an invasion of the rights of privacy ordinarily attached to a home, whether it be a dwelling house or a room in a college dormitory. . . .

3. In the instant case, we are far from satisfied that the evidence is sufficient to sustain the trial court's finding that defendant's conduct was wilful and lewd rather than the result of carelessness or thoughtlessness. Defendant has denied the intent. He is a man without a previous blemish against his record. He is a combat veteran of four major campaigns of the South Pacific, honorably discharged as a staff sergeant, seeking a college education, and working part time to help defray his expenses. He concedes that on occasions he may have been careless. His room is small and fairly close to the sidewalk. His ordinary activity therein at about the times in question, when it was his custom to remove his clothing preparatory to bathing, might easily be misinterpreted by passers-by looking into his room.

There is no evidence whatsoever that he endeavored to attract the attention of passers-by by motioning, signaling, or calling to them, unless his act of raising the shade on one occasion might be thus regarded. This would seem rather flimsy evidence upon which to convict a man of the charge specified and to forever blemish his name and character as a result.

The testimony of Dr. Hugo Thompson, professor of Religion and Philosophy at Macalester College, characterizes defendant as a man of good reputation and high standing in the seminar. All the testimony in the case is consistent with defendant's testimony that he may have been careless or heedless, but that he did not intentionally expose himself. In our opinion, the evidence as submitted is insufficient to sustain a finding that defendant wilfully and intentionally indecently exposed himself in violation of either the ordinance or the statute above designated.

Reversed with directions to enter judgment discharging defendant.

PETERSON, JUSTICE (dissenting). Because I think that the evidence was sufficient to justify a finding of intentional indecent exposure, I dissent.

There is no dispute concerning certain facts such as those that defendant was nude in the room in question under such circumstances as to be visible through the windows to casual passers-by on the sidewalk outside; that the room is on the first floor at the northwest corner of the building; that there is a window on the north side opening onto the street lying to the north; that there is a window on the west side opening onto the sidewalk; that the bottom sills of the windows are only knee-high from the floor; that if a man stood nude in front of a window his private parts would be exposed to public view; and that girls employed in the vicinity passed on the sidewalk outside the window in going to and from their work. . . .

The majority holding simply amounts to saying that it is lawful for a man to stand nude in front of a window knowing that passers-by will see him. I cannot subscribe to such a doctrine, because I think it is not the law.

LIMICY v. STATE

Court of Criminal Appeals of Texas, 1945.
148 Tex.Cr.R. 130, 185 S.W.2d 571.

BEAUCHAMP, JUDGE. The appeal is from a conviction on a charge of committing an abortion. The sentence was four years in the penitentiary.

The court in the indictment upon which conviction was had alleges that John Limicy did "willfully and designedly in and upon Lula May Howard, a women [sic] then and there pregnant, did make an assault, and did then and there unlawfully, and designedly without the consent of the said Lula May Howard, procure an abortion by then and there striking, kicking, beating and violently using the person of her, the said Lula May Howard, during her pregnancy." It becomes necessary under the charge to show that appellant "designedly" committed the offense, with the intention to force an abortion. The principal question raised by the appeal is on the sufficiency of the evidence to support a finding in accordance with the indictment.

The prosecuting witness, Lula May Howard, a twenty-year-old girl, had lived with appellant since 1940 without being married to him. They had a child born of this illegitimate cohabitation and, if we properly understand the record, she had a miscarriage at a previous time. Some five months before the date of the alleged offense they had discovered that she was again pregnant and this fact was frequently discussed between them. There is, however, no intimation that any trouble had arisen about it or that appellant was displeased because she was pregnant and the fact of her being pregnant was not mentioned or considered in any way at the time of the fight which gave rise to the prosecution. He used no language that would indicate any intention to force an abortion and the jury had only the facts and circumstances involved in the fight upon which they could find him guilty under the court's charge. The prosecutrix describes the "fight" between her and the appellant as beginning on July 8th. He first beat her with a chair. That was during the night time. After she succeeded in getting the chair away from him he grabbed a rub board and broke it over her head. He also broke the broom handle in striking her. . . . They fussed and fought intermittently until Monday, July 10th, following the Saturday night when she describes the fight as beginning. The wounds were principally on her shoulders and head. When the fighting ceased they went up town together and later returned home after which she began to suffer. The appellant had gone and she sent for a negro woman who was known as being "kind of a granny woman." A doctor was called during the night. Whatever he did and the condition which he found is not in the record. The next day Dr. Wilson was called and he testifies in the case that in his opinion the premature birth of the child, after it had died in the mother's womb, was brought about by the injuries which he found inflicted on the prosecutrix.

The record does not disclose the origin of the trouble between the parties nor is it contended that he alone engaged in the conflict. It was a fight between them in which she was the loser by considerable odds. She testified in behalf of the State and said "we just had a fight that time and he beat me up." They were fussing over the little boy and she told him she was tired of living the way they were. . . . She further says that nothing was said during all of that time about the unborn baby other than that she remarked the way he was doing he did not want her to have the baby. She does not remember what he said about that.

The facts of this case present an aggravated and brutal attack made upon the woman in a delicate condition. That he has subjected himself to a penalty quite as severe as that inflicted by the jury will be conceded. We can, however, find no evidence supporting the conclusion reached by the jury of an intent to commit an abortion. Intent may be presumed from all of the facts and circumstances of a case, as charged by the court, but the mere fact of the premature birth of the child as a result of the things done, considered with all of the circumstances of this case, will not suffice because of the very nature of the fight between them. He struck her on the head and and [sic] the shoulders, and inflicted a slight wound on the leg, all of which were calculated to inflict injuries of a serious nature but none of which were directed in a manner to indicate an intention to bring about the death of the unborn child or to cause a miscarriage. . . . The conflict seems to have arisen as a result of their quarrel in which the prosecutrix took an active part and possibly the lead. If he originated the fight without cause support would be given to the

State's contention, at least to some degree. As we find the record we believe it to be insufficient to support the jury's finding.

The judgment of the trial court is reversed and the cause is remanded.

SECTION 2. CRIMINAL NEGLIGENCE

Statements can be found to the effect that "negligence is a state of mind" or on the other hand that it is "not a state of mind." The difference is largely in the use of terms. Thus if negligence is said to be a state of mind it is conceded that to have juridical consequences it must be "manifested." If it is said not to be a state of mind, this is to emphasize that "the state of mind, which is the cause, must be distinguished from the actual negligence, which is its effect." The tendency is to use the word "negligence" as a synonym for "negligent conduct." This implies something done (or not done under circumstances involving a breach of duty to perform) with a state of mind involving this type of blameworthiness.

Intentional harm falls into quite a different category; and an act may be done with such a wanton and wilful disregard of a socially-harmful consequence known to be likely to result, that the attitude of mind will be more blameworthy than is imported by the word "negligence." Hence attention must be directed to risks of harm created by a state of mind different from either of these. Since some element of risk is involved in many kinds of useful conduct, socially-acceptable conduct cannot be limited to acts which involve no risk at all. To distinguish risks not socially acceptable from those regarded as fairly incident to our mode of life, the former are spoken of as "unreasonable." Even an unreasonable risk, (from the standpoint of the one endangered), may have been created without social fault, if the one who created the risk did not know or have reason to know of the existence of such risk under the circumstances. Hence a distinction is made between risks that are "realizable" and those that are not. Conduct, therefore, may be said to fall below the line of social acceptability if it involves a realizable and unreasonable risk of social harm. With this preface the following definition may be offered: Negligence is any conduct, except conduct intentionally harmful or recklessly disregardful of an interest of others, which falls below the standard established by law for the protection of others against unreasonable risk of harm.[1]

1. This follows rather closely the definition adopted for torts by the American Law Institute: "In the Restatement of this Subject, negligence is any conduct, which falls below the standard established by law for the protection of others against unreasonable risk of harm. It does not include conduct recklessly disregardful of an interest of others." Restatement, Second, Torts § 282 (1965).

The torts definition does not include intentional harm. Id. at comment d. For our purposes it seems better to express this exlusion than to leave it to inference.

The social purpose underlying the requirement of compensation to the person harmed is not identical with that which forms the basis of punishment. Conceivably, therefore, the standard adopted in the criminal law of negligence might be entirely different from that used in civil cases. This is not exactly the answer since the "measuring stick" here, as well as there, is the conduct of a reasonable person under like circumstances. But whereas the civil law requires conformity to this standard, a very substantial deviation is essential to criminal guilt according to the common law. To express this greater degree of deviational behavior it has been common to modify the word "negligence" with some such epithet as "criminal," "culpable," "gross" or "wicked." Needless to say this is a field not subject to exact measurement. What it amounts to as a practical matter is a caution to the jury not to convict of crime, where other elements of culpability are lacking, except where the conduct causing the harm represents a rather extreme case of negligence. The format in some states is to recognize as criminal a standard of negligent conduct denominated as "criminal negligence" and to also punish more severely under a standard of recklessness.[2]

Under some of the statutes guilt may be established by proof of negligence without showing that the conduct fell so far short of social acceptability as to merit the label "criminal" negligence. And a few jurisdictions seem to have taken this position as a matter of common law. On the other side of the picture, many offenses require something more than negligence of any degree in order to establish the *mens rea.*

GIAN-CURSIO v. STATE

District Court of Appeal of Florida, Third District, 1965.
180 So.2d 396.

CARROLL, JUDGE. The appellants, who are chiropractic physicians, were informed against in Dade County, charged with manslaughter by having caused the death of one Roger Mozian through culpable negligence.[1] The defendants were tried together and convicted. Dr. Gian-Cursio was sentenced to confinement for a period of five years, and sentence was suspended as to Dr. Epstein. Motions for new trial filed by defendants were denied, and they appealed. The two appeals were consolidated for presentation in this court.

Appellants contend the evidence was insufficient to support the verdicts and judgments of conviction. In addition, appellant Gian-

2. Model Penal Code § 2.02(2)(c) and (d) (1962).

1. § 782.07, Fla.Stat., F.S.A., provides as follows: "The killing of a human being by the act, procurement or culpable negligence of another, in cases where such killing shall not be justifiable or excusable homicide nor murder, according to the provisions of this chapter, shall be deemed manslaughter, and shall be punished by imprisonment in the state prison not exceeding twenty years, or imprisonment in the county jail not exceeding one year, or by fine not exceeding five thousand dollars."

Cursio, in a second point in his brief, claims errors at trial which he lists as allowing introduction of certain inadmissible evidence and improper impeachment of a witness, and prejudicial remarks by the prosecutor in argument. We have examined the voluminous record of the proceedings on the trial, and on consideration thereof and of the briefs and arguments we conclude that the contentions of the appellants are without merit. In our view the evidence adequately supports the verdicts and judgments against the appellants, and we find no reversible error in the rulings or action of the trial court as referred to in the second point in the brief of appellant Gian-Cursio.

The record discloses that one Roger Mozian died of pulmonary tuberculosis in May of 1963. His disease had been diagnosed in 1951 by Dr. Matis, a New York medical doctor in whose charge he remained for some ten years, during which his tuberculosis continued dormant or arrested. An X-ray examination of Mozian by Dr. Matis in January of 1962 showed his disease had become active. Dr. Matis recommended hospitalization and drug treatment, which Mozian refused. Mozian went under the care of Dr. Gian-Cursio, a licensed chiropractic physician in the State of New York, who practiced Natural Hygiene. Dr. Gian-Cursio was advised that Mozian was suffering from tuberculosis. His treatment of the patient was without drugs and by a vegetarian diet, interspersed with fasting periods. Evidence was in conflict as to length of fasting. There was testimony that on occasion the fasting continued 14 days. Dr. Epstein was a licensed chiropractic physician of Florida. Acting with Dr. Gian-Cursio and under his direction, Dr. Epstein operated a home or establishment for patients in Dade County, Florida. Beginning in the winter of 1962, on the advice of Dr. Gian-Cursio, Mozian went there and was treated by the appellant doctors, in the manner stated above. Eventually, in May of 1963 he was hospitalized, where through other doctors he was given drugs and other approved treatment for the disease but within a matter of days he died, on May 16, 1963. There was testimony that the treatment given Mozian was not approved medical treatment for one with active tuberculosis, and that had he been treated by approved medical methods and given available drugs his disease could have been arrested or controlled. From the evidence the jury could, and no doubt did, conclude that the treatment afforded by the appellants advanced rather than retarded the patient's tuberculosis infection and caused his death, and that their method of treatment of this tuberculosis patient amounted to culpable negligence as it has been defined in the decisions of the Supreme Court of this State. In State v. Heines, 144 Fla. 272, 197 So. 787, 788 the Florida Supreme Court reversed an order quashing a manslaughter information which charged a chiropractic physician with causing the death of a patient who suffered from diabetes, by culpable negligence through treatment which included taking him off insulin. After citing and discussing the earlier Florida decision, the Florida Supreme Court said:

"We need add little more to what has been written in the three cases cited to show how one who is proven to have offended as detailed in the information has violated the law against manslaughter. If a person undertakes to cure those who search for health and who are, because of their plight, more or less susceptible of following the advice of any one who claims the knowledge and means to heal, he cannot escape the consequence of his gross ignorance of accepted and established remedies and methods for the treatment of diseases, from which he knows his patients suffer and if his wrongful acts, positive or negative, reach the degree of grossness he will be answerable to the State."

In the earlier case of Hampton v. State, the Florida Court went into the matter at greater length, and what they held there is applicable to the situation presented by this record. In that case the Court said (39 So. at 424):

"We do not agree with this contention of the able counsel for the defendant. The law seems to be fairly well settled, both in England and America, that where the death of a person results from the criminal negligence of the medical practitioner in the treatment of the case the latter is guilty of manslaughter, and that this criminal liability is not dependent on whether or not the party undertaking the treatment of the case is a duly licensed practitioner, or merely assumes to act as such, acted with good intent in administering the treatment, and did so with the expectation that the result would prove beneficial, and that the real question upon which the criminal liability depends in such cases is whether there was criminal negligence; that criminal negligence is largely a matter of degree, incapable of precise definition, and whether or not it exists to such a degree as to involve criminal liability is to be determined by the jury; that criminal negligence exists where the physician or surgeon, or person assuming to act as such, exhibits gross lack of competency, or gross inattention, or criminal indifference to the patient's safety, and that this may arise from his gross ignorance of the science of medicine or surgery and of the effect of the remedies employed, through his gross negligence in the application and selection of remedies and his lack of proper skill in the use of instruments, or through his failure to give proper instructions to the patient as to the use of the medicines; that where the person treating the case does nothing that a skillful person might not do, and death results merely from an error of judgment on his part, or an inadvertent mistake, he is not criminally liable."

We reject as unsound the arguments of appellants that because their treatment conformed to generally accepted practice of drugless healers and was rendered in good faith in an effort to help Mozian, it was proper and could not be found to constitute criminal negligence. That, and appellants' further argument that their treatment of Mozian could not have been tested through testimony of medical doctors, is answered adversely to appellants by Hampton v. State, supra. In Hampton it was held to be immaterial "whether or not the party undertaking the treatment of the case is a duly licensed practitioner, or merely assumes to act as such, acted with good intent in administering the treatment, and did so with the expectation that the results would prove beneficial." Additionally, appellants argue that proximate cause was not established. The issue of proximate cause was one for the jury, and the record furnished substantial evidence upon which that issue was submitted for jury determination.

Under the applicable law as enunciated in the cited Florida cases, the trial court was eminently correct in denying defendants' motions for directed verdict and in submitting the issue of their alleged culpable negligence to the jury. No reversible error having been made to appear, the judgments in appeals numbered 64–514 and 64–561 should be and hereby are affirmed.

Affirmed.[1]

STATE v. PETERSEN

Court of Appeals of Oregon, 1974.

17 Or.App. 478, 522 P.2d 912. Aff'd in part, rev'd in part 526 P.2d 1008.

[This is the case, reported in part in the section on Causation, in which a drag-race which reached speeds of 60–80 miles an hour in a 35-mile zone resulted in the collision of one of the cars, causing the death of the passenger in that vehicle. It was there pointed out that the driver of the other competing vehicle was a proximate cause of the death of the deceased.]

Before SCHWAB, C.J., and FORT and TANZER, JJ.

TANZER, JUDGE. . . .

A person commits criminal homicide if without justification or excuse, he intentionally, knowingly, recklessly or with criminal negligence causes the death of another human being. ORS 163.005. Criminal homicide constitutes manslaughter when it is committed "recklessly," ORS 163.125(1)(a), which is defined in ORS 161.085(9) as follows:

" 'Recklessly,' when used with respect to a result or to a circumstance described by a statute defining an offense, means that a person is aware of and consciously disregards a substantial and unjustifiable risk that the result will occur or that the circumstance exists. The risk must be of such nature and degree that disregard thereof constitutes a gross deviation from the standard of care that a reasonable person would observe in the situation."

1. Accord, Commonwealth v. Pierce, 138 Mass. 165 (1884).

It must be culpable or criminal negligence to support a conviction of manslaughter. Frey v. State, 97 Okl.Cr. 410, 265 P.2d 502 (1953).

Thus, in order for defendant's conviction to be upheld, there must be proof from which the fact-finder can infer that defendant acted "recklessly" and that defendant's reckless conduct "caused" Warren's death.

There can be no question that the risk created by the race at its inception was "substantial and unjustifiable" and that disregard of such a risk would constitute a "gross deviation from the standard of care that a reasonable person would observe in the situation." The testimony indicated that defendant's pickup truck reached a speed of 70–80 miles per hour before decelerating, and that the decedents' car was only slightly behind defendant. The posted speed limit on the street was 35 miles per hour. The area through which the drivers raced was a residential area, and in the course of the race they passed a number of houses, three intersections with cross-streets (Clinton, Taggart and Woodrow), a school and a playground. The risk to the lives of other motorists, pedestrians, bystanders, and even residents of the houses along the route was obvious.

There is also evidence in the record that defendant was aware of the risk to human life which his conduct created and consciously disregarded it. The testimony indicated that defendant was familiar with automobiles and automobile racing, and defendant himself acknowledged that he knew at the time of the race that he should not have engaged in the race. Thus, defendant acted recklessly in entering into the race and in racing with Wille down the street.

Defendant contends that even if he was reckless while actively engaged in racing with Wille, his act of slowing down and stopping prior to reaching the intersection where the collision occurred was an act of prudence which terminated his recklessness. A similar contention was rejected by the Supreme Court in Lemons v. Kelly, 239 Or. 354, 360, 397 P.2d 784, 787 (1964):

". . . One who does participate in setting in motion such hazardous conduct cannot thereafter turn his liability off like a light switch. From the authorities cited we conclude that one who participates in setting such hazardous conduct in motion cannot later be heard to say: 'Oh! I withdrew before harm resulted even though no one else was aware of my withdrawal.' It would be a reasonable probability that the excitement and stimulus created by this race of several miles had not dissipated nor, in fact, terminated at all, in the fraction of a minute in time between the act of passing and the accident. The state of mind of the participants was material. We cannot gauge that state of mind to the point of saying that the stimulus or intent had ended. . . ."

While *Lemons* was a civil case, its factual analysis is equally applicable to the case at bar. The fact-finder was not required to find that the defendant's unilateral and uncommunicated act of slowing and stopping was such an act of termination as would purge his earlier initiation of the race of its quality of recklessness. The evidence authorized a finding that defendant's setting the race in motion was reckless or that there was no effective withdrawal so long as the acts which defendant helped impel had not yet ceased. The substantial and unjustifiable risk to the lives of other motorists and pedestrians created in part by his conduct could be found to have continued unabated up to and including the time of the collision. . . .

Affirmed. . . . [1]

STATE v. HOWARD

Supreme Court of Utah, 1979.
597 P.2d 878.

MAUGHAN, JUSTICE. Defendant was convicted in a jury trial of two counts of criminal homicide, viz., second degree murder and manslaughter. His sole contention before us is the district court erred by refusing his requested instruction on the lesser included offense of negligent homicide. We affirm. All statutory references are to Utah Code Ann., 1953, as amended.

The facts are essentially undisputed. In late summer of 1977, animosity developed between two former friends, Marilyn Rust and Tammy Johnson. The feud between the girls involved their friends, including the defendant, who was a friend of Marilyn Rust.

In November of 1977, Marilyn found two threatening notes on her automobile. Defendant thereafter brought a 30–06 rifle and a .22 pistol to Marilyn's apartment, leaving them there fully loaded.

Late in November, defendant slashed the tires on Tammy Johnson's car; subsequently, the tires on Marilyn's car were slashed. On January 13, 1978, defendant slashed tires on various automobiles belonging to Tammy and her husband, Danny Johnson.

The next day defendant, expecting trouble, brought a loaded 12-gauge shotgun to Marilyn's apartment. Defendant and a friend, Paul Onstadt, remained at the apartment with Marilyn throughout the evening of January 14. At approximately midnight, Tammy and Danny Johnson, Decie Johnson, and Eddy Foy came to the apartment to see Marilyn. An argument over the tire slashing ensued which lasted approximately one hour. During the argument, two friends of Marilyn and defendant, Liz Stoker and Stan Crager, arrived at the apartment. During the entire argument, defendant stood by the couch in the living room holding the shotgun in plain view at his side, indicating at one point that it was loaded.

1. Defendant, a psychiatric nurse in a psychiatric unit, killed a patient by the use of a choke hold when the patient, a violent person, was harassing an elderly patient. It was held that "criminal negligence" had not been shown since the defendant's action occurred during an emergency with little time for reflection or the opportunity to weigh alternatives. People v. Futterman, 86 A.D.2d 70, 449 N.Y.S.2d 108 (1982). See Treiman, Recklessness and the Model Penal Code, 9 Am.Jnl. of Crim.L. 281 (1981).

After the argument, as Tammy, Danny, Decie, and Eddy were leaving, Tammy made an obscene remark to defendant. He in turn made an obscene suggestion to her which was heard by her husband, Danny, as he was walking downstairs. Danny ran back to the apartment door and told Marilyn to open it, which she did. Danny stood in the doorway and demanded that defendant come out and fight; defendant, however, had no intention of fighting Danny since Danny was larger than defendant. Danny then stated he would count to five and if defendant did not come out in the hall, Danny would come in and get him. When Danny reached the count of five, he lunged through the door toward defendant, who in turn aimed the shotgun toward Danny and fired. At that second, Stan Crager, who had been standing in the room in front of defendant, jumped in front of Danny in an effort to prevent a fight, and was hit in the back by the shotgun blast. Danny, knocked off balance when Stan fell against him, veered in the direction of the kitchen door on the other side of the room by which stood the 30–06 rifle. As he did so, defendant pumped the shotgun and fired again, hitting Danny in the back. Both Stan and Danny subsequently died from their wounds.

Defendant was charged with first degree murder on two counts in the amended information. He pleaded not guilty to both counts, contending at trial he acted in self-defense.

In its instructions to the jury, the court included the definitions of the lesser included offenses of second degree murder and manslaughter, but refused to include defendant's requested instruction on negligent homicide. The relevant definitional provisions of the code are as follows:

76–5–203. Murder in the second degree.—(1) Criminal homicide constitutes murder in the second degree if the actor:

(a) Intentionally or knowingly causes the death of another; or

(b) Intending to cause serious bodily injury to another, he commits an act clearly dangerous to human life that causes the death of another; or

(c) Acting under circumstances evidencing a depraved indifference to human life, he recklessly engaged in conduct which creates a grave risk of death to another and thereby causes the death of another; or

(d) . . .

76–5–205. Manslaughter.—(1) Criminal homicide constitutes manslaughter if the actor:

(a) Recklessly causes the death of another; or

(b) Causes the death of another under the influence of extreme mental or emotional disturbance for which there is a reasonable explanation or excuse;

(c) Causes the death of another under circumstances where the actor reasonably believes the circumstances provide a moral or legal justification or extenuation for his conduct although the conduct is not legally justifiable or excusable under the existing circumstances.

76–5–206. Negligent homicide.—(1) Criminal homicide constitutes negligent homicide if the actor, acting with criminal negligence, causes the death of another.

76–2–103. Definitions of "intentionally, or with intent or willfully"; "knowingly, or with knowledge"; "recklessly, or maliciously"; and "criminal negligence or criminally negligent."—A person engages in conduct:

(1) Intentionally, or with intent or willfully with respect to the nature of his conduct or to a result of his conduct, when it is his conscious objective or desire to engage in the conduct or cause the result.

(2) Knowingly, or with knowledge, with respect to his conduct or to circumstances surrounding his conduct when he is aware of the nature of his conduct or the existing circumstances. A person acts knowingly, or with knowledge, with respect to a result of his conduct when he is aware that his conduct is reasonably certain to cause the result.

(3) Recklessly, or maliciously, with respect to circumstances surrounding his conduct when he is aware of but consciously disregards a substantial and unjustifiable risk that the circumstances exist or the result will occur. The risk must be of such a nature and degree that its disregard constitutes a gross deviation from the standard of care that an ordinary person would exercise under all the circumstances as viewed from the actor's standpoint.

(4) With criminal negligence or is criminally negligent with respect to circumstances surrounding his conduct or the result of his conduct when he ought to be aware of a substantial and unjustifiable risk that the circumstances exist or the result will occur. The risk must be of such a nature and degree that the failure to perceive it constitutes a gross deviation from the standard of care that an ordinary person would exercise in all the circumstances as viewed from the actor's standpoint.

Also relevant is the following provision:

76–5–204. Death of other than intended victim no defense.—In any prosecution for criminal homicide, evidence that the actor caused the death of a person other than the intended victim shall not constitute a defense for any purpose to criminal homicide.

We have often stated our position where the contention is that an instruction on a lesser included offense should have been given. In State v. Dougherty, Utah, 550 P.2d 175, 176 (1976), we stated:

> When an appellant makes an issue of a refusal to instruct on included offenses, we will survey the evidence, and the inferences which admit of rational deduction, to determine if there exists reasonable basis upon which a conviction of the lesser offense could rest.

In State v. Hendricks, 596 P.2d 633 (1979), we noted:

> It is a basic legal premise that a defendant in a criminal case is entitled to have his theory of the case presented to the jury. However, the right is not absolute, and a defense theory must be supported by a certain quantum of evidence before an instruction as to an included offense need be given.

Applying these principles to the case at hand, we believe there is no reasonable basis under the facts in this case which would justify a conviction of negligent homicide. As to Count I, defendant's conviction for second degree murder, the facts leave no room to suggest that, according to a reasonable view of the evidence, defendant negligently fired the shotgun when he pumped the gun, aimed at Danny Johnson, and fired as Johnson was heading toward the kitchen door of the apartment. Defendant himself presented no evidence tending to show he was unaware of a "substantial and unjustifiable risk" that the death of Johnson would occur by firing the shotgun at him. The evidence clearly does not support a negligent homicide instruction as to Count I.

Regarding Count II, defendant contends evidence presented established that the jury reasonably could have concluded defendant was unaware of a substantial and unjustifiable risk that Stan Crager would be killed in the affray. Specifically, defendant contends he was solely concerned with defending himself for an expected attack by Danny Johnson, as Johnson stood at the apartment door and counted to five. Defendant testified he knew Crager was in the room when he fired at Johnson, but he did not know where.

Thus, he asserts, since he testified he was unaware at the time he shot at Johnson that Crager would jump in the line of fire, the jury could have reasonably come to the conclusion he ought to have been, but in fact was unaware of a substantial and unjustifiable risk that Crager would be killed.

We must reject defendant's argument for the following reason: The difference between the minimum required *mens rea* of recklessness for manslaughter and criminal negligence for negligent homicide is simply whether the defendant was *aware, but consciously disregarded* a substantial risk the result would happen, or was *unaware but ought to have been aware* of a substantial risk the result would happen. This distinction is purely one of subjective intent in the mind of the actor; and, as we have noted a question of fact to be decided by the jury if any reasonable view of the evidence supports the lesser included offense. However, the question before us is not defendant's state of mind as to Crager, whom he accidentally shot, but as to Johnson at whom defendant admits he aimed the shotgun when he fired the first time. Section 76–5–204, given above, requires the focus of the intent question not upon the actual victim, but upon the *intended* victim, who in this case was Danny Johnson. Thus, the question before us is whether under any reasonable view of the evidence, defendant was unaware, but ought to have been aware, of a substantial risk that Danny Johnson, the intended victim, would be killed by the shotgun blast.

We believe that question must be answered in the negative, since no evidence supports the conclusion that the defendant was unaware of a substantial risk of death to Johnson, if he fired the shotgun at him. Indeed, it is consistent with defendant's assertion of self-defense that he intended to shoot Johnson, believing he was justified in so doing to protect his own life. No evidence was presented which would warrant an instruction of negligent homicide, especially since defendant himself admitted at trial he aimed at Johnson, and that "I usually hit what I aim at."

The jury could have reasonably come to the conclusion that defendant was at least reckless in shooting at Johnson and hitting Crager, or that defendant intentionally or knowingly shot at Johnson and hit Crager in the mistaken belief he was justified, according to the definition of manslaughter. Applying § 76–5–204, the fact that Crager instead of Johnson was shot becomes irrelevant. The court instructed the jury regarding § 76–5–204 and properly refused the requested instruction on negligent homicide.

CROCKETT, C. J., and WILKINS, HALL and STEWART, JJ., concur.[a]

SECTION 3. SPECIFIC INTENT

Despite the loose phrases "criminal intent" and "general criminal intent" courts have not lost sight of the fact that the word "intent" in its strict sense has the same meaning as "intention." Hence we find them reiterating that intent means purpose or design. The effort to assign the exact meaning has not been free from difficulty. "Intention then," writes Markby, "is the attitude of mind in which the doer

a. It was held that the statute which defines manslaughter in terms of a person who "recklessly causes the death of another person" constitutes a distinction without a sufficiently pragmatic difference from the less culpable counterpart, criminally negligent homicide, and hence is unconstitutional. The conviction of manslaughter was reversed and the case remanded with directions to resentence defendant for violation of the lesser offense. People v. Webb, 189 Colo. 400, 542 P.2d 77 (1975).

The instruction that malice might be found if defendant showed "a reckless disregard for human life" was not improper in a murder trial. This was not equivalent to an instruction that gross negligence equalled malice. State v. Kelly, 112 Ariz. 468, 543 P.2d 780 (1975).

of an act adverts to a consequence of the act and desires it to follow. But the doer of an act may advert to a consequence and not desire it: and therefore not intend it." [1] At the other extreme, Austin says that a result is intended if it is contemplated as a probable consequence, whether it is desired or not.[2] Salmond requires the element of desire but gives this word a somewhat forced construction. He says that a man desires not only the end but also the means to the end, and hence desires, although he may "deeply regret" the necessity for, the means.[3]

So far as actual intention is concerned, more is required than an expectation that the consequence is likely to result from the act. On the other hand it is not necessary that the consequence should be "desired" in the usual sense of the word, although this element may become important. If one acts for the purpose of causing a certain result he intends that result whether it is likely to happen or not. On the other hand he intends a consequence which he knows is bound to result from his act whether he desires it, regrets it or is quite indifferent as to it. And to avoid philosophical imponderables as to what is or is not "bound to happen" it is customary to speak of consequences "substantially certain to be produced." Stated in terms of a formula: Intended consequences are those which (a) represent the very purpose for which an act is done (regardless of likelihood of occurrence), or (b) are known to be substantially certain to result (regardless of desire).[4]

Use of the phrases "criminal intent" and "general criminal intent," in the broad sense of blameworthiness, has caused some confusion when actual intention was the idea to be expressed. At times the phrase "specific intent" has been employed for this purpose. In this sense "specific intent" indicates actual intention as distinguished from "general criminal intent" which includes the whole field of blameworthiness. Actual intention, however, can be expressed without the use of this phrase and there is a more important meaning for which "specific intent" should be reserved.

Some crimes require a specified intention in addition to an intended act. For example, the physical part of the crime of larceny is the trespassory taking and carrying away of the personal goods of anoth-

1. Markby, Elements of Law, § 220 (4th ed. 1889).

2. 1 Austin, Jurisprudence 424 (5th ed. 1885).

3. Salmond, Jurisprudence 395 (8th ed. 1930).

4. "The word 'intent' is used throughout the Restatement of this Subject to denote that the actor desires to cause the consequences of his act, or that he believes that the consequences are substantially certain to result from it". Restatement, Second, Torts § 8A (1965).

X handed money to **D** in payment for a mattress. **D** refused to deliver the mattress and applied the money to a pre-existing debt owed by **X** to **D**. This was held not to prove an intent to defraud. City of Cincinnati v. Young, 20 Ohio App. 2d 92, 252 N.E.2d 173 (1969).

There are three essential elements of forgery: a false writing or material alteration of an instrument; the instrument as made must be apparently capable of defrauding, and there must be an intent to defraud.

er. But this may be done intentionally, deliberately, with full knowledge of all the facts and complete understanding of the wrongfulness of the act without constituting larceny. If this wilful misuse of another's property is done with the intention of returning it (with no change of mind in this regard) the state of mind needed for larceny is lacking. Such a wrongdoer is answerable in a civil suit, and may be guilty of some special statutory offense, such as operating a motor vehicle without the owner's consent. For guilt of common-law larceny, however, he must not only intentionally take the other's property by trespass, and carry it away; he must also have an additional intention in mind—the intent to steal. Burglary, moreover, cannot be defined as "intentionally breaking and entering the dwelling house of another in the nighttime," because this may be done without committing this felony. For common-law burglary there is required, not only the intentional breaking and entering of the dwelling house of another in the nighttime, but also an additional intent,—which is to commit a felony. This additional requirement is a "specific intent." It is an additional intent specifically required for guilt of the particular offense.

STATE v. MAY

Supreme Court of Idaho, 1969.
93 Idaho 343, 461 P.2d 126.

McQuade, Justice. The defendant-appellant, Glenn C. May found himself in need of money in the early part of June, 1964. In an effort to assuage that difficulty, he approached Brigham Horrocks for the purpose of obtaining a loan. Horrocks, the complaining witness, had lent money to the appellant on prior occasions, but he at first refused May's entreaty. The next day, however, Horrocks relented and, on the appellant's suggestion, told May that he would lend the money provided that he obtain his father as a co-signer on a note which Horrocks prepared. May then went to his father's ranch to obtain his father's signature on the note. Upon reaching his father's ranch and finding him not there, appellant then signed his father's name to the note, copying his father's handwriting in an effort to make the signature appear authentic. Although May's father had previously co-signed several notes, he had never given permission or authority for appellant to sign his name for him. Appellant's father had been obliged to pay on the last note which he had cosigned with the appellant, and had counseled Glenn against getting too far into debt.

The next day, June 9, 1964, the appellant presented the $4,000 note to Horrocks, bearing his own signature and the "copy" of his father's signature, whereupon the complaining witness gave the appellant a check for $4,000.

Three years later, upon Horrocks' complaint, appellant was charged upon information of the acts of "uttering and passing" and "forging" the note with intent to defraud under I.C. § 18–3601 and on September 18 and 19, 1967, he was tried before a jury and convicted of that charge. On November 28, 1967, District Judge Boyd R. Thomas, sitting in the place of the late Judge Paul Crane who had tried the case, pronounced sentence upon the defendant. From that conviction and sentence appellant prosecutes this appeal.

The defendant presents this Court with twenty-seven assignments of error. The principal complaint throughout this lengthy bill of particulars is that appellant was never proved to have the intent to defraud which is a necessary element of the crime of forgery.[1] It is not entirely clear what the appellant understands to be comprehended by the requirement of this special intent. He argues, for instance, that he should have been able to prove his financial condition at the time of the forgery. It is difficult to understand how this may have tended to prove a lack of a specific intent to defraud. An impecunious forger is no less a forger merely because of his poverty.[2] He also argues that he has no intention to defraud either Horrocks or his own father because he intended to pay the money back. And he further contends that he had no intention to defraud because he honestly thought that his father would ratify his "copied" signature and stand behind him on the debt. These contentions evidence a profound confusion as to the quality of the intent which is necessary for conviction of forgery under our statutes. The "intent to defraud" required by I.C. § 18–3601 is simply a purpose to use a false writing as if it were genuine in order to gain some advantage, generally at someone else's expense.[3] It, thus, does not matter that the defendant meant to repay the loan or thought that his father would stand by him. As Professor Perkins says, in the most recent edition of his treatise on criminal law,

"The actual accomplishment of fraud is not a necessary element of forgery, and the intent itself does not require the contemplation of inflicting a monetary loss. . . . An intent to use a false writing to gain some advantage is an intent to defraud even if the wrongdoer has an intent to make reparation at some future time. Thus, it is no defense to a charge of forging a promissory note that the forger intended to take up the paper at maturity, or even that he has actually done so. And an intent to use an instrument to which the signature of another is wrongfuly attached is fraudulent even if that other actually owes the forger the amount of money represented and this is merely a device used to collect the debt. These results are necessary because the social interest in the integrity of instruments is violated

1. I.C. § 18–3601. See also 2 R. Anderson, Wharton's Criminal Law and Procedure §§ 621, 623, 649, at 396, 397, 440 (1957); R. Perkins, Criminal Law 339–341, 352–354. (2nd ed. 1969).

2. See Tacoronte v. United States, 323 F.2d 772 (10th Cir. 1963): State v. Christopherson, 36 Wis.2d 574, 153 N.W.2d 631 (1967).

3. Accord, cases cited supra n. 2; People v. Gill, 8 Mich.App. 89, 153 N.W.2d 678 (1967).

by the use of false writings, even under these circumstances. Furthermore, a false writing has such an obvious tendency to accomplish fraud that the jury is warranted in inferring such an intent from the mere creation of an instrument that is false, or the alteration which changes a genuine writing into a false one, unless some adequate explanation is offered . . . .

"The fact that the one whose name was forged is willing to condone the offense and pay the obligation is no defense to forgery." [4]

The jury is, of course the final arbiter of the facts, and we cannot, as a matter of law, hold that the jury in this case could not have found beyond a reasonable doubt that the defendant had the requisite intent when he forged and uttered the note in 1964.[5]

Appellant, as his twenty-fourth assignment of error, challenges the trial court's instruction no. 16,

"If you find from the evidence beyond a reasonable doubt that the promissory note in evidence before you, as Exhibit 'A', was forged and counterfeited on or about the 8th day of June, 1964, and that the defendant had the promissory note in his possession on that day and passed it to Mr. Brig Horrocks as genuine and true, then such possession and passing of the promissory note are incriminating circumstances tending to show that the defendant either forged the promissory note or knew that it had been forged, unless the evidence satisfactorily explains the possession and passing of the promissory note by the defendant, if you find that he did possess and pass the promissory note."

This instruction appears manifestly to be a correct statement of the law. It has been held in this state,[6] and in others,[7] that a person possessing a recently forged document, or passing it, is presumed either to have forged it or to have the necessary intention to defraud. This is a rebuttable presumption, but it does shift the burden to the defendant to explain his incriminating conduct. We can see no reason to upset this well established rule of evidence. . . .

We have examined the remainder of the appellant's assignments of error, and, while they are strenuously argued, we hold them to be without merit.

The judgment and sentence of the district court is affirmed.[8]

4. R. Perkins, supra n. 1, at 353–354.

5. See State v. Booton, 85 Idaho 51, 375 P.2d 536 (1962) (this writer dissented from that opinion, but on another ground.); see also, State v. Christopherson, supra n. 2.

6. State v. Booton, supra n. 5; State v. Allen, 53 Idaho 737, 27 P.2d 482 (1933).

7. State v. Christopherson, supra n. 2; People v. Gill, supra n. 3; People v. Geibel, 93 Cal.App.2d 147, 208 P.2d 743 (1949).

8. [Added by Compiler.] "When a specific intent to commit a fraud is a necessary element of the offense, proof of such intent may not be eliminated by the loose generalization that a man is presumed to intend the natural consequences of his acts." Windisch v. United States, 295 F.2d 531, 532 (5th Cir. 1961).

"Intent, of course, is a subjective state of mind usually established only by reasonable inference from surrounding circumstances." State v. Schweppe, 306 Minn. 395, 237 N.W.2d 609, 614 (1975).

McFADDEN, C. J., DONALDSON and SHEPARD, JJ., and HAGAN, DISTRICT JUDGE, concur.

STATE v. EDGAR

Supreme Court of Arizona, In Banc, 1980.
124 Ariz. 472, 605 P.2d 450.

CAMERON, CHIEF JUSTICE. This is a petition for review from a decision and opinion of the Court of Appeals which reversed the conviction, judgment, and sentence of defendant Kenneth Edgar for knowingly procuring or offering a false or forged instrument to be recorded. A.R.S. § 39–161 [1]. We have jurisdiction pursuant to Rule 31.19, Arizona Rules of Criminal Procedure, 17 A.R.S.

There are two questions on appeal:

1. Was the instrument false or forged?
2. Did the defendant cause the instrument to be recorded?

The facts necessary for a disposition on appeal are as follows. During October and November of 1971, defendant was sales manager for Chino Valley Estates, a subdivision of Consolidated Mortgage Company. Norma Jean Reid, then a 16 year old girl working as a telephone solicitor for Consolidated, wanted to purchase property at Chino Valley. She asked defendant several times to sell her a lot but he refused because she was a minor.

Eventually, a method by which Norma Jean would purchase the lot under a fictitious name was devised. There is conflicting testimony as to who initially proposed this plan. Norma Jean Reid testified that she thought that if she purchased the lot using the fictitious name of Norma Jeanne Smith, a widow who was a non-existent person, the lot would be hers. She also testified that defendant assisted her in filling out all the appropriate documents, and, according to Norma Jean, defendant was present when she signed the fictitious

One does not commit forgery by signing his own name to a company check, the account of which had been closed. People v. Susalla, 46 Mich.App. 473, 208 N.W.2d 221 (1973).

One charged with having possession of a forged motor vehicle coupon, with intent to deceive, is not guilty if he in fact had no intent to deceive. Brend v. Wood, 62 L.T. 462 (1946). The court indicated *obiter* that the possession of a "deceptive document," such as this, is sufficient to establish a *prima facie* case of intent to deceive.

In an embezzlement case an instruction told the jury that they might infer an intent to defraud from acts which tend to produce that result; that this inference was not conclusive but that it would prevail unless the defendant introduced evidence which showed beyond a reasonable doubt that there was no such intent. This was held to be error. McKnight v. United States, 115 F. 972 (6th Cir. 1902).

In carrying out a fraudulent scheme **M** bought traveler's checks which he handed to **S** together with **M**'s driver's license. Using the license for identification, **S** signed **M**'s name on the checks, and cashed them. Thereupon **M** reported the checks as stolen, and received new checks from the issuer. As the act of **S** in signing **M**'s name was fraudulent, it was forgery despite authorization by the co-conspirator. Both **M** and **S** were convicted. United States v. McGovern, 661 F.2d 27 (3d Cir. 1981).

1. This section was revised, slightly, effective 1 October 1978.

name to the documents. Norma Jean's mother corroborated her testimony.

Defendant testified, however, that while he assisted Norma Jean in completion of the documents, he was not present when the documents were signed. He stated on direct examination that Norma Jean and her mother together brought the documents to him for completion:

> ". . . I looked the paper work over and I said, 'Hey, there's no information on the I.D. statement.' She said, 'Well, maybe you had better help me fill it out.' I went into the booth with her and Norma Jean and we sat down in the closing office or whatever you want to say and she gave me this information and I put it on here, okay? And then I signed down here, as a witness, which probably I shouldn't have signed, you know, and then I said, 'Hey, get this signed.' She said, 'You want me to sign it now?' I said, 'Hey, I don't want to see nothing.' And I left the room."

One of the documents signed by Norma Jean Reid as Norma Jeanne Smith was the realty mortgage which was later recorded along with a warranty deed. This realty mortgage was signed in blank and sent to the Phoenix office by Consolidated Mortgage. "Norma Jeanne Smith's" signature was notarized by a Monte M. Kobey and his notary seal is impressed on the mortgage. The impression of the notary seal of Kenneth Edgar is also on the mortgage but is crossed out.

Norma Jean's mother spoke to Donna Stevens, one of the persons involved in credit verification at the Phoenix office, expressing her opposition to the sale. On 27 October 1971, after this call, the transaction was allegedly canceled. Defendant testified that after that point he presumed the entire transaction was terminated. Both Norma Jean and her mother also testified they thought the agreement was canceled at that time. On 28 October 1971, however, the agreement was "accepted" by a Consolidated Mortgage officer, and on 8 November 1971 a warranty deed and the realty mortgage for the lot were filed with the Yavapai County Recorder. Defendant did not personally record the papers.

Defendant was charged with the violation of A.R.S. § 39–161 which read in part as follows:

> "A person who knowingly procures or offers a false or forged instrument to be filed, registered or recorded in a public office in this state, which, if genuine, could be filed, registered or recorded under any law of this state or the United States, is guilty of a felony."

From a jury verdict and judgment of guilt, defendant appealed.

1. *Was the mortgage false or forged?*

Defendant contends that the instrument was not a "false or forged instrument" within the meaning of the statute. Defendant first contends that there is a difference between a false instrument and a genuine instrument containing false information:

> "Forgery cannot be committed by the making of a genuine instrument, although the statements made therein are untrue. The term 'falsely' has reference not to the contracts or tenor of the writing, nor to the fact stated in the writing, but implies that the paper is false, not genuine, fictitious, not a true writing, without regard to the truth or falsehood of the statement it contains." Baldwin v. Aetna Casualty and Surety Co., 24 Conn.Sup. 498, 194 A.2d 709, 712 (1963).

We have no quarrel with the law as stated in *Baldwin,* supra, as it applies to the crime of forgery. However, even if *Baldwin,* supra, applied to the instant crime, it still would not be applicable to the facts of this case. In *Baldwin,* supra, the plaintiff issued to defendant checks signed in blank for the purchase of used automobiles. The checks, then, were genuine even though not used by the defendant for the purposes intended by the person who signed the checks. In the instant case, the signature was fictitious and the mortgage a false instrument.

Defendant further contends, however, that there must be an intent to defraud in order for there to be a forged instrument. Since there was no intent to defraud on the part of Norma Jean Reid, there is no false or forged instrument. We do not agree.

Intent to defraud may be an element of the crime of forgery. It is not an element of the crime of filing a false instrument of record. We have stated that there are four elements to the crime of filing a false instrument of record, and intent to defraud is not one of them. We have stated the elements as follows:

> "First, that the instrument in question was forged; second, that it was filed in the office of the state treasurer; third, that the defendant knew of its falsity; and, fourth, that so knowing he filed or caused it to be filed." State v. Lewis, 32 Ariz. 182, 193, 256 P. 1048, 1052 (1927).

Our statute, A.R.S. § 39–161, was adopted from the California statute. See West Annotated Penal Code, § 115. The California courts have also held that intent is not an element of the crime of filing a false instrument:

> ". . . the crime with which appellant was charged, as defined in the section of the Penal Code hereinbefore referred to, consists in the offering for recordation of an instrument, which is either false or forged, when such instrument is one which, when genuine, is capable of recordation under law. The legislative intention in the enactment of the section is clearly one to protect the integri-

ty of our system of recordation of instruments and the vice interdicted is the placing of false or fictitious instruments of record which might have the effect to cloud the record. Under the section the actual effect of the false or fictitious instrument upon the record title is immaterial to the crime charged. . . . The gist of the offense charged is the offering for record of a false or forged deed. . . ."

We find no error.

2. *Did the defendant cause the instrument to be recorded?*

Defendant argues that he cannot be guilty because he did not file the instruments himself. We do not agree. Defendant's actions caused an instrument which he knew contained false information to be placed in a situation whereby the instrument would ultimately be recorded. "Whether the document was actually filed with the County Clerk by appellant himself or at his behest is immaterial. In either event, the offense is complete." The opposite result would shield from liability those who arrange to have others actually record the false instrument. We believe, for the purposes of the statute, that defendant procured the "instrument to be filed."

Defendant further contends, however, that even admitting his participation in filling out the initial sales agreement, the cancellation broke the causal chain between the action and the eventual recording of the realty mortgage. Again we do not agree. Defendant prepared instruments he knew to contain false information. He then submitted them to people who he had reason to believe would accept and record them. The fact that a stranger to the transaction attempted a cancellation and defendant thought it had been canceled cannot constitute a defense.

Opinion of the Court of Appeals, State v. Edgar, 124 Ariz. 476, 605 P.2d 454 (App.1979) vacated.

Judgment affirmed.

DOBBS' CASE

Buckingham Assizes, 1770.
2 East, P.C. 513.

Joseph Dobbs was indicted for burglary in breaking and entering the stable of James Bayley, part of his dwelling-house, in the night, with a felonious intent to kill and destroy a gelding of one A. B. there being. It appeared that the gelding was to have run for 40 guineas, and that the prisoner cut the sinews of his fore-leg to prevent his running, in consequence of which he died.

PARKER, CH. B., ordered him to be acquitted; for his intention was not to commit the felony by killing and destroying the horse, but a trespass only to prevent his running; and therefore no burglary.

But the prisoner was again indicted for killing the horse, and capitally convicted.

THACKER v. COMMONWEALTH

Supreme Court of Appeals of Virginia, 1922.
134 Va. 767, 114 S.E. 504.

WEST, J., delivered the opinion of the court.

This writ of error is to a judgment upon the verdict of a jury finding John Thacker, the accused, guilty of attempting to murder Mrs. J. A. Ratrie, and fixing his punishment at two years in the penitentiary.

The only assignment of error is the refusal of the trial court to set aside the verdict as contrary to the law and the evidence.

The accused, in company with two other young men, Doc Campbell and Paul Kelly, was attending a church festival in Alleghany county, at which all three became intoxicated. They left the church between ten and eleven o'clock at night, and walked down the county road about one and one-half miles, when they came to a sharp curve. Located in this curve was a tent in which the said Mrs. J. A. Ratrie, her husband, four children and a servant were camping for the summer. The husband, though absent, was expected home that night, and Mrs. Ratrie, upon retiring, had placed a lighted lamp on a trunk by the head of her bed. After eleven o'clock she was awakened by the shots of a pistol and loud talking in the road near by, and heard a man say, "I am going to shoot that God-damned light out;" and another voice said, "Don't shoot the light out." The accused and his friends then appeared at the back of the tent, where the flaps of the tent were open, and said they were from Bath county and had lost their way, and asked Mrs. Ratrie if she could take care of them all night. She informed them she was camping for the summer and had no room for them. One of the three thanked her, and they turned away, but after passing around the tent the accused used some vulgar language and did some cursing and singing. When they got back in the road, the accused said again he was going to shoot the light out, and fired three shots, two of which went through the tent, one passing through the head of the bed in which Mrs. Ratrie was lying, just missing her head and head of her baby, who was sleeping with her. The accused did not know Mrs. Ratrie and had never seen her before. He testified he did not know any of the parties in the tent and had no ill will against either of them; that he simply shot at the light, without any intent to harm Mrs. Ratrie or anyone else; that he would not have shot had he been sober, and regretted his action.

The foregoing are the admitted facts in the case.

An attempt to commit a crime is composed of two elements: (1) The intent to commit it; and (2) a direct, ineffectual act done towards its commission. The act must reach far enough towards the accomplishment of the desired result to amount to the commencement of the consummation.

The law can presume the intention so far as realized in the act, but not an intention beyond what was so realized. The law does not presume, because an assault was made with a weapon likely to produce death, that it was an assault with the intent to murder. And where it takes a particular intent to constitute a crime, that particular intent must be proved either by direct or circumstantial evidence, which would warrant the inference of the intent with which the act was done.

When a statute makes an offense to consist of an act combined with a particular intent, that intent is just as necessary to be proved as the act itself, and must be found as a matter of fact before a conviction can be had; and no intent in law or mere legal presumption, differing from the intent in fact, can be allowed to supply the place of the latter.

In discussing the law of attempts, Mr. Clark, in his work on criminal law, says, at p. 111: "The act must be done with the specific intent to commit a particular crime. This specific intent at the time the act is done is essential. To do an act from general malevolence is not an attempt to commit a crime, because there is no specific intent, though the act according to its consequences may amount to a substantive crime. To do an act with intent to commit one crime cannot be an attempt to commit another crime though it might result in such other crime. To set fire to a house and burn a human being who is in it, but not to the offender's knowledge, would be murder, though the intent was to burn the house only; but to attempt to set fire to the house under such circumstances would be an attempt to commit arson only and not an attempt to murder. A man actuated by general malevolence may commit murder though there is no actual intention to kill; to be guilty of an attempt to murder there must be a specific intent to kill."

Mr. Bishop, in his Criminal Law, Vol. 1 (8th ed.), at section 729, says: "When the law makes an act, whether more or less evil in itself, punishable, though done simply from general malevolence, if one takes what, were all accomplished, would be a step towards it, yet if he does not mean to do the whole, no court can justly hold him answerable for more than he does. And when the thing done does not constitute a substantive crime, there is no ground for treating it as an attempt. So that necessarily an act prompted by general malevolence, or by a specific design to do something else, is not an attempt to commit a crime not intended. . . . When we say that a man attempted to do a given wrong, we mean that he intended to do, specifically, it; and proceeded a certain way in the doing. The intent in the mind covers the thing in full; the act covers it only in part. Thus (section 730) to commit murder, one need not intend to take life, but to be guilty of an attempt to murder, he must so intend. It is not

sufficient that his act, had it proved fatal, would have been murder (section 736). We have seen that the unintended taking of life may be murder, yet there can be no attempt to murder without the specific intent to commit it—a rule the latter branch whereof appears probably in a few of the States to have been interfered with by statutes (citing Texas cases). For example, if one from a housetop recklessly throws down a billet of wood upon the sidewalk where persons are constantly passing, and it falls upon a person passing by and kills him, this would be the common law murder, but if, instead of killing, it inflicts only a slight injury, the party could not be convicted of an assault with attempt to commit murder, since, in fact, the murder was not intended."

The application of the foregoing principals to the facts of the instant case shows clearly, as we think, that the judgment complained of is erroneous. While it might possibly be said that the firing of the shot into the head of Mrs. Ratrie's bed was an act done towards the commission of the offense charged, the evidence falls far short of proving that it was fired with the intent to murder her.

However averse we may be to disturb the verdict of the jury, our obligation to the law compels us to do so.

The judgment complained of will be reversed, the verdict of the jury set aside, and the case remanded for a new trial therein, if the Commonwealth shall be so advised.[1]

Reversed.

PEOPLE v. CONNORS

Supreme Court of Illinois, 1912.
253 Ill. 266, 97 N.E. 643.

MR. JUSTICE VICKERS delivered the opinion of the court: . . .

. . . There is, however, a general agreement among the witnesses that the plaintiffs in error and their associates, through threats of violence and by the presentation of drawn revolvers, sought to compel the members of the International Association to cease work, take off their overalls and go down and join the United Association, threatening that unless this demand was complied with they would shoot or kill the members of the International Association. Morgan H. Bell, upon whom the alleged assault to murder was

1. The common-law rule "differentiates between the intent requirements for attempted and a completed crime only where the completed crime may be committed without an intent to commit that crime in particular, as in the case of felony murder." State v. Maestas, 652 P.2d 903, 905 (Utah 1982).

"Established California authority . . . demonstrates that the concept of implied malice, insofar as it permits a conviction without proof of intent to kill, is also inapplicable to a charge of assault with intent to commit murder." People v. Johnson, 30 Cal.3d 444, 179 Cal.Rptr. 209, 637 P.2d 676, 678 (1981).

See Enker, Mens Rea and Criminal Attempt, 1977 Am.B. Foundation Research J. 845.

committed, at the time of the attack was at work on the lower floor. The evidence shows that someone of the attacking party, approaching Bell and Lefevre, said, "Get that big son-of-a-b______." The men walked up to Bell, and plaintiff in error Storgaard pulled a revolver partly out of his pocket, presented the point at Bell and told him to take off his overalls or "they would bore a hole through him." Bell succeeded in getting away at that time and went upstairs, followed by two of his pursuers. Bell gives the following account of what occurred after he got upstairs: "There was some of them got me there and put their guns up to me. One of them held two guns at my stomach and another one at my head, and told me if I didn't quit my fooling and get out of there they would fill me full of holes." Plaintiff in error Connors is identified as one of the men who held a pistol on Bell, accompanied by the threat above stated. This witness states that the revolvers were held against him until he began to remove his overalls. Plaintiff in error Gentleman is also identified as one of the men who made the attack upon Bell. The evidence shows that similar attacks were made upon other workmen, who were commanded to take off their overalls under pain of being shot, and to go down to Burke and get a permit to work. Two of plaintiffs in error, O'Connor and Connors, are shown to have made a similar attack upon one Lettker, commanding him to take off his overalls, and threatening that if he did not do so to bore a hole through him. Lettker complied with the request, as did also Bell and others, to the extent of taking off their overalls. Lettker says in his testimony: "I took the gentlemen at their word. You know they said they were going to bore a hole through me, and I didn't want to be riddled or killed, and I took the man's word." This witness identifies Kane, O'Connor, Connors, Gentleman and Storgaard as being present and participating in the assault. Pistols were also drawn upon Kapritzki, and he was commanded as were the others, and to him it was said, "If you look for trouble I shoot you like a dog;" and again, "If you don't go right away you will get killed." A police station was only a block away. Some of the workmen had apparently escaped unnoticed and notified the police, and about the time that Kapritzki was being assaulted there was a cry of "Jiggers!" and "Coppers!" and at that moment a number of policemen appeared upon the scene. When the police arrived the attacking party made a hasty exit in all directions. Some of them ran down the Illinois Central tracks, some across the coal yards, and some in other directions. As he ran, plaintiff in error Gentleman was seen to throw a revolver away, and another who went down the Illinois Central tracks, put his revolver by the fence, where it was afterwards picked up by a watchman and taken to the police station. All of the attacking party succeeded in making good their escape except plaintiff in error Storgaard, who was arrested by the police on the lower floor and a loaded revolver taken from him. The presence and participation of Storgaard and Gentleman in this affair is not denied. Connors testified that he was not present, but he is not corroborated in any substantial particular and the testimony is amply sufficient to justify a finding that he was present. Arthur O'Connor also denied that he was present, claiming that he was confined to his home at the time by illness. There is some evidence tending to corroborate O'Connor's testimony, which will be considered hereafter.

Plaintiffs in error contend that the trial court erred in giving instruction No. 9 on behalf of the prosecution. That instruction is as follows:

"The court instructs you as to the intent to kill alleged in the indictment, that though you must find that there was a specific intent to kill the prosecuting witness, Morgan H. Bell, still, if you believe, from the evidence, beyond a reasonable doubt, that the intention of the defendants was only in the alternative,—that is, if the defendants, or any of them, acting for and with the others, then and there pointed a revolver at the said Bell with the intention of compelling him to take off his overalls and quit work, or to kill him if he did not,—and if that specific intent was formed in the minds of the defendants and the shooting of the said Bell with intent to kill was only prevented by the happening of the alternative,—that is, the compliance of the said Bell with the demand that he take off his overalls and quit work,—then the requirement of the law as to the specific intent is met."

The plaintiffs in error earnestly contend that pointing a loaded revolver at another within shooting distance and threatening to shoot unless some demand made by the assaulting party is complied with cannot be held to be a felonious assault with intent to kill and murder, for the reason that the intent is in the alternative and is coupled with a condition, and for that reason is not a specific intent to kill, which is necessary to sustain a conviction for an assault with an intent to murder. All the authorities agree upon the general proposition that in a prosecution for an assault with intent to murder, or with intent to commit some other felony, the specific intent charged is the gist of the offense and must be proven as charged in the indictment. Upon this and like authorities where the general rule is stated, plaintiffs in error contend that the intent to commit the crime charged must be absolute and unconditional and that if a dangerous weapon is presented in a threatening manner, accompanied with a demand upon the assaulted party and a threat to destroy his life unless such demand is complied with, the offense can not be an assault to murder. It is argued that the condition which accompanies the threat negatives the existence of that positive and specific intent which, under the law, is a necessary element in the offense charged.

No case decided by this court is cited by either party, and we are not aware that any such case exists, that is conclusive of the precise question which is raised here. In support of the view that an assault with a loaded revolver and a threat to shoot unless the party assaulted complies with a demand is not an assault with an intent to murder, plaintiffs in error rely with great confidence upon the case of Hairston v. State, 54 Miss. 689. In that case Hairston, in company with others, attempted to remove the personal effects of a laborer from the plantation of his employer, Richards, to whom said laborer was indebted on account of advances of money or provisions made to said laborer. Hairston was in the act of hauling away the household furniture which Richards attempted to stop the wagon and took hold of Hairston's mules saying that he could not move the household goods until his debt was settled. Thereupon Hairston drew a pistol and pointed it at Richards and said, "I came here to move Charles Johnson and by God I am going to do it, and I will shoot any God damned man who attempts to stop my mules," at the same time urging his mules forward as he spoke. His manner was threatening and angry and his voice loud and boisterous. Other persons who were accompanying Hairston, some of whom were armed with guns, pressed around Richards, as if they intended to aid Hairston if necessary. Richards was deterred by the apparent danger and released the mules and the wagon moved on. Under the above facts Hairston was convicted of an assault with an intent to murder Richards. The conviction was reversed by the Supreme Court of Mississippi. The reasoning of the court in that case is as follows: Richards was in the act of committing a trespass upon Hairston's property by laying his hands upon the mules and forcibly stopping Hairston upon the public highway. Hairston had a right to protect his property from such unlawful trespass, using no more force than was necessary. His threat to shoot was conditioned upon a demand which he had a right to make. In disposing of the case the Supreme Court of Mississippi uses the following language: "Here there was only a conditional offer to shoot, based upon a demand which the party had a right to make. While the law will not excuse the assault actually committed in leveling the pistol within shooting distance, it cannot, from this fact alone, infer an intent to murder. The intent must be actual,—not conditional,—and especially not conditioned upon non-compliance with a proper demand." A careful analysis of that case will show that the court laid special stress on the circumstance that the threat to shoot was coupled with a demand which the prisoner had a lawful right to make. . . .

In McClain's Criminal Law (section 232) the rule applicable to the case at bar is thus stated: "If the threatened injury, coupled with present ability to inflict it, is conditioned upon the party assailed refusing to do something which the assailant has no right to inquire him to do, it will constitute an assault even though the conditions are complied with and therefore no violence is used." . . .

We find no error in this record requiring a reversal of the judgment below. It is therefore affirmed.

Judgment affirmed.[1]

SECTION 4. OTHER PARTICULAR STATES OF MIND

The phrase "specific intent" has been used, at times, to refer to any special state of mind required for the *mens rea* of a particular offense. The underlying thought is this: Some crimes require only the general *mens rea;* others require a specific intent. Unfortunately, this adds to the confusion attaching to the use of the word "intent." This usage is too common to be ignored. It is well to emphasize, however, that many offenses require some particular state of mind other than a "specific intent" in the strict sense of the phrase.

If guilt of a certain offense requires that an act be done "fraudulently," this means it must be done with an intent to defraud. This is a specific intent in the strict sense of the phrase, but other factors are involved if the *mens rea* requirement is "malice," "knowledge" or "wilfulness."

(A) MALICE

Many statements are to be found to the effect that malice, as it is used in the law, does not imply any feeling of hatred, grudge, anger or ill-will, but requires only an intent to do harm without lawful justification or excuse. The last clause requires some modification in the homicide cases. An intent to kill may be in such sudden heat of passion engendered by adequate provocation as to fall outside of the "malice" label. On the other side, an act may be done with such wanton and wilful disregard of an obvious and extreme risk of causing death that it will be said to be done with malice aforethought (if there was no justification, excuse or mitigation) even if there was no actual intent to kill. To say that the law will "imply" an intent to kill in such a case, or that such a wanton and wilful disregard of an obvious hazard is "equivalent" to an intent to kill, is to indulge in "double-talk." It is quite proper to bring such a killing within the category of murder. The preferable explanation, however, is a frank recognition of the possibility of malice aforethought without an actual intent to kill. This may be illustrated by the case of one who intentionally

1. Although the robber held a gun during the robbery, since he made no threatening remarks there was an issue as to whether he actually had an intent to maim, wound or kill, if resisted, and this should have been left to the jury with proper instructions. Hollon v. People, 170 Colo. 432, 462 P.2d 490 (1969).

"Assault with intent to commit murder under 18 U.S.C. § 113(a) thus requires a specific intent to kill the victim, and in the special case of this offense, acting with malice by committing a reckless and wanton act without also intending to kill the victim is not sufficient for conviction." United States v. Jones, 681 F.2d 610 (9th Cir. 1982). But see State v. Maestas, 652 P.2d 903 (Utah 1982).

If one wrongfully bites another's ear, and holds on so tightly that the ear is torn from the head when the two are separated, this was done "on purpose and with intent to disfigure." State v. Skidmore, 87 N.C. 509 (1882).

blows up a building, without justification, excuse or mitigation, hoping the place to be empty but having no way of knowing whether this is the fact or not. The wrongdoer is guilty of murder if there were people in the building who were killed by the explosion. To say he "intended" to take human life is to misuse the word, but to speak of his state of mind as "malicious" is entirely unobjectionable.

If the word as it is used in the phrase "malice aforethought" gives a reasonable clue to its meaning in other than homicide cases, it would seem to be this: "Malice" means an intent to do the very harm done, or harm of a similar nature, or a wanton and wilful disregard of an obvious likelihood of causing such harm, with an implied negation of any justification, excuse or mitigation.

STATE v. LAUGLIN

Supreme Court of North Carolina, 1861.
53 N.C. 354.

Indictment for felonious burning, tried before SAUNDERS, JUDGE, at the spring term, 1861, of Robeson Superior Court.

The indictment charged that the defendant "feloniously, wilfully, and maliciously did set fire to, and burn a certain barn then having corn in the same." The proof was that the prisoner maliciously and wilfully did set fire to a stable with fodder in it, and that a crib with corn and peas in it, which stood within twenty-six feet of the stable, was partially consumed, but by great exertion was saved from total destruction.

The Court charged as to the crib (which he sometimes in the alternative calls a barn), "that if satisfied of the burning of the stable by the prisoner, as it was an unlawful act, the prisoner was responsible for the consequences; and if they (the jury) were satisfied, beyond a reasonable doubt, that the stable was likely to and did communicate to the crib, and it was thereby burnt, they should convict; but they were to be satisfied that by the burning of the stable, the burning of the crib was a reasonable probability to follow; in which case the prisoner would be answerable." The defendant's counsel excepted.

Verdict, "guilty." Sentence was pronounced, and defendant appealed.

BATTLE, JUDGE. The bill of exceptions presents for consideration two questions, both of which are of great importance to the community, as well as to the prisoner. The first is, whether the wilful and malicious setting fire to the house of another, the burning of which is only a misdemeanor, will become a capital felony, if a dwelling-house or barn with grain in it, be thereby burnt, where such burning is the probable consequence of the first illegal act. Upon this question we concur in the opinion given in the Court below: that in such a case, the prisoner is guilty of the felonious burning of the dwelling-house or barn, upon the principle that he is to be held responsible for the natural and probable consequence of his first criminal act. In support of this proposition, the burning of one's own dwelling-house with a malicious and unlawful intent, furnishes a strong argument from analogy. Such burning is, of itself, only a high misdemeanor; but if the dwellings of other persons be situated so near to the one burnt, that they take fire and are consumed, as an immediate and necessary consequence of the first illegal act, it will amount to a felony. . . .[1]

(For other reasons the judgment was reversed.)

TERRELL v. STATE

Supreme Court of Tennessee, 1888.
86 Tenn. 523, 8 S.W. 212.

CALDWELL, J. The plaintiff in error, Ned Terrell, stands convicted of the crime of mayhem, and is under sentence of two years' confinement in the penitentiary. The indictment charges him with having unlawfully, feloniously, willfully, and maliciously made an assault upon the prosecutor, James Wilson, and struck him in one eye with a stone, or some other hard substance, whereby the eye was put out, and the prosecutor was maimed and disfigured. It is shown in the proof, and admitted by the prisoner, that he struck the prosecutor in one eye with "a half of a brick," and that the prosecutor was thereby rendered entirely blind, having previously lost the other eye. On the trial of the case his honor, the circuit judge, quoted to the jury the statute under which the prisoner is presented, and then charged them further, and among other things, that "in order to convict the defendant in this case, it must be shown by the proof that he did put out the eye of the prosecutor, as alleged in the indictment, by willfully and maliciously striking him in the eye with the brick or other hard substance and that it was done unlawfully,—that is, without lawful excuse, . . . " and that if he did this "from feelings of malice toward the prosecutor . . . he would be guilty as charged." The prisoner's counsel requested the court to instruct the jury, in addition, that unless "the defendant did of his malice aforethought inflict the blow, with purpose or intent to put out the eye, or inflict some other mayhem on the prosecutor, then the defendant would not be guilty of mayhem." This request was refused by the court, and that refusal is assigned as error.

Upon this action arises the inquiry, is a specific intent to maim a necessary element of the crime of mayhem? This precise question never having been decided in this state, its solution can be best ar-

1. In a prosecution for statutory extortion, based upon a threat to accuse **X** of arson with intent to extort money from **X**, evidence that **X** did in fact burn the building was excluded as immaterial. Commonwealth v. Buckley, 148 Mass. 27, 18 N.E. 577 (1888). One who threatens a thief with criminal prosecution unless he returns the stolen property is guilty of extortion. People v. Beggs, 178 Cal. 79, 172 P. 152 (1918).

rived at by a brief review of some of the authorities and statutes upon the general subject. "Mayhem, at common law," says Mr. East, "is such a bodily hurt as renders a man less able, in fighting, to defend himself or annoy his adversary; but if the injury be such as disfigures him only, without diminishing his corporal abilities, it does not fall within the crime of mayhem." 1 Whart.Crim.Law, (8th Ed.) § 581. . . .

The words characterizing the forbidden acts are "unlawfully and maliciously." They are used alike with respect to every offense mentioned in the section, and must be given the same significance as applied to each of them. They mean the same thing when applied to mayhem that they do when applied to malicious shooting or stabbing. "Unlawfully" always means without legal justification; but "maliciously" has different meanings, which it is not important now to give in detail. Its signification as used in the fifty-fifth section of the act of 1829 is well stated and illustrated in Wright v. State, 9 Yerg. 343, 344. Wright was indicted and convicted for malicious stabbing under that section, and on appeal in error to this court it was insisted, in his behalf, that the proof did not show that degree of malice necessary to constitute the offense charged. JUDGE TURLEY, delivering the opinion of the court, said: "It is true that the statute requires that this offense shall be committed with malice aforethought, by which is not meant such malice as is required by the third section of the same act to constitute the crime of murder in the first degree, but malice according to its common law signification, which is not confined to a particular animosity to the person injured, but extends to an evil design in general, a wicked and corrupt nature, an intention to do evil." . . . "The question then arises, is the proof in this case of a character to justify the jury in having found the existence of malice according to the definition given? We consider it unnecessary to go into a minute investigation of the testimony on this point. It shows beyond a doubt that the prisoner stabbed Lewis Underwood, the prosecutor. Upon this proof the law presumes malice." With this approved interpolation, applied, as it must be, in reference to each of the offenses enumerated, the use of the word "maliciously" in the statutes is shown to afford no justification for the contention that the crime of mayhem can be committed only when the blow is stricken for the purpose of inflicting that particular injury upon the sufferer. The character of malice necessary to the crime of mayhem has in fact been held by this court to be the same as that defined in the case of malicious stabbing just quoted. Werley v. State, 11 Humph. 175. Werley was convicted for the castration of his slave. In his defense it was shown that the slave was of very lewd character, and that his master's purpose was to reform him. Upon the facts it was argued that the necessary malice was wanting. The decision was that the act was unlawful, and, that being so, malice would be implied unless circumstances of provocation be shown to remove the legal presumption. The conviction was affirmed. . . .

It is next insisted that, even under the charge of the law as given to the jury, the verdict is not supported by the evidence. Upon this contention, the whole of the evidence has been given a very careful consideration by this court, but it is not deemed necessary to enter into a minute statement or discussion of it in this opinion. It is sufficient to say that the prosecutor's testimony makes a strong case of an unexpected, unprovoked, and violent assault upon him in the nighttime, resulting, as already stated, in the destruction of his only eye, and rendering him totally blind. The only countervailing testimony is that of the defendant himself, introduced for the purpose of showing provocation and apprehension of danger from the prosecutor when the blow was stricken. The other testimony in the record is in conflict with his statements, and corroboration of those of the prosecutor.

We are well satisfied with the verdict. Let the judgment be affirmed.

TURNEY, C. J., and SNODGRASS, J., dissent.

STATE v. JOHNSON

Supreme Court of Wyoming, 1898.
7 Wyo. 512, 54 P. 502.

B. A. Johnson was charged with malicious trespass under the statute. There was an agreed statement of the evidence, and the district court reserved four questions for the decision of this court, as follows: . . . (4) Does the information in this case, under the statement of facts as agreed upon, charge any offense under the laws of this state? The facts are, in brief, that the defendant, in driving a band of sheep from a dipping corral to a neighboring railroad station, drove them over and across certain uninclosed, unimproved, and uncultivated land of the prosecuting witness, and that the defendant did not stop to graze them thereon for any greater length of time than sheep do graze while being driven from place to place by the usual and ordinary method of so driving them.

CORN, J. (after stating the facts as above). If this were a civil action for damages, a part of the questions would become important, which in this case, involving only the construction of a criminal statute, it will be unnecessary for us to decide. It is very well settled that the mere roaming of cattle and other domestic animals upon uninclosed private lands in the Western country does not constitute a trespass. A distinction has been insisted upon in the case of sheep, which are not permitted to roam at will, but are herded and directed by a shepherd; and it is maintained that, when they are driven upon such lands for the purpose of pasturage, it constitutes a trespass, for which damages may be recovered by the owner of the land. A decision of the latter question is not required by the facts of this case. The statute invoked by the prosecution is one of a very large class, both in England and this country, and provides that "whoever maliciously or mischievously injures, or causes to be injured, any property of another or any public property, is guilty of malicious trespass." Under similar statutes in England it has been held that in order to constitute the offense the act must be done from malice against the owner. The doctrine has not been carried to that extent in this country, but the authorities are nevertheless substantially agreed that the malice necessary to constitute the offense is something more than the malice which is ordinarily inferred from the willful doing of an unlawful act without excuse. The statutes were not intended to make every willful and wrongful act punishable as a crime, but they were devised to reach that class of cases where the act is done with a deliberate intention to injure. In Com. v. Williams, 110 Mass. 401, which was a prosecution for a willful and malicious injury to a building, the court say: "The jury must be satisfied that the injury was done out of a spirit of cruelty, hostility, or revenge. This element must exist in all those injuries to real or personal property which are enumerated and made criminal in the several statutes. The injury must not only be willful (that is, intentional and by design as distinguished from that which is thoughtless or accidental), but it must, in addition, be malicious, in the sense above given. The willful doing of an unlawful act without excuse, which is ordinarily sufficient to establish criminal malice, is not alone sufficient under these statutes. The act, although intentional and unlawful, is nothing more than a civil injury, unless accompanied with that special malice which the words 'willful and malicious' imply." In Duncan v. State, 49 Miss. 331, which was an indictment for malicious mischief in killing a hog, the jury returned a verdict, "We, the jury, find the accused guilty of the willful and unlawful killing of the hog, but not out of a spirit of mischief, revenge, or wanton cruelty." And this was held to be an acquittal of the accused of the charge of the indictment. So, in Wright v. State, 30 Ga. 325, which was an indictment for malicious mischief in shooting a mule, the court say: "The question to be tried was not whether he was justified in shooting the mule, but whether his motive in shooting was malicious. The question of justification would be the issue in an action for damages against him, but on this indictment the issue was malice or no malice. If he shot from the motive of protecting his crop, and not from either ill will to the owner or cruelty to the animal, his motive was not malicious, whether it was justifiable or not, and his act was not malicious mischief." In a New Jersey case the defendant was indicted for willfully and maliciously tearing down an advertisement of sale set up by the sheriff. His defense was that he took it down for the purpose of showing it to his counsel, and from no bad motive. The court say: "The word 'maliciously,' when used in the definition of a statutory crime, the act forbidden being merely malum prohibitum, has almost always the effect of making a bad intent or evil mind a constituent of the offense. The whole doctrine of that large class of offenses falling under the general denomination of 'malicious mischief' is founded on this theory. For example, it was declared by the supreme court of Massachusetts in the case of Com. v. Walden, 3 Cush. 558, that the word 'maliciously,' as used in the statute relating to malicious mischief, was not sufficiently defined as 'the willful doing of an act prohibited by law, and for which the defendant has no lawful excuse.' But that, to the contrary, in order to justify a conviction under the act referred to, the jury must be satisfied that the injury was done either out of a spirit of wanton cruelty or wicked revenge." Folwell v. State, 49 N.J.Law 31, 6 A. 619. And it seems to be generally held that, in order to bring an offense under the head of malicious mischief, it must appear that the mischief was itself the object of the act, and not that it was incidental to some other act, lawful or unlawful. . . . No answer is made to the first, second, and the third questions, none being necessary, and the fourth is answered in the negative.[1]

POTTER, C. J., and KNIGHT, J., concur.

(B) KNOWLEDGE (SCIENTER)

The relation of knowledge to convictability is a variable factor within a wide range. At one extreme is found the type of offense for which knowledge of some particular matter is required for guilt by the very definition of the crime itself;[1] as, uttering a forged instrument with knowledge of the forgery, receipt of deposit by a banker knowing that his bank is insolvent, or transportation of a vehicle in interstate commerce, knowing it to have been stolen. At the other extreme is found the type (which should be restricted to the so-called public torts or civil offenses) in connection with which the element of knowledge or lack of knowledge is so immaterial that conviction may

1. A veterinarian caused a swelling in a mare's shoulders in order to get money by pretending to cure the animal of a disease. This intentional harm to the animal was held to constitute malicious mischief although inflicted without ill will toward either the owner or the mare. Brown v. State, 26 Ohio St. 176 (1875).

One who was driving from side to side of the road with reckless abandon ran a buggy shaft into another's horse. This wanton and wilful disregard of the obvious danger to persons and property was held sufficient to make him guilty of malicious mischief although the injury was unintentional. Porter v. State, 83 Miss. 23, 35 So. 218 (1903).

The killing of a mare by a forest ranger, in good faith discharge of his duties and in compliance with a regulation of the Secretary of Agriculture, was not malicious mischief even if the regulation was invalid. Fears v. State, 33 Ariz. 432, 265 P. 600 (1928).

During the early days of prohibition in Kansas a militant reformer wrecked a saloon with an ax. Being charged with malicious trespass she insisted that she was merely putting an unlawful establishment out of business, and had "no ill will against the owner or possessor of the property, or design to destroy property merely for the purpose of its destruction", and hence had acted without malice. In upholding her conviction the court held the word "malicious" as found in this statute is employed in "the usual sense in which it is used in criminal statutes". State v. Boies, 68 Kan. 167, 74 P. 630 (1903).

1. D was charged with unlawful acquisition of food-stamp coupons. The failure to instruct the jury that D could not be convicted unless it found that D knew his requisition was not authorized by law or regulation was reversible error. United States v. Faltico, 687 F.2d 273 (8th Cir. 1982).

result although the defendant acted under such a mistake that, had the facts been as he reasonably supposed them to be, his conduct would have been acceptable in every respect. Such "offenses" are considered under "strict liability."

Between these two extremes are found offenses, for guilt of which the matter of knowledge cannot be ignored although the definitions themselves contain no specific requirement thereof. This is because knowledge or lack of knowledge may be among the determining factors of some other attitude of mind, which is required, such as intent, wilfulness, malice or criminal negligence.

From the standpoint of the prosecution (leaving out of consideration those "offenses" which have no normal *mens-rea* requirement) knowledge may be a positive factor or the want of knowledge may be a negative factor. In some prosecutions the state must prove defendant's knowledge of some particular matter to make out even a *prima facie* case of guilt. Such knowledge may be proven, like any other fact, by circumstantial evidence. It may be established from all the facts and circumstances of the case, although denied by the defendant. But the burden is on the State. In other prosecutions the want of knowledge may be peculiarly a matter of defense.

"Absolute knowledge can be had of but few things," said the Massachusetts court, and the philosopher might add "if any." For most practical purposes "knowledge" is not confined to what we have personally observed or to what we have evolved by our own cognitive faculties. Even within the domain of the law itself the word is not always employed with exactly the same signification. Suppose a man has been told that a certain bill of exchange is a forgery and he believes the statement to be true. Does he have *knowledge* of this? Obviously not if the purpose of the inquiry is to determine whether he is qualified to take the witness stand and swear that the instrument is false. But if he passes the bill as genuine he will be uttering a forged instrument with "knowledge" of the forgery if his belief and the fact correspond.

The need, therefore, is to search for the state of mind, or states of mind, which the courts have spoken of as "knowledge" for the purpose of a particular case.[1]

STATE v. BEALE

Supreme Judicial Court of Maine, 1973.
299 A.2d 921.

Before DUFRESNE, C. J., and WEBBER, WEATHERBEE, POMEROY, WERNICK and ARCHIBALD, JJ.

1. When knowledge of the existence of a particular fact is an element of an offense, such knowledge is established if the person is aware of a high probability of its existence, unless he actually believes that it does not exist. Leary v. United States, 395 U.S. 6, 46 (note 93), 89 S.Ct. 1532 (1969).

WEATHERBEE, JUSTICE.

The Defendant, who operates an antique shop in Hallowell, was convicted under 17 M.R.S.A. § 3551 of the offense of knowingly concealing stolen property. His appeal presents us for the first time with the opportunity to construe the phrase "knowing it to be stolen" found in this statute.

One Saturday during the summer of 1971, when the Defendant was absent and his store was in Mrs. Beale's care, a prospective customer, a Mrs. Johnson, noticed that some of the displayed merchandise looked familiar. On examining it further she became convinced that several items were in fact pieces of silverware and glass which had been stolen from her several months earlier.

She left and returned after a short interval with a Hallowell police officer. She then pointed out to Mrs. Beale the items which she believed to have been stolen from her. The officer told Mrs. Beale that these items were "possibly stolen" and that they should be placed aside and not displayed or sold. She then gathered these items and put them on a shelf. The officer testified that he told Mrs. Beale to tell her husband to "contact me as soon as he got back". He later testified that he said that she "would be contacted, probably, later on that day".

There was no further contact between the Beales and the police during the weekend. The following Monday morning the investigation was apparently taken over by a deputy sheriff from the county where the theft had occurred. When he called at Defendant's store Defendant informed him that he had put the articles back in the counter for sale Sunday morning and that he had sold many of these items that day in spite of knowing that the police officer had requested that they be withdrawn from sale. Among those which the Defendant said he had sold were all the articles which bore the distinctive initials by which the owner had identified them as hers.

The Defendant testified that he had purchased these items at different times from people whom he considered to be reliable, that he had receipts for many of them and that he was entitled to sell them regardless of the officer's warning. The only testimony as to the details of the complaint by Mrs. Johnson and the officer's admonitions to Mrs. Beale which were in fact related to Mr. Beale was given by Mrs. Beale (called by the State) and the Defendant himself. The Defendant and Mrs. Beale testified that Mrs. Beale told the Defendant that Mrs. Johnson claimed that these items had been stolen from her home, and that the officer had asked Mrs. Beale to put the items aside saying that he would be back later.

The statute creating this offense—17 M.R.S.A. § 3551—reads, in pertinent part:

> "Whoever buys, receives or aids in concealing stolen property, knowing it to be stolen, shall be punished . . . ".

At the close of the testimony, Defendant's counsel made several timely requests for instructions. One of them, number 3, was not given and the issue raised by it, together with counsel's related objection, prove decisive of this appeal. It reads:

"(3) The fact that the Defendant was notified that the goods were stolen after they had been purchased and received and yet went ahead and sold them does not of itself make him guilty of the crime charged, if the Defendant in truth believed that he had a valid receipt for the goods and that he had lawful possession of them."

. . .

The jury found the Defendant guilty.

Although the Defendant's requested instruction failed to focus clearly upon the issue, his objection to the Justice's charge adequately presents the issue for our review. The issue is one of statutory interpretation of the words "knowing it to be stolen". Did the Legislature intend that the jury be satisfied as to the knowledge of the Defendant by testing it subjectively or objectively? To put it another way, must the State satisfy the jury that the Defendant himself actually had knowledge that the goods were stolen or is it enough that a reasonable person, with the information that was available to the Defendant, would have known that the goods were stolen?

We find a split of authority among the jurisdictions which have had the occasion to examine this issue, with the majority requiring that the State's proof should meet the subjective test. A representative summary of the reasoning of the majority is found in the language of Von Sprecken v. State, 70 Ga.App. 222, 225, 28 S.E.2d 341, 343 (1943):

". . . The gist of the offense is the actual state of the *defendant's* mind . . . and not what, under like circumstances, might be the state of mind of some other person . . . ". (Emphasis added.)

The Massachusetts Supreme Judicial Court took a similar position in reversing a conviction for receiving stolen property which was based upon a finding of knowledge under the reasonable man standard, saying:

". . . The infraction of this statute is not proved by negligence nor by failure to exercise as much intelligence as the ordinarily prudent man. The statute does not punish one too dull to realize that the goods which he bought honestly and in good faith had been stolen.

. . .

The knowledge or belief of the defendant must be personal to him and our statute furnishes no substitute or equivalent." Commonwealth v. Boris, 317 Mass. 309, 58 N.E.2d 8, 12 (1944).

The issue has also been before the Vermont Supreme Court. The Vermont statute did not define the offense of receiving stolen goods and the Court found that the elements were those defined by the common law. The Court rejected the State's contention that reasonable notice was sufficient to supply the common law requirement of knowledge that the goods were in fact stolen. The Court said:

"If he did not have actual or positive knowledge, the question is whether from the circumstances he—not some other person—believed they had been stolen. The circumstances must have that effect upon his mind, to constitute knowledge by him." State v. Alpert, 88 Vt. 191, 92 A. 32, 37 (1914).

A minority of jurisdictions apply the so-called objective test as to knowledge, being impressed, perhaps, by the difficulties of proof as to the actual state of a defendant's mind. The position of these courts appears to be represented by the statement of the Mississippi Court in Pettus v. State, 200 Miss. 397, 410, 27 So.2d 536, 540 (1946)—a position recently reaffirmed by that Court in Bennett v. State, Miss., 211 So.2d 520, 526 (1968):

"[T]he word, 'knowing': in its relation to receiving stolen goods means that, if a person has information from facts and circumstances which should convince him that property had been stolen, or which would lead a reasonable man to believe that property had been stolen, then in a legal sense he knew it." [1]

We consider that the distinction between the bases of the two points of view [2] was clarified by an opinion from the Circuit Court of Appeals, 2nd Circuit, written by Judge Learned Hand. He wrote:

"The defendants ask us to distinguish between 'knowing' that goods are stolen and merely being put upon an inquiry which would have led to discovery; but they have misconceived the distinction which the decisions have made. The receivers of stolen goods almost

1. In some states the statutes define the offense as being committed by one who knows or who has reasonable cause to believe that the property received had been stolen. See, e.g., 21 O.S.1971, § 1713(1); Hutton v. State, Okl.Cr., 494 P.2d 1246 (1972).

2. A third approach is that taken by the Illinois Court. The Court has followed the majority rule in construing the Illinois statute to require proof that the circumstances surrounding the transaction were such as to make the *Defendant* believe that the goods had been stolen and that guilty knowledge may be inferred from the attendant facts and circumstances. However, in People v. Rife, 382 Ill. 588, 48 N.E.2d 367, 372 (1943) the Illinois Court held that:

> ". . . In determining whether the fact existed, the jury will be justified in presuming that the accused acted rationally and that whatever would convey knowledge or induce belief in the mind of a reasonable person, would, in the absence of countervailing evidence, be sufficient to apprise him of the like fact, or induce in his mind the like impression and belief. . . ."

Some modification of this position appears in more recent cases where the rule is stated to be:

> "Guilty knowledge may be established by proof of circumstances which would induce belief in a reasonable mind that the property had been stolen *and by the receipt of such property by the accused without inquiry as to its source or the title of the one from whom it was received.* . . ." (Emphasis added.) People v. Stewart, 20 Ill.2d 387, 169 N.E.2d 796, 799 (1960); People v. Grodkiewicz, 16 Ill.2d 192, 157 N.E.2d 16, 19 (1959); People v. Piszczek, 404 Ill. 465, 89 N.E.2d 387, 391 (1949).

never 'know' that they have been stolen, in the sense that they could testify to it in a court room. The business could not be so conducted, for those who sell the goods—the 'fences'—must keep up a more respectable front than is generally possible for the thieves. Nor are we to suppose that the thieves will ordinarily admit their theft to the receivers: that would much impair their bargaining power. For this reason, some decisions even go so far as to hold that it is enough, if a reasonable man in the receiver's position would have supposed that the goods were stolen. That we think is wrong; and the better law is otherwise, although of course the fact that a reasonable man would have thought that they had been stolen, is some basis for finding that the accused actually did think so. But that the jury must find that the receiver did more than infer the theft from the circumstances has never been demanded, so far as we know; and to demand more would emasculate the statute, for the evil against which it is directed is exactly that: i.e., making a market for stolen goods which the purchaser believes to have probably been stolen." United States v. Werner, 160 F.2d 438, 441–442 (2nd Cir. 1947). . . .

It appears to us that the minority jurisdictions which follow the "ordinary reasonable man" test are failing to stress sufficiently the distinction between civil and criminal responsibility. In civil cases the failure of the defendant to act with the degree of care which a person of ordinary prudence would have used may be the test of his responsibility without any determination that the defendant, himself, was a person of ordinary prudence or that he had any wrongful intent. On the other hand, the very essence of his criminal offense is the intentional wrongdoing of the defendant.

Such was the case at common law (State v. Alpert, supra) and if the Legislature had intended something less than actual knowledge, more appropriate language could easily have been chosen.

The distinction is more than one of semantics. It is made necessary by the fact that while a defendant may have received information which would have convinced a person of ordinary intelligence and average capacity to comprehend and evaluate facts, a defendant may be a person of less than average intelligence, comprehension and reasoning powers. The true test is, did the *defendant* know the goods were stolen.

This is not to say that the defendant must have direct knowledge or positive proof that the goods were stolen, such as he would have gained by actually witnessing the theft or hearing the admission of the thief. It is enough if he was made aware of circumstances which caused him to believe that they were stolen.

The fact that the jury must be satisfied as to the state of the defendant's personal belief does not present the State with an insurmountable task when direct proof of his belief is absent. Juries have been instructed from time immemorial as to other offenses that they may draw rational inferences as to intent from a defendant's speech and conduct in relation to the subject matter and from evidence showing the information of which a defendant was aware. The state of a defendant's belief may be resolved by inference in the same manner.

While the objective test of what an ordinary intelligent man would have believed cannot serve as the absolute standard which determines the defendant's guilt or innocence, the jury, in making its determination as to the state of a defendant's belief, may properly take into consideration, among other things, the belief which the jury concludes a person of ordinary intellectual capacity would have formed from such facts and circumstances. The jury may consider this in the light of its evaluation of a defendant as an intelligent person, based upon what the jury has learned about the defendant from testimony and observation.

The Presiding Justice several times presented the issue to the jury in the alternative—that is, that the requirement of guilty knowledge was satisfied if the jury found *either* that the Defendant believed the goods had been stolen *or* that a reasonable man under those circumstances would have believed that they had been stolen.

Since we are convinced that the statute must be construed to require proof that the Defendant himself believed that the goods were stolen, the verdict must be set aside.

Appeal sustained. Remanded for new trial.[a]

All Justices concurring.

[Added by the Compiler.]

a. "A finding of either actual knowledge or a belief by the defendant that the property was stolen is essential to a conviction for theft by receiving. In the absence of direct evidence, the jury may draw reasonable inferences from the facts and circumstances of the case that the defendant either knew or believed that the property was stolen." State v. Korelis, 273 Or. 427, 541 P.2d 468, 469 (1975).

Equating "reasonably should be aware" with "knowingly" was error in an instruction on a charge of knowingly introducing contraband. People v. Etchells, 646 P.2d 950 (Colo.App.1982).

In a perjury case the state is not required to allege and prove that D knew the statement he made under oath was false. But D may exculpate himself by proving that he believed he was testifying in a truthful manner. Gauthier v. State, 496 S.W.2d 584 (Tex.Cr.App.1973).

[Some statutes are broader.]

Because the statute on receiving stolen property is worded in terms of "knowing or having reasonable cause to believe the same to have been stolen," the state need not prove actual knowledge that the property was stolen but only that D had reasonable cause so to believe. Richardson v. State, 545 P.2d 1292 (Okl.Cr.App. 1976).

The Utah statute is worded in terms of receiving stolen property "knowing that it has been stolen, or believing that it probably has been stolen." State v. Plum, 552 P.2d 124 (Utah 1976).

A defendant was properly convicted of receiving stolen property by circumstantial knowledge that the property was probably stolen. State v. Hankerson, 70 Ohio St.2d 87, 434 N.E.2d 1362 (1982).

PEOPLE v. KANAN

Supreme Court of Colorado, In Department, 1974.
186 Colo. 255, 526 P.2d 1339.

ERICKSON, JUSTICE. The defendant, John E. Kanan, was convicted of passing short checks, a felony under 1967 Perm.Supp., C.R.S. 1963, 40–14–20. He contends that his conviction should be reversed because the trial cout did not properly instruct the jury. We agree and, therefore, reverse and remand for a new trial.

Kanan wrote three separate checks totaling seventy-five dollars to the ABC Liquor Store during the course of one week in February 1972. The manager of the store deposited the checks, which were returned with the notation that Kanan's account was closed for insufficient funds in January.

There is conflicting evidence as to whether Kanan had knowledge that his checking account was overdrawn. The bank sent Kanan's monthly bank statements to Kanan's address in October, November, December and January, and each statement showed that Kanan's account was overdrawn. The bank also mailed the notice of closure of the account to the same location. The evidence established that the December and January statements were returned to the bank and were not delivered to Kanan.

The jury found Kanan guilty, and he was sentenced to the penitentiary. Defense counsel contends that the trial court committed error and deprived Kanan of the presumption of innocence when the following instruction was given:

"You are instructed that a check drawn and delivered by a person carries with it a representation that such person knows the status of his account and that there are sufficient funds on deposit to pay the check upon its presentation for payment at the bank named as drawee on such check."

We agree. The presumption of innocence, coupled with proof of each element of the charge beyond a reasonable doubt, provides the foundation for our system of criminal justice. People v. Hill, Colo., 512 P.2d 257 (1973).

Under the provisions of the Short Check Statute, the prosecution must prove that the drawer of the check knew that there were insufficient funds in his account to pay the check. 1967 Perm.Supp., C.R.S.1963, 40–14–20(6). The instruction dispensed with the prosecution's obligation to prove knowledge and reversed the burden of proof.

We will not permit the prosecution to utilize a presumption of guilt as a basis for obtaining a conviction in a bad check case. People v. Vinnola, 177 Colo. 405, 494 P.2d 826 (1972); Moore v. People, 124 Colo. 197, 235 P.2d 798 (1951). We stated in *Moore* that the law does not allow an intent to defraud to be presumed whenever a bank refuses to honor a check.

Bank operations, although efficient, are subject to ordinary mistakes which fallible employees make. To conclude that whenever a check was returned to the payee, the drawer must have known the state of his account, would be "a result [which] strikes at the very foundation of our system of criminal justice." People v. Vinnola, supra. The trial court committed reversible error by submitting an instruction which forced the defendant to meet and rebut a presumption that he had knowledge of the state of his account. . . .

The prosecution contends that even if the court improperly instructed the jury, the error was harmless. We disagree. Prejudice to the defendant is inevitable when the court instructs the jury in such a way as to reduce the prosecution's obligation to prove each element of its case beyond a reasonable doubt. Gonzales v. People, 166 Colo. 557, 445 P.2d 74 (1968).

Accordingly, we reverse and remand for a new trial.

KELLEY, GROVES and LEE, JJ., concur.[1]

UNITED STATES v. JEWELL

United States Court of Appeals, Ninth Circuit, 1976.
532 F.2d 697.

OPINION

Before CHAMBERS, KOELSCH, BROWNING, DUNIWAY, ELY, HUFSTEDLER, WRIGHT, TRASK, CHOY, GOODWIN, WALLACE, SNEED and KENNEDY, CIRCUIT JUDGES.

BROWNING, CIRCUIT JUDGE: . . .

In the course of in banc consideration of this case, we have encountered another problem that divides us.

Appellant defines "knowingly" in 21 U.S.C. §§ 841 and 960 to require that positive knowledge that a controlled substance is involved be established as an element of each offense. On the basis of this interpretation, appellant argues that it was reversible error to instruct the jury that the defendant could be convicted upon proof beyond a reasonable doubt that if he did not have positive knowledge that a controlled substance was concealed in the automobile he drove over the border, it was solely and entirely because of the conscious purpose on his part to avoid learning the truth. The majority concludes that this contention is wrong in principle, and has no support in authority or in the language or legislative history of the statute.

1. An instruction presuming an intent to defraud and knowledge of insufficient funds upon dishonor and non-payment was held to be error in the absence of a further explanation. State v. Merriweather, 625 S.W.2d 256 (Tenn.1981).

It is undisputed that appellant entered the United States driving an automobile in which 110 pounds of marihuana worth $6,250 had been concealed in a secret compartment between the trunk and rear seat. Appellant testified that he did not know the marihuana was present. There was circumstantial evidence from which the jury could infer that appellant had positive knowledge of the presence of the marihuana, and that his contrary testimony was false.[1] On the other hand there was evidence from which the jury could conclude that appellant spoke the truth—that although appellant knew of the presence of the secret compartment and had knowledge of facts indicating that it contained marihuana, he deliberately avoided positive knowledge of the presence of the contraband to avoid responsibility in the event of discovery.[2] If the jury concluded the latter was indeed the situation, and if positive knowledge is required to convict, the jury would have no choice consistent with its oath but to find

1. Appellant testified that a week before the incident in question he sold his car for $100 to obtain funds "to have a good time." He then rented a car for about $100, and he and a friend drove the rented car to Mexico. Appellant and his friend were unable to adequately explain their whereabouts during the period of about 11 hours between the time they left Los Angeles and the time they admitted arriving in Mexico.

Their testimony regarding acquisition of the load car follows a pattern common in these cases: they were approached in a Tijuana bar by a stranger who identified himself only by his first name—"Ray." He asked them if they wanted to buy marihuana, and offered to pay them $100 for driving a car north across the border. Appellant accepted the offer and drove the load car back, alone. Appellant's friend drove appellant's rented car back to Los Angeles.

Appellant testified that the stranger instructed him to leave the load car at the address on the car registration slip with the keys in the ashtray. The person living at that address testified that he had sold the car a year earlier and had not seen it since. When the Customs agent asked appellant about the secret compartment in the car, appellant did not deny knowledge of its existence, but stated that it was in the car when he got it.

There were many discrepancies and inconsistencies in the evidence reflecting upon appellant's credibility. Taking the record as a whole, the jury could have concluded that the evidence established an abortive scheme, concocted and carried out by appellant from the beginning, to acquire a load of marihuana in Mexico and return it to Los Angeles for distribution for profit.

2. Both appellant and his companion testified that the stranger identified as "Ray" offered to sell them marihuana and, when they declined, asked if they wanted to drive a car back to Los Angeles for $100. Appellant's companion "wanted no part of driving the vehicle." He testified, "It didn't sound right to me." Appellant accepted the offer. The Drug Enforcement Administration agent testified that appellant stated "he thought there was probably something wrong and something illegal in the vehicle, but that he checked it over. He looked in the glove box and under the front seat and in the trunk, prior to driving it. *He didn't find anything, and, therefore, he assumed that the people at the border wouldn't find anything either*" (emphasis added). Appellant was asked at trial whether he had seen the special compartment when he opened the trunk. He responded, "Well, you know, I saw a void there, but I didn't know what it was." He testified that he did not investigate further. The Customs agent testified that when he opened the trunk and saw the partition he asked appellant "when he had that put in." Appellant told the agent "that it was in the car when he got it."

The jury would have been justified in accepting all of the testimony as true and concluding that although appellant was aware of facts making it virtually certain that the secret compartment concealed marihuana, he deliberately refrained from acquiring positive knowledge of the fact.

appellant not guilty even though he deliberately contrived his lack of positive knowledge. Appellant urges this view. The trial court rejected the premise that only positive knowledge would suffice, and properly so.

Appellant tendered an instruction that to return a guilty verdict the jury must find that the defendant knew he was in possession of marihuana. The trial judge rejected the instruction because it suggested that "absolutely, positively, he has to know that it's there." The court said, "I think, in this case, it's not too sound an instruction because we have evidence that if the jury believes it, they'd be justified in finding he actually didn't know what it was—he didn't because he didn't want to find it."

The court instructed the jury that "knowingly" meant voluntarily and intentionally and not by accident or mistake.[3] The court told the jury that the government must prove beyond a reasonable doubt that the defendant "knowingly" brought the marihuana into the United States (count 1: 21 U.S.C. § 952(a)), and that he "knowingly" possessed the marihuana (count 2: 21 U.S.C. § 841(a)(1)). The court continued:

"The Government can complete their burden of proof by proving, beyond a reasonable doubt, that if the defendant was not actually aware that there was marihuana in the vehicle he was driving when he entered the United States his ignorance in that regard was solely and entirely a result of his having made a conscious purpose to disregard the nature of that which was in the vehicle, with a conscious purpose to avoid learning the truth."

The legal premise of these instructions is firmly supported by leading commentators here and in England. Professor Rollin M. Perkins writes, "One with a deliberate anti-social purpose in mind . . . may deliberately 'shut his eyes' to avoid knowing what would otherwise be obvious to view. In such cases, so far as criminal law is concerned, the person acts at his peril in this regard, and is treated as having 'knowledge' of the facts as they are ultimately discovered to be."[4] J. Ll. J. Edwards, writing in 1954, introduced a survey of English cases with the statement, "For well-nigh a hundred years, it has been clear from the authorities that a person who deliberately shuts his eyes to an obvious means of knowledge has sufficient *mens rea* for an offence based on such words as . . . 'knowingly.'"[5] Pro-

3. The court said:

An act is done knowingly if it's done voluntarily and intentionally and not because of mistake or accident or other innocent reason.

The purpose of adding the word "knowingly" was to insure that no one would be convicted for acts done because of an omission or failure to act due to mistake or accident or other innocent reason.

4. R. Perkins, Criminal Law 776 (2d ed. 1969).

5. Edwards, The Criminal Degrees of Knowledge, 17 Modern L.Rev. 294, 298 (1954). Later in his discussion Mr. Edwards writes, "[N]o real doubt has been cast on the proposition that connivance is as culpable as actual knowledge. We have already seen the diverse fashions in which this state of mind has been defined, ranging from the original expres-

fessor Glanville Williams states, on the basis both English and American authorities, "To the requirement of actual knowledge there is one strictly limited exception. . . . [T]he rule is that if a party has his suspicion aroused but then deliberately omits to make further enquiries, because he wishes to remain in ignorance, he is deemed to have knowledge."[6] Professor Williams concludes, "The rule that wilful blindness is equivalent to knowledge is essential, and is found throughout the criminal law."

The substantive justification for the rule is that deliberate ignorance and positive knowledge are equally culpable. The textual justification is that in common understanding one "knows" facts of which he is less than absolutely certain. To act "knowingly," therefore, is not necessarily to act only with positive knowledge, but also to act with an awareness of the high probability of the existence of the fact in question. When such awareness is present, "positive" knowledge is not required. . . .

"Deliberate ignorance" instructions have been approved in prosecutions under criminal statutes prohibiting "knowing" conduct by the Courts of Appeals of the Second, Sixth, Seventh, and Tenth Circuits. In many other cases, Courts of Appeals reviewing the sufficiency of evidence have approved the premise that "knowingly" in criminal statutes is not limited to positive knowledge, but includes the state of mind of one who does not possess positive knowledge only because he consciously avoided it. These lines of authority appear unbroken. Neither the dissent nor the briefs of either party has cited a case holding that such an instruction is error or that such evidence is not sufficient to establish "knowledge."

There is no reason to reach a different result under the statute involved in this case. Doing so would put this court in direct conflict with Courts of Appeals in two other circuits that have approved "deliberate ignorance" instructions in prosecutions under 21 U.S.C. § 841(a), or its predecessor, 21 U.S.C. § 174. Nothing is cited from the legislative history of the Drug Control Act indicating that Congress used the term "knowingly" in a sense at odds with prior authority. Rather, Congress is presumed to have known and adopted the "cluster of ideas" attached to such a familiar term of art. Congress was aware of *Leary* and *Turner*, and expressed no dissatisfaction with their definition of the term.

Appellant's narrow interpretation of "knowingly" is inconsistent with the Drug Control Act's general purpose to deal more effectively "with the growing menace of drug abuse in the United States." Holding that this term introduces a requirement of positive knowledge would make deliberate ignorance a defense. It cannot be

sion 'wilful shutting of the eyes' and its closest counterpart 'wilful blindness,' to the less forceful but equally satisfactory formulae 'purposely abstaining from ascertaining' and 'wilfully abstaining from knowing.'" Id. at 302.

6. G. Williams, Criminal Law: The General Part, § 57 at 157 (2d ed. 1961).

doubted that those who traffic in drugs would make the most of it. This is evident from the number of appellate decisions reflecting conscious avoidance of positive knowledge of the presence of contraband—in the car driven by the defendant or in which he is a passenger, in the suitcase or package he carries, in the parcel concealed in his clothing.

It is no answer to say that in such cases the fact finder may infer positive knowledge. It is probable that many who performed the transportation function, essential to the drug traffic, can truthfully testify that they have no *positive* knowledge of the load they carry. Under appellant's interpretation of the statute, such persons will be convicted only if the fact finder errs in evaluating the credibility of the witness or deliberately disregards the law.

It begs the question to assert that a "deliberate ignorance" instruction permits the jury to convict without finding that the accused possessed the knowledge required by the statute. Such an assertion assumes that the statute requires positive knowledge. But the question is the meaning of the term "knowingly" in the statute. If it means positive knowledge, then, of course, nothing less will do. But if "knowingly" includes a mental state in which the defendant is aware that the fact in question is highly probable but consciously avoids enlightenment, the statute is satisfied by such proof. . . . In the language of the instruction in this case, the government must prove, "beyond a reasonable doubt, that if the defendant was not actually aware . . . his ignorance in that regard was *solely* and *entirely* a result of . . . a conscious purpose to avoid learning the truth."

No legitimate interest of an accused is prejudiced by such a standard, and society's interest in a system of criminal law that is enforceable and that imposes sanctions upon all who are equally culpable requires it.

The conviction is affirmed.[a]

ANTHONY M. KENNEDY, CIRCUIT JUDGE, with whom ELY, HUFSTEDLER and WALLACE, CIRCUIT JUDGES, join (dissenting).

Jewell was convicted and received concurrent sentences on two counts: (1) knowingly or intentionally importing a controlled substance, 21 U.S.C. §§ 952(a), 960(a)(1); (2) knowingly or intentionally possessing, with intent to distribute, a controlled substance, id. § 841(a)(1). We agree with the majority that the jury was not required to find, as to count one, that the defendant knew *which* con-

a. "A deliberate avoidance of knowledge is culpable only when coupled with a subjective awareness of high probability." United States v. Valle-Valdez, 554 F.2d 911, 914 (9th Cir. 1977).

trolled substance he possessed. We further agree that the additional state of mind required by count two—intent to distribute the substance—must be specifically proven as an element of a section 841(a)(1) violation. . . .

The majority opinion justifies the conscious purpose jury instruction as an application of the wilful blindness doctrine recognized primarily by English authorities. A classic illustration of this doctrine is the connivance of an innkeeper who deliberately arranges not to go into his back room and thus avoids visual confirmation of the gambling he believes is taking place. The doctrine is commonly said to apply in deciding whether one who acquires property under suspicious circumstances should be charged with knowledge that it was stolen.

One problem with the wilful blindness doctrine is its bias towards visual means of acquiring knowledge. We may know facts from direct impressions of the other senses or by deduction from circumstantial evidence, and such knowledge is nonetheless "actual." Moreover, visual sense impressions do not consistently provide complete certainty.

Another problem is that the English authorities seem to consider wilful blindness a state of mind distinct from, but equally culpable, as "actual" knowledge. When a statute specifically requires knowledge as an element of a crime, however, the substitution of some other state of mind cannot be justified even if the court deems that both are equally blameworthy.

Finally, the wilful blindness doctrine is uncertain in scope. There is disagreement as to whether reckless disregard for the existence of a fact constitutes wilful blindness or some lesser degree of culpability. Some cases have held that a statute's scienter requirement is satisfied by the constructive knowledge imputed to one who simply fails to discharge a duty to inform himself. There is also the question of whether to use an "objective" test based on the reasonable man, or to consider the defendant's subjective belief as dispositive.

The approach adopted in section 2.02(7) of the Model Penal Code clarifies, and, in important ways restricts,[11] the English doctrine:

When knowledge of the existence of a particular fact is an element of an offense, such knowledge is established if a person is aware of a high probability of its existence, unless he actually believes that it does not exist.

11. Professor Perkins observes that section 2.02(7) of the Model Penal Code "covers must [much] less than 'knowledge' as it has been interpreted as a mens-rea requirement in the common law." With regard to the receipt of stolen property, he criticizes the Code for not imposing liability in "the case of the man who has no belief one way or the other, but has been put on notice that it may be stolen and 'shuts his eyes' in order not to find out." R. Perkins, supra note 1 at 799 [779].

This provision requires an awareness of a high probability that a fact exists, not merely a reckless disregard, or a suspicion followed by a failure to make further inquiry. It also establishes knowledge as a matter of subjective belief, an important safeguard against diluting the guilty state of mind required for conviction. It is important to note that section 2.02(7) is a *definition* of knowledge, not a substitute for it; as such, it has been cited with approval by the Supreme Court.

In light of the Model Penal Code's definition, the "conscious purpose" jury instruction is defective in three respects. First, it fails to mention the requirement that Jewell have been aware of a high probability that a controlled substance was in the car. It is not culpable to form "a conscious purpose to avoid learning the truth" unless one is aware of facts indicating a high probability of that truth. To illustrate, a child given a gift-wrapped package by his mother while on vacation in Mexico may form a conscious purpose to take it home without learning what is inside; yet his state of mind is totally innocent unless he is aware of a high probability that the package contains a controlled substance. Thus, a conscious purpose instruction is only proper when coupled with a requirement that one be aware of a high probability of the truth.

The second defect in the instruction as given is that it did not alert the jury that Jewell could not be convicted if he "actually believed" there was no controlled substance in the car. The failure to emphasize, as does the Model Penal Code, that subjective belief is the determinative factor, may allow a jury to convict on an objective theory of knowledge—that a reasonable man should have inspected the car and would have discovered what was hidden inside. . . .

We do not question the sufficiency of the evidence in this case to support conviction by a properly-instructed jury. As with all states of mind, knowledge must normally be proven by circumstantial evidence. There is evidence which could support a conclusion that Jewell was aware of a high probability that the car contained a controlled substance and that he had no belief to the contrary. However, we cannot say that the evidence was so overwhelming that the erroneous jury instruction was harmless. Accordingly, we would reverse the judgment on this appeal.[b]

b. In a prosecution for willfully causing false claims to be made against the United States the failure to include "balancing language" instructing the jurors that willful blindness constitutes knowledge "only where the individual is aware of a high probability that fact exists and does not subjectively disbelieve the fact" was held not to be error. The court did, however, indicate such language may provide "useful clarification." United States v. Cincotta, 689 F.2d 238, 243–244 (1st Cir. 1982).

Failure to give an instruction on "high probability" and "actual belief" in a deliberate ignorance instruction was not plain error. United States v. Glick, 710 F.2d 639 (10th Cir. 1983).

(C) WILFULNESS

The adverb "wilfully" has such extreme differences of meaning that it gives no clue to the *mens rea* requirement to which it refers if it is considered alone. It must be studied with its context and in the light of the particular offense. With reference to its meaning the Supreme Court of the United States has had this to say: "The word often denotes an act which is intentional, or knowing, or voluntary, as distinguished from accidental. But when used in a criminal statute it generally means an act done [1] with a bad purpose . . . ; [2] without justifiable excuse . . . ; [or 3] stubbornly, obstinately, perversely . . . . The word is also employed [4] to characterize a thing done without ground for believing it is lawful . . . , or [5] conduct marked by careless disregard whether or not one has the right so to act, . . . "[2]

FIELDS v. UNITED STATES

United States Court of Appeals, District of Columbia, 1947.
164 F.2d 97.

Clark, Associate Justice. Appellant was convicted by the verdict of a jury in the District Court of the United States for the District of Columbia under an indictment charging him with violation of 52 Stat. 942, Act June 22, 1938, 2 U.S.C.A. § 192 which reads as follows: "Every person who having been summoned as a witness by the authority of either House of Congress to give testimony or to produce papers upon any matter under inquiry before either House, or any joint committee established by a joint or concurrent resolution of the two Houses of Congress, or any committee of either House of Congress, willfully makes default, or who, having appeared, refuses to answer any question pertinent to the question under inquiry, shall be deemed guilty of a misdemeanor, punishable by a fine of not more than $1,000 nor less than $100 and imprisoned in a common jail for not less than one month nor more than twelve months." He appeals from the judgment of conviction. . . .

For his failure to produce the records called for by the subpoena appellant was cited by the House of Representatives, upon the recommendation of the committee, for contempt. The indictment returned

2. United States v. Murdock, 290 U.S. 389, 394–5, 54 S.Ct. 223, 225, 78 L.Ed. 381 (1933). Brackets added. And see Nabob Oil Co. v. United States, 190 F.2d 478 (10th Cir. 1951).

The word "wilful" in a criminal statute means no more than that the forbidden act was done deliberately and with knowledge. It does not require an evil intent. McBride v. United States, 225 F.2d 249 (5th Cir. 1955).

"Wilfulness", as used in the statute proscribing the wilful failure to make timely payment of income taxes, requires a specific wrongful intent. United States v. Palermo, 259 F.2d 872 (3d Cir. 1958). Even gross negligence in the failure to pay the tax does not warrant conviction under this statute. Ibid.

by the grand jury contained two counts of alleged contempt, similar in substance but referring to the separate days of August 14 and 15, 1946. The lower court granted a motion for acquittal as to the first count but appellant was convicted on the second count. He was sentenced to be confined for a term of three months and to pay a fine of two hundred and fifty dollars.

The Government charged there were at least three documents pertinent to the transaction under investigation by the committee which were available to the appellant at the time of the committee hearing. These documents were produced at the trial. The jury found that one or more of these documents had been willfully withheld from the committee by the appellant.

The principal issues raised on appeal are whether or not the court below erred in failing to direct a judgment of acquittal as to the second count; whether or not the word "willfully", as used in the statute, implies an evil or bad purpose; and the related question of whether or not good faith has any bearing on the issue of willfulness. The last two issues arise from the court's charge to the jury that an evil or bad purpose is immaterial, and the court's refusal to charge that appellant's acts assertedly constituting good faith had a bearing on the issue of willfulness.

As to the first issue we are of the opinion that the evidence presented by the Government was clearly sufficient to warrant submission of the case to the jury.

Appellant contends tht the word "willful" has a meaning which includes an evil or bad purpose when used in a criminal statute. We think the term has acquired no such fixed meaning according to the type of statute in which it is employed. The Supreme Court has said, long ago, "In construing a statute, penal as well as others, we must look to the object in view, and never adopt an interpretation that will defeat its own purpose, if it will admit of any other reasonable construction." The Emily and The Caroline, 1824, 9 Wheat. 381, 6 L.Ed. 116. . . .

The apparent objective of the statute involved here would be largely defeated if, as appellant contends, a person could appear before a congressional investigating committee and by professing willingness to comply with its requests for information escape the penalty for subsequent default. This court said, in Townsend v. United States, 1938, 68 App.D.C. 223, 229, 95 F.2d 352, 358: "The meaning of the word [willful] depends in large measure upon the nature of the criminal act and the facts of the particular case. It is only in very few criminal cases that 'willful' means 'done with a bad purpose.' Generally, it means 'no more than that the person charged with the duty knows what he is doing. It does not mean that, in addition, he must suppose that he is breaking the law.'" (Quoting Learned Hand, J., in American Surety Co. v. Sullivan, 2 Cir., 1925, 7 F.2d 605, 606.) At the trial of this case the court said, in its charge to the jury:

"The word 'willful' does not mean that the failure or refusal to comply with the order of the committee must necessarily be for an evil or a bad purpose. The reason or the purpose of failure to comply or refusal to comply is immaterial, so long as the refusal was deliberate and intentional and was not a mere inadvertence or an accident." We uphold that differentiation in our view of the purpose of the statute.

Closely related to the issue of willfulness is appellant's assertion of error in the trial court's refusal to charge that appellant's voluntary production of certain records constituted evidence that he acted in good faith and did not "willfully" default. Such an assertion does not penetrate the question whether or not appellant was guilty of deliberately failing to produce subpoenaed records subject to his control, and it was the alleged failure to do so that served as the basis for the contempt citation. That question of fact was properly referred to the jury in the trial below, and the jury returned a verdict against the appellant. . . .

In conclusion, we have carefully examined the record on appeal and find in it no reversible error. Accordingly, the judgment of the trial court is

Affirmed.[1]

(Certiorari denied 332 U.S. 851, 68 S.Ct. 355, 92 L.Ed. 421. Rehearing denied 333 U.S. 839, 68 S.Ct. 607, 92 L.Ed. 1123.)

UNITED STATES v. POMPONIO

Supreme Court of the United States, 1976.
429 U.S. 10, 97 S.Ct. 22.

Per Curiam. After a jury trial, respondents were convicted of willfully filing false income tax returns in violation of 26 U.S.C. § 7206(1).[1] Based on its reading of United States v. Bishop, 412 U.S. 346, 93 S.Ct. 2008, 36 L.Ed.2d 941 (1973), the Court of Appeals held that the jury was incorrectly instructed concerning willfulness, and remanded for a new trial. The United States petitioned for certiorari. We reverse.

The respondents were charged with falsifying tax returns in two principal ways: (1) they allegedly caused corporations they controlled to report payments to them as loans, when they knew the payments

1. In a regulatory statute the word "wilful" means intentional but does imply fraud or malice. Department of Transportation v. Transportation Commission, 111 Wis.2d 80, 330 N.W.2d 159 (1983).

1. Section 7206 provides in pertinent part:

"Any person who—

"(1) . . . Willfully makes and subscribes any return, statement, or other document, which contains or is verified by a written declaration that it is made under the penalties of perjury, and which he does not believe to be true and correct as to every material matter . . .

. . .

"shall be guilty of a felony . . . ."

were really taxable dividends; and (2) they allegedly claimed partnership losses as deductions knowing that the losses were properly attributable to a corporation. Their defense was that these transactions were correctly reported, or at least that they thought so at the time.

The jury was instructed that respondents were not guilty of violating § 7206(1) unless they had signed the tax returns knowing them to be false,[2] and had done so willfully. A willful act was defined in the instructions as one done "voluntarily and intentionally and with the specific intent to do something which the law forbids, that is to say with [the] bad purpose either to disobey or to disregard the law." Finally, the jury was instructed that "[g]ood motive alone is never a defense where the act done or omitted is a crime," and that consequently motive was irrelevant except as it bore on intent. The Court of Appeals held this final instruction improper because "the statute at hand requires a finding of a bad purpose or evil motive." In so holding, the Court of Appeals incorrectly assumed that the reference to an "evil motive" in United States v. Bishop, supra, and prior cases meant something more than the specific intent to violate the law described in the trial judge's instruction.

In *Bishop* we held that the term "willfully" has the same meaning in the misdemeanor and felony sections of the Revenue Code, and that it requires more than a showing of careless disregard for the truth.[3] We did not, however, hold that the term requires proof of any motive other than an intentional violation of a known legal duty. We explained the meaning of willfulness in § 7206 and related statutes:

> "The Court, in fact, has recognized that the word 'willfully' in these statutes generally connotes a voluntary, intentional violation of a known legal duty. It has formulated the requirement of willfulness as 'bad faith or evil intent,' or 'evil motive and want of

2. We agree with the Court of Appeals that the instructions on this point were "full and complete." 528 F.2d 247, 249–250 (1975). The jury was told that the Government contended that respondents "couldn't claim this [the partnership losses] as a deduction . . . because by so doing they would know that they were filing a false report of their total gross income." Later the jury was instructed that, if they found the loans were incorrectly reported, they must also find that the return was "made willfully and with the specific intent and knowledge at the time they made it that it was in fact a false return." In explaining intent, the trial judge said that "[t]o establish the specific intent the Government must prove that these defendants knowingly did the acts, that is, filing these returns, knowing that they were false, purposely intending to violate the law." The jury was told to "bear in mind the sole charge that you have here, and that is the violation of 7206, the willful making of the false return, and subscribing to it under perjury, knowing it not to be true and [*sic*] to all material respects, and that and that alone."

3. The Court of Appeals in *Bishop* held that the evidence under the misdemeanor statute "need only show unreasonable, capricious, or careless disregard for the truth or falsity of income tax returns filed." This Court rejected the view that this lesser degree of culpability was required for a violation of the misdemeanor statute, and held on the contrary that "Congress used the word 'willfully' to describe a constant rather than a variable in the tax penalty formula."

justification in view of all the financial circumstances of the taxpayer,' or knowledge that the taxpayer 'should have reported more income than he did.'

Our references to other formulations of the standard did not modify the standard set forth in the first sentence of the quoted paragraph. On the contrary, as the other Courts of Appeals that have considered the question have recognized, willfulness in this context simply means a voluntary, intentional violation of a known legal duty. The trial judge in the instant case adequately instructed the jury on willfulness. An additional instruction on good faith was unnecessary.

As an alternative ground for ordering a new trial, the Court of Appeals held that respondents were entitled to instructions exonerating them if they believed that the payments to them were loans and that the losses belonged to the partnership. Our inspection of the record indicates that such instructions were given and that they were adequate.[4]

The respondents' other allegations of error which the Court of Appeals found it unnecessary to reach should be considered by that court in the first instance.

The petition for certiorari is granted, the judgment of the Court of Appeals is reversed, and the case is remanded for further proceedings consistent with this opinion.

It is so ordered.

SECTION 5. STRICT LIABILITY

It has been necessary to recognize that some *offenses* are not *true crimes*. Parking overtime in a restricted zone is an extreme illustration. In the absence of legislation a properly parked car could be left where it is for three hours as justifiably as for ten minutes. In the exercise of the police power, zones have been established in moderately congested areas in which parking is permitted, but for limited periods only. The length of the period depends upon needs of the particular situation. If the limit established for a certain zone is thirty minutes this is not for the reason that it would be inherently wrong for a car to be left there for a longer period. Nothing but expediency is involved. Penalties are provided as a means of enforcement but no one considers the driver who has parked overtime a crim-

4. The instructions set forth in n. 2, supra, by requiring knowledge that the returns falsely reported the transactions, implicitly required knowledge of the true nature of the transactions. In addition, the jury was instructed with respect to the loans that "if you do find that they were not bona fide loans then you must next determine whether or not the defendants knew at the time they were withdrawing this money that it was not a loan . . .. In other words, you should determine whether they knew that, and as I have told you, that is an essential element." With respect to the partnership losses, the jury was told that the Government claimed that respondents "knew that they couldn't transfer [a certain asset] to a partnership, and, therefore, when they couldn't transfer it they couldn't take the benefits of any losses sustained by the partnership in question . . . ."

inal. His violation differs from murder or theft by more than degree. It is a different kind of a breach.

To express this difference there has been a tendency to speak of such violations as "civil offenses," "public torts," "public welfare offenses," or "administrative misdemeanors." Since they are not true crimes the normal *mens rea* requirement of crime does not attach.[1] They are enforced on the basis of "strict liability" unless the particular statute or ordinance adds some limitation.

It is necessary to give special attention to three problems: (1) Is the particular offense under consideration a "civil offense" or a true crime? (2) If it is a "civil offense," has the wording of the enactment added a *mens rea* requirement of some nature? (3) If it is a true crime, has the wording of a statute eliminated the *mens rea* requirement (and if so what is the effect)?

THE QUEEN v. STEPHENS

Queen's Bench, 1866.
L.R. 1 Q.B. 702.

INDICTMENT. First count for obstructing the navigation of a public river called the Tivy by casting and throwing, and causing to be cast and thrown, slate stone and rubbish in and upon the soil and bed of the river, and thereby raising and producing great mounts projecting and extending along the stream and waterway of the river.

Second count that the defendant was the owner of large quantities of slate quarried from certain slate quarries near the river Tivy, and that he unlawfully kept, permitted, and suffered to be and remain large quantities of slate sunk in the river, so that the navigation of the river was obstructed.

Plea, not guilty.

The indictment was tried before Blackburn, J., at the last spring assizes for Pembrokeshire, when the following facts were proved:— The Tivy is a public navigable river which flows through Llechryd Bridge, thence by Kilgerran Castle, and from thence past the town of Cardigan to the sea. About twenty years ago the Tivy was navigable to within a quarter of a mile of Llechryd Bridge, from which place a considerable traffic was carried on in limestone and culm by means of lighters.

The defendant is the owner of a slate quarry called the Castle Quarry, situated near the Castle of Kilgerran, which he has extensively worked since 1842. The defendant had no spoil bank at the quarry. The rubbish from the quarry was stacked about five or six yards from the edge of the river. Previous to 1847, the defendant

1. Kenny, Outlines of Criminal Law 44–45 (18th ed. by Turner, 1962).

"However when the sanction is regulatory, rather than punitive, it does not support the characterization of the statute as criminal." State v. Rhodes, 54 Or. App. 254, 634 P.2d 806, 808 (1981).

erected a wall to prevent it from falling into the river, but in that year a heavy flood carried away the wall, and with it large quantities of the rubbish. Quantities of additional rubbish were from time to time shot by the defendant's workmen on the same spot, and so slid into the river. By these means the navigation was obstructed, so that even small boats were prevented from coming up to Llechryd Bridge.

The defendant being upwards of eighty years of age was unable personally to superintend the working of the quarry, which was managed for his benefit by his sons. The defendant's counsel was prepared to offer evidence that the workmen at the quarry had been prohibited both by the defendant and his sons from thus depositing the rubbish; and that they had been told to place the rubbish in the old excavations and in a place provided for that purpose. The learned judge intimated that the evidence was immaterial; and he directed the jury that as the defendant was the proprietor of the quarry, the quarrying of which was carried on for his benefit, it was his duty to take all proper precautions to prevent the rubbish from falling into the river, and that if a substantial part of the rubbish went into the river from having been improperly stacked so near the river as to fall into it, the defendant was guilty of having caused a nuisance, although the acts might have been committed by his workmen, without his knowledge and against his general orders. The jury found a verdict of guilty.

A rule having been obtained for a new trial, on the ground that the judge misdirected the jury in telling them that the defendant would be liable for the acts of his workmen in depositing the rubbish from the quarries so as to become a nuisance, though without the defendant's knowledge and against his orders, . . .

MELLOR, J. In this case I am of opinion, and in my opinion my Brother Shee concurs,[1] that the direction of my Brother Blackburn was right. It is quite true that this in point of form is a proceeding of a criminal nature, but in substance I think it is in the nature of a civil proceeding, and I can see no reason why a different rule should prevail with regard to such an act as is charged in this indictment between proceedings which are civil and proceedings which are criminal. I think there may be nuisances of such a character that the rule I am applying here, would not be applicable to them, but here it is perfectly clear that the only reason for proceeding criminally is that the nuisance, instead of being merely a nuisance affecting an individual, or one or two individuals, affects the public at large, and no private individual, without receiving some special injury, could have maintained an action. Then if the contention of those who say the direction is wrong is to prevail, the public would have great difficulty

1. [Footnotes 1 and 2 are official.] Shee, J., left the court just before the conclusion of the argument.

in getting redress. The object of this indictment is to prevent the recurrence of the nuisance. The prosecutor cannot proceed by action, but must proceed by indictment, and if this were strictly a criminal proceeding the prosecution would be met with the objection that there was no mens rea: that the indictment charged the defendant with a criminal offence, when in reality there was no proof that the defendant knew of the act, or that he himself gave orders to his servants to do the particular act he is charged with; still at the same time it is perfectly clear that the defendant finds the capital, and carries on the business which causes the nuisance, and is carried on for his benefit; although from age or infirmity the defendant is unable to go to the premises, the business is carried on for him by his sons, or at all events by his agents. Under these circumstances the defendant must necessarily give to his servants or agents all the authority that is incident to the carrying on of the business. It is not because he had at some time or other given directions that it should be carried on so as not to allow the refuse from the works to fall into the river, and desired his servants to provide some other place for depositing it, that when it has fallen into the river, and has become prejudicial to the public, he can say he is not liable on an indictment for a nuisance caused by the acts of his servants. It appears to me that all it was necessary to prove is, that the nuisance was caused in the carrying on of the works of the quarry. That being so my Brother Blackburn's direction to the jury was quite right.

I agree that the authorities that bear directly upon the case are very few. In the case of Reg. v. Russell,[2] the observations of Lord Campbell might have been justified by the circumstances of that case, though as I understand it the judgment of the other judges did not proceed on the same reasons. It is therefore only the opinion of Lord Campbell as applied to that case. Whether there is or is not any distinction between that case and the present may be open to question; but if there is no distinction, I should be prepared rather to have acted upon the reasons which influenced the other judge than those which influenced Lord Campbell. Inasmuch as the object of the indictment is not to punish the defendant, but really to prevent the nuisance from being continued, I think that the evidence which would support a civil action would be sufficient to support an indictment.

The rule must be discharged. As I have said, my Brother Shee concurs with me in that opinion.

BLACKBURN, J. I need only add that I see no reason to change the opinion I formed at the trial. I only wish to guard myself against it being supposed that either at the trial or now, the general rule that a principal is not criminally answerable for the act of his agent is infringed. All that is necessary to say is this, that where a person maintains works by his capital, and employs servants, and so carries

2. 3 E. & B. 942; 23 L.J. (M.C.) 173.

on the works as in fact to cause a nuisance to a private right, for which an action would lie, if the same nuisance inflicts an injury upon a public right the remedy for which would be by indictment, the evidence which would maintain the action would also support the indictment. That is all that it was necessary to decide and all that is decided.

Rule discharged.[3]

COMMONWEALTH v. OLSHEFSKI

Pennsylvania District and County Court, 1948.
64 D. & C. 343.

KREISHER, P. J., September 9, 1948. On February 6, 1948, John Fisher, a driver for above-named defendant, at the direction of defendant, purchased a load of coal at the Gilberton Coal Company colliery and had the same loaded upon a truck owned by defendant, which had a "U" tag on it, and which, under The Vehicle Code of May 1, 1929, P.L. 905, is permitted to weigh 15,000 pounds plus five percent, or a gross weight of 15,750 pounds. The load was weighed by a licensed weighmaster at the colliery and the weight was given at 15,200 pounds. Fisher drove the truck to the home of defendant, who was out of town at the time and then placed the weigh slip from the colliery in the compartment of the truck. The following day defendant went to the Danville National Bank to do some banking business and observed the Pennsylvania State Police at the Northern end of the river bridge checking on trucks. He then returned to his home and drove his truck with the load of coal to the northern end of the river bridge on his way to the borough water department scales for the purpose of having it weighed. He states that he was selling the coal in Danville, and pursuant to the requirements of an ordinance in Danville, he had to have a Danville weigh slip. Before reaching the water department's scales a State policeman stopped him and he was directed to the scales where his load was weighed by the officer and the weigh slip was signed by a licensed weighmaster, showing that his gross weight was 16,015, and that he was, therefore, overloaded 265 pounds. The officer lodged an information for his violation of The Vehicle Code. Defendant waived a hearing and the matter is now before us for disposition. . . .

It is also contended by counsel for defendant that this prosecution should be dismissed for the reason that defendant had in his possession a weigh bill for this particular load by a duly licensed weighmaster, which was weighed the day before, showing that the gross

3. One who shot and killed a house pigeon, thinking it was a wild bird, was guilty of unlawfully and wilfully killing a house pigeon. "A person who shoots a pigeon which turns out to be a house pigeon must take the consequences of his act". Had the pigeon been killed by accident he would not be guilty. Horton v. Gwynne, [1921] 2 K.B. 661.

weight of the truck and the load was within the load allowed by law for this particular truck, and that defendant, relying upon this weigh bill, voluntarily drove to where he knew the police were weighing trucks, and was of the belief that his load was a legal load, and therefore, because of this belief, he is not guilty of the crime charged.

In criminal law we have two distinct types of crimes: The one type of crime being the common-law crimes, which are designated as crimes mala in se, which means that they are crimes because the act is bad in and of itself. The other type of crime which did not exist at common law covers those acts which are made criminal by statute, and are termed crimes mala prohibita, and simply means that they are crimes not because they are bad in and of themselves, but merely because the legislative authority makes the act criminal and penal.

In crimes that are mala in se, two elements are necessary for the commission of the crime, viz., the mental element and the physical element. In this type of crime intent is a necessary element, but in statutory crimes, which are simply mala prohibita, the mental element is not necessary for the commission of the crime, and one who does an act in violation of the statute and is caught and prosecuted, is guilty of the crime irrespective of his intent or belief. The power of the legislature to punish an act as a crime, even though it is not bad in and of itself, is an absolute power of the legislature, the only restriction being the constitutional restrictions, and it is the duty of the court to enforce these enactments irrespective of what the court might personally think about the prosecution or the wisdom of the act.

Except for constitutional limitations, the power of the State legislature is absolute. It may punish any act which in its judgment requires punishment, provided it violates no constitutional restriction, and its enactments must be enforced by the courts. The courts cannot review the discretion of the legislature, or pass upon the expediency, wisdom, or propriety of legislative action in matters within its powers. Neither can the courts pass upon the action of a prosecuting officer who prosecutes a person for the violation of a statute which is violated by that person, even though the court might be of the opinion that the officer should have not instituted the prosecution.

If the testimony shows, as in this case, that defendant violated the law, and is prosecuted for that violation, then the court is bound to enforce the legislative enactments, and cannot in good conscience set itself up as the legislature and excuse one person who has violated the law and find another person guilty for the same violation. It is true that this rule of law may seem harsh and unjustifiable, but the court is powerless to correct it, and, therefore, under our duty as judge, we are obliged to hold that this defendant violated The Vehicle Code by having his truck overloaded, and that he is guilty as charged. To this end we make the following

Order

And now, to wit, September 9, 1948, it is ordered, adjudged and decreed that Felix Olshefski is guilty as charged, and the sentence of the court is that he pay the costs of prosecution, and that he pay a fine of $25 to the Commonwealth of Pennsylvania for the use of the County of Montour, and in default of payment thereof, shall undergo imprisonment in the Montour County Jail for an indeterminate period of not less than one day nor more than two days. Said sentence to be complied with on or before September 15, 1948.[1]

SMITH v. CALIFORNIA

Supreme Court of the United States, 1959.
361 U.S. 147, 80 S.Ct. 215.

[Defendant was convicted of a violation of a Los Angeles ordinance which made it unlawful for a bookseller to have an obscene book in his shop. As interpreted by the California courts, guilt of this offense was not dependent upon awareness of the obscene nature of the book.]

MR. JUSTICE BRENNAN delivered the opinion of the Court. . . .

Almost 30 years ago, Chief Justice Hughes declared for this Court: "It is no longer open to doubt that the liberty of the press and of speech is within the liberty safeguarded by the due process clause of the Fourteenth Amendment from invasion by state action. It was found impossible to conclude that this essential personal liberty of the citizen was left unprotected by the general guaranty of fundamental rights of person and property. . . ." . . . .

California here imposed a strict or absolute criminal reponsibility on appellant not to have obscene books in his shop. "The existence of a *mens re* is the rule of, rather than the exception to, the principles of Anglo-Mexican criminal jurisprudence." Still, it is doubtless

1. Perkins, Criminal Liability Without Fault: A Disquieting Trend, 68 Iowa L.Rev. 1067 (1983).

In upholding the conviction of a dealer for possessing adulterated tobacco, although he neither knew nor had any reason to suspect the adulteration, it was said that since he knew he was in possession of the tobacco "it is not necessary that he should know that the tobacco was adulterated. . . ." Regina v. Woodrow, 15 M. & W. 404, 415, 153 Eng.Rep. 907, 912 (Ex.1846). A butcher was convicted of selling unsound meat although he was unaware of the unsoundness and could not have discovered it by any examination which he could have been expected to make. Hobbs v. Winchester Corp., [1910] 2 K.B. 471.

A strict liability standard is applicable under a statute punishing issuing a check without an account or with insufficient funds. State v. McDowell, 312 N.W.2d 301 (N.D.1981).

Strict liability applies to the delivery of a controlled substance. State v. Rippley, 319 N.W.2d 129 (N.D.1982).

The defendant was properly convicted of a violation of the Federal Food, Drug and Cosmetic Act for receiving adulterated food in interstate commerce where defendant, as the President of the company, did not do all he could to avoid the problem. United States v. Park, 421 U.S. 658, 95 S.Ct. 1903 (1975).

competent for the States to create strict criminal liabilities by defining criminal offenses without any element of scienter—though even where no freedom-of-expression question is involved, there is precedent in this Court that this power is not without limitations. See Lambert v. People of State of California, 355 U.S. 225, 78 S.Ct. 240, 2 L.Ed.2d 228. But the question here is as to the validity of this ordinance's elimination of the scienter requirement—an elimination which may tend to work a substantial restriction on the freedom of speech and of the press. . . .

These principles guide us to our decision here. We have held that obscene speech and writings are not protected by the constitutional guarantees of freedom of speech and the press. Roth v. United States, 354 U.S. 476, 77 S.Ct. 1304, 1 L.Ed.2d 1498. The ordinance here in question, to be sure, only imposes criminal sanctions on a bookseller if in fact there is to be found in his shop an obscene book. But our holding in Roth does not recognize any state power to restrict the dissemination of books which are not obscene; and we think this ordinance's strict liability feature would tend seriously to have that effect, by penalizing booksellers, even though they had not the slightest notice of the character of the books they sold. The appellee and the court below analogize this strict-liability penal ordinance to familiar forms of penal statutes which dispense with any element of knowledge on the part of the person charged, food and drug legislation being a principal example. We find the analogy instructive in our examination on the question before us. The usual rationale for such statutes is that the public interest in the purity of its food is so great as to warrant the imposition of the highest standard of care on distributors—in fact an absolute standard which will not hear the distributor's plea as to the amount of care he has used. His ignorance of the character of the food is irrelevant. There is no specific constitutional inhibition against making the distributors of food the strictest censors of their merchandise, but the constitutional guarantees of the freedom of speech and of the press stand in the way of imposing a similar requirement on the bookseller. . . .

We have said: "The fundamental freedoms of speech and press have contributed greatly to the development and well-being of our free society and are indispensable to its continued growth. Ceaseless vigilance is the watchword to prevent their erosion by Congress or by the States. The door barring federal and state intrusion into this area cannot be left ajar; it must be kept tightly closed and opened only the slightest crack necessary to prevent encroachment upon more important interests." Roth v. United States, supra, 354 U.S. at page 488, 77 S.Ct. at page 1311. This ordinance opens that door too far. The existence of the State's power to prevent the distribution of obscene matter does not mean that there can be no constitutional barrier to any form of practical exercise of that power. It is plain to us that the ordinance in question, though aimed at obscene matter, has such a tendency to inhibit constitutionally protected expression that it cannot stand under the Constitution.

Reversed.

MR. JUSTICE FRANKFURTER, concurring. . . .

The Court accepts the settled principle of constitutional law that traffic in obscene literature may be outlawed as a crime. But it holds that one cannot be made amenable to such criminal outlawry unless he is chargeable with knowledge of the obscenity. Obviously the Court is not holding that a bookseller must familiarize himself with the contents of every book in his shop. No less obviously, the Court does not hold that a bookseller who insulates himself against knowledge about an offending book is thereby free to maintain an emporium for smut. How much or how little awareness that a book may be found to be obscene suffices to establish scienter, or what kind of evidence may satisfy the how much or the how little, the Court leaves for another day. . . .

[BLACK, J. and DOUGLAS, J. also wrote concurring opinions. HARLAN, J. wrote an opinion concurring in part and dissenting in part.] [a]

PEOPLE v. WASHBURN

Supreme Court of Colorado, En Banc 1979.
197 Colo. 419, 593 P.2d 962.

ROVIRA, JUSTICE. The People appeal the ruling of the Adams County District Court which dismissed separate prosecutions of the defendants on the basis that section 18–4–402(1)(b), C.R.S.1973, and section 18–4–402(1)(b), C.R.S.1973 (1978 Repl. Vol. 8), required no culpable mental state and thus violated the constitution. For the purpose of this appeal, we have consolidated both cases. We reverse and remand with directions that the informations be reinstated.

William Washburn (Washburn) was arrested and charged with theft of rental property, section 18–4–402(1)(b), C.R.S.1973, which states:

"(1) A person commits theft of rental property if he: . . .

"(b) Having lawfully obtained possession for temporary use of the personal property of another which is available only for hire, *intentionally* fails to reveal the whereabouts of or to return said

a. Scienter to some degree, is a requisite for a constitutionally permissible prosecution under a criminal obscenity statute. "The element of scienter required by statute is defined . . . as 'knowledge of the character and content of the subject matter', which complies with the constitutional requirement." Ayre v. State, 291 Md. 155, 433 A.2d 1150, 1154–5 (1981).

Scienter in obscenity statute which defined knowledge only as having general knowledge of, or reason to know, or belief or ground for belief which warrants further inspection or inquiry is constitutionally adequate. Dugal v. Hyder, 467 F.Supp. 1119 (D.C.Ariz.1979).

property to the owner thereof or his representative or to the person from whom he has received it within seventy-two hours after the time at which he agreed to return it." (Emphasis added.)

Howard Stroh (Stroh) was arrested and charged with theft of rental property, section 18–4–402(1)(b), C.R.S.1973 (1978 Repl. Vol. 8), as amended July 1, 1977, which provides:

> "(1) A person commits theft of rental property if he: . . .
>
> "(b) Having lawfully obtained possession for temporary use of the personal property of another which is available only for hire *knowingly* fails to reveal the whereabouts of or to return said property to the owner thereof or his representative or to the person from whom he has received it within seventy-two hours after the time at which he agreed to return it." (Emphasis added.)

The trial court erroneously assumed that both defendants were charged under the statute as amended. The court, after determining that the statute, as amended, was unconstitutional because it contained no element of conscious wrongdoing or criminal intent and no requirement of criminal conduct, dismissed the charges against both defendants. The bases of the court's ruling were the opinions of the United States Supreme Court in Morissette v. United States, 342 U.S. 246, 72 S.Ct. 240, 96 L.Ed. 288 (1952), and of the Alaska Supreme Court in Speidel v. State, 460 P.2d 77 (Alaska 1969). The trial court read *Morissette,* supra, to require an element of conscious wrongdoing or criminal intent in statutes such as section 18–4–402(1)(b), C.R.S.1973, as amended, and read *Speidel,* supra, as an application of that doctrine. Although the order of the trial court did not indicate that the basis for its decision was a violation of due process of law under *U.S. Const.* Amend. XIV, counsel on appeal argued, and we now decide the issue in terms of due process requirements.

I.

Although the ruling of the trial court concerning Washburn was based on the mistaken assumption by the court and counsel that he had been charged under the statute as amended, we must address the issue of the criminal intent required in the statute under which he was charged in reality. Thus, we first address the issue of the culpable mental state required in section 18–4–402(1)(b), C.R.S.1973, both before and after amendment.

The legislature can proscribe an act without regard to a culpable mental state, but only if it does so pursuant to its police power. Such is not the statute in this case. Clearly, the theft of rental property, which is punishable by imprisonment in the state penitentiary because it is a felony, is not akin to speeding violations. As the United States Supreme Court stated in *Morissette,* offenses which have their bases in common law—such as provisions concerning theft—must be construed to require a culpable mental state.

The culpable mental state required in a statute dealing with theft must be more than mere negligence, but it need not be specific intent.

Washburn argues that section 18–4–402(1)(b), C.R.S.1973, does not require a culpable mental state because "intentionally" refers to the act, not to the intent of the actor. Such an interpretation is at odds with *Morissette,* in which the United States Supreme Court addressed a similar statute.

In *Morissette,* the defendant was convicted of converting government property to his own use under a statute which did not specify a culpable mental state.[1] The lower court held that his defense of belief that the property had been abandoned could not be submitted to the jury because a culpable mental state was not an element of the offense. The United States Supreme Court reversed, holding that where an offense has been construed in the past to require criminal intent, legislative silence indicates approval of that prior judicial interpretation. The Court then construed the statute at issue to require an element of criminal intent.

It has been well settled in this state that whenever possible a statute should be construed as to obviate or reduce any constitutional infirmities, section 2–4–201(1)(a), C.R.S.1973; not to impose them. This was the crux of *Morissette,* supra. The statute in that case was silent on the subject of a culpable mental state. The United States Supreme Court did not declare the statute to be unconstitutional; rather, it found the element of criminal intent implicit in the statute.

Similarly, the language of section 18–4–402(1)(b), C.R.S.1973, while imprecise, does require a culpable mental state. By the use of the word "intentionally" the legislature has indicated its design to require a culpable mental state as an element of the offense. Section 18–1–501(4), C.R.S.1973, states that: "'Culpable mental state' means 'intentionally' . . . or 'knowingly' . . ." The use of those terms thus indicates the requirement of a culpable mental state.

Contrary to Washburn's contentions, a defendant must do more than retain the rental property for more than three days after it is due in order to be convicted.[2] The United States Supreme Court stated in *Morissette* that:

"knowing conversion requires more than knowledge that the defendant was taking the property into his possession. He must

1. 18 U.S.C. § 641 provides in pertinent part:

"Whoever embezzles, steals, purloins, or knowingly converts to his use or the use of another, or without authority, sells, conveys or disposes of any record, voucher, money, or thing of value of the United States or of any department or agency thereof, or any property made or being made under contract for the United States or any department or agency thereof: . . .

"Shall be fined not more than $10,000 or imprisoned not more than ten years, or both; but if the value of such property does not exceed the sum of $100, he shall be fined not more than $1,000 or imprisoned not more than one year, or both."

2. Washburn errs in reading "intentionally" in its commonplace usage. The word is specifically defined in section 18–1–501 to indicate specific intent as the culpable mental state.

have had knowledge of the facts, though not necessarily the law, that made the taking a conversion."

Similarly, in order to be convicted under section 18–4–402(1)(b), C.R.S. 1973, the accused must have had the specific intent that his acts constitute a wrongful retention of the rental property.[3]

This holding is in accord with our prior decision in People v. Donelson, 194 Colo. 175, 570 P.2d 542 (1977), in which we held that the culpable mental state in section 18–4–402(1)(b), C.R.S.1973, must be proved in order to sustain a conviction under the statute. . . .

The change of the word "intentionally" to "knowingly" [4] does not remove the element of a culpable mental state from the statute. The conscious culpability required by the statute remains the wrongful retention of the rental property. Under the statute before it was amended, the wrongful retention had to be with specific intent, as stated in part I above. Under the statute as amended, the wrongful retention need only be with general intent. The change of the statute from a specific intent offense to a general intent offense does not abrogate the necessity of a culpable mental state as an element of the offense. To the contrary, it is a clear indication from the legislature that conviction under the statute requires proof of the culpable mental state.

Thus, in order to be convicted under section 18–4–402(1)(b), C.R.S. 1973 (1978 Repl. Vol. 8)—the statute as amended—the defendant must have had knowledge that his acts would constitute the wrongful retention of the rental property. To make such a determination, the jury would have to be appropriately instructed. . . .

Accordingly, the judgments of the district court are reversed and the causes remanded with directions that the informations be reinstated.

PRINGLE, J., does not participate.[a]

3. If circumstances prevented the return of the rental property despite the best efforts on the part of the accused, he must be able to raise those circumstances as a defense to his *wrongful* retention of the property, despite the fact that his failure to return the property was purposeful. It is the nature of this offense which gives rise to this issue; the bulk of criminally proscribed behavior is not reasonably subject to the defense of: "my conduct was not wrong." Homicide, assault, kidnapping, sexual assault, arson, burglary, and robbery are all *malum per se*, and protestations by the accused that such conduct is blameless is irrational.

4. Section 18–1–501, C.R.S.1973:

"(6) 'Knowingly' or 'willfully'. All offenses defined in this code in which the mental culpability requirement is expressed as 'knowingly' or 'willfully' are declared to be general intent crimes. A person acts 'knowingly' or 'willfully' with respect to conduct or to a circumstance described by a statute defining an offense when he is aware that his conduct is of such nature or that such circumstance exists. A person acts 'knowingly' or 'willfully', with respect to a result of his conduct, when he is aware that his conduct is practically certain to cause the result."

a. The flag-desecration statute creates a crime malum in se and hence mens rea is required even if not specifically mentioned in the act. State v. Turner, 78 Wash.2d 276, 474 P.2d 91 (1970).

A burglary-type statute, providing for punishment without a requirement of any

STATE v. PRINCE

Supreme Court of New Mexico, 1948.
52 N.M. 15, 189 P.2d 993.

COMPTON, JUSTICE. Defendant in error was charged by an information containing two counts, based upon Section 41–4519, New Mexico Statutes, 1941 Compilation, which reads as follows: "Any person being in the possession of the property of another, who shall convert such property to his own use, or dispose of such property in any way not authorized by the owner thereof, or by law, shall be guilty of embezzlement . . ." Sec. 2, Ch. 70, Laws 1923, N.M.Sts.

The information charged:

"That in the county of Bernalillo, State of New Mexico, the said Lewis Prince, being entrusted in the possession of certain monies of Markus and Markus, a partnership, did on the 20th day of March, 1946, fraudulently convert the sum of forty-one dollars and 41/100 ($41.41) to his own use or did dispose of such property in a way not authorized by the owner thereof or by law.

"Count 2. On the 2nd day of August, 1946, in the same county and state, the said Lewis Prince, being entrusted in the possession of certain monies of Markus and Markus, a partnership, did fraudulently convert the sum of Fifty-four and 50/100 ($54.50) dollars to his own use or did dispose of such property in a way not authorized by the owner thereof or by law."

The statute in question expressly repealed a prior statute which read: "If any person who shall be *entrusted* with any property which may be the subject of larceny, shall *embezzle or fraudulently convert* to his own use, or *shall secrete with intent to embezzle or fraudulently convert* to his own use any such property, he shall be deemed guilty of larceny." Section 1543, Code 1915. (Emphasis ours.)

From an order sustaining a motion to quash the information as unconstitutional and void, plaintiff brings the case here for review by writ of error, assigning the following as error:

unlawful intent, was held to be unconstitutional. State v. Stern, 526 P.2d 344 (Wyo.1974).

"At common law, criminal intent was an essential element of proof of every crime. It remains an essential element, today, in crimes *mala in se*, particularly ones involving the taking of another's property" (citations omitted). And where necessary it "would be read into" the statute by the courts. United States v. Parker, 522 F.2d 801 (4th Cir. 1975).

Securities law provisions are not strict liability offenses under Illinois law. People v. Whitlow, 89 Ill.2d 322, 60 Ill.Dec. 587, 433 N.E.2d 629 (1982). Accord: Hentzner v. State, 613 P.2d 821 (Alaska 1980).

Delivery of a controlled substance offense does not require knowledge that substance delivered was heroin. People v. Delgado, 404 Mich. 76, 273 N.W.2d 395 (1978).

1. The court erred in making its conclusions of law.

2. The court erred in dismissing the information.

3. The court erred in dismissing the defendant. . . .

The single question for our determination is whether the statute may be sustained when it omits certain essential elements necessary to constitute the crime of embezzlement, viz., entrustment and fraudulent appropriation.

The essential elements of the offense of embezzlement are: (a) That the property belonged to some one other than the accused. (b) That the accused occupied a designated fiduciary relationship and that the property came into his possession by reason of his employment or office. (c) That there was a fraudulent intent to deprive the owner of his property. Section 1543, supra, was before the legislature when Section 41–4519, supra, was enacted. It knew the essential elements necessary to constitute the offense of embezzlement. It expressly repealed that effective statute. . . .

A penal statute should define the act necessary to constitute an offense with such certainty that a person who violates it must know that his act is criminal when he does it. Then can it be said a person having property of another in his possession, which he believes to be his own, could possibly know that he had violated the law when he sells it or otherwise appropriates it to his own use. But it clearly appears from reading the statutes in question, such appropriation is made a crime. Under its terms there is no defense for simple conversion, and to make an act, innocent itself, a crime, and criminals of those who might perchance fall within its interdiction, is inconsistent with law. The statute is uncertian in its meaning, vague and indefinite. A person charged thereunder is deprived of due process of law, in violation of the Fourteenth Amendment of the Constitution of the United States. . . .

Plaintiff also urges that in the exercise of police power the legislature has authority to define embezzlement and declare what constitutes an offense. It must be conceded that such power inheres in the state but in order that a statute may be sustained as an exercise of such power it must appear that the enactment has for its purpose the prevention of certain manifest or anticipated evil, or the preservation of the public health, safety, morals, or general welfare. As defined by Justice Holmes: "It may be said in a general way that the police power extends to all the great public needs. . . . It may be put forth in aid of what is sanctioned by usage, or held by the prevailing morality or strong and preponderant opinion to be greatly and immediately necessary to the public welfare." Nobel State Bank v. Haskell, 219 U.S. 104, 31 S.Ct. 186, 188, 55 L.Ed. 112, 32 L.R.A.,N.S., 1062, Ann.Cas.1912A, 487.

The power thus defined, and a prior valid statute having been repealed, we are unable to determine that there existed, or was anticipated, that condition of public health, safety, morals or preponderant opinion making the statute in question immediately necessary for the public welfare. No additional power is conferred by the new statute, unless it has for its purpose to embrace within its ambits the guilty and innocent alike. This would afford no reasonable ascertainable standard of guilt, and is therefore too vague and uncertain to be enforced. The accused, though presumed to be innocent, if proven guilty of simple conversion, nevertheless is a felon under the statute, in violation of the Sixth and Fourteenth Amendments to the Constitution of the United States.[1]

To sustain the statute, we would supply by intendment, words of limitation, and this would be judicial legislation. The statute cannot be extended or sustained as a reasonable exercise of police power. . . .

Our conclusion leaves the state without a statute defining embezzlement unless we determine whether section 1543, supra, has been disturbed by the repealing clause of chapter 70, Laws of 1923, N.M. St. supra.

The public welfare impels us to decide this point. . . .

It is evident that the legislature intended to displace the embezzlement law by substituting a new one. We are not satisfied that the legislature would have repealed the former act if it had not been supposed that the new act adopted in lieu of it was valid.

This being so, under the rule announced, the repealing clause necessarily fails when the purpose of the act fails and no former act is repealed. It follows that the embezzlement law existing prior to the Act of 1923 was not repealed. The judgment of the court was correct in holding that Section 41–4519, supra, did not define embezzlement, but the information having charged a crime under the act sought to be repealed, the court erred in discharging appellant.

The judgment is reversed, with directions to the trial court to reinstate the case upon its docket and proceed in a manner not inconsistent herewith, and it is so ordered.[2]

BRICE, C.J., and LUJAN and MCGHEE, JJ., concur.

1. Chapter 192 of the Public Acts of 1973 was held to be void in its entirety. The result was that its attempted repeal of the prior law was ineffective, leaving that law in full force and effect. Harrison v. State, 527 S.W.2d 745 (Tenn.App. 1975).

2. A New York statute penalizing the receipt of stolen goods by a junk-man without a requirement either of knowledge or lack of diligent inquiry as to the rights of the party selling was held to be invalid. People v. Estreich, 272 App.Div.

SADLER, JUSTICE (dissenting). The prevailing opinion is correct in directing a reversal of the order of the trial court quashing the criminal information filed below. The holding that the statute in question is unconstitutional as denying to an accused due process of law under the Fourteenth Amendment to the Constitution of the United States is plainly erroneous. It convicts the legislature of sheer stupidity to hold that in enacting 1941 Comp. § 41–4519, it intended to authorize punishment of the innocent and well intentioned along with the venal and criminally disposed. . . .

COMMONWEALTH v. KOCZWARA

Supreme Court of Pennsylvania, 1959.
397 Pa. 575, 155 A.2d 825.

COHEN, JUSTICE. This is an appeal from the judgment of the Court of Quarter Sessions of Lackawanna County sentencing the defendant to three months in the Lackawanna County Jail, a fine of five hundred dollars and the costs of prosecution, in a case involving violations of the Pennsylvania Liquor Code. . . .

698, 75 N.Y.S.2d 267, affirmed 297 N.Y. 910, 79 N.E.2d 742 (1947).

A statute made it an offense for any person, except persons of certain specified classes, to have or possess a hypodermic syringe or needle unless such possession was authorized by prescription or certificate of a physician. Since the statute made no exception in case of possession for a lawful purpose it was held to violate the due process clause of the Fourteenth Amendment. State v. Birdsell, 235 La. 396, 104 So.2d 148 (1958).

Mary Noble, a clerk who was a notary public, worked in a branch office of the Bureau of Motor Vehicles where they processed about a thousand applications for license tags a day. Most of the applicants were strangers to the notaries and it would have been practically impossible to investigate and identify each applicant personally. Because of this production-line procedure, Miss Noble was the victim of trickery and was charged with the crime of making a false attestation as notary. The state insisted that the statute in question creates strict liability and for the violation of the statute the accused was criminally liable regardless of any mistake or lack of personal intent. The court very properly refused to hold her to a degree of care which could not in reason be required; but it reached the result in a very strange way. Making a *false* attestation as notary should certainly be characterized as a true crime and as such requires the normal mens rea even if not so specifically stated in the statute. But the court said the act charged is *malum prohibitum* and not *malum in se*, and therefore a mens rea or criminal intent must be proved to support a conviction. Noble v. State, 248 Ind. 101, 223 N.E.2d 755 (1967).

The statute requiring a contractor to apply money received in payment first to the satisfaction of claims of laborers and materialmen who otherwise would have a lien, makes his failure to do so a crime with no requirement of fraud. Since this could result in imprisonment for debt it is unconstitutional. State ex rel. Norton v. Janing, 182 Neb. 539, 156 N.W.2d 9 (1968).

Statute punishing operating a vehicle and displaying a license plate belonging to another vehicle did not violate due process in failing to specify a mens rea requirement. State v. Bentz, 2 Ohio App. 3d 352, 442 N.E.2d 90 (1981).

Conviction under a Wisconsin statute prohibiting violation of home improvement contractor regulation without proof of an element of intent was an affront to due process. Stepniewski v. Gagnon, 562 F.Supp. 329 (D.C.Wis.1983).

Defendant raises two contentions, both of which, in effect, question whether the undisputed facts of this case support the judgment and sentence imposed by the Quarter Sessions Court. Judge Hoban found as fact that "in every instance the purchase [by minors] was made from a bartender, not identified by name, and service to the boys was made by the bartender. There was *no* evidence that the defendant was present on any one of the occasions testified to by these witnesses, nor that he had any personal knowledge of the sales to them or to other persons on the premises." We, therefore, must determine the criminal responsibility of a licensee of the Liquor Control Board for acts committed by his employees upon his premises, without his personal knowledge, participation, or presence, which acts violate a valid regulatory statute passed under the Commonwealth's police power.

While an employer in almost all cases is not criminally responsible for the unlawful acts of his employees, unless he consents to, approves, or participates in such acts, courts all over the nation have struggled for years in applying this rule within the framework of "controlling the sale of intoxicating liquor." At common law, any attempt to invoke the doctrine of *respondeat superior* in a criminal case would have run afoul of our deeply ingrained notions of criminal jurisprudence that guilt must be personal and individual.[1] In recent decades, however, many states have enacted detailed regulatory provisions in fields which are essentially noncriminal, e.g., pure food and drug acts, speeding ordinances, building regulations, and child labor, minimum wage and maximum hour legislation. Such statutes are generally enforceable by light penalties, and although violations are labelled crimes, the considerations applicable to them are totally different from those applicable to true crimes, which involve moral delinquency and which are punishable by imprisonment or another serious penalty. Such so-called statutory crimes are in reality an attempt to utilize the machinery of criminal administration as an enforcing arm for social regulations of a purely civil nature, with the punishment totally unrelated to questions of moral wrongdoing or guilt. It is here that the social interest in the general well-being and security of the populace has been held to outweigh the individual interest of the particular defendant. The penalty is imposed despite the defendant's lack of a criminal intent or mens rea. . . .

In the Liquor Code, Section 493, the legislature has set forth twenty-five specific acts which are condemned as unlawful, and for

1. The distinction between *respondeat superior* in tort law and its application to the criminal law is obvious. In tort law, the doctrine is employed for the purpose of settling the incidence of loss upon the party who can best bear such loss. But the criminal law is supported by totally different concepts. We impose penal treatment upon those who injure or menace social interests, partly in order to reform, partly to prevent the continuation of the anti-social activity and partly to deter others. If a defendant has personally lived up to the social standards of the criminal law and has not menaced or injured anyone, why impose penal treatment?

which penalties are provided in Section 494. Subsections (1) and (14) of Section 493 contain the two offenses charged here. In neither of these subsections is there any language which would require the prohibited acts to have been done either knowingly, wilfully or intentionally, there being a significant absence of such words as "knowingly, wilfully, etc." That the legislature intended such a requirement in other related sections of the same Code is shown by examining Section 492(15), wherein it is made unlawful to *knowingly* sell any malt beverages to a person engaged in the business of illegally selling such beverages. The omission of any such word in the subsections of Section 494 is highly significant. It indicates a legislative intent to eliminate both knowledge and criminal intent as necessary ingredients of such offenses. To bolster this conclusion, we refer back to Section 491 wherein the Code states, "It shall be unlawful (1) For any person, by himself *or by an employe or agent,* to expose or keep for sale, or directly or *indirectly* . . . to sell or offer to sell any liquor within this Commonwealth, except in accordance with the provisions of this act and the regulations of the board." The Superior Court has long placed such an interpretation on the statute.

As the defendant has pointed out, there is a distinction between the requirement of a mens rea and the imposition of vicarious absolute liability for the acts of another. It may be that the courts below, in relying on prior authority, have failed to make such a distinction. In any case, we fully recognize it. Moreover, we find that the intent of the legislature in enacting this Code was not only to eliminate the common law requirement of a mens rea, but also to place a very high degree of responsibility upon the holder of a liquor license to make certain that neither he nor anyone in his employ commit any of the prohibited acts upon the licensed premises. Such a burden of care is imposed upon the licensee in order to protect the public from the potentially noxious effects of an inherently dangerous business. We, of course, express no opinion as to the *wisdom* of the legislature's imposing vicarious responsibility under certain sections of the Liquor Code. There may or may not be an economic-sociological justification for such liability on a theory of deterrence. Such determination is for the legislature to make, so long as the constitutional requirements are met.

Can the legislature, consistent with the requirements of due process, thus establish absolute criminal liability? Were this the defendant's first violation of the Code, and the penalty solely a minor fine of from \$100–\$300, we would have no hesitation in upholding such a judgment. Defendant, by accepting a liquor license, must bear this financial risk. Because of a prior conviction for violations of the Code, however, the trial judge felt compelled under the mandatory language of the statute, Section 494(a), to impose not only an increased fine of five hundred dollars, but also a three month sentence of imprisonment. Such sentence of imprisonment in a case where liability is imposed vicariously cannot be sanctioned by this Court consistently with the law of the land clause of Section 9, Article I of the Constitution of the Commonwealth of Pennsylvania, P.S.

The Courts of the Commonwealth have already strained to permit the legislature to carry over the civil doctrine of *respondeat superior* and to apply it as a means of enforcing the regulatory scheme that covers the liquor trade. We have done so on the theory that the Code established petty misdemeanors involving only light monetary fines. It would be unthinkable to impose vicarious criminal responsibility in cases involving true crimes. Although to hold a principal criminally liable might possibly be an effective means of enforcing law and order, it would do violence to our more sophisticated modern-day concepts of justice. Liability for all true crimes, wherein an offense carries with it a jail sentence, must be based exclusively upon personal causation. It can be readily imagined that even a licensee who is meticulously careful in the choice of his employees cannot supervise every single act of the subordinates. A man's liberty cannot rest on so frail a reed as whether his employee will commit a mistake in judgment. See Sayre, Criminal Responsibility For Acts of Another, 43 Harv.L.Rev. 689 (1930). . . . Therefore, we are only holding that so much of the judgment as calls for imprisonment is invalid, and we are leaving intact the five hundred dollar fine imposed by Judge Hoban under the subsequent offense section. . . .

Judgment, as modified, is affirmed.[2]

2. [Added by the Compiler.] Compare: Herlishy v. McFeely, 110 ILTR 6 (1975), upholding vicarious liability for a liquor offense. See also Vane v. Yiannopoullos [1965] A.C. 486; State v. Young, 294 N.W.2d 728 (Minn.1980).

A truck driver whose cargo contained undersized fish was held not guilty of violating the statute if he had no knowledge that the cargo consisted of undersized fish and the cargo was so packed that it would have been unreasonable and impracticable to require him to inspect it. State v. Williams, 94 Ohio App. 249, 115 N.E.2d 36 (1952). Conviction of violating the city ordinance by driving through a flashing red light without stopping was held to be unsupportable in the face of an express finding that the driver was unable to stop because of brake failure, having experienced no prior brake trouble and having no knowledge of the defective condition of the brake. State v. Kremer, 262 Minn. 190, 114 N.W.2d 88 (1962).

In a later case only a fine was imposed upon the employer. Commonwealth v. Wolfe, 433 Pa. 141, 249 A.2d 316 (1969). In affirming this conviction it was said:

Moreover, even if we were to overrule *Koczwara* and hold that a liquor licensee who had done all he could to instruct his servants not to sell to minors cannot be liable for sales made in his absence and without his knowledge, we would still affirm appellant's conviction. For he did not do all he could in instructing his employees. Section 4–495 of the Liquor Code, supra, provides a safeguard for the licensee or his servant, agent, or employee. Under that section, a licensee or his servant, etc., may require one whose age may be in question to fill out and sign a card wherein the person must state that he is over the age of twenty-one and give his birth date. This signed statement in the possession of the licensee may be offered as a defense in all civil and criminal prosecutions for serving a minor, and no penalty is to be imposed if the courts are satisfied that the licensee acted in good faith. Appellant did not instruct his employees to follow this procedure; in fact, he was unaware of it. Thus, even if we were to overrule *Koczwara*, it would

BELL, MUSMANNO and MCBRIDE, JJ., file separate dissenting opinions.

BELL, JUSTICE (dissenting). . . .

I would affirm the judgment and the sentence on the opinion of Judge Hirt, speaking for a unanimous Superior Court.

MUSMANNO, JUSTICE (dissenting). . . .

I conclude by saying that the Majority has been so remiss in affirming the conviction in this case that I myself would be remiss if I did not dissent against a decision which flouts the Constitution, ignores the Bill of Rights and introduces into the temple of the law the Asiatic rite of "vicarious criminal liability."

MCBRIDE, JUSTICE (dissenting). I would agree that a man who sells liquor to a minor may be punished even if he did not know that the person to whom he sold was a minor. But in my opinion, the statute does not and cannot validly create an indictable misdemeanor under which a liquor licensee is punished by a fine or imprisonment, or both, for the act of an employee in selling to a minor, where, as here, the act itself is done without the licensee's knowledge, consent, or acquiescence. I would reverse the judgment and discharge the defendant.

SECTION 6. UNLAWFUL CONDUCT

It is frequently said that one who is committing an unlawful act has "general *mens rea*" or a "general criminal intent." Care must be taken not to infer too much from such a statement In the first place the phrase "unlawful act," as used in this connection, has a very restricted meaning. The state of mind of one who is committing such an "unlawful act" may be substituted for criminal negligence in establishing the *mens rea* needed for guilt of certain crimes. This is true of manslaughter and of battery but it is not true of offenses which require a specific intent or other special mental element.

not benefit appellant, who failed to instruct his employees properly.

A statute that made a parent liable for an off-road vehicle violation of his child was held to offend due process. State v. Akers, 119 N.H. 161, 400 A.2d 38 (1979).

D was charged with a violation of the Traffic law by driving 65 miles an hour in a 55-mile zone. It was held that the fact his speedometer was defective and registered 10 miles below the actual speed plus the fact **D** did *not* know the speedometer was defective and had no reason to know, was no defense. People v. Caddy, 189 Colo. 1353, 540 P.2d 1089 (1975).

"[W]e conclude that the legislature did not intend to require intent or negligence as an element of the crime of mistreating animals . . . . Nor does the fact that conviction . . . carries a potential prison sentence require that we read those elements into the offense." State v. Stanfield, 105 Wis.2d 553, 314 N.W.2d 339, 343 (1982).

A city does not act unconstitutionally in adopting a parking ordinance which makes the registered owner of a vehicle vicariously liable for illegal parking by a person using the vehicle with the permission of the owner. City of Missoula v. Shea, ___ Mont. ___, 661 P.2d 410 (1983).

COMMONWEALTH v. MINK

Supreme Judicial Court of Massachusetts, 1877.
123 Mass. 422.

INDICTMENT for the murder of Charles Ricker at Lowell, in the county of Middlesex, on August 31, 1876. Trial before Ames and Morton, JJ., who allowed a bill of exceptions in substance as follows:

It was proved that Charles Ricker came to his death by a shot from a pistol in the hand of the defendant. The defendant introduced evidence tending to show that she had been engaged to be married to Ricker; that an interview was had between them at her room, in the course of which he expressed his intention to break off the engagement and abandon her entirely; that she thereupon went to her trunk, took a pistol from it, and attempted to use it upon herself, with the intention of taking her own life; that Ricker then seized her to prevent her from accomplishing that purpose, and a struggle ensued between them; and that in the struggle the pistol was accidentally discharged, and in that way the fatal wound inflicted upon him.

The jury were instructed on this point as follows: "If you believe the defendant's story, and that she did put the pistol to her head with the intention of committing suicide, she was about to do a criminal and unlawful act, and that which she had no right to do. It is true, undoubtedly, that suicide cannot be punished by any proceeding of the courts, for the reason that the person who kills himself has placed himself beyond the reach of justice, and nothing can be done. But the law, nevertheless, recognizes suicide as a criminal act, and the attempt at suicide is also criminal. It would be the duty of any bystander who saw such an attempt about to be made, as a matter of mere humanity, to interfere and try to prevent it. And the rule is, that if a homicide is produced by the doing of an unlawful act, although the killing was the last thing that the person about to do it had in his mind, it would be an unlawful killing, and the person would incur the responsibility which attaches to the crime of manslaughter.
. . .

GRAY, C.J. The life of every human being is under the protection of the law, and cannot be lawfully taken by himself, or by another with his consent, except by legal authority. By the common law of England, suicide was considered a crime against the laws of God and man, the goods and chattels of the criminal were forfeited to the King, his body had an ignominious burial in the highway, and he was deemed a murderer of himself and a felon, *felo de se*. . . .

Suicide has not ceased to be unlawful and criminal in this Commonwealth by the simple repeal of the Colony Act of 1660 by the St. of 1823, c. 143, which (like the corresponding St. of 4 G. IV c. 52, enacted by the British Parliament within a year before) may well have had its origin in consideration for the feelings of innocent surviving relatives; nor by the briefer directions as to the form of coroner's inquests in the Rev.Sts. c. 140, § 8, and the Gen.Sts. c. 175, § 9, which in this, as in most other matters, have not repeated at length the forms of legal proceedings set forth in the statutes codified; nor by the fact that the Legislature, having in the general revisions of the statutes measured the degree of punishment for attempts to commit offences by the punishment prescribed for each offence if actually committed, has, intentionally or inadvertently, left the attempt to commit suicide without punishment, because the completed act would not be punished in any manner. Rev.Sts. c. 133, § 12. Gen.Sts. c. 168, § 8. Commonwealth v. Dennis, 105 Mass. 162. After all these changes in the statutes, the point decided in Bowen's case was ruled in the same way by Chief Justice Bigelow and Justices Dewey, Metcalf and Chapman, in a case which has not been reported.

Since it has been provided by statute that "any crime punishable by death or imprisonment in the state prison is a felony, and no other crime shall be so considered," it may well be that suicide is not technically a felony in this Commonwealth. Gen.Sts. c. 168, § 1. St.1852, c. 37, § 1. But being unlawful and criminal as *malum in se*, any attempt to commit it is likewise unlawful and criminal. Every one has the same right and duty to interpose to save a life from being so unlawfully and criminally taken, that he would have to defeat an attempt unlawfully to take the life of a third person. And it is not disputed that any person who, in doing or attempting to do an act which is unlawful and criminal, kills another, though not intending his death, is guilty of criminal homicide, and, at the least, of manslaughter.

The only doubt that we have entertained in this case is, whether the act of the defendant, in attempting to kill herself, was not so malicious, in the legal sense, as to make the killing of another person, in the attempt to carry out her purpose, murder, and whether the instructions given to the jury were not therefore too favorable to the defendant.

Exceptions overruled.[1]

STATE v. HORTON

Supreme Court of North Carolina, 1905.
139 N.C. 588, 51 S.E. 945.

HOKE, J., after stating the case: It will be noted that the finding of the jury declares that the act of the defendant was not in itself

1. "We affirm the holding that driving a car on the public roads or highways while in an intoxicated condition is an unlawful act; therefore it was entirely proper for the court to give the instruction defining manslaughter as: '. . . being that which is done in the commission of an unlawful act, not amounting to a felony. . . .'" State v. Medicine Bull Jr., 152 Mont. 34, 445 P.2d 916 (1968).

Since the ordinance forbidding the discharge of a firearm within the city has for its purpose the protection of human life or safety, unintentional death resulting from such a discharge is involuntary manslaughter. State v. Thomas, 6 Kan. App.2d 925, 636 P.2d 807 (1981).

dangerous to human life and excludes every element of criminal negligence, and rests the guilt or innocence of the defendant on the fact alone that at the time of the homicide the defendant was hunting on another's land without written permission from the owner. The act which applies only in the counties of Orange, Franklin and Scotland, makes the conduct a misdemeanor, and imposes a punishment on conviction, of not less than five nor more than ten dollars.

The statement sometimes appears in works of approved excellence to the effect that an unintentional homicide is a criminal offense when occasioned by a person engaged at the time in an unlawful act. In nearly every instance, however, will be found the qualification that if the act in question is free from negligence, and not in itself of dangerous tendency, and the criminality must arise, if at all, entirely from the fact that it is unlawful, in such case, the unlawful act must be one that is *malum in se* and not merely *malum prohibitum*, and this we hold to be the correct doctrine. In Foster's Crown Law, it is thus stated at page 258: "In order to bring a case within this description (excusable homicide) the act upon which death ensueth must be lawful. For if the act be unlawful, I mean if it be *malum in se*, the case will amount to felony, either murder or manslaughter, as circumstances may vary the nature of it. If it be done in prosecution of a felonious intent, it will be murder; but if the intent went no further than to commit a bare trespass, it will be manslaughter." At page 259, the same author puts an instance with his comments thereon as follows: "A shooteth at the poultry of B and by accident killeth a man; if his intention was to steal the poultry, which must be collected from circumstances, it will be murder by reason of that felonious intent, but if it was done wantonly and without that intention, it will be barely manslaughter. The rule I have laid down supposeth that the act from which death ensued was *malum in se*. For if it was barely *malum prohibitum*, as shooting at game by a person not qualified by statute law to keep or use a gun for that purpose, the case of a person so offending will fall under the same rule as that of a qualified man. For the statutes prohibiting the destruction of the game under certain penalties will not, in a question of this kind, enhance the accident beyond its intrinsic moment."

One of these disqualifying statutes here referred to as an instance of *malum prohibitum* was an act passed (13 Richard II, chap. 13), to prevent certain classes of persons from keeping dogs, nets or engines to destroy game, etc., and the punishment imposed on conviction was one year's imprisonment. There were others imposing a lesser penalty.

1 Bishop, New Criminal Law, sec. 332, treats of the matter as follows: "In these cases of an unintended evil result, the intent whence the act accidentally sprang must probably be, if specific, to do a thing which is *malum in se* and not merely *malum prohibitum*." Thus Archbold says: "When a man in the execution of one act, by misfor-

tune or chance and not designedly, does another act for which if he had willfully committed it, he would be liable to be punished—in that case, if the act he were doing were lawful or merely *malum prohibitum,* he shall not be punishable for the act arising from misfortune or chance, but if it be *malum in se,* it is otherwise. To illustrate: since it is *malum prohibitum,* not *malum in se,* for an unauthorized person to kill game in England contrary to the statutes, if, in unlawfully shooting at game, he accidently kills a man, it is no more criminal in him than if he were authorized. But, to shoot at another's fowls, wantonly or in sport, an act which is *malum in se,* though a civil trespass, and thereby accidentally to kill a human being is manslaughter. If the intent in the shooting were to commit larceny of the fowls, we have seen that it would be murder."

An offense *malum in se* is properly defined as one which is naturally evil as adjudged by the sense of a civilized community, whereas an act *malum prohibitum* is wrong only because made so by statute. For the reason that acts *mala in se* have, as a rule, become criminal offenses by the course and development of the common law, an impression has sometimes obtained that only acts can be so classified which the common law makes criminal, but this is not at all the test. An act can be, and frequently is, *malum in se,* when it amounts only to a civil trespass, provided it has a malicious element or manifests an evil nature, or wrongful disposition to harm or injure another in his person or property.

The distinction between the two classes of acts is well stated in 19 Am. & Eng.Enc. (2d Ed.) at p. 705: "An offense *malum in se* is one which is naturally evil, as murder, theft, and the like. Offenses at common law are generally *malum in se.* An offense *malum prohibitum,* on the contrary, is not naturally an evil, but becomes so in consequence of being forbidden."

We do not hesitate to declare that the offense of the defendant in hunting on the land without written permission of the owner was *malum prohibitum,* and the special verdict having found that the act in which the defendant was engaged was not in itself dangerous to human life, and negatived all idea of negligence, we hold that the case is one of excusable homicide, and the defendant should be declared not guilty. . . .

There was error in holding the defendant guilty, and, on the facts declared, a verdict of not guilty should be directed and the defendant discharged.

Reversed.

WALKER, J., concurs in result only.

STATE v. SEALY

Supreme Court of North Carolina, 1961.
253 N.C. 802, 117 S.E.2d 793.

DENNY, JUSTICE. The defendant assigns as error those portions of the court's charge to the jury hereinafter set out. The court, after having read to the jury G.S. § 20–158 (the statute which requires the driver of a motor vehicle to stop before entering or crossing certain through highways), and G.S. § 20–140 (the statute defining reckless driving), charged: "If you find from the evidence in this case, ... beyond a reasonable doubt that the defendant intentionally violated one or more of the statutes read to you, designed and intended to protect human life, and . . . that such intentional violation thereof was the proximate cause of the death of the deceased, then it would be your duty to return a verdict of guilty of involuntary manslaughter."

". . . (I)f you are satisfied from the testimony beyond a reasonable doubt that the driver of this car, the defendant in this case, Mr. Howard Franklin Sealy, was operating his motor vehicle in violation of the statute, in respect to stopping at the stop sign, . . . and that such action on his part was the proximate cause of the death of these two men, you would find him guilty of involuntary manslaughter."

The above instructions are conflicting and the State concedes error in the latter. According to the provisions of G.S. § 20–158, a violation thereof is not negligence *per se* in any action at law for injury to person or property, but the failure to stop at a stop sign before entering an intersection with a dominant highway may be considered with other facts in the case in determining whether or not under all the facts and circumstances involved, such driver was guilty of negligence or contributory negligence.

"Culpable negligence in the law of crimes necessarily implies something more than actionable negligence in the law of torts." . . .

"An intentional, wilful or wanton violation of a statute or ordinance, designed for the protection of human life or limb, which proximately results in injury or death, is culpable negligence." State v. Cope, supra [204 N.C. 28, 167 S.E. 458]. But, where there is an unintentional or inadvertent violation of the statute, such violation standing alone does not constitute culpable negligence. The inadvertent or unintentional violation of the statute must be accompanied by recklessness of probable consequences of a dangerous nature, when tested by the rule of reasonable prevision, amounting altogether to a thoughtless disregard of consequences or of a heedless indifference to the safety of others.

Other assignments of error need not be considered or discussed since they may not arise on another hearing.

The defendant is entitled to a new trial and it is so ordered.

New trial.[1]

UNITED STATES v. RYBICKI

United States Court of Appeals, Sixth Circuit, 1968.
403 F.2d 599.

Defendant was charged with obstructing administration of internal revenue laws by appearing in his doorway armed with a shotgun and allegedly threatening two revenue agents who were backing his truck out of his driveway.

O'SULLIVAN, CIRCUIT JUDGE. Harry J. Rybicki appeals from judgment entered on a jury verdict, convicting him of violating § 7212(a) of Title 26, U.S.C. The information charged that on February 13, 1967, Rybicki, by threats of force, obstructed two officers of the Internal Revenue Service who were then engaged in the performance of their duties, seeking to collect from him income tax owed by him to the United States. His grounds of appeal are that the government's evidence was not sufficient to sustain the verdict, and that the District Judge erroneously failed to adequately instruct the jury as to the findings essential to a verdict of guilty.

We reverse on the second ground. . . .

2) The Court's instructions.

(a) Knowledge as an essential to guilt.

1. **D** ran into a boy and knocked him down while **D** was driving a sleigh in violation of the speed law. This was held not to be sufficient to establish guilt of assault and battery. Commonwealth v. Adams, 114 Mass. 323 (1873).

D fired a shot into the night which injured a woman 216 feet away. It was held that the fact that the shot was in violation of a city ordinance could be considered with other facts on the general question of culpable negligence. Commonwealth v. Hawkins, 157 Mass. 551, 32 N.E. 862 (1893).

Accidental death by one driving a car without a license is manslaughter. Commonwealth v. Romig, 22 Pa.D. & C. 341 (1934). Contra: Commonwealth v. Williams, 133 Pa.Super. 104, 1 A.2d 812 (1938). The mere fact that the act which caused death was a trespass is not sufficient to establish criminal homicide. Regina v. Franklin, 15 Cox C.C. 163 (1883).

An unintentional and nonnegligent violation of the Health and Safety Code which results in death is not manslaughter. People v. Stuart, 47 Cal.2d 167, 302 P.2d 5 (1956). A prescription calling (in part) for sodium citrate was filled with sodium nitrate, but the fault was with someone else who had mislabeled the bottle and not with the pharmacist who filled the prescription.

In Commonwealth v. Clowser, 212 Pa. Super. 208, 239 A.2d 870 (1968), it was said (in footnote 4): The Utah Supreme Court further stated: "There are many other rules for driving mentioned in Title 57, [The Vehicle Code], the infraction of which may constitute a misdemeanor, but not all of which would constitute the basis for a conviction for manslaughter if death should result from the infraction."

The District Judge did not tell the jury that to be guilty of the charged offense, Rybicki had to know that the men were officers and were in the performance of their duties. Appellant's brief asserts:

"The court did not even mention that Mr. Rybicki should know that they were officers. The charge was fatally deficient in that it did not require the jury to find that the defendant knew the men were federal agents, knew they were performing official duties, and intended to obstruct officers as such in the performance of their duties. The jury was charged as though the crime were a regulatory offense instead of a true crime requiring *mens rea*."

The government resists the claim by asserting that knowledge by Rybicki that the Internal Revenue Agents were government officers performing official duties at the time of the alleged offense was not an essential element of the crime. We disagree.

To substantiate its argument in this regard, the government relies upon McNabb v. United States, 123 F.2d 848 (6th Cir.1941); . . . . These authorities may be distinguished from the case at bar by the fact that the offenses there involved would have been crimes regardless of the person against whom they were committed. In *Montanaro*, the defendant was stopped by federal officers while driving his car. In resisting arrest, he struck one of the officers with his car. This would have been a crime whether or not the pedestrian was an officer. In *McNabb*, a federal officer was killed under circumstances that would have resulted in a murder charge regardless of who was killed. Here, if the car "thief" had not been an officer acting in an official capacity, Rybicki would have had the right to threaten and use reasonable force to present the theft of his property.

In United States v. Chunn, 347 F.2d 717, 721 (1965), the Fourth Circuit stated,

"Concededly, there is a wide variance and lack of unanimity among the decisions as to whether *scienter* should be alleged and/or proved."

The line of cases holding that scienter is required stems from Pettibone v. United States, 148 U.S. 197, 204–207, 13 S.Ct. 542, 37 L.Ed. 419 (1893). This Court followed and relied upon Pettibone in Sparks v. United States, 90 F.2d 61, 63 (6th Cir.1937), where a deputy marshal attempted to execute a search warrant for seizure of counterfeit molds alleged to be on defendant's premises. Defendant brandished an ax and prevented the officer from carrying on the search. On page 63 we said:

"On a trial for resisting an officer it must be shown that the person resisted was an officer, and that the accused was aware of that fact. Pettibone v. United States, 148 U.S. 197, 205, 13 S.Ct. 542, 37 L.Ed. 419."

Sparks is analogous to the instant case in that the man searching for the molds would have no right to seize them from Sparks' premises and Sparks would have a right to prevent the seizure from his property unless the "searcher" was privileged by being an officer acting in the performance of his official duties. We are of the opinion that Pettibone v. United States, supra, and Morissette v. United States, 342 U.S. 246, 263, 273, 276, 72 S.Ct. 240, 96 L.Ed. 288 (1952) command a holding by us that an element of the crime charged to Rybicki was knowledge that the Internal Revenue agents were such and were engaged in performing their duty. We so hold. . . .

Reversed and remanded for a new trial.[1]

SECTION 7. "TRANSFERRED INTENT"

A tort concept, which serves a useful purpose in that field[1] but has no proper place in criminal law, because it tends more to confusion than to clarity of thought, is the so-called "doctrine of the transfer of the intent to the unintended act." This is frequently stated in some such form as this: Whenever a man meaning one wrong does another unmeant, he is punishable unless some specific intent is required. The reason sometimes offered is that "the thing done, having proceeded from a corrupt mind, is to be viewed the same whether the corruption was of one particular form or another."[2]

Such a notion results from an imperfect analysis of certain cases. Burglary is the breaking and entering of the dwelling house of anoth-

1. "It is not necessary, in the absence of special circumstances, to prove that the defendant knew that the person he assaulted was a federal officer." United States v. Bierley, 521 F.2d 191, 192 (6th Cir.1975).

Where a defendant is charged with violating 18 U.S.C. § 111 (assaulting a federal officer) "claims that he was unaware that the victim was a federal officer, the question becomes: would the defendant have been justified, because of the agent's actions, in using force against the agent had the latter, in fact, been a 'civilian'. If the defendant made an honest mistake of fact with respect to the agent's status and the defendant's use of force would have been justified against a private citizen, then he cannot be held criminally liable under § 111. For to hold him liable would create a situation 'where legitimate conduct becomes unlawful solely because of the identity of the individual or agency affected.' If, on the other hand, the defendant would not have been justified in using force against a private citizen or if the defendant used more force than the law permitted his mistake as to the agent's status would be no defense to an action under § 111." (citations omitted) United States v. Hillsman, 522 F.2d 454, 460 (7th Cir. 1975). And see United States v. Works, 526 F.2d 940 (5th Cir.1976).

"We agree with the *Falk* court in concluding that solicitation of false testimony from a prospective witness may provide the basis for conviction under the obstruction of justice provision of § 1503." United States v. Friedland, 660 F.2d 919, 931 (3d Cir.1981).

Obstruction of justice may be committed by intentionally giving a false impression in the form of disclosure of some facts and nondisclosure of other facts. State v. Coddington, 135 Ariz. 480, 662 P.2d 155 (App.1983).

The federal offense of transporting a forged security in interstate commerce requires knowledge that the security is forged, but does not require knowledge of the involvement of interstate commerce. United States v. Eisenberg, 596 F.2d 522 (2d Cir.1979).

1. If defendant shoots at A and hits B instead, the "intent is said to be 'transferred' to the victim—which is obviously a fiction, or a legal conclusion, to accomplish the desired result of liability". Prosser, Law of Torts 33 (2d ed. 1955).

2. Bishop, Criminal Law § 327 (8th ed. 1892).

er in the nighttime with intent to commit a felony or petty larceny. In other words the intent to commit some *other* crime (which must be a felony at common law) is the very state of mind which constitutes the *mens rea* for burglary. For certain offenses the intent to commit some other offense is not essential to the *mens rea* but may suffice for this purpose. Murder is an excellent example. Certain crimes such as arson, rape, robbery and burglary have been found to involve such an unreasonable element of human risk that he who is perpetrating or attempting one of them is held to have a state of mind which falls within the label "malice aforethought." Hence if homicide is caused thereby it is murder however unintended the killing may be. This is due to the law of homicide and not to any doctrine of "transferred intent."

To test the soundness of such a doctrine it is necessary to consider offenses other than burglary (which requires an intent to commit some other crime) or murder (for which an intent to commit certain other crimes will be sufficient for the *mens rea* requirement). A man who has in his pocket a weapon he has no authority to carry is not guilty of the crime of carrying a concealed weapon if it was put there secretly by others without his knowing or having any reason to know of its presence. And a man who marries a second wife, after the death of the first, is not guilty of bigamy even if he does not know of the death and thinks the first wife is still alive. In the first case we find the *actus reus* but no *mens rea*. In the second, the *mens rea* but no *actus reus*. And if the man who contracted such a marriage happened to be wearing a coat with an unsuspected weapon concealed therein, the intent to commit bigamy could not be coupled with the unintentional carrying of the concealed weapon so as to establish guilt of either offense. If he borrowed the coat for the sole purpose of wearing it during the wedding ceremony there would be some connection between the two but the *actus reus* and the *mens rea* still would not match in such a manner as to constitute criminal guilt.

It was stated by Lord Hale, and repeated in substance by Blackstone, that "if *A*. by malice aforethought strikes at *B*. and missing him strikes *C*. whereof he dies, though he never bore any malice to *C*. yet it is murder, and the law transfers the malice to the party slain." [3] Unquestionably the slayer is guilty of murder in such a case, and if any resort is to be made to a theory of transferred intent it should be limited to this general type of situation. The general mental pattern is the same whether the malicious endeavor was to kill B or to kill C. If the word "malicious" is omitted the statement might not be true. An intent to kill B might represent a very different mental pattern than an intent to kill C. For example, B at the time might be a murderer, fleeing from lawful arrest under such circumstances that A was privileged to kill him. If such was the fact an intent by A to kill

3. 1 Hale P.C. *466; 4 Bl.Comm. *201.

B would not be a guilty state of mind. It would not constitute *mens rea*. If at the same time C was obviously an innocent bystander an intent by A to kill C would amount to malice aforethought. Under such circumstances, if A should shoot at B in the proper and prudent exercise of his privilege and should happen quite unexpectedly, by a glance of the bullet, to cause the death of C, A would be free from criminal guilt. This seems to lend support to the theory of "transferred intent." The intent to kill B did not constitute *mens rea* and this innocent intent *seems* to be transferred to the unintended victim.

The hypothetical situation, however, supposes not only the privilege to direct deadly force against B, but also the proper and prudent exercise of this privilege. If, on the other hand, he exercised this privilege so imprudently and improperly as to constitute a criminally negligent disregard of the life of the innocent bystander, C, the killing of C would be manslaughter. The intent is given due consideration, but it is not "transferred."

STATE v. MARTIN

Supreme Court of Missouri, Division Two, 1938.
342 Mo. 1089, 119 S.W.2d 298.

ELLISON, J. This case comes to the writer on reassignment. An opinion was written by Cooley, C., which failed of adoption by the court on a divided vote on a question of law. We have concluded he was right in his conclusions and shall use his statement of the facts.

The appellant, George Martin, and Joe Arvin and Harold Johnson were charged by information in the Circuit Court of Buchanan County with felonious assault with intent to maim Lloyd DeCasnett. A severance was granted and appellant Martin, whom we shall call defendant, was tried alone. He was convicted, sentenced to two years' imprisonment in the penitentiary and has appealed. Among numerous other assignments of error he claims that the evidence did not justify submission of the case to the jury.

The information is based upon Section 4014, Revised Statutes 1929 (Mo.Stat.Ann., p. 2817) making it a felony for any person to shoot at or stab another or "assault or beat another with a deadly weapon, or by any other means or force likely to produce death or great bodily harm, with intent to kill, maim, ravish or rob such person. . . ." It charges an assault by defendant and Joe Arvin and Harold Johnson upon Lloyd DeCasnett "with a certain dangerous and deadly substance likely to produce death or great bodily harm, to wit: a certain glass bulb, then and there containing sulphuric acid," with intent to maim said DeCasnett. . . .

The point upon which the case was decided in the former opinion was this. It will be remembered the State's evidence showed that shortly after midnight someone in the Chevrolet sedan owned and driven by appellant threw an electric light bulb filled with sulphuric acid against the *left* front door of the Terminal Taxicab about six inches above the lower hinge, as the two cars passed at moderate city driving speed about 8 or 10 feet apart. The windows of the taxicab were open. The prosecuting witness, DeCasnett, was riding on the *right* side and Miss Main on the left side of the back seat, and the driver, Stoneburner, on the left side of the front seat. There was nothing in the evidence to show the assailants knew DeCasnett was in the car. The acid splattered over the taxicab and some of it reached the upholstery inside, but none of the occupants was burned. The opinion held these facts failed to make a case for the jury under Sec. 4014, R.S.Mo.1929, Mo.Stat.Ann., p. 2817, on authority of State v. Mulhall, 199 Mo. 202, 214, 97 S.W. 583, 586, 7 L.R.A.,N.S., 630, 8 Ann.Cas. 781; State v. Williamson, 203 Mo. 591, 102 S.W. 519, 120 Am.St.Rep. 678; and State v. Kester, Mo., 201 S.W. 62, 64.

In the Mulhall case the defendant shot with a pistol at R but missed him and hit but did not kill M who was four or five steps away and not in line with the intended victim. The accused was prosecuted for assaulting M with intent to kill. It was ruled the statute requires a charge and proof that the accused assaulted a particular person with specific intent to kill, maim, ravish or rob *that* person; and hence the decision was that a prosecution under the statute would not lie for shooting M by mistake when the assault and felonious intent were directed at R. The gravamen of the offense, says this Mulhall case, is the felonious intent against the person assailed; and doubtless if the information had charged an assault with intent to kill R, the person shot at but missed, instead of M, the person wounded but against whom the accused had no felonious intent, the result should have been different.

In the Williamson case, likewise, the defendant shot at one person and hit another, Dorn. The opinion held the evidence was insufficient to make a case under the statute, saying, "it is clear from the evidence that the defendant did not intend to shoot Dorn, for there is no evidence that he even saw him at the time he fired the shot." In the Kester case the defendant shot from the highway into a darkened dwelling house at night wounding the housewife. There was no evidence that he could have seen her, and the conviction was reversed, Faris, J., concurring in the result with expressed reluctance.

In State v. Wansong, 271 Mo. 50, 61, 195 S.W. 999, 1003, strikers were prosecuted for assaulting with intent to kill a milk wagon driver whom they had set up in the dark. Their defense was that they had no felonious intent against *him*, but thought he was another man against whom they had a grudge. This was held to be no defense since they did intend to assault the identical person they assailed, though mistaken as to his identity. There was a similar holding in State v. Layton, 332 Mo. 216, 58 S.W.2d 454, where the defendant heard a noise behind a closed door and shot, wounding one person whom he believed to be another.

The instant case presents facts different from those in the decisions reviewed above, but the same principle applies. If a man throws a splattering acid bulb or an explosive bomb, or fires a scattering shotgun charge, at a group of persons all within range, he would be liable to prosecution under Section 4014, supra, for felonious assault upon any one of them, and he could not go acquit as to one by saying he harbored a felonious intent only against another of the group. The reasonable and probable consequences of the act being to injure the whole group, he could no more escape them by such a denial than he might by deliberately shooting at one person and disclaiming a felonious intent against that person. While the law in such cases requires a specific intent, it does not require malice in fact in the sense of actual spite or ill will against the person alleged to have been the object of the attack.

On the other hand, the intent will not be imputed, in the sense of being transferred or transposed from the person aimed at and missed to a person out of range and mistakenly hit. If A shoots at B and the bullet wounds C whose presence is unknown all the cases hold there can be no conviction under Section 4014, supra. Neither will the intent be transferred from those known to be in a group to others of whose presence the accused is ignorant. We do not mean that he must know of each individual in the group. If he knows the probable consequence of the assault will be to injure any one or all of the persons he sees or otherwise is bound to believe are before him, he will be liable as to any one of them. But if, without his knowledge there be still another person present concealed, as behind a bush or wall for illustration, he would not be liable as to that person for he could have no specific intent as to him. This, we conceive, is the crucial distinction in this case.

The statement of facts set out above says there was nothing in the evidence to show the assailants knew the prosecuting witness DeCasnett was in the taxicab. We have reexamined the record on that point. The driver, Stoneburner, and Miss Main were on the left side of the front and rear seats, respectively. This was the side next to appellant's automobile as the two cars passed, and presumably the acid throwers saw them. DeCasnett was on the right side of the rear seat, away from appellant. It was past midnight. There is testimony that Eighth Street was "pretty well lighted" right at the intersection with Seneca Street. There is no evidence as to the height and brilliance of the street lights, but some ambiguous testimony developed by appellant's counsel on cross-examination that there were two lights, one on the southeast corner and one on the northwest corner. The taxicab had made a U turn at this intersection before the acid throwing occurred. Miss Main thought it had just got straightened out and was heading back north on Eighth Street at the time. DeCasnett and Stoneburner variously estimated it was from 60 to 500 feet north of the north curb of the intersection, the latter saying it was by a telephone pole about one-third way up the block. At any rate the nearest street light at the northwest corner of the intersection was behind and on the side of the street away from DeCasnett, and the light on his side of the car at the southeast corner of the intersection was further away and almost directly behind him. . . .

. . . We cannot go so far as to extend it to a person not known to be there. Perhaps the prosecutor had some good reason for charging an assault with felonious intent upon DeCasnett, instead of upon Stoneburner or Miss Main both of whom were more directly within view of their assailants. Stoneburner was the driver of the car, sitting by the left front door where the acid bulb hit. And the assailants must have known some person was driving the car even though they could not see him. The car would not run without a driver. Whatever the reasons were for designating DeCasnett as the object of the assault, they do not appear of record. We think the State did not make a case as to him for the reasons stated.

The crime was brutal and deserves commensurate punishment. It would seem to be impossible to throw a missile like an electric light bulb filled with acid from one automobile moving 15 to 25 miles per hour against another with open windows passing in the opposite direction at the same speed so as to hit above the lower door hinges of the latter, without great danger of serious injury to the occupants. In view of the facts and conclusions we have reached, the judgment is reversed and the cause remanded. All concur.[1]

REGINA v. SMITH

Court of Criminal Appeal, 1855.
Dears. 560, 169 Eng.Rep. 845.

The following case was stated for the opinion of the Court of Criminal Appeal by MR. JUSTICE CROMPTON.

The prisoner was convicted before me at the Winchester Summer Assizes, 1855, on an indictment charging him with wounding William Taylor, with intent to murder him.

On the night in question the prisoner was posted as a sentry at Parkhurst, and the prosecutor, Taylor, was posted as a sentry at a neighbouring post.

The prisoner intended to murder one Maloney, and supposing Taylor to be Maloney, shot at and wounded Taylor.

The jury found that the prisoner intended to murder Maloney, not knowing that the party he shot at was Taylor, but supposing him to

1. Compare: State v. Shanley, 20 S.D. 18, 104 N.W. 522 (1905); State v. Gallagher, 83 N.J.L. 321, 85 A. 207 (1912).

"In some cases a man shall be said, in the judgment of the law, to kill one who is in truth actually killed by another, or by himself, as where one lays poison with an intent to kill one man, which is afterwards accidentally taken by another, who dies thereof." 1 Curw.Hawk. 92. See also the case of Rex v. Harley, ante, vol. iv. p. 369.

be Maloney, and the jury found that he intended to murder the individual he shot at supposing him to be Maloney.

I directed sentence of death to be recorded, reserving the question, whether the prisoner could be properly convicted on this state of facts of wounding Taylor with intent to murder him?

CHARLES CROMPTON.

This case was considered on 24th November 1855, by JERVIS, C.J., and PARKE, B., WIGHTMAN, J., CROMPTON, J., and WILLES, J.

No Counsel appeared either for the Crown or for the prisoner.

JERVIS, C.J. There is nothing in the objection. The conviction is good.

PARKE, B. The prisoner did not intend to kill the particular person, but he meant to murder the man at whom he shot.[2]

The other learned Judges concurred.

Conviction affirmed.

REGINA v. FAULKNER

Court of Crown Cases Reserved, Ireland, 1877.
13 Cox C.C. 550.

Case reserved by Lawson, J., at the Cork Summer Assizes, 1876, the prisoner was indicted for setting fire to the ship *Zemindar*, on the high seas, on the 26th day of June, 1876. . . . It was proved that the *Zemindar* was on her voyage home with a cargo of rum, sugar, and cotton, worth 50,000*l*. That the prisoner was a seaman on board, that he went into the forecastle hold, opened the sliding door in the bulk head, and so got into the hold where the rum was stored; he had no business there, and no authority to go there, and went for the purpose of stealing some rum, that he bored a hole in the cask with the gimlet, that the rum ran out, that when trying to put a spile in the hole out of which the rum was running, he had a lighted match in his hand; that the rum caught fire; that the prisoner himself was burned on the arms and neck; and that the ship caught fire and was completely destroyed. At the close of the case for the Crown, counsel for the prisoner asked for a direction of an acquittal on the ground that on the facts proved the indictment was not sustained, nor the allegation that the prisoner had unlawfully and maliciously set fire to the ship proved. The Crown contended that, inasmuch as the prisoner was at the time engaged in the commission of a felony, the indictment was sustained, and the allegation of the intent was immaterial.

2. D shot at W and hit both W and M. He was indicted for shooting M with intent to commit murder. A conviction was affirmed. The indictment did not say, and under the statute was not required to say, that the intent was to murder M. State v. Thomas, 127 La. 576, 53 So. 868 (1910).

At the second hearing of the case before the Court for Crown Cases Reserved, the learned judge made the addition of the following paragraph to the case stated by him for the court.

"It was conceded that the prisoner had no actual intention of burning the vessel, and I was not asked to leave any question to the jury as to the prisoner's knowing the probable consequences of his act, or as to his reckless conduct."

The learned judge told the jury that, although the prisoner had no actual intention of burning the vessel, still if they found he was engaged in stealing the rum, and that the fire took place in the manner above stated, they ought to find him guilty. The jury found the prisoner guilty on both counts, and he was sentenced to seven years' penal servitude. The question for the court was whether the direction of the learned judge was right, if not, the conviction should be quashed. . . .

FITZGERALD, J. I concur in opinion with my brother Barry, and for the reasons he has given, that the direction of the learned judge cannot be sustained in law, and that therefore the conviction should be quashed. I am further of opinion that in order to establish the charge of felony under sect. 42, the intention of the accused forms an element in the crime to the extent that it should appear that the defendant intended to do the very act with which he was charged, or that it was the necessary consequence of some other felonious or criminal act in which he was engaged, or that having a probable result which the defendant foresaw, or ought to have foreseen, he, nevertheless, persevered in such other felonious or criminal act. The prisoner did not intend to set fire to the ship—the fire was not the necessary result of the felony he was attempting; and if it was a probable result, which he ought to have foreseen, of the felonious transaction on which he was engaged, and from which a malicious design to commit the injurious act with which he is charged might have been fairly imputed to him, that view of the case was not submitted to the jury. On the contrary, it was excluded from their consideration on the requisition of the counsel for the prosecution. Counsel for the prosecution in effect insisted that the defendant, being engaged in the commission of, or in an attempt to commit a felony, was criminally responsible for every result that was occasioned thereby, even though it was not a probable consequence of his act or such as he could have reasonably foreseen or intended. No authority has been cited for a proposition so extensive, and I am of opinion that it is not warranted by law. Referring to the statute on which the prisoner is charged, it is to be observed that in several instances the sections creating substantive felonies are followed by others making an attempt to do the same thing also a felony. Now, it is obvious that an attempt to do a particular thing necessarily involves the intention to commit the act. If, in the case before us, the burning rum had been extinguished before the ship took fire, could it be contended that an indictment for a wilful and malicious attempt to set fire to the ship could have been maintained?

FITZGERALD, B. I am of opinion that the direction of the learned judge at the trial was wrong, and that the conviction cannot be sustained. There can, I think, be no doubt that malice or malicious intent (which seems to me to mean the same thing) is an essential part of the character of the felony charged in the indictment. . . .

O'BRIEN, J. I am also of opinion that the conviction should be quashed, . . .

KEOGH, J. I have the misfortune to differ from the other members of the Court. . . . I am, therefore, of opinion, that the conviction should stand, as I consider all questions of intention and malice are closed by the finding of the jury, that the prisoner committed the act with which he was charged whilst engaged in the commission of a substantive felony. . . .

PALLES, C.B. I concur in the opinion of the majority of the Court, and I do so for the reasons already stated by my brother Fitzgerald. I agree with my brother Keogh that from the facts proved the inference might have legitimately drawn that the setting fire to the ship was malicious within the meaning of the 24 & 25 Vict. c. 97. I am of opinion that that inference was one of fact for the jury, and not a conclusion of law at which we can arrive upon the case before us. . . .

DEASY, B., and LAWSON, J., concurred.

Conviction quashed.

REX v. KELLY

Monaghan Assizes, Ireland, 1832.
1 Craw. & D. 186.

INDICTMENT for maliciously killing a horse. The evidence was that the prisoner had fired at the prosecutor, and killed his horse.

BUSHE, C.J. Under this Act the offence must be proved to have been done maliciously, and malice implies intention. Here the proof negatives the intention of killing the horse. The prisoner must therefore be acquitted.

SECTION 8. MOTIVE

Although sometimes confused, motive and intent and are not synonymous terms. Motive has been said to be "that something in the mind, or that condition of the mind, which incites to the action," or the "moving power which impels to action," "induces action," or "gives birth to a purpose." The difference between intent and motive may be emphasized by illustration. If one man has caused the death of another by a pistol shot, his *intent* may have been any one of a number, such as (a) to kill the deceased, (b) to frighten the deceased by shooting near him without hitting him, (c) to intimidate the deceased by pointing the weapon at him without shooting (the trigger having been pulled by accident), (d) to shoot at a target (perhaps without realizing that any other person was present), or (e) to test the "pull" of a trigger of a gun supposed to be unloaded. If in the particular case the intent was to kill the deceased, the *motive* of the shooter may also have been one (or more) of a number of possible motives, such as (a) hatred, (b) revenge, (c) jealousy, (d) avarice, (e) fear or even (f) love (as where a loved one is slain to end the suffering from an incurable disease).

Some writers have advanced the notion that when an act is committed with more than one object in view, only the most immediate intent is called "intent" and any "ulterior intent is called the motive of the act." Stroud, for example, would say that if a burglar breaks and enters the dwelling of another in the nighttime with intent to steal, his mental attitude in regard to the contemplated larceny is not (at the time of breaking into the building) an *intent* but a *motive*.[1] This, however, is quite at variance with juridical usage of these terms. The burglar's design to steal is so far from being no intent at all that it is called a "specific intent." The search for the distinction must go much deeper than this. If in the supposed case the burglar's purpose was to steal food which he wished to eat, his intent to eat would also be an *intent* although one more step removed from his immediate intent at the time of the breaking. But his urge to satisfy his appetite would be, not an *intent*, but a *motive*. This urge might come from the immediate pangs of hunger or from the recollection of such pangs on previous occasions. The burglarious act of another may be prompted by the urge for the feeling of power which money may give, or by any other impulse which may prompt a man to desire that which he does not have.

An emotional urge, unless counteracted by other urges, "leads the mind to desire" a particular result. This desire in turn may—or may not—prompt an intent to bring about that end. If the mental activity continues until such an intent is developed (all of which might occur with lightning speed) the desire is coupled with the intention and may in a sense be a part thereof. Nevertheless it is important to distinguish between the basic urge itself and the intent which resulted in the mind of the particular person, but which might not have been generated in the mind of another. When, for example, it is said that a legatee, who was aware of a large bequest in his favor, had a motive for killing his deceased testator, it is not meant that this fact is sufficient to establish an intent to kill. No more is meant than that this fact was sufficient to generate a primitive urge in that direction, although it might be completely checked by more social impulses.

1. Stroud, Mens Rea 114 (1914).

It is frequently said that "motive is not an essential element of crime." [2] Sometimes the statement is even more positive in form: "Motive is never an essential element of a crime." [3] Such broad generalizations cannot be accepted without some reservation, but with complete assurance we may say: "Proof of motive is never necessary to support a conclusion of guilt otherwise sufficiently established." [4]

The motive with which an *actus reus* was committed is always relevant. The presence or absence of a motive on the part of the defendant which might tend to the commission of such a deed may always be considered by the jury on the question of whether he did commit it. But whenever it is clearly established that he committed it, with whatever state of mind is required for the *mens rea* of the particular offense, all the requisites of criminal guilt are present, even if no possible motive for the deed can be shown.[5]

PEOPLE ex rel. HEGEMAN v. CORRIGAN

Court of Appeals of New York, 1909.
195 N.Y. 1, 87 N.E. 792.

CULLEN, CH. J. The perjury with which the relator is charged is the verification under oath of a report to the insurance department of the state, in which, in answer to a question calling for a statement of the loans held by the company secured by the pledge of bonds, stock or other collateral, it was stated that there were none. . . .

3. Doubtless, to constitute perjury there must be criminal intent, but intent must be distinguished from motive and from ultimate object. As was said by Judge Werner in People v. Molineux (168 N.Y. 264, 297, 61 N.E. 286): "In the popular mind intent and motive are not infrequently regarded as one and the same thing. In law there is a clear distinction between them. Motive is the moving power which impels to action for a definite result. Intent is the purpose to use a particular means to effect such result." "Motive is that which incites or stimulates a person to do an act. . . . Motive is never an essential element of a crime. A good motive does not prevent an act from being a crime." There runs through the criminal law a distinction between offenses that are *mala prohibita* in which no intent to do

2. People v. Zammuto, 280 Ill. 225, 227, 117 N.E. 454, 455 (1917).

3. People ex rel. Hegeman v. Corrigan, 195 N.Y. 1, 12, 87 N.E. 792, 796 (1909).

4. State v. Guilfoyle, 109 Conn. 124, 140, 145 A. 761, 767 (1929).

5. A soldier, home on leave to visit a sick child, found that it was suffering and completely neglected by its mother. Just before the expiration of his leave he killed the child because: "I could not see it suffer any longer and have to go away and leave it". An application for leave to appeal was dismissed. Rex v. Simpson, 84 L.J.K.B. 1893 (1915). It is murder to aid in the killing of one's wife even if it is at her request and because of an impulse to end her suffering from an incurable disease. People v. Roberts, 211 Mich. 187, 178 N.W. 690 (1920).

Lack of motive is relevant on the issue of identification and also to issues of premeditation and deliberation in a murder prosecution. People v. Sears, 2 Cal.3d 180, 84 Cal.Rptr. 711, 465 P.2d 847 (1970).

wrong is necessary to constitute the offense, and offenses that are *mala in se* in which a criminal intent is a necessary ingredient of the crime. While there are to be found both in judicial decisions and in text books elaborate discussions of what is a criminal intent, no attempt has been made to accurately define the term. Very possibly the attempt to make a definition so comprehensive as to be applicable to all cases would be futile, and it has often been doubted whether the term "intent" is an accurate one. However this may be, it is very apparent that the innocence or criminality of the intent in a particular act generally depends on the knowledge or belief of the actor at the time. An honest and reasonable belief in the existence of circumstances which, if true, would make the act for which the defendant is prosecuted innocent, would be a good defense. Thus, if a man killed another under such circumstances as gave proper and reasonable grounds for the belief that the person killed was about to take the life of the slayer, although the person killed was only playing a practical joke, no crime would be committed. But if the facts and circumstances which the person believed to exist were not such as in law to justify his act, then there would be no defense to the act. In other words, it is the knowledge or belief of the actor at the time that stamps identically the same intent as either criminal or innocent, for the intent to take life, unless under circumstances that the law regards as sufficient to justify the taking, is the criminal intent and the only criminal intent that can exist in case of murder (excepting where the killing is done in the commission of an independent felony). So, ordinarily, a criminal intent is an intent to do knowingly and wilfully that which is condemned as wrong by the law and common morality of the country, and if such an intent exists, it is neither justification nor excuse that the actor intended by its commission to accomplish some ultimate good.

To constitute perjury under our law it is not necessary to establish any other intent than that specified in the statute, for by its terms it is not sufficient that the affiant testifies as to what is false, but the testimony must be given willfully and knowingly, and the affiant must know that the testimony is false; if it be given in the honest belief that it is true, or by mistake or inadvertence, the case does not fall within the statute. Therefore, if a person willfully testifies to what he knows to be false, this is the criminal intent and the only criminal intent that can exist in the crime. That the ultimate object to be attained by the perjury may be beneficent or indifferent in no way absolves or qualifies the criminality of the act. One may not commit a crime because he hopes or expects that good will come of it. It is no defense to a charge of intentionally committing an act prohibited by law even that the dictates of his religious belief require one to do the act. In Reynolds v. United States, 98 U.S. 145, 25 L.Ed. 244, the prisoner was indicted for having committed bigamy in Utah, and contended in his defense that polygamy was a duty enjoined on him by his religious belief. The court there said: "This (defense) would be introducing a new element into criminal law. Laws are made for the government of actions, and while they cannot interfere with mere religious belief and opinions, they may with practices. Suppose one believed that human sacrifices were a necessary part of religious worship, would it be seriously contended that the civil government under which he lived could not interfere to prevent a sacrifice?" In People v. Pierson (176 N.Y. 201, 68 N.E. 243) this court upheld a conviction for misdemeanor where the father, acting under the dictates of his religious faith, failed to call a physician to attend his sick child. In that case the defendant, far from intending to injure his child, sought by his conduct to preserve it, and believed that his action would most conduce to that result. . . .

If one may not violate the law with impunity in obedience to the requirements of his religious faith, much less can he justify such violation merely to escape personal inconvenience or annoyance. Therefore, the explanation offered by the relator that his act was impelled solely by the desire to escape the importunities of "Wall street," if true (and the truth of this statement was plainly a question of fact), is entirely immaterial to the charge against him. The sole questions in this prosecution are: 1st. Were the facts stated by the relator in the report true or false? 2nd. If false, did the relator know them to be false when he verified the report? Though the statements made in the return may have been incorrect, if the relator made them in good faith either by inadvertence or mistake, or in the honest belief that the statements were true, then, of course, he did not commit the offense. We think the evidence contained in the affidavits was sufficient to present a question of fact on these issues.

The order of the Appellate Division should be reversed, that of the Special Term affirmed, and the relator remanded to custody. . . .[1]

1. One who sends obscene matter through the mails is guilty of a federal offense even if his purpose is to expose, and thereby correct, sexual abuses. United States v. Harmon, 45 F. 414 (D.C. Kan.1891).

The federal obscenity statute punishing the mailing of material that is obscene does not offend constitutional safeguards against convictions based upon protected material since obscenity is not within the area of constitutionally protected speech or press. Roth v. United States, 354 U.S. 476, 77 S.Ct. 1304 (1957). "Obscene material is material which deals with sex in a manner appealing to prurient interest". 354 U.S. at 487, 77 S.Ct. at 1310. See also Miller v. California, 413 U.S. 15, 93 S.Ct. 2607 (1973); Hamling v. United States, 418 U.S. 87, 94 S.Ct. 2887 (1974).

One who carries a concealed pistol is guilty of violating the statute even if his only purpose is to exhibit it as a curiosity. Walls v. State, 7 Blackf. 572 (Ind. 1845). The intentional shooting of another was "with intent to do him some grievous bodily harm" even if the only motive was to prevent an arrest. Rex v. Gillow, 1 Moody 85, 168 Eng.Rep. 1195 (1825).

"Noble motives and pure thoughts cannot bar the conviction of one who admits intentional action which violates the proscriptions of a statute declaring that action criminal, . . ." United States v. Ragsdale, 438 F.2d 21, 26 (5th Cir.1971).

If the Government asks a citizen a question, which it should not ask, the citizen may decline to answer the question or he may answer it honestly, but he cannot with impunity knowingly and wilfully answer with a falsehood. Bryson v. United States, 396 U.S. 64, 90 S.Ct. 355 (1969). If **D**, on the claim of privilege against self-incrimination, could validly have refused to complete a certain form,

LANGFORD v. UNITED STATES

United States Court of Appeals, Ninth Circuit, 1949.
178 F.2d 48.

POPE, CIRCUIT JUDGE. Langford, the appellant, was convicted of violation of the Mann Act, 18 U.S.C.A § 398 [now § 2421]. The indictment was in two counts. Count One charged the transportation of a woman, one Carol Jones, in foreign commerce, from Los Angeles County, California, to Tiajuana, Mexico, for purposes of prostitution, debauchery and other immoral practices. The second count charged transportation of the same woman, for the same purposes, from Tiajuana to Los Angeles County. Conviction was on Count Two only.

The evidence only showed that at the time of the transportation mentioned in Count One, the parties went to Mexico to be married there, and that the transportation charged in Count Two was their return trip. It is urged upon this appeal that notwithstanding the evidence of prior and subsequent prostitution, the entire trip, both going and returning, was an innocent one under the rule of Mortensen v. United States, 322 U.S. 369, 64 S.Ct. 1037, 88 L.Ed. 1331. Therefore, it is said, the verdict is against law, and not supported by the evidence. . . .

Jones, the prosecuting witness, was white and a college graduate, with a degree in sociology and applied psychology. She had been employed as a case worker in Los Angeles. She testified that she met Langford, a Negro, at a Los Angeles night club and that she voluntarily went to his home to live with him in January, 1948. A week or so later, Langford brought four sailors home with him and asked her to perform acts of sexual intercourse with them. She refused at first, but consented when Langford slapped her. At this time there was another girl present whom Jones described as a prostitute for herself and Langford. . . .

Jones testified that, although she was in love with Langford, she left him twice in March. The first time, he saw her in a car with some men and dragged her out of it so she returned to his home. She left him the second time, because he had slapped her and beaten her with a belt. On this occasion she took a room in a private home and did not engage in prostitution for several days. On the evening of April 5, Langford telephoned her and asked permission to come to see her. He came very humbly, protesting his love for her, and proposed marriage, a subject Jones had previously broached to him. Jones accepted this proposal although Langford told her she would still have to engage in prostitution for a month or two until his car was paid for. However, at this time there was an anti-miscegenation

this would not bar a prosecution for having made a false statement on such form. United States v. Knox, 396 U.S. 77, 90 S.Ct. 363 (1969).

statute in effect in California [1] so the parties decided to drive to Tiajuana, Mexico, where the law permitted marriage between the races.

In the Mortensen case, supra, a man and wife, proprietors of a house of ill fame in Nebraska, allowed two of their prostitutes to accompany them on a vacation trip to Salt Lake City, Utah. It was charged that they had violated the Mann Act because they had brought the girls back from Salt Lake City to Nebraska and the girls had resumed their occupation upon their return. The Supreme Court, through Mr. Justice Murphy, held [2] that the language of the Mann Act "is conditioned upon the use of interstate transportation for the purpose of, or as a means of effecting or facilitating, the commission of the illegal acts. Here the interstate round trip had no such purpose and was in no way related to the subsequent immoralities in Grand Island."

The rule is conceded that the dominant motive for the interstate transportation of the victim must be the purpose proscribed by the statute,[3] but we think the jury was justified in finding that this case fell within the rule. In its argument to the jury, the government advanced two theories: (1) that Langford had married Jones primarily for the purpose of causing her to return to him and continue to work for him as a prostitute; and (2) that the dominant purpose of Langford in bringing Jones back from Tiajuana to Los Angeles was to get her back to work immediately earning money for him. In the Mortensen case there was no evidence justifying the inference that, had the Mortensens not taken the girls on the interstate vacation trip, the girls would have refused to perform the proscribed activities for the Mortensens. Here, however, the fact that Langford had used force and threats to keep Jones with him, that she had nevertheless left him again, and that he had put her back to work just a day after the "marriage", warrant the conclusion that the interstate journey and marriage were nothing but a device to, in the words of the statute, "induce, entice, or compel her to give herself up to the practice

1. Cal.Civil Code, 1941, Sec. 60. This statute was held unconstitutional on October 1, 1948 in Perez v. Lippold, 32 Cal. 2d 711, 198 P.2d 17.

2. 322 U.S. 369, 377, 64 S.Ct. 1037, 1042, 88 L.Ed. 1331.

3. Hansen v. Haff, 291 U.S. 559, 54 S.Ct. 494, 78 L.Ed. 968; Mortensen v. United States, supra. [Footnotes 1–3 are by the Court.]

[Added by the Compiler.]

A statute similar to the California statute, referred to in note 1, was held to be unconstitutional by the Supreme Court. Loving v. Virginia, 388 U.S. 1, 87 S.Ct. 1817 (1967).

It is not necessary that the sole object be for immoral purposes. It suffices if one of the efficient and compelling purposes was illicit conduct. O'Neal v. United States, 240 F.2d 700 (10th Cir.1957).

"Interstate transportation of the prosecutrix between Arkansas and Oklahoma was conceded, and the only factual issue in the case was whether petitioner's dominant purpose in making the trip was to facilitate her practice of prostitution in Tulsa, Oklahoma", or was merely an accommodation to her in connection with a business trip he was making at the time. Hawkins v. United States, 358 U.S. 74, 79–80, 79 S.Ct. 136, 139 (1958).

If prostitution was clearly one of the purposes of the interstate transportation it is not necessary to show that it was the "dominant" purpose. United States v. Dimsdale, 410 F.2d 358 (5th Cir.1969).

of prostitution". The facts here are such that the jury might well disbelieve that the reason for the marriage was the usual one.

The other cases upon which appellant relies are readily distinguishable for the same reason. In Van Pelt v. United States, 4 Cir., 240 F. 346, the object of the interstate transportation was to take defendant's mistress from Virginia to Maryland to stay in the latter state until their child was born. The trip was held to have played no part in inducing the commission of a sexual act in Maryland. In Fisher v. United States, 4 Cir., 266 F. 667, 670, the purpose of the trip was to visit the girl's mother. Although illicit relations were resumed on the return, the court held that ". . . the mere fact that a journey from one state to another is followed by such intercourse, when the journey was not for that purpose, but wholly for other reasons, to which intercourse was not related cannot be regarded as a violation of the statute." Here, in view of the unusual attitude of the appellant towards marriage, we think the jury were warranted in finding that so far as appellant was concerned his dominant motive for the marriage was to get control of Jones and re-establish a relationship of pander and prostitute from which he profited so extensively, and that the trip, marriage and all, had that primary end in view. . . .[4]

Since we find no error in the record, the judgment is affirmed. (Certiorari denied 339 U.S. 938, 70 S.Ct. 669, 94 L.Ed. 589.)

LAWS v. STATE

Court of Appeals of Texas, 1888.
26 Tex.App. 643, 10 S.W. 220.

This conviction was in the second degree for the murder of Hiram Garrison, in Franklin County, Texas, on the twenty-first day of August, 1888. A term of fifteen years in the penitentiary was the penalty imposed by the verdict and judgment. . . .

WILLSON, JUDGE. Homicide is permitted by law when inflicted for the purpose of preventing theft at night, and the homicide in such case is justifiable at any time while the offender is at the place where the theft is committed, or within reach of gunshot from such place. (Penal Code, art. 570.)

In this case no question is made as to the commission of the homicide by the defendant, but defendant claims that, at the time he shot

4. A conviction under the Mann Act was not authorized by proof that defendant took a prostitute from New York to New Jersey for a week-end of recreation and returned her to New York where she again engaged in prostitution. United States v. Ross, 257 F.2d 292 (2d Cir.1958). When one induces a woman to travel in interstate commerce for the purpose of prostitution the Mann Act has been violated the moment she crosses the state line. Wiley v. United States, 257 F.2d 900 (8th Cir.1958).

To establish guilt under the Mann Act it must be shown that the dominant motive for transporting the female was prostitution or other immoral purpose, but it is not necessary to show that this was the dominant motive for the trip. United States v. Harris, 480 F.2d 601 (6th Cir.1973).

and killed the deceased, the latter had committed theft of whisky belonging to the former, and was within gunshot of the place where the theft was committed, and that it was nighttime when the theft and homicide were committed, and that he committed the homicide for the purpose of preventing the consequences of the theft. There is evidence tending to support this defense. . . .

In this State, with reference to the crime of burglary, it is provided: "By the term 'day time' is meant any time of the twenty-four hours from thirty minutes before sun rise until thirty minutes after sun set." (Penal Code, art. 710.) Again, it is provided that "words which have their meaning specially defined shall be understood in that sense, though it be contrary to their usual meaning." (Penal Code, art. 10.) It is clear to our minds, in view of the provisions cited, that a "theft by night" is a theft committed at any time between thirty minutes after sun set and thirty minutes before sun rise, and the court should have so instructed the jury; and, having failed to do so, committed a material error calculated to injure the defendant's rights.

Relating to the defense before mentioned, the court among other instructions gave to the jury the following in substance: "If you find that the defendant killed the deceased in the execution of a previously formed intent or plan to take his life, and not to prevent theft then being committed, or to prevent the consequences of the same, such killing would not be justified though done in the night time and whilst deceased was committing or had committed a theft." This instruction was not excepted to, but was urged by defendant as error in his motion for a new trial, and is insisted upon here as error. We are of the opinion that the instruction is not erroneous. If the killing was upon malice, and not to prevent a theft or the consequences of a theft, it would not be justified under the statute, although a theft by night was actually being committed by the deceased at the time he was killed. It is not the intention of the statute to justify *murder*. Such a construction of the statute would to our minds be unreasonable and exceedingly dangerous.

Other questions presented on this appeal are not discussed and determined, because they are not likely to arise on another trial. Because the charge of the court is materially defective in not instructing the jury in the legal meaning of day time and night time, the judgment is reversed and the cause is remanded.

Reversed and remanded.

Opinion delivered December 19, 1888.

TE

ndiana, 1892.

5.

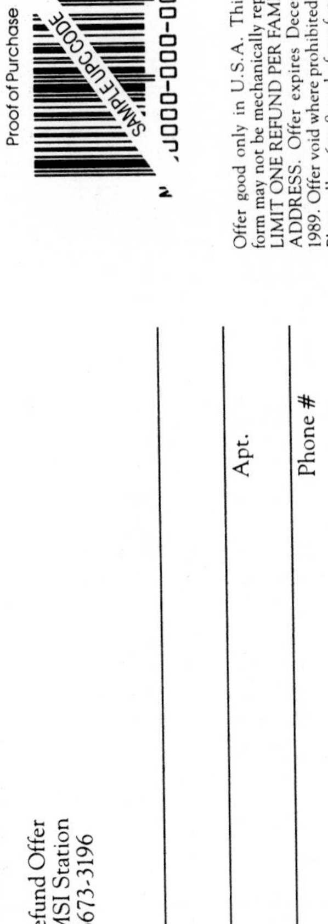

on a charge of murder in ... of voluntary manslaugh- ... ent in the State Prison for

conviction on this verdict, ... t in overruling his motion

ecedent, but insisted that ... ucted the jury very fully ... as to the general princi- ... the facts as they were ... prosecution respectively. ... xception, to be hereafter

. . .

uld have instructed the ... e accused might suffer ... the killing was justifia- ... tion of apprehension of ... nger; that one may kill ... es not apprehend dan- ... e in so doing, and may ... ense if it can be shown ... he time, knew nothing.

who is himself without ... be, to protect himself ... purpose such force as ... nd no more. The dan- ge... d by the court, in the ins... apparent necessity, as well as of the amount of force necessary to employ to resist an attack, can only be determined from the standpoint of the defendant at the time, and under all the existing circumstances." Ordinarily, one exercising the right of self-defense is compelled to act upon the instant, and with no time for deliberation or investigation, and under such circumstances a danger which exists only in appearance is to him as real and imminent as if it were actual.

It is, however, not the law that one who is in no apparent danger even, who does not, in fact, apprehend any danger, and who has no reasonable ground for such apprehension, may deliberately and maliciously kill another and successfully interpose the defense of self-defense because it subsequently appears that there was actual danger, of which he was at the time ignorant. . . .[1]

(For other reasons the judgment was reversed and a new trial directed.)

SECTION 9. CONCURRENCE OF MENS REA AND ACTUS REUS

The *mens rea* and the *actus reus* must concur to constitute a crime. The doctrine of trespass *ab initio* does not apply in criminal jurisprudence. The doctrine of continuing trespass is altogether different. *Trespass de bonis asportatis* is deemed to continue, so far as the law of larceny is concerned, as long as the trespasser keeps possession of the property so obtained. But this assumes an original trespass. It does not make a trespass out of what was not a trespass when done by any theory of "relation." And the familiar maxim "*omnis ratihabitio retrotrahitur, et mandato priori equiparatur*" (every ratification relates back, and is equivalent to a prior authorization), does not apply to criminal cases.

Concurrence, it should be emphasized, is something other than mere coincidence. The two elements of the crime must be "brought together" in the sense that the *actus reus* must be attributable to the *mens rea*.

COMMONWEALTH v. CALI

Supreme Judicial Court of Massachusetts, 1923.
247 Mass. 20, 141 N.E. 510.

BRALEY, J. The defendant having been indicted, tried and convicted under G.L. c. 266, § 10, of burning a building in Leominster belonging to Maria Cali, which at the time was insured against loss or damage by fire, with intent to injure the insurer, the case is here on his exceptions to the denial of his motion for a directed verdict, and to rulings at the trial. . . .

The only evidence as to the origin, extent and progress of the fire were the statements of the defendant to the police inspector, and as a witness. The jury who were to determine his credibility and the weight to be given his testimony could find notwithstanding his explanations of its origin as being purely accidental, that when all the circumstances were reviewed he either set it, or after the fire was

1. "One may harbor the most intense hatred toward another; he may court an opportunity to take his life; he may rejoice while he is imbruing his hands in his heart's blood; and yet, if, to save his own life, the facts showed that he was fully justified in slaying his adversary, his malice shall not be taken into account." Golden v. State, 25 Ga. 527 (1858). The fact that the fear of being caught was the sole reason for refraining from criminal conduct is unimportant so far as the law is concerned. "In the eyes of the law, a man is innocent if he did not commit the unlawful act, whatever the explanation may be for his good behavior." Evans v. United States, 257 F.2d 121, 127 (9th Cir.1958).

under way purposely refrained from any attempt to extinguish it in order to obtain the benefit of the proceeds of the policy, which when recovered, would be applied by the mortgagee on his indebtedness. If they so found, a specific intent to injure the insurer had been proved. The motion, and the defendant's requests in so far as not given were denied rightly.

The instructions to the jury that, "If a man does start an accidental fire what is his conduct in respect to it? A question might arise—as if after the fire has started accidentally, and he then has it within his power and ability to extinguish the fire and he realizes and knows that he can, and then he forms and entertains an intent to injure an insurance company he can be guilty of this offence. It is not necessary that the intent be formed before the fire is started," also show no error of law. It is true as the defendant contends, that, if he merely neglected in the emergency of the moment to act, his negligence was not proof of a purpose to commit the crime charged. The intention, however, to injure could be formed after as well as before the fire started. On his own admissions the jury were to say whether, when considered in connection with all the circumstances, his immediate departure from the premises for his home in Fitchburg, without giving any alarm, warranted the inference of a criminal intent or state of mind, that the building should be consumed. . . .

Exceptions overruled.

JACKSON v. COMMONWEALTH

Court of Appeals of Kentucky, 1896.
100 Ky. 239, 38 S.W. 422.

JUDGE HAZELRIGG delivered the opinion of the court.

The appellant was jointly indicted with one Alonzo Walling in the Campbell Circuit Court for the murder of Pearl Bryan, and on his separate trial was found guilty and sentenced to be hanged.

It will be necessary to submit only a brief summary of the facts disclosed in the voluminous record before us to render intelligible the various complaints urged on this appeal against the judgment of conviction.

On the morning of Saturday, February 1, 1896, the headless body of a woman was found on the farm of one Locke, near Newport, in Campbell county. Every effort to find the head proved futile, but the shoes the dead girl wore were marked: "Lewis & Hayes, Greencastle, Indiana," and this circumstance led to the identification of the body as that of Pearl Bryan, a young girl of that city. Her clothes were saturated with blood, particularly about the neck, and a large quantity of it was found on the ground near the neck, covering a circular spot some six or seven inches in diameter, and also a spot of similar kind some feet away. Extending near to or over this last named spot there were some privet bushes, the leaves of which were spattered with blood, and drops were discovered pending under the leaves, as though the blood had reached the under side of them by spurting from the neck, which it might do as disclosed by the testimony if the decaptitation had taken place or been commenced at the spot near the bushes, and if the victim were alive at the time.

These and other circumstances led the authorities to proceed on the theory that the murder—for such it evidently appeared to be—occurred in Campbell county. . . .

The conclusion is fairly deducible from certain portions of the testimony that an attempt was made to kill the girl by the administration of cocaine while in Cincinnati, and that this was done by the defendant or at his instance, but that she was not thereby killed. It is to be remembered that, according to the testimony of Jackson, he did not see the girl in life after Wednesday, and, according to Walling, he did not see her after that day; but the proof conduces to show that they were both with her Friday night when she was in the cab, and that they brought her over to Campbell county.

If she was then dead, as might be supposed from her making no outcry, a verdict of guilty could not have been rendered; but if she was then alive, though appearing to be dead, and by the cutting of her throat she was killed while in Campbell county, then the jury might find a verdict of guilty, although the cutting off of the head was merely for the purpose of destroying the chances for identification or for any other purpose. At least, the instruction does not authorize a verdict of conviction unless Jackson is shown to have cut off the head of his victim in Campbell county—and whilst she was in fact alive—and if he did this, he was guilty of murder, though believing her already dead, if the act succeeded and was but a part of the felonious attempt to kill her in Cincinnati. . . .

The judgment must be affirmed.

The court delivered the following response to petition for rehearing February 13, 1897:

With great earnestness, force and plausibility two contentions are made by the petitions for rehearing in this case and in the case of Walling v. Commonwealth:

1st. That no facts which occurred in the foreign jurisdiction of Ohio can be tacked on to facts which occurred in Kentucky for the purpose of supplying the elements necessary to constitute the crime of murder in Kentucky.

2d. (And this appears to be the point chiefly relied on) That in giving its instructions to the jury the trial court is not authorized to refer to any fact which occurred in the foreign jurisdiction. Other suggestions are made in the petitions, but in our judgment do not require specific response.

These two contentions may be considered together, as the first is necessarily raised and considered in the decision of the second, and so treated in the petition.

Reduced to its lowest terms, the claim of counsel is that an attempt to commit a murder in another State, supposed by the guilty party to have been there successful, but in reality completed in this State, though by an act not by him believed to be the consummation of his purpose, is not in this State punishable.

Such is not nor should it be the law. By the law of this State a crime is punishable in the jurisdiction in which it has effect. Statutes in numbers have been passed by the general assembly of this Commonwealth providing that jurisdiction should be had of crimes in the county in which the crime became effectual. (Chapter 36, article 2, Kentucky Statutes.) Such we believe to have been the common law before such enactments.

Assuming that what the jury found was true, in what State or district could the crime be punished? If not here, where? If we concede the claims of counsel for appellants no serious crime was committed in Ohio. Nothing was there done but an ineffective attempt to murder. None was committed here. What was done in this jurisdiction was only the mutilation of a supposed corpse, and yet the fact, established by overwhelming testimony, remains that the crime has been committed. Not all the refinements of counsel can lead us from the conclusion that, when a crime has been completed the result of which is a death in this Commonwealth, we can take jurisdiction of the offense.

Not for a moment can we admit as law the logical conclusion of counsel's argument, namely, that there is a variety of murder, which, by reason of error in its commission, is not anywhere in any jurisdiction punishable; not in Ohio, for the reason that the attempt there made was not successful; not in Kentucky, for the reason that the act there done, and which accomplished and completed the actual killing, was done upon the supposition that the murder had already been accomplished. . . .

We have carefully examined the immense mass of testimony in the case, and see no error to the prejudice of any substantial right of the appellant.[1]

The petition for rehearing is overruled.

1. Accord, Thabo Meli v. Regina, [1954] All E.R. 373.

"On the above facts this reference raises a single and simple question, viz., if an accused kills another by one or other of two or more different acts each of which, if it caused the death, is a sufficient act to establish manslaughter, is it necessary in order to found a conviction to prove which act caused the death? The answer to the question is No, it is not necessary to found a conviction to prove which act caused the death." Attorney General's Reference (No. 4 of 1980), [1981] 2 All E.R. 617, 619 (Ct. of App.)

MODEL PENAL CODE

Section 2.02 General Requirements of Culpability.

(1) Minimum Requirements of Culpability. Except as provided in Section 2.05, a person is not guilty of an offense unless he acted purposely, knowingly, recklessly or negligently, as the law may require, with respect to each material element of the offense.

(2) Kinds of Culpability Defined.

(a) Purposely.

A person acts purposely with respect to a material element of an offense when:

(i) if the element involves the nature of his conduct or a result thereof, it is his conscious object to engage in conduct of that nature or to cause such a result; and

(ii) if the element involves the attendant circumstances, he is aware of the existence of such circumstances or he believes or hopes that they exist.

(b) Knowingly.

A person acts knowingly with respect to a material element of an offense when:

(i) if the element involves the nature of his conduct or the attendant circumstances, he is aware that his conduct is of that nature or that such circumstances exist; and

(ii) if the element involves a result of his conduct, he is aware that it is practically certain that his conduct will cause such a result.

(c) Recklessly.

A person acts recklessly with respect to a material element of an offense when he consciously disregards a substantial and unjustifiable risk that the material element exists or will result from his conduct. The risk must be of such a nature and degree that, considering the nature and purpose of the actor's conduct and the circumstances known to him, its disregard involves a gross deviation from the standard of conduct that a law-abiding person would observe in the actor's situation.

(d) Negligently.

A person acts negligently with respect to a material element of an offense when he should be aware of a substantial and unjustifiable risk that the material element exists or will result from his conduct. The risk must be of such a nature and degree that the actor's failure to perceive it, considering the nature and purpose of his conduct and the circumstances known to him, involves a gross deviation from the standard of care that a reasonable person would observe in the actor's situation.

(3) Culpability Required Unless Otherwise Provided. When the culpability sufficient to establish a material element of an offense is not prescribed by law, such element is established if a person acts purposely, knowingly or recklessly with respect thereto.

(4) Prescribed Culpability Requirement Applies to All Material Elements. When the law defining an offense prescribes the kind of culpability that is sufficient for the commission of an offense, without distinguishing among

the material elements thereof, such provision shall apply to all the material elements of the offense, unless a contrary purpose plainly appears.

(5) Substitutes for Negligence, Recklessness and Knowledge. When the law provides that negligence suffices to establish an element of an offense, such element also is established if a person acts purposely, knowingly or recklessly. When recklessness suffies to establish an element, such element also is established if a person acts purposely or knowingly. When acting knowingly suffices to establish an element, such element also is established if a person acts purposely.

(6) Requirement of Purpose Satisfied if Purpose Is Conditional. When a particular purpose is an element of an offense, the element is established although such purpose is conditional, unless the condition negatives the harm or evil sought to be prevented by the law defining the offense.

(7) Requirement of Knowledge Satisfied by Knowledge of High Probability. When knowledge of the existence of a particular fact is an element of an offense, such knowledge is established if a person is aware of a high probability of its existence, unless he actually believes that it does not exist.

(8) Requirement of Wilfulness Satisfied by Acting Knowingly. A requirement that an offense be committed wilfully is satisfied if a person acts knowingly with respect to the material elements of the offense, unless a purpose to impose further requirements appears.

(9) Culpability as to Illegality of Conduct. Neither knowledge nor recklessness or negligence as to whether conduct constitutes an offense or as to the existence, meaning or application of the law determining the elements of an offense is an element of such offense, unless the definition of the offense or the Code so provides.

(10) Culpability as Determinant of Grade of Offense. When the grade or degree of an offense depends on whether the offense is committed purposely, knowingly, recklessly or negligently, its grade or degree shall be the lowest for which the determinative kind of culpability is established with respect to any material element of the offense.

Section 2.05 When Culpability Requirements Are Inapplicable to Violations and to Offenses Defined by Other Statutes; Effect of Absolute Liability in Reducing Grade of Offense to Violation.

(1) The requirements of culpability prescribed by Sections 2.01 and 2.02 do not apply to:

(a) offenses which constitute violations, unless the requirement involved is included in the definition of the offense or the Court determines that its application is consistent with effective enforcement of the law defining the offense; or

(b) offenses defined by statutes other than the Code, insofar as a legislative purpose to impose absolute liability for such offenses or with respect to any material element thereof plainly appears.

(2) Notwithstanding any other provision of existing law and unless a subsequent statute otherwise provides:

(a) when absolute liability is imposed with respect to any material element of an offense defined by a statute other than the Code and a conviction is based upon such liability, the offense constitutes a violation; and

(b) although absolute liability is imposed by law with respect to one or more of the material elements of an offense defined by a statute other than the Code, the culpable commission of the offense may be charged and proved, in which event negligence with respect to such elements constitutes sufficient culpability and the classification of the offense and the sentence that may be imposed therefor upon conviction are determined by Section 1.04 and Article 6 of the Code.[1]

Chapter 8

RESPONSIBILITY: LIMITATIONS ON CRIMINAL CAPACITY

SECTION 1. IMMATURITY (INFANCY)

Every civilized society must recognize criminal incapacity based upon extreme immaturity. No matter what harm is caused by one of very tender years the situation must be dealt with by some means other than the machinery established for the administration of criminal justice. This is too clear for any possibility of doubt, although there are differences of opinion as to just what should be regarded as such immaturity as to preclude criminal guilt.

While failing to develop techniques comparable to modern juvenile court and youth correction authority acts, the common law made a very reasonable approach to this problem. Because of wide differences in individuals two ages were emphasized. A child under the age of seven has no criminal capacity. At common law there is an "irrebuttable presumption of incapacity" on the part of one so young,—to use the familiar explanation of the judges. Fourteen is the other age. One who has reached the age of fourteen has criminal capacity unless incapacity is established on some entirely different basis, such as insanity. Furthermore, this means physical age and not so-called "mental age." Between the ages of seven and fourteen there is a rebuttable presumption of criminal incapacity. The common law permits the criminal conviction of a child between these ages, but only upon clear proof of such precocity as to establish a real appreciation of the wrongfulness of the thing done. This presumption is extremely strong at the age of seven and diminishes gradually until it disappears entirely at the age of fourteen.

The words of Blackstone are significant: "The law of England does in some cases privilege an infant under the age of twenty-one, as to common misdemeanors, so as to escape fine, imprisonment, and the like: and particularly in cases of omission, as not repairing a bridge, or a highway, and other similar offences; for, not having the command of his fortune till twenty-one he wants the capacity to do those things which the law requires. But where there is any notorious breach of the peace, a riot, battery, or the like (which infants, when full grown, are at least as liable as others to commit) for these an infant, above the age of fourteen, is equally liable to suffer as a person at the full age of twenty-one.

"With regard to capital crimes, the law is still more minute and circumspect; distinguishing with greater nicety the several degrees of age and discretion. . . . Thus a girl of thirteen has been burned for killing her mistress: and one boy of ten, and another of nine years old, who had killed their companions, have been sentenced to death, and he of ten years actually hanged; because it appeared, upon their trials, that the one hid himself, and the other hid the body he had killed, which hiding manifested a consciousness of guilt, and a discretion to discern between good and evil. And there was an instance in the last century where a boy of eight years old was tried at Abingdon for firing two barns; and, it appearing that he had malice, revenge, and cunning, he was found guilty, condemned, and hanged accordingly. Thus, also, in very modern times, a boy of ten years old was convicted on his own confession of murdering his bedfellow, there appearing in his whole behaviour plain tokens of a mischievous discretion; and, as the sparing this boy merely on account of his tender years might be of dangerous consequence to the public by propagating a notion that children might commit such atrocious crimes with impunity, it was unanimously agreed by all the judges that he was a proper subject of capital punishment. But, in all such cases, the evidence of that malice which is to supply age ought to be strong and clear beyond all doubt and contradiction" (4 Bl.Comm. 22–24).[a]

The age, below which there is complete criminal incapacity, has been raised by statute in some jurisdictions. Thus it has been placed at eight in England, at nine in Texas, at ten in Georgia and at twelve in Arkansas. Furthermore, the net result of some of the juvenile delinquency statutes is to raise it much higher.

Such age is omitted entirely from some of the statutes as, for example, the California section which provides in substance that children under the age of fourteen are incapable of crime "in the absence of clear proof that at the time of committing the act charged against them, they knew its wrongfulness" (Cal.Pen. Code § 26). Any provision of this nature should be read in the light of the common law. It clearly recognizes the existence of a presumption although the word is not used. And it is more logical to assume this means the established presumption of the common law than any other: that is, a presumption which is conclusive below the age of seven, extremely strong at that age, and does not disappear entirely until the age of fourteen.

a. Homicide by a boy of 10 was held not to be murder on the ground that one of his age was not shown to have the mens rea needed for murder. State in Interest of S.H., 61 N.J. 108, 293 A.2d 181 (1972).

A 13-year-old boy was convicted of murder in the second degree. In affirming the conviction the court said: "Poole hid the murder weapon as well as other pieces of evidence. He fabricated stories in attempting to establish an alibi. He claimed the shooting had been accidental; and he testified that he knew killing people was wrong. There was ample evidence that Poole knew the wrongfulness of his act." Poole v. State, 97 Nev. 175, 625 P.2d 1163, 1165 (1981).

Whether such a statute does or does not abolish the conclusive part of the common-law presumption is largely academic. This presumption applies only to one *under* the age of seven. Except where the age has been raised by statute it has always been possible, in legal theory, to rebut the presumption of incapacity of a seven-year-old child,—but it has never yet been done.

What has been said has reference to mental incapacity. An additional presumption applies in the rape cases. Under the English common law a boy under the age of fourteen is conclusively presumed to be incapable of committing this offense. If two indictments were found against a thirteen-year-old boy, one charging rape and the other charging murder, the prosecution of the rape case would be stopped the moment his age was established. The murder case would be permitted to go to the jury with an instruction emphasizing the prima-facie presumption of incapacity. Some of the states in this country have adopted the same view. In others the presumption of physical incapacity of a boy under fourteen to commit rape is rebuttable.

What amounts to a limitation of criminal capacity has been established in a few jurisdictions at a much higher age. This is in the form of a provision that no one shall be deprived of life by reason of any act done before attaining a specified age. The age so specified in Texas, for example, is seventeen, and that in California is eighteen.[1]

The problem of criminal incapacity by reason of immaturity has been disguised to some extent by the juvenile delinquency statutes, with particular emphasis upon procedure. These enactments differ widely from state to state. Some of the earlier acts merely provided an alternative procedure which might be used, in the discretion of the judge, in cases of children below a specified age. The more progressive statutes provide that what would be a crime, if committed by an older person, is not a crime but an entirely different type of misbehavior, called "juvenile delinquency," if committed by a "juvenile." Most of these statutes do not remove from the category of crime any act punishable by death or by life imprisonment. The most recent development is to enlarge the scope of "juvenile delinquency" to include even a misdeed which would be capital on the part of an older person.[2] The net result of such a provision is to raise the age of total criminal incapacity.

1. West's Ann.Cal.Pen. Code, § 190.1 (1970).

2. "No person shall be convicted of any offense unless he had attained his 13th birthday at the time the offense was committed." Smith-Hurd Ill.Anno.Stat. Ch. 38 § 6–1 (1972).

Under the New York Code, McKinney's Consol. Laws of N.Y. (1981):

"§ 30.00 Infancy

"1. A person less than sixteen years old is not criminally responsible for conduct.

Subsection 2 provides that for certain crimes persons thirteen, fourteen and fifteen are responsible.

The Federal Youth Correction Act (18 U.S.C.A. ch. 402) applies to persons under twenty-two at the time of conviction and provides that such a "youth offender" may be sentenced to the custody of

KENT v. UNITED STATES

Supreme Court of the United States, 1966.
383 U.S. 541, 86 S.Ct. 1045.

[The Juvenile Court Act of the District of Columbia gives to the Juvenile Court "exclusive jurisdiction" over a juvenile charged with a violation of law, except that it authorizes the judge of the Juvenile Court to waive jurisdiction and transfer the case to the U.S. District Court "after full investigation" in case of any child "sixteen years of age or older who is charged with an offense which would amount to a felony in the case of an adult, . . . ".

Kent, who was sixteen, was arrested for having entered the apartment of a woman, taken her wallet and raped her. He was taken to the Receiving Home for Children. As there was reason to believe the judge of the Juvenile Court might waive jurisdiction and remit the case to the District Court, Kent's counsel filed a motion for a hearing on the question of waiver. He also filed supplemental motions.]

MR. JUSTICE FORTAS delivered the opinion of the Court, ...

The Juvenile Court judge did not rule on these motions. He held no hearing. He did not confer with petitioner or petitioner's parents or petitioner's counsel. He entered an order reciting that after "full investigation, I do hereby waive" jurisdiction of petitioner and directing that he be "held for trial for [the alleged] offenses under the regular procedure of the U.S. District Court for the District of Columbia." He made no findings. He did not recite any reason for the waiver. He made no reference to the motions filed by petitioner's counsel. We must assume that he denied, *sub silentio*, the motions for a hearing, the recommendation for hospitalization for psychiatric observation, the request for access to the Social Service file, and the

the Attorney General "for treatment and supervision". If it is found necessary he may be kept in custody up to four years and under supervision for two more. C, who had committed a federal misdemeanor was sentenced under this Act. As the maximum sentence provided for this misdemeanor was one year, C objected to his sentence to the custody of the Attorney General with its four to six-year provision. He claimed that it imposed cruel and unusual punishment in violation of the Eighth Amendment and also that it violated due process of law guaranteed by the Fifth. The court rejected both claims and upheld the constitutionality of the statute. The Act, it was said, provides "not heavier penalties and punishment than are imposed upon adult offenders, but the opportunity to escape from the physical and psychological shocks and traumas attendant upon serving an ordinary penal sentence while obtaining the benefits of corrective treatment, looking to rehabilitation and social redemption and restoration". Cunningham v. United States, 256 F.2d 467 (5th Cir.1958).

Failure of the court to explain the difference between a sentence under this Act and an ordinary sentence was held, where prejudicial, sufficient to entitle defendant to withdraw his plea of guilty. Pilkington v. United States, 315 F.2d 204 (4th Cir.1963). And see Eller v. United States, 327 F.2d 639 (9th Cir.1964); Freeman v. United States, 350 F.2d 940 (9th Cir.1965).

Sentencing of a youth offender should be in accordance with the statute unless the court makes an express finding that the offender would not benefit from treatment under the Act. Dorszynski v. United States, 418 U.S. 424, 94 S.Ct. 3042 (1974).

offer to prove that petitioner was a fit subject for rehabilitation under the Juvenile Court's jurisdiction. . . .

It is to petitioner's arguments as to the infirmity of the proceedings by which the Juvenile Court waived its otherwise exclusive jurisdiction that we address our attention. Petitioner attacks the waiver of jurisdiction on a number of statutory and constitutional grounds. He contends that the waiver is defective because no hearing was held; because no findings were made by the Juvenile Court; because the Juvenile Court stated no reasons for waiver; and because counsel was denied access to the Social Service file which presumably was considered by the Juvenile Court in determining to waive jurisdiction.

We agree that the order of the Juvenile Court waiving its jurisdiction and transferring petitioner for trial in the United States District Court for the District of Columbia was invalid. There is no question that the order is reviewable on motion to dismiss the indictment in the District Court, as specified by the Court of Appeals in this case. The issue is the standards to be applied upon such review.

We agree with the Court of Appeals that the statute contemplates that the Juvenile Court should have considerable latitude within which to determine whether it should retain jurisdiction over a child or—subject to the statutory delimitation—should waive jurisdiction. But this latitude is not complete. At the outset, it assumes procedural regularity sufficient in the particular circumstances to satisfy the basic requirements of due process and fairness, as well as compliance with the statutory requirement of a "full investigation."[15] The statute gives the Juvenile Court a substantial degree of discretion as to the factual considerations to be evaluated, the weight to be given them and the conclusion to be reached. It does not confer upon the Juvenile Court a license for arbitrary procedure. The statute does not permit the Juvenile Court to determine in isolation and without the participation or any representation of the child the "critically important" question whether a child will be deprived of the special protections and provisions of the Juvenile Court Act.[16] It does not authorize the Juvenile Court, in total disregard of a motion for hearing filed by counsel, and without any hearing or statement or reasons, to decide—as in this case—that the child will be taken from the Receiving Home for Children and transferred to jail along with adults, and that he will be exposed to the possibility of a death sentence[17] instead

15. "What is required before a waiver is, as we have said, 'full investigation.' . . . It prevents the waiver of jurisdiction as a matter of routine for the purpose of easing the docket. It prevents routine waiver in certain classes of alleged crimes. It requires a judgment in each case based on 'an inquiry not only into the facts of the alleged offense but also into the question whether the *parens patriae* plan of procedure is desirable and proper in the particular case.' Pee v. United States, 107 U.S.App.D.C. 47, 50, 274 F.2d 556, 559 (1959)." Green v. United States, supra, at 350, 308 F.2d at 305.

16. See Watkins v. United States, 119 U.S.App.D.C. 409, 413, 343 F.2d 278, 282 (1964); Black v. United States, 122 U.S. App.D.C. 393, 355 F.2d 104 (1965).

17. D.C. Code § 22-2801 (1961) fixes the punishment for rape at 30 years, or death if the jury so provides in its ver-

of treatment for a maximum, in Kent's case, of five years, until he is 21.[18]

We do not consider whether, on the merits, Kent should have been transferred; but there is no place in our system of law for reaching a result of such tremendous consequences without ceremony—without hearing, without effective assistance of counsel, without a statement of reasons. It is inconceivable that a court of justice dealing with adults, with respect to a similar issue, would proceed in this manner. It would be extraordinary if society's special concern for children, as reflected in the District of Columbia's Juvenile Court Act, permitted this procedure. We hold that it does not.

1. The theory of the District's Juvenile Court Act, like that of other jurisdictions,[19] is rooted in social welfare philosophy rather than in the *corpus juris*. Its proceedings are designated as civil rather than criminal. The Juvenile Court is theoretically engaged in determining the needs of the child and of society rather than adjudicating criminal conduct. The objectives are to provide measures of guidance and rehabilitation for the child and protection for society, not to fix criminal responsibility, guilt and punishment. The State is *parens patriae* rather than prosecuting attorney and judge.[20] But the admonition to function in a "parental" relationship is not an invitation to procedural arbitrariness.

2. Because the State is supposed to proceed in respect of the child as *parens patriae* and not as adversary, courts have relied on the premise that the proceedings are "civil" in nature and not criminal, and have asserted that the child cannot complain of the deprivation of important rights available in criminal cases. It has been asserted that he can claim only the fundamental due process right to fair treatment.[21] For example, it has been held that he is not entitled to bail; to indictment by grand jury; to a speedy and public trial; to trial by jury; to immunity against self-incrimination; to confrontation of his accusers; and in some jurisdictions (but not in the District of Columbia) that he is not entitled to counsel.[22]

While there can be no doubt of the original laudable purpose of juvenile courts, studies and critiques in recent years raise serious questions as to whether actual performance measures well enough against theoretical purpose to make tolerable the immunity of the

dict. The maximum punishment for housebreaking is 15 years, D.C. Code § 22–1801 (1961); for robbery it is also 15 years, D.C. Code § 22–2901 (1961).

18. The jurisdiction of the Juvenile Court over a child ceases when he becomes 21. D.C. Code § 11–907 (1961), now § 11–1551 (Supp. IV, 1965).

19. All States have juvenile court systems. A study of the actual operation of these systems is contained in Note, Juvenile Delinquents: The Police, State Courts, and Individualized Justice, 79 Harv.L.Rev. 775 (1966).

20. See Handler, The Juvenile Court and the Adversary System: Problems of Function and Form, 1965 Wis.L.Rev. 7.

21. Pee v. United States, 107 U.S. App.D.C. 47, 274 F.2d 556 (1959).

22. See Pee v. United States, supra, at 54, 274 F.2d, at 563; Paulsen, Fairness to the Juvenile Offender, 41 Minn.L.Rev. 547 (1957).

process from the reach of constitutional guaranties applicable to adults.[23] There is much evidence that some juvenile courts, including that of the District of Columbia, lack the personnel, facilities and techniques to perform adequately as representatives of the State in a *parens patriae* capacity, at least with respect to children charged with law violation. There is evidence, in fact, that there may be grounds for concern that the child receives the worst of both worlds: that he gets neither the protections accorded to adults nor the solicitous care and regenerative treatment postulated for children.[24]

This concern, however, does not induce us in this case to accept the invitation [25] to rule that constitutional guaranties which would be applicable to adults charged with the serious offenses for which Kent was tried must be applied in juvenile court proceedings concerned with allegations of law violation. The Juvenile Court Act and the decisions of the United States Court of Appeals for the District of Columbia Circuit provide an adequate basis for decision of this case, and we go no further.

3. It is clear beyond dispute that the waiver of jurisdiction is a "critically important" action determining vitally important statutory rights of the juvenile. The Court of Appeals for the District of Columbia Circuit has so held. The statutory scheme makes this plain. The Juvenile Court is vested with "original and exclusive jurisdiction" of the child. This jurisdiction confers special rights and immunities. He is, as specified by the statute, shielded from publicity. He may be confined, but with rare exceptions he may not be jailed along with adults. He may be detained, but only until he is 21 years of age. The court is admonished by the statute to give preference to retaining the child in the custody of his parents "unless his welfare and the safety and protection of the public can not be adequately safeguarded without . . . removal." The child is protected against consequences of adult conviction such as the loss of civil rights, the use of adjudication against him in subsequent proceedings, and disqualification for public employment.

The net, therefore, is that petitioner—then a boy of 16—was by statute entitled to certain procedures and benefits as a consequence of his statutory right to the "exclusive" jurisdiction of the Juvenile Court. In these circumstances, considering particularly that decision as to waiver of jurisdiction and transfer of the matter to the District Court was potentially as important to petitioner as the difference between five years' confinement and a death sentence, we conclude that, as a condition to a valid waiver order, petitioner was entitled to a hearing, including access by his counsel to the social records and probation or similar reports which presumably are considered by the

23. Cf. Harling v. United States, 111 U.S.App.D.C. 174, 177, 295 F.2d 161, 164 (1961).

24. See Handler, op.cit. supra, note 20; Note, supra, note 19; materials cited in note 5, supra.

25. See brief of *amicus curiae*. 16–2313, 11–1586 (Supp. IV, 1965).

court, and to a statement of reasons for the Juvenile Court's decision. We believe that this result is required by the statute read in the context of constitutional principles relating to due process and the assistance of counsel. . . .

Ordinarily we would reverse the Court of Appeals and direct the District Court to remand the case to the Juvenile Court for a new determination of waiver. If on remand the decision were against waiver, the indictment in the District Court would be dismissed. However, petitioner has now passed the age of 21 and the Juvenile Court can no longer exercise jurisdiction over him. In view of the unavailability of a redetermination of the waiver question by the Juvenile Court, it is urged by petitioner that the conviction should be vacated and the indictment dismissed. In the circumstances of this case, and in light of the remedy which the Court of Appeals fashioned in Black, supra, we do not consider it appropriate to grant this drastic relief. Accordingly, we vacate the order of the Court of Appeals and the judgment of the District Court and remand the case to the District Court for a hearing *de novo* on waiver, consistent with this opinion. If that court finds that waiver was inappropriate, petitioner's conviction must be vacated. If, however, it finds that the waiver order was proper when originally made, the District Court may proceed, after consideration of such motions as counsel may make and such further proceedings, if any, as may be warranted, to enter an appropriate judgment.

Reversed and remanded.[1]

MR. JUSTICE STEWART, with whom MR. JUSTICE BLACK, MR. JUSTICE HARLAN and MR. JUSTICE WHITE join, dissenting.

This case involves the construction of a statute applicable only to the District of Columbia. Our general practice is to leave undisturbed decisions of the Court of Appeals for the District of Columbia Circuit concerning the import of legislation governing the affairs of the District. It appears, however, that two cases decided by the Court of Appeals subsequent to its decision in the present case may have considerably modified the court's construction of the statute. Therefore, I would vacate this judgment and remand the case to the Court of Appeals for reconsideration in the light of its subsequent

1. [Added by Compiler.] A minor, **H**, charged with murder and three assaults with intent to commit murder, sought a writ of mandate to direct the juvenile court to vacate its order certifying him to the superior court as a person not amenable to care and treatment available through the juvenile court. The certification had been based solely upon a doubt as to the constitutionality of the statute giving the Youth Authority power to detain a juvenile beyond his 21st birthday. The writ was issued because this was not a proper ground for the certification. The juvenile court was directed to reconsider **H**'s amenability to treatment as a juvenile, considering the crime alleged to have been committed, the circumstances and details surrounding its commission, **H**'s behavior pattern including his past record of delinquency, if any, his degree of sophistication as related to criminal activities and contradictory opinion testimony. Jimmy H. v. Superior Court of L.A. Co., 3 Cal.3d 709, 91 Cal.Rptr. 600, 478 P.2d 32 (1970).

decisions, Watkins v. United States, 119 U.S.App.D.C. 409, 343 F.2d 278, and Black v. United States, 122 U.S.App.D.C. 393, 355 F.2d 104.

APPLICATION OF GAULT

Supreme Court of the United States, 1967.
387 U.S. 1, 87 S.Ct. 1428.

[Gerald Gault, age fifteen, was taken into custody by the sheriff on the complaint of a woman who said Gerald and another boy had annoyed her with a lewd telephone call. He was taken to the Children's Detention Home. When his mother reached there she was told by a probation officer that a hearing would be held in the Juvenile Court the next day, at 3 P.M., but was not told what the specific charge would be. At the hearing, held by the Juvenile Judge in chambers, the woman who had made the complaint did not appear; no one was sworn; no transcript or recording was made; and the boy was questioned by the judge without being advised of his right to be represented by counsel or to remain silent. There was conflicting testimony as to which boy had actually spoken over the phone, but as it was a joint venture this seems not to have been significant. At a second hearing about a week later the procedure was similar. A request that the complaining party be present was denied. The probation officer's statement of what she had told him over the phone was deemed sufficient. At the conclusion of the hearing the judge committed Gerald as a juvenile delinquent to the State Industrial School "for the period of his minority [that is until 21] unless sooner discharged by due process of law." Had he been 18 the maximum punishment would have been two months.

In a habeas corpus proceeding it was claimed that the Arizona juvenile code was unconstitutional on its face and as applied to Gerald. Due process was claimed to have been violated because of the denial of (1) notice of charges, (2) right to counsel, (3) right to confrontation and cross-examination, (4) privilege against self-incrimination, (5) right to a transcript of the proceedings, and (6) right to appellate review. The Court disposed of the case without reaching the problem of appellate review.]

MR. JUSTICE FORTAS delivered the opinion of the Court. . . .

We do not in this opinion consider the impact of these constitutional provisions upon the totality of the relationship of the juvenile and the state. We do not even consider the entire process relating to juvenile "delinquents." For example, we are not here concerned with the procedures or constitutional rights applicable to the prejudicial stages of the juvenile process, nor do we direct our attention to the post-adjudicative or dispositional process. We consider only the problems presented to us by this case. These relate to the proceedings by which a determination is made as to whether a juvenile is a "delinquent" as a result of alleged misconduct on his part, with the consequence that he may be committed to a state institution. As to these proceedings, there appears to be little current dissent from the proposition that the Due Process Clause has a role to play.[11] The problem is to ascertain the precise impact of the due process requirement upon such proceedings. . . .

The history and theory underlying this development are well-known, but a recapitulation is necessary for purposes of this opinion. The Juvenile Court movement began in this country at the end of the last century. From the juvenile court statute adopted in Illinois in 1899, the system has spread to every State in the Union, the District of Columbia, and Puerto Rico.[14] The constitutionality of juvenile court laws has been sustained in over 40 jurisdictions against a variety of attacks.[15]

The early reformers were appalled by adult procedures and penalties, and by the fact that children could be given long prison sentences and mixed in jails with hardened criminals. They were profoundly convinced that society's duty to the child could not be confined by the concept of justice alone. They believed that society's role was not to ascertain whether the child was "guilty" or "innocent," but "What is he, how has he become what he is, and what had best be done in his interest and in the interest of the state to save him from a downward career." [16] The child—essentially good, as they saw it—was to be made "to feel that he is the object of [the state's]

11. See Report by the President's Commission on Law Enforcement and Administration of Justice. "The Challenge of Crime in a Free Society" (1967) (hereinafter cited as Nat'l Crime Comm'n Report), pp. 81, 85–86; Standards, p. 71; Gardner, The Kent Case and the Juvenile Court: A Challenge to Lawyers, 52 A.B.A.J. 923 (1966); Paulsen, Fairness to the Juvenile Offender, 41 Minn.L.Rev. 547 (1957); Ketcham, The Legal Renaissance in the Juvenile Court, 60 Nw.U.L.Rev. 585 (1965); Allen, The Borderland of Criminal Justice (1964), pp. 19–23; Harvard Law Review Note, p. 791; Note, Rights and Rehabilitation in the Juvenile Courts, 67 Col.L.Rev. 281 (1967); Comment, Criminal Offenders in the Juvenile Court: More Brickbats and Another Proposal, 114 U.Pa.L.Rev. 1171 (1966).

14. See National Council of Juvenile Court Judges, Directory and Manual (1964), p. 1. The number of Juvenile Judges as of 1964 is listed as 2,987, of whom 213 are full-time Juvenile Court Judges. Id., at 305. The Nat'l Crime Comm'n Report indicates that half of these judges have no undergraduate degree, a fifth have no college education at all, a fifth are not members of the bar, and three-quarters devote less than one-quarter of their time to juvenile matters. See also McCune, Profile of the Nation's Juvenile Court Judges (monograph, George Washington University, Center for the Behavioral Sciences, 1965), which is a detailed statistical study of Juvenile Court Judges, and indicates additionally that about a quarter of these judges have no law school training at all. About one-third of all judges have no probation and social work staff available to them; between eighty and ninety percent have no available psychologist or psychiatrist. Ibid. It has been observed that while "good will, compassion, and similar virtues are . . . admirably prevalent throughout the system . . . expertise, the keystone of the whole venture, is lacking." Harvard Law Review Note, p. 809. In 1965, over 697,000 delinquency cases (excluding traffic) were disposed of in these courts, involving some 601,000 children, or 2% of all children between 10 and 17. Juvenile Court Statistics—1965, Children's Bureau Statistical Series No. 85 (1966), p. 2.

15. See Paulsen, Kent v. United States: The Constitutional Context of Juvenile Cases, 1966 Sup.Ct.Review 167, 174.

16. Julian Mack, The Juvenile Court, 23 Harv.L.Rev. 104, 119–120 (1909).

care and solicitude," [17] not that he was under arrest or on trial. The rules of criminal procedure were therefore altogether inapplicable. The apparent rigidities, technicalities, and harshness which they observed in both substantive and procedural criminal law were therefore to be discarded. The idea of crime and punishment was to be abandoned. The child was to be "treated" and "rehabilitated" and the procedures, from apprehension through institutionalization, were to be "clinical" rather than punitive.

These results were to be achieved, without coming to conceptual and constitutional grief, by insisting that the proceedings were not adversary, but that the state was proceeding as *parens patriae*.[18] The Latin phrase proved to be a great help to those who sought to rationalize the exclusion of juveniles from the constitutional scheme; but its meaning is murky and its historic credentials are of dubious relevance. The phrase was taken from chancery practice, where, however, it was used to describe the power of the state to act *in loco parentis* for the purpose of protecting the property interests and the person of the child.[19] But there is no trace of the doctrine in the history of criminal jurisprudence. At common law, children under seven were considered incapable of possessing criminal intent. Beyond that age, they were subjected to arrest, trial, and in theory to punishment like adult offenders.[20] In these old days, the state was not deemed to have authority to accord them fewer procedural rights than adults.

The right of the state, as *parens patriae*, to deny to the child procedural rights available to his elders was elaborated by the assertion that a child, unlike an adult, has a right "not to liberty but to custody." He can be made to attorn to his parents, to go to school, etc. If his parents default in effectively performing their custodial functions—that is, if the child is "delinquent"—the state may intervene. In doing so, it does not deprive the child of any rights, because he has none. It merely provides the "custody" to which the child is entitled.[21] On this basis, proceedings involving juveniles were de-

17. Id., at 120.

18. Id., at 109; Paulsen, op.cit. supra, n. 15, at 173–174. There seems to have been little early constitutional objection to the special procedures of juvenile courts. But see Waite, How Far Can Court Procedure Be Socialized Without Impairing Individual Rights, 12 J.Crim.L. & Criminology, 339, 340 (1922): "The court which must direct its procedure even apparently to do something *to* a child because of what he *has done*, is parted from the court which is avowedly concerned only with doing something *for* a child because of what he *is* and *needs*, by a gulf too wide to be bridged by any humanity which the judge may introduce into his hearings, or by the habitual use of corrective rather than punitive methods after conviction."

19. Paulsen, op.cit. supra, n. 15, at 173; Hurley, Origin of the Illinois Juvenile Court Law in the Child, the Clinic, and the Court (1925), pp. 320, 328.

20. Julian Mack, The Chancery Procedure in the Juvenile Court, in the Child, the Clinic, and the Court (1925), p. 310.

21. See, e.g., Shears, Legal Problems Peculiar to Children's Courts, 48 A.B.A.J. 719, 720 (1962) ("The basic right of a juvenile is not to liberty but to custody. He has the right to have someone take care of him, and if his parents do not afford him this custodial privilege, the law must do so."); Ex parte Crouse, 4 Whart.

scribed as "civil" not "criminal" and therefore not subject to the requirements which restrict the state when it seeks to deprive a person of his liberty.[22]

Accordingly, the highest motives and most enlightened impulses led to a peculiar system for juveniles, unknown to our law in any comparable context. The constitutional and theoretical basis for this peculiar system is—to say the least—debatable. And in practice, as we remarked in the *Kent* case, supra, the results have not been entirely satisfactory.[23]

It is claimed that juveniles obtain benefits from the special procedures applicable to them which more than off-set the disadvantages of denial of the substance of normal due process. As we shall discuss, the observance of due process standards, intelligently and not ruthlessly administered, will not compel the States to abandon or displace any of the substantive benefits of the juvenile process. . . . Further, we are told that one of the important benefits of the special juvenile court procedures is that they avoid classifying the juvenile as a "criminal." The juvenile offender is now classed as a "delinquent." There is, of course, no reason why this should not continue. . . .

In any event, there is no reason why, consistently with due process, a State cannot continue if it deems it appropriate, to provide and to improve provision for the confidentiality of records of police contacts and court action relating to juveniles. . . .

Further, it is urged that the juvenile benefits from informal proceedings in the court. The early conception of the Juvenile Court proceeding was one in which a fatherly judge touched the heart and conscience of the erring youth by talking over his problems, by paternal advice and admonition, and in which, in extreme situations, benevolent and wise institutions of the State provided guidance and help

9, 11 (Sup.Ct.Pa.1839); Petition of Ferrier, 103 Ill. 367, 371–373 (1882).

22. The Appendix to the opinion of Judge Prettyman in Pee v. United States, 107 U.S.App.D.C. 47, 274 F.2d 556 (1959), lists authority in 51 jurisdictions to this effect. Even rules required by due process in civil proceedings, however, have not generally been deemed compulsory as to proceedings affecting juveniles. For example, constitutional requirements as to notice of issues, which would commonly apply in civil cases, are commonly disregarded in juvenile proceedings, as this case illustrates.

23. "There is evidence . . . that there may be grounds for concern that the child receives the worst of both worlds: that he gets neither the protections accorded to adults nor the solicitous care and regenerative treatment postulated for children." 383 U.S., at 556, 86 S.Ct., at 1054, citing Handler, The Juvenile Court and the Adversary System: Problems of Function and Form, 1965 Wis.L.Rev. 7; Harvard Law Review Note; and various congressional materials set forth in 383 U.S., at 546, 86 S.Ct., at 1050, n. 5.

On the other hand, while this opinion and much recent writing concentrate upon the failures of the Juvenile Court system to live up to the expectations of its founders, the observation of the Nat'l Crime Comm'n Report should be kept in mind:

"Although its shortcomings are many and its results too often disappointing, the juvenile justice system in many cities is operated by people who are better educated and more highly skilled, can call on more and better facilities and services, and has more ancillary agencies to which to refer its clientele than its adult counterpart." Id., at 78.

"to save him from a downward career." [36] Then, as now, goodwill and compassion were admirably prevalent. But recent studies have, with surprising unanimity, entered sharp dissent as to the validity of this gentle conception. They suggest that the appearance as well as the actuality of fairness, impartiality and orderliness—in short, the essentials of due process—may be a more impressive and more therapeutic attitude so far as the juvenile is concerned. For example, in a recent study, the sociologists Wheeler and Cottrell observe that when the procedural laxness of the "*parens patriae*" attitude is followed by stern disciplining, the contrast may have an adverse effect upon the child, who feels that he has been deceived or enticed. They conclude as follows: "Unless appropriate due process of law is followed, even the juvenile who has violated the law may not feel that he is being fairly treated and may therefore resist the rehabilitative efforts of court personnel." [37] . . .

We cannot agree with the court's conclusion that adequate notice was given in this case. Notice, to comply with due process requirements, must be given sufficiently in advance of scheduled court proceedings so that reasonable opportunity to prepare will be afforded, and it must "set forth the alleged misconduct with particularity." [52] . . . The juvenile needs counsel to cope with problems of law, to make skilled inquiry into the facts, to insist upon regularity of the proceedings, and to ascertain whether he has a defense and to prepare and submit it. The child "requires the guiding hand of counsel at every step in the proceedings against him." . . .

We conclude that the Due Process Clause of the Fourteenth Amendment requires that in respect of proceedings to determine delinquency which may result in commitment to an institution in which the juvenile's freedom is curtailed, the child and his parents must be notified of the child's right to be represented by counsel retained by them, or if they are unable to afford counsel, that counsel will be appointed to represent the child. . . .

It would be entirely unrealistic to carve out of the Fifth Amendment all statements by juveniles on the ground that these cannot lead to "criminal" involvement. In the first place, juvenile proceedings to determine "delinquency," which may lead to commitment to a state institution, must be regarded as "criminal" for purposes of the privi-

36. Mack, The Juvenile Court, 23 Harv.L.Rev. 104, 120 (1909).

37. Juvenile Delinquency—Its Prevention and Control (Russell Sage Foundation, 1966), p. 33. The conclusion of the Nat'l Crime Comm'n Report is similar: "[T]here is increasing evidence that the informal procedures, contrary to the original expectation, may themselves constitute a further obstacle to effective treatment of the delinquent to the extent that they engender in the child a sense of injustice provoked by seemingly all-powerful and challengeless exercise of authority by judges and probation officers." Id., at 85. See also Allen, The Borderland of Criminal Justice (1964), p. 19.

52. Nat'l Crime Comm'n Report, p. 87. The Commission observed that "The unfairness of too much informality is . . . reflected in the inadequacy of notice to parents and juveniles about charges and hearings." Ibid.

lege against self-incrimination. To hold otherwise would be to disregard substance because of the feeble enticement of the "civil" label-of-convenience which has been attached to juvenile proceedings. . . .

We conclude that the constitutional privilege against self-incrimination is applicable in the case of juveniles as it is with respect to adults. We appreciate that special problems may arise with respect to waiver of the privilege by or on behalf of children, and that there may well be some differences in technique—but not in principle—depending upon the age of the child and the presence and competence of parents. The participation of counsel will, of course, assist the police, Juvenile Courts and appellate tribunals in administering the privilege. If counsel was not present for some permissible reason when an admission was obtained, the greatest care must be taken to assure that the admission was voluntary, in the sense not only that it was not coerced or suggested, but also that it was not the product of ignorance of rights or of adolescent fantasy, fright or despair.[96] . . .

No reason is suggested or appears for a different rule in respect of sworn testimony in juvenile courts than in adult tribunals. Absent a valid confession adequate to support the determination of the Juvenile Court, confrontation and sworn testimony by witnesses available for cross-examination were essential for a finding of "delinquency" and an order committing Gerald to a state institution for a maximum of six years. . . .

For the reasons stated, the judgment of the Supreme Court of Arizona is reversed and the cause remanded for further proceedings not inconsistent with this opinion. It is so ordered.

Judgment reversed and cause remanded with directions.

[MR. JUSTICE HARLAN dissented in part. MR. JUSTICE STEWART filed a vigorous dissent, arguing that juvenile proceedings are not "adversary." They are, he maintained, for the "correction of a condition", not "punishment for a criminal act."]

96. The N.Y. Family Court Act § 744(b) provides that "an uncorroborated confession made out of court by a respondent is not sufficient" to constitute the required "preponderance of the evidence."

See United States v. Morales, 233 F.Supp. 160 (D.C.Mont.1964), holding a confession inadmissible in proceedings under the Federal Juvenile Deliquency Act (18 U.S.C. § 5031 et seq.) because, in the circumstances in which it was made, the District Court could not conclude that it "was freely made while Morales was afforded all of the requisites of due process required in the case of a sixteen year old boy of his experience." Id., at 170.

[Added by the Compiler.]

In a later case the Court held that the constitutional safeguard of proof beyond a reasonable doubt is as much required during the adjudicatory stage of a delinquency proceeding as are those constitutional safeguards applied in *Gault*—notice of charges, right to counsel, the rights of confrontation and examination, and the privilege against self-incrimination. In re Winship, 397 U.S. 358, 90 S.Ct. 1068 (1970).

PEOPLE v. ROPER

Court of Appeals of New York, 1932.
259 N.Y. 170, 181 N.E. 88.

LEHMAN, J. A little before two o'clock in the morning of January 20th, 1931, two youths or men, with handkerchiefs covering their faces and armed with pistols, entered a negro restaurant on Seventh avenue in New York city. At the point of the pistol, one of them compelled the people in the restaurant to go to the rear and took some money from their persons. The same youth shot and killed William Groce, a customer of the restaurant. The other bandit took money from the cash register. Then both escaped. . . .

The trial was conducted with eminent fairness, and we find no reversible error in the admission or exclusion of evidence or in the charge, if the case was tried and submitted to the jury on the proper theory. Perhaps there may be doubt as to Thorp's identification of the defendant. On that question the defendant has had a fair trial, and none of his substantial rights have been infringed by excess of zeal or fault of police, prosecuting attorney or trial judge. A majority of the court, at least, find that the verdict of the jury is not against the weight of evidence upon the issue presented to the jury. We confine discussion in this opinion to the question whether the jury's finding of guilt on these issues supports the defendant's conviction of the crime of murder in the first degree.

Thorp's testimony establishes that a negro, whom he identified as the defendant on trial, shot and killed William Groce while he and another negro were engaged in taking money at the point of a pistol from the cash register of the restaurant and from the persons of those who were present in the restaurant. The defendant's age at the time of the homicide was not determined in the manner provided by section 817 of the Penal Law. Upon the preliminary examination of the jurors, the assistant district attorney stated to them: "The defendant Louis Roper at the time of the alleged commission of the crime by him was between fifteen and sixteen years of age." Testimony that the defendant was under the age of sixteen was uncontradicted. The case was tried and submitted to the jury upon the assumption that the fact that the defendant was at the time of the homicide under the age of sixteen carries no legal consequences in a trial for murder in the first degree. We are called upon to test the validity of that assumption in this case.

Only a child under the age of seven years is incapable as matter of law of committing a crime (Penal Law, § 816), though a child "of the age of seven years, and under the age of twelve years, is presumed to be incapable of crime, but the presumption may be removed by proof that he had sufficient capacity to understand" (§ 817). Even so, not every act or omission which, if committed by an adult, would be a crime, is a crime when committed by a child, for the Legislature has expressly decreed that "a child of more than seven and less than sixteen years of age, who shall commit any act or omission which, if committed by an adult, would be a crime not punishable by death or life imprisonment, shall not be deemed guilty of any crime, but of juvenile delinquency" (Penal Law, § 2186).[1] Murder in the first degree is punishable by death. Therefore, it is clear that a child of fifteen may be guilty of the crime of murder in the first degree. When guilt of a crime has been established, its penal consequences are the same for child and adult criminal. But guilt cannot be established without proof of every essential element of the crime and, since a felonious intent is an essential element of the crime of murder, guilt of a defendant can never be established without proof of such intent. Thus, the guilt of a defendant charged with murder in the first degree may depend upon his capacity to form the felonious intent. Then the fact that a defendant is under the age of sixteen may carry legal consequences.

"There can be no murder without evidence of malice and of a felonious intent and a depraved mind. The indictment was sufficient in form when it simply accused defendant of having killed the deceased 'willfully, feloniously and with malice aforethought.' On the trial it was necessary to prove such malice and willful and felonious conduct, and this necessity was satisfied in accordance with the provisions of the statute by showing that the homicide occurred while the defendant was engaged in the commission of another felony." (People v. Nichols, 230 N.Y. 221, 226, 129 N.E. 883.)

Here, as in that case, the conviction rests upon a finding of the jury that a human being was killed by a person "engaged in the commission of another felony." True, the evidence is sufficient to support a finding that the homicide was committed by the defendant "from a deliberate and premeditated design to effect the death of the person killed," and a homicide committed in that way also would constitute murder in the first degree (Penal Law, § 1044) and might be proven under an indictment in common-law form. The jury, if such question had been presented to it, might have found that the defendant formed such a deliberate design, though under the age of sixteen; but the jury here made no such finding, for no such question was presented to it. If the trial judge in his charge had left that question to the jury, he would have been bound to charge on the degrees of homicide, and the jury would have been free to find a verdict of guilt

1. In 1967 the New York law was amended to read: "A person less than 16 years old is not criminally responsible for conduct." N.Y.Rev.Pen.Code § 30.00.

A statute providing a special penalty for an assault committed by an "adult male," upon a female or a child, refers to one of the "full age of twenty-one years." State v. Henderson, 34 Ariz. 430, 272 P. 97 (1928).

The statute gives exclusive jurisdiction of cases involving noncapital crimes to the juvenile court. If the indictment charges one under 18 with murder the district court had jurisdiction and did not lose jurisdiction by accepting a plea of murder in the second degree. State ex rel. Hinkle v. Skeen, 138 W.Va. 116, 75 S.E.2d 223 (1953), certiorari denied 345 U.S. 967, 73 S.Ct. 954 (1953). And see Hinkle v. Skeen, 117 F.Supp. 846 (1954).

in lesser degree than murder in the first degree. He chose to do otherwise. He charged the jurors that they were concerned only with the question of whether a human being was killed during the commission of a felony in which the defendant was a guilty participant, and that their verdict must be either guilty of murder in first degree or not guilty. . . .

The charge of the trial judge was fair and accurate, if the defendant's participation was with felonious intent. The crime of murder charged in the indictment is a single crime, whether committed by design or during the commission of an independent felony; "the independent felony like the deliberate and premeditated intent, being established solely for the purpose of characterizing the degree of the crime so charged, the evil mind or purpose inherent in the killing." (People v. Lytton, 257 N.Y. 310, 315, 178 N.E. 290.) The defendant may have participated in the robbery; but unless that participation was with felonious intent he was not guilty of the felony, and if he was not guilty of the independent felony, participation does not evince "the evil mind or purpose inherent in the killing." (See People v. Koerber, 244 N.Y. 147, 155 N.E. 79.)

Sometimes a spirit of innocent mischief, sometimes evil associations, not of his own choice but forced upon him by family conditions, impel a child under the age of sixteen to commit acts which constitute felonies as defined by law. The State has adopted a humane policy in its treatment of a child under the age of sixteen who commits such acts. It does not, upon proof of guilt, fasten upon him the ineffaceable stain of conviction of guilt of a felony, nor subject him to imprisonment with adult offenders. For the child's benefit, as well as for the benefit of the State, it treats a child who commits acts which, if committed by an adult would constitute a felony, not punishable by death or life imprisonment, merely as a juvenile delinquent, an unfortunate ward of the State rather than a criminal. The law, in its mercy, demands that a child should be subject to such correction as may tend to remove the causes which have led the child to commit acts inimical to society; where it might demand that an adult committing the same acts should be visited with punishment of deterrent effect.

Doubtless at times the causes which have led a child into "juvenile delinquency" are too deep-seated to be removed by such corrective treatment as the State now offers. Perhaps at times "innate depravity" is more than a fiction. The Penal Law is not concerned with such abstractions. It decrees that the acts of a child shall, in all cases other than acts constituting a felony punishable by death or life imprisonment, be treated as if done without the "evil mind" which characterizes felonious intent, and each child must be given the opportunity to benefit by corrective treatment though he be unable or unwilling to avail himself of the benefit. The law does not say that a criminal under the age of sixteen is not subject to punishment for a crime; it says that proof of acts which would establish guilt of crime if committed by an older person does not establish the guilt of a child under the age of sixteen years, of any crime, but only of juvenile delinquency.

These considerations must lead to a reversal in this case. The defendant can be convicted of murder in the first degree only upon a finding of "felonious intent." The verdict of the jury imports a finding that the defendant participated in the commission of a robbery, as defined by the statute, for the trial judge charged that without such finding the verdict must be not guilty. Upon the trial of a defendant over the age of sixteen years a finding of participation in a robbery, as defined by the statute, would import a finding of "felonious intent;" for robbery, in every degree, is a felony. Upon the trial of a child under the age of sixteen the participation of a child in a robbery, or at least in a robbery in the second or third degrees, would not establish the guilt of a felony but only of a minor offense characterized as juvenile delinquency. Hence, it is plain that the defendant's conviction rests upon no finding of guilt of a felony and thus no finding of felonious intent, and the judgment must be reversed. (People v. Moran, supra.) That is true even though no exception was taken to the charge which raises such question. A child under sixteen can be guilty of murder in the first or second degrees where he kills a man with felonious intent, but such felonious intent is not established without both proof and finding of intent to kill or of *guilt of an independent felony* during which the homicide occurred. . . .

Thus at the present time, even if not at the time of the original trial, proof that a child under the age of sixteen years participated in a robbery in the first degree cannot establish the child's guilt of a felony. Change in the punishment for that crime has the indirect result of removing the crime of robbery in the first degree from the category of crimes of which a child can be guilty if it ever was within that category. The effect is the same as if the Legislature had expressly declared that no child under the age of sixteen years can be guilty of robbery in any degree, and that upon the trial of such child for murder in the first degree, "felonious intent" may not be predicated upon guilt of robbery. In the absence of a clause excluding from its provisions offenses previously committed, the law as amended applies in all trials held thereafter, even for offenses previously committed.

Upon the new trial this defendant may be tried for murder in the first or second degrees committed through the killing of a human being with intent to effect his death. Such an action may be impelled by "evil mind" and felonious intent as evidenced by the criminal acts of the child, but not by acts which the Legislature has declared are not criminal when committed by a child. A person who with evil mind commits a crime may, in the interests of society, be punished even by death for the undesigned and unforeseen result of the crime. No person, certainly no child under the age of sixteen, is subject to death or life imprisonment because of the calamitous though undesigned result of acts which are not criminal in their inception.

The judgment of conviction should be reversed and a new trial ordered.

POUND, CH. J., CRANE, KELLOGG, O'BRIEN and HUBBS, JJ., concur.

Judgment reversed, etc.[2]

(Reargument denied 259 N.Y. 635, 182 N.E. 213.)

McKEIVER v. PENNSYLVANIA

Supreme Court of the United States, 1971.
403 U.S. 528, 91 S.Ct. 1976.

[Joseph McKeiver, age 16, was accused of robbery, larceny and receiving stolen goods. Although these are felonies under Pennsylvania law, they were not charged as such but as acts of juvenile deliquency in a juvenile court proceeding. Another boy, age 15, was charged with acts of juvenile delinquency in the form of assault and battery and conspiracy (misdemeanors). In separate proceedings, in each of which counsel's request for a jury trial had been denied, the boys were found to be juvenile delinquents. The Supreme Court of Pennsylvania consolidated the cases for the purpose of appeal, the sole question being "whether there is a constitutional right to a jury trial in juvenile court." The answer was "no" and the Supreme Court noted probable jurisdiction. This was case No. 322.

Case No. 128 was a North Carolina case in which children ranging in age from 11 to 15 had been declared to be delinquent by the juvenile court which placed them on probation for one or two years. The juvenile court had excluded the public from these proceedings, over counsel's objection, and had denied counsel's request for a jury trial.

2. A juvenile may be declared a ward of the court (1) if he needs care because of home conditions or medical deficiencies (West's Ann.Cal.Welf. & Inst.Code, § 600, (2) if found to be destitute or neglected, but without criminal conduct (id. at § 601) or (3) for the commission of a crime (id. at § 602). If the child is under 14, and the commission of a crime is relied upon to give the juvenile court jurisdiction, it must be found that there is clear proof that he possessed knowledge of the wrongfulness of his act. If the child under 14 did not appreciate the wrongfulness of his act, he did not commit a crime, (West's Cal.Pen.Code, § 26) and hence his conduct does not give the juvenile court jurisdiction under § 602. In re Gladys R., 1 Cal.3d 581, 83 Cal. Rptr. 671, 464 P.2d 127 (1970). § 600 has since been repealed, see West's Ann.Cal. Welf. & Inst.Code, § 300 (1976).

The statute empowered the court to seal the records of arrest in certain cases with the result that the arrest should be regarded as not having occurred, so the person could be permitted to answer that he had not been arrested. According this benefit to juveniles and not to adults is not arbitrary or capricious. Nor is it arbitrary or capricious to accord it to minors arrested for a misdemeanor but not to minors arrested for felony. But it does deny equal protection to accord it to a minor arrested for felony and convicted of a misdemeanor, but deny it to a minor who was arrested for felony but released without any formal charge having been filed against him. Mahon v. Municipal Court of Burbank Dist. Ct., 6 Cal.App.3d 194, 85 Cal.Rptr. 782 (1970).

The judgment of the juvenile court was affirmed by the Supreme Court of North Carolina and the Supreme Court granted certiorari and considered the two cases together.]

MR. JUSTICE BLACKMUN announced the judgment of the Court and an opinion in which THE CHIEF JUSTICE, MR. JUSTICE STEWART, and MR. JUSTICE WHITE join.

These cases present the narrow but precise issue whether the Due Process Clause of the Fourteenth Amendment assures the right to trial by jury in the adjudicative phase of a state juvenile court delinquency proceeding. . . .

1. Some of the constitutional requirements attendant upon the state criminal trial have equal application to that part of the state juvenile proceeding that is adjudicative in nature. Among these are the rights to appropriate notice, to counsel, to confrontation and to cross-examination, and the privilege against self-incrimination. Included, also, is the standard of proof beyond a reasonable doubt.

2. The Court, however, has not yet said that *all* rights constitutionally assured to an adult accused of crime also are to be enforced or made available to the juvenile in his delinquency proceeding. Indeed, the Court specifically has refrained from going that far:

"We do not mean by this to indicate that the hearing to be held must conform with all of the requirements of a criminal trial or even of the usual administrative hearing; but we do hold that the hearing must measure up to the essentials of due process and fair treatment."

3. The Court, although recognizing the high hopes and aspirations of Judge Julian Mack, the leaders of the Jane Addams School and the other supporters of the juvenile court concept, has also noted the disappointments of the system's performance and experience and the resulting widespread disaffection. *Kent*, 383 U.S., at 555–556, 86 S.Ct., at 1054–1055; *Gault*, 387 U.S., at 17–19, 87 S.Ct., at 1438–1439. There have been, at one and the same time, both an appreciation for the juvenile court judge who is devoted, sympathetic, and conscientious, and a disturbed concern about the judge who is untrained and less than fully imbued with an understanding approach to the complex problems of childhood and adolescence. There has been praise for the system and its purposes, and there has been alarm over its defects.

4. The Court has insisted that these successive decisions do not spell the doom of the juvenile court system or even deprive it of its "informality, flexibility or speed." *Winship*, 397 U.S., at 366–367, 90 S.Ct., at 1073–1074. On the other hand, a concern precisely to the opposite effect was expressed by two dissenters in *Winship*. 397 U.S., at 375–376, 90 S.Ct., at 1078–1079. . . .

We must recognize, as the Court has recognized before, that the fond and idealistic hopes of the juvenile court proponents and early reformers of three generations ago have not been realized. The devastating commentary upon the system's failures as a whole, contained in the Task Force Report: Juvenile Delinquency and Youth Crime (President's Commission on Law Enforcement and the Administration of Justice (1967)), pp. 7–9, reveals the depth of disappointment in what has been accomplished. Too often the juvenile court judge falls far short of that stalwart, protective and communicating figure the system envisaged.[4] The community's unwillingness to provide people and facilities and to be concerned, the insufficiency of time devoted, the scarcity of professional help, the inadequacy of dispositional alternatives, and our general lack of knowledge all contribute to dissatisfaction with the experiment.[5]

The Task Force Report, however, also said, page 7, "To say that juvenile courts have failed to achieve their goals is to say no more than what is true of criminal courts in the United States. But failure is most striking when hopes are highest."

Despite all these disappointments, all these failures, and all these shortcomings, we conclude that trial by jury in the juvenile court's adjudicative stage is not a constitutional requirement. We so conclude for a number of reasons:

1. The Court has refrained, in the cases heretofore decided, from taking the easy way with a flat holding that all rights constitutionally assured for the adult accused are to be imposed upon the state juvenile proceeding. . . .

2. There is a possibility, at least, that the jury trial, if required as a matter of constitutional precept, will remake the juvenile proceeding into a fully adversary process and will put an effective end to

4. "A recent study of juvenile court judges . . . revealed that half had not received undergraduate degrees; a fifth had received no college education at all; a fifth were not members of the bar." Task Force Report, p. 7.

5. "What emerges, then, is this: In theory the juvenile court was to be helpful and rehabilitative rather than punitive. In fact the distinction often disappears, not only because of the absence of facilities and personnel but also because of the limits of knowledge and technique. In theory the court's action was to affix no stigmatizing label. In fact a delinquent is generally viewed by employers, schools, the armed services—by society generally—as a criminal. In theory the court was to treat children guilty of criminal acts in noncriminal ways. In fact it labels truants and runaways as junior criminals.

"In theory the court's operations could justifiably be informal, its findings and decisions made without observing ordinary procedural safeguards, because it would act only in the best interest of the child. In fact it frequently does nothing more nor less than deprive a child of liberty without due process of law—knowing not what else to do and needing, whether admittedly or not, to act in the community's interest even more imperatively than the child's. In theory it was to exercise its protective powers to bring an errant child back into the fold. In fact there is increasing reason to believe that its intervention reinforces the juvenile's unlawful impulses. In theory it was to concentrate on each case the best of current social science learning. In fact it has often become a vested interest in its turn, loathe to cooperate with innovative programs or avail itself of forward-looking methods." Task Force Report, p. 9.

what has been the idealistic prospect of an intimate, informal protective proceeding.

3. The Task Force Report, . . . expressly recommends against abandonment of the system and against the return of the juvenile to the criminal courts.[6]

4. The Court specifically has recognized by dictum that a jury is not a necessary part even of every criminal process that is fair and equitable.

5. The imposition of the jury trial on the juvenile court system would not strengthen greatly, if at all, the fact-finding function, and would, contrarily, provide an attrition of the juvenile court's assumed ability to function in a unique manner. It would not remedy the defects of the system. Meager as has been the hoped-for advance in the juvenile field, the alternative would be regressive, would lose what has been gained, and would tend once again to place the juvenile squarely in the routine of the criminal process.

6. The juvenile concept held high promise. We are reluctant to say that, despite disappointments of grave dimensions, it still does not hold promise, and we are particularly reluctant to say, as do the Pennsylvania petitioners here, that the system cannot accomplish its rehabilitative goals. So much depends on the availability of resources, on the interest and commitment of the public, on willingness to learn, and on understanding as to cause and effect and cure. In this field, as in so many others, one perhaps learns best by doing. We are reluctant to disallow the States further to experiment and to seek in new and different ways the elusive answers to the problems of the young, and we feel that we would be impeding that experimentation by imposing the jury trial. The States, indeed, must go for-

6. "Nevertheless, study of the juvenile courts does not necessarily lead to the conclusion that the time has come to jettison the experiment and remand the disposition of children charged with crime to the criminal courts of the country. As trying as are the problems of the juvenile courts, the problems of the criminal courts, particularly those of the lower courts, which would fall heir to much of the juvenile court jurisdiction, are even graver; and the ideal of separate treatment of children is still worth pursuing. What is required is rather a revised philosophy of the juvenile court based on the recognition that in the past our reach exceeded our grasp. The spirit that animated the juvenile court movement was fed in part by a humanitarian compassion for offenders who were children. That willingness to understand and treat people who threaten public safety and security should be nurtured, not turned aside as hopeless sentimentality, both because it is civilized and because social protection itself demands constant search for alternatives to the crude and limited expedient of condemnation and punishment. But neither should it be allowed to outrun reality. The juvenile court is a court of law charged like other agencies of criminal justice with protecting the community against threatening conduct. Rehabilitating offenders through individualized handling is one way of providing protection, and appropriately the primary way in dealing with children. But the guiding consideration for a court of law that deals with threatening conduct is nonetheless protection of the community. The juvenile court, like other courts, is therefore obliged to employ all the means at hand, not excluding incapacitation, for achieving that protection. What should distinguish the juvenile from the criminal courts is greater emphasis on rehabilitation, not exclusive preoccupation with it." Task Force Report, p. 9.

ward. If, in its wisdom, any State feels the jury trial is desirable in all cases, or in certain kinds, there appears to be no impediment to its installing a system embracing that feature. That, however, is the State's privilege and not its obligation.

7. Of course there have been abuses. The Task Force Report has noted them. We refrain from saying at this point that those abuses are of constitutional dimension. They relate to the lack of resources and of dedication rather than to inherent unfairness.

8. There is, of course, nothing to prevent a juvenile court judge, in a particular case where he feels the need, or when the need is demonstrated, from using an advisory jury.

9. "The fact that a practice is followed by a large number of states is not conclusive in a decision as to whether that practice accords with due process, but it is plainly worth considering in determining whether the practice 'offends some principle of justice so rooted in the traditions and conscience of our people as to be ranked as fundamental.'" It therefore is of more than passing interest that at least 29 States and the District of Columbia by statute deny the juvenile a right to a jury trial in cases such as these. The same result is achieved in other States by judicial decision. In 10 States statutes provide for a jury trial under certain circumstances.

10. Since *Gault* and since *Duncan* the great majority of States, in addition to Pennsylvania and North Carolina, that have faced the issue have concluded that the considerations that led to the result in those two cases do not compel trial by jury in the juvenile court.

. . .

12. If the jury trial were to be injected into the juvenile court system as a matter of right, it would bring with it into that system the traditional delay, the formality and the clamor of the adversary system and, possibly, the public trial. . . .

If the formalities of the criminal adjudicative process are to be superimposed upon the juvenile court system, there is little need for its separate existence. Perhaps that ultimate disillusionment will come one day, but for the moment we are disinclined to give impetus to it.

Affirmed.

[MR. JUSTICE HARLAN concurred in the judgments in these cases because he disagrees with the theory that the constitution requires a jury in any state criminal trial in which a jury would be required in a comparable federal case. In his opinion jury trials are not required in a state criminal case either by the Sixth Amendment or by due process.

MR. JUSTICE BRENNAN seems to be of opinion that a juvenile in a juvenile court proceeding may be denied either a jury or a public hearing, but not both. Hence he concurred in the judgment in No. 322 but dissented in No. 128.

JUSTICES DOUGLASS, BLACK and MARSHALL dissented in both on the theory that appellants should have been entitled to a jury trial in both cases.] [a]

DAVIS v. ALASKA

Supreme Court of the United States, 1974.
415 U.S. 308, 94 S.Ct. 1105.

[The state statute, section 47.10.080(g), provides that the commitment of a juvenile, and the evidence given in the juvenile court "are not admissible against the minor in a subsequent case or proceedings in any other court." Based upon this statute the trial judge in a burglary trial refused to permit defense counsel, on cross-examination, to bring out the fact that a key prosecution witness, Green, was himself on probation following adjudication of juvenile delinquency relating to burglary.]

MR. CHIEF JUSTICE BURGER delivered the opinion of the Court.

We granted certiorari in this case to consider whether the Confrontation Clause requires that a defendant in a criminal case be allowed to impeach the credibility of a prosecution witness by cross-examination directed at possible bias deriving from the witness' probationary status as juvenile delinquent when such an impeachment would conflict with a State's asserted interest in preserving the confidentiality of juvenile adjudications of delinquency. . . .

(2)

The Sixth Amendment to the Constitution guarantees the right of an accused in a criminal prosecution "to be confronted with the witnesses against him." This right is secured for defendants in state as well as federal criminal proceedings under Pointer v. Texas, 380 U.S. 400, 85 S.Ct. 1065, 13 L.Ed.2d 923 (1965). Confrontation means more than being allowed to confront the witness physically. "Our cases construing the [confrontation] clause hold that a primary interest secured by it is the right of cross-examination." Douglas v. Alabama, 380 U.S. 415, 418, 85 S.Ct. 1074, 1076, 13 L.Ed.2d 934 (1965). Professor Wigmore stated:

"The main and essential purpose of confrontation is *to secure for the opponent the opportunity of cross-examination.* The opponent demands confrontation, not for the idle purpose of gazing upon the witness, or of being gazed upon by him, but for the purpose of cross-examination, which cannot be had except by the direct and personal putting of questions and obtaining immediate answers." (Emphasis

a. See Rosenberg, Constitutional Rights of Children Charged With Crime, 27 U.C.La.L.Rev. 656 (1980).

A juvenile court adjudication will operate to invoke double jeopardy protection. Breed v. Jones, 421 U.S. 519, 95 S.Ct. 1779 (1975).

in original.) 5 J. Wigmore, Evidence § 1395, p. 123 (3d ed. 1940). . . .

(3)

The claim is made that the State has an important interest in protecting the anonymity of juvenile offenders and that this interest outweighs any competing interest this petitioner might have in cross-examining Green about his being on probation. The State argues that exposure of a juvenile's record of delinquency would likely cause impairment of rehabilitative goals of the juvenile correctional procedures. This exposure, it is argued, might encourage the juvenile offender to commit further acts of delinquency, or cause the juvenile offender to lose employment opportunities or otherwise suffer unnecessarily for his youthful transgression.

We do not and need not challenge the State's interest as a matter of its own policy in the administration of criminal justice to seek to preserve the anonymity of a juvenile offender. Here, however, petitioner sought to introduce evidence of Green's probation for the purpose of suggesting that Green was biased and, therefore, that his testimony was either not to be believed in his identification of petitioner or at least very carefully considered in that light. Serious damage to the strength of the State's case would have been a real possibility had petitioner been allowed to pursue this line of inquiry. In this setting we conclude that the right of confrontation is paramount to the State's policy of protecting a juvenile offender. Whatever temporary embarrassment might result to Green or his family by disclosure of his juvenile record—if the prosecution insisted on using him to make its case—is outweighed by petitioner's right to probe into the influence of possible bias in the testimony of a crucial identification witness. . . .

The State's policy interest in protecting the confidentiality of a juvenile offender's record cannot require yielding of so vital a constitutional right as the effective cross-examination for bias of an adverse witness. The State could have protected Green from exposure of his juvenile adjudication in these circumstances by refraining from using him to make out its case; the State cannot, consistent with the right of confrontation, require the petitioner to bear the full burden of vindicating the State's interest in the secrecy of juvenile criminal records. The judgment affirming petitioner's convictions of burglary and grand larceny is reversed and the case is remanded for further proceedings not inconsistent with this opinion.

It is so ordered.

Reversed and remanded.[1] . . .

(WHITE and REHNQUIST, JJ., dissented.)

1. A statute providing that a juvenile court record shall not be used as evidence "against such child," does not bar the use of such evidence against him af-

MODEL PENAL CODE[2]

Section 4.10 Immaturity Excluding Criminal Conviction; Transfer of Proceedings to Juvenile Court.

(1) A person shall not be tried for or convicted of an offense if:

(a) at the time of the conduct charged to constitute the offense he was less than sixteen years of age, [in which case the Juvenile Court shall have exclusive jurisdiction *]; or

(b) at the time of the conduct charged to constitute the offense he was sixteen or seventeen years of age, unless:

(1) the Juvenile Court has no jurisdiction over him, or,

(2) the Juvenile Court has entered an order waiving jurisdiction and consenting to the institution of criminal proceedings against him.

(2) No court shall have jurisdiction to try or convict a person of an offense if criminal proceedings against him are barred by subsection (1) of this section. When it appears that a person charged with the commission of an offense may be of such an age that criminal proceedings may be barred under subsection (1) of this section, the Court shall hold a hearing thereon, and the burden shall be on the prosecution to establish to the satisfaction of the Court that the criminal proceeding is not barred upon such grounds. If the Court determines that the proceeding is barred, custody of the person charged shall be surrendered to the Juvenile Court, and the case, including all papers and processes relating thereto, shall be transferred.

Section 6.05 Young Adult Offenders.

(1) Specialized Correctional Treatment. A young adult offender is a person convicted of a crime who, at the time of sentencing, is sixteen but less

ter he has reached his majority. The purpose of the statute is to protect a child from the stigma of his wrongdoing in his effort to rehabilitate himself. When he is no longer a child and has demonstrated by his conviction that he has not been rehabilitated there is no reason to preclude the use of his juvenile record for the purpose of fixing his sentence. Mitchell v. Gladden, 229 Or. 192, 366 P.2d 907 (1961).

In considering the penalty issue the court may consider **D**'s juvenile court record. People v. Terry, 61 Cal.2d 137, 144 (note 3), 37 Cal.Rptr. 605, 390 P.2d 381 (1964); People v. Reeves, 64 Cal.2d 766, 51 Cal.Rptr. 691, 415 P.2d 35 (1966); State v. Manning, 149 Mont. 517, 429 P.2d 625 (1967).

The Pennsylvania statute bars the use of a juvenile court record as evidence in a criminal case to determine guilt or innocence but does not bar its use for the determination of sentence. Commonwealth ex rel. Hendrickson v. Myers, 393 Pa. 224, 144 A.2d 367 (1958); United States ex rel. Jackson v. Myers, 374 F.2d 707 (3d Cir.1967).

When a juvenile court record is used in a pre-sentence report to the judge it is not being used as "evidence". State v. Fierro, 101 Ariz. 118, 416 P.2d 551 (1966).

A sentencing court's consideration of a convicted adult offender's juvenile record does not violate due process. People v. Berry, 117 Cal.App.3d 184, 172 Cal.Rptr. 756 (1981).

2. Copyright: 1962 by the American Law Institute. Reprinted with the permission of the American Law Institute.

* The bracketed words are unnecessary if the Juvenile Court Act so provides or is amended accordingly.

than twenty-two years of age. A young adult offender who is sentenced to a term of imprisonment which may exceed thirty days [alternatives: (1) ninety days; (2) one year] shall be committed to the custody of the Division of Young Adult Correction of the Department of Correction, and shall receive, as far as practicable, such special and individualized correctional and rehabilitative treatment as may be appropriate to his needs.

(2) Special Term. A young adult offender convicted of a felony may, in lieu of any other sentence of imprisonment authorized by this Article, be sentenced to a special term of imprisonment without a minimum and with a maximum of four years, regardless of the degree of the felony involved, if the Court is of the opinion that such special term is adequate for his correction and rehabilitation and will not jeopardize the protection of the public.

[(3) Removal of Disabilities; Vacation of Conviction.

(a) In sentencing a young adult offender to the special term provided by this Section or to any sentence other than one of imprisonment, the Court may order that so long as he is not convicted of another felony, the judgment shall not constitute a conviction for the purposes of any disqualification or disability imposed by law upon conviction of a crime.

(b) When any young adult offender is unconditionally discharged from probation or parole before the expiration of the maximum term thereof, the Court may enter an order vacating the judgment of conviction.]

[(4) Commitment for Observation. If, after presentence investigation, the Court desires additional information concerning a young adult offender before imposing sentence, it may order that he be committed, for a period not exceeding ninety days, to the custody of the Division of Young Adult Correction of the Department of Correction for observation and study at an appropriate reception or classification center. Such Division of the Department of Correction and the [Young Adult Division of the] Board of Parole shall advise the Court of their findings and recommendations on or before the expiration of such ninety-day period.]

THE AMERICAN LAW INSTITUTE

YOUTH CORRECTION AUTHORITY ACT [1]

Introductory Explanation

Youthful offenders are an especially serious factor in the crime problem of the country. Young people between fifteen and twenty-one years of age constitute only 13 per cent. of our population above fifteen, but their share in the total amount of serious crime committed far exceeds their proportionate representation. Though but 13 per cent. of the population, they are responsible for approximately 26

1. Portions of the Introductory Explanation are included here by permission of The American Law Institute and Professor John B. Waite, Reporter.

per cent. of our robberies and thefts; they constitute some 40 per cent. of our apprehended burglars and nearly half of our automobile thieves. Boys from seventeen to twenty are arrested for major crimes in greater numbers than persons of any other four-year group. They come into court, not for petty offenses but for serious crime, twice as often as adults of thirty-five to thirty-nine; three times as often as those of forty-five to forty-nine; five times as often as men of fifty to fifty-nine. Nineteen-year-olds offend more frequently than persons of any other age, with eighteen-year-olds next. Moreover the proportion of youths less than twenty-one in the whole number of persons arrested has increased by 15 per cent. during the past three years; 108,857 not yet old enough to vote were arrested and fingerprinted last year.

But these figures, appalling as they are, paint only a part of the picture. A tremendous proportion of adult criminality has its inception in conviction of crime before the age of twenty-one. Every study that has ever been made indicates that if the known criminals between sixteen and twenty-one years old—those young persons actually convicted and dealt with in the courts—had somehow been prevented by that conviction from continuing a course of crime, the country's total burden of offenses would be a small fraction of what it is. The criminality of youth is an evil not limited by the boundaries of youth. It projects its social damage far into the years of maturity. If and when we manage to check the criminal propensities of any youth we shall decrease the occurrence of crime now and in the future. Youth is in this sense the focal source of the country's crime burden and is, therefore, the focus upon which crime prevention efforts must wisely be centered.

This peculiar necessity for dealing wisely and effectively with youthful wrongdoers does not of course negative the importance of proper treatment of adult offenders. Concededly the public requires adequate protection from both. And a preventive process that is effective with boys of twenty should have at least a modicum of success with men of twenty-two or forty-two. But changes in established procedures to be feasible under given conditions must often be gradual. In view of certain practical requirements of the processes set up by this proposed Act the wisdom of building slowly will be apparent as the Act is studied. Hence because of the peculiar advantages to be gained through improvement in the treatment of youthful wrongdoers especially, the Act, as a beginning, is confined in its application to youth. The age of twenty-one rather than that of twenty or twenty-two is admittedly arbitrary, but is chosen because it is the traditional end of the period of minority in the law of this country.

All crime prevention efforts, whether dealing with youth or maturity, are one or the other of two general types. On the one hand they may seek to eliminate, or ameliorate, or redirect the external conditions which impel people toward the commission of crime. Thus one crime prevention agency may strive to reduce the miseries of poverty; another to make less easily obtainable the wherewithal for intoxication. Of the other type are those activities designed to operate directly upon the individual himself and to influence his personal reaction to conditions. This proposed statute will operate upon the individual, not upon external conditions. It is not offered as a substitute for efforts to prevent crime by improvement of conditions. Neither does its advocacy depreciate in any way the activities of other agencies. It is designed to begin operation after other crime prevention activities have failed and to help strengthen resistance to criminal impulses by direct operation upon individuals.

Traditionally the criminal law has relied upon punishment and the threat of punishment as the only method of building up resistance to criminal inclinations. But with increasing knowledge of the causes of human action has come a general realization that reliance upon "punishment" as the only means of control is logically unsound. Moreover, as a practical matter, punishment as the primary method of control is not only logically unsound but obviously ineffective. It is not a satisfactory means of social protection against crime because it does not sufficiently prevent crime.

In the first place the threat of punishment does not notably prevent the commission of first offenses. As a matter of record there is now one man in jail for every 225 men over sixteen years of age who are free. And of course a great many of those who are free have previously been in jail or eventually will be in jail. Hence criminologists estimate that one or two out of every hundred males sooner or later commit a crime serious enough to call for imprisonment, undeterred by threat of punishment. . . .

Reasons for this failure are not difficult to find. Science now recognizes the existence of numerous "psychopathic personalities" whose courses of action cannot conceivably be affected by mere prospect or even experience of consequences such as the criminal law imposes. With some of them, indeed, the possible consequence, perverted in their conceptions, is an inducement rather than a deterrent. Still other people may be driven to crime by physical abnormalities whose impulsive force punishment, as such, makes no pretense of diminishing and cannot effectively counteract. More serious a defect than anything else, "punishment" takes no account whatever of the causal conditions of crime, but eventually returns its victims to social freedom not one whit better equipped than before to cope with the same necessities, incapacities, and desires to whose pressure they previously yielded.

These are negative faults in the punitive method. Even more dangerous are its positive evils. If it merely did not reform, it might be merely useless. But its worst influence is no mere innocuous failure to prevent crime; there is cogent reason to believe that it creates crime. By herding youth with maturity, the novice with the sophisticate, the impressionable with the hardened; by giving opportunity for dissemination of evil not counteracted by the prophylaxis of normal contacts; our penitentiaries actively spread the infection of crime. The penal system fosters, not checks, the plague. Small wonder therefore that punishment alone has so completely failed of its purpose. . . .

It was this unsatisfactory state of affairs which led the Institute to authorize the drafting of model statutes dealing with the treatment of youthful offenders. The Youth Correction Authority Act which is here presented for consideration is the first of two such statutes prepared. It relates only to the treatment of persons after conviction. It leaves the processes of arrest, accusation and trial unaffected. Its operation begins only after conviction and alters only post-conviction procedures.

The proposals of the Act are by no means radical. On the contrary, almost every detail of it is already the accepted law, or the approved practice, in one or more states. The Act as a whole is novel, however, because it frankly and specifically departs from the merely punitive ideas of dealing with convicted criminals and sets up the objective of rehabilitation. It is designed to protect the public from repeated crime; first, by safe segregation of dangerous persons so long as segregation is necessary; second, by such treatment of individual wrongdoers as is calculated to increase the probability that they will refrain from crime thereafter.

To these ends the Act creates a central state commission—called in the Act a Youth Correction Authority—which is invested with carefully limited and safeguarded powers to set up appropriate agencies and to determine the proper treatment for each youth committed to it by the courts. The membership of this commission and the details of its powers are discussed in connection with the various sections of the Act. Judges are left with a wide discretion as to whether they will sentence convicted youths to the custody and control of this commission or not. But no youth can merely be committed to prison. The judge of any court, except a juvenile court, before whom a youth is convicted, unless he discharges the youth or sentences him to payment of a fine only, must commit him to the Correction Authority to be dealt with by it as the statute authorizes. The Authority is given power to decide what treatment he shall be subjected to. And to the end that the treatment shall be most effective and most economically administered the Authority is authorized, within limits, to use, and thereby to bring into co-operative activity, all the facilities of the state. This is one of the most interesting features of the Act. It provides for a unified program of correctional treatment in contrast with the prevailing practice of having a variety of agencies—probation departments, parole departments, county jails and state institutions—concerned at different times in uncoordinated effort to deal with an offender.

This Act does not affect the jurisdiction or authority of existing juvenile courts. The theory upon which those courts are established is essentially the theory of this proposed Act; i.e., that corrective treatment of young persons, with segregation when necessary, is a more effective preventive of repeated crime than any mere punishment could be.

On the other hand, it seems undesirable to extend the scope of juvenile court activity to the older youths who are covered by this Act. Those courts utilize an informality of procedure wholly unsuited to the trial of older youths accused of serious crime. Moreover, there are undeniable physical and mental differences between the children, the "juveniles," with whom juvenile courts are designed to deal and the "youths" between juvenile court age and twenty-one with whose proper treatment this Act is concerned. Treatments which are sufficient when applied to children of fourteen or fifteen might be woefully inadequate for hardened young men of nineteen or twenty. Yet it would be utterly impractical to expect any juvenile court judge to administer, or even to select, treatments needed by the older youths as he selects them for children. Moreover the intermingling of juveniles and older youths which would normally result from a mere extension of juvenile court jurisdiction would be harmful. Hence, though juvenile court procedure and the proposed Act rest upon the same fundamental theories, each has its own appropriate place and the two should not be combined.

The upper age limit of juvenile court jurisdiction varies in different states. However, while in many states juvenile courts deal with delinquents over sixteen, in practice they rarely deal with youths charged with serious offenses over that age. Possibly in some states the upper age limit of the juvenile court is too high and the line of demarcation between the scope of the Act and the powers of the juvenile court will not fall in the wisest place. If this be thought true in any particular state the juvenile court law can be amended by the legislature.

Neither are the provisions of this proposed Act inconsistent with present practices and establishments relating to probation and parole. The Act extends, for reasons which have been already stated, only to persons less than twenty-one years old at the time of their apprehension. The use of probation or parole in respect to persons over twenty-one who commit crime is therefore entirely unaffected. So far as youthful offenders are concerned, the use of probation by order of criminal court judges is terminated, though it is still available to juvenile court judges. But this does not mean that probation will not be used for youths. On the contrary, it is conceivable that its use will be even more frequent; the only difference being that under the Act

orders for probation—as well as for the equivalent of parole—will be made by the Correction Authority, instead of by the trial judge or parole board.

In summation, then, this proposed Act is neither a radical departure from existing law, nor even basically novel. On the contrary, it is merely a synthesis of the theories and practices which have already been given widespread acceptance and approval, and is designed to improve public protection against crime by effective utilization of scientific knowledge and modern methods.[1]

John B. Waite,
Reporter.

SECTION 2. MENTAL DISEASE OR DEFECT (INSANITY)

The problem of insanity may become important at various points in a criminal case. The *first* is at the time of the alleged crime. Insanity of the defendant at the time of the *actus reus,* if of such character and degree as to negative criminal responsibility, will entitle him to an acquittal. The *second* point is at the time set for arraignment. If the mind of one accused of crime by indictment or information is so disordered by mental disease that he is unable to understand the charge against him, and to plead intelligently thereto, he should not be permitted to plead until his reason is restored. This problem is similar to the next and can be considered therewith. The *third* point is at the time set for trial,—or during the trial.[1] Mental disorder at this time has nothing to do with the issue of guilt or innocence (except to the extent that it may have some tendency to indicate what his mental condition was at the time of the harmful deed). But one whose mental condition is now so disordered that he is unable to understand the charge against him, and possible defenses thereto, and hence is unable properly to advise with his counsel in regard to the conduct of the trial, ought not to be tried now,—whatever his mental condition may have been at the time of the alleged crime. Hence upon such a finding the defendant is committed to

1. See Proposals for Sentencing and Treatment of the Young Adult Offender under the Model Penal Code: Paul W. Tappan, Tentative Draft No. 3 (1955). See also Criminal Justice—Youth, Proposed Final Draft No. 1 (Youth Correction Authority Act) 15 (1940). And see the companion draft, prepared by the American Law Institute, Criminal Justice—Youth, Proposed Final Draft No. 2 (Youth Court Act) (1940).

1. "One might not be insane in the sense of being incapable of standing trial and yet lack the capacity of standing trial without the benefit of counsel". Massey v. Moore, 348 U.S. 105, 108, 75 S.Ct. 145, 147, 99 L.Ed. 135 (1954).

An insane person cannot plead to an indictment, be subjected to trial, have judgment pronounced against him or undergo punishment, but a valid indictment may be found against him although no further proceedings can be had at the time. Frye v. Settle, 168 F.Supp. 7 (D.C.Mo. 1958).

Amnesia does not per se render a defendant unable to stand trial or receive a fair trial. State v. Gilder, 223 Kan. 220, 574 P.2d 196 (1977); Commonwealth v. Barky, 476 Pa. 602, 383 A.2d 526 (1978); United States v. Mota, 598 F.2d 995 (5th Cir.1979).

some proper hospital. He is to remain there until his reason is restored, at which time he is to be returned to the court for trial. If he is to be committed beyond a reasonable time, it is necessary to resort to regular commitment procedure.[1a]

The *fourth* point is at the time of allocution (when the defendant is asked by the judge, after a verdict or plea of guilty, if he knows of any reason why judgment should not be pronounced against him). In the words of Blackstone: "If, after he be tried and found guilty, he loses his senses before judgment, judgment shall not be pronounced . . . : for peradventure, says the humanity of the English law, had the prisoner been of sound memory, he might have alleged something in stay of judgment . . . ." (4 Bl.Comm. 24–25). A finding of insanity at this point requires a commitment of the defendant to a proper hospital until he regains his reason. He is then to be returned for sentence.

The *fifth* point is at the time of execution.[2] At common law this probably was limited to the execution of a sentence of death, but it is to be remembered that all felonies were capital at common law. In any event he must not be put to death while out of his mind, for if he had his reason he might be able to allege something in stay of execution.

Quite apart from a criminal case, it may be added, one who is mentally disordered to such an extent as to be a menace to himself, or to others, may be committed to a proper hospital until and unless his reason is restored. This, however, is not our present problem. As a matter of logic this section is concerned only with the first point mentioned although it will be convenient to extend the inquiry somewhat beyond this.

The nature and extent of mental disorder which will entitle the defendant to an acquittal, constitutes the outstanding problem in this

1a. Jackson v. Indiana, 406 U.S. 715, 92 S.Ct. 1845 (1972).

Where a defendant is acquitted on the grounds of insanity he may be committed pending a determination that he has regained his sanity and may be kept beyond the period for which defendant may have been kept had the defendant been convicted. The defendant's insanity must be established by a preponderance of evidence and due process standards must be satisfied in determining the need for commitment. Jones v. United States, ___ U.S. ___, 103 S.Ct. 3043 (1983).

2. One under sentence of death asked the governor to postpone execution on the ground that he had become insane after conviction. Under authority of a state statute the governor appointed three doctors who examined the convict and declared him sane. In denying relief in habeas corpus proceedings the court held that this procedure was not a denial of due process under the Fourteenth Amendment. Solesbee v. Balkcom, 339 U.S. 9, 70 S.Ct. 457 (1950). In another case in which responsibility for determining the prisoner's sanity was vested in the prison warden rather than the governor, the warden's determination being based on reports of the prison psychiatrists, there was also held to be no denial of due process. Caritativo v. California, 357 U.S. 549, 78 S.Ct. 1263, 2 L.Ed.2d 1531 (1958).

The use of a sanity commission, rather than a jury, to determine whether **D** is competent to stand trial does not violate his right to a jury trial. Commonwealth v. Bruno, 435 Pa. 200, 255 A.2d 519 (1969).

branch of the law of insanity. No distinction is made, in this inquiry, between *dementia* and *amentia.* The point here is not whether the person once had a sound mind which has deteriorated as a result of disease or injury, or was mentally deficient from birth. The sole determinant is the nature and extent of the mental abnormality. It must be emphasized that the phrase "mental disease" is employed in a very broad sense in the criminal law.[2a] Any serious mental disorder or abnormality resulting from mental disease, physical disease, physical injury or congenital deficiency often will be placed loosely under the label "mental disease." This is because the consequences of all are the same, so far as the law of crimes is concerned. At times some other phrase has been used such as "mental disease or defect." This is more precise, but it is important to keep in mind that the term "mental disease" often is used in the cases to cover the entire field.

Similarly, the phrase "insanity or idiocy" [2b] may be more precise, as a label for this department of the law, than the single word "insanity." The essential need is to distinguish deviational mental conditions due to disease, injury or congenital defect, from excitement or stupefaction resulting from intoxicating liquor or drugs. Simple labels are helpful, and the two departments are usually designated respectively as (1) "insanity" and (2) "intoxication." Only the first of these is under consideration here, but before going farther it is necessary to say more about the word "insanity" itself. It has other differences of meaning entitled to attention. At times it is used to refer to the mental condition of one who is "out of his head" from whatever cause. Thus "moral insanity" [3] has been used at times to refer to one who wilfully let his passions go until they carried him to a state of fury; and "drunken insanity" has been employed occasionally to indicate an extreme condition of intoxication. Neither of these comes within the scope of this section and it would be wise to substitute some other form of expression for the word "insanity" to convey any such idea. If this is done, and the word is accepted as broad enough to include congenital defect as well as mental disease proper, there are still two different meanings of "insanity." In one sense, any serious mental disease or defect is spoken of as "insanity," as in the sentence: "The kind and degree of insanity available as a defense to

2a. Arteriosclerosis affecting the defendant's mental functions raises a M'Naghten issue. R. v. Kemp, [1957] 1 Q.B. 399. Compulsive gambling isn't a mental disease for insanity defense purposes. United States v. Lewellyn, 723 F.2d 615 (8th Cir. 1983). Testimony on the effects of television in support of defendant's claim of "involuntary subliminal television intoxication" is not relevant on the issue of insanity. Zamora v. State, 361 So.2d 776 (Fla.App.1978).

2b. "We are of the opinion that for purposes of criminal responsibility, there is no legal difference between insanity and lunacy." State v. Billhymer, 114 Ariz. 390, 561 P.2d 311, 313 (1977). See also, In re Ramon M., 22 Cal.3d 419, 149 Cal.Rptr. 387, 584 P.2d 524 (1978).

3. "Moral insanity" should be reserved for mental disease which affects primarily the conative functions, tending toward certain compulsions with no apparent loss of perception or intelligence.

crime has many times been defined by the decisions of this court." [4] In the other sense the word "insanity" is used to express that kind and degree of mental disease or defect which establishes criminal incapacity (or contractual incapacity or testamentary incapacity or whatever the particular issue may be). The latter usage, while perhaps unfortunate, cannot be ignored because the word is found frequently in the statutes with that signification. If the two meanings are kept clearly in mind the context usually will indicate which is to be understood in the particular sentence.

While it is accepted that mental disease or defect may be so extreme as to negate criminal responsibility we do not have uniformity as to the type of disorder required for this purpose.

"M'Naghten's Case".[5] Daniel M'Naghten, who had killed Edward Drummond mistaking him for Sir Robert Peel, was found "not guilty by reason of insanity." The case was so clear on the facts that it would have been soon forgotten had it not been for a peculiar aftermath. Since the intended victim had been Sir Robert Peel there was great public excitement and the House of Lords put certain questions to the judges. The answers of the judges, given in the House of Lords, were published in connection with M'Naghten's Case and any mention of that case today has reference not to the trial of M'Naghten but to these answers of the judges. The answer of chief significance was to the effect that a defendant is not entitled to a "defence on the ground of insanity" unless at the time he "was labouring under such a defect of reason, from disease of the mind, as not to know the nature and quality of the act he was doing; or, if he did know it, that he did not know he was doing what was wrong." This is the so-called "right-wrong" test of insanity, or the "M'Naghten rule."

With reference to a question concerning an insane delusion the judges answered: "To which question the answer must of course depend on the nature of the delusion: but, making the same assumption as we did before, namely, that he labours under such partial delusion only, and is not in other respects insane, we think he must be considered in the same situation as to responsibility as if the facts with respect to which the delusion exists were real." There was also a question as to procedure, but with reference to the substantive law the two answers above are often referred to as the "M'Naghten rules." [6]

4. People v. Gilberg, 197 Cal. 306, 313, 240 P. 1000, 1003 (1925). See also: "Before the jury can acquit the prisoner on the ground of insanity, they must believe . . . that his insanity was of such character . . . ." Fisher v. People, 23 Ill. 283, 285 (1860).

5. 10 Clark & F. 200, 8 Eng.Rep. 718 (H.L.1843).

6. One who has been acquitted on the ground of insanity is entitled to be released, if he is sane now, although the evidence shows he has the same mental condition now that he had at the time of the harmful deed. Yankulov v. Bushong, 80 Ohio App. 497, 77 N.E.2d 88 (1945).

California Penal Code Secs. 1026, 1026.2 (1980), provide that one acquitted

One interesting question in this general field is this: Can evidence of some kind or grade of mental disorder, insufficient for an acquittal, be sufficient to call for conviction of a lower grade or degree of crime than would otherwise be proper? There is a trace of authority for a negative answer. Thus it has been held that mental disorder not amounting to "legal insanity" cannot negative deliberation and premeditation and thus reduce the homicide from first to second-degree murder.[7] The rule in several jurisdictions, however, is that such mental disorder may negative deliberation and premeditation,[8] leaving the question whether it may be sufficient to rule out malice aforethought. Several jurisdictions apply a rule that a mental disorder short of insanity that precludes the defendant from entertaining the required state of mind will reduce a charge to a lesser offense requiring a less demanding state of mind.[9]

STATE v. SMITH

Supreme Court of Vermont, 1978.
136 Vt. 520, 396 A.2d 126.

Before BARNEY, C.J., and DALEY, LARROW, BILLINGS, and HILL, JJ.

BARNEY, CHIEF JUDGE.

This is a prosecution for the rape of a sixteen year old babysitter and the murder of her charge, her eight year old cousin. As is so frequent in cases involving serious criminal violence, sanity is a critical issue. It is the principal concern of the appeal.

The killing is conceded, both below and here, and no issues separately contesting the rape conviction are urged here. No extended recital of facts is required. The defendant was twenty-one years old at the time of these events. The evidence disclosed that the defend-

on the ground of insanity may be confined in a state hospital for a minimum period of 90 days pending a hearing on whether he should be released to society. This is valid because this time is needed to determine if he has recovered his reason. After that period he is entitled to a full jury hearing on the question of sanity. In re Franklin, 7 Cal.3d 126, 101 Cal. Rptr. 553, 496 P.2d 465 (1972).

7. Fisher v. United States, 328 U.S. 463, 66 S.Ct. 1318 (1946).

"[U]nless psychiatric testimony is introduced for the purpose of showing insanity under the M'Naghten Rule, (a) *it is admissible only after guilt has been determined by a jury or Court, and (b) is relevant and admissible thereafter only for the limited purpose of aiding the jury or Court in fixing the penalty.*" Commonwealth v. Rightnour, 435 Pa. 104, 253 A.2d 644, 649 (1969).

"We hold, therefore, that the partial defense of diminished capacity is not recognized in Ohio and consequently, a defendant may not offer expert psychiatric testimony, unrelated to the insanity defense. . . . " State v. Wilcox, 70 Ohio St.2d 182, 436 N.E.2d 523, 533 (1982).

8. Disease of the mind, insufficient for acquittal, can prevent one from truly deliberating and from being capable of a deliberate premeditation necessary for guilt of first-degree murder. State v. Padilla, 66 N.M. 289, 347 P.2d 312 (1959).

9. "Therefore, although the State did not adopt Section 4.02 of the Model Penal Code, basic rules of evidence require that a defendant have the right to adduce evidence which would tend to disprove the existence of specific intent." State v. Sessions, 645 P.2d 643 (Utah 1982).

ant, after finding out that the babysitter was alone with her charge, went to the apartment and was admitted by the little boy while the babysitter was on the telephone. He explained his presence by claiming he had permission to borrow some records from the little boy's mother. Shortly thereafter he assaulted the babysitter and the rape occurred. Afterwards the defendant attempted to strangle the boy with a cord, then finally killed him by stabbing him with a large knife he got from the kitchen. When that happened the babysitter grabbed for the knife, cutting her hand, succeeding in knocking the defendant down, and escaped. As she ran into the street he apparently threw the knife at her but missed. The babysitter fled to a neighbor's and when the police arrived the defendant was gone. When the identity of the defendant became known, the foster family with whom he was living was contacted. He was later brought by one of them to the police station.

Almost simultaneously with the issuance of the warrant and before arraignment, the State moved for a mental examination in anticipation of a plea of insanity. That motion asserted that the defendant had a history of treatment for personality disorders at Metropolitan State Hospital in Waltham, Massachusetts; New Hampshire Hospital in Concord, New Hampshire; and Waterbury State Hospital in Waterbury, Vermont. The motion was granted at the arraignment and the examination undertaken.

The test of responsibility for criminal conduct is set out in 13 V.S.A. § 4801:

> The test when used as a defense in criminal cases shall be as follows:
>
> (1) A person is not responsible for criminal conduct if at the time of such conduct as a result of mental disease or defect he lacks adequate capacity either to appreciate the criminality of his conduct or to conform his conduct to the requirements of law.
>
> (2) The terms "mental disease or defect" do not include an abnormality manifested only by repeated criminal or otherwise antisocial conduct. The terms "mental disease or defect" shall include congenital and traumatic mental conditions as well as disease. . . .

There remains only the claim that the trial court should have charged on what is coming to be known as "diminished capacity." This issue was before the trial court and may occur on retrial, therefore it is appropriate for review on this appeal.

Contrary to the position taken by the State, our cases do not limit the application of the "diminished capacity" doctrine to the use of intoxicants. Rather, the matter of intoxication has been noted as one area of its application, where supported by appropriate facts.

The concept is directed at the evidentiary duty of the State to establish those elements of the crime charged requiring a conscious mental ingredient. There is no question that it may overlap the insanity defense in that insanity itself is concerned with mental conditions so incapacitating as to totally bar criminal responsibility. The distinction is that diminished capacity is legally applicable to disabilities not amounting to insanity, and its consequences, in homicide cases, operate to reduce the degree of the crime rather than to excuse its commission. Evidence offered under this rubric is relevant to prove the existence of a mental defect or obstacle to the presence of a state of mind which is an element of the crime, for example: premeditation or deliberation.

Since these states of mind are neither complex nor difficult to achieve, aside from special instances involving drugs, alcohol, injury or emotional frenzy, the issue frequently tends to reduce itself to situations involving lack of mental capacity itself.

For the purposes of the matter before us it is sufficient to say that where the evidence in any form supports it, a request to charge on the jury's duty to determine the existence of the states of mind required to establish the particular crime at issue in the light of any diminished capacity should be carefully reviewed by the trial court, and if appropriate, given.[1]

Reversed and remanded.

1. The California court apparently took the lead in developing the concept of diminished capacity. Thus it held "that evidence of mental infirmity, not amounting to legal insanity, is admissible and should be considered by the jury on the questions of premeditation and deliberation." People v. Baker, 42 Cal.2d 550, 569, 268 P.2d 705, 716 (1954). This means that even if defendant is not entitled to an acquittal, he may be guilty of only second-degree murder. Later it was held that by reason of diminished capacity defendant might have been unable to harbor malice aforethought, and hence be guilty of manslaughter rather than murder. People v. Henderson, 60 Cal.2d 482, 35 Cal.Rptr. 77, 386 P.2d 677 (1963). Still later this was carefully explained. "Even intentional killings can be mitigated to voluntary manslaughter if the killing occurred with sufficient provocation to arouse a reasonable man to a fit of passion or sudden quarrel or if the defendant did not attain the mental state of malice due to mental illness, mental defect or intoxication." People v. Burton, 6 Cal.3d 375, 385, 99 Cal.Rptr. 1, 7, 491 P.2d 793 (1971).

This did not meet the approval of the California legislature which recently enacted section 28 to the Penal Code, which provides:

> (a) Evidence of mental disease, mental defect, or mental disorder shall not be admitted to negate the capacity to form any mental state, including, but not limited to, purpose, intent, knowledge, or malice aforethought, with which the accused committed the act. Evidence of mental disease, mental defect, or mental disorder is admissible on the issue as to whether the criminal defendant actually formed any such mental state.
>
> (b) As a matter of public policy there shall be no defense of diminished capacity, diminished responsibility, or irresistible impulse in a criminal action.

If this statute withstands a constitutional attack it means that diminished capacity will no longer be recognized in a criminal case in California, but that will not affect other states in which it has been recognized. See, The Relevance of Innocence: Proposition 8 and The Diminished Capacity Defense, 71 Cal.L.Rev. 1197 (1983).

DAVIS v. STATE

Supreme Court of Tennessee, 1930.
161 Tenn. 23, 28 S.W.2d 993.

MR. CHIEF JUSTICE GREEN delivered the opinion of the Court.

The plaintiff in error was indicted for killing one L.R. Noe and convicted of murder in the second degree. . . .

The case was tried at length and submitted to the jury. After some deliberation, the jury returned to the courtroom and reported in substance that they found that the defendant below was insane on the subject of the relations between his late wife and Noe, but they further found that he knew the difference between right and wrong, and they asked the court what, under such circumstances, they should do.

In response, the court read to the jury a part of his charge previously given them and added some further instructions. The court rejected the contention that, if by reason of mental disease, the will power of the defendant below was so impaired, he was unable to resist the impulse to kill Noe, he would not be guilty, although he could distinguish between right and wrong as to the particular act.

(1) The charge of the court was to the effect that although plaintiff in error acted under an irresistible impulse produced by an insane delusion he would still be guilty if he could distinguish between right and wrong and knew that it was wrong to kill Noe.

Counsel contend that there may be a mental disease destroying the faculty of volition, of choosing, as well as a mental disease destroying the faculty of perception, and that either condition would relieve defendant of criminal accountability.

The court refused to recognize as a defense destroyed volition, even as a result of mental disease, apart from destroyed perception.

This difference between counsel for the defendant below and the trial judge is with respect to a matter upon which the courts of the country are divided. Irresistible impulse, coming from disease, not emotion, moral depravity, or criminal perversion, is regarded in many jurisdictions as a defense in criminal prosecutions. In other jurisdictions the idea is rejected.

The cases are collected and cited in 29 Corpus Juris, 1053. They are too numerous to justify a review, particularly in view of former decisions of this court.

It is insisted by counsel for the plaintiff in error that this court is not so far committed on the doctrine of irresistible impulse but we think that this is a mistake.

In Wilcox v. State, 94 Tenn. 106, it was said by the court that:

"The idea that an irresistible impulse is an excuse for the commission of crime, where the party is capable of knowing right from wrong, has no foundation in our jurisprudence." . . .

(2) So while upon the facts of the case, the plaintiff in error, notwithstanding his delusion, cannot be acquitted of criminal accountability, we do not approve the conviction for murder in the second degree.

We are of opinion that if as a matter of fact the deceased had debauched the wife of plaintiff in error and the plaintiff in error had been apprised of that fact and had become convinced of its truth on the day of the wedding or thereafter, and, with reasonable expedition while under the influence of passion and agitation produced by such information, had killed Noe, he would only have been guilty of voluntary manslaughter.

(3) The right and wrong test above mentioned was authoritatively laid down in McNaughten's [sic] case, 1 C. & K., 130, 8 Eng.Reprint, 718. Under that case and those following it a homicide committed under an insane delusion is excusable, if the notion embodied in the delusion and believed to be a fact, if a fact indeed, would have excused the defendant.

(4) "Manslaughter is the unlawful killing of another without malice, either express or implied, which may be either voluntary upon a sudden heat, or involuntary, but in the commission of some unlawful act." Thompson's-Shannon's Code, sec. 6444.

Such being the law, it ensues that plaintiff in error would have been guilty of manslaughter only, if when he was first obsessed by this insane conceit, acting under the passion and agitation thereby produced, he had killed Esquire Noe.

(5) In the case of a normal man who has been apprised of the violation of the chastity of a female member of his family, if sufficient time has elapsed between the receipt of the information and the homicide so that his passion has had time to cool, the killing of the seducer would be murder. Toler v. State, supra.

Cooling time affects the degree of a defendant's guilt under the law because during such an interval there is opportunity for the voice of reason, the voice of conscience, to be heard. If these voices are ignored, the killing will be attributed to deliberate revenge and punished as murder.

(6) We have before us a man found by the jury to have been insane on the subject of his wife's relations with deceased. How could his status under the law have been affected by a lapse of time between his conception of the provocation and the homicide? Possessed by this insane delusion, deranged on the subject, he remained deaf to the voice of reason and to the voice of conscience. He was beyond reason and conscience in this particular, as the record clearly shows.

It is not necessary that a defendant's reason be dethroned to mitigate a killing to manslaughter. It is error so to instruct a jury. If the excitement and passion adequately aroused obscures the reason of the defendant, the killing will be reduced to manslaughter. A defendant acting under such temporary mental stress is presumed to be incapable of malice, an essential ingredient of murder.

How then can malice be imputed to a defendant when his reason is not merely obscured but has been swept away and kept away by an insane delusion under which he acts? How can such a defendant be guilty of murder while his delusion persists? . . .

Upon the facts for the reasons stated, we conclude that the verdict of murder in the second degree is not sustained by the proof. . . .

Reversed and remanded.[1]

DURHAM v. UNITED STATES

United States of Court of Appeals, District of Columbia Circuit, 1954.
94 U.S.App.D.C. 228, 214 F.2d 862.

BAZELON, CIRCUIT JUDGE. Monte Durham was convicted of housebreaking, by the District Court sitting without a jury. The only defense asserted at the trial was that Durham was of unsound mind at the time of the offense. We are now urged to reverse the conviction (1) because the trial court did not correctly apply existing rules governing the burden of proof on the defense of insanity, and (2) because existing tests of criminal responsibility are obsolete and should be superseded. . .

II

It has been ably argued by counsel for Durham that the existing tests in the District of Columbia for determining criminal responsibility, *i.e.*, the so-called right-wrong test supplemented by the irresistible impulse test, are not satisfactory criteria for determining criminal responsibility. We are urged to adopt a different test to be applied on the retrial of this case. This contention has behind it nearly a century of agitation for reform.

A. The right-wrong test, approved in this jurisdiction in 1882,[13] was the exclusive test of criminal responsibility in the District of Columbia until 1929 when we approved the irresistible impulse test as a supplementary test in Smith v. United States.[14] The right-wrong test

1. The defense of delusional insanity can be presented under the M'Naghten rule because the delusion may have affected D's ability to distinguish right from wrong or his knowledge of the nature and quality of his act. State v. Nicholson, 1 Wash.App. 853, 466 P.2d 181 (1970).

13. 1882, 12 D.C. 498, 550, 1 Mackey 498, 550. The right-wrong test was reaffirmed in United States v. Lee, 1886, 15 D.C. 489, 496, 4 Mackey, 489, 496.

14. 1929, 59 App.D.C. 144, 36 F.2d 548, 70 A.L.R. 654.

has its roots in England. There, by the first quarter of the eighteenth century, an accused escaped punishment if he could not distinguish "good and evil," i.e., if he "doth not know what he is doing, no more than . . . a wild beast." [15] Later in the same century, the "wild beast" test was abandoned and "right and wrong" was substituted for "good and evil." [16] And toward the middle of the nineteenth century, the House of Lords in the famous M'Naghten case [17] restated what had become the accepted "right-wrong" test [18] in a form which has since been followed, not only in England [19] but in most American jurisdictions [20] as an exclusive test of criminal responsibility:

". . . the jurors ought to be told in all cases that every man is to be presumed to be sane, and to possess a sufficient degree of reason to be responsible for his crimes, until the contrary be proved to their satisfaction; and that, to establish a defence on the ground of insanity, it must be clearly proved that, at the time of the committing of the act, the party accused was labouring under such a defect of reason, from disease of the mind, as not to know the nature and quality of the act he was doing, or, if he did know it, that he did not know he was doing what was wrong." [21]

As early as 1838, Isaac Ray, one of the founders of the American Psychiatric Association, in his now classic Medical Jurisprudence of Insanity, called knowledge of right and wrong a "fallacious" test of criminal responsibility.[22] . . .

We find that as an exclusive criterion the right-wrong test is inadequate in that (a) it does not take sufficient account of psychic realities and scientific knowledge, and (b) it is based upon one symptom and so cannot validly be applied in all circumstances. We find that the "irresistible impulse" test is also inadequate in that it gives no

15. Glueck, Mental Disorder and the Criminal Law 138–39 (1925), citing Rex v. Arnold, 16 How.St.Tr. 695, 764 (1724).

16. Id. at 142–52, citing Earl Ferrer's case, 19 How.St.Tr. 886 (1760). One writer has stated that these tests originated in England in the 13th or 14th century, when the law began to define insanity in terms of intellect for purposes of determining capacity to manage feudal estates. Comment, Lunacy and Idiocy—The Old Law and Its Incubus, 18 U. of Chi.L.Rev. 361 (1951).

17. 8 Eng.Rep. 718 (1843).

18. Hall, Principles of Criminal Law 480, n. 6 (1947).

19. Royal Commission on Capital Punishment 1949–1953 Report (Cmd. 8932) 79 (1953) (hereinafter cited as Royal Commission Report).

20. Weihofen, The M'Naghten Rule in Its Present Day Setting, Federal Probation 8 (Sept. 1953); Weihofen, Insanity as a Defense in Criminal Law 15, 64–68, 109–47 (1933); Leland v. State of Oregon, 1952, 343 U.S. 790, 800, 72 S.Ct. 1002, 96 L.Ed. 1302. . . .

Mentally Defective Offenders, 43 J.Crim.L., Criminology & Police Sci. 312, 314 (1952).

21. 8 Eng.Rep. 718, 722 (1843). . . .

22. Ray, Medical Jurisprudence of Insanity 47 and 34 et seq. (1st ed. 1838). "That the insane mind is not entirely deprived of this power of moral discernment, but in many subjects is perfectly rational, and displays the exercise of a sound and well balanced mind is one of those facts now so well established, that to question it would only betray the height of ignorance and presumption." Id. at 32.

recognition to mental illness characterized by brooding and reflection and so relegates acts caused by such illness to the application of the inadequate right-wrong test. We conclude that a broader test should be adopted.

B. In the District of Columbia, the formulation of tests of criminal responsibility is entrusted to the courts and, in adopting a new test, we invoke our inherent power to make the change prospectively.

The rule we now hold must be applied on the retrial of this case and in future cases is not unlike that followed by the New Hampshire court since 1870.[47] It is simply that an accused is not criminally responsible if his unlawful act was the product of mental disease or mental defect.[48]

We use "disease" in the sense of a condition which is considered capable of either improving or deteriorating. We use "defect" in the sense of a condition which is not considered capable of either improving or deteriorating and which may be either congenital, or the result of injury, or the residual effect of a physical or mental disease.

Whenever there is "some evidence" that the accused suffered from a diseased or defective mental condition at the time the unlawful act was committed, the trial court must provide the jury with guides for determining whether the accused can be held criminally responsible. We do not, and indeed could not, formulate an instruction which would be either appropriate or binding in all cases. But under the rule now announced, any instruction should in some way convey to the jury the sense and substance of the following: If you the jury believe beyond a reasonable doubt that the accused was not suffering from a diseased or defective mental condition at the time he committed the criminal act charged, you may find him guilty. If you believe he was suffering from a diseased or defective mental condition when he committed the act, but believe beyond a reasonable doubt that the act was not the product of such mental abnormality, you may find him guilty. Unless you believe beyond a reasonable doubt either that he was not suffering from a diseased or defective mental condition, or that the act was not the product of such abnormality, you must find the accused not guilty by reason of insanity. Thus your task would not be completed upon finding, if you did find, that the accused suffered from a mental disease or defect. He would still be responsible for his unlawful act if there was no causal connection between such mental abnormality and the act.[49] These questions

47. State v. Pike, 1870, 49 N.H. 399.

48. Cf. State v. Jones, 1871, 50 N.H. 369, 398.

49. "There is no *a priori* reason why every person suffering from any form of mental abnormality or disease, or from any particular kind of mental disease, should be treated by the law as not answerable for any criminal offence which he may commit, and be exempted from conviction and punishment. Mental abnormalities vary infinitely in their nature and intensity and in their effects on the character and conduct of those who suffer from them. Where a person suffering from a mental abnormality commits a crime, there must always be some likelihood that the abnormality has played

must be determined by you from the facts which you find to be fairly deducible from the testimony and the evidence in this case. . . .

The legal and moral traditions of the western world require that those who, of their own free will and with evil intent (sometimes called *mens rea),* commit acts which violate the law, shall be criminally responsible for those acts. Our traditions also require that where such acts stem from and are the product of a mental disease or defect as those terms are used herein, moral blame shall not attach, and hence there will not be criminal responsibility.[57] The rule we state in this opinion is designed to meet these requirements.[a]

PEOPLE v. DREW

Supreme Court of California, In Bank, 1978.
22 Cal.3d 333, 149 Cal.Rptr. 275, 583 P.2d 1318.

TOBRINER, JUSTICE. For over a century California has followed the *M'Naghten* [1] test to define the defenses of insanity and idiocy. The deficiencies of that test have long been apparent, and judicial attempts to reinterpret or evade the limitations of *M'Naghten* have proven inadequate. We shall explain why we have concluded that we should discard the *M'Naghten* language, and update the California

some part in the causation of the crime; and, generally speaking, the graver the abnormality, . . . the more probable it must be that there is a causal connection between them. But the closeness of this connection will be shown by the facts brought in evidence in individual cases and cannot be decided on the basis of any general medical principle." Royal Commission Report 99.

57. An accused person who is acquitted by reason of insanity is presumed to be insane, Orencia v. Overholser, 1947, 82 U.S.App.D.C. 285, 163 F.2d 763; Barry v. White, 1933, 62 App.D.C. 69, 64 F.2d 707, and may be committed for an indefinite period to a "hospital for the insane." D.C.Code § 24–301 (1951).

We think that even where there has been a specific finding that the accused was competent to stand trial and to assist in his own defense, the court would be well advised to invoke this Code provision so that the accused may be confined as long as "the public safety and . . . [his] welfare" require. Barry v. White, 62 App.D.C. at page 71, 64 F.2d at page 709.

a. (Added by Compiler) "This Court has no desire to join the courts of New Hampshire and the District of Columbia in their 'magnificent isolation' of rebellion against M'Naghten, . . ." Andersen v. United States, 237 F.2d 118, 127 (9th Cir.1956). Accord, Sauer v. United States, 241 F.2d 640, (9th Cir. 1957); Howard v. United States, 229 F.2d 602 (5th Cir.1956).

A man who has sufficient reason to know that the act he is doing is wrong and deserves punishment is legally of sound mind and is criminally responsible for his acts. Revard v. State, 332 P.2d 967 (Okl.Cr.1958).

The court that decided *Durham* did not like the way this approach was working and attempted to modify the testimony being given. McDonald v. United States, 114 U.S.App.D.C. 120, 312 F.2d 847 (1962). Later it said that "psychiatrists should not speak directly in terms of 'product,' or even 'result' or 'cause'." Washington v. United States, 129 U.S. App.D.C. 29, 41, 390 F.2d 444, 455–56 (1967). After struggling with *Durham* for 18 years the court overruled it in favor of the substantial capacity standard of the Model Penal Code. United States v. Brawner, 153 U.S.App.D.C. 1, 471 F.2d 969 (1972).

1. Daniel M'Naghten was inconsistent in the spelling of his name, and courts and commentators ever since have shared in that inconsistency. (See Frankfurter, Of Law and Life and Other Things (1965) p. 3.) We follow the spelling in the Clark and Finnelly report of the *M'Naghten* case.

test of mental incapacity as a criminal defense by adopting the test proposed by the American Law Institute [3] and followed by the federal judiciary and the courts of 15 states.

Understandably, in view of our past adherence to *M'Naghten,* neither the psychiatrists who examined defendant nor the jury evaluated defendant's capacity in terms of the ALI test. Since the evidentiary record indicates that defendant, a former mental patient with a history of irrational assaultive behavior, lacked the capacity to conform his conduct to legal requirements, we conclude that the court's failure to instruct the jury under the ALI test was prejudicial and therefore reverse the conviction. . . .

Defendant Drew, a 22-year-old man, was drinking in a bar in Brawley during the early morning of October 26, 1975. He left $5 on the bar to pay for drinks and went to the men's room. When he returned, the money was missing. Drew accused one Truman Sylling, a customer at the bar, of taking the money. A heated argument ensued, and the bartender phoned for police assistance.

Officers Guerrero and Bonsell arrived at the bar. When Guerrero attempted to question Sylling, Drew interfered to continue the argument. Bonsell then asked Drew to step outside. Drew refused. Bonsell took Drew by the hand, and he and Officer Schulke, who had just arrived at the bar, attempted to escort Drew outside. Drew broke away from the officers and struck Bonsell in the face. Bonsell struck his head against the edge of the bar and fell to the floor. Drew fell on top of him and attempted to bite him, but was restrained by Guerrero and Schulke. Drew continued to resist violently until he was finally placed in a cell at the police station.

Charged with battery on a peace officer (Pen.Code, § 243), obstructing an officer (Pen.Code, § 148), and disturbing the peace (Pen. Code, § 415), Drew pled not guilty and not guilty by reason of insanity. . . .

This court should adopt the American Law Institute test, as stated in section 4.01, subpart (1) of the Model Penal Code, to define the defense of insanity. . . .

The purpose of a legal test for insanity is to identify those persons who, owing to mental incapacity, should not be held criminally responsible for their conduct. The criminal law rests on a postulate of free will—that all persons of sound mind are presumed capable of conforming their behavior to legal requirements and that when any such person freely chooses to violate the law, he may justly be held responsible. From the earliest days of the common law, however, the

3. "A person is not responsible for criminal conduct if at the time of such conduct as a result of mental disease or defect he lacks substantial capacity either to appreciate the criminality [wrongfulness] of his conduct or to conform his conduct to the requirements of law." (Model Pen.Code, Proposed Official Draft (1962) § 4.01, subpart (1).)

courts have recognized that a few persons lack the mental capacity to conform to the strictures of the law. . . .

The California Penal Code codifies the defense of mental incapacity. . . . "All persons are of sound mind who are neither idiots nor lunatics, nor affected with insanity." Finally section 26 specifies that "All persons are capable of commiting crimes except those belonging to the following classes" and includes among those classes "Idiots" and "Lunatics and insane persons."

Although the Legislature has thus provided that "insanity" is a defense to a criminal charge, it has never attempted to define that term. The task of describing the circumstances under which mental incapacity will relieve a defendant of criminal responsibility has become the duty of the judiciary.

Since People v. Coffman (1864) 24 Cal. 230, 235, the California courts have followed the *M'Naghten* rule to define the defense of insanity. . . .

This formulation does not comport with modern medical knowledge that an individual is a mentally complex being with varying degrees of awareness. It also fails to attack the problem presented in a case wherein an accused may have understood his actions but was incapable of controlling his behavior. Such a person has been allowed to remain a danger to himself and to society whenever, under *M'Naghten,* he is imprisoned without being afforded such treatment as may produce rehabilitation and is later, "potentially recidivistic, released."

M'Naghten's exclusive emphasis on cognition would be of little consequence if all serious mental illness impaired the capacity of the affected person to know the nature and wrongfulness of his action. Indeed, the early decision of People v. Hoin (1882) 62 Cal. 120, 123, in rejecting the defense of "irresistible impulse," rested on this gratuitous but doubtful assumption. Current psychiatric opinion, however, holds that mental illness often leaves the individual's intellectual understanding relatively unimpaired, but so affects his emotions or reason that he is unable to prevent himself from committing the act. [I]nsanity does not only, or primarily, affect the cognitive or intellectual faculties, but affects the whole personality of the patient, including both the will and the emotions. An insane person may therefore often know the nature and quality of his act, and that it is wrong and forbidden by law, and yet commit it as a result of the mental disease. . . .

Secondly, "*M'Naghten's* single track emphasis on the cognitive aspect of the personality recognizes no degrees of incapacity. Either the defendant knows right from wrong or he does not . . . . But such a test is grossly unrealistic . . . As the commentary to the American Law Institute's Model Penal Code observes, 'The law must recognize that when there is no black and white it must content itself with different shades of gray.' "

In short, *M'Naghten* purports to channel psychiatric testimony into the narrow issue of cognitive capacity, an issue often unrelated to the defendant's illness or crime. The psychiatrist called as a witness faces a dilemma: either he can restrict his testimony to the confines of *M'Naghten*, depriving the trier of fact of a full presentation of the defendant's mental state, or he can testify that the defendant cannot tell "right" from "wrong" when that is not really his opinion because by so testifying he acquires the opportunity to put before the trier of fact the reality of defendant's mental condition. . . .

In our opinion the continuing inadequacy of *M'Naghten* as a test of criminal responsibility cannot be cured by further attempts to interpret language dating from a different era of psychological thought, nor by the creation of additional concepts designed to evade the limitations of *M'Naghten*. It is time to recast *M'Naghten* in modern language, taking account of advances in psychological knowledge and changes in legal thought.

The definition of mental incapacity appearing in section 4.01 of the American Law Institute's Model Penal Code represents the distillation of nine years of research, exploration, and debate by the leading legal and medical minds of the country. It specifies that "A person is not responsible for criminal conduct if at the time of such conduct as a result of mental disease or defect he lacks substantial capacity either to appreciate the criminality [wrongfulness] of his conduct or to conform his conduct to the requirements of law."[8]

Adhering to the fundamental concepts of free will and criminal responsibility, the American Law Institute test restates *M'Naghten* in language consonant with the current legal and psychological thought. It has won widespread acceptance, having been adopted by every federal circuit except for the first circuit and by 15 states.

"In the opinion of most thoughtful observers this proposed test [the ALI test] is a significant improvement over *M'Naghten*." The advantages may be briefly summarized. First the ALI test adds a volitional element, the ability to conform to legal requirements, which is missing from the *M'Naghten* test. Second, it avoids the all-or-nothing language of *M'Naghten* and permits a verdict based on lack of substantial capacity. Third, the ALI test is broad enough to permit a psychiatrist to set before the trier of fact a full picture of the defendant's mental impairments and flexibile enough to adapt to future changes in psychiatric theory and diagnosis. Fourth, by referring to the defendant's capacity to "appreciate" the wrongfulness of his con-

8. The American Law Institute takes no position as to whether the term "criminality" or the term "wrongfulness" best expresses the test of criminal responsibility; we prefer the term "criminality."

Subpart 2 of the American Law Institute test provides that "the terms 'mental disease or defect' do not include an abnormality manifested only by repeated criminal or otherwise antisocial conduct." The language, designed to deny an insanity defense to psychopaths and sociopaths, is not relevant to the present case. The question whether to adopt subpart 2 of the ALI test is one which we defer to a later occasion.

duct the test confirms our holding that mere verbal knowledge of right and wrong does not prove sanity. Finally, by establishing a broad test of nonresponsibility, including elements of volition as well as cognition, the test provides the foundation on which we can order and rationalize the convoluted and occasionally inconsistent law of diminished capacity.

In light of the manifest superiority of the ALI test, the only barrier to the adoption of that test we perceive lies in the repeated judicial declarations that any change in the *M'Naghten* rule requires legislative action. . . .

The Legislature has never enacted the *M'Naghten* rule as a test of insanity, and its provisions relating to criminal responsibility do not incorporate the *M'Naghten* formula. (See Pen.Code, §§ 26, 1016, 1367.) Thus replacement of the *M'Naghten* rule with the ALI test will not contradict or nullify any legislative enactment. . . .

The judgment is reversed and the cause remanded for a new trial on the issue raised by defendant's plea of not guilty by reason of insanity.[1]

BIRD, C.J., and MOSK and NEWMAN, JJ., concur.

RICHARDSON, JUSTICE, dissenting.

I respectfully dissent. My objection to the majority's approach may be briefly stated. I believe that a major change in the law of the type contemplated by the majority should be made by the Legislature. . . .

1. [Added by the Compiler.] By initiative measure in 1982, the standard for the insanity defense in California was established as the traditional right/wrong test standard. West's Cal.Pen.Code § 25(b) (1982).

The Massachusetts court which had long applied *M'Naghten* supplemented by the irresistible impulse test, concluded that the Code's position was in effect a codification of its own, although it decided the wording of the Code was preferable. Commonwealth v. McHoul, 352 Mass. 544, 226 N.E.2d 556 (1967). See also United States v. Frederick, 3 M.J. 230 (C.M.A.1977).

An instruction on the "M'Naghten test supplemented by the 'irresistible impulse' principle" is in complete accordance with the Utah law and does not violate the federal constitution. Pierce v. Turner, 402 F.2d 109, 111 (10th Cir.1968).

"A person is not responsible for criminal conduct, if at the time of such conduct, as a result of mental disease or defect, his capacity either to appreciate the wrongfulness of his conduct or to conform his conduct to the requirements of the law is so substantially impaired that he cannot justly be held responsible." State v. Johnson, 121 R.I. 254, 399 A.2d 469, 476 (1979).

The British Royal Commission on Capital Punishment in 1953 proposed a test that a person would not be responsible for his unlawful act if at the time of the act "the accused was suffering from a disease of the mind to such a degree that he ought not to be held responsible."

The Utah statute reads:

"It is a defense to a prosecution under any statute or ordinance that the defendant, as a result of mental illness, lacked the mental state required as an element of the offense charged. Mental illness shall not otherwise constitute a defense." Utah Code Ann. 1953, § 76–2–305 (1983).

STATE v. WHITE

Supreme Court of Washington, En Banc, 1962.
60 Wn.2d 551, 374 P.2d 942.

DONWORTH, JUDGE. Appellant was charged, by Information, with committing two murders alleged to have been committed at different times and places on the same day (December 24, 1959). . . .

Assignment No. 9. Appellant contends that:

"The court erred in giving instruction No. 33 and further erred in failing to give the appellant's requested instructions on mental irresponsibility, which is the American Law Institute test for mental irresponsibility."

Instruction No. 33 told the jury that:

"You are instructed that the term 'mental irresponsibility', as used alternatively with the term 'insanity' in the further plea of the defendant and elsewhere in these instructions, means what is defined in law as criminal insanity. Therefore, if you find that the defendant was mentally irresponsible under the definition as contained herein, you must find the defendant not guilty by reason of mental irresponsibility.

"If the defendant is to be acquitted upon his plea of mental irresponsibility or insanity, he must convince you by a preponderance of the evidence that, at the time the crime is alleged to have been committed, his mind was diseased to such an extent that he was unable to perceive the moral qualities of the act with which he is charged, and was unable to tell right from wrong with reference to the particular act charged. A person may be sick or diseased in body or mind and yet be able to distinguish right from wrong with respect to a particular act."

Proposed instruction No. 21 (if substituted in place of No. 33) would have stated the rule as follows: . . .

" 'Mental irresponsibility means that the defendant is not responsible for the crimes charged herein if at the time of said crimes, as a result of mental disease or defect, he lacked substantial capacity either to appreciate the criminality of his act, or to conform his conduct to the requirements of law.

" 'The terms "mental disease" or "defect" do not include an abnormality manifested only by repeated criminal or otherwise anti-social conduct.' "

The essential difference between the two instructions is that the instruction which was given to the jury did not allow for an acquittal based on insanity or mental irresponsibility, if the accused had cognition (the ability to understand the nature and quality of his acts) with regard to what he did, even though his volition (his capacity "to conform his conduct to the requirements of the law") may have been substantially impaired by mental disease or defect. In other words, under the given instruction, the defense of "not guilty by reason of mental irresponsibility" is not available to a person who has the ability to understand the nature and quality of his acts, but, because of mental disease or defect, is somehow unable to control his own behavior.

The proposed but rejected instruction was based upon § 4.01 of the Model Penal Code, which test has since been adopted by the American Law Institute, on May 24, 1962. The concept that volitional control is an element of sanity for the purpose of criminal responsibility is accepted in several states. Some recognize "irresistible impulse" as a defense; others use language much like that found in the American Law Institute test.

The instruction which was assigned as error (No. 33) is based on the M'Naghten rule, which is the law in the majority of states.

The question whether the jury was correctly instructed is squarely presented by the facts of this case. There was substantial evidence from which the jury could have found that appellant could not control his own behavior, even though, at the time, he knew the difference between right and wrong. . . .

Before the two tests between which the trial court was compelled to make a choice are discussed, a third test should be mentioned. That third test is the "product" test, often called the Durham rule because of the widespread notoriety it received upon being adopted in the District of Columbia in Durham v. United States, 94 App.D.C. 228, 214 F.2d 862, 45 A.L.R.2d 1430 (1954). In essence, this rule is that a defendant in a criminal case is not responsible if his unlawful act was the product of a mental disease or mental defect. The rule in New Hampshire has been stated in the same way for over ninety years. State v. Pike, 49 N.H. 399, 6 Am.Rep. 533 (1870), and State v. Jones, 50 N.H. 369, 9 Am.Rep. 242 (1871).

However, very recently the Court of Appeals in the District of Columbia has gone far beyond the original Durham rule as it was first adopted by that court in 1954.

In Campbell v. United States, D.C.Cir., 307 F.2d 597 (March 29, 1962), the conviction of a defendant with an "emotionally unstable personality" (administratively classified by government psychiatrists as a mental disease since 1957) was reversed. It was held by the majority that the instructions of the trial court placed too much emphasis upon the defendant's capacity to control his own behavior, rather than simply instructing the jury that they must determine whether the criminal act was a product of a mental disease. They say that the test is whether he would have committed the act if he had not been the victim of a mental disease, to wit, an emotionally unstable personality. Thus, they hold that the defendant could be found innocent if his motivation was the result of such mental dis-

ease, regardless of whether or not the sanctions o
as a deterrent could have influenced him.

The fallacy in that view, as pointed out by Jud
very vigorous dissent, is that almost all criminals
such a definition of insanity. . . .

What is meant by "criminal insanity" and "men
ty" in our statute? It has consistently been held that both terms mean the same thing for purposes of criminal responsibility. The test is M'Naghten.[1] State v. Maish, 29 Wash.2d 52, 185 P.2d 486, 173 A.L.R. 382 (1947), made it especially clear that Washington has rejected the volitional test as embodied in the so-called "irresistible impulse" rule. . . .[2]

With regard to capacity to control one's behavior, it would appear that there is no more psychiatric certainty today than there was when this court decided State v. Maish, supra.

Finally, M'Naghten is preferable to the American Law Institute test in that the M'Naghten rule better serves the basic purpose of the criminal law—to minimize crime in society. The earlier quotation from Wechsler pointed out that, when M'Naghten is used, all who might possibly be deterred from the commission of criminal acts are included within the sanctions of the criminal law. Sol Rubin points out that the application of the M'Naghten rule can even help in the rehabilitation process:

". . . The M'Naghten rule declares that one who is so far removed from reality that he does not know the nature of his act does not have the mentality to be adjudged responsible. Such a holding is inevitable because of the requirement of *mens rea.* But the Durham rule would exculpate a defendant who does know the nature of his act. For the law to tell such a person that he is not responsible for his act is likely to deter and complicate his rehabilitation, because it contradicts common sense fact. To declare that such a defendant is legally responsible, but, because of his mental illness, is subject to special treatment is more consistent with reality and more likely to support his rehabilitation. . . ." "A New Approach to M'Naghten v. Durham," 45 J.Am.Jud.Soc'y 133, 136 (December, 1961).

1. "The quoted phrase will be recognized as the traditional *M'Naghten* test for criminal responsibility, which is the test applicable in this state." State v. Pyle, 216 Kan. 423, 440, 532 P.2d 1309, 1322 (1975).

"In Arizona the accepted test for criminal insanity is the rule of M'Naghten's Case." State v. Brosie, 113 Ariz. 329, 553 P.2d 1203, 1204 (1976).

"This Court has long adhered to the M'Naghten Rule and has repeatedly rejected attempts to broaden or qualify it." Jones v. State, 554 P.2d 62, 65 (Okl.Cr. 1976).

"M'Naghten rule" will still be the accepted standard for determining insanity. Clark v. State, 95 Nev. 24, 588 P.2d 1027 (1979).

2. The irresistible-impulse defense is not recognized in most jurisdictions. People v. Gorshen, 51 Cal.2d 716, 336 P.2d 492 (1959); Piccott v. State, 116 So. 2d 626 (Fla.1960).

Mr. Rubin then continues the discussion of this subject in his article and supports his position with cogent reasoning.

In summary, then, not only would any other rule be difficult to apply, but the M'Naghten rule is, for good reason, the established rule in the State of Washington. There was no error in giving the jury the instruction (No. 33) based on that test, nor in refusing to instruct on the basis of any other test of mental responsibility as requested by appellant. . . .

CONCLUSION

We have carefully considered each of appellant's assignments of error in the light of the record and the law applicable thereto. We are of the opinion that appellant had a fair trial. Finding no reversible error in the record, the judgment and sentence of the trial court entered upon the several verdicts of the jury must be affirmed. . . .

The judgment and sentence is hereby affirmed.[3]

WEAVER, OTT and ROSELLINI, JJ., concur.

HILL, JUDGE (concurring specially).

I concur in the majority opinion. However, I find myself in accord with some of the views expressed by Chief Justice Weintraub of the Supreme Court of New Jersey, in a concurring opinion in State v. Lucas (1959), 30 N.J. 37, 152 A.2d 50; he says (p. 83, 152 A.2d p. 75):

"No one will dispute that society must be protected from the insane as well as the sane. The area of disagreement is whether a civil or a criminal process should be employed when forbidden acts have been committed. If we could think of a conviction simply as a finding that the mortal in question has demonstrated his capacity for antisocial conduct, most of the battle would be decided. What would remain is the employment of such post-conviction techniques as would redeem the offender if he can be redeemed and secure him if he cannot. . . .[4]

3. "[Under the original M'Naghten language from which the California rule has been evolved] a mentally ill defendant could be found sane even though his 'knowledge' of the nature or wrongfulness of his act was merely a capacity to verbalize the 'right' (i.e., socially expected) answers to questions put to him relating to that act, without such 'knowledge' having any affective meaning for him as a principle of conduct. Such a narrow, literal reading of the M'Naughton [sic] formula has been repeatedly and justly condemned. Rather, it is urged by many that the word 'know' as used in the formula be given 'a wider definition so that it means the kind of knowing that is relevant, i.e., realization or appreciation of the wrongness of seriously harming a human being'. 'If the word "know" were given this broader interpretation, so as to require knowledge "fused with affect" and assimilated by the whole personality—so that, for example, the killer was capable of identifying with his prospective victim—much of the criticism of the knowledge test would be met.'" People v. Wolff, 61 Cal.2d 795, 800, 40 Cal.Rptr. 271, 273–74, 394 P.2d 959, 961–62 (1964).

4. "It is contended that the trial court erred in instructing on the M'Naghten rules as the test for criminal responsibility, rather than the test set forth in the Model Penal Code, § 4.01. We have con-

[Three judges expressed a preference for the position taken in Currens.]

Petition for writ of habeas corpus dismissed. White v. Rhay, 64 Wash.2d 15, 390 P.2d 535 (1964).

UNITED STATES v. HOLT

United States Court of Appeals, Fifth Circuit, 1971.
450 F.2d 868.

PER CURIAM. Appellant Holt was convicted in the court below of escaping from prison in violation of 18 U.S.C.A. § 4082(d) and 18 U.S.C.A. § 751(a). He did not contest the fact that while in trusty status he departed his place of confinement. His defense rested solely on the contention that he was insane at the time of his escape and therefore lacked the requisite intent required to commit the crimes charged. In this appeal, appellant raises only one point. He urges that the trial court erred in ruling as a matter of law that he had not produced sufficient evidence of insanity for the jury to be permitted to consider his defense.

The last word in this Circuit on the defense of insanity is Blake v. United States, 5th Cir.1969, 407 F.2d 908 (en banc). Applying *Blake,* we affirm the conviction.

The law presumes sanity. To overcome this presumption the accused must provide "some" evidence of insanity. If he does, the jury is then permitted to consider the defense of insanity along with all other evidence in the case to determine whether the prosecution has proved its case beyond a reasonable doubt. *Blake* makes clear, however, that "the question of sufficiency of the evidence necessary to make an issue for the jury on the defense of insanity . . . is for the court."

In *Blake* this Court adopted the ALI Model Penal Code test for determining criminal responsibility:

(1) A person is not responsible for criminal conduct if at the time of such conduct as a result of mental disease or defect he lacks substantial capacity either to appreciate the wrongfulness of his conduct or to conform his conduct to the requirements of law.

sidered the question of adopting a different test for criminal responsibility in this state on numerous occasions, and have consistently adhered to the M'Naghten rules. State v. Bradley, 102 Ariz. 482, 433 P.2d 273 (1967); State v. Schantz, 98 Ariz. 200, 403 P.2d 521 (1965). In Schantz we discussed § 4.01 of the Model Penal Code, and stated:

'Whatever may be the theoretical merits in the medical evaluation of the volitional aspects of the human mind, we, . . . , do not accept § 4.01 of the Model Penal Code as the test for criminal responsibility in this state.'

"As the legislature has chosen to codify the M'Naghten test in statutory form, it would be preferable to have this test presented to the jury without any elaboration." State v. Crenshaw, 98 Wn.2d 789, 659 P.2d 488, 497 (1983). (**C**'s Moscovite belief that a husband has a duty to slay a faithless wife was not an insane delusion and does not relieve **C** of responsibility for his act).

(2) As used in this Article, the terms "mental disease or defect" do not include an abnormality manifested only by repeated criminal or otherwise antisocial conduct.

It was incumbent upon Holt to provide "some" evidence to the district court that he met the ALI-*Blake* standard. This he failed to do. Holt called four witnesses, one a court-appointed psychiatrist, on the issue of his sanity. The psychiatrist described Holt as suffering from "impaired judgment," "a mental disorder," "poor judgment," "impulsivity," and as being "dissocial." When asked to explain "mental disorder," he defined it as any deviation from the normal personality. Despite vigorous interrogation by Holt's counsel, the doctor refused to describe Holt's condition as a mental disease or defect as required by the *Blake* test. Moreover, when asked if Holt's condition could prevent his knowing the wrongfulness of his act, the witness answered, "no." He also answered "no" when asked if Holt was substantially incapable of conforming his conduct to the requirements of law.

Holt thus failed to meet either part of the two-step *Blake* test. He produced adequate evidence of his abnormal personality but not even "some" evidence that he suffered from a mental disease or defect *or* that as a result of his abnormality he could not "appreciate the wrongfulness of his conduct or . . . conform his conduct to the requirements of law." The record shows that Holt's counsel questioned the psychiatrist at length, trying to elicit from him one of the magic words, "disease" or "defect." He failed. He succeeded instead in drawing from the witness a fairly clear picture of appellant as a person contemplated by paragraph (2) of the *Blake* test. Such persons are not entitled to the defense of insanity.

Since Holt failed to provide the court below with "some" evidence that he was not legally responsible for his criminal conduct, the court was correct in not permitting the jury to consider the insanity defense.

Affirmed.[1]

1. In California the burden of establishing insanity is on the defendant. People v. Drew, infra; See also Cal.Evidence Code § 522 (1966).

Placing the burden of proof of the defense of insanity on the defendant does not violate due process of law. Patterson v. New York, 432 U.S. 197, 97 S.Ct. 2319 (1977); Rivera v. Delaware, 429 U.S. 877, 97 S.Ct. 226 (1976).

"This Circuit has essentially adopted the American Law Institute standard for defining lack of mental capacity to commit a crime . . . . Once the issue of insanity has been raised, the government has the burden of proving beyond a reasonable doubt that the defendant was sane at the time of the alleged crime." United States v. Collins, 690 F.2d 431 (5th Cir.1982).

A statute withdrawing the defense of insanity from the court and jury and vesting it in a commission is unconstitutional. State v. Lange, 168 La. 958, 123 So. 639, 67 A.L.R. 1447 (1929). An accused has a constitutional right to have a jury pass upon his insanity defense. State v. Strasburg, 60 Wash. 106, 110 P. 1020 (1910).

Is a statute constitutional, which takes away from the judiciary and delegates to a branch of the executive department, the right and power to finally decide whether a person (charged with murder)

PEOPLE v. McLEOD

Court of Appeals of Michigan, 1977.
77 Mich.App. 327, 258 N.W.2d 214.

BEASLEY, JUDGE. Defendant, Joseph McLeod, was charged with arson in violation of M.C.L.A. § 750.72; M.S.A. § 28.267.

He waived a jury trial and filed notice of intention "to advance the defense of not guilty be reason of insanity." Trial commenced on May 12, 1976, continued on May 13, 1976, and was completed on May 17, 1976. The trial court found defendant guilty of arson, but mentally ill [2] and undertook on its own motion to hear the testimony of three psychiatrists regarding the treatment defendant might reasonably be anticipated to receive as a guilty but mentally ill felon.

This verdict of guilty, but mentally ill, which is new to Michigan law, was created by 1975 P.A. 180, immediate effect, July 25, 1975,[3] and requires specific findings by the trial judge as a condition precedent to the verdict of guilty but mentally ill.

Subsequently, on September 21, 1976, the trial judge filed a written opinion finding as follows:

> "It is held, therefore, that subsection (3) of Section 36 of PA 1975, No. 180 (MCLA 768.36) is legally inert and cannot be given judicial implementation for the reason that compliance with its provisions as to treatment is impossible and the Court is thereby deprived of its authority to enter a judgment of guilty but mentally ill and to sentence thereunder. Even if this were not the case,

is "sane" or "insane"? Our answer to the question is "no". Davis v. Britt, 243 Ark. 556, 420 S.W.2d 863, 865 (1967).

The "bifurcated trial" provided in some jurisdictions has been upheld. Under this procedure, if defendant pleads both not guilty and not guilty by reason of insanity, all other issues are decided in the trial under the general plea, after which if the verdict is guilty the insanity issue is determined under the special plea. See Louisell and Hazard, Insanity as a Defense: The Bifurcated Trial, 49 Cal.L. Rev. 805 (1961).

2. The file jacket shows a verdict on May 17, 1976, as follows:

"Court finds deft. guilty of burning a dwelling house or contents but mentally ill."

The record does not indicate a bench pronouncement of such verdict or a written verdict at that time. This appeal comes before this court on a record which does not include a transcript of the trial. This court assumes the trial record was not transcribed. During oral argument, request was made of counsel for a transcript of the trial judge's findings and verdict. On May 17, *1977*, subsequent to oral judgment on appeal, the trial judge made a finding that defendant was "legally sane" at the time of committing the act and that he was guilty but mentally ill.

3. 1975 P.A. 180, § 36; M.C.L.A. § 768.36; M.S.A. § 28.1059:

"(1) If the defendant asserts a defense of insanity in compliance with section 20a, the defendant may be found 'guilty but mentally ill' if, after trial, the trier of fact finds all of the following beyond a reasonable doubt:

(a) That the defendant is guilty of an offense.

(b) That the defendant was mentally ill at the time of the commission of that offense.

(c) That the defendant was not legally insane at the time of the commission of that offense."

Sections 29a(2) and 36 are unconstitutional for the reasons above stated.

"Accordingly, the verdict of guilty but mentally ill is hereby set aside and declared a nullity and a new trial is ordered."

The trial judge's opinion and order were made *sua sponte;* no petition for new trial was filed by defendant. From the order entered in accordance with the trial judge's opinion, the prosecutor filed an emergency petition for leave to appeal. Thus, the matter is here on leave to appeal granted.

For purposes of appeal, we accept the tardy findings of fact made on May 17, 1977, after oral argument on appeal, as a statutory basis for the verdict of guilty but mentally ill.

We limit our ruling to the matters before us. Consequently, in the absence of any petition by defendant delineating reasons for new trial, we only consider those matters alluded to by the trial judge in her opinion. We specifically do not express any opinion as to any matters which are not in the record furnished us. We do not believe that the cause of justice will be served by our *sua sponte* raising issues that have not been pleaded, briefed or argued.

We direct our attention to the trial judge's opinion and find that matters relating to post-sentence treatment, or lack of treatment, are prematurely raised. The reasons asserted by the trial judge for her finding of unconstitutionality are premature in that they all relate to speculation that the department of corrections or the department of mental health will not pay heed to the statute. While future events may prove the trial judge was correct in her surmise, to conclude that compliance with the statute is "impossible" is inaccurate.

It must be specifically noted that defendant has not been sentenced under the statute; therefore, it is impossible to know which portions of it will apply to him and how they will be applied. For example, if defendant is committed to the custody of the department of corrections, the statute indicates that he will receive further psychiatric evaluation. Assuming that the evaluation will result in a recommended special treatment plan,[5] the plan may be one that can be easily implemented by obtaining the services of psychiatric personnel from outside of the department of corrections or by employment of existing or additional personnel outside of the department. At this stage of the proceedings, without even the knowledge of how many defendants will be sentenced under the statute, it is not for us to guess whether or not the department of corrections will engage private psychiatrists to supplement the state facilities already available or in what other ways compliance with the statute will be possible.

5. One psychiatrist has already testified that there is no known cure for defendant's condition and that custody itself will be the only treatment possible. If that testimony gives an accurate indication of what defendant's treatment plan will be like, it would appear that the department of corrections would have to do very little for this defendant under the statute.

It is well settled that a statute must be treated with the deference due to a deliberate action of a coordinate branch of our state government and that the conflict between the statute and the constitution must be clear and inevitable before the statute will be struck down as unconstitutional. At this time and on this record, we do not find such clear and inevitable conflict between the questioned statute and the constitution. We, therefore, decline to hold this statute unconstitutional as to this defendant. In so doing, we are not without sympathy for the commendable objectives for which the trial judge has striven.

The order of the trial judge granting defendant a new trial is REVERSED and this cause REMANDED to the trial court for imposition of sentence.[a]

FULCHER v. STATE

Supreme Court of Wyoming, 1981.
633 P.2d 142.

Before ROSE, C.J., and RAPER, THOMAS, ROONEY and BROWN, JJ.

BROWN, JUSTICE.

Appellant-defendant was found guilty of aggravated assault without dangerous weapon in violation of § 6–4–506(a), W.S.1977, by the district court sitting without a jury. While appellant characterizes the issues on appeal differently, we believe the issues to be:

(1) Is it necessary for a defendant to plead "not guilty by reason of mental illness or deficiency" before evidence of unconsciousness can be presented?

(2) Was there sufficient evidence to sustain appellant's conviction?

We will affirm.

On November 17, 1979, the appellant consumed seven or eight shots of whiskey over a period of four hours in a Torrington bar, and had previously had a drink at home.

Appellant claims he got in a fight in the bar restroom, then left the bar to find a friend. According to his testimony, the last thing he remembers until awakening in jail, is going out of the door at the bar.

Appellant and his friend were found lying in the alley behind the bar by a police officer who noted abrasions on their fists and faces. Appellant and his friend swore, were uncooperative, and combative.

a. A defendant suffering from amnesia can plead guilty but mentally ill. People v. Booth, 414 Mich. 343, 324 N.W.2d 741 (1982).

One committed to the Department of Health following his acquittal of criminal charges because of insanity may not be confined beyond "the maximum period of punishment for the underlying offense, unless grounds for an extended commitment are shown." In re Moye, 22 Cal.3d 457, 149 Cal.Rptr. 491, 497, 584 P.2d 1097, 1103 (1978).

They were subsequently booked for public intoxication and disturbing the peace. During booking appellant continued to swear, and said he and his friend were jumped by a "bunch of Mexicans." Although his speech was slurred, he was able to verbally count his money, roughly $500 to $600 in increments of $20, and was able to walk to his cell without assistance.

Appellant was placed in a cell with one Martin Hernandez who was lying unconscious on the floor of the cell. After the jailer left the cell, he heard something that sounded like someone being kicked. He ran back to the cell and saw appellant standing by Hernandez. When the jailer started to leave again, the kicking sound resumed, and he observed appellant kicking and stomping on Hernandez's head. Appellant told the officer Hernandez had fallen out of bed. Hernandez was bleeding profusely and was taken to the hospital for some 52 stitches in his head and mouth. He had lost two or three teeth as a result of the kicking. . . .

At his arraignment in district court, appellant first entered a plea of "not guilty by reason of temporary mental illness." Upon being advised by the trial judge that he would have to be committed for examination pusuant to § 7–11–304, W.S.1977, he withdrew that plea and entered a plea of not guilty. . . .

At the trial Dr. LeBegue testified that in his expert medical opinion appellant suffered brain injury and was in a state of traumatic automatism at the time of his attack on Hernandez. Dr. LeBegue defined traumatic automatism as the state of mind in which a person does not have conscious and willful control over his actions, and lacks the ability to be aware of and to perceive his external environment. Dr. LeBegue further testified that another possible symptom is an inability to remember what occurred while in a state of traumatic automatism. . . .

We hold that the trial court properly received and considered evidence of unconsciousness absent a plea of "not guilty by reason of mental illness or deficiency."

The defense of unconsciousness perhaps should be more precisely denominated as the defense of automatism. Automatism is the state of a person who, though capable of action, is not conscious of what he is doing. While in an automatistic state, an individual performs complex actions without an exercise of will. Because these actions are

performed in a state of unconsciousness, they are involuntary. Automatistic behavior may be followed by complete or partial inability to recall the actions performed while unconscious. Thus, a person who acts automatically does so without intent, exercise of free will, or

knowledge of the act.

Automatism may be caused by an abnormal condition of the mind capable of being designated a mental illness or deficiency. Automatism may also be manifest in a person with a perfectly healthy mind.

In this opinion we are only concerned with the defense of automatism occurring in a person with a healthy mind. To further narrow the issue to be decided in this case, we are concerned with alleged automatism caused by concussion.

The defense of automatism, while not an entirely new development in the criminal law, has been discussed in relatively few decisions by American appellate courts, most of these being in California where the defense is statutory. Some courts have held that insanity and automatism are separate and distinct defenses, and that evidence of automatism may be presented under a plea of not guilty. Some states have made this distinction by statute. In other states the distinction is made by case law. . . .

> "The defenses of insanity and unconsciousness are not the same in nature, for unconsciousness at the time of the alleged criminal act need not be the result of a disease or defect of the mind. As a consequence, the two defenses are not the same in effect, for a defendant found not guilty by reason of unconsciousness, as distinct from insanity, is not subject to commitment to a hospital for the mentally ill." State v. Caddell, 287 N.C. 266, 215 S.E.2d 348, 360 (1975).

The principal reason for making a distinction between the defense of unconsciousness and insanity is that the consequences which follow an acquittal will differ. The defense of unconsciousness is usually a complete defense.[5] That is, there are no follow-up consequences after an acquittal; all action against a defendant is concluded.

However, in the case of a finding of not guilty by reason of insanity, the defendant is ordinarily committed to a mental institution. . . .

In some states the commitment is automatic after a finding of not guilty by reason of insanity. In Wyoming the trial judge may commit a defendant based on evidence produced at trial or the commitment may be by separate proceedings.

The mental illness or deficiency plea does not adequately cover automatic behavior. Unless the plea of automatism, separate and apart from the plea of mental illness or deficiency is allowed, certain

5. Unconsciousness is not a complete defense under all circumstances. An incomplete list of situations will illustrate. In California, "unconsciousness produced by voluntary intoxication does not render a defendant incapable of committing a crime." People v. Cox, 67 Cal.App.2d 166, 153 P.2d 362 (1944), and cases cited. In Colorado a person who participates in a fracas and as a result is hit on the head and rendered semi-conscious or unconscious cannot maintain that he is not criminally responsible. Watkins v. People, 158 Colo. 485, 408 P.2d 425 (1965). In Oklahoma a motorist is guilty of manslaughter if he drives an automobile with knowledge that he is subject to frequent blackouts. Carter v. State, Okl.Cr., 376 P.2d 351 (1962). See also, Smith v. Commonwealth, Ky., 268 S.W.2d 937 (1954). As to somnambulism, see Fain v. Commonwealth, 78 Ky. 183, 39 Am.Rep. 213 (1879); and Lewis v. State, 196 Ga. 755, 27 S.E.2d 659 (1943). See also § 6–1–116, W.S.1977.

anomalies will result. For example, if the court determines that the automatistic defendant is sane, but refuses to recognize automatism, the defendant has no defense to the crime with which he is charged. If found guilty, he faces a prison term. The rehabilitative value of imprisonment for the automatistic offender who has committed the offense unconsciously is nonexistent. The cause of the act was an uncontrollable physical disorder that may never recur and is not a moral deficiency.

If, however, the court treats automatism as insanity and then determines that the defendant is insane, he will be found not guilty. He then will be committed to a mental institution for an indefinite period. The commitment of an automatistic individual to a mental institution for rehabilitation has absolutely no value. Mental hospitals generally treat people with psychiatric or psychological problems. This form of treatment is not suited to unconscious behavior resulting from a bump on the head.

It may be argued that evidence of unconsciousness cannot be received unless a plea of not guilty by reason of mental illness or deficiency is made pursuant to Rule 15, W.R.Cr.P. We believe this approach to be illogical.

> ". . . Insanity is incapacity from disease of the mind, to know the nature and quality of one's act or to distinguish between right and wrong in relation thereto. In contrast, a person who is completely unconscious when he commits an act otherwise punishable as a crime cannot know the nature and quality thereof or whether it is right or wrong. . . . " State v. Mercer, supra, 165 S.E.2d at 335.

It does not seem that the definition of "mental deficiency" in § 7–11–301(a)(iii),[7] W.S.1977, which includes "brain damage," encompasses simple brain trauma with no permanent aftereffects. It is our view that the "brain damage" contemplated in the statute is some serious and irreversible condition having an impact upon the ability of the person to function. It is undoubtedly something far more significant than a temporary and transitory condition. The two defenses are merged, in effect, if a plea of "not guilty by reason of mental illness or deficiency" is a prerequisite for using the defense of unconsciousness. . . .

Although courts hold that unconsciousness and insanity are separate and distinct defenses, there has been some uncertainty concerning the burden of proof. We believe the better rule to be that stated in State v. Caddell, supra, 215 S.E.2d at 363: [8]

7. Section 7–11–301(a)(iii):

" 'Mental deficiency' means a defect attributable to mental retardation, brain damage and learning disabilities."

8. State v. Mercer, 275 N.C. 108, 165 S.E.2d 328, 335 (1969), held that "unconsciousness is never an affirmative defense." State v. Caddell, 287 N.C. 266, 215 S.E.2d 348, 363 (1975), overruled *Mercer*, supra, and stated that "it [unconsciousness] is an affirmative defense."

"We now hold that, under the law of this state, unconsciousness, or automatism, is a complete defense to the criminal charge, separate and apart from the defense of insanity; that *it is an affirmative defense; and that the burden rests upon the defendant to establish this defense, unless it arises out of the State's own evidence,* to the satisfaction of the jury." (Emphasis added.)

The rationale for this rule is that the defendant is the only person who knows his actual state of consciousness. Hill v. Baxter, 1 All E.R. 193 (1958), 1 Q.B. 277.

Our ruling on the facts of this case is that the defense of unconsciousness resulting from a concussion with no permanent brain damage is an affirmative defense and is a defense separate from the defense of not guilty by reason of mental illness or deficiency.

The appellant's conviction must, nevertheless, be affirmed. Dr. LeBegue was unable to state positively whether or not appellant had the requisite mental state for aggravated assault. He could not state that the character of the act was devoid of criminal intent because of the mind alteration. The presumption of mental competency was never overcome by appellant and the evidence presented formed a reasonable basis on which the trial judge could find and did find that the State had met the required burden of proof. . . .

RAPER, JUSTICE, specially concurring, with whom ROONEY, JUSTICE, joins.

I concur only in the result reached by the majority, except to the extent I otherwise herein indicate.

The reasoning of the majority with respect to the defense of unconsciousness in this case is contrary to clear legislative will and has judicially amended the statutes of this state pertaining to mental illness or deficiency excluding criminal responsibility. . . .

I am not concerned with the fact that unconsciousness may be a defense in this case but am distressed that the procedure for taking advantage of it has been cast aside. In order to reach the conclusion of the majority that it is not necessary to plead mental deficiency as a defense in the case of unconsciousness, it is indispensable that it be pretended that § 7–11–301, supra, does not exist. The appellant's disorder, if it existed, was caused by "brain damage" according to the appellant's own testimony. That is "mental deficiency" by statutory definition. The majority has feebly attempted to jump the hurdle of a statutory definition by saying "unconsciousness" is not "insanity," but we no longer use that term. It must be pointed out that under the old statutes and before adoption of the current law pertaining to mental deficiency, "insanity" was not legislatively defined. The majority is attempting to adopt the law of an era gone by-by, rather than what the authors of the new legislation considered a more informed and modern concept. . . .

MODEL PENAL CODE

Article 4. Responsibility

Section 4.01 Mental Disease or Defect Excluding Responsibility.

(1) A person is not responsible for criminal conduct if at the time of such conduct as a result of mental disease or defect he lacks substantial capacity either to appreciate the criminality [wrongfulness] of his conduct or to conform his conduct to the requirements of law.

(2) As used in this Article, the terms "mental disease or defect" do not include an abnormality manifested only by repeated criminal or otherwise anti-social conduct.

Section 4.02 Evidence of Mental Disease or Defect Admissible When Relevant to Element of the Offense; [Mental Disease or Defect Impairing Capacity as Ground for Mitigation of Punishment in Capital Cases].

(1) Evidence that the defendant suffered from a mental disease or defect is admissible whenever it is relevant to prove that the defendant did or did not have a state of mind which is an element of the offense.

[(2) Whenever the jury or the Court is authorized to determine or to recommend whether or not the defendant shall be sentenced to death or imprisonment upon conviction, evidence that the capacity of the defendant to appreciate the criminality [wrongfulness] of his conduct or to conform his conduct to the requirements of law was impaired as a result of mental disease or defect is admissible in favor of sentence of imprisonment.]

Section 4.03 Mental Disease or Defect Excluding Responsibility Is Affirmative Defense; Requirement of Notice; Form of Verdict and Judgment When Finding of Irresponsibility is Made.

(1) Mental disease or defect excluding responsibility is an affirmative defense.

(2) Evidence of mental disease or defect excluding responsibility is not admissible unless the defendant, at the time of entering his plea of not guilty or within ten days thereafter or at such later time as the Court may for good cause permit, files a written notice of his purpose to rely on such defense.

(3) When the defendant is acquitted on the ground of mental disease or defect excluding responsibility, the verdict and the judgment shall so state.[1]

SECTION 3. DRUNKENNESS (INTOXICATION)

The early common law seems to have ignored the problem of intoxication at the time of the *actus reus.*[1] Coke and Blackstone, in

1. Under the law of England until the early 19th Century voluntary intoxication was never an excuse for criminal misconduct. Director of Public Prosecutions v. Beard, [1920] App.Cas. 479.

"Intoxication" includes excitement or stupefaction induced by drugs as well as by liquor. People v. Lim Dum Dong, 26 Cal.App.2d 135, 78 P.2d 1026 (1938). A

fact, were inclined to urge that intoxication of one who committed a harmful deed should be regarded as a circumstance of aggravation. This suggestion was not adopted, but prior to the nineteenth century drunkenness, to whatever extent, was no defense in a criminal case. Since then there have been some modifications of that strict rule. Three modifications usually are mentioned: (1) Involuntary (innocent) intoxication may be so extreme as to be exculpating; (2) voluntary (culpable) intoxication may entitle the defendant to an acquittal if the crime charged requires a specific intent or special state of mind and he was too drunk to have such intent or state of mind; (3) delirium tremens is treated the same as other types of insanity although it results from overindulgence in liquor.

Firmly entrenched in the common law, although the wisdom thereof has been questioned by some, is the rule that voluntary intoxication is never exculpating. It is necessary, however, to draw a clear distinction between lack of excuse, on one hand, and disproof of some essential element of the crime charged, on the other. If the offense charged requires a specific intent, the defendant is not guilty if he was too intoxicated at the time to have any such intent, and had not entertained such an intent prior to his intoxication.[2] In such a case, proof of extreme intoxication (although "voluntary") may result in an acquittal, but it is not on any theory of exculpation. Suppose **D** has been indicted for burglary, for example. The indictment charges that **D** broke and entered the dwelling house of **X** at night with intent to steal. The evidence shows that **D** opened the front door of **X**'s house late at night, went in and was found in a drunken stupor on the floor. He was searched and it was learned that he had taken nothing. And when he is tried the jury is satisfied that while he managed to stumble into **X**'s house before he lost consciousness, his mind was too befogged with drink to be capable of entertaining any intent. Such a finding will not support a conviction of burglary.[3] This is not on any

drunken frenzy is not insanity despite the fact that it has sometimes been referred to loosely as "delirium tremens". Cheadle v. State, 11 Okl.Cr. 566, 149 P. 919 (1915); State v. Kidwell, 62 W.Va. 466, 59 S.E. 494 (1907). Delirium tremens proper is a form of mental disease and is treated on the same basis as any other form of insanity. State v. Alexander, 215 La. 245, 40 So.2d 232 (1949). The person suffering from delirium tremens is not free from fault, it is true, but the law takes notice only of the *immediate* condition which is a mental disease, and not of the excessive drinking which is *remote.* United States v. Drew, 25 Fed.Cas. No. 14,993 (C.C.D.Mass. 1828).

Voluntary intoxication is not an excuse but may be taken into consideration in determining the existence or nonexistence of malice aforethought which distinguishes murder from manslaughter. State v. Hudson, 85 Ariz. 77, 331 P.2d 1092 (1958).

2. One who drinks to "nerve" himself to commit a crime already decided upon, and who thereupon does commit that crime, is not in a position to maintain that he was too drunk at the time to entertain the intent which he executed. State v. Butner, 66 Nev. 127, 206 P.2d 253 (1949); State v. Robinson, 20 W.Va. 713 (1882).

3. State v. Phillips, 80 W.Va. 748, 93 S.W. 828 (1917). And a fumbling effort to get into a building by one too drunk to be capable of entertaining any intent is not an attempt to commit burglary. People v. Jones, 263 Ill. 564, 105 N.E. 744 (1914).

theory of excusing his conduct. One of the essential elements of the crime charged is missing. If he broke and entered the dwelling house of another at night (however wrongfully), he is still not guilty of burglary unless he did so with the intention of committing some crime therein (which crime must amount to felony at common law). Any evidence which proves the absence of such intent will disprove the charge of burglary.[4]

A person should not be convicted of larceny upon proof that he drank until his mind was so blank that he staggered away from the bar still clutching the glass from which he had been drinking, but unable to realize this fact or to entertain any intent. One who jumps from a bridge into the water below for the purpose of ending his life is punishable for an attempt to commit suicide, in some jurisdictions. But the inebriate who stumbles against the rail and tumbles over after the last spark of intelligence has faded from his mind is not guilty of such an attempt,—because an attempt requires a specific intent.[5] A drunkard (voluntarily drunk) walking with an axe on his shoulder who staggers in such a manner as to bump another with the axe is guilty of battery. This is true however intoxicated he may be because battery requires no more than criminal negligence. But he is not guilty of assault with intent to murder if he had no such intention. And proof that he was too dazed at the time to be capable of entertaining any intent will disprove the aggravated charge.

Provocation. Voluntary homicide is manslaughter rather than murder if it results from heat of passion engendered by adequate provocation and before the lapse of the "cooling time." Whether the provocation received was adequate or inadequate, and whether the time between the provocation and the fatal blow was sufficient or

4. Or any other crime requiring a specific intent, such as larceny. Johnson v. State, 32 Ala.App. 217, 24 So.2d 228 (1945); People v. Walker, 38 Mich. 156 (1878); Jamison v. State, 53 Okl.Cr. 59, 7 P.2d 171 (1932). Or assault with intent to commit rape. Whitten v. State, 115 Ala. 72, 22 So. 483 (1896). Or the "felony-murder" rule. People v. Koerber, 244 N.Y. 147, 155 N.E. 79 (1926).

"If upon retrial (for murder) the evidence indicates that defendant was unconscious at the time of the offense due to voluntary intoxication the trial judge should give the supplemental instruction on involuntary manslaughter." People v. Mosher, 1 Cal.3d 379, 391, 82 Cal.Rptr. 379, 386, 461 P.2d 659, 666 (1969).

D was entitled to an instruction on "nonstatutory" voluntary manslaughter because of evidence of diminished capacity due to intoxication. People v. Castillo, 70 Cal.2d 264, 74 Cal.Rptr. 385, 449 P.2d 449 (1969).

If D was too drunk to entertain a specific intent to murder he was not guilty of an assault with intent to kill. Avey v. State, 249 Md. 385, 240 A.2d 106 (1968).

Voluntary intoxication is not a defense to a charge of assault committed by a reckless act. State v. Rabago, 24 Or. App. 95, 544 P.2d 1061 (1976).

5. In a prosecution for attempted suicide intoxication of the prisoner at the time of the alleged attempt "is a material fact in order to arrive at the conclusion whether or not the prisoner really intended to destroy his life." Regina v. Doody, 6 Cox C.C. 463 (1854).

In a robbery trial there was evidence tending to show that D was too drunk at the time to form an intent to rob. It was reversible error for the judge to refuse to let this issue go to the jury. Womack v. United States, 336 F.2d 959 (D.C.Cir. 1964).

insufficient for passion once inflamed to subside, are both measured by an objective test,—the ordinary reasonable person. Hence the fact of intoxication has no bearing on the adequacy of the provocation or the sufficiency of the time for "cooling." [6] But whether the killing was actually in hot blood or cold blood depends upon the frame of mind of the killer himself. And if the fact of intoxication tends to throw any light upon the frame of mind of the defendant at the moment of the killing, the jury should have the benefit of this evidence with an instruction to consider it on this point only.[7]

STATE v. COOPER

Supreme Court of Arizona, In Division, 1974.
111 Ariz. 332, 529 P.2d 231.

HOLOHAN, JUSTICE. The appellant, Eugene Raymond Cooper, was convicted of kidnapping and assault with a deadly weapon for which he was sentenced to confinement for concurrent terms of 30 years to life for each offense. He appeals, raising the single issue of whether it was error for the trial court to refuse to submit the issue of insanity to the jury.

The appellant had been reported to the police as driving recklessly on the street and around a shopping center parking lot. A patrolman pursued appellant at high speed through rush-hour traffic. The appellant shot at and wounded the pursuing police officer. Shortly thereafter appellant kidnapped a man from a parking lot at gunpoint. The kidnap victim eventually wrestled the gun away from appellant, and the auto crashed into the divider on a freeway. Appellant fled on foot and was soon apprehended.

Pursuant to the request of the defense, an examination of the defendant's mental condition was ordered by the trial court. The court-appointed psychiatrists reported that the defendant was competent to assist his counsel and that the defendant understood the nature of the proceedings. A hearing was held, and the trial court found that the defendant was competent to stand trial.

The defendant gave timely notice of his intention to raise the defense of insanity at the trial.

During the trial the defense offered testimony by a psychiatrist and a psychologist as to the defendant's mental condition at the time of the offense. After hearing the evidence the trial court ruled that

6. Bishop v. United States, 71 App. D.C. 132, 107 F.2d 297 (1939); Commonwealth v. Bridge, 495 Pa. 568, 435 A.2d 151 (1981); Willis v. Commonwealth, 73 Va. 929 (1879); Rex v. Carroll, 7 Car. & P. 145, 173 Eng.Rep. 64 (1835).

Some courts have repeated Bishop's suggestion that an intent to drink may supply the malice aforethought needed for guilt of murder. See, for example, Newsome v. State, 214 Ark. 48, 50, 214 S.W.2d 778, 779 (1948); Weakley v. State, 168 Ark. 1087, 1089, 273 S.W. 374, 376 (1925).

7. Rex v. Thomas, 7 Car. & P. 817, 173 Eng.Rep. 356 (1837); Regina v. Olbey, 30 N.R. 152, 50 CCC2d 257 (S.C. Can.1979).

the evidence presented did not raise an issue as to the defendant's sanity, and the trial court refused all instructions submitted by the defense on the issue of sanity. The trial court did instruct the jury on the effect of voluntary intoxication in terms substantially the same as stated in the statute. A.R.S. § 13–132.

There is a presumption of sanity in every criminal case. To rebut that presumption and cause sanity to become an issue in the case, the defendant must introduce sufficient evidence to generate a doubt as to his sanity. If the evidence generates a reasonable doubt as to sanity, the burden falls upon the state to prove sanity beyond a reasonable doubt. Arizona has long adhered to the rule that the test of insanity is the M'Naghten rule.

The defense argues that not only did the evidence presented generate a reasonable doubt of the defendant's sanity but it would fully support a finding that the defendant was insane at the time of the commission of the criminal acts charged. The defense points out that both the psychiatrist and psychologist testified that the defendant was insane under the M'Naghten standard.

The state concedes that each of the defense experts testified that the defendant did not know the nature and quality of his acts and that he did not know he was doing wrong at the time of the acts charged, but the state points out that the condition of the defendant's mind was caused by his use of drugs and this does not constitute the defense of insanity. We agree.

The record shows that both of the defense experts testified that without the use of the drugs during the time in question the defendant would have been sane. They agreed that it was the use of drugs which induced his mental incapacity. The psychiatrist described the condition of the defendant as toxic psychosis, and the psychologist labled it as "acute drug induced psychotic episode."

The authorities have distinguished between an existing state of mental illness and a temporary episode of mental incapacity caused by the voluntary use of liquor or drugs. In the first instance the defense of insanity is available even though the state of mental illness may have been brought about by excessive or prolonged use of liquor or drugs, but in the latter instance the defense is not available. While the cases usually deal with excessive use of liquor, the same principles are applicable to drugs. Voluntary intoxication, whether by alcohol or drugs, is not a defense to crime, but evidence of such intoxication is admissible to show lack of specific intent.

It is not contested that the defendant had been voluntarily taking amphetamines for several days prior to the conduct at issue. Prior to that time the experts for the defense state that the defendant was sane. His subsequent condition, leading to his bizarre actions, was a result of an artificially produced state of mind brought on by his own hand at his own choice. The voluntary actions of the defendant do not provide an excuse in law for his subsequent, irrational conduct.

The defendant's burden to overcome the presumption of sanity was not met; therefore, the refusal of the trial court to instruct on insanity was correct.

Affirmed.[1]

CAMERON, V.C.J., and STRUCKMEYER, J., concur.

STATE v. BROWN

Supreme Court of Kansas, 1888.
38 Kan. 390, 16 P. 259.

VALENTINE, J. This was a criminal prosecution, brought in the district court of Chase county, wherein the defendant, John Brown, is charged with a violation of the provisions of chapter 104, Laws 1883 (Comp.Laws 1885, c. 31, par. 2223). The statute reads as follows: "Section 1. If any person shall be drunk in any highway, street, or in any public place or building, or if any person shall be drunk in his own house, or any private building or place, disturbing his family or others, he shall be deemed guilty of a misdemeanor, and upon conviction thereof, shall be fined in any sum not exceeding twenty-five dollars, or by imprisonment in the county jail for a period not exceeding thirty days." The information contains two counts,—in the first of which the defendant is charged with the offense of being drunk in a street in the city of Cottonwood Falls; in the second, he is charged with the offense of being drunk in the court-house in said city. A trial was had before the court and a jury, and the defendant was found guilty "as charged in the information," and was sentenced to pay a fine of $10 and the costs of suit, and to stand committed to the county jail until such fine and costs were paid. From this sentence he now appeals to this court. . . .

The next question is a more difficult one. It is whether a person may be guilty of the offense forbidden by the statute, where he innocently drinks the liquor which intoxicates him, without having any knowledge of its intoxicating qualities, and without having any idea that it would make him drunk. The court below, over his objections and exceptions, excluded nearly all the evidence offered by him to show his ignorance of the intoxicating character of the liquor, and its

1. "In our view the rule which should govern in Alaska is that voluntary intoxication will not support an insanity defense, and that all intoxication is to be regarded as voluntary unless it is unknowingly or externally compelled. . . . The better rule is one which views the accused's voluntary state of intoxication as irrelevant to the issue of insanity." Evans v. State, 645 P.2d 155, 160 (Alaska 1982).

"To constitute legal insanity, caused by intoxication, the mental disease must result from chronic alcoholism; not merely a temporary mental condition. Insanity, induced through long periods of excessive alcohol or drug consumption resulting in a continuing mental disease or defect may render a person irresponsible for his conduct; if he is deprived of the mental capacity to distinguish between right and wrong." Jones v. State, 648 P.2d 1251, 1254 (Okl.Cr.App.1982). See also Porreca v. State, 49 Md.App. 522, 433 A.2d 1204 (1981).

possible power to produce drunkenness; and the court also gave, among others, the following instruction to the jury, to-wit: "The defendant's ignorance of the intoxicating character of liquors drank by him, if he did drink any such, is no excuse for any drunkenness resulting therefrom, if any did so result." It has always been a rule of law that ignorance or mistake of law never excuses, and this, with a kindred rule that all men are conclusively presumed to know the law, is founded upon public policy, and grounded in necessity; but no such rule is invoked in this case. The question in this case is simply whether ignorance or mistake of *fact* will excuse. It is claimed by the prosecution that it will not; and this, on account of the express terms of the statute. The statute provides in express terms, and without any exception, that "if any person shall be drunk," etc., he shall be punished. And it would seem to be contended that there can be no exceptions. But are idiots, insane persons, children under seven years of age, babes, and persons who have been made drunk by force or fraud, and carried into a public place, to be punished under the statute? And if not, why not? And, if these are not to be punished, then no sufficient reason can be given for punishing those who have become drunk through unavoidable accident, or through an honest mistake. . . . Voluntary drunkenness in a public place was always a misdemeanor at common law, and it was always wrong, morally and legally. It is *malum in se.* Therefore, under either the rule enunciated by Mr. Bishop, or the one enunciated by Mr. Greenleaf, this case was erroneously tried in the court below. Whether the latter portion of said section of Mr. Greenleaf's evidence is correct or not it is not necessary for us now to decide. Whether a party, who, through an honest ignorance or mistake of fact, commits an act which is only *malum prohibitum,* may be punished for the act or not, it is not necessary now to determine. Mr. Bishop would say not; Mr. Greenleaf, following the Massachusetts supreme court decisions, would say he should be. Mr. Bishop's views are more in consonance with justice.

Before closing this opinion, it might be well to state that the fact that the defendant became intoxicated through an honest mistake might not constitute a complete defense to the action. If, after becoming drunk, he was still sufficiently in the possession of his faculties to know what he was doing, and to know the character of his acts, and went voluntarily into a public place, he would be guilty.

The judgment of the court below will be reversed, and cause remanded for a new trial.[1]

(All the justices concurring.)

1. If, having been given cocaine tablets with the statement that they were "breath fresheners", **D** took them with no notion that they were intoxicating and as a result became so intoxicated he did not know what he was doing and caused the death of another while in that condition, he is not guilty of crime. People v. Penman, 271 Ill. 82, 110 N.E. 894 (1915).

An "involuntarily intoxicated defendant's mental state must be measured by

BURROWS v. STATE

Supreme Court of Arizona, 1931.
38 Ariz. 99, 297 P. 1029.

LOCKWOOD, J. Richard N. Burrows, hereinafter called defendant, on the 7th day of June, 1929, was informed against by the county attorney of Maricopa county for the crime of murder, alleged to have been committed April 26th of that year. He was duly tried on such information, and the jury returned a verdict finding defendant guilty of murder in the first degree, fixing the penalty at death, and, from the judgment rendered on the verdict and the order overruling the motion for a new trial, this appeal has been taken. With the exception of two points, which we shall refer to in the course of this opinion, there is singularly little conflict in the evidence, and we therefor [sic] state the facts as follows:

Defendant, whose home was in Chicago, was a boy of eighteen or nineteen, and during the spring of 1929 was at a military school in Delafield, Wis. His closest friend there was one Milton Drucker. The two boys apparently came to the conclusion they would leave school for the purpose of seeing the country, and, taking a car belonging to the Drucker boy's parents, started west. They were at that time in the possession of some $55 in cash, while Drucker had a small amount of money in bank. After some days' travel they reached Phoenix, and were there detained by the police at the request of Drucker's parents. The latter's mother came on from San Diego, where she had been staying, and took her son back to Chicago. Defendant asked permission to go back with them, but was informed by Mrs. Drucker that his adopted parents had decided it would be a good lesson for him if he had to shift for himself and go to work, and for that reason she would not take him. He was alone in Phoenix, unacquainted with any one except the police who had had him in charge for a few days, and substantially, if not entirely, without money. He determined to try to get back to Chicago, and beat his way by railroad as far as Aguila, Ariz., where he discovered that he was on the way to Los Angeles instead of Chicago. He then decided to try to get back to Phoenix, where he had left a suitcase containing personal effects, and make a new start for Chicago, and seeing one Jack Martin, whom we shall hereafter call deceased, at a filling station in Aguila, and discovering the latter was going to Phoenix, asked if he might ride with him. Deceased answered affirmatively, and the two started to Phoenix in the latter's car.

Deceased was either carrying intoxicating liquor in his car, or secured some along the road, for by the time they reached Morristown, a small town some fifty miles northwest of Phoenix, he was so obvi-

the test of legal insanity, . . ."
State v. Mriglot, 15 Wash.App. 446, 448, 550 P.2d 17, 18 (1976).

ously intoxicated that the service station proprietor there suggested to the two that defendant had better drive, to which deceased assented. They left Morristown, and some few miles beyond it defendant shot and killed deceased, who was at that time sitting slumped down in the car in a drunken stupor. Defendant drove the car off the road to a small arroyo, and after taking what money deceased had on his person, placed the body in the arroyo and partially covered it with dirt, took the car, and went onto Phoenix, where he stopped at the police station and secured his personal effects. He then drove on to Denver, Colo., where he was apprehended and brought back to Phoenix. This statement of the facts is based on defendant's own testimony, and in the absence of anything further unquestionably establishes beyond the peradventure of a doubt a case of murder in the first degree.

The only defense offered at the trial was one of involuntary intoxication. Defendant testified that shortly after they left Aguila deceased began urging him to drink some beer which he was carrying in the car. Defendant had never tasted intoxicating liquor and objected most strenuously, whereupon deceased became very abusive, stating that, if defendant would not drink he would put him out of the car. Defendant, being alone, penniless, and fearing that he might be ejected and left on the desert, did drink three or four bottles of the beer, and since he was unused to intoxicating liquor, and had had little to eat in the preceding twenty-four hours, began to feel very queer.

When the parties reached Wickenburg, deceased procured some whisky, and with increasing vehemence urged defendant to partake of that. At first the latter remonstrated, but finally, as he states, through fear of what deceased might do to him, did drink some whisky. He claimed that its effect was to make him sick at the stomach and dizzy, until he had very little idea of what was happening, and that at the time the shooting occurred he was so dazed that he was unable to realize what was happening until after the fatal shot was fired, when his mind cleared up and he did realize what he had done, and that his conduct thereafter was due to panic at realizing his situation, and an effort to escape from the consequences thereof. . . .

The real issue involved is as to the manner in which involuntary intoxication must be induced, and the extent to which it must go. So far as the last point is concerned, we are of the opinion that the intoxication must be sufficient to affect the reason of a defendant to the extent that he does not understand and appreciate the nature and consequences of his act, or, as is commonly said, that he does not know right from wrong.

The other point is more difficult. It is the contention of defendant that any suggestion or influence which induces another to become intoxicated, when, if he had been left entirely to himself, he would have remained sober, excuses him from the consequences of a crime. It is the theory of the state that the influence must go to the extent of actual coercion and abuse. While this precise point has never been decided by any court, so far as the matter has been called to our attention, we are of the opinion that the true rule is that the influence exercised on the mind of a defendant must be such as to amount to duress or fraud. The law has always jealously guarded the effect of drunkenness as a defense in criminal cases, and, even with all the restrictions surrounding it, the doctrine is a dangerous one, and liable to be abused. In this case there is no suggestion of fraud, and it was for the jury to decide whether or not there was coercion and abuse to the extent of duress. While the instruction was not, perhaps as happily worded as it might have been, we are of the opinion that the jury was correctly informed as to the true rule in regard to a defense of involuntary intoxication; that (1) it must be induced by acts amounting in effect to duress; and that (2) it must go to such an extent that the mind of the defendant was incapable of understanding the criminal nature of his act. . . .

Because of the necessarily prejudicial remarks of the county attorney above discussed, the judgment is reversed, and the case remanded to the superior court of Maricopa county for a new trial.

McALISTER, C.J., and ROSS, J., concur.[1]

1. Intoxication resulting from a physician's prescription is involuntary, even if an overdose was inadvertently taken. State v. Gilchrist, 15 Wash.App. 892, 552 P.2d 690 (1976).

One could not properly be convicted of driving while under the influence of drugs, if the drug he was using had been given him by his doctor with no warning that its use while driving was prohibited. Crutchfield v. State, 627 P.2d 196 (Alaska 1981).

One who strikes a woman with a car, and does not stop and give aid, is guilty of not stopping and giving aid even if he did not know he had hit her, if the only reason he did not know was because he was drunk. Martinez v. State, 137 Tex.Cr.R. 434, 128 S.W.2d 398 (1939). The provision of West's Ann.Cal.Pen.Code § 26 exculpating persons "who committed the act charged without being conscious thereof" does not apply to one whose unconsciousness is due to voluntary intoxication. People v. Anderson, 87 Cal.App.2d 857, 197 P.2d 839 (1948).

A Massachusetts conviction of driving while "under the influence" was held not to be sufficient to authorize revocation of a chauffeur's license in New York because the New York statute spoke of driving "while intoxicated" and the two are not the same. Cashion v. Harnett, 234 App.D.C. 332, 255 N.Y.S. 169 (1932). "Under the influence" requires more than proof of sufficient alcohol to produce some effect. It requires substantial impairment of driving ability as a result of alcohol. People v. Dingle, 56 Cal.App. 445, 205 P. 705 (1922).

"Any intoxication that impairs the ability of a person to operate [a motor vehicle] is sufficient. State v. Laws, 547 S.W.2d 162, 164 (Mo.App.1977).

"It will be noticed that it is not essential to the existence of the statutory offense that the driver of the automobile should be so intoxicated that he cannot *safely* drive a car. The expression 'under the influence of intoxicating liquor' covers not only all the well-known and easily recognized conditions and degrees of intoxication, but any abnormal mental or physical condition which is the result of indulging in any degree in intoxicating liquors and which tends to deprive him of that clearness of intellect and control of himself which he would otherwise possess. So one driving an automobile upon a public street while under the influence of intoxicating liquor offends against the Disorderly Persons' act even though he drives so slowly and so skillfully and carefully that the public is not annoyed

PEOPLE v. CASTILLO

Supreme Court of California, In Bank, 1969.
70 Cal.2d 264, 74 Cal.Rptr. 385, 449 P.2d 449.

[Castillo, who had been drinking and had engaged in an argument with Rios, left the bar but returned an hour and a half later. He pointed a gun at Rios who was 14 feet away, said, "I kill you", and fired one shot which was fatal. Having been convicted of murder in the first degree, he appealed.]

TOBRINER, JUSTICE. . . .

Defendant contends that the trial court erroneously instructed the jury on the issue of voluntary manslaughter in that it failed to inform the jury that defendant could be convicted of manslaughter if he had intentionally committed the killing, yet, because of diminished capacity, did not act with malice. (People v. Conley (1966) 64 Cal.2d 310, 318, 49 Cal.Rptr. 815, 411 P.2d 911.) We conclude that defendant presented sufficient evidence of diminished capacity due to "pathological intoxication" to warrant the giving of the instruction set forth in *Conley*, and that the failure of the trial court so to instruct requires reversal. . . .

Defendant introduced expert testimony of two witnesses which tended to show that because of diminished capacity he was unable to premeditate and deliberate or to commit the homicide with malice. Dr. Lawrence, a psychologist, testified that he had examined defendant on two occasions for about an hour and a half each time. He administered several tests to defendant including the Wechsler Adult Intelligence Scale, the Rorschach Diagnostic Test, the Diagnostic Drawing Tests, and the Thematic Apperception Test. He concluded

or endangered; but such a driver is clearly not guilty of a public nuisance. To render him guilty of a public nuisance, facts not within the definition of the offense prohibited by the act of 1913 must be shown. In other words it must appear that the public was inconvenienced or endangered by the driving. This might be shown by proof that the degree of intoxication of the driver was such as to render him incapable of *properly* driving the machine; or by proof that in fact he drove it in such a manner as to endanger those using the street". State v. Rodgers, 91 N.J.L. 212, 215–16, 102 A. 433, 435 (1917).

The standard of intoxication may vary from statute to statute within a jurisdiction.

"To be under the influence within the concept of Vehicle Code section 23105, the intoxicating drug must so far affect the nervous system, the brain or muscles as to impair to an appreciable degree the ability to operate a vehicle in a manner like that of an ordinarily prudent and cautious person in full possession of his faculties, using care and under like conditions.

"On the other hand, being under the influence within the meaning of Health & Safety Code section 11550 merely requires that the person be under the influence in any detectable manner. 'The symptoms of influence are not confined to those commensurate with misbehavior, nor to demonstrate impairment of physical or mental ability.' " Gilbert v. Municipal Court of North Orange County, 73 Cal.App.3d 723, 140 Cal.Rptr. 897, 899–900 (1977).

"Self-induced intoxication by a chronic alcoholic is not involuntary intoxication within the meaning of the criminal law defense of involuntary intoxication." State v. Patch, 329 N.W.2d 836 (Minn. 1983).

from the results of the tests and from his observation of defendant that defendant was mentally retarded,[2] and that he was easily influenced. In a test designed to measure defendant's ability to form a plan and to execute that plan he obtained a low score.

Dr. Minard, a psychiatrist, testified that he had examined defendant for an hour and had reviewed the defense attorney's files in the case. He concluded that defendant had an unusual reaction to alcohol, a condition he described as alcoholic pathological intoxication. A person suffering from this condition may react exceptionally following the consumption of a small amount of alcohol and perform acts of violence without apparent motivation. The subject will almost always undergo a complete amnesia. The condition is quite similar to psychomotor epilepsy, which is caused by an electrical disturbance in the temporal lobe of the brain. Dr. Minard stated that on the basis of the facts of the homicide and his examination of defendant he believed that defendant had been unable to deliberate, premeditate, and reflect upon the gravity of the act meaningfully, and to harbor malice aforethought. Although stating that defendant's actions on the day of the homicide gave the impression that defendant was acting as a deliberating and reflecting man, Dr. Minard stated that his observation of defendant and study of his history indicated that defendant was suffering from a psychomotor seizure during the commission of the homicide and that no person so afflicted could premeditate or deliberate.[3]

Defendant primarily contends that the trial court committed error in instructing the jury. The trial court fully and correctly instructed the jury on first degree premeditated and deliberate murder and on second degree murder. The court explained that malice aforethought was an essential element of murder (Pen.Code, § 187) and that the jury should consider the evidence of diminished capacity in determining whether defendant acted with malice: "If you find from the evidence that at the time the alleged crime was committed, the defendant had substantially reduced mental capacity, whether caused by mental illness, intoxication or any other cause, you must consider what effect, if any, this diminished capacity had on the defendant's ability to form any of the specific mental states that are essential elements of murder. Thus, . . . if you find that the defendant's mental capacity was so diminished that he did not, or you have a reasonable doubt whether he did, harbor malice aforethought, as it has been defined for you, you cannot find him guilty of murder of either the first or second degree." The trial court also instructed the jury

2. Defendant scored 67 on an intelligence test on which a score of 100 is average. Ninety-nine percent of the people falling within defendant's age group would have a better score.

3. "I choose to believe that his history of blackouts in the past, his claim of amnesia at the present is amnesia at the present, his poorly motivated act of violence, his having not drinking [sic] all tie together to constitute all of the eventual things necessary to diagnose this condition."

on voluntary manslaughter upon a sudden quarrel or heat of passion and involuntary manslaughter. (Pen.Code, § 192.)

The error asserted by the defendant lies not in the language of the instructions but in their inadequacy. Although the trial court correctly instructed the jury that it must not convict defendant of *murder* without proof of malice, the court did not instruct the jury that it could convict defendant of *voluntary manslaughter* if it found that defendant had intentionally taken life but in so doing lacked malice because of diminished capacity due to mental defect, mental illness, or intoxication. Thus the trial court failed to give the instruction set out in People v. Conley, supra, 64 Cal.2d 310, 324–325 fn. 4, 49 Cal.Rptr. 815, 824, 411 P.2d 911, 920.[4] . . .

The judgment of conviction is reversed.

TRAYNOR, C.J., and PETERS and SULLIVAN, JJ., concur.

[MOSK and BURKE, JJ. concurred "in the judgment under the compulsion of" *Conley*. MCCOMB, J., dissented.]

4. In *Conley* we suggested that the jury be instructed on voluntary manslaughter in the following language: "Voluntary manslaughter [is] an intentional killing in which the law, recognizing human frailty, permits the defendant to establish the lack of malice either by a. Showing provocation such as to rouse the reasonable man to heat of passion or sudden quarrel. . . . b. Showing that due to diminished capacity caused by mental illness, mental defect, or intoxication, the defendant did not attain the mental state constituting malice."

[Added by the Compiler.]

"The Court was required, accordingly, to have instructed that if, because of diminished capacity due to defendant's voluntary intoxication, he had harbored neither malice nor an intent to kill, the offense could be no greater than involuntary manslaughter." People v. Ray, 14 Cal.3d 20, 120 Cal.Rptr. 377, 533 P.2d 1017, 1023 (1975).

Since second-degree murder does not require a specific intent to kill, intoxication to an extent precluding the formation of such intent does not prevent conviction thereof. State v. Tapia, 81 N.M. 274, 466 P.2d 551 (1970).

Voluntary intoxication is not a mitigating factor. Second-degree murder does not require an intent to kill, and hence the fact that defendant was so voluntarily intoxicated as to be unable to form an intent to kill did not entitle him to an instruction on manslaughter. State v. Lunn, 88 N.M. 64, 537 P.2d 672 (1975).

"Robbery," as used in the statute which provides that murder in the perpetration of robbery is murder in the first degree, requires a specific intent. And intoxication may be such as to negative the existence of the required specific intent. United States v. Lilly, 512 F.2d 1259 (1975).

The M'Naghten test of criminal responsibility was properly applied as to both the claim of intoxication and the claim of insanity. State v. Barry, 216 Kan. 609, 533 P.2d 1308 (1975).

"Evidence of intoxication is admissible, however, if it is relevant to negate or establish an element of the offense charged. . . . The purpose of this provision is to preclude exculpation based upon intoxication when recklessness is the standard of the offense charged. We do not think that this provision authorizes an instruction on 'reckless' manslaughter on the sole ground of intoxication." State v. Trieb, 315 N.W.2d 649, 658 (N.D.1982).

"Evidence of voluntary intoxication is admissible solely on the issue of whether or not the defendant actually formed a required specific intent, premeditated, deliberated or harbored malice aforethought, when a specific intent crime is charged." West's Ann.Cal.Penal Code § 22 (1982).

POWELL v. TEXAS

Supreme Court of the United States, 1968.
392 U.S. 514, 88 S.Ct. 2145.

MR. JUSTICE MARSHALL announced the judgment of the Court and delivered an opinion in which THE CHIEF JUSTICE, MR. JUSTICE BLACK, and MR. JUSTICE HARLAN join.

In late December 1966, appellant was arrested and charged with being found in a state of intoxication in a public place, in violation of Vernon's Ann.Texas Penal Code, Art. 477 (1952), which reads as follows:

"Whoever shall get drunk or be found in a state of intoxication in any public place, or at any private house except his own, shall be fined not exceeding one hundred dollars."

Appellant was tried in the Corporation Court of Austin, Texas, found guilty, and fined $20. He appealed to the County Court at Law No. 1 of Travis County, Texas, where a trial *de novo* was held. His counsel urged that appellant was "afflicted with the disease of chronic alcoholism," that "his appearance in public [while drunk was] . . . not of his own volition," and therefore that to punish him criminally for that conduct would be cruel and unusual, in violation of the Eighth and Fourteenth Amendments to the United States Constitution.

The trial judge in the county court, sitting without a jury, made certain findings of fact, but ruled as a matter of law that chronic alcoholism was not a defense to the charge. He found appellant guilty, and fined him $50. There being no further right to appeal within the Texas judicial system, appellant appealed to this Court; we noted probable jurisdiction. . . .

Following this abbreviated exposition of the problem before it, the trial court indicated its intention to disallow appellant's claimed defense of "chronic alcoholism." Thereupon defense counsel submitted, and the trial court entered, the following "findings of fact":

"(1) That chronic alcoholism is a disease which destroys the afflicted person's will power to resist the constant, excessive consumption of alcohol.

"(2) That a chronic alcoholic does not appear in public by his own volition but under a compulsion symptomatic of the disease of chronic alcoholism.

"(3) That Leroy Powell, defendant herein, is a chronic alcoholic who is afflicted with the disease of chronic alcoholism."

Whatever else may be said of them, these are not "findings of fact" in any recognizable, traditional sense in which that term has been used in a court of law; they are the premises of a syllogism transparently designed to bring this case within the scope of this

Court's opinion in Robinson v. State of California, 370 U.S. 660, 82 S.Ct. 1417, 8 L.Ed.2d 758 (1962). Nonetheless, the dissent would have us adopt these "findings" without critical examination; it would use them as the basis for a constitutional holding that "a person may not be punished if the condition essential to constitute the defined crime is part of the pattern of his disease and is occasioned by a compulsion symptomatic of the disease."

The difficulty with that position, as we shall show, is that it goes much too far on the basis of too little knowledge. In the first place, the record in this case is utterly inadequate to permit the sort of informed and responsible adjudication which alone can support the announcement of an important and wide-ranging new constitutional principle. We know very little about the circumstances surrounding the drinking bout which resulted in this conviction, or about Leroy Powell's drinking problem, or indeed about alcoholism itself. The trial hardly reflects the sharp legal and evidentiary clash between fully prepared adversary litigants which is traditionally expected in major constitutional cases. The State put on only one witness, the arresting officer. The defense put on three—a policeman who testified to appellant's long history of arrests for public drunkenness, the psychiatrist, and appellant himself.

Furthermore, the inescapable fact is that there is no agreement among members of the medical profession about what it means to say that "alcoholism" is a "disease." One of the principal works in this field states that the major difficulty in articulating a "disease concept of alcoholism" is that "alcoholism has too many definitions and disease has practically none." [2] This same author concludes that *"a disease is what the medical profession recognizes as such."*[3] In other words, there is widespread agreement today that "alcoholism" is a "disease," for the simple reason that the medical profession has concluded that it should attempt to treat those who have drinking problems. There the agreement stops. Debate rages within the medical profession as to whether "alcoholism" is a separate "disease" in any meaningful biochemical, physiological or psychological sense, or whether it represents one peculiar manifestation in some individuals of underlying psychiatric disorders.[4]

Nor is there any substantial consensus as to the "manifestations of alcoholism." . . .

The trial court's "finding" that Powell "is afflicted with the disease of chronic alcoholism," which "destroys the afflicted person's will power to resist the constant, excessive consumption of alcohol" covers a multitude of sins. Dr. Wade's testimony that appellant suf-

2. E. Jellinek, The Disease Concept of Alcoholism 11 (1960).

3. Id., at 12 (emphasis in original).

4. See, e.g., Joint Information Serv. of the Am. Psychiatric Assn. & the Nat. Assn. for Mental Health, The Treatment of Alcoholism—A Study of Programs and Problems 6–8 (1967) (hereafter cited as Treatment of Alcoholism).

fered from a compulsion which was an "exceedingly strong influence," but which was "not completely overpowering" is at least more carefully stated, if no less mystifying. Jellinek insists that conceptual clarity can only be achieved by distinguishing carefully between "loss of control" once an individual has commenced to drink and "inability to abstain" from drinking in the first place. Presumably a person would have to display both characteristics in order to make out a constitutional defense, should one be recognized. Yet the "findings" of the trial court utterly fail to make this crucial distinction, and there is serious question whether the record can be read to support a finding of either loss of control or inability to abstain. . . . But just as there is no agreement among doctors and social workers with respect to the causes of alcoholism, there is no consensus as to why particular treatments have been effective in particular cases and there is no generally agreed-upon approach to the problem of treatment on a large scale.[20] Most psychiatrists are apparently of the opinion that alcoholism is far more difficult to treat than other forms of behavioral disorders, and some believe it is impossible to cure by means of psychotherapy; indeed, the medical profession as a whole, and psychiatrists in particular, have been severely criticized for the prevailing reluctance to undertake the treatment of drinking problems.[21] Thus it is entirely possible that, even were the manpower and facilities available for a full-scale attack upon chronic alcoholism, we would find ourselves unable to help the vast bulk of our "visible"—let alone our "invisible"—alcoholic population.

However, facilities for the attempted treatment of indigent alcoholics are woefully lacking throughout the country.[22] It would be tragic to return large numbers of helpless, sometimes dangerous and frequently unsanitary inebriates to the streets of our cities without even the opportunity to sober up adequately which a brief jail term provides. Presumably no State or city will tolerate such a state of affairs. Yet the medical profession cannot, and does not, tell us with

20. See Treatment of Alcoholism 13–17.

21. Id., at 18–26.

22. Encouraging pilot projects do exist. See President's Commission on Law Enforcement and Administration of Justice, Task Force Report: Drunkenness 50–64, 82–108 (1967). But the President's Commission concluded that the "strongest barrier" to the abandonment of the current use of the criminal process to deal with public intoxication "is that there presently are no clear alternatives for taking into custody and treating those who are now arrested as drunks." President's Commission on Law Enforcement and Administration of Justice, The Challenge of Crime in a Free Society 235 (1967). Moreover, even if massive expenditures for physical plants were forthcoming, there is a woeful shortage of trained personnel to man them. One study has concluded that:

"[T]here is little likelihood that the number of workers in these fields could be sufficiently increased to treat even a large minority of problem drinkers. In California, for instance, according to the best estimate available, providing all problem drinkers with weekly contact with a psychiatrist and once-a-month contact with a social worker would require the full time work of *every* psychiatrist and *every* trained social worker in the United States." Cooperative Commission on Study of Alcoholism, Alcohol Problems 120 (1967) (emphasis in original).

any assurance that, even if the buildings, equipment and trained personnel were made available, it could provide anything more than slightly higher-class jails for our indigent habitual inebriates. Thus we run the grave risk that nothing will be accomplished beyond the hanging of a new sign—reading "hospital"—over one wing of the jailhouse.[23]

One virtue of the criminal process is, at least, that the duration of penal incarceration typically has some outside statutory limit; this is universally true in the case of petty offenses, such as public drunkenness, where jail terms are quite short on the whole. "Therapeutic civil commitment" lacks this feature; one is typically committed until one is "cured." Thus, to do otherwise than affirm might subject indigent alcoholics to the risk that they may be locked up for an indefinite period of time under the same conditions as before, with no more hope than before of receiving effective treatment and no prospect of periodic "freedom." [24]

Faced with this unpleasant reality, we are unable to assert that the use of the criminal process as a means of dealing with the public aspects of problem drinking can never be defended as rational. The picture of the penniless drunk propelled aimlessly and endlessly through the law's "revolving door" of arrest, incarceration, release and re-arrest is not a pretty one. But before we condemn the present practice across-the-board, perhaps we ought to be able to point to some clear promise of a better world for these unfortunate people. Unfortunately, no such promise has yet been forthcoming. If, in addition to the absence of a coherent approach to the problem of treatment, we consider the almost complete absence of facilities and manpower for the implementation of a rehabilitation program, it is difficult to say in the present context that the criminal process is utterly lacking in social value. This Court has never held that anything in the Constitution requires that penal sanctions be designed solely to achieve therapeutic or rehabilitative effects, and it can hardly be said

23. For the inadequate response in the District of Columbia following Easter v. District of Columbia, 124 U.S.App.D.C. 33, 361 F.2d 50 (1966), which held on constitutional and statutory grounds that a chronic alcoholic could not be punished for public drunkenness, see President's Commission on Crime in the District of Columbia, Report 486–490 (1966).

24. Counsel for *amici curiae* ACLU et al., who has been extremely active in the recent spate of litigation dealing with public intoxication statutes and the chronic inebriate, recently told an annual meeting of the National Council on Alcoholism:

"We have not found for two years to extract DeWitt Easter, Joe Driver, and their colleagues from jail, only to have them involuntarily committed for an even longer period of time, with no assurance of appropriate rehabilitative help and treatment. . . . The euphemistic name 'civil commitment' can easily hide nothing more than permanent incarceration. . . . I would caution those who might rush headlong to adopt civil commitment procedures and remind them that just as difficult legal problems exist there as with the ordinary jail sentence."

Quoted in Robitscher, Psychiatry and Changing Concepts of Criminal Responsibility, 31 Fed.Prob. 44, 49 (No. 3 Sept. 1967). Cf. Note, The Nascent Right to Treatment, 53 Va.L.Rev. 1134 (1967).

with assurance that incarceration serves such purposes any better for the general run of criminals than it does for public drunks.

Ignorance likewise impedes our assessment of the deterrent effect of criminal sanctions for public drunkenness. The fact that a high percentage of American alcoholics conceal their drinking problems, not merely by avoiding public displays of intoxication but also by shunning all forms of treatment, is indicative that some powerful deterrent operates to inhibit the public revelation of the existence of alcoholism. Quite probably this deterrent effect can be largely attributed to the harsh moral attitude which our society has traditionally taken toward intoxication and the shame which we have associated with alcoholism. Criminal conviction represents the degrading public revelation of what Anglo-American society has long condemned as a moral defect, and the existence of criminal sanctions may serve to reinforce this cultural taboo, just as we presume it serves to reinforce other, stronger feelings against murder, rape, theft, and other forms of antisocial conduct.

Obviously, chronic alcoholics have not been deterred from drinking to excess by the existence of criminal sanctions against public drunkenness. But all those who violate penal laws of any kind are by definition undeterred. The long-standing and still raging debate over the validity of the deterrence justification for penal sanctions has not reached any sufficiently clear conclusions to permit it to be said that such sanctions are ineffective in any particular context or for any particular group of people who are able to appreciate the consequences of their acts. Certainly no effort was made at the trial of this case, beyond a monosyllabic answer to a perfunctory one-line question, to determine the effectiveness of penal sanctions in deterring Leroy Powell in particular or chronic alcoholics in general from drinking at all or from getting drunk in particular places or at particular times.

III.

Appellant claims that his conviction on the facts of this case would violate the Cruel and Unusual Punishment Clause of the Eighth Amendment as applied to the States through the Fourteenth Amendment. The primary purpose of that clause has always been considered, and properly so, to be directed at the method or kind of punishment imposed for the violation of criminal statutes; the nature of the conduct made criminal is ordinarily relevant only to the fitness of the punishment imposed.[25]

Appellant, however, seeks to come within the application of the Cruel and Unusual Punishment Clause announced in Robinson v. State of California, 370 U.S. 660, 82 S.Ct. 1417, 8 L.Ed.2d 758 (1962), which involved a state statute making it a crime to "be addicted to

25. See generally Note, The Cruel and Unusual Punishment Clause and the Substantive Criminal Law, 79 Harv.L.Rev 635 (1966).

the use of narcotics." This Court held there that "a state law which imprisons a person thus afflicted [with narcotic addiction] * as a criminal, even though he has never touched any narcotic drug within the State or been guilty of any irregular behavior there, inflicts a cruel and unusual punishment . . . ." Id., at 667, 82 S.Ct., at 1420–1421.

On its face the present case does not fall within that holding, since appellant was convicted, not for being a chronic alcoholic, but for being in public while drunk on a particular occasion. The State of Texas thus has not sought to punish a mere status, as California did in *Robinson;* nor has it attempted to regulate appellant's behavior in the privacy of his own home. Rather, it has imposed upon appellant a criminal sanction for public behavior which may create substantial health and safety hazards, both for appellant and for members of the general public, and which offends the moral and esthetic sensibilities of a large segment of the community. This seems a far cry from convicting one for being an addict, being a chronic alcoholic, being "mentally ill, or a leper . . . ." Id., at 666, 82 S.Ct., at 1420.

Robinson so viewed brings this Court but a very small way into the substantive criminal law. And unless *Robinson* is so viewed it is difficult to see any limiting principle that would serve to prevent this Court from becoming, under the aegis of the Cruel and Unusual Punishment Clause, the ultimate arbiter of the standards of criminal responsibility, in diverse areas of the criminal law, throughout the country. . . .

Traditional common-law concepts of personal accountability and essential considerations of federalism lead us to disagree with appellant. We are unable to conclude, on the state of this record or on the current state of medical knowledge, that chronic alcoholics in general, and Leroy Powell in particular, suffer from such an irresistible compulsion to drink and to get drunk in public that they are utterly unable to control their performance of either or both of these acts and thus cannot be deterred at all from public intoxication. And in any event this Court has never articulated a general constitutional doctrine of *mens rea.*[27]

* Added by the Compiler.

Robinson held that a law making it a criminal offense to be ill is unconstitutional. In doing so the Court emphasized that the general health and welfare may require that certain human afflictions be dealt with by compulsory treatment, involving quarantine, confinement, or sequestration.

D, who had been committed as a criminal sexual psychopath, appealed. It was held that the criminal sexual psychopath law does not create a crime but is intended to protect society by sequestering the deviate so long as he remains a menace to others, and to subject him to treatment to the end that he may be rehabilitated. Since the commitment proceeding is not a criminal trial the court-appointed physician's testimony is not to be excluded for failure to give the usual Miranda warnings. State ex rel. Fulton v. Scheetz, 166 N.W.2d 874 (Iowa 1969).

27. The Court did hold in Lambert v. People of State of California, 355 U.S. 225, 78 S.Ct. 240, 2 L.Ed.2d 228 (1957), that a person could not be punished for a "crime" of omission, if that person did not know, and the State had taken no reasonable steps to inform him, of his du-

We cannot cast aside the centuries-long evolution of the collection of interlocking and overlapping concepts which the common law has utilized to assess the moral accountability of an individual for his antisocial deeds.[28] The doctrines of *actus reus, mens rea,* insanity, mistake, justification, and duress have historically provided the tools for a constantly shifting adjustment of the tension between the evolving aims of the criminal law and changing religious, moral, philosophical, and medical views of the nature of man. This process of adjustment has always been thought to be the province of the States.

Nothing could be less fruitful than for this Court to be impelled into defining some sort of insanity test in constitutional terms. Yet, that task would seem to follow inexorably from an extension of *Robinson* to this case. If a person in the "condition" of being a chronic alcoholic cannot be criminally punished as a constitutional matter for being drunk in public, it would seem to follow that a person who contends that, in terms of one test, "his unlawful act was the product of mental disease or mental defect," Durham v. United States, 94 U.S.App.D.C. 228, 241, 214 F.2d 862, 875, 45 A.L.R.2d 1430 (1954), would state an issue of constitutional dimension with regard to his criminal responsibility had he been tried under some different and perhaps lesser standard, e.g., the right-wrong test of *M'Naghten's Case.*[29] The experimentation of one jurisdiction in that field alone indicates the magnitude of the problem. But formulating a constitutional rule would reduce, if not eliminate, that fruitful experimentation, and freeze the developing productive dialogue between law and psychiatry into a rigid constitutional mold. It is simply not yet the time to write the Constitutional formulas cast in terms whose meaning, let alone relevance, is not yet clear either to doctors or to lawyers.

Affirmed.[1]

ty to act and of the criminal penalty for failure to do so. It is not suggested either that *Lambert* established a constitutional doctrine of *mens rea,* see generally Packer, Mens Rea and the Supreme Court, 1962 Sup.Ct.Rev. 107, or that appellant in this case was not fully aware of the prohibited nature of his conduct and of the consequences of taking his first drink.

28. See generally Sayre, Mens Rea, 45 Harv.L.Rev. 974 (1932).

29. 10 Cl. & Fin. 200, 8 Eng.Rep. 718 (1843).

1. [Added by the Compiler.] In Driver v. Hinnant, 356 F.2d 761 (4th Cir.1966), the conviction of being drunk in a public place in violation of the North Carolina Statute was reversed on the ground that Driver was a chronic alcoholic who did not drink voluntarily but under the compulsion of his disease. The court held it would be cruel and unusual punishment to convict one whose drunken public display was involuntary as the result of disease. The court felt that the holding of the Supreme Court in *Robinson* required the result reached here.

In Easter v. District of Columbia, 361 F.2d 50 (D.C.Cir.1966) a conviction of being drunk in a public place, in violation of the District of Columbia statute, was reversed because it was established that Easter was a chronic alcoholic. The court relied primarily upon a statute entitled "Rehabilitation of Alcoholics." "The above statutory provisions, considered in the full context of the Act of which they are a part, preclude attaching criminality in this jurisdiction to intoxication in public of a chronic alcoholic" (page 52). The court also referred to *Driver* with ap-

[MR. JUSTICE BLACK and MR. JUSTICE HARLAN, who joined in the opinion of MR. JUSTICE MARSHALL, also wrote a concurring opinion, and MR. JUSTICE WHITE wrote an opinion concurring in the result. MR. JUSTICE FORTAS, with whom MR. JUSTICE DOUGLAS, MR. JUSTICE BRENNAN and MR. JUSTICE STEWART joined, wrote a dissenting opinion.][2]

MODEL PENAL CODE

Section 2.08 Intoxication.

(1) Except as provided in Subsection (4) of this Section, intoxication of the actor is not a defense unless it negatives an element of the offense.

(2) When recklessness establishes an element of the offense, if the actor, due to self-induced intoxication, is unaware of a risk of which he would have been aware had he been sober, such unawareness is immaterial.

(3) Intoxication does not, in itself, constitute mental disease within the meaning of Section 4.01.

(4) Intoxication which (a) is not self-induced or (b) is pathological is an affirmative defense if by reason of such intoxication the actor at the time of his conduct lacks substantial capacity either to appreciate its criminality [wrongfulness] or to conform his conduct to the requirements of law.

(5) Definitions. In this Section unless a different meaning plainly is required:

(a) "intoxication" means a disturbance of mental or physical capacities resulting from the introduction of substances into the body;

(b) "self-induced intoxication" means intoxication caused by substances which the actor knowingly introduces into his body, the tendency of which to cause intoxication he knows or ought to know, unless he introduces them pursuant to medical advice or under such circumstances as would afford a defense to a charge of crime;

proval and seemed to think the reversal was required by *Robinson.*

"In Powell the Court held that it was not a violation of due process to punish the defendant for being drunk in public where defendant was a chronic alcoholic. There is no indication, however, that the Powell court intended to make the insanity defense unavailable to those who involuntarily consume alcohol because of mental disease." United States v. Henderson, 680 F.2d 659 (9th Cir.1982).

The fact that **D** was a chronic alcoholic is no defense to a charge of driving while under the influence of liquor. Shelburne v. State, 446 P.2d 56 (Okl.Cr.1968).

Evidence of **D**'s intoxication should not be considered in determining whether he committed an assault with a deadly weapon upon a peace officer or of any lesser included assault. People v. Hood, 1 Cal.3d 444, 82 Cal.Rptr. 618, 462 P.2d 370 (1969).

Criminal punishment of a chronic alcoholic for public intoxication violates the West Virginia constitutional prohibition against cruel and unusual punishment. State v. Zegeer, ___ W.Va. ___, 296 S.E.2d 873 (1982).

California public intoxication statute is constitutional. Sundance v. Municipal Court of the Los Angeles Judicial District, 141 Cal.App.3d 559, 190 Cal.Rptr. 432 (1983).

2. The dissenting justices admit that they would distinguish between a chronic alcoholic who gets drunk, and one who commits a crime such as robbery or assault while drunk, because such "offenses require independent acts or conduct and do not typically flow from and are not part of the syndrome of the disease of chronic alcoholism". (392 U.S. 559, 88 S.Ct. 2167, note 2.)

(c) "pathological intoxication" means intoxication grossly excessive in degree, given the amount of the intoxicant, to which the actor does not know he is susceptible.[1]

SECTION 4. COVERTURE

Under rather narrow limitations, to be considered in a subsequent chapter, a harmful deed which would otherwise be a crime will be excused if done under compulsion. Under the common-law "doctrine of coercion" a married woman was excused for an *actus reus* perpetrated by her under the command or coercion of her husband, without being subject to the ordinary limitations of compulsion. In fact, under the "doctrine of coercion," coverture involved a limitation of criminal capacity. The wife "cannot be guilty", says Lord Hale, if her husband is guilty of the same larceny or burglary (1 Hale P.C. * 46).

The "doctrine of coercion" did not apply in cases of treason or murder, or in offenses such as keeping a brothel which are assumed to be "generally conducted by the intrigues of the female sex." Except for these offenses (and perhaps robbery) a married woman was entitled to an acquittal if the *actus reus* was perpetrated by her under the coercion, or even the bare command, of her husband. Furthermore, the mere presence of the husband at the time of the harmful deed was sufficient to give rise to a presumption of coercion on his part. This presumption could be rebutted by evidence showing clearly the absence of coercion, but it was a powerful shield in her defense.

There may have been some reason for this doctrine in the ancient law, but there is none today. And it is definitely not recognized in the overwhelming majority of jurisdictions. It is no longer true that a married woman cannot be guilty of the very same larceny or burglary of which her husband is convicted. The presumption of coercion arising from the mere presence of the husband is usually not as strong as formerly, even where still recognized. It is a mistake, however, to assume that the "doctrine of coercion" has disappeared entirely.

PEOPLE v. STATLEY

Appellate Department, Superior Court, Los Angeles County, California, 1949.
91 Cal.App.2d Supp. 943, 206 P.2d 76.

BISHOP, J. Convicted on a charge that she had failed to yield the right of way to a pedestrian in a crosswalk, the defendant contends that the judgment of conviction should be reversed because the trial court failed to give her requested instruction that "under the laws of this State, a married woman is not capable of committing a misdemeanor while acting under threats, command or coercion of her husband." In support of her contention the defendant advances three arguments: (a) the instruction embodies a correct principle of law; (b) it was called for in this case by direct evidence that she was acting under her husband's command; (c) it was made pertinent by the common law presumption that a misdemeanor committed by a married woman in her husband's presence is done under his coercion. We have reached the conclusion that the instruction should have been given. It was a correct statement of the law, and the evidence before the jurors made it applicable. We cannot, however, square the ancient presumption with the facts of modern life. We are not ready to put our stamp of approval on the statement that, when a married woman who is operating a motor vehicle in which her husband is a passenger, neglects to make a boulevard stop, fails to signal before she turns, or commits any other violation of the traffic laws, the probability is that she did so because he made her do so.

There can be no doubt that the requested instruction is a correct statement of the law, for we find in section 26, Penal Code: "All persons are capable of committing crimes except . . . : Seven. Married women (except for felonies) acting under the threats, commands, or coercion of their husbands." [a] One of the two exceptions contained in the language of the section was eliminated in People v. Graff (1922), 59 Cal.App. 706, 708, 211 P. 829, 830, by rephrasing the quoted provision to read: "Married women are persons capable of committing all crimes, except misdemeanors committed by them when acting under the threats, command, or coercion of their husbands." It may quite properly be restated, for the purpose of this misdemeanor case, to eliminate all exceptions: "Married women are persons not capable of committing misdemeanors when acting under the threats, command, or coercion of their husbands." It was this principle of law that the defendant desired to have implanted in the minds of the jurors in order that she might have the benefit of it. The possibility that this code provision has become anachronistic does not justify the courts in disregarding it. A legislative enactment is not repealed by time or changed conditions, but only by further legislation.

The testimony which gave pertinency to this instruction came from the lips of defendant's husband. After relating how the automobile which the defendant was driving, and in which he was riding, had stopped, to permit the traffic to clear up in the lane between them and the crosswalk, defendant's husband continued by repeating the words he had addressed to her, "You have got plenty of clearance, take it." She had begun to move forward just before he spoke these words, and following their utterance she drove on and into the crosswalk, causing a pedestrian to jump back.

We find in this evidence no basis for concluding that the defendant, in driving across the lane of traffic and into the crosswalk, had

a. Repealed 1976.

acted under a threat or under the coercion of her husband, but, had the matter been submitted to the jury, it is possible that it would have been determined that she acted under his command, or at least have entertained a reasonable doubt about the matter. His declaration to her was couched in the form of a command, and while it must be conceded that the jury might have determined that the defendant paid no attention to what her husband was saying, the question was one of fact, and the defendant was entitled to have the case submitted to the jury on her theory of the facts. Of course, the husband's denial that his words "Take it" constituted a command, no more removed the possibility of a command from the case than did his denial that there was a pedestrian in the crosswalk do away with him.

The defendant contends that the requested instruction was pertinent not only because there was direct evidence of a command but for the further reason that a presumption had arisen that she was acting under the coercion or command of her husband, and she requested, vainly, a further instruction that there was such a presumption. Whether or not such a presumption arises is a question that will be involved in any retrial of this case, and so merits attention. Our determination that there is no such presumption applying in this case is not predicated on any misapprehension about the existence of the presumption at common law. It did exist. It is referred to in O'Donnell v. State (1941), 73 Okl.Cr. 1, 117 P.2d 139, 141, as being: "the rule of the common law that where a crime, with some exceptions, was committed by a married woman conjointly with or in the presence of her husband, prima facie she was not criminally liable, as it was presumed that she acted in obedience to his commands and under his coercion. This doctrine is announced by Blackstone, who says that it is a thousand years old."

"But the foregoing view of the legal relationship of husband and wife is no longer warranted, when by modern conditions and through modern statutory provisions the wife has been emancipated with respect to her personal wages and earnings. Where the reason for a rule of common law which is the spirit and soul of that law, fails, the rule itself fails." [1]

We conclude, then, that the reign of the thousand year old presumption has come to an end. In our society, where almost no bride promises to obey her husband, and where it is not accepted as the usual that a wife does what her husband wishes by way of yielding obedience to a dominant will, the basis for the presumption has disappeared. A presumption that has lost its reason must be confined to a museum; it has no place in the administration of justice. If, therefore, a wife is to escape the consequences of her disobedience of a statute on the ground that she was acting in obedience to her hus-

1. Where not hampered by statute some courts have completely repudiated the common-law doctrine of coercion of a married woman by her husband. United States v. Dege, 364 U.S. 51, 80 S.Ct. 1589, 4 L.Ed.2d 1563 (1960); State v. Turnbow, 67 N.M. 341, 354 P.2d 533 (1960).

band, the fact is not established by the mere circumstance that her husband was present when she offended. The judgment and order appealed from are reversed; the case is remanded for a new trial.

SHAW, P.J., and STEPHENS, J., concurred.[2]

MODEL PENAL CODE

Section 2.09 Duress. . . .

(3) It is not a defense that a woman acted on the command of her husband, unless she acted under such coercion as would establish a defense under this Section. [The presumption that a woman, acting in the presence of her husband, is coerced is abolished.] [3]

2. "Especially since the passage of the married woman's emancipation legislation in this State, the married woman is as capable of and as responsible for crime as if she were single. . . . She is to be regarded, in the contemplation of our criminal statutes, as an independent entity." Johnson v. State, 152 Tenn. 184, 187, 274 S.W. 12 (1925).

Chapter 9

RESPONSIBILITY: MODIFYING CIRCUMSTANCES

SECTION 1. IGNORANCE OR MISTAKE

(A) IGNORANCE OR MISTAKE OF LAW

"Ignorance of the law is no excuse," is one of the most familiar phrases in this branch of jurisprudence. It is not entirely without exception, although the exceptions are rare. What is intended to convey the same general idea in other words is this: "Every person is presumed to know the law." In order to understand either the rule itself, or the exceptions thereto, it is necessary to know what is meant by the word "presumed." And this is complicated by the fact that the words "presumed" and "presumption" are used in three different senses in the law.

One of the senses is to signify a mere inference of fact. If two men are in a small well-lighted room at the same time when no one else is there, and if both are there, fully conscious, for a substantial period of time, it can be inferred ("presumed") that each knew of the other's presence. This is not a rule of law. It is merely a common sense conclusion based upon ordinary experience. It is unfortunate that the words "presumed" and "presumption" were ever used in this sense, and such usage can be ignored for the purposes of this subsection. Nothing could be more absurd than to suggest as a common sense conclusion, based upon ordinary experience, that everyone knows all of the criminal law.[1] The fair inference is that nobody does. Hence attention here may be concentrated upon the other two meanings.

A true presumption is a rule of law which calls for a certain result unless the party adversely affected comes forward with evidence to overcome it. This (although it is the true presumption) often is referred to as a "prima facie presumption" to distinguish it from the so-called "conclusive presumption" which is a legal device in the form of a postulate used for the determination of a particular case whether it

1. A judge thinking of this presumption in terms of an inference of fact would be bound to reject it. "There is no presumption in this country that every person knows the law: it would be contrary to common sense and reason if it were so." Per Maule, J. in Martindale v. Falkner, 2 C.B. 706, 719, 135 Eng.Rep. 1129 (1846). Quoted in Ryan v. State, 104 Ga. 78, 82, 30 S.E. 678, 680 (1898).

represents the actual facts or not. A typical example is the conclusive presumption of delivery by all prior parties to a negotiable instrument which has reached the hands of a holder in due course. The net result of this "conclusive presumption" is that such a holder in due course can enforce the instrument as effectively against a prior party who did not deliver it as against one who did. It merely disguises a rule of substantive law in the language of a rule of evidence.

If "everyone is presumed to know the law" in this sense, it means that a particular case will be disposed of exactly as if the defendant actually did know the law whether such is the fact or not. And this is exactly the sense in which this word is used ordinarily in this phrase. This is the sense in which it is used in all of those cases in which "ignorance of the law is no excuse." In those rare and exceptional cases in which ignorance of the law is recognized as an excuse in a criminal case the presumption is rebuttable. In other words, while there are exceptions to the rule that "ignorance of the law is no excuse" there are none to the statement that "everyone is presumed to know the law"—except to the extent that the presumption may be overcome by evidence where this is permissible. Stated differently, knowledge of the law is presumed; in most cases this presumption is conclusive but under exceptional circumstances it is disputable.

The most obvious instance in which the presumption of knowledge of the law is rebuttable is in a prosecution for an offense requiring a specific intent. One does not commit larceny, for example, by a trespassory taking and carrying away of the chattel of another if it is done without an intent to steal. Hence one does not commit larceny by such an asportation of another's chattel if he does so under the honest belief that it belongs to him and he has the right to immediate possession of it. And under such circumstances it is immaterial whether the error which led to this bona-fide belief was due to a mistake of fact or a mistake of law. It is to be observed, however, that the ignorance or mistake in such a case concerns some other law and not the law violated. In a larceny case it may be shown that a misunderstanding of property law led to a bona-fide belief that the particular chattel belonged to the defendant and that he had a lawful right to immediate possession thereof, but not that he never heard of the law of larceny or that he mistakenly believed he could take away and appropriate another's property wrongfully without subjecting himself to the penalty of that law under the particular circumstances of the taking. To illustrate further: In a prosecution for malicious trespass based upon removing a fence from a certain path, it could be shown that a mistaken belief with reference to the law of right of way led to the opinion that the fence should not be there, but not that the defendant did not know there was a penalty for wrongfully tearing down another's property.

Problems of particular difficulty in this field are: (1) To what extent does the rule permitting evidence of a misunderstanding of some law, other than the one violated, apply to offenses requiring some particular state of mind which is not "specific intent?" and (2) may circumstances ever be so exceptional as to permit an excuse based upon ignorance or mistake of law (a) in prosecutions for offenses requiring only the "general mens rea," or (b) in prosecutions for a violation of the very law which is claimed to have been misunderstood? [2]

STATE v. CUDE

Supreme Court of Utah, 1963.
14 Utah 2d 287, 383 P.2d 399.

CALLISTER, JUSTICE. Defendant appeals from his conviction and judgment of grand larceny. It appears from the record that the defendant left his automobile at a garage in Ogden, Utah with the request that the same be repaired. The garage owner initially estimated the cost of the necessary work to be in the neighborhood of $180.00. There was evidence, however, that the defendant authorized the garage owner to fix the car, irrespective of the cost. After leaving his automobile at the garage, defendant left the state and returned a few days later. At that time he was presented with a repair bill in the amount of $345.00. Unable to pay this charge (or, for that matter, the estimate of $180.00) the defendant was refused possession of the car by the garageman. Several hours thereafter (after the garage had closed for the night) defendant returned and, using a duplicate key, drove the automobile away.

The automobile was recovered by the police a day or so later while in the possession of a friend of the defendant. It was the contention of the latter that he had taken the car for the purpose of selling the same to realize enough cash to pay off the garage bill.

This court has previously ruled that an owner of personalty in the possession of another by virtue of some special right or title, as bailee or otherwise, is guilty of larceny, if he takes such property from the person in possession *with the fraudulent intention of depriving such person of his rights.*

The defendant requested an instruction regarding his defense, namely, that he could not be found guilty if, at the time of the taking, he honestly believed that he had a right to the possession of the automobile. We are of the opinion that the lower court erred in refusing to give such an instruction.

2. Ignorance of the law of arrest was no defense to a charge of unlawfully interfering with the United States Attorney's performance of his official duties by arresting him. Finn v. United States, 219 F.2d 894 (9th Cir.1955), certiorari denied 349 U.S. 906, 75 S.Ct. 583 (1955).

"Mistake of law is no defense to the underlying crime or the conspiracy charge." United States v. Jones, 642 F.2d 909, 914 (5th Cir.1981). See Perkins, Ignorance or Mistake of Law Revisited, 1980 Utah L.Rev. 973.

It is fundamental that an essential element of larceny is the intent to steal the property of another. Consequently, if there is any reasonable basis in the evidence upon which the jury could believe that the accused thought he had a right to take possession of his automobile, or if the evidence in that regard is such that it might raise a reasonable doubt that he had the intent to steal, then that issue should be presented to the jury. The principle is correctly stated in 52 C.J.S. Larceny § 150, p. 999, that if the property was taken under any ". . . circumstances from which the jury might infer that the taking was under a claim of right, [the] accused is entitled to an appropriate charge distinguishing larceny from a mere trespass." . . .

It is held, and we think correctly so, that the general charge that the accused must have the intent to steal does not meet the request to have this particular theory of defense presented to the jury. In a prosecution for stealing sheep, the trial court had given such a general instruction but refused to give the defendant's request, similar to the one submitted here, that if the defendant believed he had a right to take the sheep, he would not be guilty of larceny. Defendant assigned the refusal to give his request as error. After discussing a number of authorities on the subject the court reversed on that ground stating:

"The foregoing authorities would seem to clearly establish that the defendant's requested instruction . . . [as to belief of right to possession] . . . or one similar to it should have been given by the district court, and that it was prejudicial error to refuse it."

It is suggested that the defendant's own evidence shows he had the necessary intent to steal at the time he took the car. This seems to argue the weight of the evidence; that the defense was not made in good faith; and that it could not be believed. This is a jury question. The defendant's position was exactly to the contrary. The testimony of the garageman is that the defendant requested permission to leave his car on the lot while he went to Salt Lake to get money. Defendant gave an explanation of his return to the lot and the removal of the car which could be considered as consistent with his theory of defense. He also testified that, "But since that I was the owner of the automobile I had never in my life believed I was committing any felony by taking the car for just a day or two, and that is what I did." That he thought he had a right to take his own car was the only avenue of defense open to the defendant and the only one he asserted. It is consistent with the testimony just quoted and with his request for the instruction referred to above. We think it inescapable that the refusal of the trial court to submit the case to the jury upon his theory deprived defendant of a fair trial, and for that reason the judgment should be reversed on that ground.

We find no merit to defendant's assignment of error relating to the cross-examination with respect to his felony record.

Reversed and remanded for a new trial.[1]

McDONOUGH, CROCKETT and WADE, JJ., concur.

HENRIOD, CHIEF JUSTICE, (dissenting). . . .

CUTTER v. STATE

Supreme Court of New Jersey, 1873.
36 N.J.L. 125.

BEASLEY, CHIEF JUSTICE. The defendant was indicted for extortion in taking fees to which he was not entitled, on a criminal complaint before him as a justice of the peace. The defence which he set up, and which was overruled, was that he had taken these moneys innocently, and under a belief that by force of the statute he had a right to exact them.

This subject is regulated by the twenty-eighth section of the act for the punishment of crimes. This clause declares that no justice or other officer of this state shall receive or take any fee or reward, to execute and do his duty and office, but such as is or shall be allowed by the laws of this state, and that "if any justice, &c., shall receive or take, by color of his office, any fee or reward whatsoever, not allowed by the laws of this state, for doing his office, and be thereof convicted, he shall be punished," &c.

On the part of the state it is argued that this statute is explicit in its terms, and makes the mere taking of an illegal fee a criminal act, without regard to the intent of the recipient. Such undoubtedly is the literal force of the language, but then, on the same principle, the officer would be guilty if he took, by mistake or inadvertence, more than the sum coming to him. Nor would the statutory terms, if taken in their exact signification, exclude from their compass, an officer who might be laboring under an insane delusion. Manifestly therefore, the terms of this section are subject to certain practical limitations. This is the case with most statutes couched in comprehensive terms, and especially with those which modify or otherwise regulate common law offences. In such instances the old and the new law are to be construed together; and the former will not be considered to be abolished except so far as the design to produce such effect appears to be clear. In morals it is an evil mind which makes the offence, and this, as a general rule, has been at the root of criminal law. The consequence is that it is not to be intended that this principle is discarded, merely on account of the generality of statutory language. It is highly reasonable to presume that the law makers did not intend to disgrace or to punish a person who should do an act under the belief that it was lawful to do it. And it is this presumption that fully justifies the statement of Mr. Bishop, "that a statute will not

1. The taking of property "under a contractual claim of right, in good faith, however ill advised, is not larceny." State v. Abbey, 13 Ariz.App. 55, 474 P.2d 62, 64 (1970).

generally make an act criminal, however broad may be its language, unless the offender's intent concurred with his act."

This doctrine applies with full force to the present case. If the magistrate received the fees in question without any corrupt intent, and under the conviction that they were lawfully his due, I do not think such act was a crime by force of that statute above recited.

But it is further argued on the part of the prosecution, that as the fees to which the justice was entitled are fixed by law, and as he cannot set up, as an excuse for his conduct his ignorance of the law, his guilty knowledge is undeniable. The argument goes upon the legal maxim *ignorantia legis neminem excusat.* But this rule, in its application to the law of crimes, is subject, as it is sometimes in respect to civil rights, to certain important exceptions. Where the act done is *malum in se,* or where the law which has been infringed was settled and plain, the maxim, in its rigor, will be applied; but where the law is not settled, or is obscure, and where the guilty intention, being a necessary constituent of the particular offense, is dependent on a knowledge of the law, this rule, if enforced, would be misapplied. To give it any force in such instances, would be to turn it aside from its rational and original purpose, and to convert it into an instrument of injustice. The judgments of the courts have confined it to its proper sphere. Whenever a special mental condition constitutes a part of the offence charged, and such condition depends on the question whether or not the culprit had certain knowledge with respect to matters of law, in every such case it has been declared that the subject of the existence of such knowledge is open to inquiry, as a fact to be found by the jury. This doctrine has often been applied to the offence of larceny. The criminal intent, which is an essential part of that crime, involves a knowledge that the property taken belongs to another; but even when all the facts are known to the accused, and so the right to the property is a mere question of law, still he will make good his defence if he can show, in a satisfactory manner, that being under a misapprehension as to his legal rights, he honestly believed the articles in question to be his own.

The adjudications show many other applications of the same principle, and the facts of some of such cases were not substantially dissimilar from those embraced in the present inquiry. In the case of The People v. Whaley, 6 Cow. 661, a justice of the peace had been indicted for taking illegal fees, and the court held that the motives of the defendant, whether they showed corruption or that he acted through a mistake of the law, were a proper question for the jury. The case in The Commonwealth v. Shed, 1 Mass. 228, was put before the jury on the same ground. This was likewise the ground of decision in the case of The Commonwealth v. Bradford, 9 Metc. 268, the charge being for illegal voting, and it being declared that evidence that the defendant had consulted counsel as to his right of suffrage, and had acted on the advice thus obtained, was admissible in his favor. This evidence was only important to show that the defendant in infringing the statute had done so in ignorance of the rule of law upon the subject. Many other cases, resting on the same basis, might be cited; but the foregoing are sufficient to mark clearly the boundaries delineated by the courts to the general rule, that ignorance of law is no defence where the mandates of a statute have been disregarded or a crime has been perpetrated.

That the present case falls within the exceptions to this general rule, appears to me to be plain. There can be no doubt that an opinion very generally prevailed that magistrates had the right to exact the fees which were received by this defendant, and that they could be legally taken under similar circumstances. The prevalence of such an opinion could not, it is true, legalize the act of taking such fees; but its existence might tend to show that the defendant, when he did the act with which he stands charged, was not conscious of doing anything wrong. If a justice of the peace, being called upon to construe a statute with respect to the fees coming to himself, should, exercising due care, form an honest judgment as to his dues, and should act upon such judgment, it would seem palpably unjust, and therefore inconsistent with the ordinary grounds of judicial action, to hold such conduct criminal if it should happen that a higher tribunal should dissent from the view thus taken, and should decide that the statute was not susceptible of the interpretation put upon it. I think the defendant had the right in this case to prove to the jury that the moneys, which it is charged he took extorsively, were received by him under a mistake as to his legal rights, and that as such evidence being offered by him was overruled, the judgment on that account must be reversed.[1]

PEOPLE v. WEISS

Court of Appeals of New York, 1938.
276 N.Y. 384, 12 N.E.2d 514.

[During the investigation of the kidnaping and murder of the Lindbergh baby in New Jersey, one of the suspects was Wendel. In the effort to solve the case, defendants assisted a New Jersey detective in seizing Wendel in New York and there confining him in an effort to extort a confession from him. They offered evidence to show that before they assisted in the arrest they were assured by the

1. The maxim "ignorance of the law is no defense" has no application to a charge of an offense in which the knowledge of some other law is a material element. United States v. Squires, 440 F.2d 859 (2d Cir.1971).

"There are however, two categories of cases in which a defense of ignorance of law is permitted even though it is not specifically written into the criminal statute. The first category involves instances where the defendant is ignorant of an independently determined legal status or condition that is one of the operative facts of the crime. . . . The second category of cases in which defense of ignorance of the law has been read into criminal statutes involves prosecution under complex regulatory schemes that have the potential of snaring unwitting violators." United States v. Fierros, 692 F.2d 1291, 1294–1295 (9th Cir.1982).

detective that he had authority to make the arrest, and power to authorize their assistance, and they believed they were authorized and were doing police work. Most of this evidence was excluded by the trial judge.]

O'BRIEN, JUDGE. . . . Counsel for defendants requested: "That if the defendants, or either of them, acted in the honest belief that his act in seizing and confining Wendel was done with authority of law, even if they were mistaken in such belief, that they cannot be convicted of seizing, confining or kidnapping Wendel, with intent, to cause him without authority of law to be confined or imprisoned within the State, and the jury must acquit such defendants or defendant." To this request the court replied: "I not only decline to charge that but I repeat that the question of good faith is no defense." The jury was also instructed that "even if they [defendants] did believe it, it is no defense in this case." If such interpretation is to prevail, then it must follow that in every instance where a defendant admits the fact that he intended to make the arrest and the courts later declare the arrest to have been made without authority of law, he must necessarily be convicted as a kidnapper, irrespective of his belief or his intentions to conform with the law. A peace officer, in the mistaken belief that he is acting with authority of law, makes an illegal arrest and later, in an effort to extort a confession, puts his prisoner through the third degree. He is guilty of the crime of assault, or of official oppression,[1] but he is certainly not a kidnapper. The question of assault is not in this case. So the trial judge charged.

The intent of defendants to seize and confine Wendel cannot be doubted, but their intent to perform these acts without authority of law depends upon the state of mind of the actors. If in good faith they believed that they were acting within the law, there could have been no intent to act "without authority of law." Their belief or disbelief indicates intent or lack of it, and they were entitled to testify in respect to their intent based upon their belief.

No matter how doubtful the credibility of these defendants may be or how suspicious the circumstances may appear, we cannot say as matter of law that, even in so strong a case as this for the prosecution, the jury was not entitled to consider the question whether defendants in good faith believed that they were acting with authority of law. We are, therefore, constrained to reverse the judgment of conviction and order a new trial for the purpose of submitting that question of fact to the jury.

The judgments should be reversed and a new trial ordered.[2]

1. A person unlawfully beaten by an arresting officer, state or city, is denied the right of due process and has an action against the officer under the federal civil rights act. Morgan v. Labiak, 368 F.2d 338 (10th Cir.1966).

2. An alien's alleged reasonable belief that he had the consent of the Attorney General to reenter the United States is a viable mistake of law defense to a charge of unlawful reentry of a deported alien. United States v. Anton, 683 F.2d 1011 (7th Cir.1982).

CRANE, CHIEF JUDGE (dissenting). I must dissent from the conclusions of JUDGE O'BRIEN in this case, upon three grounds:

First. I believe that the charge and rulings of the court were correct, and that the law has been well stated by Judge Johnston in the prevailing opinion. The fact that the defendants may have thought they had authority to confine Wendel is no excuse for the criminal act and no defense. The crime of kidnapping is committed when a person seizes and confines another with intent to cause him to be confined or imprisoned within the state, and the act is done without lawful authority. The fact that the person thought he had lawful authority has nothing to do with the matter. The intent applies to the seizing and to the confining. The defendants in this case intended to seize Wendel and to confine him within the state. In fact they confined him, bound, in Schlossman's home. Whether they thought they were acting according to law or not, or had legal authority, is no defense. They had no legal authority, and the judge so charged as matter of law. In this he was correct, for such is the law. In fact, no one claims they had any legal authority. Where, therefore, one is seized, taken away, and secretly confined, and it turns out that the person doing it had no legal authority to do it, the crime of kidnapping is committed. Of course, if there be legal authority, there is no crime, but the fact that the person mistakenly thought that they had authority does not lessen the crime. . . .

LEHMAN, LOUGHRAN, and RIPPEY, JJ., concur with O'BRIEN, J.

CRANE, C.J., dissents in opinion, in which HUBBS and FINCH, JJ., concur.

Judgments reversed, etc.

COMMONWEALTH v. BENESCH

Supreme Judicial Court of Massachusetts, 1935.
290 Mass. 125, 194 N.E. 905.

QUA, J. These two indictments are now before this court on the exceptions of the defendants Benesch, Davison and Tibbetts. . . . The second indictment charges the same persons with conspiring to have registered brokers or salesmen sell securities in accordance with an instalment or partial payment contract which was not approved by the public utilities commission. . . .

2. We now come to the second indictment. It is not disputed that the instalment plan contracts had not been approved by the public utilities commission. Under this indictment, in order to hold any one defendant, it was necessary for the Commonwealth to show as to that defendant that he entered into a combination with others for the purpose of doing the illegal act of selling securities on an instalment

plan contract which had not been approved by the commission. In the case of conspiracy, as with other common law crimes, it is necessary that criminal intent be shown. Speaking in general terms, there must be an intent to do wrong. Selling the shares on instalments was not in itself wrong. It need involve no deceit or other element detrimental to the individual purchaser or to the public interest. So long as the contracts had not been approved, sale of the shares was *malum prohibitum* because of the statute, and nothing more. While no decision in this Commonwealth directly in point has been called to our attention, it has been held by excellent authority in other jurisdictions that in order to sustain an indictment for conspiracy to commit an offence which, like that here involved, is *malum prohibitum* only, belonging to a general type of offences which has been greatly extended by modern legislation in many fields, it must appear that the defendant knew of the illegal element involved in that which the combination was intended to accomplish. We believe this is sound law, where the charge is conspiracy. We do not imply that proof of criminal intent is required to sustain a complaint or indictment for the substantive offence prohibited by the statute. To constitute the criminal intent necessary to establish a conspiracy there must be both knowledge of the existence of the law and knowledge of its actual or intended violation.

The trial judge charged the jury in accordance with these principles, but he left it for the jury to say whether all three of the defendants now before the court had a criminal intent with respect to this second indictment. We think this was error. Perhaps as to Benesch alone there was evidence of the necessary intent. He could be found to have been at the head and front of the whole enterprise. If approval of the contracts had been obtained, it could have been inferred that he would have attended to it or would have known of it and that he must have known approval had not been obtained. He contends that he had no knowledge of the act of 1924 requiring approval, but while actual knowledge cannot be predicated solely upon the maxim that every man is presumed to know the law, yet under many circumstances knowledge of important requirements of law having to do with the kind of business in which a person is engaged may be readily inferable. It appears that Benesch at least knew that there were "Blue Sky Laws," and asked his counsel to look out for them. But one cannot be a conspirator alone. We are of opinion that the evidence is insufficient to support a verdict that any of the other alleged conspirators had the knowledge, both of the existence of the prohibition and of its violation, which is necessary to prove affirmatively a criminal intent. There is no evidence that any of them knew that the contracts had not been approved or that any of them occupied such a position in the Trust that such knowledge could be inferred. It may be doubted whether there is any evidence that Davison knew even that any shares were being sold on the instalment plan. Tibbetts was a subordinate salesman taking orders from his superiors. There is nothing to show that it was his duty to see that the contracts were approved. Whether he might be found guilty, if charged with the substantive offence of making sales is not before us. We are now concerned with actual criminal intent. Simpson was treasurer and director. He was not a promoter, but was hired by Benesch on a salary. The duties performed by him seem to have been chiefly of a routine character. It would be carrying inferences of fact too far to assume without further evidence that he knew the law and also knew that those who had organized the Trust and put it in working order had failed to obey the law. Mr. Swift was a lawyer and was a director. He testified that he did not know of the statute of 1924 until November, 1927, and that these matters had been left to one Mr. Burns who had secured the incorporation of the Trust. There was evidence introduced by the Commonwealth that partial payment sales were stopped by September 20, 1927. If it can be inferred that Mr. Swift did know of the law, there was no evidence that he knew before November that it had not been complied with. There was no substantial evidence that partial payment sales were continued after that time. Wells and Robinson stand in much the same position. Both came into the office of the Trust long after it had been organized and was in full operation. There is at most no more than a scintilla of evidence that any of the alleged coconspirators with Benesch consciously and intentionally joined in a conspiracy to sell shares for instalments on unapproved contracts.

Other exceptions not here mentioned have become immaterial.

It follows that . . . the exceptions of all three defendants in the second case are sustained.

So ordered.

LAMBERT v. CALIFORNIA

Supreme Court of the United States, 1957.
355 U.S. 225, 78 S.Ct. 240.

MR. JUSTICE DOUGLAS delivered the opinion of the Court.

Section 52.38(a) of the Los Angeles Municipal Code defines "convicted person" as follows:

"Any person who, subsequent to January 1, 1921, has been or hereafter is convicted of an offense punishable as a felony in the State of California, or who has been or who is hereafter convicted of any offense in any place other than the State of California, which offense, if committed in the State of California, would have been punishable as a felony."

Section 52.39 provides that it shall be unlawful for "any convicted person" to be or remain in Los Angeles for a period of more than five days without registering; it requires any person having a place of abode outside the city to register if he comes into the city on five occasions or more during a 30-day period; and it prescribes the information to be furnished the Chief of Police on registering.

Section 52.43(b) makes the failure to register a continuing offense, each day's failure constituting a separate offense.

Appellant, arrested on suspicion of another offense, was charged with a violation of this registration law. The evidence showed that she had been at the time of her arrest a resident of Los Angeles for over seven years. Within that period she had been convicted in Los Angeles of the crime of forgery, an offense which California punishes as a felony. Though convicted of a crime punishable as a felony, she had not at the time of her arrest registered under the Municipal Code. At the trial, appellant asserted that § 52.39 of the Code denies her due process of law and other rights under the Federal Constitution, unnecessary to enumerate. The trial court denied this objection. The case was tried to a jury which found appellant guilty. The court fined her $250 and placed her on probation for three years. Appellant, renewing her constitutional objection, moved for arrest of judgment and a new trial. This motion was denied. On appeal the constitutionality of the Code was again challenged. The Appellate Department of the Superior Court affirmed the judgment, holding there was no merit to the claim that the ordinance was unconstitutional. The case is here on appeal. 28 U.S.C. § 1257(2), 28 U.S.C.A. § 1257(2). We noted probable jurisdiction, 352 U.S. 914, 77 S.Ct. 218, 1 L.Ed.2d 121, and designated *amicus curiae* to appear in support of appellant. The case, having been argued and reargued, we now hold that the registration provisions of the Code as sought to be applied here violate the Due Process requirement of the Fourteenth Amendment.

The registration provision, carrying criminal penalties, applies if a person has been convicted "of an offense punishable as a felony in the State of California" or, in case he has been convicted in another State, if the offense "would have been punishable as a felony" had it been committed in California. No element of willfulness is by terms included in the ordinance nor read into it by the California court as a condition necessary for a conviction.

We must assume that appellant had no actual knowledge of the requirement that she register under this ordinance, as she offered proof of this defense which was refused. The question is whether a registration act of this character violates Due Process where it is applied to a person who has no actual knowledge of his duty to register, and where no showing is made of the probability of such knowledge.

We do not go with Blackstone in saying that "a vicious will" is necessary to constitute a crime, 4 Bl.Comm. * 21, for conduct alone without regard to the intent of the doer is often sufficient. There is wide latitude on the law-makers to declare an offense and to exclude elements of knowledge and diligence from its definition. But we deal here with conduct that is wholly passive—mere failure to register. It is unlike the commission of acts, or the failure to act under circumstances that should alert the doer to the consequences of his deed. The rule that "ignorance of the law will not excuse" is deep in our law, as is the principle that of all the powers of local government, the police power is "one of the least limitable." On the other hand, Due Process places some limits on its exercise. Engrained in our concept of Due Process is the requirement of notice. Notice is sometimes essential so that the citizen has the chance to defend charges. Notice is required before property interests are disturbed, before assessments are made, before penalties are assessed. Notice is required in a myriad of situations where a penalty or forfeiture might be suffered for mere failure to act. . . . These cases involved only property interests in civil litigation. But the principle is equally appropriate where a person, wholly passive and unaware of any wrongdoing, is brought to the bar of justice for condemnation in a criminal case.

Registration laws are common and their range is wide. Many such laws are akin to licensing statutes in that they pertain to the regulation of business activities. But the present ordinance is entirely different. Violation of its provisions is unaccompanied by any activity whatever, mere presence in the city being the test. Moreover, circumstances which might move one to inquire as to the necessity of registration are completely lacking. At most the ordinance is but a law enforcement technique designed for the convenience of law enforcement agencies through which a list of the names and addresses of felons then residing in a given community is compiled. The disclosure is merely a compilation of former convictions already publicly recorded in the jurisdiction where obtained. Nevertheless, this registrant on first becoming aware of her duty to register was given no opportunity to comply with the law and avoid its penalty, even though her default was entirely innocent. She could but suffer the consequences of the ordinance, namely, conviction with the imposition of heavy criminal penalties thereunder. We believe that actual knowledge of the duty to register or proof of the probability of such knowledge and subsequent failure to comply are necessary before a conviction under the ordinance can stand. As Holmes wrote in The Common Law, "A law which punished conduct which would not be blameworthy in the average member of the community would be too severe for the community to bear." Id., at 50. Its severity lies in the absence of an opportunity either to avoid the consequences of the law or to defend any prosecution brought under it. Where a person did not know of the duty to register and where there was no proof of the probability of such knowledge, he may not be convicted consistently with Due Process. Were it otherwise, the evil would be as great as it is when the law is written in print too fine to read or in a language foreign to the community.

Reversed.[1]

MR. JUSTICE BURTON, dissents because he believes that, as applied to this appellant, the ordinance does not violate her constitutional rights.

MR. JUSTICE FRANKFURTER, whom MR. JUSTICE HARLAN and MR. JUSTICE WHITTAKER join, dissenting. . . .

LONG v. STATE

Supreme Court of Delaware, 1949.
44 Del. 262, 65 A.2d 489.

PEARSON, JUDGE, delivering the opinion of the court:

The defendant Long was married to his first wife in Wilmington, and resided there with her for thirty years prior to their separation in October 1945. On September 21, 1946, he went to Arkansas. He had been pensioned from the police force, and had been in bad health for a number of years. He testified that he went to Arkansas on account of his health because he "thought it would be a better climate"; also that he went there to obtain a divorce; and that he intended "to leave Delaware permanently and take up a permanent domicile in Arkansas". His health improved there. He returned to Wilmington for a few days in November "for business reasons" and spent the Christmas holidays in Wilmington. On December 3, he renewed his Delaware automobile registration for six months ending June 30, 1947. He remained in Arkansas for the statutory period of residence required for divorce in that state, and instituted divorce proceedings against his wife in the Chancery Court of Garland County. On January 7, 1947, that court entered a decree of absolute divorce. The decree recites publication of a notice and the mailing of a registered letter with a copy of the complaint to defendant's wife, a nonresident of Arkansas. She did not appear in the proceeding. She testified before the lower court here that she was not "served with any divorce papers" and did not receive any mail or a registered letter from Arkansas. On the same day the divorce decree was granted, defendant left Arkansas and returned to Wilmington where he has since resided. While in Wilmington during the Christmas holidays of 1946, he had been offered a job in a hospital there. He accepted this job after the divorce decree was granted and began work on January 13, 1947. On January 25, he was married to a second wife in Wilmington. This marriage was the subject of the bigamy prosecution under Rev.Code of Del. Sec. 5254. Defendant contends that the court below was required to recognize the Arkansas decree because of the provi-

1. On remand the Municipal Court ordered a new trial. On petition the California Supreme Court issued a writ of prohibition on the ground that the Los Angeles ordinance violated the state constitution, Art. XI, sec. 1, since it is in conflict with state legislation which has preempted this field. Lambert v. Municipal Court, 53 Cal.2d 690, 3 Cal.Rptr. 168, 349 P.2d 984 (1960).

sions of a Delaware statute, 45 Laws of Del. Chap. 225, p. 906; that recognition of the decree was required under the full faith and credit clause of the Federal Constitution, article 4, § 1; that even if not required to do so, the court should have recognized the decree on the ground of comity; that the court erred in charging the jury with respect to the time when domicile of defendant in Arkansas was required in order that the Arkansas decree be recognized as valid; that the court erred in excluding evidence of a reasonable mistake by defendant in the application of law to the facts, and in rejecting other testimony. . . .

The evidence of defendant's consulting an attorney and following his advice was refused on two grounds: (1) that it is "not proper to presume, in view of the bigamy statute and the exceptions thereto that our Legislature intended that other and additional exceptions be extended by the Courts of this State"; and (2) that defendant's mistake was one of law, and is a case "to which the maxim 'ignorantia juris non excusat' applies." Numerous authorities are cited by the court. . . .

We turn now to the ground that this is a case to which the ignorance of law maxim applies. In many crimes involving a *specific* criminal intent, an honest mistake of law constitutes a defense if it negatives the specific intent. State v. Pullen, 3 Pennewill, 184, 50 A. 538 (larceny); State v. Collins, 1 Marv. 536, 41 A. 144 (embezzlement); see list of cases in the Keedy article, supra, at p. 89; also Perkins: Ignorance and Mistake in Criminal Law, 88 Univ. of Pa.Law Rev. 35, 45, 46. As to crimes not involving a specific intent, an honest mistake of law is usually, though not invariably, held not to excuse conduct otherwise criminal. (Perkins article, pp. 41–45 and cases cited.) A mistake of law, where not a defense, may nevertheless negative a general criminal intent as effectively as would an exculpatory mistake of fact. Thus, mistake of law is disallowed as a defense in spite of the fact that it may show an absence of the criminal mind. The reasons for disallowing it are practical considerations dictated by deterrent effects upon the administration and enforcement of the criminal law, which are deemed likely to result if it were allowed as a general defense. As stated in the Perkins article, supra, p. 41: ". . . But if such ignorance were available as a defense in every criminal case, this would be a constant source of confusion to juries, and it would tend to encourage ignorance at a point where it is peculiarly important to the state that knowledge should be as widespread as is reasonably possible. In the language of one of the giants of the profession, this is a point at which 'justice to the individual is rightly outweighed by the larger interests on the other side of the scales.'" Quoting from Holmes: The Common Law, p. 48.

Similar considerations are involved when we disallow ignorance or mistake of law as a defense to a defendant who engages in criminal conduct (even though not obviously immoral or anti-social) where his ignorance or mistake consists merely in (1) unawareness that such conduct is or might be within the ambit of any crime; or (2) although aware of the existence of criminal law relating to the subject of such conduct, or to some of its aspects, the defendant erroneously concludes (in good faith) that his particular conduct is for some reason not subject to the operation of any criminal law. But it seems to us significantly different to disallow mistake of law where (3) together with the circumstances of the second classification, it appears that before engaging in the conduct, the defendant made a bona fide, diligent effort, adopting a course and resorting to sources and means at least as appropriate as any afforded under our legal system, to ascertain and abide by the law, and where he acted in good faith reliance upon the results of such effort. It is inherent in the way our legal system functions that the criminal law consequences of any particular contemplated conduct cannot be determined in advance with certainty. Not until after the event, by final court decision, may the consequences be definitely ascertained. Prior to the event, the ultimate that can be ascertained about the legal consequences consists of predictions of varying degrees of probability of eventuation. Hence, in the sense in which we are concerned with the expression, a "mistake of law" of the second or third classification refers to the failure of predictions of legal consequences to come to pass. No matter how logical, plausible and persuasive may be the bases for a prediction (assumptions, abstract legal rules, reasoning, etc.,) a mistake of law arises if the prediction does not eventuate; and there is no mistake of law if the prediction eventuates. . . .

We find nothing about the crime of bigamy under our statute which calls for a contrary holding. As previously decided, an absence of general criminal intent is a defense to this crime. As to the acts involved in the crime, remarriage is obviously neither immoral nor anti-social in our culture. These aspects lie in the circumstance that the defendant has a spouse living from whom a divorce has not been obtained which our courts will recognize as valid. The matters to which a mistake of law might relate are legal questions concerning marriage and divorce. It is a gross understatement to say that such questions are more frequently perplexing than obvious to a layman. For these reasons, the defense seems appropriate and we hold it available in prosecutions for bigamy.

Here, from the evidence rejected by the lower court, the jury might have found substantially as follows: (1) that prior to his second marriage, defendant consulted a reputable Delaware attorney for the purpose of ascertaining whether such marriage would be lawful or unlawful in Delaware, and so that he might abide by the law; (2) that the attorney advised him that the proposed remarriage would not be unlawful; (3) that he relied on this advice, honestly believing his remarriage lawful; (4) that his efforts to ascertain the law were at all times diligent and in good faith, not by way of subterfuge, and such that there was no better course for ascertaining the law than that which he followed; and hence, that he made a full disclosure to the attorney of the relevant circumstances as well as of what he proposed to do, and that he had no substantial reason to believe that the advice received was ill-founded, such as circumstances reasonably indicating that the attorney was incompetent to give advice about this matter, or had not given the question sufficient consideration, or that the advice was lacking in candor. Assuming that the Arkansas decree be held invalid here, such findings would constitute a defense to the present charge as a mistake of law of the third classification. They would meet the test of bona fide, diligent efforts, as well designed to accomplish ascertainment of the law as any available under our system. The conditions indicated furnish safeguards against pretext and fraud. The defendant would have the burden of demonstrating that his efforts were well nigh exemplary. It would not be enough merely for him to say that he had relied on advice of an attorney, unless the circumstances indicated that his conduct throughout in seeking to ascertain the law and in relying on advice received manifested good faith and diligence beyond reproach. We see no occasion to assume that recognizing such a defense would foster dishonest practices among attorneys. These might well be expected to be deterred by the availability of disciplinary measures for non-professional conduct. Moreover, although erroneous advice might save a defendant from criminal responsibility for acts in reliance on it, the same acts would in many instances incur substantial civil responsibility and financial loss. The risk of possible disingenuous resort to the defense does not seem to us sufficient to warrant withholding it from those acting in good faith. Accordingly, the evidence should have been submitted to the jury under proper instructions.

A new trial should be awarded for the reasons set forth in this opinion.

An order accordingly will be entered.[1]

1. Selling securities without a permit is *malum prohibitum*, not *malum in se*. Hence one who was advised by the Corporation Commissioner that no permit was required for certain sales, and who relied upon that advice in good faith, could not properly be convicted for making such sales even if the advice was wrong. People v. Ferguson, 134 Cal. App. 41, 24 P.2d 965 (1933).

Reliance upon advice of counsel is an element of good faith where the applicability of a statute to a factual situation is doubtful. United States v. McMillan, 114 F.Supp. 638 (D.C.D.C.1953).

In a case involving the Watergate "footsoldiers" charged with a civil rights statute, 18 U.S.C. § 241, the court held the defendants were entitled to have the jury instructed on mistake of law as a defense. The court observed: ". . . surely two laymen cannot be faulted for acting on a known and represented fact situation and in accordance with a legal theory espoused by this and all past Attorneys General for forty years." United States v. Barker, 546 F.2d 940, 952 (D.C.Cir.1976).

Defendant was charged and convicted of possession of a concealable firearm by a convicted felon (Cal.Penal Code § 12021). She claimed mistake as to her legal status as a defense. The conviction was upheld, the court observing: "Thus regardless of what she reasonably believed, or what her attorney may have told her, defendant was deemed to know *under the law* that she was a convicted felon forbidden to possess concealable firearms. Her asserted mistake regarding her correct legal status was a mistake of law, not fact. It does not consti-

STATE v. STRIGGLES

Supreme Court of Iowa, 1926.
202 Iowa 1318, 210 N.W. 137.

ALBERT, J. We gather from the record and arguments of counsel the following history of the case at bar: It appears that in the early part of 1923 there was installed in several places of business in the city of Des Moines a gum- or mint- vending machine. The machine and its workings are fully set out in the opinion in the case of State v. Ellis, 200 Iowa 1228, 206 N.W. 105. In that opinion it was judicially determined that such machine was a gambling device, within the inhibition of the statute.

On August 1, 1923, in several proceedings then pending in the municipal court of the city of Des Moines, a decision was rendered holding that such machine was not a gambling device. The distributors of the machine in question thereupon secured a certified copy of said decree, and equipped themselves with a letter from the county attorney's office, and also one from the mayor of the city, which stated that such machine was not a gambling device. Thus equipped, they presented themselves to appellant, Striggles, who conducted a restaurant in the city of Des Moines, and induced him to allow them to install a machine in his place of business.

Subsequent thereto, in the early part of 1925, the Polk County grand jury returned an indictment against appellant, in which it charged that he did "willfully and unlawfully keep a house, shop, and place . . . resorted to for the purpose of gambling, and he, . . . did then and there willfully and unlawfully permit and suffer divers persons, . . . in said house, shop, and place . . . to play a certain machine . . . being then and there a gambling device." On entering a plea of not guilty, the appellant was put on trial. He offered in evidence the aforesaid certified copy of the judgment decree of the court, and the letters from the county attorney and the mayor, which were promptly objected to, and the objection sustained. The appellant, while testifying, was permitted by the court to say that the exhibits had been presented to him before he permitted the machine to be installed. He was then asked by his counsel whether he relied on the contents of the papers when he gave his permission for installation of the machine. Objection to this line of testimony was sustained. He was also asked whether he would have permitted the machine to be installed, had he believed it to be a gambling device. He was not permitted to answer this question.

It is first urged in this case that the certified copy of the judgment from the municipal court was admissible in evidence, on the strength of the case of State v. O'Neil, 147 Iowa 513, 126 N.W. 454.

tute a defense to section 12021." People v. Snyder, 32 Cal.3d 590, 186 Cal.Rptr. 485, 652 P.2d 42, 44 (1982).

A careful reading of the case, however, shows that it has no application to the case at bar. A certain statute of this state was held to be violative of the Constitution of the United States, and therefore void, in State v. Hanaphy, 117 Iowa 15, 90 N.W. 601, and State v. Bernstein, 129 Iowa 520, 105 N.W. 1015. The United States Supreme Court then decided Delamater v. South Dakota, 205 U.S. 93, 27 S.Ct. 447, 51 L.Ed. 724. On the strength of this opinion by the United States Court, we then overruled the Hanaphy and Bernstein cases, in McCollum v. McConaughy, 141 Iowa 172, 119 N.W. 539.

The crime with which O'Neil was charged, was committed by him between the time of the filing of the opinion of this court and the filing of the opinion of the United States Supreme Court. We held in that case that the appellant could not be guilty, because he was entitled to rely on the decision of this court which held the law in question unconstitutional.

Cases cited from other jurisdictions in appellant's argument are in line with the O'Neil case. There is no case cited, nor can we find one, on diligent search, holding that the decision of an inferior court can be relied upon to justify the defendant in a criminal case in the commission of the act which is alleged to be a crime. We are disposed to hold with the O'Neil case, that, when the court of highest jurisdiction passes on any given proposition, all citizens are entitled to rely upon such decision; but we refuse to hold that the decisions of any court below, inferior to the Supreme Court, are available as a defense, under similar circumstances. . . .

The matters of which complaint is made should have been taken into consideration by the district court in passing sentence on a verdict of guilty, and this was apparently done in this case, as the fine assessed was the minimum.—Affirmed.

EVANS, STEVENS, FAVILLE, and MORLING, JJ., concur.[1]

MODEL PENAL CODE

Section 2.04 Ignorance or Mistake.

(1) Ignorance or mistake as to a matter of fact or law is a defense if:

(a) the ignorance or mistake negatives the purpose, knowledge, belief, recklessness or negligence required to establish a material element of the offense; or

1. "Ignorance of the provision of this Code or of any criminal statute is not a defense to any criminal prosecution. However, mistake of law which results in the lack of an intention that consequences which are criminal shall follow, is a defense to a criminal prosecution under the following circumstances: (2) Where the offender reasonably relied on a final judgment of a competent court of last resourt that a provision making the conduct in question criminal was unconstitutional." La.Rev.Stat. 14:17 (1974).

In refusing to take the position that reliance could not be had upon the opinions of lesser courts during its own silence the Supreme Court said that "unless we are to hold that parties may not reasonably rely upon any legal pronouncement

(b) the law provides that the state of mind established by such ignorance or mistake constitutes a defense.

(2) Although ignorance or mistake would otherwise afford a defense to the offense charged, the defense is not available if the defendant would be guilty of another offense had the situation been as he supposed. In such case, however, the ignorance or mistake of the defendant shall reduce the grade and degree of the offense of which he may be convicted to those of the offense of which he would be guilty had the situation been as he supposed.

(3) A belief that conduct does not legally constitute an offense is a defense to a prosecution for that offense based upon such conduct when:

(a) the statute or other enactment defining the offense is not known to the actor and has not been published or otherwise reasonably made available prior to the conduct alleged; or

(b) he acts in reasonable reliance upon an official statement of the law, afterward determined to be invalid or erroneous, contained in (i) a statute or other enactment; (ii) a judicial decision, opinion or judgment; (iii) an administrative order or grant of permission; or (iv) an official interpretation of the public officer or body charged by law with responsibility for the interpretation, administration or enforcement of the law defining the offense.

(4) The defendant must prove a defense arising under Subsection (3) of this Section by a preponderance of evidence.

Section 2.02 (9) Culpability as to Illegality of Conduct. Neither knowledge nor recklessness or negligence as to whether conduct constitutes an offense or as to the existence, meaning or application of the law determining the elements of an offense is an element of such offense, unless the definition of the offense or the Code so provides.[1]

(B) IGNORANCE OR MISTAKE OF FACT

Ignorance or mistake of fact is very often an excuse for what would otherwise be a crime. A street car conductor, for example, who ejects a passenger from the car (without the use of unreasonable force) under the honest and reasonable, though mistaken, belief that his fare has not been paid, is liable to the passenger in a civil action but not guilty of criminal assault and battery. *"Ignorantia facti excusat,"* however, is too sweeping even for a general statement of law, because it is clear (to mention only one point for the moment) that if a certain deed would constitute exactly the same crime under either of two factual situations, it will be no excuse that one was mistaken for the other.

A general statement which will apply to the ordinary situation, although it is subject to important qualifications, is this: Mistake of fact will disprove a criminal charge if the mistaken belief is (a) hon-

emanating from sources other than this Court, we cannot regard as blameworthy, those parties who conform their conduct to the prevailing statutory or constitutional norm." United States v. Peltier, 422 U.S. 531, 542, 95 S.Ct. 2313, 2320 (1975).

1. Copyright 1962 by the American Law Institute. Reprinted with the permission of the American Law Institute.

estly entertained, (b) based upon reasonable grounds, and (c) of such a nature that the conduct would have been lawful had the facts been as they were reasonably supposed to be. This general rule is subject to many exceptions and these exceptions may cut in either direction, so to speak. (1) At times an honest mistake of fact may be exculpating although not based upon reasonable grounds. (2) In other prosecutions a well-grounded belief of a fact which would entitle the defendant to an acquittal if true may not save him from conviction if erroneous.

Typical instances of the first kind of exception are found in prosecutions of those offenses, such as larceny, requiring a specific intent. There is no such thing in the common law as larceny by negligence. One does not commit this crime by carrying away the chattel of another in the mistaken belief that it is his own, no matter how great may have been the fault leading to this belief, if the belief itself is genuine. And the defendant is entitled to an acquittal in the prosecution for any crime requiring a specific intent or other special mental element, if such intent or other element is lacking,—even if the reason for its absence is a mistaken belief as to some fact. Such a belief must be genuine and sincere but it is not necessary for it to be based upon due care.[1]

Offenses enforced on the basis of strict liability give opportunity for exceptions of the second type. Cases holding that a mistake of fact can never be a defense to a prosecution for a civil offense go too far, but even a well-grounded mistake of fact is not exculpating if the mistake could have been discovered by the use of greater care which it is not unreasonable to require of one in such a situation.

THE KING v. EWART

Court of Appeal of New Zealand, 1905.
25 N.Z.L.R. 709.

(A newspaper vendor sold a copy of a paper containing obscene matter and was indicted for violation of the statute on that subject.)

1. The Texas statute (Vernon's Ann. Pen.Code art. 41) provided that for an act, otherwise criminal, to be excusable because of mistake of fact, it had to be a mistake that "does not arise from a want of proper care on the part of the person so acting." Even under this statute one who takes what he honestly believes to be his is not guilty of theft whether this belief did or did not result from want of due care. Green v. State, 153 Tex.Cr.R. 442, 221 S.W.2d 612 (1949).

"There is, of course, no question about the proposition: if the defendant took the property under an honest but mistaken belief that he was entitled to do so, that would negative his intent to steal; and he would not be guilty of theft; . . . ." State v. Kazda, 545 P.2d 190, 192 (Utah 1976).

"As a general principle of law a person is not guilty of robbery in forcibly taking property from the person of another, if he does so under a bona fide belief that he is the owner of the property. The reason for this rule is that one who takes his own property or that which he believes to be his own property lacks the felonious intent required for larceny or robbery." United States v. Mack, 6 M.J. 598, 599 (ACMR 1978).

STOUT, C.J.: The first question that arises in this case is whether the provisions of section 3 of "The Offensive Publications Act, 1892," require that, before a conviction can be affirmed against an accused person, there must be proof that he knew the publication he sold to be indecent, and whether there can be no conviction if the jury believes he did not know that the newspaper he sold was indecent; in fact, whether *mens rea* is required to be proved under this Act. . . .

The sole questions, in my opinion, that the jury had to determine were, 1, whether the prisoner did sell the newspaper, and, 2, whether the newspaper sold was indecent, immoral, or obscene. The jury found both these questions in the affirmative.

I am therefore of opinion that the conviction should be affirmed.

WILLIAMS, J.: . . . Exactly similar considerations apply to subsection 5 of section 82 of "The Post Office Act, 1900." That subsection makes it penal without any qualification to post any postal packet containing indecent or obscene matter.[1] A bishop who was obliging enough to post such a packet for a stranger would have to be convicted if knowledge were immaterial. In my opinion, therefore, honest ignorance is a defence to the charge in the present case. The act forbidden having been done, it lay upon the defendant to show that he did it unwittingly and without a guilty mind. If he knew the publication contained indecent matter, or if he suspected that it contained such matter and abstained from ascertaining whether it did or not, the tainted mind would be present. It would be, however, competent for him to establish its absence, and if the jury were satisfied upon the evidence that it was absent he was entitled to be acquitted, and I think the jury should have been so directed. As to the other questions raised, I agree with His Honour. I think, therefore, the conviction should be quashed, and that there should be a new trial.

EDWARDS, J. . . . There are, therefore, two classes of cases under the statute law—1, those in which, following the common-law rule, a guilty mind must either be necessarily inferred from the nature of the act done or must be established by independent evidence; 2, those in which, either from the language or the scope and object of

1. In A Book v. Attorney General, 383 U.S. 413, 418, 83 S.Ct. 975, 977 (1966), it was held: "Under this definition [of obscenity], . . . three elements must coalesce: it must be established that (a) the dominant theme of the material taken as a whole appeals to a prurient interest in sex; (b) the material is patently offensive because it affronts contemporary community standards relating to the description or representation of sexual matters, and (c) the material is utterly without redeeming social value."

The requirement that to be obscene the material must be "utterly without redeeming social value" has been rejected in favor of "taken as a whole, lacks serious literary, artistic, political or scientific value." See Hamling v. United States, 418 U.S. 87, 102, 94 S.Ct. 2887, 2900 (1974) (quoting from Miller v. California, 413 U.S. 15, 24, 93 S.Ct. 2607, 2615 (1973)).

In judging obscenity pursuant to a state statute, a state-wide community standard must be applied. People v. Tabron, 190 Colo. 149, 544 P.2d 380 (1976).

the enactment to be construed, it is made plain that the Legislature intended to prohibit the act absolutely, and the question of the existence of a guilty mind is only relevant for the purpose of determining the quantum of punishment following the offence. There is also a third class in which, although from the omission from the statute of the words "knowingly" or "wilfully" it is not necessary to aver in the indictment that the offence charged was "knowingly" or "wilfully" committed, or to prove a guilty mind, and the commission of the act in itself *prima facie* imports an offence, yet the person charged may still discharge himself by proving to the satisfaction of the tribunal which tries him that in fact he had not a guilty mind. . . .

The case does, I think, clearly come within the third class of cases to which I have referred. The act charged is, I think, clearly an act which, upon the true construction of the statute, is made in itself *prima facie* to import a guilty mind, but as to which the presumption arising from the doing of the act may be rebutted by evidence adduced by the person charged. This, I think, is the result of the authorities, and it is one which will insure justice being done in all such cases.

I desire to guard myself from appearing to suggest that a person charged with this offence can in all cases discharge himself from the consequences simply by swearing that he did not know the contents of what he was selling. In any case it will be for the jury to decide whether they will believe the prisoner's evidence upon that point or not. Further, I think that if the prosecution can in any such case establish that any particular newspaper or serial publication has acquired the reputation of publishing indecent, immoral, or obscene matter, and that nevertheless the person charged has sold any issue of that paper or serial publication which does contain indecent, immoral, or obscene matter, the jury would be justified in inferring, and indeed ought to infer, that if the person charged did not take the precaution to see that what he sold did not contain such matter, it was because he wilfully abstained from making an inquiry which it was his duty to make. It may, I think, be safely laid down that it is the duty of a news-vendor to know at least the general character of the newspapers and serial publications which he sells, and either to abstain altogether from selling those which in their previous issues have acquired a doubtful character or to ascertain with respect to each copy that he sells that it contains nothing indecent, immoral, or obscene.

In my opinion the case, as it stood, ought to have been left to the jury, with the direction that if they believed that the prisoner was honestly ignorant of the contents of the newspaper in question then they should acquit him. The prisone[r] is therefore, in my opinion, entitled to a new trial, and there should be an order accordingly.

. . .

New Trial Ordered.

(COOPER, J., wrote an opinion in favor of upholding the conviction. CHAPMAN, J., wrote an opinion in favor of granting a new trial.)

PEOPLE v. VOGEL

Supreme Court of California, In Bank, 1956.
46 Cal.2d 798, 299 P.2d 850.

[In a bigamy trial the court refused to admit evidence to show that defendant's wife had told him she was going to get a divorce, and that some time thereafter she married Earl Heck, lived with him, and received mail and telephone calls as Mrs. Earl Heck. The reason for the refusal was that "defendant's good faith belief that she had divorced him and married Heck was immaterial".]

TRAYNOR, JUSTICE. Defendant appeals from a judgment of conviction entered on a jury verdict finding him guilty of bigamy and from an order denying his motion for a new trial. . . .

We have concluded that defendant is not guilty of bigamy, if he had a bona fide and reasonable belief that facts existed that left him free to remarry. As in other crimes, there must be a union of act and wrongful intent. So basic is this requirement that it is an invariable element of every crime unless excluded expressly or by necessary implication. Sections 281 and 282 do not expressly exclude it nor can its exclusion therefrom be reasonably implied.

Certainly its exclusion cannot be implied from the mere omission of any reference to intent in the definition of bigamy, for the commissioners' annotation to section 20 makes it clear that such an omission was not meant to exclude intent as an element of the crime but to shift to defendant the burden of proving that he did not have the requisite intent. The commissioners quote at length from People v. Harris, 29 Cal. 678, 681–682. That case involved a conviction for twice voting at the same election. The defendant sought to defend upon the ground that he was so drunk at the time he voted the second time that he did not know what he was doing and that he therefore had no criminal intent. The court held that the trial court erred in excluding from the jury any consideration of the mental state of the defendant by reason of his intoxicated condition, stating: "It is laid down in the books on the subject, that it is a universal doctrine that to constitute what the law deems a crime there must concur both an evil act and an evil intent. *Actus non facit reum nisi mens sit rea.*—1 Bish. on Cr.Law, Secs. 227, 229; 3 Greenl.Ev., Sec. 13. Therefore the intent with which the unlawful act was done must be proved as well as the other material facts stated in the indictment; which may be by evidence either direct or indirect, tending to establish the fact, or by inference of law from other facts proved. When the act is proved to have been done by the accused, if it be an act in itself unlawful, the law in the first instance presumes it to have been intended, and the proof of justification or excuse lies on the defendant to overcome this legal and natural presumption. . . .

The "correct and authoritative exposition of Sec. 20" as applied in People v. Harris to the crime of twice voting in the same election applies with even greater force to the crime of bigamy and compels the conclusion that guilty knowledge, which was formerly a part of the definition of bigamy was omitted from section 281 to reallocate the burden of proof on that issue in a bigamy trial. Thus, the prosecution makes a prima facie case upon proof that the second marriage was entered into while the first spouse was still living, and his bona fide and reasonable belief that facts existed that left the defendant free to remarry is a defense to be proved by the defendant.

Nor must the exclusion of wrongful intent be implied from the two exceptions set forth in section 282. Obviously they are not all inclusive, for it cannot be seriously contended that an insane person or a person who married for the second time while unconscious, Pen. Code, § 26, subds. 3, 5, could be convicted of bigamy. Moreover, the mere enumeration of specific defenses appropriate to particular crimes does not exclude general defenses based on sections 20 and 26 (see, 2 Lewis' Sutherland, Statutory Construction, § 495, p. 924; 23 Cal.Jur., Statutes, § 118, p. 742), for the enumerated defenses in no way conflict with such general defenses. . . .

The foregoing construction of sections 281 and 282 is consistent with good sense and justice. (See, dissenting opinion of McComb, J., in People v. Kelly, 32 Cal.App.2d 624, 628, 90 P.2d 605.) The severe penalty imposed for bigamy, the serious loss of reputation conviction entails, the infrequency of the offense, and the fact that it has been regarded for centuries as a crime involving moral turpitude, make it extremely unlikely that the Legislature meant to include the morally innocent to make sure the guilty did not escape. . . .

In a prosecution for bigamy evidence that a person is generally reputed to be married is admissible as tending to show actual marriage. The same evidence that would tend to prove an actual marriage, if offered by the People, could reasonably form the basis for an honest belief by a defendant that there was such marriage, that it was legally entered into, and that he was, therefore, free to remarry. The evidence offered to show that Peggy had married Earl Heck should therefore have been admitted. The statement allegedly made by Peggy that she was going to divorce defendant was admissible on the issue of his belief that she had done so and it was also admissible to impeach her testimony that she did not tell him that she was going to divorce him. The exclusion of this evidence was clearly prejudicial, for it deprived defendant of the defense of a bona fide and reasonable belief that facts existed that left him free to remarry. . . .

The judgment and order are reversed.[1]

1. Contra: Braun v. State, 230 Md. 82, 185 A.2d 905 (1962). In State v. Crosby, 148 Mont. 307, 420 P.2d 431 (1966), **D**, who had married

GIBSON, C.J., and CARTER, SCHAUER, SPENCE and MCCOMB, JJ., concur.

SHENK, JUSTICE. I dissent. . . .

Bigamy is a statutory crime, defined in section 281 of the Penal Code, as follows: "Every person having a husband or wife living, who marries any other person, except in the cases specified in the next section, is guilty of bigamy." The exceptions contained in section 282 are as follows:

"The last section does not extend—

"1. To any person by reason of any former marriage, whose husband or wife by such marriage has been absent for five successive years without being known to such person within that time to be living; nor

"2. To any person by reason of any former marriage which has been pronounced void, annulled, or dissolved by the judgment of a competent Court."

While the legislature has provided a condition and a term of years after which a person may in good faith reasonably conclude that an absent spouse is dead, it has provided no such condition or term for concluding that an absent spouse has procured a divorce. The legislature has not, either expressly or by reasonable implication, made a mere belief in the existence of a prior divorce a defense to a bigamy prosecution. . . .

PEOPLE v. HERNANDEZ

Supreme Court of California, In Bank, 1964.
61 Cal.2d 529, 39 Cal.Rptr. 361, 393 P.2d 673.

PEEK, JUSTICE. By information defendant was charged with statutory rape. (Pen.Code, § 261, subd. 1.) Following his plea of not guilty he was convicted as charged by the court sitting without a jury and the offense determined to be a misdemeanor.

Section 261 of the Penal Code provides in part as follows: "Rape is an act of sexual intercourse, accomplished with a female not the wife of the perpetrator, under either of the following circumstances: 1. Where the female is under the age of 18 years; . . . ."

three times was indicted for bigamy in two counts based (1) upon the second marriage and (2) upon the third marriage. The prosecution under the second count was barred by the statute of limitations and **D** claimed that the third marriage was not bigamous because his second marriage was void since he was already married at the time and he had obtained a divorce from his first wife before the third marriage. Held, this is not a defense. To be entitled to be married again the so-called void marriage must be declared void by judicial decree.

It is beyond the power of the legislature to punish a junk dealer who purchased stolen property without knowing it was stolen and without even a failure to use due diligence in this regard. People v. Estreich, 272 App.Div. 698, 75 N.Y.S.2d 267 (1947). Aff'd 297 N.Y. 910, 79 N.E.2d 742.

The sole contention raised on appeal is that the trial court erred in refusing to permit defendant to present evidence going to his guilt for the purpose of showing that he had in good faith a reasonable belief that the prosecutrix was 18 years or more of age.

The undisputed facts show that the defendant and the prosecuting witness were not married, and had been companions for several months prior to January 3, 1961—the date of the commission of the alleged offense. Upon that date the prosecutrix was 17 years and 9 months of age and voluntarily engaged in an act of sexual intercourse with defendant.

In support of his contention defendant relies upon Penal Code, § 20, which provides that "there must exist a union, or joint operation of act and intent, or criminal negligence" to constitute the commission of a crime. He further relies upon section 26 of that code which provides that one is not capable of committing a crime who commits an act under an ignorance or mistake of fact which disproves any criminal intent.

Thus the sole issue relates to the question of intent and knowledge entertained by the defendant at the time of the commission of the crime charged.

Consent of the female is often an unrealistic and unfortunate standard for branding sexual intercourse a crime as serious as forcible rape. Yet the consent standard has been deemed to be required by important policy goals. We are dealing here, of course, with statutory rape where, in one sense, the lack of consent of the female is not an element of the offense. In a broader sense, however, the lack of consent is deemed to remain an element but the law makes a conclusive presumption of the lack thereof because she is presumed too innocent and naive to understand the implications and nature of her act. The law's concern with her capacity or lack thereof to so understand is explained in part by a popular conception of the social, moral and personal values which are preserved by the abstinance from sexual indulgence on the part of a young woman. An unwise disposition of her sexual favor is deemed to do harm both to herself and the social mores by which the community's conduct patterns are established. Hence the law of statutory rape intervenes in an effort to avoid such a disposition. This goal, moreover, is not accomplished by penalizing the naive female but by imposing criminal sanctions against the male, who is conclusively presumed to be responsible for the occurrence.

The assumption that age alone will bring an understanding of the sexual act to a young woman is of doubtful validity. Both learning from the cultural group to which she is a member and her actual sexual experiences will determine her level of comprehension. The sexually experienced 15-year old may be far more acutely aware of the implications of sexual intercourse than her sheltered cousin who is beyond the age of consent. A girl who belongs to a group whose members indulge in sexual intercourse at an early age is likely to rapidly acquire an insight into the rewards and penalties of sexual indulgence. Nevertheless, even in circumstances where a girl's actual comprehension contradicts the law's presumption, the male is deemed criminally responsible for the act, although himself young and naive and responding to advances which may have been made to him.

The law as presently constituted does not concern itself with the relative culpability of the male and female participants in the prohibited sexual act. Even where the young woman is knowledgeable it does not impose sanctions upon her. The knowledgeable young man, on the other hand, is penalized and there are none who would claim that under any construction of the law this should be otherwise. However, the issue raised by the rejected offer of proof in the instant case goes to the culpability of the young man who acts *without* knowledge that an essential factual element exists and has, on the other hand, a positive, reasonable belief that it does not exist.

The primordial concept of *mens rea,* the guilty mind, expresses the principle that it is not conduct alone but conduct accompanied by certain specific mental states which concerns or should concern the law. In a broad sense the concept may be said to relate to such important doctrines as justification, excuse, mistake, necessity and mental capacity, but in the final analysis it means simply that there must be a "joint operation of act and intent," as expressed in section 20 of the Penal Code, to constitute the commission of a criminal offense. The statutory law, however, furnishes no assistance to the courts beyond that, and the casebooks are filled to overflowing with the courts' struggles to determine just what state of mind should be considered relevant in particular contexts. In numerous instances culpability has been completely eliminated as a necessary element of criminal conduct in spite of the admonition of section 20 to the contrary. More recently, however, this court has moved away from the imposition of criminal sanctions in the absence of culpability where the governing statute, by implication or otherwise, expresses no legislative intent or policy to be served by imposing strict liability. (People v. Stuart, 47 Cal.2d 167, 302 P.2d 5, 55 A.L.R.2d 705; People v. Vogel, 46 Cal.2d 798, 299 P.2d 850; People v. Winston, 46 Cal.2d 151, 293 P.2d 40.)

Statutory rape has long furnished a fertile battleground upon which to argue that the lack of knowledgeable conduct is a proper defense. The law in this state now rests, as it did in 1896, with this court's decision in People v. Ratz, 115 Cal. 132, at pages 134 and 135, 46 P. 915, at page 916, where it is stated: "The claim here made is not a new one. It has frequently been pressed upon the attention of courts, but in no case, so far as our examination goes, has it met with favor. The object and purpose of the law are too plain to need comment, the crime too infamous to bear discussion. The protection of society, of the family, and of the infant, demand that one who has carnal intercourse under such circumstances shall do so in peril of the fact, and he will not be heard against the evidence to urge his belief that the victim of his outrage had passed the period which would make his act a crime." The age of consent at the time of the Ratz decision was 14 years, and it is noteworthy that the purpose of the rule, as there announced, was to afford protection to young females therein described as "infants." The decision on which the court in Ratz relied was The Queen v. Prince, L.R. 2 Crown Cas. 154. However England has now, by statute, departed from the strict rule, and excludes as a crime an act of sexual intercourse with a female between the ages of 13 and 16 years if the perpetrator is under the age of 24 years, has not previously been charged with a like offense, and believes the female "to be of the age of sixteen or over and has reasonable cause for the belief." (Halsburg's Statutes of England, 2d Ed., Vol. 36, Continuation Volume 1956, at page 219.)

The rationale of the Ratz decision, rather than purporting to eliminate intent as an element of the crime, holds that the wrongdoer must assume the risk; that, subjectively, when the act is committed, he consciously intends to proceed regardless of the age of the female and the consequences of his act, and that the circumstances involving the female, whether she be a day or a decade less than the statutory age, are irrelevant. There can be no dispute that a criminal intent exists when the perpetrator proceeds with utter disregard of, or in the lack of grounds for, belief that the female has reached the age of consent. But if he participates in a mutual act of sexual intercourse, believing his partner to be beyond the age of consent, with reasonable grounds for such belief, where is his criminal intent? In such circumstances he has not consciously taken any risk. Instead he has subjectively eliminated the risk by satisfying himself on reasonable evidence that the crime cannot be committed. If it occurs that he has been misled, we cannot realistically conclude that for such reason alone the intent with which he undertook the act suddenly becomes more heinous.

While the specific contentions herein made have been dealt with and rejected both within and without this state, the courts have uniformly failed to satisfactorily explain the nature of the criminal intent present in the mind of one who in good faith believes he has obtained a lawful consent before engaging in the prohibited act. As in the Ratz case the courts often justify convictions on policy reasons which, in effect, eliminate the element of intent. The Legislature, of course, by making intent an element of the crime, has established the prevailing policy from which it alone can properly advise us to depart.

We have recently given recognition to the legislative declarations in sections 20 and 26 of the Penal Code, and departed from prior decisional law which had failed to accord full effect to those sections as applied to charges of bigamy. (People v. Vogel, supra, 46 Cal.2d 798, 299 P.2d 850.) . . .

We are persuaded that the reluctance to accord to a charge of statutory rape the defense of a lack of criminal intent has no greater justification than in the case of other statutory crimes, where the Legislature has made identical provision with respect to intent. " 'At common law an honest and reasonable belief in the existence of circumstances, which, if true, would make the act for which the person is indicted an innocent act, has always been held to be a good defense. . . . So far as I am aware it has never been suggested that these exceptions do not equally apply to the case of statutory offenses unless they are excluded expressly or by necessary implication.' " (Matter of Application of Ahart, 172 Cal. 762, 764–765, 159 P. 160, 161–162, quoting from Regina v. Tolson, [1889] 23 Q.B.D. 168, s. c., 40 Alb.L.J. 250.) Our departure from the views expressed in Ratz is in no manner indicative of a withdrawal from the sound policy that it is in the public interest to protect the sexually naive female from exploitation. No responsible person would hesitate to condemn as untenable a claimed good faith belief in the age of consent of an "infant" female whose obviously tender years preclude the existence of reasonable grounds for that belief. However, the prosecutrix in the instant case was but three months short of 18 years of age and there is nothing in the record to indicate that the purposes of the law as stated in Ratz can be better served by foreclosing the defense of a lack of intent. This is not to say that the granting of consent by even a sexually sophisticated girl known to be less than the statutory age is a defense. We hold only that in the absence of a legislative direction otherwise, a charge of statutory rape is defensible wherein a criminal intent is lacking.[1]

For the foregoing reasons People v. Ratz, supra, 115 Cal. 132, 46 P. 915, and People v. Griffin, supra, 117 Cal. 583, 49 P. 711 are overruled, and People v. Sheffield, 9 Cal.App. 130, 98 P. 67, is disapproved to the extent that such decisions are inconsistent with the views expressed herein.

Some question has been raised that the offer of proof of defendant's reasonable belief in the age of the prosecutrix was insufficient to justify the pleading of such belief as a defense to the act. It is not our purpose here to make a determination that the defendant entertained a reasonable belief. Suffice to state that the offer demonstrated a sufficient basis upon which, when fully developed, the trier

1. Those engaged in commercialized vice must determine the age of the females at their peril. People v. Zeihm, 40 Cal.App.3d 1085, 1089, 115 Cal.Rptr. 528, 531 (1974).

Where defendant was charged with inducing a minor to use marijuana he was entitled to a jury instruction on the defense issue of a reasonable belief that the victims were adults. People v. Goldstein, 130 Cal.App.3d 1024, 182 Cal.Rptr. 207 (1982).

of fact might have found in defendant's favor. We conclude that it was reversible error to reject the offer.

The judgment is reversed.

GIBSON, C.J., and TRAYNOR, SCHAUER, MCCOMB, PETERS and TOBRINER, JJ., concur.[2]

STATE v. RANDOLPH

Court of Appeals of Washington, Division 1, 1974.
12 Wash.App. 138, 528 P.2d 1008.

SWANSON, CHIEF JUDGE.

QUAERE: Is a reasonable and good faith—although mistaken—belief that the consenting female was 18 years of age or over a defense to a charge of carnal knowledge? The trial court said "No," rejecting the proffered defense, and found Gregory Lee Randolph guilty. He appeals on the sole basis of the trial court's refusal to consider the defense of a good faith belief that the prosecutrix was over the age of consent.

Appellant points out that his claim of error presents a matter of first impression in the appellate courts of this state and urges us to depart from the traditional and almost uniform rule that reasonable mistake as to the age of the victim of statutory rape is not a defense to a prosecution for that crime. Although a few jurisdictions in this country have adopted statutes recognizing such a defense, the general rule to the contrary was uniformly followed by the courts of this nation until the decision in People v. Hernandez, 61 Cal.2d 529, 39 Cal.Rptr. 361, 393 P.2d 673 (1964), which overruled prior California decisions and held that in the absence of a legislative direction otherwise, the reasonable belief that the prosecutrix was over the age of consent is a defense to a prosecution for statutory rape. Thus, the *Hernandez* court, which placed considerable reliance upon opinions of scholars who have criticized the "strict liability" rule generally applied in cases of carnal knowledge, rejected the notion that the protection of society, the family, and the infant required, as a matter of sound public policy, the elimination of criminal intent as a defense in such cases.

Appellant has failed to cite any decision from a jurisdiction other than that of the State of California wherein a court has adopted the rule stated in *Hernandez* and, in the absence of an appropriate affirmative statutory change by our state legislature, we decline the invitation to be the first jurisdiction to do so. Indeed, it appears that every jurisdiction which has had the opportunity to consider the *Hernandez* rule has likewise rejected it. State v. Silva, 53 Haw. 232, 491

2. A mistake of fact instruction is proper on the question of whether the defendant in a forcible rape and kidnaping case reasonably believed the victim consented to the defendant's acts. People v. Mayberry, 15 Cal.3d 143, 125 Cal.Rptr. 745, 542 P.2d 1337 (1975).

P.2d 1216 (1971) [but see dissenting opinion, contra]; Kelley v. State, 51 Wis.2d 641, 187 N.W.2d 810 (1971); Commonwealth v. Moore, 359 Mass. 509, 269 N.E.2d 636 (1971); State v. Vicars, 186 Neb. 311, 183 N.W.2d 241 (1971); State v. Superior Court of Pima County, 104 Ariz. 440, 454 P.2d 982 (1969); State v. Moore, 105 N.J.Super. 567, 253 A.2d 579 (1969); People v. Doyle, 16 Mich.App. 242, 167 N.W.2d 907 (1969); State v. Morse, 281 Minn. 378, 161 N.W.2d 699 (1968); State v. Fulks, 83 S.D. 433, 160 N.W.2d 418 (1968); Eggleston v. State, 4 Md.App. 124, 241 A.2d 433 (1968). See Nelson v. Moriarty, 484 F.2d 1034 (1st Cir.1973).

It may well be the case, as the court stated in People v. Doyle, supra, that "[c]urrent social and moral values make more realistic the California view that a reasonable and honest mistake of age is a valid defense to a charge of statutory rape . . ." 16 Mich.App. at 243, 167 N.W.2d at 908. Nevertheless, statutory rape or carnal knowledge as proscribed in RCW 9.79.020 is a recognized judicial exception to the general rule that a mistake of fact is a defense to a criminal charge. We therefore disagree with the view expressed in *Hernandez* that such exception may not be sustained except by legislation so directing; rather, we believe the converse, that the exception must be sustained unless the legislature decides otherwise. As the court in State v. Superior Court of Pima County, supra, stated, 104 Ariz. at 443, 454 P.2d at 985, "We do not think the predatory nature of man has changed in the last decade. If mistake of fact is to be the standard of permissive conduct, the legislature is the appropriate forum to indulge in that decision."

In light of the foregoing, there can be no doubt as to the proper interpretation to be given our state carnal knowledge statute, RCW 9.79.020, which provides in part:

> Every male person who shall carnally know and abuse any female child under the age of eighteen years, not his wife, and every female person who shall have sexual intercourse with any male child under the age of eighteen years, not her husband, shall be punished as follows:
>
> . . .
>
> (3) When such act is committed upon a child of fifteen years of age and under eighteen years of age, by imprisonment in the state penitentiary for not more than fifteen years.

In Laws of 1919, ch. 132, § 1, p. 368, the state legislature amended the above quoted statute by omitting "and of previously chaste character" after the words "under eighteen years of age" in subdivision (3). Accordingly, our state Supreme Court in State v. Linton, 36 Wash.2d 67, at 86, 87, 216 P.2d 761, at 773 (1950), stated:

> From 1909 to 1919, there was a reference to chaste character in the rape statute, although with respect to the punishment only. . . .

. . .

Evidence as to previous chaste character was, therefore, directly pertinent in prosecutions under the 1909 statute. In 1919, the legislature reenacted and amended the 1909 statute, retaining subsection 3, above quoted, except that it omitted those words ["and of previously chaste character"]. Laws of 1919, chapter 132, p. 368. But it is not pertinent to any issue under the statute now in force, which is the statute of 1919.

In the most recent amendment, Laws of 1973, 1st Ex.Sess., ch. 154, § 123, the legislature omitted the words originally in the first paragraph of the statute "have sexual intercourse with" which followed "every female person who shall" and substituted "carnally know and abuse." Significantly, although the legislature has amended RCW 9.79.020 on several occasions, it has not seen fit to require that an element of criminal intent be proven by the state in the prosecution of one accused of violating the statute. We must presume that the legislature is aware of the general view discussed herein that legislation such as RCW 9.79.020 does not leave room for the possible defense of reasonable mistake of fact by the accused as to the victim's age, and therefore the failure of the legislature specifically to depart from the view makes it inappropriate for us to do so. The state of the law in Washington on this subject is quite literally the same as it was when our state Supreme Court observed in State v. Melvin, 144 Wash. 687, at page 690, 258 P. 859, at page 860 (1927), "What the legislature has virtually said by this statute . . . is, that the male or female, as the case may be, who is prosecuted, is guilty, where the other one involved in the transaction is under the age of 18 years . . ." For the reason stated, the trial court correctly refused to consider appellant's defense insofar as it was based upon an asserted mistake of fact as to the victim's age.

Judgment affirmed.[1]

HOROWITZ and JAMES, JJ., concur.

1. "It has long been the law of this Commonwealth that it is no defense that the defendant did not know that the victim was under the statutory age of consent. Further, it is immaterial that the defendant reasonably believed that the victim was sixteen years of age or older or that he may have attempted to ascertain her age." Commonwealth v. Miller, 385 Mass. 521, 432 N.E.2d 463 (1982).

"The object of the proposed testimony, was to show that defendant believed, or had good reason to believe, that the prosecuting witness was, at the time of taking or enticing away, over fifteen years of age. Would such proof aid the defendant, if in fact the female was under the age named? We think not. It is not like the case stated by appellant, and found in the books, of a married man, through a mistake of the person, having intercourse with a woman, whom he supposed to be his wife, when she was not. In such a case there is no offense, for none was intended either in law or morals. In the case at bar, however, if defendant enticed the female away, for the purpose of defilement or prostitution, there existed a criminal or wrongful intent—even though she was over the age of fifteen. The testimony offered was, therefore, irrelevant—for the only effect of it would have been, to show that he intended one wrong, and by mistake committed another. The wrongful intent to do the one act, is only transposed to the

MODEL PENAL CODE

Section 213.6 Provisions Generally Applicable to Article 213. [Sexual Offenses.]

(1) Mistake as to Age. Whenever in this Article the criminality of conduct depends on a child's being below the age of 10, it is no defense that the actor did not know the child's age, or reasonably believed the child to be older than 10. When criminality depends on the child's being below a critical age other than 10, it is a defense for the actor to prove by a preponderance of the evidence that he reasonably believed the child to be above the critical age.

. . .

Section 230.1 Bigamy and Polygamy.

(1) Bigamy. A married person is guilty of bigamy, a misdemeanor, if he contracts or purports to contract another marriage, unless at the time of the subsequent marriage:

(a) the actor believes that the prior spouse is dead; or

(b) the actor and the prior spouse have been living apart for five consecutive years throughout which the prior spouse was not known by the actor to be alive; or

(c) a Court has entered a judgment purporting to terminate or annul any prior disqualifying marriage, and the actor does not know that judgment to be invalid; or

(d) the actor reasonably believes that he is legally eligible to remarry.

(2) Polygamy. A person is guilty of polygamy, a felony of the third degree, if he marries or cohabits with more than one spouse at a time in purported exercise of the right of plural marriage. The offense is a continuing one until all cohabitation and claim of marriage with more than one spouse terminates. This section does not apply to parties to a polygamous marriage, lawful in the country of which they are residents or nationals, while they are in transit through or temporarily visiting this State.

(3) Other Party to Bigamous or Polygamous Marriage. A person is guilty of bigamy or polygamy, as the case may be, if he contracts or purports to contract marriage with another knowing that the other is thereby committing bigamy or polygamy.[1]

other. And though the wrong intended is not indictable, the defendant would still be liable, if the wrong done is so." State v. Ruhl, 8 Iowa 447, 450 (1859).

The federal offense of transporting a kidnaped person across a state line is violated by one who willfully transports a kidnaped person from one point to another, and in doing so crosses a state line, even if this was done without knowledge of the state line. United States v. Napier, 518 F.2d 316 (9th Cir.1975).

SECTION 2. IMPELLED PERPETRATION

A command or order, not backed by public authority, will not excuse a deed which would otherwise be a crime (except to the decreasing extent that a husband's command may excuse his wife). Under certain circumstances one who has carried out a private command or order may be free from guilt although the criminal law was violated, but the excuse will be based upon some other ground. If, for example, the thing commanded is not obviously wrongful, and the order is carried out in innocence of the criminal purpose intended, the "innocent agent" is not guilty of crime. This may happen in various ways, such as where an employer commits larceny by directing an employee to take a certain chattel (which actually belongs to another) and place it in the employer's house or store. The employee is not guilty of crime if he carries out this order in the innocent belief that the chattel belongs to his employer. In such cases, however, it is the mistake of fact, and not the command, which constitutes the excuse.

If a command or order is accompanied by violence or threat of violence, the real problem is not the command but the compulsion. An "act" is a willed movement. Hence if one's body is propelled against his will, this is not his act. The classic example is this: **A, B** and **C** are standing near the edge of a precipice. Suddenly **A** shoves **B** violently against **C**, causing **C** to fall to his death. **A** has caused the death of **C**, but **B** whose body was used as a tool by **A**, so to speak, has not caused this death. **B** did not act, he was acted upon.

Such a situation is mentioned to avoid any possible misunderstanding, but "compulsion" has quite a different meaning. "Compulsion," as used in this connection, applies where it is the *will* rather than the *body* which is coerced. If, in a case similar to the one mentioned, **A** had not touched **B**, but had pointed a loaded pistol at him and threatened to kill him unless he pushed **C** over the edge, and **B** had done this to save his own life, it would have been a case of compulsion. In this case **B** had a choice. It was not an easy choice, to be sure, but when he decided to push **C** to his death rather than risk his own life, this was a willed movement and hence an "act." And the resulting death is legally imputable to him as well as to **A**. Whether he is criminally responsible for this death he has caused depends upon whether or not this compulsion will be recognized as an excuse.

Statements can be found by some of the early writers indicating that no man is ever criminally answerable for what he was compelled to do in order to save his own life. And unquestionably such compulsion or necessity will be recognized as an excuse for most deeds which would otherwise be criminal. But Blackstone asserted: ". . . though a man be violently assaulted, and hath no other possible means of escaping death but by killing an innocent person, this fear and force shall not acquit him of murder; for he ought rather to die himself than escape by the murder of an innocent."[1] No sound analogy can be drawn from the "self defense" cases because such defense does not involve the killing of an *innocent* person. And the very few cases of this nature which have reached the courtroom show that the common law does not justify or excuse such a killing.[2] Strangely enough the possibility of manslaughter rather than murder in such cases seems never to have had adequate consideration. The killing is intentional to be sure, and there is no legally recognized *provocation.* But the circumstances are extremely *mitigating.* The mitigation in such a case is entitled to greater recognition than that in most instances of voluntary manslaughter committed in the sudden heat of passion. The state of mind of one who reluctantly takes the life of an innocent person as the only means of saving his own, while not guiltless, is certainly not malice aforethought.

The statement above refers to the common law. In some of the new penal codes it is provided that such a killing is manslaughter.[2a]

One of the most sordid cases of compulsion is that of the brute who tried, at the point of a gun, to force his wife and another man to have sexual intercourse. He was convicted of an assault with intent to commit rape on his own wife. On appeal it was urged that the male victim of the assault would not have been guilty of rape had the act been completed and hence there was no intent to commit rape. The court, in affirming the conviction, did not rest the decision entirely upon this point but was inclined to the view that not even the fear of immediate death would be a defense to a charge of rape.[3]

For most offenses, however, a well-grounded fear of immediate death or great bodily injury is recognized as an excuse. One is not punishable for robbery because of having driven the get-away car for robbers if it is done at the point of a pistol and under the threat of immediate death.[4] And one who damaged a threshing machine with a sledge hammer was held not guilty of crime when it was found that

1. 4 Bl.Comm. 30.

"[C]oercion is not a defense to murder." United States v. Buchanan, 529 F.2d 1148, 1153 (7th Cir.1976).

The House of Lords has ruled that the defense of compulsion or duress is available to a principal in the second degree to homicide although not necessarily to a principal in the first degree. Lynch v. D.P.P. [1975] 1 All E.R. 913 (H.L.). The Canadian Supreme Court has taken the same position. Regina v. Paquette, 30 CCC 2d 417 (S.C.Can.1976).

2. The leading case is Brewer v. State, 72 Ark. 145, 78 S.W. 773 (1904). An Alabama opinion goes into the subject rather thoroughly although the actual decision turns on another point. Arp v. State, 97 Ala. 5, 12 So. 301 (1893).

In Axtell's Case, J. Kelyng, 13, 84 Eng. Rep. 1060 (1660), arising out of the conviction and execution of Charles I, it was held that Axtell, the soldier "who commanded the guards at the King's tryal, and at his murder" was guilty although he claimed "that all he did was as a soldier, by the command of his superiour officer, whom he must obey or die" because "where the command is traiterous, there the obedience to that command is also traiterous".

2a. E.g. Wis.Stat.Ann. § 940.05.

3. State v. Dowell, 106 N.C. 722, 11 S.E. 525 (1890).

4. People v. Merhige, 212 Mich. 601, 180 N.W. 418 (1920).

he had been compelled to do so by a violent mob.[5] It was even recognized that one who joins the enemy forces in time of war is not guilty of treason if he does so in fear of death or great bodily injury, and escapes at the first reasonable opportunity [6]—provided he has not caused death in the meantime.[7]

It has been argued that if such compulsion will excuse treason it should excuse any crime, and therefore murder.[8] The answer, however, is obvious. Joining enemy forces, with mental reservation, and leaving at the earliest opportunity causes no lasting harm. Homicide does.

The word "compulsion," as it is used in the criminal law, is limited usually to situations in which the unwilling action is compelled by some other person. Quite similar emergencies may arise in which the pressure is exerted by some other agency, and the result is the same. Here also it is necessary to distinguish between forcing the body and forcing the will. Treating physical impossibility and extreme pressure of circumstances as if they were identical "is one of the oldest fallacies of the law." [9] If a tornado hurls the body of **A** against **B,** with fatal results to **B,** this death is not caused by the act of **A.** But if **A** and **B** are adrift in a small boat 1000 miles from land and without food, and **A** kills **B** and eats his flesh as the only means of saving his own life, this death is caused by **A.** Furthermore, no matter how great the necessity, the law will not excuse the intentional killing of an *innocent* person on the plea that it was necessary to save the life of the slayer. In the boat case mentioned the English court insisted that the crime was murder and pronounced sentence of death,[10] but the sentence was afterward commuted by the crown to six months' imprisonment. It would seem that circumstances so obviously and extremely mitigating as to cause such a reduction by the pardoning power should have been recognized by the court as reducing the

5. Rex v. Crutchley, 5 Car. & P. 133, 172 Eng.Rep. 909 (1831).

6. Oldcastle's Case, 3 Co.Inst. *10, 1 Hale, P.C. 50, 1 East, P.C. 70. "An American . . . charged with playing the role of the traitor may defend by showing that force or coercion compelled such conduct". Kawakita v. United States, 343 U.S. 717, 736, 72 S.Ct. 950, 962, 96 L.Ed. 1249 (1952). As to what constitutes compulsion see D'Aquino v. United States, 192 F.2d 338 (9th Cir. 1951).

Respublica v. McCarty, 2 Dallas 86, 1 L.Ed. 300 (Pa.1781). In this case defendant was not excused because he was still with the British forces eleven months after he claimed to have been compelled to join them.

7. The soldier "who commanded the guards at the king's tryal, and at his murder" had no defense although "all that he did was as a soldier, by the command of his superior officer, whom he must obey or die". Axtell's Case, Kelyng 13, 84 Eng.Rep. 1060 (1660).

Compulsion, as a defense to a charge of crime, must involve a threat of "imminent" infliction of death or great bodily harm. Such a threat directed at some indefinite time in the future is not a defense. State v. Milum, 213 Kan. 581, 516 P.2d 984 (1973).

8. 1 East, Pleas of the Crown 294 (1803).

9. Per Mr. Justice Holmes in the Eliza Lines, 199 U.S. 119, 130, 26 S.Ct. 8, 10, 50 L.Ed. 115 (1905).

10. Regina v. Dudley and Stephens, 14 Q.B.D. 273 (1884).

grade of the crime itself. In the famous case of "human jettison," the actual verdict was guilty of manslaughter. In this case a leaking boat loaded with survivors after a ship-wreck was in grave danger of sinking in a storm. It was not a modern life-boat and all would have been lost if it had gone down. The sailors threw some passengers overboard to lighten the load. As thus lightened the boat was kept afloat during the storm and the survivors were picked up by a passing vessel the following day. The judge charged the jury that the sailors had no privilege to sacrifice passengers even in such extreme peril.[11] He intimated, although it was quite beside the point, that if several are in such peril that some must be sacrificed in order for any to be saved—and none of the group owes any duty to others in this emergency—choice by lot would be proper.

What seems to be the accepted view today, although the cases are very few, is that no one is privileged to choose the death of some other innocent person in order to preserve his own life. In extreme emergencies, however, the field of legally-recognized causation may be somewhat narrow. One may not wilfully plunge a knife into an obviously guiltless breast, but it does not follow that in a race, or even a struggle, for means of safety, adequate to preserve the life of only one, the winner shall under all circumstances be said to have killed the loser.

On the other hand, where the necessity is great a deed not involving death or great bodily harm may be excused, even if otherwise it would be a crime. For example, if merchant vessels are forbidden to enter a certain port, and such a ship is forced to take refuge there during a violent storm, for the safety of the vessel and those on board, there has been no violation of the embargo.[12] And what might otherwise constitute attempted revolt by sailors on the high seas may be excused by the unseaworthiness of the vessel.[13]

The problem that seems to have aroused the most discussion and the least litigation is that of taking food to avoid starvation. Although Lord Bacon said that "if a man steals viands to satisfy a present hunger, this is no felony nor larceny," [14] the books are full of statements indicating that "economic necessity" is no defense to a criminal charge. And it has been so held.[15] But "economic necessity," as this phrase has been used, falls far short of an actual need to prevent starvation. And mere convenience will not excuse the intentional deprivation of another's property. Under ordinary circumstances in the modern community it is not *necessary* to take anoth-

11. United States v. Holmes, 1 Wall. Jr. 1, Fed.Cas. No. 15,383 (1842). The judge emphasized the duty owed by sailors to passengers.

12. The William Gray, 1 Paine 16, Fed.Cas. No. 17,694 (1810). Compare Commonwealth v. Brooks, 99 Mass. 434 (1868).

13. United States v. Ashton, 2 Sumn. 13, Fed.Cas. No. 14,470 (1834).

14. Bacon: Maxims, reg. 5.

15. State v. Moe, 174 Wash. 303, 24 P.2d 638 (1933).

er's food, without his consent, because an appeal may be made to th public authorities. But if a ship should be disabled on the high seas and its wireless destroyed, and those on board, after exhausting the ship's provisions, should find that part of the cargo was food and should break open boxes of freight and eat the contents as the only means of saving themselves from starvation, they would not be guilty of larceny. Doubtless the lack of any case holding such an appropriation not to be larceny (or *contra*) is because the result is too obvious to have resulted in prosecution.

The bank cashier who hands over money to an armed bandit, under threat of immediate death if he refuses, thereby appropriates the bank's money to save his own life. But this is not embezzlement.[16]

The Model Penal Code [17] and statutes of some states [18] have adopted a standard for duress that is more liberal than the traditional rule. The standard recognizes a defense to any crime if the actor was coerced to commit the offense by use or threat to use unlawful force against him or another, "which a person of reasonable firmness in his situation would have been unable to resist." The Model Penal Code [19] also recognizes that conduct may be justifiable if the actor believes it to be necessary to avoid a harm or evil to himself or another and the harm or evil to be avoided is greater than the conduct sought to be prevented. This embodies a choice of evils for the actor and a defense so long as the actor has not made an inappropriate choice. The concept of choice of evils does not necessarily rule out the alternative defense of duress. Some courts have recognized the availability of a defense of choice of evils or necessity in proper circumstances but a real emergency must be shown, not merely a choice of courses of action, before the defense is available.[20]

STATE v. BURNEY

Court of Appeals of Oregon, 1980.
49 Or.App. 529, 619 P.2d 1336.

GILLETTE, PRESIDING JUDGE. This is a criminal case in which the defendant was charged with the offense of being an ex-convict in possession of a firearm. ORS 166.270.[1] He was found guilty after a

16. State v. McGuire, 107 Mont. 341, 88 P.2d 35 (1938).

17. § 2.09.

18. Ariz.Rev.Stat.Ann. § 13–412 (1978); Utah Code Ann.1953, § 76–2–302.

19. § 3.02.

20. United States v. Seward, 687 F.2d 1270 (10th Cir.1982).

"[W]here a criminal defendant is charged with escape and claims that he is entitled to an instruction on the theory of duress or necessity, he must proffer evidence of a bona fide effort to surrender or return to custody as soon as the claimed duress or necessity had lost its coercive force." United States v. Bailey, 444 U.S. 394, 100 S.Ct. 624, 637 (1980).

1. ORS 166.270 provides that

"(1) Any person who has been convicted of a felony under the law of this state or any other state, or who has been convicted of a felony under the laws of the Government of the United States, who owns, or has in his possession or under his custody or control any pistol, revolver, or other firearms capable of being concealed upon the

trial to the court. The sole issue on his appeal is whether the trial court erred in refusing to consider the "choice of evils" defense, ORS 161.200, in assessing the evidence presented at trial. We reverse and remand.

The principal facts are not in dispute. Defendant, who is an ex-convict, moved from Boise, Idaho, to Portland on November 6, 1979. The weekend prior to moving, he had been fishing with a friend. That friend left a pistol in defendant's pickup, without defendant's knowledge. Several weeks later, on the evening of the incident in question, the defendant found the pistol. The circumstances surrounding its discovery led to the crime charged in this case.

Shortly after midnight on December 2, 1979, defendant was returning home from a birthday celebration. He pulled into the lot behind the Burger King, at Broadway and Burnside in Portland, to have a hamburger. The Burger King was closed. When defendant went back to his pickup, it would not start.

Thinking the pickup would start again if he let it sit for awhile, defendant went to call his wife to let her know what was happening. While waiting, he had a glass of wine and played a few games of pool for money in Mary's Club, a nearby establishment. Defendant won ten to sixteen dollars and decided to leave. He had just left Mary's when he noticed Griffin, one of the persons from whom he had won money, coming out of the club with a broken-down cue stick. Because Griffin had been belligerent and was acting strangely, defendant was afraid of him. Specifically, defendant feared Griffin would try to take his money back.

Defendant stopped and asked what Griffin wanted. He walked beside Griffin for a short distance. Griffin became involved in an altercation with an unknown person who bumped into him on the sidewalk. Another unknown person intervened. Defendant left as Griffin and the other two were straightening things out.

Defendant had crossed Burnside and was in the parking lot where his pickup was parked when he heard running footsteps behind him.

person, or machine gun, commits the crime of exconvict in possession of a firearm.

"(2) For the purposes of this section, a person 'has been convicted of a felony' if, at the time of his conviction for an offense, that offense was a felony under the law of the jurisdiction in which it was committed. Provided, however, that such conviction shall not be deemed a conviction of a felony if:

"(a) At the time of conviction, and pursuant to the law of the jurisdiction in which the offense occurred, the offense was made a misdemeanor by the type or manner of sentence actually imposed; or

"(b) The offense was for possession of marijuana.

"(3) Subsection (1) of this section shall not apply to any person who has been convicted of only one felony under the law of this state or any other state, or who has been convicted of only one felony under the laws of the United States, which felony did not involve the possession or use of a firearm, and who has been discharged from imprisonment, parole or probation for said offense for a period of 15 years prior to the date of alleged violation of subsection (1) of this section.

"(4) Exconvict in possession of a firearm is Class C felony."

He turned as he reached his truck and saw Griffin "coming out" at him. Defendant reached under the seat of the pickup for a tire iron to protect himself from what he feared was an impending attack. Instead of the tire iron, he felt his friend's pistol. He had not known until that moment that the pistol was there. Defendant pointed the pistol at Griffin's legs and told him to get away. Griffin left. Defendant tossed the pistol back under the seat and tried to restart his truck. Before he could start it the police arrived.

James Powell, a Portland police officer, testified that on December 2, 1979, at 2:40 a.m. he received a radio call to go to the Sealander Restaurant. When Officer Powell arrived he observed Patrick Griffin, who had a cue stick in his hand, pointing to the defendant's vehicle and saying the defendant had a gun on his person. The police immediately approached the defendant's vehicle and ordered him out of his truck. Once outside the defendant denied having a gun.[2] The police searched the vehicle and found the handgun under the passenger seat. The defendant was then advised of his rights, whereupon he admitted he pointed the gun at Griffin because Griffin was threatening him with a cue stick. He also admitted to the officers at the scene that he had been convicted of rape in Utah.

After considering all of the evidence, and indicating that he believed the defendant's story with respect to the circumstances under which the incident occurred, the trial judge found the defendant guilty of the charge. He specifically ruled that the defense of "choice of evils" was not available in a case in which the defendant is charged with being an ex-convict in possession of a firearm. The defendant argues that, because the evidence showed (and the trial judge apparently believed) that the defendant feared for his safety, the defense was applicable.

The "choice of evils" defense is set out in ORS 161.200 as follows:

> "(1) Unless inconsistent with other provisions of chapter 743, Oregon Laws 1971, defining justifiable use of physical force, or with some other provision of law, conduct which would otherwise constitute an offense is justifiable and not criminal when:
>
> "(a) That conduct is necessary as an emergency measure to avoid an imminent public or private injury; and
>
> "(b) The threatened injury is of such gravity that, according to ordinary standards of intelligence and morality, the desirability and urgency of avoiding the injury clearly outweigh the desirability of avoiding the injury sought to be prevented by the statute defining the offense in issue.
>
> "(2) The necessity and justifiability of conduct under subsection (1) of this section shall not rest upon considerations pertain-

2. The police testified that defendant denied having a gun. Defendant testified that he denied having a gun *on his person,* because he understood the officer's question to be directed at that possibility. The trial judge specifically stated that he believed defendant's testimony.

ing only to the morality and advisability of the statute, either in its general application or with respect to its application to a particular class of cases arising thereunder."

We think that the trial judge's conclusion that ORS 161.200 is inapplicable to the offense of being an ex-convict in possession of a firearm is incorrect. The statute contains no such express exception, and we see no justification for implying one. To the contrary, one who has been previously convicted of a felony is just as entitled to defend himself from an imminent threat of injury as is any other private citizen. We hold that the defense is available to those who have been previously convicted of a felony and, in appropriate circumstances, may justify their resort to a weapon which it would otherwise be unlawful for them to possess.

We have previously stated that a defendant is entitled to the choice of evils defense if there is evidence that

> "(1) . . . [H]is conduct was necessary to avoid a threatened injury; (2) . . . the threatened injury was imminent; and (3) . . . it was reasonable for defendant to believe that the need to avoid the injury was greater than the need to avoid the injury which the [other statute] seeks to prevent." State v. Matthews, 30 Or.App. 1133, 1136, 569 P.2d 662 (1977); State v. Lawson, 37 Or.App. 739, 588 P.2d 110 (1978).

The trial judge apparently found all of those elements present in this case, but declined to apply the defense solely because he believed it was unavailable in this kind of charge. Inasmuch as he was mistaken in this premise, his rationale in convicting the defendant was erroneous.

A question remains as to whether or not this error requires reversal. The state argues that, even if we decide that the choice of evils defense was available to the defendant, all of the testimony establishes that the defendant maintained control of the gun far beyond the time it was necessary to do so in order to protect himself. In fact, the gun was hidden away in the defendant's pickup and was only discovered after a police search. In light of this evidence, the state argues, the defendant is guilty in any event, and we should affirm.

We agree with the state that there was sufficient evidence from which the trial court could find that the defendant was guilty of being an ex-convict in possession of a firearm for the period of time during which, by his own admission, he retained the gun after the threat to his person had ended. However, the evidence was not such as to *require* the trial court to find the defendant guilty. The reason for defendant's hiding of the gun is not established. He may have intended to return it to its owner in Idaho. On the other hand, he may have intended to turn it over to a policeman as soon as possible. If the former was his intent, he is guilty. If the latter was, he may not be; it would be unconscionable to hold defendant guilty for continuing to possess a gun which came into his possession rightfully, unless and until he thereafter had a reasonable opportunity to divest himself of it in a manner which would not create a public peril.

Defendant was never asked what his intent was. There are permissible inferences both ways. The question is one for a trier of fact.

Reversed and remanded for a new trial.[a]

MODEL PENAL CODE

Section 2.09 Duress.

(1) It is an affirmative defense that the actor engaged in the conduct charged to constitute an offense because he was coerced to do so by the use of, or a threat to use, unlawful force against his person or the person of another, which a person of reasonable firmness in his situation would have been unable to resist.

(2) The defense provided by this Section is unavailable if the actor recklessly placed himself in a situation in which it was probable that he would be subjected to duress. The defense is also unavailable if he was negligent in placing himself in such a situation, whenever negligence suffices to establish culpability for the offense charged.

. . .

(4) When the conduct of the actor would otherwise be justifiable under Section 3.02, this Section does not preclude such defense.

Section 3.02 Justification Generally: Choice of Evils.

(1) Conduct which the actor believes to be necessary to avoid a harm or evil to himself or to another is justifiable, provided that:

(a) the harm or evil sought to be avoided by such conduct is greater than that sought to be prevented by the law defining the offense charged; and

(b) neither the Code nor other law defining the offense provides exceptions or defenses dealing with the specific situation involved; and

(c) a legislative purpose to exclude the justification claimed does not otherwise plainly appear.

(2) When the actor was reckless or negligent in bringing about the situation requiring a choice of harms or evils or in appraising the necessity for his

a. A seventeen-year-old boy in an Industrial School who submitted to an act of sodomy with a guard, under threats that the guard would "slap him down" every time he saw him, acted under compulsion. Perryman v. State, 63 Ga.App. 819, 12 S.E.2d 388 (1940).

One is not guilty of killing moose without a license and out of season if this was reasonably necessary to protect his property. Cross v. State, 370 P.2d 371, 93 A.L.R.2d 1357 (Wyo.1962).

In defense against a charge of sale of amphetamine tablets, D claimed duress in that his friends had been threatened with death if he did not sell. The court apparently would have recognized this threat to D's friends as a defense except that: "Avenues of escape were always available, . . ." United States v. Gordon, 526 F.2d 406, 408 (9th Cir.1975).

"We hold that the duress defense is available in Michigan whenever a defendant offers evidence that his escape was necessitated by an immediate threat of death or seriously bodily injury, including a threat of homosexual attack." People v. Mendoza, 108 Mich.App. 733, 310 N.W.2d 860, 864 (1981).

conduct, the justification afforded by this Section is unavailable in a prosecution for any offense for which recklessness or negligence, as the case may be, suffices to establish culpability.[a]

SECTION 3. CONSENT OF THE OTHER PARTY

The problem of consent in the criminal law requires particular attention to two different matters: (1) What is the legal effect of consent or non-consent? (2) What will be regarded as consent within the legal meaning of the term?

In studying the legal effect of consent or non-consent it is important to recognize three different categories of crime.

(1) In certain offenses the *want* of consent of the person harmed is an essential ingredient of the crime by the very words of the definition, or the necessary implication of other terms. Thus in common-law rape the phrase "without her consent" (or "against her will") is found in the definition itself. The finding of consent on the part of the person alleged to have been harmed completely disproves the commission of such a crime.

(2) At the other extreme will be found those offenses which can be committed even with the consent of the person harmed, such as "statutory rape" (carnal knowledge of a child) or murder. Furthermore, touching a girl under the age of consent with intent to have intercourse with her is an assault with intent to commit rape,[1] or an attempt to commit rape[2] although no force or violence is intended and she is entirely willing. And the sound view is that such a girl is just as incapable of giving a legally-recognized permission to an indecent fondling of her person as she is of giving such license to the act of intercourse itself, and hence her consent to such liberties is no defense.[3] A girl under the age of consent is frequently said to be incapable of giving consent to such misdeeds. What is meant, of course, is that her consent is incapable of giving a legally-recognized permission.

(3) Between these two extremes is a third category in which consent or non-consent will determine whether the conduct was lawful or unlawful within certain limits,—but not beyond. The typical example is battery. What is called a "fond embrace" when gladly accepted by a sweetheart is called "assault and battery" when perpetrated upon another without her consent. And the act of one who grabs another

1. People v. Babcock, 160 Cal. 537, 117 P. 549 (1911); Commonwealth v. Murphy, 165 Mass. 66, 42 N.E. 504 (1895); Fannin v. State, 65 Okl.Cr. 444, 88 P.2d 671 (1939); Steptoe v. State, 134 Tex.Cr.R. 320, 115 S.W.2d 916 (1938). Contra: State v. Pickett, 11 Nev. 255 (1876).

2. Alford v. State, 132 Fla. 624, 181 So. 839 (1938); Rainey v. Commonwealth, 169 Va. 892, 193 S.E. 501 (1937); Regina v. Martin, 9 Car. & P. 213, 169 Eng.Rep. 49 (1840).

3. People v. Gibson, 232 N.Y. 458, 134 N.E. 531 (1922); Carter v. State, 121 Tex. Cr. 493, 51 S.W.2d 316 (1932).

by the ankles and causes him to fall violently to the ground may result in a substantial jail sentence under some circumstances, but receive thunderous applause if it stops a ball carrier on the gridiron. The difference is because one who engages in a game such as football consents to such physical contact as is normally and properly to be expected in playing the game.

There are limits, however, to the extent to which the law will recognize a license based on such consent. Just as there can be no legally-valid permission to be killed, so the law will not recognize a license unnecessarily to be maimed. One may permit an amputation made necessary by accident or disease. But he who struck off the hand of a "lustie rogue" to enable him to beg more effectively was guilty despite the other's request.[4] A wrongdoer effectively may give consent to moderate chastisement and he who inflicts such permitted punishment is not guilty of assault and battery although he would be guilty without consent.[5] On the other hand, if two engage in a fist fight, by mutual consent, exchanging blows intended or likely to cause great bodily injury, both are guilty of assault and battery.[6]

In a prosecution for any offense falling within the second category, or one beyond the permitted limits in the third category, it is futile to talk of consent because this will not be exculpating even if established. If the crime falls within the first category the prosecution must negative consent to make out even a prima-facie case. A prima-facie case does not necessarily require positive evidence of non-consent, if the offense is within the third category, but within the limits permitted by law proof of consent will disprove the charge. This invites inquiry as to just what will be regarded as consent within the legal meaning of the term.

It has been said: "A 'compelled consent' is in law no consent at all." [7] And this is beyond question if the duress employed was sufficient. Submission under extreme pain or fear is not that positive concurrence with the desire of another which is implied by the word "consent" as it is used in the law. What is claimed to have been duress in a particular case may be inadequate for this purpose. This will depend upon all the circumstances including the offense alleged to have been committed. In no case, however, will "consent" be recognized if it was induced by threats of immediate death or great bodily harm imposed by one apparently able and willing to enforce his threats if frustrated.

Certain of the statutory additions to the crime of extortion are enlightening on this point. They provide a punishment for the ob-

4. Wright's Case, Co. Litt. 127a (1604).

5. State v. Beck, 19 S.C.L. (1 Hill) 363 (1833).

6. State v. Newland, 27 Kan. 764 (1882); Commonwealth v. Collberg, 119 Mass. 350 (1876); King v. Donovan, [1934] 2 K.B. 498.

7. Shehany v. Lowry, 170 Ga. 70, 72, 152 S.E. 114, 115 (1929).

taining of property from another "with his consent, induced by a wrongful use of force or fear." [8] The fear may be induced by a threat to harm the person or his relative or member of his family, by injury to person or property, accusation of crime, imputation of deformity or disgrace, exposure of a secret,[9] or kidnaping. If the force or fear generates a well-grounded belief that the property must be handed over to avoid immediate death or great bodily injury, the submission thereto is not "consent," in the legal view, and the obtaining of the property by such means is robbery,—not extortion. If the property is freely and voluntarily handed over without any coercion it is a gift,—not extortion. Only between these extremes is the other's property obtained "with his consent by a wrongful use of force and fear."

Conditional consent is no consent beyond the terms of the condition. If one places an article in the hands of another for inspection with the understanding that he will either return it or pay for it now, there is no consent for him to run off with it without payment.[10] And the proprietor of a store who placed a large box of matches on the counter, for the convenience of customers in lighting pipes and cigars in the store, did not consent that the whole box of matches should be carried away.[11] Consent to one thing, moreover, is not consent to a different or additional thing. The girl who willingly ate a fig did not consent to eat a deleterious drug added without her knowledge.[12] Nor would her consent have included some entirely different article if it had been substituted by sleight of hand undetected by her.

Consent obtained by fraud has given rise to some of the most difficult problems in this field.

REX v. TURVEY

Court of Criminal Appeal, 1946.
[1946] 2 All E.R. 60.

LORD GODDARD, L.C.J. [delivering the judgment of the court]: In this case the court is of the opinion that the conviction must be quashed. The appellant appeals against his conviction on count 1 of the indictment only.

The circumstances were these: The appellant was charged that on Dec. 12, 1945, being a servant of His Majesty's Minister of Works, he stole from the Minister a considerable number of table knives, spoons, and so forth. He had got into touch with some foreigner living at Newton Abbot, and found that he would be a ready receiver of goods which could be stolen from the Ministry of Works. Then, be-

8. West's Ann.Cal.Pen.Code § 518 (1970).

9. Id. at § 519.

10. Rex v. Chisser, T.Raym. 275, 83 Eng.Rep. 142 (1678).

11. Mitchum v. State, 45 Ala. 29 (1871).

12. Commonwealth v. Stratton, 114 Mass. 303 (1873).

ing in charge at that time of a depot of the Ministry of Works at Torquay, he approached one Ward, who was in charge of a depot at Exeter. Ward was tempted to steal the property of the Ministry of Works and hand it to the appellant, who would in turn hand it to the man at Newton Abbot. Ward at once communicated with his superiors at Bristol, the people who were really in control of the property, and told them of this plan which had been suggested to him. The officials of the Ministry of Works said it would be a good thing to let this plan go on and catch them at a suitable time, which would enable them to prosecute this appellant for stealing. What they did was this: They told Ward to hand over the property to the appellant, and Ward handed over the property to the appellant. He intended to hand it to the appellant and did hand it to the appellant.

That being so, the question arose whether or not the appellant could be charged with stealing. He could have been charged with conspiracy that he was inciting to commit a felony and other charges, there is no doubt, but could he be charged with the felony of stealing? In this case it is perfectly clear that if he stole the goods, he stole them at Exeter, but he did not take them there against the will of the owner because the owner handed them to him and meant to hand them to him. The chairman in his ruling, when counsel submitted no case, set out his findings, and it appears that he decided principally on the authority of R. v. Eggington [sic] (1), an old case, but perfectly good law, and also because he took a certain view with regard to the control the owner was exercising over the goods.

R. v. Egginton [1] was a case in which a servant told his master that someone was going to rob the premises. "Very well," said the master, "let them rob the premises and we will catch them"; in other words, to put a homely illustration, a man, knowing that somebody is going to break into his house, leaves the bolts drawn and so makes it easy for the man to come into the house, and when he comes in he catches him and a crime has been committed; he commits the crime none the less that the servant has been told to make things easy.[2] In this case, if Ward had been told by the person who really had control of these matters, "Let the appellant come in and take the goods," that would have been one thing, but he told him to take the goods and hand them to the appellant, and that makes all the difference.

One matter to which the chairman seems to have attached considerable importance was this, that Ward said to the appellant at the time when he was handing over the goods: "You must give me a receipt, I must have a receipt for these goods," and the appellant said he quite understood that and he would give a receipt for the goods. Thereupon, a perfectly fictitious document is made out, which both

1. [By the Compiler.] R. v. Egginton (1801), 2 Bos. & P. 508; 15 Digest 883, 9693.

2. But it is otherwise if the servant opened the door for D at the master's direction. Smith v. State, 362 P.2d 1071 (Alaska 1961).

parties knew and intended to be fictitious, under which it is made to look as though the goods were handed over to the appellant to take to the Palace Hotel at Torquay, but, of course, that was not an authority by Ward to the appellant to take the goods to Torquay because everybody knew that the appellant was meaning to steal these goods and they were to go to the receiver at Newton Abbot. No one intended that they were to go to Torquay, and this document was simply manufactured as a blind, or whatever word you like to use; it is not a genuine document, and therefore it is as if it did not exist.

The other point on which the chairman in his direction to the jury, as we think, went wrong was that he told the jury that these goods always remained under the control of the Ministry, because apparently the police had been warned, and the police were to follow the prisoner once he had stolen them, either to follow him or go immediately to Newton Abbot and find them in the possession of the receiver. But that will not do. Once the goods were handed over to the appellant the goods were under his control and nobody else's. What was to happen supposing, while he was driving along being followed by the police, the police car broke down? Of course, he would cheerfully drive away with these goods. Of course the goods were under the appellant's control as soon as he went away with the goods.

The charge that was put against the appellant was the wrong charge, a charge of which he could not have been convicted because there was no evidence here of what, to use a technical expression, is termed asportation. He did not carry away the goods against the will of the owner but because the owner was willing that he should have the goods and gave them to him. In those circumstances, the conviction will be quashed, so far as this charge is concerned, and the appeal allowed on count 1.

Appeal allowed.

PEOPLE v. COOK

District Court of Appeal, Second District, Division 4, California, 1964.
228 Cal.App.2d 716, 39 Cal.Rptr. 802.

BURKE, PRESIDING JUSTICE. Frank Billy Ray Cook, defendant, was charged by information with violation of section 487, subd. 3 of the Penal Code (Grand Theft Auto) and Vehicle Code, section 10851. He was acquitted by a jury of Grand Theft Auto, but found guilty of violating Vehicle Code, section 10851. A new trial was denied, probation was denied, and defendant was sentenced to the state prison for the term prescribed by law. . . .

The first ground of appeal is that the Mercury was taken with the consent of Frahm Pontiac, and even though such consent be deemed to have been induced by trick and device and under false pretenses, nevertheless, it constituted consent. The arrangements were made to register the Mercury in the buyer's name which would entitle him to possession and use of the vehicle. Frahm Pontiac acquired defendant's Buick as a trade-in and part consideration for the Mercury. Having acquired the Mercury with Frahm's consent, possession cannot be held to have been obtained in violation of section 10851 of the Vehicle Code.[1] The point appears to be novel in California but defendant offers persuasive authority from other jurisdictions to the effect that fraudulent inducement does not vitiate the consent given to the extent of creating the crime of auto theft.

In Perkins on Criminal Law, p. 859, it is stated:

"It has been held, it may be emphasized, that one who obtains the owner's consent to drive his car by fraudulently misrepresenting the use to be made of it, is not guilty of operating a car without the consent of the owner although the owner would not have consented to the use actually made."

One of the earliest cases holding that fraudulently induced consent is consent nonetheless and that such consent prevents a violation of a vehicle joy ride statute is State v. Boggs, 181 Iowa 358, 164 N.W. 759 (1917), the court stating: "The gist of the offense charged is taking and driving of the motor car in question without the consent of the owner."

The court then noted: "It is contended on behalf of appellant that consent obtained by trick, deceit, or misrepresentation is not consent in fact." In rejecting this contention, the court concluded: "The statute was not designed to punish one who [by misrepresentation or for a fraudulent purpose], obtains consent of the owner to take and operate his motor vehicle . . . ."

In State v. Mularky, 195 Wis. 549, 218 N.W. 809 (1928), State v. Boggs, supra, was discussed with approval, and the court there held that consent, however obtained, presented a violation of the Wisconsin Joy Ride Statute.

In United States v. One 1941 Chrysler, 74 F.Supp. 970 (E.D.Mich. 1947), the court was called upon to construe sections 413 and 414 of the Michigan Penal Statutes. These two sections are the equivalent of California's Penal Code, section 499b (the Misdemeanor Joy Ride Statute) and Vehicle Code, section 10851, the court holding:

"The provisions of such statutes as Sections 413 and 414 are not designed to punish one who obtains consent of the owner to take and operate his motor vehicle by misrepresentations or for a fraudulent purpose. They are directed against one who takes possession of such

1. Section 10851 of the Vehicle Code reads in part as follows:

"Any person who drives or takes a vehicle not his own, without the consent of the owner thereof, and with intent either permanently or temporarily to deprive the owner thereof of this title to or possession of the vehicle, whether with or without intent to steal the same, or any person who is a party or accessory to or an accomplice in the driving or unauthorized taking or stealing is guilty of a felony, ..." (Stats.1959, c. 3, p. 1597, § 10851.)

a vehicle without the consent of the owner." (See also People v. Smith, 213 Mich. 351, 182 N.W. 64.)

The above mentioned cases constitute specific applications of the basic common law rule that, unless there is statutory language to the contrary, whenever lack of consent is a necessary element of a crime, the fact that consent is obtained through misrepresentation will not supply the essential element of non-consent.

Perkins on Criminal Law, at page 859, states:

"Except for this, (larceny by trick) if it is truly an exception, and except where the result has been changed by statute, an offense which requires the absence of consent is not committed if there was consent to exactly what was done, even if such consent was induced by fraud." . . .

People v. Perez, 203 Cal.App.2d 397, 21 Cal.Rptr. 422, has been cited as supporting defendant's conviction of a violation of Vehicle Code, § 10851. In that case, the defendant attained possession of an automobile under the false representation that he had a buyer for it. He was given permission by the owner to keep the car for three days to make the sale to his buyer. Defendant never returned the car. The court stated (p. 399, 21 Cal.Rptr. p. 424): "Even though his original possession had been lawful, he had no authority to keep [the automobile] more than three days and then only for the purpose of consummating a sale to [his purported buyer.] . . . Actually, his original possession, his keeping the car beyond three days, his driving the car to Arizona . . . were all unlawful and, . . . if believed, could not be construed in any other way than intentionally taking and depriving the owner of possession, to say the least. Intent to deprive the owner may be established from the circumstances of the case, [citation] and is a question for the trier of fact. [Citations.] Each time defendant drove the car without the consent of the owner it was a violation of the statute. [Citation.]"

There is a generally recognized distinction, however, between *fraud in the factum,* which gives rise to no consent at all, and *fraud in the inducement,* which does not vitiate consent. Perez, supra, is an example of *fraud in the factum,* since the owner never intended that the defendant would acquire possession of the car for his own use.

Here, there was *fraud in the inducement;* the owner intended to sell defendant the car and consented to the taking of possession of it by him and, unlike Perez, the fraud did not vitiate consent.

No authorities are cited in opposition to defendant's contentions that consent, albeit falsely induced, bars prosecution under such section 10851 of the Vehicle Code. Respondent argues only that the facts conclusively establish an intent on defendant's part, defendant having been an accomplice, to deprive Frahm Pontiac of its title or possession of the 1959 Mercury, which is the essence of the charge;

that the fraud in obtaining consent vitiates the consent and does not excuse the criminal act.

Fraud, vitiating consent, as indicated, is a completely tenable principle in contract law, and when specifically incorporated in a penal statute determines the operation of the section, as in the case of Penal Code, section 484. However, section 10851 of the Vehicle Code makes no reference to fraud, false pretense or trick and device but is specifically based upon the taking without consent. . . .

The judgment of conviction is reversed and the cause remanded to the trial court with directions to dismiss.[1]

JEFFERSON and KINGSLEY, JJ., concur.

STATE v. LANKFORD

Court of General Sessions of Delaware, Sussex County, 1917.
6 Boyce 594, 102 A. 63.

. . . Harry S. Lankford was indicted for an assault upon Alice M. Lankford, his wife. Verdict guilty. . . .

BOYCE, J., charging the jury, in part: It is admitted that the accused and the prosecuting witness were married on the tenth day of June, 1916, and that the former communicated syphilis to his wife.

A husband may commit an assault and battery upon his wife, notwithstanding the marriage relation.

A wife in confiding her person to her husband does not consent to cruel treatment, or to infection with a loathsome disease. A husband, therefore, knowing that he has such a disease, and concealing the fact from his wife, by accepting her consent, and communicating the infection to her, inflicts on her physical abuse, and injury, resulting in great bodily harm; and he becomes, notwithstanding his marital rights, guilty of an assault, and indeed, a completed battery.

If the accused knew he was infected with syphilis, and his infection was unknown to his wife, the intent to communicate the disease to her by having sexual intercourse with her, may be inferred from the actual results.

If the jury should find from the evidence that the accused, knowing that he was infected with a venereal disease, and, without informing his wife of the fact, had sexual intercourse with her after such knowledge had been communicated to him, and thereby infected her with the disease, their verdict should be guilty.

If the jury should find that the accused, during the period he had sexual relations with his wife, did not know that he was infected with a venereal disease, and that he did not communicate with his wife

1. *Cook* was reaffirmed in People v. Donell, 32 Cal.App.3d 613, 108 Cal.Rptr. 232 (1973).

after being informed that he was infected, their verdict should be not guilty.

Verdict, guilty.[1]

REGINA v. DEE

Court for Crown Cases Reserved, Ireland, 1884.
15 Cox C.C. 579.

MAY, C.J. The question which arises on the case is whether, in point of law, the prisoner should be considered as guilty of rape. There is not, I think, any doubt or dispute as to the facts and circumstances of the case. Upon the report of the judge, who was myself, and the findings of the jury, it is, I think, established, that Judith Gorman, the wife of one J. Gorman, who was absent, having gone out to fish, lay down upon a bed in her sleeping room in the evening when it was dark; that the prisoner came into the room, personating her husband, lay down upon her and had connection with her; that she did not at first resist, believing the man to be her husband, but that on discovering that he was not her husband, which was after the commencement, but before the termination of the proceeding, her consent or acquiescence terminated, and she ran downstairs. It appeared, I think manifestly, that the prisoner knew the woman was deceived, as she said to the prisoner in his presence and hearing when he came into the room, "You are soon home to-night," to which he made no reply. At the time my own opinion, founded upon well-known cases in England, was that the prisoner was not guilty of rape, but at the request of the counsel for the Crown I left certain questions to the jury, and upon their findings directed them to find a verdict of guilty, reserving the case for the consideration of this court, which is now called upon to decide the question which arises. There have been several cases in England which have arisen on the point, whether the having connection with a married woman by personation of her husband amounts to the crime of rape. Rape may be defined as sexual connection with a woman forcibly and without her will: (Reg. v. Fletcher, 8 Cox C.C. 134). It is plain, however, "forcibly" does not mean violently, but with that description of force which must be exercised in order to accomplish the act, for there is no doubt that unlawful connection with a woman in a state of unconsciousness, produced by profound sleep, stupor, or otherwise, if the man knows that the

1. A doctor of theology, by falsely pretending to be a surgeon, induced a woman to permit him to make an intimate examination of her body under pretense of examining the working of an artificial limb. A conviction of assault and battery, and indecent assault, was affirmed on the ground that her consent was obtained by fraud. Commonwealth v. Gregory, 132 Pa.Super. 507, 1 A.2d 501 (1938).

D obtained a woman's consent to sexual intercourse with her under the false and fraudulent pretense that he was an officer and would otherwise arrest her. It was held that this was not rape because of her consent to the act. People v. Cavanaugh, 30 Cal.App. 432, 158 P. 1053 (1916).

woman is in such a state, amounts to a rape. The case which the court has to deal with is that of connection with a married woman obtained by personation of the husband while the woman is awake. On this point subtle distinctions have been drawn. The earliest reported case appears to be that of Rex v. Jackson (Russ. & Ry. 487). There the prisoner was convicted of burglary with intent to commit a rape on a married woman. It appeared in evidence that the prisoner got into the woman's bed as if he had been her husband, and had partial connection with her. The case was considered by the twelve judges. Four of the judges thought having carnal knowledge of a woman whilst she was under the belief that the man is her husband would be a rape, but the other eight judges thought it would not; but several of the eight judges intimated that if the case should occur again they would advise the jury to find a special verdict. This case cannot be regarded as one of much authority. Doubts seem to have existed in the minds even of the majority. However, in Reg. v. Saunders (8 C. & P. 265), in the year 1838, a married woman, a Mrs. Cleasby, in like manner submitted to connection with a man believing him to be her husband, but on discovering the mistake she ran and hanged herself, but was cut down and recovered. Gurney, B. directed the jury that the evidence did not establish a rape, as she consented, but that if they found that it was a fraud on her, and that she did not consent as to the person, they might find the prisoner guilty of an assault, which was accordingly so found, the court proceeding on the enactment of 7 Will. 4 & 1 Vict. c. 85, s. 11, which provides that on the trial of any person for any felony which includes an assault, the jury may acquit of the felony and find the party guilty of an assault, if the evidence should warrant such finding. I do not myself understand the application of the statute. If the consent of the woman prevented the crime being a rape, it would seem that it would also prevent it being an assault, which consent excludes. The same point arose in the case of Reg. v. Clarke (1 Dears.C.C. 397), where, under similar circumstances, the jury having found the prisoner guilty, the judge reserved the case, and upon argument the judges held that they were bound by the decision in R. v. Jackson, and that they ought not to allow the question to be opened, and the conviction was quashed. Reg. v. Barrow is reported in 1 L.Rep.C.C.R. 156. All the judges, Bovill, C.J., Channell, B., Byles, Blackburn, and Lush, JJ., there held, under similar circumstances, that when the consent is obtained by fraud, the act does not amount to rape; contrary, however, to the opinion of Kelly, C.B., before whom the case was tried, expressed at the trial. The case of Reg. v. Flattery was not a case of personation of a husband, but of sexual connection by a medical man, under pretence of his performing a surgical operation on a woman. In that case the prisoner was adjudged guilty of rape, it being clear that the woman did not submit knowingly to connection but to a different act, Kelly, C.B. saying "the case is therefore not within the authority of those cases which have been decided, decisions which I regret, that where a man by fraud induces a woman to submit to sexual connection it is not rape." Mellor, Denman, and Field, JJ. and Huddleston, B. all expressed their dissatisfaction with the dictum of Rex v. Jackson, and their desire that the case should be reconsidered. The last case on the subject of personation appears to be that of Reg. v. Young (14 Cox C.C. 114). Though the prisoner was held to have been properly convicted in that case, it does not clearly illustrate the precise point which is now before us, for on the facts as explained by the judge who tried the case it appeared that the commencement of the sexual connection in that case, which was one of personation, took place while the woman was asleep. Before its completion, however, she awoke and called out to her husband. It would seem that the criminal and felonious act of penetration was completed while the woman was asleep, and therefore unconscious. It is well settled, as I have observed, that connection with a woman while unconscious does constitute rape. The question arises now for our consideration, are we bound to follow the decisions in England to which I have referred? The series of cases to which I have drawn attention appear to be an echo of the first case of Rex v. Jackson. The others followed, no further argument being treated as necessary. Nevertheless, if the doctrine thus established had been adopted by the judges in England without objection, I do not think that this court should establish a different legal determination, unanimity on such points being of great importance. In its inception, however, that original case of Rex v. Jackson was dissented from by four of the twelve judges who heard it, while on the majority several apparently doubted the doctrine there contended for. In the case of Reg. v. Flattery all the judges desired that this doctrine should be reconsidered. In Ireland, until the present case, no similar question seems to have arisen; and it appears to me, under all the circumstances, that it is competent for us, and it is our duty, to consider the doctrine of those English decisions upon their merits. Now, rape being defined to be sexual connection with a woman without her consent, or without and therefore against her will, it is essential to consider what is meant and intended by consent. Does it mean an intelligent, positive concurrence of the will of the woman, or is the negative absence of dissent sufficient? In these surgical cases it is held that the submission to an act believed to be a surgical operation does not constitute consent to a sexual connection, being of a wholly different character; there is no *consensus quoad hoc.* In the case of personation there is no *consensus quoad hanc personam.* Can it be considered that there is a consent to the sexual connection, it being manifest that, had it not been for the deceit or fraud, the woman would not have submitted to the act? In the cases of idiocy, of stupor, or of infancy, it is held that there is no legal consent, from the want of an intelligent and discerning will. Can a woman, in the case of personation, be regarded as consenting to the act in the exercise of an intelligent will? Does she consent, not knowing the real nature of the act? As observed by Mr. Curtis, she intends to consent to a lawful and marital act, to which it is her duty to submit. But did she consent to an act of adultery? Are not the acts themselves wholly different in their moral nature? The act she permitted cannot properly be regarded as the real act which took place. Therefore the connection was done, in my opinion, without her consent, and the crime of rape was constituted. I therefore, am of opinion that the conviction should stand confirmed.

PALLES, C.B. . . . The person by whom the act was to be performed was part of its essence. The consent of the intellect, the only consent known to the law, was to the act of the husband only, and of this the prisoner was aware. As well put by Mr. Curtis, what the woman consented to was not adultery, but marital intercourse. The act consented to was not a crime in law; it would not subject her to a divorce. Were adultery criminally punishable by our law she would not be guilty. Compare the case now with Reg. v. Flattery (2 Q.B. Div. 410), a decision subsequent to any of those relied on for the prisoner. In it the act to which the consent was given, one of medical treatment, was different in nature from the act committed, and on this difference in nature the case turned. Viewing man as an animal, it might be said that the act here consented to and the act committed were of the same nature. Thus, the case might be distinguished from Reg. v. Flattery, and the animal instinct of the idiot held to be consent. But if I be right in holding that, in determining the legal relations of man to man, we regard him not as the animal but as the rational being, and if in administering the common law of this country, we are, as I believe us to be, at liberty to remember that it is the law of a Christian country, the growth of centuries of Christian wisdom—a law which, on the one hand, constituted the crime of rape as the protection of virtue, and on the other hand gave effect to the divine institution of marriage, by subjecting the wife to the will of the husband—I cannot entertain any doubt that the violation by a stranger of the person of a married woman is, in the view of that law, as it is in morality, an act different in nature from the lawful act of the husband. If this be so, Reg. v. Flattery (2 Q.B.Div. 410) rules this case. For these reasons, I am of opinion that the conviction should stand. . . .[1]

(LAWSON, O'BRIEN, ANDREWS, and MURPHY, JJ., also give opinions affirming the conviction.)

1. "If a woman be beguiled into her consent by marrying a man who had another wife living, or by causing the nuptials to be illegally celebrated, and persuading her that the directions of the law had been observed; in neither case will the pretended husband be guilty of a rape." State v. Murphy, 6 Ala. 765, 770 (1844).

Procuring sexual intercourse with a single woman by the device of a sham marriage is rape by fraud under the Texas statute. Lee v. State, 44 Tex.Cr. 354, 72 S.W. 1005 (1902). Oklahoma held otherwise on the ground that the artifice meant by the statute is such as deceives the woman as to the identity of the man with whom she is having intercourse. Draughn v. State, 12 Okl.Cr. 479, 158 P. 890 (1916).

Where the victim of a homosexual assault arranged for, aided, and en-

MODEL PENAL CODE

Section 2.11 Consent.

(1) In General. The consent of the victim to conduct charged to constitute an offense or to the result thereof is a defense if such consent negatives an element of the offense or precludes the infliction of the harm or evil sought to be prevented by the law defining the offense.

(2) Consent to Bodily Harm. When conduct is charged to constitute an offense because it causes or threatens bodily harm, consent to such conduct or to the infliction of such harm is a defense if:

(a) the bodily harm consented to or threatened by the conduct consented to is not serious; or

(b) the conduct and the harm are reasonably foreseeable hazards of joint participation in any concerted activity of a kind not forbidden by law; or

(c) the consent establishes a justification for the conduct under Article 3 of the Code.

(3) Ineffective Consent. Unless otherwise provided by the Code or by the law defining the offense, assent does not constitute consent if:

(a) it is given by a person who is legally incompetent to authorize the conduct charged to constitute the offense; or

(b) it is given by a person who by reason of youth, mental disease or defect or intoxication is manifestly unable or known by the actor to be unable to make a reasonable judgment as to the nature or harmfulness of the conduct charged to constitute the offense; or

(c) it is given by a person whose improvident consent is sought to be prevented by the law defining the offense; or

(d) it is induced by force, duress or deception of a kind sought to be prevented by the law defining the offense.

Section 3.08 Use of Force by Persons with Special Responsibility for Care, Discipline or Safety of Others.

The use of force upon or toward the person of another is justifiable if: . . .

(4) the actor is a doctor or other therapist or a person assisting him at his direction, and:

(a) the force is used for the purpose of administering a recognized form of treatment which the actor believes to be adapted to promoting the physical or mental health of the patient; and

(b) the treatment is administered with the consent of the patient or, if the patient is a minor or an incompetent person, with the consent of his parent or guardian or other person legally competent to consent in his behalf, or the treatment is administered in an emergency when the actor believes that no one competent to consent can be consulted and that a reasonable person, wishing to safeguard the welfare of the patient, would consent; or. . . .

couraged the assailant to use force against the victim the victim's consent prevented the assailant's conviction for forcible sexual assault. State v. Booher, 305 N.C. 554, 290 S.E.2d 561 (1982).

Section 213.1 Rape and Related Offenses. . . .

(2) Gross Sexual Imposition. A male who has sexual intercourse with a female not his wife commits a felony of the third degree if: . . .

(c) he knows that she is unaware that a sexual act is being committed upon her or that she submits because she falsely supposes that he is her husband.[a]

SECTION 4. GUILT OF THE INJURED PARTY

Guilt of the injured party will be a complete defense as to acts, which would otherwise be criminal, if such acts were committed in self-defense or otherwise to prevent crime and did not exceed the privilege recognized by law for such a purpose. In such a case the person has no wrongful purpose in mind but is merely seeking to frustrate a crime attempted by another. On the other hand it is an established principle of law that one crime is no excuse for another. The fact that the person killed was himself a murderer is no defense to a charge of murder. And it is just as much larceny to steal from a thief as to steal from anyone else,—[1] although needless to say the recapture of stolen property from the thief, by or for the lawful owner, is not stealing. It is also larceny to steal liquor or drugs from one who violated the law by possessing it.[2] And the fact that counterfeit coin was paid to a prostitute for unlawful intercourse is no defense to a charge of uttering counterfeit coin.[3]

COMMONWEALTH v. MORRILL & ANOTHER

Supreme Judicial Court of Massachusetts, 1851.
62 Mass. 571.

This was an indictment, which alleged that the defendants, Samuel G. Morrill and John M. Hodgdon, on the 17th of September, 1850, at Newburyport, "devising and intending one James Lynch by false pretences to cheat and defraud of his goods, did then and there unlawfully, knowingly and designedly falsely pretend and represent to said Lynch that a certain watch which said Morrill then and there had, and which said Morrill and Hodgdon then and there proposed and offered to exchange with said Lynch for two other watches belonging to said Lynch, was a gold watch of eighteen carats fine, and was of great value, to wit, of the value of eighty dollars; and the said Lynch, then and there believing the said false pretences and repre-

a. Copyright 1962 by the American Law Institute. Reprinted with the permission of the American Law Institute.

1. Ward v. People, 3 Hill 395 (N.Y. 1842). And it is no defense to a charge of embezzling money from a city that the city acquired the money illegally. State v. Patterson, 66 Kan. 447, 77 P. 860 (1903).

2. State v. Donovan, 108 Wash. 276, 183 P. 127 (1919). And it is malicious mischief wilfully to destroy liquor so held by another. State v. Stark, 63 Kan. 529, 66 P. 243 (1901).

3. The Queen v. ___, 1 Cox C.C. 250 (1845).

sentations so made as aforesaid by said Morrill and Hodgdon, and being deceived thereby, was induced by reason of the false pretences and representations so made as aforesaid to deliver, and did then and there deliver, to the said Morrill the two watches aforesaid, belonging to said Lynch, and of the value of twenty dollars, and the said Morrill & Hodgdon did then and there receive and obtain the two said watches, the property of said Lynch, as aforesaid, in exchange for the said watch, so represented as a gold watch as aforesaid, by means of the false pretences and representations aforesaid, and with intent to cheat and defraud the said Lynch of his said two watches, as aforesaid; whereas in truth and in fact said watch so represented by said Morrill and Hodgdon as a gold watch, eighteen carats fine, and of the value of eighty dollars, was not then and there a gold watch, and was not then and there eighteen carats fine, and was then and there of trifling value," & c.

At the trial in the court of common pleas, before Hoar, J., it appeared in evidence, that Lynch represented his watches, one of which was of silver, and the other of yellow metal, as worth fifty dollars; and on the testimony of the only witness for the commonwealth, who was a judge of the value of watches, they were worth not exceeding fifteen dollars. Lynch testified, that his silver watch cost him fifteen dollars; that he received the other in exchange for two, which cost him respectively seven dollars and thirteen dollars; and that he believed it to be worth thirty dollars.

The defendant requested the presiding judge to instruct the jury, that if Lynch's watches were not worth fifty dollars, or some considerable part of that sum, but were of merely trifling value, this indictment could not be maintained. But the judge instructed the jury, that if they supposed that each of the parties was endeavoring to defraud the other, and Lynch knew that his watches were of little value, the jury should not convict the defendants merely because they had the best of the bargain; but that if the defendants made the false representations charged in the indictment, with the intent to defraud, knowing them to be false, and they were such as would mislead and deceive a man of ordinary prudence, and Lynch, by reason of the representations, and trusting in them, parted with his property and was defrauded, it was not necessary to show that he was defrauded to the extent charged in the indictment, provided he, in good faith, parted with property which he believed to be valuable, and was defrauded to any substantial amount, for example, to the amount of five dollars; and that the defendants might be convicted, although from the mistake of Lynch, in over-estimating his property, he might not have been cheated to so great an extent as he at the time supposed.

The jury found the defendants guilty, who thereupon moved in arrest of judgment, on the ground that the indictment was insufficient; and this motion being overruled, they alleged exceptions to the order of the court, overruling the same, and also to the instructions aforesaid.

DEWEY, J. The exceptions taken to the instructions of the presiding judge cannot be sustained. If it were true that the party, from whom the defendants obtained goods by false pretences, also made false pretences as to his goods, which he exchanged with the defendants, that would be no justification for the defendants, when put on trial upon an indictment, charging them with obtaining goods by false pretences, knowingly and designedly in violation of a statute of this commonwealth. Whether the alleged misrepresentation of Lynch, being a mere representation as to the value or worth of a certain watch, and an opinion rather than a statement of a fact, would be such false pretence as would render him amenable to punishment under this statute, might be questionable, but supposing that to be otherwise, and it should appear that Lynch had also violated the statute, that would not justify the defendants. If the other party has also subjected himself to a prosecution for a like offence, he also may be punished. This would be much better than that both should escape punishment, because each deserved it equally. . . .[a]

Judgment on the verdict.

SECTION 5. CONDUCT OF THE INJURED PARTY

The rules of law concerning negligence as a defense in civil actions for personal injuries have no application to criminal prosecu-

a. Prosecutions for obtaining money or property by false pretenses have raised this issue frequently. The leading case for the minority view (although the New York rule is now otherwise as a result of legislation) is McCord v. People, 46 N.Y. 470 (1871). In this case defendant obtained a gold watch and a diamond ring as a "bribe" by falsely pretending to be an officer with a warrant for the victim's arrest. In reversing a conviction of false pretenses the court said that neither law nor public policy designs the protection of rogues in their dealing with one another. The Wisconsin court reached a similar result under other facts. State v. Crowley, 41 Wis. 271 (1876). The majority view is that *particeps criminis* applies only to civil actions, and that the guilt of one is not sufficient to establish the innocence of the other in a criminal prosecution. Horton v. State, 85 Ohio St. 13, 96 N.E. 797 (1911). Thus convictions have been upheld where money was obtained by altering a number punched from an illegal punch board, State v. Mellenberger, 163 Or. 233, 95 P.2d 709 (1939); by falsely pretending to have an unlawful plan to tap wires coming from horse races, Gilmore, Munger and Klein v. People, 87 Ill. App. 128 (1899); and by a confidence game in which the victim was induced to place a bet under the belief that a trick had been practiced whereby he was to cheat the other party, Regina v. Hudson, 8 Cox C.C. 305 (1860). In another case the suggestion that the victim of false pretenses thought he was buying stolen property was rejected as unimportant. Frazier v. Commonwealth, 291 Ky. 467, 165 S.W.2d 33 (1942).

The New York court felt bound to follow McCord, but suggested to the legislature that the rule be changed. People v. Thompkins, 186 N.Y. 413, 417, 79 N.E. 326, 327 (1906). The change was made the following year. N.Y.Laws 1907, c. 581, § 1. The rule was changed by statute in Wisconsin much more recently. Wis.Stat.Ann. 939.14 (1982). "It is no defense to a prosecution for crime that the victim also was guilty of crime. . . ."

There is no legal recognition of the claim that a dishonest man cannot be defrauded. Barbee v. United States, 392 F.2d 532 (5th Cir.1968).

tions.[1] "It is enough to say that contributory negligence, if shown, is never a defense or excuse for crime, nor can it in any degree serve to purge an act otherwise constituting a public offense of its criminal character." [2] In one case a man threw a handful of blasting powder into an open fireplace. A resulting explosion set fire to the building and the wife and 19 year old son of the host were burned to death. Several others, some of them younger and less able to take care of themselves than those who were killed, were able to get out of the house in safety. But this did not entitle defendant to an instruction that he was excused if those who did not reach safety had failed to use due care in the effort.[3] In another case defendants had run over and killed a pedestrian while they were driving a horse and carriage at an excessive rate and were somewhat intoxicated. They thought they should be excused because deceased, who was deaf, had the habit of walking in the middle of the road at various times of the day and night. But the court held otherwise.[4]

It does not follow, however, that the conduct of the injured party must be ignored. His conduct may have a bearing on whether or not the one who caused the injury was culpably negligent.[5] Or it may be found that the negligence of the injured party was the *sole* cause of his injury.[6] "If the decedents were negligent," said the Washington court, "and such negligence was the sole cause of their death, then the appellant would not be guilty of manslaughter." [7]

HUBBARD v. COMMONWEALTH

Court of Appeals of Kentucky, 1947.
304 Ky. 818, 202 S.W.2d 634.

Opinion of the court by STANLEY, COMMISSIONER—Reversing.

R.W. Dyche died of a heart attack. Robert Hubbard has been adjudged guilty of killing him and sentenced to two years' imprisonment on a charge of voluntary manslaughter. The trial was had in Jackson County on a change of venue.

1. Bowen v. State, 100 Ark. 232, 140 S.W. 28 (1911); People v. McKee, 80 Cal. App. 200, 251 P. 675 (1926); State v. Campbell, 82 Conn. 671, 74 A. 927 (1910); State v. Medlin, 355 Mo. 564, 197 S.W.2d 626 (1946); Click v. State, 144 Tex.Cr.R. 468, 164 S.W.2d 664 (1942).

2. State v. Moore, 129 Iowa 514, 519 106 N.W. 16, 17 (1906). Accord: Penix v. Commonwealth, 313 Ky. 587, 233 S.W.2d 89 (1950). See Wis.Stat.Ann. 939.14 (1982).

3. Embry v. Commonwealth, 236 Ky. 204, 32 S.W.2d 979 (1930).

4. Regina v. Longbottom and Another, 3 Cox C.C. 439 (1849). See also Regina v. Kew, 12 Cox C.C. 355 (1872).

5. Held v. Commonwealth, 183 Ky. 209, 208 S.W. 772 (1919); People v. Campbell, 237 Mich. 424, 212 N.W. 97 (1927).

6. In some instances the decedent's negligence may have intervened between the conduct of D and the fatal result so as to have been the sole proximate cause of the death. State v. Gordon, 219 Kan. 643, 549 P.2d 886 (1976).

7. State v. Ramser, 17 Wash.2d 581, 590, 136 P.2d 1013, 1017 (1943). And see Commonwealth v. Aurick, 138 Pa.Super. 180, 10 A.2d 22 (1939).

Hubbard was at home on furlough from the army in August, 1945. He was arrested for being drunk in a public place and taken before the County Judge of Laurel County. Being too drunk to be tried, he was ordered to jail, but refused to go peaceably. Dyche, the jailer, and Newman, a deputy, took hold of him. The prisoner resisted and struck Newman. In the scuffle both fell to the floor and Hubbard lay on his back "kicking at" anybody or anything within reach. Dyche had hold of him. He said, "I have done all I can; you will have to help me," or "Somebody is going to have to take my place; I am done." Judge Boggs took hold of the prisoner and persuaded him to get up; but he continued to resist as he was being taken to jail by Newman and another person. Dyche followed them out of the courthouse. He put his hand over his heart and sat down. In a few minutes he got down on the ground where he "rolled and tumbled" until he died within a half hour. Hubbard never struck Dyche at all, and he received no physical injury. He had been suffering for some time with a serious condition of the heart, and had remarked to a friend several hours before that he was feeling bad. Three doctors testified that his death was due to acute dilation of the heart, but that the physical exercise and excitement was calculated to accelerate his death.

The defendant testified that he had no memory of what had occurred. He and the deceased were friends.

The only inquiry we need make is whether the facts constitute involuntary manslaughter. It seems manifest that under any proper view of the case the defendant could be guilty of no higher degree of homicide, although the court did not give an instruction on that offense. The death of Dyche was charged to have resulted from the commission by Hubbard of a misdemeanor not of a character likely to endanger life. The Attorney General frankly concedes that the defendant was at least entitled to an instruction on involuntary manslaughter, and expresses grave doubt whether he is guilty of any culpable homicide. The only theory of guilt is that his unlawful act in resisting arrest contributed to Dyche's death or accelerated it.

There is a close line of distinction between criminal responsibility and innocence where the facts approach or are similar to those presented here. One cannot escape culpability because factors other than his act contributed to the death of another or hastened it, such as where he was suffering from some fatal malady or had a predisposed physical condition, as being in feeble health, without which a blow or other wound would not have been fatal. Under most modern decisions death caused or accomplished through fright, fear or nervous shock may form a basis for criminal responsibility. On the other hand, it is held that to warrant a conviction of homicide the act of the accused must be the proximate cause of death; that if there was an intervening cause for which the accused was not responsible and but for which death would not have occurred, he is blameless. . . .

In the present case the misdemeanor of the defendant must be regarded as too remote—not in time, to be sure, but as the cause. The failure of the man's diseased heart was the cause. The deceased knowing he had a serious condition of the heart undertook a task which he knew would excite him or create an emotional state of mind, which he also well knew he should have avoided. The evidence is that he had theretofore exercised such wise discretion. His intervening act in rolling and tumbling in pain on the courthouse yard, instead of lying quiet and still, was probably as much responsible for his ensuing death as was the initial excitement caused by the conduct of the accused. It was suggested in reference to the death of the woman in the Couch case that it may have been due to improper or want of attention following her confinement, or to some unrelated disease, hence the indictment which described the facts in detail was held not to state a criminal offense. It is, at least, speculative to say that the act of the defendant in this case was sufficiently proximate to impose criminal responsibility upon him for the unfortunate death. We are of opinion, therefore, that the court should have directed an acquittal.

The judgment is reversed.

REGINA v. HOLLAND

Liverpool Assizes, 1841.
2 Moody & R. 351, 174 Eng.Rep. 313.

Indictment for murder. The prisoner was charged with inflicting divers mortal blows and wounds upon one Thomas Garland, and (amongst others) a cut upon one of his fingers.

It appeared by the evidence that the deceased had been waylaid and assaulted by the prisoner, and that, amongst other wounds, he was severely cut across one of his fingers by an iron instrument. On being brought to the infirmary, the surgeon urged him to submit to the amputation of the finger, telling him, unless it were amputated, he considered that his life would be in great hazard. The deceased refused to allow the finger to be amputated. It was thereupon dressed by the surgeon, and the deceased attended at the infirmary from day to day to have his wounds dressed; at the end of a fortnight, however, lockjaw came on, induced by the wound on the finger; the finger was then amputated, but too late, and the lockjaw ultimately caused death. The surgeon deposed, that if the finger had been amputated in the first instance, he thought it most probable that the life of the deceased would have been preserved.

For the prisoner, it was contended that the cause of death was not the wound inflicted by the prisoner, but the obstinate refusal of the deceased to submit to proper surgical treatment, by which the fatal result would, according to the evidence, have been prevented.

MAULE, J., however, was clearly of opinion that this was no defence, and told the jury that if the prisoner wilfully, and without any justifiable cause, inflicted the wound on the party, which wound was ultimately the cause of death, the prisoner was guilty of murder; that for this purpose it made no difference whether the wound was in its own nature instantly mortal, or whether it became the cause of death by reason of the deceased not having adopted the best mode of treatment; the real question is, whether in the end the wound inflicted by the prisoner was the cause of death?

Guilty.[a]

SECTION 6. CONDONATION BY INJURED PARTY

"Of a nature somewhat similar to the two last is the offence of *theft bote,* which is where the party robbed not only knows the felon, but also takes his goods again, or other amends, upon agreement not to prosecute. This is frequently called compounding of felony, and formerly was held to make a man an accessory; but is now punished only with fine and imprisonment. . . . By statute 25 Geo. II, c. 36, even to advertise a reward for the return of things stolen, with no questions asked, or words to the same purport, subjects the advertiser and the printer to a forfeiture of 50*l.* each." 4 Bl.Comm. 133–4.

The owner's reacquisition of a chattel previously stolen from him is not of itself sufficient to taint him with criminal guilt. It is his act of obtaining it under agreement or understanding to abstain from prosecution or to withhold evidence of the larceny that is illegal. This is merely a particular instance of a general crime. For anyone to obtain anything of value, or a promise thereof, upon such an agreement or understanding in regard to any felony is a common-law offense known as compounding a felony. The ancient classification of such an offender as an accessory to the crime after the fact suggests that it was limited to cases of felony in the early days. But that limitation has tended to disappear. It has been said that to take a reward to forbear or stifle a criminal prosecution for a misdemeanor is also indictable at common law, except for offenses largely of the nature of private injuries or of low grade.[1] The chief exception to the rule has been in the category of the so-called "civil offense." And it has not been uncommon for statutes to forbid the compounding of any criminal offense.[2]

a. After a violent attack by **D, X** was in bed in a prison hospital in a semiconscious condition. He fell out of bed several times and died five days after the attack. **D's** conviction of second-degree murder was affirmed. He was the cause of the death even if it was the falls out of bed that proved fatal. State v. Little, 57 Wash.2d 516, 358 P.2d 120 (1961).

The victim of a criminally negligent traffic accident was moved from the hospital, by his mother, contrary to the doctor's orders. There was no evidence that this actually hastened the death but the court indicates that it would not have been superseding had it done so. People v. Clark, 106 Cal.App.2d 271, 235 P.2d 56 (1951).

For the rule under a Texas statute see Noble v. State, 54 Tex.Cr.R. 436, 113 S.W. 281 (1908).

1. State v. Carver, 69 N.H. 216, 39 A. 973 (1897).

2. 211 Crim.Law & Proc., § 32–1 (1977). Murphy v. Rochford, 55 Ill.App. 3d 695, 13 Ill.Dec. 543, 371 N.E.2d 260 (1977).

Discussions of the subject often suggest that an attempt by the offender and the offended to settle the offense outside of the criminal court room is usually a crime and always quite ineffective. This is far from the true picture.[3] To begin with, a multitude of offenses, including a substantial number of serious crimes, are not prosecuted because they are settled between the two persons involved and never reach the attention of the prosecuting authorities. This, of course, is merely a factual matter and does not dispute the statement as to the law. The law itself, however, has taken definite strides in this direction. The most sweeping provision of this nature is a statute expressly authorizing the compromise of a misdemeanor for which the injured person has a civil action (unless there are special circumstances of aggravation).[4] The court may have discretion to permit the prosecution to proceed notwithstanding such a compromise,[5] but it will be exercised rarely and only under unusual circumstances.

There are also certain specific provisions to be considered. The most common is the statute providing that intermarriage of the parties shall bar a prosecution for seduction,[6] although important differences in statutes do exist. Much rarer is the enactment under which such marriage will bar a prosecution for rape.[7] Some statutes invite a settlement by the parties, such as a bad check act providing a penalty for the issuance of such an instrument unless it is paid within five days after written notice;[8] or a statute making the refusal of an officer, clerk or agent to hand over money or property in his care, on demand, prima-facie evidence of embezzlement.[9]

Any such provision gives to the person harmed by a crime more or less power to control whether prosecution shall or shall not be brought. Beyond any of the foregoing in this regard is the enactment found in some states providing that no prosecution for adultery shall be brought except upon complaint of the aggrieved spouse.[10]

These exceptions have been mentioned because of their importance, but they are definitely exceptions. A criminal offense is a public wrong. The act which constitutes a crime may also be a private wrong, such as larceny or battery, or be a public wrong only, such as joining enemy forces in time of war or making fraudulent misstatements in an income tax return. Insofar as an act constitutes a pri-

3. For an elaborate consideration of the field see Miller, The Compromise of Criminal Cases, 1 So.Cal.L.Rev. 1 (1927).

4. For example, West's Ann.Cal.Pen. Code, §§ 1377–1379 (1970).

5. Id. at § 1378.

6. West's Ann.Cal.Pen.Code, § 269 (1970); Ill.Rev.Stats., c. 38, § 537 (1957); New York Penal Law § 2176. As to an offer of marriage see Lasater v. State, 77 Ark. 468, 94 S.W. 59 (1906).

7. Ill.Rev.Stats., c. 38, § 490 (1957), repealed 1961.

8. Tenn.Code Ann. § 39–1960 (1975). Under some of the statutes payment on written notice does not bar the prosecution but merely negatives the presumption of fraudulent intent. Cook v. Commonwealth, 178 Va. 251, 16 S.E.2d 635 (1941). See also 10 U.S.C.A. § 923a.

9. Id. at § 39–4233 (1955).

10. For example, Iowa Code Ann. § 702.1. Whether or not consent given by filing the complaint can be withdrawn later, so as to stop the prosecution, is discussed in State v. Allison, 175 Minn. 218, 220 N.W. 563 (1928).

vate wrong the injured individual is free to make a settlement with the wrongdoer, or to forgive him entirely without any reparation. But the general rule is that a private individual has no power to ratify, settle or condone a public wrong even if it was a wrong which injured his person or harmed his property. If he is able to do so it is only because of some exception to the general rule and in the exact manner provided.[11] In the absence of such exception the victim of rape cannot excuse the ravisher by ratifying or forgiving the act [12] or even by marrying him.[13] The owner of money or property, even after complete restitution has been made, cannot forgive the crime of embezzlement [14] or larceny.[15] If is even beyond the power of a mother's love to wipe out the criminal guilt of a son who maliciously burned her barn.[16]

HOLSEY v. STATE

Court of Appeals of Georgia, 1908.
4 Ga.App. 453, 61 S.E. 836.

POWELL, J. The defendant, who did odd jobs around a livery stable, drove one of the horses on a certain Sunday without the consent of the proprietor. On the next day, when the proprietor discovered this fact, he gave the defendant the choice of taking a whipping or paying for the horse; the defendant chose the latter horn of the dilemma and bought the horse on satisfactory terms. Afterwards his prosecution was instituted and the defendant was convicted.

The old and well-recognized rule is that where one person interferes with the property of another and converts it to his own use, the latter, upon discovery of the fact, may elect to reclaim the property,

11. Commonwealth v. Heckman, 113 Pa.Super. 70, 172 A. 28 (1934).

The "misdemeanor compromise statute" A.R.S. § 13–3981 (1978) does not apply. The damage to another vehicle was only incidental to the crime of leaving the scene of an accident. Hence the fact that defendant reached a settlement with the driver of the other vehicle does not bar a prosecution for leaving the scene of an accident. State ex rel. Baumert v. Municipal Court, 125 Ariz. 429, 610 P.2d 63 (1980).

"A.R.S. § 13–3981 applies only when a misdemeanor offense invariably creates a civil cause of action." As this is not true of indecent exposure, it cannot be compromised. State ex rel. Baumert v. Superior Court, 130 Ariz. 256, 635 P.2d 849, 850 (1981).

12. Commonwealth v. Slattery, 147 Mass. 423, 18 N.E. 399 (1888).

13. State v. Newcomer, 59 Kan. 668, 54 P. 685 (1898).

14. Fleener v. State, 58 Ark. 98, 23 S.W. 1 (1893).

15. Breaker v. State, 103 Ohio St. 670, 134 N.E. 479 (1921).

16. State v. Craig, 124 Kan. 340, 259 P. 802 (1927).

D could be guilty of assault with intent to rape if the woman's consent was after the assault but before penetration. Such consent does not undo the previous wrongdoing. Copeland v. State, 55 Ala. App. 99, 313 So.2d 219 (1975), reh. denied, 294 Ala. 755, 313 So.2d 223 (1975).

A conviction of manslaughter was proper when the evidence showed, in D's own words, that he injected the victim with heroin when she was already so "bombed out" that she could not walk or talk straight, and he realized a further injection would cause her to "fall out." It is no defense that the victim importuned D to administer the injection. People v. Cruciana, 36 N.Y.2d 304, 367 N.Y.S.2d 758, 327 N.E.2d 803 (1975).

treating the taking as wrongful, or he may waive the wrongful character of the taking and treat the matter as a purchase of the property by the taker, and sue him for the price. In the latter event the law looks upon the transaction just as if it were originally a regular sale between the parties. In the case at bar, when the owner of the animal discovered that it had been used,—that is to say, that the defendant had made a wrongful interference with it, and then took pay for the entire value of the animal, neither law nor justice should give the transaction any other interpretation than that it was the intention of the owner of the animal to acquiesce in the defendant's act of using it on the day before. Indeed, we think it may be said, as a general rule, that in no event will a prosecution under section 225 of the Penal Code lie, where, before the institution of the prosecution, the owner of the animal, either for or without a consideration, has given acquiescence, or, so to speak, ex post facto consent to the previously unauthorized use of his property. This ruling is to be taken, however, with the understanding that the principle is applicable only in that class of cases where the offense involves no crime against society or good morals, but relates solely to the redressing of private-property wrongs. Of course the ex post facto consent of the owner could not render a larceny, with all its elements complete, any the less a crime; but as to the offenses of the nature involved in § 225 of the Penal Code there is a different principle.

Judgment reversed.[1]

PEOPLE v. GOULD

Supreme Court of Michigan, 1888.
70 Mich. 240, 38 N.W. 232.

LONG, J. The respondent in this cause was convicted in the circuit court for the county of Shiawassee, for seducing and debauching one Kate Morrow, and brings the case here on writ of error.

The action was brought under section 9283, How.Stat., which provides:

"If any man shall seduce and debauch any unmarried woman, he shall be punished by imprisonment in the State prison not more than five years," etc.

The information charges—

"That on October 10, 1886, at the township of Shiawassee, in the county of Shiawassee, [said William Gould] did seduce and debauch

1. Under the Oregon statutes any class C felony which can be punished as a misdemeanor may be civilly compromised. The power to compromise a misdemeanor rests solely in the court's discretion. Consent of the injured party is not essential. State v. Dumond, 270 Or. 854, 530 P.2d 32 (1974).

As to the effect of the termination of a criminal proceeding because of a compromise see Restatement, Torts § 660 and comment c (1938); Orndorff v. Bond, 185 Va. 497, 39 S.E.2d 352 (1946); Leonard v. George, 178 F.2d 312 (4th Cir. 1949).

one Kate Morrow; she, the same Kate Morrow, being then and there an unmarried woman," etc.

The cause was tried before a jury.

It appeared on the trial of the case that on April 19, 1887, said Kate Morrow made complaint, under How.Stat. § 9283, before George A. Parker, a justice of the peace of the township of Shiawassee, in said county, charging the respondent with seducing and debauching her. A warrant was issued on said complaint; the respondent was arrested, and brought before said justice; and the examination set down for April 27, 1887. On said day the case was called, the respondent being present, and a recess taken to 1 o'clock in the afternoon of the same day. During such recess the respondent sought and obtained an interview with Kate and her mother, and finally went to their home, where Kate and respondent were married, during such recess, by Mr. Carruthers, a justice of the peace of said township. On the afternoon of the same day, about 7 o'clock, the respondent took the east-bound train for Port Huron, and deserted and abandoned his wife, and did not live or cohabit with her after said marriage, nor did he return to said county of Shiawassee till brought there under arrest as a disorderly person, under How.Stat. § 1985. . . .

The court voluntarily charged the jury, among other matters, as follows:

"On this subject of marriage, I charge you that, if the marriage (and there is no dispute about that) took place, with the intention on respondent's part, at that time, to perform in good faith all the duties which the relation of marriage imposed, and which naturally grew out of such relation, then the complaint would not be warranted; but if the marriage was resorted to as a piece of legal trickery to stop the voice of the girl, Kate, and prevent her from being a witness, with the intention, fixed and determined on in his mind at that time, not to live with her, nor to assume any of the duties and obligations of the marriage relation, and with the intention to abandon this girl, then the offense would be one against public decency and order, and would not be condoned by such marriage, and would be subject to prosecution."

We do not agree with the learned circuit judge in what he states the law to be, or in the reasons which he gives for so holding. Under this charge the jury were told that the guilt or innocence of the respondent must be made to depend, not upon the facts which go to make up the offense charged,—the seducing and debauching, and, as in this case, the surrender by Kate Morrow of her person to the respondent, in reliance upon his promise of marriage,—but upon the good faith or want of good faith of the respondent in entering into the marriage relation with her after the offense with which he was charged was committed.

It would not be claimed that, had the respondent married this girl at any time previous to the complaint being made against him, public policy or public decency would have required his prosecution. But, on the other hand, it will be conceded that public morals and public decency would be much better subserved by the marriage of the parties in this class of cases, as well as in bastardy proceedings under the statute, and thus make legitimate the children begotten by such illicit intercourse, and save, in part at least, the shame and disgrace of the injured female. The statute, in other sections, provides some punishment for the offense of deserting and abandoning the female after such marriage.

The *gravamen* of the offense under the statute under which respondent was convicted, is not the mere fact of intercourse. Two elements enter into it, and both must concur and exist at the same time,—seduction and debauchery; and, if there is no such concurrence, the offense would not be complete. Debauchery and carnal intercourse, without seduction, is no offense under this statute. The offense which this statute is aimed at is the seduction and debauchery accomplished by the promises and blandishments the man brings to his aid in effecting the ruin and disgrace of the female; and where the seduction and debauchery is accomplished by promises of marriage, upon which the female relies, and thus surrenders her person, and gives to the man the brightest jewel in the crown of her womanhood, it is the broken promise which the law will regard as the *gravamen* of the offense. It must therefore be held that, where seduction and debauchery is accomplished under promise of marriage, and the promise has been kept and performed, no prosecution can be allowed or conviction had after such marriage; and the question of the good faith or want of good faith upon the part of the man in entering into such marriage cannot enter into the question of his guilt or innocence. The promise has been kept and performed, and it would be against public policy and public decency to permit prosecutions to be carried forward in the courts of justice thereafter.

This question came before the courts of Pennsylvania in Com. v. Eichar, 1 Am.Law Jour. 551. In that case, Knox, P.J., delivering the opinion of the court, says:

"Can he now be convicted and punished for her seduction before marriage? It is not the carnal connection, even when induced by the solicitation of the man, that is the object of this statutory penalty, but it is the *seduction under promise* of marriage, which is an offense of so grievous a nature as to require this exemplary punishment. What promise? One that is kept and performed? Clearly not, but a false promise, broken and violated after performing its fiendish purpose. The evil which led to the enactment was not that females were seduced, and then made the wives of the seducers; but that, after the ends of the seducer were accomplished, his victim was abandoned to her disgrace. An objection to this construction is that it places within the power of the seducer a means of escaping the penalty. This is far better than, by a contrary construction, to remove ducement to a faithful adherence to the promise which obtained the consent."

Prosecutions under similar statutes in New York are prohibited by statute after the marriage of the parties. 3 Rev.St.N.Y. (5th ed.) 942.

We think this better reasoning than that of the learned circuit judge before whom this case was tried.

The respondent's fifth request to charge should have been given. It follows that the verdict and judgment of the court below must be reversed, and set aside, and the respondent discharged.[1]

CHAMPLIN and MORSE, JJ., concurred with LONG, J.

SHERWOOD, C.J. I concur in the result in this case, on the ground that the marriage is not repudiated by the wife, nor claimed to be fraudulent. Were it otherwise, I should agree with the circuit judge.

CAMPBELL, J., did not sit.

MODEL PENAL CODE

Section 213.3 Corruption of Minors and Seduction.

(1) Offense Defined. A male who has sexual intercourse with a female not his wife, or any person who engages in deviate sexual intercourse or causes another to engage in deviate sexual intercourse, is guilty of an offense if: . . .

(d) the other person is a female who is induced to participate by promise of marriage which the actor does not mean to perform.[1]

1. "It is true, as stated, that society approves the act of defendant when he endeavors to make amends for the wrong done the injured female, by marrying her, and usually a good faith marriage between the parties to the wrong, prevents or terminates a prosecution; but the statute which defines the offense and declares the punishment therefor, makes no such provision. If the defendant has acted in good faith in marrying the girl, and honestly desires to perform the marital obligations resting upon him, and is prevented from doing so by the influence and interference of persons other than his wife, it may constitute a strong appeal to the prosecution to discontinue the same, or to the governor for the exercise of executive clemency, but as the law stands it furnishes no defense to the charge brought against the defendant.

"The judgment of the District Court will be affirmed." State v. Newcomer, 59 Kan. 668, 670, 54 P. 685, 686 (1898).

"If any man against whom a prosecution has begun, either before a justice of the peace or by indictment by a grand jury, for the crime of seduction, shall marry the female alleged to have been seduced, such prosecution shall not then be terminated, but shall be suspended; provided, that if at any time thereafter the accused shall wilfully and without such cause, as now constitutes a legal cause for divorce, desert and abandon such female, then at such time said prosecution shall be continued and proceed as though no marriage had taken place between such female and the accused." Ark. Stats. § 41-3409 (1947). The following section expressly provides that the wife shall be competent as a witness against the accused.

Compare Harp v. State, 158 Tenn. 510, 14 S.W.2d 720 (1928).

If the victim of rape marries the offender before trial she is incompetent, under the Iowa statute, to be a witness against him. State v. McKay, 122 Iowa 658, 98 N.W. 510 (1904).

Chapter 10

SPECIAL DEFENSES

SECTION 1. PUBLIC AUTHORITY

Nothing done under valid public authority is a crime if such authority is in no way exceeded or abused. Deeds which would otherwise be crimes, such as taking or destroying property, taking hold of a person by force and against his will, placing him in confinement, or even taking his life, are not criminal if done with proper public authority. The typical instances in which even the extreme act of taking human life is done by public authority are (1) the killing of an enemy as an act of war and within the rules of war, and (2) the execution of a sentence of death pronounced by a competent tribunal.

Any unauthorized departure from the authority given destroys the privilege which would otherwise be present. Even in time of war an alien enemy may not be killed needlessly after he has been disarmed and securely imprisoned.[1] No one other than the proper officer or his duly appointed deputy may lawfully execute the sentence of death.[2] And that officer may not substitute one method of execution for another.[3] Suppose, for example, in a state in which the electric chair is used for capital punishment, the officer in charge should discover that no electric current was available at the time set for execution. The sentence of the court would specify that particular means of carrying out the sentence, and if the officer should shoot the prisoner, or hang him, the officer would be guilty of criminal homicide.

"And, further, if judgment of death be given by a judge not authorized by lawful commission, and execution is done accordingly, the judge is guilty of murder. And upon this account Sir Matthew Hale himself, though he accepted the place of a judge of the common pleas

1. "That it is legal to kill an alien enemy in the heat and exercise of war, is undeniable; but to kill such an enemy after he has laid down his arms, and especially when he is confined in prison, is murder." State v. Gut, 13 Minn. (Gil. ed.) 315, 330 (1868).

" . . . an order to kill unresisting Vietnamese would be an illegal order, and that if Calley knew the order was illegal or should have known it was illegal, obedience to an order was not a valid defense." Calley v. Callway, 519 F.2d 184, 193 (5th Cir.1975), cert. denied 425 U.S. 911, 96 S.Ct. 1505.

2. " . . . even though it be the judge himself." 4 Bl.Comm. 179.

3. "If an officer beheads one who is adjudged to be hanged, or *vice versa*, it is murder, . . . " Ibid.

under Cromwell's government, (since it is necessary to decide the disputes of civil property in the worst of times,) yet declined to sit on the crown side at the assizes and try prisoners, having very strong objections to the legality of the usurper's commission; a distinction perhaps rather too refined, since the punishment of crimes is at least as necessary to society as maintaining the boundaries of property."[4]

Wilful abuse of authority will also destroy the privilege. Thus obviously excessive flogging of a disobedient convict, by a guard, constituted criminal assault and battery.[5]

The exercise of public authority most commonly resulting in an application of force to the person is the making of an arrest, or the detention of one already in custody. A peace officer, or even a private person, may have authority to arrest a certain individual. This authority is sometimes under a warrant and at other times without a warrant.[6] The amount of force that may lawfully be used in the apprehension depends upon all of the facts in the particular case, including the conduct of the arrestee and the nature of the offense for which the arrest is being made. If the arrest itself is authorized, and the force used in making it is not excessive, there is no assault, battery or false imprisonment.[7] On the other hand, a battery results from any laying on of hands to make an unauthorized arrest,[8] or

4. Id. at 178.

5. State v. Mincher, 172 N.C. 895, 90 S.E. 429 (1916).

6. Professor Wilgus, in his very scholarly analysis, has reached this conclusion: At common law either officer or private person was privileged to arrest without a warrant for treason, felony or breach of the peace committed in his presence,—except that the arrest for breach of the peace was not privileged without a warrant unless it was effected while the breach was being committed or on immediate and continuous pursuit thereafter. Wilgus, Arrest Without a Warrant, 22 Mich.L.Rev. 673 (1924). Compare Restatement, Second, Torts, §§ 119, 121 (1965).

At common law, moreover, either officer or private person is privileged, without a warrant, to arrest one who is reasonably believed to be guilty of felony, with one important distinction: The officer is protected if he believes upon reasonable grounds (1) that a felony has been committed and (2) that the arrestee is the guilty person; whereas for the protection of a private person it is necessary (1) that a felony has in fact been committed and (2) that he has reasonable grounds for believing the arrestee guilty of committing it. Ibid; A.L.I. Code of Criminal Procedure, 236–40 (official draft with commentaries, 1931).

Changes have been made by statutes, usually enlarging the scope of the privilege to arrest without a warrant, especially in cases involving misdemeanors. McKinney's Consol.L.N.Y. § 140–10 (1971).

7. State v. Fuller, 96 Mo. 165, 168, 9 S.W. 583, 584 (1888).

8. Restatement, Second, Torts § 118, comment *b* (1965).

West's Ann.Cal.Pen.Code § 196 (1970). "Homicide is justifiable when committed by public officers and those acting by their command in their aid and assistance, either . . . When necessarily committed in retaking felons who have been rescued or have escaped, or when necessarily committed in arresting persons charged with felony, and who are fleeing from justice or resisting such arrest." § 197. "Homicide is also justifiable when committed by any person in any of the following cases: . . .

"4. When necessarily committed in attempting, by lawful ways and means, to apprehend any person for any felony committed, . . .".

People v. Curtis, 70 Cal.2d 347, 74 Cal. Rptr. 713, 450 P.2d 33 (1969), involved one who injured a police officer while resisting an unlawful arrest. One statute prohibits forceful resistance to an arrest by a known officer even if unlawful. An-

from the use of excessive force in making an arrest that would otherwise be lawful.[9]

REGINA v. LESLEY

Court for Crown Cases Reserved, 1860.
Bell C.C. 220, 169 Eng.Rep. 1236.

ERLE, C.J. In this case the question is, whether a conviction for false imprisonment can be sustained upon the following facts.

The prosecutor and others, being in Chili, and subjects of that state, were banished by the government from Chili to England.

The defendant, being master of an English merchant vessel lying in the territorial waters of Chili, near Valparaiso, contracted with that government to take the prosecutor and his companions from Valparaiso to Liverpool, and they were accordingly brought on board the defendant's vessel by the officers of the government, and carried to Liverpool by the defendant under his contract. Then, can the conviction be sustained for that which was done within the Chilian waters? We answer no.

We assume that in Chili the act of the government towards its subjects was lawful; and, although an English ship in some respects carries with her the laws of her country in the territorial waters of a foreign state, yet in other respects she is subject to the laws of that state as to acts done to the subjects thereof.

We assume that the government could justify all that it did within its own territory, and we think it follows that the defendant can justify all that he did there as agent for the government, and under its authority. In Dobree v. Napier (2 Bing.N.C. 781) the defendant, on behalf of the Queen of Portugal, seized the plaintiff's vessel for violating a blockade of a Portuguese port in time of war. The plaintiff brought trespass; and judgment was for the defendant, because the Queen of Portugal, in her own territory, had a right to seize the vessel and to employ whom she would to make the seizure; and therefore the defendant, though an Englishman seizing an English vessel, could justify the act under the employment of the Queen.

We think that the acts of the defendant in Chili become lawful on the same principle, and therefore that there is no ground for the conviction.

The further question remains, can the conviction be sustained for that which was done out of the Chilian territory? And we think it can.

other statute provides that a battery on a police officer "engaged in the performance of his duties" is a felony. It was held that forceful resistance to a known officer who was attempting an unlawful arrest was a battery because of the first statute, but it was a misdemeanor rather than a felony because an officer attempting an unlawful arrest is not "engaged in the performance of his duties."

9. Moody v. State, 120 Ga. 868, 48 S.E. 340 (1904); Reyonlds v. Griffith, 126 W.Va. 766, 30 S.E.2d 81 (1944).

It is clear that an English ship on the high sea, out of any foreign territory, is subject to the laws of England; and persons, whether foreign or English, on board such ship, are as much amenable to English law as they would be on English soil. In Regina v. Sattler (Dears. & Bell's C.C.R. 525) this principle was acted on, so as to make the prisoner, a foreigner, responsible for murder on board an English ship at sea: the same principle has been laid down by foreign writers on international law, among which it is enough to cite Ortolan, sur la Diplomatic de la Mer, liv. 2, cap. 13.

The Merchant Shipping Act, 17 & 18 Vict. c. 104, s. 267, makes the master and seamen of a British ship responsible for all offences against property or person committed on the sea out of her Majesty's dominions as if they had been committed within the jurisdiction of the Admiralty of England.

Such being the law, if the act of the defendant amounted to a false imprisonment he was liable to be convicted. Now, as the contract of the defendant was to receive the prosecutor and the others as prisoners on board his ship, and to take them, without their consent, over the sea to England, although he was justified in first receiving them in Chili, yet that justification ceased when he passed the line of Chilian jurisdiction, and after that it was a wrong which was intentionally planned and executed in pursuance of the contract, amounting in law to a false imprisonment.

It may be that transportation to England is lawful by the law of Chili, and that a Chilian ship might so lawfully transport Chilian subjects; but for an English ship the laws of Chili, out of the state, are powerless, and the lawfulness of the acts must be tried by English law.

For these reasons, to the extent above mentioned, the conviction is affirmed.

Conviction confirmed accordingly.[1]

COMMONWEALTH ex rel. WADSWORTH v. SHORTALL

Supreme Court of Pennsylvania, 1903.
206 Pa. 165, 55 A. 952.

[Wadsworth was a private in a division of the National Guard that had been ordered out by the governor to suppress disorder and violence which was beyond the control of local authorities. He was posted to guard a house at night and told to halt all prowlers or persons approaching the house. He was ordered to "shoot to kill" any person who refused to halt when challenged. About 11:30 o'clock a stranger

1. The ship went very near Peru and the prosecutor asked to be put ashore there offering to pay the captain the amount the Chilian government paid him. The captain refused on the ground that he was under contract to take him to Liverpool. The ship touched at the Azores and the captain had holes made in the boats to prevent the men getting away.

appraoched the house. Wadsworth called "halt" four times. The stranger ignored the command, opened the gate, continued into the yard, and was then shot and killed by Wadsworth. Wadsworth was arrested and held in custody on a charge of manslaughter. To inquire into the legality of his imprisonment the presiding justice of this court allowed a writ of habeas corpus.]

Opinion by MR. JUSTICE MITCHELL, April 17, 1903: . . .

And while the military are in active service for the suppression of disorder and violence, their rights and obligations as soldiers must be judged by the standard of actual war. No other standard is possible, for the first and overruling duty is to repress disorder, whatever the cost, and all means which are necessary to that end are lawful. The situation of troops in a riotous and insurrectionary district approximates that of troops in an enemy's country, and in proportion to the extent and violence of the overt acts of hostility shown is the degree of severity justified in the means of repression. The requirements of the situation in either case, therefore, shift with the circumstances, and the same standard of justification must apply to both. The only difference is the one already adverted to, the liability to subsequent investigation in the courts of the land after the restoration of order.

Coming now to the position of the relator, in regard to responsibility, we find the law well settled. "A subordinate stands as regards the application of these principles, in a different position from the superior whom he obeys, and may be absolved from liability for executing an order which it was criminal to give. The question is, as we have seen, had the accused reasonable cause for believing in the necessity of the act which is impugned, and in determining this point, a soldier or member of the posse comitatus may obviously take the orders of the person in command into view as proceeding from one who is better able to judge and well informed; and if the circumstances are such that the command may be justifiable, he should not be held guilty for declining to decide that it is wrong with the responsibility incident to disobedience, unless the case is so plain as not to admit of a reasonable doubt. A soldier, consequently, runs little risk in obeying any order which a man of common sense so placed would regard as warranted by the circumstances:" Hare, Const. Law, p. 920.

The cases in this country have usually arisen in the army and been determined in the United States courts. But by the Articles of War (art. 59) under the acts of congress, officers or soldiers charged with offenses punishable by the laws of the land, are required (except in time of war) to be delivered over to the civil (i.e., in distinction from military) authorities; and the courts proceed upon the principles of the common (and statute) law: 31 F. 711. The decisions therefore are precedents applicable here.

A leading case is U.S. v. Clark, 31 F. 710. A soldier on the military reservation at Fort Wayne had been convicted by court martial and when brought out of the guardhouse with other prisoners at "retreat," broke from the ranks and was in the act of escaping when Clark, who was the sergeant of the guard, fired and killed him. Clark was charged with homicide and brought before the United States district judge, sitting as a committing magistrate. Judge Brown, now of the Supreme Court of the United States, delivered an elaborate and well considered opinion, which has ever since been quoted as authoritative. In it he said, "The case reduces itself to the naked legal proposition whether the prisoner is excused in law in killing the deceased." Then after referring to the common-law principle that an officer having custody of a prisoner charged with felony may take his life if it becomes absolutely necessary to do so to prevent his escape, and pointing out the peculiarities of the military code which practically abolish the distinction between felonies and misdemeanors, he continued, "I have no doubt the same principle would apply to the acts of a subordinate officer, performed in compliance with his supposed duty as a soldier; and unless the act were manifestly beyond the scope of his authority, or were such that a man of ordinary sense and understanding would know that it was illegal, that it would be a protection to him, if he acted in good faith and without malice."

In McCall v. McDowell, 1 Abb. (U.S.) 212, where an action was brought by plaintiff against Gen. McDowell and Capt. Douglas for false imprisonment under a general order of the former for the arrest of persons publicly exulting over the assassination of President Lincoln, the court said, "Except in a plain case of excess of authority, where at first blush it is apparent and palpable to the commonest understanding that the order is illegal, I cannot but think that the law will excuse a military subordinate, when acting in obedience to the order of his commander, otherwise he is placed in a dangerous dilemma of being liable to damages to third persons, for obedience to the order, or for the loss of his commission and disgrace for disobedience thereto. . . . Between an order plainly legal and one palpably otherwise there is a wide middle ground where the ultimate legality and propriety of orders depends or may depend upon circumstances and conditions, of which it cannot be expected that the inferior is informed or advised. In such cases justice to the subordinate demands, and the necessities and efficiency of the public service require that the order of the superior should protect the inferior, leaving the responsibility to rest where it properly belongs, upon the officer who gave the command." The court sitting without a jury accordingly gave judgment for Capt. Douglas, though finding damages against Gen. McDowell.

In U.S. v. Carr, 1 Woods 480, which was a case of the shooting of a soldier in Fort Pulaski by the prisoner who was sergeant of the guard, Woods, J., afterwards of the Supreme Court of the United States, charged the jury: "Place yourselves in the position of the prisoner at the time of the homicide. Inquire whether at the moment he fired his piece at the deceased, with his surroundings at the time, he had reasonable ground to believe, and did believe, that the killing or serious wounding of the deceased was necessary to the suppression of a mutiny then and there existing, or of a disorder which threatened to ripen into mutiny. If he had reasonable ground so to believe, then the killing was not unlawful. But if on the other hand the mutinous conduct of the soldiers, if there was any such, had ceased, and it so appeared to the prisoner, or if he could reasonably have suppressed the disorder without the resort to such violent means as the taking of the life of the deceased, and it would so have appeared to a reasonable man under like circumstances, then the killing was unlawful. But it must be understood that the law will not require an officer charged with the order and discipline of a camp or fort to weigh with scrupulous nicety the amount of force necessary to suppress disorder. The exercise of a reasonable discretion is all that is required."

In Riggs v. State, 4 Cold. 85, the Supreme Court of Tennessee held to be correct an instruction to the jury that "any order given by an officer to his private which does not expressly and clearly show on its face, or in the body thereof, its own illegality, the soldier would be bound to obey, and such order would be a protection to him."

These are the principal American cases and they are in entire accord with the long line of established authorities in England.

Applying these principles to the act of the relator, it is clear that he was not guilty of any crime. The situation as already shown was one of martial law, in which the commanding general was authorized to use as forcible military means for the repression of violence as his judgment dictated to be necessary. The house had been dynamited at night and threatened again. With an agent so destructive, in hands so lawless, the duty of precaution was correspondingly great. There was no ground therefore for doubt as to the legality of the order to shoot. The relator was a private soldier and his first duty was obedience. His orders were clear and specific, and the evidence does not show that he went beyond them in his action. There was no malice for it appears affirmatively that he did not know the deceased, and acted only on his orders when the situation appeared to call for action under them. The unfortunate man who was killed was not shown to have been one of the mob gathered in the vicinity, though why he should have turned into the gate is not known. The occurrence, deplorable as it was, was an illustration of the dangers of the lawless condition of the community, or of the minority who were allowed to control it, and must be classed with the numerous instances in riots and mobs, where mere spectators and even distant non-combatants get hurt without apparent fault of their own. . . .

The relator, Arthur Wadsworth, is discharged from further custody under the warrant held by respondent.[1]

1. If a military detail was sent to kill an officer unlawfully the order given would not excuse the killing. But a member of the detail who did *not* know the mission and did not participate in the killing would not be guilty of the homi-

MODEL PENAL CODE

Section 2.10 Military Orders.

It is an affirmative defense that the actor, in engaging in the conduct charged to constitute an offense, does no more than execute an order of his superior in the armed services which he does not know to be unlawful.

cide. The rule that all conspirators are guilty by reason of the act of one in carrying out their unlawful agreement has no application to a soldier obeying orders with no knowledge of an intended unlawful purpose. Riggs v. State, 43 Tenn. 85 (1866). An order to a sentry to kill anyone using opprobrious words to him would be obviously illegal and void, and would not justify or excuse such a killing. United States v. Bevans, 24 Fed. Cas. 1183, No. 14,589 (1816), reversed on other grounds 3 Wheat. 336 (1818). An order to assist in the perpetration of rape is not a military command. State v. Roy, 233 N.C. 558, 64 S.E.2d 840 (1951).

"The acts of a subordinate done in compliance with an unlawful order given him by his superior are excused and impose no criminal liability upon him unless the superior's order is one which a man of *ordinary sense and understanding* would, under the circumstances, know to be unlawful, or if the order in question is actually known to the accused to be unlawful." United States v. Calley, 483 F.2d 1401 (4th Cir.1973).

An officer may shoot, if necessary, to arrest one who has committed a felony in his presence. Stinnett v. Virginia, 55 F.2d 644 (4th Cir.1932). Even under the statute an officer is not privileged to shoot a fleeing misdemeanant who cannot otherwise be arrested. The statute reads: "If, after notice of the intention to arrest the defendant, he either flee or forcibly resist, the officer may use all the necessary means to effect the arrest." Johnson v. State, 173 Tenn. 134, 114 S.W. 819 (1938).

One being arrested for a misdemeanor resisted the officer and was shot. For this shooting the officer was convicted of assault and battery. This conviction was reversed because of an instruction to the effect that an officer arresting for a misdemeanor has no right to go to the extremity of shedding blood except in self-defense. Territory v. Machado, 30 Haw. 487 (1928).

"If he have a warrant for any crime, from the highest to the lowest, whether a felony or a misdemeanor, and the party resist, and the constable have no means of making him amenable except by killing him, he is justified in so doing. But the case of flight is different from resistance. If the warrant be for felony, flight is tantamount to resistance, and the flying felon may be justifiably killed, if he cannot be otherwise secured. In cases of misdemeanor, resistance will justify killing, though flight will not; for in such cases the law considers it better, that the accused should escape than that a life should be taken." Rex v. Finnerty, 1 Cr. & Dix 167, n. (Ireland, 1830). This is dictum as to the misdemeanant since the person to be arrested was charged with a felony. A number of cases which seem to authorize deadly force to overcome resistance on the part of one being arrested for a misdemeanor, were actually self-defense cases. Pearson, The Right to Kill in Making Arrests, 28 Mich. L.Rev. 957 (1930).

In a study of this subject it is helpful to compare different provisions of the statutes such, for example, as the following sections of the California Penal Code:

§ 843. "When the arrest is being made by an officer under the authority of a warrant, after information of the intention to make the arrest, if the person to be arrested either flees or forcibly resists, the officer may use all necessary means to effect the arrest."

§ 196. "Homicide is justifiable when committed by public officers and those acting by their command in their aid and assistance, either— . . .

"2. When necessarily committed in overcoming actual resistance to the execution of some legal process, or in the discharge of any other legal duty; or,

"3. When necessarily committed in retaking felons who have been rescued or have escaped, or when necessarily committed in arresting persons charged with felony, and who are fleeing from justice or resisting such arrest."

One who responds to the call of an officer to aid in making an arrest, and uses such force as is reasonably necessary to carry out the officer's orders, is justified even if the officer is not. Common-

Section 3.03 Execution of Public Duty.

(1) Except as provided in Subsection (2) of this Section, conduct is justifiable when it is required or authorized by:

(a) the law defining the duties or functions of a public officer or the assistance to be rendered to such officer in the performance of his duties; or

(b) the law governing the execution of legal process; or

(c) the judgment or order of a competent court or tribunal; or

(d) the law governing the armed services or the lawful conduct of war; or

(e) any other provision of law imposing a public duty.

(2) The other sections of this Article apply to:

(a) the use of force upon or toward the person of another for any of the purposes dealt with in such sections; and

(b) the use of deadly force for any purpose, unless the use of such force is otherwise expressly authorized by law or occurs in the lawful conduct of war.

(3) The justification afforded by Subsection (1) of this Section applies:

(a) when the actor believes his conduct to be required or authorized by the judgment or direction of a competent court or tribunal or in the lawful execution of legal process, notwithstanding lack of jurisdiction of the court or defect in the legal process; and

(b) when the actor believes his conduct to be required or authorized to assist a public officer in the performance of his duties, notwithstanding that the officer exceeded his legal authority.

wealth v. Sadowsky, 80 Pa.Super. 496 (1923).

Section 131(a) of the Restatement of Torts limited the use of deadly force in making an arrest to cases where "the arrest is made for treason or for a felony which normally causes or threatens death or serious bodily harm, or which involves the breaking and entry of a dwelling place". This was so far out of line with existing law that it was amended to read "treason or felony" without restriction as to the type of felony. Restatement, 1948 Supp. 628. See now Restatement, Second, Torts § 131 (1965).

The court, assuming that the common law authorized a private person to use deadly force if necessary to effect the arrest of any fleeing felon, announced that for the future this would be limited to "treason, murder, voluntary manslaughter, mayhem, arson, robbery, common law rape, common law burglary, kidnapping, assault with intent to murder, rape or rob, or a felony which normally causes or threatens death or great bodily harm." And the private person must know that the arrestee is guilty and acts at his peril on this point. Commonwealth v. Chermansky, 430 Pa. 170, 242 A.2d 237 (1968).

"[A]t common law an officer may use deadly force where necessary to apprehend the fleeing perpetrator of any felony." But he may "use deadly force only when he reasonably believes that such force is necessary to effect an arrest." Clark v. Ziedonis, 513 F.2d 79, 82–83 (7th Cir.1975). But compare Mattis v. Schnarr, 547 F.2d 1007 (8th Cir.1976) with Wiley v. Memphis Police Department, 548 F.2d 1247 (6th Cir.1977), cert. denied 434 U.S. 822, 98 S.Ct. 65; Garner v. Memphis Police Department, 710 F.2d 240 (6th Cir.1983).

Section 3.07 Use of Force in Law Enforcement.

(1) Use of Force Justifiable to Effect an Arrest. Subject to the provisions of this Section and of Section 3.09, the use of force upon or toward the person of another is justifiable when the actor is making or assisting in making an arrest and the actor believes that such force is immediately necessary to effect a lawful arrest.

(2) Limitations on the Use of Force.

(a) The use of force is not justifiable under this Section unless:

(i) the actor makes known the purpose of the arrest or believes that it is otherwise known by or cannot reasonably be made known to the person to be arrested; and

(ii) when the arrest is made under a warrant, the warrant is valid or believed by the actor to be valid.

(b) The use of deadly force is not justifiable under this Section unless:

(i) the arrest is for a felony; and

(ii) the person effecting the arrest is authorized to act as a peace officer or is assisting a person whom he believes to be authorized to act as a peace officer; and

(iii) the actor believes that the force employed creates no substantial risk of injury to innocent persons; and

(iv) the actor believes that:

(1) the crime for which the arrest is made involved conduct including the use or threatened use of deadly force; or

(2) there is a substantial risk that the person to be arrested will cause death or serious bodily harm if his apprehension is delayed.

(3) Use of Force to Prevent Escape from Custody. The use of force to prevent the escape of an arrested person from custody is justifiable when the force could justifiably have been employed to effect the arrest under which the person is in custody, except that a guard or other person authorized to act as a peace officer is justified in using any force, including deadly force, which he believes to be immediately necessary to prevent the escape of a person from a jail, prison, or other institution for the detention of persons charged with or convicted of a crime.

(4) Use of Force by Private Person Assisting an Unlawful Arrest.

(a) A private person who is summoned by a peace officer to assist in effecting an unlawful arrest, is justified in using any force which he would be justified in using if the arrest were lawful, provided that he does not believe the arrest is unlawful.

(b) A private person who assists another private person in effecting an unlawful arrest, or who, not being summoned, assists a peace officer in effecting an unlawful arrest, is justified in using any force which he would be justified in using if the arrest were lawful, provided that (i) he believes the arrest is lawful, and (ii) the arrest would be lawful if the facts were as he believes them to be.

Section 3.09 Mistake of Law as to Unlawfulness of Force or Legality of Arrest; Reckless or Negligent Use of Otherwise Justifiable Force; Reckless or Negligent Injury or Risk of Injury to Innocent Persons.

(1) The justification afforded by Sections 3.04 to 3.07, inclusive, is unavailable when:

(a) the actor's belief in the unlawfulness of the force or conduct against which he employs protective force or his belief in the lawfulness of an arrest which he endeavors to effect by force is erroneous; and

(b) his error is due to ignorance or mistake as to the provisions of the Code, any other provision of the criminal law or the law governing the legality of an arrest or search.

(2) When the actor believes that the use of force upon or toward the person of another is necessary for any of the purposes for which such belief would establish a justification under Sections 3.03 to 3.08 but the actor is reckless or negligent in having such belief or in acquiring or failing to acquire any knowledge or belief which is material to the justifiability of his use of force, the justification afforded by those Sections is unavailable in a prosecution for an offense for which recklessness or negligence, as the case may be, suffices to establish culpability.

(3) When the actor is justified under Sections 3.03 to 3.08 in using force upon or toward the person of another but he recklessly or negligently injures or creates a risk of injury to innocent persons, the justification afforded by those Sections is unavailable in a prosecution for such recklessness or negligence towards innocent persons.[a]

SECTION 2. DOMESTIC AUTHORITY

References may be found to an ancient authority of a husband to chastise his wife[1] with a "whip or rattan no bigger than my thumb, in order to inforce the salutary restraints of domestic discipline."[2] This was doubted in Blackstone's time,[3] and is definitely not recognized in the modern common law. Hence a husband who strikes his wife, even to enforce obedience to his just commands, is guilty of battery,[4] although he may use moderate force to *restrain* her from committing crimes or torts.[5] Spouse beating is frequently made punishable by express statutory provision; several states have enacted statutes for the prevention of domestic violence and protection of the victims.[6]

Firmly recognized in the law, however, is the right of the parent to discipline his minor child by means of moderate chastisement.[7]

1. "They refuse to bind him to keep the peace at her suit unless her life be in danger, because by the law he hath the power of castigation; . . . " Bradley v. His Wife, 1 Keb. 637, 83 Eng.Rep. 1157 (1663).

2. Bradley v. State, Walker 156, 157 (Miss.1824).

3. 1 Bl.Comm. 444–5.

4. Fulgham v. State, 46 Ala. 143 (1871).

5. See People v. Winters, 2 Park.Cr. 10 (N.Y.1823).

6. West's Ann.Cal.Pen.Code, § 273.5 (1977); Mass.Gen.Laws Ann., c. 208 § 34c (1978).

7. Richardson v. State Board, 98 N.J.L. 690, 121 A. 457 (1923).

The right to correct an adopted child is the same as the right of a natural parent in this regard;[8] and this authority has been extended even to one who has taken a child into his home to be brought up as a member of the family without formal adoption.[9] Similarly, a guardian may lawfully administer moderate chastisement for the correction of his ward.[10]

The common law authorized a master to punish his apprentice in the same manner; but true apprenticeship is a special relation. An employer has no authority to administer corporal punishment to an ordinary servant merely because the particular employee happens to be a minor.[11] The father's authority to punish a minor child may be delegated to an employer; but the employer has no such privilege unless he has received permission from the parent.[12]

"By law as well as immemorial usage, a schoolmaster is regarded as standing in loco parentis, and, like the parent, has the authority to moderately chastise pupils under his care."[13] A statute, ordinance, or school-board regulation may restrict the privilege of the teacher in this regard, or may forbid the teacher to resort to corporal punishment in any form, but in the absence of such restriction the ordinary whipping of a pupil, for wilful disobedience of lawful rules, is not an assault and battery by the teacher, if administered for discipline and not in anger or with undue severity.[14]

The authority of a parent or teacher to punish a child will not justify immoderate punishment, and any excess of this nature will constitute an assault and battery; [15] but the test of unreasonableness in this regard should be found, not in some slight error of judgment as to the force to be used, but in the substitution of a malicious desire to inflict pain in place of a genuine effort to correct the child by proper means.[16]

Those in charge of trains, boats, theaters, stadia and similar places, while without authority to punish members of the public for misbehavior, may use reasonable and moderate force to expel a person who refuses to pay his fare or admission,[18] or is guilty of serious misconduct even after he has paid. But even one with authority to

8. State v. Koonse, 123 Mo.App. 655, 101 S.W. 139 (1907).

9. See the instruction in State v. Gillett, 56 Iowa 459, 9 N.W. 362 (1881).

10. Stanfield v. State, 43 Tex. 167 (1875).

11. Tinkle v. Dunivant, 84 Tenn. 503 (1886). "The rule obtaining in this state is that a master has no authority to chastise his servant, no matter how flagrant his violation of duty may be." Cook v. Cook, 232 Mo.App. 994, 996, 124 S.W.2d 675, 676 (1939).

12. Cooper v. State, 67 Tenn. 324 (1874).

13. Roberson v. State, 22 Ala.App. 413, 414, 116 So. 317, 318 (1928). See discussion Ingraham v. Wright, 430 U.S. 651, 664, 97 S.Ct. 1401, 1408–1409 (1977).

14. Danenhoffer v. State, 69 Ind. 295 (1879).

15. State v. Mizner, 50 Iowa 145 (1878); Clasen v. Pruhs, 69 Neb. 278, 95 N.W. 640 (1903).

16. See Boyd v. State, 88 Ala. 169, 172, 7 So. 268, 269 (1890).

18. Carpenter v. Washington & G.R. Co., 121 U.S. 474, 7 S.Ct. 1002, 30 L.Ed. 1015 (1887).

remove such a person will be guilty of assault and battery if he does so improperly as by ejecting a passenger from a moving train.[19]

CLEARY v. BOOTH

Queen's Bench Division, 1893.
[1893] 1 Q.B. 465.

LAWRENCE, J. The question in this case is not an easy one; there is no authority, and it is a case of first impression. The question for us is whether the head master of a board school is justified in inflicting corporal punishment upon one of his scholars for an act done outside the limits of the school, and the appellant's counsel has in his argument relied on what might happen if a boy were not punished by the master for such acts. The facts seem to be that a boy while coming to the appellant's school was assaulted by another boy belonging to the same school; that complaint was made to the appellant, who then and there punished the boy who had committed the assault and also the respondent, who was in his company. The first observation that occurs to one to make is that one of the greatest advantages of any punishment is that it should follow quickly on the offence. The cases cited to us shew that the schoolmaster is in the position of the parent. What is to become of a boy between his school and his home? Is he not under the authority of his parent or of the schoolmaster? It cannot be doubted that he is; and in my opinion among the powers delegated by the parent to the schoolmaster, such a power as was exercised by the appellant in this case would be freely delegated. If we turn to the Code we find that there are several things for which a grant may be given, including discipline and organization, and that the children are to be brought up in habits of good manners and language, and of consideration for others. Can it be reasonably argued that the only right of a schoolmaster to inflict punishment is in respect of acts done in the school, and that it is only while the boys are there that he is to see that they are well-mannered, but that he has exceeded all the authority delegated to him by the parent if he punishes a boy who within a yard of the school is guilty of gross misbehaviour? It is difficult to express in words the extent of the schoolmaster's authority in respect to the punishment of his pupils; but in my opinion his authority extends, not only to acts done in school, but also to cases where a complaint of acts done out of school, at any rate while going to and from school, is made to the schoolmaster. In the present case I think that weight may properly be placed on the fact that the act for which the boy was punished was done to another pupil of the same school. I think, therefore, that the justices were wrong in convicting the appellant as they did, and that the case must be sent back to them to find as a fact whether the punishment was excessive.

19. State v. Kinney, 34 Minn. 311, 25 N.W. 705 (1885).

Collins, J. I am of the same opinion. It is clear law that a father has the right to inflict reasonable personal chastisement on his son. It is equally the law, and it is in accordance with very ancient practice, that he may delegate this right to the schoolmaster. Such a right has always commended itself to the common sense of mankind. It is clear that the relation of master and pupil carries with it the right of reasonable corporal chastisement. As a matter of common sense, how far is this power delegated by the parent to the schoolmaster? Is it limited to the time during which the boy is within the four walls of the school, or does it extend in any sense beyond that limit? In my opinion the purpose with which the parental authority is delegated to the schoolmaster, who is entrusted with the bringing up and discipline of the child, must to some extent include an authority over the child while he is outside the four walls. It may be a question of fact in each case whether the conduct of the master in inflicting corporal punishment is right. Very grave consequences would result if it were held that the parent's authority was exclusive up to the door of the school, and that then, and only then, the master's authority commenced; it would be a most anomalous result to hold that in such a case as the present the boy who had been assaulted had no remedy by complaint to his master, who could punish the assailant by a thrashing, but must go before the magistrate to enforce a remedy between them as citizens. Not only would such a position be unworkable in itself, but the Code, which has the force of an Act of Parliament, clearly contemplates that the duties of the master to his pupils are not limited to teaching. A grant may be made for discipline and organization, and it is clear that he is entrusted with the moral training and conduct of his pupils. It cannot be that such a duty or power ceases the moment that the pupil leaves school for home; There is not much opportunity for a boy to exhibit his moral conduct while in school under the eye of the master: the opportunity is while he is at play or outside the school; and if the schoolmaster has no control over the boys in their relation to each other except when they are within the school walls, this object of the Code would be defeated. In such a case as the present, it is obvious that the desired impression is best brought about by a summary and immediate punishment. In my opinion parents do contemplate such an exercise of authority by the schoolmaster. I should be sorry if I felt myself driven to come to the opposite conclusion, and am glad to be able to say that the principle shews that the authority delegated to the schoolmaster is not limited to the four walls of the school. It is always a question of fact whether the act was done outside the delegated authority; but in the present case I am satisfied, on the facts, that it was obviously within it. The question of excess is one for the magistrates.

STATE v. MIZNER

Supreme Court of Iowa, 1876.
45 Iowa 248.

DAY, J. The prosecuting witness, Ida Brumer, in substance testified that the defendant taught a district school in Rossville, and that she commenced attending his school in the forepart of November, 1874. That, on the 22nd day of December, 1874, whilst she was a pupil in defendant's school, defendant whipped her, in a manner which, from her testimony, appears to be unreasonable and immoderate. She further testified that, at the time she commenced going to school, which was about the 10th day of November, she told the defendant she was twenty years of age, and that, in fact, she was twenty-one years of age on the 25th day of that month.

No testimony was introduced on the part of the State but that of the prosecuting witness. The State having rested, the defendant made the following admissions and offer, to-wit: "It is hereby conceded by the defendant that he whipped Ida Brumer, at the time and place alleged in the information, and that he is guilty of an assault and battery, unless he can show, as he offers to do, that such whipping was reasonable chastisement of said Ida Brumer, in the school, as his pupil, for misconduct in school. Defendant further concedes that said Ida Brumer, at the time of such whipping, had attained her majority." Thereupon the court refused to allow the defendant to prove that the alleged whipping was reasonable chastisement of said Ida Brumer in school, as his pupil, for misconduct in school, holding that, as it was conceded that Ida Brumer had attained her majority at the time of the whipping, the facts which the defendant offered to prove constituted no defense. To this ruling the defendant excepted. No further evidence being introduced, the court instructed the jury as follows: "If you find from the evidence that the defendant committed an assault and battery upon the prosecutrix, and you further find from the evidence that at the time of the assault the prosecutrix had attained the age of twenty-one years, you are instructed that the defendant had not the lawful right to make the assault and battery as a punishment for disobedience of the orders of the teacher or of the rules of the school." The defendant excepted to this instruction.

The court seems to have recognized the general doctrine that a teacher may, for the maintenance of his authority and the enforcement of discipline, legally inflict reasonable chastisement upon a pupil. Whilst the authorities upon the subject are not numerous, there can, it seems to us, be no doubt of the existence of this right. In 3 Greenleaf on Evidence, section 63, it is said the criminality of a charge of assault and battery may be disproved by evidence showing that the act was lawful; as, if a parent in a reasonable manner corrects his child, or a schoolmaster his scholar.

The court denied the right of the defendant in this case to inflict corporal punishment to any extent upon the prosecuting witness, because she was twenty-one years of age. A parent may lawfully correct his child, being under age, in a reasonable manner. 1 Blackstone, 452; 2 Kent's Commentaries, 203. If the court intended to deny the right of the defendant to chastise the prosecuting witness because the same limitation is imposed upon a teacher as upon a parent, the right to inflict corporal punishment should, in this case, have been denied upon reaching the age of eighteen, for then the prosecuting witness attained her majority. Code, 2237. Schools are provided for the instruction of youth between the ages of five and twenty-one years. Code, section 1727. If the right of a teacher to inflict corporal punishment is correlative simply with the right of a parent, it follows that in every school there may be a privileged class of young ladies, between the ages of eighteen and twenty-one years, entitled to all the privileges of the school, but not subject to the same discipline and authority as the other pupils. It is quite apparent that such a condition of things might destroy the authority of the teacher and be utterly subversive of good order. But, as the court fixed the age of twenty-one years, it is probable that he had in view, not any analogy between teacher and parent, but the ages of those who might lawfully attend school. Only youth between the ages of five and twenty-one years are, of right, entitled to attend the public schools.

But, if a child a few months younger than five years should, by misrepresenting his age, or by mere sufferance, be allowed to attend school and enjoy its privileges and advantages, would a teacher be liable to a prosecution for assault and battery, if he should inflict reasonable and moderate chastisement upon such pupil for conduct tending to destroy the order of the school and lessen the means of imparting instruction to others? Manifestly, it seems to us, he would not. And, if a person a few months more than twenty-one years of age should, by the like sufferance or misrepresentation, be allowed to become a pupil in a school, upon what principle could such person claim all the privileges and advantages which belong only to persons under the age of twenty-one years, and at the same time be granted immunity from the reasonable corporal inflictions which may legally be imposed upon a person under twenty-one years of age? A person over twenty-one years of age becomes a pupil only of his own voluntary act. If he does so, and thus of his own will creates the relation of teacher and pupil, and claims privileges and advantages belonging only to those under age, he thereby waives any privilege which his age confers. These views are fully sustained by the case of Stevens v. Fassett, 27 Maine 266. In this case, on page 287, the court say: "But it is insisted that, if such is the authority of the teacher over one who is in legal contemplation a scholar, the same cannot apply to the case of one who has no right to attend the school as a pupil. It is not necessary to settle the question whether one living in the district and not being between the ages of four and twenty-one years can, with propriety, require the instruction of town schools. If such does present himself as a pupil, is received and instructed by the master, he cannot claim the privilege, and receive it, and at the same time be subject to none of the duties incident to a scholar. If disobedient, he is not exempt from the liability to punishment, so long as he is treated as having the character which he assumes. He cannot plead his own voluntary act, and insist that it is illegal, as an excuse for creating disturbances, and escape consequences which would attach to him either as a refractory, incorrigible scholar, or as one who persists in interrupting the ordinary business of the school."

The prosecuting witness in this case, although within fifteen days of being twenty-one years old, told the defendant that she was twenty years of age. This could have been done for no other purpose but that of deceiving the defendant as to her age, and securing privileges and advantages to which the law did not entitle her. She voluntarily assumed the position of pupil, claimed its rights, and took upon herself it duties, and she thereby conferred upon her teacher his correlative rights and duties. The court should have permitted the defendant to prove that the whipping was a reasonable chastisement of the prosecuting witness, as his pupil, for misconduct in school, and should have left it to the jury to determine whether or not the whipping was, under all the circumstances, reasonable.

In rejecting the testimony offered, and in giving the instruction complained of, the court erred.

Reversed.[1]

MODEL PENAL CODE

Section 3.08 Use of Force by Persons with Special Responsibility for Care, Discipline or Safety of Others.

The use of force upon or toward the person of another is justifiable if:

(1) the actor is the parent or guardian or other person similarly responsible for the general care and supervision of a minor or a person acting at the request of such parent, guardian or other responsible person and:

(a) the force is used for the purpose of safeguarding or promoting the welfare of the minor, including the prevention or punishment of his misconduct; and

1. On retrial Mizner was unable to prove that the whipping was reasonable chastisement and was again convicted of assault and battery. This conviction was affirmed. State v. Mizner, 50 Iowa 145 (1878).

A teacher who allegedly banged a student's head against a wall and pulled hair was guilty of assault. There was no reasonable basis for a claim of defense of the right to use force for correction of a student. Reg. v. Kannal, 60 CCC 2d 71 (Sask.Dist.Ct.1981).

See also Ingraham v. Wright, 430 U.S. 651, 664, 97 S.Ct. 1401, 1408–1409 (1977). A teacher's right to maintain discipline may go beyond the age of majority. Baker v. Owen, 395 F.Supp. 294 (D.C. N.C.1975), affirmed 423 U.S. 907, 96 S.Ct. 210.

(b) the force used is not designed to cause or known to create a substantial risk of causing death, serious bodily harm, disfigurement, extreme pain or mental distress or gross degradation; or

(2) the actor is a teacher or a person otherwise entrusted with the care or supervision for a special purpose of a minor and:

(a) the actor believes that the force used is necessary to further such special purpose, including the maintenance of reasonable discipline in a school, class or other group, and that the use of such force is consistent with the welfare of the minor; and

(b) the degree of force, if it had been used by the parent or guardian of the minor, would not be unjustifiable under Subsection (1)(b) of this Section; or . . .[a]

[There are also provisions for certain other persons such as guardians, doctors, wardens, and persons responsible for the safety of vessels or aircraft, or authorized to maintain order or decorum in a train or in a place where others are assembled.]

SECTION 3. PREVENTION OF CRIME

Two important privileges overlap. They are the privilege (1) to intervene for the purpose of preventing the perpetration of crime and (2) to defend person or property. To the extent of the overlap both privileges are available to the one thus benefited. "It is not necessary that he should intervene solely for the purpose of protecting the public order or of protecting the private interests imperiled. His act, though a single one, may well be done for both purposes. If so, either privilege is available to him." [1]

Perhaps it should be said that any unoffending person may intervene for the purpose of preventing the commission or consummation of any crime if he does so without resorting to measures which are excessive under all of the facts of the particular case. No such statement has been found because, perhaps, the measures permissible for the prevention of minor misdemeanors are so mild as scarcely to require a privilege for their support.

In the absence of legislative authority, the privilege to intervene for the purpose of preventing the commission or consummation of a crime does not authorize the use of force in case of a misdemeanor which is not a breach of the peace.[2] In considering statutory enlargements of this field it is important to bear in mind that the "privilege to use force to prevent the commission of crime is usually co-extensive with the privilege to make an arrest therefor without a warrant." [3] It is not uncommon for modern statutes to authorize either a peace officer [4] or a private person [5] to arrest without a warrant for

a. Copyright 1962 by the American Law Institute. Reprinted with the permission of the American Law Institute.

1. Restatement, Second, Torts, Scope Note to c. 5, Topic 2 (1965).

2. Id. at § 140.

3. Id. at § 140, comment *a*.

4. For example, West's Ann.Cal.Pen. Code, § 836 (1970).

5. Id. at § 837.

any public offense committed or attempted in his presence, and such an enactment *may* be held to make a corresponding enlargement in the field of crime prevention.

No legislative authority is needed for the privilege other than that indicated above. The common law recognizes the privilege to use force to prevent the commission or consummation, not only of a felony, but also of a misdemeanor amounting to a breach of the peace.[6] As to all such offenses the question is not whether force may be used but only under what circumstances and to what extent.

The use of deadly force for crime prevention is limited. Restricting attention for the moment to force neither intended nor likely to cause death or serious bodily harm, and to offenses within the general scope of the preventive privilege (whether by common law or by legislative enlargement), the following generalization may be offered: Any amount of such force is privileged to prevent the commission or consummation of such an offense if it is reasonably believed to be necessary for this purpose.[7] The use of force, although not intended or likely to cause death or serious bodily harm, constitutes a battery if it is clearly in excess of that reasonably believed necessary for the prevention.

This takes us to the most difficult part of the field, which is the use of deadly force for crime prevention.[8]

6. Ward v. De Martini, 108 Cal.App. 745, 292 P. 192 (1930); Spicer v. People, 11 Ill.App. 294 (1882). As so used a "breach of the peace" means a public offense done by violence or one causing or likely to cause an immediate disturbance of public order. Restatement, Second, Torts § 116 and § 140, comment *a* (1965).

7. Restatement, Second, Torts §§ 141–143 (1965).

8. Statutes on this point differ widely. For example, compare the following:

West's Ann.Cal.Pen.Code, § 197. "Homicide is also justifiable when committed by any person in either of the following cases:

"1. When resisting any attempt to murder any person or to commit a felony, or to do some great bodily injury upon any person; or,

"2. When committed in defense of habitation, property or person, against one who manifestly intends or endeavors, by violence or surprise, to commit a felony, or against one who manifestly intends and endeavors, in a violent, riotous or tumultuous manner, to enter the habitation of another for the purpose of offering violence to any person therein; . . . ."

"But the right to kill is based upon the law of necessity or apparent necessity. . . . The doctrine of the right to protect one's habitation gives no moral right to kill another, unless necessity or apparent necessity, for purposes countenanced by law, exists. . . . after the deceased had entered, though burglariously, and after he was in the house, the defendant had no right to kill him for the act of entry already committed. . . . The right of defendant, in other words, was limited (1) to the protection of himself, (2) to prevent a felony in the bedroom and, probably, (3) to prevent the deceased from entering that room at all." State v. Sorrentino, 31 Wyo. 129, 137–8, 224 P. 420, 422 (1924).

See Kadish, Respect for Live and Regard for Rights in the Criminal Law, 64 Cal.L.Rev. 871 (1976).

COMMONWEALTH v. EMMONS

Superior Court of Pennsylvania, 1945.
157 Pa.Super. 495, 43 A.2d 568.

Opinion by ARNOLD, J., July 19, 1945:

The defendant, Mildred E. Emmons, on September 21, 1943 shot one Edward Gray with a rifle and seriously injured him. She was indicted in three counts,—assault and battery with intent to murder, aggravated assault and battery and simple assault and battery. The jury found her guilty of aggravated assault and battery. The court overruled defendant's motion for new trial and sentenced, and this appeal followed.

The defendant lived in a second floor apartment of a house in Sacone, Upper Darby, Delaware County, Pa. The apartment house fronted on a forty foot wide improved street known as Broadway Avenue. On the side of the house was an unopened street known as Beechwood Avenue, which was a cul-de-sac ending at the rear of the apartment house premises, and was used by the defendant as a way to a garage on the premises.

The defendant had purchased under a bailment lease a Chevrolet Sedan automobile, and on September 21, 1943 was in default thereunder in the amount of $115.66, being two monthly installments. The bailment lease gave the bailor the right to repossess upon default. The lease had been assigned by the seller-bailor to a finance company, which determined to repossess. Its representative came to defendant's second floor apartment on September 21, 1943 at about 11:00 o'clock A.M., knocked on the door and also rang the door bell. There was no response, the defendant later claiming she was asleep.

Defendant's automobile was at this time parked on the unopened cul-de-sac street called Beechwood Avenue. With the aid of Gray (an employee of a commercial garage) defendant's automobile was pushed backwards onto Broadway Avenue and parked near the curb, and the hood of the automobile was raised in order to check the serial numbers. Two shots were fired and the left femur bone in the leg of Edward Gray was badly shattered.

Circumstances led the police officers to interview the defendant who stated that she had fired with a .22 rifle, but did not recall how many shots. She said that she believed the men were stealing her automobile, and that she fired at a point near the intersection of the unopened street and Broadway Avenue, and did not aim at or intend to shoot anyone. There was, however, evidence on the part of the Commonwealth upon which the jury may well have found that the defendant intentionally shot Gray.

The various assignments of error raise but one question, viz.:—

Where in good faith and upon reasonable grounds, one believes her automobile is being stolen from where it was parked in broad daylight on an unopened street (or private way),—may one shoot the person believed to be the thief in order to prevent the supposed larceny? The learned court below answered this question in the negative, and so do we.

While it has been asserted that some rule of law exists which justifies killing in order to prevent the commission of a felony,—we are convinced that no such broadly stated rule exists. There is no right to kill in order to prevent *any* felony. To justify the killing it must be to prevent the commission of a felony which is either an atrocious crime or one attempted to be committed by force (or surprise) such as murder, arson, burglary, rape, kidnapping, sodomy or the like.

While we are unable to discover any Pennsylvania cases on the subject, all writers seem to be in accord, both where the death of the supposed felon results, and where some form of assault and battery is committed.

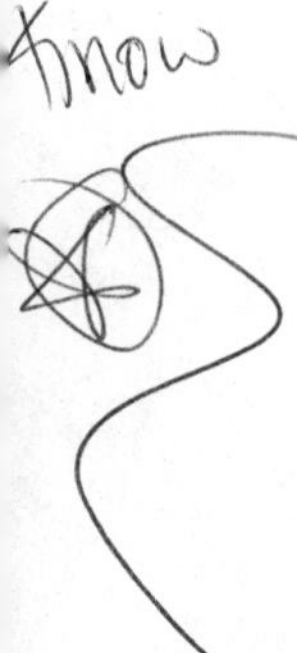

40 C.J.S., Homicide, Section 101, states the rule: "The taking of human life is justifiable when done for the prevention of any *atrocious* crime attempted to be committed with force. . . . A homicide is justifiable when committed by necessity and in good faith in order to prevent a felony attempted by *force* or surprise, such as murder, robbery, burglary, arson, rape, sodomy and the like. . . . Killing to prevent a felony is not justifiable if the felony is a secret one, or *unaccompanied by force,* or if it *does not involve the security of the person or home.* . . . (Emphasis supplied.)

26 Am.Jur., Homicide, Section 172, states the rule: "In general, it may be said that the law countenances the taking of human life in connection with the defense of property *only where an element of danger to the person of the slayer* is present. . . ." (Emphasis supplied.) "The mere fact that such (personal) property is being wrongfully taken . . . does not justify a homicide committed in an attempt to prevent the taking or detention."

1 Bishop Criminal Law, 9th Ed., Section 876, states the rule: "A felonious homicide is committed by one who inflicts death in opposing an unlawful endeavor to carry away his property. There is here the right to resist, but not to the taking of life."

The rule is the same where the supposed felon does not die and the indictment is for some form of assault and battery: 6 C.J.S., Assault and Battery, Section 94, "It is only in extreme cases that a person is entitled to inflict great bodily harm or endanger human life in protecting (personal) property, although *where the defense of person or of a dwelling, is involved, it would seem that the use of a deadly weapon may sometimes be justified.*" (Emphasis supplied.)

Likewise in 4 Am.Jur., Assault and Battery, Section 63: "While a man may use as much force as is necessary in the defense of his property, it is generally held *that in the absence of the use of force on the part of the intruder,* he is not justified in inflicting great bodily harm or endangering life." (Emphasis supplied.) "The preservation of human life and limb from grievous harm is of more importance to society than the protection of property." . . .

In the present case the defendant was not defending her person, or her home or "castle". There was no felony by force or any atrocious crime to be prevented. There was no danger to her or her habitation. There was no force by an intruder for her to repel. There was no justification in law for her infliction of grievous bodily harm.

The assignments of error are overruled, the judgment of the court below is affirmed, and defendant is directed to appear in the court below at such time as she may be there called, and that she be by that court committed until she has complied with her sentence or any part of it that had not been performed at the time the appeal was made a supersedeas.[1]

RHODES, DITHRICH and ROSS, JJ., dissent.

VILIBORGHI v. STATE

Supreme Court of Arizona, 1935.
45 Ariz. 275, 43 P.2d 210.

[Tried for murder, defendant was convicted of manslaughter. He conducted a store in the front of the building in which he lived. The evidence was conflicting but the testimony of defendant indicated the following: The store had been burglarized on several occasions, during one of which a shot had been fired at him. On the night in question he was awakened by noises in the front of the building and went to investigate, taking a revolver with him, thinking that burglars were attempting to break into the building. Seeing a human hand reaching through the front window, and believing that his life and property were in danger, he fired through the window and immediately heard footfalls of persons running away. After the noise ceased he investigated and found the body of deceased lying on the sidewalk and beside it a jar of preserves and a bottle of pickles which had evidently been taken from a shelf adjacent to the broken window through which he saw the hand entering. The defense was based upon a claim of justification, and an appeal was taken on the ground

1. Compare State v. Metcalfe, 206 N.W. 620 (Iowa 1925), superseded by the opinion in State v. Metcalfe, 203 Iowa 155, 212 N.W. 382 (1927).

"The use of force or the imposition of a confinement intended or likely to cause death or serious bodily harm is privileged if the felony for the prevention of which the actor is intervening is of a type threatening death or serious bodily harm or involving the breaking and entry of a dwelling place." Restatement, Second, Torts § 143(2) (1965).

To be within the privilege the force must be used for the purpose of preventing a felony. One who actually prevented the consummation of a felony by shooting the felon was not protected in a case in which the fact of the intended felony was unknown to the shooter at the time. Regina v. Dadson, 4 Cox C.C. 360 (1850).

(among several others) that error was committed in the instructions to the jury.]

LOCKWOOD, CHIEF JUSTICE. . . . It was the contention of defendant, sustained by evidence offered in his behalf, that the deceased was, at the time the fatal shot was fired, actually engaged in a first-degree burglary, with the intent to commit petit larceny. Section 4746, R.C.1928. Petit larceny is the stealing of any goods under the value of $50, unless they belong to certain specified classes, regardless of value. Section 4757, R.C.1928. This offense of itself is merely a misdemeanor, and the killing of a thief who is engaged merely in a misdemeanor is not justifiable. It may be urged that, since under our statute the burglary is completed as soon as the felonious entry is made, the actual taking of property as a result of and immediately after the entry is not burglary, but merely petit larceny, and therefore the owner of the premises can only resist such taking in the manner allowed for the prevention of a misdemeanor. We think this is a most unreasonable limitation of the law of justifiable homicide. If this be the law, all a burglar needs to do is to complete his entry, and he may then with impunity continue his burglarious purpose without fear of being shot by the justly incensed home owner, so long as he tells the latter that he has no intention of taking more than $50 worth of property. We cannot conceive such to be the law, and hold that so far as the question of justifiable homicide is concerned, when goods are stolen during the commission of a burglary, the entire act from beginning to end is a felony, and any one who may kill the perpetrator before he has fully completed his purpose is to be tried by the rules applying to homicides committed to prevent felonies, and not those which govern misdemeanors. It therefore follows that the owner of the premises burglarized may, at any stage of a burglary, kill the burglar if it be reasonably necessary to prevent the final completion of his felonious prupose, regardless at what stage of the crime the shooting occurs. He may, even after the burglary has been completed, and the burglar is withdrawing from the scene of his crime, if the latter attempts to resist or flee from arrest, use such force as is reasonably necessary for the apprehension of the offender, even to the taking of life. Section 4590, R.C.1928. And in all of such cases the question of the necessity of the killing depends upon the reasonable apprehension and belief of the defendant, and not whether such apprehension and belief was justified by the facts as they actually existed. With these tests it clearly appears that the instructions complained of were erroneous in several respects.

The first one states positively that, regardless of what the circumstances would lead the defendant, as a reasonable man, to believe, if as a matter of fact the deceased was not actually engaged in an attempt to burglarize the defendant's store, the latter would be guilty of either murder or manslaughter in killing him. It omits entirely the test of reasonable grounds for belief, and directs the jury to return their verdict on the facts as they actually existed, and not as they appeared to the reasonable apprehension of the defendant.

The second instruction is correct, for under no circumstance may one person shoot another as a punishment for a crime which has been committed.

The third instruction is somewhat ambiguous in that it might be construed to mean that, after the entry had been completed, even though the burglary is still in progress, the owner of the premises may not kill to prevent the completion of the attempted crime. This, as we have said, is not the law. This instruction alone, however, in view of the general instructions, would probably not be reversible error, for the ambiguity is hardly of such a serious nature that, taking the instructions as a whole, it would mislead the jury.

The fourth instruction, however, is fatally erroneous. It states flatly that if the defendant killed the deceased to prevent the loss of the canned goods which are referred to in the evidence, even though the deceased was in the act of stealing them, he would be guilty of manslaughter. As we have stated, had the stealing been a simple misdemeanor, the instruction would have been correct, but the whole evidence shows beyond doubt that if the deceased did steal the canned goods referred to, it must have been done in the perpetration of a burglary, and the stealing was therefore part of a felony and the defendant was justified in killing the deceased if it was reasonably necessary to prevent its completion. In no possible way can this instruction be reconciled with the law, and it is obvious that it, considered with the evidence which appears in the record, was in the highest degree prejudicial, and could not be cured by a reference to the general instructions.

Because of the various errors which we have discussed, we are of the opinion that the defendant did not have that fair and impartial trial guaranteed him by the law, and the judgment of the superior court is therefore reversed, and the case remanded for a new trial.[1]

McAlister and Ross, JJ., concur.

1. It is reversible error to instruct that in order to establish a defense the defendant's act must have been to prevent a felony and the force used by him no more than necessary to prevent the felony. He might have been mistaken as to a felony actually impending, or as to the force needed to repel it. Spicer v. People, 11 Ill.App. 294 (1882).

X proposed sexual intercourse to Mrs. D which she refused. X said he would be back next morning to compel her. She told D. D pretended to leave for work next morning but returned and concealed himself near the bedroom. X came, found Mrs. D in the kitchen, led her to the bedroom; whereupon D stabbed X to death. D was indicted for murder and convicted of manslaughter. The conviction was affirmed because a killing to prevent a felony cannot be justified unless there was reason to believe it was necessary for that purpose. Luttrell v. State, 178 Miss. 877, 174 So. 53 (1937).

Mrs. Moore found deceased with his arm around her daughter and his other hand under her clothes. She shot and killed him. The daughter was under the age of consent and Mrs. Moore's defense was that she shot to prevent the crime of rape. A conviction of murder was reversed because the judge failed to instruct the jury that defendant was privileged to kill if necessary to prevent

PEOPLE v. CEBALLOS

Supreme Court of California, In Bank 1974.
12 Cal.3d 470, 116 Cal.Rptr. 233, 526 P.2d 241.

BURKE, JUSTICE.

Don Ceballos was found guilty by a jury of assault with a deadly weapon (Pen.Code, § 245). Imposition of sentence was suspended and he was placed on probation. He appeals from the judgment, contending primarily that his conduct was not unlawful because the alleged victim was attempting to commit burglary when hit by a trap gun mounted in the garage of defendant's dwelling and that the court erred in instructing the jury. We have concluded that the former argument lacks merit, that the court did not commit prejudicial error in instructing the jury, and that the judgment should be affirmed.

Defendant lived alone in a home in San Anselmo. The regular living quarters were above the garage, but defendant sometimes slept in the garage and had about $2,000 worth of property there.

In March 1970 some tools were stolen from defendant's home. On May 12, 1970, he noticed the lock on his garage doors was bent and pry marks were on one of the doors. The next day he mounted a loaded .22 caliber pistol in the garage. The pistol was aimed at the center of the garage doors and was connected by a wire to one of the doors so that the pistol would discharge if the door was opened several inches.

The damage to defendant's lock had been done by a 16-year-old boy named Stephen and a 15-year-old boy named Robert. On the afternoon of May 15, 1970, the boys returned to defendant's house while he was away. Neither boy was armed with a gun or knife. After looking in the windows and seeing no one, Stephen succeeded in removing the lock on the garage doors with a crowbar, and, as he pulled the door outward, he was hit in the face with a bullet from the pistol.

Stephen testified: He intended to go into the garage "[f]or musical equipment" because he had a debt to pay to a friend. His "way

statutory rape. Moore v. State, 91 Tex. Cr.R. 118, 237 S.W. 931 (1922).

It was error to instruct that under no circumstances of aggravation would a man be justified in taking the life of another who attempts seduction of the slayer's wife. Biggs v. State, 29 Ga. 723 (1860).

A woman is not privileged to kill a man who is attempting to rape her if she is obviously and safely able to prevent the rape without the use of deadly force. Tolbert v. State, 31 Ala.App. 301, 15 So. 2d 745 (1943).

The statute which provides that a homicide is justifiable when committed by a person "in defense of habitation or property, against one who manifestly intends and endeavors, by violence or surprise, to commit a felony", does not give carte blanche to shoot another simply because the other is committing an act which might be considered a felony. "Rather, it is necessary that the act 'reasonably creates a fear of great bodily injury.' " State v. McIntyre, 106 Ariz. 439, 445, 477 P.2d 529, 535 (1970).

of paying that debt would be to take [defendant's] property and sell it" and use the proceeds to pay the debt. He "wasn't going to do it [i.e., steal] for sure, necessarily." He was there "to look around," and "getting in, I don't know if I would have actually stolen."

Defendant, testifying in his own behalf, admitted having set up the trap gun. He stated that after noticing the pry marks on his garage door on May 12, he felt he should "set up some kind of a trap, something to keep the burglar out of my home." When asked why he was trying to keep the burglar out, he replied, ". . . Because somebody was trying to steal my property . . . and I don't want to come home some night and have the thief in there . . . usually a thief is pretty desperate . . . and . . . they just pick up a weapon . . . if they don't have one . . . and do the best they can."

When asked by the police shortly after the shooting why he assembled the trap gun, defendant stated that "he didn't have much and he wanted to protect what he did have."

As heretofore appears, the jury found defendant guilty of assault with a deadly weapon. (Pen.Code, § 245.) An assault is "an unlawful attempt, coupled with a present ability, to commit a violent injury on the person of another." (Pen.Code, § 240.)

Defendant contends that had he been present he would have been justified in shooting Stephen since Stephen was attempting to commit burglary (Pen.Code, § 459), that under cases such as United States v. Gilliam, 25 Fed.Cas. p. 1319, No. 15,205a, defendant had a right to do indirectly what he could have done directly, and that therefore any attempt by him to commit a violent injury upon Stephen was not "unlawful" and hence not an assault. The People argue that the rule in *Gilliam* is unsound, that as matter of law a trap gun constitutes excessive force, and that in any event the circumstances were not in fact such as to warrant the use of deadly force.

The issue of criminal liability under statutes such as Penal Code section 245 where the instrument employed is a trap gun or other deadly mechanical device appears to be one of first impression in this state, but in other jurisdictions courts have considered the question of criminal and civil liability for death or injuries inflicted by such a device. . . .

In the United States, courts have concluded that a person may be held criminally liable under statutes proscribing homicides and shooting with intent to injure, or civilly liable, if he sets upon his premises a deadly mechanical device and that device kills or injures another. However, an exception to the rule that there may be criminal and civil liability for death or injuries caused by such a device has been recognized where the intrusion is, in fact, such that the person, were he present, would be justified in taking the life or inflicting the bodily harm with his own hands. The phrase "were he present" does not hypothesize the actual presence of the person (see Rest. 2d Torts,

§ 85, coms. (a), (c) & (d)), but is used in setting forth in an indirect manner the principle that a person may do indirectly that which he is privileged to do directly.

Allowing persons, at their own risk, to employ deadly mechanical devices imperils the lives of children, firemen and policemen acting within the scope of their employment, and others. Where the actor is present, there is always the possibility he will realize that deadly force is not necessary, but deadly mechanical devices are without mercy or discretion. Such devices "are silent instrumentalities of death. They deal death and destruction to the innocent as well as the criminal intruder without the slightest warning. The taking of human life [or infliction of great bodily injury] by such means is brutally savage and inhuman."

It seems clear that the use of such devices should not be encouraged. . . .

. . . Penal Code section 197 provides: "Homicide is . . . justifiable . . . 1. When resisting any attempt to murder any person, or to commit a felony, or to do some great bodily injury upon any person; or, 2. When committed in defense of habitation, property, or person, against one who manifestly intends or endeavors, by violence or surprise, to commit a felony . . . ." (See also Pen. Code, § 198.) Since a homicide is justifiable under the circumstances specified in section 197, *a fortiori* an attempt to commit a violent injury upon another under those circumstances is justifiable.

By its terms subdivision 1 of Penal Code section 197 appears to permit killing to prevent any "felony," but in view of the large number of felonies today and the inclusion of many that do not involve a danger of serious bodily harm, a literal reading of the section is undesirable. People v. Jones, 191 Cal.App.2d 478, 481, 12 Cal.Rptr. 777, in rejecting the defendant's theory that her husband was about to commit the felony of beating her (Pen.Code, § 273d) and that therefore her killing him to prevent him from doing so was justifiable, stated that Penal Code section 197 "does no more than codify the common law and should be read in light of it." *Jones* read into section 197, subdivision 1, the limitation that the felony be "some atrocious crime attempted to be committed by force." *Jones* (at p. 482, 12 Cal.Rptr. at p. 780) further stated, "the punishment provided by a statute is not necessarily an adequate test as to whether life may be taken for in some situations it is too artificial and unrealistic. We must look further into the character of the crime, and the manner of its perpetration (see Storey v. State [71 Ala. 329]). *When these do not reasonably create a fear of great bodily harm,* as they could not if defendant apprehended only a misdemeanor assault, *there is no cause for the exaction of a human life.*" (Italics added.)

Jones involved subdivision 1 of Penal Code section 197, but subdivision 2 of that section is likewise so limited. The term "violence of [sic] surprise" in subdivision 2 is found in common law authorities and, whatever may have been the very early common law the rule developed at common law that killing or use of deadly force to prevent a felony was justified only if the offense was a forcible and atrocious crime. (See Storey v. State, supra; II Cooley's Blackstone, p. 1349; Perkins on Criminal Law, supra, pp. 989–993; 1 Hale, Pleas of the Crown (1847), p. 487.) "Surprise" means an unexpected attack—which includes force and violence (see Perkins, supra, p. 1026, fn. 3), and the word thus appears redundant.

Examples of forcible and atrocious crimes are murder, mayhem, rape and robbery. In such crimes "from their atrocity and violence human life [or personal safety from great harm] either is, or is presumed to be, in peril".

Burglary has been included in the list of such crimes. However, in view of the wide scope of burglary under Penal Code section 459, as compared with the common law definition of that offense, in our opinion it cannot be said that under all circumstances burglary under section 459 constitutes a forcible and atrocious crime.[2]

Where the character and manner of the burglary do not reasonably create a fear of great bodily harm, there is no cause for exaction of human life or for the use of deadly force. The character and manner of the burglary could not reasonably create such a fear unless the burglary threatened, or was reasonably believed to threaten, death or serious bodily harm.

In the instant case the asserted burglary did not threaten death or serious bodily harm, since no one but Stephen and Robert was then on the premises. . . .

We thus conclude that defendant was not justified under Penal Code section 197, subdivisions 1 or 2, in shooting Stephen to prevent him from committing burglary. . . .

We recognize that our position regarding justification for killing under Penal Code section 197, subdivisions 1 and 2, differs from the position of section 143, subdivision (2), of the Restatement Second of Torts, regarding the use of deadly force to prevent a "felony . . . of a type . . . involving the breaking and entry of a dwelling place" [5] (see also Perkins on Criminal Law, supra, p. 1030, which is in

2. At common law burglary was the breaking and entering of a mansion house in the night with the intent to commit a felony. (People v. Barry, 94 Cal. 481, 482, 29 P. 1026; see 1 Witkin, Cal. Crimes (1963) p. 414; 1 Cooley's Blackstone, pp. 223–228; comment, 25 So.Cal. L.Rev. 75.) Burglary under Penal Code section 459 differs from common law burglary in that the entry may be in the daytime and of numerous places other than a mansion house (see 1 Witkin, supra, pp. 416–418), and breaking is not required (see People v. Allison, 200 Cal. 404, 408, 253 P. 318). For example, under section 459 a person who enters a store with the intent of committing theft is guilty of burglary. (See People v. Corral, 60 Cal.App.2d 66, 140 P.2d 172.) It would seem absurd to hold that a store detective could kill that person if necessary to prevent him from committing that offense. (See 13 Stan.L.Rev. 566, 579.)

5. Section 143, subdivision (2), of Restatement Second of Torts, reads, "The use of force . . . intended or likely to cause death or serious bodily harm is privileged if the actor reasonably be-

accord with the foregoing section of the Rest. 2d Torts) but in view of the supreme value of human life we do not believe deadly force can be justified to prevent all felonies of the foregoing type, including ones in which no person is, or is reasonably believed to be, on the premises except the would-be burglar. . . .

We conclude that as a matter of law the exception to the rule of liability for injuries inflicted by a deadly mechanical device does not apply under the circumstances here appearing. . . .

The judgment is affirmed.

WRIGHT, C.J., and MCCOMB, TOBRINER, MOSK, SULLIVAN and CLARK, JJ., concur.

MODEL PENAL CODE

Section 3.07 . . .

(5) Use of Force to Prevent Suicide or the Commission of a Crime.

(a) The use of force upon or toward the person of another is justifiable when the actor believes that such force is immediately necessary to prevent such other person from committing suicide, inflicting serious bodily harm upon himself, committing or consummating the commission of a crime involving or threatening bodily harm, damage to or loss of property or a breach of the peace, except that:

(i) any limitations imposed by the other provisions of this Article on the justifiable use of force in self-protection, for the protection of others, the protection of property, the effectuation of an arrest or the prevention of an escape from custody shall apply notwithstanding the criminality of the conduct against which such force is used; and

(ii) the use of deadly force is not in any event justifiable under this Subsection unless:

(1) the actor believes that there is a substantial risk that the person whom he seeks to prevent from committing a crime will cause death or serious bodily harm to another unless the commission or the consummation of the crime is prevented and that the use of such force presents no substantial risk of injury to innocent persons; or

(2) the actor believes that the use of such force is necessary to suppress a riot or mutiny after the rioters or mutineers have been ordered to disperse and warned, in any particular manner that the law may require, that such force will be used if they do not obey.

(b) The justification afforded by this Subsection extends to the use of confinement as preventive force only if the actor takes all reasonable

lieves that the commission or consummation of the felony cannot otherwise be prevented and the felony for the prevention of which the actor is intervening is of a type threatening death or serious bodily harm or *involving the breaking and entry of a dwelling place.*" (Italics added.)

The comment to that subsection states:

The Statement in this Subsection permits the use of means intended or likely to cause death or serious bodily harm for the purpose of preventing such crimes as murder, voluntary manslaughter, mayhem, robbery, common law rape, kidnapping, and *burglary.*" (Italics added.)

measures to terminate the confinement as soon as he knows that he safely can, unless the person confined has been arrested on a charge of crime.

Section 3.06 Use of Force for the Protection of Property. . . .

(3) Limitations on Justifiable Use of Force. . . .

(d) Use of Deadly Force. The use of deadly force is not justifiable under this Section unless the actor believes that: . . .

(ii) the person against whom the force is used is attempting to commit or consummate arson, burglary, robbery or other felonious theft or property destruction and either:

(1) has employed or threatened deadly force against or in the presence of the actor; or

(2) the use of force other than deadly force to prevent the commission or the consummation of the crime would expose the actor or another in his presence to substantial danger of serious bodily harm.[1]

SECTION 4. SELF-DEFENSE

It is convenient to discuss problems of self-defense in terms of deadly force (force either intended or likely to cause death or great bodily injury) and nondeadly force (force neither intended nor likely to cause death or great bodily injury). It is important also to distinguish between reasonable force and unreasonable force, these being complex concepts dependent upon the nature of the force itself and the circumstances under which it is employed. It is misleading to speak of a division of the field into (1) deadly force and (2) reasonable force because these terms are neither mutually exclusive nor collectively exhaustive. Either deadly force or nondeadly force may be either reasonable or unreasonable, depending upon the circumstances of its use. Deadly force is unreasonable if nondeadly force is obviously sufficient to prevent the threatened harm.[1] And nondeadly force is unreasonable if it is obviously and substantially in excess of what is needed for the particular defense.[2]

There are some indications of an original requirement of actual necessity[3] but they do not represent the modern common law of self-defense. The privilege to use force in the effort to avert harm threatened (actually or apparently) by the wrongful act of another is based upon the reasonable belief of the defender under the circum-

1. Etter v. State, 185 Tenn. 218, 205 S.W.2d 1 (1947).

2. People v. Moody, 62 Cal.App.2d 18, 143 P.2d 978 (1943); Restatement, Second, Torts § 70 (1965). A kick is not a justifiable method of turning a trespasser out of the house. Wild's Case, 2 Lewin C.C. 214, 168 Eng.Rep. 1132 (1837).

"Use of excessive force constitutes battery." Coleman v. State, 320 A.2d 740 (Del.1974).

3. Scott v. State, 203 Miss. 349, 34 So. 2d 718 (1948); Regina v. Smith, 8 Car. and P. 160, 173 Eng.Rep. 441 (1837); Regina v. Bull, 9 Car. and P. 22, 173 Eng. Rep. 723 (1939).

stances as they appear at the moment.[4] He is neither limited by, nor entitled to the benefit of, secret intentions or other unknown factors. One who has knocked down another, in the reasonable belief that this was necessary to prevent being stabbed, is not guilty of battery because it is learned later that the other intended no harm but was merely playing too realistic a joke with a rubber dagger.[5] On the other hand, proof that a fatal shot actually saved the life of the slayer is no defense if he fired in cold blood while utterly unaware of the impending danger.[6] One caution should be added. A bona-fide belief which is correct will not be held to be unreasonable merely because the defender is unable to paint a word-picture explaining exactly how he knew what the real facts were.[7]

One who is himself free from fault is privileged to use whatever nondeadly force reasonably seems to him to be necessary to prevent being harmed by the wrongful act of another.[8] This is true whether the threatened harm is deadly or nondeadly. And he may use this force without yielding ground unless the endangering conduct of the other is negligent rather than intentional.[9] Deadly force is not privileged in defense against nondeadly force.[10] One, for example, must submit to a box on the ear and seek redress in the courts if he is unable to prevent it by means other than resort to deadly force.[11] One who is at fault in bringing on the encounter, or in engaging in it, is not privileged to use any force to defend himself against nondeadly force.

There is a sharp split with reference to the privilege of using deadly force in self-defense. Some states follow the "retreat rule" and others the "no retreat rule." These labels are not precise because no jurisdiction either requires retreat, or permits a standing of

4. People v. Anderson, 44 Cal. 65 (1872); People v. Toledo, 85 Cal.App.2d 570, 577, 193 P.2d 953 (1948); Territory v. Yadao, 35 Hawaii 198 (1939); Weston v. State, 167 Ind. 324, 78 N.E. 1014 (1906); State v. Anderson, 230 N.C. 54, 51 S.E.2d 895 (1949); United States v. Ah Chong, 15 Philippine, 448 (1910). One whose life has been threatened by another, and who sees that other apparently reaching for a weapon, may shoot in self-defense although the other does not have a weapon in hand or in sight at the moment. Lomax v. State, 205 Miss. 635, 39 So.2d 267 (1949). As to the rule under the Texas statute see Brown v. State, 152 Tex.Cr.R. 440, 214 S.W.2d 792 (1948).

5. Restatement, Second, Torts § 63, Illustrations 5, 9 (1965).

6. Trogden v. State, 133 Ind. 1, 32 N.E. 725 (1892); Josey v. United States, 77 U.S.App.D.C. 321, 135 F.2d 809 (1943); Restatement, Second, Torts § 63, Comment *f* (1965).

7. The American Law Institute has stated this result in other words:

". . . correctly or reasonably believes . . ."

Restatement, Second, Torts §§ 63(2), 70(1) (1965).

8. State v. Gough, 187 Iowa 363, 174 N.W. 279 (1919); State v. Evenson, 122 Iowa 88, 97 N.W. 979 (1904); People v. Katz, 263 App.Div. 883, 32 N.Y.S.2d 157 (1942); State v. Sherman, 16 R.I. 631, 18 A. 1040 (1889).

9. Restatement, Second, Torts § 64 (1965).

10. State v. Doherty, 52 Or. 591, 98 P. 152 (1908); United States v. Hawk Wing, 694 F.2d 1115 (8th Cir.1982). Compare State v. Bartlett, 170 Mo. 658, 71 S.W. 148 (1902). As to the rule under a particular statute see Witty v. State, 150 Tex. Cr.R. 555, 203 S.W.2d 212 (1947).

11. Restatement, Second, Torts § 65, Illustration 1 (1965).

ground, under all circumstances. To understand the difference between the two rules it is necessary to think in terms of three situations. (1) One, entirely free from fault, is the victim of an assault which was murderous from the beginning. (2) One who was the aggressor in an ordinary fist fight, or other nondeadly encounter, or who willingly engaged therein, finds that his adversary has suddenly and unexpectedly changed the nature of the contest and is resorting to deadly force. (3) One who started an encounter with a murderous assault upon another, or who willingly engaged in mutual combat of a deadly nature, changes his mind in the midst of the fight and would like to stop. According to Sir Michael Foster the common law made a different provision for each of the three.[12] Under his analysis the person identified above as "one" is in situation—(1) entitled to stand his ground and defend himself with deadly force if this reasonably seems necessary for his protection there; (2) required to retreat rather than to use deadly force in his defense if a reasonably safe retreat is available, unless in his "castle" at the time; (3) required to "withdraw" before resorting to deadly force. As to (3) there seems to be little disagreement. The murderous assailant has not lost his privilege of self-defense forever, [13] but he has forfeited it for the moment. He cannot reacquire it by "retreat to the wall." He must bring his attack to an end.[14] And if he is unable to get entirely away from his adversary, he must in some manner convey to him the information that the fight is over.[15] If circumstances do not permit him to do so this is his own misfortune for bringing such a predicament upon himself.[16]

The chief controversy has been in regard to situation (1). Professor Joseph H. Beale took the position that the innocent victim of a murderous assault is always required to take advantage of an obviously safe retreat, rather than to resort to deadly force unless he is

12. Foster, Crown Law 273–277 (1762).

13. State v. Goode, 271 Mo. 43, 195 S.W. 1006 (1917).

A murderous assailant who had abandoned his purpose, withdrawn from the conflict, and fled into his house had regained the privilege of self-defense and could use deadly force when the other broke into the house to kill him. Stoffer v. State, 15 Ohio St. 47 (1864). It is an assault for the victim of an attack to hunt up his assailant and strike him after he has withdrawn completely. Wendler v. State, 128 Fla. 618, 175 So. 255 (1937).

West's Ann.Cal.Pen.Code, § 197 (1970). "Homicide is also justifiable when committed by any person in any of the following cases: . . .

"(3) When committed in the lawful defense of such person . . . ; but such person . . . if he was the assailant or engaged in mutual combat, must really and in good faith have endeavored to decline any further struggle before such homicide was committed; . . . ".

14. People v. Button, 106 Cal. 628, 39 P. 1073 (1895). For the distinction between "retreat" and "withdrawal" see State v. Mayberry, 360 Mo. 35, 226 S.W.2d 725 (1950).

15. State v. Smith, 10 Nev. 106 (1875); State v. Jones, 56 N.C.App. 259, 289 S.E.2d 383 (1982).

16. People v. Button, 106 Cal. 628, 39 P. 1073 (1895).

(a) the victim of attempted robbery, (b) attacked by a person he is lawfully attempting to arrest, or (c) in his "castle" at the time.[17]

The so-called "no retreat rule" jurisdictions tend to follow the analysis of Foster. The "retreat rule" jurisdictions tend to accept Beale's position with reference to situation (1). This has tended to cause confusion in regard to situation (2). Foster thought of one in this situation as having an "imperfect" right of self-defense because required to retreat rather than use deadly force if a safe retreat was available. Some courts have interpreted this "imperfect" right of self-defense to mean that it is only partly exculpatory. One killing under an "imperfect" right of self-defense is not guilty of murder, but is guilty of manslaughter, under this analysis.[18]

The phrase "retreat to the wall," although derived from the facts of an ancient case, [19] is used strictly as a metaphor. One who is subject to this requirement is bound to elect an obviously safe retreat in preference to the use of deadly force, if such an avenue of escape is available. Whenever the circumstances are such that no obviously safe retreat is available the person is "at the wall" and no retreat (or further retreat) is required.

STATE v. REALINA

Intermediate Court of Appeals of Hawaii, 1980.
1 Hawaii 167, 616 P.2d 229.

Before HAYASHI, C.J., and PADGETT and BURNS, JJ.

BURNS, JUDGE.

Defendant Marcelino Realina appeals from a district court judgment convicting him of the offense of terroristic threatening in violation of HRS § 707–715(a).[1]

At the time of the alleged offense, complainant Steve Hardisty was 24 years old, approximately 5 feet 6 inches to 5 feet 9 inches and 200 pounds. Defendant Realina was 44 years old. The record fails to indicate his height and weight. Realina sometimes testified through an Ilocano dialect interpreter and sometimes directly in English.

The relationship between Hardisty and Realina preceded the evening of the alleged offense.

Hardisty testified that during a period when he was still living with his wife, he found Realina at his home and told Realina "if I

17. Beale, Retreat from a Murderous Assault, 16 Harv.L.Rev. 567 (1903).

18. State v. Partlow, 90 Mo. 608, 4 S.W. 14 (1887); People v. Filippelli, 173 N.Y. 509, 66 N.E. 402 (1903).

19. Anonymous, Fitzh.Abr.Corone, pl. 284 (1328).

1. This section was substantially amended by Act 184, Session Laws 1979. For purposes of this appeal, we refer only to the offense as it was defined at the time of arrest and trial.

ever catch you again, you better watch out. . . . You better stay out of my way."

Realina testified that in July or August 1977 Hardisty telephoned Realina and twice said, "Y___ f___. You fool around with my wife. I'm going to kill you." Realina reported these threats to the police and was told that he did not have to worry because they would talk to Hardisty.

Thereafter, but prior to the alleged offense, Hardisty separated from his wife in contemplation of eventual divorce.

On December 8, 1977, just prior to 7 p.m., while driving in Hilo, Hardisty saw Realina also driving. Hardisty concluded that Realina was going to visit Hardisty's wife and got upset. Hardisty followed Realina, who, seeing Hardisty following him, drove to the Hilo police station.[2]

When they reached the police station parking lot, they stopped their cars. Hardisty got out of his car and approached Realina, telling Realina, "You come out you f___ Filipino. I'll kill you." The situation continued with Realina silent in his car and Hardisty outside repeating his threats. After a while Realina started his car's engine, preparing to drive away. To prevent Realina from leaving, Hardisty reached in the car and grabbed Realina by the shirt. Realina turned off his car's engine and Hardisty let go of his shirt. Realina looked in his car for a weapon, found a cane knife, and came out of the car with it in his hand. Hardisty turned and ran to the police station, approximately 100 yards away. Realina ran after him, about 30 yards behind. Hardisty entered the police station and in a very excited state reported that he was being chased by a man who was trying to kill him. A police officer listened to Hardisty's story and then went to the doorway and saw Realina running toward the police station, still at least 30 feet away, with the cane knife held in an upward position. As Realina approached, the officer placed his hand on his gun and ordered Realina to drop the cane knife. Realina immediately complied.

The Police Lieutenant in the station then instructed the officer to arrest Realina for terroristic threatening, which he did.

Although he had no prior record, Realina was sentenced to 30 days confinement.

Our standard of review is prescribed in State v. Hernandez, 61 Haw. 475, 605 P.2d 75.

> On appeal, the test to ascertain the legal sufficiency of the evidence is whether, viewing the evidence in the light most favorable

2. [DEFENSE COUNSEL:] Q. . . . If you have any idea, could you tell us why Mr. Realina drove to the police station?

[HARDISTY:] A. I guess maybe he was afraid or something.

to the State, there is substantial evidence to support the conclusion of the trier of fact. [Citations omitted.]

To determine whether there is substantial evidence to support the conviction, we must first determine the elements of the crime of which Realina was convicted and the available defenses. To do that, we have to wind our way through the penal code's statutory maze.

§ 707–715[3] *Terroristic threatening.*

(1) A person commits the offense of terroristic threatening if he threatens, by word or conduct, to cause bodily injury to another person . . . :

(a) With the intent to terrorize, or in reckless disregard of the risk of terrorizing, another person; . . .

. . .

§ 703–300. *Definitions relating to justification.* In this chapter, unless a different meaning is plainly required:

(1) "Believes" means reasonably believes.

(2) "Force" means any bodily impact, restraint, or confinement, or the threat thereof.

(3) "Unlawful force" means force which is employed without the consent of the person against whom it is directed and the employment of which constitutes an offense or would constitute an offense except for a defense not amounting to a justification to use the force. . . .

(4) "Deadly force" means force which the actor uses with the intent of causing or which he knows to create a substantial risk of causing death or serious bodily harm. . . . A threat to cause death or serious bodily injury, by the production of a weapon or otherwise, so long as the actor's intent is limited to creating an apprehension that he will use deadly force if necessary, does not constitute deadly force.

. . .

§ 703–301 *Justification a defense; civil remedies unaffected.* (1) In any prosecution for an offense, justification, as defined in sections 703–302 through 703–309, is a defense.

. . .

COMMENTARY ON § 703–301

. . . Subsection (1) merely establishes that justification is a defense. This places the burden of producing some credible evidence of the existence of justification on the defendant. If he produces such evidence, or if it appears as part of the prosecution's case, the defendant is entitled to have the defense considered by

3. See n. 1, supra.

the jury. The prosecution, however, must prove beyond a reasonable doubt, facts which negative the defense.

. . .

§ 703–304 *Use of force in self-protection.* (1) . . . [T]he use of force upon or toward another person is justifiable when the actor believes that such force is immediately necessary for the purpose of protecting himself against the use of unlawful force by the other person on the present occasion.

(2) The use of deadly force is justifiable under this section if the actor believes that deadly force is necessary to protect himself against death, serious bodily injury, kidnapping . . .

. . .

§ 701–115 *Defenses.* (1) A defense is a fact or set of facts which negatives penal liability.

(2) No defense may be considered by the trier of fact unless evidence of the specified fact or facts has been presented. If such evidence has been presented, then:

(a) If the defense is not an affirmative defense, the defendant is entitled to an acquittal if the trier of fact finds that the evidence, when considered in the light of any contrary prosecution evidence, raises a reasonable doubt as to the defendant's guilt . . .

. . .

Since, by definition, "force", as enumerated in HRS § 703–300, includes "the threat" of force and since the essence of terroristic threatening is a threat, it follows that the authorization to use force or deadly force contained in HRS §§ 703–304(1) and (2) may be available in a justification defense to a charge of terroristic threatening. Whether deadly force may be used depends upon whether the defendant reasonably believed such force was necessary to protect him from certain dangers enumerated in HRS § 703–304(2). Whether non-deadly force may be used depends upon whether the defendant reasonably believed it necessary to prevent unlawful force from being used against him. Those conclusions lead to the following inquiry.

What kind of force did Realina use? With respect to deadly force, certainly Realina's cane knife could have been used to cause serious bodily harm. Whether his use of it in this case created a substantial risk of causing serious bodily harm is not so certain. Further, if Realina's intent in wielding the knife was limited to creating an *apprehension* that he would use deadly force if necessary,[4] his conduct

4. [REALINA:] A. . . . So, in order to defend myself, I look at the knife—just to defend myself in case.

[DEFENSE COUNSEL:] Q. So you—

[REALINA:] A. I came out of my car and then he run away and just as (inaudible) I know that he going reach by the police station.

[DEFENSE COUNSEL:] Q. So you followed him because you knew he was going to reach the police station.

[REALINA:] A. Yeah.

would not have constituted "deadly force" within the meaning of HRS § 703–300(4).

According to HRS § 703–304(2), the use of deadly force was justifiable if Realina believed it necessary to protect himself against kidnapping. According to HRS § 707–720, ". . . . A person commits the offense of kidnapping if he intentionally restrains another person with intent to: . . . (d) Inflict bodily injury upon him . . . ; or (e) Terrorize him . . ." In the present case, the testimony seems to establish a *prima facie* showing that Hardisty violated HRS § 707–720 before Realina reached for the knife. Therefore, the record contains sufficient evidence to initially justify Realina's resort to deadly force. It, of course, follows that if Realina used only nondeadly force, justification was available as a defense, since the force previously used by Hardisty was clearly unlawful, and Realina could reasonably have believed force was immediately necessary to protect himself.

Thus, whether the force he used was deadly or nondeadly, Realina clearly met the burden imposed on him by HRS § 701–115 to come forward with evidence of justification. Justification is not an affirmative defense under the Penal Code. The burden was on the prosecution to prove facts negativing the justification defense beyond a reasonable doubt. See HRS § 701–115(2)(a) and Commentary to HRS § 703–301, supra. On review, the question is whether there is substantial evidence negativing the defense.

The State contends that Realina's justification defense "evaporated in the long chase of the victim." In other words, the State concedes that Realina's actions were lawful until some point between his car and the police station, at which point the State contends his actions became unlawful. In view of the special and unusual facts of this case, and especially in view of the facts that it was Realina who drove to the police station and that the chase was into the police station from the police station parking lot, we do not think the length of the chase is substantial evidence negativing Realina's justification defense.

We hold that the record lacks substantial evidence to support the trier of facts' conclusion of guilt.

Reversed.[a]

[DEFENSE COUNSEL:] Q. Did you ever threaten him?

[REALINA:] A. No.

[DEFENSE COUNSEL:] Q. Did you intend to hurt him with the knife?

[REALINA:] A. No. In fact, as I said I was only trying to defend myself just in case.

a. Conviction of assault in the third degree was affirmed although the initial attack was by the other against defendant. The evidence showed that after defendant knocked his assailant down, he kicked him three times in the face while he was down. It was held that the evidence supported the conclusion that defendant did not reasonably believe these kicks were necessary in his defense. State v. Sanchez, 2 Hawaii App. 577, 636 P.2d 1365 (1981).

PEOPLE v. LA VOIE

Supreme Court of Colorado, 1964.
155 Colo. 551, 395 P.2d 1001.

MOORE, JUSTICE. The defendant in error, to whom we will refer as defendant, was accused of the crime of murder in an information filed in the district court of Jefferson county. He entered a plea of not guilty and a jury was selected to try the case. At the conclusion of the evidence, the trial court, on motion of counsel for defendant, directed the jury to return a verdict of not guilty. It was the opinion of the trial court that the evidence was insufficient to warrant submission of any issue to the jury in that the sum total thereof established a clear case of justifiable homicide. The district attorney objected, and the case is here on writ of error requesting this court to render an opinion expressing its disapproval of the action of the trial court in directing the verdict of not guilty.

Eighteen witnesses testified during the trial; thirteen were called as witnesses for the prosecution and five for the defense, including the defendant himself. We have read the record and have found nothing therein which would warrant the submission of any issue to the jury for determination.

For purposes of focus and clarity we will summarize the pertinent facts leading up to the homicide. The defendant was employed as a pharmacist at the Kincaid Pharmacy, 7024 West Colfax Avenue, Lakewood, Colorado. His day's work ended at about 12:30 A.M. After leaving his place of employment, he obtained something to eat at a nearby restaurant and started on his way home. He was driving east on West Colfax Avenue, toward the city of Denver, at about 1:30 A.M. An automobile approached his car from the rear. The driver of this auto made contact with the rear bumper of defendant's car and thereupon forcibly, unlawfully, and deliberately accelerated his motor, precipitating the defendant forward for a substantial distance and through a red traffic light. There were four men in the automobile who were under the influence of intoxicating liquor in varying degrees. Prior to ramming the car of the defendant they had agreed to shove him along just for "kicks." The defendant applied his brakes to the full; but the continuing force from behind precipitated him forward, causing all four wheels to leave a trail of skid marks. When defendant's car ultimately came to a stop the auto containing the four men backed away a few feet. The defendant got out of his car and as he did so he placed a revolver beneath his belt. He had a permit to carry the gun. The four men got out of their auto and advanced toward the defendant threatening to "make you eat that damn gun," to "mop up the street with you," and also directed vile, profane and obscene language at him. The man who was in advance of his three companions kept moving toward defendant in a menacing manner. At this point the defendant shot him. As a result, he died at the scene of the affray.

In upholding the action of the trial court we think it sufficient to direct attention to the opinion of this court in People v. Urso, 129 Colo. 292, 269 P.2d 709, where we find, inter alia, the following pertinent language:

". . . It is our opinion, and we so state, that if it is within the power of a trial court to set aside a verdict, not supported by competent legal evidence, then it is equally within the province and power of the court to prevent such a verdict ever coming into existence. In either position, before or after the verdict, the trial court is compelled to survey and analyze the evidence, and from the same evidence, his analysis would undoubtedly be the same before or after a verdict. If it is to the end that the evidence is insufficient or incompetent, and no part of it is convincing beyond a reasonable doubt, then he should be courageous enough to prevent a miscarriage of justice by a jury. . . ."

The law of justifiable homicide is well set forth by this court in the case of Young v. People, 47 Colo. 352, 107 P. 274:

". . . When a person has reasonable grounds for believing, and does in fact actually believe, that danger of his being killed, or of receiving great bodily harm, is imminent, he may act on such appearances and defend himself, even to the extent of taking human life when necessary, although it may turn out that the appearances were false, or although he may have been mistaken as to the extent of the real or actual danger. . . ."

The defendant was a stranger to all four occupants of the auto. He was peaceably on his way home from work, which terminated after midnight. Under the law and the circumstances disclosed by the record, defendant had the right to defend himself against the threatened assault of those whose lawlessness and utter disregard of his rights resulted in the justifiable killing of one of their number.

The judgment is affirmed.[1]

SUTTON and HALL, JJ., concur.

1. Dwyer was partially disabled by arthritis. He was hemmed in by a wall at his back and a bar at his side. In this helpless position he was approached by an alleged karate expert who invited Dwyer to fight. As the assailant continued his charge upon Dwyer, Dwyer cut the other several times with a knife, inflicting injuries which resulted in death. A conviction of manslaughter was reversed on the ground that this was justifiable self-defense. State v. Dwyer, 317 So.2d 149 (Fla.App.1975).

"Perfect self-defense excuses a killing altogether and is established when it is shown that, at the time of the killing:

(1) it appeared to defendant and he believed it to be necessary to kill the deceased in order to save himself from death or great bodily harm; and

(2) defendant's belief was reasonable in that the circumstances as they appeared to him at the time were sufficient to create such a belief in the mind of a person of ordinary firmness; and

(3) defendant was not the aggressor in bringing on the affray, i.e., he did

BROWN v. UNITED STATES

Supreme Court of the United States, 1921.
256 U.S. 335, 41 S.Ct. 501, 65 L.Ed. 961.

MR. JUSTICE HOLMES delivered the opinion of the court.

The petitioner was convicted of murder in the second degree committed upon one Hermes at a place in Texas within the exclusive jurisdiction of the United States, and the judgment was affirmed by the Circuit Court of Appeals. 257 F.R. 46. A writ of certiorari was granted by this Court. 250 U.S. 637, 39 S.Ct. 494, 63 L.Ed. 1183. . . .

The other question concerns the instructions at the trial. There had been trouble between Hermes and the defendant for a long time. There was evidence that Hermes had twice assaulted the defendant with a knife and had made threats communicated to the defendant that the next time one of them would go off in a black box. On the day in question the defendant was at the place above mentioned superintending excavation work for a postoffice. In view of Hermes's threats he had taken a pistol with him and had laid it in his coat upon a dump. Hermes was driven up by a witness, in a cart to be loaded, and the defendant said that certain earth was not to be removed, whereupon Hermes came toward him, the defendant says, with a knife. The defendant retreated some twenty or twenty-five feet to where his coat was and got his pistol. Hermes was striking at him and the defendant fired four shots and killed him. The judge instructed the jury among other things that "it is necessary to remember, in considering the question of self-defense, that the party assaulted is always under the obligation to retreat, so long as retreat is open to him, provided he can do so without subjecting himself to the danger of death or great bodily harm." The instruction was reinforced by the further intimation that unless "retreat would have appeared to a man of reasonable prudence, in the position of the defendant, as involving danger of death or serious bodily harm" the defendant was not entitled to stand his ground. An instruction to the effect that if the defendant had reasonable grounds of apprehension that he was in danger of losing his life or of suffering serious bodily

not aggressively and willingly enter into the fight without legal excuse or provocation; and

(4) defendant did not use excessive force, i.e., did not use more force than was necessary under the circumstances to protect himself from death or great bodily harm."

State v. Bush, 307 N.C. 152, 297 S.E.2d 563, 568 (1982).

If sufficient evidence has been presented to raise the issue of self-defense, the prosecution must prove beyond a reasonable doubt that the defendant did not act in self-defense. Commonwealth v. Rodriguez, 370 Mass. 684, 352 N.E.2d 203 (1976). Accord, State v. Turner, 29 N.C. App. 33, 222 S.E.2d 745 (1976).

An instruction requiring a defendant to prove a claim of self-defense by a preponderance of evidence did not unconstitutionally shift from the state its burden of proving all elements of a murder charge. Thomas v. Leeke, 547 F.Supp. 612 (D.C. S.C.1982).

harm from Hermes he was not bound to retreat was refused. So the question is brought out with sufficient clearness whether the formula laid down by the Court and often repeated by the ancient law is adequate to the protection of the defendant's rights.

It is useless to go into the developments of the law from the time when a man who had killed another no matter how innocently had to get his pardon, whether of grace or of course. Concrete cases or illustrations stated in the early law in conditions very different from the present, like the reference to retreat in Coke, Third Inst. 55, and elsewhere, have had a tendency to ossify into specific rules without much regard for reason. Other examples may be found in the law as to trespass *ab initio*. Rationally the failure to retreat is a circumstance to be considered with all the others in order to determine whether the defendant went farther than he was justified in doing; not a categorical proof of guilt. The law has grown, and even if historical mistakes have contributed to its growth it has tended in the direction of rules consistent with human nature. Many respectable writers agree that if a man reasonably believes that he is in immediate danger of death or grievous bodily harm from his assailant he may stand his ground and that if he kills him he has not exceeded the bounds of lawful self-defence. That has been the decision of this Court. Beard v. United States, 158 U.S. 550, 559, 15 S.Ct. 962, 39 L.Ed. 1086. Detached reflection cannot be demanded in the presence of an uplifted knife. Therefore in this Court, at least, it is not a condition of immunity that one in that situation should pause to consider whether a reasonable man might not think it possible to fly with safety or to disable his assailant rather than to kill him. Rowe v. United States, 164 U.S. 546, 558, 17 S.Ct. 172, 41 L.Ed. 547. The law of Texas very strongly adopts these views as is shown by many cases, of which it is enough to cite two. Cooper v. State, 49 Tex.Crim.Rep. 28, 38, 89 S.W. 1068. Baltrip v. State, 30 Tex.Ct.App. 545, 549, 17 S.W. 1106.

It is true that in the case of Beard he was upon his own land (not in his house), and in that of Rowe he was in the room of a hotel, but those facts, although mentioned by the Court, would not have bettered the defence by the old common law and were not appreciably more favorable than that the defendant here was at a place where he was called to be, in the discharge of his duty. There was evidence that the last shot was fired after Hermes was down. The jury might not believe the defendant's testimony that it was an accidental discharge, but the suggestion of the Government that this Court may disregard the considerable body of evidence that the shooting was in self-defence is based upon a misunderstanding of what was meant by some language in Battle v. United States, 209 U.S. 36, 38, 28 S.Ct. 422, 52 L.Ed. 670. Moreover if the last shot was intentional and may seem to have been unnecessary when considered in cold blood, the defendant would not necessarily lose his immunity if it followed close upon the others while the heat of the conflict was on, and if the defendant believed that he was fighting for his life.

The Government presents a different case. It denies that Hermes had a knife and even that Brown was acting in self-defence. Notwithstanding the repeated threats of Hermes and intimations that one of the two would die at the next encounter, which seem hardly to be denied, of course it was possible for the jury to find that Brown had not sufficient reason to think that his life was in danger at that time, that he exceeded the limits of reasonable self-defence or even that he was the attacking party. But upon the hypothesis to which the evidence gave much color, that Hermes began the attack, the instruction that we have stated was wrong.

Judgment reversed.[1]

MR. JUSTICE PITNEY and MR. JUSTICE CLARKE dissent.

1. "The doctrine of 'retreat to the wall' had its origin before the general introduction of guns. Justice demands that its application have due regard to the present general use and to the type of firearms. It would be good sense for the law to require, in many cases, an attempt to escape from a hand to hand encounter with fists, clubs, and even knives, as a condition of justification for killing in self-defense; while it would be rank folly to so require when experienced men, armed with repeating rifles, face each other in an open space, removed from shelter, with intent to kill or to do great bodily harm. What might be a reasonable chance for escape in the one situation might in the other be certain death. Self-defense has not, by statute nor by judicial opinion, been distorted by an unreasonable requirement of the duty to retreat, into self-destruction." State v. Gardner, 96 Minn. 318, 104 N.W. 971 (1905).

Although there is no duty to retreat in this jurisdiction, "once having retreated from a place of danger, an act of voluntarily returning which is deliberately calculated to lead to further conflict deprives the defendant of his claim of self-defense." State v. Britson, 130 Ariz. 380, 636 P.2d 628, 634 (1981).

One who finds trouble by going out of his way to look for it does not have the privilege of self-defense. Valentine v. State, 108 Ark. 594, 159 S.W. 26 (1913). But the mere fact that a man has been threatened and has reason to expect an assault does not deprive him of the right to go about his business as usual, even if this will take him where he has reason to expect the other. People v. Gonzales, 71 Cal. 569, 12 P. 783 (1887). And if he does meet the other, and is attacked by him, he has the privilege of self-defense, in spite of the fact that he took the precaution of arming himself to be prepared for such an emergency. State v. Evans, 124 Mo. 397, 28 S.W. 8 (1894). A man cannot be said to be seeking a difficulty, in the sense of being deprived of the privilege of self-defense, merely because he is attempting to restrain a trespasser from unwarranted control over his property. And this is true even if he armed himself with a weapon to be prepared to defend himself if necessary. Ayers v. State, 60 Miss. 709 (1883). The fact that one is carrying a weapon unlawfully does not deprive him of the privilege of using it if necessary to defend himself from death or great bodily injury. State v. Doris, 51 Or. 136, 94 P. 44 (1908). The fact that a difficulty arose out of an unlawful gambling game does not deprive the innocent victim of a murderous assault of the privilege of self-defense. State v. Leaks, 114 S.C. 257, 103 S.E. 549 (1919). Compare Shack v. State, 236 Ala. 667, 184 So. 688 (1938).

A trespasser has the right of self-defense after he has availed himself of every means of retreat. Thompson v. State, 462 P.2d 299, 302 (Okl.Cr.1969).

PEOPLE v. LIGOURI

Court of Appeals of New York, 1940.
284 N.Y. 309, 31 N.E.2d 37.

SEARS, J. The defendants, Giro Ligouri and William Panaro, were indicted together for the crime of murder in the first degree. They have been found guilty by the verdict of a jury of the crime of murder in the second degree. Their convictions have been unanimously affirmed by the Appellate Division in the second department, and are brought before this court by an order granted by one of the judges of this court.

It is not disputed by either appellant that Ligouri, on October 24, 1938, shot and killed Nicholas Cosaluzzo. In fact, Ligouri, himself, sworn in his own behalf, testified to the shooting. The affair occurred about three o'clock in the afternoon in a public street in the borough of Brooklyn, New York City, at or near the corner of McDonald avenue and Avenue X. . . .

The defendant Ligouri urges that the trial court in its charge in respect to justification committed error. The court was requested on behalf of Ligouri to charge in this language: "If the defendant Ligouri was attacked feloniously by the deceased, Cosaluzzo, the defendant Ligouri had a right to shoot Cosaluzzo." The court declined to charge as requested, stating that it had already been covered. Defendant continued, "I ask Your Honor to charge the jury that a person who is feloniously attacked is under no obligation to retreat but may stand his ground, and if necessary, kill his opponent." This the court declined, saying, "If a person kills another whom he claims assaults him, he is under an obligation to retreat as far as possible, unless the circumstances are such that unless he acted as he did he would be the recipient of irreparable and grievous bodily harm." Exceptions were taken to the court's declining to charge as requested and to the charge. In the main charge the court had said on the subject of self-defense: "The defendant Ligouri claims that while he discharged these revolvers, what he did was done in self-defense. As I have alredy said, the law is that an act otherwise criminal is justified when done to protect the person committing it, or another whom he is bound to protect from inevitable and irreparable personal injury, and the injury could only have been prevented by the act, nothing more being done than is necessary to prevent the injury. A person who is attacked before he can resort to acts which result in death, is bound to retreat and to avoid the attack, unless the circumstances be such that he believes that he is in such imminent danger of irreparable injury, and the only thing he could do to protect himself and prevent that injury being inflicted upon him, would be to act as he did, and to do no more to prevent it than was necessary. If the circumstances justified the belief on his part that he is in danger of inevitable and irreparable injury, although it should turn out he was mistaken, an ordinarily prudent man under the same circumstances would be justified in doing what he did, if he thinks he is in danger of death. If you believe that Nick unexpectedly pulled this gun and snapped it on him, and under those circumstances he felt the only thing for him to do was to do what he did, discharge and empty both of his guns into him, even though death resulted, that would be justifiable under the law, but he could not do more than necessary, more than what an ordinarily prudent man under the same circumstances would be justified in doing. He does not have to satisfy you that the situation existed, but if, upon considering all the evidence in the case, there is a reasonable doubt, he must have the benefit of it, and your verdict will be not guilty, because the People must establish to your satisfaction beyond a reasonable doubt that this was a wilful, wanton killing, and was not excusable and not justifiable. That is their burden."

The applicable statute, Penal Law, section 1055, contains the following language:

"Homicide is also justifiable when committed:

"1. In the lawful defense of the slayer, or of his or her husband, wife, parent, child, brother, sister, master or servant, or of any other person in his presence or company, when there is reasonable ground to apprehend a design on the part of the person slain to commit a felony, or to do some great personal injury to the slayer, or to any such person, and there is imminent danger of such design being accomplished; or,

"2. In the actual resistance of an attempt to commit a felony upon the slayer, in his presence, or upon or in a dwelling or other place of abode in which he is."

The language employed by the court in the main charge is that applicable in the usual case of self-defense and falls within the first subdivision as above cited. This is not, however, the ordinary case. Here, on the assumption in the request, a felony was in process of being committed. So in substance the court charged. To avoid the felonious aggression against his person, if it occurred, Ligouri was justified under the second division of the section in standing his ground and, if necessary, destroying the person making the felonious attack. . . .

We reach the conclusion that error occurred in the refusal of the trial court to charge as requested. It may be argued that the charge amounted to granting the request as no one could consider escape as reasonably possible from a pistol purposefully and directly aimed at the assailed. The charge, however, left this matter to deduction. The defendants were on trial for crimes punishable by death. They were entitled to have the judge charge the jury definitely and directly that if they found that the felonious assault, assumed in the request, was occurring, the defendant against whom it was being perpetrated was justified in killing the felonious aggressor if such were necessary in resisting the assault. This error goes to the very foundation of the defense, and necessitates a reversal of the conviction of Ligouri. . . .

For these reasons the judgments should be reversed and a new trial ordered as to both defendants. . . .[1]

LEHMAN, CH. J., LOUGHRAN and RIPPEY, JJ., concur with SEARS, J.; LEWIS, J., dissents in opinion in which FINCH, J., concurs as to Ligouri but concurs in the grant of a new trial to Panaro; CONWAY, J., concurs in the opinion of LEWIS, J., as to Ligouri but votes to affirm as to both defendants.

Judgments reversed, etc.

STATE v. DAVIS

Supreme Court of South Carolina, 1948.
214 S.C. 34, 51 S.E.2d 86.

OXNER, JUSTICE. Appellant, Mack Davis, was indicted and tried for the murder of Norman Gordon, Jr. He sought to excuse the homicide on the ground of self-defense. The trial resulted in a verdict of guilty with recommendation to the mercy of the Court and he was sentenced to imprisonment for life. The only question to be determined on this appeal is whether in establishing his plea of self-defense, appellant had the right to claim immunity from the law of retreat.

About 11 o'clock on Saturday night, August 2, 1947, appellant shot the deceased in a cornfield near a filling station and store operated by W. H. Hinds in a rural section of Florence County. Some time late that afternoon these two [men] had an argument at a tobacco barn where the deceased was working, as a result of which the deceased, apparently without much, if any, provocation, slapped or struck appellant and knocked him down. Appellant immediately left the scene. That night about 9 o'clock he came to the store of Mr. Hinds. About an hour and a half later the deceased arrived and asked Hinds to lend him a gun, stating, according to Hinds, "I believe Mack (appellant) is going to shoot me." Hinds refused to do so and told the deceased that he didn't "want any shooting around here." The deceased replied that he had a gun at the tobacco barn which he

1. "We would further note the holding of this court in Gillaspy v. State, 96 Okl.Cr. 347, 255 P.2d 302 (1953), in which this court upheld the accuracy of an instruction which read in part as follows: 'It is the duty of a person so threatened with danger to his life or person to use at the time all reasonable means apparent to a reasonable person under the circumstances shown to avoid such danger before taking human life, except that he is not bound to retreat to avoid the necessity or apparent necessity of killing, if he is in a place where he has a right to be and has done no act on his part to bring about the necessity for killing.' 255 P.2d, at 309." Thompson v. State, 462 P.2d 299, 302 (Okl.Cr.1969).

It was error not to include in the charge that if the defendant had a reasonable belief he was about to be killed or suffer great bodily injury, he had no duty to retreat but could stand his ground and shoot his assailant in self-defense. State v. Ward, 26 N.C.App. 159, 215 S.E.2d 394 (1975).

could get and then left. About the same time or shortly thereafter, appellant went across the road in the direction of his home. Approximately a half hour later Hinds and several of those in the store heard the sound of a shotgun. They made an investigation and found the deceased lying fatally wounded in the cornfield at a point about 25 or 30 yards from the store and about 15 feet from the road, with a rifle near his body. He died shortly thereafter while being carried to the office of a physician.

Appellant testified that after hearing the conversation between the deceased and Hinds, he became alarmed and went home for the purpose of securing his shotgun, intending to return to the store where he had several matters to attend to. He said that he planned to approach the store from the rear through the cornfield because the deceased might see him first if he entered through the front. According to his testimony, while in the cornfield he saw the deceased approaching and squatted to escape observation but that the deceased when within close range recognized him and raised his rifle, whereupon he (appellant) shot in defense of his life. The theory of the State was that appellant concealed himself in the cornfield for the purpose of shooting the deceased as the latter returned to the store.

Appellant lived at the home of his sister and brother-in-law, a distance of about four-tenths of a mile from the scene of the homicide. The field in question was owned by Hinds and cultivated by appellant's brother-in-law as a sharecropper. Appellant worked for him and had assisted in cultivating this corn, which had been laid by at the time of the homicide, but the record does not disclose whether his compensation was in the form of wages or a share in the crop. The deceased also worked on some farm in the same community.

Counsel for appellant requested the Court "to charge the jury that the defendant was on the premises on which he was working and the law of retreat would not apply to him." The request was refused and the jury was instructed that it was incumbent upon appellant to establish all of the elements of self-defense, including that of retreating, which the Court then qualified as follows: "I charge you as a matter of law that if a person is threatened with a gun, any kind of firearms, within shooting range, why, obviously there is no duty to retreat; and it is only in cases where a person can with safety avoid a difficulty that he is required to retreat under the law to avoid committing murder." . . .

It is now well established in this State that if a person is assaulted while on his own premises and is without fault in bringing on the difficulty, he is not bound to retreat in order to invoke the benefit of the doctrine of self-defense, but may stand his ground and repel the attack with as much force as is reasonably necessary. . . . This is true whether the attack occurs in defendant's home, place of business, or elsewhere on property owned or lawfully occupied by him. It was also held in State v. Marlowe, 120 S.C. 205, 112 S.E. 921, 922, that a member of a club, wrongfully attacked by another in the club rooms, was under no duty to retreat, the Court observing: "A man is no more bound to allow himself to be run out of his rest room than his workshop." In some jurisdictions the rule has been extended so as to relieve the defendant from the necessity of retreating if attacked in any place where he has a right to be, as when he is lawfully on a public street or highway. We have not gone that far. In State v. McGee, 185 S.C. 184, 193 S.E. 303, 306, the Court stated that "The fact that the defendant was on a public highway, where all men have equal rights, and in his automobile, did not constitute any one of those special privileges obviating the necessity of retreating before killing." It was held in State v. Gordon, supra [128 S.C. 422, 122 S.E. 503], that where a foreman on a farm was assaulted by one of the employees under him at the place where they were working, he was not required to retreat. The Court concluded that the place of work "was the defendant's place of business within the meaning of that term as employed in the law of retreat."

In the case at bar, we do not think under the circumstances that appellant is entitled to claim immunity from the law of retreat. The homicide did not occur at or within the curtilage of the home in which he resided. This house was located across the public road and at some distance from the scene of the shooting. Nor was appellant attacked while working at his "place of business". It is true that he had assisted during the year in cultivating the corn in this field but his presence there on the night in question was wholly unrelated to his employment. There is no showing that he even had any interest in the corn crop. Whether his brother-in-law, the sharecropper, would have been required to retreat if attacked in this cornfield under similar circumstances is a question that is not before us.

All exceptions are overruled and judgment affirmed.[1]

BAKER, C.J., and FISHBURNE, STUKES and TAYLOR, JJ., concur.

1. Defendant on his own land acting in a legal manner need not retreat after being threatened before using deadly force. State v. Hendrix, 270 S.C. 653, 244 S.E.2d 503 (1978). The jury should have been instructed that since defendant was in her home she had no duty to retreat or escape but was entitled to stand her ground and take the life of the assailant if that became necessary. Jackson v. State, 31 Md.App. 518, 357 A.2d 845 (1976).

Where defendant was in his own home there was no duty to retreat. Collier v. State, 57 Ala.App. 375, 328 So.2d 626 (1975), cert. denied 295 Ala. 397, 328 So. 2d 629 (1976).

A garage owner, attacked in the private driveway to his garage, was under no duty to retreat. State v. Sipes, 202 Iowa 173, 209 N.W. 458 (1926).

When a man is on his own premises other than his house or within the curtilage thereof the reasons for not retreating do not apply. Lee v. State, 92 Ala. 15, 9 So. 407 (1890).

The right to stand his ground applies to one while in his dwelling house, office, or place of business, or within the curtilage thereof. Bryant v. State, 252 Ala. 153, 39 So.2d 657 (1949).

PEOPLE v. McGRANDY

Court of Appeals of Michigan, 1967.
9 Mich.App. 187, 156 N.W.2d 48.

BURNS, JUDGE. A circuit court jury found Mrs. Edna Marie McGrandy guilty of manslaughter. The facts of this case for the purposes of this opinion can be stated as follows.

On May 1, 1965, defendant and her husband, both of whom had been out drinking much beer and some whiskey, returned to their second floor apartment. Without getting into the details of what occurred upon their arrival, suffice it to say that Mr. McGrandy stood in the kitchen doorway with a loaded rifle in his hands. It is defendant's claim that her husband cocked the rifle and intended to use it on her. Mrs. McGrandy then grabbed a butcher knife, and in an alleged attempt to "get him out of my way so I [Mrs. McGrandy] could get out," Mr. McGrandy was fatally stabbed.

Defendant might have avoided a confrontation with her husband by retreating out another kitchen doorway which led to the apartment's rear porch and stairway. The jury was made very aware of this alternative route of escape.

In support of defendant's argument of self-defense counsel for defendant, citing People v. Stallworth (1961), 364 Mich. 528, 111 N.W.2d 742, requested a jury instruction that a person is not obliged to retreat from his dwelling. The trial court, however, gave the following instruction.

"Now, in justification of the offense herein charged, the defendant interposed a plea of self-defense. Under certain circumstances this is a good defense. To make a plea of self-defense, it must appear that the defendant was without fault on her part. If she herself was the aggressor in the conflict, she cannot invoke the doctrine of self-defense as an excuse for the killing unless she was at that time, as she saw it, in imminent danger of losing her own life or suffering some grievous bodily injury, and *there was no way open for her to retreat, as he saw it.*[a] Self-defense will not justify the taking of a human life unless you jurors shall be satisfied from the testimony, first that the defendant was not the aggressor bringing on the difficulties as has just been pointed out. Secondly, that there existed at the time of striking the fatal blow in Marie McGrandy's mind a present and impending necessity to save herself from death or some great bodily harm, and third, *there must be no way open whereby she could have retreated, as it appeared to her, at that time, to a place of safety and thus avoid the conflict.*

a. Under the retreat rule the innocent victim of a murderous attack is not deprived of the right to use deadly force in his defense by reason of an avenue of escape which he did not know existed. Commonwealth v. Palmer, 467 Pa. 476, 359 A.2d 375 (1976).

"Unless you find all three of these elements in the case, then the plea of self-defense fails." (Emphasis supplied.)

The general rule in cases where self-defense is asserted is that the defendant must do "all which is reasonably in his power to avoid the necessity of extreme resistance, by retreating where retreat is safe." Pond v. People (1860), 8 Mich. 150, 176. The *Pond* case, supra, page 177, also recognized an exception to this rule:

"A man is not however, obliged to retreat if assaulted in his dwelling, but may use such means as are absolutely necessary to repel the assailant from his house, or to prevent his forcible entry, even to the taking of life."

There is a split of authority throughout the country in the applicability of this exception when the assailant and the assailed share the same living quarters where the alleged attack occurred. Justice Cardozo in People v. Tomlins (1914), 213 N.Y. 240, 107 N.E. 496 reasoned:

"It is not now and never has been the law that a man assailed in his own dwelling is bound to retreat. If assailed there, he may stand his ground and resist the attack. He is under no duty to take to the fields and the highways, a fugitive from his own home. . . . The rule is the same whether the attack proceeds from some other occupant or from an intruder. It was so adjudged in Jones v. State [1884], 76 Ala. 8, 14. 'Why,' it was there inquired, 'should one retreat from his own house, when assailed by a partner or cotenant, any more than when assailed by a stranger who is lawfully upon the premises? Whither shall he flee, and how far, and when may he be permitted to return?' " . . .

In People v. Stallworth, supra, the defendant killed her husband by stabbing him when the deceased attempted to put her out of the home forcibly. The Court quoted from the *Pond* case, supra:

" 'a man is not . . . obliged to retreat if assaulted in his [own] dwelling.' "

The Court continued:

"If the testimony of Mrs. Stallworth at the trial which bore directly on the fatal episode were to be accepted at face value, it would appear to meet the tests of self-defense spelled out above."

In our opinion the *Stallworth* case, supra, aligns Michigan jurisprudential thinking with the above cited authorities.

The failure to give defendant's requested instruction resulted in prejudicial error. Defendant's other assignments of error are without merit or do not require consideration because of our disposition of the case.

Reversed and remanded for new trial.[1]

1. A wife, attacked by her husband in the home in which each had an equal right to be, had no duty to flee from the home but could use such force as she perceived to be needed to prevent harm to herself. People v. Lenkevich, 394 Mich. 117, 229 N.W.2d 298 (1975).

STATE v. FISCHER

Court of Appeals of Washington, Division 2, 1979.
23 Wn.App. 756, 598 P.2d 742.

PETRIE, JUDGE. Defendant, Eugene Victor Fischer, appeals from his conviction of second-degree assault. RCW 9A.36.020. At trial, he readily acknowledged striking the alleged victim with a flashlight, but asserted his actions were justified because he was lawfully defending himself and his employees. We hold that the trial court's instruction regarding the circumstances under which defendant was entitled to use force to defend himself and others did not provide the jury with an adequate standard upon which to measure the defendant's action. Accordingly, we reverse his conviction and remand the cause for new trial.

Shortly after midnight on December 11, 1977, Nick Lester and two friends entered the Bull & Bash Tavern in Bremerton. Defendant, who is part-owner of the Bull & Bash, was on duty at the entrance. He first noticed the three men when they walked past him without paying the cover charge and without letting him check their identification. Before he had an opportunity to confront them, he received a complaint from a female patron concerning Lester's behavior. Defendant decided to ask him to leave the tavern. Defendant and one of the bouncers, Bob Haney, approached Lester for this purpose. At this point two different versions of the incident emerge.

Accordingly to defendant, Lester started fighting with Haney; Haney was thrown to the floor; and Ray Jaworski, another bouncer, joined in the fray. Lester became more and more aggressive, and Jaworski had a difficult time controlling him. He deliberately threw a pull-tab machine at the bartender, Patricia Watson, who then sprayed him with mace. By this time, Lester was enraged. He was attempting to climb over the bar to "get" Watson when Jaworski called for help. Two policemen entered the bar on a routine "walk

If one is attacked in his home by another legal occupant of the same home, the privilege of non-retreat does not apply. State v. Bobbitt, 415 So.2d 724 (Fla.1982).

Some courts have taken a different position.

There is a duty to retreat if both live in the house. Commonwealth v. Johnson, 213 Pa. 432, 62 A. 1064 (1906); State v. Grierson, 96 N.H. 36, 69 A.2d 851 (1950). There is a duty to retreat if assailant entered as an invited guest. Oney v. Commonwealth, 225 Ky. 590, 9 S.W.2d 723 (1928). There is no duty to retreat if "he is attacked within his dwelling place which is not also the dwelling place of the other, . . . " Restatement, Second, Torts § 65(2)(a) (1965).

It has never been the law of Massachusetts that one assaulted in his own home need not retreat before resorting to the use of deadly force. The right to use deadly force by way of self defense is not available to one threatened until he has availed himself of all reasonable and proper means in the circumstance to avoid combat. This has equal application to one assaulted in his own home. The fact that the accused was attacked in his own home is one factor to be considered by the jury, but there is no rule in this state that one attacked in his own home has no duty to retreat. Commonwealth v. Shaffer, 367 Mass. 508, 326 N.E.2d 880 (1975).

N.B. This seems to be the only state ever to take such a position.

through" just as defendant hit Lester on the head with his large metal flashlight.

Lester's version of the encounter is, of course, quite different. It indicates the defendant and his employees were the aggressors. Nevertheless, as long as the record contains substantial evidence which, if believed by a jury, would justify defendant's actions, the jury must be properly advised of the law of self-defense and defense of others.

Defendant asserts that the trial court erred in refusing to instruct the jury as follows:

> If at the time of the alleged assault defendant as a *reasonably and ordinarily prudent man believed* he and/or another were in danger of great bodily harm, he would have the right to resort to self-defense and *his conduct is to be judged by the conditions appearing to him at that time, not by the conditions as they might appear when the threat of harm no longer exists.*

(Emphasis added.)

In place of defendant's proposed instruction, the court gave the following charge:

> It is a defense to a charge of Second Degree Assault that the force used was lawful as defined in this instruction.
>
> The use of force upon or toward the person of another is lawful when used by someone lawfully aiding a person about to be injured in preventing or attempting to prevent an offense against the person, and when the force is not more than is necessary.
>
> *Necessary means that no reasonably effective alternative to the use of force appeared to exist and that the amount of force used was reasonable to effect the lawful purpose intended.*

(Emphasis added.)

The italicized portion of the court's instruction is a direct quote from RCW 9A.16.010 and WPIC § 16.05; and the remainder is consistent with WPIC § 17.02. Another division of this court has recently held, and we agree, that the provisions of the new criminal code were not intended to abrogate common law self-defense requirements. Therefore, the court's instruction can stand only if it included the essential element that the person using the force need only reasonably believe, in light of all the facts and circumstances known to him, that he or another person is in danger. As the court noted in State v. Bailey, supra, 22 Wash.App. at 650, 591 P.2d at 1214:

> Necessity must . . . be considered by the jury standing in the shoes of the defendant. The applicable standard is that persons may use that degree of force necessary to protect themselves as a reasonably prudent man or woman would use under the conditions appearing to them at the time.

The trial judge refused the proposed instruction not because he believed it was an improper statement of the law, but because he was satisfied that the "subjective" common law standard was "inherent" in the instruction given. We appreciate that this argument is appealing to the trained legal mind. However, the instruction can be said to be sufficient only if it makes the subjective standard manifestly apparent to the average juror. In our view, it does not meet that test. The prejudice to the defendant is apparent. Accordingly, we reverse the conviction and remand for new trial.

Although our resolution of this issue is determinative of this appeal, it seems prudent to briefly address defendant's other two assignments of error. Defendant contends that the trial court erred by instructing the jury that one who comes to the aid of an aggressor cannot claim that he acted in the defense of himself or another. The Supreme Court recently overruled prior case law and declared that an individual who acts in defense of another person, reasonably believing him to be the "innocent party," is justified in using force to protect that person even if, *in fact,* the party protected was the aggressor. If an issue regarding defendant's right to defend an aggressor is raised on retrial, instructions consistent with the holding of State v. Penn, supra, should be given.

Finally, defendant argues that the trial court erred in not instructing the jury regarding his right to use force to defend his *property.* Defendant bases this argument on his analysis of RCW 9.01.200.[1] Although this issue was not raised at trial, it now appears that it may be raised on retrial.

We have only recently observed that this statute merely provides a means of indemnification and reimbursement for damages sustained by an individual who is acquitted on a self-defense theory. The statute does not expressly or impliedly expand the common law and statutory right to use reasonable force to protect one's property. The reasonableness of that force is measured by the common law of this state, limitations imposed by RCW 9A.16.020, and judicial interpretations of that statute. If defense of property becomes an issue on retrial, instructions should be drawn from the appropriate sources.

Judgment is reversed and the cause is remanded for new trial.[a]

REED, ACTING C.J., and SOULE, J., concur.

1. RCW 9.01.200 states:

"No person in the state shall be placed in legal jeopardy of any kind whatsoever for protecting by any reasonable means necessary, himself, his family, *or his real or personal property,* or for coming to the aid of another who is in imminent danger of or the victim of aggravated assault, armed robbery, holdup, rape, murder, or any other heinous crime.

"When a substantial question of self defense in such a case shall exist which needs legal investigation or court action for the full determination of the facts, and the defendant's actions are subsequently found justified under the intent of this section, the state of Washington shall indemnify or reimburse such defendant for all loss of time, legal fees, or other expenses involved in his defense." (Emphasis added.)

a. "To claim self-defense, a defendant's belief about the necessity of defending himself must be based on reason-

STATE v. RUMMELHOFF

Court of Appeals of Washington, Division 1, Panel Two, 1969.
1 Wn.App. 192, 459 P.2d 976.

STAFFORD, JUDGE. This is an appeal from a judgment of the trial court which found defendant Walter Rummelhoff guilty of assault in the second degree. . . .

The victim, a cabdriver, drove defendant to a restaurant during the evening. He was asked to wait outside. The defendant emerged a short time later and walked away from the cab without paying. The victim followed him a short distance on foot, tapped him on the shoulder and said, "Hey, where are you going? You are going the wrong way; come back to the cab." At that point the defendant whirled, stabbed the victim, and said, "You've had it now, . . . " and walked away.

The defendant does not deny the stabbing. He argues that he had twice been assaulted on the streets, was justifiably apprehensive, and thus had a right to act in the belief that he was defending himself. This contention has been answered in State v. Hill, 76 Wash.Dec.2d 728, 458 P.2d 171 (1969), at 736:

Appellant argues that it was error to instruct the jury that the amount of force that may be lawfully used in self-defense is to be measured by what a reasonably prudent man would have done under the existing circumstances. Although he submitted no proposed instruction on the subject, he criticizes the instruction given because it did not make him the sole judge as to existence of the peril of great bodily harm confronting him and the amount of force necessary to protect himself against it.

If we were to agree with appellant's position, there would be no limit to the amount of force which a person could use in defending himself against such alleged peril. (Italics ours.)

One's right to resist force with force is dependent upon what a reasonably cautious and prudent man would have done under the conditions then existing.[1] Under the facts of this case the defendant did not meet the test.

able grounds. A subjective belief of danger will not alone suffice; the defendant's belief of danger must also be reasonable." Scheikofsky v. State, 636 P.2d 1107, 1110 (Wyo.1981).

Defendant must show not only that he actually believed he was in danger of death or serious bodily harm, but that the belief was reasonable based on circumstances as perceived by the defendant, not as they actually existed. People v. Green, 113 Mich.App. 699, 318 N.W.2d 547 (1982).

1. Accord: State v. Lawton, 4 Or.App. 109, 476 P.2d 821 (1970).

"In determining whether the actor's apprehension of the intentional infliction of bodily harm or an offensive contact is reasonable, the circumstances which are known, or should be known, to the actor must be such as would lead a reasonable man to entertain such an apprehension.

The defendant asserts the trial court erred by refusing to recognize that he was the victim, rather than the original aggressor. The trial court chose to believe the testimony of the victim. There was substantial evidence, based upon conflicting testimony, to support the trial court's determination. We will not substitute our judgment.

The trial court's refusal to accept defendant's theory of self-defense was entirely correct. One who initially is an aggressor cannot invoke the doctrine of self-defense until he, in good faith, endeavors to withdraw from and abandon the conflict. There was no evidence that Mr. Rummelhoff ever sought to avoid or withdraw from the conflict.

STATE v. HANTON

Supreme Court of Washington, En Bank, 1980.
94 Wn.2d 129, 614 P.2d 1280.

WILLIAMS, JUSTICE. Petitioner Solomon Hanton seeks review of a jury conviction of first-degree manslaughter while armed with a deadly weapon. The Court of Appeals affirmed the conviction in an un-

In this connection the qualities which primarily characterize a 'reasonable man' are ordinary firmness and courage." Restatement, Second, Torts § 63, Comment *i* (1965).

The instruction should not speak in terms of an "ordinarily prudent and courageous man," but of an "ordinarily prudent and cautious man." State v. Sipes, 202 Iowa 173, 185, 209 N.W. 458, 463 (1926). Accord: People v. Smith, 164 Cal. 451, 129 P. 785 (1913).

". . . the fears of a reasonable man that his life is in danger, or that a felony is about to be perpetrated upon him." Jarrard v. State, 206 Ga. 112, 114, 55 S.E.2d 706, 709 (1949).

In Kansas the statutory justification for the use of deadly force in self-defense "requires the trier of fact to determine reasonableness of the accused's actions by an objective rather than a subjective standard." State v. Simon, 231 Kan. 572, 646 P.2d 1119 (1982).

The question is not apparent danger as seen by the jury at the trial, but as it appeared to the defendant at the moment. Wireman v. Commonwealth, 290 Ky. 704, 162 S.W.2d 557 (1942); Patillo v. State, 22 Tex.App. 586, 3 S.W. 766 (1886).

The fact that defendant was intoxicated at the time would not justify a killing in alleged self-defense if the need for deadly force would not have seemed necessary to a reasonably prudent man under the circumstances. Springfeld v. State, 96 Ala. 81, 11 So. 250 (1892). Contra: His condition may be taken into account in considering whether he apprehended an assault. Regina v. Gamlin, 1 Fost. and F. 90, 175 Eng.Rep. 639 (1858).

One who has received information of threats against his life made by another is justified in acting more quickly, and taking harsher measures for his protection against that other, than in the absence of such information. People v. Torres, 94 Cal.App.2d 146, 210 P.2d 324 (1949).

If D, charged with murder genuinely believed the circumstances to be such that the killing would be justified, this will not excuse the killing if the belief was unreasonable; but even so, the killing may be voluntary manslaughter rather than murder. People v. Vaughn, 26 Ill.App.3d 247, 324 N.E.2d 697 (1975).

In a murder trial in which the defense claimed was self-defense, and the evidence indicated the possibility that D acted recklessly or upon provocation, it was error not to give a manslaughter instruction. This was not a case where the failure to establish malice would necessarily require complete exculpation. Pendergrast v. United States, 332 A.2d 919 (D.C. App.1975).

published opinion. We reverse the Court of Appeals and remand the case for a new trial.

Petitioner and the victim were driving their respective automobiles in Bellevue, Washington on February 25, 1977. While leaving an intersection, petitioner pulled in front of the victim's car in such a manner as to cut him off, causing him to apply his brakes to avoid an accident. This apparently made the victim quite angry, for he followed close behind petitioner's car until they stopped at the next stoplight. There the victim left his car, came up to petitioner's car, opened the door, and attempted to pull him out. Petitioner thereupon drew a pistol and shot him. He died several days later as a result of the wound.

Petitioner was charged with and convicted of first-degree manslaughter. RCW 9A.32.060(1)(a). At trial he requested the following instruction on self-defense:

> When a defendant claims he killed another in defense of his person or property, the burden is upon that defendant only to produce some evidence, no matter how slight, tending to prove that the homicide was done in self-defense. It is not necessary for the defendant to prove this to you beyond a reasonable doubt, nor by a preponderance of the evidence. The defendant sustains this burden of proof, if from a consideration of the evidence in the case you have a reasonable doubt as to whether or not the killing was done in self-defense.
>
> It is the duty of the State to prove beyond a reasonable doubt the lack of self-defense.

The court gave the following instruction:

> When a defendant claims he killed another in defense of his person or property, the burden is upon that defendant only to produce some evidence tending to prove that the homicide was done in self-defense. It is not necessary for the defendant to prove this to you beyond a reasonable doubt, nor by a preponderance of the evidence. The defendant sustains this burden of proof, if from a consideration of the evidence in the case you have a reasonable doubt as to whether or not the killing was done in self-defense.

Instruction No. 13.

On appeal, petitioner argued that the instruction as given unconstitutionally placed on him the burden of proving self-defense and that such an allocation of the burden had been disapproved by this court in State v. Roberts, 88 Wash.2d 337, 562 P.2d 1259 (1977). The Court of Appeals rejected the applicability of this reasoning to homicide offenses under the new criminal code, RCW 9A.32, relying on State v. Bradley, 20 Wash.App. 340, 581 P.2d 1053 (1978).

We agree with petitioner that the effect of the challenged instruction was to shift to petitioner the burden of proof on self-defense. The instruction as given was substantially the same as the one at issue in *Roberts.* We found that instruction defective because it impermissibly shifted the burden to the accused. The same shift in the allocation of the burden occurred here. Therefore, the only question here is whether the burden may be allocated to an accused under the present statute.

We begin by noting that the due process clause of the fourteenth amendment to the United States Constitution requires the prosecution to prove beyond a reasonable doubt every fact necessary to constitute the crime with which an accused is charged. This principle has been reaffirmed recently by the United States Supreme Court in Sandstrom v. Montana, 442 U.S. 510, 99 S.Ct. 2450, 61 L.Ed.2d 39, 48 (1979). See also Patterson v. New York, 432 U.S. 197, 206–07, 97 S.Ct. 2319, 2324–25, 53 L.Ed.2d 281 (1977).

In order to determine which facts the prosecution must prove beyond a reasonable doubt, it is necessary to analyze each element of the crime charged. The Court of Appeals cited State v. Bradley, supra, in support of its holding that absence of self-defense is not an element of a *homicide offense* under the new criminal code and that the State may therefore impose on an accused the burden of proving it. But the court did not analyze the elements of the crime of manslaughter either in *Bradley* or in the present case. Since murder and manslaughter are clearly separate homicide offenses under the statutory scheme, we must analyze *each* element of first-degree manslaughter in our consideration of petitioner's claim.

RCW 9A.32.060(1)(a) states, in pertinent part:

> (1) A person is guilty of manslaughter in the first degree when:
>
> (a) He recklessly causes the death of another person . . .

Since recklessness is expressly made an element of the crime of first-degree manslaughter, the prosecution must prove it beyond a reasonable doubt. State v. Roberts, supra. The statute provides:

> (c) *Recklessness.* A person is reckless or acts recklessly when he knows of and disregards a substantial risk that a wrongful act may occur and his disregard of such substantial risk is a gross deviation from conduct that a reasonable man would exercise in the same situation.

RCW 9A.08.010(1)(c).

Self-defense is explicitly made a lawful act by at least two provisions of the criminal code. First, homicide is justifiable when committed either:

> (1) In the lawful defense of the slayer, or his or her husband, wife, parent, child, brother, or sister, or of any other person in his presence or company, when there is reasonable ground to apprehend a design on the part of the person slain to commit a felony or to do some great personal injury to the slayer or to any such per-

son, and there is imminent danger of such design being accomplished; or

(2) In the actual resistance of an attempt to commit a felony upon the slayer, in his presence, or upon or in a dwelling, or other place of abode, in which he is.

RCW 9A.16.050(1) and (2). Moreover, use of force is not unlawful when used "by a party about to be injured . . . in preventing or attempting to prevent an offense against his person." RCW 9A.16.020(3).

A person acting in self-defense cannot be acting recklessly as that term is defined in RCW 9A.08.010(1)(c). There can be no recklessness without disregard of risk of a wrongful act, and self-defense, as defined, is not "wrongful." Moreover, since self-defense is not wrongful, it cannot be "a gross deviation from conduct that a reasonable man would exercise in the same situation." RCW 9A.08.010(1)(c).

In short, an action taken in self-defense is inconsistent with the statutory definition of recklessness. Since proof of self-defense negates the element of recklessness in first-degree manslaughter, requiring an accused to prove self-defense places on him or her the burden of proving absence of recklessness. Such a result is proscribed by *Winship* and *Mullaney.* Accordingly, we hold that in a prosecution for first-degree manslaughter the State must bear the burden of proving absence of self-defense beyond a reasonable doubt. This conclusion makes it unnecessary to consider petitioner's statutory construction argument that the legislature intended to place the burden on the State.

It does not necessarily follow, however, that the court must instruct the jury that the burden of proof on self-defense rests on the prosecution. When recklessness is an element of the crime charged, and the court properly instructs the jury on the elements of recklessness, the jury must determine, before it may convict, that the accused knew of and disregarded a substantial risk that a wrongful act would occur and that such disregard was a gross deviation from the conduct of a reasonable person in the same situation. Such a finding is totally inconsistent with self-defense. A person acting in self-defense cannot be acting recklessly. Thus, if the jury is able to find that a defendant acted recklessly, it has already precluded a finding of self-defense. We hold, therefore, that an instruction allocating the burden of proof to the State to disprove self-defense is not necessary when there is adequate instruction on the elements of recklessness.

If a defendant presents sufficient evidence to raise an issue of self-defense, the court need only instruct on it without allocating the burden of proof. Such an instruction permits a defendant to fully argue his theory of the case. The jury may then consider the evidence of self-defense in determining whether a defendant was acting recklessly.

We reverse and remand for a new trial.

UTTER, C.J., and ROSELLINI, STAFFORD, WRIGHT, BRACHTENBACH, HOROWITZ, DOLLIVER and HICKS, JJ., concur.

STATE v. BROADHURST

Supreme Court of Oregon, 1948.
184 Or. 178, 196 P.2d 407.

(Defendant, who had "married" Dr. Broadhurst although she was the wife of another, asked Williams to kill her "husband." Williams pretended to have car trouble at a spot on a lonely road where he knew Dr. Broadhurst would be driving. Dr. Broadhurst stopped to give help and Williams hit him over the head with a heavy wrench. At that point, according to Williams' testimony, he changed his mind and decided to leave without killing the other. But Dr. Broadhurst came at him and he was forced to kill to save his own life. Defendant was convicted of first degree murder and appeals.)

ROSSMAN, C.J. . . . Finally, under this contention the defendant argues that the testimony of Williams shows that he shot in self-defense and that Williams' testimony is binding upon the State. She, therefore, claims that the crime of murder was not committed.

In a preceding paragraph we showed that Williams swore that he struck Dr. Broadhurst only once with the wrench. He claimed that at that juncture he underwent a change of heart and decided to quit. His actual words were: "I had quit. . . . I decided I was going to leave the country right away." By reverting to the preceding paragraph, the testimony can be read upon which the defendant depends for a contention that two affrays occurred at the Succor Creek junction: (a) one in which Williams was the aggressor, and (b) a second in which Dr. Broadhurst was the aggressor. The defendant claims that Williams abandoned the first before the second purported affray was begun.

Dr. Joseph Beeman, whose qualifications are admitted, performed an autopsy upon Dr. Broadhurst's remains. He found three wounds upon the forehead. One was three-eights of an inch in diameter, another was an inch and a half in diameter. He said: "This wound had gone down to the skull." The third wound "was one and five-eighths of an inch long and three-fourths of an inch wide." According to the witness it "had gone through the skull and had torn the frontal part . . . had fractured the skull bone over the right eye." We call attention to the fact that two of the blows penetrated the skull and that one of them fractured the skull bone. Dr. Beeman testified that the shotgun wounds were in the right chest. We quote from him:

"He had the shotgun wounds in his right chest which was going from left to right, just slightly upwards and slightly backwards." . . .

An aggressor, in a combat which led to the death of the assaulted party, can not claim that he struck the fatal blow in self-defense unless, before the blow, he withdrew in good faith from the combat, and, in addition, brought home to the assaulted man notice of his intention in such a way that the adversary, as a reasonable man, must have known that the assault was ended. Abandonment of the assault and reasonable notice thereof are essential to restore to the aggressor the right of self-defense. Vol. 40, C.J.S., Homicide, § 121, page 995, in stating the rule to which we are adverting says:

". . . He must also in some manner make known his intention to his adversary; and if the circumstances are such that he cannot notify his adversary, as where the injuries inflicted by him are such as to deprive his adversary of his capacity to receive impressions concerning his assailant's design and endeavor to cease further combat, it is the assailant's fault and he must bear the consequences. As long as a person keeps his gun in his hand prepared to shoot, the person opposing him is not expected or required to accept any act or statement as indicative of an intent to discontinue the assault. . . ."

In 26 Am.Jur., Homicide, § 135, page 247, we find:

". . . Nor is this all; the aggressor must inform his antagonist of his purpose to withdraw from the conflict. If the circumstances are such that he cannot do this, it is attributable to his own fault and he must abide by the consequences."

Both of the treatises from which we quoted cite in partial support of their statements People v. Button, 106 Cal. 628, 39 P. 1073, 28 L.R.A. 591, 46 Am.St.Rep. 259. That decision is carefully reasoned and fully supports the claims made for it.

If Williams had quit the combat before he shot Dr. Broadhurst, he did not manifest that fact in any way whatever, with the exception of walking a few steps to his automobile. But upon the seat of the car lay his gun ready to be fired. At the moment when he claims Dr. Broadhurst advanced upon him he still had the wrench in his hand. His own words are, "When he started after me I had the wrench in my hand." There is no evidence that Dr. Broadhurst, upon whose head three vicious blows had rained, one of which fractured his skull bone, had regained consciousness when he is said to have begun an attack upon his assailant. Unless Dr. Broadhurst in some miraculous manner had regained consciousness and had discovered the secret purpose of Williams to abandon the assault, the right of Williams to act in self-defense had not been restored. Williams was asked: "Was he pretty well recovered when you handed the shirt to him?" He answered, "No." The nearest he came to attributing consciousness to the battered, bloody victim of his brutal blows was made in the following answer: "I had just got to the door and he started to come after me, so I imagine he was coming out of it." If Dr. Broadhurst advanced upon Williams, then we think that the following, taken from People v. Button, supra, is applicable:

"While the deceased had eyes to see and ears to hear, he had no mind to comprehend, for his mind was taken from him by the defendant at the first assault. Throughout the whole affray, it must be conceded that the deceased was guilty of no wrong, no violation of the law. When he attempted to kill the defendant, he thought he was acting in self-defense, and, according to his lights, he was acting in self-defense."

We are certain that the fifth and sixth contentions are without merit. . . .

The judgment of the circuit court is affirmed.[1]

(Certiorari denied 337 U.S. 906, 69 S.Ct. 1046, 93 L.Ed. 1718.)

MODEL PENAL CODE

Section 3.04. Use of Force in Self-Protection.

(1) Use of Force Justifiable for Protection of the Person. Subject to the provisions of this Section and of Section 3.09, the use of force upon or toward another person is justifiable when the actor believes that such force is immediately necessary for the purpose of protecting himself against the use of unlawful force by such other person on the present occasion.

(2) Limitations on Justifying Necessity for Use of Force.

(a) The use of force is not justifiable under this Section:

(i) to resist an arrest which the actor knows is being made by a peace officer, although the arrest is unlawful; or

(ii) to resist force used by the occupier or possessor of property or by another person on his behalf, where the actor knows that the person using the force is doing so under a claim of right to protect the property, except that this limitation shall not apply if:

(1) the actor is a public officer acting in the performance of his duties or a person lawfully assisting him therein or a person making or assisting in a lawful arrest; or

(2) the actor has been unlawfully dispossessed of the property and is making a re-entry or recaption justified by Section 3.06; or

1. "The right of self-defense is available only to one who is without fault. If a person voluntarily, i.e., aggressively and willingly, without legal provocation or excuse, enters into a fight, he cannot invoke the doctrine of self-defense unless he abandons the fight, withdraws from it, and gives notice to his adversary that he has done so." State v. Jones, 56 N.C. App. 259, 289 S.E.2d 383, 397 (1982).

"However, it is well settled . . . that self-defense is not available to a person who is committing or attempting to commit a forcible felony." State v. Marks, 226 Kan. 704, 602 P.2d 1344, 1351 (1979).

(3) the actor believes that such force is necessary to protect himself against death or serious bodily harm.

(b) The use of deadly force is not justifiable under this Section unless the actor believes that such force is necessary to protect himself against death, serious bodily harm, kidnapping or sexual intercourse compelled by force or threat; nor is it justifiable if:

(i) the actor, with the purpose of causing death or serious bodily harm, provoked the use of force against himself in the same encounter; or

(ii) the actor knows that he can avoid the necessity of using such force with complete safety by retreating or by surrendering possession of a thing to a person asserting a claim of right thereto or by complying with a demand that he abstain from any action which he has no duty to take, except that:

(1) the actor is not obliged to retreat from his dwelling or place of work, unless he was the initial aggressor or is assailed in his place of work by another person whose place of work the actor knows it to be; and

(2) a public officer justified in using force in the performance of his duties or a person justified in using force in his assistance or a person justified in using force in making an arrest or preventing an escape is not obliged to desist from efforts to perform such duty, effect such arrest or prevent such escape because of resistance or threatened resistance by or on behalf of the person against whom such action is directed.

(c) Except as required by paragraphs (a) and (b) of this Subsection, a person employing protective force may estimate the necessity thereof under the circumstances as he believes them to be when the force is used, without retreating, surrendering possession, doing any other act which he has no legal duty to do or abstaining from any lawful action.

(3) Use of Confinement as Protective Force. The justification afforded by this Section extends to the use of confinement as protective force only if the actor takes all reasonable measures to terminate the confinement as soon as he knows that he safely can, unless the person confined has been arrested on a charge of crime.[a]

SECTION 5. DEFENSE OF OTHERS

"Ordinarily,—if not always," says Bishop, "one may do in another's defence whatever the other might in the circumstances do for himself."[1] But while this has been repeated now and then[2] it is broader than the special privilege granted to one to use force in the aid of another.[3] This special privilege seems to have had its roots in

1. Bishop, Criminal Law § 877 (9th Ed. 1923).

2. Stanley v. Commonwealth, 86 Ky. 440, 6 S.W. 155 (1887).

3. Morrison v. Commonwealth, 74 S.W. 277, 24 Ky.Law Rep. 2493 (1903); Restatement, Second, Torts § 76 (1965).

the law of property.[4] The privilege of one to protect what is "his" was extended to include the protection of his wife, his children and his servants. In the course of time this privilege outgrew the property analogy and came to be regarded as a "mutual and reciprocal defence."[5] The household was regarded as a group. Any member of the family had the privilege of defending another member; the master could defend the servant, or the servant defend the master.[6] Even this concept of the privilege has been outgrown. It now includes the members of one's immediate family or household and any other whom he is under a legal or socially-recognized duty to protect.[7] Thus a conductor is privileged to defend his passenger, and a person is privileged to defend a friend whom he is with at the moment.[8] The special privilege of using force for the defense of others has now been extended to include even the protection of a stranger.[9]

The privilege to use force in defense of another is subject to the same general limitations and restrictions as the privilege to use force in self-defense. Hence deadly force may not be used to save another from non-deadly force,[10] and even non-deadly force must not be obviously in excess of what is needed for the purpose.[11]

This special privilege to use force in the defense of persons does not supersede the privilege to use force for the prevention of crime. It is in addition thereto.[12] One person may be in a position to claim both privileges.[13] Another may have the benefit of one only,—or of neither.

4. Restatement, Second, Torts § 76, Comment *e* (1965).

5. 3 Bl.Comm. 3.

6. "A man may defend his family, his servants or his master, whenever he may defend himself." Pond v. People, 8 Mich. 150, 176 (1860).

7. Restatement, Second, Torts § 76, Comments *e, f* (1965).

8. Ibid.

9. "It may safely be assumed that at the present day . . . every man has the right of defending any man by reasonable force against unlawful force." Salmond, Torts 375 (11th Ed. 1953).

10. Id. at Comment *b*.

11. Ibid.

12. In a case in which the relation between the parties was not emphasized the court said: "The law makes it the duty of every one, who sees a felony attempted by violence, to prevent it, if possible, and allows him to use the necessary means to make his resistance effectual. One may kill in defense of another under the same circumstances that he would have the right to kill in defense of himself." State v. Hennessey, 29 Nev. 320, 344, 90 P. 221, 227 (1907).

13. "As to the defendant Wendell Reed, the court failed to charge the law with respect to both (a) his right to fight in the necessary defense of his step-father, and (b) his right and duty as a private citizen to interfere to prevent a felonious assault. Each right is recognized in the decisions of this court." State v. Robinson, 213 N.C. 273, 281, 195 S.E. 824, 829–30 (1938).

West's Ann.Cal.Pen.Code, § 197. "Homicide is also justifiable when committed by any person in any of the following cases: . . .

"3. When committed in the lawful defense of . . . a wife or husband, parent, child, master, mistress, or servant of such person, when there is reasonable ground to apprehend a design to commit a felony or to do some great bodily injury, and imminent danger of such design being accomplished; but such person, or the person in whose behalf the defense was made, if he was the assailant or engaged in mutual combat must really and in good faith have endeavored to decline any further

MITCHELL v. STATE

Supreme Court of Florida, 1901.
43 Fla. 188, 30 So. 803.

MABRY, J. Plaintiffs in error were tried and convicted in the Criminal Court of Record for Duval County of the crime of manslaughter, upon an information filed against them in that court charging them with the commission of that offence. They have sued out a writ of error to this court and have specified six assignments of error, only two of which—the fourth and fifth—have been argued. . . .

The fourth assignment of error imputes to the court error in refusing to give the seventh request on behalf of plaintiffs in error. This request sought to have the jury instructed that if they believed from the evidence the defendant Mitchell, at the time he fired the fatal shot that killed the deceased, the latter, from all indications present to the observations of said defendant, was in the act of striking at the sister of defendant with an open knife in an angry manner; and, further, that defendant had good reason to believe and did believe that his sister was then in imminent danger of being killed or of receiving great bodily harm from deceased, then, as matter of law, the defendant had the right to use whatever means he had at command to prevent the infliction of such harm upon his sister, and if in doing so it was necessary to take the life of deceased, defendant would be justified in doing so, and the verdict should be not guilty. The avowed object of this request was to place defendant Mitchell in a position to avail himself of the defence of justifiable homicide embraced in the second head of the second division of section 2378 Revised Statutes, to the effect that a homicide is justifiable when committed not only in lawful defence of the person killing, but also in defence of his or her husband, wife, parent, child, master, mistress, or servant, when there shall be reasonable ground to apprehend a design to commit a felony or to do some great personal injury, and there shall be imminent danger of such design being accomplished. Neither brother nor sister is included among the domestic relations enumerated in the statute in defence of whom life may be taken, not merely when an actual necessity to kill to prevent a felony, but when there shall be reasonable ground to apprehend a design to commit a felony or to do some great personal injury and there shall be imminent danger of such design being accomplished, but we are earnestly requested to include them by construction. In the specific enumeration of the persons in the statute the legislature has employed no terms under which the courts are authorized to include other persons

struggle before the homicide was committed; . . .".

"The statutory justification for the use of deadly force in defense of a person as contained in K.S.A. 21–3211 is to be determined by the trier of fact using an objective standard, i.e., from the viewpoint of a reasonable man in accused's position." State v. Simon, 231 Kan. 572, 646 P.2d 1119 (1982) (Syllabus by the court).

of similar relation, and until the statute is amended, brother and sister cannot be included. We reached this conclusion after mature deliberation in the case of Richard v. State, decided at the last term, and still think our conclusion correct.

At common law any person might take the life of another to prevent him from committing a known forcible felony, and this right is recognized by our statute. By the third head of the second division of section 2378, homicide is justifiable when necessarily committed in attempting by lawful ways and means to apprehend any person for any felony committed, or in lawfully suppressing any riot, or in lawfully keeping and preserving the peace. The felony of unlawfully taking of life or inflicting serious bodily harm is a violent breach of the peace, and it may be prevented by slaying the perpetrator. A brother is not, of course, excluded from the right to slay to prevent the felony upon his sister, as he may to prevent it upon any other person. The right to slay in such case, however, rests upon necessity. It was so at common law when one not assaulted himself slayed to prevent a felony, and our statute expressly provides that homicide is justifiable "when necessarily committed . . . in lawfully suppressing any riot or in lawfully keeping and preserving the peace." When called upon to define the right to slay to prevent a felony by one not himself assaulted or endangered, and not standing within the relations enumerated by the statute, the court should not extend it beyond necessity, and a request broader than this should be refused. In this case the court instructed the jury, at the request of defendants, that the law "permits one who sees another in the act of committing a felony to use every means in his power to prevent its commission, and, if in doing so, it becomes necessary to take the life of the person so offending, the law holds him who so takes human life blameless." According to the testimony in the case the defendants, before Mitchell commenced to shoot at the deceased, were not assaulted or in any way threatened with injury. By the testimony of the State it appeared that deceased and a brother of Mitchell had a difficulty, and also the sister of deceased and the sister of Mitchell had quarreled, and that some ten or fifteen minutes after these disturbances had been stopped and quieted the defendants came up and Mitchell commenced to fire on deceased who was making no demonstrations of harm towards any one at the time. The deceased was shot twice in the back and once in the breast and [died] in a short time thereafter. Witnesses for the defence state that when the defendants came up the deceased was approaching the sister of Mitchell with a drawn knife in his hand and used language indicating a design to kill her. Some of the witnesses say that deceased was five or six feet from Mitchell's sister when the firing commenced, and others indicate that he was still closer. Mitchell said nothing, but entered the field by rapidly firing his pistol at deceased who soon fell mortally wounded. The correct view of the law upon the facts is whether the killing was necessarily done to prevent a felony, and as the seventh request was not entirely consistent with this view it was properly refused.

The next error assigned is that the verdict is not sustained by the evidence. It is conceded that the witnesses in the case for the respective parties are in direct conflict and about equal in number. If the testimony of the State is to be believed, defendants can have no ground of complaint for being convicted of manslaughter. The question of conflict in the evidence was for the jury, and there is no ground for disturbing the verdict on this account. . . .

The judgment must be affirmed, and it is so ordered.[1]

STATE v. BERNARDY

Court of Appeals of Washington, Division 1, 1980.
25 Wn.App. 146, 605 P.2d 791.

ANDERSEN, JUDGE.

FACTS OF CASE

Kenneth Bernardy (defendant) appeals from a jury conviction of second-degree assault and judgment and sentence entered thereon.

On September 4, 1977, Steven Wilson became involved in a fight with Larry Curtis Harrison, a friend of the defendant. Testimony introduced at trial indicated that Wilson started the altercation and then was knocked to the ground by Harrison. While lying on the ground, Wilson was kicked in the head several times by the defendant.

The defendant testified that he kicked Wilson in order to protect his friend, Harrison, because Wilson was trying to get up and another participant, one Greg Gowens, was coming to Wilson's assistance. He also testified that he was wearing tennis shoes at the time. Wilson sustained serious head injuries as a result of the fight.

The defendant argues that he was not afforded effective representation of counsel and that his conviction was not supported by sufficient evidence. Our review of the entire record, including the defend-

1. The Florida statute now provides for a general right of defense as well as a right to prevent the commission of a felony against the person. Fla.Stat.Ann. § 782.02 (1976).

"Thus a wife . . . is entitled to employ force or violence not more than sufficient to ward off an offense against the person of her husband should that offense or assault be unlawful. The same would hold true were she attempting to defend herself or a stranger. However, as with self-defense, so also with the defense of any other one is not justified in using force for protection unless she *reasonably* believes that there is immediate danger of unlawful bodily harm." State v. Grimes, 90 S.D. 43, 237 N.W.2d 900, 902 (1976).

"Although a person had the right to use deadly force to defend his spouse and children as well as himself from the infliction of great bodily injury, the exercise of that right must be grounded upon a reasonable apprehension of imminent harm, and a reasonable belief that the killing is necessary to protect against such injury. I.C. 18–4009 . . . " State v. Carter, 103 Idaho 917, 655 P.2d 434 (1982).

ant's personal restraint petition and his pro se brief, reveals that these contentions are without merit.

The defendant also assigns as error on this appeal that the trial court refused his proposed instruction concerning the legal privilege of defending another.

One issue is determinative.

ISSUE

Should the trial court have instructed the jury regarding the legal privilege of defending another?

DECISION

CONCLUSION. Evidence was presented which, if believed, would have allowed the jury to conclude that the defendant acted reasonably in defense of another. The trial court therefore erred in not instructing the jury on the legal privilege of defending another.

An individual who acts in defense of another person, reasonably believing him to be the innocent party and in danger, is justified in using force necessary to protect that person even if, in fact, the party whom he is defending was the aggressor. If properly requested by the defense, a "defense of others" instruction must be given whenever there is evidence from which the jury could conclude that, under the circumstances, the actor's apprehension of danger and use of force were reasonable.

As to the apprehension of danger in this case, the defendant testified that he believed Gowens was coming to the assistance of Wilson, that Wilson was trying to get up and that together they were a danger to Harrison. With regard to the force used, the defendant testified that he was wearing tennis shoes, used the sides of his feet and did not believe the kicks would cause Wilson any serious damage. Although we are satisfied that the evidence clearly supports the verdict, a trial court is bound to give an instruction on a party's theory of the case when, as in this situation, there is evidence to support it. The failure to do so constitutes reversible error.

Reversed and remanded for a new trial.[a]

JAMES and RINGOLD, JJ., concur.

a. One is privileged to go to the defense of his brother if this reasonably seems to be necessary to save the brother from death or great bodily injury. And in doing so he is not charged with knowledge of the fact that the brother had no privilege to defend himself unless he knew or should have known that his brother was the aggressor. Snell v. State, 29 Tex.App. 236, 15 S.W. 722 (1890).

PEOPLE v. CURTIS

Supreme Court of Michigan, 1884.
52 Mich. 616, 18 N.W. 385.

CAMPBELL, J. Curtis was tried in the Cass county circuit court and convicted of murder in the second degree. Errors are assigned on rulings during the trial and in instructions to the jury. Macon Wilson was the person killed. . . .

The respondent was entitled and bound to take an interest in the life and safety of his brother. There was no difference in the testimony as to his being in danger, and all the instructions which confined the right of respondent to helping him only when he was entirely without fault were unwarranted. The court refused to charge that a brother might interpose against a felonious or serious bodily harm, unless the assailed party was entirely blameless, and this was contrary to the well-settled principle that a dangerous felony may be prevented by one who is not himself in the wrong, directly or by complicity. . . .[1]

The judgment must be reversed and a new trial ordered. The prisoner must be remanded to the custody of the sheriff of Cass county, and must be allowed bail if he desires it, in a moderate amount.

The other Justices concurred.

MODEL PENAL CODE

Section 3.05 Use of Force for the Protection of Other Persons.

(1) Subject to the provisions of this Section and of Section 3.09, the use of force upon or toward the person of another is justifiable to protect a third person when:

(a) the actor would be justified under Section 3.04 in using such force to protect himself against the injury he believes to be threatened to the person whom he seeks to protect; and

(b) under the circumstances as the actor believes them to be, the person whom he seeks to protect would be justified in using such protective force; and

(c) the actor believes that his intervention is necessary for the protection of such other person.

(2) Nothwithstanding Subsection (1) of this Section:

(a) when the actor would be obliged under Section 3.04 to retreat, to surrender the possession of a thing or to comply with a demand before using force in self-protection, he is not obliged to do so before using force for the protection of another person, unless he knows that he can thereby secure the complete safety of such other person; and

1. One may kill if necessary to save his brother's life even if the latter started the difficulty unless he did so with felonious intent. Little v. State, 87 Miss. 512, 40 So. 165 (1906).

(b) when the person whom the actor seeks to protect would be obliged under Section 3.04 to retreat, to surrender the possession of a thing or to comply with a demand if he knew that he could obtain complete safety by so doing, the actor is obliged to try to cause him to do so before using force in his protection if the actor knows that he can obtain complete safety in that way; and

(c) neither the actor nor the person whom he seeks to protect is obliged to retreat when in the other's dwelling or place of work to any greater extent than in his own.[a]

SECTION 6. DEFENSE OF THE HABITATION

The concept of a man's habitation as his "castle" runs throughout the law and the privilege of defending the habitation must not be confused with the privilege of defending property which stands upon a much lower level. At common law the dweller is privileged to use deadly force if this reasonably seems necessary to prevent the commission or consummation of burglary. At this point no greater advantage is given than would be available under the privilege of crime prevention—the prevention of an atrocious felony or a so-called dangerous felony of which burglary is a typical example. And the same may be said of the dweller's privilege to use deadly force if this reasonably seems necessary to save his habitation from arson.

The defense of the dwelling may be for the purpose of saving the house itself from damage or destruction,[1] or it may be to preserve its character as a place of refuge and repose by preventing the unlawful intrusion of outsiders. The dweller is privileged to use reasonable nondeadly force to prevent any unlawful harm or injury to his place of abode, or to prevent any unlawful intrusion therein. The dweller is not privileged to use deadly force to prevent any and every trespass to the dwelling, but although there is authority otherwise [a] the trend seems to be in the direction of holding that an unlawful entry of the dwelling for the purpose of an assault upon any person therein may be resisted by deadly force if this reasonably seems necessary for the purpose, "although the circumstances may not be such as to justify a belief that there was actual peril of life or great bodily harm." [b]

1. Where there was evidence that D acted in defense of his home, an instruction on his right to act in self-defense without an instruction also on his right to act in defense of his home was prejudicial error. State v. Edwards, 28 N.C.App. 196, 220 S.E.2d 158 (1975).

a. Carroll v. State, 23 Ala. 28 (1853).

b. People v. Eastman, 405 Ill. 491, 498, 91 N.E. 387, 390 (1950). Accord, Leverette v. State, 104 Ga.App. 743, 122 S.E.2d 745 (1961).

"The doctrine of the right to protect one's habitation gives no moral right to kill another, unless necessity, or apparent necessity, for purposes countenanced by law exists, . . .

STATE v. MITCHESON

Supreme Court of Utah, 1977.
560 P.2d 1120.

CROCKETT, JUSTICE. The defendant, Gary Alfred Mitcheson, was convicted of murder in the second degree for shooting Richard Herrera in the front yard of 432 South Fourth East, Price, Utah, at about 3:30 a.m. on February 7, 1976. He was sentenced to a term of five years to life in the state prison.

On his appeal the point of critical concern is his charge that the trial court erred in refusing his request to instruct the jury on the defense of using force in the protection of one's habitation.

The deceased, Richard Herrera, sold his car (a 1967 Chevrolet van) to Alfred Mitcheson, defendant's father, on December 15, 1975. The original wheels and tires had been changed for what are called "Mag Wheels" and tires, which have a wider tread. Some time after the father had taken possession of the van, a dispute arose between the parties over those wheels. The father, supported by the defendant, claimed that they had been included in the sale, but the deceased and his brother, Ernie Herrera, claimed they only agreed to loan the "Mag Wheels" and tires temporarily.

On several occasions in January, 1976, the two brothers requested that the wheels and tires be returned, but the defendant and his father did not comply. On one of those occasions the Herrera brothers and some friends went to the father's home to remove the wheels. The father protested and called the police. When they arrived they told the Herreras, the deceased and his brother, to leave the wheels alone and that any disagreement should be settled by going to court.

A few days thereafter, on February 6, 1976, the defendant was parked in the van at a drive-in restaurant when the deceased came up to the van, opened the door and hit the defendant on the jaw and eye; and made threats to the defendant to the effect that I will "put you under." A couple of hours later the defendant and some of his friends went to the home of Jerry Giraud, where they saw the deceased's car parked. There was a conversation in which the defendant offered to fight the deceased, which was then refused. But, they agreed to meet in the town park and fight at 2:00 o'clock the next afternoon.

Defendant and his friend, Wendell Johnson, drove to his father's house, where the defendant obtained a rifle. He and Johnson then arranged for a poker game to be held at the home of defendant's sister, Debbie, and went there in the van where they proceeded to play cards. Still later that night, at about 3:30 a.m., the deceased, Richard Herrera, and some of his friends drove up to this house for the stated purpose of removing the wheels from the van. When they entered upon her premises Debbie told them to leave. They did not comply. A considerable commotion ensued, including her screaming at them to get off her premises. Defendant came to the doorway of the house with the rifle. He fired a shot and Richard Herrera fell with a bullet wound in his neck from which he shortly expired.

The essence of the defense, and the basis for the requested instructions, was that the defendant was using the rifle as a backup resource in protection of the peace and security of his habitation and that its discharge and the striking of the deceased was an accident. The argument that the defendant was not entitled to that instruction is: (1) that the sister's home was not his habitation; . . .

Defense of Habitation

The pertinent statute is 76–2–405, U.C.A. 1953, which provides in part:

> A person is justified in using force against another when and to the extent that he reasonably believes . . . necessary to prevent . . . other's unlawful entry into or attack upon his habitation; however, he is justified in the use of force which is intended to cause death or serious bodily injury only if:
>
> (1) The entry is made or attempted in a violent and tumultuous manner and he reasonably believes that the entry is attempted or made for the purpose of assaulting or offering personal violence to any person, dwelling or being therein . . . .

That statute has its roots in the ancient and honored doctrine of the common law that a man's home is his castle, and that even the peasant in his cottage, may peaceably abide within the protective cloak of the law, and no one, not even the king nor all his armies can enter to disturb him.[2]

In view of the salutary purpose of that statute, of preserving the peace and good order of society, it should be interpreted and applied in the broad sense to accomplish that purpose. Thus it would include not only a person's actual residence, but also whatever place he may be occupying peacefully as a substitute home or habitation, such as a hotel, motel, or even where he is a guest in the home of another;[4] and so would apply to the defendant in his sister's home. . . .

2. See Semayne's Case (1604) 5 Coke 91, 77 Eng. Reprint 194, where it was stated that "the house of everyone is to him his castle and fortress, as well for his defense against injury and violence, as for his repose; and although the life of a man is a thing precious and favored in law . . . if thieves come to a man's house to rob him, or murder, and the owner or his servants kill any of the thieves in defense of himself and his house, it is not felony and he shall lose nothing . . . (citing other older authorities)."

4. As to the guest in another's home, see State v. Osborne, 200 S.C. 504, 21 S.E.2d 178 (1942).

The right of defendant, in other words, was limited (1) to the protection of himself, (2) to prevent a felony in the bedroom and, probably, (3) to prevent the deceased from entering that room at all." State v. Sorrentino, 31 Wyo, 129, 137–38, 224 P. 420, 422 (1924).

In a criminal case the defendant need not specially plead his defenses. The entry of a plea of not guilty places upon the State the burden of proving every element of the offense beyond a reasonable doubt. This gives the defendant the benefit of every defense thereto which may cause a reasonable doubt to exist as to his guilt, arising either from the evidence, or lack of evidence, in the case; and this is true whether his defenses are consistent or not.

On the basis of what has been said herein, it is our opinion that if the requested instruction had been given and the jury had so considered the evidence, there is a reasonable likelihood that it may have had some effect upon the verdict rendered. Therefore the defendant's request should have been granted. Accordingly, it is necessary that the judgment be reversed.

SECTION 7. DEFENSE OF PROPERTY

Criminal cases, in which defense of property has been relied upon as an exculpating circumstance, have seldom been entirely divorced from some other privilege, such as self-defense, crime prevention, or defense of habitation,[1] and the fact that the exercise of such other privilege may result incidentally in the protection of property, does not in any way narrow its scope. Hence property protection is usually overshadowed by self-defense, crime prevention or even the privilege of arrest. In fact, the chief importance of the privilege of protecting property is frequently that its exercise does not make one an "aggressor", or in any way at fault, and hence leaves all other privileges unimpaired.[2]

One is privileged to use nondeadly force when this reasonably appears to be necessary to protect his property, real or personal, from unprivileged interference by another,—provided he does not employ more force than reasonably appears to be necessary for the purpose.[3]

1. For example, State v. Pollard, 139 Mo. 220, 40 S.W. 949 (1897).

2. Ayers v. State, 60 Miss. 709 (1883).

3. Restatement, Second, Torts § 77 (1965). No force is privileged if a mere request would obviously be sufficient. Ibid.

"A man may use force to defend his real or personal property in his actual possession against one who endeavors to dispossess him with right, taking care that the force used does not exceed what reasonably appears to be necessary for the purpose of defense and prevention." Carpenter v. State, 62 Ark. 286, 310, 36 S.W. 900, 907 (1896). And see Turpen v. State, 89 Okl.Cr. 6, 204 P.2d 298 (1949).

If the reasonable use of nondeadly force unexpectedly results in accidental death, it does not constitute criminal homicide. Morgan v. Durfee, 69 Mo. 469 (1897); Hinchcliffe's Case, 1 Lewin 161, 168 Eng.Rep. 998 (1823).

It was held unreasonable to beat an old man with a cane merely because he was picking a few flowers. Chapell v. Schmidt, 104 Cal. 511, 58 P. 892 (1894).

The owner may use reasonable force to eject a trespasser from his home, after notice to withdraw is ignored. Phelps v. Arnold, 112 Cal.App. 518, 297 P. 31 (1931).

A kick is not a justifiable mode of putting a mere trespasser out of the house and death resulting from such unreasonable force is criminal homicide. Wild's Case, 2 Lewin 214, 168 Eng.Rep. 1132 (1837), and see Fortune v. Commonwealth, 133 Va. 669, 112 S.E. 861 (1922).

There is no justification for an assault in revenge for the breaking of a mirror, after the harm has been done. State v.

This privilege does not include the use of deadly force, at least if the habitation is not involved, even if the trespass cannot be prevented otherwise.[4] Bishop says, "it may now be deemed reasonably clear that, to prevent an unlawful entrance into a dwelling-house, the occupant may make defence to the taking of life, without being liable even for manslaughter." [5] But this seems not to be the accepted view where the defender has no reason to fear that the trespasser intends to commit a felony or to inflict personal harm upon him or some other person in the house.[6] Clearly, if the defender reasonably believes that the intruder intends to kill him, or to inflict great bodily harm upon him, or upon anyone else in the house, he may make his defense at the threshold.[7] He is not bound to stay the use of deadly force until the other has gained the advantage of an entrance. But

Allen, 131 W.Va. 667, 49 S.E.2d 847 (1948).

4. Turpen v. State, 89 Okl.Cr. 6, 204 P.2d 298 (1949); State v. Patterson, 45 Vt. 308 (1873).

"But, in the absence of an attempt to commit a felony, he cannot defend his property, except his habitation, to the extent of killing the aggressor for the purpose of preventing the trespass; and if he should do so, he would be guilty of a felonious homicide." Carpenter v. State, 62 Ark. 286, 310, 36 S.W. 900, 907 (1896).

"Life being superior to property, no one has the right to kill in defence of the latter; yet by less extreme means, one may defend his own." 2 Bishop, Criminal Law § 706 (9th ed. 1923).

The defendant drew a knife which he threatened to use (but did not use) in defense of his property. A conviction of assault was reversed on the ground that a *threat* to use a weapon may be privileged when its actual use would not be. State v. Yancey, 74 N.C. 244 (1876). See State v. Realina, 1 Hawaii App. 167, 616 P.2d 229 (1980).

The court said, *obiter*, that death resulting from the accidental discharge of a gun used only as a bluff, would not necessarily be criminal. People v. Hubbard, 64 Cal.App. 27, 220 P. 315 (1923).

5. 2 Bishop, Criminal Law § 707 (9th ed. 1923).

In speaking of the conduct of the prosecuting witness the court said: "It was his house and he had a right to protect it against any peace-disturbing, profane intruder, even if necessary to the taking of his life." State v. Raper, 141 Mo. 327, 329, 42 S.W. 935, 936 (1897). The knife had actually been drawn but not used except as a bluff.

In affirming a conviction of murder for the shooting of a trespasser who refused to leave the house, the court said *obiter* that one may prevent an aggressor from entering his home when the door is closed, even to the extent of killing him. Russell v. State, 219 Ala. 567, 122 So. 683 (1929).

6. Carroll v. State, 23 Ala. 28 (1853); Miller v. Commonwealth, 188 Ky. 435, 222 S.W. 96 (1920); State v. Taylor, 143 Mo. 150, 44 S.W. 785 (1898); State v. Patterson, 45 Vt. 308 (1873).

"One is no more privileged to use such force to prevent another from intruding upon his dwelling place than he is to use similar force to prevent the other from intruding upon his possession of any other land. In either case, he may use such force if the intrusion threatens death or serious bodily harm to the occupiers or users of the land." Restatement, Second, Torts § 79, Comment *d* (1965).

"The broad rule invoked that one is justified in killing to prevent entrance of his residence against his protest is approved in this State in accordance with the weight of authority, subject to the qualification that the entrance is either with a felonious purpose to do bodily harm, or under circumstances justifying a reasonable apprehension of such purpose." Wooten v. State, 171 Tenn. 362, 365, 103 S.W.2d 324, 325 (1937).

"He can kill intentionally only in defense of life or person, or to prevent a felony." People v. Hubbard, 64 Cal.App. 27, 35, 220 P. 315, 319 (1923).

7. Bailey v. People, 54 Colo. 337, 130 P. 832 (1913); Cooper's Case, Cro.Car. 554, 79 Eng.Rep. 1069 (K.B.1639).

the accepted view does not permit the use of deadly force merely to prevent a relatively unimportant trespass, even if it takes the form of an entrance of the dwelling. The difference between this and Bishop's view is not so wide as might seem at first glance. When an intruder insists upon an unlawful entrance into the building with such violence that only deadly force can stop him, the defender will usually have good reason to fear for his safety or the safety of others. And no more than this is needed for his privilege to use deadly force. But he might know the facts to be otherwise. A householder who is on the outside, for example, and too far away at the moment to make use of nondeadly force would not be privileged to shoot to prevent the entrance of one he knew did not intend to commit a felony or to inflict personal harm.[8]

Deadly force is privileged, if apparently necessary, not only to prevent a felonious intrusion of the dwelling house, but also to prevent a felonious attack upon the house itself, such as an attempt to commit arson or malicious mischief.[9] But in all such cases the privilege is rather that of crime prevention than property protection.[10]

COMMONWEALTH v. DONAHUE

Supreme Judicial Court of Massachusetts, 1889.
148 Mass. 529, 20 N.E. 171.

HOLMES, J. This is an indictment for robbery, on which the defendant has been found guilty of an assault. The evidence for the Commonwealth was, that the defendant had bought clothes, amounting to twenty-one dollars and fifty-five cents, of one Mitchelman, who called at the defendant's house, by appointment, for his pay; that some discussion arose about the bill, and that the defendant went upstairs, brought down the clothes, placed them on a chair, and put twenty dollars on a table, and told Mitchelman that he could have the money or the clothes; that Mitchelman took the money and put it in his pocket, and told the defendant he owed him one dollar and fifty-five cents, whereupon the defendant demanded his money back, and, on Mitchelman refusing, attacked him, threw him on the floor, and choked him until Mitchelman gave him a pocket-book containing twenty-nine dollars. The defendant's counsel denied the receiving of the pocket-book, and said that he could show that the assault was justifiable, under the circumstances of the case, as the defendant believed that he had a right to recover his own money by force, if neces-

8. "A comes to B's premises during a severe storm and asks permission to take shelter in B's dwelling house. B refuses to permit him to do so, although he knows that A neither intends nor is likely to harm any person or thing in the house. A, a much larger man than B, attempts to overcome B's resistance by physical force which B is unable to resist except by shooting A. B is not privileged to do so to prevent A from entering his dwelling place." Restatement, Second, Torts § 79, Illustration 1 (1965).

9. State v. Couch, 52 N.M. 127, 193 P.2d 405 (1948).

10. Restatement, Second, Torts § 79, Comment *c* (1965).

sary. The presiding justice stated that he should be obliged to rule, that the defendant would not be justified in assaulting Mitchelman to get his own money, and that he should rule as follows: "If the jury are satisfied that the defendant choked and otherwise assaulted Mitchelman, they would be warranted in finding the defendant guilty, although the sole motive of the defendant was by this violence to get from Mitchelman by force money which the defendant honestly believed to be his own." Upon this the defendant saved his exceptions, and declined to introduce evidence; the jury were instructed as stated, and found the defendant guilty.

On the evidence for the Commonwealth, it appeared, or at the lowest the jury might have found, that the defendant offered the twenty dollars to Mitchelman only on condition that Mitchelman should accept that sum as full payment of his disputed bill, and that Mitchelman took the money, and at the same moment, or just afterwards, as part of the same transaction, repudiated the condition. If this was the case,—since Mitchelman, of course, whatever the sum due him, had no right to that particular money except on the conditions on which it was offered, Commonwealth v. Stebbins, 8 Gray 492,—he took the money wrongfully from the possession of the defendant, or the jury might have found that he did, whether the true view be that the defendant did not give up possession, or that it was obtained from him by Mitchelman's fraud. . . .

It is settled by ancient and modern authority, that, under such circumstances, a man may defend or regain his momentarily interrupted possession by the use of reasonable force, short of wounding or the employment of a dangerous weapon. . . . To this extent the right to protect one's possession has been regarded as an extension of the right to protect one's person, with which it is generally mentioned. . . .

We need not consider whether this explanation is quite adequate. There are weighty decisions which go further than those above cited, and which hardly can stand on the right of self-defence, but involve other considerations of policy. It has been held, that, even where a considerable time had elapsed between the wrongful taking of the defendant's property and the assault, the defendant had a right to regain possession by reasonable force, after demand upon the third person in possession, in like manner as he might have protected it without civil liability. Whatever the true rule may be, probably there is no difference in this respect between the civil and the criminal law. The principle has been extended to a case where the defendant had yielded possession to the person assaulted, through the fraud of the latter. On the other hand, a distinction has been taken between the right to maintain possession and the right to regain it from another who is peaceably established in it, although the possession of the latter is wrongful. It is unnecessary to decide whether, in this case, if Mitchelman had taken the money with a fraudulent intent, but had not repudiated the condition until afterwards, the defendant would have had any other remedy than to hold him to his bargain if he could, even if he knew that Mitchelman still had the identical money upon his person.

If the force used by the defendant was excessive, the jury would have been warranted in finding him guilty. Whether it was excessive or not was a question for them; the judge could not rule that it was not, as matter of law. Therefore the instruction given to them, taken only literally, was correct. But the preliminary statement went further, and was erroneous; and coupling that statement with the defendant's offer of proof, and his course after the rulings, we think if fair to assume that the instruction was not understood to be limited, or, indeed, to be directed to the case of excessive force, which, so far as appears, had not been mentioned, but that it was intended and understood to mean that any assault to regain his own money would warrant finding the defendant guilty. Therefore the exceptions must be sustained.

It will be seen that our decision is irrespective of the defendant's belief as to what he had a right to do. . . . There is no question here of the effect of a reasonable but mistaken belief with regard to the facts. The facts were as defendant believed them to be.

Exceptions sustained.[1]

PEOPLE v. CEBALLOS

Supreme Court of California, In Bank, 1974.
12 Cal.3d 470, 116 Cal.Rptr. 233, 526 P.2d 241.

[This is the case, supra p. 742, in which a conviction of assault with a deadly weapon was affirmed. In the daytime, when no one else was near, two boys with larceny in mind, attempted to force open the door of a garage and one was shot in the face by a trap-gun that had been set by defendant to keep out intruders. Defendant's claim that the use of deadly force in this case was within the privilege of crime prevention, was rejected. The privilege of protecting property was not raised by defendant.]

BURKE, JUSTICE. . . .

Defendant also does not, and could not properly, contend that the intrusion was in fact such that, were he present, he would be justified

1. "Force may be used by the owner to retake property from a person who has obtained possession of it by force or fraud and is overtaken while carrying it away." Riffel v. Letts, 31 Cal.App. 426, 428, 160 P. 845, 846 (1916).

The Iowa Criminal Code Sec. 704.4, provides that a "person is justified in the use of reasonable force to prevent or terminate criminal interference with his or her possession or other right in property." It was held that this has no application to a defendant who has, at an earlier time been deprived of possession of his property by a wrongful taking committed out of his presence, and who then attempts by use of force to recover the property, although it is elsewhere. State v. Nelson, 329 N.W.2d 643 (Iowa 1983).

under Civil Code section 50 in using deadly force. That section provides, "Any necessary force may be used to protect from wrongful injury the person or property of oneself. . . . ." This section also should be read in the light of the common law, and at common law in general deadly force could not be used solely for for the protection of property. (See Model Penal Code, supra, § 3.06, com. 8; Perkins on Criminal Law, supra, p. 1026, fn. 6; 13 Stan.L.Rev. 566, 575–576.) " 'The preservation of human life and limb from grievous harm is of more importance to society than the protection of property.' " Thus defendant was not warranted under Civil Code section 50 in using deadly force to protect his personal property.

The opinion of Justice McKee in Dinan v. Fitz Gibbon, 63 Cal. 387, contains language indicating that deadly force, if necessary, may be used to protect property against a trespasser. However, the other justices concurred in the judgment on the ground of an error in instructions and did not give their approval to that language. Thus Justice McKee's language has no controlling weight.

At common law an exception to the foregoing principle that deadly force could not be used solely for the protection of property was recognized where the property was a dwelling house in some circumstances. (See Simpson v. State, supra, 59 Ala. 1, 14; Perkins on Criminal Law, supra, pp. 1022–1025; Model Penal Code, supra, § 3.06, com. 8, pp. 38–41.) "According to the older interpretation of the common law, even extreme force may be used to prevent dispossession [of the dwelling house]." (See Model Penal Code, supra, com. 8.) Also at common law if another attempted to burn a dwelling the owner was privileged to use deadly force if this seemed necessary to defend his "castle" against the threatened harm. Further, deadly force was privileged if it was, or reasonably seemed, necessary to protect the dwelling against a burglar. (See Perkins on Criminal Law, supra, p. 1023.)

Here we are not concerned with dispossession or burning of a dwelling, and, as heretofore concluded, the asserted burglary in this case was not of such a charcter as to warrant the use of deadly force. . . .[1]

1. Defendant set a spring gun in an unoccupied building with the intent to kill anyone who should force an entrance. This was done to protect his furniture. Two brothers went to this building and one of them gained an entrance, merely to satisfy his curiosity, by breaking the lock. He was killed by the spring gun as he entered. A conviction of manslaughter was affirmed. State v. Green, 118 S.C. 279, 110 S.E. 145 (1921). See also Falco v. State, 407 So.2d 203 (Fla.1981).

The privilege to use deadly force by means of a spring gun, to protect property, is measured by the extent of the privilege the owner would have to use deadly force for this purpose, in person, if he were present. Restatement, Second, Torts, § 85 (1965).

A spring gun placed in a trunk in such a manner as to kill anyone who opened it, caused the death of a maid who looked in just as a matter of curiosity. A conviction of murder was reversed because the judge had approved the view of the prosecuting attorney that killing by means of a spring gun is privileged only to prevent the commission of a capital crime. State v. Marfaudille, 48 Wash. 117, 92 P. 939 (1907).

MODEL PENAL CODE

Section 3.06 Use of Force for the Protection of Property.

(1) Use of Force Justifiable for Protection of Property. Subject to the provisions of this Section and of Section 3.09, the use of force upon or toward the person of another is justifiable when the actor believes that such force is immediately necessary:

(a) to prevent or terminate an unlawful entry or other trespass upon land or a trespass against or the unlawful carrying away of tangible, movable property, provided that such land or movable property is, or is believed by the actor to be, in his possession or in the possession of another person for whose protection he acts; or

(b) to effect an entry or re-entry upon land or to retake tangible movable property, provided that the actor believes that he or the person by whose authority he acts or a person from whom he or such other person derives title was unlawfully dispossessed of such land or movable property and is entitled to possession, and provided, further, that:

(i) the force is used immediately or on fresh pursuit after such dispossession; or

(ii) the actor believes that the person against whom he uses force has no claim of right to the possession of the property and, in the case of land, the circumstances, as the actor believes them to be, are of such urgency that it would be an exceptional hardship to postpone the entry or re-entry until a court order is obtained.

(2) Meaning of Possession. . . .

(3) Limitations on Justifiable Use of Force.

(a) Request to Desist. The use of force is justifiable under this Section only if the actor first requests the person against whom such force is used to desist from his interference with the property, unless the actor believes that:

(i) such request would be useless; or

(ii) it would be dangerous to himself or another person to make the request; or

The setting of spring guns in open fields or outhouses, not within the curtilage of the dwelling house, without notice, will not justify or excuse resulting homicide. United States v. Gilliam, 25 Fed.Cas.1319, No. 15,205a (1882).

A trespasser in a vineyard, who was injured by a spring gun, was entitled to damages. Hooker v. Miller, 37 Iowa 613 (1873).

If one sets a deadly spring gun on open land and thereby kills a trespasser it is criminal homicide. But a device set merely to alarm a trespasser or to inflict slight chastisement is privileged. Simpson v. State, 59 Ala. 1 (1877).

A statute provided that whoever set a spring gun for the purpose of killing game "or for any other purpose" should be guilty of manslaughter in the second degree if it caused the death of any human being. Defendant set a spring gun in his orchard to prevent persons from stealing his apples. A trespasser, who pulled the wire just out of curiosity, was killed. The court affirmed a conviction of second degree murder. Schmidt v. State, 159 Wis. 15, 149 N.W. 388 (1914).

(iii) substantial harm will be done to the physical condition of the property which is sought to be protected before the request can effectively be made.

(b) Exclusion of Trespasser. The use of force to prevent or terminate a trespass is not justifiable under this Section if the actor knows that the exclusion of the trespasser will expose him to substantial danger of serious bodily harm.

(c) Resistance of Lawful Re-entry or Recaption. . . .

(d) Use of Deadly Force. The use of deadly force is not justifiable under this Section unless the actor believes that:

(i) the person against whom the force is used is attempting to dispossess him of his dwelling otherwise than under a claim of right to its possession; or

(ii) the person against whom the force is used is attempting to commit or consummate arson, burglary, robbery or other felonious theft or property destruction and either:

(1) has employed or threatened deadly force against or in the presence of the actor; or

(2) the use of force other than deadly force to prevent the commission or the consummation of the crime would expose the actor or another in his presence to substantial danger of serious bodily harm.

(4) Use of Confinement as Protective Force. . . .

(5) Use of Device to Protect Property. The justification afforded by this Section extends to the use of a device for the purpose of protecting property only if:

(a) the device is not designed to cause or known to create a substantial risk of causing death or serious bodily harm; and

(b) the use of the particular device to protect the property from entry or trespass is reasonable under the circumstances, as the actor believes them to be; and

(c) the device is one customarily used for such a purpose or reasonable care is taken to make known to probable intruders the fact that it is used.

(6) Use of Force to Pass Wrongful Obstructor. . . .[1]

SECTION 8. ENTRAPMENT

Officers have sometimes gone too far in their zeal to secure convictions,—so far, in fact, as to defeat their own purpose. The most obvious cases are those in which the plot to trap an offender has been laid in such a manner as to leave out some element essential to guilt. In one case, for example, officers planned to catch the person who had been aiding prisoners of war to escape. A prisoner, who was willing to cooperate with the officers, was directed what to do. The

1. Copyright 1962 by the American Law Institute. Reprinted with the permission of the American Law Institute.

defendant took this prisoner, in her vehicle, beyond the ordinary prison limits to a point where she was arrested under the prearranged plan. A conviction of aiding a prisoner of war to escape was held to be improper because there had been no escape,—since the prisoner had gone only where he was directed to go by those in charge.[1] Furthermore a detective who seemingly joins a criminal venture, not to promote its success but to secure evidence of the crime, is not a real conspirator and his acts cannot be imputed to the others.[2] And if such a detective himself unlocks and opens the door through which the others enter there can be no conviction of common-law burglary. Since his intent was to frustrate the crime, he is not guilty. And since he is not guilty, his opening of the door cannot be imputed to the others and hence an essential element of common-law burglary is lacking.[3] Or if a detective placed an obstruction on a railroad track, with authority from the company and with the intent to remove it before any harm was done, which he did, another could not properly be convicted on the theory that he was present aiding and abetting the commission of a crime.[4]

More difficult are those cases in which every element of the offense is present but it is claimed that there should be no conviction because of "entrapment" by a public officer. Providing an opportunity for those criminally inclined to perpetrate an offense in the presence of an officer will not bar conviction. It is no defense to an indictment for larceny, for example, that the money was stolen from a constable who feigned drunkenness with the intention of making an arrest if his money should be taken.[5]

The distinction is between detection and instigation. Traps may be laid or "decoys" employed to secure the conviction of those who intend to commit crime; but the zeal for enforcement must not induce officers to implant criminal ideas in innocent minds.[6] And for some reason the word "entrapment," which might well refer to the former situation, has come to be applied only the second.[7]

1. Rex v. Martin, Russ. and R.C.C. 196, 168 Eng.Rep. 757 (1811).

2. State v. Neely, 90 Mont. 199, 300 P. 561 (1931).

"The defendant is not to be charged with what was done by the detective, as the two were not acting together for a common purpose." State v. Currie, 13 N.D. 655, 661, 102 N.W. 875, 877 (1905).

In a jurisdiction that recognizes a unilateral conspiracy the result may be different. State v. La Forge, 183 N.J. Super. 118, 443 A.2d 269 (1981).

3. Love v. People, 160 Ill. 501, 43 N.E. 710 (1896).

An even clearer case was the one where the "burglar" waited on the outside while a supposed accomplice, acting under directions of the sheriff, opened the door, went in, took some money, marked it so it could be identified, and then went out and delivered it. People v. Collins, 53 Cal. 185 (1878).

4. State v. Douglass, 44 Kan. 618, 26 P. 476 (1890).

5. People v. Hanselman, 76 Cal. 460, 18 P. 425 (1888).

6. "Decoys are permissible to entrap criminals, but not to create them; . . . ." United States v. Healy, 202 F. 349 (D.C.Mont.1913).

7. "Entrapment is the conception and planning of an offense by an officer and his procurement of its commission by one who would not have perpetrated it except for the trickery, persuasion, or fraud of

The mere fact that officers have led the defendant to furnish a specific instance of an habitual course of criminal conduct is not a defense.[8] Thus one may be convicted of using the United States mails to give information telling where obscene matter can be obtained, although his letter was in response to a request written by a post office inspector under a fictitious name.[9] And evidence of liquor purchased by officers may be used to convict the seller of a violation of the prohibition law.[10]

Recently, a minority of courts have adopted a concept of entrapment that focuses on the conduct of the police rather than the predisposition of the offender.[11] If police employ methods of persuasion of inducement which create a substantial risk that an offense will be committed by persons other than those who are ready to commit it the defense of entrapment is available.[12]

UNITED STATES v. RUSSELL

Supreme Court of the United States, 1973.
411 U.S. 423, 93 S.Ct. 1637.

MR. JUSTICE REHNQUIST delivered the opinion of the Court.

Respondent Richard Russell was charged in three counts of a five-count indictment returned against him and codefendants John and Patrick Connolly. After a jury trial in the District Court, in which his sole defense was entrapment, respondent was convicted on all three counts of having unlawfully manufactured and processed methamphetamine ("speed") and of having unlawfully sold and delivered that drug in violation of 21 U.S.C. §§ 331(q)(1), (2), 360a(a), (b)

the officer." People v. Lindsey, 91 Cal. App.2d 914, 916, 205 P.2d 1114, 1115 (1949). "The law does not frown upon the entrapment of a criminal but will not tolerate the seduction of innocent people into a career of crime by its officers." People v. Crawford, 105 Cal.App.2d 530, 536, 537, 234 P.2d 181, 185 (1951).

A conviction was reversed because of evidence that an immigration officer had suggested to defendant a plan to bring Chinese over the border illegally. Woo Wai v. United States, 223 F. 412, 137 C.C.A. 604 (9th Cir. 1915).

The Iowa court refused to reverse a conviction of burglary, although the plan had been suggested to defendant by a constable. But the court expressed disapproval of the practice and reduced the sentence from three years to six months. State v. Abley, 109 Iowa 61, 80 N.W. 225 (1899).

Compare Saunders v. People, 18 Mich. 218 (1878). In this case a policeman complied with defendant's request to leave a door to the courthouse unlocked so the defendant could remove public records. The officer had communicated the request to his superiors and had been directed to comply. This practice was denounced by the court, and two of the judges apparently would have been willing to reverse the conviction on this ground alone.

8. People v. Lindsey, 91 Cal.App.2d 914, 205 P.2d 1114 (1949).

9. Grimm v. United States, 156 U.S. 604, 15 S.Ct. 470, 39 L.Ed. 550 (1895).

10. Moss v. State, 4 Okl.Cr. 247, 111 P. 950 (1910).

11. People v. Barraza, 23 Cal.3d 675, 153 Cal.Rptr. 459, 591 P.2d 947 (1979); State v. Provard, 63 Hawaii 536, 631 P.2d 181 (1981); State v. Mullen, 216 N.W.2d 375 (Iowa 1974); People v. Turner, 390 Mich. 7, 210 N.W.2d 336 (1973); State v. Taylor, 599 P.2d 496 (Utah 1979).

12. Model Penal Code § 2.13(1)(b).

(1964 ed., Supp. V). He was sentenced to concurrent terms of two years in prison for each offense, the terms to be suspended on the condition that he spend six months in prison and be placed on probation for the following three years. On appeal, the United States Court of Appeals for the Ninth Circuit, one judge dissenting, reversed the conviction solely for the reason that an undercover agent supplied an essential chemical for manufacturing the methamphetamine which formed the basis of respondent's conviction. The court concluded that as a matter of law "a defense to a criminal charge may be founded upon an intolerable degree of governmental participation in the criminal enterprise." 459 F.2d 671, 673 (1972). We granted certiorari, and now reverse that judgment.

There is little dispute concerning the essential facts in this case. On December 7, 1969, Joe Shapiro, an undercover agent for the Federal Bureau of Narcotics and Dangerous Drugs, went to respondent's home on Whidbey Island in the State of Washington where he met with respondent and his two codefendants, John and Patrick Connolly. Shapiro's assignment was to locate a laboratory where it was believed that methamphetamine was being manufactured illicitly. He told the respondent and the Connollys that he represented an organization in the Pacific Northwest that was interested in controlling the manufacture and distribution of methamphetamine. He then made an offer to supply the defendants with the chemical phenyl-2-propanone, an essential ingredient in the manufacture of methamphetamine, in return for one-half of the drug produced. This offer was made on the condition that Agent Shapiro be shown a sample of the drug which they were making and the laboratory where it was being produced.

During the conversation, Patrick Connolly revealed that he had been making the drug since May 1969 and since then had produced three pounds of it.[2] John Connolly gave the agent a bag containing a quantity of methamphetamine that he represented as being from "the last batch that we made." Shortly thereafter, Shapiro and Patrick Connolly left respondent's house to view the laboratory which was located in the Connolly house on Whidbey Island. At the house, Shapiro observed an empty bottle bearing the chemical label phenyl-2-propanone.

By prearrangement, Shapiro returned to the Connolly house on December 9, 1969, to supply 100 grams of propanone and observe the manufacturing process. When he arrived he observed Patrick Connolly and the respondent cutting up pieces of aluminum foil and placing them in a large flask. There was testimony that some of the foil pieces accidentally fell on the floor and were picked up by the respondent and Shapiro and put into the flask.[3] Thereafter, Patrick Connol-

2. At trial Patrick Connolly admitted making this statement to Agent Shapiro but asserted that the statement was not true.

3. Agent Shapiro did not otherwise participate in the manufacture of the drug or direct any of the work.

ly added all of the necessary chemicals, including the propanone brought by Shapiro, to make two batches of methamphetamine. The manufacturing process having been completed the following morning, Shapiro was given one-half of the drug and respondent kept the remainder. Shapiro offered to buy, and the respondent agreed to sell, part of the remainder for $60.

About a month later, Shapiro returned to the Connolly house and met with Patrick Connolly to ask if he was still interested in their "business arrangement." Connolly replied that he was interested but that he had recently obtained two additional bottles of phenyl-2-propanone and would not be finished with them for a couple of days. He provided some additional methamphetamine to Shapiro at that time. Three days later Shapiro returned to the Connolly house with a search warrant and, among other items seized an empty 500-gram bottle of propanone and a 100-gram bottle, not the one he had provided, that was partially filled with the chemical.

There was testimony at the trial of respondent and Patrick Connolly that phenyl-2-propanone was generally difficult to obtain. At the request of the Bureau of Narcotics and Dangerous Drugs, some chemical supply firms had voluntarily ceased selling the chemical.

At the close of the evidence, and after receiving the District Judge's standard entrapment instruction,[4] the jury found the respondent guilty on all counts charged. On appeal, the respondent conceded that the jury could have found him predisposed to commit the offenses, but argued that on the facts presented there was entrapment as a matter of law. The Court of Appeals agreed, although it did not find the District Court had misconstrued or misapplied the traditional standards governing the entrapment defense. Rather, the court in effect expanded the traditional notion of entrapment, which focuses on the predisposition of the defendant, to mandate dismissal of a criminal prosecution whenever the court determines that there has been "an intolerable degree of governmental participation in the criminal enterprise." In this case the court decided that the conduct of the agent in supplying a scarce ingredient essential for the manufacture of a controlled substance established that defense.

This new defense was held to rest on either of two alternative theories. One theory is based on two lower court decisions which have found entrapment, regardless of predisposition, whenever the government supplies contraband to the defendants. The second theory, a nonentrapment rationale, is based on a recent Ninth Circuit deci-

4. The District Judge stated the governing law on entrapment as follows: "Where a person already has the willingness and the readiness to break the law, the mere fact that the government agent provides what appears to be a favorable opportunity is not entrapment." He then instructed the jury to acquit respondent if it had a "reasonable doubt whether the defendant had the previous intent or purpose to commit the offense . . . and did so only because he was induced or persuaded by some officer or agent of the government." No exception was taken by respondent to this instruction.

sion that reversed a conviction because a government investigator was so enmeshed in the criminal activity that the prosecution of the defendants was held to be repugnant to the American criminal justice system. The court below held that these two rationales constitute the same defense, and that only the label distinguishes them. In any event, it held that "[b]oth theories are premised on fundamental concepts of due process and evince the reluctance of the judiciary to countenance 'overzealous law enforcement.'" 459 F.2d, at 674, quoting Sherman v. United States, 356 U.S. 369, 381, 78 S.Ct. 819, 825, 2 L.Ed.2d 848 (1958) (Frankfurter, J., concurring in result).

This Court first recognized and applied the entrapment defense in Sorrells v. United States, 287 U.S. 435, 53 S.Ct. 210, 77 L.Ed. 413 (1932).[5] In *Sorrells,* a federal prohibition agent visited the defendant while posing as a tourist and engaged him in conversation about their common war experiences. After gaining the defendant's confidence, the agent asked for some liquor, was twice refused, but upon asking a third time the defendant finally capitulated, and was subsequently prosecuted for violating the National Prohibition Act.

Mr. Chief Justice Hughes, speaking for the Court, held that as a matter of statutory construction the defense of entrapment should have been available to the defendant. Under the theory propounded by the Chief Justice, the entrapment defense prohibits law enforcement officers from instigating a criminal act by persons "otherwise innocent in order to lure them to its commission and to punish them." Thus, the thrust of the entrapment defense was held to focus on the intent or predisposition of the defendant to commit the crime. "[I]f the defendant seeks acquittal by reason of entrapment he cannot complain of an appropriate and searching inquiry into his own conduct and predisposition as bearing upon that issue."

Mr. Justice Roberts concurred but was of the view "that courts must be closed to the trial of a crime instigated by the government's own agents."[6] The difference in the view of the majority and the concurring opinions is that in the former the inquiry focuses on the predisposition of the defendant, whereas in the latter the inquiry focuses on whether the government "instigated the crime."

In 1958 the Court again considered the theory underlying the entrapment defense and expressly reaffirmed the view expressed by the *Sorrells* majority. Sherman v. United States, supra. In *Sherman* the defendant was convicted of selling narcotics to a Government informer. As in *Sorrells,* it appears that the Government agent gained the confidence of the defendant and, despite initial reluctance, the defendant finally acceded to the repeated importunings of the agent to

5. The first case to recognize and sustain a claim of entrapment by government officers as a defense was apparently Woo Wai v. United States, 223 F. 412 (CA9 1915).

6. Justices Brandeis and Stone concurred in this analysis.

commit the criminal act. On the basis of *Sorrels,* (*sic*) this Court reversed the affirmance of the defendant's conviction.

In affirming the theory underlying *Sorrells,* Mr. Chief Justice Warren for the Court, held that "[t]o determine whether entrapment has been established, a line must be drawn between the trap for the unwary innocent and the trap for the unwary criminal." Mr. Justice Frankfurter stated in an opinion concurring in the result that he believed Mr. Justice Roberts had the better view in *Sorrells* and would have framed the question to be asked in an entrapment defense in terms of "whether the police conduct revealed in the particular case falls below standards . . . for the proper use of governmental power." [7] . . .

Respondent's concession in the Court of Appeals that the jury finding as to predisposition was supported by the evidence, is, therefore, fatal to his claim of entrapment. He was an active participant in an illegal drug manufacturing enterprise which began before the Government agent appeared on the scene, and continued after the Government agent had left the scene. He was, in the words of *Sherman,* supra, not an "unwary innocent" but an "unwary criminal." The Court of Appeals was wrong, we believe, when it sought to broaden the principle laid down in *Sorrells* and *Sherman.* Its judgment is therefore reversed.

Reversed.

MR. JUSTICE DOUGLAS, with whom MR. JUSTICE BRENNAN concurs, dissenting.

A federal agent supplied the accused with one chemical ingredient of the drug known as methamphetamine ("speed") which the accused manufactured and for which act he was sentenced to prison. His defense was entrapment, which the Court of Appeals sustained and which the Court today disallows. Since I have an opposed view of entrapment, I dissent.

. . .

Federal agents play a debased role when they become the instigators of the crime, or partners in its commission, or the creative brain behind the illegal scheme. That is what the federal agent did here when he furnished the accused with one of the chemical ingredients needed to manufacture the unlawful drug.

MR. JUSTICE STEWART, with whom MR. JUSTICE BRENNAN and MR. JUSTICE MARSHALL join dissenting. . . .

The concurring opinion of Mr. Justice Roberts, joined by Justices Brandeis and Stone, in the *Sorrells* case, and that of Mr. Justice Frankfurter, joined by Justices Douglas, Harlan, and Brennan, in the

7. Justices Douglas, Harlan, and Brennan shared the views of entrapment expressed in the Frankfurter opinion.

Sherman case, took a different view of the entrapment defense. In their concept, the defense is not grounded on some unexpressed intent of Congress to exclude from punishment under its statutes those otherwise innocent persons tempted into crime by the Government, but rather on the belief that "the methods employed on behalf of the Government to bring about conviction cannot be countenanced." Thus, the focus of this approach is not on the propensities and predisposition of a specific defendant, but on "whether the police conduct revealed in the particular case falls below standards, to which common feelings respond, for the proper use of governmental power." Phrased another way, the question is whether—regardless of the predisposition to crime of the particular defendant involved—the governmental agents have acted in such a way as is likely to instigate or create a criminal offense.[1] Under this approach, the determination of the lawfulness of the Government's conduct must be made—as it is on all questions involving the legality of law enforcement methods—by the trial judge, not the jury. . . .[a]

The purpose of the entrapment defense, then, cannot be to protect persons who are "otherwise innocent." Rather, it must be to prohibit unlawful governmental activity in instigating crime. As Mr. Justice Brandeis stated in Casey v. United States, supra, 276 U.S., at 425, 48 S.Ct., at 376: "This prosecution should be stopped, not because some right of Casey's has been denied, but in order to protect the government. To protect it from illegal conduct of its officers. To preserve the purity of its courts." If that is so, then whether the particular defendant was "predisposed" or "otherwise innocent" is irrelevant; and the important question becomes whether the Government's conduct in inducing the crime was beyond judicial toleration. . . .

It is the Government's duty to prevent crime, not to promote it. Here, the Government's agent asked that the illegal drug be pro-

1. Both the Proposed New Federal Criminal Code (1971), Final Report of the National Commission on Reform of Federal Criminal Laws § 702, and the American Law Institute's Model Penal Code § 2.13 (Proposed Official Draft, 1962), adopt this objective approach.

a. [Added by the Compiler.] "The duty to determine whether or not the issue of entrapment exists is that of the judge and not the jury." Hence "refusal to give an instruction on the subject of entrapment was proper in this case since there was no evidence of entrapment." United States v. Teeslink, 421 F.2d 768, 771 (9th Cir. 1970).

"Entrapment exists only when the government has implanted the criminal design in the mind of the defendant; the central issue of predisposition is a fact question for the jury." United States v. Martin, 533 F.2d 268, 269 (5th Cir. 1976).

Since the politicians known as the ABSCAM defendants showed predisposition by their ready acceptance of large bribes, they were not entrapped. And the government's actions were not so outrageous as to involve due-process concerns of "fundamental fairness." United States v. Jannotti, 673 F.2d 578 (3d Cir. 1982).

". . . there is no constitutionally imposed requirement of reasonable suspicion before an undercover operation, e.g. ABSCAM, can be commenced." United States v. Vanzandt, 14 M.J. 332, 343 (CMA 1982).

"Since police knew defendant was not a cocaine dealer, yet induced him to make purchases and sales of cocaine, it would appear the police agents impermissibly manufactured or instigated a crime." People v. LaBate, 122 Mich.App. 644, 332 N.W.2d 555 (1983).

duced for him, solved his quarry's practical problems with the assurance that he could provide the one essential ingredient that was difficult to obtain, furnished that element as he had promised, and bought the finished product from the respondent—all so that the respondent could be prosecuted for producing and selling the very drug for which the agent had asked and for which he had provided the necessary component. Under the objective approach that I would follow, this respondent was entrapped, regardless of his predisposition or "innocence."

In the words of Mr. Justice Roberts:

"The applicable principle is that courts must be closed to the trial of a crime instigated by the government's own agents. No other issue, no comparison of equities as between the guilty official and the guilty defendant, has any place in the enforcement of this overruling principle of public policy."

I would affirm the judgment of the Court of Appeals.[b]

PEOPLE v. BARRAZA

Supreme Court of California, In Bank, 1979.
23 Cal.3d 675, 153 Cal.Rptr. 459, 591 P.2d 947.

MOSK, JUSTICE. We confront in this criminal appeal two separate issues: . . . and (2) the proper test to be applied to the defense of entrapment.

Defendant appeals from his conviction on two counts of selling heroin (Health & Saf. Code, § 11352).

Count II charged a second sale of heroin on September 11, 1975; both the female agent and the defendant testified that the agent tried to contact defendant by telephoning the Golden State Mental Health Detoxification Center, where he worked as a patient care technician, several times during the three weeks between the dates of the two alleged heroin sale transactions. On September 11, the agent finally succeeded in speaking to defendant and asked him if he had "anything"; defendant asked her to come to the detoxification center. The two then met at the center and talked for some time—a few minutes according to the agent, more than an hour by the defendant's account.

The agent's version of this encounter described defendant as hesitant to deal because "he had done a lot of time in jail and he couldn't afford to go back to jail and . . . he had to be careful about what he was doing." She further testified that after she convinced defend-

b. "*Pascu* (577 P.2d 1064) undeniably expanded the scope of the entrapment defense by abandoning the objective, 'average person' standard of entrapment previously adopted by the court . . . . However, we do not think that *Pascu* can correctly be read to have abandoned the need for police conduct involving inducement, persuasion or instigation as an essential component of the entrapment defense." Municipality of Anchorage v. Flanagan, 649 P.2d 957, 961 (Alaska App. 1982).

ant she "wasn't a cop," he gave her a note, to present to a woman named Stella, which read: "Saw Cheryl [the agent]. Give her a pair of pants [argot for heroin]. [signed] Cal." The agent concluded her testimony by stating that she then left defendant, used the note to introduce herself to the dealer Stella, and purchased an orange balloon containing heroin.

Defendant described a somewhat different pattern of interaction with the agent at their September 11th meeting. He related that he had asked her to come and see him because he was "fed up with her" and wanted her to quit calling him at the hospital where he worked because he was afraid she would cause him to lose his job. He insisted he told her during their conversation that he did not have anything; that he had spent more than 23 years in prison but now he had held a job at the detoxification center for four years, was on methadone and was clean, and wanted the agent to stop "bugging" him. He testified that the agent persisted in her efforts to enlist his aid in purchasing heroin, and that finally—after more than an hour of conversation—when the agent asked for a note to introduce her to a source of heroin he agreed to give her a note to "get her off . . . [his] back." According to the defendant, he told the agent that he did not know if Stella had anything, and gave her a note which read: "Saw Cheryl. If you have a pair of pants, let her have them." . . .

Defendant urges that his conviction on the second count must be reversed because the trial court erred in failing to instruct the jury sua sponte on the defense of entrapment. His contention requires that we reexamine the entrapment doctrine to determine the manner in which the defense must be raised.

Though long recognized by the courts of almost every United States jurisdiction,[1] the defense of entrapment has produced a deep schism concerning its proper theoretical basis and mode of application. The opposing views have been delineated in a series of United States Supreme Court decisions. The court first considered the entrapment defense in Sorrells v. United States (1932) 287 U.S. 435, 53 S.Ct. 210, 77 L.Ed. 413. The majority held that entrapment tended to establish innocence, reasoning that Congress in enacting the criminal statute there at issue could not have intended to punish persons otherwise innocent who were lured into committing the proscribed conduct by governmental instigation. This focus on whether persons were "otherwise innocent" let the majority to adopt what has become known as the subjective or origin-of-intent test under which entrapment is established only if (1) governmental instigation and induce-

1. The defense appears to have first been asserted by Eve, who complained, when charged with eating fruit of the tree of knowledge of good and evil: "The serpent beguiled me, and I did eat." (Genesis 3:13.) Though Eve was unsuccessful in asserting the defense, it has been suggested that the defense was unavailable to her because the entrapping party was not an agent of the punishing authority. (Groot, The Serpent Beguiled Me and I (Without Scienter) Did Eat—Denial of Crime and the Entrapment Defense, 1973 U.Ill.L.F. 254.)

ment overstep the bounds of permissibility, and (2) the defendant did not harbor a preexisting criminal intent. Under the subjective test a finding that the defendant was predisposed to commit the offense would negate innocence and therefore defeat the defense. Finally, because entrapment was viewed as bearing on the guilt or innocence of the accused, the issue was deemed proper for submission to the jury.

Justice Roberts wrote an eloquent concurring opinion, joined by Justices Brandeis and Stone, in which he argued that the purpose of the entrapment defense is to deter police misconduct. He emphatically rejected the notion that the defendant's conduct or predisposition had any relevance: "The applicable principle is that courts must be closed to the trial of a crime instigated by the government's own agents. No other issue, no comparison of equities as between the guilty official and the guilty defendant, has any place in the enforcement of this overruling principle of public policy." (Id. at p. 459, 53 S.Ct. at p. 219.) Because he viewed deterrence of impermissible law enforcement activity as the proper rationale for the entrapment defense, Justice Roberts concluded that the defense was inappropriate for jury consideration: "It is the province of the court and of the court alone to protect itself and the government from such prostitution of the criminal law." (Id. at p. 457, 53 S.Ct. at p. 218.)

In Sherman v. United States (1958) 356 U.S. 369, 78 S.Ct. 819, 2 L.Ed.2d 848, the majority refused to adopt the "objective" theory of entrapment urged by Justice Roberts, choosing rather to continue recognizing as relevant the defendant's own conduct and predisposition. The court held that "a line must be drawn between the trap for the unwary innocent and the trap for the unwary criminal." (Id. at p. 372, 78 S.Ct. at p. 821.) Justice Frankfurter, writing for four members of the court in a concurring opinion, argued forcefully for Justice Roberts' objective theory: "The courts refuse to convict an entrapped defendant, not because his conduct falls outside the proscription of the statute, but because, even if his guilt be admitted, the methods employed on behalf of the Government to bring about conviction cannot be countenanced." (Id. at p. 380, 78 S.Ct. at p. 824.) He reasoned that "a test that looks to the character and predisposition of the defendant rather than the conduct of the police loses sight of the underlying reason for the defense of entrapment. No matter what the defendant's past record and present inclinations to criminality, or the depths to which he has sunk in the estimation of society, certain police conduct to ensnare him into further crime is not to be tolerated by an advanced society. . . . Permissible police activity does not vary according to the particular defendant concerned . . . ." (Id. at pp. 382–383, 78 S.Ct. at p. 826.) "Human nature is weak enough," he wrote, and "and sufficiently beset by temptations without government adding to them and generating crime." (Id. at p. 384, 78 S.Ct. at p. 826.) Justice Frankfurter concluded that guidance as to appropriate official conduct could only be provided if the court reviewed police conduct and decided the entrapment issue.

The United States Supreme Court recently reviewed the theoretical basis of the entrapment defense in United States v. Russell (1973) 411 U.S. 423, 93 S.Ct. 1637, 36 L.Ed.2d 366, and once again the court split five votes to four in declining to overrule the subjective theory adopted in *Sorrells*. . . .

For all the foregoing reasons we hold that the proper test of entrapment in California is the following:[3] was the conduct of the law enforcement agent likely to induce a normally law-abiding person to commit the offense? For the purposes of this test, we presume that such a person would normally resist the temptation to commit a crime presented by the simple opportunity to act unlawfully. Official conduct that does no more than offer that opportunity to the suspect—for example, a decoy program—is therefore permissible; but it is impermissible for the police or their agents to pressure the suspect by overbearing conduct such as badgering, cajoling, importuning, or other affirmative acts likely to induce a normally law-abiding person to commit the crime.

Although the determination of what police conduct is impermissible must to some extent proceed on an ad hoc basis, guidance will generally be found in the application of one or both of two principles. First, if the actions of the law enforcement agent would generate in a normally law-abiding person a motive for the crime other than ordinary criminal intent, entrapment will be established. An example of such conduct would be an appeal by the police that would induce such a person to commit the act because of friendship or sympathy, instead of a desire for personal gain or other typical criminal purpose. Second, affirmative police conduct that would make commission of the crime unusually attractive to a normally law-abiding person will likewise constitute entrapment. Such conduct would include, for example, a guarantee that the act is not illegal or the offense will go undetected, an offer of exorbitant consideration, or any similar enticement.[4]

Finally, while the inquiry must focus primarily on the conduct of the law enforcement agent, that conduct is not to be viewed in a vacuum; it should also be judged by the effect it would have on a normally law-abiding person situated in the circumstances of the case at hand. Among the circumstances that may be relevant for this pur-

3. The wording of this test is derived from the proposed new federal criminal code (Nat.Com. on Reform of Fed.Crim. Laws, Final Rep.—Proposed New Fed. Crim. Code (1971) § 702(2)) and Chief Justice Traynor's dissenting opinion in People v. Moran (1970) supra, 1 Cal.3d 755, 765, 83 Cal.Rptr. 411, 463 P.2d 763.

4. There will be no entrapment, however, when the official conduct is found to have gone no further than necessary to assure the suspect that he is not being "set-up." The police remain free to take reasonable, though restrained, steps to gain the confidence of suspects. A contrary rule would unduly hamper law enforcement; indeed, in the case of many of the so-called "victimless" crimes, it would tend to limit convictions to only the most gullible offenders.

pose, for example, are the transactions preceding the offense, the suspect's response to the inducements of the officer, the gravity of the crime, and the difficulty of detecting instances of its commission. (See Grossman v. State (Alaska 1969) supra, 457 P.2d 226, 230.) We reiterate, however, that under this test such matters as the character of the suspect, his predisposition to commit the offense, and his subjective intent are irrelevant.[5] . . .

The judgment is reversed.

BIRD, C. J., and TOBRINER, MANUEL and NEWMAN, JJ., concur.

RICHARDSON, JUSTICE, concurring and dissenting.

I concur in that portion of the majority's opinion which holds that defendant's conviction on count I should be reversed because of the prejudicial "mini-*Allen*" instruction erroneously given to the jury. . . .

CLARK, JUSTICE, dissenting.

The most significant question presented by this case is whether this court should adopt the "hypothetical-person" ("objective") test of entrapment.

The test now applied in California, in all but seven of the other states, and in the federal courts is the "origin-of-intent" ("subjective") standard. This test focuses, quite properly, upon the guilt of the particular defendant, asking whether he was predisposed to commit the crime charged. If he was ready and willing to commit the offense at any favorable opportunity, then the entrapment defense fails even if the police used an unduly persuasive inducement.

The guilt of the particular defendant is irrelevant under the hypothetical-person test. It focuses instead upon the conduct of the police. If the police use an inducement likely to cause a hypothetical person to commit the crime charged, then the fact that the particular defendant was ready and willing to commit it does not defeat the entrapment defense. The evil of the hypothetical-person test is apparent—it leads to acquittal of persons who are in fact guilty. By focusing on police conduct rather than the defendant's predisposition, it creates a risk of acquitting dangerous chronic offenders.

That risk is strikingly illustrated by the facts of this case. The evidence would support the conclusion that defendant is one of the most cynical manipulators of the criminal justice system imaginable, that he abused the trust placed in him as an employee of a drug detoxification program to sell heroin to the patients with whom he worked, nullifying the program's slight chances of success and wasting countless thousands of tax dollars, that he initially refused to sell heroin to the deputy solely because he suspected she was an under-

5. Because the test of entrapment we adopt herein is designed primarily to deter impermissible police conduct, it will be applicable, except for the present defendant, only to trials that have not yet begun at the time this decision becomes final.

cover officer, and that, before finally agreeing to make the sale through his wife, he sought to immunize himself by "entrapping" the deputy into the conduct he now relies upon as the basis of his entrapment defense. If the factfinder takes this view of the evidence, but also concludes the officer's conduct would have induced a hypothetical person to commit the offense, defendant goes free. . . .[a]

MODEL PENAL CODE

Section 2.13 Entrapment.

(1) A public law enforcement official or a person acting in cooperation with such an official perpetrates an entrapment if for the purpose of ob-

a. [Compiler's footnote.] Conduct of the police in stocking a warehouse with television sets and in thereafter informing the defendant of the contents, security, and location of the warehouse was not sufficiently gross to warrant a conclusion that due process was violated. People v. Peppars, 140 Cal.App.3d 677, 189 Cal. Rptr. 879 (1983). "Police methods designed to tempt innocent persons into crime are as objectionable as the coerced confession and the unlawful search." Accardi v. United States, 227 F.2d 168, 172 (5th Cir. 1958).

" 'Entrapment' is the planning of an offense by an officer, or someone acting under his direction, and his procurement by improper inducement of its commission by one who would not have perpetrated it, except for the trickery of the *officer*." Crosbie v. State, 330 P.2d 602, 606 (Okl.Cr.1958).

"The controlling question in entrapment is whether an unwary innocent, having no disposition to commit a crime, is trapped into an offense that is the product of the creative activity of the government's own agents. Sorrells and Sherman hold that this is a question for the jury, unless the evidence is so clear that the Court should decide it as a matter of law." Lathem v. United States, 259 F.2d 393, 396 (5th Cir. 1958).

"This defense (entrapment) requires admission of guilt of the crime charged and all of its elements, including the required mental state." United States v. Hill, 655 F.2d 512, 514 (3d Cir. 1981).

"The general rule of this Circuit is that a defendant cannot both plead entrapment and deny committing the acts on which the prosecution is predicated." United States v. Sedigh, 658 F.2d 1010, 1014 (5th Cir. 1981); United States v. Smith, 629 F.2d 650 (10th Cir. 1980); People v. Bradley, 73 Ill.App.3d 347, 29 Ill. Dec. 395, 391 N.E.2d 1078 (1979); State v. Amodei, 222 Kan. 140, 563 P.2d 440 (1977); Norman v. State, 588 S.W.2d 340 (Tex.Cr.App.1979); Annotation, Availability in State Court of Defense of Entrapment Where Accused Denies Committing Acts Which Constitute Offense Charged, 5 A.L.R. 4th 1128 (1981); Annotation, Availability in Federal Court of Defense of Entrapment Where Accused Denies Committing Acts Which Constitute Offense Charged, 54 A.L.R.Fed. 644 (1981).

A defendant may assert entrapment without being required to concede that he committed the crime charged or any of its elements. United States v. Demma, 523 F.2d 981 (9th Cir. 1975).

The defense of entrapment is not available and does not extend to an act of inducement or solicitation by private citizens who are not public officers or acting as agents of public officers. State v. Farris, 218 Kan. 136, 542 P.2d 725 (1975).

An exhaustive note points out that the "subjective" test for entrapment has been generally accepted. This is the so-called "origin of intent" test which means that one was not entrapped to commit an offense if he was "predisposed" to commit it. It is added that a few states have criticized the "subjective test" and have adopted the "objective test." Under this test the only question is whether the nature of police activity involved was so improper that it was likely to induce one to commit a crime he had not previously intended. Note, Entrapment to Commit Narcotic Offense, 62 A.L.R.3d 110 (1975).

Because Michigan rejects the subjective test of entrapment and adopts the objective test, it was reversible error to submit the issue of entrapment to the jury. This must be decided by the trial judge. People v. Van Riper, 65 Mich. App. 230, 237 N.W.2d 262 (1976).

taining evidence of the commission of an offense, he induces or encourages another person to engage in conduct constituting such offense by either:

(a) making knowingly false representations designed to induce the belief that such conduct is not prohibited; or

(b) employing methods of persuasion or inducement which create a substantial risk that such an offense will be committed by persons other than those who are ready to commit it.

(2) Except as provided in Subsection (3) of this Section, a person prosecuted for an offense shall be acquitted if he proves by a preponderance of evidence that his conduct occurred in response to an entrapment. The issue of entrapment shall be tried by the Court in the absence of the jury.

(3) The defense afforded by this Section is unavailable when causing or threatening bodily injury is an element of the offense charged and the prosecution is based on conduct causing or threatening such injury to a person other than the person perpetrating the entrapment.[1]

Part 2

PROCEDURE AND ENFORCEMENT

Chapter 11

THE LIMITATIONS OF PROSECUTION

SECTION 1. JURISDICTION

(A) THE EXTENT OF THE AUTHORITY OF THE STATE

Criminal prosecutions are subject to certain limitations. Four distinct kinds, namely, jurisdiction, lapse of time, former jeopardy and what is known as the *ex post facto rule,* are entitled to special consideration.

"The power of a sovereign to affect the rights of persons, whether by legislation, by executive decree, or by the judgment of a court, is called *jurisdiction.*"[1] As relates to the power of a sovereign to affect the rights of persons by the judgment of a court, jurisdiction is the power to hear and determine a cause of action. Thus we use the word jurisdiction first, to mean the scope of authority of a state; and second, within the state, to signify the scope of authority of its various tribunals. To have jurisdiction over a criminal prosecution means to have power, first, to inquire into the facts; second, to apply the law to the facts; and third, if the law as applied to these facts requires it, to pronounce the appropriate sentence. Any given court may lack these powers either because they are not within the judicial machinery of the state at all, or because they are lodged exclusively in some other part of this machinery. If any such question arises we have first to decide whether the state has the power to try the accused for the alleged crime. The different theories of criminal jurisdiction are entitled to first consideration.

1. Beale, The Jurisdiction of a Sovereign State, 36 Harv.L.Rev. 241 (1923).

TITLE 18—UNITED STATES CODE
CRIMES AND CRIMINAL PROCEDURE

§ 1651. Piracy under law of nations [2]

Whoever, on the high seas, commits the crime of piracy as defined by the law of nations, and is afterwards brought into or found in the United States, shall be imprisoned for life.

§ 1652. Citizens as pirates

Whoever, being a citizen of the United States, commits any murder or robbery, or any act of hostility against the United States, or against any citizen thereof, on the high seas, under color of any commission from any foreign prince, or state, or on pretense of authority from any person, is a pirate, and shall be imprisoned for life.

§ 2381. Treason

Whoever, owing allegiance to the United States, levies war against them or adheres to their enemies, giving them aid and comfort within the United States or elsewhere, is guilty of treason and shall suffer death, or be imprisoned not less than five years and fined not less than $10,000; and shall be incapable of holding any office under the United States.

§ 953. Private correspondence with foreign governments

Any citizen of the United States, wherever he may be, who, without authority of the United States, directly or indirectly commences or carries on any correspondence or intercourse with any foreign government or any officer or agent thereof, with intent to influence the measures or conduct of any foreign government or of any officer or agent thereof, in relation to any disputes or controversies with the United States, or to defeat the measures of the United States, shall be fined not more than $5,000 or imprisoned not more than three years, or both.

This section shall not abridge the right of a citizen to apply, himself or his agent, to any foreign government or the agents thereof for redress of any injury which he may have sustained from such government or any of its agents or subjects.

§ 2112. Personal property of United States

Whoever robs another of any kind or description of personal property belonging to the United States, shall be imprisoned not more than fifteen years.

2. Constitution of the United States, Art. I, § 8: 1. The Congress shall have power. . . . 10. To define and punish piracies and felonies committed on the high seas, and offenses against the law of nations.

§ 471. Obligations or securities of United States

Whoever, with intent to defraud, falsely makes, forges, counterfeits, or alters any obligation or other security of the United States, shall be fined not more than $5,000 or imprisoned not more than fifteen years, or both.

(i) In General

IN RE CARMEN'S PETITION

United States District Court, N.D. California, S.D., 1958.
165 F.Supp. 942.

Goodman, Chief Judge. Petitioner is confined at the California State Penitentiary at San Quentin pursuant to a judgment of conviction of murder and a sentence of death imposed by the Superior Court of the State of California in and for the County of Madera, on October 30, 1951. By an application for the writ of habeas corpus, he seeks his discharge on the ground that the California Superior Court lacked jurisdiction to try him for the murder of which he was convicted because exclusive jurisdiction to try him for such offense was vested by federal statute in the United States District Court.

The statute relied upon by petitioner is often referred to as the Ten Major Crimes Act [2] and is now incorporated in Sections 1151, 1153, and 3242 of Title 18 of the United States Code. It provides in substance that an Indian who commits any of the ten listed crimes, among which is murder, in Indian Country shall be subject to the same laws and penalties and tried in the same courts as persons committing such crime within the exclusive jurisdiction of the United States. During petitioner's trial in the Superior Court apparently he and his counsel, the prosecution, and the court were all unaware of this statute. There was testimony at the trial indicating that both petitioner and his victim were Indians, but this testimony was given as background information and not for the purpose of questioning the court's jurisdiction. There was evidence that the scene of the crime was the victim's residence, but this evidence did not establish that his residence was in Indian Country. . . .

The testimony at petitioner's trial was that both he and his victim were Indians, and that the murder occurred at the victim's residence. Although these facts alone did not fully demonstrate the lack of jurisdiction in the trial court, they should have put the State Court on inquiry as to its own jurisdiction. The right to be tried in a Federal Court accorded petitioner by the Ten Major Crimes Act, was not a

2. As originally enacted in 1885, 23 Stat. 385, this Act dealt only with seven crimes and was then referred to as the Seven Major Crimes Act. In 1909, the crime of assault with a dangerous weapon was included. 35 Stat. 1151. And, in 1932, incest and robbery were added, 47 Stat. 337.

Currently see 18 U.S.C.A. 1153 (1976).

mere procedural right, waived unless asserted.[3] It could not have been waived even by express agreement. The Ten Major Crimes Act was enacted for the protection of the Indian wards of the United States. Both the trial court and the state's attorneys had a duty to uphold this federal statute. They had a responsibility to see to it that the court did not improperly assume jurisdiction over an Indian ward of the Federal government.

When the matter came to the attention of the United States, its representative promptly advised the California Supreme Court of the jurisdictional question while the appeal was pending. The stipulation of the parties that petitioner was an Indian by blood, and that the locus of the crime was an Indian allotment, the title to which was held in trust, constituted at the least a prima facie showing of the lack of jurisdiction in the State court. If, in the opinion of the California Supreme Court, the exclusive federal jurisdiction also depended upon the fact that petitioner was a tribal Indian and had not received a fee patent to an allotment under the Dawes Act, these were facts which were a matter of public record and easily ascertainable. They were in fact ascertained by the Referee appointed by the California Supreme Court upon petitioner's application for the writ of habeas corpus, which was promptly presented to that court after his unsuccessful appeal. Yet the California Supreme Court deemed itself powerless to remedy an assumption of jurisdiction clearly in violation of a federal statute.

Under these circumstances, it becomes the plain duty of this Court to protect the jurisdiction vested in the Federal Courts by the Ten Major Crimes Act. . . .

The writ of Habeas Corpus will issue and it is Ordered that petitioner be discharged from custody.[4]

3. [By the Compiler] Except for offenses enumerated in the Major Crimes Act, all crimes committed by enrolled Indians against other Indians in Indian Country are within the jurisdiction of the tribal courts, but a non-Indian charged with committing a crime against a non-Indian in Indian Country is subject to prosecution under state law. United States v. Antelope, 430 U.S. 641, 97 S.Ct. 1395 (1977).

Tribal courts do not have jurisdiction over non-Indians who violate a tribal law. Oliphant v. Suquamish Indian Tribe, 435 U.S. 191, 98 S.Ct. 1011 (1978).

"It has been repeatedly held in cosidering objections to the jurisdiction of the court in criminal prosecutions, a distinction must be made between those which involve jurisdiction of fundamental rights of the accused and those which involve mere personal privileges of the accused. The former cannot be waived, but the latter can." In re Duty, 318 P.2d 900, 902 (Okl.Cr.1957).

4. The president of a national bank was charged with violation of a state statute which made it a felony for an officer of a bank to accept a deposit when his bank was insolvent and with knowledge of such insolvency. His conviction, affirmed by the state court, was reversed by the Supreme Court on the ground that Congress, having created a system of national banks, has the sole power to regulate and control the exercise of their operations. Easton v. Iowa, 188 U.S. 220, 23 S.Ct. 288, 47 L.Ed. 452 (1903).

Title 18 of the United States Code (Crimes and Criminal Procedure) has this provision:

Section 3231. District Courts.

The district courts of the United States shall have original jurisdiction, exclusive

(ii) BASIS OF CRIMINAL JURISDICTION

REGINA v. WAINA AND SWATOA

Supreme Court of New South Wales, 1874.
2 N.S.W.L.R. 403.

[The Plato, a British ship, was wrecked. The crew of ten men then rigged up the longboat of some eight tons, and sailed it into a harbor of the savage island of Mallatta or Mallantha. Six of the crew went on shore and while on the beach were attacked by natives, and killed before the eyes of the four men in the longboat, who immediately decided to leave. They were pursued by canoes full of natives who fired arrows at them, wounding the captain. The boat soon went ashore on a reef, and the natives waded out to plunder it. After taking what they wanted from the boat, they killed two more of the crew, stripped the captain and remaining member of the crew, and then sank a tomahawk in the captain's skull.]

SIR J. MARTIN, C.J. . . . I am of opinion that the prosecution must fail for several reasons. If it depended simply on the point whether a boat is a "ship" within the meaning of the cases, I might reserve the decision. The case, however, does not depend on that alone. Whether a boat is a "ship" within the meaning of the cases there is no authority to show. My own opinion, however, is that a Judge would not be allowed to extend the law so as to stretch the jurisdiction of the Court in such a manner. The cases clearly show that the general principle is that a British ship is part of British territory, wherever she is *waterborne,* and that every foreigner on board, committing a crime on the high seas, is amenable to our law.[1] It is equally clear, however, that our jurisdiction does not extend one inch outside of the ship. It is strictly confined to the vessel, and there is no area surrounding the ship, however small, over which it can be made to extend. I admit that it is not the size of the vessel that would alone make it a ship, and I will not say that if this boat had started originally on a voyage, registered as a ship, that it would not be one within the meaning of the cases. I do not think, however, that a boat of the character disclosed in the evidence, sailing under the

of the courts of the States, of all offenses against the laws of the United States.

Nothing in this title shall be held to take away or impair the jurisdiction of the courts of the several States under the laws thereof.

The fact that one is on probation under a federal conviction does not deprive the state, which has arrested him, of jurisdiction to try him for the state offense. Strand v. Schmittroth, 251 F.2d 590 (9th Cir. 1957).

1. "If it be committed on board of a foreign vessel by a citizen of the United States, or on board of a vessel of the United States by a foreigner, the offender is to be considered, *pro hac vice,* and in respect to this subject as belonging to the nation under whose flag he sails." United States v. Holmes, 18 U.S. 412, 417 (1820).

A ship is "floating territory" of the nation whose flag she flies. Skiriotes v. Florida, 313 U.S. 69, 78, 61 S.Ct. 924 (1941).

circumstances narrated, comes within the description of a ship. I have taken considerable trouble in looking into all the cases, and I can find none, either American or English, which would justify me in holding it to be a ship. Here, however, supposing it were a ship, was this boat on shore on this island? and under the circumstances described, could it be held to be within our jurisdiction? I am of opinion that it could not.

The Attorney-General had referred to the Merchant Seaman's Act as conferring jurisdiction, but the Imperial Parliament could not pass a statute affecting foreigners outside the British dominions. No foreign nation would allow such an assumption of authority, nor would the British nation allow a similar power to be assumed by foreigners. We might pass statutes affecting our own subjects wherever they might be; but where a foreigner committed an offence outside the British dominions, no statute of ours couid [sic] make him amenable to British laws. If the jurisdiction contended for could be extended to a boat there is no saying to what lengths the argument might lead. If the jurisdiction extended to a boat, it might be held to extend to a raft, or to anything that floated on the water. I am of opinion, supposing that the murder was committed in the boat whilst on shore on this island, and that the arrows were fired either from the shore or from the canoes, that the Court would have no jurisdiction—neither the shore nor the canoes being British territory. The onus of proving that the crime was committed within British territory lay upon the Crown; but here the evidence showed that the prisoners were foreigners in their own country, and there was no British law that could touch them. . . . Being of opinion, therefore, that this boat on shore on a foreign island was not a "ship on the high seas," and that the crime committed was by foreigners in their own country, I hold that this Court has no jurisdiction whatever to try the case.

His Honor then directed the jury to acquit the prisoners, which they as once did in compliance with his Honor's direction, and the prisoners were both *discharged.*

UNITED STATES v. SMILEY

United States Circuit Court, N.D. California, 1864.
27 Fed.Cas. 1132, No. 16,317.

[The steamer Golden Gate, belonging to the Pacific Mail Steamship Company caught fire off the Mexican Coast and was completely destroyed. The underwriter sent a ship to recover lost treasure but this venture was unsuccessful. Then Thomas J.L. Smiley and others fitted up an expedition with complete equipment. They obtained from the Mexican government a license to explore for the lost treasure and recovered over three hundred thousand dollars in money. As Smiley and the original shippers were unable to agree upon what the recovering party should retain as compensation for the recovery of the specie, none of it was given up and Smiley and the others were indicted for plundering and stealing the treasure from the Golden Gate in violation of the federal statute against stealing money or goods from, or belonging to, a wrecked ship.]

FIELD, CIRCUIT JUSTICE. We are not prepared to decide that the statute does not apply to a case where the vessel has gone to pieces, to which the goods belonged, of which larceny is alleged. It would fail of one of its objects if it did not extend to goods which the officers and men of a stranded or wrecked vessel had succeeded in getting ashore, so long as a claim is made by them to the property, though before its removal the vessel may have been broken up. We are inclined to the conclusion that, until the goods are removed from the place where landed, or thrown ashore, from the stranded or wrecked vessel, or cease to be under the charge of the officers or other parties interested, the act would apply if a larceny of them were committed, even though the vessel may in the meantime have gone entirely to pieces and disappeared from the sea. But in this case the treasure taken had ceased to be under the charge of the officers of the Golden Gate, or of its underwriters, when the expedition of Smiley was fitted out, and all efforts to recover the property had been given up by them. The treasure was then in the situation of derelict or abandoned property, which could be acquired by any one who might have the energy and enterprise to seek its recovery. In our judgment the act was no more intended to reach cases where property thus abandoned is recovered, than to reach property voluntarily thrown into the sea, and afterwards fished from its depths.

But if the act covered a case where the property was recovered after its abandonment by the officers of the vessel and others interested in it, we are clear that the circuit court has no jurisdiction of the offense here charged. The treasure recovered was buried in the sand, several feet under the water, and was within one hundred and fifty feet from the shore of Mexico. The jurisdiction of that country over all offenses committed within a marine league of its shore, not on a vessel of another nation, was complete and exclusive.

Wheaton, in his treatise on International Law, after observing that "the maritime territory of every state extends to the ports, harbors, bays, and mouths of rivers and adjacent parts of the sea inclosed by headlands, belonging to the same state," says: "The general usage of nations superadds to this extent of territorial jurisdiction a distance of a marine league, or as far as a cannon-shot will reach from the shore, along all the coasts of the state. Within these limits its rights of property and territorial jurisdiction are absolute, and exclude those of every other nation." Part 2, c. 4, § 6.

The criminal jurisdiction of the government of the United States—that is, its jurisdiction to try parties for offenses committed against its laws—may in some instances extend to its citizens everywhere. Thus, it may punish for violation of treaty stipulations by its citizens abroad, for offenses committed in foreign countries where, by treaty, jurisdiction is conceded for that purpose, as in some cases in China and in the Barbary States; it may provide for offenses committed on deserted islands, and on an uninhabited coast, by the officers and seamen of vessels sailing under its flag. It may also punish derelictions of duty by its ministers or consuls, and other representatives abroad. But in all such cases it will be found that the law of congress indicates clearly the extraterritorial character of the act at which punishment is aimed. Except in cases like these, the criminal jurisdiction of the United States is necessarily limited to their own territory, actual or constructive. Their actual territory is co-extensive with their possessions, including a marine league from their shores into the sea.

This limitation of a marine league was adopted because it was formerly supposed that a cannon-shot would only reach to that extent. It is essential that the absolute domain of a country should extend into the sea so far as necessary for the protection of its inhabitants against injury from combating belligerents while the country itself is neutral. Since the great improvement of modern times in ordnance, the distance of a marine league, which is a little short of three English miles, may, perhaps, have to be extended so as to equal the reach of the projecting power of modern artillery. The constructive territory of the United States embraces vessels sailing under their flag; wherever they go they carry the laws of their country, and for a violation of them their officers and men may be subjected to punishment. But when a vessel is destroyed, and goes to the bottom, the jurisdiction of the country over it necessarily ends, as much so as it would over an island which should sink into the sea.

In this case it appears that the Golden Gate was broken up; not a vestige of the vessel remained. Whatever was afterwards done with reference to property once on board of her, which had disappeared under the sea, was done out of the jurisdiction of the United States, as completely as though the steamer had never existed.

We are of opinion, therefore, that the circuit court has no jurisdiction to try the offense charged, even if, under the facts admitted by the parties, any offense was committed According to the stipulation, judgment sustaining the demurrer will be, therefore, entered and the defendants discharged.[1]

1. Federal law does not prohibit California's assertion of penal jurisdiction over its citizens even though at the time of their commission of the charged offenses they were outside of California's territorial limits. The state had a proper interest in controlling fishing near its limits, and its law was not in conflict with any federal rule. People v. Weeren, 26 Cal.3d 654, 163 Cal.Rptr. 255, 607 P.2d 1279 (1980).

FELTON v. HODGES

United States of Appeals, Fifth Circuit, 1967.
374 F.2d 337.

[Felton brought a civil rights action [1] against Florida officials claiming that under color of Florida law they had deprived him of his constitutional rights. This was based upon the fact that he had been arrested, his personal property confiscated, and so forth, for activities of his beyond the territorial limits of Florida. The officials had acted under a Florida law which expressly undertook to regulate such activities of Florida fishermen "within or without the boundaries of such state waters". On defendant's motion the district court dismissed the suit. On appeal the question was whether this Florida law was valid.]

TUTTLE, CHIEF JUDGE. . . .

That critical question has been authoritatively answered, and the answer is affirmative. In Skiriotes v. State of Florida, 313 U.S. 69, 61 S.Ct. 924, 85 L.Ed. 1193 (1941), the issue was whether a Florida statute forbidding the use of diving equipment in the taking of commercial sponges had been unconstitutionally applied to convict the appellant, who claimed immunity from Florida regulation by reason of the fact that he was operating outside the territorial limits of the state. Florida contended that her boundaries did in fact encompass the territory in question. The Supreme Court found it unnecessary to decide this question. Instead, it said:

"Appellant's attack thus centers in the contention that the State has transcended its power simply because the statute has been applied to his operations inimical to its interests outside the territorial waters of Florida. The State denies this, pointing to its boundaries as defined by the state constitution of 1868, which the State insists had the approval of Congress and in which there has been acquiescence over a long period.

. . .

"[W]e do not find it necessary to resolve the contentions as to the interpretation and effect of the Act of Congress of 1868. *Even if it were assumed that the locus of the offense was outside the territorial waters of Florida, it would not follow that the State could not prohibit its own citizens from the use of the described divers' equipment at that place.* No question as to the authority of the United States over these waters, or over the sponge fishery, is here

1. Section 1983. Civil Action for Deprivation of Rights. Every person who, under color of any statute, ordinance, regulation, custom, or usage, of any State or Territory, subjects, or causes to be subjected, any citizen of the United States or other person within the jurisdiction thereof to the deprivation of any rights, privileges, or immunities secured by the Constitution and laws, shall be liable to the party injured in an action at law, suit in equity, or other proper proceeding for redress. R.S. § 1979. See currently 42 U.S.C.A. § 1983 (1981).

involved. No right of a citizen of any other State is here asserted. The question is solely between appellant and his own State. . . .

"If the United States may control the conduct of its citizens upon the high seas, we see no reason why the State of Florida may not likewise govern the conduct of its citizens upon the high seas with respect to matters in which the State has a legitimate interest and where there is no conflict with acts of Congress." Id. at 75–77, 61 S.Ct. at 929. (Emphasis added.)

Following the approach dictated by *Skiriotes,* we must inquire whether Florida has a legitimate interest in controlling the activities which it sought to regulate here. It appears from the complaint, and from the concessions made by appellant's counsel in oral argument, that appellant's crawfish traps were located in a group of reefs adjacent to the Florida Keys, and that the crawfish in this area move freely in and out of Florida's territorial waters, so that any taking of them would clearly have an effect upon the State's conservation efforts. Under these circumstances, we think it apparent that the State has an interest sufficient to enable it to subject appellant, one of its own citizens, to the conservation regulations which it sought to enforce here.

One further point requires discussion. As we read it, *Skiriotes* clearly holds that a state, given the requisite interest in a particular subject, may subject its citizens to extra-territorial regulation in order to protect that interest. It does not, however, explicitly hold that the state's officers may make arrests outside its boundaries in their efforts to effectuate such extra-territorial regulation. In his complaint, appellant has arguably, if inartfully, alleged that at least one of the arrests to which he was subjected took place beyond Florida's three mile seaward boundary. We must, therefore, consider the effect of such an allegation.

Obviously, no state is at liberty to abridge the rights of persons not subject to its jurisdiction by indiscriminate arrests effected beyond its territorial limits, under the guise of attempted exercise of the extra-territorial regulatory powers which it enjoys under the rule of *Skiriotes.* Here, however, as in *Skiriotes,* the question is solely between appellant and his own state. The arrests to which appellant alleges he was subjected were an integral part of the efforts of the State of Florida to regulate the conduct of one of its own citizens in a matter in which the State clearly had a legitimate interest. In our opinion, the added fact that one or more of these arrests may have taken place a few miles outside Florida's three mile seaward boundary line cannot transmute the otherwise proper efforts of these State officials into a violation of appellant's constitutional rights.

As we have noted, the predicate of appellant's complaint is simply that the State of Florida had no jurisdiction over his activities because his crawfish traps were set beyond the State's seaward boundary. This, in the light of *Skiriotes,* is untenable; and without that predicate, appellant's complaint fails, for its allegations demonstrate no deprivation of any right secured to him by the Constitution.

The judgment is affirmed.[2]

HANKS v. STATE

Texas Court of Appeals, 1882.
13 Tex.App. 289.

WHITE, P.J. There is but a single question which we think is involved in and requires discussion on this appeal.

Appellant and one P.F. Dillman were jointly indicted in the District Court of Travis county for the forgery of a transfer of a land

2. An English statute authorized the trial of any English subject charged in England with murder or manslaughter "whether committed within the King's dominions or without". Under this statute a conviction of murder was held to be proper, since the defendant was an English subject, although the crime was committed abroad. Regina v. Azzopardi, 1 Car. & K. 203, 174 Eng.Rep. 776 (1843).

In MacLeod v. Attorney General for New South Wales [1891] A.C. 455, the defendant, having first married in New South Wales and later married another wife in St. Louis, Missouri, was convicted of bigamy in the colony of New South Wales. The conviction was under this statute: "Whosoever being married marries another person during the life of the former husband or wife, wheresoever such second marriage takes place, shall be liable to penal servitude for seven years." This conviction was reversed by the Judicial Committee of the Privy Council. It was suggested that "whosoever" as here used means whosoever etc., "and who is amenable, at the time of the offence committed, to the jurisdiction of the colony of New South Wales," and that "wheresoever" as used in the statute means "wheresoever in this colony the offence is committed."

In other words, it is within the power of a nation to provide for the punishment of misconduct by its national wherever such misconduct may be committed, but since the common law limits criminal jurisdiction to that included within the territorial principle, any extension by statute must be clearly expressed.

The nature of the crime itself might be such as to indicate very clearly an intent to extend it beyond the territorial theory, such as the law making it an offense for a United States consul knowingly to certify a false invoice, which is used for illustration in United States v. Bowman, 43 S.Ct. 39, 260 U.S. 94, 99 (1922). See also the other illustrations given there and the statute actually involved in the case.

Jurisdiction was upheld over a defendant for federal crimes related to the killing of a United States Congressman in Guyana. The Court observed:

> "Courts have generally inferred such jurisdiction for two types of statutes: (1) statutes which represent an effort by the government to protect itself against obstructions and frauds; and (2) statutes where the vulnerability of the United States outside its own territory to the occurrence of the prohibited conduct is sufficient because of the nature of the offense to infer reasonably that Congress meant to reach those extraterritorial offenses." United States v. Layton, 509 F.Supp. 212 (N.D.Cal. 1981).

This interpretation was recently applied to a statute reading: "It is unlawful to use or operate or assist in using or operating any net, trap, line, spear, or appliance other than in connection with angling, in taking fish, except as provided in this chapter or Chapter 4 of this part." (Cal.Fish & Game Code, § 8603). People v. Foretich, 14 Cal.App.3d Supp. 6, 92 Cal.Rptr. 481 (1970). This very questionable application was assumed to be supported by *Skiriotes,* in which the Supreme Court made no attempt to interpret the Florida statute but held only that the statute, as interpreted by the state court did not "transcend the limits of" state power.

See Blakesley, United States Jurisdiction Over Extraterritorial Crime, 73 Jnl. Crim.L. & Crim. 1109 (1982).

certificate for a league and labor of land in the State of Texas. It is alleged in the indictment that the acts constituting the forgery were all committed in Caddo parish, in the State of Louisiana. No act or thing connected with the execution of the forgery is charged to have been done in Texas; but the crime and injury, so far as this State is concerned, are averred to consist in the fact that the said forgery in Louisiana "did then and there relate to and affect an interest in land in the State of Texas, . . . and would, if the same were true and genuine, have transferred and affected certain property, to-wit, a certain land certificate, number 222, for one league and labor of land in the State of Texas," etc.

This indictment was brought under Article 451 of the Penal Code.

By Article 454 of the Code it is declared that "persons out of the State may commit and be liable to indictment and conviction for committing any of the offenses enumerated in this chapter which do not in their commission necessarily require a personal presence in this State, the object of this chapter being to reach and punish all persons offending against its provisions, whether within or without this State," etc.

It was made a ground both in the motion to quash the indictment and in arrest of judgment, and is again urgently insisted upon in the able brief of counsel for appellant, that the facts alleged, if true, would constitute an offense against the sovereign State of Louisiana alone, and one of which the courts of this State would have no jurisdiction.

If the position thus assumed in behalf of appellant be correct, then the Legislature had no authority to pass the act quoted, and the same is an absolute nullity. Can this proposition be maintained? It certainly cannot be found in any constitutional inhibition, State or Federal, depriving the Legislature of the authority, and unless there is some authority of law superior to the right of a State Legislature, which could and should control the action of the latter within the scope of its constitutional powers, we cannot well conceive how its enactments, if reasonable and consistent with that power, could be held inoperative and nugatory.

Two authorities, which are to the effect that "the Legislature of one State cannot define and punish crimes committed in another State," are mainly relied upon. The leading one is the case of The State v. Knight, taken from 2 Haywood, and reported in Taylor's North Carolina Reports, page 44. The other is People v. Merrill, 2 Park's Criminal Reports, 590. The defendant in the first case was indicted under a statute the words of which were: "And whereas there is reason to apprehend that wicked and ill disposed persons resident in the neighboring States make a practice of counterfeiting the current bills of credit of this State, and by themselves or emissaries utter or vend the same, with an intention to defraud the citizens of this State: Be it enacted, etc., that all such persons shall be subject to the same mode of trial, and on conviction liable to the same pains and penalties as if the offense had been committed within the limits of this State and prosecuted in the superior court of any district of this State." It was held that the jurisdiction to try in North Carolina was doubtful, and the prisoner was discharged.

Mr. Wharton, in his work on the Conflict of Laws, says: "The sturdiest advocates of the hypothesis that the *locus delicti* alone confers jurisdiction have admitted that there are cases in which a person whose residence is outside the territory may make himself, by conspiring extra-territorially to defeat its laws, infra-territorially responsible. If, for instance, a forger should establish on the Mexican side of the boundary between the United States and Mexico a manufactory for the forgery of United States securities, for us to hold that when the mischief is done he can take up his residence in the United States without even liability to arrest, would not merely expose our government to spoliation, but bring its authority into contempt. To say that in such a case the Mexican government can be relied upon to punish is no answer; because, first, in countries of such imperfect civilization, penal justice is uncertain; secondly, in cases where, in such country, the local community gains greatly by the fraud and suffers by it no loss, the chances of conviction and punishment would be peculiarly slight; and, thirdly, because all that the offender would have to do to escape justice in such a case would be to walk over the boundary line into the United States, where on this hypothesis he would go free." (Whart. Conflict of Laws, sec. 876.) Again he says: "Thus it has been held that the originator of a nuisance to a stream in one country which affects such stream in another country is liable to prosecution in the latter country; that the author of a libel uttered by him in one country and published by others in another country from which he is absent at the time is liable in the latter country; that he who on one side of a boundary shoots a person on the other side is amenable in the country where the blow is received; that he who in one State employs an innocent agent to obtain goods by false pretenses in another State is amenable in the latter State; and that he who sells through agents, guilty or innocent, lottery tickets in another State is amenable in the State of the sale, though he was absent from such State personally. In England we have the same principle affirmed by the highest judicial authority." And he quotes Lord Campbell as saying, "that a person may, by the employment as well of a conscious as of an unconscious agent, render himself amenable to the law of England when he comes within the jurisdiction of our courts;" and Cir. R. Phillimore as saying, "It is a monstrous thing that any technical rule of venue should prevent justice from being done in this country on a criminal for an offense which was perpetrated here but the execution of which was concocted in another country." (Whart. Conflict of Laws, sec. 877.)

Mr. Cooley, in his great work on Constitutional Limitations, treating of territorial limitation to legislative authority, says: "The legislative authority of every State must spend its force within the territorial limits of the State. . . . It cannot provide for the punishment as crimes of acts committed beyond the State boundary, because such acts, if offenses at all, must be offenses against the sovereignty within whose limits they have been done." But, after laying down this doctrine, in the very next sentence he says: "But if the consequences of an unlawful act committed outside the State have reached their ultimate and injurious result within it, it seems that the perpetrator may be punished as an offender against such State." (Cooley's Const.Lim., 4 ed., pp. 154–5.) If this latter rule be the law, then it is a solecism to say that the Legislature cannot so declare it by express enactment.

Story, in his Conflict of Laws, says: "Although the penal laws of every country are in their nature local, yet an offense may be committed in one sovereignty in violation of the laws of another, and if the offender be afterwards found in the latter State, he may be punished according to the laws thereof, and the fact that he owes allegiance to another sovereignty is no bar to the indictment." (Story on the Conflict of Laws, 4 ed., section 625b.)

The offense charged in the indictment against appellant comes clearly within the terms of Article 454 of the Penal Code. Had it been committed by one of our own citizens within this State, there then could be no question as to his liability. Here, the defendant in effect says: "You may try and convict your own citizens for the same act I have committed, but you cannot try and punish me, because what I have done, though equally as violative of the spirit and letter of the law, is still not triable in your court because it was committed in another State, and your Legislature could not pass a law which could embrace me within its pains and penalties." We can see no valid reason why the Legislature of the State of Texas could not assert, as it has done in Article 454 supra, her jurisdiction over wrongs and crimes with regard to the land titles of the State, no matter whether the perpetrator of the crime was at the time of its consummation within or without her territorial limits. Such acts are offenses against the State of Texas and her citizens only, and can properly be tried only in her courts. It may in fact be no crime against the State in which it is perpetrated; and if it is under such circumstances as we are considering, that other State would have no interest in punishing it and would rarely, if ever, do so. When this forgery was committed in Louisiana, *eo instanti* a crime was committed against, and injury done to, the State of Texas, because it affected title to lands within her sovereignty.

Our conclusion is that the Legislature had authority to adopt the act in question; that the same is in violation of no law superior thereto; and that the jurisdiction thereby conferred can be rightly exercised by the courts of this State. The defendant appears to us to come clearly within the scope of that jurisdiction. He has been, as far as we can see, fairly and impartially tried under the law, and legally convicted according to the evidence exhibited in the record. We have found no error for which a reversal of the judgment should be had, and it is therefore affirmed.

Affirmed.[1]

HURT, J., dissents upon the ground that the Legislature had no authority to pass Article 454, Penal Code.

Opinion delivered November 22, 1882.

(iii) THE SITUS OF CRIME

STATE v. HALL

Supreme Court of North Carolina, 1894.
114 N.C. 909, 19 S.E. 602.

INDICTMENT for murder, tried at Spring Term, 1893, of Cherokee, before GRAVES, J., and a jury.

The defendants (Hall, as principal and Dockery, as accessory before the fact), were charged with the killing of Andrew Bryson on 11 July, 1892, in Cherokee County. The testimony tended to show that when the shooting occurred by which deceased was killed the defendants were in North Carolina and the deceased in Tennessee.

The defendants asked for the following instructions (among others):

"1. That it devolves upon the State to satisfy the jury beyond a reasonable doubt that the killing took place in the State of North Carolina; and if the State has failed to satisfy the jury beyond a reasonable doubt that the deceased received the wound from which he died whilst he was in the State of North Carolina, the defendants are not guilty.

"2. That if the prisoners were in North Carolina and the deceased was in Tennessee and the prisoners, or either of them, shot the deceased whilst he, the deceased, was in the State of Tennessee, and the deceased died from the effects of the wounds so received, the defendants are not guilty."

The instructions were refused, and after a verdict of guilty the defendants appealed from the judgment rendered thereon.

SHEPHERD, C.J. . . . It is a general principle of universal acceptation that one State or sovereignty can not enforce the penal or

1. Under the statute (18 U.S.C.A. § 1546) the United States District Court had jurisdiction to convict an alien of the crime of knowingly making a false statement under oath in a visa application to an American consular official located in a foreign country. The fact that the alien came into this country is no part of the offense. It was complete the moment he perjured himself in the foreign country. United States v. Pizzarusso, 388 F.2d 8 (2d Cir. 1967).

criminal laws of another, or punish crimes or offenses committed in and against another State or sovereignty. . . .

It seems to have been a matter of doubt in ancient times whether, if a blow was struck in one county and death ensued in another, the offender could be prosecuted in either, though according to Lord Hale (Pleas of the Crown, 426) "the more common opinion was that he might be indicted where the stroke was given." This difficulty, as stated by Mr. Starkie, was sought to be avoided by the legal device "of carrying the dead body back into the the county where the blow was struck, and the jury might there," he adds, "inquire both of the stroke and death." 1 Starkie Cr.Pl., 2 Ed., 304; 1 Hawk, P.C., ch. 13; 1 East, 361. But to remove all doubt in respect to a matter of such grave importance, it was enacted by the statute 2 and 3 Edward VI that the murder might be tried in the county where the death occurred.[1] This statute, either as a part of the common law or by reenactment, is in force in many of the States of the Union, and as applicable to counties within the same State its validity has never been questioned, but where its provisions have been extended so as to affect the jurisdiction of the different States its constitutionality has been vigorously assailed. Such legislation, however, has been very generally, if not indeed uniformly, sustained. . . .

Statutes of this character "are founded upon the general power of the Legislature, except so far as restrained by the Constitution of the Commonwealth and the United States to declare any willful or negligent act which causes an injury to person or property within its territory, to be a crime." Kerr on Homicide, 47. In many of the States there are also statutes substantially providing that where the death occurs outside of one State, by reason of a stroke given in another, the latter State may have jurisdiction. See our act, The Code, sec. 1197. The validity of these statutes seems to be undisputed, and indeed it has been held in many jurisdictions that such legislation is but in affirmance of the common law. It is manifest that statutes of this nature are only applicable to cases where the stroke and the death occur in different jurisdictions, and it is equally clear that where the stroke and the death occur in the same State the offense of murder at

1. Where defendant inflicted injuries upon a victim in New York which resulted in the latter's death two days later, in New Jersey, the crime was not punishable in New Jersey. State v. Carter, 27 N.J.L. 499 (1859).

Where deceased died in Texas as a result of a blow struck by defendant in Quay County, New Mexico, venue of murder prosecution was properly laid in Quay County. State v. Justus, 65 N.M. 195, 334 P.2d 1104 (1959).

Under a statute providing: "If any such mortal wound shall be given, or other violence or injury shall be inflicted, or poison administered, on the high seas, or on any other navigable waters, or on land, either within or without the limits of this state, by means whereof death shall ensue in any county thereof, such offense may be prosecuted and punished in the county where such death may happen," defendant was convicted of murder, for inflicting, outside of Michigan, wounds of which the victim died within the state. Tyler v. People, 8 Mich. 320 (1860).

common law is there complete, and the courts of that State can alone try the offender for that specific common law crime.

The turning point, therefore, in this case is whether the stroke was, in legal contemplation, given in Tennessee, the alleged place of death; and upon this question the authorities all seem to point in one direction. . . .

In Simpson v. State, 92 Ga. 41, 17 S.E. 984, it was held by the Supreme Court of Georgia that one who, in the State of South Carolina, aims and fires a pistol at another who at the time is in the State of Georgia, is guilty of the offense of "shooting at another" although the ball did not take effect, but struck the water in the latter State. The Court said: "Of course the presence of the accused within this State is essential to make his act one which is done in this State, but the presence need not be actual; it may be constructive. The well-established theory of the law is that where one puts in force an agency for the commission of crime, he in legal contemplation accompanies the same to the point where it becomes effectual. . . . So, if a man in the State of South Carolina criminally fires a ball into the State of Georgia the law regards him as accompanying the ball and as being represented by it up to the point where it strikes. If an unlawful shooting occurred while both the parties were in this State the mere fact of missing would not render the person who shot any the less guilty; consequently, if one shooting from another State goes, in a legal sense, where his bullet goes, the fact of his missing the object at which he aims can not alter the legal principle." . . .

In view of the foregoing authorities it can not be doubted that the place of the assault or stroke in the present case was in Tennessee, and it is also clear that the offense of murder at common law was committed within the jurisdiction of that State. If this be so it must follow that unless we have some statute expressly conferring jurisdiction upon the courts of this State, or making the act of shooting under the circumstances a substantive murder, the offense with which the prisoners are charged can only be tried by the tribunals of Tennessee. . . .

The fact that the prisoners and the deceased were citizens of the State of North Carolina can not affect the conclusion we have reached. If, as we have seen, the offense was committed in Tennessee, the personal jurisdiction generally, claimed by nations over their subjects who have committed offenses abroad or on the high seas can not be asserted by this State. Such jurisdiction does not exist as between the States of the Union under their peculiar relation to each other (Rorer Interstate Law, 308), and even if it could be rightfully claimed it could not in a case like the present be enforced in the absence of a statute providing that the offense should be tried in North Carolina. Even in England, where it seems the broadest claim to such jurisdiction is asserted, a statute (33 Hen. VIII) appears to have been necessary in order that the courts of that country could try a

murder committed in Lisbon by one British subject upon another. In People v. Merrill, 2 Parker Cr.Cases, 600, it is said that by the common law offenses were local and the jurisdiction in such case depends upon statutory provisions. Granting, however, that in some instances the jurisdiction may exist without statute, it is not exercised in all cases. Dr. Wharton says: "It has already been stated that as to crimes committed by subjects in foreign civilized States, with the single exception in England of homicides, the Anglo-American practice is to take cognizance only of offenses directed against the sovereignty of the prosecuting State; perjury before consuls and forgery of government documents being included in this head." To the same effect is 3 A. & E. Enc., 539, in which it is said: "As to offenses committed in foreign civilized lands the country of arrest has jurisdiction only of offenses distinctively against its sovereignty." See also Dr. Wharton's article upon the subject in 1 Criminal Law Magazine, 715. As between the States the question is so clear to us that we forbear a general discussion of the subject. We may further remark that, while it is true that the criminal laws of a State can have no extra-territorial force, we are of the opinion that it is competent for the Legislature to determine what acts within the limits of the State shall be deemed criminal, and to provide for their punishment. Certainly, there could be no complaint where all the parties concerned in the homicide are citizens of North Carolina. It may also be observed that in addition to its common-law jurisdiction the State of Tennessee has provided by statute for the trial of an offender under the circumstances of this case.

For the reasons given we are constrained to say that the prisoners are entitled to a

New trial.[2]

2. Accord, State v. Carter, 27 N.J.L. 499 (1859).

The same principle applies to other offenses. Thus the offense of obtaining property by false pretenses is committed where the property is obtained and not where the false pretense is made, Connor v. State, 29 Fla. 455, 10 So. 891 (1892); robbery is committed where the property is taken from the person, not where the person is first seized, if he is carried to another place before compelled to surrender his property, Sweat v. State, 90 Ga. 315, 17 S.E. 273 (1892), nor where the property is carried subsequently, 2 Hale P.C. *163; forgery is committed where the false instrument is made and the offense of uttering a forged instrument is committed where the instrument is uttered, State v. Hudson, 13 Mont. 112, 32 P. 413 (1893); the offense of receiving stolen goods is committed where they are received, State v. Rider, 46 Kan. 332, 26 P. 745 (1891); libel is committed at the place of publication, Commonwealth v. Blanding, 20 Mass. 304 (1825); contra: United States v. Smith, 173 F. 227 (D.Ind. 1909); and bigamy is committed where the bigamous marriage is performed, 1 Hale P.C. *693.

The defendants were indicted for manslaughter of a man who died within the county in consequence of injuries inflicted by them upon him in a British merchant ship on the high seas. The statute provided "if a mortal wound is given, or other violence or injury inflicted, or poison is administered, on the high seas, or on land either within or without the limits of this state, by means whereof death ensues in any county thereof, such offence may be prosecuted and punished in the county where the death happens." This statute was upheld. Commonwealth v. Macloon, 101 Mass. 1 (1869).

The federal court had jurisdiction over a drug conspiracy case where the evi-

BEATTIE v. STATE

Supreme Court of Arkansas, 1904.
73 Ark. 428, 84 S.W. 477.

George Beattie, a resident of Missouri, was arrested, tried and convicted on a charge that, being a resident of the State of Missouri, he did, in the county of Sharp and State of Arkansas, in May, 1904, herd, graze and permit to run at large about nineteen head of cattle. He was convicted and fined $100 before a justice of the peace. . . .

RIDDICK, J., (after stating the facts.) This is an appeal from a judgment convicting a nonresident defendant and assessing a fine of $100 against him for permitting his cattle to run at large in this State.

Now, it is clear that our statute on that subject does not forbid a nonresident, whose cattle have strayed or come of their own volition into this State, from driving them out again. It is equally clear that it does not subject a resident of Missouri, who turns his cattle at large in that State, to a criminal prosecution and fine if the cattle afterwards come into this State; for the Legislature of this State has no power to punish a resident of Missouri for a lawful act done in that State. Nor do we think that it would alter the case if the defendant knew, at the time he turned them at large in Missouri, that they would probably come into Arkansas, for the Legislature of this State cannot compel the residents of Missouri who live near the State line to keep their cattle in inclosed lots or fields in order to prevent them from coming into this State, and we do not think that it was the intention of this statute to do so. The people of Missouri have the right to permit their cattle to run at large in that State, unless forbidden by the law of that State; and if the people of this State desire to keep such cattle from entering this State, they can do so by putting up a fence along the line between this State and Missouri or by a statute authorizing the cattle of nonresidents which stray into this State to be impounded and kept at the costs of the owners. But to undertake to arrest and fine a resident of Missouri because he does not prevent his cattle from straying into this State would be to assume a jurisdiction over the residents of that State never intended by the statute and beyond the power of the Legislature to confer.

dence indicated that the defendants intended to consummate the conspiracy within the territorial limits of the United States, even if no overt act of conspiracy had occurred within the territorial limits of the United States. Defendants had been arrested on the high seas. United States v. Gray, 659 F.2d 1296 (5th Cir. 1981).

A "Ponzi" scheme involving oil wells in the United States was enough for federal court jurisdiction on mail fraud and securities violations for defrauding foreign investors. United States v. Cook, 573 F.2d 281 (5th Cir. 1978).

Where Indians were charged with standing in Indian country and shooting at police officers who were outside of Indian country, the crime of assault with a dangerous weapon was consummated outside of Indian country and the South Dakota Court had jurisdiction. State v. Winckler, 260 N.W.2d 356 (S.D.1977).

The evidence in the case was conflicting, and some of it, if true, might have warranted a finding that the defendant was guilty, but the finding of facts by the court has evidence to support it, and, taking that as true, no crime was committed.

The judgment will therefore be reversed, and the cause remanded for a new trial.

PEOPLE v. BOTKIN

Supreme Court of California, In Bank, 1901.
132 Cal. 231, 64 P. 286.

GAROUTTE, J. Defendant has been convicted of the crime of murder, and prosecutes this appeal. The charge of the court given to the jury upon the law contained declarations which were held to be unsound in People v. Vereneseneckockockhoff, 129 Cal. 497, 58 P. 156. In view of the decision in that case, the attorney-general concedes that the judgment should be reversed and the cause remanded to the trial court for further proceedings. But defendant claims that she is not triable at all by the courts of this state, and this contention should now be passed upon. For if maintainable, a second trial becomes a useless expenditure of money, time, and labor, and necessarily should not be had.

For the purposes of testing the claim of lack of jurisdiction in the courts of California to try defendant, the facts of this case may be deemed as follows: Defendant, in the city and county of San Francisco, state of California, sent by the United States mail to Elizabeth Dunning, of Dover, Delaware, a box of poisoned candy, with intent that said Elizabeth Dunning should eat of the candy and her death be caused thereby. The candy was received by the party to whom addressed, she partook thereof, and her death was the result. Upon these facts may the defendant be charged and tried for the crime of murder in the courts of the state of California? We do not find it necessary to declare what the true rule may be at common law upon this state of facts, for, in our opinion, the statute of this state is broad enough to cover a case of the kind here disclosed. There can be no question but that the legislature of this state had the power to declare that the acts here pictured constitute the crime of murder in this state, and we now hold that the legislative body has made that declaration.

Section 27 of the Penal Code reads as follows:—

"The following persons are liable to punishment under the laws of this state:—

"1. All persons who commit, in whole or in part, any crime within this state;

"2. All who commit larceny or robbery out of this state, and bring to, or are found with the property stolen, in this state;

"3. All who, being out of this state, cause or aid, advise or encourage, another person to commit a crime within this state, and are afterwards found therein."

Subdivision 1 covers the facts of this case. The acts of defendant constituted murder, and a part of those acts were done by her in this state. Preparing and sending the poisoned candy to Elizabeth Dunning, coupled with a murderous intent, constituted an attempt to commit murder, and defendant could have been prosecuted in this state for that crime, if, for any reason, the candy had failed to fulfill its deadly mission. That being so—those acts being sufficient, standing alone, to constitute a crime, and those acts resulting in the death of the person sought to be killed—nothing is plainer than that the crime of murder was in part committed within this state. The murder being committed *in part* in this state, the section of the law quoted declares that persons committing murder under those circumstances, "are liable to punishment under the laws of this state." The language quoted can have but one meaning, and that is: a person committing a murder in part in this state is punishable under the laws of this state, the same as though the murder was wholly committed in this state.

Counsel for defendant insist that this section contemplates only offenses committed by persons who, at the time, are without the state. This construction is not sound. For as to subdivision 1, it is not at all plain that a person without the state could commit, in whole, a crime within the state. Again, if the crime in whole is committed within the state by a person without the state, such a person could not be punished under the laws of this state, for the state has not possession of his body, and there appears to be no law by which it may secure that possession. Indeed, all of the subdivisions of the section necessarily contemplate a case where the person is, or comes, within the state. If the framers of the section had intended by subdivision 1 to cover the case of persons only who were without the state when the acts were committed which constitute the crime, they would have inserted in the section the contingency found in the remaining subdivisions, which subdivisions contemplate a return to the state of the person committing the crime. It is plain that the section, by its various provisions, was intended to embrace *all persons* punishable under the laws of the state of California. The defendant, having committed a murder in part in the state of California, is punishable under the laws of the state, exactly in the same way, in the same courts and under the same procedure, as if the crime was committed entirely within the state.

For the foregoing reasons the judgment and orders are reversed and the cause remanded.[1]

McFarland, J., Van Dyke, J., Henshaw, J., Beatty, C. J., and Temple, J., concurred.

1. Cf. People v. Licenziata, 199 App. Div. 106, 191 N.Y.S. 619 (2nd Dep't 1921). In this case the defendant purchased a large quantity of wood alcohol in New

PEOPLE v. UTTER

[California] Court of Appeal, Second District, Division 4, 1972.
24 Cal.App.3d 535, 101 Cal.Rptr. 214.

[The indictment against Utter had several counts but we are concerned here primarily with the first, which charged him with the murder of Norma Wilson. One of the other counts charged robbery. There was evidence which was intended to show that Utter, while in California and with intent to murder Mrs. Wilson, induced her to make a trip to Europe; that while still in California he purchased the tickets and the murder weapon; that he and Mrs. Wilson did make the trip to Europe; that he killed her in Spain; and returned to California bringing with him valuable jewelry she had been wearing when she left. He was convicted on several counts including those for murder and robbery.]

JEFFERSON, ACTING PRESIDING JUSTICE.

. . .

Defendant contends that the court lacked jurisdiction to conduct the trial with respect to the charges of murder and robbery. . . .

For the reasons set forth below we conclude that defendant is correct as to the lack of jurisdiction over the murder charge, but that the other contentions are without merit.

The defendant first contends that, because the physical acts relating to the murder and robbery took place outside the state of California, the courts of this state had no jurisdiction with respect to those charges. We conclude that, under the present state of decisional law in California, the trial court had jurisdiction over the robbery count, but not over the murder count.

Two sections of the Penal Code are applicable to the problem before us. They are sections 27 and 778a of the Penal Code, which read as follows:

York. This he put into mixtures called "whisky" and "brandy", which he sold for beverage purposes. A customer from Connecticut purchased part of it and this purchase found its way to a hotel at Chicopee Falls, Massachusetts, where a man died as a result of drinking it. It was shown that defendant knew of the poisonous nature of the mixture when he sold it in New York. A conviction of manslaughter in the first degree in New York was affirmed under the statutes of that state.

In People v. Zayas, 217 N.Y. 78, 111 N.E. 465 (1916), defendant was held triable in New York for there making false pretenses by means of which he obtained property which was delivered to him in Pennsylvania.

United States has jurisdiction over one who, while in a foreign country, conspires with persons within the United States, if an overt act in furtherance of the conspiracy is committed within the United States. Melia v. United States, 667 F.2d 300 (2d Cir. 1981).

See Cook, The Logical and Legal Bases of the Conflict of Laws, 33 Yale L.J. 457, 462 (1924).

Section 27: "The following persons are liable to punishment under the laws of this state:

"1. All persons who commit, in whole or in part, any crime within this state;

"2. All who commit any offense without this state which, if committed within this state, would be larceny, robbery, or embezzlement under the laws of this state, and bring the property stolen or embezzled, or any part of it, or are found with it, or any part of it, within this state;

"3. . . . "

Section 778a: "Whenever a person, with intent to commit a crime, does any act within this state in execution or part execution of such intent, which culminates in the commission of a crime, either within or without this state, such person is punishable for such crime in this state in the same manner as if the same had been committed entirely within this state."

The evidence shows that defendant brought the jewelry to California, where he turned it over to Forget. The express language of subdivision (2) of section 27 confers jurisdiction on the trial court over the robbery count. The case law so holds. (People v. Case (1967) 49 Cal.2d 24, 313 P.2d 840.)[1]

However, although a literal reading of subdivision (1) of section 27, and of section 778a, would seem to support jurisdiction over the murder count also, those sections have a history of judicial construction, binding on us in the case at bench, which requires us to read the statutory language in a manner more restrictive than a literal reading would suggest.

1. [Compiler's note.] Without the aid of statute it was held that D, who stole a horse in Missouri and took it into Iowa, was guilty of larceny in Iowa as a matter of common law. State v. Bennett, 14 Iowa 479 (1863).

Accord, State v. Ellis, 3 Conn. 185 (1819); Ferrill v. Commonwealth, 62 Ky. 153 (1864); Thomas v. Commonwealth, 15 S.W. 861, 12 Ky.L.Rep. 903 (1891); Cummings v. State, 1 Harr. & J. 340 (Md. 1802); Worthington v. State, 58 Md. 403 (1882); Commonwealth v. Andrews, 2 Mass. 14 (1806); Commonwealth v. Holder, 75 Mass. 7 (1857); Hamilton v. State, 11 Ohio 435 (1842); State v. Johnson, 2 Or. 115 (1864); State v. Hill, 19 S.C. 435 (1883).

Contra: Lee v. State, 64 Ga. 203 (1879); Beal v. State, 15 Ind. 378 (1860); State v. Reonnals, 14 La.Ann. 278 (1859); People v. Loughridge, 1 Neb. 11 (1871); State v. LeBlanch, 31 N.J.L. 82 (1864); People v. Gardner, 2 Johns. 477 (N.Y.1807); People v. Schenck, 2 Johns. 479 (N.Y.1807); State v. Brown, 2 N.C. 100 (1794); Simmons v. Commonwealth, 5 Binn. 617 (Pa. 1813); Simpson v. State, 23 Tenn. 456 (1844). This has been changed by statute see Henry v. State, 47 Tenn. 331 (1870).

Whatever may be the rule at common law, it is clear that a state statute may make it a punishable offense, under the name of larceny, for a thief to bring into the state, goods stolen elsewhere by him. State v. Adams, 14 Ala. 486 (1848); La Vaul v. State, 40 Ala. 44 (1866); McFarland v. State, 4 Kan. 68 (1866); People v. Williams, 24 Mich. 156 (1871); State v. Butler, 67 Mo. 59 (1877); State v. Hickle, 268 N.W.2d 826 (S.D.1978).

In People v. Muffum (*sic*) (1953) 40 Cal.2d 709, 256 P.2d 317, the Supreme Court construed the two sections above quoted and held that they required the doing, in California, of an act amounting to an "attempt" to commit the offense charged, within the definition of attempt in criminal cases generally—i.e., that there must be acts beyond mere preparation. Although there can be no doubt that there is no constitutional objection to a broader interpretation and although the *Buffum* decision has been strongly criticized, that case remains the law of California and we have no choice but to apply it in the case at bench.

The only acts of defendant which this record discloses which relate to the murder count are the act of inducing Mrs. Wilson to undertake the fatal trip, inferentially the act of purchasing the tickets, and the aquisition of the assumed murder weapon. The only direct evidence on the formation of the intent to kill is in Forget's testimony concerning a conversation in Spain, although from other things in the record it might be inferred that defendant had held that intent before the party left Los Angeles for Montreal. Giving the fullest possible effect to the whole record, clearly it falls short of an "attempt." It follows that, on the record before us, the trial court had no jurisdiction over the murder count. . . .

The judgment is modified, reversed in part and affirmed in part, as follows: (1) the judgment on count I is reversed; (2) the judgment on counts, II, IV and V is affirmed; (3) the judgment is modified by deleting the reference to count III; the sentence contained in said judgment is vacated and the case is remanded to the trial court for further proceedings consistent with this opinion.

KINGSLEY and DUNN, JJ., concur.

STATE v. SEEKFORD

Supreme Court of Utah, 1981.
638 P.2d 525.

GOULD, DISTRICT JUDGE. Defendant appeals from his nonjury conviction of theft, a second degree felony.

Defendant rented a car on February 4, 1980, in Utah County, and immediately traveled with friends named Revoir to Price and Cleveland, Utah, and then to Las Vegas, Nevada, arriving in Las Vegas on February 5, 1980. They then traveled to Arizona and then Texas. During the course of their travel, defendant and Cary Revoir had several discussions regarding the rented car. During one of these conversations, Revoir said, "We ought to take the car back. We could get in trouble over it." Defendant's responses were that he would "handle it." Defendant and Revoirs then were separated, with defendant keeping the car. Revoirs located him a few days later by telephone, and asked if he was going to return the car, to which defendant replied he would "handle it." Defendant then indicated to Michelle Revoir that he had "some friends who could make him some license plates."

The vehicle was located and recovered several months later.

Defendant's attack is that the Utah court was without jurisdiction. U.C.A., 1953, 76–1–201 provides:

> (1) A person is subject to prosecution in this state for an offense which he commits, while either within or outside the state, by his own conduct or that of another for which he is legally accountable, if:
>
> (a) The offense is committed either wholly or partly within the state; or
>
> (b) The conduct outside the state constitutes an attempt to commit an offense within the state; or
>
> (c) The conduct outside the state constitutes a conspiracy to commit an offense within the state and an act in furtherance of the conspiracy occurs in the state; or
>
> (d) The conduct within the state constitutes an attempt, solicitation, or conspiracy to commit in another jurisdiction an offense under the laws of both this state and such other jurisdiction.
>
> (2) An offense is committed partly within this state if either the conduct which is an element of the offense, or the result which is such an element, occurs within this state. . . .

The court made no specific written finding that an element of the offense occurred in Utah, but did have the following exchange with counsel:

> THE COURT: . . . It may have been that at the time the Rental Agreement was made here, he knew very well he was never going to bring the car back.
>
> MR. SCHUMACHER: But there is no evidence of that before the Court.
>
> THE COURT: I don't know. Maybe there is. Maybe I could infer from what I heard of the entire chain of events, very reasonably, that he had that intent at the time he took it. I think there is stronger evidence along other lines. I think it's something that may be accumulated.

It is clear from this exchange that the court had in mind that the element of "intent" had to have existed in defendant's mind while he was in Utah.

Subsequently, the court found defendant guilty. In view of the exchange between the court and counsel as shown above, we must conclude that the court's finding of guilt encompassed a finding that defendant harbored an "intent to deprive the owner of his property" while in the State of Utah. The offense therefore was committed in this state, and the Utah courts have jurisdiction to try defendant for the offense. . . .

Defendant next contends that the state charged defendant improperly under the general theft statute when it had available a specific statute covering thefts pursuant to rental agreements. The present Utah theft statute consolidates the offenses known under prior law as larceny, embezzlement, extortion, receiving stolen property, and false pretenses into a single offense entitled "theft." All that is now required is simply to plead the general offense of theft and the accusation may be supported by evidence that it was committed in any manner specified in 404 through 410 of the Code.

The judgment of the trial court is affirmed.

HALL, C.J., HOWE and OAKS, JJ.

STEWART, J., concurs in the result.

(iv) JURISDICTION OVER BOUNDARY RIVERS

NIELSON v. OREGON

Supreme Court of the United States, 1909.
212 U.S. 315, 29 S.Ct. 383.

[Nielson, a citizen of Washington, had a license from the Fish Commissioner of Washington to operate a purse net on the Columbia River and was on said river, within the limits of the State of Washington, operating a purse net when he was arrested by Oregon officers. An Oregon statute prohibited fishing with a purse net on the Columbia River and Nielson was convicted for a violation of that law. From that judgment the case was taken to the Supreme Court on error.

Before the territories had been admitted into the Union it had been provided by Act of Congress "that the Territory of Oregon and the Territory of Washington, shall have concurrent jurisdiction over all offenses committed on the Columbia River, where said river forms the common boundary between said territories". And the Act of Congress admitting Oregon into the Union provides that it shall have "jurisdiction in civil and criminal cases upon the Columbia River and Snake River, concurrently with the states and territories of which those rivers form a boundary in common with this State".]

MR. JUSTICE BREWER. . . . Undoubtedly one purpose, perhaps the primary purpose, in the grant of concurrent jurisdiction was to avoid any nice question as to whether a criminal act sought to be prosecuted was committed on one side or the other of the exact boundary in the channel, that boundary sometimes changing by reason of the shifting of the channel. Where an act is *malum in se* prohibited and punishable by the laws of both States, the one first acquiring jurisdiction of the person may prosecute the offense, and its judgment is a finality in both States, so that one convicted or acquitted in the courts of the one State cannot be prosecuted for the same offense in the courts of the other. But, as appears from the quotation we have just made, it is not limited to this. It extends to civil as well as criminal matters, and is broadly a grant of jurisdiction to each of the States.

The present case is not one of the prosecution for an offense *malum in se,* but for one simply *malum prohibitum.* Doubtless the same rule would apply if the act was prohibited by each State separately, but where as here the act is prohibited by one State and in terms authorized by the other, can the one State which prohibits, prosecute and punish for the act done within the territorial limits of the other? Obviously, the grant of concurrent jurisdiction may bring up from time to time many and some curious and difficult questions, so we properly confine ourselves to the precise question presented. The plaintiff in error was within the limits of the State of Washington, doing an act which that State in terms authorized and gave him a license to do. Can the State of Oregon, by virtue of its concurrent jurisdiction, disregard that authority, practically override the legislation of Washington, and punish a man for doing within the territorial limits of Washington an act which that State had specially authorized him to do? [a] We are of opinion that it cannot. It is not at all impossible that in some instances the interests of the two States may be different. Certainly, as appears in the present case, the opinion of the legislatures of the two States is different, and the one State cannot enforce its opinion against that of the other, at least as to an act done within the limits of that other State. Whether, if the act of the plaintiff in error had been done within the territorial limits of the State of Oregon, it would make any difference we need not determine, nor whether, in the absence of any legislation by the State of Washington authorizing the act, Oregon could enforce its statute against the act done anywhere upon the waters of the Columbia. Neither is it necessary to consider whether the prosecution should be in the names of the two States jointly. It is enough to decide, as we do, that for an act done within the territorial limits of the State of Washington under authority and license from that State one cannot be prosecuted and punished by the State of Oregon. . . .

The judgment of the Supreme Court of the State of Oregon is reversed and the case remanded for further proceedings not inconsistent with this opinion.[1]

a. "*(S)ubstantive law* is that which declares what acts are crimes and proscribes the punishment therefor; whereas *procedural law* is that which provides or regulates the steps by which one who violates the law is punished." State v. Augustine, 197 Kan. 207, 209, 416 P.2d 281, 283 (1966).

1. In many cases the courts of one state have punished crimes committed upon that part of the river within the boundaries of another state: Carlisle v. State, 32 Ind. 55 (1869); Dougan v. State, 125 Ind. 130, 25 N.E. 171 (1890); Lemore v. Commonwealth, 127 Ky. 480, 105 S.W. 930 (1907); State v. Cunningham, 102

MODEL PENAL CODE

Section 1.03 Territorial Applicability.

(1) Except as otherwise provided in this Section, a person may be convicted under the law of this State of an offense committed by his own conduct or the conduct of another for which he is legally accountable if:

(a) either the conduct which is an element of the offense or the result which is such an element occurs within this State; or

(b) conduct occurring outside the State is sufficient under the law of this State to constitute an attempt to commit an offense within the State; or

(c) conduct occurring outside the State is sufficient under the law of this State to constitute a conspiracy to commit an offense within the State and an overt act in furtherance of such conspiracy occurs within the State; or

(d) conduct occurring within the State establishes complicity in the commission of, or an attempt, solicitation or conspiracy to commit, an offense in another jurisdiction which also is an offense under the law of this State; or

(e) the offense consists of the omission to perform a legal duty imposed by the law of this State with respect to domicile, residence or a relationship to a person, thing or transaction in the State; or

(f) the offense is based on a statute of this State which expressly prohibits conduct outside the State, when the conduct bears a reasonable relation to a legitimate interest of this State and the actor knows or should know that his conduct is likely to affect that interest.

(2) Subsection (1)(a) does not apply when either causing a specified result or a purpose to cause or danger of causing such a result is an element of an offense and the result occurs or is designed or likely to occur only in another jurisdiction where the conduct charged would not constitute an offense, unless a legislative purpose plainly appears to declare the conduct criminal regardless of the place of the result.

(3) Subsection (1)(a) does not apply when causing a particular result is an element of an offense and the result is caused by conduct occurring outside the State which would not constitute an offense if the result had occurred

Miss. 237, 59 So. 76 (1912); State v. Metcalf, 65 Mo.App. 681 (1896); State v. Cameron, 2 Pin. 490 (Wis.1850); see Commonwealth v. Garner, 3 Grat. 655 (Va. 1846). In Wiggins Ferry Co. v. Reddig, 24 Ill.App. 260 (1887), the court at page 265 said: "Undoubtedly it would be held that the judicial tribunal first taking cognizance of the cause would, under well established and understood principles, retain its jurisdiction to the end of the controversy, applying the law of the *forum* to the facts of the case in settling the rights of the parties."

Defendant was charged in Minnesota with larceny from the person. The evidence showed that the offense was committed on a bridge which spans the Mississippi River, at a point between Minnesota and Wisconsin, and was committed on a part of the bridge over an island which is on the Wisconsin side of the main channel of the river. It was held that the Minnesota court had jurisdiction. State v. George, 60 Minn. 503, 63 N.W. 100 (1895).

Where a river which forms a boundary line between two states suddenly leaves its old bed and forms a new one by the process of avulsion there is no change of the boundary line. State v. Jacobs, 93 Ariz. 336, 380 P.2d 998 (1963).

there, unless the actor purposely or knowingly caused the result within the State.

(4) When the offense is homicide, either the death of the victim or the bodily impact causing death constitutes a "result", within the meaning of Subsection (1)(a) and if the body of a homicide victim is found within the State, it is presumed that such result occurred within the State.

(5) This State includes the land and water and the air space above such land and water with respect to which the State has legislative jurisdiction.[2]

(B) VENUE

If an alleged offense is triable within the state it is then necessary to determine which of the courts in the state may try it. To decide this it is necessary to ascertain the particular area (or areas) of the state within which it may be tried. This area will usually be a county, although in some states it may be some other subdivision such as a district. And the county (or other area) appropriate for this trial is called the "venue." The word "venue" originally meant the neighborhood from which the jurors were to come. It still has that meaning except that the place of trial is the same whether it is to be by a jury or without a jury.

Statutory provisions with reference to venue differ from state to state. The American Law Institute included the following suggestions in its proposed Code of Criminal Procedure, after an exhaustive study of all of the existing statutes:

Section 238. Right to try where offense committed within state. Any person who commits within this state an offense against this state, whether he is within or without the state at the time of its commission, may be tried in this state.

Section 239. Offense in or against aircraft. Any person who commits an offense in or against any aircraft while it is in flight over this state may be tried in this state. The trial in such case may be in any county over which the aircraft passed in the course of such flight.

Section 240. Place of trial generally. In all criminal prosecutions the trial shall be in the county where the offense was committed unless otherwise provided in this Code.

Section 241. Where accessory in one county and offense committed in another. Where a person in one county aids, abets or procures the commission of an offense in another county he may be tried for the offense in either county.

Section 242. Where offense committed partly in one and partly in another county. Where several acts are requisite to the com-

2. Copyright: 1962 by the American Law Institute. Reprinted with the permission of the American Law Institute.

mission of an offense, the trial may be in any county in which any of such acts occurs.

Section 243. Where offense committed on or near county boundary. Where an offense is committed on or within five hundred yards of the boundary of two or more counties the trial may be in any one of such counties.

Section 244. Where person in one county commits offense in another. Where a person in one county commits an offense in another county the trial may be in either county.

Section 245. Where offense committed on railroad train or other vehicle. Where an offense is committed on a railroad train or other public or private vehicle while in the course of its trip the trial may be in any county through which such train or other vehicle passed during such trip.

Section 246. Where offense committed on vessel. Where an offense is committed on board a vessel in the course of its voyage, the trial may be in any county through which the vessel passed during such voyage.

Section 247. Where injury inflicted in one county and death occurs in another. Where a person inflicts an injury upon another person in one county from which the injured person dies in another county, the trial for the homicide may be in either county.

Section 248. Where stolen property brought into another county. Where a person obtains property by larceny, robbery, false pretenses or embezzlement in one county and brings the property so obtained into any other county or counties, he may be tried in the county in which he obtains the property or in any other county into which he brings it.

Section 249. Conviction or acquittal in one county bar to prosecution in another. Where a person may be tried for an offense in two or more counties, a conviction or acquittal of the offense in one county shall be a bar to a prosecution for the same offense in another county.

Where the evidence as to venue is disputed the jury should pass upon it as one of the issues of the case. If it is clear that the court has no jurisdiction over the offense the prosecution should be dismissed. But if the lack of jurisdiction is because the offense is within the exclusive jurisdiction of the court of some other county of the state the usual procedure is not to discharge the defendant, but to have him committed, or admitted to bail, to await transfer to the proper county for trial there.

STATE v. FAVORS

Supreme Court of Arizona, En Banc, 1962.
92 Ariz. 147, 375 P.2d 260.

UDALL, VICE CHIEF JUSTICE. Bobby Favors was convicted in the Superior Court of Pima County of the crime of wilfully and unlawfully robbing Jack Weylor on December 7, 1960. He appeals to this court.

With two other men Favors entered upon Weylor's property and with a 30–30 rifle forced him to give up his wallet along with its contents. The identity of Favors as one of the three men was established to the satisfaction of the jury, notwithstanding the fact that he claimed to have been elsewhere at the time of the commission of the crime.

The errors urged by the defendant relate to four different matters. First it is argued that the court erred in reopening the state's case to hear evidence on the question of venue, when the state failed to establish venue before the time that the court was to instruct the jury. When defendant had finished his own closing argument he asked the court to instruct the jury that there was no evidence in the trial that the crime had been committed in Pima County. Thereupon plaintiff moved the court for permission to reopen the case for the purpose of hearing evidence regarding the question of venue, which motion was granted. Deputy Sheriff Norman Ranger was recalled and he testified that the alleged robbery was committed in Pima County at the place specified in the information.

Such a ruling was within the sound discretion of the court. In State v. Cassady, 67 Ariz. 48, 190 P.2d 501, we said:

"Our rules of criminal procedure should be construed so as to promote justice—not to thwart it. To have refused to permit the state to reopen its case would have been an abuse of legal discretion and an 'assist' to the obstruction of justice." . . .

Judgment of conviction affirmed.[1]

BERNSTEIN, C.J., and STRUCKMEYER, JENNINGS and LOCKWOOD, JJ., concur.

1. Where defendant did not know that venue would not be proved he could move for an acquittal at the conclusion of the evidence. United States v. Brothman, 191 F.2d 70 (2d Cir.1951).

"The venue was a jurisdictional fact, . . ." People v. Adams, 300 Ill. 20, 24, 132 N.E. 765, 767 (1921). ". . . it has always been the law requiring the government or state, as the case might be, to prove the venue in order to show jurisdiction of the court to try and determine the issue." State v. Jackson, 187 Ind. 694, 699, 121 N.E. 114, 116 (1918). "'It is a maxim in the law that consent can never confer jurisdiction; by which is meant that the consent of parties cannot empower a Court to act upon subjects which are not submitted to its determination and judgment by the law.' Cooley on Const.Lim. p. 575. . . . The general rule undoubtedly is that the objection that a court has no jurisdiction of the person of the accused may be waived. . . . This court holds that 'the right to object to the locality of trial is a personal privilege which the party may waive and thereby confer jurisdiction.' Brown v. Brown, 155 Tenn. 530, at page 537, 296 S.W. 356, 358, citing cases." State ex

STATE v. ZIMMER

Supreme Court of Kansas, 1967.
198 Kan. 479, 426 P.2d 267.

HARMAN, COMMISSIONER. William Frederick Zimmer was convicted of the offenses of kidnaping in the first degree, with harm inflicted (K.S.A. 21–449) and of murder in the first degree (K.S.A. 21–401). As punishment the jury imposed the death penalty for the kidnaping charge and life imprisonment for the murder. The trial court denied appellant's motion for new trial, and adjudged sentences in accordance with the jury verdict, from which defendant Zimmer has appealed. . . .

Appellant urges as ground for reversal of his conviction that proper venue as to the murder offense was never established in Shawnee county, inasmuch as there was no evidence the killing occurred therein. He argues the state produced evidence the victim was last seen alive in Wamego in Pottawatomie county and her body was found in Pottawatomie county; therefore the murder offense could be prosecuted only in that county.

Section 10 of the bill of rights to our Kansas constitution provides in part:

rel. Lea v. Brown, 166 Tenn. 669, 694–5, 64 S.W.2d 841, 849 (1933). Accord, Hildebrand v. United States, 304 F.2d 716 (10th Cir.1962).

The federal statute provides (18 U.S.C.A. § 3231): "The district courts of the United States shall have original jurisdiction, exclusive of the courts of the States, of all offenses against the laws of the United States". Hence the question in regard to a particular court of the United States is one of venue rather than jurisdiction. Bickford v. Looney, 219 F.2d 555 (10th Cir.1955).

The right guaranteed by the Constitution to be tried in the county in which the crime is alleged to have been committed relates to venue rather than jurisdiction and is waived by a plea of guilty. Key v. Page, 424 P.2d 99 (Okl.Cr.1967).

D has a constitutional right to a trial by jury in the district in which the crime was committed. There is no constitutional guaranty that the accused has a right to be tried in the division of the district in which the crime was committed. Franklin v. United States, 384 F.2d 377 (5th Cir.1967).

Where the only reference from which venue might be inferred was testimony relating to certain named streets and business establishments the conviction was reversed. Morris v. State, 363 P.2d 377 (Okl.Cr.1961). The court said it would take judicial notice of the boundaries of the counties and the geographical locations of the cities and towns of the state, but not of streets and buildings where there is no evidence as to the town or city in which they are located.

Permitting either trial or appellate court to decide venue from facts judicially noticed but not communicated to the jury would deprive defendant of trial by jury on the issue of fact alleged in the indictment. State v. Jones, 240 Or. 129, 400 P.2d 524 (1965).

Venue for the trial of a criminal case need not be proved beyond a reasonable doubt, but only by a preponderance of the evidence, and it may be established by circumstantial evidence. People v. Erb, 235 Cal.App.2d 650, 45 Cal.Rptr. 503 (1965). Contra, State v. Jones, 240 Or. 129, 400 P.2d 524 (1965).

"Proof of venue is an essential element of the Government's case. It may be established either by direct or circumstantial evidence. Furthermore, unlike other elements of a crime which must be proved beyond a reasonable doubt, venue need only be proved by a preponderance of the evidence." United States v. Massa, 686 F.2d 526, 527–528 (7th Cir.1982).

"In all prosecutions, the accused shall be allowed to appear and defend in person, or by counsel . . . and a speedy public trial by an impartial jury of the county or district in which the offense is alleged to have been committed. . . ."

This is implemented by the following statutes:

"Offenses committed against the laws of this state shall be punished in the county in which the offense is committed, except as may be otherwise provided by law." (K.S.A. 62–401.)

"When a public offense has been committed, partly in one county and partly in another, or the act or effects constituting or requisite to the consummation of the offense occur in two or more counties, the jurisdiction is in either county." (K.S.A. 62–404.)

And our statute denouncing kidnaping provides:

". . . Any person or persons charged with such offense may be tried in any county into or through which the person so seized, inveigled, decoyed, kidnaped, or otherwise taken shall have been carried or brought." (K.S.A. 21–449).

It is true as contended there was no evidence as to where the fatal blows were struck.

Appellant was charged in the information with felony murder, that is, killing while engaged in the perpetration of a felony, namely, kidnaping. The jury was instructed upon this type of murder and appellant stands convicted thereof. Hence the kidnaping was an essential element of the murder offense. Inasmuch as the initial abduction occurred in Shawnee county and the kidnaping was triable there, venue on the murder charge became permissible there under 62–404.

It may be noteworthy that the general area in Pottawatomie county where the victim was last seen alive other than by her killer and where her body was found, is so situated it lies within five or six minutes driving distance from three adjoining counties, including Shawnee, and no more than fifteen minutes from at least two others. A murderer should not escape punishment because the exact place of his crime is concealed.

The Supreme Court of Washington was confronted with an identical factual situation where the same legal contention was made as here in State v. Wilson, 38 Wash.2d 593, 231 P.2d 288, cert. den. 342 U.S. 855, 72 S.Ct. 81, 96 L.Ed. 644, cert. den. 343 U.S. 950, 72 S.Ct. 1044, 96 L.Ed. 1352. The defendants there were convicted of kidnaping in the first degree and murder in the first degree and the death penalty imposed. The facts were that the victim was kidnaped in Clark County, Washington, and a week later her body was found in Skamania County, Washington, fifty-five miles from the scene of the kidnaping. She had been brutally beaten, cut behind her ear and sexually violated. Death was caused by carbon monoxide poisoning. The evidence did not reveal where the cause of death occurred.

The state of Washington has a constitutional provision respecting place of trial essentially identical to that quoted from our own bill of rights and an implementing statute identical to our 62–404.

Under a statute similar to our own the defendants in Wilson were charged with felony murder. The court held the county wherein the kidnaping occurred had jurisdiction to try the murder charge, stating:

"Nor does the fact that no one can say with certainty whether the death occurred in Clark county, where the kidnaping occurred, or in Skamania county, where the body was found, present any bar to the prosecution for murder in Clark county."

We hold venue on the murder charge was properly established in Shawnee county.

At the conclusion of the prosecution evidence appellant moved for his discharge upon the venue issue already mentioned and upon the ground appellee had failed to prove the kidnaping charge. Denial of this motion is assigned as error. This contention is based upon the argument there was no evidence that the girl Gladys was confined against her will.

The child was taken under such circumstances as to cause crying and screaming in her younger brother and sister, she was crying when seen in appellant's company in the field northwest of Topeka and appellant admitted to officers he slapped her because she was crying. She was found brutally murdered. The contention is wholly without merit. Moreover, as a matter of law, a child of tender years may not consent to its seizure. At 1 Am.Jur., 2d Abduction and Kidnapping, § 16, the rule is stated:

"A child of tender years is ordinarily regarded as incapable of consenting to its seizure and abduction and, when taken from its rightful guardian, is deemed to have been taken without its consent as a matter of law."

The jury here was later instructed in accordance with the foregoing and properly so. The evidence was sufficient to support the charges, including the element of wilfulness, and the court committed no error in denying the motion to discharge.

The judgment and sentences are affirmed.

Approved by the court.[1]

1. See also State v. Duvaul, 223 Kan. 718, 576 P.2d 653 (1978).

STATE v. REESE

Supreme Court of Washington, Department One, 1920.
112 Wash. 507, 192 P. 934.

MAIN, J. The defendant was charged by information, by the prosecuting attorney of Spokane county, with the crime of grand larceny. The trial resulted in a verdict of guilty. A motion in arrest of judgment was made and sustained. The state appeals.

The information, omitting the formal parts, is as follows:

"That on or about August 31st, 1919, on a railway train of the Northern Pacific Railroad, arriving in, and passing through, Spokane county, Washington, the said defendant, Arthur Reese, whose other or true name is to the prosecuting attorney unknown, then and there being, did then and there, wilfully, unlawfully and feloniously, take, steal and carry away one certain gold watch of the value of $50 and one certain gold bougat [sic] watch fob of the value of $50, the property of, and belonging to, Chas. E. Roediger, with the intent to deprive and defraud the owner thereof."

It should be noted that, in this charge, it is not alleged that the offense was committed in Spokane county. Upon the trial it appeared from testimony that the respondent was a porter on the Northern Pacific train leaving Tacoma, Washington, on the evening of the 30th or 31st of August, 1919. The train arrived in Spokane the following morning. Among the passengers on the train was one C.E. Roediger, who occupied a berth in a sleeping car just in front of the car which was in charge of the respondent. Roediger retired about midnight, and at the time the train was near Yakima, Washington. At this time he had in his vest pocket a watch and fob. He awoke near Lind, Washington, and his watch and fob were missing. About a month later the respondent pawned the watch in the city of Spokane. Thereafter he was arrested, with the result as above indicated. The charge in this case is laid under § 2293 of Rem. & Bal.Code, which provides:

"The route traversed by any railway car, coach, train or other public conveyance, and the water traversed by any boat shall be criminal districts; and the jurisdiction of all public offenses committed on any such railway car, coach, train, boat or other public conveyance, or at any station or depot upon such route, shall be in any county through which said car, coach, train, boat or other public conveyance may pass during the trip or voyage, or in which the trip or voyage may begin or terminate."

By this statute, it is attempted to make the route traversed by a railway train a criminal district and to provide that the court in any county through which the train may pass during its trip shall have jurisdiction of any offense committed upon the train, regardless of whether, at the time the crime was committed, the train was in the county where the prosecution is attempted to be had. If this statute is constitutional, the judgment of the superior court cannot be sustained. On the other hand, if the statute is unconstitutional, the trial court ruled correctly on the motion in arrest of judgment. It should be kept in mind that this is not a case where property stolen in one county is carried by the thief into another, and in the latter county is charged with having committed an offense therein. As already pointed out, the information in this case does not charge that the offense was committed in Spokane county. Neither is it a case where an act done in one county contributes to the offense in another. The question is the constitutionality of the law under which the accused was tried and convicted. Const., art. 1, § 22, provides:

"In criminal prosecutions, the accused shall have the right to . . . a speedy public trial by an impartial jury of the county in which the offense is alleged to have been committed. . . ."

Under this section of the constitution one accused of crime has a right to be tried in the county in which the offense is alleged to have been committed. It requires no argument to show that the offense, being alleged in a particular county, the proof must show that it was committed in that county. Comparing the provisions of the statute with the requirements of the constitution, it appears that the statute goes beyond the constitutional limitation. Under the statute, the route traversed by a railway train is made a criminal district, and an offender may be prosecuted in any county in such district. Under the constitution, he can only be prosecuted in the county where the offense has been committed. In State v. Carroll, 55 Wash. 588, 104 Pac. 814, 133 Am.St. 1047, the court had before it a statute providing that, when property taken by burglary in one county had been brought into another county, the jurisdiction was in either county. It was there held that the statute violated Const., art. 1, § 22, which guaranteed to the accused a right to a trial in the county in which the offense was alleged to have been committed. While that case can hardly be said to be exactly in point upon the question presented upon this appeal, yet the analogy is very close. . . . In People v. Brock, 149 Mich. 464, 112 N.W. 1116, the question was before the supreme court of Michigan, and it was there held that such a statute cannot be sustained under a constitutional provision which guarantees to the accused the right to a trial in the county in which the offense has been committed. It was there said:

"It would be a startling innovation should we say that the legislature has power to subject a person charged with crime to prosecution in any one of several counties, covering a strip of territory coextensive with the length or breadth of the state, at the prosecutor's election, and yet that is what this statute authorizes if it is valid. It cannot be said that this offense was in 'contemplation of law' committed in each of said counties, as in a case where property stolen in one county is carried by the thief into another, or possibly where an act done in one county contributes to the commission of the offense in another."

In Watt v. People, 126 Ill. 9, 18 N.E. 340, the question was before the supreme court of Illinois and a different conclusion was there reached, though not by a unanimous court. The holding in that case seems to be influenced by the fact that the constitutional provision there being considered was less restrictive than were the similar provisions in either of the two earlier constitutions, and this fact led to the conclusion that it was the intention "to release in some degree the rigid rule formerly prevailing." As already stated, none of the other cases cited in the notes of Corpus Juris, or in the brief, discuss or decide the question here presented. Under this state of the authorities, we are constrained to disagree with the writer of the text upon where the weight of authority lies. It seems to us that reason and authority both support the view that the statute cannot take away from an accused a right guaranteed by the constitution.

The judgment will be affirmed.[1]

HOLCOMB, C.J., MITCHELL, PARKER, and MACKINTOSH, JJ., concur.

1. In 1922 the constitution of the State of Washington was amended as follows: "The route traversed by any railway coach, train or public conveyance, and the water traversed by any boat shall be criminal districts; and the jurisdiction of all public offenses committed on any such railway car, coach, train, boat or other public conveyance, or at any station or depot upon such route, shall be in any county through which the said car, coach, train, boat or other public conveyance may pass during the trip or voyage, or in which the trip or voyage may begin or terminate." Art. I, § 22. See now Amendment 10.

A statute authorizing trial in either county if the offense was committed within one-quarter mile of the county line was held to be unconstitutional. Armstrong v. State, 41 Tenn. 338 (1860).

Accord, State v. Montgomery, 115 La. 155, 38 So. 949 (1905); State v. Hatch, 91 Mo. 568, 4 S.W. 502 (1887). A similar statute was held valid in Michigan, but the constitutional provisions were different. People v. Donaldson, 243 Mich. 104, 219 N.W. 602 (1928). In Oregon a statute authorizing trial in either county, if the offense is committed within a mile of the county line, was held not to violate defendant's right to be tried in the county in which the crime was committed. This statute was said merely to enlarge the boundaries of the county for judicial purposes. State v. Lehman, 130 Or. 132, 279 P. 283 (1929).

Where an offense is committed partly in one county and partly in another, a trial in either satisfies the constitutional provision which entitles the accused to be tried in the county in which the offense was committed. Kneefe v. Sullivan, 2 Or.App. 152, 465 P.2d 741 (1970).

In Commonwealth v. Macloon, 101 Mass. 1 (1869), it was held that death within the state, resulting from injuries inflicted elsewhere, was sufficient to authorize trial and conviction in the state, under an express statutory provision to that effect. Accord, as to death in one county resulting from an injury inflicted in another county in the same state, under a statute expressly so providing. State v. Criqui, 105 Kan. 716, 185 P. 1063 (1919). In State v. Carter, 27 N.J.L. 499 (1859) it was held that an indictment charging a fatal assault committed in New York and resulting in death in New Jersey charged no crime in the latter state. Apparently New Jersey had a statute somewhat similar to the Massachusetts act, but the court held that it applied only to murder and not to manslaughter. The opinion indicates that it is beyond the power of the state to punish for acts done exclusively in another state, even if death results therefrom and occurs in New Jersey.

In Washington it was held that taking a girl from one county and placing her in another county authorized conviction (of placing a girl in a house of prostitution) in the county *from which* she was taken.

UNITED STATES v. DIXON

United States District Court, E.D. New York, 1947.
73 F.Supp. 683.

Theodore Dixon was charged by indictments with manslaughter and assault committed on board a merchant vessel of the United States, and he moves to dismiss both indictments.

Motion denied.

BYERS, DISTRICT JUDGE. This is a motion, pursuant to Rule 12 of the Federal Rules of Criminal Procedure, 18 U.S.C.A. following section 687, to dismiss both indictments, made after plea of not guilty as to each. The motion was permitted pursuant to paragraph (b)(3) of said Rule.

The grounds are:

1, 2 and 3. That both indictments fail to show jurisdiction in the court. The respective charges involve one transaction; and as to the first, the defendant is charged with manslaughter according to Title 18 U.S.C.A. § 453; as to the second, he is charged with assault under Title 18 U.S.C.A. §§ 451 and 455.

It will be assumed from the motion papers, pro and con, that the proof will show that the defendant is a citizen of Great Britain, who was chief cook on the S.S. Benjamin Silliman, a merchant vessel of the United States which on March 27, 1947, was in command of W.S. Evans as master, and was proceeding out of the port of Ceuta, Spanish Morocco.

That between midnight and 2:00 A.M. of that day a fracas occurred in defendant's cabin, during the course of which one Elmo Martin was shot and the defendant Dixon was wounded. The master at once arranged for a doctor and a launch to attend the two men and take them ashore.

State v. Ashe, 182 Wash. 598, 48 P.2d 213 (1935). And a prosecution for obtaining property by false pretenses could be maintained in the county in which the false and fraudulent representation was made, although the property was obtained in another county. State v. Knutson, 168 Wash. 633, 12 P.2d 923 (1932). Both of these decisions were under a statute declaring the venue to be in either county if the offense was committed partly in each.

But a similar statute was held not to authorize a prosecution for attempted abortion in the county in which the miscarriage occurred if the unlawful operation was performed in a different county. State v. Hollenbeck, 36 Iowa 112 (1873). And a statute, authorizing a prosecution for burglary in a county into which was taken the loot from a house broken into in another county, was held to be unconstitutional. State v. McGraw, 87 Mo. 161 (1885).

The offense of filing a false income-tax return may be tried either in the district in which the return was prepared or in the district in which it was filed. United States v. United States District Court, 209 F.2d 575 (6th Cir.1954).

Although B's shooting of the witness occurred in the Middle District of Tennessee, venue for prosecution of obstruction of justice could lie in the Northern District of Alabama, where the case was pending in which the witness was scheduled to testify. United States v. Barham, 666 F.2d 521 (11th Cir.1982).

That at about 8:00 A.M., the master gave the British Consul at that port written authority to place a guard over both men, and to make a formal report to the United States Consul at Tangier.

That on April 2, 1947, the British Vice-Consul handed over the defendant to the master of the United States merchant ship Richardson to transport him to this country. He was so brought to the port of New York and there arrested and taken into custody, on or about April 15, 1947, and is now held to answer these indictments which were filed in this court on August 27 and September 2, 1947, respectively.

The alleged crimes having been committed on the high seas or elsewhere out of the jurisdiction of any particular state or district, trial is proper in the district where the offender is found, or into which he is first brought, Title 28 U.S.C.A. § 102.

It is a reasonable inference that the master of the Silliman sought the aid of the British Consul in Ceuta in the absence of a United States Consul, and that the former acted on behalf of the master in keeping Dixon under guard, and in causing him to be transported to the United States, and there to answer to a charge of having committed a crime on a merchant ship of the United States.

The court is not called upon to inquire how the defendant got here, so long as he was found in or was first brought to this district.

It is the present view that the master of the Silliman could have brought Dixon here in custody, and that he merely accomplished that purpose by securing the assistance of the British Vice-Consul and that of the master of the Richardson.

Dixon was not entitled to any intervention of the courts of Spanish Morocco, or of Great Britain. He had signed on a merchant ship of the United States and thereby subjected himself to the laws of this country, and he has been duly indicted, and must stand trial.

The foregoing disposes as well of the second and third points urged for him as of the first.

He was never in the custody of the British Vice-Consul as such, but the latter was requested by the master of the defendant's ship to assist in the discharge of the latter's duty and authority; no necessity for extradition arose, as the defendant never sought asylum in any country.

4. That the indictments fail to set forth a crime under the laws of the United States. This is contradicted by the language of the Statutes to which reference has been made.

It is no answer to the manslaughter charge that the alleged victim died ashore in the hospital, and not on the ship where seemingly he was shot. Title 18 U.S.C.A. § 553. See also Bostic v. Rives, 71 App. D.C. 2, 107 F.2d 649, at page 651.

This court is not called upon to direct which indictment is to be tried first.

Motion to dismiss denied. Settle order.[a]

UNITED STATES v. CORES

Supreme Court of the United States, 1958.
356 U.S. 405, 78 S.Ct. 875.

MR. JUSTICE CLARK delivered the opinion of the Court.

The sole issue in this appeal is whether an alien crewman who willfully remains in the United States in excess of the 29 days allowed by his conditional landing permit, in violation of § 252(c) of the Immigration and Nationality Act,[1] is guilty of a continuing offense which may be prosecuted in the district where he is found. Discovering that appellee's permit had expired before he entered the district where he was apprehended and where the prosecution was begun, the District Court dismissed the criminal information, holding that a violation of § 252(c) was not a continuing crime. The Government brought direct appeal, 18 U.S.C. § 3731, 18 U.S.C.A. § 3731, and we noted probable jurisdiction. 1957, 355 U.S. 866, 78 S.Ct. 123, 2 L.Ed. 2d 72. Since we conclude that the District Court was in error, the judgment is reversed and the case is remanded for further proceedings.

The information, filed in the United States District Court for the District of Connecticut, charged that appellee entered the United States at Philadelphia on April 27, 1955, and that 29 days later, at the

a. Where two or more courts have concurrent jurisdiction of the same offense the established rule is that the court first acquiring jurisdiction of the prosecution, retains it to the end. State v. Parker, 234 N.C. 236, 66 S.E.2d 907 (1951), unless it voluntarily dismisses or abandons the prosecution, Rogers v. State, 101 Miss. 847, 58 So. 536 (1912), or the defendant waives his right to insist upon trial there, State v. Van Ness, 109 Vt. 392, 199 A. 759 (1938). Actual jurisdiction of the prosecution (as distinguished from potential jurisdiction of the offense) ordinarily requires jurisdiction of the person. Sherrod v. State, 197 Ala. 286, 72 So. 540 (1916). Hence if indictments for the same offense are found properly in two or more counties the case normally will be tried in the court first acquiring jurisdiction of the person by arrest. Smithey v. State, 93 Miss. 257, 46 So. 410 (1908). If, however, in the absence of any collusion on the part of the defendant, he is tried and acquitted in a court other than the one first acquiring jurisdiction, this is a complete bar to a subsequent trial in the first court. State v. Howell, 220 S.C. 178, 66 S.E.2d 701 (1951). On the other hand the state has a right to elect the forum in which it will proceed and is not to be deprived of this choice by the machinations of the defendant or his friends. McDaniel, Sheriff v. Sams, 259 Ky. 56, 82 S.W.2d 215 (1935).

1. [Footnotes by the Court.] 66 Stat. 221, 8 U.S.C. § 1282(c), 8 U.S.C.A. § 1282(c). Subsection (a) authorizes immigration officers to grant permits, on certain conditions, allowing alien crewmen to land for periods up to 29 days. Subsection (b) details procedures for revocation of permits. Subsection (c) sets out the criminal penalties involved in this case:

> "Any alien crewman who willfully remains in the United States in excess of the number of days allowed in any conditional permit issued under subsection (a) of this section shall be guilty of a misdemeanor, and upon conviction thereof shall be fined not more than $500 or shall be imprisoned for not more than six months, or both."

expiration of his conditional landing permit, he "did wilfully and knowingly remain in the United States, to wit: Bethel, Connecticut," in violation of § 252(c) of the Immigration and Nationality Act. A plea of guilty was entered, but a government attorney informed the court prior to sentencing that appellee was not in Connecticut at the expiration of his permit as charged in the information, but that in fact he came to Connecticut only after spending about a year in New York. The judge permitted withdrawal of the guilty plea and dismissed the case. He cited an earlier decision of the same court holding that § 252(c) did not define a continuing crime. United States v. Tavares, No. 9407 Crim., May 6, 1957, and indicated that the information was brought in an improper district since appellee was not in Connecticut at the time his permit expired.[2]

The Constitution makes it clear that determination of proper venue in a criminal case requires determination of where the crime was committed.[3] This principle is reflected in numerous statutory enactments, including Rule 18, Fed.Rules Crim.Proc., which provides that except as otherwise permitted, "the prosecution shall be had in a district in which the offense was committed . . . ." In ascertaining this locality we are mindful that questions of venue "raise deep issues of public policy in the light of which legislation must be construed." The provision for trial in the vicinity of the crime is a safeguard against the unfairness and hardship involved when an accused is prosecuted in a remote place. Provided its language permits, the Act in question should be given that construction which will respect such considerations.

Unlike some statutory offenses,[4] there is an absence here of any specific provision fixing venue, save the general language of the Act providing for venue "at any place in the United States at which the violation may occur . . . ."[5] In such cases the Court must base

2. Appellee suggests that the inconsistency in the date of the offense as alleged in the information and as represented by government counsel provides additional reason for upholding the dismissal. This phase of the case, however, is not before us, United States v. Borden Co., 1939, 308 U.S. 188, 206–207, 60 S.Ct. 182, 191–192, 84 L.Ed. 181, so we confine our opinion to the point of statutory construction which clearly prompted the dismissal. Any inconsistency may be asserted by appellee on remand. See Fed. Rules Crim.Proc. [Rule] 7(e), 18 U.S.C.A.

3. "The Trial of all Crimes, except in Cases of Impeachment, shall be by Jury; and such Trial shall be held in the State where the said Crimes shall have been committed . . . ." U.S. Const. Art. III, § 2, cl. 3.

"In all criminal prosecutions, the accused shall enjoy the right to a speedy and public trial, by an impartial jury of the State and district wherein the crime shall have been committed . . . ." U.S. Const. Amend. VI.

4. See e.g., 18 U.S.C. § 659, 18 U.S.C.A. § 659 (theft of goods in interstate commerce); 18 U.S.C. § 1073, 18 U.S.C.A. § 1073 (flight to avoid prosecution or giving testimony); 18 U.S.C. § 3236, 18 U.S.C.A. § 3236 (murder or manslaughter); 18 U.S.C. § 3239, 18 U.S.C.A. § 3239 (transmitting or mailing threatening communications); 32 Stat. 847, 34 Stat. 587, 49 U.S.C. § 41(1), 49 U.S.C.A. § 41(1) (certain violations of Interstate Commerce Act). See Barron, Federal Practice and Procedure, § 2061.

5. § 279, Immigration and Nationality Act, 66 Stat. 230, 8 U.S.C. § 1329, 8 U.S.C.A. § 1329.

its determination on "the nature of the crime alleged and the location of the act or acts constituting it." United States v. Anderson, 1946, 328 U.S. 699, 703, 66 S.Ct. 1213, 1216, 90 L.Ed. 1529, and if the Congress is found to have created a continuing offense, "the locality of [the] crime shall extend over the whole area through which force propelled by an offender operates."

Section 252(c) punishes "[a]ny alien crewman who willfully remains in the United States in excess of the number of days allowed." The conduct proscribed is the affirmative act of willfully remaining, and the crucial word "remains" permits no connotation other than continuing presence. Nor does the section necessarily pertain to any particular locality, such as the place of entry, for the Act broadly extends to willfully remaining "in the United States." [6] Appellee urges, however, that the offense is completed the moment the permit expires, and that even if the alien remains thereafter, he no longer commits the offense. It is true that remaining at the instant of expiration satisfies the definition of the crime, but it does not exhaust it. It seems incongruous to say that while the alien "wilfully remains" on the 29th day when his permit expires, he no longer does so on the 30th, though still physically present in the country. Given the element of willfulness, we believe an alien "remains," in the contemplation of the statute, until he physically leaves the United States. The crime achieves no finality until such time. Since an offense committed in more than one district "may be inquired of and prosecuted in any district in which such offense was . . . continued," 18 U.S.C. § 3237, 18 U.S.C.A. § 3237, venue for § 252(c) lies in any district where the crewman willfully remains after the permit expires. Appellee entered Connecticut and was found there, so that district has venue for the prosecution.

The legislative history is not inconsistent with this interpretation of the statute. After a thorough investigation of our immigration laws completed some two years prior to the enactment of § 252(c), the Senate Committee on the Judiciary reported, "The problems relating to seamen are largely created by those who desert their ships, remain here illegally beyond the time granted them to stay, and become lost in the general populace of the country." S.Rep. No. 1515, 81st Cong., 2d Sess., 550. The tracing of such persons is complicated

6. The offense here is unlike crimes of illegal entry set out in § 275 and § 276 of the Act. 66 Stat. 229, 8 U.S.C. §§ 1325, 1326, 8 U.S.C.A. §§ 1325, 1326. Those offenses are not continuing ones, as "entry" is limited to a particular locality and hardly suggests continuity. Hence a specific venue provision in § 279 of the Act was required before illegal entry cases could be prosecuted at the place of apprehension. 66 Stat. 230, 8 U.S.C. § 1329, 8 U.S.C.A. § 1329. This reasoning underlay the request for specific legislation by the Immigration and Naturalization Service. See Analysis of S. 3455, 81st Cong., prepared by the General Counsel of the Service, p. 276–2. In contrast to illegal entry, the § 252(c) offense of willfully remaining is continuing in nature. A specific venue provision would be mere surplusage, since prosecutions may be instituted in any district where the offense has been committed, not necessarily the district where the violation first occurred. The absence of such provision, therefore, is without significance.

by the obscuration worked both by their own movement and by the passage of time. In this atmosphere the Congress sought to establish sanctions for alien crewmen who "willfully remain," the Senate Committee having observed that traditional remedies for the problem were inadequate because many crewmen "do not have the necessary documents to permit deportation." Ibid. It is hardly likely that the Congress would create the new sanction only to strip it of much of its effectiveness by compelling trial in the district where the crewman was present when his permit expired—a place which months or years later might be impossible of proof.

Moreover, we think it not amiss to point out that this result is entirely in keeping with the policy of relieving the accused, where possible, of the inconvenience incident to prosecution in a district far removed from his residence. Forcing an alien crewman to trial in the district where he was present at the expiration of his permit could entail much hardship. By holding the crime here to be a continuing one we make a valuable tool of justice available to the crewman. Rule 21(b) of the Federal Rules of Criminal Procedure provides for transfer of the proceeding to another district on motion of the defendant if it appears that the offense was committed in more than one district, and "if the court is satisfied that in the interest of justice the proceeding should be transferred to another district or division in which the commission of the offense is charged." The rule, with its inherent flexibility, would be inapplicable absent characterization of the offense as continuing in nature.

Reversed and remanded.[7]

MR. JUSTICE DOUGLAS, with whom THE CHIEF JUSTICE and MR. JUSTICE BLACK concur, dissenting.

The decision seems to me to be out of harmony with the statutory scheme of venue which Congress designed for immigration cases. We are here concerned with a crime under § 252 of the Immigration and Nationality Act of 1952, 66 Stat. 163, 220, 8 U.S.C. § 1282, 8 U.S.C.A. § 1282; *viz.* unlawfully remaining in the United States. Sections 275 and 276 describe crimes of unlawful entry. Section 279 gives the District Courts jurisdiction over the trial of both types of crimes; and as to venue it provides:

"Notwithstanding any other law, such prosecutions or suits may be instituted at any place in the United States at which the violation

7. [Added by the Compiler.] The Taft-Hartley Act did not require union officers to file non-Communist affidavits but it did make such filing a condition precedent to a union's use of the procedures of the National Labor Relations Board. Such affidavits were required to be filed in the District of Columbia. It was held that if a false affidavit was executed in Colorado, there deposited in the mail, received in the District of Columbia and there placed on file, the offense was committed only in the District of Columbia. Hence a trial in the federal district court of Colorado was invalid for lack of venue. Travis v. United States, 364 U.S. 631, 81 S.Ct. 358, 5 L.Ed.2d 340 (1961). It was intimated that the result would have been otherwise if the officers had been required to file non-Communist affidavits.

may occur or at which the person charged with a violation of sections 275 or 276 of this title may be apprehended."

When Congress wanted to lay venue in the district where the accused was "apprehended," it said so. It would seem, therefore, that venue may be laid in the district where the alien was "apprehended" only in case of the crimes of unlawful entry. All other crimes are to be prosecuted in the district where the violation first occurred. It is no answer to say that this crime is different because it was "continuous." See In re Snow, 120 U.S. 274, 281, 7 S.Ct. 556, 559, 30 L.Ed. 658. As District Judge Smith said, the distinction drawn by § 279 between venue at the place of violation and venue at the place of apprehension "would be meaningless if violations such as the one in issue were regarded as continuous." *

Moreover, the crime is completed when the conditional permit expires. All elements of the crime occur then. Nothing more remains to be done. It is then and there, Congress says, that the crime is "committed" in the sense that term is employed in Art. III, § 2, cl. 3 of the Constitution and in the Sixth Amendment.

I would affirm the judgment of the District Court.

(C) COURTS

Having determined the county (or other area) in which the accused may be tried, the final inquiry in the matter of jurisdiction is to ascertain which one of the tribunals sitting there is the proper one for this particular case. This is seldom a difficult problem although differences in the various jurisdictions tend to complicate any generalized statement.

To speak in very broad terms we may say that the ordinary criminal case will be tried in the court of general jurisdiction unless some other tribunal has been provided for this purpose. The name will vary from state to state, the labels "circuit court", "district court" and "superior court" being the most common. In many of the large cities the trial will be in the "criminal court," which may be a separate tribunal, or may be merely the name applied to the division (or divisions), of the district, circuit or superior court to which the criminal cases are assigned.

If the prosecution is for the violation of a city ordinance it will be in a city tribunal which may be called a "police court" or "municipal court" or may have some other name. Such a court (or some other) may have concurrent jurisdiction with the circuit, district or superior

* [Footnote by Mr. Justice Douglas.] Congress has made its intent equally clear in analogous situations, see, e.g., 18 U.S.C. § 659, 18 U.S.C.A. § 659, where the possession of certain stolen goods, certainly a continuing illegal status similar to remaining, is made a crime. Section 659 provides in pertinent part: "The offense shall be deemed to have been committed . . . in any district in which the defendant may have taken or been in possession of the said money, baggage, goods, or chattels."

court over part of the criminal field,—usually limited to misdemeanor cases.

If the accusation charges a petty offense it may be triable summarily before a magistrate, and in some states the magistrate may have exclusive jurisdiction over the case at this stage of the proceedings. Where this is true such a case can reach the court of general jurisdiction only on appeal,—although the provision may be for a trial *de novo* upon such appeal. It is important to distinguish the trial of a petty offense by a magistrate (which may or may not be appealed to the court of general jurisdiction) from a preliminary hearing by a magistrate which does not determine guilt or innocence but merely decides whether there is sufficient evidence of guilt to require that the accused be bound over to the other court.

If the defendant is a "juvenile" (a term having a special definition for this purpose which varies from state to state), and the misdeed charged is not expressly excluded by the statute authorizing this type of procedure, the case may be tried in the "juvenile court." Whether it *must* be tried there, or may be tried either there or in the ordinary courts, depends upon the legislation in the particular state The more progressive statutes on the subject give the juvenile court exclusive jurisdiction over cases falling within its field.

STATE v. SHULTS

Supreme Court of Montana, 1976.
169 Mont. 33, 544 P.2d 817.

HASWELL, JUSTICE. The question in this case is whether a Montana district court retains jurisdiction of a criminal case in which the state amends an Information charging a single felony to one charging only a lesser included misdemeanor.

This appeal was submitted on an agreed statement of fact pursuant to section 95–2408(d), R.C.M.1947:

"On June 3, 1975, a one count Information was filed in the District Court of the First Judicial District of the State of Montana, in and for the County of Lewis and Clark, charging the defendant, Daniel Marcus Shults, with the offense of Theft, § 94–6–302(1)(a), R.C.M.1947, a felony. Arraignment was set for June 6, 1975. At the arraignment, upon motion of Deputy County Attorney Charles A. Graveley, the Information was amended to charge the Defendant with the offense of Unauthorized Use of a Motor Vehicle, § 94–6–305, R.C.M.1947, a misdemeanor. The Defendant was then arraigned in the District Court and plead guilty to the misdemeanor. Upon questioning by the Court, Defendant acknowledged his awareness that by entering such a plea he was risking the full punishment of imprisonment in the County Jail for a term not to exceed six (6) months, or a fine not to exceed Five Hundred Dollars ($500.00), or both. Whereupon the

Court accepted Defendant's plea of guilty and sentenced him to serve a term of six (6) months in the Lewis and Clark County Jail.

"On June 9, 1975, the Defendant filed a motion in the District Court to set aside the judgment of conviction and to dismiss the amended Information on the grounds that the District Court lacked jurisdiction over the misdemeanor offense charged. The motion was briefed, a hearing was held and the District Court denied Defendant's motion on July 9, 1975. On July 17, 1975, Defendant filed a notice appealing the denial of said motion to the Supreme Court of the State of Montana."

The district court has original jurisdiction in all criminal cases amounting to a felony (Art. VII, Section 4, 1972 Montana Constitution) and ". . . of all public offenses not otherwise provided for" (section 95–301, R.C.M.1947). The justice court has ". . . such original jurisdiction as may be provided by law" (Art. VII, Section 5, 1972 Montana Constitution) which jurisdiction includes ". . . all misdemeanors punishable by a fine not exceeding five hundred dollars ($500.00) or imprisonment not exceeding six (6) months, or both such fine and imprisonment . . ." (subject to exceptions not pertinent here). Section 95–302, R.C.M.1947.

Here the original charge carried a penalty of imprisonment up to ten years (section 94–6–302(4)) and was clearly a felony because of the potential sentence. Section 94–1–105(1), R.C.M.1947. The amended charge carried a penalty of a fine up to $500 or imprisonment in the county jail for a term not exceeding six months (section 94–6–305(2), R.C.M.1947) and was clearly a misdemeanor. Section 94–2–101(31), R.C.M.1947.

The misdemeanor here is a lesser included offense in the felony. Section 95–1711(1)(b)(i), R.C.M.1947. Unauthorized use of the automobile is the common element in both the original charge and the amended charge, the former requiring the additional element of an intent or purpose to deprive the owner of his property. Cf. section 94–6–302(1)(a), R.C.M.1947, and section 94–6–305(1), R.C.M.1947.

In the instant case it is conceded that had the amended charge been filed originally, the district court would have had no subject matter jurisdiction over the crime. But because the original charge was a felony, the jurisdiction of the district court attached at the commencement of the action. Was the district court's jurisdiction divested when the state later amended the information to charge only a lesser included misdemeanor?

It has been held in a similar case from another jurisdiction that where the district court's jurisdiction is invoked by an indictment charging felony theft, it is not lost by the fact that the state subsequently reduces the charge to a lesser included misdemeanor theft. Bruce v. Texas (Tex.1967) 419 S.W.2d 646.

We consider this a sound rule. Here the parties concede that where a defendant is charged with a felony, tried by jury, and convicted of a lesser included misdemeanor, the district court does not lose jurisdiction. This conforms to the applicable general rule which has been stated in 22 C.J.S. Criminal Law § 169:

"As a general rule, where the court has jurisdiction of the crime for which accused is indicted, sometimes by reason of statute, it is not lost if on the evidence he is convicted of a crime of an inferior grade of which it would not have jurisdiction originally . . . ."

We see no difference in principle or result where the state amends the original charge prior to trial, and the defendant pleads guilty to the lesser included offense. If the rule were otherwise, the court of original jurisdiction would lose its ability to conclude the case with a just result.

The order of the district court refusing to set aside the conviction and dismiss the amended information is affirmed.[1]

JAMES T. HARRISON, C.J., and JOHN C. HARRISON, CASTLES and DALY, JJ., concur.

MODEL PENAL CODE

Section 1.03 Territorial Applicability.

(1) Except as otherwise provided in this Section, a person may be convicted under the law of this State of an offense committed by his own conduct or the conduct of another for which he is legally accountable if:

(a) either the conduct which is an element of the offense or the result which is such an element occurs within this State; or

(b) conduct occurring outside the State is sufficient under the law of this State to constitute an attempt to commit an offense within the State; or

(c) conduct occurring outside the State is sufficient under the law of this State to constitute a conspiracy to commit an offense within the State and an overt act in furtherance of such conspiracy occurs within the State; or

1. A conviction in the magistrate court must be reversed if the charge is one within the exclusive subject-matter jurisdiction of the district court. State v. Lynch, 82 N.M. 532, 484 P.2d 374 (1971).

A conviction in the superior court must be reversed if the offense charged was in the exclusive jurisdiction of an inferior court. People v. Fiene, 226 Cal.App.2d 305, 37 Cal.Rptr. 925 (1964).

On a trial for felonious assault in the district court the defendant may be convicted of a simple assault, although had the information charged only a simple assault the jurisdiction to try this misdemeanor would have been in an inferior court. People v. Spreckels, 125 Cal.App. 2d 507, 270 P.2d 513 (1954); In re McKinney, 70 Cal.2d 8, 73 Cal.Rptr. 580, 447 P.2d 972 (1968).

As carrying a concealed firearm is now a felony the circuit court cannot refuse jurisdiction because the Civil and Criminal Court of Pinellas County has jurisdiction only of misdemeanors. State v. Hardy, 239 So.2d 279 (Fla.App.1970).

Cal.Penal Code, § 1462 (1976) provides: "The jurisdiction of the municipal and justice courts is the same and concurrent." § 1462.1 (1983).

(d) conduct occurring within the State establishes complicity in the commission of, or an attempt, solicitation or conspiracy to commit, an offense in another jurisdiction which also is an offense under the law of this State; or

(e) the offense consists of the omission to perform a legal duty imposed by the law of this State with respect to domicile, residence or a relationship to a person, thing or transaction in the State; or

(f) the offense is based on a statute of this State which expressly prohibits conduct outside the State, when the conduct bears a reasonable relation to a legitimate interest of this State and the actor knows or should know that his conduct is likely to affect that interest.

(2) Subsection (1)(a) does not apply when either causing a specified result or a purpose to cause or danger of causing such a result is an element of an offense and the result occurs or is designed or likely to occur only in another jurisdiction where the conduct charged would not constitute an offense, unless a legislative purpose plainly appears to declare the conduct criminal regardless of the place of the result.

(3) Subsection (1)(a) does not apply when causing a particular result is an element of an offense and the result is caused by conduct occurring outside the State which would not constitute an offense if the result had occurred there, unless the actor purposely or knowingly caused the result within the State.

(4) When the offense is homicide, either the death of the victim or the bodily impact causing death constitutes a "result", within the meaning of Subsection (1)(a) and if the body of a homicide victim is found within the State, it is presumed that such result occurred within the State.

(5) This State includes the land and water and the air space above such land and water with respect to which the State has legislative jurisdiction.[a]

SECTION 2. EXTRADITION

If the courts of the state in which the accused is found have not the power to try him for the crime of which he is accused, the question arises whether the state or nation in which such person could be tried for the offense, has the right to ask the first state to arrest the accused and deliver him over to the second state for trial by it. The surrender of an accused person in this way is called "extradition;" and where it is between the states of the Union it is frequently referred to as "interstate rendition." [1] The demand for extradition is called a "requisition." [2] The "demanding state" makes the demand upon the "asylum state,"—in which the fugitive has taken refuge.

1. "Interstate rendition" was rejected in favor of the phrase "interstate extradition" in the uniform act on this subject.

2. "We hold that once the governor of the asylum state has acted on a requisition for extradition based on the demanding state's judicial determination that probable cause existed, no further judicial inquiry may be had on that issue in the asylum state." Michigan v. Doran, 439 U.S. 282, 290, 99 S.Ct. 530 (1978).

The Constitution of the United States provides (Art. IV, § 2, cl. 2) that "[a] person charged in any State with Treason, Felony or other Crime, who shall flee from Justice, and be found in another State, shall on Demand of the executive Authority of the State from which he fled, be delivered up, to be removed to the State having Jurisdiction of the Crime", and Congress has enacted (18 U.S.C.A. § 3182) that "Whenever the executive authority of any State or Territory demands any person as a fugitive from justice, of the executive authority of any State, District or Territory to which such person has fled, and produces a copy of an indictment found or an affidavit made before a magistrate of any State or Territory, charging the person demanded with having committed treason, felony, or other crime, certified as authentic by the governor or chief magistrate of the State or Territory from whence the person so charged has fled, the executive authority of the State, District or Territory to which such person has fled shall cause him to be arrested and secured, and notify the executive authority making such demand, . . . " (See also the following section.) In any case authorized by those provisions the governor of a state may appoint an agent to demand of the executive authority of another state or territory any fugitive from justice charged with any crime if its own statute is broad enough. The Tennessee statute, for example, authorizes the governor to "appoint an agent to demand and receive any fugitive from justice and return such person to this state.[3] The Iowa Code at one time, authorized the demand only in the case of a "fugitive from justice charged with treason or felony."[4] The Iowa statute authorized the governor to appoint agents to demand fugitives from justice, not only from the executive authority of another state or territory, but also "from the executive authority of a foreign government." But the clause just quoted was void. International extradition depends upon treaties and no state of the Union can enter into treaties with foreign nations. Furthermore international extradition is a matter of foreign relations, belonging exclusively to the national government.[5]

3. Tenn.Code Ann. § 4–9–121 (1982).

4. Iowa Code Ann. § 759.1 (1946). This has been changed by enactment of the Uniform Criminal Extradition Act. See Iowa Code Ann. Chap. 820.1 (1978).

5. "The laws of nations embrace no provision for the surrender of persons who are fugitives from the offended laws of one country to the territory of another. It is only by treaty that such surrender can take place." 4 Moore, Digest of International Law 245, (1906) quoting Mr. Rush, Sec. of State, to Mr. Hyde de Newville, Apr. 9, 1817. As the state of Iowa cannot enter into a treaty with a foreign government (U.S.Const. Art. I, § 10, cl. 1) it would never be in a position to demand the surrender of a fugitive as a matter of right from a foreign government. Clearly it could do no more than to request it as a matter of comity. But, "[a]lthough the question whether the several States of the United States possess the power to surrender fugitive criminals to foreign governments has never been actually decided by the Supreme Court, yet it may now be regarded as settled doctrine that they do not possess such power, but that it belongs exclusively to the National Government. The question has, however, been by no means free from controversy, and the present accepted view is the result of a gradual evolution of opinion and practice." 4 Moore, Digest of International Law 240 (1906). If Iowa cannot surrender a fugitive to a foreign government it would have little ground upon which to

The Constitution and statutes of the United States authorize extradition of a fugitive from justice charged with "treason, felony or other crime," but this is only "on demand of the executive authority of the state from which he fled." The federal law imposes no duty upon the offended state to make a demand if it does not choose to do so. Hence a state statute limiting the authority of the governor, in his demand for the return of fugitives from other states, to those charged with treason or felony (as once did the Iowa statute) is entirely valid. The legislative body is free to establish a policy of not demanding the return of misdemeanants if it sees fit to do so. The mandate of the Constitution of the United States, however, does not permit a state legislature to establish a policy of not surrendering fugitive misdemeanants to other states. The Texas statute purports to do this [6] but the limitation is unconstitutional. Despite the wording of this statute a fugitive may be extradited from Texas for a misdemeanor as well as for a felony.[7]

PACILEO v. WALKER

Supreme Court of the United States, 1980.
449 U.S. 86, 101 S.Ct. 308.

PER CURIAM. The United States Constitution provides that "A person charged in any State with Treason, Felony or other Crime, who shall flee from Justice, and be found in another State, shall on Demand of the executive Authority of the State from which he fled, be delivered up, to be removed to the State having Jurisdiction of the Crime." Art. IV, § 2, cl. 2.

In this case, there is no dispute as to the facts necessary to resolve the legal question presented. In 1975, respondent James Dean Walker escaped from the Arkansas Department of Corrections and remained at large until he was apprehended in California in 1979. In December 1979, the Governor of Arkansas requested the arrest and rendition of respondent, alleging that respondent was a fugitive from justice. In February 1980, the Governor of California honored the

make requisition as a matter of comity. But more than that, if it lacks the power to make such a rendition it would seem equally to lack the power to make the demand. As said by Mr. Justice Miller in United States v. Rauscher, 119 U.S. 407, 414, 7 S.Ct. 234, 30 L.Ed. 425 (1886): "[I]t can hardly be admitted that, even in the absence of treaties or acts of Congress on the subject, the extradition of fugitives from justice can become the subject of negotiation between a state of this Union and a foreign government."

The truth is that as far as we are concerned with foreign countries, extradition is governed, exclusively by the treaties of the United States with such countries, and by Acts of Congress in furtherance of the provisions thereof. 18 U.S.C.A. §§ 752, 1502, 3051, 3181, 3185–6, 3188–93 (1969). As a matter of procedure all applications for requisitions should be addressed to the Secretary of State accompanied by the necessary papers. 18 U.S.C.A. § 3184 (1969).

6. Vernon's Ann. Texas Code Crim. Proc. Art. 5101 (1979).

7. Ex parte Wells, 108 Tex.Cr.R. 57, 298 S.W. 904 (1927). Guilt or innocence of the fugitive cannot be determined in the asylum state. In re Wheeler, 46 Wash.2d 277, 280 P.2d 673 (1955).

request of the Governor of Arkansas and duly issued a warrant of arrest and rendition. This warrant was then served upon respondent by the Sheriff of El Dorado County, Cal. Respondent thereafter challenged the Governor's issuance of the warrant in both state and federal courts. He was unsuccessful until he reached the Supreme Court of California, which, on April 9, 1980, issued a writ of habeas corpus directing the Superior Court of El Dorado County to "conduct hearings to determine if the penitentiary in which Arkansas seeks to confine petitioner is presently operated in conformance with the Eighth Amendment of the United States Constitution and thereafter to decide the petition on its merits."

Petitioner Sheriff contends that Art. IV, § 2, cl. 2, and its implementing statute, 18 U.S.C. § 3182, do not give the courts of the "asylum" or "sending" state authority to inquire into the prison conditions of the "demanding" state. We agree. In Michigan v. Doran, 439 U.S. 282, 99 S.Ct. 530, 58 L.Ed.2d 521 (1978), our most recent pronouncement on the subject, we stated that "interstate extradition was intended to be a summary and mandatory executive proceeding derived from the language of Article IV, § 2, cl. 2 of the Constitution." Id. at 288, 99 S.Ct. at 535. We further stated that:

> "A governor's grant of extradition is prima facie evidence that the constitutional and statutory requirements have been met . . . . Once the governor has granted extradition, a court considering release on habeas corpus can do no more than decide (a) whether the extradition documents on their face are in order; (b) whether the petitioner had been charged with a crime in the demanding state; (c) whether the petitioner is the person named in the request for extradition; and (d) whether the petitioner is a fugitive. These are historic facts readily verifiable." Id., at 289, 99 S.Ct., at 535.

In Sweeney v. Woodall, 344 U.S. 86, 73 S.Ct. 139, 97 L.Ed. 114 (1952), this Court held that a fugitive from Alabama could not raise in the federal courts of Ohio, the asylum state, the constitutionality of his confinement in Alabama. We stated:

> "Considerations fundamental to our federal system require that the prisoner test the claimed unconstitutionality of his treatment by Alabama in the courts of that State. Respondent should be required to initiate his suit in the courts of Alabama, where all parties may be heard, where all pertinent testimony will be readily available, and where suitable relief, if any is necessary, may be fashioned." Id., at 90, 73 S.Ct., at 140.

We think that the Supreme Court of California ignored the teachings of these cases when it directed one of its own trial courts of general jurisdiction to conduct an inquiry into the present conditions of the Arkansas penal system. Once the Governor of California issued the warrant for arrest and rendition in response to the request of the Governor of Arkansas, claims as to constitutional defects in the Arkansas penal system should be heard in the courts of Arkansas, not those of California. "To allow plenary review in the asylum state of issues that can be fully litigated in the charging state would defeat the plain purposes of the summary and mandatory procedures authorized by Art. IV, § 2." Michigan v. Doran, 439 U.S., at 290, 99 S.Ct., at 536.

The petition for certiorari is granted, the judgment of the Supreme Court of California is reversed, and the case is remanded for further proceedings not inconsistent with this opinion.

Reversed and remanded.

JUSTICE MARSHALL, dissenting.

Because Michigan v. Doran, 439 U.S. 282, 99 S.Ct. 530, 58 L.Ed.2d 521 (1978) did not involve a claimed violation of the Eighth Amendment, and because Sweeney v. Woodall, 344 U.S. 86, 73 S.Ct. 139, 97 L.Ed. 114 (1952) did not involve a state court's decision to grant state habeas corpus relief, I do not believe that they control the question raised here, and I would set the case for plenary review.

STATE v. HALL

Supreme Court of North Carolina, 1894.
115 N.C. 811, 20 S.E. 729.

AVERY, J. The defendants were arrested, and are now held under the statute (The Code, sec. 1165), which provides that any one of certain judicial officers therein named, "on satisfactory information laid before him that any fugitive in the State has committed, out of the State and within the United States, any offense which by the law of the State in which the offense was committed is punishable, either capitally or by imprisonment for one year or upwards in any State prison, shall have full power and authority, and is hereby required to issue a warrant for said fugitive, and commit him to jail within the State for the space of six months, unless sooner demanded by the authorities of the State wherein the offense may have been committed, pursuant to the Act of Congress in that case made and provided," etc. It is manifest that the prisoners cannot be lawfully detained, under the unmistakable language of the law, unless it has been made to appear that they are liable to extradition under the Act of Congress, passed in pursuance of Art. IV, sec. 2, clause 2, of the Constitution of the United States, in order to provide for the surrender of persons charged with criminal offenses "who shall flee from justice and be found in another State."

The prisoners were tried for murder in Cherokee County, and, upon appeal, it was held (114 N.C. 909, 19 S.E. 602) that if the deceased, at the time of receiving the fatal injury, was in the State of Tennessee, and the prisoners were in the State of North Carolina, the courts of the former Commonwealth alone had jurisdiction of the offense. The prisoners, if such were the facts, were deemed by the law to have accompanied the deadly missile sent by them across the border, and to have been constructively present when the fatal wound was actually inflicted. As our statute confers no power to detain in custody, or to surrender at the demand of the Executive of another State, any person who does not fall within the definition of a fugitive from justice according to the interpretation given by the courts of the United States to the clause of the Federal Constitution providing for interstate extradition, and the Act of Congress passed in pursuance of it, the only question before us is, whether a person can, in contemplation of law, "flee from justice" in the State of Tennessee when he has never been actually but only constructively within its territorial limits. Upon this question there is abundant authority, emanating not only from the foremost textwriters and some of the ablest jurists of the most respectable State courts, but from the Supreme Court of the United States, whose peculiar province it is to declare what interpretation shall be given to the Federal Constitution and the statutes enacted by Congress in pursuance of its provisions, which are declared by that instrument to be the supreme law of the land. If we can surrender under our statute only fugitives within the meaning of the Act of Congress, it would seem sufficient to cite Ex-parte Reggel, where it is held that a person arrested as a fugitive has a right "to insist upon proof that he was within the demanding State at the time he is alleged to have committed the crime charged, and consequently withdrew from her jurisdiction so that he could not be reached by her criminal process." It is admitted that the prisoners have never withdrawn from the jurisdiction of the courts of Tennessee, and have never been, either at the time when the homicide was committed, or since, exposed to arrest under process issuing from them. . . .

To hold that a person, who is liable to indictment only by reason of his constructive presence, is a fugitive from the justice of a State within whose limits he has never gone since the commission of the offense, involves as great an error as to maintain that one who has stood still and never ventured within the reach of another has fled from him to avoid injury. One who has never fled cannot be a fugitive. 2 Moore Extradition, sec. 582, et seq., after quoting the extract already given from Reggel's case, cites a number of other cases wherein Governors of States, under well-considered opinions of their legal advisers, have recognized and acted upon the principle that a person cannot be said to flee from a place where he has never actually been, but to which, by a legal fiction, he is deemed to have followed an agency or instrumentality, put in motion by him, to accomplish a criminal purpose. Spear (Extradition, pp. 396 to 400) cites and discusses the authorities bearing upon the question whether a person can be a fugitive from a State into which he has never entered, and not only reaches the same conclusion at which we have arrived, but maintains *arguendo* that a person who has been extradited as a fugitive cannot be sent back from the demanding State on requisition of the Executive who surrendered him, to answer a crime committed while he was a fugitive, because one who is forcibly taken away does not, in contemplation of law or in fact, flee from justice. The author says that, to assume that an abduction by force, though under legal process, is fleeing, "is a gross absurdity, quite as bad as the theory of fugitives by construction." . . .

While a statute passed now, and making it murder to wilfully put in motion within the State of North Carolina any force which should kill a human being in a neighboring State, might not be amenable to such constitutional objection as that discussed in State v. Knight, 1 N.C. 143, it would, as to this case, be an *ex post facto* law. But in the exercise of its reserved sovereign powers the State may, as an act of comity to a sister State, provide by statute for the surrender, upon requisition, of persons who, like the prisoners, are indictable for murder in another State, though they have never fled from justice.[1] If it shall be proved that the prisoners were in fact in North Carolina and the deceased in Tennessee when the fatal wound was inflicted, a law may still be enacted giving the Governor the authority to issue his warrant and deliver them on requisition. Meantime, it may be asked, what can be done to provide for this *casus omissus?* We may answer, in the language of Spear, supra, p. 400: "Nothing by any extradition process, until there is some authority of law for it. . . . State statutes may be enacted to furnish a remedy not now supplied by either Federal or State law." Were the courts, without any semblance of right, to supply the legislative omission, it would be a criminal usurpation of authority, more pernicious to the public interests than the escape of, not two, but scores of criminals. Appellate courts cannot deliberately legislate for the punishment of crime without incurring a moral accountability as grave as that of the criminal who suffers by the usurpation. . . .

In State v. Spier, 12 N.C. 491, the Supreme Court declared the prisoner entitled to his discharge upon a writ of *habeas corpus,* where the term of the Court expired pending his trial for murder, because he could not be again put in jeopardy for that offense. The defect in the law was subsequently remedied by statute, allowing the Court to continue into the next week if a felony were being tried when the week expired. But the Court, composed of *Taylor, Hall* and *Henderson,* did not hesitate for a moment because a guilty man might escape. On the contrary, *Judge Hall* said: "The guilt or innocence of the prisoner is as little the subject of inquiry as the merits of any case can be, when it is brought before this Court on a collateral question of law." Courts enforce laws not simply to punish the guilty, but as well to protect the innocent. The law which fails to provide for the extradition of a guilty man must be understood and adhered to, because it may be invoked as a protection to the innocent who are prosecuted without cause, against the annoyance, expense

1. In re Hayes, 101 Cal.App.2d 416, 225 P.2d 272 (1950); Ex parte Bledsoe, 93 Okl.Cr. 302, 227 P.2d 680 (1951).

and invasion of a personal liberty involved in being extradited. There was error. The prisoners should have been discharged.

Error.[2]

(CLARK, J., filed a dissenting opinion in which MACRAE, J., joined.)

HYATT v. PEOPLE ex rel. CORKRAN

Supreme Court of the United States, 1903.
188 U.S. 691, 23 S.Ct. 456.

This proceeding by *habeas corpus* was commenced by the relator, defendant in error, to obtain his discharge from imprisonment by the plaintiff in error, the chief of police in the city of Albany, State of New York, who held the relator by means of a warrant issued in extradition proceedings by the governor of New York. The justice of the Supreme Court of New York, to whom the petition for the writ was addressed, and also upon appeal, the Appellate Division of the Supreme Court of New York, refused to grant the relator's discharge, but the Court of Appeals reversed their orders and discharged him. 172 N.Y. 176, 64 N.E. 825. A writ of error has been taken from this court to review the latter judgment.

The relator stated in his petition for the writ that he was arrested and detained by virtue of a warrant of the governor of New York,

2. Accord, In re Mohr, 73 Ala. 503 (1883).

In Kentucky v. Dennison, 24 How. 66, 16 L.Ed. 717 (U.S.1860), a motion was made in behalf of the State of Kentucky for a rule on the Governor of Ohio to show cause why a mandamus should not be issued by this Court commanding him to cause Willis Lago, a fugitive from justice, to be delivered up, to be removed to the State of Kentucky. The charge was that Lago "a colored freeman" had aided and abetted a female slave of a citizen of Kentucky to escape from her master. This was a crime in Kentucky but no such offense was known to the laws of Ohio. After holding that notwithstanding this fact it was the duty of the Governor of Ohio to honor this requisition from the Governor of Kentucky, Mr. Chief Justice Taney speaking for the Supreme Court said at pages 109–110: "But if the Governor of Ohio refuses to discharge this duty, there is no power delegated to the General Government, either through the Judicial Department or any other department, to use any coercive means to compel him.

"And upon this ground the motion for a mandamus must be overruled."

"It is true, that under present legal conditions, the general government, as was decided in the case of the Commonwealth of Kentucky v. Dennison, 24 How. 66, cannot enforce the performance of this constititutional obligation. But this results entirely from the fact that the act of congress which regulates these proceedings, directs the constitutional demand to be made upon the governor of the state to which the fugitive has fled; but as the executive of a state is not a federal officer, the general government cannot compel the performance of a function which it has no right to annex to the office. This was the extent of the decision just referred to; but I can entertain no doubt of the power of congess to vest in any national officer the authority to cause the arrest in any state of a fugitive from the justice of another state, and to surrender such fugitive on the requisition of the executive of the latter state. The national right to require the surrender, under the terms of the constitution, seems to me to be clear, and all that is necessary to render such right enforceable, in every case, is the necessary organ of the federal government." Beasley, C.J., In re Voorhees, 32 N.J.L. 141, 145–6 (1867). See also State of South Dakota v. Brown, 20 Cal.3d 765, 144 Cal.Rptr. 758, 576 P.2d 473 (1978).

granted on a requisition from the governor of Tennessee, reciting that relator had been indicted in that State for the crime of grand larceny and false pretences, and that he was a fugitive from the justice of that State; that the warrant under which he was held showed that the crimes with which he was charged were committed in Tennessee, and the relator stated that nowhere did it appear in the papers that he was personally present within the State of Tennessee at the time the alleged crimes were stated to have been committed; that the governor had no jurisdiction to issue his warrant in that it did not appear before him that the relator was a fugitive from the justice of the State of Tennessee, or had fled therefrom; that it did not appear that there was any evidence that relator was personally or continuously present in Tennessee when the crimes were alleged to have been committed; that it appeared on the face of the indictments accompanying the requisition that no crime under the laws of Tennessee was charged or had been committed. Upon this petition the writ was issued and served.

The return of the defendant in error, the chief of police, was to the effect that the relator was held by virtue of a warrant of the governor of New York, and a copy of it was annexed. . . .

Upon the hearing before the judge on March 17, 1902, the relator was sworn without objection, and testified that he had been living in the State of New York for the past fourteen months; that his residence when at home was in Lutherville, Maryland; that he was in the city of Nashville, in the State of Tennessee, on July 2, 1901, and (under objection as immaterial) had gone there on business connected with a lumber company in which he was a heavy stockholder; that he arrived in the city on July 2, in the morning, and left about half-past seven in the evening of the same day, and while there he notified the Union Bank and Trust Company (the subsequent prosecutor herein) that the resignation of the president of the lumber company had been demanded and would probably be accepted that day. That after such notification, and on the same day, the resignation was obtained, and the Union Bank and Trust Company was notified thereof by the relator before leaving the city on the evening of that day; that he passed through the city of Nashville on the 16th or 17th of July thereafter on his way to Chattanooga, but did not stop at Nashville at that time, and had not been in the State of Tennessee since the 16th day of July, 1901, at the time he went to Chattanooga; that he had never lived in the State of Tennessee, and had not been in that State between the 26th or 27th of May, 1899, and the 2d day of July, 1901.

Upon this state of facts the judge, before whom the hearing was had, dismissed the writ and remanded the relator to the custody of the defendant Hyatt, as chief of police. This order was affirmed without any opinion by the Appellate Division of the Supreme Court, 72 App.Div. 629, but, as stated, it was reversed by the Court of Appeals, 172 N.Y. 176, and the relator discharged. . . .

MR. JUSTICE PECKHAM, after making the foregoing statement of facts, delivered the opinion of the court. . . .

The subsequent presence for one day (under the circumstances stated above) of the relator in the State of Tennessee, eight days after the alleged commission of the act, did not, when he left the State, render him a fugitive from justice within the meaning of the statute. There is no evidence or claim that he then committed any act which brought him within the criminal law of the State of Tennessee, or that he was indicted for any act then committed. The proof is uncontradicted that he went there on business, transacted it and came away. The complaint was not made nor the indictments found until months after that time. His departure from the State after the conclusion of his business cannot be regarded as a fleeing from justice within the meaning of the statute. He must have been there when the crime was committed, as alleged, and if not, a subsequent going there and coming away is not a flight.

We are of opinion that as the relator showed without contradiction and upon conceded facts that he was not within the State of Tennessee at the times stated in the indictments found in the Tennessee court, nor at any time when the acts were, if ever committed, he was not a fugitive from justice within the meaning of the Federal statute upon that subject, and upon these facts the warrant of the governor of the State of New York was improperly issued, and the judgment of the Court of Appeals of the State of New York discharging the relator from imprisonment by reason of such warrant must be

Affirmed.[1]

1. This rule does not prevail in international extradition. Rex v. Godfrey, 39 T.L.R. 5 (K.B.1922). For a discussion of the Godfrey case see 32 Yale L.J. 287 (1923).

"To be regarded as a fugitive from justice it is not necessary that one shall have left the State in which the crime is alleged to have been committed for the very purpose of avoiding prosecution." Hogan v. O'Neill, 255 U.S. 52, 56, 41 S.Ct. 222, 223, 65 L.Ed. 497, 500 (1921). Cf. Roberts v. Reilly, 116 U.S. 80, 97, 6 S.Ct. 291, 300, 29 L.Ed. 544, 549 (1885); Bassing v. Cady, 208 U.S. 386, 28 S.Ct. 392, 52 L.Ed. 540 (1907).

Ignorance of having violated the law does not prevent one who leaves the State from being a fugitive: Appleyard v. Massachusetts, 203 U.S. 222, 27 S.Ct. 122, 51 L.Ed. 161 (1906).

"It is upon the petitioner under such circumstances to prove that he is not in fact a fugitive from justice and the burden requires evidence which is practically conclusive." Seely v. Beardsley, 194 Iowa 863, 866, 190 N.W. 498, 500 (1922). The question of insanity will not be tried in such proceedings: Drew v. Thaw, 235 U.S. 432, 35 S.Ct. 137, 59 L.Ed. 302 (1914). Nor will the court pass on the statute of limitations. Biddinger v. Commissioner of Police of City of New York, 245 U.S. 128, 38 S.Ct. 41, 62 L.Ed. 193 (1917).

The court will not pass upon an alleged alibi of a fugitive who admits he was within the demanding state at the time of the alleged offense. Edmunds v. Griffin, 177 Iowa 389, 156 N.W. 353 (1916).

With the principal case, cf. Leonard v. Zweifel, 171 Iowa 522, 151 N.W. 1054 (1915); Taylor v. Wise, 172 Iowa 1, 126 N.W. 1126 (1910).

One, constructively present only at the time of the crime, who enters the jurisdiction voluntarily, gives bail and then departs, has waived his immunity. Kay v. State, 34 Ala.App. 8, 37 So.2d 525 (1948), rehearing denied 251 Ala. 419, 37 So.2d 529 (1948).

If **D** was within the state when he took steps which were intended to, and did, re-

APPLICATION OF O'RIORDAN

Court of Appeals of Kansas, 1982.
7 Kan.App. 460, 643 P.2d 1147.

Before FOTH, C.J., and REES and PARKS, JJ.

PARKS, JUDGE. This is a habeas corpus proceeding in which the petitioner Louis O'Riordan challenges the lawfulness of his restraint under a governor's extradition warrant.

On December 18, 1980, a governor's warrant was issued for the arrest of O'Riordan, who was arrested and released on his own recognizance on December 24, 1980. O'Riordan filed a petition for writ of habeas corpus on January 2, 1981, alleging that he was unlawfully deprived of his liberty by James H. Fountain, sheriff of Reno County, Kansas.

At the hearing on January 6, 1981, Judge Porter K. Brown found that the extradition documents on their face were not in order because there was no notation that the magistrate issuing the warrant for the arrest of the petitioner made a finding of probable cause. The court recessed the hearing to February 6, 1981 to allow the State of Arkansas time to show that the warrant was issued upon the proper finding. On February 6, Judge Brown, after examining an order of the Circuit Court of Polk County, Arkansas dated January 13, found he still could not determine the question left open on January 6 and recessed the hearing until March 6, at which time he considered an order nunc pro tunc filed by the circuit judge of Polk County. He then found that all requirements for extradition of the petitioner were satisfied. Accordingly, Judge Brown dissolved the writ of habeas corpus and dismissed the action with costs assessed to the petitioner O'Riordan. This appeal followed.

Petitioner contends that because the extradition procedure entails a restraint of liberty, the Fourth and Fifth Amendment rights are invoked and probable cause must be found before extradition may be permitted.

Concerning the issue of probable cause, we are reminded that an asylum state in an extradition proceeding may not conduct its own investigation into the sufficiency of the facts supporting a finding of probable cause but must accept the conclusion of the demanding state if the documents reveal that a probable cause determination was made. Michigan v. Doran, 439 U.S. 282, 289, 99 S.Ct. 530, 535, 58 L.Ed.2d 521 (1978). *Doran* also determined that the scope of review of an extradition request in a habeas corpus proceeding is limited to determining (a) whether the extradition documents on their face

sult in a crime his departure from the state makes him a "fugitive" in the constitutional sense even if he left the state before the crime was complete. Strassheim v. Daily, 221 U.S. 280, 31 S.Ct. 558, 55 L.Ed. 735 (1911). If **D** left the state after setting a bomb to murder **X**, although before the fatal explosion, he is a "fugitive".

are in order; (b) whether the petitioner has been charged with a crime in the demanding state; (c) whether the petitioner is the person named in the request for extradition; and (d) whether the petitioner is a fugitive.

The original extradition documents included an arrest warrant and information couched entirely in the language of the statute. The certificates did not state that the judge who issued the bench warrant heard evidence prior to its issuance and at that time found that probable cause existed. However, the nunc pro tunc order considered at the March 6 hearing reflects proceedings by the Arkansas court on January 13, 1981 and a contemporaneous finding of probable cause based on examination of the victim and the charging documents. The order also states that this probable cause had existed since February 14, 1980 and ordered the court files amended to reflect that probable cause did exist at the time the information was filed.

In Zambito v. Blair, 610 F.2d 1192, 1196 (4th Cir.1979), the court concluded as follows:

> "[6] In such circumstances, we conclude that the fourth amendment, as applied to the states by the fourteenth amendment, requires only that, prior to an extradition, there in fact have been a finding of probable cause by a neutral judicial officer, not that the demanding papers, additionally, must say so. Where such a finding has actually been made in the demanding state before extradition, and where the person executing the governor's warrant has no substantial basis for doubting that it has been made, execution of that warrant is not constitutionally invalid merely because the documents which were presented to the governor of the asylum state did not, at the time of their presentation, specify that the finding had been made."

In view of the holding in *Zambito,* we conclude that when, as here, the demanding papers presented do not specify that a finding of probable cause had been made prior to issuance of the warrant but such a finding is made prior to extradition, the requirements for extradition are met.

Petitioner also complains that the documents should have revealed sufficient facts to notify him of the crime charged. He relies in part on Wilbanks v. State, 224 Kan. 66, 579 P.2d 132 (1978) and In re Simpson, 2 Kan.App.2d 713, 586 P.2d 1389 (1978), which preceded the holding of *Doran* and its restrictions on the review of extradition requests. Because of the limited review permitted by *Doran,* it makes little difference whether the defendant is notified of the facts behind the warrant if he is the subject of a proper extradition and probable cause has been found in the demanding state. Since the asylum state cannot inquire into the facts behind the warrant, defendant's remedy would be to request a bill of particulars once extradited. . . .

Affirmed.

APPLICATION OF ROBINSON

Supreme Court of Nevada, 1958.
74 Nev. 58, 322 P.2d 304.

EATHER, JUSTICE. . . . Upon two grounds appellant asserts that the court below was in error in denying him discharge from custody under his writ.

First he contends that he was not a fugitive from justice of the state of Oregon.

In May, 1942 appellant was convicted of burglary in Oregon and sentenced to a term of five years in the state prison. In June, 1944 he was granted parole under the terms of which he was released to the custody of officers of Lincoln County, Nebraska, for the purpose of standing trial for felony. He was convicted in Nebraska and sentenced to serve 20 months in the state prison. He was released in August, 1945. On January 3, 1946, with a balance of his Oregon sentence remaining to be served, the Oregon parole board revoked his parole. The record before us is silent as to the basis for the revocation. We may assume it was for violation of the conditions of the parole. It was for the purpose of requiring him to serve the balance of his sentence that his return to Oregon was sought by the executive warrant here in question.

Appellant contends that in delivering him to Nebraska, Oregon has waived further service of sentence; that since he was compelled to leave Oregon under these circumstances he cannot be regarded as a fugitive from justice of that state. In support of his contention he relies upon In re Whittington, 34 Cal.App. 344, 167 P. 404.[a]

Authorities are divided upon this proposition. In our view the better rule and the weight of authority today is to the effect that the mode or manner of a person's departure from a demanding state generally does not affect his status as a fugitive from justice and that the fact that his departure was involuntary or under legal compulsion will not preclude his extradition. Brewer v. Goff, 10 Cir., 138 F.2d

a. [By the Compiler.] The theory of implied waiver by sending a prisoner to another state was expressly disapproved. In re Patterson, 64 Cal.2d 357, 49 Cal. Rptr. 801, 411 P.2d 897 (1966).

Oklahoma takes the position that if a person in custody in one state is surrendered on extradition to another state this operates as a waiver of jurisdiction over the person and he cannot be considered a fugitive from justice from the surrendering state so as to be returned there on extradition. But if he is released on probation, and violates his probation which is then revoked, he is extraditable to the state from which he was surrendered. Application of Brown, 432 P.2d 358 (Okl. Cr.1967).

One may be a fugitive in the constitutional sense although he did not leave the demanding state voluntarily. Johnson v. Peterson, 1 Wash.App. 856, 466 P.2d 183 (1970).

The Oklahoma court held that if one in custody on a criminal charge was released to another jurisdiction, on extradition proceedings, this constituted a waiver of a demand that he be returned on extradition, but was not a waiver of a right to try the person if he was once more in the original jurisdiction. Peoples v. State, 523 P.2d 1123 (Okl.Cr.1974).

710, holding that the Whittington decision is against the weight of authority.[1]

The essential fact remains that having committed an act which the law of Oregon constitutes a crime and having been convicted and sentenced therefor, appellant departed from Oregon jurisdiction and, when sought for enforcement of his penal obligation to that state, was found in another state.

Nor do we feel that Oregon can be said to have waived its right to insist upon service of sentence. Delivery to Nebaska was under parole from Oregon. Under these circumstances appellant continued while in Nebraska and until revocation of parole to serve the Oregon sentence. It was for Oregon to fix the conditions under which its sentence might be served. Oregon's act was not a suspension of sentence or abandonment of the prisoner. The appellant was not prejudiced in any constitutional right by Oregon's action in aid of the administration of justice in a sister state.

Second: Appellant contends that Oregon's right of requisition is barred by res judicata. Following Oregon's revocation of parole in 1946, Oregon on two occasions (prior to the present proceeding) has laid claim to a right to take appellant into custody as a parole violator. On both occasions appellant has secured discharge through habeas corpus.

The first occasion was in Nebraska. Local authorities took appellant into custody at Oregon's request. Appellant sought habeas corpus. The writ was summarily denied. On appeal the Nebraska

1. [Footnote by the Court.] California amendment of Penal Code, § 1549 (St. 1937, p. 1583) destroyed the effect of the Whittington case by expressly giving authority to the Governor to surrender any person charged with crime in another state, even though such person left the demanding state involuntarily.

[Compiler's note]. A prisoner awaiting trial for crime in Texas was extradited to California where he was wanted on a much more serious charge (murder). For some reason the murder charge was dropped whereupon an effort was made to extradite him back to Texas, but he was released on habeas corpus. In re Whittington, 34 Cal.App. 344, 167 P. 404 (1917).

The Governor of Oregon honored a requisition made by the Governor of Texas for the delivery of the plaintiff in error for removal to Texas as a fugitive from the justice of that State. The accused was taken to Texas, tried for murder and a conspiracy to commit murder and acquitted. She was, however, not released from custody because she was ordered by the Governor of Texas under a requisition of the Governor of Georgia, to be held for delivery to an agent of the State of Georgia for removal to that State as a fugitive from justice. Held, that the failure of Congress when enacting the interstate extradition provisions to provide for the case of a fugitive from justice who has not fled into the state where he is found, but was brought into it involuntarily by a requisition from another state, does not take the matters within the unprovided area out of possible state action, but leaves the state free to deliver the accused to any state from whose justice he has fled. Innes v. Tobin, 240 U.S. 127, 36 Sup.Ct. 290, 60 L.Ed. 562 (1916). Accord: Hackney v. Welsh, 107 Ind. 253, 8 N.E. 141 (1886). Contra: In re Hope, 7 N.Y.Cr. 406, 10 N.Y.Supp. 28 (1889). See Spear, A Lawyer's Question, 13 Alb.L.Q. 230; Larremore, Inadequacy of the Present Federal Statute Regulating Interstate Rendition, 10 Col.L.Rev. 208 (1910).

See note, Fugitives from Justice under the Federal Rendition Clause, 18 Col.L. Rev. 70 (1918).

Supreme Court, Application of Robinson, 150 Neb. 443, 34 N.W.2d 887, directed the lower court to issue the writ and proceed to hearing. Oregon failed to press its rights. No hearing was had. Appellant was discharged, without hearing, on Oregon's default.

The second occasion was in Kansas. Appellant had been convicted of a federal offense and sentenced to the federal prison at Leavenworth. Oregon placed a detainer against him with the prison authorities. Appellant through habas corpus attacked Oregon's right to custody. Oregon withdrew the detainer. No hearing was had.

It cannot be said that appellant's discharges under habeas corpus in these two occasions resulted from judicial determinations which now bar Oregon from asserting the right of requisition. Appellant's discharges resulted simply from Oregon's failure to press its rights. Although appellant contends that the failure of a state to assert or press its extradition rights at a given time would result in a waiver of these rights, no authority is cited in support of this contention, and none has come to the attention of the court. Never has any hearing been had upon the merits of appellant's contentions until the hearing before the court below. Never were those rights judicially determined until the present proceeding. Res judicata does not apply.[a]

On motion to dismiss: Motion denied.

On appeal: Affirmed.

BADT, C.J., and MERRILL, J., concur.

HARDY v. BETZ

Supreme Court of New Hampshire, 1963.
105 N.H. 169, 195 A.2d 582.

[**D**, a resident of New Hampshire, was indicted in Massachusetts for nonsupport of an illegitimate child. A requisition from Massachusetts was honored by the governor of New Hampshire, who issued his warrant of arrest and extradition. Pursuant thereto defendant arrested plaintiff, who petitioned for a writ of habeas corpus.]

DUNCAN, JUSTICE. These proceedings relate to the support of a minor male child born April 29, 1953 in Boston, Massachusetts, shortly after his mother's removal thereto from Portsmouth, New Hampshire. Soon after the birth of the child the mother married, and has continued to reside in Boston. In 1962 as a result of a request for public support, a proceeding was brought in the Roxbury District Court in Massachusetts, seeking support for the child from the plaintiff herein under the provisions of the Uniform Reciprocal Enforcement of Support Act. RSA ch. 546. Following a hearing before the Superior Court in Rockingham County on November 26, 1962, the pe-

a. One who has been extradited from Florida to Connecticut can be brought back by extradition to serve the balance of a term for which he had received a conditional pardon that was later revoked. United States v. Matus, 218 F.2d 466 (2d Cir.1954).

tition was denied upon the ground that the plaintiff herein was under no duty to support the child. See RSA 168:1 requiring a paternity charge to be instituted within one year of the birth of the child. Thereafter the proceedings culminating in the petition now before us were instituted.[1]

The reserved case states that the plaintiff "has at no time seen [the mother of the child] since she departed from Portsmouth," that he denies that he is the father of the child, and that "he is not and never has been a fugitive from justice in the Commonwealth of Massachusetts." His application for a writ of habeas corpus alleges that he "was not in Massachusetts on the thirtieth day of May 1959 [the date alleged in the indictment] or at any time subsequent thereto."

At the outset it may be pointed out that we are not concerned with the contention that the plaintiff is not a fugitive from justice. The requisition papers disclose that it is conceded that at the time of the commission of the alleged crime the plaintiff was in Portsmouth, and that it is alleged that acts committed by him in Portsmouth intentionally resulted in a crime in Massachusetts. The answer of the Commonwealth of Massachusetts to the plaintiff's petition clearly indicates that the extradition proceedings are grounded upon the provisions of section 6 of the Uniform Extradition Act. RSA ch. 612.[2]

This section provides: "Extradition of Persons Not Present in Demanding State at Time of Commission of Crime. The governor of this state may also surrender, on demand of the executive authority of any other state, any person in this state charged in such other state in the manner provided in section 3 with committing an act in this state, or in a third state, intentionally resulting in a crime in the state whose executive authority is making the demand, and the provisions of this chapter not otherwise inconsistent, shall apply to such cases, even though the accused was not in that state at the time of the commission of the crime, and has not fled therefrom." RSA 612:6.

1. The threat of a criminal punishment is a coercive measure to induce a man to perform his civil duty by supporting his family, but execution of the threat tends to frustrate the purpose of such legislation because it usually makes it impossible for the support to be given. This led to the Uniform Reciprocal Enforcement of Support Act, which has been very widely adopted, and provides for an alternative demand in the form of a support order and permits extradition to be avoided by compliance with this support order. See West's Ann.Cal.Code Civ.Proc. §§ 1650–1699 (1974); 2 U.C.L.A.L.Rev. 267 (1955).

2. Although the federal constitution and statute require extradition only of one who has fled from the demanding state they do not prohibit the states from doing more. And the provision of the Uniform Extradition Act which authorizes the governor to issue his warrant of arrest and extradition of one who did an act intentionally resulting in a crime in the demanding state, although he was not therein, is constitutional and valid. Sheriff v. Thompson, 85 Nev. 211, 452 P.2d 911 (1969); Miller v. Decker, 411 F.2d 302 (1969).

All states have adopted this Uniform Act which has its own provisions for extradition. In re Morgan, 244 Cal.App.2d 903, 53 Cal.Rptr. 642 (1966).

The recital in the warrant of the governor of this state that the plaintiff herein is "charged . . . with having fled from said Commonwealth of Massachusetts" may be regarded as surplusage and presents no issue for determination here. Additionally, no issue is presented with respect to the form of the requisition papers, which include the required copy of an indictment, and of an affidavit before a magistrate.

The issue to be determined is whether a crime under the law of Massachusetts is substantially charged. Mass.G.L., c. 273, § 15 provides in part: "Any father of an illegitimate child, whether begotten within or without the Commonwealth, who neglects or refuses to contribute reasonably to its support and maintenance, shall be guilty of a misdemeanor." The section further provides that if there has been no final adjudication of paternity "the question of paternity shall be determined in proceedings hereunder." It thus appears that although it has never been determined that the plaintiff herein is the father of the minor child in question the Massachusetts statute provides for such determination upon trial of the indictment. Under the Massachusetts statute the offense alleged is a continuing one and establishment of paternity is not a prerequisite to indictment.

The essential question before us is whether the indictment returned in Massachusetts can be held to charge a crime committed in that jurisdiction, when the affidavits establish that the plaintiff was not there present at the time of the crime for which he was indicted. By the sworn statement of the District Attorney for Suffolk District the plaintiff is charged with "having committed in Portsmouth, New Hampshire an act or acts intentionally resulting in the commission of said crime in this Commonwealth." The papers contain no specification of the nature of the "act or acts" so alleged to have been committed in this state, but it is plainly inferable that reliance is placed upon "acts of omission" committed in this state which are claimed to have "intentionally resulted" in a crime in Massachusetts. . . .

It has already been found by the Superior Court in the 1962 proceedings that the plaintiff is under no duty here to support the child, his paternity never having been established. Under the law of this jurisdiction no obligation to support an illegitimate child exists where paternity has been neither established nor acknowledged. See RSA 168:1 requiring a paternity charge to be instituted within one year of the birth of the child.

We come then to the question of whether Massachusetts can by legislative act impose upon a resident of New Hampshire, not present in Massachusetts, an obligation to support an illegitimate child in Massachusetts; and more particularly, impose criminal liability for failure to support such a child, when the father has never been within the jurisdiction of that Commonwealth so that it could impose such an obligation or liability upon him. . . .

"The criminal law of a state or nation has no operation or effect beyond its geographical or territorial limits." Anderson, Wharton's Criminal Law and Procedure, s. 23. Restatement, Conflict of Laws, s. 457. See Hartford v. Superior Court, 47 Cal.2d 447, 454, 304 P.2d 1. "The crime of failure to furnish support, however, is committed where the defendant should have furnished the support[3] . . . if the defendant was once subject to the jurisdiction so that the obligation exists." 2 Beale, The Conflict of Laws, s. 428.4. . . .

An order should be entered discharging the plaintiff from custody.

Remanded.

BLANDIN and WHEELER, JJ., concurred.

KENISON, C.J., and LAMPRON, J., dissented.

KENISON, CHIEF JUSTICE (dissenting). . . . The majority opinion in effect holds that section 6 of the Uniform Extradition Act is unconstitutional and cannot be applied in support cases where it is most needed. If there was authority for this view in the rigid dogma of Beale (2 Beale, The Conflict of Laws, s. 428.4) or in the worry of Lord Ellenborough a century and a half ago ("Can the island of Tobago pass a law to bind the rights of the whole world?", Buchanan v. Rucker, 9 East. 192 [K.B.1808]), it is not impressive today. In re Harris, 170 Ohio St. 151, 163 N.E.2d 762. The continuing crime of neglecting to support an illegitimate child in Massachusetts "whether begotten within or without the commonwealth" (Mass.G.L., c. 273, § 15) is an extraditable offense under section 6 of the Uniform Extradition Act. RSA 612:6. Ehrenzweig, Conflict of Laws, s. 82 (1962).

LAMPRON, J., concurs in this dissent.

3. **K**, who lived in Montana, was the father of two small children who lived with their mother in Washington. A Montana court had ordered **K** to pay $12.50 a month for the support of his children, which order had been almost completely ignored. **K** was extradited to Washington where he was convicted of criminal nonsupport. He was placed on probation conditioned on his support of his children until they reached the age of twenty-one. This conviction was affirmed. The situs of the crime of nonsupport is where the minor children are located. By his wilful failure to provide the required support, **K** did an act which intentionally resulted in the crime in Washington and hence was properly extraditable under the special provision of the statute. State v. Klein, 4 Wash.App. 736, 484 P.2d 455 (1971).

If **D** committed grand theft by embezzlement, having a duty to account for the money in Arizona, that state had jurisdiction over the crime. State v. Roderick, 9 Ariz.App. 19, 448 P.2d 891 (1969).

STATE v. ANDERSON

Supreme Court of Utah, 1980.
618 P.2d 42.

WILKINS, JUSTICE. This is an appeal by Defendant Leslie Clark Anderson from his conviction in the District Court for Weber County for theft of an automobile.

Defendant was arrested in California on the Utah charge and was detained there pending extradition to stand trial in Utah. He resisted extradition in California by filing a petition for writ of habeas corpus in the Santa Barbara Superior Court. Prior to proceedings on that petition he was returned to Utah by Utah police officers pursuant to a Governor's Extradition Warrant.

In attacking his conviction, defendant argues that because his petition for habeas corpus was pending in California, the Utah District Court lacked jurisdiction to try him. Thus, he contends, it was a denial of due process for the District Court to refuse to stay all proceedings pending the outcome of the habeas corpus action in California.

In Frisbie v. Collins [1] the Supreme Court stated:

> This Court has never departed from the rule announced in Ker v. Illinois, 119 U.S. 436, 444, 7 S.Ct. 225, 229, 30 L.Ed. 421, that the power of a court to try a person for crime is not impaired by the fact that he had been brought within the court's jurisdiction by reason of a "forcible abduction." No persuasive reasons are now presented to justify overruling this line of cases. They rest on the sound basis that due process of law is satisfied when one present in court is convicted of crime after having been fairly apprized of the charges against him and after a fair trial in accordance with constitutional procedural safeguards. There is nothing in the Constitution that requires a court to permit a guilty person rightfully convicted to escape justice because he was brought to trial against his will.[2] (footnote omitted)

Here the record reflects that defendant was convicted "after a fair trial in accordance with constitutional procedural safeguards." That he was brought before the Utah court in the face of a pending proceeding in California attacking his extradition does not impair his conviction.

Affirmed.[a]

CROCKETT, C.J., and MAUGHAN, HALL and STEWART, JJ., concur.

1. 342 U.S. 519, 72 S.Ct. 509, 96 L.Ed. 541 (1952).

2. Id., at 522, 72 S.Ct. at 511.

a. If **D** was assaulted by the officer of another state and brought here unlawfully, the state nevertheless had jurisdiction over him and his conviction is affirmed. State v. Crump, 82 N.M. 487, 484 P.2d 329 (1971).

"[F]orcible return to the jurisdiction of the United States constitutes no bar to prosecution once the defendant is found within the United States." United States

STATE v. KEALY

Supreme Court of Iowa, 1893.
89 Iowa 94, 56 N.W. 283.

ROTHROCK, J. The defendant was indicted for the crime of obtaining money under false pretenses. After the crime was committed, he left this state, and went to the state of New York. A requisition was made upon the governor of that state for the extradition of the defendant, upon the ground that he had been indicted in this state, and he was returned to this state in pursuance of the requisition. After he was brought to this state, and while he was in custody under that indictment, he was indicted for forging a promissory note. When he was brought into court on the last indictment, he made a motion to be discharged from restraint on the indictment for forgery, on the ground that he was not extradited on that charge, and that, being in restraint on the first charge, he could not be required to plead to the second indictment, nor could he be restrained of his liberty by reason thereof, he never having had an opportunity to return to the state of New York. The court overruled the motion, and required the defendant to plead to the indictment. A plea of guilty was entered, and the defendant was sentenced to imprisonment in the penitentiary for two years.

It appears from the abstract in the case that the two indictments were founded upon wholly different and distinct charges, and, as we understand it, they did not involve the same transaction. The record does not show what disposition was made of the indictment of obtaining money under false pretenses. It is stated in argument that the defendant was sentenced to imprisonment for one year on that charge.

The question presented for decision is stated by counsel for the appellant in the following language: "Can a party taken from one country or state to another, upon proceedings of extradition, legally be held to answer to another and different offense than that upon which he was so extradited, without being given an opportunity to return to the state of his asylum?"

This case does not involve any question of international extradition. The defendant's removal from the state of New York to this state was not procured by any fraudulent pretense or representation made to him for the purpose of bringing him within the jurisdiction of our courts. It is provided by section 2, article 4, of the constitution of the United States, that "a person charged in any state with treason, felony or other crime, who shall flee from justice and be found in another state, shall on demand of the executive authority of the state

v. Lovato, 520 F.2d 1270, 1271 (9th Cir. 1975).

"Once the defendant is before the court, the court will not inquire into the circumstances surrounding his presence there." United States v. Marzano, 357 F.2d 257, 271 (7th Cir.1976); Quiver v. State, 339 N.W.2d 303 (S.D.1983).

from which he fled be delivered up to be removed to the state having jurisdiction of the crime." There was no abuse of this constitutional provision in this case. Extradition was not resorted to as a means of procuring the presence of the defendant in this state for the purpose of serving him with process in a civil action. There can be no question that the grand jury of Jones county, in this state, had the power to find the second indictment against the defendant, and there was the same right of extradition upon that charge that there was on the first indictment. His counsel states in argument that he was sentenced to the penitentiary for one year on the first indictment, and the imprisonment of two years on the second indictment was to commence at the expiration of the imprisonment on the first. It will be observed that what the defendant demanded was that the second indictment should be held in abeyance until he was discharged from imprisonment on the first, and until a reasonable time and opportunity had been given him after his release on the first charge to return to New York, from which asylum he was forcibly taken on the first charge.

There is a conflict of authority upon this question. This court is committed to the doctrine that, when a person is properly charged with a crime, the courts will not inquire into the circumstances under which he as brought into this state, and within the jurisdiction of the court. State v. Ross, 21 Iowa 467. It is true that the defendants in that case were not brought to this state under a requisition upon the executive of another state. They were arrested in the state of Missouri without legal warrant, and after being forcibly brought to this state they were rearrested, and turned over to the civil authorities, and indicted. It is said in that case that, "the officers of the law take the requisite process, find the persons charged within the jurisdiction, and this, too, without force, wrong, fraud, or violence on the part of any agent of the state, or officer thereof. And it can make no difference whether the illegal arrest was made in another state or another government. The violation of the law of the other sovereignty, so far as entitled to weight, would be the same in principle in the one case as the other. That our own laws have been violated is sufficiently shown by the indictment. For this the state had a right to detain the prisoners, and it is of no importance how or where their capture was effected." In the case at bar the defendant was properly indicted, and when process was issued on the indictment, it is of no importance by what authority he was brought into this state. In support of this doctrine: State v. Stewart, 60 Wis. 587, 19 N.W. 429; Ham v. State, 4 Tex.App. 645; State v. Brewster, 7 Vt. 118; Dow's Case, 18 Pa.St. 37; State v. Wensel, 77 Ind. 428; Kerr v. People, 110 Ill. 627. The first two cases above cited are founded on facts substantially the same as the case at bar. As we have said, there is a conflict of authority upon the question. The cases will be found collected in 7 Am. and Eng. Encyclopedia of Law, 648. We have no disposition to depart from the rule adopted by this court in State v. Ross, supra, and the judgment of the district court is Affirmed.[1]

1. Accord, Lascelles v. Georgia, 148 U.S. 537, 13 S.Ct. 687, 37 L.Ed. 549 (1893); State v. Rowe, 104 Iowa 323, 73 N.W. 833 (1898); Knox v. State, 164 Ind. 226, 73 N.E. 255 (1905); In re Flack, 88 Kan. 616, 129 P. 541 (1913) overruling State v. Hall, 40 Kan. 338, 19 P. 918 (1888); People v. Martin, 188 Cal. 281, 205 P. 121 (1922).

"In Knox v. State, at page 231, Montgomery, J., stated the following: 'The right of the person extradited to return to the country from which he has been surrendered is not a natural and inherent right of his own, but is based upon the right of his adopted sovereign to afford asylum to the fugitive, and to refuse to give him up to another except upon such terms as it is pleased to impose. The criminal himself never acquires a personal right of asylum or refuge anywhere, but all such rights as he may claim in this respect flow entirely out of the rights of the government to whose territory he has fled.' "

A defendant returned to the United States after being kidnapped in Uruguay and tortured in Brazil was held to be entitled to release if he could prove his charges. The court relied on due process grounds to find a divestiture of jurisdiction. United States v. Toscanino, 500 F.2d 267 (2d Cir.1974). The case has not been followed and was limited to its facts in United States ex rel. Lujan v. Gengler, 510 F.2d 62 (2d Cir.1975). In Gerstein v. Pugh, 420 U.S. 103, 95 S.Ct. 854 (1975), the Supreme Court restated the rule that an illegal arrest or detention does void a subsequent conviction.

"A long and almost unbroken line of authority holds that a state has jurisdiction to try a person for a crime if that person is within the state, even if his presence there was obtained by force, fraud, or violation of the laws of this or another state or country." Warmbo v. State, 578 P.2d 582, 584 (Alaska 1978).

"See note, Extradition-Prosecution for Other Offenses, 61 U. of Pa.Law Rev. 496 (1913).

"See Ex parte Wilson, 63 Tex.Cr.R. 281, 140 S.W. 98 (1911); Dominguez v. State, 90 Tex.Cr.R. 92, 234 S.W. 79 (1921); In re Jones, 54 Cal.App. 423, 201 P. 944 (1921)." Keedy, Cases on the Administration of The Criminal Law, 272–3, n. 14 (1928).

In United States v. Rauscher, 119 U.S. 407, 7 S.Ct. 234, 30 L.Ed. 425 (1886), it was held that one extradited from England on an indictment for murder could not be put on trial for inflicting cruel and unusual punishment. Apparently it was assumed, when extradition was demanded, that the victim would die, but the death did not occur. Miller, J., said:

> "That right, as we understand it, is that he shall be tried only for the offence with which he is charged in the extradition proceedings, and for which he was delivered up, and that if not tried for that, or after trial and acquittal, he shall have a reasonable time to leave the country before he is arrested upon the charge of any other crime committed previous to his extradition." Id. at 424.

"Therefore, international law recognizes that the asylum state may limit the trial of the fugitive in the demanding state to those crimes which have been found to be extraditable offenses in law and where probable cause to believe the petitioner committed the crime has been shown by the evidence." Freedman v. United States, 437 F.Supp. 1252, 1259 (D.C.N.D.Ga.1977).

See Jacob, International Extradition: Implications of the Eisler Case, 59 Yale L.J. 622 (1950).

See In re Hope, 7 N.Y.Cr. 406, 10 N.Y.S. 28 (1889). See note, Limitations in Trial of Extradition and Interstate Rendition Prisoners, 6 Col.L.Rev. 522 (1906).

Until an extradited person has had reasonable time in which to return to the state from which he was brought, he is privileged from the service of civil process. Murray v. Wilcox, 122 Iowa 188, 97 N.W. 1087 (1904); Compton, Ault & Co. v. Wilder, 40 Ohio St. 130 (1883). In some jurisdictions an extradited person is not immune from civil process. Reid v. Ham, 54 Minn. 305, 56 N.W. 35 (1893); In re Walker, 61 Neb. 803, 86 N.W. 510 (1901), especially where extradition was not procured by connivance or in bad faith. Williams v. Bacon, 10 Wend. 636 (N.Y.1834). Where one who was brought here on extradition, is admitted to bail and returns to his home state, he is exempt here from civil process when he comes back for his trial. Murray v. Wilcox, supra.

BLOOM v. MARCINIAK

Kansas City Court of Appeals, Missouri, 1934.
76 S.W.2d 712.

SHAIN, PRESIDING JUDGE. . . . There is a question which presents itself to this court in this cause that, in so far as this court has been able to ascertain, presents in some respects a question of first impression not only in this state but in the other states of the Union as well, and, in so far as our research of the federal authorities is concerned, we have been unable to find any precedent directly in point.

The facts before us are clearly to the effect that a requisition regular in every respect has been made by the Governor of the state of Michigan on the Governor of the state of Kansas for the return from Kansas, the asylum state, of the petitioner, Bloom. It further is shown that the Governor of the state of Kansas has honored the requisition of the Governor of the state of Michigan and made a finding of fact to the effect that petitioner, Bloom, is a fugitive from justice, and in accordance with due form and due process has turned the petitioner over to the accredited agent of the state of Michigan, who in fulfillment of this lawful mission brings the petitioner en route into the state of Missouri, where his progress has been interrupted by the process issued out of this court.

This question presents itself: What authority have the courts of Missouri to interrupt this process of law so set in force and so being executed?

This court recognizes that a writ of habeas corpus is a writ of right, and we are not unmindful of the rights of citizenship.

In this case the usual feature, to wit, a requisition granted by the Governor of our own state, is absent. Had the Governor of our own state honored a requisition for the petitioner, then the issue of fact as to whether or not the petitioner is a fugitive could be determined by this court and the petitioner released if the finding of this court was to the effect that the petitioner was not a fugitive from justice.[1] Under the facts as above set forth, Missouri would unquestionably be the asylum state, and it is universally held that the courts of the asylum state have full jurisdiction to determine the issue involved.

As between the states of this Union, the Federal Constitution and the laws passed by Congress must control. The courts of this state, as well as the courts of all the states of this Union, should respect the laws of other states or else the very purposes of the Union of states must fail. It is especially important that the above course be fol-

1. No hearing is required before the governor of the asylum state issues his warrant of extradition. Application of Dugger, 17 Ariz.App. 297, 497 P.2d 413 (1973).

lowed concerning such laws and process of laws as are controlled by our national Constitution and acts of Congress.

While, as between a demanding and an asylum state, questions of comity must yield to the questions of the constitutional rights of the citizen of the asylum state, still we conclude that, as to the constitutional rights of one en route from an asylum state to a demanding state in due course of law and procedure, the courts of this state have no jurisdiction to disturb or overthrow the quasi judicial procedure of the sister asylum state.

While we find no expression of authority on all fours with the language above, still we conclude that our language is in logical sequence with well-established principles of law. While some earlier decisions are to the contrary, it is now a well-settled principle of law that the defense that a prisoner is not a fugitive from justice must be raised before he is taken from the asylum state.

For the law to be other than above would bring confusion. The authorities of one state must indulge in the presumption that the authorities of a sister state have awarded to a prisoner apprehended within its borders all due process of law to which he is entitled under the Constitution.

The documents presented in this case all bear evidence of regularity, and there is nothing from which we can conclude that the petitioner was not awarded every opportunity in Kansas, the fugitive state, to avail himself of his every constitutional right.

Based upon the conclusions above, the release of the petitioner is denied, our writ is quashed, and the said H. Henry Bloom, petitioner herein, is remanded to the custody of W.J. Marciniak, agent of the state of Michigan, free from interference in the performance of his official duty.[2]

2. Joseph B. Mora was charged in California with the crimes of kidnaping and murder. His fingerprints were taken and he was bound over to stand trial after a preliminary hearing. He left California and the Governor of that state sent to the Governor of Utah extradition papers in proper form and requested a return of Joseph B. Mora. The Governor of Utah issued a rendition warrant and petitioner was arrested. He filed a petition for a writ of habeas corpus. He admitted that his name was Joseph B. Mora, but claimed he was not the one sought by California. He offered no evidence. Fingerprint experts had testified that his prints matched those on the extradition papers. Without emphasizing this, the court held that the state had made out a prima facie case and the burden was on petitioner to prove he was not the one intended. Mora v. Larson, 540 P.2d 520 (Utah 1975).

A "claim of mistaken identity is a question that can be raised by habeas corpus in the asylum state. . . .

"The state has the burden of proving that the person arrested is the person named in the extradition papers. The state makes a prima facie case on that issue by showing that the arrested person has (or is known by) the same name as that appearing on the extradition papers." Langley v. Hayward, 656 P.2d 1020, 1021, 1022 (Utah 1982).

See DeGraffenreid, The Law of Extradition, 2 Ala.L.Rev. 207 (1950).

See a case note in 34 Minn.L.Rev. 565 (1950).

SECTION 3. STATUTE OF LIMITATIONS

"With regard to limitations as to time, it is one of the peculiarities of English law that no general law of prescription in criminal cases exists among us. The maxim of our law has always been 'Nullum tempus occurrit regi,' and as a criminal trial is regarded as an action by the king, it follows that it may be brought at any time. This principle has been carried to great lengths in many well-known cases. In the middle of the last century Aram was convicted and executed for the murder of Clarke, fourteen years after his crime. Horne was executed for the murder of his bastard child (by his own sister) thirty-five years after his crime. In 1802 Governor Wall was executed for a murder committed in 1782. Not long ago a man named Sheward was executed at Norwich for the murder of his wife more than twenty years before; and I may add as a curiosity that, at the Derby Winter Assizes in 1863, I held a brief for the Crown in a case in which a man was charged with having stolen a leaf from a parish register in the year 1803. In this instance the grand jury threw out the bill." [1]

But although this was true at common law [2] statutory limitations of the time in which prosecutions may be instituted, are quite general.[3]

1. 2 Stephen, History of the Criminal Law of England 1–2 (1883).

2. See the statement in Brightman v. Hatzel, 183 Iowa 385, 395, 167 N.W. 89, 92 (1918).

3. In 1944 Patriarca was indicted as an accessory before the fact to the murders of two persons in 1930. The statute provided that "no person shall be convicted of any offense, except treason against the state, murder, arson, burglary, counterfeiting, forgery, robbery, larceny, rape, or bigamy, unless indictment be found against him therefor within 3 years from the time of committing the same." The indictment was held to be too late on the ground that "a felony and being accessory before the fact to that felony are two separate and distinct offenses." State v. Patriarca, 71 R.I. 151, 43 A.2d 54, 57 (1945). The court emphasized that under Rhode Island law an accessory before the fact must be indicted as such and not as a principal. In People v. Mather, 4 Wend. 229 (N.Y.1830) it is said at page 255: "Whatever is murder is included in it. If the crime of accessory to a murder before the fact is not a murder, it is without a specific name." For this reason the statutory exception was held to include the accessory to murder before the fact and not to bar such a prosecution.

A statute limiting the time within which indictments may be found and filed has no reference to prosecutions in the police courts of municipalities. And such a prosecution will not be barred by lapse of time unless some statute or ordinance so provides. Battle v. Mayor, Etc., of City of Marietta, 118 Ga. 242, 44 S.E. 994 (1903).

An indictment charged that defendant made a false statement in a naturalization proceeding and thereby procured naturalization unlawfully. It was held that this indictment was not controlled by the three-year period of the general statute relating to non-capital offenses, but came under the five-year period of the Nationality Act. United States v. Bridges, 86 F.Supp. 922 (N.D.Cal.1949).

Although the conviction was reversed on other grounds the court took the position that a felony-murder instruction is proper in a murder trial although a trial for the constituent felony would have been barred by the statute of limitations. People v. Lilliock, 265 Cal.App.2d 419, 71 Cal.Rptr. 434 (1968).

The fact that a robbery prosecution had been barred by the statute of limitations does not preclude the introduction of evidence of that robbery in the penalty trial of a capital case. People v. Terry,

CALIFORNIA PENAL CODE

§ 799. [No limitation for murder, embezzlement of public moneys or falsification of public records: When prosecution may be commenced.] There is no limitation of time within which a prosecution for murder, the embezzlement of public moneys, a violation of Section 209, or the falsification of public records must be commenced. Prosecution for murder may be commenced at any time after the death of the person killed. Prosecution for the embezzlement of public money, a violation of Section 209, or the falsification of public records may be commenced at any time after the discovery of the crime.

§ 800. (a) An indictment for any felony, except murder, the embezzlement of public money, or a violation of Section 209 of the Penal Code, and except as provided in subdivisions (b) and (c), shall be found, an information filed, or case certified to the superior court within three years after its commission.

(b) An indictment for a violation of Section 261, 264.1, 288, or 289 of, or subdivision (c), (d), or (f) of Section 286, or subdivision (c), (d), or (f) of Section 288a, or for the acceptance of a bribe by a public official or a public employee, a felony, shall be found, an information filed, or case certified to the superior court within six years after its commission.

(c) An indictment for grand theft, felony welfare fraud in violation of Section 11483 of the Welfare and Institutions Code, felony Medi-Cal fraud in violation of Section 14017 of the Welfare and Institutions Code, forgery, voluntary manslaughter, or involuntary manslaughter, a violation of Section 72, 118, 118a, 132 or 134, of the Penal Code, Section 25540 or 25541 of the Corporations code, or Section 1090 or 27443 of the Government Code, shall be found, an information filed, or case certified to the superior court within three years after its discovery.*

§ 801. [Misdemeanors: One Year limitation.] Except as provided, an indictment for any misdemeanor shall be found or an information or complaint filed within one year after its commission.

§ 802. [Limitation where defendant out of State when or after offense was committed: Time of absence from State excluded.] If, when or after the offense is committed, the defendant is out of the State, an indictment may be found, a complaint or an information filed or a case certified to the superior court, in any case originally triable in the superior court, or a com-

70 Cal.2d 410, 77 Cal.Rptr. 460, 454 P.2d 36 (1969).

Where defendant was charged with murder but convicted of the lesser-included offense of involuntary manslaughter which was barred by the statute of limitations, the conviction could not stand. People v. Morgan, 75 Cal.App.3d 32, 141 Cal.Rptr. 863 (1977).

* A magistrate conducting a preliminary examination of **D** accused of an offense, triable only in a higher court, has no power to convict or acquit. He may order **D** released if the evidence is insufficient to "bind him over" to the court having jurisdiction of the offense, but this is not an acquittal and does not prevent further proceedings against **D**. In California if **D** offers to plead guilty to the offense charged, or to a lesser included offense or an attempt to commit the offense, the magistrate may (if **D**'s counsel is present and the prosecuting attorney consents) accept the plea and certify the case to the superior court (Cal.Pen. Code, § 859a). This has the same effect as if **D** had pleaded guilty in the superior court and is what is meant by a "case certified to the superior court" in the statute of limitations.

plaint may be filed, in any case originally triable in any other court, within the term limited by law; and no time during which the defendant is not within this State, is a part of any limitation of the time for commencing a criminal action.

§ 802.5. The time limitations provided in this chapter for the commencement of a criminal action shall be tolled upon the issuance of an arrest warrant or the finding of an indictment, and no time during which a criminal action is pending is a part of any limitation of the time for recommencing that criminal action in the event of a prior dismissal of that action, subject to the provisions of Section 1387.

§ 803. Indictment found, when presented and filed. An indictment is found, within the meaning of this chapter, when it is presented by the grand jury in open court, and there received and filed.

PEOPLE v. McGEE

Supreme Court of California, In Bank, 1934.
1 Cal.2d 611, 36 P.2d 378.

LANGDON, J. On November 3, 1930, an information was filed charging defendant with the crime of rape, and alleging the commission of the offense on or about March 30, 1926. A prior conviction of second degree burglary was also charged. Defendant appeared without counsel, pleaded guilty and was sentenced to imprisonment in the state prison. On March 18, 1933, defendant filed a motion to set aside the judgment, which was denied. This appeal is from the order denying the motion.

Section 800 of the Penal Code provides: "An indictment for any other felony than murder, the embezzlement of public money, or the falsification of public records, must be found, or an information filed, within three years after its commission." Section 802 of the same code provides: "If, when the offense is committed, the defendant is out of the state, indictment may be found or an information filed within the term herein limited after his coming within the state, and no time during which the defendant is not an inhabitant of, or usually resident within this state, is part of the limitation." On the face of the information herein it clearly appears that it was not filed within the period of the statute of limitations, and no allegations setting forth an exception to the running of the statute are made. If defendant had set up the bar of limitation, he would, so far as the record shows, have been entitled to a dismissal. But he failed to do so and raises the defense now for the first time after conviction and sentence. His contention is that the court lacked jurisdiction after the expiration of the three-year period, and that the judgment was therefore void.

Whether the statute of limitations in criminal cases is jurisdictional, or a matter of defense to be affirmatively pleaded by the defendant, is a question upon which there exists some diversity of opinion. In California the law is in a most confused state. This court, in Ex parte Blake, 155 Cal. 586 [102 P. 269, 18 Ann.Cas. 815], declared that the statute was a mere matter of defense, and not ground for discharge on habeas corpus. The District Court of Appeal, in Ex parte Vice, 5 Cal.App. 153 [89 P. 983], came to the opposite conclusion; and in People v. Hoffman, 132 Cal.App. 60 [22 P.2d 229], the court held that a motion to set aside a judgment would lie where the information showed on its face that the statute had run. A hearing in the Hoffman case was denied by this court. The early case of People v. Miller, 12 Cal. 291, also lends support to this conclusion.

It is necessary that this confusion be eliminated, and that the rule which shall govern prosecutions in this state be declared. In our view, the more desirable rule is that the statute is jurisdictional, and that an indictment or information which shows on its face that the prosecution is barred by limitations fails to state a public offense. The point may therefore be raised at any time, before or after judgment.[1]

This is, of course, a rule essentially different from that governing civil actions, and it results from the different character of the statute in the two kinds of proceedings. In civil actions the statute is a privilege which may be waived by the party. In criminal cases, the state, through its legislature, has declared that it will not prosecute crimes after the period has run, and hence has limited the power of the courts to proceed in the matter. It follows that where the pleading of the state shows that the period of the statute of limitations has run, and nothing is alleged to take the case out of the statute, for example, that the defendant has been absent from the state, the power to proceed in the case is gone. . . .

The order appealed from is reversed.[2]

SEAWELL, J., CURTIS, J., WASTE, C.J., SHENK, J., and PRESTON, J., concurred.

1. The statute of limitations in criminal cases is jurisdictional and hence may be raised at any time. It is not waived by failure to assert it. In re Demillo, 14 Cal.3d 598, 121 Cal.Rptr. 725, 535 P.2d 1181 (1975).

2. "[I]n the administration of criminal justice, the statute of limitations must be held to affect not only the remedy, but to operate as a jurisdictional limitation upon the power to prosecute and punish". Waters v. United States, 328 F.2d 739, 743 (10th Cir.1964).

The statute of limitations is merely one of repose. It gives a right that is waived if not asserted. Hence the indictment need not negate the running of the period. People v. Brady, 257 App.Div. 1000, 13 N.Y.S.2d 789 (1939).

One may be a person "Fleeing from justice" so as to toll the federal statute of limitations although he was not within the federal district when the crime was committed. Brouse v. United States, 68 F.2d 294 (1st Cir.1933).

D was informed against for forceable rape. The information was later amended to charge statutory rape (intercourse with a female under 18). This amendment was at a time when the statute of limitations barred the prosecution. Since statutory rape was not an offense

STATE v. DISBROW

Supreme Court of Iowa, 1906.
130 Iowa 19, 106 N.W. 263.

[**D** appealed from a conviction of embezzlement. The evidence had shown several acts of embezzlement over a period of six years. The conviction was under a second indictment after an earlier one found against **D** had been set aside as defective. The judge instructed the jury that **D** could be convicted of all his acts of embezzlement which had occurred within three years prior to the return of the first indictment. This ruling was assigned as error.]

WEAVER, J. . . .

It is said, however, on the part of the State, that it is settled law that "the time during which an indictment which has been quashed or set aside was pending is not, in case a new indictment is found, computed as a part of the period of limitation, provided the same offense and the same offender are charged in both indictments." We find this general proposition stated in some of the text-books and cyclopedias; but reference to the cases relied upon, so far as we have been able to examine them, reveals in each instance that the decision turns upon a local statute expressly or impliedly providing that upon the setting aside of an indictment or the entry of a *nol. pros.* the right of the State to present a new indictment within a limited time shall not be prejudiced. . . .

It seems to us a reasonable and just proposition that, in the absence of any statute saving such right to the State, the running of the statute of limitations ought not to be interrupted or suspended by the return and pendency of an indictment upon which no valid conviction or judgment can be founded. Such an indictment is no indictment. It is a nullity, and while it may serve as authority for the trial court to continue the defendant in custody and cause a resubmission of the case to the grand jury, such order is in effect the mere direction that the original inquiry shall be resumed as if the defective indictment had never been voted or returned into court. It is no more than a restoration of the case to the status it occupied at the time it was originally submitted. The grand jury takes it up anew, and may present or ignore the bill, without any reference whatever to the fact that one indictment has been presented and set aside. Cases are not wanting which tend to sustain this view. . . . But, without reference to the precedents from other States, our statute admits of no other conclusion than the one we have indicated. . . .

intended to be charged in the original information, nor necessarily included therein, the amendment could not relate back to the time of the original information. Prosecution for statutory rape was barred. People v. Chapman, 47 Cal.App. 3d 597, 121 Cal.Rptr. 315 (1975).

Other questions argued are not likely to arise on a retrial and we need not discuss them. For the reasons stated, the case must be remanded to the district court for a new trial.

Reversed.[1]

UNITED STATES v. GANAPOSKI

District Court of the United States, M.D. Pennsylvania, 1947.
72 F.Supp. 982.

[After Ganaposki, a bankrupt, had fraudulently concealed his assets from the trustee in bankruptcy in violation of federal law, the applicable statute of limitations which had provided that the indictment must be found "within three years after the commission of the offense", was amended to read that such concealment "shall be deemed to be a continuing offense until the bankrupt shall have been finally discharged, and the period of limitations herein provided shall not begin to run until such final discharge". Eight years after the concealment Ganaposki, who had been denied a discharge in bankruptcy, was indicted for that offense.]

MURPHY, DISTRICT JUDGE. . . . Defendant argues that the statute of limitations had expired long before the date of the indictment; that although the bankruptcy proceedings were pending when the Chandler Act of 1938 went into effect on September 22, 1938, the proviso of Section 52, sub. d, should not affect proceedings then pend-

1. The statute is tolled while an indictment for the offense is pending, even if it is defective. Hickey v. State, 131 Tenn. 112, 174 S.W. 269 (1915).

"Whenever an indictment is dismissed for any error, defect or irregularity . . . after the period prescribed by the applicable statute of limitations has expired, a new indictment may be returned . . . (within six months) which new indictment shall not be barred by any statute of limitations." 18 U.S.C.A. § 3288 (1969).

Reinstating an inadvertently dismissed information reinstates the standing which such information had prior to the dismissal, even though such reinstatement was made at a time when more than a year had elapsed since the commission of the offense. City of Keokuk v. Shultz, 188 Iowa 937, 176 N.W. 946 (1920). The due filing of an information arrests the statute of limitations and it is not necessary that the trial be held within the prescribed period. Ibid.

E and three fellow-employees of a bank co-operated in the embezzlement of its money and the falsification of its records to conceal the shortages. This continued year after year until **E**, no longer with the bank, was not in a position to aid in the concealment. At that time he told the others that he "was absolutely through and would have nothing further to do with the shortage at the" bank. Having been indicted for embezzlement, **E** claimed that the prosecution was barred because more than the period of limitations had elapsed since the communication. The others had continued their unlawful activities until just a few weeks prior to the indictment. It was held that if a conspirator effectively withdraws from a conspiracy he is not liable for the further acts of his former associates and the statute of limitations begins to run from the date of his withdrawal. But **E**'s withdrawal was not effective. Although he received no part of the money embezzled after the communication, he did not tell his co-conspirators to stop falsifying the records. He did not want them to stop because that would have resulted in an immediate disclosure of the crime. Hence their continuing wrongful acts were imputable to him and he is not protected by the statute. Eldredge v. United States, 62 F.2d 449 (10th Cir. 1932).

ing. Says defendant, if it did affect the proceedings it was an ex post facto law and invalid; also because it did not treat all debtors alike. With this we cannot agree.

When a right of acquittal has not been absolutely acquired by the completion of the period of limitation, that period is subject to enlargement without being obnoxious to the constitutional prohibition against ex post facto laws.

Such an extension makes no change in the rules of evidence or quantum of proof. An act of limitation is an act of grace purely on the part of the sovereign and especially is this so in the matter of criminal prosecution. Such enactments are measures of public policy. They are entirely subject to the will of Congress. . . .

Defendant finally relies upon the case of United States v. Fraidin, supra, and particularly the reasoning and conclusion of that court. Confronted with a situation similar to that before us, the court in a very learned and exhaustive opinion referred to the discussion in 2 Collier on Bankruptcy, 14th Ed., Section 29.15, p. 1206, where the author in discussing Section 29, sub. d, states: "Now the period of limitations is governed completely by events outside the acts of the defendant in concealing his property, namely, discharge. In view of the fact that a discharge might be refused because there was concealment, or for numerous other reasons, it is quite possible that the period in which an indictment could be brought for concealment of assets might run interminably. It would seem that the general objective sought by the proviso *could have been attained* by making the concealment of assets a continuing offense until discharged or *denial thereof.*" (Italics supplied.) It will be noted that the author states that "the general objective sought by the proviso could have been attained by making the concealment of assets a continuing offense until discharge or denial thereof." We do not disagree with the able author of the text of that valuable book, but surely it was not made as a suggestion to the courts to make an addition to the legislation as it was written by Congress.

The Court in the Fraidin case reasoned that it was proper to make such an addition and concluded (see Id., 63 F.Supp. at page 285) that "the proviso in this section as amended should be construed as though the words 'or until denial thereof' appeared at the very end of the proviso." We do not feel the court had the right to make such an addition. We refuse to do so.

In United States v. Newman, supra, 63 F.Supp. at page 270, the court stated inter alia, construing Section 29, sub. d;

"(3) Difficulties such as are anticipated are an insufficient justification for refusing to adopt an interpretation of Section 29 which its language plainly demands. (4) Unwise public policy is not the equivalent of lack of power or if (as here) Congress possess the authority to legislate as it has done in the two sections named, that is not the business of this court."

United States v. Nazzaro, supra, 65 F.Supp. 457: "The provisions of Section 29, sub. d, are not ambiguous. Congress and not the courts must determine if and when prosecution for an offense should be barred by limitation. No legislative history has been found or called to the attention of the court indicating that Congress intended otherwise than it expressly provided." The court followed United States v. Newman, supra, in the conclusion that the only remedy available for any asserted injustice or hardship created by this provision is an appeal to Congress to modify the statute.

"The general rule respecting statutes of limitation is that the language of the act must prevail, and no reasons based on apparent inconvenience or hardship can justify a departure from it." Amy v. Watertown, 1889, 130 U.S. 320, 9 S.Ct. 537, 538, 32 L.Ed. 953. . . .

For the foregoing reasons, we feel that the defendant's motion to dismiss should be denied. An order to that effect will be filed forthwith.[1]

1. A statute is unconstitutional if it authorizes punishment for an offense as to which the statute of limitations has already run, or an amnesty been given. Thompson v. State, 54 Miss. 740 (1887); State v. Keith, 63 N.C. 140 (1869); State v. Sneed, 25 Tex.Supp. 66 (1860).

The most elaborate discussion of this point to be found in the cases is in two opinions involving the same case. State v. Hart Moore, 42 N.J.L. 208 (1880); Moore v. State, 43 N.J.L. 203 (1881).

The statute of limitations on a charge of conspiracy to violate the Internal Revenue Law begins to run from the last overt act alleged in the indictment. United States v. Albanese, 123 F.Supp. 732 (D.C.N.Y.1954), affirmed 224 F.2d 879 (2d Cir.1955), certiorari denied 350 U.S. 845, 76 S.Ct. 87, 100 L.Ed. 753 (1955).

Cores, supra, was decided on the issue of venue. Since the foreign sailor who violated his landing permit, by remaining in this country after the 29-day authorization had elapsed, was guilty of a continuing offense he was triable in any federal district in which he was found. For the same reason the statute of limitations would not start to run in his favor while he was unlawfully remaining here.

The Universal Military Training and Service Act (50 U.S.C.A.App. § 453) makes it the duty of every male citizen between the ages of 18 and 26 to register at such times and places as determined by proclamation of the President and regulations prescribed. The proclamation provides that persons born on or after September 19, 1930, shall be registered on the day they attain the 18th anniversary of their birth, or within five days thereafter. **T**, who was born on June 23, 1941, was under duty to register between June 23 and June 28, 1959. He did not register then or later. His indictment on May 3, 1967, was held to have been barred by the 5-year period of limitations which was held to have started to run when he had failed to register by June 28, 1959. The contention of the government that **T** had a duty to register which continued until he was 26, and that the offense continued until that time, was rejected. Toussie v. United States, 397 U.S. 112, 90 S.Ct. 858 (1970).

White, J., joined by Burger, C.J. and Harlan, J., dissented on the ground that the regulations expressly provide that the duty "of every person subject to registration to present himself for and submit to registration shall continue at all times, ..."

"We hold . . . that either concealing or possessing stolen goods is a continuing offense for purpose of the statute of limitations." State v. Lawrence, 312 N.W.2d 251, 253 (Minn.1981).

STATE v. RUSSELL

Supreme Court of Hawaii, 1980.
62 Hawaii 474, 617 P.2d 84.

LUM, JUSTICE. This appeal involves the statutory interpretation of Hawaii's New Penal Code (New Code) and its application to an offense triable under Hawaii's Pre-Penal Code (Old Code); it also involves the statutory interpretation of Hawaii's detainer agreement, under chapter 834, HRS. The circuit court had dismissed an indictment charging both defendants, Robert Taylor Russell and Lawrence Frederick Carlson, with two counts of obtaining money under fraudulent and false pretenses under HRS § 750–21 (Old Code). The court had ruled that the statute of limitations of the New Code barred prosecutions of both defendants, and that a violation of the detainer agreement by the State against Defendant Carlson also required a dismissal of his case with prejudice. The State of Hawaii has appealed the court's ruling and raises the question of whether the trial judge was correct in his interpretation of the applicable statutory provisions of the New Code. . . . We have carefully examined these provisions of law and have come to the conclusion that the trial judge was incorrect. We therefore reverse.

During the period between November 28, 1972 to February 26, 1973, defendants are accused of having committed false representations and pretense to fraudulently obtain from THC Financial Corporation approximately $800,000. It was during this period, on January 1, 1973, that the New Code became law. After February 26, 1973, defendants concede they have been continuously absent from this State.

The indictment was not returned against defendants until March 22, 1978, more than five years after their departure. . . .

We first take up the issue of whether the statute of limitations had actually expired to bar prosecution of the defendants.

Defendants are required to be prosecuted under the Old Code.[1] The statute of limitations of the Old Code[2] does not bar prosecution of "any person who absents himself from the State."

1. HRS § 701–101 *Applicability to offenses committed before the effective date.* (1) Except as provided in subsections (2) and (3), this Code does not apply to offenses committed before its effective date. Prosecutions for offenses committed before the effective date are governed by the prior law, which is continued in effect for that purpose, as if this Code were not in force. For purposes of this section, an offense is committed before the effective date if any of the elements of the offense occurred before that date.

2. HRS § 701–1 *Two years; exceptions.* No person shall be prosecuted for any offense under the laws of the State, except murder in the first and second degrees, manslaughter, rape, assault with intent to ravish, carnal abuse of a minor under the age of twelve years, kidnapping, arson in the first and second degrees, burglary in the first and second degrees, forgery, robbery in the first and second degrees, larceny in the first degree, giving, promising, or receiving a bribe, extortion in the first and second degrees, compounding an offense punish-

Turning to the New Code, we find that § 701–101(2) provides in part:

> (2) In any case pending on or commenced after the effective date of this Code, involving an offense committed before that date:
>
> (a) Upon the request of the defendant a *defense* or mitigation *under this Code,* whether specifically provided for herein or based upon the failure of the Code to define an applicable offense, *shall apply;* . . . . (Emphasis added.)

The New Code then defines "defenses":

> § 701–115 *Defenses.* (1) A defense is a fact or set of facts which negatives penal liability.

In their motion to dismiss, defendants requested the application of the New Code statute of limitations under § 701–108 [3] as a "defense."

able by imprisonment for life, and embezzlement, unless the prosecution for the offense is commenced within two years next after the commission thereof. *Nothing herein contained shall bar any prosecution against any person who* flees from justice, or *absents himself from the State,* or so secretes himself that he cannot be found by the officers of the law, so that process cannot be served upon him. (Emphasis added.)

3. HRS § 701–108 *Time limitations.*

(1) A prosecution for murder may be commenced at any time.

(2) Except as otherwise provided in this section and in section 707–740, prosecutions for other offenses are subject to the following periods of limitation:

(a) A prosecution for a class A felony must be commenced within six years after it is committed;

(b) A prosecution for any other felony must be commenced within three years after it is committed;

(c) A prosecution for a misdemeanor or a parking violation must be commenced within two years after it is committed;

(d) A prosecution for a petty misdemeanor or a violation other than a parking violation must be commenced within one year after it is committed.

(3) If the period prescribed in subsection (2) has expired, a prosecution may nevertheless be commenced for:

(a) Any offense an element of which is either fraud or a breach of fiduciary obligation within one year after discovery of the offense by an aggrieved party or by a person who has a legal duty to represent an aggrieved party and who is himself not a party to the offense, but in no case shall this provision extend the period of limitation otherwise applicable by more than three years; and

(b) Any offense based on misconduct in office by a public officer or employee at any time when the defendant is in public office or employment or within two years thereafter, but in no case shall this provision extend the period of limitation otherwise applicable by more than three years.

(4) An offense is committed either when every element occurs, or, if a legislative purpose to prohibit a continuing course of conduct plainly appears, at the time when the course of conduct or the defendant's complicity therein is terminated. Time starts to run on the day after the offense is committed.

(5) A prosecution is commenced either when an indictment is found or an information filed, or when an arrest warrant or other process is issued, provided that such warrant or process is executed without unreasonable delay.

(6) *The period of limitation does not run:*

(a) *During any time when the accused is continuously absent from the State or has no reasonably ascertainable place of abode or work within the State, but in no case shall this provision extend the period of limitation otherwise applica-*

Specifically, they were able to convince the trial judge that New Code § 701–108(6)(a) applied as a "defense" to their case. The ingenuity of defense resulted in the application of part of the statute of limitations of the Old Code and part of the New Code. In effect, the two-year running limitation of the Old Code was used for the offense of false pretense [4] and the three-year tolling limitation of the New Code was used to cover defendants' absence from this State. Such an application limited the prosecutable period to five years; thus, the court was able to find that the statute had expired by 24 days before the indictment was returned to justify his dismissal of the indictment.

Defendants argue that they are entitled to use any "defense" as provided by the New Code. We do not disagree, but we do not see that as the issue. The central issue is whether the statute of limitations of the New Code is applicable to the instant case. If it is not, then its three-year tolling limitation cannot be applied as a "defense"; in which case the unlimited tolling provision of the Old Code must govern.

Statutes of limitations are acts of grace conferred by the sovereign which limit its right to prosecute criminal offenders.

In its adoption of the statute of limitations of both the old and new codes, the Hawaii legislature constructed a statute which first sets out the periods of limitation for various offenses; it then sets out certain exceptions—the circumstances in which the limitation periods are to be tolled.

Therefore, the statute of limitations is simply a rule of law with certain exceptions created by the legislature. The rule and its exceptions are a cohesive unit; they are reasonably related and represent a scheme by the legislature to carry out its wisdom of legislative grace. The exceptions are part of the rule and do not operate independently from the rule.

Defendants argue that the statute permits them to use the exception of the New Code as a "defense." We disagree. The importation of exceptions into statutes properly affected with a public interest is not lightly to be made. Statutes are to be construed with reference to the whole system of law of which they form a part.

It is a well settled rule of statutory construction that exceptions to legislative enactments must be strictly construed. One who claims the benefit of such an exception has the burden of bringing himself clearly within it.

Defendants argue, and we concur, that the offense of false pretense for which they stand indicted is not covered by the New Code.

ble by more than three years; (Emphasis added) or

(b) During any time when a prosecution against the accused for the same conduct is pending in this State.

4. We agree with defendants that the two-year statute of limitations is applicable. We do not find merit in the State's argument that the crime of false pretense has the same statute of limitations as larceny.

It is for this reason that the statute of limitations of the New Code does not cover the offense of the instant case. Without such coverage, the exception suffers the same fate and cannot serve as a "defense."

For the foregoing reasons, we find that the trial court erred in ruling that the three-year tolling provision of the New Code can be applied to the two-year limitation period of the Old Code. We hold that § 707–1 of the Old Code is the only statute of limitations to be used in this case and because of defendants' absence from the State, their prosecutions are not barred.

We believe that the construction we have adopted complies with § 701–104[5] of the New Code. . . .

Reversed and remanded for action consistent with this opinion.

PEOPLE v. SIEGEL

District Court of Appeal, Second District, Division 2, California, 1965.
235 Cal.App.2d 522, 45 Cal.Rptr. 530.

FLEMING, JUSTICE. May a probationer who received a suspended sentence in 1946 and whose probation was revoked in 1948 be required to serve his sentence in 1965?

In April 1946 defendant Siegel pleaded guilty to the crime of issuing a check without sufficient funds. He was sentenced to imprisonment for one year in the Los Angeles county jail, sentence was suspended, and he was placed on three years' probation. By the terms of his probation Siegel was ordered to follow all rules and regulations of the probation department and was granted permission to leave the state.

Subsequently Siegel left the state—with assurances, he now claims, that he need not report periodically to the probation department in order to remain in good standing. Since the original probation records in this case have been destroyed—Penal Code, § 1203.10, permits destruction of probation papers five years after the termination of probation—the only evidence of this alleged assurance consists of Siegel's own statement to that effect.

In May 1948 Siegel's probation officer recommended that the court revoke probation on the ground of desertion and issue a bench warrant for his arrest. The officer's report stated, "Probationer last reported on Jan. 2, 1948 . . . and Probation Officer has been unable to locate said probationer since that time. It now appears that said probationer has deserted." On the recommendation of the pro-

5. § 701–104 *Principles of construction.* The provisions of this Code cannot be extended by analogy so as to create crimes not provided for herein; however, in order to promote justice and effect the objects of the law, all of its provisions shall be given a genuine construction, according to the fair import of the words, taken in their usual sense, in connection with the context, and with reference to the purpose of the provision.

bation officer probation was revoked in May 1948 and a bench warrant issued for defendant's arrest.

Fifteen years passed.

In July 1963 Siegel again appeared before the Superior Court to answer a charge of issuing checks without sufficient funds, and at that time his 1946 sentence and 1948 revocation of probation were brought before the court. The court ordered a supplemental probation report to cover Siegel's activities during the intervening years. This report showed that in February 1948 Siegel had been convicted in Florida of vagrancy; in November 1948, convicted in Chicago of passing bad checks; in August 1949, convicted in New York of grand larceny; in June 1952, convicted in Chicago federal court of transporting bad checks across state lines; in September 1958, again convicted of a federal offense involving bad checks; in October 1961, again convicted in a Florida federal court of transporting forged checks across state lines. In July 1963, as previously noted, he appeared before the California Superior Court on bad check charges.

After considering this report the court found that the defendant had violated the terms of his probation, the revocation of probation was confirmed, and the 1946 sentence of one year in the county jail was ordered into execution.

Siegel appeals from the order requiring him to serve his original sentence, and he has obtained bail pending appeal. He contends the trial court was without jurisdiction to sentence him some 17 years after the original judgment, and that in any event the trial court abused its discretion in so doing.

(1) *The Court Had Jurisdiction*

The law is settled that when a court revokes probation within the probationary period, the defendant may be arrested and sentenced any time thereafter even though the probationary period has expired. The jurisdictional fact is the timely revocation of probation. Resentencing or execution of the judgment may occur at any time after revocation of probation, regardless of lapse of time. In People v. Brown, 111 Cal.App.2d 406, 244 P.2d 702, resentencing occurred 15 years after defendant had been placed on probation; in People v. Daugherty, 233 Cal.App.2d 284, 43 Cal.Rptr. 446, 11 years after judgment; and in People v. Mason, 184 Cal.App.2d 182, 7 Cal.Rptr. 525, 11 years after judgment.

Siegel's probation was revoked in 1948 while the original three-year probationary term was in effect, and thus the court in 1963 possessed jurisdiction to order the sentence into execution, even though 17 years had elapsed from the date of the original sentence.

(2) *No Abuse of Discretion*

The trial court did not abuse its legal discretion in revoking probation. When judgment has been pronounced and sentence suspended upon the grant of probation, probation may be revoked without notice and hearing, and defendant ordered committed pursuant to the judgment.[1] Although the court may not arbitrarily revoke probation, it is not required to hold a hearing under rules which are applicable to formal trials and revocation may be based upon the probation officer's report alone.

The supplemental probation report on Siegel showed violations of probation during the probationary period, for example, the conviction for vagrancy in Florida in February 1948. Since the commission of further crimes within the probationary period is good ground for revocation of probation the court acted within its authority in confirming the revocation of probation and ordering the previously-imposed sentence into execution.

There remains the question whether as a matter of sound public policy stale proceedings such as these should be further pursued. At some point every old judgment, even in criminal cases, becomes archaic and obsolete. Judgments should not be asserted to the surprise of the parties or their representatives when all proper vouchers of evidence are destroyed and facts have become obscured by lapse of time or death of witnesses. Obviously at some point the books must be balanced, and old debts written off. Thus, the doctrine of laches, the rule of adverse possession, the ten-year statute of limitations for execution on a civil judgment (Code Civ.Proc. § 681), and the three-year statute of limitations for commencing most felony actions (Penal Code, § 800), all reflect a policy of repose in dealing with past events.

Here we are concerned with a one-year sentence of imprisonment ordered into execution 17 years after the original judgment. The probation files in the case have been destroyed, the original probation officer is dead, and the reasons for the original revocation of probation cannot be ascertained by direct evidence. Although during the intervening years the defendant bounced from bad check to bad check and from prison to prison, for these other crimes he has paid his penalty. In the light of these considerations the trial court might well have determined that the public interest would be better served by the application of a general policy of repose to stale criminal judgments, no matter how unworthy the individual beneficiary of such a policy might be, rather than by enforcement of an antiquated criminal sentence which through lapse of time carries substantial risk of injustice and can have little deterrent effect on crime.

1. Contrast the situation where no judgment has been given and pronouncement of sentence has been suspended; in that event there is no basis on which a defendant could be directly committed to prison on revocation. He is therefore entitled to notice and hearing and counsel in what is equivalent to an arraignment for judgment. (In re Levi, 39 Cal.2d 41, 244 P.2d 403; In re Klein, 197 Cal.App.2d 58, 17 Cal.Rptr. 71.)

Yet, presumptively, these considerations were fully weighed by the trial court and its decision went the other way. As an appellate court we cannot say on this record that the result reached was clearly erroneous.

Judgment affirmed.

ROTH, P.J., and HERNDON, J., concur.

MODEL PENAL CODE

Section 1.06 Time Limitations.

(1) A prosecution for murder may be commenced at any time.

(2) Except as otherwise provided in this Section, prosecutions for other offenses are subject to the following periods of limitation:

(a) a prosecution for a felony of the first degree must be commenced within six years after it is committed;

(b) a prosecution for any other felony must be commenced within three years after it is committed;

(c) a prosecution for a misdemeanor must be commenced within two years after it is committed;

(d) a prosecution for a petty misdemeanor or a violation must be commenced within six months after it is committed.

(3) If the period prescribed in Subsection (2) has expired, a prosecution may nevertheless be commenced for:

(a) any offense a material element of which is either fraud or a breach of fiduciary obligation within one year after discovery of the offense by an aggrieved party or by a person who has legal duty to represent an aggrieved party and who is himself not a party to the offense, but in no case shall this provision extend the period of limitation otherwise applicable by more than three years; and

(b) any offense based upon misconduct in office by a public officer or employee at any time when the defendant is in public office or employment or within two years thereafter, but in no case shall this provision extend the period of limitation otherwise applicable by more than three years.

(4) An offense is committed either when every element occurs, or, if a legislative purpose to prohibit a continuing course of conduct plainly appears, at the time when the course of conduct or the defendant's complicity therein is terminated. Time starts to run on the day after the offense is committed.

(5) A prosecution is commenced either when an indictment is found [or an information filed] or when a warrant or other process is issued, provided that such warrant or process is executed without unreasonable delay.

(6) The period of limitation does not run:

(a) during any time when the accused is continuously absent from the State or has no reasonably ascertainable place of abode or work within the State, but in no case shall this provision extend the period of limitation otherwise applicable by more than three years; or

(b) during any time when a prosecution against the accused for the same conduct is pending in this State.[a]

SECTION 4. FORMER JEOPARDY

Litigation would never end if the issues determined in one action could be raised anew between the same parties by the mere commencement of another proceeding. In the words of the ancient maxim: *"Nemo debet bis vexari pro eadem causa"* (No one ought to be twice tried for the same cause). This found expression in the common law in the form of the plea of *res judicata* in civil suits and in the pleas of the *autrefois acquit* and *autrefois convict* in criminal prosecutions. Such a plea in a criminal case, in the words of Blackstone, "is grounded on this universal maxim of the common law of England, that no man is to brought into jeopardy of his life more than once for the same offence." 4 Bl.Comm. *335. The actual foundation is the broader maxim mentioned above, but it is from statements such as Blackstone's that we derive our phrases "former jeopardy," "double jeopardy" and "twice in jeopardy."

The Fifth Amendment says: ". . . nor shall any person be subject for the same offense to be twice put in jeopardy of life or limb; . . . " Similar language is to be found in the constitutions of many states, but it is important to keep in mind that there was no such common-law plea as "former jeopardy." The plea was either "former acquittal" (autrefois acquit) or "former conviction" (autrefois convict). There is no reason to believe that the phrase "twice put in jeopardy" was used in the Fifth Amendment for the purpose of introducing a change into this department of the law. In all likelihood the framers of the Constitution had no more in mind than embodiment of the common-law prohibition against placing a defendant in jeopardy a second time for the same offense after *acquittal* or *conviction.* An enlargement has resulted from judicial interpretation, however. The courts have held that a defendant is "in jeopardy" as soon as the jury has been impaneled and sworn (if the court has jurisdiction and the indictment is sufficient to support a conviction) and that the bar against a second trial begins at this point.[1] This position has tended to introduce new difficulties into this branch of the law. The common-law principle (to repeat) was that an accused person should not be prosecuted again for the same offense after he had once been convicted or acquitted thereof. The word "jeopardy" merely happened to be used by Blackstone and others in explanation of this principle. The principle itself was quite independent of the meaning of the word "jeopardy." And this word, apart from the meaning engrafted upon it by the courts, signifies danger or peril. It comes from the same source as the word "jeopardize" which means "to expose to loss or injury." In a very real sense a man is in

1. Crist v. Bretz, 437 U.S. 28, 98 S.Ct. 2156 (1978).

jeopardy when he has been charged with crime by a valid indictment. Neither precedent nor policy forbids a second indictment for the same offense merely because of the finding of a prior one, and the bar of "former jeopardy" has never been carried to that extent.

The bar known as "former jeopardy" is grounded partly upon expediency and partly upon "fair play." Expediency alone requires some device which will prevent the same issues being tried time and again by the same parties. "Fair play" may require more than this. It would be quite unfair to the defendant in a criminal case, for example, if either the prosecuting attorney or the judge could arbitrarily withdraw the case from the jury after the trial started, merely in the hope of obtaining another jury which might be more likely to find a verdict of guilty. Any such unfairness could have been prevented, without material change from the common-law concept by treating as the "equivalent of an acquittal" any disposition of a criminal case by which a jury which had been duly impaneled and sworn to try it was not permitted to bring in a verdict, by any act of the prosecuting attorney, or by any violation of judicial discretion on the part of the judge. Some of the cases approach the problem from this point of view.

Another solution, however, was reached by many courts. This was grounded upon the premise that a defendant was "in jeopardy" when a jury was duly impaneled and sworn to try his case and that the trial of this same case by any other jury would be placing him "twice in jeopardy." [2] Such a position required certain exceptions to

2. Jeopardy attaches when the jury has been selected and sworn, even though no evidence has been taken. Downum v. United States, 372 U.S. 734, 83 S.Ct. 1033 (1963).

Although some state courts had held that more is required, the Supreme Court held that the Constitution requires the holding that jeopardy attaches in a state case when the jury is impaneled and sworn. Crist v. Bretz, 437 U.S. 28, 98 S.Ct. 2156 (1978).

In a case tried without a jury, jeopardy was held to attach when the court begins to hear evidence. United States v. Choate, 527 F.2d 748 (9th Cir. 1975).

However, it has been held that the testimony of the witness is immaterial to jeopardy and it attaches in a bench trial when the first witness is sworn. Goolsby v. Hutto, 691 F.2d 199 (4th Cir.1982).

The double jeopardy clause does not prevent one who commits illegal acts while on probation from being accountable for those acts both through parole violation proceedings and by criminal prosecution. State v. Montgomery, 3 Or.App. 555, 474 P.2d 780 (1970).

Although the Court had distinguished between the pronouncement of sentence, which is not final, and an acquittal, which is, so that an enhanced penalty on appeal from the sentence is constitutionally permissible. United States v. DiFrancesco, 449 U.S. 117, 101 S.Ct. 426 (1980). It held that a sentence of life imprisonment imposed in the sentencing stage of a bifurcated trial under the Missouri statute, may not be increased to death upon retrial. Bullington v. Missouri, 451 U.S. 430, 101 S.Ct. 1852 (1981).

"Because probation is a form of punishment and a person cannot be placed twice in jeopardy of punishment, we now hold that the reimposition of a sentence after a defendant has been placed on probation, absent a violation of a condition of probation, is a violation of both the United States and Wisconsin Constitutions' double jeopardy clauses." State v. Dean, 111 Wis.2d 361, 330 N.W.2d 630, 632 (App.1983).

avoid obvious miscarriages of justice. The two views reach the same result in most cases but there are important shades of difference.

Because of these facts some of the problems in this field arise out of peculiarities in the proceedings themselves,—of which the following are merely examples. Was the case withdrawn from the jury after it had been duly impaneled and sworn but before it had rendered a verdict, and if so why? Has a retrial been ordered after a verdict was rendered, and if so what was the verdict and why was the retrial ordered?

Apart from problems arising out of the peculiarities of procedure in the particular case are those arising out of interpretations of the phrase "the same offense" as used in the former jeopardy rule. These two sets of problems require separate attention although both may happen to be involved in the same case.

(A) PROBLEMS PECULIAR TO THE PROCEEDINGS

No "jeopardy" is involved if the court lacked jurisdiction to try the case or if the indictment was insufficient to support a conviction. If, because of some fatal defect the indictment was quashed before trial [1] or set aside during the trial or afterwards, the defendant may be prosecuted upon a proper indictment subsequently found against him [2] (provided it is not barred for some other reason such as the statute of limitations).

Furthermore, jeopardy attaches only when there has been a real prosecution for crime. If a wrongdoer, not having been accused, hastens before a magistrate, confesses to having committed a certain offense and pays the fine imposed, the state is not barred from a subsequent prosecution. Such voluntary confession and payment of fine is not a criminal prosecution.[3] The burden of proof is upon the prosecution when it seeks to avoid a plea of former jeopardy on the claim of fraud or collusion.[4] And where the prosecuting attorney starts the prosecution, and carries it through, this has been held to bar a subsequent prosecution even if the prosecuting attorney was corrupted during the pendency of the prosecution. Such a judgment may be voidable, but it is not void and cannot be attacked in a collateral proceeding.[5]

1. Reddan v. State, 4 G. Greene 137 (Iowa, 1853); State v. Scott, 99 Iowa 36, 68 N.W. 451 (1896).

2. State v. Smith, 88 Iowa 178, 55 N.W. 198 (1893).

3. State v. Bartlett, 181 Iowa 436, 164 N.W. 757 (1917).

4. State v. Maxwell, 51 Iowa 314, 1 N.W. 666 (1879).

5. Shideler v. State, 129 Ind. 523, 28 N.E. 537, 29 N.E. 36 (1891).

Conviction under a city ordinance for carrying a concealed weapon was held not to bar a subsequent prosecution under a state statute prohibiting possession of a pistol by one who has been convicted of a felony. Barwood v. State, 198 Kan. 659, 426 P.2d 151 (1967).

HUDSON v. LOUISIANA

Supreme Court of the United States, 1981.
450 U.S. 40, 101 S.Ct. 970.

JUSTICE POWELL delivered the opinion of the Court.

The question in this case is whether Louisiana violated the Double Jeopardy Clause, as we expounded it in Burks v. United States, 437 U.S. 1, 98 S.Ct. 2141, 57 L.Ed.2d 1 (1978), by prosecuting petitioner a second time after the trial judge at the first trial granted petitioner's motion for new trial on the ground that the evidence was insufficient to support the jury's verdict of guilty.

I

Petitioner Tracy Lee Hudson was tried in Louisiana state court for first-degree murder, and the jury found him guilty. Petitioner then moved for a new trial, which under Louisiana law was petitioner's only means of challenging the sufficiency of the evidence against him.[1] The trial judge granted the motion, stating: "I heard the same evidence the jury did[;] I'm convinced that there was no evidence, certainly not evidence beyond a reasonable doubt, to sustain the verdict of the homicide committed by this defendant of this particular victim." The Louisiana Supreme Court denied the State's application for a writ of certiorari.

At petitioner's second trial, the State presented an eyewitness whose testimony it had not presented at the first trial. The second jury also found petitioner guilty. The Louisiana Supreme Court affirmed the conviction.

1. Louisiana's Code of Criminal Procedure does not authorize trial judges to enter judgments of acquittal in jury trials. La.Code Crim.Proc.Ann., Art. 778 (West); State v. Henderson, 362 So.2d 1358, 1367 (1978). Accordingly, a criminal defendant's only means of challenging the sufficiency of evidence presented against him to a jury is a motion for new trial under La.Code Crim.Proc.Ann., Art. 851 (West), which provides in pertinent part:

"The Court, on motion of the defendant, shall grant a new trial whenever:

"(1) The verdict is contrary to the law and the evidence;

"(2) The court's ruling on a written motion, or an objection made during the proceedings, shows prejudicial error;

"(3) New and material evidence that, notwithstanding the exercise of reasonable diligence by the defendant, was not discovered before or during the trial, is available, and if the evidence had been introduced at the trial it would probably have changed the verdict or judgment of guilty;

"(4) The defendant has discovered, since the verdict or judgment of guilty, a prejudicial error or defect in the proceedings that, notwithstanding the exercise of reasonable diligence by the defendant, was not discovered before the verdict or judgment; or

"(5) The court is of the opinion that the ends of justice would be served by the granting of a new trial, although the defendant may not be entitled to a new trial as a matter of strict legal right."

We think it clear that the trial judge in this case acted under paragraph (1) in granting a new trial. See infra, at 972.

Petitioner then sought a writ of habeas corpus in a Louisiana state court, contending that the Double Jeopardy Clause barred the State from trying him the second time. Petitioner relied on our decision in *Burks* [2] that "the Double Jeopardy Clause precludes a second trial once the reviewing court has found the evidence legally insufficient" to support the guilty verdict.[3] The trial court denied a writ, and the Louisiana Supreme Court affirmed. The Supreme Court read *Burks* to bar a second trial only if the court reviewing the evidence—whether an appellate court or a trial court—determines that there was *no* evidence to support the verdict. Because it believed that the trial judge at petitioner's first trial had granted petitioner's motion for new trial on the ground that there was *insufficient* evidence to support the verdict, although some evidence, the Louisiana Supreme Court concluded that petitioner's second trial was not precluded by the Double Jeopardy Clause.

We granted a writ of certiorari, and we now reverse.

II

We considered in *Burks* the question "whether an accused may be subjected to a second trial when conviction in a prior trial was reversed by an appellate court solely for lack of sufficient evidence to sustain the jury's verdict." We held that a reversal "due to a failure of proof at trial," where the State received a "fair opportunity to offer whatever proof it could assemble," bars retrial on the same charge. We also held that it makes "no difference that the *reviewing* court, rather than the trial court, determined the evidence to be insufficient." (Emphasis in original), or that "a defendant has sought a new trial as one of his remedies, or even as the sole remedy."

Our decision in *Burks* controls this case, for it is clear that petitioner moved for a new trial on the ground that the evidence was legally insufficient to support the verdict and that the trial judge granted petitioner's motion on that ground. In the hearing on the motion, petitioner's counsel argued to the trial judge that "the verdict of the jury is contrary to the law and the evidence." After reviewing the evidence put to the jurors, the trial judge agreed with petitioner "that there was no evidence, certainly not evidence beyond a reasonable doubt, to sustain the verdict"; and he commented, "[H]ow they concluded that this defendant committed the act from that evidence when no weapon was produced, no proof of anyone who saw a blow struck, is beyond the Court's comprehension." The Louisiana Supreme Court recognized that the trial judge granted the new trial on the ground that the evidence was legally insufficient. The Supreme

2. We decided *Burks* before the Louisiana Supreme Court entered its judgment affirming petitioner's conviction.

3. *Burks* involved a federal prosecution, but the Court held in Greene v. Massey, 437 U.S. 19, 24, 98 S.Ct. 2151, 2154, 57 L.Ed.2d 15 (1978), that the double jeopardy principle in *Burks* fully applies to the States. See Benton v. Maryland, 395 U.S. 784, 89 S.Ct 2056, 23 L.Ed.2d 707 (1969); Crist v. Bretz, 437 U.S. 28, 98 S.Ct. 2156, 57 L.Ed.2d 24 (1978).

Court described the trial judge's decision in these words: "[T]he trial judge herein ordered a new trial pursuant to LSA–C.Cr.P. art. 851(1) solely for lack of *sufficient evidence* to sustain the jury's verdict . . . ." (emphasis in original). This is precisely the circumstance in which *Burks* precludes retrials. Nothing in *Burks* suggests, as the Louisiana Supreme Court seemed to believe, that double jeopardy protections are violated only when the prosecution has adduced no evidence at all of the crime or an element thereof.

The State contends that *Burks* does not control this case. As the State reads the record, the trial judge granted a new trial only because he entertained personal doubts about the verdict. According to the State, the trial judge decided that he, as a "13th juror," would not have found petitioner guilty and he therefore granted a new trial even though the evidence was not insufficient as a matter of law to support the verdict. The State therefore reasons that *Burks* does not preclude a new trial in such a case, for the new trial was not granted "due to a failure of proof at trial."

This is not such a case, as the opinion of the Louisiana Supreme Court and the statements of the trial judge make clear. The trial judge granted the new trial because the State had failed to prove its case as a matter of law, not merely because he, as a "13th juror," would have decided it differently from the other 12 jurors. Accordingly there are no significant facts which distinguish this case from *Burks,* and the Double Jeopardy Clause barred the State from prosecuting petitioner a second time.

III

The judgment of the Louisiana Supreme Court is reversed.

It is so ordered.

UNITED STATES v. KLANDE

United States Court of Appeals, Eighth Circuit, 1979.
602 F.2d 180.

ROSS, CIRCUIT JUDGE. Defendants appeal an order of the district court denying their motions to dismiss the indictment on grounds of double jeopardy. We affirm.

Defendants, Darrell Lee Schaapveld, Barbara Ann Klande and Emma Lou Klande were indicted on charges of conspiring to import and distribute marijuana in violation of 21 U.S.C. §§ 952(a), 963 and 841(a)(1), 846. Defendant Schaapveld was also indicted on charges of unlawful possession of marijuana in violation of 21 U.S.C. § 841(a)(1).

The Mexican Government seized and retained possession of the alleged marijuana relating to the conspiracy charges. Because the United States Government at no time acquired possession of the substance seized, the possibility arose of a demonstration at trial by the

United States Customs' dog that allegedly had detected the marijuana.

On the fourth day of trial, a newspaper article concerning the dog's planned appearance was published in a local paper. During the jury's absence, the district court brought the article to the attention of counsel. The article cited comments by the district court judge, the government prosecutor and counsel for Schaapveld regarding the dog.[2]

Based on the article, the Klandes moved for a mistrial arguing, *inter alia,* that the prosecutor had attested to the dog's reliability. Counsel for Schaapveld indicated that he wanted to talk with his client and question the jury before deciding whether to move for a mistrial. The district court also indicated a desire to question the jury. The district court then granted a mistrial as to the Klandes. After consulting with his client, counsel for Schaapveld also moved for and was granted a mistrial. Later questioning of the jury indicated that no juror had seen the article.

Defendants then moved to dismiss the indictment on grounds of double jeopardy. The district court denied the motions, finding that the prosecutor's comments in the article did not amount to prosecutorial overreaching or result in actual prejudice to the defendants.

The issue on appeal[3] is whether the double jeopardy clause bars reprosecution of the defendants in light of the factual circumstances leading to the district court's mistrial order.

First, defendants contend that this appeal should be reviewed as a *sua sponte* declaration of mistrial by the district court. Defendants base this claim mainly on the actions of the district court judge in bringing the article to the attention of counsel and indicating he would "accept whatever guidance" counsel offered regarding the article. If the actions of the district court were viewed as a *sua sponte* declaration of mistrial without the defendants' consent, the Supreme Court requires a showing of "manifest necessity" for the mistrial, and absent such a showing the double jeopardy clause would bar retrial. United States v. Scott, 437 U.S. 82, 93, 98 S.Ct. 2187, 57 L.Ed. 2d 65 (1978); United States v. Jorn, 400 U.S. 470, 484–85, 91 S.Ct. 547,

2. Judge Lord's comments, sometimes humorous, concerned the logistics of having a dog in the courtroom, the media requests to cover the demonstration, and his desire that the proceedings remain serious.

The prosecutor's comments concerned the dog's behavior in the prosecutor's office, the location and purpose of the demonstration, and the prosecutor's recollection of a previous demonstration by the dog.

Counsel for Schaapveld commented that he did not know what the government would prove with the demonstration and he also related a story concerning a previous demonstration where another dog had attacked an attorney.

3. Jurisdiction of this court is based on 28 U.S.C. § 1291, and an expedited appeal was permitted in accordance with Rule 2, Federal Rules of Appellate Procedure. See Abney v. United States, 431 U.S. 651, 662, 97 S.Ct. 2034, 52 L.Ed.2d 651 (1977).

27 L.Ed.2d 543 (1970); United States v. Perez, 22 U.S. (9 Wheat.) 579, 580, 6 L.Ed. 165 (1824).

However the record does not support defendants' claim of a *sua sponte* declaration of mistrial. Rather, the record clearly indicates that each defendant moved for a mistrial [4] and argued vigorously the possible prejudice caused by the article.

Where a *defendant* successfully moves for a mistrial, the double jeopardy clause generally does not bar reprosecution, "even if defendant's motion is necessitated by a prosecutorial or judicial error." However, retrial is barred where the error is "intended to provoke mistrial" or is "motivated by bad faith or undertaken to harass or prejudice" the defendant. In the absence of such "prosecutorial or judicial overreaching," the double jeopardy clause is not a barrier to reprosecution, even if the error may justify disciplinary action. "[M]ere negligence" alone is not the type of conduct which would amount to prosecutorial overreaching.

Defendants contend that the circumstances surrounding the publication of the newspaper article constituted prosecutorial overreaching. However, defendants Klande concede that the prosecutor's actions were not intentional.

We believe the prosecutor's comments quoted in the article, even if improper, cannot reasonably be construed as intended to harass the defendants. Also, there appears no intent to provoke a mistrial, because the district court found that both the prosecutor and counsel for defendant Schaapveld believed the article would not be published until after trial. Finally, we agree with the district court that the defendants were not actually prejudiced, especially in view of the fact that no juror had seen the article.

When, as in this case, the prosecutor's conduct does not prejudice the defendants or constitute prosecutorial overreaching or even gross negligence, we hold that the double jeopardy clause does not bar reprosecution. . . .

The order of the district court is affirmed.[a]

4. Defendant Schaapveld argues that he was forced to make his motion for mistrial because the district court had already granted a mistrial as to the Klandes. In United States v. Dinitz, 424 U.S. 600, 609, 96 S.Ct. 1075, 47 L.Ed.2d 267 (1976) the Supreme Court indicated that the important question is not whether defendant faces a "Hobson's choice" but rather whether the defendant "retain[s] primary control over the course to be followed . . . ." The record shows that counsel for Schaapveld requested and was granted a recess for the specific purpose of determining whether to move for a mistrial. Immediately following the recess Schaapveld made his motion, thus establishing his control over the decision.

a. Defendant was prosecuted for theft. The prosecutor in examining an expert witness asked if the witness had ever done business with the defendant and witness said he had not. The prosecutor asked if this was because the defendant "is a crook?" Defendant obtained a mistrial. The Supreme Court held jeopardy did not bar a retrial. "Prosecutorial conduct that might be viewed as harassment or overreaching, even if sufficient to justify a mistrial on defendant's motion, therefore, does not bar retrial absent intent on the part of

ILLINOIS v. SOMERVILLE

Supreme Court of the United States, 1973.
410 U.S. 458, 93 S.Ct. 1066.

MR. JUSTICE REHNQUIST delivered the opinion of the Court.

We must here decide whether declaration of a mistrial over the defendant's objection, because the trial court concluded that the in-

the prosecutor to subvert the protections afforded by the Double Jeopardy Clause. . . ."

Only where the governmental conduct in question is intended to "goad" the defendant moving for a mistrial may a defendant raise a bar of Double Jeopardy to a second trial after having succeeded in aborting the first on his own motion. Oregon v. Kennedy, 456 U.S. 667, 674–676, 102 S.Ct. 2083, 2089 (1982).

Burton and Mack were charged jointly with robbing Sam Lawhon. They elected to be tried separately. Burton was tried first and was acquitted. During the trial of Mack, his attorney questioned the alleged victim of the robbery in regard to his testimony in Burton's trial, and then said: "and in spite of your testimony he was acquitted?" The prosecuting attorney immediately moved to discharge the jury and this motion was sustained. Mack was later tried and convicted by another jury over his objection that the proceeding before the first jury barred any subsequent trial for the same offense. In affirming the conviction the court said that the second trial resulted from the prejudicial misconduct of defendant's attorney. Mack v. Commonwealth, 177 Va. 921, 15 S.E.2d 62 (1941).

A soldier was charged with rape and put on trial before a general court-martial in time of war. After hearing evidence and arguments of counsel, the court-martial closed to consider the case. Later the same day the court-martial reopened and announced that it would be continued until a later day to hear other witnesses not then available. A week later the commanding general of the division withdrew the charges from the court-martial and transferred them to the commanding general of the Third Army with recommendations for trial by a new court-martial. The reason given was that the "tactical situation" made it impracticable to complete the case within a reasonable time. For a similar reason it was transferred on to the commanding general of the Fifteenth Army, who convened a court-martial to try the case. The soldier was convicted after his plea of former jeopardy had been overruled. The case was then taken to the federal court by habeas corpus proceedings. In upholding the conviction the court said: "The double-jeopardy provision of the Fifth Amendment, however, does not mean that every time a defendant is put to trial before a competent tribunal he is entitled to go free if the trial fails to end in a final judgment. Such a rule would create an insuperable obstacle to the administration of justice in many cases in which there is no semblance of the type of oppressive practices at which the double-jeopardy prohibition is aimed. There may be unforeseeable circumstances that arise during a trial making its completion impossible, such as the failure of a jury to agree upon a verdict. In such event the purpose of the law to protect society from those guilty of crimes frequently would be frustrated by denying courts power to put the defendant to trial again." Wade v. Hunter, Warden, 336 U.S. 684, 688–9, 69 S.Ct. 834, 837, 93 L.Ed. 974 (1949). Mr. Justice Murphy, Mr. Justice Douglas and Mr. Justice Rutledge dissented.

The quashing of a bad indictment is no bar to a prosecution upon a good one. And if the first indictment was quashed upon defendant's motion, he cannot later maintain that it was valid. He cannot "blow hot and cold". United States v. Narvaez-Granillo, 119 F.Supp. 556 (D.C. Cal.1954).

If a conviction was vacated because defendant was not competent to stand trial there is no bar to another trial after he becomes competent. Flynn v. United States, 217 F.2d 29 (9th Cir.1954) cert. denied, 348 U.S. 930, 75 S.Ct. 344 (1955).

During the trial it became necessary to discharge one juror. **D** agreed to proceed with eleven jurors but the prosecution insisted on a twelve-man jury. Over the protest of **D**'s counsel the jury was discharged. Former jeopardy was held to prevent another trial. Hutchins v. District Court, 423 P.2d 474 (Okl.Cr. 1967).

dictment was insufficient to charge a crime, necessarily prevents a State from subsequently trying the defendant under a valid indictment. We hold that the mistrial met the "manifest necessity" requirement of our cases, since the trial court could reasonably have concluded that the "ends of public justice" would be defeated by having allowed the trial to continue. Therefore, the Double Jeopardy Clause of the Fifth Amendment, made applicable to the States through the Due Process Clause of the Fourteenth Amendment, did not bar retrial under a valid indictment.

I

On March 19, 1964, respondent was indicted by an Illinois grand jury for the crime of theft. The case was called for trial and a jury impaneled and sworn on November 1, 1965. The following day, before any evidence had been presented, the prosecuting attorney realized that the indictment was fatally deficient under Illinois law because it did not allege that respondent intended to permanently deprive the owner of his property. Under the applicable Illinois criminal statute, such intent is a necessary element of the crime of theft,[1] and failure to allege intent renders the indictment insufficient to charge a crime. But under the Illinois Constitution at that time,[2] an indictment was the sole means by which a criminal proceeding such as this may be commenced against a defendant. Illinois further provides that only formal defects, of which this was not one, may be cured by amendment. The combined operation of these rules of Illinois procedure and substantive law meant that the defect in the indictment was "jurisdictional"; it could not be waived by the defendant's failure to object, and could be asserted on appeal or in a post-conviction proceeding to overturn a final judgment of conviction.

Faced with this situation, the Illinois trial court concluded that further proceedings under this defective indictment would be useless and granted the State's motion for a mistrial. On November 3, the grand jury handed down a second indictment alleging the requisite intent. Respondent was arraigned two weeks after the first trial was aborted, raised a claim of double jeopardy which was overruled, and the second trial commenced shortly thereafter. The jury returned a verdict of guilty, sentence was imposed, and the Illinois courts upheld the conviction. Respondent then sought federal habeas corpus, alleging that the conviction constituted double jeopardy contrary to the

Rule 23, Federal Rules of Criminal Procedure:

"(a) . . . .

"(b) Jury of Less Than Twelve. Juries shall be of 12 but at any time before verdict the parties may stipulate in writing with the approval of the court that the jury shall consist of any number less than 12 or that a valid verdict may be returned by a jury of less than 12 should the court find it necessary to excuse one or more jurors for any just cause after trial commences."

1. Ill.Rev.Stat., c. 38, § 16–1(d)(1) (1963).

2. See Constitution of Illinois, Art. II, § 8 (1967). When the State Constitution was amended in 1970, this provision was retained as the first paragraph of Art. I, § 7.

prohibition of the Fifth and Fourteenth Amendments. The Seventh Circuit affirmed the denial of habeas corpus prior to our decision in United States v. Jorn, 400 U.S. 470, 91 S.Ct. 547, 27 L.Ed.2d 543 (1971). The respondent's petition for certiorari was granted, and the case remanded for reconsideration in light of *Jorn* and Downum v. United States, 372 U.S. 734, 83 S.Ct. 1033, 10 L.Ed.2d 100 (1963). On remand, the Seventh Circuit held that respondent's petition for habeas corpus should have been granted because, although he had not been tried and *acquitted* as in United States v. Ball, 163 U.S. 662, 16 S.Ct. 1192, 41 L.Ed. 300 (1896), and Benton v. Maryland, 395 U.S. 784, 89 S.Ct. 2056, 23 L.Ed.2d 707 (1969), jeopardy had attached when the jury was impaneled and sworn, and a declaration of mistrial over respondent's objection precluded a retrial under a valid indictment. For the reasons stated below, we reverse that judgment.

II

The fountainhead decision construing the Double Jeopardy Clause in the context of a declaration of a mistrial over a defendant's objection is United States v. Perez, 9 Wheat. 579 (1824). Mr. Justice Story, writing for a unanimous Court, set forth the standards for determining whether a retrial, following a declaration of a mistrial over a defendant's objection, constitutes double jeopardy within the meaning of the Fifth Amendment. In holding that the failure of the jury to agree on a verdict of either acquittal or conviction did not bar retrial of the defendant, Mr. Justice Story wrote: "We think, that in all cases of this nature, the law has invested Courts of justice with the authority to discharge a jury from giving any verdict, whenever, in their opinion, taking all the circumstances into consideration, there is a manifest necessity for the act, or the ends of public justice would otherwise be defeated. They are to exercise a sound discretion on the subject; and it is impossible to define all the circumstances, which would render it proper to interfere. To be sure, the power ought to be used with the greatest caution, under urgent circumstances, and for very plain and obvious causes; and, in capital cases especially, Courts should be extremely careful how they interfere with any of the chances of life, in favour of the prisoner. But, after all, they have the right to order the discharge; and the security which the public have for the faithful, sound, and conscientious exercise of this discretion, rests, in this, as in other cases, upon the responsibility of the Judges, under their oaths of office." Id., at 580.

This formulation, consistently adhered to by this Court in subsequent decisions, abjures the application of any mechanical formula by which to judge the propriety of declaring a mistrial in the varying and often unique situations arising during the course of a criminal trial. The broad discretion reserved to the trial judge in such circumstances has been consistently reiterated in decisions of this Court. . . .

In Downum v. United States, the defendant was charged with six counts of mail theft, and forging and uttering stolen checks. A jury was selected and sworn in the morning, and instructed to return that afternoon. When the jury returned, the Government moved for the discharge of the jury on the ground that a key prosecution witness, for two of the six counts against defendant, was not present. The prosecution knew, prior to the selection and swearing of the jury, that this witness could not be found and had not been served with a subpoena. The trial judge discharged the jury over the defendant's motions to dismiss two counts for failure to prosecute and to continue the other four. This Court, in reversing the convictions on the ground of double jeopardy, emphasized that "[e]ach case must turn on its facts," 372 U.S., at 737, 83 S.Ct., at 1035 and held that the second prosecution constituted double jeopardy, because the absence of the witness and the reason therefor did not there justify, in terms of "manifest necessity," the declaration of a mistrial.

In United States v. Jorn, supra, the Government called a taxpayer witness in a prosecution for willfully assisting in the preparation of fraudulent income tax returns. Prior to his testimony, defense counsel suggested he be warned of his constitutional right against compulsory self-incrimination. The trial judge warned him of his rights, and the witness stated that he was willing to testify and that the Internal Revenue Service agent who first contacted him warned him of his rights. The trial judge, however, did not believe the witness' declaration that the IRS had so warned him, and refused to allow him to testify until after he had consulted with an attorney. After learning from the Government that the remaining four witnesses were "similarly situated," and after surmising that they, too, had not been properly informed of their rights, the trial judge declared a mistrial to give the witnesses the opportunity to consult with attorneys. In sustaining a plea in bar of double jeopardy to an attempted second trial of the defendant, the plurality opinion of the Court, emphasizing the importance to the defendant of proceeding before the first jury sworn, concluded:

"It is apparent from the record that no consideration was given to the possibility of a trial continuance; indeed, the trial judge acted so abruptly in discharging the jury that, had the prosecutor been disposed to suggest a continuance, or the defendant to object to the discharge of the jury, there would have been no opportunity to do so. When one examines the circumstances surrounding the discharge of this jury, it seems abundantly apparent that the trial judge made no effort to exercise a sound discretion to assure that, taking all the circumstances into account, there was a manifest necessity for the *sua sponte* declaration of this mistrial. United States v. Perez, 9 Wheat., at 580. Therefore, we must conclude that in the circumstances of this case, appellee's reprosecution would violate the double jeopardy provision of the Fifth Amendment." 400 U.S., at 487, 91 S.Ct., at 558. . . .

In the instant case, the trial judge terminated the proceeding because a defect was found to exist in the indictment that was, as a matter of Illinois law, not curable by amendment. The Illinois courts have held that even after a judgment of conviction has become final, the defendant may be released on habeas corpus, because the defect in the indictment deprives the trial court of "jurisdiction." The rule prohibiting the amendment of all but formal defects in indictments is designed to implement the State's policy of preserving the right of each defendant to insist that a criminal prosecution against him be commenced by the action of a grand jury. The trial judge was faced with a situation similar to those in *Simmons, Lovato,* and *Thompson,* in which a procedural defect might or would preclude the public from either obtaining an impartial verdict or keeping a verdict of conviction if its evidence persuaded the jury. If a mistrial were constitutionally unavailable in situations such as this, the State's policy could only be implemented by conducting a second trial after verdict and reversal on appeal, thus wasting time, energy, and money for all concerned. Here, the trial judge's action was a rational determination designed to implement a legitimate state policy, with no suggestion that the implementation of that policy in this manner could be manipulated so as to prejudice the defendant. This situation is thus unlike *Downum,* where the mistrial entailed not only a delay for the defendant, but also operated as a post-jeopardy continuance to allow the prosecution an opportunity to strengthen its case. Here, the delay was minimal, and the mistrial was, under Illinois law, the only way in which a defect in the indictment could be corrected. Given the established standard of discretion set forth in *Perez, Gori,* and *Hunter,* we cannot say that the declaration of a mistrial was not required by "manifest necessity" or the "ends of public justice." . . .

The determination by the trial court to abort a criminal proceeding where jeopardy has attached is not one to be lightly undertaken, since the interest of the defendant in having his fate determined by the jury first impaneled is itself a weighty one. Nor will the lack of demonstrable additional prejudice preclude the defendant's invocation of the double jeopardy bar in the absence of some important countervailing interest of proper judicial administration. But where the declaration of a mistrial implements a reasonable state policy and aborts a proceeding that at best would have produced a verdict that could have been upset at will by one of the parties, the defendant's interest in proceeding to verdict is outweighed by the competing and equally legitimate demand for public justice.

Reversed.[a]

[JUSTICES WHITE, DOUGLAS, BRENNAN and MARSHALL dissented.]

a. [Added by the Compiler.] If the trial court enters a judgment of acquittal no retrial is possible no matter how "egregiously erroneous" the decision may have been. Sanabria v. United States, 437 U.S. 54, 98 S.Ct. 2170 (1978).

After the jury had been empaneled and sworn, D filed a motion that he be given

BENTON v. MARYLAND

Supreme Court of the United States, 1969.
395 U.S. 784, 89 S.Ct. 2056.

[Benton was tried in a Maryland state court on charges of burglary and larceny. The jury found him not guilty of larceny but convicted him on the burglary count. Because both the grand and petit juries in his case had been selected under an invalid law, Benton was given the option of demanding reindictment and retrial. He chose to have his conviction set aside and a new indictment and new trial followed. Being again charged with both larceny and burglary, he moved to have the larceny count dismissed on the ground that to try him again for larceny would violate the constitutional prohibition against double jeopardy. His motion was denied and on the second trial he was convicted of both burglary and larceny. His appeals to the Maryland courts proved fruitless but the Supreme Court granted certiorari limited to the consideration of two issues:

"(1) Is the double jeopardy clause of the Fifth Amendment applicable to the States through the Fourteenth Amendment?

"(2) If so, was the petitioner 'twice put in jeopardy' in this case?"] *

MR. JUSTICE MARSHALL delivered the opinion of the Court. . . .

In 1937, this Court decided the landmark case of Palko v. Connecticut, 302 U.S. 319, 58 S.Ct. 149, 82 L.Ed. 288. Palko, although indicted for first-degree murder, had been convicted of murder in the second degree after a jury trial in a Connecticut state court. The State

a psychiatric examination. This motion was granted, and the jury dismissed. A superseding indictment was returned, containing the same two counts as were included in the first indictment, together with four additional counts. A new jury was selected and D was placed on trial. Counts five and six were dismissed and D was convicted on the first four. This conviction was affirmed. D's motion was held to be analogous to conduct calculated to necessitate a new trial. "In such a situation, where the mistrial is not attributable to prosecutorial or judicial overreaching, the defendant is barred from relying upon double jeopardy." United States v. White, 524 F.2d 1249, 1252 (5th Cir.1975).

The double-jeopardy provision of the constitution does not prevent an appeal by the government in a case in which the trial judge rules in favor of D after the jury has returned a verdict of guilty. Reversal on appeal would merely reinstate the jury's verdict of guilty. United States v. Wilson, 420 U.S. 332, 95 S.Ct. 1013 (1975).

If the judge orders the indictment dismissed at the conclusion of a trial without a jury, this is the equivalent of an acquittal, and further proceedings would violate the double-jeopardy clause. United States v. Jenkins, 420 U.S. 358, 95 S.Ct. 1006 (1975).

If the judge dismisses the indictment before trial, the government may appeal. There is no double jeopardy involved because in this case jeopardy had never attached. Serfass v. United States, 420 U.S. 377, 95 S.Ct. 1055 (1975).

* [Compiler's note.] The sentence on the second conviction was longer than that in the first but this was not dealt with in this case. The two sentences were pronounced to run concurrently—the burglary sentence being the longer but the Court felt that Benton should not have the larceny conviction on his record, if it was invalid, and refused to follow the "concurrent sentence doctrine" which had been used in the past to dodge the consideration of an issue such as this.

appealed and won a new trial. Palko argued that the Fourteenth Amendment incorporated, as against the States, the Fifth Amendment requirement that no person "be subject for the same offense to be twice put in jeopardy of life or limb." The Court disagreed. Federal double jeopardy standards were not applicable against the States. Only when a kind of jeopardy subjected a defendant to "a hardship so acute and shocking that our polity will not endure it," did the Fourteenth Amendment apply. The order for a new trial was affirmed. In subsequent appeals from state courts, the Court continued to apply this lesser *Palko* standard.

Recently, however, this Court has "increasingly looked to the specific guarantees of the [Bill of Rights] to determine whether a state criminal trial was conducted with due process of law." In an increasing number of cases, the Court "has rejected the notion that the Fourteenth Amendment applies to the States only a 'watered-down, subjective version of the individual guarantees of the Bill of Rights . . . .' " Malloy v. Hogan, 378 U.S. 1, 10–11, 84 S.Ct. 1489, 1495, 12 L.Ed.2d 653 (1964).[12] Only last Term we found that the right to trial by jury in criminal cases was "fundamental to the American scheme of justice," Duncan v. Louisiana, 391 U.S. 145, 149, 88 S.Ct. 1444, 1447, 20 L.Ed.2d 491 (1968), and held that the Sixth Amendment right to a jury trial was applicable to the States through the Fourteenth Amendment.[13] For the same reasons, we today find that the double jeopardy prohibition of the Fifth Amendment represents a fundamental ideal in our constitutional heritage, and that it should apply to the States through the Fourteenth Amendment. Insofar as it is inconsistent with this holding, Palko v. Connecticut is overruled.

. . .

Our recent cases have thoroughly rejected the *Palko* notion that basic constitutional rights can be denied by the States as long as the totality of the circumstances do not disclose a denial of "fundamental fairness." Once it is decided that a particular Bill of Rights guarantee is "fundamental to the American scheme of justice," the same constitutional standards apply against both the State and Federal Governments. *Palko's* roots had thus been cut away years ago. We today only recognize the inevitable.

The fundamental nature of the guarantee against double jeopardy can hardly be doubted. Its origins can be traced to Greek and Roman times, and it became established in the common law of England long before this Nation's independence.[14] As with many other elements of the common law, it was carried into the jurisprudence of this Country through the medium of Blackstone, who codified the

12. Quoting from Ohio ex rel. Eaton v. Price, 364 U.S. 263, 275, 80 S.Ct. 1463, 1469–1470, 4 L.Ed.2d 1708 (1960) (Brennan, J., dissenting).

13. A list of those Bill of Rights guarantees which have been held "incorporated" in the Fourteenth Amendment can be found in *Duncan*, supra, at 148, 88 S.Ct., at 1446.

14. J. Sigler, Double Jeopardy 1–37 (1969).

doctrine in his Commentaries. "[T]he plea of *autrefoits acquit,* or a former acquittal," he wrote, "is grounded on this universal maxim of the common law of England, that no man is to be brought into jeopardy of his life more than once for the same offence." [15] Today, every State incorporates some form of the prohibition in its constitution or common law.[16] As this Court put it in Green v. United States, 355 U.S. 184, 187–188, 78 S.Ct. 221, 223, 2 L.Ed.2d 199 (1957), "[t]he underlying idea, one that is deeply ingrained in at least the Anglo-American system of jurisprudence, is that the State with all its resources and power should not be allowed to make repeated attempts to convict an individual for an alleged offense, thereby subjecting him to embarrassment, expense and ordeal and compelling him to live in a continuing state of anxiety and insecurity, as well as enhancing the possibility that even though innocent he may be found guilty." This underlying notion has from the very beginning been part of our constitutional tradition. Like the right to trial by jury, it is clearly "fundamental to the American scheme of justice." The validity of petitioner's larceny conviction must be judged not by the watered-down standard enunciated in *Palko,* but under this Court's interpretations of the Fifth Amendment double jeopardy provision.

It is clear that petitioner's larceny conviction cannot stand once federal double jeopardy standards are applied. Petitioner was acquitted of larceny in his first trial. Because he decided to appeal his burglary conviction, he is forced to suffer retrial on the larceny count as well. As this Court held in Green v. United States, supra, at 193–194, 78 S.Ct. at 227, "[c]onditioning an appeal of one offense on a coerced surrender of a valid plea of former jeopardy on another offense exacts a forfeiture in plain conflict with the constitutional bar against double jeopardy."

Maryland argues that *Green* does not apply to this case because petitioner's original indictment was absolutely void. One cannot be placed in "jeopardy" by a void indictment, the State argues. This argument sounds a bit strange, however, since petitioner could quietly have served out his sentence under this "void" indictment had he not appealed his burglary conviction. Only by accepting the option of a new trial could the indictment be set aside; at worst the indictment would seem only voidable at a defendant's option, not absolutely void. . . . Petitioner was acquitted of larceny. He has, under *Green,* a valid double jeopardy plea which he cannot be forced to waive. Yet Maryland wants the earlier acquittal set aside, over petitioner's objections, because of a defect in the indictment. This it cannot do. Petitioner's larceny conviction cannot stand. . . . The judgment is va-

15. 4 Blackstone, Commentaries *334.

16. J. Sigler, supra, n. 14, at 78–79; Brock v. North Carolina, 344 U.S. 424, 435, n. 6, 73 S.Ct. 349, 354, 97 L.Ed. 456 (1953) (Vinson, C.J., dissenting).

cated and the case is remanded for further proceedings not inconsistent with this opinion.

It is so ordered.

Judgment vacated and case remanded.[b]

MR. JUSTICE WHITE, concurring. . . .

[MR. JUSTICE HARLAN, joined by MR. JUSTICE STEWART filed a dissenting opinion.]

NORTH CAROLINA v. PEARCE

Supreme Court of the United States, 1969.
395 U.S. 711, 89 S.Ct. 2072.

[Two cases were consolidated because both raised issues in regard to the sentence to be pronounced on reconviction after the original conviction had been set aside. In each case a federal district judge, in a habeas corpus proceeding, had held that the sentence pronounced by the state court was unconstitutional. One issue dealt with the time actually served under the reversed conviction. Due process was held to require that in pronouncing the new sentence full credit must be given for the time thus served. This is because "the Constitution was designed as much to prevent the criminal from being twice punished for the same offence as from being twice tried for it." Former jeopardy forbids both.]

MR. JUSTICE STEWART delivered the opinion of the Court. . . .

We hold that the constitutional guarantee against multiple punishments for the same offense absolutely requires that punishment al-

b. The rule announced in *Benton*, that the former jeopardy clause of the Fifth Amendment is incorporated in the Due Process clause of the Fourteenth, is to be fully retroactive in its application. Ashe v. Swenson, 397 U.S. 436, 90 S.Ct. 1189 (1970).

In a later case **P** was convicted of voluntary manslaughter in a trial for murder. That conviction was reversed because of improper instructions and **P** was again put on trial for murder over his claim of former jeopardy. This trial also resulted in a conviction of voluntary manslaughter. In reversing this conviction the Supreme Court held that conviction of a lesser included offense amounts to an acquittal of everything charged which is above the offense represented by the conviction. Hence to place **P** on trial for murder a second time violated the prohibition against former jeopardy. The fact that the second conviction was the same as the first did not save it because it was constitutionally impermissible to place him on trial for murder the second time. Price v. Georgia, 398 U.S. 323, 90 S.Ct. 1757 (1970).

A juvenile court hearing was held to determine whether **M**, a juvenile, should be declared a ward of the court because of having stolen a motor vehicle. The judge was not satisfied that **M** had committed the alleged theft and dismissed the petition. Later another petition was filed against **M** on the same charge. It was held that the dismissal was the equivalent of an acquittal and that former jeopardy was a bar to the second hearing. Richard M. v. Superior Court of Shasta County, 4 Cal.3d 370, 93 Cal.Rptr. 752, 482 P.2d 664 (1971). The fact that **M** had testified without having been placed under oath did not prevent the dismissal from operating as an acquittal.

Double jeopardy standards are applicable to juvenile proceedings. Breed v. Jones, 421 U.S. 519, 95 S.Ct. 1779 (1975).

ready exacted must be fully "credited" [13] in imposing sentence upon a new conviction for the same offense. If, upon a new trial, the defendant is acquitted, there is no way the years he spent in prison can be returned to him. But if he is reconvicted, those years can and must be returned—by subtracting them from whatever new sentence is imposed.

To hold that the second sentence must be reduced by the time served under the first is, however, to give but a partial answer to the question before us. We turn, therefore, to consideration of the broader problem of what constitutional limitations there may be upon the general power of a judge to impose upon reconviction a longer prison sentence than the defendant originally received.

Long-established constitutional doctrine makes clear that, beyond the requirement already discussed, the guarantee against double jeopardy imposes no restrictions upon the length of a sentence imposed upon reconviction. At least since 1896, when United States v. Ball, 163 U.S. 662, 16 S.Ct. 1192, 41 L.Ed. 300, was decided, it has been settled that this constitutional guarantee imposes no limitations whatever upon the power to *retry* a defendant who has succeeded in getting his first conviction set aside. . . . And at least since 1919, when Stroud v. United States, 251 U.S. 15, 40 S.Ct. 50, 64 L.Ed. 103, was decided, it has been settled that a corollary of the power to retry a defendant is the power, upon the defendant's reconviction, to impose whatever sentence may be legally authorized, whether or not it is greater than the sentence imposed after the first conviction.[16] "That a defendant's conviction is overturned on collateral rather than direct attack is irrelevant for these purposes."

Although the rationale for this "well-established part of our constitutional jurisprudence" has been variously verbalized, it rests ultimately upon the premise that the original conviction has, at the defendant's behest, been wholly nullified and the slate wiped clean. As to whatever punishment has actually been suffered under the first conviction, that premise is, of course, an unmitigated fiction, as we have recognized in Part I of this opinion.[17] But, so far as the convic-

13. Such credit must, of course, include the time credited during service of the first prison sentence for good behavior, etc.

16. In *Stroud* the defendant was convicted of first degree murder and sentenced to life imprisonment. After reversal of this conviction, the defendant was retried, reconvicted of the same offense, and sentenced to death. This Court upheld the conviction against the defendant's claim that his constitutional right not to be twice put in jeopardy had been violated. See also Murphy v. Massachusetts, 177 U.S. 155, 20 S.Ct. 639, 44 L.Ed. 711; Robinson v. United States, 324 U.S. 282, 65 S.Ct. 666, 89 L.Ed. 944, affirming, 144 F.2d 392. The Court's decision in Green v. United States, 355 U.S. 184, 78 S.Ct. 221, 2 L.Ed.2d 199, is of no applicability to the present problem. The *Green* decision was based upon the double jeopardy provision's guarantee against retrial for an offense of which the defendant was acquitted.

17. Cf. King v. United States, 69 App. D.C. 10, 98 F.2d 291, 293–294: "The Government's brief suggests, in the vein of The Mikado, that because the first sentence was void appellant 'has served no sentence but has merely spent time in the penitentiary;' that since he should not have been imprisoned as he was, he was not imprisoned at all."

tion itself goes, and that part of the sentence that has not yet been served, it is no more than a simple statement of fact to say that the slate *has* been wiped clean. The conviction *has* been set aside and the unexpired portion of the original sentence will never be served. A new trial may result in an acquittal. But if it does result in a conviction, we cannot say that the constitutional guarantee against double jeopardy of its own weight restricts the imposition of an otherwise lawful single punishment for the offense in question. To hold to the contrary would be to cast doubt upon the whole validity of the basic principle enunciated in United States v. Ball, supra, and upon the unbroken line of decisions that have followed that principle for almost 75 years. We think those decisions are entirely sound, and we decline to depart from the concept they reflect.

The other argument advanced in support of the proposition that the Constitution absolutely forbids the imposition of a more severe sentence upon retrial is grounded upon the Equal Protection Clause of the Fourteenth Amendment. The theory advanced is that, since convicts who do not seek new trials cannot have their sentences increased, it creates an invidious classification to impose that risk only upon those who succeed in getting their original convictions set aside. The argument, while not lacking in ingenuity, cannot withstand close examination. In the first place, we deal here not with increases in existing sentences, but with the imposition of wholly new sentences after wholly new trials. Putting that conceptual nicety to one side, however, the problem before us simply cannot be rationally dealt with in terms of "classifications." A man who is retried after his first conviction has been set aside may be acquitted. If convicted, he may receive a shorter sentence, he may receive the same sentence, or he may receive a longer sentence than the one originally imposed. The result may depend upon a particular combination of infinite variables peculiar to each individual trial. It simply cannot be said that a State has invidiously "classified" those who successfully seek new trials, any more than that the State has invidiously "classified" those prisoners whose convictions are *not* set aside by denying the members of that group the opportunity to be acquitted. To fit the problem of this case into an equal protection framework is a task too Procrustean to be rationally accomplished.

We hold, therefore, that neither the double jeopardy provision nor the Equal Protection Clause imposes an absolute bar to a more severe sentence upon reconviction. A trial judge is not constitutionally precluded, in other words, from imposing a new sentence, whether greater or less than the original sentence, in the light of events subsequent to the first trial that may have thrown new light upon the defendant's "life, health, habits, conduct, and mental and moral propensities." Such information may come to the judge's attention from evidence adduced at the second trial itself, from a new presentence investigation, from the defendant's prison record, or possibly from other sources. The freedom of a sentencing judge to consider the defendant's conduct subsequent to the first conviction in imposing a new sentence is no more than consonant with the principle that a State may adopt the "prevalent modern philosophy of penology that the punishment should fit the offender and not merely the crime."

To say that there exists no absolute constitutional bar to the imposition of a more severe sentence upon retrial is not, however, to end the inquiry. There remains for consideration the impact of the Due Process Clause of the Fourteenth Amendment.

It can hardly be doubted that it would be a flagrant violation of the Fourteenth Amendment for a state trial court to follow an announced practice of imposing a heavier sentence upon every reconvicted defendant for the explicit purpose of punishing the defendant for his having succeeded in getting his original conviction set aside. Where, as in each of the cases before us, the original conviction has been set aside because of a constitutional error, the imposition of such a punishment, "penalizing those who choose to exercise" constitutional rights, "would be patently unconstitutional." And the very threat inherent in the existence of such a punitive policy would, with respect to those still in prison, serve to "chill the exercise of basic constitutional rights." But even if the first conviction has been set aside for nonconstitutional error, the imposition of a penalty upon the defendant for having successfully pursued a statutory right of appeal or collateral remedy would be no less a violation of due process of law.[19] "A new sentence, with enhanced punishment, based upon such a reason, would be a flagrant violation of the rights of the defendant." A court is "without right to . . . put a price on an appeal. A defendant's exercise of a right of appeal must be free and unfettered. . . . [I]t is unfair to use the great power given to the court to determine sentence to place a defendant in the dilemma of making an unfree choice." "This Court has never held that the States are required to establish avenues of appellate review, but it is now fundamental that, once established, these avenues must be kept free of unreasoned distinctions that can only impede open and equal access to the courts. . . .

Due process of law, then, requires that vindictiveness against a defendant for having successfully attacked his first conviction must play no part in the sentence he receives after a new trial. And since the fear of such vindictiveness may unconstitutionally deter a defendant's exercise of the right to appeal or collaterally attack his first conviction, due process also requires that a defendant be freed of apprehension of such a retaliatory motivation on the part of the sentencing judge.[20]

19. See Van Alstyne, In Gideon's Wake: Harsher Penalties and the "Successful" Criminal Appellant, 74 Yale L.J. 606 (1965); Note, Unconstitutional Conditions, 73 Harv.L.Rev. 1595 (1960).

20. The existence of a retaliatory motivation would, of course, be extremely difficult to prove in any individual case. But data have been collected to show that increased sentences on reconviction

In order to assure the absence of such a motivation, we have concluded that whenever a judge imposes a more severe sentence upon a defendant after a new trial, the reasons for his doing so must affirmatively appear. Those reasons must be based upon objective information concerning identifiable conduct on the part of the defendant occurring after the time of the original sentencing proceeding. And the factual data upon which the increased sentence is based must be made part of the record, so that the constitutional legitimacy of the increased sentence may be fully reviewed on appeal.

We dispose of the two cases before us in the light of these conclusions. In No. 418 Judge Johnson noted that "the State of Alabama offers no evidence attempting to justify the increase in Rice's original sentences . . . ." He found it "shocking that the State of Alabama has not attempted to explain or justify the increase in Rice's punishment—in these three cases, over threefold." And he found that "the conclusion is inescapable that the State of Alabama is punishing petitioner Rice for his having exercised his post-conviction right of review . . . ." In No. 413 the situation is not so dramatically clear. Nonetheless, the fact remains that neither at the time the increased sentence was imposed upon Pearce, nor at any stage in his habeas corpus proceeding, has the State offered any reason or justification for that sentence beyond the naked power to impose it. We conclude that in each of the cases before us, the judgment should be affirmed.

It is so ordered.[a]

Judgment in each case affirmed.

are far from rare. See Note, Constitutional Law: Increased Sentence and Denial of Credit on Retrial Sustained Under the Traditional Waiver Theory, [1965] Duke L.J. 395. A touching bit of evidence showing the fear of such a vindictive policy was noted by the trial judge in Patton v. North Carolina, 256 F.Supp. 225, who quoted a letter he had recently received from a prisoner:

"Dear Sir:

"I am in the Mecklenburg County jail. Mr. ___ chose to re-try me as I knew he would.

. . .

"Sir the other defendant in this case was set free after serving 15 months of his sentence, I have served 34 months and now I am to be tried again and with all probability I will receive a heavier sentence then before as you know sir my sentence at the first trile was 20 to 30 years. I know it is usuelly the courts prosedure to give a large sentence when a new trile is granted I guess this is to discourage Petitioners.

"Your Honor, I don't want a new trile. I am more afraid of more time . . . .

Your Honor, I know you have tried to help me and God knows I appreciate this but please sir don't let the State try me if there is any way you can prevent it.

Very truly yours"

Id. at 231, n. 7.

a. California went further and held that conviction on retrial could not result in a penalty greater than that first imposed. Thus if the conviction was on two counts, with sentences first pronounced to run concurrently, the conviction on retrial after reversal might not result in sentences pronounced to run consecutively. People v. Ali, 66 Cal.2d 277, 57 Cal. Rptr. 348, 424 P.2d 932 (1966).

The state statute forbids a more severe sentence as a result of a second trial than was imposed under the conviction that was reversed on appeal. State v. Sorenson, 639 P.2d 179 (Utah 1981).

MR. JUSTICE BLACK, concurring and dissenting. . . .

MR. JUSTICE WHITE, concurring in part.

I join the Court's opinion except that in my view Part II–C should authorize an increased sentence on retrial based on any objective, identifiable factual data not known to the trial judge at the time of the original sentencing proceeding.

[HARLAN, DOUGLAS and MARSHALL, JJ., concurred in the result but thought that former jeopardy would preclude a longer sentence on retrial.]

(B) "THE SAME OFFENSE"

The underlying principle is that when an issue has once been settled between two parties as the result of a fair trial it should not be possible to reopen it by starting a new proceeding. Much of the difficulty in this field would have been avoided if attention had been focused upon this basic precept. But the precept has often been concealed behind words which were intended to express it. And just as the other aspect of the field was confused by overemphasis upon the word "jeopardy," so this part has been complicated by the use of the words "the same offense." [1]

MISSOURI v. HUNTER

Supreme Court of the United States, 1983.
___ U.S. ___, 103 S.Ct. 673.

CHIEF JUSTICE BURGER delivered the opinion of the court.

We granted certiorari to consider whether the prosecution and conviction of a criminal defendant in a single trial on both a charge of "armed criminal action" and a charge of first degree robbery—the underlying felony—violates the Double Jeopardy Clause of the Fifth Amendment.

On the evening of November 24, 1978, respondent and two accomplices entered an A & P supermarket in Kansas City, Missouri. Respondent entered the store manager's office and ordered the manager, at gun point, to open two safes. While the manager was complying with the demands of the robbers, respondent struck him twice with the butt of his revolver. While the robbery was in progress, an employee who drove in front of the store observed the robbery and went to a nearby bank to alert an off-duty police officer. That officer arrived at the front of the store and ordered the three

California's "statutory rape" law does not violate the equal protection clause although it is only sex with a female under the age of 18 that is punished. Michael M. v. Superior Court, 450 U.S. 464, 101 S.Ct. 1200 (1981).

1. Extrinsic evidence is admissible on the trial to identify the crime of which defendant has been convicted previously. People v. Braddock, 41 Cal.2d 794, 264 P.2d 521 (1953).

men to stop. Respondent fired a shot at the officer and the officer returned the fire but the trio escaped.

Respondent and his accomplices were apprehended. In addition to being positively identified by the store manager and the police officer at trial and in a line-up, respondent made an oral and written confession which was admitted in evidence. At his trial, respondent offered no direct evidence and was convicted of robbery in the first degree, armed criminal action and assault with malice. . . .

Mo.Stat.App. § 559.225 (Vernon 1979) proscribes armed criminal action and provides in pertinent part:

> "[A]ny person who commits any felony under the laws of this state by, with, or through the use, assistance, or aid of a dangerous or deadly weapon is also guilty of the crime of armed criminal action and, upon conviction, shall be punished by imprisonment by the division of corrections for a term of not less than three years. The punishment imposed pursuant to this subsection shall be in addition to any punishment provided by law for the crime committed by, with, or through the use, assistance, or aid of a dangerous or deadly weapon. No person convicted under this subsection shall be eligible for parole, probation, conditional release or suspended imposition or execution of sentence for a period of three calendar years."

Pursuant to these statutes respondent was sentenced to concurrent terms of (a) ten years' imprisonment for the robbery; (b) 15 years for armed criminal action; and (c) to a consecutive term of five years' imprisonment for assault, for a total of 20 years.

On appeal to the Missouri Court of Appeals, respondent claimed that his sentence for both robbery in the first degree and armed criminal action violated the Double Jeopardy Clause of the Fifth Amendment of the United States Constitution made applicable to the states by the Fourteenth Amendment. The Missouri Court of Appeals agreed and reversed respondent's conviction and 15-year sentence for armed criminal action. The Court of Appeals relied entirely upon the holding of the Missouri Supreme Court. . . . The State's timely alternative motion for rehearing or transfer to the Missouri Supreme Court was denied by the Court of Appeals on September 15, 1981. The Missouri Supreme Court denied review on November 10, 1981. . . .

The Double Jeopardy Clause is cast explicitly in terms of being "twice put in jeopardy." We have consistently interpreted it " 'to protect an individual from being subjected to the hazards of trial and possible conviction more than once for an alleged offense.' " Because respondent has been subjected to only one trial, it is not contended that his right to be free from multiple trials for the same offense has been violated. Rather, the Missouri court vacated respondent's conviction for armed criminal action because of the statements of this Court that the Double Jeopardy Clause also "protects against multiple punishments for the same offense." Particularly in light of recent precedents of this Court, it is clear that the Missouri Supreme Court has misperceived the nature of the Double Jeopardy Clause's protection against multiple punishments. With respect to cumulative sentences imposed in a single trial, the Double Jeopardy Clause does no more than prevent the sentencing court from prescribing greater punishment than the legislature intended.

In Whalen v. United States, 445 U.S. 684, 100 S.Ct. 1432, 63 L.Ed. 2d 715 (1980), we addressed the question whether cumulative punishments for the offenses of rape and of killing the same victim in the perpetration of the crime of rape was contrary to federal statutory and constitutional law. A divided Court relied on Blockburger v. United States, 284 U.S. 299, 52 S.Ct. 180, 76 L.Ed. 306 (1932), in holding that the two statutes in controversy proscribed the "same" offense. The opinion in *Blockburger* stated:

> "The applicable rule is that where the same act or transaction constitutes a violation of two distinct statutory provisions, the test to be applied to determine whether there are two offenses or only one, is whether each provision requires proof of a fact which the other does not."

In *Whalen* we also noted that *Blockburger* established a rule of statutory construction in these terms:

> "The assumption underlying the rule is that Congress *ordinarily* does not intend to punish the same offense under two different statutes. Accordingly, where two statutory provisions proscribe the 'same offense,' they are construed not to authorize cumulative punishments *in the absence of a clear indication of contrary legislative intent.*"

We went on to emphasize the qualification on that rule:

> "[W]here the offenses are the same . . . cumulative sentences are not permitted, *unless elsewhere specially authorized by Congress.*"

It is clear, therefore, that the result in *Whalen* turned on the fact that the Court saw no "clear indication of contrary legislative intent." Accordingly, under the rule of statutory construction, we held that cumulative punishment could not be imposed under the two statutes.

In Albernaz v. United States, 450 U.S. 333, 101 S.Ct. 1137, 67 L.Ed.2d 275 (1981), we addressed the issue whether a defendant could be cumulatively punished in a single trial for conspiracy to import marihuana and conspiracy to distribute marihuana. There, in contrast to *Whalen,* we concluded that the two statutes did not proscribe the "same" offense in the sense that " 'each provision requires proof of a fact [that] the other does not.' " We might well have stopped at that point and upheld the petitioners' cumulative punishments under the challenged statutes since cumulative punishment can presumptively be assessed after conviction for two offenses that are not the "same" under *Blockburger.* However, we went on to state that because:

> "The *Blockburger* test is a 'rule of statutory construction,' and because it serves as a means of discerning congressional purpose *the rule should not be controlling where, for example, there is a clear indication of contrary legislative intent.*"

We found "[n]othing . . . in the legislative history which . . . discloses an intent contrary to the presumption which should be accorded to these statutes after application of the *Blockburger* test." Ibid. We concluded our discussion of the impact of clear legislative intent on the *Whalen* rule of statutory construction with this language:

> [T]he question of what punishments are constitutionally permissible is no different from the question of what punishment the Legislative Branch intended to be imposed. *Where Congress intended, as it did here, to impose multiple punishments, imposition of such sentences does not violate the Constitution.*"

Here, the Missouri Supreme Court has construed the two statutes at issue as defining the same crime. In addition, the Missouri Supreme Court has recognized that the legislature intended that punishment for violations of the statutes be cumulative. We are bound to accept the Missouri court's construction of that State's statutes. However, we are not bound by the Missouri Supreme Court's legal conclusion that these two statutes violate the Double Jeopardy Clause, and we reject its legal conclusion.

Our analysis and reasoning in *Whalen* and *Albernaz* lead inescapably to the conclusion that simply because two criminal statutes may be construed to proscribe the same conduct under the *Blockburger* test does not mean that the Double Jeopardy Clause precludes the imposition, in a single trial, of cumulative punishments pursuant to those statutes. The rule of statutory construction noted in *Whalen* is not a constitutional rule requiring courts to negate clearly expressed legislative intent. Thus far, we have utilized that rule only to limit a federal court's power to impose convictions and punishments when the will of Congress is not clear. Here, the Missouri Legislature has made its intent crystal clear. Legislatures, not courts, prescribe the scope of punishments.[5]

Where, as here, a legislature specifically authorizes cumulative punishment under two statutes, regardless of whether those two statutes proscribe the "same" conduct under *Blockburger,* a court's task of statutory construction is at an end and the prosecutor may seek and the trial court or jury may impose cumulative punishment under such statutes in a single trial.

5. This case presents only issues under the Double Jeopardy Clause.

Accordingly, the judgment of the Court of Appeals of Missouri, Western District, is vacated and the case is remanded for further proceedings not inconsistent with this opinion.

So ordered.

JUSTICE MARSHALL, with whom JUSTICE STEVENS joins, dissenting.

. . .[1]

1. On May 16, 1977, the Court of Criminal Appeals of Oklahoma decided a case in which it expressed a view that had been widely held. It took the position that felony-murder and the underlying felony are separate and distinct offenses. Hence conviction of the underlying felony does not bar prosecution and conviction for the felony-murder. Johnson v. Hampton, 564 P.2d 641 (Okl. Cr.1977). The very next month the Supreme Court had before it another Oklahoma case. Harris had been convicted of felony-murder, the underlying felony being armed robbery. Later, based upon the same event, his claim of former jeopardy was denied and he was convicted of armed robbery. This conviction was reversed on the ground that the second trial was barred by double jeopardy. Harris v. Oklahoma, 443 U.S. 682, 97 S.Ct. 2912 (1977). The case of Johnson v. Hampton, infra, was thereafter vacated by the United States Supreme Court, 434 U.S. 947, 98 S.Ct. 471 (1977) for reconsideration in light of Brown v. Ohio, 432 U.S. 161, 97 S.Ct. 2221 (1977) and Harris v. Oklahoma, 433 U.S. 682, 97 S.Ct. 2912 (1977).

"An act or omission which is made punishable in different ways by different provisions of this code may be punished under either of such provisions, but in no case can it be punished under more than one; an acquittal or conviction and sentence under either one bars a prosecution for the same act or omission under any other. . . ." West's Ann.Cal.Pen. Code § 654 (1977).

The statute has involved some problems of interpretation. **D** threw gasoline into the bedroom of Mr. and Mrs. **R** and ignited it. He was convicted of two counts of attempted murder and one count of arson. It was held that arson was the means used in the attempt to murder and hence **D** could not be punished for both. But an act depends upon the objective and if the intent is to kill two persons unlawfully it is two offenses. Hence **D** could properly be punished for the two attempts to murder but the sentence for arson must be dismissed. Neal v. State, 55 Cal.2d 11, 9 Cal.Rptr. 607, 357 P.2d 839 (1961).

The California statute does not bar the prosecution or conviction of the different offenses involved—it bars only the double punishment. Hence **D** could be convicted of burglary and the larceny for which the burglary was committed, but he could be punished only for one. People v. McFarland, 58 Cal.2d 748, 376 P.2d 449 (1962). That this statute is distinct from former jeopardy has been emphasized. Thus where an unlawful abortion resulted in death of the woman the offender could not be punished for both the abortion and the murder, but a conviction of abortion (although the woman was already dead) did not bar a conviction and punishment for the murder, since no punishment had been imposed upon the earlier conviction. People v. Tideman, 57 Cal. 2d 574, 21 Cal.Rptr. 207, 370 P.2d 1007 (1962).

Since the objective of the burglary of which **D** was convicted and sentenced was the commission of a grand theft of which he was also convicted, the sentence for grand theft was set aside. In re Romano, 64 Cal.2d 826, 51 Cal.Rptr. 910, 415 P.2d 798 (1966).

Convicting **D** of driving after his license had been suspended and driving while intoxicated based upon one act of driving did not violate this provision. In re Hayes, 70 Cal.2d 604, 75 Cal.Rptr. 790, 451 P.2d 430 (1969).

In the absence of such a statute, since larceny is not an offense which is included in burglary **D** could properly be convicted and sentenced for both crimes. State v. McAfee, 78 N.M. 108, 428 P.2d 647 (1967); State v. Deats, 82 N.M. 711, 487 P.2d 139 (1971).

Where **D** committed the offense of burglary and attempted theft arising from the same episode **D** could only be convicted and sentenced for one offense. State v. Cloutier, 286 Or. 579, 596 P.2d 1278 (1979).

Under the so-called habitual criminal act a former conviction may be used to enhance the punishment imposed in a lat-

WINN v. STATE

Supreme Court of Wisconsin, 1892.
82 Wis. 571, 52 N.W. 775.

LYON, C.J. 1. The special plea in bar of this prosecution sufficiently avers that the charge of the murder of Coates in the first information, and the charge of an assault with intent to murder Defoy in the present information, are predicated upon one and the same act of *Winn.* It is correctly argued in the plea, as it was at the bar, that if he committed the alleged felonious assault upon Defoy, and in doing so killed Coates, although unintentionally, he is guilty of murder. But the jury acquitted him of the crime of murder, and from that fact the inference is plausibly drawn that the jury must necessarily have negatived the alleged felonious assault upon Defoy, for otherwise they would have convicted *Winn* of the murder charged. It was very earnestly and ingeniously contended in argument by the learned counsel for *Winn* that in substance and legal effect such acquittal is an acquittal of the charge of felonious assault in the present information, and that by compelling the accused to trial therefor he was put twice in jeopardy of punishment for the same offense, in violation of the constitutional and statutory declaration of rights in that behalf. Const. art. I, sec. 8; R.S. sec. 4610.

The arguments for and against the sufficiency of this special plea are very full and able, and numerous adjudications are cited on either side in support of the respective propositions of counsel. To review the cases would call for a treatise on this branch of the law. We do not feel called upon to undertake the task of writing one. We adopt as the law on this subject the rule laid down by Chief Justice Shaw in Comm. v. Roby, 12 Pick. 496. The rule is that the offenses charged in two indictments are not identical unless they concur both in *law* and in *fact,* and that the plea of *autrefois acquit* or *convict* is bad if the offenses charged in the two indictments be distinct in law, no matter how closely they are connected in fact. In order to determine whether there is a concurrence in law, that is, whether a conviction or acquittal on one indictment is a good bar to a prosecution on another, the true inquiry is whether the first indictment was such that the accused might have been convicted under it by proof of the facts alleged in the other indictment.[1] If he could not, the conviction or acquittal under the first indictment is no bar. The result of an applica-

er case. The fact that the former conviction is used for this purpose more than once does not constitute former jeopardy. Fischer v. State, 483 P.2d 1162 (Okl.Cr. 1971).

1. If two offenses are the same successive prosecutions are barred. Under Ohio law joyriding and auto theft are lesser included and a greater offense and conviction for one bars prosecution for the other. Brown v. Ohio, 432 U.S. 161, 97 S.Ct. 2221 (1977).

Assault with a machete, entering a military reservation for the purpose of breaking into a building, and rape, although all growing out of occurrences on a single evening, were distinct offenses and the defendant could properly be convicted of all three. United States v. Quinones, 516 F.2d 1309 (1st Cir.1975).

tion of this test to the present inquiry is obvious. *Winn* could not have been convicted of the murder of Coates merely upon proof that he made a felonious assault upon Defoy. Proof that he killed Coates would also be required. Hence an acquittal on the information charging the murder of Coates is no bar to this information for a felonious assault on Defoy, and the special plea was properly overruled. To the same effect is the English case of Queen v. Morris, L.R. 1 Cr.Cas. 90, in which the accused was convicted of an assault and battery, and suffered punishment therefor, and afterwards, the injured party died of the wounds inflicted upon him by the accused. A subsequent indictment for manslaughter was upheld on the ground that the two prosecutions, though founded on the same assault, were for different offenses. The same question has frequently arisen in prosecutions for violations of excise laws, and the rule above stated seems to have been invariably applied by the courts. Black, Intox.Liq. 648, ch. 21, § 555, and cases cited in notes.

The reasonableness and justice of the above rule is shown and emphasized by the testimony on the trial of this case. It appears quite satisfactorily, if not conclusively, therefrom that *Winn* made a distinct felonious assault upon Defoy when he pointed his loaded revolver at him and snapped it, which had no connection with the killing of Coates, and that such killing resulted from the struggle to disarm *Winn*, and was purely accidental. Very likely *Winn* was acquitted of the murder of Coates on similar proofs, and the jury may not have considered,—probably did not consider,—whether *Winn* intended to kill Defoy or not when the revolver missed fire. Had issue been taken upon the special plea, and tried on the testimony in this record, we should expect the jury to find that the first assault, to wit, the attempt by *Winn* to shoot Defoy, had nothing to do with the acquittal of *Winn* of the murder of Coates, and that the question whether such attempt was or was not a felonious assault upon Defoy was not involved in such acquittal. This shows that *Winn* may be guilty of the felonious assault on Defoy and yet not guilty of the murder of Coates. A rule which would absolve *Winn* from conviction and punishment for the assault upon Defoy, of which he was guilty, merely because he was acquitted of the murder of Coates, of which he was not guilty, would be a most vicious one, and would shock all sensible and just ideas of the proper administration of criminal justice. We do not hesitate to reject such a rule. The demurrer to the special plea was properly sustained. . . .

By the Court.—The judgment of the circuit court is affirmed.[2]

2. "Manifestly, appellee, if first tried for the shooting and wounding of Caywood, could not be convicted on proof that he shot Stewart, though both Caywood and Stewart were wounded by one and the same shot. As well might it be argued that, in the killing of several members of the same family by putting poison in the food eaten by them, conviction of the poisoner for the death of one of them would bar a prosecution for the killing of the others.

"If one should throw a bomb into a crowd, and kill several persons, it could not be maintained that his conviction for

SPANNELL v. STATE

Court of Criminal Appeals of Texas, 1918.
83 Tex.Cr.R. 418, 203 S.W. 357.

MORROW, JUDGE. Appellant was convicted of the murder of M.C. Butler. Appellant, his wife and deceased were in an automobile together, at night, and Major Butler and Mrs. Spannell were killed. Appellant claimed, and testified, that Major Butler assaulted him, and that several shots were fired by him at Major Butler with no intent to injure Mrs. Spannell. He was indicted in separate indictments for each of the homicides, was tried and acquitted for the murder of his wife, and filed in this case a plea of former acquittal based upon the proposition that the two homicides, resulting from a single act and volition, constituted but one offense. The court's refusal to submit the plea to the jury is made the basis of complaint. If in shooting at Major Butler with malice appellant unintentionally killed his wife, he would be guilty and could be prosecuted for murdering her. Richards v. State, 35 Tex.Cr.R. 38, 30 S.W. 805; McCullough v. State, 62 Tex.Cr.R. 126, 136 S.W. 1055, in which the court says: "If appellant shot at Ollie Jamison with either his express or implied malice, and killed his wife without intending to kill her, his offense would be murder in the second degree."

If in defending his life against an unlawful attack by Major Butler appellant accidentally killed his wife, he was guilty of no offense. Plummer v. State, 4 Tex.App. 310; Clark v. State, 19 Tex.App. 495; Vining v. State, 66 Tex.Cr.R. 316, 146 S.W. 909. From the Plummer case, supra, we quote, as follows:

"We take the law to be that if the jury believed that the defendant found himself in a condition where he would have been justified in taking the life of Smelser in order to save himself from death or the infliction of great bodily harm, and, in so defending himself from such danger, he, by mistake or accident, shot Mrs. Smelser, then he would not only not be guilty of an assault with intent to murder Mrs. Smelser, but he would not be guilty of any offense whatever."

If he shot at Butler and in the same act killed Mrs. Spannell unintentionally, his guilt or innocence of each of the homicides would depend on whether in shooting at Butler he acted with malice or in self-defense. Assuming that the shots were fired at Butler only, and

the death of one of them would bar a prosecution against him for the killing of any of the others. It seems to us that the mere statement of appellee's contention constitutes its refutation.

"The offenses committed by appellee were not included within one another, though resulting from the same act, but were separate and distinct offenses." Commonwealth v. Browning, 146 Ky. 770, 772–3, 143 S.W. 407, 408 (1912). See also Ciucci v. Illinois, 356 U.S. 571, 78 S.Ct. 839 (1958).

Where the same act constitutes a violation of two distinct statutes the test to determine whether there are two offenses or only one is whether each requires proof of a fact which the other does not. United States v. Brisbane, 239 F.2d 859 (3d Cir.1956).

killed Mrs. Spannell, appellant having no intent, or volition to injure her, to determine whether he was guilty or innocent on his trial for her murder, it was necessary to decide whether in shooting at Butler he acted in self-defense or with malice. On this state of facts the decision that he was innocent of the murder of Mrs. Spannell necessarily involves the finding that appellant's act in firing at Butler was not such as to constitute murder.

It follows that, whether in shooting at Butler appellant acted with malice, or was justified, if in the same act, with no volition to injure his wife, he killed her, there could be but one offense, and the State, prosecuting under separate indictments for each of the homicides, would be concluded as to both by the judgment rendered in one of them. . . .

Where two persons are killed or injured in one transaction, the fact that more than one shot was fired does not, as a matter of law, render it insusceptible of proof that they were both killed by one act. A series of shots may constitute one act, in a legal sense, where they are fired with one volition. In cases where two persons have been killed or wounded by a series of shots, and under the general issue of not guilty it is urged as a defense that one of the homicides or injuries resulted from shots aimed at one striking another, the issue of singleness of the act and intent bringing the double result has not been made to depend on the number of shots fired.

If Major Butler killed Mrs. Spannell, or if appellant, with separate acts and volition, killed her, the offenses were not identical. The statute, article 572, C.C.P., designates as the special pleas available, former conviction, former acquittal, which include former jeopardy. Powell v. State, 17 Tex.App. 345. We infer that the plea of res adjudicata, in so far as it is distinct from these, is not to be entertained. This per force of the statute, article 572, supra, which names as one of the two special pleas permitted, "that he has been before acquitted by a jury of the accusation against him, in a court of competent jurisdiction, whether the acquittal was regular or irregular." It is the judgment of acquittal for the identical act and volition which will operate to sustain his plea, and the evidence, lack of evidence or reasons which impelled the court to enter the judgment are not important further than as they bear on the issue of identity. . . .

The failure of the court to admit evidence and submit to the jury the issues raised by the plea of former acquittal requires a reversal of the judgment, which is ordered.

Reversed and remanded.[1]

1. A conviction of manslaughter, based upon a traffic accident, was held to bar a conviction of assault and battery on another person injured in the same accident, but not to bar a conviction of driving while intoxicated. Smith v. State, 159 Tenn. 674, 21 S.W.2d 400 (1929).

Killing three passengers in an automobile in one accident constituted three offenses for which three consecutive sentences could be imposed. State v. Miranda, 3 Ariz.App. 550, 416 P.2d 444 (1966).

(The concurring opinion of DAVIDSON, P.J., and the opinions given in overruling a motion for a rehearing are omitted.)

ASHE v. SWENSON

Supreme Court of the United States, 1970.
397 U.S. 436, 90 S.Ct. 1189.

MR. JUSTICE STEWART delivered the opinion of the Court.

In Benton v. Maryland, 395 U.S. 784, 89 S.Ct. 2056, 23 L.Ed.2d 707, the Court held that the Fifth Amendment guarantee against double jeopardy is enforceable against the States through the Fourteenth Amendment. The question in this case is whether the State of Missouri violated that guarantee when it prosecuted the petitioner a second time for armed robbery in the circumstances here presented.

Where basically the same evidence was used in a prosecution for criminal negligence in the operation of a vehicle resulting in death as had been introduced in a prior prosecution for driving while intoxicated, reckless driving and leaving the scene of an accident, which prior prosecution had resulted in an acquittal, the second prosecution was barred by double jeopardy. People v. Martinis, 46 Misc.2d 1066, 261 N.Y.S.2d 642 (1965).

Joyriding is a lesser included offense of automobile theft, and a conviction of joyriding bars a subsequent prosecution for automobile theft based upon the same wrongful possession of the car. Brown v. Ohio, 432 U.S. 161, 97 S.Ct. 2221 (1977).

D wrongfully took **X**'s car in California and drove it to Salem, Oregon, where he was arrested for violation of Oregon's special statute prohibiting the unauthorized use of a motor vehicle. After he had been convicted and sentenced in Oregon, he was arrested in California charged with grand theft auto and joyriding, based upon the same transaction. It was held that the prosecution was barred by the special provisions of the California Penal Code (sections 656, 793). People v. Comingore, 20 Cal.3d 142, 141 Cal.Rptr. 542, 570 P.2d 723 (1977).

It was held that the subsequent prosecution was barred in these cases: State v. Waterman, 87 Iowa 255, 54 N.W. 359 (1893), (obstruction of a highway shown by parol to be the same obstruction in both cases); State v. Egglesht, 41 Iowa 574 (1875), (uttering forged checks, the former conviction having been for uttering one at the same time and in the same transaction, though another check); State v. Sampson, 157 Iowa 257, 138 N.W. 473 (1912), (holding to the same effect in case of several articles stolen at the same time, even though the articles were owned by different persons).

It was held that the subsequent prosecution was not barred in these cases: State v. Blodgett, 143 Iowa 578, 121 N.W. 685 (1909), (forgery and uttering forged instrument); State v. White, 123 Iowa 425, 98 N.W. 1027 (1904), (gambling and keeping a gambling house); State v. Graham, 73 Iowa 553, 35 N.W. 628 (1887), (maintaining a nuisance in the form of a building used for the unlawful sale of liquor and keeping liquor for the purpose of unlawful sale); State v. Brown, 75 Iowa 768, 39 N.W. 829 (1888), (follows State v. Graham, supra); State v. Boever, 203 Iowa 86, 210 N.W. 571 (1926), (maintaining a liquor nuisance and unlawful possession of the same liquor); State v. Cleaver, 196 Iowa 1278, 196 N.W. 19 (1923), (maintaining liquor nuisance and bootlegging); State v. Ingalls, 98 Iowa 728, 68 N.W. 445 (1896), (larceny and breaking and entering); State v. Broderick, 191 Iowa 717, 183 N.W. 310 (1921), (breaking and entering a building and feloniously receiving property stolen from the same building by means of breaking and entering); State v. Brown, 95 Iowa 381, 64 N.W. 277 (1895), (acquittal of a crime does not bar a prosecution for conspiracy to commit the crime); State v. Dericks, 42 Iowa 196 (1875), (permitting **W**, a minor, to play billiards in a saloon at one time and permitting **M**, another minor, to play in the saloon at another time); State v. Norman, 135 Iowa 483, 113 N.W. 340 (1907), (larceny of fowls from the premises of **A** and larceny of fowls from the premises of **B**).

Sometime in the early hours of the morning of January 10, 1960, six men were engaged in a poker game in the basement of the home of John Gladson at Lee's Summit, Missouri. Suddenly three or four masked men, armed with a shotgun and pistols, broke into the basement and robbed each of the poker players of money and various articles of personal property. The robbers—and it has never been clear whether there were three or four of them—then fled in a car belonging to one of the victims of the robbery. Shortly thereafter the stolen car was discovered in a field, and later that morning three men were arrested by a state trooper while they were walking on a highway not far from where the abandoned car had been found. The petitioner was arrested by another officer some distance away.

The four were subsequently charged with seven separate offenses—the armed robbery of each of the six poker players and the theft of the car. In May 1960 the petitioner went to trial on the charge of robbing Donald Knight, one of the participants in the poker game. At the trial the State called Knight and three of his fellow poker players as prosecution witnesses. Each of them described the circumstances of the holdup and itemized his own individual losses. The proof that an armed robbery had occurred and that personal property had been taken from Knight as well as from each of the others was unassailable. The testimony of the four victims in this regard was consistent both internally and with that of the others. But the State's evidence that the petitioner had been one of the robbers was weak. Two of the witnesses thought that there had been only three robbers altogether, and could not identify the petitioner as one of them. Another of the victims, who was the petitioner's uncle by marriage, said that at the "patrol station" he had positively identified each of the other three men accused of the holdup, but could say only that the petitioner's voice "sounded very much like" that of one of the robbers. The fourth participant in the poker game did identify the petitioner, but only by his "size and height, and his actions."

The cross-examination of these witnesses was brief, and it was aimed primarily at exposing the weakness of their identification testimony. Defense counsel made no attempt to question their testimony regarding the holdup itself or their claims as to their losses. Knight testified without contradiction that the robbers had stolen from him his watch, $250 in cash, and about $500 in checks. His billfold, which had been found by the police in the possession of one of the three other men accused of the robbery, was admitted in evidence. The defense offered no testimony and waived final argument.

The trial judge instructed the jury that if it found that the petitioner was one of the participants in the armed robbery, the theft of "any money" from Knight would sustain a conviction. He also instructed the jury that if the petitioner was one of the robbers, he was guilty under the law even if he had not personally robbed Knight.

The jury—though not instructed to elaborate upon its verdict—found the petitioner "not guilty due to insufficient evidence."

Six weeks later the petitioner was brought to trial again, this time for the robbery of another participant in the poker game, a man named Roberts. The petitioner filed a motion to dismiss, based on his previous acquittal. The motion was overruled, and the second trial began. The witnesses were for the most part the same, though this time their testimony was substantially stronger on the issue of the petitioner's identity. For example, two witnesses who at the first trial had been wholly unable to identify the petitioner as one of the robbers, now testified that his features, size, and mannerisms matched those of one of their assailants. Another witness who before had identified the petitioner only by his size and actions now also remembered him by the unusual sound of his voice. The State further refined its case at the second trial by declining to call one of the participants in the poker game whose identification testimony at the first trial had been conspicuously negative. The case went to the jury on instructions virtually identical to those given at the first trial. This time the jury found the petitioner guilty, and he was sentenced to a 35-year term in the state penitentiary.

The Supreme Court of Missouri affirmed the conviction, holding that the "plea of former jeopardy must be denied." A collateral attack upon the conviction in the state courts four years later was also unsuccessful. The petitioner then brought the present habeas corpus proceeding in the United States District Court for the Western District of Missouri, claiming that the second prosecution had violated his right not to be twice put in jeopardy. Considering itself bound by this court's decision in Hoag v. New Jersey, 356 U.S. 464, 78 S.Ct. 829, 2 L.Ed.2d 913, the District Court denied the writ, although apparently finding merit in the petitioner's claim. The Court of Appeals for the Eighth Circuit affirmed, also upon the authority of Hoag v. New Jersey, supra. We granted certiorari to consider the important constitutional question this case presents.

As the District Court and the Court of Appeals correctly noted, the operative facts here are virtually identical to those of Hoag v. New Jersey, supra. In that case the defendant was tried for the armed robbery of three men who, along with others, had been held up in a tavern. The proof of the robbery was clear, but the evidence identifying the defendant as one of the robbers was weak, and the defendant interposed an alibi defense. The jury brought in a verdict of not guilty. The defendant was then brought to trial again, on an indictment charging the robbery of a fourth victim of the tavern hold-up. This time the jury found him guilty. After appeals in the state courts proved unsuccessful, Hoag brought his case here.

Viewing the question presented solely in terms of Fourteenth Amendment due process—whether the course that New Jersey had pursued had "led to fundamental unfairness," this Court declined to reverse the judgment of conviction, because "in the circumstances shown by this record, we cannot say that petitioner's later prosecution and conviction violated due process." [6] The Court found it unnecessary to decide whether "collateral estoppel"—the principle that bars relitigation between the same parties of issues actually determined at a previous trial—is a due process requirement in a state criminal trial, since it accepted New Jersey's determination that the petitioner's previous acquittal did not in any event give rise to such an estoppel. And in the view the Court took of the issues presented, it did not, of course, even approach consideration of whether collateral estoppel is an ingredient of the Fifth Amendment guarantee against double jeopardy.

The doctrine of Benton v. Maryland, 395 U.S. 784, 89 S.Ct. 2056, puts the issues in the present case in a perspective quite different from that in which the issues were perceived in Hoag v. New Jersey, supra. The question is no longer whether collateral estoppel is a requirement of due process, but whether it is a part of the Fifth Amendment's guarantee against double jeopardy. And if collateral estoppel is embodied in that guarantee, then its applicability in a particular case is no longer a matter to be left for state court determination within the broad bounds of "fundamental fairness," but a matter of constitutional fact we must decide through an examination of the entire record.

"Collateral estoppel" is an awkward phrase, but it stands for an extremely important principle in our adversary system of justice. It means simply that when an issue of ultimate fact has once been determined by a valid and final judgment, that issue cannot again be litigated between the same parties in any future lawsuit. Although first developed in civil litigation, collateral estoppel has been an established rule of federal criminal law at least since this Court's decision more than 50 years ago in United States v. Oppenheimer, 242 U.S. 85, 37 S.Ct. 68, 61 L.Ed. 161. As Mr. Justice Holmes put the matter in that case, "It cannot be that the safeguards of the person, so often and so rightly mentioned with solemn reverence, are less than those that protect from a liability in debt." As a rule of federal law, therefore, "[i]t is much too late to suggest that this principle is not fully applicable to a former judgment in a criminal case, either

6. The particular "circumstance" most relied upon by the Court was "the unexpected failure of four of the State's witnesses at the earlier trial to identify petitioner, after two of these witnesses had previously identified him in the course of the police investigation. Indeed, after the second of the two witnesses failed to identify petitioner, the State pleaded surprise and attempted to impeach his testimony. We cannot say that, after such an unexpected turn of events, the State's decision to try petitioner for the Yager robbery was so arbitrary or lacking in justification that it amounted to a denial of those concepts constituting 'the very essence of a scheme of order justice, which is due process.'" 356 U.S., at 469–470, 78 S.Ct. at 833.

In the case now before us, by contrast, there is no claim of any "unexpected turn of events" at the first trial, unless the jury verdict of acquittal be so characterized.

because of lack of 'mutuality' or because the judgment may reflect only a belief that the Government had not met the higher burden of proof exacted in such cases for the Government's evidence as a whole although not necessarily as to every link in the chain." United States v. Kramer, 289 F.2d 909, at 913.

The federal decisions have made clear that the rule of collateral estoppel in criminal cases is not to be applied with the hypertechnical and archaic approach of a 19th century pleading book, but with realism and rationality. Where a previous judgment of acquittal was based upon a general verdict, as is usually the case, this approach requires a court to "examine the record of a prior proceeding, taking into account the pleadings, evidence, charge, and other relevant matter, and conclude whether a rational jury could have grounded its verdict upon an issue other than that which the defendant seeks to foreclose from consideration." The inquiry "must be set in a practical frame, and viewed with an eye to all the circumstances of the proceedings." Sealfon v. United States, 332 U.S. 575, 579, 68 S.Ct. 237, 240. Any test more technically restrictive would, of course, simply amount to a rejection of the rule of collateral estoppel in criminal proceedings, at least in every case where the first judgment was based upon a general verdict of acquittal.

Straightforward application of the federal rule to the present case can lead to but one conclusion. For the record is utterly devoid of any indication that the first jury could rationally have found that an armed robbery had not occurred, or that Knight had not been a victim of that robbery. The single rationally conceivable issue in dispute before the jury was whether the petitioner had been one of the robbers. And the jury by its verdict found that he had not. The federal rule of law, therefore, would make a second prosecution for the robbery of Roberts wholly impermissible.

The ultimate question to be determined, then, in the light of Benton v. Maryland, supra, is whether this established rule of federal law is embodied in the Fifth Amendment guarantee against double jeopardy. We do not hesitate to hold that it is. For whatever else that constitutional guarantee may embrace, it surely protects a man who has been acquitted from having to "run the gantlet" a second time. Green v. United States, 355 U.S. 184, 190, 78 S.Ct. 221, 225, 2 L.Ed.2d 199.

The question is not whether Missouri could validly charge the petitioner with six separate offenses for the robbery of the six poker players.[a] It is not whether he could have received a total of six pun-

a. [Compiler's note.]

Collateral estoppel does not apply if the issue involved in the two cases was not fully contested in the first. State v. Harris, 78 Wash.2d 894, 480 P.2d 484 (1971). Reversed, Harris v. Washington, 404 U.S. 55, 92 S.Ct. 183 (1971). When an issue has once been determined by final judgment, it cannot be litigated again between the same parties.

If **D** was convicted in the first trial he has no claim to collateral estoppel because no issue has been decided in his

ishments if he had been convicted in a single trial of robbing the six victims. It is simply whether, after a jury determined by its verdict that the petitioner was not one of the robbers, the State could constitutionally hale him before a new jury to litigate that issue again.

After the first jury had acquitted the petitioner of robbing Knight, Missouri could certainly not have brought him to trial again upon that charge. Once a jury had determined upon conflicting testimony that there was at least a reasonable doubt that the petitioner was one of the robbers, the State could not present the same or different identification evidence in a second prosecution for the robbery of Knight in the hope that a different jury might find that evidence more convincing. The situation is constitutionally no different here, even though the second trial related to another victim of the same robbery. For the name of the victim, in the circumstances of this case, had no bearing whatever upon the issue of whether the petitioner was one of the robbers.

In this case the State in its brief has frankly conceded that following the petitioner's acquittal, it treated the first trial as no more than a dry run for the second prosecution: "No doubt the prosecutor felt the state had a provable case on the first charge, and, when he lost, he did what every good attorney would do—he refined his presentation in light of the turn of events at the first trial." But this is precisely what the constitutional guarantee forbids.

The judgment is reversed, and the case is remanded to the Court of Appeals for the Eighth Circuit for further proceedings consistent with this opinion.

It is so ordered.

Reversed and remanded.[b]

[There were three concurring opinions and one dissent.]

favor. State v. Tanton, 88 N.M. 333, 540 P.2d 813 (1975).

b. In State v. Cormier, 46 N.J. 494, 218 A.2d 138 (1966), after **D** had been acquitted of conspiracy he was placed on trial for the offense which had been alleged to be the target of the alleged conspiracy. Since the evidence on the second trial was essentially the same as that introduced in the conspiracy trial, it was held that **D** was protected under the principle of collateral estoppel.

"Whenever on the trial of an accused person it appears that upon a criminal prosecution under the laws of another state, government or country, founded upon the act or omission in respect to which he is on trial, he has been acquitted or convicted, it is a sufficient defense". West's Ann.Cal.Pen.Code, § 656 (1949).

Conviction of conspiracy in a state court will not bar a federal conviction based upon the same unlawful combination. Since it violated both state and federal law it constituted two offenses. Abbate v. United States, 359 U.S. 187, 79 S.Ct. 666, 3 L.Ed.2d 729 (1959). Compare Bartkus v. Illinois, 359 U.S. 121, 79 S.Ct. 676, 3 L.Ed.2d 684 (1959).

After **D** was convicted of violating the federal Bank Robbery Act, he was convicted in a state court based upon the same robbery. This was held not to be former jeopardy because **D's** act violated the laws of two separate sovereigns. Hill v. Beto, 340 F.2d 640 (5th Cir.1968). Accord, Bartkus v. Illinois, 359 U.S. 121, 79 S.Ct. 676 (1959); Commonwealth v. Mills, 217 Pa.Super. 269, 269 A.2d 322 (1970).

STATE v. CARROLL

Supreme Court of Hawaii, 1981.
63 Hawaii 345, 627 P.2d 776.

Before RICHARDSON, C.J., and OGATA, MENOR, LUM and NAKAMURA, JJ.

PER CURIAM. The State appeals from a circuit court order granting defendant-appellee Alfred Kapala Carroll's motion to dismiss an indictment charging him with a violation of HRS §§ 705–500 and 708–821(1)(b) (Attempted Criminal Property Damage in the Second Degree). In an earlier district court trial, defendant had been acquitted of the charge of violating Revised Ordinances of Honolulu (R.O.H.) § 13–21.3(a) (1969) (Possession of an Obnoxious Substance). The issue on appeal is whether the separate charges against defendant

State prosecution in Tennessee is not barred by prior conviction for the same crime in Massachusetts. State v. Straw, 626 S.W.2d 286 (Tenn.Cr.App.1981).

The bar against double jeopardy did not prevent federal conviction for aggravated robbery of a post office, notwithstanding the prior conviction of robbery in the state court based upon the same criminal conduct. It was said: "It is well settled that double jeopardy does not bar a federal conviction for violation of federal law arising from the same criminal act or occurrence which has resulted in a state conviction. Abbate v. United States, 359 U.S. 187, 79 S.Ct. 666, 3 L.Ed. 2d 729 (1959); . . . " Speed v. United States, 518 F.2d 75, 76 (8th Cir.1975).

The same act may constitute two offenses, one against the United States and one against a state, but for the same offense a trial in the municipal court is former jeopardy, which bars another trial in the state court because the "dual sovereignty" theory has no application to this situation. Waller v. Florida, 397 U.S. 387, 90 S.Ct. 1184 (1970).

Conviction of a lesser-included offense bars a subsequent trial for the inclusive offense. But *conviction* of driving while intoxicated does not bar a trial for homicide by vehicle based upon the same transaction. The one is not a less-included offense of the other. State v. Tanton, 88 N.M. 333, 540 P.2d 813 (1975).

Acquittal of the co-principal does not prevent **D** from being found guilty of the rape of his wife which was actually committed by the co-principal while **D** held his wife. Rozell v. State, 502 S.W.2d 16 (Tex.Cr.App.1973).

Acquittal of the principal does not necessarily foreclose prosecution of an alleged aider and abettor. United States v. Coppola, 526 F.2d 764 (10th Cir.1975).

D's conviction for Murder, premised on the existence of a conspiracy, can stand even though the person who allegedly perpetrated the homicide has been found not guilty. Commonwealth v. Jackson, 463 Pa. 301, 344 A.2d 842 (1975).

"Having reviewed these Alaska cases, we have come to the conclusion that a judgment in a criminal case favorable to one defendant should not bar prosecution of a codefendant in a subsequent proceeding. . . . We therefore reject nonmutual collateral estoppel in such criminal cases." State v. Kott, 636 P.2d 622, 624 (Alaska App.1981). The court relied on Standefer v. United States, 447 U.S. 10, 100 S.Ct. 1999 (1980), holding that nothing in the double jeopardy clause prevents the trial of a defendant as an aider and abettor simply because the principal was not guilty of the offense charged.

The so-called "Petite policy," announced in Petite v. United States, 361 U.S. 529, 530, 80 S.Ct. 450, 451 (1960), is that the federal government will not prosecute after a conviction or acquittal in a state court under circumstances in which former jeopardy would bar the prosecution except for "dual sovereignty"—unless there is some impelling reason for the prosecution. It was held that the prosecution should be dismissed in such a case although the government did not seek dismissal until after conviction. Rinaldi v. United States, 434 U.S. 22, 98 S.Ct. 81 (1977).

arose from the same "episode." If so, HRS §§ 701–109(2) [1] and 701–111(1)(b) [2] bar the State from bringing defendant to trial for Attempted Criminal Property Damage in the Second Degree after prosecuting him on the possessory charge. We find that the two charges did not arise from the same episode and therefore, we reverse.

I.

Defendant was arrested on October 19, 1978 at 2:40 a.m. for starting a fire at Jefferson School. Police Officer Mossman, who was alerted to the scene by a private citizen, conducted a routine search of defendant for weapons and found a cannister. Believing it was a container of nasal spray, he returned it to defendant.

Defendant was then transported to the police station and booked for Attempted Criminal Property Damage in the Second Degree. During a custodial search by Police Officer Hee, the cannister was again recovered. This time, however, the police officer identified it as Mace. Defendant was subsequently charged at 3:20 a.m. for Possession of an Obnoxious Substance.

On December 26, 1978, defendant was brought to trial in the district court and acquitted of the misdemeanor charge of Possession of an Obnoxious Substance. On March 2, 1979, he was brought to trial in the circuit court on the felony charge of Attempted Criminal Property Damage in the Second Degree.[3] Defendant argued that the two offenses were part of a single "episode" within the context of HRS § 701–109(2), supra, and should have been prosecuted in the same proceeding.

Defendant moved to dismiss the indictment for Attempted Criminal Property Damage in the Second Degree on the ground that he had been prosecuted previously for Possession of an Obnoxious Substance, an offense arising from the same episode. He argued that

1. HRS § 701–109(2) provides as follows:

Except as provided in subsection (3) of this section, a defendant shall not be subject to separate trials for multiple offenses based on the same conduct or arising from the same episode, if such offenses are known to the appropriate prosecuting officer at the time of the commencement of the first trial and are within the jurisdiction of a single court.

2. HRS § 701–111(1)(b) provides:

When prosecution is barred by former prosecution for a different offense. Although a prosecution is for a violation of a different statutory provision or is based on different facts, it is barred by a former prosecution under any of the following circumstances:

(1) The former prosecution resulted in an acquittal which has not subsequently been set aside or in a conviction as defined in section 701–110(3) and the subsequent prosecution is for:

. . . .

(b) Any offense for which the defendant should have been tried on the first prosecution under section 701–109 unless the court ordered a separate trial of the offense[.]

3. On October 24, 1978, this case was bound over to the circuit court from the district court. The indictment charging defendant with Attempted Criminal Property Damage in the Second Degree was filed on January 16, 1979.

the prosecution for Attempted Criminal Property Damage in the Second Degree was prohibited by HRS § 701–111(1)(b), supra.

The trial court concluded that the Attempted Criminal Property Damage offense was "closely related enough [to the possessory offense] so that it can be considered as part of a series and stemming from one incident or transaction that resulted in separate arrests." After finding that both charges were properly within its jurisdiction, the trial court granted defendant's motion to dismiss the indictment, based primarily on State v. Aiu, 59 Haw. 92, 576 P.2d 1044 (1978).

The question presented on appeal is whether HRS §§ 701–109(2) and 701–111(1)(b) prohibit the State from bringing defendant to trial for Attempted Criminal Property Damage in the Second Degree after defendant had been acquitted of the possessory charge.

II.

This court has previously addressed the issue of whether a subsequent prosecution must be barred by HRS § 701–109(2) in State v. Aiu, supra. However, in *Aiu,* it was conceded that the offenses charged arose from the same conduct or episode. Id., 59 Haw. at 96, 576 P.2d at 1048. *Aiu* is therefore not precedential authority for the case at bar.

Section 701–109(2), HRS, prohibits the State from subjecting a defendant to separate trials for offenses arising from the same conduct or "episode," provided that the offenses are known to the prosecutor at the commencement of the first trial and are within the jurisdiction of a single court. Under HRS § 701–111(1)(b), the State is barred from subsequently prosecuting a defendant for any offense which should have been joined in a prior trial under HRS § 701–109(2). . . .

III.

All of the preconditions required for the application of HRS § 701–109(2) are satisfied in this case. It is uncontested that the appropriate prosecuting officer was aware of the existence of the Attempted Criminal Property Damage charge at the time that the possessory charge was prosecuted.[5] Furthermore, both charges are clearly within the jurisdiction of a single court.

We begin with consideration, and rejection, of the State's interpretation of the word "episode." First, the State contends erroneously that HRS § 701–109(2) was derived from Model Penal Code § 1.08(2) (Tent. Draft No. 5, 1956) and therefore assumes that the Model Penal

5. Since the record on appeal does not contain a copy of the complaint charging defendant with Possession of an Obnoxious Substance, there is no evidence as to whether that complaint enumerated facts concerning the Attempted Criminal Property Damage charge. However, Officer Hee testified that the police report on the possessory charge mentioned that defendant had been initially arrested for Attempted Criminal Property Damage in the Second Degree.

TRANSACTION RECORD Completed offline

0103 10APR89 ACC# 01066558100 1296 106

DEPOSIT

TRANSACTION AMOUNT $ 596.99

#106
1296
APR 10 1989
CITICORP SAVINGS

Thank you!

See **Notice of Hold** on reverse if funds availability is delayed.
Any Questions? Please call our Customer Service Center at 1-800-248-9696.*

CITICORP ®
SAVINGS
A Federal Savings and Loan Association

CCS 678 (7/88)

*In order to ensure that you always receive the highest quality customer service, Citicorp Savings randomly monitors incoming calls to our 800 number.

NOTICE OF HOLD

Amount of Funds Held	Number of Business Days Held (Includes Day of Deposit)	Reason Code For Extended Hold (see below) A	B	C	D
______	______	☐	☐	☐	☐
______	______	☐	☐	☐	☐
______	______	☐	☐	☐	☐

We are delaying the availability of the amounts shown above from this deposit. These funds will be available on the first business day after the expiration of the hold days shown above.

If you have Checks As Cash℠ the amounts indicated above are immediately available, even though a hold has been placed, up to the unused portion of your Checks As Cash pledged amount.

If you did not receive this notice at the time you made the deposit and the check you deposited is paid, we will refund to you any fees for overdrafts or returned checks that result solely from the additional delay that we are imposing. To obtain a refund of such fees, contact your branch.

EXTENDED HOLD REASON CODES

A = New Account
B = The check(s) you deposited today exceeds $5,000.
This hold applies only to the amount over $5,000.
C = You have overdrawn your account repeatedly in the last six months.
D = The check you deposited was previously returned unpaid.

IF NO BOX IS CHECKED NORMAL HOLD PERIODS APPLY

TRANSACTION RECORD

0103 10APR89 ACC# 01066558100 1296 106

DEPOSIT

TRANSACTION AMOUNT $ 50.00

#106
1296
APR 10 1989
CITICORP SAVINGS

See **Notice of Hold** on reverse if funds availability is delayed.
Any Questions? Please call our Customer Service Center at 1-800-248-9696.*

CITICORP ®
SAVINGS
A Federal Savings and Loan Association

CCS 678 (7/88)

*In order to ensure that you always receive the highest quality customer service, Citicorp Savings randomly monitors incoming calls to our 800 number.

NOTICE OF HOLD

Amount of Funds Held	Number of Business Days Held (Includes Day of Deposit)	Reason Code For Extended Hold (see below) A	B	C	D
________	________	☐	☐	☐	☐
________	________	☐	☐	☐	☐
________	________	☐	☐	☐	☐

We are delaying the availability of the amounts shown above from this deposit. These funds will be available on the first business day after the expiration of the hold days shown above.

If you have Checks As Cash[SM] the amounts indicated above are immediately available, even though a hold has been placed, up to the unused portion of your Checks As Cash pledged amount.

If you did not receive this notice at the time you made the deposit and the check you deposited is paid, we will refund to you any fees for overdrafts or returned checks that result solely from the additional delay that we are imposing. To obtain a refund of such fees, contact your branch.

EXTENDED HOLD REASON CODES

A = New Account
B = The check(s) you deposited today exceeds $5,000.
This hold applies only to the amount over $5,000.
C = You have overdrawn your account repeatedly in the last six months.
D = The check you deposited was previously returned unpaid.

IF NO BOX IS CHECKED NORMAL HOLD PERIODS APPLY

Code does not use the word "episode." Thus, the State hypothesizes that the Legislature coined the word "episode" as a shorthand means of encompassing subsections (b) and (c) of Model Penal Code § 1.08(2).

We note that the provision upon which the State relies was amended and renumbered as Model Penal Code § 1.07(2) in the 1962 Proposed Official Draft and that the amended provision contained the word "episode." Model Penal Code § 1.07, status of section (Proposed Official Draft, 1962). Furthermore, the Table of Derivation accompanying the Hawaii Penal Code indicates that HRS § 701–109 was derived from Model Penal Code § 1.07 (Proposed Official Draft, 1962), rather than its predecessor. 7A HRS at 497, app. § 3. Model Penal Code § 1.07(2) provides:

> (2) *Limitation on Separate Trials for Multiple Offenses.* Except as provided in Subsection (3) of this Section, a defendant shall not be subject to separate trials for multiple offenses based on the same conduct or arising from the same criminal episode, if such offenses are known to the appropriate prosecuting officer at the time of the commencement of the first trial and are within the jurisdiction of a single court.

Second, the comment accompanying Model Penal Code § 1.07(2) reveals that the drafters of the code did not intend "episode" to encompass the situations described in Model Penal Code § 1.08(2)(b) and (c) (Tent. Draft No. 5, 1956). Model Penal Code § 1.07(2), as originally drafted, was considerably broader and would have required joinder of offenses where it is now merely permissible. Although the Model Penal Code Advisory Committee favored broadening the formulation to include offenses "based on a course of conduct having a common criminal purpose or plan or involving repeated commission of the same kind of offense," the Model Penal Code Council viewed both this and the original language in Model Penal Code § 1.08(2) (Tent. Draft No. 5, 1956) as too inclusive. Model Penal Code § 1.07, status of section (Proposed Official Draft, 1962). Model Penal Code § 1.07(2), limiting the requirement to "multiple offenses based on the same conduct or arising from the same criminal episode," was designed to meet the Council's view. *Id.* Thus, we can infer from the commentary to Model Penal Code § 1.07(2) that the Legislature, in formulating HRS § 701–109(2), did not intend a determination of a single criminal "episode" to be based solely upon a defendant's singular criminal objective or common purpose or plan.

Although we reject the State's interpretation of "episode," we acknowledge that evidence of one crime is admissible in the trial of another crime if it tends to prove motive, intent, common scheme or plan, or design involving the commission of two or more crimes so related that proof of one tends to prove the other. However, mere allegations of a defendant's subjective intent are insufficient to require joinder of offenses that are otherwise unrelated.

IV.

Section 701–109(2), HRS, reflects a policy that a defendant should not have to face the expense and uncertainties of multiple trials based on essentially the same conduct or episode. *Commentary* on HRS § 701–109. It is designed to prevent the State from harassing a defendant with successive prosecutions where the State is dissatisfied with the punishment previously ordered or where the State has previously failed to convict the defendant.

We agree with defendant that proximity in time, place and circumstances of the offenses will necessarily enter into the policy considerations underlying HRS § 701–109(2). Where the offenses occur at the same time and place and under the same circumstances, it is likely that the facts and issues involved in the charges will be similar. The witnesses to be used and the evidence to be offered will probably overlap to the extent that joinder of the charges would be justified. Compulsory joinder of offenses which share a proximity in time, place and circumstances would not only protect the defendant from successive prosecutions based on the same conduct or episode, but it would also save the defendant and the State time and money required in the presentation of repetitive evidence.

In view of the dual considerations of fairness to the defendant and society's interest in efficient law enforcement, we hold that the test for determining the singleness of a criminal episode should be based on whether the alleged conduct was so closely related in time, place and circumstances that a complete account of one charge cannot be related without referring to details of the other charge. We do not, of course, by our holding in this case, preclude a defendant from asserting his right to separate trials where joinder of the offenses would be unjust and prejudicial.

Applying the test to the facts before us, we reject defendant's contention that the offenses occurred concurrently. Defendant argues that it would be unreasonable to conclude that the possessory offense did not occur until the arrest at the police station. He points to the arresting officer's initial discovery of the cannister as evidence that he was in possession of the Mace at the schoolyard.

Defendant also attempts to draw an analogy between his predicament and the situation in State v. Matischeck, 20 Or.App. 332, 531 P.2d 737 (1975). In *Matischeck,* the defendant had been arrested for Driving Under the Influence of Intoxicating Liquor and a vial of tablets was recovered from his person during a routine search. Two days later, the tablets were identified as amphetamines and an information was filed charging the defendant with Criminal Activity in Drugs. Id. at 738. Defendant emphasizes that in *Matischeck,* the possessory charge was effective as of the arrest for Driving Under the Influence of Intoxicating Liquor, rather than at the time the substance was identified. Therefore, he argues that the possessory charge in the instant case should be effective as of the arrest for Attempted Criminal Property Damage in the Second Degree, rather than at the time the Mace was identified at the police station.

We find that defendant was charged with the commission of offenses which occurred at different times and places and under different circumstances. Our rationale is based primarily on the fact that the arresting officer failed to recognize the illegal nature of the canister at the time of the search for weapons. As a result, defendant's possession of the Mace continued after his initial arrest, until the subsequent discovery and identification at the police station.

While it is true that the possessory offense can be traced to the time of the first arrest, we cannot say that the possessory charge should be deemed effective as of the time of that arrest. The point in time at which the Mace was identified is important because prior to the identification, the facts and circumstances within the first arresting officer's knowledge did not afford probable cause to believe that an offense other than Attempted Criminal Property Damage in the Second Degree had been committed. The facts can be distinguished from those in State v. Matischeck, 20 Or.App. 332, 531 P.2d 737 (1975), where the police officer's immediate seizure of the vial indicated that he had probable cause to suspect contraband. In contrast to the case at bar, the identification of the contraband in *Matischeck* served to verify the earlier suspicion.

Furthermore, under HRS § 701–108(4), an offense of a continuing nature such as the possession of Mace is deemed to be committed at the time when the course of conduct is terminated.

Not only did the offenses occur at different times and places, but they were discovered under different circumstances which resulted in arrests by different police officers. We therefore conclude that the offenses were so separate in time and place and so distinct in circumstances that the acquittal on the possessory charge did not bar prosecution for the Attempted Criminal Property Damage in the Second Degree.

Reversed and remanded for further proceedings not inconsistent with this opinion.[a]

a. Citations for drunk driving, driving without a safety sticker, and driving without a registration certificate charged separate, independent offenses where they were committed at different times and were entirely unrelated to each other were not committed to accomplish a "single criminal objective" and a prosecution for drunk driving was not barred by guilty pleas to the other citations. Hupp v. Johnson, 606 P.2d 253 (Utah 1980).

MODEL PENAL CODE

Section 1.08 When Prosecution Barred by Former Prosecution for the Same Offense.

When a prosecution is for a violation of the same provision of the statutes and is based upon the same facts as a former prosecution, it is barred by such former prosecution under the following circumstances:

(1) The former prosecution resulted in an acquittal. There is an acquittal if the prosecution resulted in a finding of not guilty by the trier of fact or in a determination that there was insufficient evidence to warrant a conviction. A finding of guilty of a lesser included offense is an acquittal of the greater inclusive offense, although the conviction is subsequently set aside.

(2) The former prosecution was terminated, after the information had been filed or the indictment found, by a final order or judgment for the defendant, which has not been set aside, reversed, or vacated and which necessarily required a determination inconsistent with a fact or a legal proposition that must be established for conviction of the offense.

(3) The former prosecution resulted in a conviction. There is a conviction if the prosecution resulted in a judgment of conviction which has not been reversed or vacated, a verdict of guilty which has not been set aside and which is capable of supporting a judgment, or a plea of guilty accepted by the Court. In the latter two cases failure to enter judgment must be for a reason other than a motion of the defendant.

(4) The former prosecution was improperly terminated. Except as provided in this Subsection, there is an improper termination of a prosecution if the termination is for reasons not amounting to an acquittal, and it takes place after the first witness is sworn but before verdict. Termination under any of the following circumstances is not improper:

(a) The defendant consents to the termination or waives, by motion to dismiss or otherwise, his right to object to the termination.

(b) the trial court finds that the termination is necessary because:

(1) it is physically impossible to proceed with the trial in conformity with law; or

(2) there is a legal defect in the proceedings which would make any judgment entered upon a verdict reversible as a matter of law; or

(3) prejudicial conduct, in or outside the courtroom, makes it impossible to proceed with the trial without injustice to either the defendant or the State; or

(4) the jury is unable to agree upon a verdict; or

(5) false statements of a juror on voir dire prevent a fair trial.

Section 1.09 When Prosecution Barred by Former Prosecution for Different Offense.

Although a prosecution is for a violation of a different provision of the statutes than a former prosecution or is based on different facts, it is barred by such former prosecution under the following circumstances:

(1) The former prosecution resulted in an acquittal* or in a conviction as defined in Section 1.08 and the subsequent prosecution is for:

(a) any offense of which the defendant could have been convicted on the first prosecution; or

(b) any offense for which the defendant should have been tried on the first prosecution under Section 1.07, unless the Court ordered a separate trial of the charge of such offense; or

(c) the same conduct, unless (i) the offense of which the defendant was formerly convicted or acquitted and the offense for which he is subsequently prosecuted each requires proof of a fact not required by the other and the law defining each of such offenses is intended to prevent a substantially different harm or evil, or (ii) the second offense was not consummated when the former trial began.

(2) The former prosecution was terminated, after the information was filed or the indictment found, by an acquittal or by a final order or judgment for the defendant which has not been set aside, reversed or vacated and which acquittal, final order or judgment necessarily required a determination inconsistent with a fact which must be established for conviction of the second offense.

(3) The former prosecution was improperly terminated, as improper termination is defined in Section 1.08, and the subsequent prosecution is for an offense of which the defendant could have been convicted had the former prosecution not been improperly terminated.

Section 1.10 Former Prosecution in Another Jurisdiction: When a Bar.

When conduct constitutes an offense within the concurrent jurisdiction of this State and of the United States or another State, a prosecution in any such other jurisdiction is a bar to a subsequent prosecution in this State under the following circumstances:

(1) The first prosecution resulted in an acquittal or in a conviction as defined in Section 1.08 and the subsequent prosecution is based on the same conduct, unless (a) the offense of which the defendant was formerly convicted or acquitted and the offense for which he is subsequently prosecuted each requires proof of a fact not required by the other and the law defining each of such offenses is intended to prevent a substantially different harm or evil or (b) the second offense was not consummated when the former trial began; or

* See footnote, supra, Sec. 1.08(1).

(2) The former prosecution was terminated, after the information was filed or the indictment found, by an acquittal or by a final order or judgment for the defendant which has not been set aside, reversed or vacated and which acquittal, final order or judgment necessarily required a determination inconsistent with a fact which must be established for conviction of the offense of which the defendant is subsequently prosecuted.

Section 1.11 Former Prosecution Before Court Lacking Jurisdiction or When Fraudulently Procured by the Defendant.

A prosecution is not a bar within the meaning of Sections 1.08, 1.09 and 1.10 under any of the following circumstances:

(1) The former prosecution was before a court which lacked jurisdiction over the defendant or the offense; or

(2) The former prosecution was procured by the defendant without the knowledge of the appropriate prosecuting officer and with the purpose of avoiding the sentence which might otherwise be imposed; or

(3) The former prosecution resulted in a judgment of conviction which was held invalid in a subsequent proceeding on a writ of habeas corpus, coram nobis or similar process.[a]

SECTION 5. EX POST FACTO LAWS

Another limitation placed upon criminal prosecutions is that a person shall not be punished on a criminal charge for an act which was no offense at the time it was performed. Such a law is known as an *ex post facto* law and is prohibited both by The Constitution of the United States and by State Constitutions.[1] The term *ex post facto* "applies only to criminal laws; such laws as make acts, innocent when done, criminal; or, if criminal when done, aggravate the crime, or increase the punishment, or reduce the measure of proof.[2] Every *ex post facto* law is necessarily retrospective; but the converse is not true. . . . Retrospective laws, as distinguished from *ex post facto* laws, are not in conflict with the United States Constitution, nor are they in conflict with our State Constitution." [3]

a. Copyright 1962 by the American Law Institute. Reprinted with the permission of the American Law Institute.

1. "No . . . ex post facto Law shall be passed." U.S. Const. Art. I, § 9, cl. 3. "No State shall . . . pass any . . . ex post facto Law . . . ." U.S. Const. Art. I, § 10. "No . . . ex post facto law . . . shall ever be passed." Iowa Const. Art. I, § 21.

2. A statute creating a presumption of driving under the influence of liquor, on evidence of a prescribed quantum of alcohol in the driver's blood, amounted to an ex-post-facto law as applied to a driver involved in an accident after the bill had been signed by the governor but before the date on which the law became effective (60 days after it was signed). DeWoody v. Superior Court, 8 Cal.App.3d 52, 87 Cal.Rptr. 210 (1970). The presumption would permit conviction on less proof than would otherwise be required.

3. State v. Squires, 26 Iowa 340, 346–7 (1868). Cf. Polk Co. v. Hierb, 37 Iowa 361 (1873); Kring v. Missouri, 107 U.S. 221, 2 S.Ct. 443, 27 L.Ed. 506 (1882); In re Medley, 134 U.S. 160, 10 S.Ct. 384, 33 L.Ed. 835 (1890); Duncan v. Missouri, 152 U.S. 377, 14 S.Ct. 570, 38 L.Ed. 485

UNITED STATES v. RAMIREZ

United States Court of Appeals, Ninth Circuit, 1973.
480 F.2d 76.

Before DUNIWAY and HUFSTEDLER, CIRCUIT JUDGES, and ANDERSON,* DISTRICT JUDGE.

PER CURIAM. In a single count indictment returned September 16, 1971, appellants Ballan and Ramirez and sixteen others were

(1894). A statute which increases the punishment for an existing offense is not applicable to a violation occurring prior to the enactment of the punishment. State v. Marx, 200 Iowa 884, 205 N.W. 518 (1925). Hence a jail sentence on conviction of maintaining a liquor nuisance, at a time before the statute authorizing such jail sentence became effective, was erroneous. Ibid. A change in the law relating to murder, by which degrees of murder with fixed penalties are substituted for the prior rule under which the jury determined whether the punishment should be death or life imprisonment, is *ex post facto.* Marion v. State, 16 Neb. 349, 20 N.W. 289 (1884). A change from death to one year's imprisonment at hard labor, followed by death, or from death to death preceded by solitary confinement is *ex post facto* as to offenses committed prior to the statutory change. Hartung v. People, 22 N.Y. 95 (1860), 26 N.Y. 167 (1863); In re Petty, 22 Kan. 477 (1879); In re Medley, 134 U.S. 160, 10 S.Ct. 384, 33 L.Ed. 835 (1890). Cf. State v. Rooney, 12 N.D. 144, 95 N.W. 513 (1903), in which a change of place of incarceration pending execution and a longer period of imprisonment prior to execution was held to be a mitigation of sentence. A change from fine "or" imprisonment to fine "and" imprisonment is *ex post facto.* Flaherty v. Thomas, 94 Mass. 428 (1866); Commonwealth v. McDonough, 95 Mass. 581 (1866).

Application of 1979 parole guidelines to offenses committed in 1975 and 1976 did not violate the ex post facto clause where it could not be said that the 1975 guidelines would have been less severe. Johnson v. United States Parole Commission, 555 F.Supp. 461 (D.C.Minn.1982).

Corrections in the method of calculating parole eligibility to conform to a correct interpretation of a state statute because of a decision by the state's highest court did not violate the ex post facto clause. Holguin v. Raines, 695 F.2d 372 (9th Cir.1982).

A statute reducing the punishment, which was enacted after the offense but prior to the conviction, applies to that conviction. People v. McGowan, 199 Misc. 1, 104 N.Y.S.2d 652 (1951).

A statute is not *ex post facto* because it attaches to a subsequent crime an increased punishment on account of former convictions, even though such former convictions were had prior to the enactment of the statute. State v. Dowden, 137 Iowa 573, 115 N.W. 211 (1908); State v. Norris, 203 Iowa 327, 210 N.W. 922 (1926); McDonald v. Massachusetts, 180 U.S. 311, 21 S.Ct. 389, 45 L.Ed. 542 (1901); People v. Stanley, 47 Cal. 113 (1874); Commonwealth v. Marchand, 155 Mass. 8, 29 N.E. 578 (1891); Commonwealth v. Graves, 155 Mass. 163, 29 N.E. 579 (1891); Ex parte Allen, 91 Ohio St. 315, 110 N.E. 535 (1915).

A statute denying to convicts under sentence for a second offense the same reductions from their sentence for good behavior that are allowed to other convicts is not *ex post facto* as applied to the punishment of an offense subsequently committed, although the offender had been convicted of his first offense before the passage of the act. In re Miller, 110 Mich. 676, 68 N.W. 990 (1896).

A statute providing for a determination of guilt and then a separate determination as to penalty where the sentence may be death or imprisonment for life, is not *ex post facto* as to murder previously committed. People v. Ward, 50 Cal.2d 702, 328 P.2d 777 (1958).

A statute forbidding deductions for good conduct during the first six months reincarceration following parole violation, enacted before **D** was sentenced but after **D** was paroled, was ex post facto as to **D**. Greenfield v. Scafati, 277 F.Supp. 644 (1967). Aff'd Scafati v. Greenfield, 390 U.S. 713, 88 S.Ct. 1409 (1967).

---

* See note * on page 942.

charged with conspiracy to import, receive, conceal and transport marijuana in violation of 21 U.S.C. § 176a. Defendants were found guilty by a jury on June 19, 1972, and sentence was pronounced the next morning, June 20, 1972. Ramirez received a sentence of seven years and a fine of $15,000.00. Ballan was sentenced for five years and a fine of $5,000.00. The sentences were imposed under Sec. 176a, which was repealed effective May 1, 1971. Comprehensive Drug Abuse Prevention and Control Act of 1970 (the Act), Pub.L. 91–513, 84 Stat. 1236, 21 U.S.C. Sec. 801 et seq. The acts charged against the appellants extended over a period of time from approximately March to November of 1970.

Appellants' main thrusts on this appeal are four-fold:

First: The government cannot initiate a prosecution after the effective date of repeal for alleged criminal acts occurring prior thereto;

Second: Assuming that the first proposition is answered adversely to appellants, they cannot be punished under the repealed provisions, but must be punished under the new and less severe penalty provisions;

Third: Sentencing under the harsher penalties of the repealed act amounts to cruel and unusual punishment proscribed by the Eighth Amendment. This point is raised only by Ramirez; . . .

FIRST ISSUE

The first issue was not raised in the recent case of Bradley v. United States, 410 U.S. 605, 93 S.Ct. 1151, 35 L.Ed.2d 528 (1973), affirming 455 F.2d 1181 (CA 1st Cir.), since the prosecution there was commenced before May 1, 1971. Nevertheless, this court has squarely ruled on the question and the reasoning is directly applicable to this case. United States v. Cummings, 468 F.2d 274 (9 Cir.1972). In *Cummings* as here, the interdicted acts took place before the repeal of the statute and the indictment was returned after the repeal. These prosecutions for violations of the law occurring before were saved by the general saving statute, 1 U.S.C. Sec. 109, and the special saving clauses of the Act, Sections 702 and 1103. *Cummings,* supra, pp. 276–277. It could not have been the intent of Congress to grant amnesty to the unapprehended as of May 1, 1971, while continuing

Making the possession of a pistol, by one who has been convicted of robbery, a crime is not ex post facto as to such possession after the statute even if the robbery conviction was prior to its enactment. Salazar v. State, 423 S.W.2d 297 (Tex.1968).

Statutory amendment providing that if a plea of guilty is entered to a murder charge, without specification of the degree, a three-judge panel shall determine the degree of the crime and give sentence, replacing such determination by a single judge, is not ex post facto. Rainsberger v. Fogliani, 380 F.2d 783 (9th Cir. 1967).

* Honorable J. Blaine Anderson, United States District Judge, District of Idaho, sitting by designation.

interdiction and punishment for essentially the same conduct for violations occurring after May 1, 1971.

SECOND ISSUE

While it may be argued that if the prosecution had begun after May 1, 1971, punishment should be under the new Act, we do not believe the rationale of *Bradley* supports this notion, but on the contrary, supports the conclusion that the sentences were properly imposed under the provisions of the repealed Act, as saved. As stated in *Bradley* (93 S.Ct. p. 1155), "As we have said, sentencing is part of prosecution. The mandatory minimum sentence of five years must therefore be imposed on offenders who violated the law before May 1, 1971."

THIRD ISSUE

Ramirez alone raises the Eighth Amendment violation because of sentencing under the harsher provisions of the repealed Act. We conclude this is not cruel and unusual punishment. While United States v. Fithian, 452 F.2d 505, 506 (9th Cir.1971) does not speak in terms of cruel and unusual punishment, it unmistakeably directs that sentencing under the repealed provision "was the only course available." Further, 1 U.S.C. § 109 provides that repeal "shall not have the effect to release or extinguish any penalty . . ." and remains in force to sustain "the enforcement of such penalty". The sentence imposed on Ramirez was well within and below the maximum sentence which could have been imposed. He is in the same class as all persons convicted and sentenced under the repealed provisions. Sentences under Sec. 176a were not cruel and unusual punishment prior to repeal. They do not become so by the later promulgation of less severe penalties for similar prohibited conduct.

The district judge was correct in proceeding and sentencing appellants under 21 U.S.C. § 176a repealed effective May 1, 1971. . . .

After careful review we find nothing in appellants' other assignments of error justifying a reversal.

Appellants' bonds are revoked as of now.

Affirmed.[1]

1. [By the Compiler.] "We find it unnecessary to decide the question of the effective date of the indictment, since the general savings clause found in 1 U.S.C.A. § 109, coupled with judicial construction of that section, disposes of the issue in this case.

"The general savings clause provides in part:

" 'The repeal of any statute shall not have the effect to release or extinguish any penalty, forfeiture, or liability incurred under such statute, unless the repealing act shall so expressly provide, and such statute shall be treated as still remaining in force for the purpose of sustaining any proper action or prosecution for the enforcement of

HUFSTEDLER, CIRCUIT JUDGE (dissenting):

I dissent solely from the disposition of the second issue: Does the penalty provision under the new Act apply to a prosecution under section 176a initiated after the repeal of section 176a? In my view, the majority's negative response is contrary to the teaching of Bradley v. United States (1973) 410 U.S. 605, 93 S.Ct. 1151, 35 L.Ed.2d 528.

Section 1103(a) of the Comprehensive Drug Abuse Prevention and Control Act of 1970 provides in pertinent part: "Prosecutions for any violation of law occurring prior to the effective date of [the Act] shall not be affected by the repeals . . . made by [it] or abated by reason thereof." The keystone of the *Bradley* rationale is its construction of the word "prosecutions" in section 1103(a) as "clearly imports a beginning and an end." The "end," as *Bradley* squarely held, is the conclusion of sentencing. The "beginning" of a prosecution is the return of an indictment. These indictments were returned after section 176a had been repealed. There was no prosecution to be saved by section 1103(a). *Bradley* means that any prosecution initiated before repeal of the statute carries with it the old section 176a

such penalty, forfeiture, or liability. . . .'

"Under this section, penalties accruing while a statute was in force may be prosecuted after its repeal, unless there is an express provision to the contrary in the repealing statute." United States v. Brown, 429 F.2d 566, 568 (9th Cir.1970).

When a penal statute is amended so as to lessen the punishment for the offense, the legislature could provide either that the old punishment or the new should apply to offenses already committed. If no provision is made either way this is a clear manifestation of legislative intent that the lighter punishment is the proper penalty for the prohibited act. This will prevail over a general saving clause and hence only the lighter sentence can be applied in any case in which the judgment had not become final before the amendment. In re Estrada, 63 Cal.2d 740, 48 Cal.Rptr. 172, 408 P.2d 948 (1965). See also In re Ring, 64 Cal.2d 450, 50 Cal. Rptr. 530, 413 P.2d 130 (1966).

A statute was amended so as to leave no penalty for the offense of which D had been convicted and sentenced for life. D's conviction had been affirmed by the state court but was being considered by the Supreme Court on a petition for certiorari at the time the amendment became effective. It was held that the conviction cannot stand. Webb v. Beto, 457 F.2d 346 (5th Cir.1972).

D was convicted of a narcotic offense which was repealed by a substitute statute with a saving clause saying prosecutions for prior violations were not affected by the change. Held, the mandatory sentence under the old law must be imposed. Bradley v. United States, 410 U.S. 605, 93 S.Ct. 1151 (1973).

"The purpose of the abatement and pardon doctrine is to prevent the injustice manifest in continuing to prosecute for an activity after the legislature has declared that activity to be lawful." United States v. Chiarizio, 525 F.2d 289, 295 (2d Cir.1975). The court held it did not apply to the case at bench because no outright repeal was involved. The old statute was replaced by another incorporating the same substantive offense. But there is no "abatement and pardon" doctrine so far as the repeal of a criminal statute is concerned. If a criminal statute is repealed with no saving clause, general or special, no sentence can be imposed for a prior violation for the simple reason that there is no law to authorize it. There is no manifest injustice in the punishment of one who has violated the law, even if the same act could be done now without transgressing the law. This is emphasized by the fact that many states have a general saving clause to the effect that the repeal of a criminal statute shall not bar prosecution for offenses already committed.

penalty. Conversely, any prosecution under section 176a begun after repeal of section 176a for the substantive offense committed before repeal carries with it the milder penalties of the successor statute.

The substantive offense was specifically saved. Prosecutions initiated before repeal were "not . . . affected" or "abated." Prosecutions begun after repeal of section 176a could be neither affected nor abated, because they were nonexistent when the old statute was repealed.

I would vacate the sentence and remand for resentencing under the new statute.

PLACHY v. STATE

Court of Criminal Appeals of Texas, 1922.

91 Tex.Cr.R. 405, 239 S.W. 979.

LATTIMORE, JUDGE. Appellant was convicted in the District Court of Wharton County of the offense of selling intoxicating liquor, and his punishment fixed at four years in the penitentiary. . . .

It was alleged and proved on the trial that whisky was sold by appellant to said Wooley. The latter testified as a witness for the State. The Dean Law which was in operation on November 2, 1921, made the purchaser of intoxicating liquor punishable, and when used as a witness this court has uniformly held such purchaser to be an accomplice. This construction of the law must continue to prevail as to all violations thereof which occurred prior to the taking effect of said Chapter 61, supra. An examination of said amendatory statute discloses that Sec. 2c thereof reads as follows:

"Upon a trial for a violation of any of the provisions of this Chapter, the purchaser, transporter, or possessor of any of the liquors prohibited herein shall not be held in law or in fact to be an accomplice, when a witness in any such trial." Said amendatory Act became effective November 15, 1921, or about two weeks after date of the alleged offense herein charged against appellant. An exception was taken to the charge of the court below in this case because same did not submit to the jury the law of accomplice testimony as applicable to the witness Wooley, and in this connection we observe that the trial court refused a special instruction on the law of accomplice testimony telling the jury that the witness Wooley was an accomplice and must be considered by them as such. We are not informed by any qualification to any bill of exceptions as to the reason for such failure and refusal on the part of the trial court. It may have been that the learned trial judge was of the opinion that the amendatory act, supra, having gone into effect prior to the time of the instant trial, that Sec. 2c above quoted was applicable. We are of opinion that such a conclusion would be error.

It seems well settled in this State that a law which alters the rules of evidence applicable in a given case, so that under the new law less or different testimony is required to convict the offender than was required at the time of the commission of the offense, must be held an ex post facto law and not applicable upon the trial of one for an offense committed prior to the taking effect of such new enactment.

Section 16, Article 1 of our Constitution inhibits ex post facto laws. Supporting its definition by reference to numerous decisions of most of the states of the Union, as well as of the Supreme Court of the United States, Cyc. gives the following: "An ex post facto law is one which imposes a punishment for an act which was not punishable when it was committed, or imposes additional punishment, or changes the rules of evidence by which less or different testimony is sufficient to convict." See 8 Cyc. p. 1027. In Hart v. State, 40 Ala. 32, 88 Am. Dec. 752, the passage of a statute doing away with the requirement that an accomplice be corroborated, was held ex post facto in a prosecution for an offense committed prior to the enactment of such law. So in Goode v. State, 50 Fla. 45, 39 So. 461, a law which modified an existing rule of evidence by making proof of delivery of intoxicating liquor to a person by the accused, prima facie proof of ownership, was held to be ex post facto. So also in State v. Grant, 79 Mo. 113, 49 Am.Rep. 218, a law removing the incompetence to testify of one who had been convicted of petty larceny was held ex post facto when such evidence was offered on the trial of one for an offense committed prior to the enactment of such statute.

Agreeing to the definition of ex post facto law as above given, and applying the rule of reason to its application in the instant case, we observe that the removal of the purchaser of intoxicating liquor from the ranks of accomplice testimony by statute, clearly makes possible a conviction on less evidence. A, the seller, could not formerly be convicted on the testimony of B, the purchaser, except some other person corroborate B. Under the rule now obtaining since the passage of said amendatory act, supra, A, the seller can be convicted on the testimony of B, the purchaser, alone. This brings the instant case squarely within the rule laid down in Calloway et al. cases, supra, and will necessitate a reversal herein because of the failure and refusal of the court to apply the law of accomplice testimony to the witness Wooley. . . .

For the error above mentioned the judgment of the trial court will be reversed and the cause remanded.[1]

Reversed and remanded.

1. Accord, Phillips v. State, 92 Tex.Cr. R. 317, 244 S.W. 146 (1922); Hart v. State, 40 Ala. 32 (1866). A law which changes the rules of evidence in such a way as to allow a conviction on less evidence or proof than was previously required, is unconstitutional. Calder v. Bull, 3 Dall. 386, 1 L.Ed. 648 (U.S.1798); Duncan v. Missouri, 152 U.S. 377, 14 S.Ct. 570, 38 L.Ed. 485 (1894); Cummings v. Missouri, 4 Wall. 277, 325, 18 L.Ed. 356 (U.S.1866).

THOMPSON v. MISSOURI

Supreme Court of the United States, 1898.
171 U.S. 380, 18 S.Ct. 922.

MR. JUSTICE HARLAN delivered the opinion of the court.

The record suggests many questions of law, but the only one that may be considered by this court is whether the proceedings against the plaintiff in error were consistent with the provision in the Constitution of the United States forbidding the States from passing *ex post facto* laws.

Thompson was indicted in the St. Louis Criminal Court at its November term 1894 for the murder, in the first degree, of one Joseph M. Cunningham, a sexton at one of the churches in the city of St. Louis. Having been tried and convicted of the offence charged, he prosecuted an appeal to the Supreme Court of Missouri, and by that court the judgment was reversed and a new trial was ordered. State v. Thompson, 132 Mo. 301, 34 S.W. 31. At the second trial the accused was again convicted; and a new trial having been denied, he prosecuted another appeal to the Supreme Court of the State. That court affirmed the last judgment, and the present appeal brings that judgment before us for reëxamination. State v. Thompson, 141 Mo. 408, 42 S.W. 949.

The evidence against the accused was entirely circumstantial in its nature. One of the issues of fact was as to the authorship of a certain prescription for strychnine, and of a certain letter addressed to the organist of the church containing threatening language about the sexton. The theory of the prosecution was that the accused had obtained the strychnine specified in the prescription and put it into food that he delivered or caused to be delivered to the deceased with intent to destroy his life. The accused denied that he wrote either the prescription or the letter to the organist, or that he had any connection with either of those writings. At the first trial certain letters written by him to his wife were admitted in evidence for the purpose of comparing them with the writing in the prescription and with the letter to the organist. The Supreme Court of the State, upon the first appeal, held that it was error to admit in evidence for purposes of comparison the letters written by Thompson to his wife, and for that error the first judgment was reversed and a new trial ordered.

And a provision in the constitution of the state of Utah for the trial of criminal cases (other than capital) by a jury of eight persons only, was held to be *ex post facto* as to offenses committed before the territory became a state. Thompson v. Utah, 170 U.S. 343, 18 S.Ct. 620, 42 L.Ed. 1061 (1898).

Change in rule of evidence as to corroboration of prosecutrix's testimony in a rape case could not be applied retroactively. State v. Byers, 102 Idaho 159, 627 P.2d 788 (1981).

Subsequently, the general assembly of Missouri passed an act which became operative in July, 1895, providing that "comparison of a disputed writing with any writing proved to the satisfaction of the judge to be genuine shall be permitted to be made by witnesses, and such writings and the evidence of witnesses respecting the same may be submitted to the court and jury as evidence of the genuineness or otherwise of the writing in dispute." Laws Missouri, April 8, 1895, p. 284.[a]

This statute is in the very words of section 27 of the English Common Law Procedure Act of 1854, 17 & 18 Vict. c. 125. And by the 28 Vict. c. 18, §§ 1, 8, the provisions of that act were extended to criminal cases.

At the second trial, which occurred in 1896, the letters written by the accused to his wife were again admitted in evidence, over his objection, for the purpose of comparing them with the order for strychnine and the letter to the organist. This action of the trial court was based upon the above statute of 1895.

The contention of the accused is that as the letters to his wife were not, *at the time of the commission of the alleged offence,* admissible in evidence for the purpose of comparing them with other writings charged to be in his handwriting, the subsequent statute of Missouri changing this rule of evidence was *ex post facto* when applied to his case.

It is not to be denied that the position of the accused finds apparent support in the general language used in some opinions. . . .

Applying the principles announced in former cases—without attaching undue weight to general expressions in them that go beyond the questions necessary to be determined—we adjudge that the statute of Missouri relating to the comparison of writings is not *ex post facto* when applied to prosecutions for crimes committed prior to its passage. If persons excluded, upon grounds of public policy, at the time of the commission of an offence, from testifying as witnesses for or against the accused, may, in virtue of a statute, become competent to testify, we cannot perceive any ground upon which to hold a statute to be *ex post facto* which does nothing more than admit evidence of a particular kind in a criminal case upon an issue of fact which was not admissible under the rules of evidence as enforced by judicial decisions at the time the offence was committed. The Missouri statute, when applied to this case, did not enlarge the punishment to which the accused was liable when his crime was committed, nor make any act involved in his offence criminal that was not criminal at the time he committed the murder of which he was found

a. When ordered by a court to provide handwriting exemplars, D has no right to refuse, and if he does refuse the fact of his refusal may be admitted into evidence. State v. Haze, 218 Kan. 60, 542 P.2d 720 (1975).

guilty. It did not change the quality or degree of his offence. Nor can the new rule introduced by it be characterized as unreasonable—certainly not so unreasonable as materially to affect the substantial rights of one put on trial for crime. The statute did not require "less proof, in amount or degree," than was required at the time of the commission of the crime charged upon him. It left unimpaired the right of the jury to determine the sufficiency or effect of the evidence declared to be admissible, and did not disturb the fundamental rule that the State, as a condition of its right to take the life of an accused, must overcome the presumption of his innocence and establish his guilt beyond a reasonable doubt. Whether he wrote the prescription for strychnine, or the threatening letter to the church organist, was left for the jury, and the duty of the jury, in that particular, was the same after as before the passage of the statute. The statute did nothing more than remove an obstacle arising out of a rule of evidence that withdrew from the consideration of the jury testimony which, in the opinion of the legislature, tended to elucidate the ultimate, essential fact to be established, namely, the guilt of the accused. Nor did it give the prosecution any right that was denied to the accused. It placed the State and the accused upon an equality; for the rule established by it gave to each side the right to have disputed writings compared with writings proved to the satisfaction of the judge to be genuine. Each side was entitled to go to the jury upon the question of the genuineness of the writing upon which the prosecution relied to establish the guilt of the accused. It is well known that the adjudged cases have not been in harmony touching the rule relating to the comparison of handwritings: and the object of the legislature, as we may assume, was to give the jury all the light that could be thrown upon an issue of that character. We cannot adjudge that the accused had any vested right in the rule of evidence which obtained prior to the passage of the Missouri statute, nor that the rule established by that statute entrenched upon any of the essential rights belonging to one put on trial for a public offence.

Of course, we are not to be understood as holding that there may not be such a statutory alteration of the fundamental rules in criminal trials as might bring the statute in conflict with the *ex post facto* clause of the Constitution. If, for instance, the statute had taken from the jury the right to determine the sufficiency or effect of the evidence which it made admissible, a different question would have been presented. We mean now only to adjudge that the statute is to be regarded as one merely regulating procedure and may be applied to crimes committed prior to its passage without impairing the substantial guarantees of life and liberty that are secured to an accused by the supreme law of the land.

The judgment of the Supreme Court of Missouri is affirmed.[1]

1. A law is not *ex post facto* which makes certain matters admissible in evidence. State v. Dowden, 137 Iowa 573, 115 N.W. 211 (1908). A law is not *ex*

PEOPLE v. GILL

Supreme Court of California, 1856.
6 Cal. 637.

MR. CHIEF JUSTICE MURRAY delivered the opinion of the Court. MR. JUSTICE TERRY concurred.

The prisoner was indicted for murder, charged to have been committed on the 22d day of March, 1856, and was found "guilty of the crime of murder in the second degree."

post facto which enlarges the class of persons who can testify. Hopt v. Utah, 110 U.S. 574, 4 S.Ct. 202, 28 L.Ed. 262 (1884). Cf. Mrous v. State, 31 Tex.Cr.R. 597, 21 S.W. 764 (1893); Wester v. State, 142 Ala. 56, 38 So. 1010 (1905).

Laws do not come within the *ex post facto* rule if they merely regulate the mode of procedure in criminal cases and do not interfere with substantial protections theretofore granted to the accused. Cooley, Constitutional Limitations 372–83 (7th ed., Lane, 1903); Kring v. Missouri, 107 U.S. 221, 2 S.Ct. 443, 27 L.Ed. 506 (1882); People v. Mortimer, 46 Cal. 114 (1873); Marion v. State, 20 Neb. 233, 29 N.W. 911 (1886). Thus the legislature may change the place of trial or the tribunal. Cook v. United States, 138 U.S. 157, 11 S.Ct. 268, 34 L.Ed. 906 (1891); Commonwealth v. Phelps, 210 Mass. 78, 96 N.E. 349 (1911); Commonwealth v. Phillips, 28 Mass. 28 (1831); State v. Jackson, 105 Mo. 196, 16 S.W. 829 (1891); People v. Green, 201 N.Y. 172, 94 N.E. 658 (1911); State v. Cooler, 30 S.C. 105, 8 S.E. 692 (1889); State v. Welch, 65 Vt. 50, 25 A. 900 (1892). A statute authorizing an appeal by the State in proceedings for condemnation of liquors, relates only to procedure, and is not *ex post facto* as to such proceedings instituted before the act went into effect. State v. Taggart, 186 Iowa 247, 172 N.W. 299 (1919). It is not *ex post facto* to substitute proceedings by information for indictment. Lybarger v. State, 2 Wash. 552, 27 P. 449 (1891); In re Wright, 3 Wyo. 478, 27 P. 565 (1891). Contra: State v. Kingsly, 10 Mont. 537, 26 P. 1066 (1891); McCarty v. State, 1 Wash. 377, 25 P. 299 (1890). These two cases hold otherwise as to crimes committed when the state was a territory and hence governed by the federal constitution.

The statute conferring authority on the board of parole to mitigate sentences and grant paroles to persons convicted before the law took effect is not objectionable as *ex post facto*. Ware v. Sanders, 146 Iowa 233, 124 N.W. 1081 (1910); People ex rel. Liebowitz v. Warden, 186 App.Div. 730, 174 N.Y.S. 823 (1st Dep't 1919). An indeterminate sentence law is not *ex post facto* if it does not increase prior maximum and minimum penalties. Davis v. State, 152 Ind. 34, 51 N.E. 928 (1898); Commonwealth v. Kalck, 239 Pa. 533, 87 A. 61 (1913). The same is true of a law which merely remits a portion of the punishment or otherwise mitigates it. Commonwealth v. Wyman, 66 Mass. 237 (1853); Commonwealth v. Gardner, 77 Mass. 438 (1858); People v. Hayes, 140 N.Y. 484, 35 N.E. 951 (1894). Thus a change may be made from fine "and" imprisonment to fine "or" imprisonment. Hartung v. People, 22 N.Y. 95 (1860). And the death penalty may be changed to imprisonment for life at hard labor. Commonwealth v. Wyman, 66 Mass. 237 (1853); Commonwealth v. Gardner, 77 Mass. 438 (1858). See McInturf v. State, 20 Tex.App. 335 (1886). The contrary was held in New York. Shepherd v. People, 25 N.Y. 406 (1862). Removal of the minimum limit of a penalty is not *ex post facto*. People v. Hayes, 70 Hun 111, 24 N.Y.S. 194 (1893). And mere changes in the details of carrying out the punishment are unobjectionable if no substantial right of the prisoner is affected. Holden v. Minnesota, 137 U.S. 483, 11 S.Ct. 143, 34 L.Ed. 734 (1890). In re Tyson, 13 Colo. 482, 22 P. 810 (1889); State v. Rooney, 12 N.D. 144, 95 N.W. 513 (1903); Gilreath v. Commonwealth, 136 Va. 709, 118 S.E. 100 (1923).

Mere changes of prison discipline or penal administration are not *ex post facto*. People v. Bodjack, 210 Mich. 443, 178 N.W. 228 (1920); Commonwealth v. Kalck, 239 Pa. 533, 87 A. 61 (1913).

A change in the method of selecting grand jury lists is not unconstitutional as applied to a crime already committed. State v. Pell, 140 Iowa 655, 119 N.W. 154 (1909). Nor is a change in the number of

At the time of the killing, charged in the indictment, there was no such crime known to the law as murder in the second degree, and the party could only have been convicted of murder or manslaughter.

The Act defining the offence of which the prisoner is found guilty, was not passed until the 16th of April, 1856, and provides that, upon trials for crimes committed previous to its passage, the party shall be tried by the laws in force at the time of the commission of such crime.

It is supposed, however, that this case presents an exception to the rule thus established. The blow was given before, but the death ensued after, the passage of the last statute. The death must be made to relate back to the unlawful act which occasioned it, and as the party died in consequence of wounds received on a particular day,

grand jurors. State v. Ah Jim, 9 Mont. 167, 23 P. 76 (1890); Hallock v. United States, 185 F. 417 (8th Cir.1911). Nor is a law which changes the mode of summoning or impaneling the jury. Gibson v. Mississippi, 162 U.S. 565, 16 S.Ct. 904, 40 L.Ed. 1075 (1896); Stokes v. People, 53 N.Y. 164 (1873). Nor is one which limits the time for challenging the jurors. State v. Taylor, 134 Mo. 109, 35 S.W. 92 (1896). Nor is one which gives the state additional peremptory challenges. State v. Ryan, 13 Minn. 370 (1868); Walston v. Commonwealth, 16 B.Mon. 15 (Ky.1855). Nor is one which gives the accused fewer peremptory challenges. South v. State, 86 Ala. 617, 6 So. 52 (1889); Mathis v. State, 31 Fla. 291, 12 So. 681 (1893). Nor is one which changes the grounds for challenge. Stokes v. People, 53 N.Y. 164 (1873). Nor is one which changes the requirements as to the pleadings. State v. Manning, 14 Tex. 402 (1855); Perry v. State, 87 Ala. 30, 6 So. 425 (1889). Nor is one which regulates the procedure on appeal. Jacquins v. Commonwealth, 63 Mass. 279 (1852).

Where at the time of defendant's conviction statute provided for a death penalty, which statute was declared unconstitutional, a new statute also applying a death penalty under proper procedures could be applied to prior crime for which defendant was again convicted without violating *ex post facto* provisions. Dobbert v. Florida, 432 U.S. 282, 97 S.Ct. 2290 (1977).

For a position distinguishing *Dobbert*, see People v. Harvey, 76 Cal.App.3d 441, 142 Cal.Rptr. 887 (1978).

A law which provides for separate trials of persons jointly indicted, only when granted by the court for good cause shown, is not *ex post facto* as to pending prosecutions, although the prior law authorized separate trials as a matter of right. Beazell v. Ohio, 269 U.S. 167, 46 S.Ct. 68, 70 L.Ed. 216 (1925).

The change in the mode of execution from hanging to electrocution, though after a verdict of guilty and before sentence does not come within the *ex post facto* rule. Ex parte Johnson, 96 Tex.Cr. R. 473, 258 S.W. 473 (1924).

A statute providing for the seizure and destruction of liquor is not *ex post facto* as to liquor which was lawfully acquired before the law was passed. Samuels v. McCurdy, 267 U.S. 188, 45 S.Ct. 264, 69 L.Ed. 568 (1925).

A statute authorizing the admission of evidence of defendant's history and background, and other matters, in mitigation or aggravation may be applied to an offense committed prior to its enactment without violating the constitutional prohibition against *ex post facto* laws. People v. Feldkamp, 51 Cal.2d 237, 331 P.2d 632 (1958).

The statute provided that by good conduct a convict could earn "good time" and thereby advance the actual date of his release. This statute was amended by substantially reducing the amount of "good time" a convict could earn. In holding that the amended statute could not be applied to a convict whose offense was committed before the effective date of the statute, the Court said: "Thus, even if a statute merely alters penal provisions accorded by the grace of the legislature, it violates the Clause if it is both retrospective and more onerous than the law in effect on the date of the offense." Weaver v. Graham, 450 U.S. 24, 101 S.Ct. 960, 965 (1981).

the day on which the act was committed, and not the one on which the result of the act was determined, is the day on which the murder is properly to be charged.

Besides this, although it is not absolutely necessary to state the precise day on which the killing took place, still, a conviction in a case like the present, where the party was called upon, by the indictment, to answer an offence under one statute, and was found guilty under another, would be bad, and ought to be arrested on motion.

The judgment is reversed, and the Court below directed to re-try the prisoner for murder.[1]

BOUIE v. CITY OF COLUMBIA

Supreme Court of the United States, 1964.
378 U.S. 347, 84 S.Ct. 1697.

[A South Carolina statute provided: "Every entry upon the lands of another . . . after notice from the owner or tenant prohibiting such entry, shall be a misdemeanor and punished. . . . " Petitioners who had received no such notice entered a restaurant where they were not wanted and sat down at the counter. Having refused to leave when ordered to do so, they were arrested and charged with criminal trespass under the statute quoted above. On this charge they were convicted and this conviction was affirmed by the state court which construed the statute to cover not only "the act of entry on the premises of another after receiving notice not to enter, but also the act of remaining on the premises of another after receiving notice to leave." The Supreme Court granted certiorari.]

MR. JUSTICE BRENNAN delivered the opinion of the Court. . . .

We think it clear that the South Carolina Supreme Court, in applying its new construction of the statute to affirm these convictions, has deprived petitioners of rights guaranteed to them by the Due Process Clause. If South Carolina had applied to this case its new statute prohibiting the act of remaining on the premises of another after being asked to leave, the constitutional proscription of *ex post*

1. On the second trial the defendant was convicted of manslaughter. He appealed on the claim that the old law had been repealed. This contention was rejected because the repealing statute contained a saving clause. The conviction was affirmed. People v. Gill, 7 Cal. 356 (1857).

The statute of limitations does not begin to run on the crime of manslaughter until the death of the victim. People v. Rehman, 62 Cal.2d 135, 41 Cal.Rptr. 457, 396 P.2d 913 (1964).

The repeal of a statute subsequent to conviction does not prevent reliance upon that conviction for prosecution under the habitual offender statute. State v. Darrah, 76 N.M. 671, 417 P.2d 805 (1966).

If D was convicted of a crime that was then a felony, this conviction may be relied upon as a prior felony even if because of an amendment it is now a misdemeanor. Ibid.

Enhancement of defendant's sentence under California determinate sentence law was not in violation of bar against ex post facto laws where convictions which occurred prior to the new law were used to enhance the sentence. People v. Williams, 140 Cal.App.3d 445, 189 Cal.Rptr. 497 (1983).

facto laws would clearly invalidate the convictions. The Due Process Clause compels the same result here, where the State has sought to achieve precisely the same effect by judicial construction of the statute. While such a construction is of course valid for the future, it may not be applied retroactively, any more than a legislative enactment may be, to impose criminal penalties for conduct committed at a time when it was not fairly stated to be criminal. Application of this rule is particularly compelling where, as here, the petitioners' conduct cannot be deemed improper or immoral. . . .

In the last analysis the case is controlled, we think, by the principle which Chief Justice Marshall stated for the Court in United States v. Wiltberger, 5 Wheat. 76, 96, 5 L.Ed. 37:

"The case must be a strong one indeed, which would justify a Court in departing from the plain meaning of words, especially in a penal act, in search of an intention which the words themselves did not suggest. To determine that a case is within the intention of a statute, its language must authorise us to say so. It would be dangerous, indeed, to carry the principle, that a case which is within the reason or mischief of a statute, is within its provisions, so far as to punish a crime not enumerated in the statute, because it is of equal atrocity, or of kindred character, with those which are enumerated. . . ."

The crime for which these petitioners stand convicted was "not enumerated in the statute" at the time of their conduct. It follows that they have been deprived of liberty and property without due process of law in contravention of the Fourteenth Amendment.

Reversed.

Chapter 12

PROCEEDINGS PRELIMINARY TO TRIAL

SECTION 1. STEPS BY THE PROSECUTION PRIOR TO INDICTMENT

(A) INTRODUCTION

The presence of one accused of crime is not essential to the finding of an indictment against him and he has no right to be present during this stage of the proceedings. The grand jury can decide whether he should be tried for some particular crime even if he is still at large,—and this is frequently done. On the other hand it is not necessary to wait for the indictment before making an arrest and frequently it is not wise to do so because the one accused might disappear during the deliberations of the grand jury.

If the indictment is found before the accused has been taken into custody a bench warrant will be issued for his arrest. If it is deemed desirable to have the arrest precede the indictment it will be necessary to have a complaint or information made before a magistrate to secure the issuance of a warrant, unless the circumstances are such as to authorize an arrest without a warrant. If the arrest precedes the indictment, and is made in obedience to a warrant, the procedure may follow this general outline (although variations will be found in some jurisdictions): (1) A complaint (or information or affidavit—the procedure varies in different jurisdictions) will be made or filed before a magistrate (or other officer having authority to issue warrants) charging the accused with a specified crime. (2) If the jurisdiction does not require the complaint itself to be in the form of a sworn written document the magistrate will put the complainant under oath while the facts are being stated, after which he may have the statement reduced to writing in the form of an affidavit. In any event the magistrate may require the complainant to answer questions, under oath, and may obtain the sworn statements of other witnesses if available. (3) If the magistrate finds "probable cause" for the charge made against the accused he will issue a warrant for his arrest (unless the magistrate decides that a summons will be sufficient to cause the accused to be present for trial and the law of the jurisdiction authorizes the use of a summons under the facts of the particular case.) (4) This warrant will be delivered to some peace officer for execution. (5) This officer will arrest the accused by virtue of this warrant. (6) The accused will then be taken before the magistrate for preliminary examination. (7) The result of the preliminary examination will be that the defendant is either discharged or "held to answer." (8) If held to answer he will be either bailed or committed to jail. (9) If he is committed to jail the magistrate (in many jurisdictions) will make out a warrant of commitment which he will deliver with the defendant to the officer. (10) The prosecuting attorney (unless he files an information against the accused, if the law of the jurisdiction permits such procedure) will file a bill of indictment to be presented to the grand jury. (11) The grand jury will hear evidence in support of the charge against the accused and will either find it to be a "true bill" or they will "ignore" it (fail to find it to be a true bill). (12) If the bill of indictment is found by the grand jury to be a "true bill" it will be properly indorsed and filed (whereupon the accused stands indicted for the crime charged against him). (13) The defendant (he was not strictly speaking a "defendant" until a formal pleading had been filed against him by the state) will be arraigned (called to the bar of the court to answer to the accusation contained in the indictment). (14) If the defendant pleads not guilty he will be tried by a petit jury (unless the jurisdiction authorizes the waiver of a jury in such a case and the jury is waived by defendant,—in which event he will be tried by the judge without a jury). (15) As a result of this trial the jury (if able to agree) will bring in a verdict of "guilty" (of the offense charged or of some lesser "included" offense) or "not guilty." (16) After the verdict of the jury the judge will pronounce the judgment (unless the verdict was "guilty" and the judgment is "arrested," or the pronouncement of judgment is suspended,—where this is permitted). The judgment will be one of acquittal if the verdict was "not guilty," and of conviction if the verdict was "guilty."

Various other steps may follow if the judgment is one of conviction, depending upon whether the defendant accepts this pronouncement as final or asks for a new trial or an appeal or a pardon, and so forth. But it is not necessary for the moment to carry this outline beyond the judgment of the trial court. It should be added that if the judgment is one of conviction the judge will also pronounce the penalty imposed upon the convicted defendant, unless a new trial has been granted or an appeal taken. This is the "sentence." In some jurisdictions, if the conviction is for felony, the "sentence" pronounced by the court may be in general terms and the actual term of incarceration may be determined later by some board or "authority."

Under sound theory these two pronouncements—(i.e. that of conviction and the sentence) are both judgments, although they are frequently referred to as "judgment and sentence." Both may be pronounced at the same time or the judgment of conviction may be entered at once and the sentence be pronounced at a later time.[1]

It should also be mentioned that other steps may or may not be involved, such as an application for bail, an attack upon the validity of the indictment, an application for a change of venue, and so forth.

In some jurisdictions, if probation is indicated after guilt has been established by verdict or plea, the judge may either pronounce sentence and suspend the execution thereof, or he may postpone the pronouncement of sentence. One judge, years ago before probation officers had been provided for him, began the practice of suspending the sentence on condition that the defendant get a job, go to work and save his earnings above his reasonably necessary expenses by depositing a stipulated amount each week with the clerk, to be returned to him later if he lived up to the condition. Willingness or unwillingness to work, he concluded, was the best test to divide the sheep from the goats. His study of nonsupport cases brought to light the fact that frequently failure to support the family resulted from getting drunk after receiving the week's pay and spending the money while in that condition. If, as was frequently the fact, the man did not indulge in excessive drinking during the week, the judge added special conditions to his probation. His pay check was to be delivered to some responsible agency to be used for the benefit of the entire family, including himself. And from the end of the work week until Monday morning he was to be in jail.[a]

(B) THE COMPLAINT

To secure the issuance of a warrant of arrest (of one who has not been indicted or informed against) it is necessary to go before a magistrate or other officer authorized to issue warrants, and satisfy him in the manner prescribed by law that proper ground exists. This involves making a "complaint", and although the common law did not require it to be in written form, this is required today. For example: "The complaint is a written statement of the essential facts constituting the offense charged. It shall be made upon oath before a magistrate.[1] And in the words of the Federal Rules of Criminal Procedure:

1. After the Supreme Court had held that existing statutes providing for capital punishment, as enforced, were unconstitutional, the Governor of Tennessee commuted two death sentences to 99 years imprisonment. After this was affirmed by the state Court of Criminal Appeals, and the Supreme Court of the State had denied certiorari, the prisoners petitioned for habeas corpus in the United States District Court. The District Court dismissed but this was reversed by the United States Court of Appeals on the ground that there were no viable death sentences to commute. This in turn was reversed by the Supreme Court on the ground that no federal question was involved. If the state law allows the governor to reduce a death sentence to a term of years this does not violate the constitution. Rose v. Hodges, 423 U.S. 19, 96 S.Ct. 175 (1975).

a. For an interesting study of probation see Gwyn, Work, Earn and Save, published by Institutes for Civic Education, Extension Division, University of North Carolina, Chapel Hill.

1. Fed.R.Crim.P. 3.

"If it appears from the complaint, or from an affidavit or affidavits filed with the complaint, that there is probable cause to believe that an offense has been committed and that the defendant has committed it, a warrant for the arrest of the defendant shall issue to any officer authorized by law to execute it." [2]

(C) THE WARRANT

Criminal procedure stems from the machinery developed for the handling of felony cases when all felonies were punishable by death. Many important changes have been made but all too frequently the steps now taken are still dominated by theories which should have been modified when milder punishments were provided for most felonies and which never should have applied in misdemeanor cases. This is well illustrated at this point in our procedure in many jurisdictions.

If complaint has been made before a magistrate charging a person with a capital crime, and it is sufficient to constitute "probable cause" of his guilt thereof, the first effort should be directed toward getting the supposed felon into custody. This is important first because it may be necessary to protect the community from other felonies that might be perpetrated by the same offender and second because there is no other way to assure his presence when it may be needed for the trial.

Many offenses are committed, however, under such circumstances that no more is needed than an official communication to the person accused thereof to appear for trial at a specified time and place. Where this is true it is an unnecessary burden upon officers charged with the enforcement of the law to require them to arrest the accused and take him before a magistrate for the purpose of giving bail. It is also an unnecessary hardship to be inflicted upon the accused himself,—particularly if he happens to be innocent of the offense charged. Hence the time has long passed when a warrant of arrest should be regarded as the logical result of every complaint. Except in the case of more serious crimes it might well be regarded as the exception rather than the rule. More will be said of this in the subsection entitled "Summons."

Reflecting the ancient theory a number of the statutes make it mandatory upon the magistrate to issue a warrant of arrest if "probable cause" or "reasonable ground to believe" is established supported by oath or affirmation. The following is an example:

If the "magistrate is satisfied from the complaint that the offense complained of has been committed and that there is reasonable ground to believe that the defendant has committed it, he must issue his warrant for the arrest of the defendant." [1]

2. Fed.R.Crim.P. 4.

1. West's Ann.Cal.Pen.Code, § 813 (1978). An amendment provides that a "judge of the justice court who is not a member of the State Bar may issue such a warrant only upon the concurrence of

The Model Code of Criminal Procedure recommends the issuance of a summons in certain situations and the direction that the magistrate issue a warrant has an appropriate exception.[2]

Anciently any official command or order which authorized an arrest was spoken of as a "warrant of arrest." This included the oral order of a magistrate to arrest one who had committed a felony or breach of the peace in his presence.[3] This usage has left a trace still to be observed. Many statutes make provision for arrest on the oral order of a magistrate for an offense committed in his presence and also for arrests without a warrant (as well as for arrests in obedience to a warrant). And an arrest on such an oral order of a magistrate is not within the limitations provided for an arrest *without a warrant.*

What is now known as a "warrant of arrest," however, must be in writing. It has been defined as a "written order directing the arrest of a person or persons, issued by a court, body or official, having authority to issue warrants." [4]

The American Law Institute, after an exhaustive study of various statutes included the following as section 3 of its model Code of Criminal Procedure:

> *Section 3. Form and contents of warrant.* The warrant of arrest shall
>
> (a) be in writing and in the name of the State [Commonwealth or People];
>
> (b) set forth substantially the nature of the offense;
>
> (c) command that the person against whom the complaint was made be arrested and brought before the magistrate issuing the warrant or, if he is absent or unable to act, before the nearest or most accessible magistrate in the same county;
>
> (d) specify the name of the person to be arrested or, if his name is unknown to the magistrate, shall designate such person by any name or description by which he can be identified with reasonable certainty;
>
> (e) state the date when issued and the municipality or county where issued; and
>
> (f) be signed by the magistrate with the title of his office.

the district attorney" or the Attorney General. See also the statutes in Alabama, Arizona, Idaho, Oklahoma, South Dakota, Tennessee. For mandatory provisions in somewhat different form see the statutes in Indiana, Michigan, Missouri, Nebraska, Nevada, New Mexico, Wisconsin and Wyoming.

2. American Law Institute, Code of Criminal Procedure, § 2 (1930).

A recent proposal provides that a warrant "may" issue and authorizes a warrant for an offense of serious bodily injury or where defendant would not respond to a summons. Unif. Rules of Crim. Procedure, Second Tent.Draft, Rule 3(b) (1973).

3. Lord Hale, writing in the seventeenth century, speaks of such an oral order of a magistrate as "a good warrant without writing." 2 Hale P.C. *86.

4. Restatement, Second, Torts, § 113 (1965).

The customary statutory provision is much more general than this with a suggested form to be followed in substance. The following are given in the Federal Rules of Criminal Procedure:

Rule 4. . . . (c) Form. (1) Warrant. The warrant shall be signed by the magistrate and shall contain the name of the defendant or, if his name is unknown, any name or description by which he can be identified with reasonable certainty. It shall describe the offense charged in the complaint. It shall command that the defendant be arrested and brought before the nearest available magistrate.

(2) . . . .

Federal Rules of Criminal Procedure

Form 12

Warrant For Arrest Of Defendant

In the United States District Court for the ______ District ______ of ______ Division.

United States of America
v. } No. ______
John Doe

To ______________________[5]

You are hereby commanded to arrest John Doe and bring him forthwith before the District Court for the ______ District of ______ in the city of ______ to answer to an indictment charging him with robbery of property of the First National Bank of ______ in violation of 12 U.S.C.A. § 588b.

____
Clerk

By ______________________
Deputy Clerk

5. Insert designation of officer to whom warrant is issued, e.g., "any United States Marshal or any other authorized officer"; or "United States Marshal for __ District of __"; or "any United States Marshal"; or "any Special Agent of the Federal Bureau of Investigation"; or "any United States Marshal or any Special Agent of the Federal Bureau of Investigation" or "any agent of the Alcohol Tax Unit". [This is note 1 to the official form.]

"An arrest warrant that correctly names the person to be arrested generally satisfies the fourth amendment's particularity requirement, . . . On the other hand . . . an arrest warrant that incorrectly names the person to be arrested will usually be deemed insufficient . . . unless it includes some other description of the intended arrestee that is sufficient to identify him." Powe v. City of Chicago, 664 F.2d 639, 645 (7th Cir. 1981). It was held that the giving of one or two of several names by which the person is familiarly known is insufficient without identifying description.

The Fourth Amendment to the Constitution of the United States provides:

> The right of the people to be secure in their persons, houses, papers, and effects, against unreasonable searches and seizures, shall not be violated, and no Warrants shall issue, but upon probable cause, supported by Oath or affirmation, and particularly describing the place to be searched, and the persons or things to be seized.

Such a provision does not forbid every arrest (or search) without a warrant, since this part of it merely bars "unreasonable searches and seizures." It does forbid an arrest (or search) without a warrant wherever this would be unreasonable, and it places limitations upon the issuance of warrants.

The validity of a warrant is not dependent upon the fact of crime having been committed or the guilt of the person accused.[6] It is dependent entirely upon three other factors which are: (1) compliance with all of the legal requirements for the issuance of a warrant, (2) jurisdiction of the magistrate or other issuing authority, and (3) regularity in the form of the warrant.[7] For obvious reasons one who properly executes a valid warrant is fully protected.[8] The protection may go even beyond this. So far as the executing officer is concerned the inquiry is not whether the warrant was actually valid or not, but whether it was "fair on its face" or *obviously* invalid.[9] As said by the California Court: "Where a warrant valid in form and issued by a court of competent jurisdiction is placed in the hands of an officer for execution, it is his duty without delay to carry out its commands. The law is well settled that for the proper execution of such process the officer incurs no liability, however disastrous may be the effect of its execution upon the person against whom it is issued." [10]

The constitutional provision quoted, and the corresponding clauses of the state constitutions, bar unreasonable searches and seizures of both persons and property, and the limitations upon the issuance of warrants apply to warrants of arrest and to search warrants. One type of warrant commands the seizure of a person, the other commands a search for property with the direction that it be seized if

6. Restatement, Second, Torts § 123, comment *a* (1965).

7. Id. at § 123.

8. Id. at § 122.

9. Id. at § 124.

10. Malone v. Carey, 17 Cal.App.2d 505, 506–7, 62 P.2d 166, 167 (1936).

A warrant can have no authority beyond the territorial boundaries of the issuing jurisdiction. Hence an arrest in Kansas by a deputy sheriff of Oklahoma under a warrant from a district court of Oklahoma was unlawful. Stuart v. Mayberry, 105 Okl. 13, 231 P. 491 (1924). But a Kentucky warrant charging a specified felony constituted "reasonable information" to a Virginia officer that accused was charged in the other state with a crime punishable by imprisonment for more than a year and authorized the officer to arrest the accused without a warrant. Mullins v. Sanders, 189 Va. 624, 54 S.E.2d 116 (1949).

found. Aside from the purpose to be accomplished they have much in common. The most outstanding difference is in regard to the life of the warrant issued. A warrant of arrest is good until executed or withdrawn,[11] whereas a search warrant is valid for a very short period only frequently expiring, if not executed, in three [12] or ten days.[13]

Where a bench warrant has been authorized by the court the actual issuance of the warrant is a ministerial act.[14]

No warrant is valid unless there was "probable cause" for its issuance, and in the case of an arrest warrant this means there was "probable cause", or reasonable ground to believe, that a crime has been, or is being, committed by the person accused. A warrant may be issued on the basis of credible hearsay evidence.[15] It has been held that information received through an informant is acceptable so long as the informant's statement is reasonably corroborated by other matters within the officer's knowledge.[16]

Since it is the magistrate, or other issuing officer who must find probable cause for the issuance of the warrant, the complaint together with the accompanying affidavits, if any, must contain information needed for this purpose. And as this problem is the same in regard to the issuance of arrest warrants and search warrants the cases are interchangeable, so to speak.

11. A warrant of arrest does not expire by lapse of time but remains in effect until executed. State v. Bell, 334 So. 2d 385 (La.1976).

It was held that a deportation warrant, which is a warrant of arrest and deportation, was prima facie valid although it had been outstanding for 11 years. Belaskus v. Crossman, 164 F.2d 412 (5th Cir. 1947).

12. Swanson v. State, 113 Tex.Cr.R. 104, 18 S.W.2d 1082 (1929).

13. McClary v. State, 34 Okl.Cr. 403, 246 P. 891 (1926).

"It shall command the officer to search within a specified period of time not to exceed 10 days. . . ." Rule 41(c)(1) F.R.Cr.P.

14. State v. Gordon, 18 La.Ann. 528 (1866).

15. Jones v. United States, 362 U.S. 257, 80 S.Ct. 725 (1960); Draper v. United States, 358 U.S. 307, 79 S.Ct. 329 (1959).

16. Jones v. United States, 362 U.S. 257, 80 S.Ct. 725 (1960).

Through a glass front door of D's apartment an officer saw a yellow hand-rolled cigarette which he reasonably believed to be marijuana. The officer had knocked at the door to request the occupant to turn down the volume of the stereo, which was annoying other occupants of the building. When the door was opened the officer detected the odor of burning marijuana. He requested permission to enter, and when this was denied he forced his way in because he had "seen it and smelled it." He seized the cigarette he had seen from the outside, and two others, and it was found they were in fact marijuana. It was held error not to suppress this evidence. The court held that the officer had sufficient evidence to secure a search warrant, but this would not authorize a warrantless search in the absence of "exigent circumstances" which were held to be lacking in this case. The court seems not to have been impressed by the claim that the evidence would have been disposed of before a search warrant could be obtained. State v. Schur, 217 Kan. 741, 538 P.2d 689 (1975).

For the difference between a warrantless search, which requires "exigent circumstances," and a warrantless arrest, which does not, see United States v. Watson, 423 U.S. 411, 96 S.Ct. 820 (1976).

ILLINOIS v. GATES

Supreme Court of the United States, 1983.
___ U.S. ___, 103 S.Ct. 2317.

JUSTICE REHNQUIST delivered the opinion of the Court.

Respondents Lance and Susan Gates were indicted for violation of state drug laws after police officers, executing a search warrant, discovered marijuana and other contraband in their automobile and home. Prior to trial the Gates' moved to suppress evidence seized during this search. The Illinois Supreme Court, 85 Ill.2d 376, 53 Ill. Dec. 218, 423 N.E.2d 887 (1981) affirmed the decisions of lower state courts, 82 Ill.App.3d 749, 38 Ill.Dec. 62, 403 N.E.2d 77 (1980) granting the motion. It held that the affidavit submitted in support of the State's application for a warrant to search the Gates' property was inadequate under this Court's decisions in Aguilar v. Texas, 378 U.S. 108, 84 S.Ct. 1509, 12 L.Ed.2d 723 (1964) and Spinelli v. United States, 393 U.S. 410, 89 S.Ct. 584, 21 L.Ed.2d 637 (1969).

We granted certiorari to consider the application of the Fourth Amendment to a magistrate's issuance of a search warrant on the basis of a partially corroborated anonymous informant's tip. . . .

We now turn to the question presented in the State's original petition for certiorari, which requires us to decide whether respondents' rights under the Fourth and Fourteenth Amendments were violated by the search of their car and house. A chronological statement of events usefully introduces the issues at stake. Bloomingdale, Ill., is a suburb of Chicago located in DuPage County. On May 3, 1978, the Bloomingdale Police Department received by mail an anonymous handwritten letter which read as follows:

> "This letter is to inform you that you have a couple in your town who strictly make their living on selling drugs. They are Sue and Lance Gates, they live on Greenway, off Bloomingdale Rd. in the condominums. Most of their buys are done in Florida. Sue his wife drives their car to Florida, where she leaves it to be loaded up with drugs, then Lance flys down and drives it back. Sue flys back after she drops the car off in Florida. May 3 she is driving down there again and Lance will be flying down in a few days to drive it back. At the time Lance drives the car back he has the trunk loaded with over $100,000.00 in drugs. Presently they have over $100,000.00 worth of drugs in their basement.
>
> They brag about the fact they never have to work, and make their entire living on pushers.

I guarantee if you watch them carefully you will make a big catch. They are friends with some big drugs dealers, who visit their house often.

Lance & Susan Gates

Greenway

In Condominiums"

The letter was referred by the Chief of Police of the Bloomingdale Police Department to Detective Mader, who decided to pursue the tip. Mader learned, from the office of the Illinois Secretary of State, that an Illinois driver's license had been issued to one Lance Gates, residing at a stated address in Bloomingdale. He contacted a confidential informant, whose examination of certain financial records revealed a more recent address for the Gates, and he also learned from a police officer assigned to O'Hare Airport that "L. Gates" had made a reservation on Eastern Airlines flight 245 to West Palm Beach, Fla., scheduled to depart from Chicago on May 5 at 4:15 p.m.

Mader then made arrangements with an agent of the Drug Enforcement Administration for surveillance of the May 5 Eastern Airlines flight. The agent later reported to Mader that Gates had boarded the flight, and that federal agents in Florida had observed him arrive in West Palm Beach and take a taxi to the nearby Holiday Inn. They also reported that Gates went to a room registered to one Susan Gates and that, at 7:00 a.m. the next morning, Gates and an unidentified woman left the motel in a Mercury bearing Illinois license plates and drove northbound on an interstate frequently used by travelers to the Chicago area. In addition, the DEA agent informed Mader that the license plate number on the Mercury registered to a Hornet station wagon owned by Gates. The agent also advised Mader that the driving time between West Palm Beach and Bloomingdale was approximately 22 to 24 hours.

Mader signed an affidavit setting forth the foregoing facts, and submitted it to a judge of the Circuit Court of DuPage County, together with a copy of the anonymous letter. The judge of that court thereupon issued a search warrant for the Gates' residence and for their automobile. The judge, in deciding to issue the warrant, could have determined that the *modus operandi* of the Gates had been substantially corroborated. As the anonymous letter predicted, Lance Gates had flown from Chicago to West Palm Beach late in the afternoon of May 5th, had checked into a hotel room registered in the name of his wife, and, at 7:00 a.m. the following morning, had headed north, accompanied by an unidentified woman, out of West Palm Beach on an interstate highway used by travelers from South Florida to Chicago in an automobile bearing a license plate issued to him.

At 5:15 a.m. on March 7th, only 36 hours after he had flown out of Chicago, Lance Gates, and his wife, returned to their home in Bloomingdale, driving the car in which they had left West Palm Beach some

22 hours earlier. The Bloomingdale police were awaiting them, searched the trunk of the Mercury, and uncovered approximately 350 pounds of marijuana. A search of the Gates' home revealed marijuana, weapons, and other contraband. The Illinois Circuit Court ordered suppression of all these items, on the ground that the affidavit submitted to the Circuit Judge failed to support the necessary determination of probable cause to believe that the Gates' automobile and home contained the contraband in question. This decision was affirmed in turn by the Illinois Appellate Court and by a divided vote of the Supreme Court of Illinois.

The Illinois Supreme Court concluded—and we are inclined to agree—that, standing alone, the anonymous letter sent to the Bloomingdale Police Department would not provide the basis for a magistrate's determination that there was probable cause to believe contraband would be found in the Gates' car and home. The letter provides virtually nothing from which one might conclude that its author is either honest or his information reliable; likewise, the letter gives absolutely no indication of the basis for the writer's predictions regarding the Gates' criminal activities. Something more was required, then, before a magistrate could conclude that there was probable cause to believe that contraband would be found in the Gates' home and car.

The Illinois Supreme Court also properly recognized that Detective Mader's affidavit might be capable of supplementing the anonymous letter with information sufficient to permit a determination of probable cause. In holding that the affidavit in fact did not contain sufficient additional information to sustain a determination of probable cause, the Illinois court applied a "two-pronged test," derived from our decision in Spinelli v. United States, 393 U.S. 410, 89 S.Ct. 584, 21 L.Ed.2d 637 (1969). The Illinois Supreme Court, like some others, apparently understood *Spinelli* as requiring that the anonymous letter satisfy each of two independent requirements before it could be relied on. J.A., at 5. According to this view, the letter, as supplemented by Mader's affidavit, first had to adequately reveal the "basis of knowledge" of the letter writer—the particular means by which he came by the information given in his report. Second, it had to provide facts sufficiently establishing either the "veracity" of the affiant's informant, or, alternatively, the "reliability" of the informant's report in this particular case.[a]

a. [Added by the Compiler.] A confidential informant who had frequently given the police information resulting in narcotics arrests, and whose information had always been reliable, telephoned L, a detective. The informant said that in approximately 15 minutes D would be driving to a specified parking lot, that he would be driving a black & gray Buick Riviera, license No. BB–6400 and would have several balloons of heroin with him. L went to the specified parking lot, saw D arrive there at the time indicated, driving a black & gray Buick Riviera, license No. BB–6400, and drive slowly from aisle to aisle as if looking for someone. L then arrested D and seized several balloons of heroin which were found in the car. It was held that the tip was so replete with detail as to be self-verifying. The court held the *Aguilar-Spinelli* test was satisfied relying upon *Draper.* Peo-

The Illinois court, alluding to an elaborate set of legal rules that have developed among various lower courts to enforce the "two-pronged test," found that the test had not been satisfied. First, the "veracity" prong was not satisfied because, "there was simply no basis [for] . . . conclud[ing] that the anonymous person [who wrote the letter to the Bloomingdale Police Department] was credible." J.A., at 7a. The court indicated that corroboration by police of details contained in the letter might never satisfy the "veracity" prong, and in any event, could not do so if, as in the present case, only "innocent" details are corroborated. J.A., at 12a. In addition, the letter gave no indication of the basis of its writer's knowledge of the Gates' activities. The Illinois court understood *Spinelli* as permitting the detail contained in a tip to be used to infer that the informant had a reliable basis for his statements, but it thought that the anonymous letter failed to provide sufficient detail to permit such an inference. Thus, it concluded that no showing of probable cause had been made.

We agree with the Illinois Supreme Court that an informant's "veracity," "reliability" and "basis of knowledge" are all highly relevant in determining the value of his report. We do not agree, however, that these elements should be understood as entirely separate and independent requirements to be rigidly exacted in every case, which the opinion of the Supreme Court of Illinois would imply. Rather, as detailed below, they should be understood simply as closely intertwined issues that may usefully illuminate the commonsense, practical question whether there is "probable cause" to believe that contraband or evidence is located in a particular place.

This totality of the circumstances approach is far more consistent with our prior treatment of probable cause than is any rigid demand that specific "tests" be satisfied by every informant's tip. . . .

If, for example, a particular informant is known for the unusual reliability of his predictions of certain types of criminal activities in a locality, his failure, in a particular case, to thoroughly set forth the basis of his knowledge surely should not serve as an absolute bar to a finding of probable cause based on his tip. Likewise, if an unquestionably honest citizen comes forward with a report of criminal activity—which if fabricated would subject him to criminal liability—we have found rigorous scrutiny of the basis of his knowledge unnecessary. Conversely, even if we entertain some doubt as to an informant's motives, his explicit and detailed description of alleged wrongdo-

ple v. Williams, 189 Colo. 311, 541 P.2d 76 (1975).

Where the informer was a witness to the crime it was reversible error to refuse to disclose his identity on demand at the trial. Roviaro v. United States, 353 U.S. 53, 77 S.Ct. 623 (1957). The identity of the informer must be disclosed (or the prosecution dismissed) if there is a reasonable possibility that he could give evidence on the issue of guilt which might exonerate **D**. Honore v. Superior Court, 70 Cal.2d 162, 74 Cal.Rptr. 233, 449 P.2d 169 (1969).

But where the informer was relied upon only to establish probable cause for the arrest of **D** his identity need not be disclosed. McCray v. Illinois, 386 U.S. 300, 87 S.Ct. 1056 (1967).

ing, along with a statement that the event was observed first-hand, entitles his tip to greater weight than might otherwise be the case. Unlike a totality of circumstances analysis, which permits a balanced assessment of the relative weights of all the various indicia of reliability (and unreliability) attending an informant's tip, the "two-pronged test" has encouraged an excessively technical dissection of informants' tips, with undue attention being focused on isolated issues that cannot sensibly be divorced from the other facts presented to the magistrate. . . .

For all these reasons, we conclude that it is wiser to abandon the "two-pronged test" established by our decisions in *Aguilar* and *Spinelli.* In its place we reaffirm the totality of the circumstances analysis that traditionally has informed probable cause determinations. The task of the issuing magistrate is simply to make a practical, common-sense decision whether, given all the circumstances set forth in the affidavit before him, including the "veracity" and "basis of knowledge" of persons supplying hearsay information, there is a fair probability that contraband or evidence of a crime will be found in a particular place. And the duty of a reviewing court is simply to ensure that the magistrate had a "substantial basis for . . . conclud[ing]" that probable cause existed. We are convinced that this flexible, easily applied standard will better achieve the accommodation of public and private interests that the Fourth Amendment requires than does the approach that has developed from *Aguilar* and *Spinelli.*

Our earlier cases illustrate the limits beyond which a magistrate may not venture in issuing a warrant. A sworn statement of an affiant that "he has cause to suspect and does believe that" liquor illegally brought into the United States is located on certain premises will not do. An affidavit must provide the magistrate with a substantial basis for determining the existence of probable cause, and the wholly conclusory statement at issue in *Nathanson* failed to meet this requirement. An officer's statement that "affiants have received reliable information from a credible person and believe" that heroin is stored in a home, is likewise inadequate. As in *Nathanson,* this is a mere conclusory statement that gives the magistrate virtually no basis at all for making a judgment regarding probable cause. Sufficient information must be presented to the magistrate to allow that official to determine probable cause; his action cannot be a mere ratification of the bare conclusions of others. In order to ensure that such an abdication of the magistrate's duty does not occur, courts must continue, to conscientiously review the sufficiency of affidavits on which warrants are issued. But when we move beyond the "bare bones" affidavits present in cases such as *Nathanson* and *Aguilar,* this area simply does not lend itself to a prescribed set of rules, like that which had developed from *Spinelli.* Instead, the flexible, common-sense standard articulated in *Jones, Ventresca,* and *Brinegar* better serves the purposes of the Fourth Amendment's probable cause requirement. . . .

Our decision in Draper v. United States, 358 U.S. 307, 79 S.Ct. 329, 3 L.Ed.2d 327 (1959), however, is the classic case on the value of corroborative efforts of police officials. There, an informant named Hereford reported that Draper would arrive in Denver on a train for Chicago on one of two days, and that he would be carrying a quantity of heroin. The informant also supplied a fairly detailed physical description of Draper, and predicted that he would be wearing a light colored raincoat, brown slacks and black shoes, and would be walking "real fast". Hereford gave no indication of the basis for his information.

On one of the stated dates police officers observed a man matching this description exit a train arriving from Chicago; his attire and luggage matched Hereford's report and he was walking rapidly. We explained in *Draper* that, by this point in his investigation, the arresting officer "had personally verified every facet of the information given him by Hereford except whether petitioner had accomplished his mission and had the three ounces of heroin on his person or in his bag. And surely, with every other bit of Hereford's information being thus personally verified, [the officer] had 'reasonable grounds' to believe that the remaining unverified bit of Hereford's information—that Draper would have the heroin with him—was likewise true."

The showing of probable cause in the present case was fully as compelling as that in *Draper*. . . .

Finally, the anonymous letter contained a range of details relating not just to easily obtained facts and conditions existing at the time of the tip, but to future actions of third parties ordinarily not easily predicted. The letter writer's accurate information as to the travel plans of each of the Gates was of a character likely obtained only from the Gates themselves, or from someone familiar with their not entirely ordinary travel plans. If the informant had access to accurate information of this type a magistrate could properly conclude that it was not unlikely that he also had access to reliable information of the Gates' alleged illegal activities. Of course, the Gates' travel plans might have been learned from a talkative neighbor or travel agent; under the "two-pronged test" developed from *Spinelli*, the character of the details in the anonymous letter might well not permit a sufficiently clear inference regarding the letter writer's "basis of knowledge." But, as discussed previously, supra, 2332, probable cause does not demand the certainty we associate with formal trials. It is enough that there was a fair probability that the writer of the anonymous letter had obtained his entire story either from the Gates or someone they trusted. And corroboration of major portions of the letter's predictions provides just this probability. It is apparent, therefore, that the judge issuing the warrant had a "substantial basis for . . . conclud[ing]" that probable cause to search the Gates' home and car existed. The judgment of the Supreme Court of Illinois therefore must be

Reversed.[b]

JUSTICE WHITE, concurring in the judgment.

b. [Added by the Compiler.] In a prior case it was held that reputation attributes could be considered in determining probable cause and that statements against an informant's penal interest were entitled to be credited in determining reliability. United States v. Harris, 403 U.S. 573, 91 S.Ct. 2075 (1971).

An affidavit that is insufficient cannot be rehabilitated by testimony concerning information possessed by the affiant when the warrant was sought but not at that time disclosed to the magistrate. Whiteley v. Warden, 401 U.S. 560, 91 S.Ct. 1031 (1971).

An affidavit stating that affiant personally searched the informant in advance, observed the informant entering specified premises and returning with marijuana, was sufficient to authorize the issuance of a search warrant. Glantz v. District Court, 154 Mont. 132, 461 P.2d 193 (1969).

An affidavit stating that an informant showed affiant where several burglaries had been committed and told exactly what had been taken, which proved to be correct when checked with police records, and also stated that a suit stolen from one particular address (which also proved on checking to be correct) was hanging in the bedroom of **D**, was sufficient to authorize the issuance of a search warrant. State v. Scott, 11 Ariz.App. 68, 461 P.2d 712 (1969).

Officers who saw **D** run by, and who heard a bystander shouting "Stop thief", had probable cause to arrest **D** without a warrant. It was not necessary to find the victim and establish the theft before giving chase. State v. Franklin, 104 Ariz. 324, 452 P.2d 498 (1969).

If there is some evidence of a possibility that the informer is a material witness to the crime charged against **D**, the People must either disclose the informer's identity or incur a dismissal. Price v. Superior Court, 1 Cal.3d 836, 83 Cal.Rptr. 369, 463 P.2d 721 (1970).

An affidavit in support of a warrant may be challenged by showing a false statement by the affiant knowingly and intentionally made, with reckless disregard for the truth, was included in the affidavit, if the statement was necessary to the finding of probable cause. On such a showing a hearing must be held and if it is determined that such circumstances exist, the fruits of a search must be excluded. Franks v. Delaware, 438 U.S. 154, 98 S.Ct. 2674 (1978).

Applying state law, it was held that an affidavit containing deliberately false statements requires the court to void the warrant regardless of the statement's effect on probable cause. People v. Cook, 22 Cal.3d 67, 148 Cal.Rptr. 605, 583 P.2d 130 (1978).

Good faith error in a carefully prepared search warrant affidavit does not require suppression of the evidence seized, even where the erroneous allegation was essential to the establishment of probable cause. The purpose of the exclusionary rule is to deter police misconduct, and good faith errors cannot be deterred. United States v. Luna, 525 F.2d 4 (6th Cir. 1975).

A crime victim who witnessed the crime was presumptively reliable as "citizen-informant," for purposes of testing sufficiency of search warrant affidavit, though his reliability had not been previously tested, and police officers were also presumed to be reliable, and thus statements of the victim and of officers could be relied upon to the extent they were based on their personal observations. People v. Hill, 12 Cal.3d 731, 117 Cal. Rptr. 393, 528 P.2d 1 (1974).

The Affidavit was held to be sufficient. People v. MacLeish, 16 Cal.App.3d 96, 93 Cal.Rptr. 679 (1971).

PEOPLE v. MONTOYA

Court of Appeal, First District, Division 2, 1967.
255 Cal.App.2d 137, 63 Cal.Rptr. 73.

[A search of the defendant, after his arrest, had revealed two $100 bills. The introduction of this evidence at the trial was insisted upon as error.]

TAYLOR, ASSOCIATE JUSTICE. Defendant, Thomas Montoya, appeals from a judgment of conviction entered on a jury verdict finding him guilty of robbery (Pen.Code, § 211), arguing that he was arrested pursuant to an invalid warrant that did not contain any description of the person to be seized and was therefore in violation of article I, section 19, of the state Constitution, as well as the Fourth Amendment of the Constitution of the United States. Defendant also contends that the warrant did not state the time of its issuance, as required by section 815 of the Penal Code. . . .

Defendant first argues that the warrant violates article I, section 19 of the state Constitution, which provides, so far as pertinent: ". . . no warrant shall issue, but on probable cause, supported by oath or affirmation, particularly describing the place to be searched and the persons and things to be seized." This provision, with two slight and wholly unimportant verbal differences, is identical with the Fourth Amendment to the United States Constitution, and like the Fourth Amendment, applies to warrants of arrest as well as search warrants. The warrant here described the person to be seized as "John Doe, white male adult, 30 to 35 years, 5′ 10″ 175 lbs. dark hair, medium build." Defendant argues that the warrant is void because the description is general and did not contain any information by which he could be identified with reasonable certainty. The People, with commendable objectivity, concede that a warrant which merely identifies a defendant by the use of a fictitious name without any description whatsoever is void. They argue, however, that a warrant using "any name" is authorized by section 815 of the Penal Code (set forth below)[1] and, in the alternative, that the description here was sufficient to meet the constitutional standards. The question is one of first impression on both points.

As to section 815 of the Penal Code, Elliott v. Haskins, 20 Cal. App.2d 591, 67 P.2d 698, supports the People's position. However, that case is of doubtful authority since it ignored the pertinent constitutional provisions and was decided before Mapp v. Ohio, 367 U.S.

1. Penal Code section 815: "A warrant of arrest must specify the name of the defendant or, if it is unknown to the magistrate, judge or justice, the defendant may be designated therein by any name. It must also state the time of issuing it, and the city and county, county, city, town or township where it is issued and be signed by the magistrate, judge or justice issuing it with the title of his office."

643, 81 S.Ct. 1684, 6 L.Ed.2d 1081, established that the Fourth Amendment of the United States Constitution applied to the states.[2]

The weight of authority holds that to meet the constitutional requirements, a "John Doe" warrant must describe the person to be seized with reasonable particularity. The warrant should contain sufficient information to permit his identification with reasonable certainty. This may be done by stating his occupation, his personal appearance, peculiarities, place of residence or other means of identification. Where a name that would reasonably identify the subject to be arrested cannot be provided, then some other means reasonable to the circumstances must be used to assist in the identification of the subject of the warrant.

We hold, therefore, that when read with the constitutional provisions, section 815 does not obviate the necessity of describing the person to be arrested.[3] If a fictitious name is used the warrant should also contain sufficient descriptive material to indicate with reasonable particularity the identification of the person whose arrest is ordered.

We turn, therefore, to the question of whether the description of defendant as a "white male adult, 30 to 35 years, 5′ 10″ 175 lbs. dark hair, medium build" meets the constitutional requirement of "reasonable particularity." There is very little authority on this question, as most of the cases deal with search warrants. However, a useful analogy is presented by the cases relating to search warrants issued pursuant to statutes similar to section 1525 of the Penal Code,[4] which authorizes a warrant for the search of the person.

The authorities agree that the constitutional requirement is not met where only characteristics of age, weight, height and race are mentioned.[5] Although the warrant here also indicated that the person to be seized had dark hair, we think it was nevertheless too general a description. It could be applied to a great number of persons in a city the size of Oakland. Accordingly, we hold that the description of defendant in the warrant did not meet the constitutional re-

2. The case has been properly criticized (11 So.Cal.L.Rev., 520; 15 So.Cal.L. Rev., 142).

3. As with affidavits for search warrants, federal standards apply since the constitutional provisions apply to both kinds of warrants.

4. Penal Code section 1525: "A search warrant cannot be issued but upon probable cause, supported by affidavit, naming or describing the person, and particularly describing the property and the place to be searched." Oddly, the arrest warrant statutes (Pen.Code, §§ 813–815) contain no similar language.

5. In Dow v. State, 207 Md. 80, 113 A.2d 423, 49 A.L.R.2d 1205, Wilson v. State, 200 Md. 187, 88 A.2d 564, and Giordano v. State, 203 Md. 174, 100 A.2d 31, the race, age, height and weight descriptions were held sufficient where accompanied by an indication that the person to be arrested could be identified by the arresting officer. However, in United States v. Swanner, supra, it was held that the subjective knowledge or intention of the executing officer lends no support to the warrant and that its validity must be tested from the identifying information on its face.

In Martini v. State, 200 Md. 609, 92 A.2d 456, a description referring to "a white man, 25 years of age," was held insufficient as the court concluded there must be in the city about 18,000 persons who answered the description.

quirement, and the warrant was void for that reason.[a] In view of this conclusion, we need not discuss defendant's other contention that the warrant was also invalid as it failed to state the time of its issuance as required by the second sentence of section 815, quoted above (fn. 1).

It does not follow, however, that defendant's arrest was unlawful simply because the warrant underlying it was void. As indicated in the statement of facts, prior to the arrest, the Oakland police had the teletype referring to the warrants. Section 850 of the Penal Code provides that a teletype of a warrant has the same effect as the original. In this case, however, the teletype from the San Francisco Police Department contained more information than the warrant. It contained the additional facts that defendant had a large mustache,

a. [Added by the Compiler.] A warrant for the arrest of "John Doe or Richard Roe, whose other or true name is to your complainant unknown" with nothing added for identification, is invalid. Commonwealth v. Crotty and Others, 92 Mass. 403 (1865).

Where a magistrate signs warrants in blank, and delivers them to a police officer to be filled up with the names of persons to be arrested, as occasion may require, and the police officer fills up one of them for the arrest of an individual without any charge under oath being first made, the warrant will be a nullity, as not issuing in the ordinary course of justice from a court or magistrate. Rafferty v. People, 69 Ill. 111 (1873). A warrant issued with a blank for the name is not illegal where the name is unknown. Bailey v. Wiggins, 5 Har. 462 (Del.1854). A warrant must either name or describe the person to be arrested. Robison v. United States, 4 Okl.Cr. 336, 111 P. 984 (1910). A warrant for the arrest of an unnamed person is void unless it contains such a *descriptio personae* as will supply the lack of the name by which the accused is known. People ex rel. Prisk v. Allison, 6 Colo.App. 80, 39 P. 903 (1895).

A "John Doe" warrant which adequately describes the person to be arrested is valid. United States v. Altiere, 343 F.2d 115 (7th Cir. 1965).

"Appellant's contention that the place of possession to be searched was not sufficiently described in the search warrant is not well founded. It was described in both the affidavit and search warrant as a 'Scripps-Booth automobile touring car, license No. 232504'. . . . It is difficult to imagine a more definite description of the thing or possession to be searched under this search warrant than that given.

"Appellant insists that since the search warrant commanded the search of the automobile 'now being used and occupied and controlled by John Doe et al.,' there is not a sufficient description of the person to make the search warrant valid. That contention cannot be sustained because this search warrant did not command that any person be searched, and, acting under it, the peace officers did not search the person of any one." Prater v. Commonwealth, 216 Ky. 451, 287 S.W. 951 (1926). Accord as to a warrant for the search of a building, adequately described but said to belong to "John Doe." State ex rel. Henderson v. Cuniff, 30 Tenn.App. 347, 206 S.W.2d 32 (1947).

If the name of the owner or occupant is unknown no name is required in a search warrant. Harvey v. Drake, 40 So. 2d 214 (Fla.1949).

A warrant ordering officers to search for and seize "books, records, pamphlets, cards, receipts, lists, memoranda, pictures, recordings and other written instruments concerning the Communist Party of Texas and the operations of the Communist Party in Texas" is a general warrant and violates the constitutional requirement that a warrant particularly describe the things to be seized. Stanford v. Texas, 379 U.S. 476, 85 S.Ct. 506, 13 L.Ed.2d 813 (1965).

Warrant authorizing seizure of documents on an attached list "together with other fruits, instrumentalities and evidence of crime at this [time] unknown" was not a general warrant and general language would be read as limited to items pertaining to the authorized subject matter of the warrant. Andresen v. Maryland, 427 U.S. 463, 96 S.Ct. 2737 (1976).

was of a Latin type, as well as the address of Rosalie who had been previously identified by the victim. Information provided by one police department to another is presumed to be reliable. Thus, when the Oakland officers found defendant fitting the teletyped description at Rosalie's, they were presented with a state of facts that would lead a reasonable person to conclude that defendant should be held to answer. It follows that the Oakland officers here had sufficient probable cause for the arrest of defendant even without the warrant. His arrest and the subsequent search were lawful,[b] and the two $100 bills were properly introduced into evidence.

The judgment of conviction is affirmed.

SHOEMAKER, P.J. and AGEE, J., concur.

PEOPLE v. WARREN

Supreme Court of New York, 1843.
5 Hill 440.

CERTIORARI to the Oneida general sessions, where the defendant was convicted of an assault and battery upon one Johnson, a constable. Johnson arrested the defendant on a warrant issued by the inspectors of election of the city of Utica for interrupting the proceedings at the election by disorderly conduct in the presence of the inspectors. (1 R.S. 137, § 37.) The warrant was regular and sufficient upon its face. The defendant resisted the officer, and for that assault he was indicted. The defendant offered to prove that he had not been in the presence or hearing of the inspectors at any time during the election, and *that Johnson knew it.* The court excluded the evidence, and the defendant was convicted. He now moved for a new trial on a bill of exceptions.

W. Hunt, for the defendant, said the evidence should have been admitted. It would have shown that the inspectors had no jurisdic-

b. "LaBelle's arrest, although made pursuant to an invalid warrant, is nonetheless lawful because it was supported by probable cause independent of the defective warrant." United States ex rel. LaBelle v. LaVallee, 517 F.2d 750, 753 (2d Cir. 1975).

It has been held that nothing will excuse the arrest of one other than the arrestee designated in the warrant. Holmes v. Blyler, supra. This is unnecessarily extreme and some statutes expressly provide that there shall be no liability if the arrest is made in the good faith belief that the one taken into custody is the one referred to in the warrant. See West's Ann.Cal.Civ.Code, § 43.5(a). See also Hill v. California, 401 U.S. 797, 91 S.Ct. 1106 (1971).

A warrant was issued for the arrest of "John Doe alias Ortegas". Before the officer arrested the accused he asked: "Are you Artegas?" and the accused answered: "Yes". The arrest was held to have been lawful. Otey v. United States, 417 F.2d 559 (D.C. Cir. 1969).

Under the statute a police officer may lawfully arrest a person without a warrant if he has probable cause to believe an offense is being committed in his presence, even though it is a misdemeanor. House v. Ane, 56 Hawaii 383, 538 P.2d 320 (1975).

tion of the subject matter; and if the officer knew it, his process was no justification of the arrest. But,

PER CURIAM. Although the inspectors had no jurisdiction of the subject matter, yet as the warrant was regular upon its face, it was a sufficient authority for Johnson to make the arrest, and the defendant had no right to resist the officer. The knowledge of the officer that the inspectors had no jurisdiction is not important. He must be governed and is protected by the process, and cannot be affected by any thing which he has heard or learned out of it. There are some *dicta* the other way; but we have held on several occasions that the officer is protected by process regular and legal upon its face, whatever he may have heard going to impeach it.

And without hearing *T. Jenkins,* (district attorney,) who was to have argued for the people,

New trial denied.[3]

(D) ARREST

The "slightest touching of another, or of his clothes, or cane, or anything else attached to his person" is a battery unless privileged.[1] In one case the privilege may have been granted by consent (and within the field in which consent to physical contact is recognized by law), such as the consent impliedly given by a football player to the rather violent physical contact properly incident to the game, or the consent of one who mingles in a crowd to the less violent jostling which must be expected when many people are very close together. In other situations the privilege may exist notwithstanding the lack of consent of the one concerned, as where another is authorized by law to arrest him. But anyone, even an officer, "who would justify laying hands on a person for the purpose of making an arrest, must come protected by the shield provided by law." [2] In fact, even without touching the other, the officer may subject himself to liability for assault or false imprisonment if he undertakes to make an arrest without being privileged by law to do so.[3]

3. According to the definition of a warrant "fair on its face" adopted by the American Law Institute in Restatement, Second, Torts § 124 (1965), such a warrant is always protection to the officer executing it. However, a "warrant" which names a person over whom or states a crime over which the court or body issuing it does not have jurisdiction is not a warrant "fair on its face," by definition, and offers no protection to the officer executing it. This results from the fact that the person undertaking the execution of the warrant takes the risk of knowing the general nature of the jurisdiction of the court or body whose process he serves.

1. Crosswhite v. Barnes, 139 Va. 471, 477, 124 S.E. 242, 244 (1924).

2. Ibid; State v. Small, 184 Iowa 882, 885, 169 N.W. 116, 117 (1918).

3. For example, an officer might be guilty of an assault because of an attempted arrest, without privilege, even if the other succeeded in avoiding him without being touched. Furthermore, if the other submitted to such an arrest without physical contact, the officer would be liable for false imprisonment. See Gold v. Bissell, 1 Wend. 210 (N.Y.1828).

(i) What Constitutes Arrest

"An arrest is the taking of another into . . . custody . . . for the actual or purported purpose of bringing the other before a court, or of otherwise securing the administration of the law." [4] It is made by an actual restraint of the person arrested, or by his submission to the custody of the person making the arrest. As explained by an English court: "Mere words will not constitute an arrest; and if the officer says, 'I arrest you,' and the party runs away, it is no escape; but if the party acquiesces in the arrest, and goes with the officer, it will be a good arrest." [5] The court had in mind a case in which the officer did not touch the other, because touching for the manifested purpose of arrest by one having lawful authority completes the apprehension, "although he does not succeed in stopping or holding him even for an instant." [6] Stated in other terms, words alone, however, appropriate, will not be sufficient for an arrest unless accompanied either by actual physical contact or by submission of the other person.

The word "arrestee," although not found in many of the dictionaries, at least with this meaning, is a very useful term employed to signify the person who has been arrested or whose arrest is being sought or attempted.[7] The one making or attempting the arrest, whether an officer or a private person, may be spoken of as the "arrester."

An arrest must be for the actual or purported *purpose* of bringing the other before a court, body, or official or of otherwise securing the administration of the law. If there is no intent to take the other anywhere and his detention is a mere incident to the proper exercise of some other privilege, it is not an arrest.[8] If, for example, a peace

4. Restatement, Second, Torts § 112 (1965).

Blackstone stated that an arrest was ". . . the apprehending or restraining of one's person in order to be forthcoming to answer an alleged or suspected crime." 4 Bl.Comm. 288.

"To constitute an arrest, there must be an actual or constructive seizure or detention of the person, performed with the intention to effect an arrest, and so understood by the person detained." Jenkins v. United States, 161 F.2d 99, 101 (10th Cir. 1947); Brinegar v. United States, 165 F.2d 512, 514 (10th Cir. 1948).

5. Russen v. Lucas, 1 Car. and P. 153, 171 Eng.Rep. 1141 (N.P.1824).

On the other hand one who goes with an officer at the latter's request is not necessarily under arrest. Williams v. United States, 189 F.2d 693 (D.C.Cir. 1951).

6. State ex rel. Sadler v. District Court, 70 Mont. 378, 386, 225 P. 1000, 1002 (1924).

7. See State ex rel. Wong You v. District Court, 106 Mont. 347, 351, 78 P.2d 353, 354 (1938).

8. The act of stopping a motorist to see his driver's license does not constitute an arrest. State v. Hobson, 95 Idaho 920, 523 P.2d 523 (1974).

"[N]o arrest takes place when a police officer makes an investigatory stop and detention of a person . . . ." State v. Sinclair, 11 Wash.App. 523, 528–29, 523 P.2d 1209, 1213 (1974).

"Arrest connotes restraint and not temporary detention for routine questioning." Shook v. United States, 337 F.2d 563, 566 (8th Cir. 1964).

The act of a policeman in stopping a motorist to see if he has a driver's license is a permissible police practice not

officer is privileged by law to require a motorist to show his operator's license,[9] and requires a driver to stop his car for this purpose,[10] whereupon he examines the license, finds it in order, and permits the driver to proceed on his way without undue delay, there has been no arrest. There has been "confinement" in the technical sense because the driver was detained by authority of an officer; but since it was momentary and a mere incident to the proper exercise of a privilege, the word "arrest" is not used. It would have constituted an arrest if the officer had violated his privilege in requiring the motorist to stop.[11]

(ii) Who May Arrest

Arrests are made either (1) in obedience to a warrant, (2) upon the oral order of a magistrate for an offense committed in his presence, (3) in aid of an officer who has requested assistance in making an arrest, or (4) "without a warrant" which has survived as an inept phrase meaning an arrest under circumstances other than any of the three first mentioned.

(1) Under a Warrant ("Warranted Arrest")

At common law a warrant of arrest might be directed either to an officer or to a private person.[1] Modern statutes frequently authorize the issuance of warrants directed to "any peace" or "law enforcement officer." [2] At one time it was not uncommon to authorize direction to a private person.[3] Few of the statutes now have this express

amounting to an arrest. Commonwealth v. Mitchell, 355 S.W.2d 686 (Ky.1962).

An officer was privileged to stop a minor driving a car with out-of-state license plates to determine if he had a driver's license, and finding that he did not, had probable cause to arrest the minor for driving without a license. Lipton v. United States, 348 F.2d 591 (9th Cir. 1965).

It was implied that if officers approached a standing car for the purpose of routine investigation, with no intent to detain the person beyond the momentary requirements of such a mission, this would not constitute an arrest. Rios v. United States, 364 U.S. 253, 262, 80 S.Ct. 1431, 1437, 4 L.Ed.2d 1688 (1960).

If police stop a moving car, not for a routine investigation but to question the occupants about a suspected felony, this is an arrest and is unlawful if made without probable cause. Bowling v. United States, 350 F.2d 1002 (D.C.Cir.1965).

See, infra, under The Frisk and Held for Questioning.

9. Uniform Motor Vehicle Operators' and Chauffeurs' License Act, § 15(b); West's Ann.Cal.Vehicle Code § 12951(6) (1971); Tenn.Code Ann. § 55–7–109 (1980).

10. A state highway patrolman is empowered by the Tennessee statute to stop a car at any time and require the driver to show his license. Cox v. State, 181 Tenn. 344, 181 S.W.2d 338 (1944). Cf. Robedeaux v. State, 94 Okl.Cr. 171, 232 P.2d 642 (1951).

A constitutional limitation exists on the manner in which a motorist is stopped for a license check. Delaware v. Prouse, 440 U.S. 648, 99 S.Ct. 1391 (1979).

11. Robertson v. State, 184 Tenn. 277, 198 S.W.2d 633 (1947). In this case the officers stopped the car and asked to see the driver's license, not because they wanted to inspect the license but merely as a device to enable them to see what was in the car.

1. 2 Hale P.C. *110.

2. Iowa Code § 804.2 (1979); Kan.Stat.Ann. § 22–2202(17) (1981).

3. Tenn.Code Ann. § 11529 (Williams, 1934).

authorization but the common-law authority will not be abrogated unless the statute is very clear upon this point.[4]

The common law required one arresting under a warrant to have the warrant in his possession at the time,[5] unless he was assisting another who had the warrant and who was then actively cooperating in the effort to make the arrest, and was actually or constructively present at the time.[6] This may have been suited to the conditions of the time in which the rule developed, but it is quite unsuited to the needs of the present day. Some of the modern statutes provide that "the officer need not have the warrant in his possession at the time of the arrest, but after the arrest, if the person arrested so requires, the warrant shall be shown to him as soon as practicable." [7] Some statutes authorize a telegraphic copy of a warrant of arrest.[8]

(2) On Oral Order of a Magistrate

Under the common law a magistrate who saw the commission of a felony or a breach of the peace was authorized either to arrest the offender himself or to order any peace officer or private person to do so.[1] This order might be given orally and was sufficient authority for the arrest. Such authority is seldom exercised but it is commonly included in modern statutes on arrest, frequently being enlarged to

4. Meek v. Pierce, 19 Wis. 300, 318 (1865).

5. 1 Hale P.C. *583. An officer with a warrant for the arrest of Shaw on a misdemeanor charge left the warrant in his buggy while he went to Shaw's house about 150 or 200 yards away and arrested him. The arrest was effected only after a struggle, and Shaw was found guilty of resisting an officer and assault and battery. On defendant's motion this verdict was set aside "on the ground that at the time of making the arrest the officer had not such possession of the warrant as is required by law." This order was reversed on appeal and the case was remanded for the purpose of having sentence imposed. State v. Shaw, 104 S.C. 359, 89 S.E. 322 (1916).

When a valid warrant has been issued for the arrest of the accused for a misdemeanor and police officers make the arrest but do not have the warrant in their possession, the arrest is unlawful; and the officers are liable in damages to the accused. Crosswhite v. Barnes, 139 Va. 471, 124 S.E. 242 (1924). However, in Cabell v. Arnold, 86 Tex. 102, 23 S.W. 645 (1893), a valid warrant was issued and retained by a United States marshal, who telegraphed his deputy to make the arrest. The deputy, without the warrant in his possession and after informing the arrestee that a warrant had been issued, made the arrest. The court held that the one arrested could recover no damages in a civil action against the marshal.

See notes, Necessity of possession of warrant by officer claiming arrest privileged as under warrant, 25 Iowa L.Rev. 660 (1940); Necessity of showing warrant upon making arrest under warrant, 40 A.L.R. 62 (1926); 100 A.L.R. 188 (1936); What information is the accused person entitled to at the time of his arrest, 42 L.R.A. 673 (1899); and Using handcuffs in arresting for a misdemeanor, 3 A.L.R. 1172 (1919).

6. **G,** a policeman in Kalamazoo, Michigan, had a warrant for the arrest of **M** on a misdemeanor charge. Learning that **M** was in Battle Creek, **G** telephoned to an officer there to hold **M** until **G** reached that city. This was done and **M** was held for about three hours and then turned over to **G.** It was held that **M** was falsely imprisoned until **G** arrived with the warrant. McCullough v. Greenfield, 133 Mich. 463, 95 N.W. 532 (1903).

7. This is the provision of A.L.I. Code of Criminal Procedure, § 24. The provision of the Federal Rules of Criminal Procedure is the same in substance. Rule 4.

8. West's Ann.Cal.Pen.Code, §§ 850, 851 (1970).

1. 4 Bl.Comm. *292.

permit the magistrate to order the arrest of one who has committed any "public offense" in his presence.[2]

(3) Assisting an Officer

The sheriff, being the officer particularly charged by common law with keeping the peace and apprehending wrongdoers, was authorized, whenever necessary for such purposes, to "command all the people of his county to attend him; which is called the *posse comitatus,* or power of the county; . . ."[1] The power to require such assistance by all able-bodied males, over the age of fifteen and under the rank of Peer, included the power to call upon any such individual. In the course of time it was recognized that any peace officer is authorized to call upon private persons to aid him in making arrests or preventing crimes.[2] And a person so required to give such assistance is guilty of a misdemeanor if he wrongfully refuses to comply.[3] Such a provision is frequently included in the modern statutes.[4] Some of the enactments speak only in terms of aid to an officer in executing a warrant,[5] whereas others codify the common-law rule,[6] and still others go to the length of authorizing any person making a lawful arrest to summon assistance.[7]

2. See, for example, West's Ann.Cal. Pen.Code, § 838 (1970). Defendant, a magistrate, on seeing the plaintiff commit a misdemeanor in his presence, ordered a policeman to arrest plaintiff and to "take him to the station house." Plaintiff was so arrested and imprisoned and brings an action for false imprisonment against the defendant. The court said: "While, therefore, a magistrate may order the arrest of any one for a public offense committed in his presence, he has no power to at once, without an examination or hearing, or without informing the offender of the charge against him, commit him to prison. If there be good cause for postponing the hearing, and the offender fail to give bail in a bailable case, then he may be committed until the hearing. But for a magistrate to order the arrest of any one for a misdemeanor committed in his presence, and at once without a hearing, or without cause postponing the hearing to another time, or giving him an opportunity to have counsel or give bail, peremptorily order him to prison is contrary to the very spirit of our bill of rights and the pointed provisions of our statutes." Toughey v. King, 77 Tenn. 422, 428 (1882).

1. 1 Bl.Comm. *343.

2. 1 Wharton, Criminal Procedure, § 41 (10th ed., Kerr, 1918).

3. 1 Hale P.C. *588; 1 Bl.Comm. *343.

4. The provision in the American Law Institute's Code of Criminal Procedure is as follows:

> Section 27. *Officer may summon assistance.* Any officer making a lawful arrest may orally summon as many persons as he deems necessary to aid him in making the arrest. Every person when required by an officer shall aid him in the making of such arrest.

5. This is true of the statutes in Oklahoma, and Tennessee.

6. Alabama, Arkansas, Indiana, Iowa, Kentucky, Mississippi, North Dakota.

7. California, Idaho. Note, Right and duty of bystander, when summoned either directly or by hue and cry, to assist officer in making arrest without warrant, 18 Am. and Eng.Ann.Cas. 932 (1911). Note, Posse Comitatus, 44 Am.St.Rep. 136 (1895).

"If the officer has no warrant, or authority that will justify him, he may be liable as a trespasser; but the person who is called upon for aid, having no means of knowing what the warrant is by which the officer acts, and who relies upon the official character and call of the sheriff as his security for doing what is required, is clearly entitled to protection against suits by the person arrested." McMahan v. Green, 34 Vt. 69, 70 (1861).

But where the party making the arrest is not a known public officer, the person

(4) "Without a Warrant" ("Warrantless Arrest")

Three special types of authority to make an arrest have been shown: (1) A warrant in the strict sense of written process issued by a magistrate, judge, or other official or body having authority to issue warrants; (2) the oral order of a magistrate to arrest for an offense committed in his presence and (3) the request for assistance by an officer who is himself undertaking to make the arrest. The common law recognized the authority of an officer to arrest, under certain other circumstances. Four types of circumstances were recognized as giving an officer a general power to arrest without any special authorization: (1) For a felony or a breach of the peace committed or attempted in his presence; (2) on a "charge" of felony made to the officer by a private person accusing another of a felony; (3) upon reasonable grounds for believing that a felony has been committed by the arrestee (often spoken of as "reasonable suspicion of felony" or "probable cause"); (4) for a felony actually committed by the arrestee but not in the officer's presence. These four are occasionally included in a statute, in modified form.

Modern statutes are more simply drawn and authorize arrest for a felony only where there is reasonable cause to believe a felony has been committed and reasonable cause that the person arrested committed the felony.[8] Some states have also expanded the power of police officers to make warrantless arrests in misdemeanor cases on probable cause to believe the offense has been committed and that the failure to arrest may result in injury to person or property, loss of evidence, or flight.

(a) Committed in his presence

At common law either an officer [1] or a private citizen [2] was authorized to arrest, without a warrant, for a felony committed in his pres-

aiding him is not protected under this rule if the arrest is unauthorized. Dietrichs v. Schaw, 43 Ind. 175 (1873). See note, Liability for assisting in unlawful arrest or subsequent detention. 14 L.R.A.,N.S., 1123 (1908). There is authority contra. In Mitchell v. State, 12 Ark. 50 (1851) the court speaking of the rights of one summoned to assist an officer said, "It is most clearly his right to refuse in case the officer has no legal authority to do the act, and it is equally clear that he has no such right in case the officer has such authority. He must, therefore, act or decline to act at his peril. If it be a hardship for a person, called by an officer to assist him, to decide at his peril, it is quite as hard that the rights of innocent individuals should be invaded with impunity." Id. at 59.

A private person has no right to refuse to assist an officer in making an arrest merely because some danger is involved; but if the effort would be dangerous and futile he may be entitled to refuse under extreme circumstances. Dougherty v. State, 106 Ala. 63, 17 So. 393 (1895).

An officer who assists another in an obviously unlawful arrest is not protected by the mere fact that the other requested his assistance. Roberts v. Commonwealth, 284 Ky. 365, 144 S.W.2d 811 (1940).

8. § 77–7–2(2), Utah Code Ann. 1953.

1. A.L.I. Code of Criminal Procedure 231 (Official Draft with Commentaries, 1931).

2. Id. at 238.

ence. Either might also arrest, without a warrant, for a misdemeanor committed in his presence provided (1) the misdemeanor constituted a breach of the peace (in the narrow sense of the phrase, meaning a public offense done by violence or one causing or likely to cause an immediate disturbance of public order) and (2) the arrest was made immediately or on fresh pursuit.[3] The statutes in most of the states now permit an officer to arrest, without a warrant, for any public offense (felony or misdemeanor) committed in his presence.[4] About twenty states have legislation extending this same authority to any private person.[5] In other states the authority of a private person to arrest for an offense committed in his presence is either retained as it was at common law (felony or a misdemeanor amounting to a breach of the peace),[6] broadened a little to include also a misdemeanor in the form of petit larceny,[7] or narrowed by being limited to felony cases only.[8]

3. 9 Halsbury, Laws of England 86–9 (2nd ed., Hailsham, 1933).

4. A.L.I. Code of Criminal Procedure 232–3 (Official Draft with Commentaries, 1931). The Institute lists all of the states as having such legislation *except* Colorado, Maryland, Massachusetts, New Mexico, North Carolina, Texas, Vermont, West Virginia and Wisconsin.

"It is true that the authority of FBI agents to arrest without a warrant is limited to cases where they have reasonable ground to believe that the person to be arrested has committed a felony." United States v. Digilio, 538 F.2d 972, 984 (3rd Cir. 1976).

5. Id. at 239. The states listed are Alabama, Arizona, California, Georgia, Idaho, Illinois, Iowa, Michigan, Minnesota, Mississippi, Montana, Nevada, New York, North Dakota, Oklahoma, Oregon, Rhode Island, South Dakota, Tennessee, Utah.

A citizen may arrest another if a felony has in fact been committed and he has reasonable cause to believe that the person arrested committed it. As we have explained, defendant did commit a felony; further Lasko had reasonable cause to believe defendant was the culprit. Thus, when Lasko first restrained him by holding his arms, it was defendant's duty not to resist." People v. Fosselman, 33 Cal. 3d 572, 189 Cal.Rptr. 855, 659 P.2d 1144, 1148 (1983).

6. Id. at 239.

7. Ibid.

8. Id. at 238. The reasonable mistake of fact doctrine applies, and the officer is protected if he acts on a bona fide belief, based upon reasonable grounds, that an offense is being committed in his presence, even if no offense is in fact committed. Cave v. Cooley, 48 N.M. 478, 152 P.2d 886 (1944). An officer who makes an arrest for public drunkenness, without a warrant, is protected if the arrestee appears to be drunk even if not drunk as a matter of fact. Goodwin v. State, 148 Tenn. 682, 257 S.W. 79 (1924); Morris v. Combs' Administrator, 304 Ky. 187, 200 S.W.2d 281 (1947); see Kelley v. State, 184 Tenn. 143, 149, 197 S.W.2d 545, 547 (1946).

"In passing upon the right of an officer to make an arrest of one who is in possession of a pistol on the public street of a city, where the possession of a pistol makes a prima facie case, the possession in the presence of an officer determines the right of the officer to make an arrest, even though upon the trial of the case the accused might present a legal defense." Reed v. State, 195 Ga. 842, 851, 25 S.E.2d 692, 698 (1943).

"We therefore conclude that . . . the act of fishing was committed by plaintiff (who admitted that he had no license) in the presence of defendants and that they were not required to know that the admitted fishing was done at a place or under circumstances where a license was not required under some exemption contained in the statute," and hence they were authorized to arrest the plaintiff without a warrant. Giannini v. Garland, 296 Ky. 361, 367, 177 S.W.2d 133, 136 (1944).

In Stearns v. Titus, 193 N.Y. 272, 85 N.E. 1077 (1908), it is stated: "To justify an arrest without a warrant for the commission of that offense, the crime must be actually committed or attempt be

STATE v. GONZALES

Court of Appeals of Washington, Division 1, 1979.
24 Wn.App. 437, 604 P.2d 168.

FARRIS, JUDGE. Robert Walter Gonzales appeals his convictions for assault in the second degree while armed with a deadly weapon and possession of stolen property in the third degree. We affirm.

On October 19, 1977, a plainclothes security officer for a downtown department store saw Gonzales emerge from the rear of the men's outerwear department with a bulge under his overcoat and leave the store. The security officer, who had arrested Gonzales for shoplifting on two prior occasions, followed him to a barber shop. Gonzales entered the shop and sat down. The security officer returned to the department store where he determined that a leather coat was missing from the men's outerwear department.

Returning toward the barber shop, the security officer approached Gonzales on the street, identified himself as a store security officer and asked for the coat. Gonzales produced the leather coat from under his overcoat and the security officer, who was not armed, asked Gonzales to accompany him back to the store. When Gonzales tried to run away, the security officer grabbed him by the arm. Gonzales then displayed a knife and waved it at the security officer, who released Gonzales. Gonzales fled, but was subsequently arrested by police.

Gonzales contends that his arrest was unlawful and, therefore, (1) he had a legal privilege to use force in resisting his arrest by the security officer and (2) the evidence of his possession of the coat should have been suppressed.

At common law in general, a private person may arrest for a misdemeanor only if it constitutes a breach of the peace and is committed in his presence. Numerous states, however, have statutes which permit the owner of a mercantile establishment or his employee to arrest for shoplifting committed in his presence. In states without such laws, courts have recently indicated that such arrests may be made under a common law right. While Washington has no statute concerning citizen arrests, the common law is applicable where not repugnant to the provisions of the state constitution or statutes. The owner of a mercantile establishment or his employee may make a warrantless arrest of a thief who he has observed shoplifting, even though no breach of the peace has occurred. This interpretation of

made to commit it in the presence of the officer. Reasonable suspicion, or probable cause to believe its commission is not sufficient." Also the misdemeanor is not committed in the "presence" of the officer unless he knows it is committed. State v. Gartland, 304 Mo. 87, 263 S.W. 165 (1924).

"A peace officer cannot legally make an arrest without a warrant for an offense claimed to have been committed in his presence which he himself provokes or brings about." Scott v. Feilschmidt, 191 Iowa 347, 351, 182 N.W. 382, 384 (1921).

the common law is in conformity with the Washington statutes granting civil and criminal immunity from liability to owners and authorized employees of mercantile establishments in actions arising from the reasonable detention of suspected shoplifters.

Here the security officer observed Gonzales leaving the store with a bulge under his overcoat. His conclusions were confirmed when Gonzales produced the missing leather coat from under his overcoat upon request. His subsequent arrest of Gonzales was lawful.

Further, Gonzales exceeded his legal privilege to resist the arrest even if it was unlawful. As stated in State v. Rousseau, 40 Wash.2d 92, 95, 241 P.2d 447, 449 (1952):

> [T]he force used in resisting an unlawful arrest must be reasonable and proportioned to the injury attempted upon the party sought to be arrested, and he cannot use or offer to use a deadly weapon if he has no reason to apprehend a greater injury than a mere unlawful arrest.

There is nothing in the record which would justify Gonzales' threat to use his knife.

The arrest was lawful and therefore the trial court properly denied Gonzales' motion to suppress evidence of his possession of the leather coat. Further, the fourth amendment to the United States Constitution, and the exclusionary rule thereunder, applies to state action only and not to the actions of private citizens. There is no prohibition against the State's use of evidence or information obtained by a private citizen, even though by unlawful means, unless the actions of the private citizen were in some way "instigated, encouraged, counseled, directed, or controlled" by the State or its officers. There is nothing in the record which indicates or even suggests that the State instigated, encouraged, counseled, directed or controlled the actions of the security officer here.

Affirmed.[a]

DORE and WILLIAMS, JJ., concur.

a. "Where an officer is apprised by any of his senses that a crime is being committed, it is committed in his presence so as to justify an arrest without a warrant." (It was the sense of smell in this case.) Massa v. State, 159 Tenn. 428, 430, 19 S.W.2d 248, 249 (1929). See note, 15 Minn.L.Rev. 359 (1931).

But in People v. Johnson, 86 Mich. 175, 48 N.W. 870 (1891) shouting on the public street amounting to a breach of the peace, which was heard by a policeman 150 feet away was not committed in the "presence" of the officer because the one shouting was not in view.

The fact that the arrestee was carrying a concealed weapon at the time of the arrest will not justify the apprehension if the officer did not know of the presence of the weapon until a search was made. People v. Henneman, 373 Ill. 603, 27 N.E.2d 448 (1940), noted in 31 J.Crim.L. & Criminology 465 (1940). See note, 92 A.L.R. 490 (1934). Cf. James v. State, 94 Okl.Cr. 239, 234 P.2d 422 (1951).

Loud talking in the kitchen of one's home, heard by officers in passing but not a word of which was understood by them, was not the commission of an offense in their presence, there being no showing that the occupants were intoxicated or disorderly. Lucarini v. State, 159 Tenn. 373, 19 S.W.2d 239 (1929).

(b) On charge preferred by another

At one time in the development of the law of arrest it seemed as if the authority of an officer to arrest on a charge of felony preferred by another person would be given almost the scope of that arising under a warrant. Lord Hale says: "And it appears by the books before-mentioned that in cases of arrests of this or like nature, the constable may execute his office upon information and request of others, that suspect and charge the offenders, ..."[1] The most extreme statement of the point is by Mr. Justice Buller, in Williams v. Dawson,[2] to the effect that if an officer "received a person into custody, on a charge preferred by another of felony or a breach of the peace, there he is to be considered as a mere conduit; and if no felony or breach of the peace was committed, the person who preferred the charge alone is answerable." The phrase "receives a person into custody" suggests that the arrest may have been made by a private person who merely turned the arrestee over to an officer to take before a magistrate. If so the case is not unusual. Where an arrest is made by a private person upon his own responsibility the arrestee should be taken before a magistrate without undue delay and an officer who merely assists in causing this to be done does not incur liability thereby. This authority of the officer is frequently incorporated in a special statute.[3] The statement quoted from Mr. Justice Buller was approved, however, in Hobbs v. Branscomb[4] in which case the arrest had not been made by a private person but was made by the officers on a charge preferred by a private person. This seems to suggest complete protection to the officer who makes an arrest on a charge preferred by another with the sole responsibility resting upon that other. Some qualification was to be expected and was made very shortly. Just a few years after Hobbs v. Branscomb an officer, without a warrant, made an arrest for receiving stolen property on a charge preferred by a young thief. It was held unlawful for him to

Police who encounter an accident, and observe the defendant's intoxication in a public place, may arrest for an offense committed in their presence. Kincannon v. State, 541 P.2d 1339 (Okl.Cr.1975); State v. Bryan, 16 Utah 2d 47, 395 P.2d 539 (1964).

One fleeing from another state to avoid prosecution for a robbery committed by him there is violating the federal Fugitive Felon Act. Hence an officer who finds him may arrest him for an offense committed in the presence of such officer. Bircham v. Commonwealth, 238 S.W.2d 1008 (Ky.1951).

1. 2 Hale P.C. *89–90.

2. Nisi Prius (1788), quoted in Hobbs v. Branscomb, 3 Camp. 420, 421, 170 Eng.Rep. 1431, 1432 (K.B.1813).

Lord Mansfield had said much the same a few years earlier: ". . . if a man charges another with felony, and requires an officer to take him into custody, and carry him before a magistrate, it would be most mischievous that the officer should be bound first to try, and at his peril exercise his judgment on the truth of the charge. He that makes the charge should alone be answerable. The officer does his duty in carrying the accused before a magistrate, who is authorized to examine, and commit or discharge." Samuel v. Payne, 1 Dougl. 359, 360, 99 Eng.Rep. 230, 231 (K.B.1780).

3. See Tenn.Code Ann. § 40–7–113(b) (1982).

4. See note 2 supra.

deprive a person of his liberty on such information, without further evidence.[5]

Thus the statement of the common law upon this point cannot be given in the unqualified terms suggested by Mr. Justice Buller, but must be in some such form as this: An officer arresting without a warrant upon a charge of felony preferred by another, and accusing the arrestee thereof, is protected if he acts reasonably.[6] This is expressly incorporated into a number of the statutes by including in the section authorizing an officer to arrest without a warrant, as one of the clauses: "On a charge made, upon reasonable cause, of the commission of a felony by the person arrested." [7] The word "charge" in such a statute, as at common law, does not mean a formal written charge made to a magistrate but an oral accusation made to the peace officer himself.[8]

An officer has reasonable ground for believing a person guilty of felony if he has received information to this effect from a person who is reasonably entitled to be believed.[9] This would seem to permit the inclusion of this basis for arrest without a warrant in the "probable cause" category and render a separate clause unnecessary. But because of a special limitation injected into the "probable cause" section in many of the statutes (to be considered in the next subsection) this clause serves a useful purpose. "[W]e understand the law to be now well settled," said the Tennessee court, "that a *peace officer* may make an arrest on a charge of felony, upon a reasonable cause of suspicion, without a warrant, although it should afterwards turn out that no felony had, in fact, been committed. . . . And this principle of the common law is distinctly incorporated in our Code." [10]

An additional element is added by the Texas statute, to the effect that where it is shown by satisfactory proof to a peace officer, upon the representation of a credible person, that a felony has been committed, *and that the offender is about to escape, so that there is no time to procure a warrant, such peace officer may, without warrant, pursue and arrest the accused.*[11]

Many of the statutes have no such clause in any form.

5. Isaacs v. Brand, 2 Stark. 167, 171 Eng.Rep. 609 (N.P.1817).

6. Mr. Justice Buller's reference to a "breach of the peace" as well as a felony is understandable if the arrest was actually made by a private person for such an offense committed in his presence and the officer merely received the custody of the person after the arrest had been made.

7. See the statutes of California, Idaho, Mississippi, Oklahoma, Tennessee.

8. Haggard v. First Nat. Bank of Mandan, 72 N.D. 434, 8 N.W.2d 5 (1942).

9. Vaughn v. State, 178 Tenn. 384, 158 S.W.2d 715 (1942); Lee v. State, 148 Tex.Cr.R. 220, 185 S.W.2d 978 (1945).

10. Lewis v. State, 40 Tenn. 127, 146 (1859).

11. Vernon's Ann.Tex.Code Cr.Proc. art. 14.04 (1977).

(c) On probable cause

An arrest without a warrant on a bare suspicion, not supported by reasonable grounds, is clearly unlawful;[1] but both the common law and the statutes authorize an arrest on "reasonable suspicion of felony" subject to certain qualifications. What came to be the accepted view of the common law is that either an officer or a private person is privileged to arrest one who is reasonably believed to be guilty of felony, with this important distinction: the officer is protected if he believes, upon reasonable grounds (1) that a felony has been committed and (2) that the arrestee is the guilty party; whereas for the protection of a private person it is necessary (1) that a felony has in fact been committed and (2) that he has reasonable grounds for believing the arrestee guilty of committing it.[2] The reason for this difference is that while either an officer or a private person is privileged to make an arrest for a felony not committed in his presence if he has reasonable grounds for believing the arrestee guilty thereof,—the private person is under no *duty* to do so.[3] To deter private persons from officious interference with the liberty of others it is quite proper to require them to act at their peril on the question whether a felony

1. People v. Chatman, 322 Ill.App. 519, 54 N.E.2d 631 (1944).

2. Holley v. Mix, 3 Wend. 350, 353 (N.Y.1829); Beckwith v. Philby, 6 B. & C. 635, 638–9, 108 Eng.Rep. 585, 586 (K.B.1827); Walters v. Smith [1914] 1 K.B. 595; 1 Stephen, History of the Criminal Law 193 (1883); 9 Halsbury, Laws of England 84–87 (2d ed. Hailsham, 1933); A.L.I. Code of Criminal Procedure 236–42 (Official Draft with Commentaries, 1931).

Professor Jerome Hall has taken the position that the common law, prior to the Revolution, required an actual felony plus reasonable cause to believe the arrestee guilty thereof, to authorize an arrest without a warrant by an officer, as well as by a private person. Legal and Social Aspects of Arrest Without a Warrant, 49 Harv.L.Rev. 566 (1936). Without doubt the generalizations of the early writers lend support to this theory; but Professor Hall was unable to produce any early case in which an officer, having made an arrest on reasonable grounds for believing the arrestee guilty of felony, was held to have acted unlawfully because no felony had in fact been committed. Probably the most that can be said is that some of the early writers were thinking in terms of this requirement but that when the point was actually raised in the cases it was held that a peace officer is not required to act at his peril on the question whether a felony has in fact been committed or not. See Restatement, Second, Torts § 121(b) (1965).

A valid arrest without a warrant is one based upon "probable cause", which means that the arresting officer had "reasonable grounds for believing the arrestee guilty." Martinez v. People, 168 Colo. 314, 451 P.2d 293 (1969).

"In Brinegar v. United States, 338 U.S. 160, 175–76, 69 S.Ct. 1302, 93 L.Ed. 1879 (1949), the Supreme Court stated that probable cause to arrest existed where the facts and circumstances within an officer's knowledge and of which he has reasonably trustworthy information are sufficient in themselves to warrant a man of reasonable caution in the belief that an offense has been or is being committed. United States v. Lemmons, 527 F.2d 662, 664 (6th Cir. 1976).

For the purpose of determining probable cause to arrest, a different standard applies to a citizen informer than a paid, undisclosed informer. People v. Anaya, 545 P.2d 1053 (Colo.App.1975).

"It may therefore be stated as a general proposition that private citizens who are witnesses to or victims of a criminal act, absent some circumstance that would cast doubt upon their information, should be considered reliable." People v. Ramey, 16 Cal.3d 263, 269, 127 Cal.Rptr. 629, 632, 545 P.2d 1333, 1336 (1976).

3. McCrackin v. State, 150 Ga. 718, 722, 105 S.E. 487, 489 (1920).

has or has not been committed, when they undertake to arrest for such an offense not occurring in their presence. With the officer it is different because in his case the privilege to arrest for felony carries with it a corresponding duty. Unfortunately, however, a number of the statutes authorizing an officer to arrest without a warrant have worded this part of the enactment in some such form as: "When a felony has in fact been committed, and he has reasonable cause to believe that the person to be arrested has committed it." [4]

It is in jurisdictions in which the general authority of an officer to arrest on reasonable suspicion of felony has such a limitation that there is real need for an additional clause authorizing him to arrest on a charge of felony preferred by another.[5]

Some states have expressly codified the common-law rule whereby a peace officer is authorized to arrest without a warrant where he has reasonable cause to believe (a) that a felony has been committed and (b) that the person arrested committed it,[6] and the decisions have tended to recognize this rule where the courts have not been hampered by restrictive enactments.[7]

For the most part the statutes have not changed the authority of a private person to arrest on reasonable suspicion of felony but have

4. Idaho, Oklahoma. Compare subdivisions 3 and 5 of Idaho Code, § 19–603 (1948).

5. The states mentioned in the preceding note have this additional clause.

6. Alabama, Kentucky, Michigan, Utah.

7. "Today's decision is the first square holding that the Fourth Amendment permits a duly authorized law enforcement officer to make a warrantless arrest in a public place even though he had adequate opportunity to procure a warrant after developing probable cause for arrest." United States v. Watson, 423 U.S. 411, 426–27, 96 S.Ct. 820, 829 (1976).

N.B. The quotation is from the concurring opinion of Mr. Justice Powell who emphasizes that this differs from a warrantless search which is authorized only "in exigent circumstances."

Officers who had probable cause to arrest S, found her standing in the open doorway of her house. Hence she was in a "public place" for the purpose of the Fourth Amendment and subject to arrest without a warrant. When officers undertook to arrest her she retreated into the house; but she could not by this device thwart an arrest which had been set in motion in a public place, and hence the warrantless entry into the house to make the arrest was lawful, as was also the ensuing search incident thereto. United States v. Santana, 427 U.S. 38, 96 S.Ct. 2406 (1976).

Mr. Justice White, in a concurring opinion, states that an officer, with probable cause to make an arrest of one reasonably believed to be in the house, does not need a warrant to enter the house and make the arrest, at least if force is not required for the entry. This he states "has been the longstanding statutory or judicial rule in the majority of jurisdictions in the United States . . . and has been deemed consistent with state constitutions, as well as the Fourth Amendment." 96 S.Ct. at 2410.

Warrantless arrests within the home are per se unreasonable in the absence of exigent circumstances. People v. Ramey, 16 Cal.3d 263, 127 Cal.Rptr. 629, 545 P.2d 1333 (1976).

An officer may enter the home of a suspect to arrest on probable cause to believe the suspect is within the home without a warrant only on consent or when exigent circumstances are present. Payton v. New York, 445 U.S. 573, 100 S.Ct. 1371 (1980).

If the home of a third person is to be entered to search for and arrest a suspect a search warrant must be obtained in absence of consent or exigent circumstances. Steagald v. United States, 451 U.S. 204, 101 S.Ct. 1642 (1981).

left it as it was at common law with the requirement that (a) a felony has in fact been committed and (b) he has reasonable ground for believing the arrestee guilty. New York requires an actual felony by the arrestee himself, to authorize such an arrest by a private person;[8] a few statutes authorize the arrest on reasonable ground to believe the arrestee guilty of felony, even if no felony has in fact been committed,[9] while the Texas enactment does not authorize a private person without a warrant to arrest for an offense not committed in his presence.[10]

LEWIS v. UNITED STATES

United States Court of Apepals, District of Columbia Circuit, 1969.
135 U.S.App.D.C. 187, 417 F.2d 755.

Before FAHY, SENIOR CIRCUIT JUDGE, and BURGER and TAMM, CIRCUIT JUDGES.

TAMM, CIRCUIT JUDGE: On April 5, 1966, Mr. Louis Brodsky was shot fatally while working in his liquor store. Appellants were each indicted and charged with felony murder (22 D.C.Code § 2401), robbery (22 D.C.Code § 2901), unauthorized use of an automobile (22 D.C.Code § 2204) and carrying a dangerous weapon (22 D.C.Code § 3204). Appellants were tried in a joint trial by jury which resulted in Elroy Lewis being convicted of felony murder, robbery, unauthorized use and carrying a dangerous weapon. He was sentenced to life imprisonment. Bobby Lewis was found not guilty of felony murder but was convicted of robbery, unauthorized use and carrying a dangerous weapon. He was sentenced to 5 to 15 years for robbery and one to three years for unauthorized use, these two sentences to run consecutively. He also received a concurrent sentence of four months to one year for carrying a dangerous weapon. Both appellants seek reversal of their convictions. We find that neither appellant merits such relief.

At approximately 3:00 p.m. on April 5, 1966, Mr. and Mrs. Lewis (no relation to appellants) left their apartment in the northeast section of Washington, D.C., and proceeded to Edgewood Liquors, a nearby store. They testified that as they approached the entrance of the store, they encountered a man leaving the store wearing a ski mask and carrying a gun. They testified further that this man brushed by them and walked rapidly toward a parked car occupied by three males. At this point the Lewises entered a gas station located at the corner and the aforementioned car drove away hastily. The

8. N.Y.Code Cr.Proc. § 140.30 (1981).

9. Kentucky, Mississippi, Utah.

10. Lacy v. State, 7 Tex.App. 403 (1879), construing the Texas statute which is now Vernon's Ann.Tex.Code Cr. Proc. art. 14.01 (1977).

For a collection of cases and a discussion of the subjects covered by footnotes 10, 11, and 12, see note, 133 A.L.R. 608 (1941).

Note, on arrest without warrant on suspicion for unlawful possession of weapons, 92 A.L.R. 490 (1934).

only information communicated to the police (Scout Car 121) was that a holdup and a robbery had just occurred at Fourth Street and Rhode Island Avenue, N.E. As the officers approached the area of the crime they observed a Mr. Taylor waving his arms at their vehicle. Mr. Taylor testified that he had been working in the gas station located at Fourth Street and Rhode Island Avenue when the Lewises "came running into the shop there and asked to call the police. . . . ." Mr. Taylor testified further that he saw a green car "going around the corner at a tremendous pace of speed" and that he "flagged . . . down" the police car. According to the testimony of both the two officers in the squad car and Mr. Taylor, a high speed chase ensued. The police car did not always maintain sight of this green car but various citizens along the route pointed out the direction it was taking. Finally, as the police car was rapidly racing (50–60 mph) up Rhode Island Avenue, one of the officers noticed a green car turning onto V Street. Mr. Taylor testified that he immediately recognized the vehicle as "the car that left the liquor store." Since their car was going too fast to enable them to turn onto V Street, the officers proceeded into the next intersection and, as they went around the corner, they saw the green car "in the middle of the street" and four males about 50 feet away. The officers promptly placed the four men under arrest. The entire chase encompassed only four minutes, the radio alert of the robbery was broadcast at approximately 3:01 p.m. and the arrest was accomplished at 3:05 p.m.

Incident to this arrest apellants were searched. On the person of Bobby Lewis was found a red ski mask, a .45 caliber pistol, $80 in cash and a manila envelope containing change. On the person of Elroy Lewis was found a black ski mask and $90 in cash. In addition, as appellants were being searched a witness (Mrs. Warren) testified that from the vantage point of her second floor window she saw Elroy Lewis toss a gun into the car in front of which appellants were being searched. She informed the police of this and they recovered a .38 caliber pistol from the car. An FBI ballistics report confirmed the fact that this gun was the murder weapon.

A hearing on a pretrial motion to suppress was conducted at which appellants argued for the suppression of all the items taken from them. After hearing oral argument by counsel, the trial judge denied appellants' motion to suppress. . . .

I

Both appellants argue forcefully that the police lacked probable cause to arrest them and that consequently all the items seized from them must be suppressed. As to this issue both appellants propound the same argument; indeed, they recognize that the money, the masks, the manila envelope and the murder weapon constitute "key prosecution evidence". In order to determine whether probable cause existed at the time of appellants' arrest we must follow the applicable standard set out by the Supreme Court:

Probable cause exists where 'the facts and circumstances within . . . (the officers') knowledge and of which they had reasonably trustworthy information (are) sufficient in themselves to warrant a man of reasonable caution in the belief that' an offense has been or is being committed.[4]

Thus the conduct of the police in this case must be gauged by a test of *reasonableness.* In this regard we must not lose sight of the fact that, in order to establish probable cause, "[m]uch less evidence . . . is required [than that necessary] to establish guilt." [5] We must also remember that

[t]he test of probable cause is not what reaction victims—or judges—might have but what the totality of the circumstances means to police officers. Conduct innocent in the eyes of the untrained may carry entirely different 'messages' to the experienced or trained observer (footnote omitted).[6]

We now must apply the standards enunciated above to the particular facts and circumstances of the case before us. Upon close inspection, the record reveals two police officers responding to a radio alert that a holdup and a robbery had just occurred. Upon arrival at the scene of the crime, they encounter a citizen who tells them, at the very least, that he saw a "speeding green car" leave the scene of the robbery. The police follow his directions, aided by two different citizens who are in the street pointing the way, and then observe a green car turning a corner. As the officers proceed around the block they come upon a green car abandoned in the middle of the street and four males walking away from the car, less than one-half block in distance. From these facts we conclude that the police were obviously in "hot pursuit" of their suspects and consequently we feel that any course of action, other than arresting appellants, would have constituted a dereliction of their duty to the public. . . .

We have thoroughly considered each of appellants' other allegations of error and we find that they do not warrant extended discussion. Since the officers had probable cause to arrest appellants and

4. Brinegar v. United States, 338 U.S. 160, 175–176, 69 S.Ct. 1302, 93 L.Ed. 1879 (1949). Accord, Carroll v. United States, 267 U.S. 132, 45 S.Ct. 280, 69 L.Ed. 543 (1925). While the Supreme Court's opinion in *Brinegar* is generally recognized as the standard-bearer in the probable cause area it is interesting to note that as early as 1813 the eminent Chief Justice Marshall counseled us that "the term 'probable cause,' according to its usual acceptation, means less than evidence which would justify condemnation. . . ." Locke v. United States, 11 U.S. (7 Cranch) 339, 348, 3 L.Ed. 364 (1813).

5. Bailey v. United States, 128 U.S. App.D.C. 354, 357–358, 389 F.2d 305, 308–309 (1967).

6. Davis & Sams v. United States, 133 U.S.App.D.C. 172, at 174, 409 F.2d 458, at 460 (decided February 18, 1969).

since their trial was fairly conducted in all aspects, the convictions of each must be

Affirmed.[1]

(d) For felony by arrestee

Under the English common law an officer arresting for felony who apprehended an innocent person was not justified unless he had probable ground to believe him guilty, but proof that the arrestee was the felon was justification in itself.[1] This has sometimes been codified, as in a statute providing that a peace officer "may, without a warrant, arrest a person; . . . (2) When a person arrested has committed a felony, although not in his presence. (3) Whenever he has reasonable cause to believe that the person to be arrested has committed a felony, whether or not a felony has in fact been committed." [2] At the present time, on the other hand, at least in the absence of express statutory authority therefor, it "is an elementary maxim that a search, seizure or arrest cannot be retroactively justified by what is uncovered".[3] And the trend of the case law is such as to cast serious doubt about the validity of a statute purporting to authorize an arrest without either a warrant or probable cause to believe the arrestee guilty.

(e) On official information

The common law of arrest developed before the appearance of the telephone, the telegraph, the radio, and the official law-enforcement bulletin. These, together with changes such as the substitution of the automobile for the horse as the common means of transportation, require certain additions to the authority of an officer to arrest without a warrant.

1. The weight of authority seems to be: ". . . it is expressly declared in all of the authorities that the constitutional provision against search and seizure has reference only to general searches for the purpose of obtaining evidence, and has no reference to, nor does it prevent, arrests in proper cases without warrant." United States v. Rembert, 284 F. 996, 1001 (S.D.Tex.1922); Commonwealth v. Phelps, 209 Mass. 396, 95 N.E. 868 (1911). See note, 1 A.L.R. 585 (1919).

Warrantless arrest of a suspect for a felony in his home when officers enter in hot pursuit is constitutional. Warden v. Hayden, 387 U.S. 294, 87 S.Ct. 1642 (1967).

1. 2 Hale, P.C. *85. Even a private person was justified in the arrest if his arrestee was in fact the felon. Id. at *78. And see State v. Williams, 14 S.W.2d 434, 435–6 (Mo.1929).

"A private citizen, on the other hand, is privileged to make an arrest only where he has reasonable grounds for believing in the guilt of the person arrested and a felony has in fact been committed." United States v. Hillsman, 522 F.2d 454, 461 (7th Cir. 1975).

2. West's Ann.Cal.Pen.Code, § 836 (1970).

3. United States v. Como, 340 F.2d 891, 893 (2d Cir. 1965).

"[A]n arrest is not justified by what the subsequent search discloses." Henry v. United States, 361 U.S. 98, 104, 80 S.Ct. 168, 4 L.Ed.2d 134 (1959).

It is commonplace today for important parts of the instructions issued by the headquarters of a law-enforcement unit to be sent to the various officers by radio and by an official bulletin issued periodically. It is also commonplace for one officer to receive an official communication from another officer by telephone, telegraph or letter. Due recognition should be given to such official communications. As yet very little has been done in this direction. Louisiana has pointed the way with a statute authorizing an officer to arrest without a warrant when "the peace officer has received positive and reliable information that another peace officer from this state holds an arrest warrant, or a peace officer of another state or the United States holds an arrest warrant for a felony offense." [a]

(iii) Place of Arrest

The chief peace officer of the ancient village was a bailiff; and the village itself was called a "wick." In the course of time "bailiff's wick" was contracted into "bailiwick" and came to mean the territory or area throughout which a peace officer exercises his authority as such as a matter of law. Thus, in the absence of some special provision, the bailiwick of a member of the state police or state highway patrol is the state itself, the bailiwick of a sheriff is his county, and the bailiwick of a policeman is his town or city. The possibility of broader authority by some special provision of law must not be overlooked. The Alabama statute, for example, expressly authorizes a policeman or marshal to arrest anywhere within the limits of the county in which his city, town or village is situated.[1] It must not be assumed that an officer may never act in an official capacity outside of his bailiwick, because this may be authorized by some special statute.[2] For example, some states expressly authorize a peace officer to execute a warrant anywhere in the state,[3] and any state having the Uniform Act on Fresh Pursuit expressly authorizes peace officers of other states to follow a fleeing felon across its boundary and arrest him within its territory. Any such special enactment will extend the authority of a peace officer in the particular situation specified, but it does not enlarge his bailiwick. It enables him to perform certain acts in an official capacity outside of his bailiwick. It is strictly construed, and hence legislative authorization for an officer to execute a warrant in any part of the state does not empower him to arrest *without a warrant* outside of his own bailiwick.[4]

Under the English common law a warrant issued by a judge of the King's Bench extended all over the kingdom, and was dated merely "England," but a warrant issued by a justice of the peace was good only in his county unless it was "backed" (endorsed) by the justice of another county, whereupon it could be executed therein.[5] In this country it is necessary to examine the statutes of each particular

a. La.Stat.Ann.—C.Cr.Proc. Art. 213(4) (1981).

1. Ala.Code, tit. 15, § 15–10–1 (1977).

2. Utah Code Ann., 1953, § 77–9–3.

3. Tenn.Code Ann. § 40–6–212 (1982).

4. Henson v. State, 120 Tex.Cr.R. 176, 49 S.W.2d 463 (1932).

5. 4 Bl.Comm. *291–2.

state. Some of these statutes are very similar to the English common law,[6] some require the warrant to be directed to a peace officer of the county in which the prosecution is brought but authorize him to execute it in any county in the state,[7] some authorize the direction to be to officers of the state generally so that the warrant may be executed in any county in the state, but limit each officer to his own bailiwick so far as execution is concerned,[8] while many others have the sweeping provision that a warrant of arrest may be executed in any part of the state by any peace officer of the state.[9]

By a rather common provision, if a person who has been lawfully arrested escapes, or is rescued, the person from whose custody he has unlawfully departed may immediately pursue him and retake him without a warrant in any place within the state.[10] An occasional suggestion for statutory change would authorize an officer, as such, to arrest without a warrant, outside of his bailiwick, for an offense committed in his presence, whether the officer was outside of his bailiwick when the offense was committed or was within his bailiwick at that time and followed the offender outside on fresh pursuit.[11]

(iv) Arrest of Fugitive From Another Jurisdiction [1]

Most jurisdictions authorize law enforcement officers to arrest a person for a serious offense on reasonable grounds that the person arrested is a fugitive from a foreign jurisdiction.[2] Individuals who

6. Or.Rev.Stats. 133.150, 133.160 (1957). Now see Or.Rev.Stat. 133.120 (1981).

7. Del.Rev.Code, §§ 4468, 4477 (1935). And see the interpretation of the Washington statute in Nadeau v. Conn, 142 Wash. 243, 252 P. 913 (1927). The Delaware statute now authorizes the arrest "by any officer authorized by law". Del. Code Ann., Super.Court Rule 4(c)(1) (1975).

8. Such a provision was construed in York v. Commonwealth, 82 Ky. 360 (1884).

9. Ariz.Rev.Stats.; Cr.Proc.Rule 3.3 (1973).

10. See the statutes of Alabama, Arizona, California, Iowa and New York.

11. See United States v. Braggs, 189 F.2d 367 (10th Cir. 1951). Utah Code Ann., 1953, § 77–9–3.

1. A bench warrant was issued in the District of Wyoming for the arrest of plaintiff. Relying upon this warrant, a United States marshal for the District of Columbia arrested plaintiff without a warrant in the latter jurisdiction. The court, speaking through Brandeis, J., upheld the arrest: "The original arrest and detention were lawful. A person duly charged with a felony in one State, may, if he flees to another, be arrested, without a warrant, by a peace officer in the State in which he is found and be detained for the reasonable time necessary to enable a requisition to be made. . . . The rule is not less liberal where the fugitive stands charged by an indictment found in one federal district and flees to another. . . . If the bench warrant issued in Wyoming was not effective as a warrant within the District of Columbia, the possession of it did not render illegal an arrest which could lawfully have been made without it. It would, at least serve as evidence that . . . [the marshal] . . . had reasonable cause to believe that a felony had been committed by [the plaintiff]." Stallings v. Splain, 253 U.S. 339, 341–2, 40 S.Ct. 537, 538, 64 L.Ed. 940 (1920). See notes, 46 Am.St.Rep. 414 (1895); 26 L.R.A. 33 (1895). As to a violation of the federal Fugitive Felon Act see Bircham v. Commonwealth, 238 S.W.2d 1008 (Ky. 1951).

2. § 14 of the Uniform Criminal Extradition Act, 11 U.La. p. 252 (1974) provides: "The arrest of a person may be lawfully made also by any peace officer or a private person, without a warrant upon reasonable information that the accused stands charged in the courts of a

are fugitives from justice from one state may be arrested in another state pursuant to a request from the demanding state for the arrest of the fugitive;[3] however, frequently, police officers in a jurisdiction other than the one from which the suspect fled have occasion to discover that an individual is wanted by another jurisdiction where no request for arrest has been made. This occurs frequently when the person who is a fugitive is lawfully stopped for some reason in the jurisdiction to which the person has fled and the investigating officer has run a National Crime Information Center computer check to determine whether there is an outstanding warrant for the suspect. Upon being advised that a warrant is outstanding or receiving other probable cause to establish the person to be a fugitive, the officer may affect an arrest to hold the fugitive pending extradition to the jurisdiction where the individual is sought and where charges are pending. This process has been upheld by the courts.[4]

(v) Time of Arrest

In the absence of some statutory restriction an arrest for crime, lawful in other respects, may be made on any day and at any hour of the day or night. Most of the statutes which mention time grant this authority, but a few of them make some restrictions in misdemeanor cases. Statutes in a few states do not authorize arrest for a misdemeanor at night unless upon the direction of the Magistrate endorsed upon the warrant;[a] a few others do not authorize arrest for a misdemeanor at night unless there is such authority in the warrant or the arrest is for an offense committed in the presence of the apprehending officer;[b] and a few do not authorize arrest for a misdemeanor either at night or on Sunday unless upon the direction of the Magistrate endorsed upon the warrant.[c] Some statutes provide that any arrest warrant may be served at anytime of the day or night.[d]

(vi) Rights, Privileges and Duties

---

(1) Manifestation of Purpose and Authority

Whatever crime one may have committed in the past, if he is engaged in no offense at the moment, he is privileged to use force if

state with a crime punishable by death or imprisonment for a term exceeding one year. . . ."

3. The asylum state will, on proper request, issue a warrant for the arrest of the fugitive pending extradition to the demanding state. §§ 6, 7, 13 Uniform Criminal Extradition Act, 11 U.La. p. 166, 180, 249 (1974).

4. Where the defendant was stopped by an officer who had previously seen a National Crime Information Center (NCIC) printout showing an outstanding warrant for the defendant and an F.B.I. wanted flyer on the defendant, the officer had probable cause to arrest the defendant. United States v. McDonald, 606 F.2d 552 (5th Cir. 1979).

a. Idaho Code Ann. § 19–607 (1979).

b. West's Ann.Cal.Pen.Code, § 840 (1976) (10 p.m. to 6 a.m.).

c. Minn.Stats.Ann. § 629.31 (1971).

d. McKinney's Consol.L.N.Y.Cr.Proc. § 120.80 (1981).

necessary to defend himself against any unlawful act which threatens him with death or injury or deprivation of his liberty.[1] And because of the mistake of fact doctrine it is important for him to know whether he is confronted with such danger or is dealing with a "minister of justice." Hence there is a common-law requirement that one about to be arrested is entitled to notice, if he does not already know, of (1) the intention to take him into the custody of the law, (2) the authority for the arrest, and (3) the reason therefor. This manifestation of purpose and authority is the so-called "Notice of arrest." The common law does not require this manifestation of purpose and authority if the making thereof is reasonably believed by the arrester to be: (a) dangerous to the arrester or to a third person, or (b) likely to imperil the making of the arrest or (c) useless or unnecessary.[2] A statutory provision substantially as follows is not uncommon:

"The person making the arrest must inform the person to be arrested of the intention to arrest him, of the cause of arrest, and the authority to make it, except when the person to be arrested is actually engaged in the commission of or attempt to commit an offense, or is pursued immediately after its commission, or after an escape. If the person making the arrest is acting under the authority of a warrant, he must show the warrant, if required." [3]

The American Law Institute, in restating the common law, says:

"If a peace officer makes an arrest without a warrant, the fact that he is in uniform, or so displays his badge of office as to be reasonably visible to the other, is a sufficient manifestation that he is making an arrest upon suspicion of felony or for a breach of the peace or other conduct for which by common law or by statute he is authorized to arrest the other." [4]

More than this, however, is required by many of the statutes.[5]

(2) Use of Force

The authority to arrest carries with it the privilege of using reasonable force if necessary to accomplish this purpose. Unless the arrester has authority to make the particular arrest, any force used by him to effect the apprehension will be unlawful. Hence it is necessary to distinguish between the authority to arrest and the authority to

1. Starr v. United States, 153 U.S. 614, 14 S.Ct. 919, 38 L.Ed. 841 (1894); State v. Phillips, 118 Iowa 660, 92 N.W. 876 (1902); State v. Belk, 76 N.C. 10 (1877).

2. Restatement, Second, Torts § 128 (1965).

3. For example, see the statutes in California, Idaho, Nevada.

4. Restatement, Second, Torts § 128, comment *d* (1965).

5. Ala.Code, 15–10–4 (1977); West's Ann.Cal.Pen.Code, § 841 (1970); Tenn. Code Ann. § 40–7–106 (1982).

use force in accomplishing the arrest. The general rule is that the arrester is privileged to use reasonable force in order to make an authorized arrest. It assumes lawful authority for the arrest itself, and states in substance that in making or attempting such an arrest the arrester is privileged to make use of reasonable force, and is not privileged to employ any greater degree of force. Hence an arrester acts unlawfully if he uses more than reasonable force in making or attempting an arrest, however much authority he might have for the arrest itself.

The courts should not, as stated by a federal judge, "lay down rules which will make it so dangerous for officers to perform their duties that they will shrink and hesitate from action which the proper protection of society demands." [1] Hence in distinguishing the degree of force permitted for the purpose of making an arrest from that which is unlawful the question is not whether it exceeded the actual necessity in some slight way, but whether it was reasonable under all of the circumstances or grossly excessive.[2] To quote from a Missouri case: "An officer in making an arrest should use no unnecessary violence; but it being his duty to make an arrest, the law clothes him with the power to accomplish that result. His duty is to overcome all resistance and bring the party to be arrested under physical restraint and the means he may use must be co-extensive with the duty, and so the law is written." [3]

In a very general way it is said to be lawful to kill if necessary to arrest for felony but not if the person is to be arrested for a misdemeanor only.[4] Defensive force must be distinguished from force employed solely for the purpose of apprehension. The arrester, if placed in danger by the violence of the arrestee, may use whatever force reasonably seems necessary to save himself from death or great bodily harm,—and he may do this without abandoning the effort to arrest, and whether the arrest is for felony or misdemeanor.[5] "The officer must of necessity be the aggressor; his mission is not accomplished when he wards off the assault; he must press forward and accomplish his object, he is not bound to put off the arrest until a more favorable time. Because of these duties devolved upon him the law throws around him a special protection".[6] Hence he may "freely and without retreating repel force by force".[7]

1. Stinnett v. Virginia, 55 F.2d 644, 647 (4th Cir. 1932).

2. "It is when excessive force has been used maliciously, or to such a degree as amounts to a wanton abuse of authority that criminal liability will be imputed." State v. Dunning, 177 N.C. 559, 562, 98 S.E. 530, 531 (1919).

3. State v. Fuller, 96 Mo. 165, 168, 9 S.W. 583, 584 (1888).

4. 1 Bishop, New Criminal Procedure § 159 (2d ed., Underhill, 1913). See note, Homicide by official action or by officers of justice, 67 L.R.A. 292 (1905).

5. Restatement, Second, Torts §§ 65, 131, comment *d* (1965).

6. State v. Dierberger, 96 Mo. 666, 675, 10 S.W. 168, 171 (1888); State v. Ford, 344 Mo. 1219, 130 S.W.2d 635 (1939).

7. Foster, Crown Law 321 (2d ed. 1791).

The American Law Institute originally took the position that no one, officer or private person, with or without a warrant, is privileged to use deadly force merely to stop the flight of one whose arrest is sought for a nondangerous felony.[8] This was so obviously not a restatement of the law that the Institute felt obliged to amend the wording in 1948.[9] The modern common law does not authorize a private person to use deadly force to effect an arrest unless it is for a felony of violence such as murder, arson, rape, robbery, burglary or mayhem. But it authorizes a peace officer to use deadly force if this reasonably seems necessary in making an arrest for felony. This goes too far and the Model Penal Code would limit the use of deadly force to the officer who is arresting for felony and believes that the arrestee has used or threatened to use deadly force or will probably cause death or serious bodily harm if his apprehension is delayed. (Section 3.7(2)(b)). This position has been adopted in some of the new penal codes.

An apprehending officer has the privilege of taking reasonable steps to protect himself from harm and to prevent escape of his prisoner. Hence if he believes, and has reasonable grounds for believing, such precaution necessary, he may handcuff or otherwise manacle his prisoner. This privilege depends upon all of the facts of each particular case, and an officer may be acting unlawfully if he should handcuff one arrested on a minor traffic charge if there was no resistance and no other reason for believing handcuffing necessary.[10] There is, however, support for an officer routinely handcuffing a prisoner who has been formally arrested and is to be transported.[11]

The mere fact that the arrest is on a traffic charge, however, or for some other relatively minor offense, is not of itself conclusive of the precautions the officer may take. An officer has been killed by one arrested on a minor traffic charge who happened to be a gangster wanted for murder although not recognized as such by the arrester. Hence an apprehending officer is entitled to consider not only the offense for which the arrest is made, but the prisoner himself—his reputation if known, and in any case his appearance and his con-

8. Restatement, Torts § 131 and particularly illustration 1 (1934).

9. Restatement, 1948 Supp. p. 628. See now Restatement, Second, Torts § 131 (1965).

Ex parte Warner, 21 F.2d 542, 543 (N.D.Okl.1927); Stinnett v. Virginia, 55 F.2d 644, 646–7 (4th Cir. 1932); Jackson v. State, 66 Miss. 89, 5 So. 690, 692 (1888); Thompson v. Norfolk & W.R. Co., 116 W.Va. 705, 182 S.E. 880, 883 (1935). The Warner case involved a violation of the prohibition law. In the Jackson case the court did not deem it necessary to disclose what the felony was but the inference is that it was larceny. In the Stinnett case the court expressly referred to the limitation suggested (to dangerous felonies) and held that this is not the common law.

"Where a felony of violence has been committed, moreover, a private citizen may use reasonable force, including deadly force, to prevent the felon's escape from the scene," United States v. Hillsman, 522 F.2d 454, 461 (7th Cir. 1975).

10. 1 Wharton, Criminal Procedure § 102 (10th ed., Kerr, 1918).

11. Healy v. City of Brentwood, 649 S.W.2d 916 (Mo.App.1983).

duct—together with any other facts which may indicate whether violence or attempted escape is to be expected.

If the arrest is for felony the officer is privileged to handcuff his prisoner even if there has been no actual resistance or attempt to escape or evidence indicating the probability of either.[12]

(3) Arrest in the Home

In *Payton* the Supreme Court said: "We now . . . hold that the Fourth Amendment to the United States Constitution, made applicable to the States by the Fourteenth Amendment, prohibits the police from making a warrantless and nonconsensual entry into a suspect's home in order to make a routine felony arrest." [1] Three dissenting Justices presented a rather convincing argument in support of the claim that from ancient times the common law has authorized an officer, having lawful authority to make a warrantless arrest for felony, to break into the arrestee's home if necessary to accomplish his mission. And this seems to have been the prevailing view. Thus a distinguished scholar, speaking of the English law said: "In cases directly involving the crown, the rule was that 'the King's keys unlocked all doors.' " [2] And the American Law Institute in drafting a Code of Criminal Procedure worded one section as follows, in the belief that it represented the sound view: "An officer, in order to make an arrest either by virtue of a warrant, or when authorized to make such arrest for felony without a warrant, as provided in section 21, may break open a door or window of any building in which the person to be arrested is or is reasonably believed to be, if he is refused admittance after he has announced his authority and purpose." [3]

12. "There must be some discretion reposed in a sheriff or other officer, making an arrest for felony, as to the means taken to apprehend the supposed offender, and to keep him safe and secure after such apprehension:" Firestone v. Rice, 71 Mich. 377, 384, 38 N.W. 885, 888 (1888).

"The sheriff cannot stop, when the man is unknown to him, at the moment of arrest, to inquire into his character, or his intentions as to escape, or his guilt or innocence of the offense charged against him. His duty is to take him, to safely keep him, and to bring his body before a magistrate. If he does this without wantonness or malice, it is not for a jury to find that his precautions were useless and unnecessary in the light of after-acquired knowledge of the true character and intent of the accused, and to punish the sheriff in damages for what honestly appeared to him at the time to be reasonable and right." Id. at 387, 38 N.W., at 889.

"Where a private person undertakes to arrest a felon or an escaped felon, and has made his purpose and reason for the arrest known, he must then proceed in a peaceable manner to make the arrest and if he is resisted he may use such force as is necessary to overcome the resistance, if used for that purpose alone." State v. Stancill, 128 N.C. 606, 610, 38 S.E. 926, 928 (1901).

As to the liability of a state officer who deals with his prisoner in such a way as to violate the prisoner's rights under the Fourteenth Amendment see Lynch v. United States, 189 F.2d 476 (5th Cir. 1951).

1. Payton v. New York, 445 U.S. 573, 100 S.Ct. 1371, 1374–75 (1980).

2. Wilgus, Arrest Without a Warrant, 22 Mich.L.Rev. 798, 800 (1924).

3. A.L.I. Code of Criminal Procedure, Section 28 (1931). And see A.L.I. A Model Code of Pre-Arraignment Procedure, App. XI (1975).

Furthermore: "A majority of the States that have taken a position on the question permit warrantless entry into the home to arrest even in the absence of exigent circumstances." [4] A majority of the Court, however, has established that at least this is no longer true in this country. In the absence of a warrant or "exigent circumstance," [5] there can be no entry into a dwelling to make an arrest without consent. No attempt was made to indicate what is included within the term "exigent circumstances," but there can be no doubt that imminent danger to human life [6] or an arrest on hot pursuit [7] would qualify. The risk of death cannot wait upon the issuance of a warrant, nor can a fleeing felon avoid arrest by running into his house a few steps ahead of a pursuing officer. It seems that impending loss of important evidence will also be included.[8]

It was noted later that "an arrest warrant alone will suffice to enter a suspect's own residence to effect his arrest." [9] But it was held that a valid arrest warrant does not authorize the arrest to be made in the home of another. In the absence of either "exigent circumstances" or consent the officer with valid arrest warrant will need also a search warrant in order to go into the house of another where the arrestee is reasonably believed to be. The Court added: "Finally, the exigent circumstances doctrine significantly limits the situations in which a search warrant would be needed. For example, a warrantless entry of a home would be justified if the police were in 'hot pursuit' of a fugitive. Thus, to the extent that searches for persons pose special problems, we believe that the exigent circumstances doctrine is adequate to accommodate legitimate law enforcement needs." [10]

UNITED STATES v. WICKIZER

United States Court of Appeals, Sixth Circuit, 1980.
633 F.2d 900.

NATHANIEL R. JONES, CIRCUIT JUDGE.

Norman Earl Wickizer appeals from a conviction for unlawfully receiving or possessing unregistered firearms in violation of 26 U.S.C. §§ 5861(d) and 5871.

4. 445 U.S., at 598, 100 S.Ct., at 1386.

5. "Accordingly, we have no occasion to consider the sort of emergency or dangerous situation, described in our cases as 'exigent circumstances,' that would justify a warrantless entry into the home for the purpose of either arrest or search." 445 U.S., at 583, 100 S.Ct. at 1378.

6. Warden v. Hayden, 387 U.S. 294, 298–99, 87 S.Ct. 1642, 1645–46 (1967).

7. United States v. Santana, 427 U.S. 38, 42–43, 96 S.Ct. 2406, 2409–10 (1976).

8. Schmerber v. California, 384 U.S. 757, 770–71, 86 S.Ct. 1826, 1835–36 (1966). "Generally, if there is a reasonable possibility of injury or death if the entry not be made, or if there is a likelihood that the suspect will escape if the entry not be made, 'exigent circumstances' exist." Weddle v. State, 621 P.2d 231, 240 (Wyo.1980).

9. Steagald v. United States, 451 U.S. 204, 101 S.Ct. 1642, 1652 (1981).

10. Ibid. (Citations omitted).

On October 26, 1979, the sheriff for Madison County, Indiana, wrote the Kentucky State Police to advise them that Ernest Smith and David Taylor had escaped from jail. The letter stated the sheriff's belief that Smith was going to the Harlan County area in Kentucky.

On November 13, 1979, the Kentucky State Police filed a criminal complaint alleging that Smith was a fugitive from justice with the Trial Commissioner in the Harlan County District Court. The Trial Commissioner was given the Indiana Sheriff's letter at this time. An arrest warrant was issued for Smith.

On December 6 or 7, 1979, two state police officers received a tip that Smith was staying at a cabin with another man and woman and that both men were armed. The cabin was owned by Smith's stepbrother. The police were told that Smith said he wouldn't be taken alive. The police believed the man with Smith was Taylor.

On December 7, 1979, five state police officers and two Harlan County Deputy Sheriffs went to the cabin to arrest Smith. Although they had the arrest warrant, they had not acquired a search warrant for the premises.

When the police arrived at the cabin they found the door was locked. The police then kicked in the door without knocking or announcing their identity. After kicking in the door an officer shouted "police, take it easy."

There were four people inside the cabin: Smith, Wickizer, and two women. They were asleep on two mattresses.

Smith and Wickizer were taken outside and handcuffed. The officers noticed two guns propped up against the wall near the mattresses. One was a sawed-off .30 calibre carbine; the other was a sawed-off .22 calibre rifle. These rifles were in the plain view of the officers.

Wickizer filed a motion to suppress the firearms alleging an unlawful search and seizure. The motion was denied.

Wickizer appeals from the denial of the motion to suppress.

Wickizer contends that the government had the burden of justifying the search and seizure of the firearms because an arrest warrant was not issued in his name and the police did not have a search warrant. He asserts that the district court improperly allocated the burden of proof.

The burden of establishing a *prima facie* case of an unlawful search and seizure is on the movant, once he makes out a *prima facie* case the burden shifts to the government. Wickizer made a prima facie case, but the district court concluded that the government carried its burden. The evidence presented by Wickizer's witnesses about the facts of the arrest was ample to conclude the arrest was not improper.

Wickizer asserts that the arrest warrant issued for Smith was improper. He contends the district court erred in considering the letter from the Indiana State Police in upholding the warrant.

In determining that there was probable cause to support the arrest warrant the district court considered both the affidavit of the detective who swore Smith was a fugitive from justice and the letter sent by the Indiana State Police. The court concluded: "as the letter was tendered at the same time [as the affidavit], although it, is not specifically incorporated by reference, it is logical to consider it as an addendum to the complaint."

Wickizer contends that Kentucky law requires that a determination of probable cause be confined to the affidavit. He relies on Robinson v. Commonwealth, 550 S.W.2d 496 (Ky.1977). *Robinson* is not on point. Although it does state that the determination of probable cause is confined to the affidavit, this language was intended to state that if a warrant is valid on its face, the court will not go behind these allegations to determine if they were based on sufficient evidence.

The district court's consideration of the Indiana Police letter was not error. The evidence supports the conclusion that the letter was given to the Trial Commissioner before the warrant was issued. It was proper to consider information before a magistrate other than that contained in the affidavit. In this case, the letter and the affidavit were sufficient to justify the issuance of the arrest warrant.

Wickizer's next contention is that even if the arrest warrant was valid, it did not authorize the police to enter the cabin. There is no merit to this argument.

In Payton v. New York, 445 U.S. 573, 100 S.Ct. 1371, 63 L.Ed.2d 639 (1980), the Supreme Court stated "For Fourth Amendment purposes, an arrest warrant founded on probable cause implicitly carries with it the limited authority to enter a dwelling in which the suspect lives when there is reason to believe the suspect is within." 100 S.Ct. at 1388. We believe the police were properly authorized to enter the cabin.

The seizure of the rifles was also valid under the plain view doctrine. Coolidge v. New Hampshire, 403 U.S. 443, 91 S.Ct. 2022, 29 L.Ed.2d 564 (1971). Although there was a conflict in the testimony about when the rifles were seen, one police officer testified that the rifles were seen when the police first entered the cabin. The district court found this was true. The rifles were leaning against the wall in plain view. Both rifles were sawed off to an illegal length and the court found they were "obviously contraband." This was a fact question and the court concluded the officers saw the rifles when they entered the cabin. In these circumstances, we hold that the seizure of the rifles was proper.

The police also had probable cause to arrest Wickizer. The police were entitled to ask Wickizer to go outside the cabin because "[a] brief stop of a suspicious individual in order to determine his identity or to maintain the status quo momentarily while obtaining mere information, may be most reasonable in light of the facts known to the officer at the time." The district court found that "when the officers had Smith and Wickizer get out of the cabin, they had seen firearms propped against the wall near the mattresses." Once the rifles were seized the police had probable cause to arrest Wickizer for possession of the sawed-off rifle nearest him.

We have examined Wickizer's other contentions and we find none of them has merit.

AFFIRMED.

(4) Search of Prisoner

The common law authorizes any person making a lawful arrest to search the arrestee (unless such a search is obviously uncalled for) and to take from him any (a) offensive weapons or articles that might be useful in effecting an escape, or (b) fruits of the crime for which he was arrested or other evidence tending to prove him guilty thereof.[1] A very large discretion is extended to the arrester in this regard, particularly if he is an officer. Thus it has been held that an officer may remove the clothing of his prisoner if this is necessary under the circumstances for an effective search of his person.[2] Reasonable doubts must be resolved in favor of the officer, but obviously unreasonable steps must be avoided. It has been held, for example, that a male officer exceeded his privilege, after an arrest of a servant girl, on a charge of larceny, by requiring her to strip and stand naked before him.[3] Such procedure should be left to the police matron,—or to some matron called upon to assist the officer for this special purpose, if no police matron is available. Recent cases have questioned the propriety of strip searches of persons arrested for minor offenses.[4]

Few of the statutes express the full scope of the common-law privilege of search and seizure incidental to a lawful arrest.[5] Many of

1. Hughes v. State, 145 Tenn. 544, 238 S.W. 588 (1922); Harris v. United States, 331 U.S. 145, 67 S.Ct. 1098, 91 L.Ed. 1399 (1947); Fischer v. State, 195 Md. 477, 74 A.2d 34 (1950).

2. "We think that the coroner, the sheriff, or a policeman, when he arrests a person charged with crime, has a right to search that person for evidences of his guilt, and if, in the prosecution of this search, it becomes necessary to remove the clothing of such person, the officer has a right to do so, . . . " Woolfolk v. State, 81 Ga. 551, 562, 8 S.E. 724, 728 (1889).

3. Hebrew v. Pulis, 73 N.J.L. 621, 64 A. 121 (1906). The girl was not under technical arrest when the search was ordered; however the court stated, "But, even if the case had been such that the officer would have been justified in arresting without a warrant, we think he was not justified in compelling the plaintiff to strip naked." 625, 64 A. at 122.

4. Tinetti v. Wittke, 479 F.Supp. 486 (E.D.Wis.1979), affirmed 620 F.2d 160 (7th Cir.).

5. The Michigan statute provides for taking from the arrestee "all offensive weapons or incriminating articles," which

the codes have no provision on the subject thus leaving it entirely to the common law. As said by the Missouri court: "We find no statute of this State giving the arresting officer authority to search a prisoner, but no statute is necessary. The power exists from the nature and objects of the public duty the officer is required to perform. Such authority is directly given to a committing magistrate by statute (section 4308), but unless the arresting officer has the authority immediately, on making the arrest, all evidence of crime and of identification of the criminal might be destroyed before the prisoner could be taken before the magistrate." [6]

Some of the statutes express part only of the common-law authority, such as this: "Any person making a lawful arrest may take from the person arrested all offensive weapons which he may have about his person and shall deliver them to the magistrate before whom he is taken." [7] "We do not think," said the Iowa court, "that an officer making an arrest is precluded by this statute from taking from the person of the prisoner any property other than 'offensive weapons.' " [8]

CHIMEL v. CALIFORNIA

Supreme Court of the United States, 1969.
395 U.S. 752, 89 S.Ct. 2034.

MR. JUSTICE STEWART delivered the opinion of the Court.

This case raises basic questions concerning the permissible scope under the Fourth Amendment of a search incident to a lawful arrest.

seems to cover the field. Mich.Stats. Ann. § 28.884 (1978).

6. Holker v. Hennessey, 141 Mo. 527, 540, 42 S.W. 1090, 1093 (1897).

7. Such a provision, in substance, is found in the statutes of California, Idaho, Nevada, Oklahoma.

8. Commercial Exchange Bank v. McLeod, 65 Iowa 665, 667, 19 N.W. 329 (1884), 22 N.W. 919 (1885).

"It is a general rule that whenever officers have authority to conduct a search, their search can extend to portable effects, such as the contents of baggage, box, or bundle." Wright v. State, 177 Md. 230, 233, 9 A.2d 253, 255 (1939).

It may extend to the automobile the arrestee is driving at the time of the arrest. Arthur v. State, 227 Ind. 493, 86 N.E.2d 698 (1950); State v. Ragland, 171 Kan. 530, 233 P.2d 740 (1951); Callahan v. State, 42 Okl.Cr. 425, 276 P. 494 (1929); Fuqua v. State, 175 Tenn. 11, 130 S.W.2d 125 (1939).

Search of the automobile cabin area of a vehicle incident to arrest of the operator is proper. New York v. Belton, 453 U.S. 454, 101 S.Ct. 2860 (1981).

As to the involuntary use of the stomach pump to obtain evidence see Rochin v. California, 342 U.S. 165, 72 S.Ct. 205, 96 L.Ed. 183 (1952).

Obtaining evidence from the mouth by means of a "judo choke" was held to violate due process because it was dangerous. People v. Sanders, 268 Cal.App.2d 802, 74 Cal.Rptr. 350 (1969).

"When officers, in the course of a bona fide effort to execute a valid search warrant, discover articles which, although not included in the warrant, are reasonably identifiable as contraband, they may seize them whether they are initially in plain sight or come into plain sight subsequently, as a result of the officers' efforts." Skelton v. Superior Court of Orange County, 1 Cal.3d 144, 81 Cal.Rptr. 613, 622, 460 P.2d 485 (1969).

Seizure of a tied off opaque balloon on the seat beside a driver of a vehicle that

The relevant facts are essentially undisputed. Late in the afternoon of September 13, 1965, three police officers arrived at the Santa Ana, California, home of the petitioner with a warrant authorizing his arrest for the burglary of a coin shop. The officers knocked on the door, identified themselves to the petitioner's wife, and asked if they might come inside. She ushered them into the house, where they waited 10 or 15 minutes until the petitioner returned home from work. When the petitioner entered the house, one of the officers handed him the arrest warrant and asked for permission to "look around." The petitioner objected, but was advised that "on the basis of the lawful arrest," the officers would nonetheless conduct a search. No search warrant had been issued.

Accompanied by the petitioner's wife, the officers then looked through the entire three-bedroom house, including the attic, the garage, and a small workshop. In some rooms the search was relatively cursory. In the master bedroom and sewing room, however, the officers directed the petitioner's wife to open drawers and "to physically move contents of the drawers from side to side so that [they] might view any items that would have come from [the] burglary." After completing the search, they seized numerous items—primarily coins, but also several medals, tokens, and a few other objects. The entire search took between 45 minutes and an hour.

At the petitioner's subsequent state trial on two charges of burglary, the items taken from his house were admitted into evidence against him, over his objection that they had been unconstitutionally seized. He was convicted, and the judgments of conviction were affirmed by both the California District Court of Appeal, 61 Cal.Rptr. 714, and the California Supreme Court, 68 Cal.2d 436, 67 Cal.Rptr. 421, 439 P.2d 333. Both courts accepted the petitioner's contention that the arrest warrant was invalid because the supporting affidavit was set out in conclusory terms, but held that since the arresting officers had procured the warrant "in good faith", and since in any event they had had sufficient information to constitute probable cause for the petitioner's arrest, that arrest had been lawful. From this conclusion the appellate courts went on to hold that the search of the petitioner's home had been justified, despite the absence of a search warrant, on the ground that it had been incident to a valid arrest. We granted certiorari in order to consider the petitioner's substantial constitutional claims.

Without deciding the question, we proceed on the hypothesis that the California courts were correct in holding that the arrest of the petitioner was valid under the Constitution. This brings us directly to the question whether the warrantless search of the petitioner's entire house can be constitutionally justified as incident to that arrest. The decisions of this Court bearing upon that question have been far

has been lawfully stopped is proper under the plain view doctrine. Texas v. Brown, ___ U.S. ___, 103 S.Ct. 1535 (1983).

from consistent, as even the most cursory review makes evident. . . .

When an arrest is made, it is reasonable for the arresting officer to search the person arrested in order to remove any weapons that the latter might seek to use in order to resist arrest or effect his escape. Otherwise, the officer's safety might well be endangered, and the arrest itself frustrated. In addition, it is entirely reasonable for the arresting officer to search for and seize any evidence on the arrestee's person in order to prevent its concealment or destruction. And the area into which an arrestee might reach in order to grab a weapon or evidentiary items must, of course, be governed by a like rule. A gun on a table or in a drawer in front of one who is arrested can be as dangerous to the arresting officer as one concealed in the clothing of the person arrested. There is ample justification, therefore, for a search of the arrestee's person and the area "within his immediate control"—construing that phrase to mean the area from within which he might gain possession of a weapon or destructible evidence.

There is no comparable justification, however, for routinely searching rooms other than that in which an arrest occurs—or, for that matter, for searching through all the desk drawers or other closed or concealed areas in that room itself. Such searches, in the absence of well-recognized exceptions, may be made only under the authority of a search warrant. The "adherence to judicial processes" mandated by the Fourth Amendment requires no less. . . .

It would be possible, of course, to draw a line between *Rabinowitz* and *Harris* [a] on the one hand, and this case on the other. For *Rabinowitz* involved a single room, and *Harris* a four-room apartment, while in the case before us an entire house was searched. But such a distinction would be highly artificial. The rationale that allowed the searches and seizures in *Rabinowitz* and *Harris* would allow the searches and seizures in this case. No consideration relevant to the Fourth Amendment suggests any point of rational limitation, once the search is allowed to go beyond the area from which the person arrested might obtain weapons or evidentiary items. The only reasoned distinction is one between a search of the person arrested and the area within his reach on the one hand, and more extensive searches on the other.

The petitioner correctly points out that one result of decisions such as *Rabinowitz* and *Harris* is to give law enforcement officials the opportunity to engage in searches not justified by probable cause, by the simple expedient of arranging to arrest suspects at home rather than elsewhere. We do not suggest that the petitioner is necessarily correct in his assertion that such a strategy was utilized here, but the fact remains that had he been arrested earlier in the day, at his

a. [By the Compiler.] United States v. Rabinowitz, 339 U.S. 56, 70 S.Ct. 430 (1950); Harris v. United States, 331 U.S. 145, 67 S.Ct. 1098 (1947).

place of employment rather than at home, no search of his house could have been made without a search warrant. In any event, even apart from the possibility of such police tactics, the general point so forcefully made by Judge Learned Hand in United States v. Kirschenblatt, 2 Cir., 16 F.2d 202, 51 A.L.R. 416, remains:

"After arresting a man in his house, to rummage at will among his papers in search of whatever will convict him, appears to us to be indistinguishable from what might be done under a general warrant; indeed, the warrant would give more protection, for presumably it must be issued by a magistrate. True, by hypothesis the power would not exist, if the supposed offender were not found on the premises; but it is small consolation to know that one's papers are safe only so long as one is not at home." Id., at 203.

Rabinowitz and *Harris* have been the subject of critical commentary for many years, and have been relied upon less and less in our own decisions. It is time, for the reasons we have stated, to hold that on their own facts, and insofar as the principles they stand for are inconsistent with those that we have endorsed today, they are no longer to be followed.

Application of sound Fourth Amendment principles to the facts of this case produces a clear result. The search here went far beyond the petitioner's person and the area from within which he might have obtained either a weapon or something that could have been used as evidence against him. There was no constitutional justification, in the absence of a search warrant, for extending the search beyond that area. The scope of the search was, therefore, "unreasonable" under the Fourth and Fourteenth Amendments and the petitioner's conviction cannot stand.

Reversed.[b]

MR. JUSTICE HARLAN, concurring. . . .

[JUSTICES WHITE and BLACK dissented.]

b. *Chimel* applies only to searches conducted after that case was decided. Hill v. California, 401 U.S. 797, 91 S.Ct. 1106 (1971).

An officer lawfully arrested D for a *traffic violation*. The officer then conducted a full-scale search which resulted in finding heroin in a crumpled cigarette package in an inside pocket. This evidence was introduced over D's objection and resulted in a conviction of violation of the federal statute. The claim that this evidence was obtained by unlawful search and seizure was rejected. An officer making a lawful arrest may make a full search of the person arrested. He is not limited to a Terry-type frisk. And he does not need to establish any basis for the search other than the lawful arrest. United States v. Robinson, 414 U.S. 218, 94 S.Ct. 467 (1973). The same result was reached in Gustafson v. Florida, 414 U.S. 260, 94 S.Ct. 488 (1973).

"Accordingly, we hold that when a policeman has made a lawful custodial arrest of the occupant of an automobile, he may, as a contemporaneous incident of that arrest search the passenger compartment of that automobile . . . the police may also examine the contents of any containers found within the passenger compartment. . . ." New York v. Belton, 453 U.S. 454, 460, 101 S.Ct. 2860 (1981).

A state officer should not overinterpret these cases. They mean only that there is nothing in the Constitution to bar a

(5) The "Frisk"

It is common practice for an officer to pass his hands over the clothing of an arrestee in order to determine quickly whether or not any deadly weapons are concealed there. This is known as the "frisk." In one case a "frisk" may be preliminary to a thorough search; in another it may satisfy the officer that no more is needed. A "frisk" following a lawful arrest is clearly privileged—unless, in some jurisdictions, it is an arrest on a minor charge under circumstances showing plainly no reason for any search at all. The important question is whether "frisking" one who has not been arrested may be privileged in proper situations.

The law dealing with the privilege of an officer to touch the person of another had its development before the invention of a tiny deadly weapon which might be concealed in the pocket and fired without even being removed therefrom. And rules quite suitable for the day when an armed man carried a sword or a "blunderbuss," plain for everyone to see, do not give the officer adequate opportunity to protect himself against a gangster armed with a concealed weapon.

Since the constitutional bar is only against unreasonable searches and seizures it would clearly not prohibit a "frisk" *reasonably* necessary for the officer's own protection. Such authority could be granted by statute and the uniform "Arrest Act", drafted by the Interstate Commission on Crime, includes a section which will authorize a peace officer, whenever he reasonably believes it necessary for his own pro-

full-scale search incident to any lawful custodial arrest. But his state law may be more restrictive, as it is, for example in California. Thus a camper was arrested for a violation of the fire code by having an open campfire in a "high fire hazard area." A full search resulted in finding marijuana in the camper's possession. It was held that under the circumstances a pat-down, Terry-type search for weapons was authorized but the full search was not. Hence the marijuana was found as a result of unlawful search and seizure and the conviction of possession of that drug was reversed. People v. Brisendine, 13 Cal.3d 528, 119 Cal. Rptr. 315, 531 P.2d 1099 (1975).

The court reaffirmed the position taken in *Brisendine* that the California Constitution gives greater protection than the Constitution of the United States, to an arrestee. One arrested for a traffic violation is not even subject to a pat-down search unless there is probable cause to believe that weapons may be found. An exception is added. A pat-down search of the arrestee for weapons is always permissible if he is to be transported in a patrol car. People v. Norman, 14 Cal.3d 929, 123 Cal.Rptr. 109, 538 P.2d 237 (1975).

A police officer may not exceed a pat-down search of a person arrested for public intoxication when the only justification for the search is transportation in a public vehicle. A full body search may be conducted immediately prior to incarceration to prevent entry of contraband into the jail facility. People v. Longwill, 14 Cal.3d 943, 123 Cal.Rptr. 297, 538 P.2d 753 (1975).

On the other hand the Utah court, citing *Robinson*, said: "It is well settled that in making a lawful arrest an officer may make a search of the person arrested and the immediate surroundings to check for evidence of crime or dangerous weapons." State v. Lopes, 552 P.2d 120, 121–22 (Utah 1976).

A handbag carried by the defendant may be inventoried by jailers preliminary to the booking and jailing of the defendant. Illinois v. Lafayette, ___ U.S. ___, 103 S.Ct. 2605 (1983).

tection, to "frisk" for dangerous weapons any person he is lawfully questioning as a criminal suspect.[1]

TERRY v. OHIO

Supreme Court of the United States, 1968.
392 U.S. 1, 88 S.Ct. 1868.

[A police detective, McFadden, saw Terry (and others) whose conduct was strongly suggestive of criminal activity. The officer stopped Terry, identified himself, passed his hands quickly over Terry's clothing and when he felt what was obviously a revolver he reached into the pocket, seized the weapon and arrested Terry. This case was brought to test the validity of the familiar "stop and frisk". The Court rejected the claim that stopping a person for questioning is not a "seizure" and that the "frisk" is not a "search". Such procedure must be tested against the constitutional privilege to be free from unreasonable searches and seizures.]

MR. CHIEF JUSTICE WARREN delivered the opinion of the Court. . . .

We must still consider, however, the nature and quality of the intrusion on individual rights which must be accepted if police officers are to be conceded the right to search for weapons in situations where probable cause to arrest for crime is lacking. . . .

Our evaluation of the proper balance that has to be struck in this type of case leads us to conclude that there must be a narrowly drawn authority to permit a reasonable search for weapons for the protection of the police officer, where he has reason to believe that he is dealing with an armed and dangerous individual, regardless of whether he has probable cause to arrest the individual for a crime. The officer need not be absolutely certain that the individual is armed; the issue is whether a reasonably prudent man in the circumstances would be warranted in the belief that his safety or that of others was in danger. And in determining whether the officer acted reasonably in such circumstances, due weight must be given, not to his inchoate and unparticularized suspicion or "hunch," but to the specific reasonable inferences which he is entitled to draw from the facts in light of his experience. Cf. Brinegar v. United States, supra.

We must now examine the conduct of Officer McFadden in this case to determine whether his search and seizure of petitioner were

1. "A peace officer may search for a dangerous weapon any person whom he has stopped to question as provided in section 2, whenever he has reasonable ground to believe that he is in danger if the person possesses a dangerous weapon." The Uniform Arrest Act, § 3.

See Gisske v. Sanders, 9 Cal.App. 13, 98 P. 43 (1908); People v. Didonna, 124 Misc. 872, 210 N.Y.S. 135 (Sp.Sess.1925); People v. Rivera, 14 N.Y.2d 441, 252 N.Y.S.2d 458, 201 N.E.2d 32 (1964), certiorari denied 379 U.S. 978, 85 S.Ct. 679, 13 L.Ed.2d 568 (1965); People v. Pugach, 15 N.Y.2d 65, 255 N.Y.S.2d 833, 204 N.E.2d 176 (1964), certiorari denied 380 U.S. 936, 85 S.Ct. 946 (1965).

reasonable, both at their inception and as conducted. He had observed Terry, together with Chilton and another man, acting in a manner he took to be preface to a "stick-up." We think on the facts and circumstances Officer McFadden detailed before the trial judge a reasonably prudent man would have been warranted in believing petitioner was armed and thus presented a threat to the officer's safety while he was investigating his suspicious behavior. The actions of Terry and Chilton were consistent with McFadden's hypothesis that these men were contemplating a daylight robbery—which, it is reasonable to assume, would be likely to involve the use of weapons—and nothing in their conduct from the time he first noticed them until the time he confronted them and identified himself as a police officer gave him sufficient reason to negate that hypothesis. Although the trio had departed the original scene, there was nothing to indicate abandonment of an intent to commit a robbery at some point. Thus, when officer McFadden approached the three men gathered before the display window at Zucker's store he had observed enough to make it quite reasonable to fear that they were armed; and nothing in their response to his hailing them, identifying himself as a police officer, and asking their names served to dispel that reasonable belief. We cannot say his decision at that point to seize Terry and pat his clothing for weapons was the product of a volatile or inventive imagination, or was undertaken simply as an act of harassment; the record evidences the tempered act of a policeman who in the course of an investigation had to make a quick decision as to how to protect himself and others from possible danger, and took limited steps to do so. . . .

We need not develop at length in this case, however, the limitations which the Fourth Amendment places upon a protective seizure and search for weapons. These limitations will have to be developed in the concrete factual circumstances of individual cases. See Sibron v. New York, 392 U.S. 40, 88 S.Ct. 1889, 1912, 20 L.Ed.2d 917 decided today.[1] Suffice it to note that such a search, unlike a search without

1. *Sibron* was a companion case before the Court at the same time as *Terry*. When the officer approached Sibron with the remark: "You know what I am after", Sibron began to reach into his pocket, whereupon his hand was intercepted by the officer who reached into the same pocket and discovered envelopes containing heroin. The conviction of Sibron for unauthorized possession of narcotics was reversed. The Court found that the officer had no reason to believe Sibron was armed, and in any event the search was not a "pat-down" for weapons but a reaching into a pocket in a search for narcotics. Such a search would be authorized only by an officer who had probable cause to arrest for crime, which this officer did not have.

Nine days after a woman was murdered in an apartment building where **D**'s mother lived, she told **D** the police wanted to talk with him. He said he would be there that night, and when he arrived the police took him to the police station. His confession made at the station was admitted over his objection, and his conviction was affirmed by the New York courts, holding that the officers had authority, without probable cause for arrest, to detain **D** briefly for interrogation. In vacating the judgment and remanding the case for further proceedings the Court held that the case goes beyond *Terry* but that there may be merit in the State's position. Hence the Court desires a "record which squarely and necessarily presents the issue and fully illuminates

a warrant incident to a lawful arrest, is not justified by any need to prevent the disappearance or destruction of evidence of crime. The sole justification of the search in the present situation is the protection of the police officer and others nearby, and it must therefore be confined in scope to an intrusion reasonably designed to discover guns, knives, clubs, or other hidden instruments for the assault of the police officer.

The scope of the search in this case presents no serious problem in light of these standards. Officer McFadden patted down the outer clothing of petitioner and his two companions. He did not place his hands in their pockets or under the outer surface of their garments until he had felt weapons, and then he merely reached for and removed the guns. He never did invade Katz' person beyond the outer surfaces of his clothes, since he discovered nothing in his pat-down which might have been a weapon. Officer McFadden confined his search strictly to what was minimally necessary to learn whether the men were armed and to disarm them once he discovered the weapons. He did not conduct a general exploratory search for whatever evidence of criminal activity he might find.

V.

We conclude that the revolver seized from Terry was properly admitted in evidence against him. At the time he seized petitioner and searched him for weapons, Officer McFadden had reasonable grounds to believe that petitioner was armed and dangerous, and it was necessary for the protection of himself and others to take swift measures to discover the true facts and neutralize the threat of harm if it materialized. The policeman carefully restricted his search to what was appropriate to the discovery of the particular items which he sought. Each case of this sort will, of course, have to be decided on its own facts. We merely hold today that where a police officer observes unusual conduct which leads him reasonably to conclude in light of his experience that criminal activity may be afoot and that the persons with whom he is dealing may be armed and presently dangerous, where in the course of investigating this behavior he identifies himself as a policeman and makes reasonable inquiries, and where nothing in the initial stages of the encounter serves to dispel his reasonable fear for his own or others' safety, he is entitled for the protection of himself and others in the area to conduct a carefully limited search

the factual context in which the question arises [concerning] the legality of custodial questioning on less than probable cause for a full-fledged arrest". Morales v. New York, 396 U.S. 102, 90 S.Ct. 291 (1969).

Picking up a suspect for questioning at police headquarters, absent probable cause, was held not to be supportable under a stop and frisk argument and a confession obtained from such action was suppressed. Dunaway v. New York, 442 U.S. 200, 99 S.Ct. 2248 (1979).

The test for an investigatory stop is based "not on the policeman's subjective theory, but whether the record discloses articulable objective facts were available to the ofifcer to justify the stop." State v. Peck, 329 N.W.2d 680, 686 (Iowa 1982).

of the outer clothing of such persons in an attempt to discover weapons which might be used to assault him. Such a search is a reasonable search under the Fourth Amendment, and any weapons seized may properly be introduced in evidence against the person from whom they were taken.

Affirmed.

[BLACK, HARLAN and WHITE, JJ., wrote concurring opinions. DOUGLAS, J., dissented.]

Terry established that some seizures significantly less intrusive than an arrest may be permitted even in the absence of probable cause. This was applied in the following case. As officers were about to execute a warrant to search a house for narcotics, they encountered the owner descending the front steps and detained him while they searched the house. After finding narcotics therein, they arrested and searched him and found 8.5 grams of heroin in his pocket. He was charged with possession of the heroin found on his person and moved to suppress on the claim that the heroin was found by an illegal search. The only question was whether the original detention was lawful. In holding it lawful the Court said: "Thus, for Fourth Amendment purposes, we hold that a warrant to search for contraband founded on probable cause implicitly carries with it the limited authority to detain the occupants of the premises while a proper search is conducted."[2]

(6) "Held for Questioning"

There is no authority (without consent or special statute) to lock a man in jail for questioning or for investigation if the circumstances are not sufficient to arrest him on a criminal charge, except that a court or magistrate may be authorized to commit a material *witness* in a criminal case who refuses to enter into an undertaking to appear and testify in court after having been directed to do so.[1]

Under our system of justice no person is bound to incriminate himself, but there is no immunity which entitles a mere witness to refuse to give information relative to the guilt of some one else, unless there is some special protection in the particular case, as for example where the two are husband and wife.[2] Anciently, witnesses were punishable for a failure to give to officers outside of the courtroom information of any felony known to them.[3] While this is not common at the

2. Michigan v. Summers, 452 U.S. 692, 101 S.Ct. 2587, 2595 (1981).

Where law enforcement officers had reason to believe **D** was carrying luggage containing contraband they could temporarily detain the luggage, located in a public place, until a trained sniffer dog could examine the luggage. Use of a sniffer dog in such cases is not a search within the 4th Amendment. However, 90 minute detention was too long under the circumstances. United States v. Place, ___ U.S. ___, 103 S.Ct. 2637 (1983).

1. Markwell v. Warren County, 53 Iowa 422, 5 N.W. 570 (1880).

2. Jin Fuey Moy v. United States, 254 U.S. 189, 41 S.Ct. 98, 65 L.Ed. 214 (1920).

3. 4 Bl.Comm. * 119–21.

present time it is still the right of the officer to demand such information, and the moral duty of the citizen to answer fully so long as what he says does not tend to incriminate himself or his spouse, or improperly to divulge a privileged communication.[4] The temporary detention of one being questioned for information in regard to a crime is not an arrest on the one hand, and if properly conducted is not unlawful, on the other.[5]

4. "The duty of every good citizen is, when called upon, to give all information in his power to the proper officers of the law as to persons connected with crime (Miller v. Fano, 134 Cal. 106, 66 P. 183); and this should be held to require that all proper information be given upon request of a personal nature, as affecting the one of whom inquiry is made, when the circumstances are such as to warrant an officer in making inquiry." Gisske v. Sanders, 9 Cal.App. 13, 16, 98 P. 43, 44–5 (1908). Accord, United States v. First National Bank of Mobile, 67 F.Supp. 616, 625 (S.D.Ala.1946).

5. "In this state, however, we have consistently held that circumstances short of probable cause to make an arrest may still justify an officer's stopping pedestrians or motorists on the streets for questioning. If the circumstances warrant it, he may in self-protection request a suspect to alight from an automobile or to submit to a superficial search for concealed weapons. Should the investigation then reveal probable cause to make an arrest, the officer may arrest the suspect and conduct a reasonable incidental search. . . . We do not believe that our rule permitting temporary detention for questioning conflicts with the Fourth Amendment." People v. Mickelson, 59 Cal.2d 448, 450–51, 452, 30 Cal.Rptr. 18, 380 P.2d 658 (1963).

One who willingly accompanies officers to police headquarters and talks with them freely in the belief that he will be able to beguile them into exculpating him, is not under arrest. United States v. Vita, 294 F.2d 524 (2d Cir.1961), certiorari denied 369 U.S. 823, 82 S.Ct. 837, 7 L.Ed.2d 788 (1962). Compare a case in which under somewhat similar facts it was held that a 19-year-old **D** considered that he was under restraint and therefore was under arrest. Seals v. United States, 117 U.S.App.D.C. 79, 325 F.2d 1006 (1963), certiorari denied 376 U.S. 964, 84 S.Ct. 1123, 11 L.Ed.2d 982 (1964).

See supra, under What Constitutes Arrest.

Stopping a car to determine the identity of the occupant and the vehicle was not an arrest and could be made without probable cause to make an arrest. State v. Cloman, 254 Or. 1, 456 P.2d 67 (1969).

O stopped a car driven by **D** because the license plate showed that it was a rented car and **O** wanted to check **D**'s authority to drive the car. When **O** discovered that the rental agreement had been altered he detained **D** long enough to check with the rental agency about the altered agreement. It was held that this detention was not an arrest and that it was reasonable although the officer had no probable cause to arrest **D**. State v. Lewis, 80 N.M. 274, 454 P.2d 360 (1969).

Within minutes after an armed robbery, a police dispatcher broadcast an all-points bulletin telling of the robbery and giving a description of the get-away car. Officers stopped a car meeting that description, searched the occupants and found weapons and the victim's wallet. In affirming a conviction of robbery, the court said (Johnson v. State, 86 Nev. 52, 464 P.2d 465, 466 (1970)):

> The police officers had every right to stop Johnson's vehicle, for they had reason to believe a felony had been committed, and the vehicle they stopped closely resembled the description provided by Kramer.
>
> As we said in Robertson v. State, 84 Nev. 559, 562, 445 P.2d 352, 353 (1968):
>
> > "It is now the settled law of this state that an officer may stop the occupants of an automobile for legitimate police investigation so long as there is probable cause for that action. [Citations.] This action is proper even though there is not probable cause for arrest at the moment. But if the investigation conducted, together with knowledge originally available to the officers combines to supply probable cause for arrest, it may then be made, and a reasonable, incidental search conducted."
>
> Since the officers had every legal right to stop Johnson's vehicle, they had the right to search it. We ruled in Barnes v.

The "Arrest Act," drafted by the Interstate Commission on Crime includes a provision under which a peace officer may question any person abroad whom he has reason to suspect of committing a crime and may demand of him his name, address, business abroad and whither he is going. If such person does not satisfactorily identify himself and explain his actions, the officer shall have authority to detain him for two hours or less for further questioning and investigation.[6]

Approaching a suspect to ask questions is proper, a detention of the suspect requires reasonable suspicion,[7] and an arrest may only take place on probable cause.[8] The provisions of the Arrest Act are now probably unconstitutional.[9]

(7) Disposition of Prisoner

Since the purpose of lawful arrest is to take the prisoner before a magistrate, court, body or official or otherwise secure the administration of the law, this is exactly what must be done. And even if an arrest is lawful when made the detention of the prisoner will become unlawful if this disposition is not made with reasonable promptness.

If the arrest is in obedience to a warrant the disposition of the prisoner will be directed therein, and this direction must be obeyed [a] unless the statute requires otherwise in some special situation. For example, if the warrant follows the familiar pattern it will command the officer to arrest the person named and take him before the issuing magistrate or some other magistrate of the same county.[b]

State, supra, 85 Nev. at 72, 450 P.2d at 152:

> "In a recent decision of this court, Robertson v. State [supra], we held that a police officer may 'stop the occupants of an automobile for legitimate police investigation so long as there is probable cause for that action. [Citations.]' We think that same rule applies to individuals where, as here, appellant was reasonably within the area of the robbed office and met a reasonable description of the robber.
>
> *"Once the suspect has been detained, if the officer has reason to believe that the suspect is armed and presently dangerous to the officer or to others, he may 'take necessary measures to determine whether the person is in fact carrying a weapon and to neutralize the threat of physical harm.'* Terry v. Ohio, 392 U.S. 1, 88 S.Ct. 1868, 20 L.Ed.2d 889 (1967)." (Emphasis added.)

Police officers who have detained but not arrested the occupant of a vehicle that has been properly stopped, may under Terry v. Ohio, conduct a warrantless search of the automobile's passenger compartment, where a weapon could be, if the officers have specific and articulate facts that the occupant is dangerous and may obtain a weapon. Michigan v. Long, ___ U.S. ___, 103 S.Ct. 3469 (1983).

6. The Uniform Arrest Act, § 2.

7. United States v. Mendenhall, 446 U.S. 544, 100 S.Ct. 1870 (1980); Reid v. Georgia, 448 U.S. 438, 100 S.Ct. 2752 (1980).

8. Florida v. Royer, ___ U.S. ___, 103 S.Ct. 1319 (1983).

9. A California statute required persons who loiter or wander on the streets to provide "credible and reliable" identification and to account for their presence when requested by a peace officer. The statute was held to be unconstitutionally vague. Kolender v. Lawson, ___ U.S. ___, 103 S.Ct. 1855 (1983). A detention of a citizen must be based on "objective facts." Brown v. Texas, 443 U.S. 47, 99 S.Ct. 2637 (1979).

a. 2 Hale P.C. * 119.

b. Ida.Code § 19–616 (1979); § 77–35–7, 1953, Utah Code Ann.

If the arrest is without a warrant the arrester must, without unreasonable delay, take the prisoner before a magistrate of the county in which the arrest is made.[c] The cases often speak of the arrester's duty in such terms as that he must take the prisoner before the magistrate "immediately" or "forthwith."[d] On the other hand, delay may be unavoidable, and hence unlawfulness at this point arises not from delay as such, but from unreasonable delay.[e] If an arrest is made at night, at an hour when the normal facilities for obtaining bail are not available, and the arrest itself is quite reasonable under the circumstances, the prisoner may be locked up for the night, and taken before the magistrate at a reasonable hour in the morning.[f]

(8) Rights and Duties of Arrestee

It is the duty of every person, whether guilty of any offense or not, to submit to arrest if the one arresting is duly authorized to do so under the circumstances and the arrest is made in a lawful manner[1]. An arrest which is unauthorized or is made in an unlawful manner may be resisted[2] unless there has been some statutory change in this regard such as is mentioned below. Where one has reason to believe that an unlawful attempt is being made to convey him by force beyond the reach of the law, or to carry him out of the country, he is justified in resisting, even to the death of his adversary if that becomes necessary.[3] But a man is not justified if he intentionally kills in defense against an illegal arrest of ordinary character.[4]

An unlawful arrest, however, may be such provocation as will reduce a killing in the resistance of such an arrest to manslaughter.[5]

c. If there is such great excitement at the time and place of arrest as to indicate the possibility of mob action there the arresting officer is privileged to carry the prisoner before a magistrate of some other county. Wiggins v. Norton, 83 Ga. 148, 9 S.E. 607 (1889).

d. Rutledge v. Rowland, 161 Ala. 114, 126–7, 49 So. 461, 466 (1909); Hogg v. Lorenz, 234 Ky. 751, 754, 29 S.W.2d 17, 18 (1930). Rule 5(a) F.R.Cr.P. "Without unnecessary delay."

e. Oxford v. Berry, 204 Mich. 197, 170 N.W. 83 (1918); State v. Freeman, 86 N.C. 683 (1882).

f. Ibid.; King v. Robertson, 227 Ala. 378, 150 So. 154 (1933); Tschuor v. Meck, 72 Ariz. 200, 232 P.2d 848 (1951). Brown v. State, 276 Ark. 20, 631 S.W.2d 829 (1982).

1. King v. State, 89 Ala. 43, 8 So. 120 (1890).

2. "He [the officer] has no protection from his office, or from the fact that the other is an offender." 1 Bishop, Criminal Law § 868 (9th ed. 1923). As to the change made by the Uniform Arrest Act see footnote 6.

3. Ibid.

4. In resisting an unlawful arrest the citizen is not justified in taking the life of the trespasser, unless it is necessary to save his own life or to save his person from great bodily harm. Creighton v. Commonwealth, 84 Ky. 103 (1886).

5. Rex v. Chapman, 12 Cox C.C. 4 (1871). See note, Homicide in resisting arrest, 66 L.R.A. 353 (1905).

"And it is too well settled to be discussed, that an assault and resisting one in the execution of any authority or power, is indictable at common law." State v. Downer, 8 Vt. 424, 429 (1836).

An important change in regard to the privilege of resisting arrest is found in certain recent statutes such as the following:

"If a person has knowledge, or by the exercise of reasonable care, should have knowledge, that he is being arrested by a peace officer, it is the duty of such person to refrain from using force or any weapon to resist such arrest".[6]

No such provision is needed where the arrest is lawful because it has always been illegal to resist a lawful arrest. The purpose of such a provision is to impose upon the citizen a duty to submit to apprehension by a known officer, even if the latter is actually exceeding his authority, and seek redress in the courts, rather than to resort to self-help.[7] The arrestee's belief that the arrest is in excess of the officer's authority, it may be added, is often a mistaken notion and this provision discourages the attempt to settle such a dispute by force.

(vii) The Third Degree

Any force or violence used for the purpose of extorting a confession from a prisoner is unlawful. The confession so obtained is not admissible in evidence,[1] and the officer who employed such force is guilty of assault and battery. He may be liable under the federal "Civil Rights Act," [2] or under the corresponding provision of the federal criminal code.[3]

The Supreme Court has held that "real evidence" obtained from a defendant by the violent use of a stomach pump, to which he did not consent, may not be used to convict him even in a state court, because of the due process clause.[4]

(E) SUMMONS

The primitive method of bringing a defendant into court was by force, but as civilization advances there is an increasing tendency to procure his presence by persuasion whenever such procedure seems reasonably adequate for the purpose. Although almost forgotten now, arrest was anciently the normal procedure for procuring the

6. West's Ann.Cal.Pen.Code, § 834a (1957 amendt.). This was adapted from section 5 of the Uniform Arrest Act. And see Model Penal Code Sec. 3.04(2)(a)(i).

7. See Warner, The Uniform Arrest Act, 28 Va.Law Rev. 315, 330–31 (1942).

1. Brown v. Mississippi, 297 U.S. 278, 56 S.Ct. 461 (1936).

2. 42 U.S.C.A. § 1983 (1981); Refoule v. Ellis, 74 F.Supp. 336 (N.D.Ga.1947). The federal courts have jurisdiction over suits brought under this section without allegation or proof of any jurisdictional amount. Douglas v. City of Jeannette, 319 U.S. 157, 63 S.Ct. 877, 87 L.Ed. 1324 (1943).

For an extensive review of the Civil Rights Act, see Note, 43 Ill.L.Rev. 105 (1948); Anteau, Federal Civil Rights Act 2nd Ed. (1980).

3. 18 U.S.C.A. § 242 (1969); Screws v. United States, 325 U.S. 91, 65 S.Ct. 1031, 89 L.Ed. 1495 (1945); Williams v. United States, 341 U.S. 97, 71 S.Ct. 576, 95 L.Ed. 774 (1951).

4. Rochin v. California, 342 U.S. 382, 72 S.Ct. 205, 96 L.Ed. 183 (1952).

presence of the defendant in a civil case.[1] Such usage has become so nearly obsolete that it is greatly restricted [2] if not entirely prohibited. It is almost as absurd to rely upon arrest as the normal procedure in cases of minor infractions as it would be to do so in civil proceedings.

"It is provided by statute in England that upon complaint made of the commission of any offense the justice may, if he think fit, issue a summons instead of a warrant of arrest; and upon the failure of the person summoned to appear the justice may issue a warrant of arrest. 11 & 12 Vict. ch. 42, sec. 1.

"The summons is frequently used in England, even in felony cases if the magistrate is satisfied the person summoned will appear." [4]

The Federal Rules of Criminal Procedure provide that "upon the request of the attorney for the government a summons instead of a warrant shall issue." [5] Some states have adopted provisions allowing a summons to be used in lieu of arrest where the accused will appear on a summons and there is no danger of breach of the peace or injury to persons, property or danger to the community.[6] Some statutes express a preference for a summons in misdemeanor cases where the defendant will appear.[7] Other jurisdictions provide for the use of a summons as an alternative to arrest in misdemeanor or municipal ordinances cases.[8] One of the urgent needs for the improvement of the machinery of law enforcement is the enlarged use of the summons in lieu of arrest in all cases in which there is reason to believe it will be effective in having the defendant in court at the proper time.[9]

1. One author has insisted that a "discriminating and scholarly use of these terms" limits the words "arrest" and "arrested" to civil cases and employs "apprehend" and "apprehension" in criminal proceedings. 1 Wharton, Criminal Procedure, § 1 (10th ed., Kerr, 1918).

2. "No person shall be imprisoned for debt arising out of, or founded on a contract, express or implied, except in cases of fraud or breach of trust, ..." Mich. Const. Art. I § 21 (1963).

4. A.L.I.Code of Criminal Procedure 217 (Official Draft with Commentaries, 1931).

5. Rule 4 F.R.Cr.P.; See also Ariz. Rev.Stat., Rules of Cr.P. 3.1 and 2.

6. § 77–35–6(b), 1953, Utah Code Ann.

7. Fla.Stat.Ann. § 901.9 (1973).

8. Ohio Rev.Code § 2935.10 (1982).

9. The American Law Institute, Code of Criminal Procedure, includes the following sections:

Section 12. *When summons shall be issued.* (1) Where the complaint is for the commission of an offense which the magistrate is empowered to try summarily he shall issue a summons instead of a warrant of arrest, unless he has reasonable ground to believe that the person against whom the complaint was made will not appear upon a summons, in which case he shall issue a warrant of arrest.

(2) Where the complaint is for a misdemeanor, which the magistrate is not empowered to try summarily, he shall issue a summons instead of a warrant of arrest, if he has reasonable ground to believe that the person against whom the complaint was made will appear upon a summons.

(3) The summons shall set forth substantially the nature of the offense, and shall command the person against whom the complaint was made to appear before the magistrate issuing the summons at a time and place stated therein.

Section 13. *How summons served.* The summons may be served in the same manner as the summons in a civil action.

Section 14. *Effect of not answering summons.* If a person summoned fails, without good cause, to appear as commanded by the summons, he shall

The greatest use of procedure of this general nature, in other than civil cases, has resulted from an extra-legal device,—the traffic ticket. While this special type of "summons" is strictly legal now as a result of municipal ordinance or state law [10] it seems to have had its origin and early development as a result of police practice in certain communities with no legislative foundation whatever.

The traffic "ticket" is not a true summons because it is not a writ issued by a court or magistrate. It is usually either a "notice" issued by the officer to the motorist, that he will be arrested if he does not appear, or it is an agreement, signed by the motorist, that he will do so. Some statutes, or ordinances have provided for the release of a traffic violator, *after* arrest, by this device, but a much better provision authorizes the officer who has stopped such a motorist to release him *without* arrest if he will *agree* to appear voluntarily. The average traffic violator is not a "criminal" in any sense of the word, and anything which seems to place him in that category not only does him an injustice but is likely to confuse the attitude of the public toward those who commit true crimes.

The use of tickets and citations save so much time that they have been authorized for use in other misdemeanor or minor infraction cases where the circumstances do not require a more drastic approach.[11]

(F) SUMMARY TRIAL AND PRELIMINARY EXAMINATION

Under English statutes, old enough to be common law in this country, magistrates were authorized to try certain petty offenses, without waiting for an indictment by the grand jury and without calling in the aid of a trial jury. Such a proceeding was spoken of as a summary trial. In this country magistrates, or other inferior courts, are authorized to try certain petty offenses without waiting for an indictment by the grand jury. And it is convenient to speak of these as "summary trials" although in many of them the defendant may demand a jury trial if he sees fit to do so.

The summary trial of a petty offense is quite different from a preliminary hearing or examination, although the two are sometimes confused by the layman. In a summary trial the magistrate is making a determination of guilt or innocence, and this determination is final unless an appeal is taken from a judgment of conviction. In a

be considered in contempt of court, and may be punished by a fine of not more than twenty dollars. Upon such failure to appear, the magistrate shall issue a warrant of arrest. If after issuing a summons the magistrate becomes satisfied that the person summoned will not appear as commanded by the summons he may at once issue a warrant of arrest.

For another approach favoring the use of a summons as an alternative to arrest see, National Advisory Commission on Criminal Justice Standards and Goals-Correction 4.3 (1973); American Bar Association Standards for Criminal Justice 10–3.1–3.2 (1980).

10. Iowa Code Ann. § 321.485 (1946).

11. West Ann.Calif.Pen.Code § 853.6 (1981).

preliminary hearing or examination the magistrate has no power to make the determination of guilt or innocence and is merely called upon to determine whether there is sufficient ground to bind the defendant over to trial by a higher court.[12] Sufficient ground to bind him over is found if it appears from the examination that a public offense, triable by a higher court, has been committed, and there is probable cause for believing the defendant guilty thereof.[1]

Two early English statutes [2] provided that the magistrate before whom a person was brought charged with felony, "shall take the examination of such prisoner and information of those that bring him, of the fact and circumstances thereof, and the same or as much thereof as shall be material to prove the felony, shall be put in writing within two days after the said examination." [3]

Under these statutes it was the practice of magistrates, for several centuries, to conduct secret inquisitions in which the accused, as well as others, was interrogated. In the early part of the nineteenth century this inquisitorial practice gave way in England to the custom of giving the accused the opportunity of making a voluntary statement after being cautioned that it might be used in evidence against him. This practice was crystallized in the statute of 1848 [4] which provided that the examination of all witnesses for the prosecution should precede this opportunity given to the accused, after caution, to make a voluntary statement if he should so desire.

Provisions against self-incrimination would prevent any inquisitorial practice in this country which included any pressure to compel the accused to answer questions. A rather common statutory provision is in substance as follows:

"When the accused is brought before the magistrate upon an arrest, either with or without a warrant, on a charge of having committed a public offense which the magistrate is not competent to try and determine, the magistrate shall immediately inform him of the charge

12. T was charged with first-degree murder. At the conclusion of the preliminary hearing the magistrate ordered T bound over to the district court on a charge of murder in the second degree. Dissatisfied with that order, the district attorney dismissed the first charge and filed a new charge of first-degree murder. T's motion to dismiss the second charge was overruled. On a new preliminary hearing he was bound over on a charge of first-degree murder, and was tried and convicted of that offense. The conviction was affirmed. In such a proceeding the magistrate's function is to determine probable cause. If he fails to bind over on a charge that is warranted by the evidence, the state's remedy is to dismiss and file anew. As the defendant has not been in jeopardy he has no complaint. State v. Turner, 223 Kan. 707, 576 P.2d 644 (1978).

1. People v. Sears, 124 Cal.App.2d 839, 269 P.2d 683 (1954).

Probable cause to hold D to answer does not require evidence sufficient for conviction. Williams v. Superior Court, 71 Cal.2d 1144, 80 Cal.Rptr. 747, 458 P.2d 987 (1967).

2. 1 and 2 Phil. and M., c. 13, sec. 4 (1554); 2 and 3 Phil. and M., c. 10, sec. 2 (1555).

3. A.L.I. Code of Criminal Procedure 266 (Official Draft with Commentaries, 1931).

4. 11 and 12 Vict., ch. 42, sec. 18. See now the Criminal Practice Act of 1925, 15 and 16 Geo.V., ch. 86, sec. 12.

against him, and of his right to the aid of counsel in every stage of the proceedings." [5]

The rights of an accused receive special attention in Chapter 13.

(G) DISCHARGE, COMMITMENT AND BAIL

If, as a result of a summary trial for a petty offense the defendant is acquitted, he must be discharged immediately and has the benefit of the rules of former jeopardy. But if the discharge is because, on preliminary examination, the magistrate does not find that an offense was committed, or finds that an offense was committed but that there is not sufficient reason to believe defendant guilty thereof, there has been no acquittal and the rules of former jeopardy do not apply. If as a result of a summary trial the defendant is found guilty (or if he entered a plea of guilty instead of standing trial) the magistrate renders such judgment as the case may require. And unless an appeal is taken this judgment is executed by an appropriate officer. When, as a result of a preliminary examination, the defendant is bound over to answer the charge filed against him,[1] he is admitted to bail unless the offense is not bailable. If the offense is not bailable, or defendant is unable to give bail, the defendant is committed to jail to await trial in the higher court.

SECTION 2. THE INDICTMENT OR INFORMATION

(A) THE GRAND JURY

The grand jury, one of the ancient English institutions, is a body of persons summoned from all parts of the county to pass upon accusations of crime therein. The number was variable at common law, but could not exceed twenty-three nor be less than twelve. It could not be less than twelve because a common-law indictment required the favorable vote of twelve grand jurors. It could not exceed twenty-three because the requirement of unanimity was limited to the trial jury and had no application to the grand jury. Since the vote of twelve grand jurors was sufficient to find an indictment it would not do to permit a body of such size that an indictment could be found although as many, or more, voted against than in favor. Some statutes have reduced the size of the grand jury and have substituted a

5. See the statutes of Idaho, Missouri, Oklahoma. For another form see Iowa Code 813.2, Rule 2 (1979). The right to a preliminary examination may be waived. Flowers v. State, 95 Okl.Cr. 27, 238 P.2d 841 (1951).

1. If the magistrate has jurisdiction over the subject matter he may bind the defendant over even if the complaint is insufficient as a matter of law. Tschuor v. Meck, 72 Ariz. 200, 232 P.2d 848 (1951).

All that is required to hold a defendant to answer to the superior court is a reasonable probability of guilt. People v. Platt, 124 Cal.App.2d 123, 268 P.2d 529 (1954).

new requirement as to the number of votes needed to find an indictment. Proceedings before the grand jury are secret except that some statutes permit a court to order public sessions of the grand jury when the subject matter of its investigation is one affecting the general public welfare,—such as corruption in public office or dereliction of duty by public officials.

A bill of indictment is a written accusation of crime submitted to the grand jury for its consideration. In this country this bill ordinarily is drawn by a prosecuting attorney, whose title varies from jurisdiction to jurisdiction, the more common being "district attorney," "county attorney," or in the federal system, "United States attorney." If this bill of indictment is found by the grand jury to be a "true bill," and is duly presented by them as such, it then becomes an indictment and the accused stands indicted. If the required number of grand jurors do not vote that the bill of indictment shall be found to be a true bill, the grand jury is said to "ignore" it. Such a bill does not become an indictment and the accused is not indicted.

If the grand jurors of their own knowledge, or of their own motion on information from others, take notice of a public offense, this is spoken of as a "presentment." In some jurisdictions such a presentment has been held sufficient to support a prosecution. The common practice, on the other hand, is for this presentment to be regarded as a mere instruction to the prosecuting attorney to draw a bill of indictment. Such a bill is submitted to the grand jury, the same as any other bill of indictment, and if found to be a true bill it becomes the basis of the prosecution.

(B) THE INDICTMENT *

The legal mind of the sixteen and seventeen hundreds, together with other more worthy accomplishments, was master of the art of making two words grow where only one had ever been seen before. This art was applied with unusual diligence in the drawing of indictments and with the accretion of generations such pleadings became increasingly cumbersome. The ancient theory required every essential element of the offense charged to be stated directly and positively in the indictment and permitted no omission to be cured or aided by inference or intendment. So rigid were the requirements of technical exactness that many guilty defendants escaped on the most subtle distinctions.

Back of the apparent absurdity in these decisions there was in the beginning a useful purpose which was subsequently lost sight of entirely. Blackstone lamented the existence, in his day, of one hundred and sixty capital offenses. In the face of such atrocious severity of

* In part this section is adapted, by permission, from an article by the compiler of these cases, entitled "Short Indictments and Informations," 15 American Bar Association Journal 292, and to some extent from an article entitled "The Short Indictment Act," 14 Iowa Law Review 385.

punishment one might well expect to find humane judges searching for technicalities merely to save miserable offenders from penalties which were outrageously excessive in particular cases. This practice seems not to have been uncommon. Furthermore, the procedure was scarcely less barbarous than the penalties. This was in the days when one who stubbornly refused to plead did not have a plea of not guilty entered for him. It was even prior to the time when a plea of guilty was entered in such a case. The practice then was to pass judgment that he suffer *peine fort et dure* by which he was slowly starved and crushed to death if his obstinancy continued. It is not surprising to find, associated with such methods, a procedure which did not permit the defendant to see the indictment or to have a copy of it, but forced him to rely entirely upon what he could gather from having the pleading read to him.[1] This was his sole source of information relative to the charge against him prior to the introduction of evidence in the trial itself. It was only natural for such rigorous procedure to receive an interpretation and application which was harsh from the standpoint of pleaders but mitigating so far as defendants were concerned. And when a judge occasionally went farther and required some mere evidentiary fact to be included in the indictment, it was not because this is required by good pleading (which in fact forbids it) but rather because a humane impulse had been forced to crack a piece of judicial machinery which would not yield otherwise to the proper administration of justice in the particular case. Unfortunately, however, every such decision became a precedent for all future cases, even after undue severity had been eliminated from the penal provisions and unreasonable harshness had been removed from the procedure itself. For every defendant who had been saved from paying the death penalty for some trivial offense by legalistic acumen, there remained an additional word, clause or phrase which all future indictments for such offenses would have to contain. More and more such pleadings became complicated and formidable. These fossilized relics of the age of punitive savagery were brought over to this country. Even the common-sense pioneers accepted them as a matter of course. Thus in a decision handed down in the middle of the last century,[2] reference is made to an indictment containing eight counts, only one of which is set forth in the opinion. This one contains over five hundred words. If the others were of equal length, as is more than probable, the entire pleading ran well over four thousand words. And the purpose of all this wilderness of language was merely to charge the defendants with the murder of Boyd Wilkinson.

The impetus in the direction of insisting upon technical perfection in criminal pleading—of "trying the record" instead of the defendant—not only outlived the original underlying purpose of serving as a safeguard against over-severity of punishment, but was carried to its most absurd extremes after the need for such manipulation had van-

1. Chitty, Criminal Law, 403.

2. State v. Shelledy, 8 Iowa 477 (1859).

ished. An outstanding example of justice being completely submerged in the formalism of the proceedings, is State v. Campbell, decided in 1907.[3] In this case a conviction of rape was reversed because the concluding sentence of the indictment was "against the peace and dignity of State" whereas the court held it should have been "against the peace and dignity of *the* State." Another verdict of guilty was set at naught because the indictment concluded "against the peace and dignity of the State of W. Virginia," the court being of the opinion that the word *West* should have been written in full.[4] Another classic, this time in the field of technical variance, is the case in which a conviction of stealing a pair of shoes was reversed because the proof established the larceny of two shoes both for the right foot and hence not a pair.[5] A fourth illustration of what should be avoided in the administration of criminal justice is the decision which upset a conviction under a statute making it grand larceny to steal any "cow or animal of the cow kind." The evidence had disclosed the theft of a steer, which was not "of the cow kind," said the appellate court, because a steer is a male.[6]

On the other hand, under statutes passed long ago it became possible to eliminate much of the needless verbosity and repetition with which common-law indictments were burdened. In fact the common legislative command was to use "ordinary and concise language, without repetition, and in such a manner as to enable a person of common understanding to know what is intended." But while the purpose was to simplify the wording of indictments to some extent, no change was made in the general plan, which required the indictment to include both the accusation of the offense itself and the particulars of the offense. The unfortunate result of retaining the same general plan was the retention of most of the verbosity and archaism of expression, because prosecuting attorneys preferred to follow the old precedents rather than to venture the use of simpler language which was authorized by the legislature, without any guiding suggestions.

The modern trend is in the direction of simplified indictments. The most progressive step in this direction reduces the indictment to a very simple and direct statement of the charge against the defendant, and entitles him to move for a bill of particulars if he wishes more information. This motion will be granted if additional information is needed. The brevity of such an indictment is well illustrated

3. 210 Mo. 202, 109 S.W. 706.

4. Lemons v. State, 4 W.Va. 755 (1870).

5. State v. Harris, 3 Har. 559 (Del. 1841).

6. Marsh v. State, 3 Ala.App. 80, 57 So. 387 (1912).

Where the defendant was charged with prostitution but the information failed to specify the type of "sexual conduct" defendant was alleged to have offered or agreed to or engaged in the information was defective and the case dismissed. Kass v. State, 642 S.W.2d 463 (Tex.Cr. App.1981).

by one of the forms appended to the federal rules of criminal procedure.[7]

Indictment for Murder in the First Degree of Federal Officer

In the District Court of the United States
for the ______ District of ______,
______ Division

United States of America v. John Doe } No. ______ (18 U.S.C.A. §§ 1111, 1114)

The grand jury charges:

On or about the ______ day of ______ 19__, in ______ District of ______, John Doe, with premeditation and by means of shooting murdered John Roe, who was then an officer of the Federal Bureau of Investigation of the Department of Justice engaged in the performance of his official duties.[8]

A True Bill

____
Foreman

____
United States Attorney

Not all jurisdictions have simplified the indictment to this extent, but is is desirable that it should be done. The defendant gets more information from such a direct statement (plus a bill of particulars if there is any reason therefor) than he ever received from the most verbose indictment drawn in "legalistic" language.

(C) THE CORONER'S INQUEST

A coroner's inquest is an inquiry by the coroner, with the aid of a jury, into the death of a person. Under the English common law a person could be tried for murder or manslaughter on the finding of a coroner's jury, the same as upon indictment by a grand jury. This

7. "In a number of cases the Court has emphasized two of the protections which an indictment is intended to guarantee, reflected by two of the criteria by which the sufficiency of an indictment is to be measured. These criteria are, first, whether the indictment 'contains the elements of the offense intended to be charged, "and sufficiently apprises the defendant of what he must be prepared to meet,"' and, secondly, 'in case any other proceedings are taken against him for a similar offence, whether the record shows with accuracy to what extent he may plead a former acquittal or conviction.'" Russell v. United States, 369 U.S. 749, 763–764, 82 S.Ct. 1038 (1962).

8. "The specificity formerly held necessary to charge an offense is no longer required or sanctioned." Hence it was not necessary for the indictment to mention that the officer was a "human being." Donnelly v. United States, 185 F.2d 559 (10th Cir.1950).

has not been the practice in this country. But the accusation returned by the coroner's jury usually authorizes the coroner to order the arrest and commitment of the accused, and is the equivalent of an examination and commitment by a magistrate.

(D) THE INFORMATION

An information is a written accusation of crime preferred by the public prosecuting officer without the intervention of the grand jury.

Under the English common law there could be no trial for felony on an information, because all felonies were punishable by death and it was felt that no one should be put on trial for his life except upon the sworn accusation of a jury,—either the grand jury or a coroner's jury. But the right of the attorney-general of Great Britain or of the solicitor-general during a vacancy in the other office, to file an information charging a misdemeanor was so well established that on several occasions Lord Mansfield denied applications by this official for leave to proceed in this way,—on the ground that he had the right *ex officio,* and no leave of court was needed. In this country the powers which were exercised by those officers in England are distributed to a large extent among the district attorneys (or county attorneys) of the state, an office which did not exist in England. Hence these officers are entitled to prosecute by information as a right inhering in their office, in the absence of some express limitation.

In most of the states there are constitutional limitations upon the power to prosecute by information. A few of the constitutions expressly authorize the legislature to modify or abolish the grand jury.[1] A few place the indictment and the information upon an equal basis,[2] and a slightly larger number have a similar provision with the qualification that the prosecution by information shall be only after examination and commitment by a magistrate, or the waiver of such examination.[3]

At the other extreme the Fifth Amendment to the Constitution of the United States provides: "No person shall be held to answer for a capital, or otherwise infamous crime, unless on presentment or indictment of a grand jury, except in cases arising in the land or naval forces, or in the militia, when in actual service in time of war or public danger; . . . "

Whether a crime is infamous within the meaning of this Amendment is determined by the punishment provided for it,[4] and it has been held that any offense punishable by imprisonment in a peniten-

1. See, for example, the constitutions of Colorado, Illinois, Indiana, Iowa, Nebraska, North Dakota, South Dakota and Wyoming. Such legislation has been enacted in these states.

2. See, for example, the constitutions of Missouri, Nevada and Washington.

3. See, for example, the constitutions of Arizona, California, Idaho, Louisiana (except for a capital crime), Montana (or after leave granted by court), New Mexico, Oklahoma, Utah.

4. Ex parte Wilson, 114 U.S. 417, 5 S.Ct. 935, 29 L.Ed. 89 (1885).

tiary or at hard labor is infamous [5] (and any person sentenced to a term of more than one year for a federal offense may be imprisoned in a United States penitentiary).[6]

The Fifth Amendment provision for grand jury indictment is a limitation upon the federal government only, and does not apply to prosecutions in the state courts,[7] but very smilar provisions are found in some of the state constitutions.[8] Under federal procedure, it may be added, the requirement that the prosecution for an infamous crime shall be only by indictment by a grand jury can be waived in other than capital cases. The rule is: "An offense which may be punished by imprisonment for a term exceeding one year or at hard labor may be prosecuted by information if the defendant, after he has been advised of the nature of the charge and of his rights, waives in open court prosecution by indictment." [9]

There has been a definite trend in modern times, with the aid of statutes and constitutional amendments, to make an increasingly larger use of the information.[10] This is entirely proper. The grand jury served a very important function in the transition from the rough and ready "justice" of the Hue and Cry to modern criminal procedure. It was also one of the safeguards of the subject against the king. But at the present time it should be reserved as a body to be called upon in emergencies rather than one whose action is needed in every felony prosecution.

SECTION 3. STEPS BY THE PROSECUTION AFTER INDICTMENT

After the indictment or the information for an indictable offense, there are several steps which may be taken by the prosecution before trial, one of which—the arraignment, is of such a nature that the trial cannot proceed without it unless it has been waived or the defendant is a corporation (or a different procedure has been established by statute).

(A) THE BENCH WARRANT

The person indicted, or informed against, may or may not be in the custody of the law at the time. If he is not, and does not voluntarily submit to the jurisdiction of the court, it is necessary that he be brought in. By the early English practice, if the offense charged was

5. United States v. Moreland, 258 U.S. 433, 42 S.Ct. 368, 66 L.Ed. 700 (1922).

6. 18 U.S.C.A. § 4083.

7. Hurtado v. California, 110 U.S. 516, 4 S.Ct. 111 (1884).

8. See, for example, the constitutions of Maine, New York, Ohio and Rhode Island.

9. Federal Rules of Criminal Procedure, Rule 7(b), 18 U.S.C.A.

10. Where a criminal complaint in legal form is verified as true in positive terms, such verification constitutes a sufficient showing to authorize the issuance of a warrant of arrest. And if the defendant waives a preliminary hearing such verified complaint is sufficient to authorize holding him for trial and the filing of an information in the district court. State v. Hendricks, 80 Idaho 344, 330 P.2d 334 (1958).

a misdemeanor only, *venire facias ad respondendum* was issued. This was a writ summoning the defendant to appear and be arraigned for the offense. If the offense charged was a felony, or if the defendant failed to respond to the *venire facias* issued in a misdemeanor case, the court issued a *capias* which commanded the sheriff to take the defendant and have him at the next assizes. If the magistrate had reason to believe one charged with a misdemeanor would not respond to a *venire facias,* a *capias* could be issued in the first instance as in felony cases. And, quite unfortunately it seems, the practice of issuing the *venire facias* tended to fall into disuse and the *capias* came to be used as the regular procedure for misdemeanors as well as for felonies. The *capias* satisfies the definition of an arrest warrant and this process frequently goes under the name of a "warrant" at the present time. The label "bench warrant" is common because this writ is issued from the bench, in legal theory, although ordinarily it is prepared and handed over by the clerk. By means of arrest or by summons or by merely transferring the accused from the jail if he is already in custody, he is brought before the court for arraignment.

(B) THE ARRAIGNMENT

"To arraign is nothing else but to call the prisoner to the bar of the court, to answer the matter charged upon him in the indictment." 4 Bl.Comm. 322.

The ancient ceremony consisted of four parts. First, the prisoner was called to the bar by name and commanded to raise his hand. The raising of the hand was merely for the purpose of identification and was not indispensable. Usually today the step by which the prisoner is brought before the bar of the court and identified is regarded as something preliminary to the arraignment rather than a part thereof. Second, the indictment was read to the prisoner distinctly in English,—and this was true in the early days when all other proceedings in court were in Latin. There was no thought of giving him a copy because usually he would not have been able to read it. The usual procedure today is to read the indictment or information, but a few of the statutes stipulate that it shall either be read or the substance stated. It is very generally provided that a copy shall be delivered to the defendant. Third, it was "demanded of him" whether he was guilty or not guilty of the crime charged. In form this seems inadequate since it has always been possible for the defendant to answer in some form other than a plea of guilty or a plea of not guilty. This was unimportant, however, because the form did not result in an actual limitation. And the usual provision today is that defendant shall be asked "whether he pleads guilty or not guilty." Fourth, (if the plea was "not guilty") the prisoner was asked how he would be tried.

This last part of the original arraignment goes back to the very origin of trial by jury. The more ancient method of trial for criminal offenses was trial by ordeal. In the words of Blackstone (4 Bl. Comm. 342–3): "Fire-ordeal was performed either by taking up in the hand, unhurt, a piece of red-hot iron of one, two, or three pounds' weight; or else by walking barefoot, and blindfold, over nine red-hot plough-shares laid lengthwise at unequal distances; and if the party escaped unhurt he was adjudged innocent; but if it happened otherwise, as without collusion it usually did, he was then condemned as guilty. . . .

"Water-ordeal was performed either by plunging the bare arm up to the elbow in boiling water, and escaping unhurt thereby, or by casting the person suspected into a river or pond of cold water; and if he floated therein without any action of swimming, it was deemed an evidence of his guilt, but if he sank he was acquitted."

The theory of trial by ordeal was that "God would always interpose miraculously to vindicate the guiltless." Hence, when trial by jury was added as a method of determining guilt or innocence, the defendant was given his choice of these methods of trial by asking him: "How will you be tried—by God or by country?" If he answered: By God," he was tried by ordeal. If he answered: "By country," he was given a jury trial. After trial by ordeal became obsolete this question still was asked as a part of the arraignment although the defendant, at that time, had no choice as to how he would be tried for an indictable offense. Because there was no choice the approved answer of the defendant came to be: "By God and my country."

The fourth part of the ancient arraignment has tended to disappear in this country. In a few states the statutes expressly provide that it shall not be necessary to ask the prisoner how he will be tried. In the others this question is merely omitted from the statutory provisions for arraignment. On the other hand, there is very real reason for restoring this question to the arraignment,—in changed form. Today, in all but a very few states, one charged by indictment or equivalent information is permitted to waive the jury and be tried by the judge without a jury (either in all cases or in certain cases). In every instance in which this waiver is permitted the arraignment might well include this question (if the plea is not guilty): "How will you be tried—by a jury or without a jury?"

Under the early procedure the trial followed the arraignment very promptly if the defendant's plea was not guilty. In this country today the usual practice is to have the arraignment follow promptly after the indictment or information, if the defendant is available, although the trial may not be expected to be held until a later time. Many of the statutes permit the defendant to "appear" for arraignment by counsel if the indictment or information is for a misdemeanor.

Rule 10 of the Federal Rules of Criminal Procedure is as follows: "Arraignment shall be conducted in open court and shall consist of reading the indictment or information to the defendant or stating to him the substance of the charge and calling on him to plead thereto. He shall be given a copy of the indictment or information before he is called upon to plead."

(C) MOTIONS

A motion is an application made to a judge or court to obtain some rule or order deemed necessary or desirable in the progress of a cause. There are no peculiar motions by the prosecution, subject to special rules and provisions, but if an occasion arises which entitles the prosecution to some special rule or order it may file a motion therefor. If, for example, special circumstances should entitle the prosecution to a postponement of the date set for trial, this would be secured by the filing of an appropriate motion.[a]

(D) DEMURRER

If the defendant files a plea which, as a matter of law, is insufficient on its face for the purpose for which it is filed, the common law permitted a demurrer thereto. The modern statutory forms of pleas leave little occasion for a demurrer by the prosecution. Probably its most frequent use has been in connection with pleas of former conviction or former acquittal. Where the demurrer has been abolished, by statute or by rule, any objection to the defendant's plea is raised by motion.

(E) NOLLE PROSEQUI

The rule of the common law was that "at any time, at least before the traverse jury was impaneled and sworn to try the cause, it was competent for the prosecutor to *nol. pros.* the entire indictment, without prejudice to a further or fresh proceeding for the same offense".[1] It was said that "the power to enter a *nolle prosequi* exists in the prosecuting officer. He exerts it upon his official responsibility. The court has no right to interfere in its exercise." [2]

If the nolle prosequi resulted in the withdrawal of a legally sufficient indictment, after the trial commenced and without the consent of the defendant, it had the effect of an acquittal. Otherwise it was without prejudice to a further or fresh proceeding for the same offense.

In a number of the states today, no prosecution can be discontinued or abandoned, after the indictment or information has been filed, without an order of the court. In such a jurisdiction the prosecuting

a. As to whether or not the prosecution may have a change of venue or of *venire* see Newberry v. Commonwealth, 192 Va. 819, 66 S.E.2d 841 (1951).

1. State v. McPherson, 9 Iowa 53 (1859).

2. State v. Smith, 49 N.H. 155 (1870). And see United States v. Foster, 226 A.2d 164 (D.C.Ct.App.1967).

officer wishing to have the prosecution dismissed, after the filing of the indictment or information, files a "motion to dismiss." The frequency with which such a motion, by the prosecuting officer, is granted by the court as a matter of course causes it to have much the appearance of a nolle prosequi. And it frequently goes under that name, unofficially. But a dismissal by the court on motion of the prosecuting officer is quite different in fact from the common-law nolle prosequi,—which was a dismissal by that officer himself.

In some jurisdictions prosecutors may "divert" a defendant who has been charged, or one that the police believe has committed an offense although not formally charged, by placing the defendant or suspect on probation. Sometimes court approval is required and in other cases the prosecutor acts on his own authority. If the defendant or suspect completes the diversion probation all charges or potential charges are abandoned.

SECTION 4. STEPS BY THE DEFENDANT

(A) BAIL

Probably no step more frequently takes first place in the mind of one who finds himself in the custody of the law than that of being released on bail. It is properly considered at this point, therefore, although by no means limited to proceedings prior to the trial.[3]

The word "bail" comes from the Old French "baillier" (to deliver). As a verb (in this connection) it means the delivery of the accused. In its origin it meant the delivery of the body of the accused by the public officer to "private jailers" who were bound to produce him when required by the court. As a noun (in this connection) it refers to his "private jailers" (now commonly called his "sureties") and also to the security given for his release (more commonly called a "bail bond" or "recognizance"—depending upon the form—or simply an "undertaking").

The sureties of one who has been released on bail are not required or expected to keep him in confinement, but only to produce him when needed. But the ancient theory that they were "private jailers" prevailed to the extent of giving them authority to arrest the accused and surrender him to the public officer even before he was needed for purposes of the prosecution, if they deemed this necessary to insure his presence when required. This common-law authority is very generally incorporated in the statutes.

3. The provision of the state constitution that a person shall be released on bail except for capital crimes when facts are evident or presumption great ensures availability of release on bail as a matter of right only before conviction. In re Podesto, 15 Cal.3d 921, 127 Cal.Rptr. 97, 544 P.2d 1297 (1976).

As to bail after conviction see Herzog v. United States, 75 S.Ct. 349 (1955).

The purpose of committing to jail one who has been *charged* with crime is not to punish him. So far the state has no right to punish him because his guilt has not been established.[4] The purpose is merely to secure his presence in order that he may be tried and, if found guilty, punished. The object of bail, therefore, is to provide a means of relief from an imprisonment which is imposed merely as a matter of precaution. From this it follows that it should be so regulated as reasonably to insure that the accused will be present when he is needed and that his liberty will not be restrained beyond the extent reasonably required for this purpose. Thus at common law, the matter of bail being entirely within the discretion of the magistrate or judge, it was felt that ordinarily there was no way to insure the appearance of one charged with a capital offense other than by keeping him in custody, and bail was commonly denied in these cases. On the other hand the probability that one charged with a misdemeanor could be produced by friends, under sufficient financial pressure, was considered so great that bail was almost never denied to one so accused. When, beginning with the device of "benefit of clergy," it was possible to have one charged with a felony for which he would not be executed, there was not thought to be any definite indication either way.

In this country most of the states have a provision in their constitutions which is in substance as follows: All persons shall be bailable by sufficient sureties, unless for capital offenses when the proof is evident or the presumption great. This greatly narrows the discretion of the magistrate or judge in this field, but such discretion still exists in the matter of deciding what will be sufficient financial pressure to procure the presence of the accused when needed. This is subject to the general limitation that "excessive bail shall not be required" and in some jurisdictions to more specific restrictions.

Before an accused was delivered from the custody of the official jailer into the "friendly custody" of his "private jailers" at common law, security was required in the form of either a bail bond or a recognizance. A bail bond is a sealed instrument executed by the "bail" (now frequently by the accused, the principal, and his sureties), binding them to pay to the state a specified sum of money if the accused fails to appear as therein stipulated. A recognizance, at common law, was an obligation acknowledged by the obligor in open court and entered upon the order book. Being witnessed by the record itself it did not require the signature or seal of the obligor. A recognizance, when used in lieu of a bail bond, acknowledged an obligation to pay a specified sum of money if the accused failed to appear as therein specified. Anciently the accused himself was not a party to this acknowledgment, but this exclusion tended to disappear. In more recent times the acknowledgment—depending upon the jurisdic-

4. Bell v. Wolfish, 441 U.S. 520, 99 S.Ct. 1861 (1979).

tion and the gravity of the offense—might be by (1) both the accused and one or more sureties, (2) only the accused, (3) only a surety or sureties. In other words, the obligation is to pay a specified sum of money to the state if the accused fails to appear as specified,—whether it is in the form of a bail bond or a recognizance. The "undertaking" under some of the statutes is not exactly either the bail bond or the recognizance of the common law, but it is intended for the same purpose.

The so-called "cash bail," a deposit of money in lieu of a bail bond or recognizance, seems to have been unknown to the common law, but is quite common under the statutes. Several jurisdictions now allow a deposit of cash of a percentage of the total bond set, which deposit is returnable to the defendant on compliance with the terms of release.

Confusion will be avoided if care is taken to distinguish four phrases—(1) entitled to bail, (2) admitted to bail, (3) taking of bail, and (4) release on bail. In most of the jurisdictions one not charged with a capital offense is *entitled* to bail as a constitutional right before conviction. If the charge is a capital one he is still *entitled* to bail unless the "proof is evident or the presumption great." But as this must be determined by the court an order must be made *admitting* the defendant to bail or refusing to do so. If the defendant is *admitted* to bail, or *entitled* to bail as a matter of right without a hearing, and tenders an undertaking for this purpose, some authorized court or official must determine whether the offer is or is not satisfactory. The *taking* of bail is the acceptance of the tendered undertaking or cash deposit by an authorized court or official. The determination of whether such an offer is or is not sufficient does not have reference to the amount involved, which was fixed in advance, but depends upon whether or not the sureties can "qualify." If the bail is accepted and the prisoner is permitted to go at large he has then been *released* on bail. Sometimes the phrase is that he has been "enlarged" on bail.

If one who has been released on bail fails to appear at the stipulated time, steps will be taken to forfeit his undertaking or cash deposit. No final order of forfeiture will be entered at that time because the failure to appear may have resulted from excusable circumstances. In one form or another (the procedure varies under the different statutes) an opportunity will be given to show cause why the undertaking or cash deposit should not be forfeited. If such cause cannot be shown the actual forfeiture will follow.[a]

a. "Under Rule 46 Federal Rules of Criminal Procedure, 18 U.S.C.A. an obligor or surety on a bond becomes liable on a breach of condition of a bond. The district court, in its discretion, may set aside the forfeiture if justice does not require its enforcement. United States v. Davis, 202 F.2d 621 (7th Cir. 1953). See Rule 46(e)(2) F.R.Cr.P.

Even the final forfeiture of the undertaking or cash deposit does not interfere with the prosecution of the accused. If he is later brought into court he will be tried and, if convicted, punished.

If a prisoner is dissatisfied with an order refusing to admit him to bail, or refusing to accept an offer of bail made by him or in his behalf, or if he thinks the amount fixed for his bail is excessive, his remedy is by habeas corpus or in some jurisdictions an appeal or summary application for review by a higher court.

The ancient theory that one arrested on a criminal charge must, pending trial, either remain in jail or be released on bail, results in needless hardship in many cases. The indigent prisoner may languish in jail because of inability to provide bail. And if he does provide bail it will usually be necessary for him to purchase a bail bond or undertaking from a professional bondsman which is expensive. If the indigent prisoner is one who is not likely to appear for trial if released, he may be unable to provide bail and this presents a situation for which no adequate solution has yet been presented. But in many cases there is no reason to believe the prisoner will not appear for trial if released, and for such a one provision should be made for releasing him on his own recognizance. The President's Commission on Law Enforcement and Administration of Justice recommended:

"Bail projects should be undertaken at the State, county, and local levels to furnish judicial officers with sufficient information to permit the pre-trial release without financial condition of all but that small portion of defendants who present a high risk of flight or dangerous acts prior to trial." [1]

As amended by the Bail Reform Act of 1966 the federal statute (18 U.S.C.A.) now provides:

§ 3146. Release in noncapital cases prior to trial.

(a) Any person charged with an offense, other than an offense punishable by death, shall, at his appearance before a judicial officer, be ordered released pending trial on his personal recognizance or upon the execution of an unsecured appearance bond in an amount specified by the judicial officer, subject to the condition that such person not commit an offense under section 1503, 1512, or 1513 of this title, unless the officer determines, in the exercise of his discretion, that such a release will not reasonably assure the appearance of the person as required. When such a determination is made, the judicial officer shall, either in lieu of or in addition to the above methods of release, impose a condition of release that such person not commit an offense under section 1503, 1512, or 1513 of this title and impose the

1. See the general discussion of the problem, including this recommendation. The Challenge of Crime in a Free Society, 131–133 (U.S. Govt. Printing Office, 1967).

first of the following conditions of release which will reasonably assure the appearance of the person for trial or, if no single condition gives that assurance, any combination of the following conditions:

(1) place the person in the custody of a designated person or organization agreeing to supervise him;

(2) place restrictions on the travel, association, or place of abode of the person during the period of release;

(3) require the execution of an appearance bond in a specified amount and the deposit in the registry of the court, in cash or other security as directed, of a sum not to exceed 10 per centum of the amount of the bond, such deposit to be returned upon the performance of the conditions of release;

(4) requires the execution of a bail bond with sufficient solvent sureties, or the deposit of cash in lieu thereof; or

(5) impose any other condition deemed reasonably necessary to assure appearance as required, including a condition requiring that the person return to custody after specified hours. . . .[2]

(B) HABEAS CORPUS

Habeas corpus is a Latin phrase meaning literally: "have the body." The import is that you have the one before the court in person (and explain by what authority you are detaining him). It is a legal device to give summary relief against illegal restraint of personal liberty. The legal process employed for this purpose is the *writ of habeas corpus.* It is a high prerogative common-law writ esteemed for centuries as the best and only sufficient safeguard of personal freedom. It has for its object the speedy release by judicial decree, of a person who is illegally restrained of his liberty, or is illegally detained from the control of those entitled to his custody. It is a writ of inquiry directed to the person in whose custody the prisoner is detained, requiring the custodian to bring the prisoner before the judge or court, that appropriate judgment may be rendered upon judicial inquiry into the alleged unlawful restraint.

The Constitution of the United States provides (Art. I, sec. 9, par. 2): "The privilege of the writ of habeas corpus shall not be suspended, unless in cases of rebellion or invasion the public safety may require it."

An outline of the proceedings may be helpful to an understanding of the law of habeas corpus. The starting point is a petition. The person in custody or someone on his behalf, prepares a petition for a writ of habeas corpus and presents it to some court or the judge thereof. By so doing he "files a petition for a writ of habeas

2. The Bail Reform Act of 1966 provides for the pretrial release of an accused if there is reasonable assurance that he will appear when required. Absolute certainty is not demanded. United States v. Alston, 420 F.2d 176 (D.C.Cir. 1969).

corpus." This petition may be either denied or granted, but it is important to bear in mind that granting the petition does not entitle the prisoner to a discharge. This is the preliminary step and the actual hearing does not take place until after the petition is granted. The petition must give the name or description of the custodian, the cause or pretense for the imprisonment (if known) and the ground upon which it is claimed to be illegal. The petition will be denied if it does not satisfy the legal requirements as to form, if it is not presented to the proper court or judge, or if it does not state facts sufficient to authorize release of the prisoner. On the other hand, if the petition is in proper form presented to a proper court or judge, and states a cause which if true, would entitle the prisoner to be released, it must be granted. The court or judge has very little discretion at this point of the proceedings. If the writ is granted, the petitioner is often said to have "sued out a writ of habeas corpus."

The writ of habeas corpus is directed to the custodian and commands him to have the body of the prisoner before the court or judge at a specified time, and to bring with him the writ itself with a return thereon showing what he has been doing with the prisoner (meaning whether or not he has been detaining the person said to be a prisoner, and if so by what authority). If the return, or answer, of the custodian does not state a lawful authority for the confinement of the prisoner, his discharge will be ordered forthwith. If it states an adequate cause of detention the disputed facts will be determined at a hearing, and the court or judge, as a result of this hearing, will determine whether the detention is lawful or unlawful. If it is found to be lawful the prisoner will be remanded to the custody of the custodian. If it is found to be unlawful the discharge of the prisoner will be ordered, subject to the possibility that the court or judge may find proper cause for his commitment now despite the fact that his previous detention has been irregular.

Where one is deprived of his liberty without even the color of legal authority, the availability of the writ of habeas corpus is obvious. If the imprisonment is claimed to be by virtue of legal process, the validity and present force of such process are the only subjects of investigation in this type of proceeding. The dual nature of our government must be considered in this connection. If the imprisonment is claimed to be by virtue of federal authority, the validity and present force of such authority can be tested only by federal proceedings. Imprisonment claimed to be under state authority, on the other hand, may be inquired into by either state or federal proceedings, although it is only in rare instances that the federal courts or judges will discharge a prisoner held under color of state authority unless the prisoner has first exhausted his remedies in the state courts.[1]

1. This does not require repetitious applications to state courts. Brown v. Allen, 344 U.S. 443, 73 S.Ct. 397 (1953). Denial of certiorari by the Supreme Court imports no expression of opinion on the merits of the case but means only that there were not four members of the

A writ of habeas corpus cannot be used as a substitute for an appeal.[2] And such a proceeding does not have all the strength of an appeal. Thus Rule 52(b) of the Federal Rules of Criminal Procedure provides: "Plain errors or defects affecting substantial rights may be noticed although they were not brought to the attention of the court." This was held to apply to a direct appeal but not to a collateral attack. In a 1979 habeas proceeding, plain error in an instruction, unchallenged during the trial, could not be relied upon, without more, to reverse a 1963 conviction.[3]

If he claims that error was committed by the trial judge in admitting or excluding evidence or in giving or refusing instructions, or in any other manner, he must raise such an issue by a motion directed to the trial court or by an appeal to a higher court,—or in extreme cases by a writ of certiorari.

There is, however, a margin of common ground on which a prisoner may question the legality of his imprisonment either by appeal or

Court who thought the case should be heard. Ibid.

2. Dromiack v. Warden, 96 Nev. 269, 607 P.2d 1145 (1980); Morishita v. Morris, 621 P.2d 691 (Utah 1980).

The fact that the prisoner has not completed a proper sentence on one count does not preclude him from bringing habeas corpus on another count. In re Chapman, 43 Cal.2d 385, 273 P.2d 817 (1954).

"The general rule is that habeas corpus cannot serve as a substitute for an appeal, and in the absence of special circumstances constituting an excuse for failure to employ that remedy, the writ will not lie where the claimed errors could have been, but were not, raised upon a timely appeal from a judgment of conviction." (Quoted from earlier cases). In re Black, 66 Cal.2d 881, 59 Cal.Rptr. 429, 432, 428 P.2d 293, 296 (1967).

"Although habeas corpus ordinarily cannot serve as a second appeal, that general rule is primarily a discretionary policy which may be overlooked where 'special circumstances' are deemed to exist." In re Coughlin, 16 Cal.3d 52, 127 Cal.Rptr. 337, 545 P.2d 249 (1976). Accord, Cardarella v. United States, 375 F.2d 222 (8th Cir. 1967).

As far as federal prisoners are concerned there has been a change of procedure in making a collateral attack based upon an alleged lack of jurisdiction. Under the "jurisdiction act", 28 U.S.C. § 2255, this is to be by motion rather than by resort to habeas corpus. With reference to this change of procedure see United States v. Hayman, 342 U.S. 205, 72 S.Ct. 263, 96 L.Ed. 232 (1952).

The availability of the writ of habeas corpus does not depend on actual detention in prison. One who has been released on parole is constructively a prisoner subject to restraint by penal authorities and the writ is available to him to test the validity of that restraint. In re Petersen, 51 Cal.2d 177, 331 P.2d 24 (1958). Accord: Jones v. Cunningham, 371 U.S. 236, 83 S.Ct. 373 (1963).

A person released on his own recognizance after conviction pending appeal is still in custody within the meaning of 28 U.S.C.A. § 2241(e)(3). Hensley v. Municipal Court, 411 U.S. 345, 93 S.Ct. 1571 (1973).

A writ of habeas corpus does not entitle petitioner to a release if the only illegality of his detention is that he is being held in the wrong institution under a felony conviction when the sentence should have been for a misdemeanor. In such a case the order will direct that petitioner be taken before the district court to await a valid sentence. Lawton v. Hand, 183 Kan. 694, 331 P.2d 886 (1958).

Habeas corpus is available to one who has been released on parole or on bail. In re Smiley, 66 Cal.2d 606, 58 Cal.Rptr. 579, 427 P.2d 179, (1967). This applies to one who has been released on his own recognizance since this is simply an alternative to bail in appropriate cases and the one so released is subject to restraints. Ibid.

3. United States v. Frady, 456 U.S. 152, 102 S.Ct. 1584 (1982).

by habeas corpus. If his claim is that the court did not have jurisdiction over the subject matter, or over his person, or did not have authority to pronounce the sentence under which he is being confined, he may have the issue tested by either method,—with this limitation: ordinarily he must appeal if this remedy is still available to him.

Our criminal jurisdiction is based largely upon the so-called territorial theory of jurisdiction. If a particular criminal case did not involve any exception to the normal requirement, and a case should go to conviction although the crime clearly had not been committed within the territorial jurisdiction of the trial court, the defendant could be released from imprisonment under the sentence pronounced in such a case by habeas corpus proceedings, if necessary, because the trial, conviction, and sentence were utterly void by reason of lack of jurisdiction. The same might be true if the defendant had been indicted, tried, and convicted on a charge of a non-indictable offense. Although such an offense was committed within the territorial jurisdiction of the district court, for example, the law of the jurisdiction might be such that it would have to be prosecuted by complaint and summary trial before a magistrate and could come within the legal jurisdiction of the district court only on appeal. Hence a person in the penitentiary serving a sentence under a conviction based upon an indictment charging a non-indictable offense would be entitled to be released on a petition for habeas corpus [4] (if it is too late to appeal).

Furthermore, even though a court starts with jurisdiction over the subject matter and the defendant, it may lose that jurisdiction before sentence is pronounced. If it does lose such jurisdiction, the sentence is utterly void, and a prisoner serving such a sentence is entitled to release on habeas corpus if no other remedy is available.

A typical case is one in which a proper indictment was filed and the defendant arrested, after which the indictment was altered by an unauthorized amendment charging a different crime than that found by the grand jury. When the proper indictment was found the court had jurisdiction over the subject matter and when the defendant was arrested the court had jurisdiction over his person. At that point jurisdiction was complete so far as that case was concerned. But when the indictment was unlawfully altered to charge a different crime the court lost jurisdiction because there was no longer any lawful charge against the defendant. The alteration destroyed the original indictment and the altered writing had no standing in law. Hence the trial was of a man not legally charged with any crime and no court has jurisdiction to conduct such a criminal trial. For this reason he was able to secure his release by habeas corpus.[5]

Another typical case of loss of jurisdiction is the Arkansas case in which a violent mob moved into the court room and completely dominated the trial, intimidating witnesses, counsel, jurors and even the

4. Conkling v. Hollowell, 203 Iowa 1374, 214 N.W. 717 (1927).

5. In re Bain, 121 U.S. 1, 7 S.Ct. 781, 30 L.Ed. 849 (1877).

judge himself so that no one dared to do anything other than let the case proceed to a hasty conviction. When this mob moved in and took over the situation the jurisdiction of the court moved out. What remained was the empty form of a trial having no legal validity whatever. The prisoner serving a sentence pronounced by that state court was released by federal habeas corpus proceedings.[6]

Furthermore, a court otherwise having jurisdiction of the case may pronounce a sentence it has no authority to pronounce under the law. The court acts without jurisdiction in the pronouncement of such a sentence, and the sentence itself is void and can be attacked either directly or indirectly. This is well illustrated in *Medley.* In that case the court inadvertently pronounced a sentence based on a statute passed after the crime was committed, and hence *ex post facto* as to that particular prosecution. So the prisoner serving that sentence was entitled to release on habeas corpus.[7]

This brings us to one of the most famous habeas corpus cases of modern times: Mooney v. Holohan.[8] Tom Mooney had been convicted of first-degree murder in the California court, as a result of the fatal bombing of the San Francisco Preparedness Parade on July 22, 1916. After the conviction it was clearly established that perjury had been committed by witnesses for the prosecution during Mooney's trial. This would have entitled Mooney to a new trial, if the discovery had been made in time, but it was not a ground for release by habeas corpus because it did not affect the jurisdiction of the court or the authority of the court to pronounce sentence in the case.

The question may be asked: "If an innocent man has been convicted on perjured testimony, why should he not be released by habeas corpus?" But the flaw in this question is rather obvious. It cannot be determined judicially that perjury has been committed in a particular case without a thorough judicial investigation of the facts. Since the court is bound to issue a writ of habeas corpus if a petition presenting a proper ground therefor is presented in proper form to the appropriate court, it follows that every convict could secure a retrial of his case, in effect, by filing a petition for habeas corpus and alleging perjury by witnesses for the prosecution,—if this was recognized as a ground for release by this form of proceeding. Furthermore, a prisoner might be guilty of the crime of which he was convicted despite the fact that witnesses for the prosecution misstated facts on the witness stand in their zeal to put him "behind the bars." Hence it cannot be assumed that a convict is innocent merely because perjury on the part of prosecuting witnesses is established. For this reason, proof of such perjury should be used for other purposes. It should be used to secure a new trial if the discovery is made in time;

6. Moore v. Dempsey, 261 U.S. 86, 43 S.Ct. 265, 67 L.Ed. 543 (1923).

7. In re Medley, 134 U.S. 160, 10 S.Ct. 384, 33 L.Ed. 835 (1890).

8. Mooney v. Holohan, 294 U.S. 103, 55 S.Ct. 340, 79 L.Ed. 791 (1935). Cf. Coggins v. O'Brien, 188 F.2d 130 (1st Cir. 1951). Noted 65 Harv.L.Rev. 510 (1952).

and if not, it should be the basis of a petition for a pardon. Since the issuance of a pardon is within the discretion of the governor (or other pardoning authority,—depending upon the jurisdiction) it is possible for proper cases to be handled in this way without the risk of opening up every criminal case to a re-trial in collateral form.

Mooney was in the courts time and again, but the case which introduced a new element into the law of habeas corpus was when he filed an application in the Supreme Court of the United States for leave to file a petition for a writ of habeas corpus to be issued out of the High Court itself. His claim in this application was that he was being confined in violation of the "due process clause," of the Fourteenth Amendment to the Constitution of the United States, for the reason (as he alleged) that the *sole basis* of his conviction was perjured testimony *knowingly used by the prosecuting authorities* in order to obtain a conviction. The extreme nature of this claim must be emphasized: (1) The perjured testimony was alleged to be the sole basis of his conviction, which means in substance that he would have been entitled to an advice to the jury to acquit if this evidence had been lacking; (2) The perjured testimony was knowingly and purposely used against him by the prosecuting attorney. It may be added parenthetically that this extreme claim was never established and that Mooney was never released by habeas corpus; he was ultimately released by a governor who was satisfied that perjury had actually been committed by prosecuting witnesses and that there was at least grave doubt about his guilt.

The Supreme Court of the United States not only refused to order Mooney's release from imprisonment, it even refused to issue the writ of habeas corpus. It did not investigate the facts behind the extreme claim in his petition for the reason that he had not applied to the California courts for a writ of habeas corpus *on that ground.* But the Court said in substance, "If you can substantiate this claim and the California courts will not release you from imprisonment on that proof, *we will.*" The Court took the position that if the prosecuting authority of the state contrived to procure a criminal conviction through a deliberate deception of the court and the jury by the presentation of testimony known to be perjured, this was not due process of law but the mere pretense of a trial. And since, in such a case, there was no conviction based on due process of law, the judge would be wholly without authority to pronounce any sentence based upon such apparent conviction. Hence such a sentence, being beyond the jurisdiction of the court and utterly void, would give no authority for the defendant's confinement, so that a release might properly be ordered in habeas corpus proceedings,—even in the federal courts if the prisoner had exhausted his remedies in the state courts without avail.

This case will stand out in history as a benchmark in the law of habeas corpus because it suggested that any conviction in a case in which any agency of the government had deprived the convict of his constitutional right to due process of law, is in legal effect utterly void and incapable of authorizing the judge to pronounce any valid sentence thereon, so that imprisonment under a sentence purporting to be based on such a conviction is without authority of law and will entitle the prisoner to release on habeas corpus proceedings if it is too late to raise the question by motion or appeal.

The Mooney case was decided only a few years after the famous *Scottsboro Rape* case.[9] This was not a habeas corpus case but had a bearing on the problem because it was held to show a violation of due process. Several young negroes were charged with rape in the state of Alabama. They were young and illiterate and obviously surrounded by hostile sentiment. The judge appointed all of the members of the bar to represent the accused. This had the appearance of a magnificent gesture; but what was everyone's business turned out to be nobody's business (as is so usually the case) and as a result no one of the trials lasted as long as a day although rape is a capital offense in that state. The conviction was affirmed on appeal by the Supreme Court of Alabama, and was taken to the Supreme Court of the United States by a writ of certiorari. The High Court reversed the Alabama court on the ground that the failure of the trial judge to make effective appointment of counsel to assist the defendants in their defense, coupled with the judge's failure to acquaint the defendants with their right to counsel, and his failure to give them time and opportunity to secure counsel, was a denial of due process of law in violation of the Fourteenth Amendment.

Scottsboro plus *Mooney* clearly suggested the possibility of habeas corpus in a case in which it was claimed the defendant had been denied the right of counsel, and this was soon put to the test. And the Supreme Court of the United States held, that while a defendant may waive his right of counsel and try his own case, he will be entitled to a release on habeas corpus if he was convicted in a case in which he was improperly denied the right of counsel, because such a conviction was based upon a violation of his constitutional right to due process of law and the court had no jurisdiction to pronounce any sentence upon such a void conviction.[10]

The Supreme Court has also held that if a confession and a plea of guilty have been obtained by threats made by officers of the law, the judge has no jurisdiction to pronounce judgment of conviction and sentence upon such a plea, and hence imprisonment under such a sentence may be terminated by habeas corpus proceedings if a more direct remedy is not available.[11] The court also held that if prison officials suppress a convict's appeal documents until too late for him to

9. Powell v. Alabama, 287 U.S. 45, 53 S.Ct. 55, 77 L.Ed. 158 (1932).

10. Johnson v. Zerbst, 304 U.S. 458, 58 S.Ct. 1019, 82 L.Ed. 1461 (1938); Walker v. Johnston, 312 U.S. 275, 61 S.Ct. 574, 85 L.Ed. 830 (1941).

11. Waley v. Johnson, 316 U.S. 101, 62 S.Ct. 964, 86 L.Ed. 1302 (1942).

perfect an appeal under state law, this amounts to a violation of his constitutional rights and will entitle him to have the validity of his conviction tested by habeas corpus proceedings.[12]

The result of these cases was to suggest that any one in a state penitentiary has a chance for release under federal habeas corpus proceedings, and a flood of such petitions followed. The vast majority of them were entirely without success. The federal courts had made it clear in the cases mentioned above that they intended to preserve and maintain the constitutional safeguards of persons accused of crime, by the use of federal habeas corpus if necessary. They next made it equally clear that this device is not a haven of refuge for those properly convicted of crime in the state courts.

It may be added that the Supreme Court has held that it is improper for prison authorities to require a petition for habeas corpus to be submitted for approval to some agency designated by them, such as the legal investigator of the parole board, and that such a regulation is invalid; but also, that such a regulation is not a ground for the release of an otherwise legally convicted and confined prisoner.[13]

The effect of the Supreme Court's holdings in the mentioned cases and in many others is to subject state and federal court convictions to post conviction review in federal courts for any violation of federal constitutional rights that may have prevented a fair trial. Courts no longer speak only in terms of lack of jurisdiction but address the question of whether the alleged violation denies a fair trial.[14] Habeas corpus is now available for a state prisoner to test in federal court the sufficiency of evidence to support his conviction.[15]

The statute defining federal habeas corpus jurisdiction (28 U.S. C.A. section 2241) provides:

"Power to grant writ

"(a) Writs of habeas corpus may be granted by the Supreme Court, and any justice thereof, the district courts and any circuit judge within their respective jurisdictions. The order of a circuit

12. Cochran v. Kansas, 316 U.S. 255, 62 S.Ct. 1068, 86 L.Ed. 1453 (1942).

It was held that the prosecution's use of a coerced confession in a state case called for a reversal of a conviction obtained thereby. Brown v. Mississippi, 297 U.S. 278, 56 S.Ct. 461 (1936). And this is true whether the coercion is physical or mental. Payne v. Arkansas, 356 U.S. 560, 78 S.Ct. 844 (1958). On the other hand the mere evidence of a threat of lynching will not bar the use of a confession if it was freely and voluntarily given at another time and place in the absence of any coercive influence. Thomas v. Arizona, 356 U.S. 390, 78 S.Ct. 885 (1958).

13. Ex parte Hull, 312 U.S. 546, 61 S.Ct. 640 (1941). It has been held that 28 U.S.C.A. § 2255, which is the substantial equivalent of a writ of habeas corpus in more convenient form is not unconstitutional. To limit defendant to this remedy except where it is inadequate or ineffective does not suspend the writ of habeas corpus. United States v. Anselmi, 207 F.2d 312 (3d Cir. 1953).

14. See discussion Fay v. Noia, 372 U.S. 391, 83 S.Ct. 822 (1963) (habeas corpus from state conviction); Kaufman v. United States, 394 U.S. 217, 89 S.Ct. 1068 (1969) (federal remedy under 28 U.S.C. § 2255).

15. Jackson v. Virginia, 443 U.S. 307, 99 S.Ct. 2781 (1979).

judge shall be entered in the records of the district court of the district wherein the restraint complained of is had.

"(b) The Supreme Court, any justice thereof, and any circuit judge may decline to entertain an application for a writ of habeas corpus and may transfer the application for hearing and determination to the district court having jurisdiction to entertain it.

"(c) The writ of habeas corpus shall not extend to a prisoner unless—

"(1) He is in custody under or by color of the authority of the United States or is committed for trial before some court thereof; or

"(2) He is in custody for an act done or omitted in pursuance of an Act of Congress, or an order, process, judgment or decree of a court or judge of the United States; or

"(3) He is in custody in violation of the Constitution or laws or treaties of the United States; or

"(4) He, being a citizen of a foreign state and domiciled therein is in custody for an act done or omitted under any alleged right, title, authority, privilege, protection, or exemption claimed under the commission, order or sanction of any foreign state, or under color thereof, the validity and effect of which depend upon the law of nations; or

"(5) It is necessary to bring him into court to testify or for trial."

(It should be observed that clause (5) provides for *habeas corpus ad testificandum* and has nothing to do with alleged unlawfulness of restraint. In such a case the prisoner is restored to the custody from which he was taken as soon as he is no longer needed as a witness.)

The most famous case under clause (2) of the federal statute is *In re Neagle.*[16] Neagle, a deputy United States marshal appointed to protect Mr. Justice Field of the United States Supreme Court while the Justice was on judicial duties in California, shot and killed one Terry while the latter was in the act of making a dangerous assault upon the Justice. Neagle was charged with murder in California and was arrested by state authorities there who insisted they were going to place him on trial for murder to determine whether or not the killing was under circumstances sufficient to justify the homicide. Upon federal habeas corpus proceedings it was held that the deputy marshal was acting under the authority of a law of the United States and hence not liable to answer to the courts of California for his act. He was therefore ordered released from the custody of the state authorities.

This case suggests two comments: (1) A federal officer committing homicide while in the performance of his duties as such officer is guilty of no offense if he is acting within the scope of his legal privi-

16. In re Neagle, 135 U.S. 1, 10 S.Ct. 658, 34 L.Ed. 55 (1890).

lege under the circumstances, but is guilty of criminal homicide if he takes life by the use of deadly force which is clearly not privileged by the facts of the particular case. (2) The federal government has the right and power to determine this issue in its own courts, and it is quite proper that it should do so.

It is very questionable, however, whether habeas corpus is the desirable remedy. Under one of the sections providing for the removal of causes (28 U.S.C.A. section 1442) the deputy marshal could have such a case removed to the federal court for trial there, as was done in the somewhat similar case of Tennessee v. Davis.[17]

(C) DEMURRER

A demurrer is a challenge by one party to his opponent's pleading. A demurrer to an indictment is a pleading by the defendant attacking the sufficiency of the indictment for a defect which is apparent from its face. This demurrer admits the truth of every fact sufficiently alleged but insists that as a matter of law the facts so alleged do not constitute an offense. In fact, at common law, this demurrer brings the whole record before the court so that any defect upon the face of either could be reached in this way.

In the early days a decision in favor of the defendant, on his demurrer to the indictment, resulted in his discharge unless the defect was obviously one of form rather than substance, in which case he was detained until a new indictment could be found. Even his discharge, however, did not bar the finding of a subsequent indictment charging the same offense as that intended by the first. Many of the modern statutes provide that the defendant shall not be discharged, as a result of sustaining his demurrer, if the judge orders the case resubmitted to the same or another grand jury;—or (if such procedure is available under the facts in the particular jurisdiction) if he

17. Tennessee v. Davis, 100 U.S. 257, 25 L.Ed. 648 (1879).

The provision of 28 U.S.C.A. § 2255 which is the substantial equivalent of a writ of habeas corpus in more convenient form is not unconstitutional. To limit defendant to this remedy except where it is inadequate or ineffective does not suspend the writ of habeas corpus. United States v. Anselmi, 207 F.2d 312 (3d Cir. 1953), cert. denied, and a motion for leave to file a petition for a writ of habeas corpus was also denied. 345 U.S. 947, 73 S.Ct. 868 (1953).

§ 2255 is an independent civil action. United States v. Hayman, 342 U.S. 205, 72 S.Ct. 263 (1952); Heflin v. United States, 358 U.S. 415, 79 S.Ct. 451 (1959).

It was held in one case that at least under certain circumstances the writ of habeas corpus is available to one who is at liberty on bail. Commonwealth ex rel. Levine v. Fair, 394 Pa. 262, 146 A.2d 834 (1958). Jones, C. J., dissented on the ground that the writ is not available to one who has been released on bail. The authority has been so strongly in favor of the position taken by the dissent that it has been held habeas corpus is not available to one who had been released on bail and surrendered himself into custody for the sole purpose of applying for the writ. Baker v. Grice, 169 U.S. 284, 18 S.Ct. 323 (1898).

However, authority today clearly supports a determination of custody based on a petitioner's being released on bail or recognizance. Hensley v. Municipal Court, 411 U.S. 345, 93 S.Ct. 1571 (1973); Davis v. Muellar, 643 F.2d 521 (8th Cir. 1981).

orders or permits an amendment, or directs the filing of an information against the defendant.

Since the demurrer admits the truth of the allegations made, inquiry is invited as to what will happen if the court decides that the indictment is legally sufficient and proper. There is no reason why this admission should be of any more force than "for the sake of argument" to determine the validity of the pleading, but anciently it was far more than this. It was said by an early writer: ". . . . if a person be indicted or appealed of felony and he will demur to the appeal or indictment and it be judged against him, he shall have judgment to be hanged, for it is a confession of the indictment, ..."[1] The severity of this rule was modified in the course of time. Permission to enter a plea after the demurrer was overruled came to be granted commonly in felony cases. And modern statutes grant this permission in all cases,—felony or misdemeanor.

Under modern statutes, if a defendant fails or refuses to answer an indictment or information against him, a plea of not guilty is entered in his behalf.[2] It is doubtful if the ancient rule could be applied constitutionally today in light of the requirements for a valid guilty plea.[3]

The demurrer is a superfluous device,—at this point as elsewhere in procedure. It was pointed out in the Seventeenth Century that there was nothing to be accomplished by a demurrer to the indictment that could not be obtained in some other way.[4] Demurrers have been abolished in federal proceedings[5] and most jurisdictions have followed the trend in that direction.[6]

(D) MOTIONS

(i) MOTION TO QUASH

If it could be seen from the face of the indictment that it was insufficient as a matter of law a proper mode of attack was by a

1. 2 Hale P.C. *257. ". . . if he demurre in law, and it be adjudged against him, he shall have judgment to be hanged." 2 Co.Inst. *178.

2. In California a plea of not guilty must be entered. West's Ann.Cal.Pen. Code, § 1024 (1970).

3. Boykin v. Alabama, 395 U.S. 238, 89 S.Ct. 1709 (1969). See also Rule 11(f) Federal Rules of Criminal Procedure.

4. ". . . he may have all the advantages of exception to the insufficiency of the indictment or appeal by way of exception either before his plea of *not guilty*, or after his conviction and before judgment, . . ." 2 Hale P.C. *257. The original publication was in 1678. While Lord Hale is not specific at this point, what he has reference to is a *motion to quash* before his plea of not guilty, or a *motion in arrest of judgment* after conviction. At common law any objection which could be raised by a demurrer to the indictment could also be raised by either of these motions.

5. Federal Rules of Criminal Procedure, Rule 12, 18 U.S.C.A. Federal Rules of Civil Procedure, Rule 7(a), 28 U.S.C.A.

6. The American Law Institute has recommended that demurrers to the indictment or information be abolished. Code of Criminal Procedure § 209 (official draft, 1930).

motion to quash. Any objection to the indictment which could be raised by demurrer could be raised also by the motion to quash, at common law.

The quashing of an indictment was not a bar to another indictment for the same offense. Hence the defendant gained no advantage by it, other than delay, unless it was a prosecution which should not have been brought at all. If defendant was indicted for the stealing of a dog, in the early days before this was a crime, the motion to quash was the proper remedy. It could be made at any time after the indictment was found (and before verdict) whereas a demurrer could not be filed prior to arraignment. And the motion did not involve any admission by the defendant. Hence it was more advantageous than a demurrer. If it was a different kind of case, on the other hand, and the objection raised by the motion could be cured by a new and more carefully drawn indictment, it was to the advantage of the defendant to wait before urging it. He could force the prosecution to disclose its case in full, he could take his chances, with one jury, and if the verdict was against him he could raise, by a motion in arrest of judgment, any objection he could have urged earlier by a demurrer or a motion to quash. Hence the motion to quash and the demurrer to the indictment tended more and more to fall into disuse while increased reliance was placed upon the motion in arrest of judgment. To prevent this statutes were passed in some states providing that the motion in arrest of judgment could not be sustained on any ground which could have been urged by a motion to quash or by a demurrer, other than lack of jurisdiction or the failure of the indictment or information to charge an offense. The net result of such a provision (sometimes expressly stated) is that any error or defect in the proceedings, other than lack of jurisdiction or failure to charge an offense, which properly could be raised by the defendant before going to trial, is waived by him if he goes to trial without objection. This is the provision of Rule 12 of the Federal Rules of Criminal Procedure except that the court is authorized to grant relief from the waiver for cause shown.

Another legislative effort to improve criminal procedure, in some jurisdictions, took the form of extending the motion to quash to cover other purposes and providing that it should not be used for any objection which could be raised by demurrer. The more modern trend, although it still has far to go, is to abolish both the demurrer and the motion to quash and substitute for both a motion to dismiss.

(ii) Motion to Dismiss

The motion to quash was greatly enlarged by statute. Some of the enactments changed the label to "motion to set aside the indictment" (or the information). But no motion under either label is appropriate for all of the possible need in this regard. Such a motion is completely ineffective, for example, if no indictment or information has been filed. But one arrested for crime cannot be kept in jail or on bail indefinitely by the mere absence of such formal accusation.[a] After the lapse of too great a period of time (the statutory provisions differ) the defendant is entitled to be released from jail or to have his undertaking discharged (or his cash deposit returned) if he is on bail. And one device by which he obtains this relief has been a "motion to dismiss." The result, if the motion is granted, is the dismissal of the pending prosecution although it does not bar subsequent proceedings against him for the same offense unless this is so stated in the statute.

Some states have simplified the procedure by using the motion to dismiss not only for this purpose but also to quash the indictment or information. Simplification at this point has been carried to its logical conclusion in the Federal Rules of Criminal Procedure. Rule 12 abolishes the demurrer, the motion to quash, the plea in abatement, the plea to the jurisdiction, the plea of former conviction or former acquittal, and all other but the basic pleas. If there is *any* reason why a prosecution should be disposed of otherwise than on a plea of guilty, a plea of not guilty or a plea of *nolo contendere*, this is accomplished in a federal case by a motion to dismiss.

(iii) FOR CHANGE OF VENUE

The common law permitted the defendant to obtain a change of the place of trial to an adjoining county if for any reason a fair and impartial trial could not be had in the county in which the offense was committed.[1] This transfer was known as a change of venue. For the most part now it is regulated by statute. The defendant's application for a change of venue is referred to as a "petition" in some of the statutes. Essentially it is a motion and under the more simplified types of procedure it is so called.

a. Gerstein v. Pugh, 420 U.S. 103, 95 S.Ct. 854 (1975).

1. ". . . the law is clear and uniform as far back as it can be traced . . . where an impartial trial cannot be had in the proper county, it shall be tried in the next." Rex v. Cowle, 2 Burr. 834, 859, 97 Eng.Rep. 587, 602 (1759). By the Crown and *a fortiori* by the defendant.

A state statute which prevents a change of venue for a criminal jury trial, regardless of local prejudice against the accused, on the sole ground that the offense charged is a misdemeanor, is constitutionally invalid as violative of the 14th Amendment right to trial by an impartial jury. Groppi v. Wisconsin, 400 U.S. 505, 91 S.Ct. 490 (1971).

In a proper case mandamus will issue from an appellate court to compel a change of venue in a criminal case. Maine v. Superior Court of Mendocino County, 68 Cal.2d 375, 66 Cal.Rptr. 724, 438 P.2d 372 (1968).

The community had been exposed to massive publicity attendant upon **D**'s trial, conviction, appeal and reversal of the penalty (death). And **D**'s recent escape from the county jail had catapulted the case onto front pages again and had provoked a wave of alarm and concern throughout the community, and the fact that **D** had recanted and confessed at the first penalty trial had been reiterated and emphasized in newspaper reports preceding retrial. In view of this a change of venue was necessary to guarantee **D** an unbiased jury in the pending penalty trial and mandamus was granted to compel such an order. Fain v. Superior Court of Stanislaus County, 2 Cal.3d 46, 84 Cal. Rptr. 135, 465 P.2d 23 (1970).

The defendant's petition or motion for a change of venue is a waiver of his right to have the trial in the county in which the offense is alleged to have been committed. Hence no such question is involved where the motion is filed by him. It is otherwise where the prosecution seeks a change of venue. In several states such a change is authorized by express constitutional provision. In the absence of such a provision in the constitution uniformity is lacking. In a number of states the need of having an impartial trial has been held sufficient to authorize a change on motion of the prosecuting attorney.[2] In others, even a statute providing for such a change has been held unconstitutional.[3]

(iv) For Change of Judge

A recusation is a challenge, directed against the judge before whom the case is to be tried, based upon the ground of prejudice or some other disqualification. In the beginning it was a request that the judge excuse (recuse) himself. Under modern statutes it is much more than this. The transfer of a case from one judge to another often has been called loosely a "change of venue." This inaccurate terminology has come about in part, no doubt, by reason of the fact that the judicial machinery in some parts of the country has been such that the simplest and most obvious method of obtaining a change of the judge to try the case has been by transferring it from one county to another. The proper designation is "change of judge." The defendant's effort to secure such a change in the early days was very definitely an "application" or a "petition," and it still, at times, carries such a label. But under the statutes it is essentially a motion and under the more simplified types of procedure it is designated a "motion for a change of judge."

(v) For Other Purposes

A motion, it should be remembered, must of necessity be an instrument that can be adapted to any peculiar need that arises. If the defendant is entitled to a postponement of the date set for trial, to a bill of particulars, or to relief of any other nature, his request therefor should be by motion. The desirable procedure would provide simply that if an occasion arises which entitles the defendant to some special rule or order he may file a motion therefor. This would include any of the motions mentioned above and any other for which a need might be found. Rule 12 of the Federal Rules of Criminal Procedure, for example, provides that except for the basic pleas, defendant's request for anything to which he thinks he is entitled "shall be raised only by motion to dismiss or to grant appropriate relief." [4]

2. See Newberry v. Commonwealth, 192 Va. 819, 66 S.E.2d 841 (1951). And see State v. Dryman, 127 Mont. 579, 269 P.2d 796 (1954).

3. Wheeler v. State, 24 Wis. 52 (1869).

4. This chapter deals with Proceedings Preliminary to Trial and the statement in the text is made with this in mind. To correct a judgment that the court had no power to pronounce, if no

(E) PLEAS

A trial, at law, is for the determination of an issue. And the issue, under our procedure, is formed by the pleadings. In a criminal case the pleading by the prosecution is the indictment or information, and that by the defendant is his plea. Without the defendant's plea there would be no issue and hence nothing to try.

In ancient times, if a person indicted for felony "stood mute," an inquest of office was taken to determine whether his silence was wilful or the result of incapacity to speak,—unless he had already spoken in court on the same day. If it was determined that he wilfully stood mute, judgment of *peine fort et dure* was given against him. This was: "That he be sent to the prison from whence he came, and put into a dark, lower room, and there to be laid naked upon the bare ground upon his back without any clothes or rushes under him or to cover him except his privy members, his legs and arms drawn and extended with cords to the four corners of the room, and upon his body laid as great a weight of iron, as he can bear, and more. And the first day he shall have three morsels of barley bread without drink, the second day he shall have three draughts of water, of standing water next the door of the prison, without bread, and this to be his diet till he die. . . .

"This judgment is given for his contempt in refusing his legal trial, and therefore he forfeits his goods, but it is no attainder, nor gives any escheat or corruption of blood. . . .

"The severity of the judgment is to bring men to put themselves upon their legal trial, and tho sometimes it hath been given and executed, yet for the most part men bethink themselves and plead." (2 Hale P.C. *319).

In the course of time the defendant who refused to plead was dealt with a little more humanely by the rule that the obstinate refusal to plead amounted to a plea of guilty. Under modern statutes such refusal by the defendant results in a plea of not guilty being entered for him by the court. In effect such refusal *is* itself a plea of not guilty and the entry by the judge is a mere matter of form.

At common law all of defendant's pleas, in a criminal case, were oral. Some of the statutes incorporate this requirement. Others permit the pleas to be either oral or in writing, and a few of them *require* certain pleas to be in writing.

(i) PLEA OF SANCTUARY

Anciently an offender who had fled to a church, or church yard, was immune from arrest while he remained in this sanctuary. And,

other remedy is available, the defendant may apply for a writ of error coram nobis even after the sentence has been served. United States v. Morgan, 346 U.S. 502, 74 S.Ct. 247 (1954).

unless his offense was treason or sacrilege, he was entitled to depart from the country if he took certain steps to confess his guilt and abjure the realm. He was given forty days to leave from a designated port. And if he was arrested and arraigned during this time his relief was by pleading his privilege of sanctuary. This saved his life, but by this abjuration his blood was attainted, and he forfeited all his goods and chattels. The plea of sanctuary was abrogated in the early 1600s.

(ii) Plea of Benefit of Clergy

In the very early days a cleric, charged with felony, was entitled to have his case transferred from the king's court to the ecclesiastical court. Originally this transfer was effected by a demand made by the bishop or ordinary. Later the procedure was for the cleric to file a plea of benefit of clergy and to support this plea by proof of his qualification. After the procedure of transferring such a case to the ecclesiastical court was abolished, benefit of clergy came to be a device by which one so entitled was spared the penalty of death in the king's court. It was extended, moreover, to include any man who could read. At this time the plea of benefit of clergy was available, but rapidly fell into disuse. A literate defendant could plead not guilty, with the possibility of acquittal, and still have the benefit of clergy, if convicted, by insisting upon it at the time of allocution. That is, when the judge asked him if he knew of any reason why judgment of death should not be pronounced against him, he could answer in the affirmative because entitled to benefit of clergy. Benefit of clergy is of historical interest only, but it is a mistake to assume that it was never recognized in this country.[1]

(iii) Plea to the Jurisdiction

By this plea the defendant questions the authority of the court to try him for the offense charged. If the lack of jurisdiction is shown on the face of the indictment, or information, it is demurrable or quashable. And if the lack is established by the evidence the defendant is entitled to an acquittal. This plea, therefore, was seldom used and has been omitted by many of the statutes. There is no proper place for it in simplified procedure. A motion should be adequate to raise any objection to the jurisdiction which can be determined without the aid of a jury. This is accomplished by Rule 12 of the Federal Rules of Criminal Procedure.

(iv) Plea in Abatement

At common law any objection to the prosecution which could not be raised properly by a plea in bar could be raised by a plea in abatement. This plea could be used for any defect, either apparent on the

1. It was allowed, for example, in State v. Sutcliffe, 4 Strob. 372 (S.C.1850).

face of the indictment or founded on some matter extrinsic of the record. Thus to a large extent it tended merely to duplicate the demurrer or the motion to quash. It was purely a dilatory device for it was "a rule upon all pleas in abatement that he who takes advantage of a flaw must at the same time show how it may be amended" (4 Bl. Comm. 335). Its most frequent use came to be in cases of misnomer. If the defendant was indicted by the wrong name he could force a new indictment by filing this plea and proving his true name. Modern statutes have very generally simplified the procedure at this point. In one form or another they require defendant to state his true name at the time of arraignment, if he has been misnamed. If he fails to do so the prosecution may proceed under the name originally used. If he gives his true name this is duly entered in the record and included in subsequent proceedings without the delay of a new indictment or information. There is no room for a plea in abatement in simplified procedure.

(v) Plea of Pardon

It was a rule of the common law that an offender could not be tried for an offense for which he had been pardoned. But unless the pardon was in such form that the court could take judicial notice thereof, a special plea was required—the plea of pardon. If the defendant did not enter this plea he could be tried and convicted, though his pardon would still protect him from punishment. Only the most formalistic procedure would provide for such a plea because a pardon can be brought to the attention of the court in the most informal manner. It may be added that in some states the constitutional provision for pardon applies only "after conviction."

(vi) Pleas of Former Conviction, Former Acquittal or Former Jeopardy

The pleas of former conviction and former acquittal played an important part in the development of the law of "former jeopardy." Some of the states added a third plea—the plea of former jeopardy. This addition was due to the notion that without it the protection to which a defendant was entitled might be defeated by the simple device of stopping the first prosecution before it reached the point of conviction or acquittal. Courts, however, have tended to reach the same results whether this third plea was included in the statute or not. Without the addition of this plea the tendency has been to hold that if the case is withdrawn from a jury, after it has been sworn and "charged with the deliverance of the defendant," and *without proper reason,* this is "equivalent to an acquittal" and bars a subsequent prosecution for that reason. Where this plea is included in the statute, on the other hand, the withdrawal of a case from a jury after "jeopardy has attached" has been held not to bar a subsequent prosecution if it was because of "manifest necessity." [1] Thus a plea of former jeopardy has been held not to bar a trial by a second jury if the case was withdrawn from the first because of illness of a juror, or of the defendant, or of the judge; because of impossibility of the jurors to agree upon a verdict; or because of other extreme physical or legal necessity.

There is no need, however, for any of these three pleas. The defendant is to be protected against double punishment and against an *improper* second trial, but no special plea is needed for this purpose. If the determination can be made without the aid of a jury a motion to dismiss should be sufficient to raise the point. And proper instructions to the jury in a trial under a plea of not guilty can complete the safeguard. These pleas (or at least the first two of them) are to be found in a number of the statutes but the trend is in the direction of abolishing them, as is done in Rule 12 of the Federal Rules of Criminal Procedure.

(vii) Plea of Agreement to Turn State's Evidence

Efficient enforcement of the law often makes it important for officers to enlist the aid of certain offenders in order to convict others. At times this has taken the form of an agreement by the prosecuting attorney not to prosecute a certain offender if he will testify against other parties to the same crime. This practice should be limited to cases of necessity and should be used with care to insure that the net result is the conviction of those most deserving punishment. The prosecuting attorney seldom will violate such an agreement on his part, but if he should the matter can be brought to the attention of the court. Since the prosecuting attorney has no pardoning power this cannot be an absolute bar to the prosecution, but it should be sufficient for the court to dismiss the prosecution if this is consistent with the ends of justice. Texas recognized a plea of agreement to turn state's evidence.[a] It was held that the plea was addressed solely to the court and did not present a jury question.[b] It is a matter much more appropriately handled by a motion to dismiss and this plea has had no general recognition.

(viii) Plea of Not Guilty by Reason of Insanity

Although the trend has been in the direction of reducing the pleas to be used in criminal cases, one new plea has been added by legislation [1] adopted in a substantial number of states. This is the plea of not guilty by reason of insanity. The hope was to simplify the trial

1. See Illinois v. Somerville, 410 U.S. 458, 93 S.Ct. 1066 (1973).

a. Camron v. State, 32 Tex.Cr.R. 180, 22 S.W. 682 (1893).

b. Cameron [sic] v. State, 25 S.W. 288 (Tex.Cr.App.1894). See Prosecuting Attorney's Promise of Immunity, 46 Harv. L.Rev. 714 (1933).

1. See West's Ann.Cal.Pen.Code, § 1016 (1982).

by limiting this issue to a trial under this plea, and determining every other issue of guilt or innocence under the general plea of not guilty. It is doubtful that the added plea achieved the desired result. If this plea is joined with the plea of not guilty, under the California statutes, the defendant is tried first under the plea of not guilty and in that trial he is conclusively presumed to have been sane at the time of the alleged offense. If the verdict is guilty he is then tried on the plea of not guilty by reason of insanity, either before the same jury or a new jury.[2] A defendant who pleads not guilty by reason of insanity, without pleading not guilty in general, admits the commission of the offense charged.

(ix) PLEA OF NOT GUILTY

Where a claim is made against the defendant in a civil action on certain alleged facts, the existence of which the defendant intends to deny on the trial, his pleading is framed in such a way as to deny generally the facts alleged against him. If, on the contrary, the defendant intends to admit that the facts alleged by the plaintiff are true, but to defend by proving other facts which constitute a defense under the particular circumstances, the common law of civil procedure requires him to disclose this by the nature of his pleading, called one of confession and avoidance. He is not entitled to introduce such proof under a plea which merely purports to deny the facts alleged. There was no such distinction in the common law of criminal procedure. If a defendant, charged with having feloniously stolen, taken and carried away the goods of another and so forth, intends to defend on the ground that he did not take the goods at all, his plea is "not guilty." But he enters the same plea if he intends to admit that he took and carried away the goods but did so (1) because they belonged to him and he had the right of immediate possession, (2) because he had the owner's consent to take them, (3) because he reasonably and in good faith believed that he had the owner's consent to take them, (4) because he took them as an officer of the law under proper authority to do so, or for any other reason which would constitute a defense to the charge. In truth, the plea of "not guilty" does not purport to say whether the facts charged in the indictment or information are untrue, or whether there are additional facts which nullify the effect of those charged so far as the defendant is concerned. It purports no more than its face value—that the defendant is "not guilty" of the offense charged.

The rule that a plea of not guilty in a criminal case raises every possible issue of guilt or innocence still prevails in general. Statutes creating some special plea such as "not guilty by reason of insanity" withdraw one particular issue from the general plea of "not guilty." But such special plea is not one of confession and avoidance. It usually admits nothing. (If this plea is filed without also the filing of a

2. Id. at § 1026 (1978).

plea of not guilty, the net result is an admission that the defendant did the act charged.)

(x) Plea of Guilty

The plea of guilty does not give rise to any issue. It is a formal confession of guilt before the court, and is the equivalent of a verdict of guilty except for the possibility of withdrawal. At common law the court, *in its discretion*, might refuse or permit the withdrawal of a plea of guilty and the substitution of another plea therefor, at any time before sentence was pronounced. This is the general rule today, but an occasional decision (misinterpreting a statute intending to codify the common law rule) has held that the defendant has an absolute right to withdraw his plea of guilty, if he does so in time.[1] The most astounding case on this point is in Iowa. The defendant pleaded guilty. The judge, after assuring himself that defendant fully understood the charge against him and meant to confess his guilt, accepted the plea. Later the judge, after giving defendant an opportunity to offer any reason why judgment should not be pronounced against him, sentenced him to a term in the penitentiary. After the defendant had spent a few days in the penitentiary he formed a dislike for the place and appealed to his lawyer to get him out at once. The lawyer found that the sentence had not yet been entered in the court's record book and announced in open court that the defendant withdrew his plea of guilty. The judge refused to permit the withdrawal but he was reversed by the Supreme Court of Iowa.[2] The notion that the judgment of the court is not the official pronouncement from the bench, but the manual act of the clerk in entering it in the record book is questionable although as a matter of common law it is not a "final judgment" until such entry. Prior thereto it is within the control of the judge, but it should not be within the unlimited control of the defendant. In a later case the court soundly overruled its long list of cases giving the defendant an absolute right to withdraw his plea and gave the statute its proper interpretation, which leaves the granting or refusing of the withdrawal in the discretion of the court.[3]

In order for a plea to be valid, before it is accepted it must be shown that the plea was voluntarily made based on a knowing and understanding assessment of guilt. If a plea is based upon a plea bargain the terms of the bargain must be disclosed and the bargain kept or the defendant afforded appropriate relief.[4]

At common law the defendant may plead guilty to any offense. The court cannot refuse to accept the plea even in a capital case. It

1. State v. Hale, 44 Iowa 96 (1876).

2. State v. Wieland, 217 Iowa 887, 251 N.W. 757 (1933).

3. State v. Machovec, 236 Iowa 377, 17 N.W.2d 843 (1945).

4. Santobello v. New York, 404 U.S. 257, 92 S.Ct. 495 (1971). See also Rule 11(e) F.R.Cr.P.

may, however, advise him to withdraw a plea of guilty, and will usually do so in a case punishable by death. Moreover, the court may give the defendant an opportunity to consider the matter and retract his plea by postponing either the entrance of the plea or the judgment pronounced upon it. A few of the statutes do not permit the acceptance of a plea of guilty in a capital case.[5]

Several jurisdictions now recognize a conditional plea of guilty. The defendant admits guilt but reserves a legal challenge for appellate review which if successful will allow the plea to be withdrawn and in proper cases the charge to be dismissed.[6]

(xi) PLEA OF NOLO CONTENDERE

If the defendant was indicted for a non-capital offense he might, at common law, offer a plea which did not expressly confess his guilt but impliedly did so by throwing himself on the king's mercy. This plea differed from the plea of guilty in two important respects. It could not be entered unless it was accepted by the court. Even if accepted by the court the filing of such a plea could not be used in a civil action for the same injury as a confession of guilt.[7] This plea is no longer recognized in England, in Canada, or (for the most part at least) in state cases in this country; but it has always been recognized in the federal courts. It is expressly included in Rule 11 of the Federal Rules of Criminal Procedure. In explaining this inclusion it was said:

"Historically the plea of *nolo contendere* was made only as a preliminary to an arrangement or an expectation that the punishment would be a fine and nothing more; but that, at least in recent years, has disappeared, and the plea of *nolo contendere* has exactly the same effect so far as punishment is concerned as a plea of guilty.

5. A statute may require the court to refuse to accept a plea of guilty in a capital case if defendant is not represented by counsel. People v. Ballentine, 39 Cal. 2d 193, 246 P.2d 35 (1952).

Even if **D**'s counsel is present when he offers to plead guilty in a federal court the judge must not accept the plea without first personally addressing **D** and determining that the plea is offered voluntarily with understanding of the nature of the offense charged against him. This was based upon Rule 11 of the Federal Rules of Criminal Procedure and without reaching any constitutional question. McCarthy v. United States, 394 U.S. 459, 89 S.Ct. 1166 (1969).

Later the Court held that a state criminal conviction based on a guilty plea cannot stand unless there is an affirmative showing on the record that the plea was offered voluntarily and understandingly. To satisfy the due process requirement the judge must personally canvass the matter with the defendant. Boykin v. Alabama, 395 U.S. 238, 89 S.Ct. 1709 (1969).

Forfeiture of bail as a means of disposing of a traffic citation, frequently used as a matter of convenience only, may not be treated as a plea of guilty. Kirkendall v. Korseberg, 247 Or. 75, 427 P.2d 418 (1967).

D, charged with first-degree murder which carried the death sentence, offered to plead guilty to second-degree murder although insisting he was not guilty. This plea had been advised by counsel in face of very strong evidence of guilt. It was held that the plea was voluntary and valid and properly accepted by the Court. North Carolina v. Alford, 400 U.S. 25, 91 S.Ct. 160 (1970).

6. Rule 11(a)(2) F.R.Cr.P.; Conditional Guilty Pleas, 93 Harv.L.Rev. 564 (1980).

7. 1 Hawk.P.C. c. 31, § 3.

"However, it was thought by the Committee that this particular plea should be retained because of the effect of a plea of guilty in an antitrust case, for instance, and the implication that arises from the Clayton Act and all those things." [8]

The official notes prepared by the committee add:

"While at times criticized as theoretically lacking in logical basis, experience has shown that it performs a useful function from a practical standpoint." [9]

(xii) PLEA OF GUILTY TO A LESSER OFFENSE

If the charge in the indictment or information is of a crime which has lower degrees, or other included offenses, the defendant may *offer* to plead guilty to any such offense of which he could be convicted on a trial under this indictment or information. Such a plea cannot be entered as a matter of right, and the judge ordinarily will refuse to accept it unless the prosecuting attorney so recommends.

If the defendant offers to plead guilty to some offense not named in the indictment, and not an "included offense," this is in substance a request that the original indictment or information be dismissed and a new one filed. This is entirely outside of the formal procedure.

The whole practice of "bargaining for pleas" has the possibility of abuse and should be handled with caution by prosecuting authorities.[10]

8. VI New York University School of Law Institute Proceedings 162 (1946).

Recently there has been a tendency to re-establish the plea of nolo contendere. For example, a 1963 amendment to the California Penal Code, section 1016, authorizes the defendant to file a plea of nolo contendere "subject to the consent of the district attorney and with the approval of the court". The current statute does not require the consent of the district attorney only "approval of the the court." Cal.Pen.Code § 1016 (1982).

A plea of guilty or nolo contendere is not rendered involuntary because it is the product of plea bargaining between the defendant and the state. And the court may accept a bargained plea of guilty or nolo contendere to any lesser offense reasonably related to the offense charged in the accusatory pleading even if it is not an included offense. People v. West, 3 Cal.3d 595, 91 Cal.Rptr. 385, 477 P.2d 409 (1970).

9. Notes to Rule 11, Federal Rules of Criminal Procedure, 18 U.S.C.A.

Another form of this plea is *non vult contendere* (he does not wish to contend). In a California murder case the court refused to permit defendant to withdraw a plea of not guilty and plead *non vult contendere,* but later permitted him to withdraw his original plea and plead guilty. People v. Lennox, 67 Cal. 113, 7 P. 260 (1885).

The plea of nolo contendere was added to the California Penal Code by a 1963 amendment to section 1016. See note 6.

10. Alschuler, Plea Bargaining and its History, 79 Cal.L.Rev. 1 (1979); Alschuler, The Changing Plea Bargaining Debate, 69 Cal.L.Rev. 647 (1981); O'Brien, Plea Bargaining and the Supreme Court, 9 Hast.Con.L.Q. 109 (1981).

YORK v. STATE

Supreme Court of Wyoming, 1980.
619 P.2d 391.

ROONEY, JUSTICE. Defendant-appellant appeals from an order of the district court denying appellant's petition for post-conviction relief. The petition was filed pursuant to § 7–14–101 et seq., W.S.1977 [1] and alleged violation of appellant's constitutional rights in the particulars which are contained in the issues presented on this appeal.

Appellant words those issues as follows:

"1. Is there a substantial denial of constitutional rights when the prosecution fails to fulfill completely its portion of a criminal plea bargain agreement where the defendant, who was offered the plea bargain, has fulfilled his portion by a plea of guilty?

"2. Did the court improperly inform the defendant that he would lose his right to appeal by entering a plea of guilty?

"3. Is it mandatory for the court before accepting a plea of guilty to notify a defendant as required by Rule 15(c)(5) W.R.Cr. P., even though the defendant is not placed under oath and is not asked questions about the offense?

"4. Was a factual substantial basis for a plea of guilty presented to the court in this case?

"5. Did the court err by not giving the defendant the opportunity to give his side of the story?

"6. Did the court err by not assuring itself that the defendant possessed an understanding of the law in relation to the facts before accepting the plea of guilty?"

We affirm.

PERFORMANCE OF PLEA BARGAIN

On October 18, 1978, appellant pleaded not guilty to the charge of murder in the second degree. On November 30, 1978, the plea was changed to "not guilty" and "not guilty by reason of mental illness or deficiency." Examination of appellant was made by a psychiatrist at the Wyoming State Hospital and by a court appointed psychiatrist at Rapid City, South Dakota. Each gave an opinion that appellant did not have a mental illness or deficiency which would result in a lack of capacity to comprehend his position, to understand the nature and object of the proceedings against him, to cooperate with his counsel and

1. Section 7–14–101 et seq., W.S.1977 provide a remedy for persons convicted and imprisoned who assert violation of constitutional rights. Section 7–14–101 begins: "Any person imprisoned in the penitentiary who asserts that in the proceedings which resulted in his conviction there was a substantial denial of his rights under the constitution of the United States or of the state of Wyoming, or both, may institute proceedings under this act . . . ."

conduct his defense in a rational manner, to appreciate the wrongfulness of his conduct at the time of the offense, and to conform his conduct to the requirements of law at the time of the offense.

As a result of the plea bargaining efforts, the county attorney offered to reduce the charge against appellant to *voluntary* manslaughter and to secure dismissal of a felony indictment charging larceny or receiving stolen property with a value of over $100, which was outstanding in New Mexico. By letter, the district attorney's office for the Second Judicial District, State of New Mexico, agreed to such dismissal if appellant "enters a plea of guilty to the charge of *Voluntary* Manslaughter" (emphasis supplied) in this case.

Appellant refused the offer of the State, but agreed to plead guilty to the charge of *involuntary* manslaughter. The written plea agreement signed by the deputy county attorney, by appellant, and by his attorney, dated March 9, 1979, makes no reference to the New Mexico charge or to the dismissal thereof.

At the change of plea proceedings, the trial court requested the deputy county attorney to state his understanding of the agreement. The trial court then requested appellant's attorney to do likewise. They said that it required the withdrawal of appellant's not guilty pleas made to the second degree murder charge, the reduction of the charge to involuntary manslaughter, and appellant's plea of guilty to it. The court then inquired of the defendant as follows:

"Q. Now, Mr. York, what's your understanding of this agreement?

"A. What they said is correct, sir.

"Q. Well, I'd like to hear it from you. What are you going to do and what's the State going to do in this matter?

"A. I don't understand what you mean, sir.

"Q. Well, you signed this plea agreement, didn't you?

"A. Yes, sir.

"Q. And did you read it before you signed it?

"A. Yes sir.

"Q. I want you to answer this, Mr. York, without talking to Mr. Sowada, and I want you to answer without Mr. Sowada talking to you. Now, you can read the agreement again if you wish, but I want you to tell me what you're going to do and what the State's going to do in regard to this agreement.

"A. Well, I'm pleading guilty to the charge of manslaughter because I feel that there is a possibility of acts that would constitute this charge on the basis of the evidence that I've seen and the pictures and so forth, and therefore, I feel that I possibly am guilty of this charge and that's the reason I want to plead guilty to it.

"Q. Now, Mr. York, you entered a plea here several months ago of not guilty and you entered a plea of not guilty by reason of mental illness or deficiency. Now, what are you going to do about that plea of not guilty by reason of mental illness or deficiency?

"A. Well, sir, the reason that plea was originally was because part of this I just simply cannot remember.

"Q. What are you going to do with that plea, what have you agreed to do about that plea?

"A. Well, what I agreed to do with this is drop that plea, is—well, withdraw, I'd drop—I mean, withdraw, okay, because although I still can't remember parts—my memory hasn't improved any.

"Q. When did you first look at this instrument, this plea agreement? When did you first look at it?

"A. Today.

"Q. Just a little while ago?

"A. Yes, but we talked about it a little bit.

"Q. Court's going to be in recess for ten minutes, and I want you to go over it again real thoroughly with your attorney. I want you to make sure you understand what's in it.

"THE COURT: Court will be in recess for ten minutes.

"(At this time, the Court recessed at 3:25 p.m., returning to the courtroom at 3:50 p.m.)

"Q. Mr. York, have you had time to go over this plea agreement during this recess?

"A. Yes, sir.

"Q. Now, would you tell the Court your understanding of the agreement, please?

"A. Well, I'm going to withdraw my plea of not guilty to second degree murder by reason of mental illness or deficiency and the State will—now, wait a minute,—and the State agrees to reduce the charge to manslaughter, involuntary manslaughter.

"Q. And when the State does that, how are you going to plead to the reduced charge?

"A. Guilty, sir.

"Q. Did you and Mr. Sowada talk about this plea bargaining?

"A. Yes, we did, sir.

"Q. When Mr. Sowada announced to you that he had reached this agreement with the State, what did you tell him?

"A. Well, he announced to me yesterday he reached an agreement with the State and I says, 'Fine, let's go ahead with it.'

"Q. You were in agreement?

"A. Yes, sir.

"Q. You understand this agreement?

"A. Yes, sir.

"Q. Now, Mr. York, Mr. Sowada is your legal advisor, he's your lawyer and counselor and he presents you and has. He'd represent you at the trial, he'd conduct the trial, he'd make most all the decisions. But when it comes time for a person charged with a crime to plead guilty to the original charge or to a reduced charge, that person, the defendant, in this case you, you have to make the decision to enter the plea of guilty and it has to be your sole decision. Do you understand that?

"A. Yes, I do, sir.

"Q. Now, is this your decision to enter into this plea agreement?

"A. Yes, sir."

Although there was no mention of the New Mexico charge during the trial court's inquiry and although it was not included in the written plea agreement, appellant now complains that the prosecution failed to fulfill its portion of the agreement in not securing dismissal of the New Mexico charge and that the procedure was, therefore, improper. The trial court's findings that appellant "understood the plea agreement with regard to the charges in New Mexico," and that the "written plea agreement . . . shows no mention of the New Mexico charges nor any disposition thereof," were supported by substantial evidence. The terms and conditions of the plea agreement as presented to the court and as thoroughly discussed in detail before the court were fully performed.

Further, appellant was not substantially prejudiced by such inasmuch as the New Mexico charge was actually dismissed. Accordingly, even though the procedure be erroneous, it would not be subject to reversal if prejudice is not established.

PROPRIETY OF PROCEEDINGS AT WHICH APPELLANT CHANGED HIS PLEA

Appellant's last five contentions of error concern the propriety of the proceedings at which he changed his plea from "not guilty" and "not guilty by reason of mental illness and deficiency" to the charge of second degree murder to that of "guilty to the charge of involuntary manslaughter."

A review of the transcript of such proceedings reflects an exhaustive and detailed effort by the trial court to ascertain the voluntariness of appellant's action and appellant's understanding of the consequences of it. Such is necessary. After ascertaining appellant's understanding of the plea agreement (see transcript quotation, supra), the trial court inquired concerning appellant's access to drugs, alcohol, or prescription medicine and was told that there was no such access. He inquired of appellant's attorney concerning his knowledge of grounds to believe appellant was not competent to understand and enter the plea agreement. The attorney said he knew of none and that in his opinion appellant understood "what he's doing." The trial court then asked appellant the following questions and received the following answers:

"Q. Now, Mr. York, you've entered a plea of not guilty in this matter and you can persist in that plea of not guilty throughout all these proceedings. Did you know that you had that right?

"A. Yes, sir.

"Q. Now, Mr. York, this amended Information charges a felony also, and you're entitled to a jury trial. That would be a trial before twelve men and women who would sit in that jury box to your left and hear all of the case, hear the State's side and your side and listen to the Judge give them instructions on the law, and then would retire to render a verdict. Now, at any such trial, the State would have the burden of proving that you were guilty beyond a reasonable doubt. You would not have to prove your innocence. You would be presumed innocent throughout the trial and until the verdict of the jury was otherwise. Now, the jury, all twelve would have to agree before you could be convicted of any crime. You would not have to assist the State in presenting its evidence. The State must prove the charges by its evidence. You could take the witness stand and testify if you wanted to, or you could remain silent and not take the stand. If you did the latter, not take the stand, the State couldn't comment on that or use it against you in any way, because to do so would be to violate your right against self-incrimination.

"Do you understand your constitutional right to a trial and against incriminating yourself and being represented at this trial by your attorney?

"A. Yes, I do, sir.

"Q. Now, by entering a plea of guilty, you admit in this particular case that you've killed a human being by your culpable neglect or criminal carelessness. Do you understand that, sir?

"A. Yes, sir.

"Q. And by entering a plea of guilty, you will also waive your right to trial by jury and waive your right to cross-examine the State's witnesses and to call witnesses in your behalf. You waive your right against self-incrimination, because you're admitting the offense. Mr. York, you waive any legal defense that you might have or that might exist in law against this charge, and the sole remaining issue will be the sentence of the Court. Do you know what the maximum penalty is for manslaughter in Wyoming?

"A. Twenty years, sir.

"Q. You're right, Mr. York, the maximum is twenty, the minimum is one year. In addition to any prison sentence, the Court can impose a fine of a thousand dollars, which can be added to any period of incarceration. Now, have you thought about this penalty before you entered into the plea agreement?

"A. Yes, sir.

"Q. Now, a plea of guilty to a felony has some indirect consequences, Mr. York. In Wyoming, you lose your right to vote at all elections, you lose the right to serve on juries, you lose the right to be appointed or elected to positions of trust in the state and any of its subdivisions. The conviction could be used against you in another criminal case if there be one. A conviction could affect your credibility as a witness, that is, your giving testimony in another case, whether it be a civil case or a criminal case.

"The Federal Government has laws pertaining to the possession of firearms by those who have been convicted of felonies. That would apply to you. It may lead to difficulty in obtaining a job in the future. I want you to have somewhat of a general understanding that there are these indirect consequences. Do you have any questions about those?

"A. No, sir."

Appellant then responded negatively to several questions of the trial court concerning promises, threats, harassment, and suggestions of leniency in connection with the plea bargain.

After the plea of "not guilty" and "not guilty by reason of mental illness or deficiency" was withdrawn, and the appellant pled guilty to the amended information charging involuntary manslaughter, the court asked the deputy county attorney what the evidence of the State would be if the matter were to go to trial.

The deputy county attorney advised that an autopsy reflected the death to have been caused by a bullet passing through the heart. The deputy county attorney presented testimony of the undersheriff. Under oath, he testified to the result of his investigation of the homicide. He related his findings at the scene of the crime; that the deceased had his left hand in his pocket; that the path of the bullet through the body was from the left chest sternum area to the lower right part; to the recovery of the bullet; that "[t]he gun would have had to have been held at an elevated position above the shoulder for the bullet to travel in the path that it did through the body"; that a paraffin test found primer powder on appellant's hand in a manner to indicate he had discharged the gun; that he (the undersheriff) was advised by Doug O'Farrell that he went to the trailer in which the homicide occurred upon hearing a shot and found appellant bending over the body and appellant then told him, "I just shot the sucker," and "they're going to hang me for this"; that appellant made a similar statement to him (the undersheriff); that the gun found at the crime scene belonged to appellant and that it fired the bullet which caused the death; that the trigger pull on the gun was tested and found to be such that it would not have discharged accidentally; and that appellant was intoxicated at the time.

The trial court then asked appellant and his attorney if they had any comment with reference to that which was stated, and they answered in the negative. The trial court asked the deputy county attorney why the State entered into the plea agreement, and the lengthy response was to the effect that while a guilty verdict could possibly result on the original charge, the "more realistic" result would be one of involuntary manslaughter and that justice would be accomplished by the plea bargain at a saving in time and expense. The court then asked the following questions and received the following answers:

> "THE COURT: Mr. York, I want to advise you once more of the constitutional rights that you have waived by your guilty plea. I want you to consider them carefully. By entering a plea of guilty, Mr. York, you waive—and by that, I mean, the Court understands you to say, 'I understand my rights, I know what they are, but I don't want to exercise them, I'm going to disregard those rights and plead guilty.' Is that your understanding of 'waiver'?
>
> "DEFENDANT: Yes, sir.
>
> "THE COURT: Thank you, sir. The constitutional rights that you waive by pleading guilty are, the right to a speedy and a public trial, the right to trial by jury, the right to see, hear and question all witnesses, the right to present evidence in your favor and to testify or to remain silent at the trial, the right to have the Judge order into court all evidence and all witnesses in your favor. You waive the right to have a competent lawyer defend you throughout the trial; the right not to be convicted except by proof beyond a reasonable doubt is also waived. And lastly, you waive and lose the right to appeal to the Supreme Court of Wyoming if convicted.
>
> "Now, having those rights in mind and all the other matters that the Court has advised you of, do you still wish to plead guilty?
>
> "DEFENDANT: Yes, sir.
>
> "THE COURT: Mr. York, would you mind telling the Court why you entered into this plea agreement and why you have entered a plea of guilty?
>
> "DEFENDANT: Well, originally, sir, because I was charged with a very serious offense and with the opportunity to lower it made available to me, and I thought it was my advantage to take that. And I think by the evidence that's presented to me, if I was like an outsider looking in on this thing, I think I am probably guilty of this.
>
> "THE COURT: Anything else you wish to say, Mr. York?

"DEFENDANT: No, sir.

"THE COURT: Do you have any questions at all about your rights?

"DEFENDANT: No, I don't, sir."

The foregoing lengthy quotations from the proceedings in which appellant changed his plea refute his contentions of error in connection with such proceedings.

There was a factual basis presented to the court for a plea of guilty. Appellant's argument that there was insufficient evidence of culpable negligence or criminal neglect in view of appellant's intoxication fails to recognize the impact of the evidence that places the gun in appellant's hand with a trigger pull that will not allow an accidental discharge. A deliberate intent to kill or other specific intent need not be established for the crime of manslaughter. Voluntary intoxication is not a defense to a general intent crime. Criminal carelessness was established in connection with a manslaughter case under facts similar to this case in Eagan v. State, 58 Wyo. 167, 128 P.2d 215 (1942).

The record does not support appellant's argument that the court did not give him an opportunity "to give his side of the story." Appellant was asked several times if he desired to comment on that said. The undersheriff related the story given to him by appellant, and appellant was asked for his comment on it. He had none.

Nor does the record support appellant's argument that the court did not assure itself that appellant possessed an understanding of the law in relation to the facts before accepting the plea of guilty. The fact that the plea was to be to involuntary manslaughter and not to voluntary manslaughter was discussed. Appellant acknowledged that he killed a human being and that it was a result of culpable neglect or criminal carelessness. The elements of the offense and appellant's actions relative thereto were considered during the proceeding in more than one fashion.[3] Appellant's answer to the court's inquiry as to the reason for the change of plea, the recess for consultation by appellant with his attorney concerning such, the reading of the information, and the reasons given by appellant for pleading guilty were sufficient for the purpose of establishing appellant's understanding of the law in relation to the facts.

Appellant argues that the court "informed the defendant that by pleading guilty he would . . . waive and lose the right to appeal to the Supreme Court of Wyoming if convicted." The discourse in which the statement was made is quoted supra. It reflects that it was in context of an explanation of the trial rights which appellant would lose by virtue of a guilty plea. It referred to the appeal right

3. We recommend that the elements of the offense be specifically set forth as such before a plea of guilty is accepted to avoid any potential for misunderstanding in this respect. See Standard 14–1.4 of the American Bar Association Standards for Criminal Justice.

"if convicted." Its practical effect would be to encourage the appellant to not plead "guilty." Error and prejudice are not established.

Appellant's only other contention of error is the failure of the trial court to advise him as required by Rule 15(c)(5), W.R.Cr.P., that the court may ask him questions under oath if he pleads guilty and that the answers may be used against him in a proceeding for perjury or false statement.[4] The trial court did not comply with this requirement of Rule 15(c)(5). While we do not approve of the noncompliance with the rule and again direct strict compliance therewith in the future, we must note that appellant was not asked any questions under oath and, thus, was not prejudiced by the failure of the trial court to give the admonition required by Rule 15(c)(5).

We have already referred supra to the proposition that erroneous procedure is not subject to reversal if prejudice is not established.

Inasmuch as we do not find reversible error on the issues presented by appellant, the action of the trial court is affirmed.

(F) DISCOVERY*

The procedure by which one litigant is enabled to force his opponent to make certain of his evidence available for examination has come to be known as "discovery", and if this authorization is granted prior to the trial itself it is often referred to as "pre-trial discovery". The modern trend in civil cases has been to go very far in this direction.

Limiting our attention to criminal procedure it may be said without hesitation that the common law of England prior to the Revolution made no provision for discovery by a criminal defendant. What seems to have been the first effort in this direction occurred shortly after the Revolution, when a motion was made for an order requiring the prosecution to make a report available for inspection by the defendant.[1] The Attorney-General said: "There never yet was an instance of such an application as the present, to give the defendant an

4. The pertinent portion of Rule 15 reads:

"(c) *Advice to defendant.*—Before accepting a plea of guilty or nolo contendere, the court must address the defendant personally in open court and inform him of, and determine that he understands, the following:

. . .

"(5) That if he pleads guilty or nolo contendere, the court may ask him questions about the offense to which he has pleaded, and if he answers these questions under oath, on the record, and in the presence of counsel, his answers may later be used against him in a prosecution for perjury or false statement."

* See Fletcher, Pretrial Discovery in State Criminal Cases, 12 Stan.L.Rev. 293 (1960); Louisell, Criminal Discovery, Real or Apparent, 49 Calif.L.Rev. 56 (1961); Louisell, The Theory of Criminal Discovery and Practice of Criminal Law, 14 Vand.L.Rev. 921 (1961); Note, 63 Colum. L.Rev. 361 (1963); Note, 15 Stan.L.Rev. 700 (1963); Moore, Criminal Discovery, 19 Hastings L.J. 865 (1968); Ostrow, The Case for Preplea Disclosure, 90 Yale L.J. 1581 (1981); Prosecutorial Discovery, 83 W.Va. 187 (1980).

1. The King v. Holland, 4 T.R. 691, 100 Eng.Rep. 1248 (K.B.1792).

opportunity of inspecting the evidence intended to be used against him upon a public prosecution". The motion was made upon two grounds: first, as a matter of right; and second, as within the discretion of the court. It was denied upon both grounds, Lord Kenyon saying: "There is no principle to warrant it . . . . : and if we were to grant it, it would subvert the whole system of criminal law".

Some years later a different position was taken by the English court. Thus in 1833 the prosecution was directed to permit the defendant to examine a threatening letter allegedly written by him, in order to give his witnesses an opportunity to study the handwriting.[2] And in 1861 a defendant charged with false pretenses was given permission to inspect letters written by him to the alleged victim.[3] It is probable that in each case the court was thinking of this as something within its power to grant rather than a right belonging to the defendant. Without question this was the position taken in a recent Pennsylvania case.[4] The trial judge had ordered the prosecution to permit a pre-trial inspection by defendant of the alleged murder weapon, and pictures of the bedroom which was the scene of the killing, and the prosecution sought a writ of prohibition to prevent the carrying out of this order. In denying the writ the Supreme Court of Pennsylvania emphasized that the trial judge had exercised his discretionary power and was not enforcing any right of the defendant. A vigorous dissent asserted that even the recognition of such a discretionary power in the court was a "disastrous precedent-shattering decision".

The dissenting justice would have avoided this phrase if his research of the cases had been a little more extensive. As early as 1927 the Missouri court had recognized that the defendant in a criminal case has a right of discovery when circumstances make this important for the proper preparation of his defense.[5] This was a prosecution for leaving the scene of a fatal traffic accident without stopping and an eye-witness had given the prosecution a written statement of the accident. The trial judge denied defendant's motion for a pre-trial inspection of the statement and this was held to be error. The defendant had a right to this discovery. Even earlier than this Iowa had a statute permitting such discovery but this had been held not to be mandatory.[6]

California has gone farther than most states in recognizing the defendant's right to pre-trial inspection of evidence in the hands of

2. Rex v. Harrie, 6 Car. & P. 105, 172 Eng.Rep. 1165 (1833).

3. Regina v. Colucci, 3 F. & F. 103, 176 Eng.Rep. 46 (1861).

4. In re Di Joseph's Petition, 394 Pa. 19, 145 A.2d 187 (1958).

5. State v. Tippet, 317 Mo. 319, 296 S.W. 132 (1927). In the same year the New York court, with an elaborate discussion of pre-trial discovery, refused to order the district attorney to make available to defendant documents and memoranda which were not themselves admissible in evidence. People ex rel. Lemon v. Supreme Court, 245 N.Y. 24, 156 N.E. 84, 52 A.L.R. 200 (1927).

6. State v. Howard, 191 Iowa 728, 183 N.W. 482 (1921).

the prosecution. In Powell[7] often regarded the leading California case on the point, D made a motion for an order authorizing D and his attorney to inspect and copy a signed statement made by D in the office of the Chief of Police, and also of a typewritten transcript of a tape recording made later in the same office. The motion was supported by affidavits of D and his attorney which set forth that D was not able to recall his statements nor relate them to his attorney; that the documents might be necessary to refresh D's recollection; that the evidence in the statements was material to the issue of liability, if any, and would be admissible at the trial. No counter affidavits were filed. The trial judge denied the motion on the ground that in a criminal prosecution the accused is not entitled to a pre-trial inspection of his written confession. The Supreme Court of California issued a writ of mandamus requiring the respondent court to set aside its original order and to issue an appropriate order of inspection with the right to make copies as requested.

Where discovery in a criminal case is recognized it has included not only confessions but such subjects as guns and bullets,[8] reports of scientific analyses,[9] autopsies,[10] photographs of persons and places,[11] breath test materials and samples.[12]

Rule 16 of the Federal Rules of Criminal Procedure formerly provided that upon motion of a defendant at any time after the filing of an indictment or information the court might order the attorney for the government to permit the defendant to inspect and copy or photograph designated books, papers, documents or tangible objects obtained from or belonging to the defendant, or obtained from others by seizure or process, upon a showing that the items sought may be material to the preparation of his defense and that the request is reasonable.[13] It is noteworthy that this did not include signed or tape-recorded confessions or statements made by the defendant, nor physical objects not belonging to the defendant which were found by the police or turned over to them voluntarily by others.

7. Powell v. Superior Court In and For Los Angeles County, 48 Cal.2d 704, 312 P.2d 698 (1957).

8. State ex rel. Mahoney v. Superior Court, 78 Ariz. 74, 275 P.2d 887 (1954).

9. Walker v. Superior Court In and For Mendocino County, 155 Cal.App.2d 134, 317 P.2d 130 (1957).

10. State v. Thompson, 54 Wash.2d 100, 338 P.2d 319 (1959).

11. Norton v. Superior Court In and For San Diego County, 173 Cal.App.2d 133, 343 P.2d 139 (1959).

In juvenile court proceedings the juvenile has a right to pre-trial discovery of his statements, admissions and conversations solely in the control of the authorities and necessary for the preparation of his defense. Joe Z. a Minor v. Superior Court of L.A. Co., 3 Cal.3d 797, 91 Cal. Rptr. 594, 478 P.2d 26 (1970).

12. Police have a duty to preserve a breath test ampule for defendant's analysis in a drunk driving case. People v. Hitch, 12 Cal.3d 641, 117 Cal.Rptr. 9, 527 P.2d 361 (1974).

Duty to preserve breath sample. Garcia v. District Court, 197 Colo. 38, 589 P.2d 924 (1979).

Contra: State v. Helmer, 278 N.W.2d 808 (S.D.1979); State v. Canaday, 90 Wn. 2d 808, 585 P.2d 1185 (1978).

13. For a somewhat similar rule see State v. Johnson, 28 N.J. 133, 145 A.2d 313 (1958).

Jencks[14] established the right of the defendant in a criminal case to inspect written reports such as FBI records, *after the witness has testified in court,* to aid in cross-examination. And the so-called Jencks Act, 18 U.S.C.A. § 3500 provides: "In any criminal prosecution . . . no statement or report . . . made by a Government witness or prospective Government witness (other than the defendant) . . . shall be subject of subpoena, discovery or inspection until said witness has testified on direct examination in the trial of the case".[15]

Rule 26.2 Federal Rules of Criminal Procedure (1980) now implements the Jencks Act by providing for a motion for production of a statement of a witness who has testified other than a defendant.[16]

Rule 16 of the Federal Rules of Criminal Procedure now gives the defendant a substantial right of pre-trial discovery. It is as follows:

Rule 16. Discovery and inspection. (a) Disclosure of Evidence by the Government. (1) Information Subject to Disclosure. (A) Statement of Defendant. Upon request of a defendant the government shall permit the defendant to inspect and copy or photograph any relevant written or recorded statements made by the defendant, or copies thereof, within the possession, custody or control of the government, the existence of which is known, or by the exercise of due diligence may become known, to the attorney for the government; the substance of any oral statement which the government intends to offer in evidence at the trial made by the defendant whether before or after arrest in response to interrogation by any person then known to the defendant to be a government agent; and recorded testimony of the defendant before a grand jury which relates to the offense

14. Jencks v. United States, 353 U.S. 657, 77 S.Ct. 1007, 1 L.Ed.2d 1103 (1957).

A 600-word memorandum summarizing parts of a 3½-hour interrogation of witnesses is not a "statement" of the kind required to be produced by the so-called "Jencks Act" (18 U.S.C.A. § 3500). Palermo v. United States, 360 U.S. 343, 79 S.Ct. 1217, 3 L.Ed.2d 1287 (1959). An appendix to the opinion gives a partial summary of the legislative history bearing on the proper construction of the statute.

15. An FBI agent interviewed a witness, taking notes at the time. The agent then repeated back to the witness what had been said, referring to his notes. The witness indicated that the agent's oral presentation was correct. The agent then incorporated the substance of the notes in an "interview report" and destroyed the original notes. The trial judge found that this report was producible as a written statement made by said witness and adopted by him within the meaning of section 3500(e)(1). Prior to this finding the judge had denied a motion for the production of this statement in a trial resulting in conviction. The conviction was reversed. Campbell v. United States, 373 U.S. 487, 83 S.Ct. 1356, 10 L.Ed.2d 501 (1963).

"We hold that a writing prepared by a Government lawyer relating to the subject matter of the testimony of a Government witness that has been 'signed or otherwise adopted or approved' by the Government witness is producible under the Jencks Act [18 U.S.C.A. § 3500]." Goldberg v. United States, 425 U.S. 94, 98, 96 S.Ct. 1338 (1976).

16. Burkland, Federal Rule of Criminal Procedure 26.2: The Impact on Unsettled Jencks Act Issues, 1981 U.Ill.L. Rev. 897 (1981).

charged. Where defendant is a corporation, partnership, association or labor union . . . .

(B) Defendant's Prior Record. . . .

(C) Documents and Tangible Objects. . . .

(D) Reports of Examinations and Tests. . . .

(b) Disclosure of Evidence by the Defendant. . . .

It has often been assumed that the prosecution would have no right of pre-trial discovery in a criminal case, but the California court has held that where important it is entitled to such discovery as will violate neither defendant's privilege against self-incrimination nor the attorney-client privilege.[17] **D**, charged with rape, asked for a continuance on the ground that he needed time to gather medical evidence to prove he was impotent. After the continuance was granted the district attorney filed a motion requesting discovery of the names and addresses of physicians who would testify on behalf of **D**, the names and addresses of all physicians who had examined **D** prior to the trial, and all X-rays taken immediately following injuries which were claimed to have rendered **D** impotent. The motion having been granted by the trial court **D** sought prohibition on the ground that the forced disclosure of such information would violate his privilege against self-incrimination and also the attorney-client privilege. The order requiring discovery was upheld in part and reversed in part by the Supreme Court of California. The Court started with the premise that discovery should not be a "one-way street" and that the defendant in a criminal case has no valid interest in denying the prosecution access to evidence which will facilitate the ascertainment of the facts, except so far as necessary to protect his privilege against self-incrimination or some other recognized privilege. It held that the prosecution was entitled to discover the names of the witnesses who were to be called by **D** at the trial and such X-rays as he intended to introduce in evidence. The Court reasoned that this would violate no privilege of **D** since it did not require disclosure of anything that **D** did not himself intend to have brought out during the trial. But insofar as the trial court's order had required **D** to disclose the names of doctors he did not intend to use as witnesses and to furnish X-rays he did not intend to introduce as evidence, the forced disclosure would violate his privilege against self-incrimination and possibly also his attorney-client privilege.

In a later case an order directing **D**'s attorney to disclose to the prosecution the names, addresses and expected testimony of all witnesses he intended to call at the trial, and with no showing that compliance with this order would not give information tending to incriminate **D**, was held to be too broad, violative of **D**'s constitutional rights and hence void and unenforceable.[18] Recently, however, the Califor-

17. Jones v. Superior Court of Nevada County, 58 Cal.2d 56, 22 Cal.Rptr. 879, 372 P.2d 919 (1962).

18. Prudhomme v. Superior Court of Los Angeles County, 2 Cal.3d 320, 85 Cal. Rptr. 129, 466 P.2d 673 (1970). See also

nia Supreme Court held that trial courts could not order prosecution discovery from the defense in the absence of legislative authorization and direction.[19] The Court held the trial court could not order production of a witness's prior statement. The Court expressed concern for proper attention to considerations of self-incrimination and the attorney-client privilege. The status of prior decisions is at least rendered inoperative and the decision is a step backward. Other states have not been as restrictive as to prosecution discovery.

Discovery was provided by an Act of Congress of 1874 which authorized a court in revenue cases, on motion of the government attorney, to require **D** to produce in court his private books, invoices and papers, or else the allegations of the attorney were to be taken to be confessed. The result would be a forfeiture of **D**'s goods. It was held that such a compulsory production of a man's private papers, to be used in evidence against him, is in effect an unreasonable search and seizure in violation of the Fourth Amendment; and that it also compelled him to give evidence against himself in violation of the Fifth Amendment.[20] The holding of the case has been significantly undermined by more recent decisions finding neither a Fourth nor a Fifth Amendment objection to a grand jury subpoena for personal papers.[21] The Supreme Court has expressly sanctioned production of a defense witness's statement where discovery was of potentially impeaching value.[22] Rule 16, Federal Rules of Criminal Procedure, provides for wide defense and prosecution discovery before trial, and Rule 26.2 provides for the production of witness's statements from both prosecution and defense.

A recent Utah provision provides for wide open discovery by both prosecutor and defense subject to constitutional limitations.[23]

Rule 17.1 of the Federal Rules of Criminal Procedure is as follows:

Pretrial Conference

At any time after the filing of the indictment or information the court upon motion of any party or upon its own motion may order one or more conferences to consider such matters as will promote a fair and expeditious trial. At the conclusion of a conference the court shall prepare and file a memorandum of the matters agreed upon. No admissions made by the defendant or his attorney at the conference shall be used against the defendant unless the admissions are reduced to writing and signed by the defendant and his attorney.

Reynolds v. Superior Court, 12 Cal.3d 834, 117 Cal.Rptr. 437, 528 P.2d 45 (1974).

19. People v. Collie, 30 Cal.3d 43, 177 Cal.Rptr. 458, 634 P.2d 534 (1981).

20. Boyd v. United States, 116 U.S. 616, 6 S.Ct. 524 (1886).

21. Fisher v. United States, 425 U.S. 391, 96 S.Ct. 1569 (1976).

22. United States v. Nobles, 422 U.S. 225, 95 S.Ct. 2160 (1975).

23. Utah Code Ann.1953, § 77–35–16 (1982). See Blumenson, Constitutional Limitations on Prosecutorial Discovery, 18 Harv. Civil Rights and Civ.Lib.L.Rev. 125 (1983).

This rule shall not be invoked in the case of a defendant who is not represented by counsel. Added Feb. 28, 1966, eff. July 1, 1966.[24]

OMNIBUS HEARINGS

Under the authority of a federal court to hold a pretrial conference and to utilize needed procedures in criminal cases, several federal courts have, in appropriate cases, held an "Omnibus Hearing" to allow counsel the widest latitude in discovery and pretrial preparation. This procedure was initiated in the Southern District of California [1] and has been successfully utilized in other districts. The effect of the hearing is to grant a joint discovery motion, and matters of procedure and evidence can also be resolved at such a hearing. Stipulations are entered into as well as plea bargaining explored.[2] The trial judge is an active participant in the hearing which insures greater cooperation between counsel as well as the opportunity to rule on issues before trial. Often the process is expedited by the exchange of forms among the parties which result in the exchange of information and the narrowing of issues. One or more conferences may be held. At the conclusion of the hearing, an appropriate order is entered indicating disclosures made, rulings and orders of the court, stipulations and any other matter determined or left pending for later resolution.[3] The American Bar Association Standards on Criminal Justice early recommended such a procedure [4] and the process has been employed with success in some states.

PROSECUTOR'S DUTY TO DISCLOSE

Independent of statutes and rules a prosecutor may have a constitutional and ethical obligation to make disclosures of certain matters to a defendant. The Supreme Court has held "that the suppression by the prosecution of evidence favorable to an accused upon request violates due process where the evidence is material either to guilt or to punishment, irrespective of the good faith or bad faith of the prosecution." [5] This establishes a prosecutor's constitutional duty to disclose material matter to the defense. The failure to meet this obligation may lead to reversal or collateral relief from a conviction in some circumstances.[6] Therefore, in most jurisdictions a defendant may

24. See the Tentative Draft of Standards Relating to Discovery and Procedure Before Trial, by the American Bar Association (1969).

1. Weninger, Criminal Discovery and Omnibus Procedure in a Federal Court: A Defense View, 49 S.Cal.L.Rev. 514 (1976). The procedure was first employed by the late Judge James M. Carter.

2. Defender Newsletter, July 1967, Volume IV, No. 4.

3. Wright, Federal Practice and Procedure, Criminal 2d § 293.

4. ABA Standards on Discovery and Procedure Before Trial, § 5.1(a) (1970).

5. Brady v. Maryland, 373 U.S. 83, 83 S.Ct. 1194 (1963).

6. The burden of proof for relief from a conviction is set forth in United States v. Agurs, 427 U.S. 97, 96 S.Ct. 2392 (1976).

make a demand on the prosecution to produce specific favorable evidence including matters that would bear on credibility.[7]

A prosecutor may not sit back and let evidence which he knows is erroneous to remain uncorrected.[8] The prosecutor must disclose the truth when he is aware that a prosecution witness is giving false testimony.

In addition to a prosecutor's constitutional and statutory obligation to disclose information the American Bar Association Model Rules of Professional Conduct provide:

> The prosecutor in a criminal case shall:
>
> * * *
>
> (d) make timely disclosure to the defense of all evidence or information known to the prosecutor that tends to negate the guilt of the accused or mitigates the offense, and, in connection with sentencing, disclose to the defense and to the tribunal all unprivileged mitigating information known to the prosecutor, except when the prosecutor is relieved of this responsibility by a protective order of the tribunal. (Rule 3.8, 1983).

7. Failure to disclose evidence that effected the credibility of a witness required a new trial. Giglio v. United States, 405 U.S. 150, 92 S.Ct. 763 (1972).

8. Alcorta v. Texas, 355 U.S. 28, 78 S.Ct. 103 (1957); Napue v. Illinois, 360 U.S. 264, 79 S.Ct. 1173 (1959).

Chapter 13

CERTAIN RIGHTS AND PRIVILEGES OF THE ACCUSED

The voir dire examination, challenges to jurors, conduct of the trial, rules of evidence, instructions, and proceedings after verdict are matters normally dealt with in general practice and procedure courses, and in the course on evidence. Space limitations do not permit their inclusion here. Certain rights and privileges of the accused, however, are entitled to attention.

SECTION 1. THE RIGHT TO COUNSEL

Under the English common law one on trial for a capital crime had no right to the aid of counsel so far as matters of fact were concerned.[1] If a point of law arose it would be argued for him by counsel although originally this was due more to the desire of the judges to have the point clarified than to the recognition of any right belonging to the defendant. He did not have the aid of counsel in the examination or cross-examination of witnesses. In 1698 a statute was passed by which persons accused of high treason were given the right to have the assistance of counsel.[2] Not until 1836 did an English statute accord a similar right to those on trial for felony [3], although for some years prior to that time the judges had tended "to allow a prisoner counsel to instruct him what questions to ask, or even to ask questions for him, . . . " [4] In this country, however, the denial of assistance of counsel to those accused of crime, felony included, was rejected by the Colonies, and the right to such assistance was a part of our concept of due process of law at the time of the adoption of the Constitution.[5]

As it was not recognized under the early English law in felony cases, and no such right had been formally granted in England when the Sixth Amendment was proposed in 1789,[6] the assistance-of-counsel clause was added to insure that he should have such a right in federal prosecutions. For nearly one hundred and fifty years the right-to-counsel guarantee of the Sixth Amendment was understood to mean only that an accused person who appeared with counsel was entitled to have the assistance of this attorney in his defense against the charge. When Congress, for example, enacted a statute in 1790

1. 4 Bl.Comm. *355.

2. 7 & 8 Wm. III, c. 3, sec. 1.

3. 6 & 7 Wm. IV, c. 114.

4. 4 Bl.Comm. 355–56.

5. Powell v. Alabama, 287 U.S. 45, 53 S.Ct. 55, 77 L.Ed. 158, 84 A.L.R. 527 (1932).

6. The first ten amendments, the first eight of which are known as the "Bill of Rights", were proposed on September 25, 1789, and ratified on December 15, 1791.

requiring the court to assign counsel to represent defendants in capital cases [7] no one doubted that this was something in addition to the constitutional guarantee. But in 1938 the Supreme Court took the position that the Sixth Amendment guarantee of assistance of counsel means not only that defendant's counsel must be permitted to assist him in his defense, but that an indigent defendant has the right to have counsel assigned to him.[8] This arose out of a trial for a non-capital felony. The right, it was explained, could be waived but the court lacked jurisdiction to try an uncounseled defendant who had not intelligently waived this right.

Rule 44 of the Federal Rules of Criminal Procedure, considered a restatement of case law as to proceedings in the federal courts [9] is as follows: "Every defendant who is unable to obtain counsel shall be entitled to have counsel assigned to represent him at every stage of the proceedings from his initial appearance before the federal magistrate or the court through appeal, unless he waives such appointment."

For the most part the state courts took the position that a defendant who appeared with counsel could not be denied the right to have his assistance in the case, but that it was not necessary to assign counsel to an indigent defendant, at least in a non-capital case. And the Supreme Court held that the due-process requirement of the Fourteenth Amendment did not require a state to furnish counsel to the defendant in every criminal case in which he was unable to employ an attorney.[10] In other words, whether an indigent defendant in a non-capital case was entitled to have counsel assigned to him was held to depend upon the facts of the particular case.[11]

After several *dicta* to the effect that it would be a denial of due process to refuse to appoint counsel for an indigent defendant in a capital case in a state court, this was the square holding in *Hamilton*.[12] At this point the position seemed to be that except in a capital case an indigent defendant in a state criminal case was entitled to have counsel appointed for him if there were special circumstances which made this important, but not otherwise.[13]

7. 1 Stat. 118. This statute is still in the books. 18 U.S.C.A. § 3005.

8. Johnson v. Zerbst, 304 U.S. 458, 58 S.Ct. 1019, 82 L.Ed. 1461, 146 A.L.R. 357 (1938).

9. Holtzoff, The Right of Counsel Under the Sixth Amendment, 20 N.Y.U.L.Q. Rev. 1 (1944).

10. Betts v. Brady, 316 U.S. 455, 62 S.Ct. 1252, 86 L.Ed. 1595 (1942). The conviction was affirmed in a robbery case in which the defendant did not have counsel and had not waived his right.

11. A defendant in a criminal case who has exhausted his means in the employment of private counsel, has the right to employ an expert and take depositions at public expense. English v. Missildine, 311 N.W.2d 292 (Iowa 1981).

12. Hamilton v. Alabama, 386 U.S. 52, 82 S.Ct. 157, 7 L.Ed.2d 114 (1961).

13. See Chewning v. Cunningham, 368 U.S. 443, 82 S.Ct. 498, 7 L.Ed.2d 442 (1962).

GIDEON v. WAINWRIGHT

Supreme Court of the United States, 1963.
372 U.S. 335, 83 S.Ct. 792.

MR. JUSTICE BLACK delivered the opinion of the Court.

Petitioner was charged in a Florida state court with having broken and entered a poolroom with intent to commit a misdemeanor. This offense is a felony under Florida law. Appearing in court without funds and without a lawyer, petitioner asked the court to appoint counsel for him, whereupon the following colloquy took place:

"The COURT: Mr. Gideon, I am sorry, but I cannot appoint Counsel to represent you in this case. Under the laws of the State of Florida, the only time the Court can appoint Counsel to represent a Defendant is when that person is charged with a capital offense. I am sorry, but I will have to deny your request to appoint Counsel to defend you in this case.

"The DEFENDANT: The United States Supreme Court says I am entitled to be represented by Counsel."

Put to trial before a jury, Gideon conducted his defense about as well as could be expected from a layman. He made an opening statement to the jury, cross-examined the State's witnesses, presented witnesses in his own defense, declined to testify himself, and made a short argument "emphasizing his innocence to the charge contained in the Information filed in this case." The jury returned a verdict of guilty, and petitioner was sentenced to serve five years in the state prison. Later, petitioner filed in the Florida Supreme Court this habeas corpus petition attacking his conviction and sentence on the ground that the trial court's refusal to appoint counsel for him denied him rights "guaranteed by the Constitution and the Bill of Rights by the United States Government." Treating the petition for habeas corpus as properly before it, the State Supreme Court, "upon consideration thereof" but without an opinion, denied all relief. Since 1942, when Betts v. Brady, 316 U.S. 455, 62 S.Ct. 1252, 86 L.Ed. 1595, was decided by a divided Court, the problem of a defendant's federal constitutional right to counsel in a state court has been a continuing source of controversy and litigation in both state and federal courts. To give this problem another review here, we granted certiorari. Since Gideon was proceeding *in forma pauperis,* we appointed counsel to represent him and requested both sides to discuss in their briefs and oral arguments the following: "Should this Court's holding in Betts v. Brady, 316 U.S. 455, 62 S.Ct. 1252, 86 L.Ed. 1595, be reconsidered?" . . .

Treating due process as "a concept less rigid and more fluid than those envisaged in other specific and particular provisions of the Bill of Rights," the Court held that refusal to appoint counsel under the particular facts and circumstances in the Betts case was not so "offensive to the common and fundamental ideas of fairness" as to amount to a denial of due process. Since the facts and circumstances of the two cases are so nearly indistinguishable, we think the Betts v. Brady holding if left standing would require us to reject Gideon's claim that the Constitution guarantees him the assistance of counsel. Upon full reconsideration we conclude that Betts v. Brady should be overruled. . . .

We accept Betts v. Brady's assumption, based as it was on our prior cases, that a provision of the Bill of Rights which is "fundamental and essential to a fair trial" is made obligatory upon the States by the Fourteenth Amendment. We think the Court in Betts was wrong, however, in concluding that the Sixth Amendment's guarantee of counsel is not one of these fundamental rights. Ten years before Betts v. Brady, this Court, after full consideration of all the historical data examined in Betts, had unequivocally declared that "the right to the aid of counsel is of this fundamental character." Powell v. Alabama, 287 U.S. 45, 68, 53 S.Ct. 55, 63, 77 L.Ed. 158 (1932). While the Court at the close of its Powell opinion did by its language, as this Court frequently does, limit its holding to the particular facts and circumstances of that case, its conclusions about the fundamental nature of the right to counsel are unmistakable. . . .

Not only these precedents but also reason and reflection require us to recognize that in our adversary system of criminal justice, any person haled into court, who is too poor to hire a lawyer, cannot be assured a fair trial unless counsel is provided for him. This seems to us to be an obvious truth. Governments, both state and federal, quite properly spend vast sums of money to establish machinery to try defendants accused of crime. Lawyers to prosecute are everywhere deemed essential to protect the public's interest in an orderly society. Similarly, there are few defendants charged with crime, few indeed, who fail to hire the best lawyers they can get to prepare and present their defenses. That government hires lawyers to prosecute and defendants who have the money hire lawyers to defend are the strongest indications of the widespread belief that lawyers in criminal courts are necessities, not luxuries. The right of one charged with crime to counsel may not be deemed fundamental and essential to fair trials in some countries, but it is in ours. From the very beginning, our state and national constitutions and laws have laid great emphasis on procedural and substantive safeguards designed to assure fair trials before impartial tribunals in which every defendant stands equal before the law. This noble ideal cannot be realized if the poor man charged with crime has to face his accusers without a lawyer to assist him. A defendant's need for a lawyer is nowhere better stated than in the moving words of Mr. Justice Sutherland in Powell v. Alabama:

"The right to be heard would be, in many cases, of little avail if it did not comprehend the right to be heard by counsel. Even the intelligent and educated layman has small and sometimes no skill in the science of law. If charged with crime, he is incapable, generally, of determining for himself whether the indictment is good or bad. He is unfamiliar with the rules of evidence. Left without the aid of counsel he may be put on trial without a proper charge, and convicted upon incompetent evidence, or evidence irrelevant to the issue or otherwise inadmissible. He lacks both the skill and knowledge adequately to prepare his defense, even though he have a perfect one. He requires the guiding hand of counsel at every step in the proceedings against him. Without it, though he be not guilty, he faces the danger of conviction because he does not know how to establish his innocence." 287 U.S., at 68–69, 53 S.Ct., at 64, 77 L.Ed. 158.

The Court in Betts v. Brady departed from the sound wisdom upon which the Court's holding in Powell v. Alabama rested. Florida, supported by two other States, has asked that Betts v. Brady be left intact. Twenty-two States, as friends of the Court, argue that Betts was "an anachronism when handed down" and that it should now be overruled. We agree.

The judgment is reversed and the cause is remanded to the Supreme Court of Florida for further action not inconsistent with this opinion.

Reversed.[1]

1. [By the Compiler.] The right to counsel means effective counsel. It is not sufficient that **D** was represented by a member of the bar, or even by a lawyer who is very competent in other fields. If the attorney was so unfamiliar with the crucial problems of the case as to be unable to make an effective defense **D** has been deprived of his right to counsel. People v. Ibarra, 60 Cal.2d 460, 34 Cal. Rptr. 863, 386 P.2d 487 (1963). The fact that counsel advised **D** to plead guilty although there were technical defenses that might have handicapped the prosecution was held not to entitle him to relief. Edwards v. United States, 103 U.S.App. D.C. 152, 256 F.2d 707 (1958).

The right to counsel is not satisfied by a standard which requires the trial to be reduced to a farce or sham before there has been ineffective assistance of counsel. People v. Pope, 23 Cal.3d 412, 152 Cal.Rptr. 732, 590 P.2d 859 (1979).

"Counsel furnishing representation under the plan shall be selected from a panel of attorneys designated or approved by the court, or from a bar association, legal aid agency, or defender organization furnishing representation pursuant to the plan. In every criminal case in which the defendant is charged with a felony or a misdemeanor (other than a petty offense as defined in section 1 of this title) or with juvenile delinquency by the commission of an act which, if committed by an adult, would be such a felony or misdemeanor or with a violation of probation and appears without counsel, the United States magistrate or the court shall advise the defendant that he has the right to be represented by counsel and that counsel will be appointed to represent him if he is financially unable to obtain counsel. Unless the defendant waives representation by counsel, the United States magistrate or the court, if satisfied after appropriate inquiry that the defendant is financially unable to obtain counsel, shall appoint counsel to represent him. Such appointment may be made retroactive to include any representation furnished pursuant to the plan prior to appointment. The United States magistrate or the court shall appoint separate counsel for defendants having interests that cannot properly be represented by the same counsel, or when other good cause is shown." Criminal Justice Act of 1964, sec. 3006A(b).

If **D** entered a plea of guilty of forgery acting upon the advice of the deputy public defender, whereas under the pleadings he should not have been charged with forgery, **D** was denied due process be-

MR. JUSTICE DOUGLAS. . . . My brother Harlan is of the view that a guarantee of the Bill of Rights that is made applicable to the States by reason of the Fourteenth Amendment is a lesser version of that same guarantee as applied to the Federal Government. Mr. Justice Jackson shared that view. But that view has not prevailed and rights protected against state invasion by the Due Process Clause of the Fourteenth Amendment are not watered-down versions of what the Bill of Rights guarantees.

MR. JUSTICE CLARK, concurring in the result. . . .

cause he was not assigned effective counsel and a conviction based upon that plea must be reversed. In re Williams, 1 Cal. 3d 168, 81 Cal.Rptr. 784, 460 P.2d 984 (1969).

The federal constitutional right to counsel applies for indigents to misdemeanor and petty offenses where there is a sentence of imprisonment. Argersinger v. Hamlin, 407 U.S. 25, 92 S.Ct. 2006 (1972). "We therefore hold that the Sixth and Fourteenth Amendments to the United States Constitution require only that no indigent criminal defendant be sentenced to a term of imprisonment unless the State has afforded him the right to assistance of appointed counsel in his defense." Scott v. Illinois, 440 U.S. 367, 373, 374, 99 S.Ct. 1158 (1979).

A misdemeanor theft conviction, where counsel was not provided even where only a fine was imposed, may not be used to enhance a subsequent conviction to a felony. Baldasar v. Illinois, 446 U.S. 222, 100 S.Ct. 1585 (1980).

The fact that **D** was represented by retained counsel does not preclude claim of inadequate representation. Where retained counsel, unknown to **D**, was related to the complaining witness and such counsel failed to challenge jurors who were related to the complaining witness, and failed to represent **D** properly in other respects, **D** was as much without counsel as if he were represented by ineffectual appointed counsel. State v. Moser, 78 N.M. 212, 430 P.2d 106 (1967).

The public defender's determination that **D** is not financially able to employ counsel is not subject to review by the trial court even if the public defender's services are sought for a collateral attack on a final judgment rather than a defense to a pending charge. Ingram v. Justice Court, 69 Cal.2d 832, 73 Cal.Rptr. 410, 447 P.2d 650 (1968).

A defendant in a state criminal trial has a constitutional right to proceed without counsel when he voluntarily and intelligently elects to do so. And it is reversible error to force a lawyer upon him if he prefers to conduct his own defense. Faretta v. California, 422 U.S. 806, 95 S.Ct. 2525 (1975).

Even against the desire of a defendant who wants to defend himself, a standby counsel may be appointed to be present if desired. But if such standby interferes and conducts the defense against the desire of the defendant this constitutes an unconstitutional interference with his right to defend himself. Wiggins v. Estelle, 681 F.2d 266 (5th Cir. 1982).

An inmate has a conditional right to counsel where parole may be rescinded. Gee v. Brown, 14 Cal.3d 571, 122 Cal. Rptr. 231, 536 P.2d 1017 (1975). See also Morrissey v. Brewer, 408 U.S. 471, 92 S.Ct. 2593 (1972).

The trial judge sequestered all witnesses and before each recess instructed each testifying witness not to discuss his testimony with *anyone*. This was within sound judicial discretion as to non-party witnesses; but as to the defendant who testified this impinged upon his right to the assistance of counsel. He had a right to consult his attorney during the overnight recess. Geders v. United States, 425 U.S. 80, 96 S.Ct. 1330 (1976).

An indigent defendant does not have an unqualified right to counsel of his own choosing. Where defendant's original appointed defender was hospitalized and a new defender, who was prepared and willing and able to Act, was appointed six days before trial, the defendant was not entitled to a continuance in order to obtain the first appointed defender. ". . . 'the right to a *meaningful attorney-client relationship*' is without basis the law." Morris v. Slappy, ___ U.S. ___, 103 S.Ct. 1610 (1983).

MR. JUSTICE HARLAN, concurring.

I agree that Betts v. Brady should be overruled, but consider it entitled to a more respectful burial than has been accorded, at least on the part of those of us who were not on the Court when that case was decided. . . .

In agreeing with the Court that the right to counsel in a case such as this should now be expressly recognized as a fundamental right embraced in the Fourteenth Amendment, I wish to make a further observation. When we hold a right or immunity, valid against the Federal Government, to be "implicit in the concept of ordered liberty" and thus valid against the States, I do not read our past decisions to suggest that by so holding, we automatically carry over an entire body of federal law and apply it in full sweep to the States. Any such concept would disregard the frequently wide disparity between the legitimate interests of the States and of the Federal Government, the divergent problems that they face, and the significantly different consequences of their actions. Cf. Roth v. United States, 354 U.S. 476, 496–508, 77 S.Ct. 1304, 1315–1321, 1 L.Ed.2d 1498 (separate opinion of this writer). In what is done today I do not understand the Court to depart from the principles laid down in Palko v. Connecticut, 302 U.S. 319, 58 S.Ct. 149, 82 L.Ed. 288, or to embrace the concept that the Fourteenth Amendment "incorporates" the Sixth Amendment as such.

On these premises I join in the judgment of the Court.

DOUGLAS v. CALIFORNIA

Supreme Court of the United States, 1963.
372 U.S. 353, 83 S.Ct. 814.

MR. JUSTICE DOUGLAS delivered the opinion of the Court. . . .

Although several questions are presented in the petition for certiorari, we address ourselves to only one of them. The record shows that petitioners requested, and were denied, the assistance of counsel on appeal, even though it plainly appeared they were indigents. In denying petitioners' requests, the California District Court of Appeal stated that it had "gone through" the record and had come to the conclusion that "no good whatever could be served by appointment of counsel." The District Court of Appeal was acting in accordance with a California rule of criminal procedure which provides that state appellate courts, upon the request of an indigent for counsel, may make "an independent investigation of the record and determine whether it would be of advantage to the defendant or helpful to the appellate court to have counsel appointed. . . . After such investigation, appellate courts should appoint counsel if in their opinion it would be helpful to the defendant or the court, and should deny the appointment of counsel only if in their judgment such appointment would be of no value to either the defendant or the court." People v. Hyde, 51 Cal.2d 152, 154, 331 P.2d 42, 43. . . .

In spite of California's forward treatment of indigents, under its present practice the type of an appeal a person is afforded in the District Court of Appeal hinges upon whether or not he can pay for the assistance of counsel. If he can the appellate court passes on the merits of his case only after having the full benefit of written briefs and oral argument by counsel. If he cannot the appellate court is forced to prejudge the merits before it can even determine whether counsel should be provided. At this stage in the proceedings only the barren record speaks for the indigent, and, unless the printed pages show that an injustice has been committed, he is forced to go without a champion on appeal. Any real chance he may have had of showing that his appeal has hidden merit is deprived him when the court decides on an *ex parte* examination of the record that the assistance of counsel is not required.

We are not here concerned with problems that might arise from the denial of counsel for the preparation of a petition for discretionary or mandatory review beyond the stage in the appellate process at which the claims have once been presented by a lawyer and passed upon by an appellate court. We are dealing only with the first appeal, granted as a matter of right to rich and poor alike (Cal.Penal Code §§ 1235, 1237), from a criminal conviction. We need not now decide whether California would have to provide counsel for an indigent seeking a discretionary hearing from the California Supreme Court after the District Court of Appeal had sustained his conviction (see Cal. Const., Art. VI, § 4c; Cal.Rules on Appeal, Rules 28, 29), or whether counsel must be appointed for an indigent seeking review of an appellate affirmance of his conviction in this Court by appeal as of right or by petition for a writ of certiorari which lies within the Court's discretion. But it is appropriate to observe that a State can, consistently with the Fourteenth Amendment, provide for differences so long as the result does not amount to a denial of due process or an "invidious discrimination." [1] Absolute equality is not required; lines

1. [By the Compiler.] It was not improper for the public defender to move to withdraw as appellate counsel on the ground that the claims were legally frivolous. "It is the obligation of any lawyer—whether privately retained or publicly appointed—not to clog the courts with frivolous motions or appeals." Polk County v. Dodson, 454 U.S. 312, 102 S.Ct. 445, 453 (1981).

The federal constitutional right to appellate counsel does not include the right to appointed counsel for discretionary appeals. Ross v. Moffitt, 417 U.S. 600, 94 S.Ct. 2437 (1974).

There is no violation of a defendant's right to counsel where retained counsel is ineffective in pursuing discretionary review. Wainwright v. Torna, 455 U.S. 586, 102 S.Ct. 1300 (1982).

A "no merit" letter is an insufficient basis on which to excuse appointed appellate counsel from further participation. A request to be relieved as appellate counsel must be accompanied by a brief referring to anything in the record that would support the appeal. A copy of the brief must be furnished the indigent and time given for such person to raise any points he chooses. The appellate court must make a full examination of the record and if it is determined the appeal is wholly frivolous the appellate court may dismiss the appeal or decide the matter

can be and are drawn and we often sustain them. But where the merits of the one and only appeal an indigent has as of right are decided without benefit of counsel, we think an unconstitutional line has been drawn between rich and poor. . . .

The present case, where counsel was denied petitioners on appeal, shows that the discrimination is not between "possibly good and obviously bad cases," but between cases where the rich man can require the court to listen to argument of counsel before deciding on the merits, but a poor man cannot. There is lacking that equality demanded by the Fourteenth Amendment where the rich man, who appeals as of right, enjoys the benefit of counsel's examination into the record, research of the law, and marshalling of arguments on his behalf, while the indigent, already burdened by a preliminary determination that his case is without merit, is forced to shift for himself. The indigent, where the record is unclear or the errors are hidden, has only the right to a meaningless ritual, while the rich man has a meaningful appeal.

We vacate the judgment of the District Court of Appeal and remand the case to that court for further proceedings not inconsistent with this opinion. It is so ordered.

Judgment of the District Court of Appeal vacated and case remanded.

MR. JUSTICE CLARK, dissenting.

I adhere to my vote in Griffin v. Illinois, 351 U.S. 12, 76 S.Ct. 585, 100 L.Ed. 891 (1956), but, as I have always understood that case, it does not control here. It had to do with the State's obligation to furnish a record to an indigent on appeal. There we took pains to point out that the State was free to "find other means of affording adequate and effective appellate review to indigent defendants." Id., at 20, 76 S.Ct., at 591. Here California has done just that in its procedure for furnishing attorneys for indigents on appeal. We all know that the overwhelming percentage of *in forma pauperis* appeals are frivolous. Statistics of this Court show that over 96% of the petitions filed here are of this variety.[1] California, in the light of a like experience, has provided that upon the filing of an application for the appointment of counsel the District Court of Appeal shall make "an independent investigation of the record and determine whether it would be of advantage to the defendant or helpful to the appellate court to

on the merit. Anders v. California, 386 U.S. 738, 87 S.Ct. 1396 (1967). In California the case will be affirmed rather than dismissed. People v. Wende, 25 Cal.3d 436, 158 Cal.Rptr. 839, 600 P.2d 1071 (1979).

Counsel has no duty to argue every nonfrivolous issue requested to be argued by a client. Jones v. Barnes, ___ U.S. ___, 103 S.Ct. 3308 (1983).

1. [By Mr. Justice Clark.] Statistics from the office of the Clerk of this Court reveal that in the 1961 Term only 38 of 1093 *in forma pauperis* petitions for certiorari were granted (3.4%). Of 44 *in forma pauperis* appeals, all but one were summarily dismissed (2.3%).

have counsel appointed." People v. Hyde, 51 Cal.2d 152, 154, 331 P.2d 42, 43 (1958). California's courts did that here and after examining the record certified that such an appointment would be neither advantageous to the petitioners nor helpful to the court. It, therefore, refused to go through the useless gesture of appointing an attorney. In my view neither the Equal Protection Clause nor the Due Process Clause requires more. I cannot understand why the Court says that this procedure afforded petitioners "a meaningless ritual." To appoint an attorney would not only have been utter extravagance and a waste of the State's funds but as surely "meaningless" to petitioners.

With this new fetish for indigency the Court piles an intolerable burden on the State's judicial machinery. Indeed, if the Court is correct it may be that we should first clean up our own house. We have afforded indigent litigants much less protection than has California. Last Term we received over 1,200 *in forma pauperis* applications in none of which had we appointed attorneys or required a record. Some were appeals of right. Still we denied the petitions or dismissed the appeals on the moving papers alone. At the same time we had hundreds of paid cases in which we permitted petitions or appeals to be filed with not only records but briefs by counsel, after which they were disposed of in due course. On the other hand, California furnishes the indigent a complete record and if counsel is requested requires its appellate courts either to (1) appoint counsel or (2) make an independent investigation of that record and determine whether it would be of advantage to the defendant or helpful to the court to have counsel appointed. Unlike Lane v. Brown, 372 U.S. 477, 83 S.Ct. 768, decision in these matters is not placed in the unreviewable discretion of the Public Defender or appointed counsel but is made by the appellate court itself.

California's concern for the rights of indigents is clearly revealed in People v. Hyde, supra. There, although the Public Defender had not undertaken the prosecution of the appeal, the District Court of Appeal nevertheless referred the application for counsel and the record to the Los Angeles Bar Association. One of its members reviewed these papers, after which he certified that no meritorious ground for appeal was disclosed. Despite this the California District Court of Appeal made its own independent examination of the record.

There is an old adage which my good Mother used to quote to me, i.e., "People who live in glass houses had best not throw stones." I dissent.

MR. JUSTICE HARLAN, whom MR. JUSTICE STEWART joins, dissenting.

In holding that an indigent has an absolute right to appointed counsel on appeal of a state criminal conviction, the Court appears to rely both on the Equal Protection Clause and on the guarantees of fair procedure inherent in the Due Process Clause of the Fourteenth Amendment, with obvious emphasis on "equal protection." In my view the Equal Protection Clause is not apposite, and its application to cases like the present one can lead only to mischievous results. This case should be judged solely under the Due Process Clause, and I do not believe that the California procedure violates that provision.

Equal Protection

To approach the present problem in terms of the Equal Protection Clause is, I submit, but to substitute resounding phrases for analysis. I dissented from this approach in Griffin v. Illinois, and I am constrained to dissent from the implicit extension of the equal protection approach here—to a case in which the State denies no one an appeal, but seeks only to keep within reasonable bounds the instances in which appellate counsel will be assigned to indigents.

The States, of course, are prohibited by the Equal Protection Clause from discriminating between "rich" and "poor" *as such* in the formulation and application of their laws. But it is a far different thing to suggest that this provision prevents the State from adopting a law of general applicability that may affect the poor more harshly than it does the rich, or, on the other hand, from making some effort to redress economic imbalances while not eliminating them entirely.

Every financial exaction which the State imposes on a uniform basis is more easily satisfied by the well-to-do than by the indigent. Yet I take it that no one would dispute the constitutional power of the State to levy a uniform sales tax, to charge tuition at a state university, to fix rates for the purchase of water from a municipal corporation, to impose a standard fine for criminal violations, or to establish minimum bail for various categories of offenses. Nor could it be contended that the State may not classify as crimes acts which the poor are more likely to commit than are the rich. And surely there would be no basis for attacking a state law which provided benefits for the needy simply because those benefits fell short of the goods or services that others could purchase for themselves.

Laws such as these do not deny equal protection to the less fortunate for one essential reason: the Equal Protection Clause does not impose on the States "an affirmative duty to lift the handicaps flowing from differences in economic circumstances." To so construe it would be to read into the Constitution a philosophy of leveling that would be foreign to many of our basic concepts of the proper relations between government and society. The State may have a moral obligation to eliminate the evils of poverty, but it is not required by the Equal Protection Clause to give to some whatever others can afford.

Thus it should be apparent that the present case is not one properly regarded as arising under this clause. California does not discriminate between rich and poor in having a uniform policy permitting everyone to appeal and to retain counsel, and in having a separate rule dealing *only* with the standards for the appointment of counsel for those unable to retain their own attorneys. The sole classification established by this rule is between those cases that are believed to have merit and those regarded as frivolous. And, of course, no matter how far the state rule might go in providing counsel for indigents, it could never be expected to satisfy an affirmative duty—if one existed—to place the poor on the same level as those who can afford the best legal talent available.

Parenthetically, it should be noted that if the present problem may be viewed as one of equal protection, so may the question of the right to appointed counsel at trial, and the Court's analysis of that right in Gideon v. Wainwright, 372 U.S. 335, 83 S.Ct. 792, is wholly unnecessary. The short way to dispose of Gideon v. Wainwright, in other words, would be simply to say that the State deprives the indigent of equal protection whenever it fails to furnish him with legal services, and perhaps with other services as well, equivalent to those that the affluent defendant can obtain. . . .

SECTION 2. THE PRIVILEGE AGAINST SELF-INCRIMINATION

The Fifth Amendment provides: "No person shall . . . be compelled in any criminal case to be a witness against himself, . . ." It seems that this provision was "originally intended only to prevent return to the hated practice of compelling a person, in a criminal proceeding directed at him, to swear against himself".[1] It has been extended by interpretation, however, to protect not only the defendant, but also the witness, in all methods of interrogation before a court, grand jury or coroner's inquest, in investigations by a legislative body or administrative official.[2] The Fifth Amendment applies *per se* only in federal proceedings, but almost all state constitutions have a like or similar provision and this is one of the provisions of the Bill of Rights which is so basic to a free society that it is incorporated into the Due Process Clause of the Fourteenth Amendment and thereby made applicable to state proceedings.[3]

1. 8 Wigmore, Evidence, sec. 2252, p. 324 (McNaughton rev. 1961).

2. Id. at pp. 326–328.

3. D was held in contempt of court for refusing to answer certain questions in a state proceeding. He claimed that he was privileged not to answer because the questions called for answers that would tend to be incriminating. The state court upheld the conviction on a finding that the questions did not call for incriminating answers. The Supreme Court held that the questions did call for incriminating answers and reversed the conviction on the ground that the Fifth Amendment's exemption from self-incrimination is also protected by the Fourteenth against abridgment by the states. Malloy v. Hogan, 378 U.S. 1, 84 S.Ct. 1489, 12 L.Ed.2d 653 (1964).

The state may compel a witness to testify, notwithstanding the fact that such testimony might tend to incriminate him of a federal offense, but the federal government would not be permitted to make any use of the testimony thus compelled. Murphy v. Waterfront Commission of New York Harbor, 378 U.S. 52, 84 S.Ct. 1594, 12 L.Ed.2d 678 (1964). The Court held that the privilege protects either a

In 1628 the King of England, Charles I, asked the lord chief justice if a reluctant prisoner in the Tower of London could be "racked" to make him talk. After consultation with all the judges the lord chief justice replied that the law did not permit a man to be tortured by the rack.[4] In this country today it is a matter of common knowledge (1) that any police brutality in the effort to coerce a confession is unlawful, and (2) that harsh police practices have not entirely disappeared. Years ago "the third degree" became a byword to symbolize violence by which officers extorted a confession. As such use of violence tended to disappear under the impact of public indignation some departments substituted other forms of torture, such as the "sweatbox". The prisoner was placed in a small box, which was kept entirely dark, and there he remained as long as necessary, which might be several days. He was allowed no communication with any person except an officer who would approach now and then to interrogate him. He was told he could get out whenever he was ready "to tell the truth"—nothing but a full confession being accepted as the "truth".[5] Then it was discovered that psychological torture might be as effective as physical torture. This often took the form of tiresome questioning carried on by officers acting in relays for excessively long hours, with the prisoner having little or no rest or refreshment.

It has long been the rule that an involuntary confession is not admissible in evidence against the defendant, and a confession is deemed involuntary if obtained by any form of compulsion, and also if it is obtained by promises.[6] Until recently the only explanation for exclusion was the fact that an involuntary confession is untrustworthy.

JACKSON v. DENNO, WARDEN

Supreme Court of the United States, 1964.
378 U.S. 368, 84 S.Ct. 1774.

[Some time after Jackson had robbed the desk clerk of a hotel, he encountered an officer on the street. They exchanged shots resulting in the death of the officer and the wounding of Jackson. At the hospital to which he was taken Jackson gave an oral confession and about two hours later a more complete and damaging written confes-

state or a federal witness against incrimination under either state or federal law. It expressly overruled United States v. Murdock, 284 U.S. 141, 52 S.Ct. 63, 76 L.Ed. 210 (1933), which held that the federal government could compel a witness to give testimony that might incriminate him under state law. The implication is that the witness can be compelled to testify but that because of the privilege the state will not be permitted to make any use of compelled testimony. Compare Adams v. Maryland, 347 U.S. 179, 74 S.Ct. 442, 98 L.Ed. 608 (1954).

4. Proceedings Against John Felton for the Murder of the Duke of Buckingham, 3 How.St.Tr. 367 (1628).

5. See, for example, Ammons v. State, 80 Miss. 592, 32 So. 9 (1902).

6. An incriminating statement given on officer's promise that it would not be used against **D** is not admissible against him. Killough v. United States, 336 F.2d 929 (D.C.Cir. 1964).

sion. Both confessions were introduced in evidence without objection although there was a dispute as to the circumstances under which the latter was obtained.]

MR. JUSTICE WHITE delivered the opinion of the Court.

Petitioner, Jackson, has filed a petition for habeas corpus in the Federal District Court asserting that his conviction for murder in the New York courts is invalid because it was founded upon a confession not properly determined to be voluntary. The writ was denied, 206 F.Supp. 759 (D.C.S.D.N.Y.), the Court of Appeals affirmed, 309 F.2d 573 (C.A.2d Cir.), and we granted certiorari to consider fundamental questions about the constitutionality of the New York procedure governing the admissibility of a confession alleged to be involuntary. . . .

In his closing argument, Jackson's counsel did not ask for an acquittal but for a verdict of second degree murder or manslaughter. Counsel's main effort was to negative the premeditation and intent necessary to first degree murder and to separate the robbery felony from the killing. He made much of the testimony tending to show a substantial interval between leaving the hotel and the beginning of the struggle with the policeman. The details of that struggle and the testimony indicating the policeman fired the first shot were also stressed.

Consistent with the New York practice where a question has been raised about the voluntariness of a confession, the trial court submitted that issue to the jury along with the other issues in the case. The jury was told that if it found the confession involuntary, it was to disregard it entirely, and determine guilt or innocence solely from the other evidence in the case; alternatively, if it found the confession voluntary, it was to determine its truth or reliability and afford it weight accordingly. . . .

II.

It is now axiomatic that a defendant in a criminal case is deprived of due process of law if his conviction is founded, in whole or in part, upon an involuntary confession, without regard for the truth or falsity of the confession, and even though there is ample evidence aside from the confession to support the conviction. Equally clear is the defendant's constitutional right at some stage in the proceedings to object to the use of the confession and to have a fair hearing and a reliable determination on the issue of voluntariness, a determination uninfluenced by the truth or falsity of the confession. In our view, the New York procedure employed in this case did not afford a reliable determination of the voluntariness of the confession offered in evidence at the trial, did not adequately protect Jackson's right to be free of a conviction based upon a coerced confession and therefore cannot withstand constitutional attack under the Due Process Clause of the Fourteenth Amendment. We therefore reverse the judgment below denying the writ of habeas corpus.

Under the New York rule, the trial judge must make a preliminary determination regarding a confession offered by the prosecution and exclude it if in no circumstances could the confession be deemed voluntary. But if the evidence presents a fair question as to its voluntariness, as where certain facts bearing on the issue are in dispute or where reasonable men could differ over the inferences to be drawn from undisputed facts, the judge "must receive the confession and leave to the jury, under proper instructions, the ultimate determination of its voluntary character and also its truthfulness." Stein v. New York, 346 U.S. 156, 172, 73 S.Ct. 1077, 1086, 97 L.Ed. 1522. If an issue of coercion is presented, the judge may not resolve conflicting evidence or arrive at his independent appraisal of the voluntariness of the confession, one way or the other. These matters he must leave to the jury.

This procedure has a significant impact upon the defendant's Fourteenth Amendment rights. In jurisdictions following the orthodox rule, under which the judge himself solely and finally determines the voluntariness of the confession, or those following the Massachusetts procedure, under which the jury passes on voluntariness only after the judge has fully and independently resolved the issue against the accused, the judge's conclusions are clearly evident from the record since he either admits the confession into evidence if it is voluntary or rejects it if involuntary. Moreover, his findings upon disputed issues of fact are expressly stated or may be ascertainable from the record. In contrast, the New York jury returns only a general verdict upon the ultimate question of guilt or innocence. It is impossible to discover whether the jury found the confession voluntary and relied upon it, or involuntary and supposedly ignored it. Nor is there any indication of how the jury resolved disputes in the evidence concerning the critical facts underlying the coercion issue. Indeed, there is nothing to show that these matters were resolved at all, one way or the other. . . .

A defendant objecting to the admission of a confession is entitled to a fair hearing in which both the underlying factual issues and the voluntariness of his confession are actually and reliably determined. But did the jury in Jackson's case make these critical determinations, and if it did, what were these determinations?

Notwithstanding these acknowledged difficulties inherent in the New York procedure, the Court in Stein found no constitutional deprivation to the defendant. The Court proceeded to this conclusion on the basis of alternative assumptions regarding the manner in which the jury might have resolved the coercion issue. Either the jury determined the disputed issues of fact against the accused, found the confession voluntary and therefore properly relied upon it; or it found the contested facts in favor of the accused and deemed the confession involuntary, in which event it disregarded the confession in accordance with its instructions and adjudicated guilt based solely on the other evidence. On either assumption the Court found no error in the judgment of the state court. . . .

It is now inescapably clear that the Fourteenth Amendment forbids the use of involuntary confessions not only because of the probable unreliability of confessions that are obtained in a manner deemed coercive, but also because of the "strongly felt attitude of our society that important human values are sacrificed where an agency of the government, in the course of securing a conviction, wrings a confession out of an accused against his will," and because of "the deep rooted feeling that the police must obey the law while enforcing the law; that in the end life and liberty can be as much endangered from illegal methods used to convict those thought to be criminals as from the actual criminals themselves." . . .

Under the New York procedure, the evidence given the jury inevitably injects irrelevant and impermissible considerations of truthfulness of the confession into the assessment of voluntariness. Indeed the jury is told to determine the truthfulness of the confession in assessing its probative value. As a consequence, it cannot be assumed, as the Stein Court did, that the jury reliably found the facts against the accused. This unsound assumption undermines Stein's authority as a precedent and its view on the constitutionality of the New York procedure. The admixture of reliability and voluntariness in the considerations of the jury would itself entitle a defendant to further proceedings in any case in which the essential facts are disputed, for we cannot determine how the jury resolved these issues and will not assume that they were reliably and properly resolved against the accused. And it is only a reliable determination on the voluntariness issue which satisfies the constitutional rights of the defendant and which would permit the jury to consider the confession in adjudicating guilt or innocence.

But we do not rest on this ground alone, for the other alternative hypothesized in Stein—that the jury found the confession involuntary and disregarded it—is equally unacceptable. Under the New York procedure, the fact of a defendant's confession is solidly implanted in the jury's mind, for it has not only heard the confession, but it has been instructed to consider and judge its voluntariness and is in position to assess whether it is true or false. If it finds the confession involuntary, does the jury—indeed, can it—then disregard the confession in accordance with its instructions? If there are lingering doubts about the sufficiency of the other evidence, does the jury unconsciously lay them to rest by resort to the confession? Will uncertainty about the sufficiency of the other evidence to prove guilt beyond a reasonable doubt actually result in acquittal when the jury knows the defendant has given a truthful confession? . . .

We turn to consideration of the disposition of this case. Since Jackson has not been given an adequate hearing upon the voluntariness of his confession he must be given one, the remaining inquiry being the scope of that hearing and the court which should provide it. . . .

However, we think that the further proceedings to which Jackson is entitled should occur initially in the state courts rather than in the federal habeas corpus court. Jackson's trial did not comport with constitutional standards and he is entitled to a determination of the voluntariness of his confession in the state courts in accordance with valid state procedures; the State is also entitled to make this determination before this Court considers the case on direct review or a petition for habeas corpus is filed in a Federal District Court. . . .

It is New York, therefore, not the federal habeas corpus court, which should first provide Jackson with that which he has not yet had and to which he is constitutionally entitled—an adequate evidentiary hearing productive of reliable results concerning the voluntariness of his confession. It does not follow, however, that Jackson is automatically entitled to a complete new trial including a retrial of the issue of guilt or innocence. Jackson's position before the District Court, and here, is that the issue of his confession should not have been decided by the convicting jury but should have been determined in a proceeding separate and apart from the body trying guilt or innocence. So far we agree and hold that he is now entitled to such a hearing in the state court. But if at the conclusion of such an evidentiary hearing in the state court on the coercion issue, it is determined that Jackson's confession was voluntarily given, admissible in evidence, and properly to be considered by the jury, we see no constitutional necessity at that point for proceeding with a new trial, for Jackson has already been tried by a jury with the confession placed before it and has been found guilty. True, the jury in the first trial was permitted to deal with the issue of voluntariness and we do not know whether the conviction rested upon the confession; but if it did, there is no constitutional prejudice to Jackson from the New York procedure if the confession is now properly found to be voluntary and therefore admissible. If the jury relied upon it, it was entitled to do so. Of course, if the state court, at an evidentiary hearing, redetermines the facts and decides that Jackson's confession was involuntary, there must be a new trial on guilt or innocence without the confession being admitted in evidence. . . .

Reversed.[1]

1. Oregon, which had followed the New York rule changed to the Massachusetts rule after Jackson. State v. Brewton, 238 Or. 590, 395 P.2d 874 (1964).

A defendant who entered a plea of guilty on advice of competent counsel cannot attack his conviction collaterally by petition for a writ of habeas corpus which merely alleges that his plea was the result of a previously-coerced confession. In such a case his conviction is not based upon the allegedly-coerced confession but upon his admission of guilt in

MR. JUSTICE BLACK, with whom MR. JUSTICE CLARK joins as to Part I of this opinion, dissenting in part and concurring in part.

In Stein v. New York, 346 U.S. 156, 177–179, 73 S.Ct. 1077, 1089–1090, this Court sustained the constitutionality of New York's procedure under which the jury, rather than the trial judge, resolves disputed questions of fact as to the voluntariness of confessions offered against defendants charged with crime. I think this holding was correct and would adhere to it. While I dissented from affirmance of the convictions in Stein, my dissent went to other points; I most assuredly did not dissent because of any doubts about a State's constitutional power in a criminal case to let the jury, as it does in New York, decide the question of a confession's voluntariness. In fact, I would be far more troubled about constitutionality should either a State or the Federal Government declare that a jury in trying a defendant charged with crime is compelled to accept without question a trial court's factual finding that a confession was voluntarily given. Whatever might be a judge's view of the voluntariness of a confession, the jury in passing on a defendant's guilt or innocence is, in my judgment, entitled to hear and determine voluntariness of a confession along with other factual issues on which its verdict must rest. . . .

MR. JUSTICE CLARK, dissenting. . . .

But even if the trial judge had instructed the jury to consider truth or falsity, the order here should be for a new trial, as in Rogers v. Richmond, supra. There the Court of Appeals was directed to hold the case a reasonable time "in order to give the State opportunity to *retry* petitioner . . . ." 365 U.S. at 549, 81 S.Ct. at 744. (Emphasis supplied.) But the Court does not do this. It strikes down New York's procedure and then tells New York—not to retry the petitioner—but merely to have the trial judge hold a hearing on the admissibility of the confession and enter a definitive determination on that issue, as under the Massachusetts rule. This does not cure the error which the Court finds present. If the trial court did so err, this Court is making a more grievous error in amending New York's rule here

open court. McMann v. Richardson, 397 U.S. 759, 90 S.Ct. 1441 (1970).

The federal kidnaping act, 18 U.S.C.A. § 1201(a), provides for the death penalty if the jury so directs and for imprisonment for any term of years or for life, if the death penalty is not imposed. The Supreme Court held the statute valid but held that the death penalty could not be imposed because the law, by authorizing the death penalty to be imposed by the jury but not by the court if the jury was waived or a plea of guilty entered, placed an unconstitutional burden upon the exercise of constitutional rights. United States v. Jackson, 390 U.S. 570, 88 S.Ct. 1209 (1968). But it held that a plea of guilty, entered before *Jackson*, was not involuntary even if entered to avoid the possibility of a death sentence. Many guilty pleas are motivated by the hope of a lesser penalty than otherwise. Brady v. United States, 397 U.S. 742, 90 S.Ct. 1463 (1970).

The voluntariness of a confession may be established by a preponderance of the evidence. Lego v. Twomey, 404 U.S. 477, 92 S.Ct. 619 (1972).

Some states require proof beyond a reasonable doubt under state law.

and then requiring New York to apply it *ex post facto* without benefit of a full trial. Surely under the reasoning of the Court, the petitioner would be entitled to a new trial.

Believing that the constitutionality of New York's rule is not ripe for decision here, I dissent. If I am in error on this, then I join my Brother Harlan. His dissent is unanswerable.

MR. JUSTICE HARLAN, whom MR. JUSTICE CLARK and MR. JUSTICE STEWART join, dissenting.

Even under the broadest view of the restrictive effect of the Fourteenth Amendment, I would not have thought it open to doubt that the States were free to allocate the trial of issues, whether in criminal or civil cases, between judge and jury as they deemed best. The Court now holds, however, that New York's long-standing practice of leaving to the jury the resolution of reasonably disputed factual issues surrounding a criminal defendant's allegation that his confession was coerced violates due process. It is held that the Constitution permits submission of the question of coercion to the trial jury only if preceded by a determination of "voluntariness" by the trial judge—or by another judge or another jury not concerned with the ultimate issue of guilt or innocence.

The Court does make one bow to federalism in its opinion: New York need not retry Jackson if it, rather than the federal *habeas corpus* court, now finds, in accordance with the new ground rules, the confession to have been voluntary. I doubt whether New York, which in Jackson's original trial faithfully followed the teachings of this Court which were then applicable, will find much comfort in this gesture. . . .

GRIFFIN v. CALIFORNIA

Supreme Court of the United States, 1965.
380 U.S. 609, 85 S.Ct. 1229.

[Griffin was convicted of first-degree murder in a jury trial during which his failure to testify was the subject of comment by the district attorney and an instruction by the judge. The conviction having been affirmed by the Supreme Court of California was carried to this Court by certiorari.]

MR. JUSTICE DOUGLAS delivered the opinion of the Court. . . .

If this were a federal trial, reversible error would have been committed. Wilson v. United States, 149 U.S. 60, 13 S.Ct. 765, 37 L.Ed. 650, so holds. It is said, however, that the Wilson decision rested not on the Fifth Amendment, but on an Act of Congress. 18 U.S.C. § 3481. That indeed is the fact, as the opinion of the Court in the Wilson case states. But that is the beginning, not the end of our inquiry. The question remains whether, statute or not, the comment rule, approved by California, violates the Fifth Amendment.

We think it does. It is in substance a rule of evidence that allows the State the privilege of tendering to the jury for its consideration the failure of the accused to testify. No formal offer of proof is made as in other situations; but the prosecutor's comment and the court's acquiescence are the equivalent of an offer of evidence and its acceptance. The Court in the Wilson case stated:

". . . the Act was framed with a due regard also to those who might prefer to rely upon the presumption of innocence which the law gives to every one, and not wish to be witnesses. It is not every one who can safely venture on the witness stand, though entirely innocent of the charge against him. Excessive timidity, nervousness when facing others and attempting to explain transactions of a suspicious character, and offenses charged against him, will often confuse and embarrass him to such a degree as to increase rather than remove prejudices against him. It is not every one, however, honest, who would therefore willingly be placed on the witness stand. The statute, in tenderness to the weakness of those who from the causes mentioned might refuse to ask to be witnesses, particularly when they may have been in some degree compromised by their association with others, declares that the failure of a defendant in a criminal action to request to be a witness shall not create any presumption against him."

If the words "Fifth Amendment" are substituted for "Act" and for "statute" the spirit of the Self-Incrimination Clause is reflected. For comment on the refusal to testify is a remnant of the "inquisitorial system of criminal justice," which the Fifth Amendment outlaws.[5] It is a penalty imposed by courts for exercising a constitutional privilege. It cuts down on the privilege by making its assertion costly. It is said, however, that the inference of guilt for failure to testify as to facts peculiarly within the accused's knowledge is in any event natural and irresistible, and that comment on the failure does not magnify that inference into a penalty for asserting a constitutional privilege. People v. Modesto, 62 A.C. 452, 468–469, 42 Cal.Rptr. 417, 398 P.2d

5. Our decision today that the Fifth Amendment prohibits comment on the defendant's silence is no innovation, for on a previous occasion a majority of this Court indicated their acceptance of this proposition. In Adamson v. People of State of California, 332 U.S. 46, 67 S.Ct. 1672, the question was, as here, whether the Fifth Amendment proscribed California's comment practice. The four dissenters (Black, Douglas, Murphy and Rutledge, JJ.) would have answered this question in the affirmative. A fifth member of the Court, Justice Frankfurter, stated in a separate opinion: "For historical reasons a limited immunity from the common duty to testify was written into the Federal Bill of Rights, and I am prepared to agree that, as part of that immunity, comment on the failure of an accused to take the witness stand is forbidden in federal prosecutions." Id., at 61, 67 S.Ct. at 1680. But, though he agreed with the dissenters on this point, he also agreed with Justices Vinson, Reed, Jackson, and Burton that the Fourteenth Amendment did not make the Self-Incrimination Clause of the Fifth Amendment applicable to the States; thus he joined the opinion of the Court which so held (the Court's opinion assumed that the Fifth Amendment barred comment, but it expressly disclaimed any intention to decide the point. Id., at 50, 67 S.Ct. at 1674).

753. What the jury may infer given no help from the court is one thing. What they may infer when the court solemnizes the silence of the accused into evidence against him is quite another. That the inference of guilt is not always so natural or irresistible is brought out in the Modesto opinion itself:

"Defendant contends that the reason a defendant refuses to testify is that his prior convictions will be introduced in evidence to impeach him ([Cal.] Code Civ.Proc. § 2051) and not that he is unable to deny the accusations. It is true that the defendant might fear that his prior convictions will prejudice the jury, and therefore another possible inference can be drawn from his refusal to take the stand."

We said in Malloy v. Hogan, supra, 378 U.S. p. 11, 84 S.Ct. p. 1495, that "the same standards must determine whether an accused's silence in either a federal or state proceeding is justified." We take that in its literal sense and hold that the Fifth Amendment, in its direct application to the federal government and its bearing on the States by reason of the Fourteenth Amendment, forbids either comment by the prosecution on the accused's silence or instructions by the court that such silence is evidence of guilt.[6]

Reversed.

THE CHIEF JUSTICE took no part in the decision of this case.

MR. JUSTICE HARLAN concurring.

I agree with the Court that within the federal judicial system the Fifth Amendment bars adverse comment by federal prosecutors and judges on a defendant's failure to take the stand in a criminal trial, a right accorded him by that amendment. And given last Term's decision in Malloy v. Hogan, 378 U.S. 1, 84 S.Ct. 1489, 12 L.Ed.2d 653, that the Fifth Amendment applies to the States in all its refinements, I see no legitimate escape from today's decision and therefore concur in it. I do so, however, with great reluctance, since for me the decision exemplifies the creeping paralysis with which this Court's recent adoption of the "incorporation" doctrine is infecting the operation of the federal system. . . .

6. We reserve decision on whether an accused can require, as in Bruno v. United States, 308 U.S. 287, 60 S.Ct. 198, 84 L.Ed. 257, that the jury, be instructed that his silence must be disregarded.

[Added by compilers.]

The answer given later was affirmative. It is reversible error for the judge in a state case to refuse to give such an instruction. Carter v. Kentucky, 450 U.S. 288, 101 S.Ct. 1112 (1981). Earlier the Court had held that giving such an instruction over the objection of the defendant did not violate the federal constitution. Lakeside v. Oregon, 435 U.S. 333, 98 S.Ct. 1091 (1978). The Indiana Court held that giving a "no adverse inferences" instruction over defendant's objections was reversible error under state law. Hill v. State, 267 Ind. 480, 371 N.E.2d 1303, 1306 (1978).

A prosecutor's argument constituting improper comment on an accused's silence is to be evaluated under the standard of harmless error beyond a reasonable doubt. United States v. Hasting, ___ U.S. ___, 103 S.Ct. 1974 (1983).

[By Mr. Justice Stewart.]

MR. JUSTICE STEWART, with whom MR. JUSTICE WHITE joins, dissenting. . . .

Moreover, no one can say where the balance of advantage might lie as a result of counsels' discussion of the matter. No doubt the prosecution's argument will seek to encourage the drawing of inferences unfavorable to the defendant. However, the defendant's counsel equally has an opportunity to explain the various other reasons why a defendant may not wish to take the stand, and thus rebut the natural if uneducated assumption that it is because the defendant cannot truthfully deny the accusations made.

I think the California comment rule is not a coercive device which impairs the right against self-incrimination, but rather a means of articulating and bringing into the light of rational discussion a fact inescapably impressed on the jury's consciousness. The California procedure is not only designed to protect the defendant against unwarranted inferences which might be drawn by an uninformed jury; it is also an attempt by the State to recognize and articulate what it believes to be the natural probative force of certain facts. Surely no one would deny that the State has an important interest in throwing the light of rational discussion on that which transpires in the course of a trial, both to protect the defendant from the very real dangers of silence and to shape a legal process designed to ascertain the truth.

The California rule allowing comment by counsel and instruction by the judge on the defendant's failure to take the stand is hardly an idiosyncratic aberration. The Model Code of Evidence, and the Uniform Rules of Evidence both sanction the use of such procedures.[6] The practice had been endorsed by resolution of the American Bar Association and the American Law Institute,[7] and has the support of the weight of scholarly opinion.[8] . . .

6. Model Code of Evidence, Rule 201 (1942); Uniform Rules of Evidence, Rule 23(4) (1953).

7. 56 A.B.A.Rep. 137–159 (1931); 59 A.B.A.Rep. 130–141 (1934); 9 Proceedings A.L.I. 202, 203 (1931).

8. See Bruce, The Right to Comment on the Failure of the Accused to Testify, 31 Mich.L.Rev. 226; Dunmore, Comment on Failure of Accused to Testify, 26 Yale L.J. 464; Hadley, Criminal Justice in America, 11 A.B.A.J. 674, 677; Hiscock, Criminal Law and Procedure in New York, 26 Col.L.Rev. 253, 258–262; Note, Comment on Defendant's Failure to Take the Stand, 57 Yale L.J. 145.

[By the Compiler.]

Comment by prosecutor regarding the failure of accused to testify violates the federal constitutional privilege against self-incrimination but does not require a reversal unless it resulted in a miscarriage of justice. People v. Bostick, 62 Cal.2d 820, 44 Cal.Rptr. 649, 402 P.2d 529 (1965). Comment by court and prosecuting attorney on D's failure to testify violated his constitutional privilege against self-incrimination and requires reversal where it was so extensive as to suggest that without it the result might have been more favorable to him. People v. Odom, 236 Cal.App.2d 876, 46 Cal.Rptr. 453 (1965). Improper argument and instruction on D's failure to testify constituted error but not such a denial of due process and fair trial that it could be raised retroactively on collateral attack by habeas corpus. In re Gaines, 63 Cal. 2d 234, 45 Cal.Rptr. 865, 404 P.2d 473 (1965).

In a joint trial it is reversible error to permit counsel for one defendant to comment on co-defendant's failure to testify.

KASTIGAR v. UNITED STATES

Supreme Court of the United States, 1972.
406 U.S. 441, 92 S.Ct. 1653.

(In the effort to make needed evidence available without either being unfair to the individual or imposing unnecessary handicaps upon the Government, Congress enacted a new immunity statute (18 U.S.C. § 6002). This did not bar a subsequent prosecution for the offense involved, but provided that in any subsequent prosecution of one who had testified under grant of such immunity, there could be no use of the testimony given by him, or of any other evidence which had been made available because of such testimony (use or derivative use). Persons before the grand jury who had been granted such immunity refused to testify on the ground that the statute did not give them adequate protection and was hence unconstitutional. The District Court rejected this claim, found them in contempt, and ordered them imprisoned until either they testified or the term of the grand jury expired. This was affirmed by the Court of Appeals of the Ninth Circuit (440 F.2d 954), and the Supreme Court granted certiorari.)

MR. JUSTICE POWELL delivered the opinion of the Court. . . .

Syllabus

The United States can compel testimony from an unwilling witness who invokes the Fifth Amendment privilege against compulsory self-incrimination by conferring immunity, as provided by 18 U.S.C. § 6002, from use of the compelled testimony and evidence derived therefrom in subsequent criminal proceedings, as such immunity from use and derivative use is coextensive with the scope of the privilege and is sufficient to compel testimony over a claim of the privilege. Transactional immunity would afford broader protection than the Fifth Amendment privilege, and is not constitutionally required. In a subsequent criminal prosecution, the prosecution has the burden

De Luna v. United States, 308 F.2d 140 (5th Cir. 1962).

In United States ex rel. Lewis v. Yaeger, 285 F.Supp. 780 (D.C.N.J.1968), **D** did not testify, but counsel had him get up and stand in front of the jury alongside another man in an attempt to demonstrate marked resemblance and thereby raise the issue of mistaken identity. This was held to open the door to comment on **D**'s failure to testify.

D, arrested for robbery, was advised of his constitutional rights, including his right to remain silent. He was then questioned and remained silent. It was reversible error for the prosecutor, on cross-examination, to impeach D's credibility of alibi by inquiring into his silence at the police station. United States v. Hale, 422 U.S. 171, 95 S.Ct. 2133 (1975).

The rule is applicable to the states. Doyle v. Ohio, 426 U.S. 610, 96 S.Ct. 2240 (1976).

Pre-arrest silence of a suspect, not in custody, who has not been warned that he need not make a statement, may be used in a criminal prosecution without violating his constitutional rights. Jenkins v. Anderson, 447 U.S. 231, 100 S.Ct. 2124 (1980). Post arrest silence of a suspect who has not been given the Miranda warnings may be used to impeach the suspect. Fletcher v. Weir, 455 U.S. 603, 102 S.Ct. 1309 (1982).

of proving affirmatively that evidence proposed to be used is derived from a legitimate source wholly independent of the compelled testimony.[1]

SECTION 3. THE RIGHT OF PRIVACY (TO BE FREE FROM UNREASONABLE SEARCH AND SEIZURE)

The Fourth Amendment provides: "The right of the people to be secure in their persons, houses, papers and effects, against unreasonable searches and seizures, shall not be violated, ..." It was clear that any unlawful arrest, search or seizure by a federal officer was a violation of this constitutional right, but for a century and a quarter evidence which was relevant, material and otherwise competent was admitted against the defendant even if it had been obtained by such a violation. In 1914 *Weeks*[1] held that the Fourth Amendment barred the use of evidence, so procured, in a federal prosecution. This came to be known as the "exclusionary rule". In *Wolf*[2] the Supreme Court, for the first time, discussed the effect of the operation of the Due Process Clause of the Fourteenth Amendment upon such evidence. It held that security of privacy against unlawful intrusion by the police is implicit in the concept of ordered liberty and as such enforceable against the states under the protection of that Clause. Hence no state could affirmatively sanction such police intrusion. But finding that most of the English-speaking world did not regard the "exclusionary rule" as an essential ingredient of the right, it held that a state court was not required to exclude evidence merely because it was obtained by unlawful search and seizure. Twelve years later *Wolf* was expressly overruled by *Mapp*[3] wherein it was stated: "We hold that all evidence obtained by searches and seizures in violation of the Constitution is, by that same authority, inadmissible in a state court".[4]

The Court found at the time *Wolf* was decided that 30 states had rejected the "exclusionary rule". After that decision some of those states changed position as to this, such as *Cahan*[5] in California. Now, of course, the "exclusionary rule" applies in all our courts, state and federal.[6]

1. See also Ullmann v. United States, 350 U.S. 422, 76 S.Ct. 497 (1956). See Strachan, Self-Incrimination, Immunity and Watergate, 56 Tex.L.Rev. 791 (1978).

1. Weeks v. United States, 232 U.S. 383, 34 S.Ct. 341, 58 L.Ed. 652 (1914).

2. Wolf v. Colorado, 338 U.S. 25, 69 S.Ct. 1359, 93 L.Ed. 1782 (1949).

3. Mapp v. Ohio, 367 U.S. 643, 81 S.Ct. 1684, 6 L.Ed.2d 1081, 84 A.L.R.2d 933 (1961).

4. Id. at 655, 81 S.Ct. at 1691.

5. People v. Cahan, 44 Cal.2d 434, 282 P.2d 905, 50 A.L.R.2d 513 (1955).

6. *Mapp* does not apply retrospectively to state cases which had been finally decided before the *Mapp* decision was rendered. It applies to cases which were pending on direct review at that time (Ker v. California, 374 U.S. 23, 83 S.Ct. 1623, 10 L.Ed.2d 726 (1963)), but not to those in which the point can be raised only by collateral attack (habeas corpus in this case). Linkletter v. Walker, 381 U.S. 618, 85 S.Ct. 1731, 14 L.Ed.2d 601 (1965). "Thus the accepted rule today is that in appropriate cases the Court may in the interest of justice make the rule prospective. And 'there is much to be said in favor of such a rule for cases arising in

The purpose of this rule is commonly stated to be the deterrence of police misconduct; but its chief accomplishment has been the release of obviously guilty defendants. The Court has begun to place limitations on its application. Thus in a civil case evidence was not to be excluded which had been obtained by a state officer in good faith reliance upon a warrant later held to be defective.[7] In another case,[8] of much greater importance particularly to the states, the Court held that in Fourth Amendment decisions, the second-guessing of state courts by federal district courts is not warranted. In other words, when the state has provided an opportunity for full and fair litigation of a Fourth Amendment claim and decided that the search and seizure were lawful, a state prisoner may not be granted federal habeas corpus on the repeated claim that evidence introduced at his trial had been obtained by an unconstitutional search and seizure. In this context, if the exclusionary rule would make any contribution to the effectuation of the Fourth Amendment, it would be minimal as compared to the societal costs of applying the rule.[9]

The language of the opinions suggest that the Court will be inclined to enforce the rule vigorously in any case in which officers have wilfully violated the right of the defendant, but not necessarily in a case in which they acted in the good faith belief that their conduct was duly authorized.

WONG SUN v. UNITED STATES

Supreme Court of the United States, 1963.
371 U.S. 471, 83 S.Ct. 407.

[Toy and Wong Sun were convicted in the federal district court of the offense of fraudulent and knowing transportation and concealment of illegally imported heroin. Federal officers had broken into Toy's bedroom and searched for narcotics which were not found. Toy told the officers he had not been selling narcotics but that "Johnny" had. He took them to Johnny Yee's place where they found about an ounce of heroin. Yee then implicated Toy and Wong Sun who later made incriminating, unsigned statements. Over timely objections, the original statement by Toy, the heroin taken from Yee and the pre-trial statements were admitted in evidence. It was found that the officers' uninvited entrance into Toy's bedroom had been unlawful.]

MR. JUSTICE BRENNAN delivered the opinion of the Court. . . .

the future.'" Id. at 628, 85 S.Ct. at 1737.

7. United States v. Janis, 428 U.S. 433, 96 S.Ct. 3021 (1976).

8. Stone v. Powell, 428 U.S. 465, 96 S.Ct. 3037 (1976).

Where defendant asserted that he was illegally arrested after which a confession was made, where a state court passed on and upheld the validity of the arrest it was not thereafter subject to challenge in federal court. Cardwell v. Taylor, ___ U.S. ___, 103 S.Ct. 2015 (1983).

9. 96 S.Ct. at 3055.

We believe that significant differences between the cases of the two petitioners require separate discussion of each. We shall first consider the case of petitioner Toy.

It is conceded that Toy's declarations in his bedroom are to be excluded if they are held to be "fruits" of the agents' unlawful action.

In order to make effective the fundamental constitutional guarantees of sanctity of the home and inviolability of the person, this Court held nearly half a century ago that evidence seized during an unlawful search could not constitute proof against the victim of the search. The exclusionary prohibition extends as well to the indirect as the direct products of such invasions. Silverthorne Lumber Co. v. United States, 251 U.S. 385, 40 S.Ct. 182, 64 L.Ed. 319. Mr. Justice Holmes, speaking for the Court in that case, in holding that the Government might not make use of information obtained during an unlawful search to subpoena from the victims the very documents illegally viewed, expressed succinctly the policy of the broad exclusionary rule:

"The essence of a provision forbidding the acquisition of evidence in a certain way is that not merely evidence so acquired shall not be used before the Court but that it shall not be used at all. Of course this does not mean that the facts thus obtained become sacred and inaccessible. If knowledge of them is gained from an independent source they may be proved, like any others, but the knowledge gained by the Government's own wrong cannot be used by it in the way proposed." 251 U.S. at 392, 40 S.Ct. at 183.

The exclusionary rule has traditionally barred from trial physical, tangible materials obtained either during or as a direct result of an unlawful invasion. It follows from our holding in Silverman v. United States, 365 U.S. 505, 81 S.Ct. 679, 5 L.Ed.2d 734, that the Fourth Amendment may protect against the overhearing of verbal statements as well as against the more traditional seizure of "papers and effects." Similarly, testimony as to matters observed during an unlawful invasion has been excluded in order to enforce the basic constitutional policies. Thus, verbal evidence which derives so immediately from an unlawful entry and an unauthorized arrest as the officers' action in the present case is no less the "fruit" of official illegality than the more common tangible fruits of the unwarranted intrusion.[11] Nor do the policies underlying the exclusionary rule invite any logical distinction between physical and verbal evidence. Either in terms of deterring lawless conduct by federal officers, or of closing the doors of the federal courts to any use of evidence unconstitutionally obtained, the danger in relaxing the exclusionary rules in the case of

[Footnote by the Court.]

11. See Kamisar, Illegal Searches or Seizures and Contemporaneous Incriminating Statements: A Dialogue on a Neglected Area of Criminal Procedure, 1961 U. of Ill.Law Forum 78, 84–96. But compare Maguire, Evidence of Guilt (1959), 187–190.

verbal evidence would seem too great to warrant introducing such a distinction.

The Government argues that Toy's statements to the officers in his bedroom, although closely consequent upon the invasion which we hold unlawful, were nevertheless admissible because they resulted from "an intervening independent act of a free will." This contention, however, takes insufficient account of the circumstances. Six or seven officers had broken the door and followed on Toy's heels into the bedroom where his wife and child were sleeping. He had been almost immediately handcuffed and arrested. Under such circumstances it is unreasonable to infer that Toy's response was sufficiently an act of free will to purge the primary taint of the unlawful invasion.

The Government also contends that Toy's declarations should be admissible because they were ostensibly exculpatory rather than incriminating. There are two answers to this argument. First, the statements soon turned out to be incriminating, for they led directly to the evidence which implicated Toy. Second, when circumstances are shown such as those which induced these declarations, it is immaterial whether the declarations be termed "exculpatory." Thus we find no substantial reason to omit Toy's declarations from the protection of the exclusionary rule.

We now consider whether the exclusion of Toy's declarations requires also the exclusion of the narcotics taken from Yee, to which those declarations led the police. The prosecutor candidly told the trial court that "we wouldn't have found those drugs except that Mr. Toy helped us to." Hence this is not the case envisioned by this Court where the exclusionary rule has no application because the Government learned of the evidence "from an independent source," nor is this a case in which the connection between the lawless conduct of the police and the discovery of the challenged evidence has "become so attenuated as to dissipate the taint." Nardone v. United States, 308 U.S. 338, 341, 60 S.Ct. 266, 268, 84 L.Ed. 307. We need not hold that all evidence is "fruit of the poisonous tree" simply because it would not have come to light but for the illegal actions of the police. Rather, the more apt question in such a case is "whether, granting establishment of the primary illegality, the evdience to which instant objection is made has been come at by exploitation of that illegality or instead by means sufficiently distinguishable to be purged of the primary taint." Maguire, Evidence of Guilt, 221 (1959). We think it clear that the narcotics were "come at by the exploitation of that illegality" and hence that they may not be used against Toy.

It remains only to consider Toy's unsigned statement. We need not decide whether, in light of the fact that Toy was free on his own recognizance when he made the statement, that statement was a fruit of the illegal arrest. Since we have concluded that his declarations in the bedroom and the narcotics surrendered by Yee should not have been admitted in evidence against him, the only proofs remaining to sustain his conviction are his and Wong Sun's unsigned statements. Without scrutinizing the contents of Toy's ambiguous recitals, we conclude that no reference to Toy in Wong Sun's statement constitutes admissible evidence corroborating any admission by Toy. We arrive at this conclusion upon two clear lines of decisions which converge to require it. One line of our decisions establishes that criminal confessions and admissions of guilt require extrinsic corroboration; the other line of precedents holds that an out-of-court declaration made after arrest may not be used at trial against one of the declarant's partners in crime.

It is a settled principle of the administration of criminal justice in the federal courts that a conviction must rest upon firmer ground than the uncorroborated admission or confession of the accused. . . .

We turn now to the case of the other petitioner, Wong Sun. We have no occasion to disagree with the finding of the Court of Appeals that his arrest, also, was without probable cause or reasonable grounds. At all events no evidentiary consequences turn upon that question. For Wong Sun's unsigned confession was not the fruit of that arrest, and was therefore properly admitted at trial. On the evidence that Wong Sun had been released on his own recognizance after a lawful arraignment, and had returned voluntarily several days later to make the statement, we hold that the connection between the arrest and the statement had "become so attenuated as to dissipate the taint." The fact that the statement was unsigned, whatever bearing this may have upon its weight and credibility, does not render it inadmissible; Wong Sun understood and adopted its substance, though he could not comprehend the English words. The petitioner has never suggested any impropriety in the interrogation itself which would require the exclusion of this statement.

We must then consider the admissibility of the narcotics surrendered by Yee. Our holding, supra, that this ounce of heroin was inadmissible against Toy does not compel a like result with respect to Wong Sun. The exclusion of the narcotics as to Toy was required solely by their tainted relationship to information unlawfully obtained from Toy, and not by any official impropriety connected with their surrender by Yee.[a] The seizure of this heroin invaded no right of privacy of person or premises which would entitle Wong Sun to object to its use at his trial.

However, for the reasons that Wong Sun's statement was incompetent to corroborate Toy's admissions contained in Toy's own statement, any references to Wong Sun in Toy's statement were incompe-

a. [Compiler's note.] The rule of "standing" is reaffirmed and applied to elecronic surveillance. Only one whose own constitutional right was violated is in a position to exclude the evidence so obtained. Alderman v. United States, 394 U.S. 165, 89 S.Ct. 961 (1969).

tent to corroborate Wong Sun's admissions. Thus, the only competent source of corroboration for Wong Sun's statement was the heroin itself. We cannot be certain, however, on this state of the record, that the trial judge may not also have considered the contents of Toy's statement as a source of corroboration.

Surely, under the narcotics statute, the discovery of heroin raises a presumption that someone—generally the possessor—violated the law. As to him, once possession alone is proved, the other elements of the offense—transportation and concealment with knowledge of the illegal importation of the drug—need not be separately demonstrated, much less corroborated. 21 U.S.C. § 174, 21 U.S.C.A. § 174. Thus particular care ought to be taken in this area, when the crucial element of the accused's possession is proved solely by his own admissions, that the requisite corroboration be found among the evidence which is properly before the trier of facts. We therefore hold that petitioner Wong Sun is also entitled to a new trial.

The judgment of the Court of Appeals is reversed and the case is remanded to the District Court for further proceedings consistent with this opinion.

It is so ordered.

Judgment of Court of Appeals reversed and case remanded to the District Court.[b]

b. A chain of causation that began with an illegal search and seizure by officers led them, four months later, to H who turned out to be the chief witness in the criminal trial of C. H was willing to help the officers and, more than a year later, voluntarily testified against C. After C had been found guilty, the judge set aside that finding on the ground that without the testimony of H there was insufficient evidence of guilt and that H's testimony must be suppressed because it was the result of an illegal search. It was held that this was error and that the finding of guilt should be reinstated. The Court reaffirmed *Wong Sun* to the extent of holding that evidence which is the "fruit of the forbidden tree" must be excluded, but rejected the further conclusion that no logical distinction can be drawn between verbal and physical evidence. The rule must be "invoked with much greater reluctance" to exclude the evidence of a "live witness" than to support the suppression of an inanimate object. The testimony of this witness, under the circumstances of this case, was sufficiently independent of the constitutional violation to permit its introduction. United States v. Ceccolini, 435 U.S. 268, 98 S.Ct. 1054 (1978).

Officers with authority to enter a house to make an arrest must first give "notice" which includes identification and statement of purpose. But the Court upheld a state law which made an exception in exigent circumstances, as when giving the notice would probably result in the loss of important evidence. Ker v. California, 374 U.S. 23, 83 S.Ct. 1623 (1963).

Defendant gave a confession six hours after an illegal arrest and after being advised of his rights three times. The confession was held to be the product of the illegal arrest and inadmissible. Taylor v. Alabama, 457 U.S. 687, 102 S.Ct. 2664 (1982).

Passengers who asserted neither a property nor a possessory interest in a car, and established no legitimate expectation of privacy in the glove compartment or area under the front seat, were not entitled to suppression of items seized from those places. Rakas v. Illinois, 439 U.S. 128, 99 S.Ct. 421 (1978).

"A closed piece of luggage found in a lawfully searched car is constitutionally protected to the same extent as are closed pieces of luggage found anywhere else." Robbins v. California, 453 U.S. 420, 101 S.Ct. 2841, 2843 (1981).

MR. JUSTICE DOUGLAS, concurring.

While I join the Court's opinion I do so because nothing the Court holds is inconsistent with my belief that there having been time to get a warrant, probable cause alone could not have justified the arrest of petitioner Toy without a warrant. . . .

MR. JUSTICE CLARK, with whom MR. JUSTICE HARLAN, MR. JUSTICE STEWART and MR. JUSTICE WHITE join, dissenting.

The Court has made a Chinese puzzle out of this simple case involving four participants: Hom Way, Blackie Toy, Johnny Yee and "Sea Dog" Sun. In setting aside the convictions of Toy and Sun it has dashed to pieces the heretofore recognized standards of probable cause necessary to secure an arrest warrant or to make an arrest without one. Instead of dealing with probable cause as involving "probabilities," "the factual and practical considerations of everyday life on which reasonable and prudent men, not legal technicians, act," the Court sets up rigid, mechanical standards, applying the 20–20 vision of hind-sight in an area where the ambiguity and immediacy inherent in unexpected arrest are present. While probable cause must be based on more than mere suspicion, it does not require proof sufficient to establish guilt. The sole requirement heretofore has been that the knowledge in the hands of the officers at the time of arrest must support a "man of reasonable caution in the belief" that the subject had committed narcotic offenses. Carroll v. United States, 267 U.S. 132, 162, 45 S.Ct. 280, 288, 69 L.Ed. 543 (1925). . . .

WAYNE v. UNITED STATES

United States Court of Appeals, District of Columbia Circuit, 1963.
115 U.S.App.D.C. 234, 318 F.2d 205.

[W, on trial under an indictment charging attempted abortion terminating in death, objected to the introduction in evidence of the autopsy report on the victim and expert testimony as to the cause of death. He claimed that these were the product of an unlawful entry into his apartment by the police. The evidence was admitted over his objection and a conviction resulted.]

BURGER, CIRCUIT JUDGE. . . .

When an officer has made a lawful custodial arrest of the occupants of an automobile, he may as an incident of that arrest, search the passenger compartment of the car, and any container found therein, whether locked or not, may be seized and searched even absent probable cause to believe that contraband or evidence of crime will be found. New York v. Belton, 453 U.S. 454, 101 S.Ct. 2860 (1981). (Six Justices agreed that both cases should be decided the same way, but did not agree which way.) Note that the factual difference is that in *Belton* the occupants of the car had been arrested prior to the search whereas in *Robbins* they had not.

The Louisiana Supreme Court said *obiter* that its own state constitution gives more protection than is provided in *Belton.* State v. Hernandez, 410 So.2d 1381 (La.1982).

(3)

(a) Appellant's third contention will be treated in two parts. The contention is that the entry of the police into his apartment, which had been found by a District Judge on a pre-trial motion to have been illegal, and the seizure of the body immediately following such illegal entry, precluded the introduction of the coroner's testimony about the condition of the body and the cause of death. The doctrine invoked is that commonly known as the "fruit of the poisonous tree." The government challenges the finding that the entry was illegal and argues further that, even if it was, it did not preclude the coroner from testifying.

Without now reaching the legality of the entry, we agree with the government that, in the circumstances of this case, the testimony objected to could not be considered as the "fruit of the poisonous tree." The Supreme Court has recently had occasion to discuss and clarify this difficult doctrine. Wong Sun v. United States, 371 U.S. 471, 83 S.Ct. 407, 9 L.Ed.2d 441 (1963). It stated that the exclusionary rule has no application when the government obtains evidence "from an independent source." Silverthorne Lumber Co. v. United States, 251 U.S. 385, 392, 40 S.Ct. 182, 64 L.Ed. 319 (1920). The Court added that the question to be asked in applying the doctrine is " 'whether, *granting establishment of the primary illegality*, the evidence to which the instant objection is made has been come at by exploitation of that illegality or instead by means sufficiently distinguishable to be purged of the primary taint.' Maguire, Evidence of Guilt, 221 (1959)."

It appears to us that the standards set forth in Wong Sun call for admission of the coroner's testimony. It is undisputed that the deceased's sister had told the police, prior to their entry into appellant's apartment, that her sister was there. No one seeking entry "knew" as a fact that she was dead and no one had a right to assume it was a "body" rather than a dying or unconscious person, as the police thought. Accordingly, it is clear that this information came from an independent source, and it cannot reasonably be said that the evidence embodied in the coroner's testimony was acquired "by exploitation of . . . [the] illegality," see Maguire, supra, or that it can be regarded as "gained by the Government's own wrong," Silverthorne, supra, 251 U.S. at 392, 40 S.Ct. at 183. It was inevitable that, even had the police not entered appellant's apartment at the time and in the manner they did, the coroner would sooner or later have been advised by the police of the information reported by the sister,[6] would have obtained the body, and would have conducted the post mortem examination prescribed by law. See D.C.Code Ann. § 11–1203 (1961).

[Footnote by the Court.]

6. Rules and Regulations of the Metropolitan Police Chapter II, Section 55, p. 33, Chapter XXIV, Section 12, p. 104a (eff. Nov. 1948).

Thus, the necessary causal relation between the illegal activity and the evidence sought to be excluded is lacking in this case.

JUDGE WASHINGTON considers that the discussion in the preceding pages amply justifies the admission of the coroner's testimony, and that it is not necessary for us to pass upon the legality of the police entry, the reviewability of the pre-trial order, or the need (or not) to remand the case for further hearings on the circumstances of the entry. Accordingly, the discussion which follows reflects my own views. Judge Washington concurs in this opinion up to this point, and concurs in the affirmance of the conviction. . . .[1]

Affirmed.

EDGERTON, CIRCUIT JUDGE (dissenting).

It is hard for me to disregard the conduct and consider the rights of an unlicensed drunken doctor who seems to have bungled his work and killed his patient.

Since Judge Burger thinks the police entered Wayne's apartment legally and I think they entered illegally, while Judge Washington does not reach this question, it is not decided. Judge Washington and Judge Burger think the coroner's testimony was rightly admitted and therefore affirm the conviction. I disagree. . . .

Since the body, which made it possible for the coroner to testify, was illegally obtained, I think his testimony should have been excluded. That the police learned legally from Joan that Jean was dead is immaterial because this knowledge did not, without the aid of the subsequent illegal entry, enable the coroner to testify. The "indepen-

[Added by the Compiler.]

1. An assault victim's in-court identification is not tainted by an illegal arrest of the defendant and subsequent identification procedures (evidence of the latter was excluded at trial). United States v. Crews, 445 U.S. 463, 100 S.Ct. 1244 (1980). "Wong Sun v. United States, 371 U.S. 471, 83 S.Ct. 407, 9 L.Ed.2d 441, is the most recent case involving the extent of the 'poisonous tree' doctrine. There the Court held that the declarations of Toy made in his bedroom simultaneously with the arrest were inadmissible. In the same case the Court held that the unsigned confession of Wong Sun made upon his voluntary return to police headquarters several days after he had been released on his own recognizance was admissible. Following Nardone v. United States, 308 U.S. 338, 341, 60 S.Ct. 266, 268, 84 L.Ed. 307, the Court held that the connection between the arrest and the statement had 'become so attenuated as to dissipate the taint.' . . .

"In the Wong Sun case the statements of Toy made simultaneously with the illegal arrest and the unsigned confession of Wong Sun made several days thereafter are at opposite ends of the pole in considering the fruit of the poisonous tree. Between these two extremes there is a line, on one side of which the fruit is contaminated by the illegal arrest, and on the other side of which the taint has been dissipated. Where this line shall be drawn is a question of fact to be determined in each case." United States v. McGavic, 337 F.2d 317, 318–19 (6th Cir.1964).

The fact that officers entered **D**'s car unlawfully would not prevent a later search of the car under a search warrant if the warrant was based entirely upon other and independent information. United States v. Radford, 361 F.2d 777 (4th Cir.1966).

Testimony of a witness who was discovered by exploitation of illegal police conduct is generally not admissible, but if the witness becomes known to the police by means independent of the illegal conduct his testimony is admissible. Lockridge v. Superior Court, 3 Cal.3d 166, 89 Cal.Rptr. 731, 474 P.2d 683 (1970).

dent source" principle is simply that evidence obtained *without use of illegal means* is not excluded on the ground that the same evidence has also been obtained by use of illegal means. Since the body, and consequently the coroner's testimony, were not obtained without use of illegal means, the principle has no application here.

The majority of the court take the position that legal acquisition of information *leading to* an illegal entry makes evidence *resulting from* the illegal entry admissible, if by using the legally acquired information in a *different* way the government *could have* got the resulting evidence legally. . . .

LOPEZ v. UNITED STATES

Supreme Court of the United States, 1963.
373 U.S. 427, 83 S.Ct. 1381.

[A federal agent, investigating possible evasion of excise taxes on cabarets, was in L's office at L's request. Unknown to L the agent had a tape recorder in his pocket which recorded L's offer to bribe the agent. L was indicted for attempted bribery of a federal officer and at the trial the agent testified to what was said in the office on that occasion and, over timely objection, the tape recording thereof was admitted in evidence.]

MR. JUSTICE HARLAN delivered the opinion of the Court. . . .

Petitioner's remaining contentions concern the admissibility of the evidence relating to his conversation with Davis on October 24. His argument is primarily addressed to the recording of the conversation, which he claims was obtained in violation of his rights under the Fourth Amendment. Recognizing the weakness of this position if Davis was properly permitted to testify about the same conversation, petitioner now challenges that testimony as well, although he failed to do so at the trial. His theory is that, in view of Davis' alleged falsification of his mission, he gained access to petitioner's office by misrepresentation and all evdience obtained in the office, i.e., his conversation with petitioner, was illegally "seized." . . .

We need not be long detained by the belated claim that Davis should not have been permitted to testify about the conversation of October 24. Davis was not guilty of an unlawful invasion of petitioner's office simply because his apparent willingness to accept a bribe was not real. He was in the office with petitioner's consent, and while there he did not violate the privacy of the office by seizing something surreptitiously without petitioner's knowledge. The only evidence obtained consisted of statements made by Lopez to Davis, statements which Lopez knew full well could be used against him by Davis if he wished. We decline to hold that whenever an offer of a bribe is made in private, and the offeree does not intend to accept, that offer is a constitutionally protected communication.

Once it is plain that Davis could properly testify about his conversation with Lopez, the constitutional claim relating to the recording of that conversation emerges in proper perspective. The Court has in the past sustained instances of "electronic eavesdropping" against constitutional challenge, when devices have been used to enable government agents to overhear conversations which would have been beyond the reach of the human ear. It has been insisted only that the electronic device not be planted by an unlawful physical invasion of a constitutionally protected area. The validity of these decisions is not in question here. Indeed this case involves no "eavesdropping" whatever in any proper sense of that term. The Government did not use an electronic device to listen in on conversations it could not otherwise have heard. Instead, the device was used only to obtain the most reliable evidence possible of a conversation in which the Government's own agent was a participant and which that agent was fully entitled to disclose. And the device was not planted by means of an unlawful physical invasion of petitioner's premises under circumstances which would violate the Fourth Amendment. It was carried in and out by an agent who was there with petitioner's assent, and it neither saw nor heard more than the agent himself.

The case is thus quite similar to Rathbun v. United States, 355 U.S. 107, 78 S.Ct. 161, 2 L.Ed.2d 134, in which we sustained against statutory attack the admission in evidence of the testimony of a policeman as to a conversation he overheard on an extension telephone with the consent of a party to the conversation. The present case, if anything, is even clearer, since in Rathbun it was conceded by all concerned "that either party may *record* the conversation and publish it." 355 U.S. at 110, 78 S.Ct. at 163. (Emphasis added.)

Stripped to its essentials, petitioner's argument amounts to saying that he has a constitutional right to rely on possible flaws in the agent's memory, or to challenge the agent's credibility without being beset by corroborating evidence that is not susceptible of impeachment. For no other argument can justify excluding an accurate version of a conversation that the agent could testify to from memory.[11] We think the risk that petitioner took in offering a bribe to Davis fairly included the risk that the offer would be accurately reproduced in court, whether by faultless memory or mechanical recording.

It is urged that whether or not the recording violated petitioner's constitutional rights, we should prevent its introduction in evidence in this federal trial in the exercise of our supervisory powers. But the court's inherent power to refuse to receive material evidence is a power that must be sparingly exercised. Its application in the present case, where there has been no manifestly improper conduct by federal officials, would be wholly unwarranted.[12]

11. [Footnotes by the Court.] The trustworthiness of the recording is not challenged.

12. Since Agent Davis himself testified to the conversation with petitioner which was the subject matter of the re-

The function of a criminal trial is to seek out and determine the truth or falsity of the charges brought against the defendant. Proper fulfillment of this function requires that, constitutional limitations aside, all relevant, competent evidence be admissible, unless the manner in which it has been obtained—for example, by violating some statute or rule of procedure—compels the formulation of a rule excluding its introduction in a federal court.

When we look for the overriding considerations that might require the exclusion of the highly useful evidence involved here, we find nothing. There has been no invasion of constitutionally protected rights, and no violation of federal law or rules of procedure. Indeed, there has not even been any electronic eavesdropping on a private conversation which government agents could not otherwise have overheard. There has, in short, been no act of any kind which could justify the creation of an exclusionary rule. We therefore conclude that the judgment of the Court of Appeals must be affirmed.

Affirmed.

MR. CHIEF JUSTICE WARREN, concurring in the result.

In concur in the result achieved by the Court but feel compelled to state my views separately. As pointed out in the dissenting opinion of Mr. Justice Brennan, the majority opinion may be interpreted as reaffirming *sub silentio* the result in On Lee v. United States, 343 U.S. 747, 72 S.Ct. 967, 96 L.Ed. 1270. Since I agree with Mr. Justice Brennan that On Lee was wrongly decided and should not be revitalized, but base my views on grounds different from those stated in the dissent, I have chosen to concur specially. Although the dissent assumes that this case and On Lee are in all respects the same, to me they are quite dissimilar constitutionally and from the viewpoint of what this Court should permit under its supervisory powers over the administration of criminal justice in the federal courts.

I also share the opinion of Mr. Justice Brennan that the fantastic advances in the field of electronic communication constitute a great danger to the privacy of the individual; that indiscriminate use of such devices in law enforcement raises grave constitutional questions under the Fourth and Fifth Amendments; and that these considerations impose a heavier responsibility on this Court in its supervision of the fairness of procedures in the federal court system. However, I do not believe that, as a result, all uses of such devices should be proscribed either as unconstitutional or as unfair law enforcement methods. One of the lines I would draw would be between this case and On Lee.

As MR. JUSTICE HARLAN sets out in greater detail, Agent Davis, upon entering the premises of the petitioner, gave full notice of both his authority and purpose—to investigate possible evasion or delin-

cording, the question whether there may be circumstances in which the use of such recordings in evidence should be limited to purposes of "corroboration" is not presented by this case.

quency in the payment of federal taxes. In the course of this investigation, the petitioner offered Davis a bribe and promised more in the future if Davis would conceal the facts of the petitioner's tax evasion. Davis accepted the money and promptly reported it to his superiors. On a return visit to the petitioner's place of business to complete the investigation, Davis was outfitted with a concealed recorder to tape his conversation with the petitioner. At trial, Davis testified to both of his conversations with the petitioner, and the tape recording was introduced to corroborate this testimony. The petitioner did not claim he was entrapped into the bribery or that the purpose of the investigation from the start was to induce the bribe. On the contrary, he admitted giving the money to Davis but claimed that it was for the purpose of having the latter prepare his tax return. The only purpose the recording served was to protect the credibility of Davis against that of a man who wished to corrupt a public servant in the performance of his public trust. I find nothing unfair in this procedure. . . .

MR. JUSTICE BRENNAN, with whom MR. JUSTICE DOUGLAS and MR. JUSTICE GOLDBERG join, dissenting.

In On Lee v. United States, 343 U.S. 747, 72 S.Ct. 967, 96 L.Ed. 1270, the Court sustained the admission in evidence of the testimony of a federal agent as to incriminating statements made by the accused, a laundryman, on trial for narcotics offenses. The statements were made by the accused while at large on bail pending trial in a conversation in his shop with an acquaintance and former employee, who, unknown to the accused, was a government informer and carried a radio transmitter concealed on his person. The federal agent, equipped with a radio receiver tuned to the transmitter, heard the transmitted conversation while standing on the sidewalk outside the laundry. The Court rejected arguments invoking the Fourth Amendment and our supervisory power against the admissibility of the agent's testimony. I believe that that decision was error, in reason and authority, at the time it was decided; that subsequent decisions and subsequent experience have sapped whatever vitality it may once have had; that it should now be regarded as overruled; that the instant case is rationally indistinguishable; and that, therefore, we should reverse the judgment below. . . .

(6) The Olmstead decision caused such widespread dissatisfaction that Congress in effect overruled it by enacting § 605 of the Federal Communications Act, which made wiretapping a federal crime. . . . The passive and the quiet, equally with the active and the aggressive, are entitled to protection when engaged in the precious activity of expressing ideas or beliefs. Electronic surveillance destroys all anonymity and all privacy; it makes government privy to everything that goes on.

In light of these circumstances I think it is an intolerable anomaly that while conventional searches and seizures are regulated by the

Fourth and Fourteenth Amendments and wiretapping is prohibited by federal statute, electronic surveillance as involved in the instant case, which poses the greatest danger to the right of private freedom, is wholly beyond the pale of federal law.[20] . . .

PEOPLE v. MAYBERRY

Supreme Court of California, In Bank, 1982.
31 Cal.3d 335, 182 Cal.Rptr. 617, 644 P.2d 810.

RICHARDSON, JUSTICE. May law enforcement officers use police-trained dogs to detect the odor of narcotics emanating from transported containers in the baggage areas of public airports? Under the circumstances herein presented we conclude that they may and that the limited and nonintrusive olfactory investigation performed in this case did not constitute a "search" thereby invoking the constitutional limitations imposed by the Fourth Amendment to the United States Constitution or article I, section 13, of the California Constitution. Accordingly, we will affirm defendant's judgment of conviction.

An amended information filed in the San Diego Superior Court December 12, 1979, charged defendant with: (1) transporting marijuana (Health & Saf.Code, § 11360, subd. (a)); (2) possessing marijuana for sale (id., § 11359); and (3) possessing concentrated cannabis (id., § 11357, subd. (a)).

Following the denial of defendant's motion to suppress under Penal Code section 1538.5, he entered a plea of guilty to the charge of transporting marijuana. He was given a three-year suspended sen-

20. Senator Hennings has termed electronic eavesdropping more insidious and more prevalent than wiretapping. The Wiretapping-Eavesdropping Problem: A Legislator's View, 44 Minn.L.Rev. 813, 815 (1960). Another observer has called the problem "far graver" than wiretapping. Williams, The Wiretapping-Eavesdropping Problem: A Defense Counsel's View, 44 Minn.L.Rev. 855, 862 (1960).

[Added by compiler.]

A government undercover agent transmitted to narcotics agents several conversations with the defendant that were held in various places. The testimony of the agents was held admissible. United States v. White, 401 U.S. 745, 91 S.Ct. 1122 (1971).

That evidence of a crime being committed, or to be committed, is recorded on tape without the knowledge of the wrongdoer does not constitute entrapment. United States v. Osborn, 350 F.2d 497 (6th Cir.1965).

There is a tendency to extend the statutory prohibition of wire tapping to bar electronic surveillance without physical contact. See West's Ann.Cal.Pen.Code, § 653j (now § 632) added in 1963. This was interpreted not to apply to a communication if such surveillance was with the consent of one of the parties. People v. Fontaine, 237 Cal.App.2d 320, 46 Cal. Rptr. 855 (1965).

"Neither the federal constitution nor state law requires the suppression of evidence obtained by the warrantless recording of a telephone conversation between a consenting police informant and a non-consenting defendant." State v. Geraldo, 68 Ohio St.2d 120, 429 N.E.2d 141, 142 (1981).

A tape recording of a conversation between conspirators, in the office of one after the other had agreed to co-operate with the police, may be used to corroborate the testimony of the accomplice. What was said was not mere evidence of crime; it was an attempt to procure subornation of perjury and hence was itself a crime. United States v. Mancusi, 370 F.2d 601 (2d Cir.1967).

tence with 60 days' confinement, and required to register pursuant to Health and Safety Code section 11590 and to submit to other conditions of probation. Defendant appeals from the denial of the section 1538.5 motion to suppress.

On August 8, 1979, Officers Cooper and Flores of the San Diego Police Department's Narcotics Task Force (NTF) were on duty in the nonpublic portion of the baggage area at the San Diego Airport. With full permission of the airport authority and the airlines, Officer Cooper, assisted by a fully trained and qualified narcotics dog, "Corky," was checking, for evidence of narcotics, all luggage from certain inbound aircraft flights originating in Florida. Defendant, flying to San Diego from Dayton, Ohio, at the Dallas-Fort Worth Airport had boarded a flight originating in Miami. The officers had no previous information that defendant's luggage contained any contraband, nor was there any other reason to be suspicious of his luggage.

After Corky "alerted" to defendant's suitcase, an identifying tape was placed on it and it was transported to the baggage claim area with the rest of the luggage from the flight. When defendant picked up the suitcase, Officer Cooper identified himself and requested that defendant accompany him to an airport office for an investigation. Defendant agreed, and after having been informed of Corky's "alert," was asked to consent to a search of his luggage. Defendant orally agreed, but before he signed a written consent form Officer Cooper told him that the officer had never failed to get a warrant under similar circumstances. Defendant was advised of his *Miranda* rights; the suitcase was opened and found to contain marijuana.

The trial court made the following findings:

1. On the day in question, law enforcement officers and Corky were allowed to be anywhere at the airport including the baggage handling areas.

2. Both Corky and his handler, Officer Cooper, were fully trained in narcotics detection.

3. Based on information as to the flow of narcotics from Florida to San Diego, the agents had reason to believe narcotics could be found in the luggage of incoming passengers from planes originating in Florida.

4. Law enforcement officers did not have specific information regarding defendant.

5. The sniffing of the luggage by Corky in the baggage area, and away from public view, was a minimal intrusion justified by the agents' reasonable efforts to protect the public from the flow of narcotics from Florida.

6. The use of Corky to alert the agents to the suitcase was reasonable.

7. Defendant voluntarily consented to a search of his suitcase after being contacted by law enforcement.

8. The motion to suppress should be denied.

To the extent these findings resolve questions of fact, they must be upheld on appeal if supported by substantial evidence; yet we exercise our independent judgment in reviewing the legal question whether the officer's conduct was reasonable under the Constitution. (See People v. Leyba (1981) 29 Cal.3d 591, 596–597, 174 Cal.Rptr. 867, 629 P.2d 961.)

The NTF justifies its search of all luggage off incoming flights originating in Florida on its experience with a "high" frequency of narcotics seizures in luggage from such flights. During 1979, 25 narcotics cases involved incoming flights to San Diego. Of those 25 cases, 14, or 56 percent, were from flights originating in Florida. During the same period there were 5 flights a day from Florida to San Diego, or a total of 1,825 flights. Accordingly, less than 1 percent of these (approximately .76 percent) of such flights were found to have narcotics aboard. The record also demonstrates that the NTF has established excellent contacts in Florida, both among law enforcement officers and informants.

Defendant contends that Corky's smelling of his luggage constituted an unreasonable exploratory search. His claim is supported by several California appellate cases which have invalidated similar canine procedures unless preceded by prior information or a reasonable suspicion that narcotics may be present in the subject area. Defendant argues that, standing alone, statistics disclosing a high relative frequency of drug traffic from Florida afford an insufficient basis for subjecting his luggage to an exploratory warrantless sniff.

All of the foregoing cases are premised upon the proposition that similar canine olfactory investigations constituted a "search," the propriety of which would be governed by Fourth Amendment principles. A recent appellate case, however, People v. Matthews (1980) 112 Cal.App.3d 11, 19–20, 169 Cal.Rptr. 263, noting a series of recent contrary federal decisions, has cast doubt upon this conclusion. In upholding a warrantless sniff of narcotics at a Long Beach storage terminal, the *Matthews* court observed, "The use of narcotic trained detector dogs is not uncommon, and federal courts have . . . held that sniffing the air surrounding an object *is neither an intrusion nor a search.*" (P. 19, 169 Cal.Rptr. 263, italics added.) There is substantial authority supporting this conclusion.

We recognize that one recent federal case has departed from the foregoing line of authorities and has held that the use of trained police dogs to sniff luggage is a search for Fourth Amendment purposes. (United States v. Beale (9th Cir.1982) 674 F.2d 1327). No petition for certiorari has yet been filed in *Beale,* and, with due respect, we disagree with its conclusion. *Beale* stressed the sanctity of private luggage, and opined that "One who reposes his personal effects, *including contraband,* in a locked suitcase is surely entitled to assume that a trained canine will not broadcast its incriminating contents to the authorities." (P. 1334 [filed opn., at p. 11], italics added.) To the contrary, one who secrets illegal narcotics in his suitcase has no *protectible* privacy interest in those narcotics, nor any legitimate objection to an unintrusive method of detection which reacts *only* to such contraband. As *Beale* itself acknowledges, detection of narcotics by trained sniffer dogs is a "minimal invasion of privacy," involving "no risk that an innocent person's privacy will be intruded upon." (P. 1334, quoting from earlier authorities.)

It is commonly accepted that a "search" is a governmental intrusion upon, or invasion of, a citizen's personal security in an area in which he has a reasonable expectation of privacy. Most of the foregoing federal cases have concluded that dog-sniffing investigations of the type here employed are neither intrusions nor invasions of anyone's reasonable expectation of privacy. The courts so holding have stressed that such procedures involve no physical entry into one's home or possessions, or invasion of one's person, or use of mechanical or electronic equipment, or examination of, or prying into, one's private communications or noncriminal personal affairs. Additionally, as the Second Circuit Court of Appeals stressed in *Bronstein,* supra, police dogs are trained to "alert" or react *only to contraband,* unlike mechanical investigatory aids or devices (magnetometers, telescopes, recorders etc.) which intrude in sweeping and *indiscriminate* fashion into one's private affairs and personal effects. (521 F.2d at p. 463.

Did Corky breach any reasonable, protectible expectation of privacy as to any odors emanating from defendant's concealed contraband? We think not. Rather, we share the views recently expressed by the Fifth Circuit Court of Appeals in *Goldstein,* supra. In rejecting such expectation, it held that although an airline passenger may reasonably anticipate that the *contents* of his luggage will not be exposed in the absence of consent or a search warrant, "the passenger's reasonable expectation of privacy does not extend to the airspace surrounding that luggage" (stressing that narcotic-trained dogs are used "in response to the need to control the rise in illegal drug trafficking, while preserving, at the same time, an airline passenger's reasonable expectation of privacy.")

In our view, the escaping smell of contraband from luggage may be likened to the emanation of a fluid leaking from a container. The odor is detectable by the nose, as the leak is visible to the eye. We discern no constitutionally significant difference in the manner of escape, and conclude that any privacy right is lost when either escapes into the surrounding area. Given Corky's training, our conclusion is not altered by the fact that it is his nose and not his handler's which detected the odor.

From the foregoing, we conclude that, at least within the context of an airport luggage search, passengers (and others transporting narcotics) have no reasonable expectation of privacy which would preclude the use of sniffer dogs such as Corky even when there is an absence of prior specific suspicion that narcotics are present.

We add two cautionary notes. Prior appellate cases quite properly have required an adequate demonstration of the dog's training and experience in narcotics detection before the dog's reaction to a particular suitcase or other object is admitted into evidence. Such condition was met in the present case, as reflected in the trial court's findings, and defendant does not challenge this.

Moreover, as the People readily acknowledge, a police dog's positive reaction to a suitcase ordinarily is not sufficient cause to search and seize it without a warrant. In the absence of either *exigent circumstances or consent* by the owner, the investigating officers must first obtain a search warrant upon a proper showing of probable cause.

The trial court found that defendant had consented to a search of his luggage after Corky "alerted" to the presence of narcotics therein. Although defendant maintains that his consent was involuntary, being a "mere submission to authority," this was a factual matter which the trial court, in light of all the circumstances, resolved adversely to defendant. Nor, in our view, was the defendant's consent to the search nullified by the officer's comment to defendant that a search warrant could readily be obtained. Rather, our review of the record discloses substantial evidence supporting the trial court's finding of consent.

The judgment is affirmed.[1]

MOSK, NEWMAN, KAUS and BROUSSARD, JJ., concur.

BIRD, CHIEF JUSTICE, dissenting.

A rose by any other name would *not* make this a "plain smell" case. The odor which the dog Corky perceived was *not* "detectable by the nose" of any police officer. In holding that no search occurs when the government uses specially trained animals to detect that which is undetectable to human senses, the majority casts its lot with

1. "Third, the state has not touched on the question whether it would have been feasible to investigate the contents of Royer's bags in a more expeditious way. The courts are not strangers to the use of trained dogs to detect the presence of controlled substances in luggage. There is no indication here that this means was not feasible and available. If it had been used, Royer and his luggage could have been momentarily detained while this investigative procedure was carried out. Indeed, it may be that no detention at all would have been necessary. A negative result would have freed Royer in short order; a positive result would have resulted in his justifiable arrest on probable cause." The Court said the facts would appear to show at least reasonable suspicion and the use of a sniffer dog would have been proper. Florida v. Royer, ___ U.S. ___, 103 S.Ct. 1319, 1328–29 (1983).

Subsequently the court held the detention of a suspect's luggage on reasonable suspicion it contained contraband and the use of a sniffer dog to determine if a prohibited substance was contained therein was proper, although the detention for a period of 90 minutes, under the circumstances, was improper. United States v. Place, ___ U.S. ___, 103 S.Ct. 2637 (1983).

a number of courts, mostly federal, whose decisions on this issue have been justly criticized as "short on reasoning" and "unsound."

It is neither wise nor necessary for this court to join this "unfortunate tendency." Unwise, because the "[t]otally unrestrained use of trained dogs . . . would not be consistent with the kind of open society to which we are committed. It would be intolerable if the police, in no way limited by the Fourth Amendment, were free to utilize dogs to undertake 'a wholesale examination of all baggage in the hope that a crime might be detected' or 'to roam the streets at will with trained dogs or sensor instruments, detecting the odor of marijuana and arresting persons at will as a result.'"

Nor is today's holding justified by logic or precedent. The majority's conclusion has been rejected by virtually all of the commentators nationwide and is a sharp, unexplained break with a consistent line of decisions by the courts of appeal of this state.

I must respectfully dissent.

. . .

SECTION 4. RIGHTS AS TO THE TIME OF TRIAL

When the defendant has been indicted or informed against, has been arraigned and has entered his plea of not guilty (or had this plea entered for him by the court), the proceedings are in shape for trial. But although the proceedings are ready for trial the parties may not be. Two rights inhere in the defendant which protect him on both sides in this regard. The first of these is the right to a speedy trial; the other is the right not to be forced to trial until he has had due time for preparation.

The right of a person charged with a public offense to demand a speedy trial dates back to Magna Carta. A "speedy trial" does not mean a trial forthwith.[1] The machinery of justice is not so adapted that every person accused of crime can be tried on the very day he is taken into custody under an indictment or information,—or on the day the formal charge is filed if he is in custody at that time. Due regard must be given to the terms of court, in other than metropolitan areas. More than this, the prosecution is entitled to a reasonable time to prepare its case and get ready for trial. The purpose of this right is not to embarrass the prosecuting officer in the performance of his duty, but only to prevent unreasonable imprisonment without trial, which was anciently a means of great oppression. The defendant cannot insist that his trial be set at a date too early to allow a

1. For a note on the right to speedy trial see 21 L.Ed.2d 905 (1969).

An unexplained delay of 140 days between the filing of a misdemeanor complaint for a traffic violation and **D**'s arrest was an unreasonable deprivation of his right to a speedy trial, and a writ of prohibition was issued to bar the prosecution. Rost v. Municipal Court, 184 Cal. App.2d 507, 7 Cal.Rptr. 869, 85 A.L.R.2d 974 (1960).

reasonable opportunity to prepare the case against him.[2] Even after the date is set if, without the fault of the prosecution, delay becomes necessary in order to procure the attendance of material witnesses, or for some other proper purpose, a reasonable continuance will be granted. But negligence or want of due diligence in the preparation of its case will not entitle the prosecution to a delay in the setting of the case for trial or for a postponement of the date after it has been set.

At common law there was nothing to prevent the prosecution from putting the defendant on trial immediately after his arraignment unless he could show sufficient cause for a continuance. Statutes frequently entitle a defendant to a certain period after his plea is entered (such as three days or five days) without any showing on his part. And with or without such a statutory provision he will be given such reasonable time as he can show is necessary for the preparation of his defense. Upon proper showing he will be entitled to a continuance even after the date for the trial has been set. He is not entitled to a continuance just for the purpose of delay, but courts are reluctant to force a defendant to a criminal trial for which he insists he is not ready.

The first comprehensive analysis of the Sixth Amendment right to a speedy trial is found in Barker v. Wingo, 407 U.S. 514, 92 S.Ct. 2182 (1972). More than five years had elapsed between the arrest and the trial, but the Court held that under the circumstances of this case the right to a speedy trial had been waived or in any event did not result in prejudice. The Court's opinion made it clear that any detailed implementation of the right would need to be made by legislation rather than by judicial decision. This was followed by the Speedy Trial Act of 1974, 18 U.S.C. § 3161 et seq., 88 Stat. 2076 et seq. The time specified for the various steps of the prosecution, together with numerous periods of delay that are excluded in computing the time, are detailed at length in 18 U.S.C. § 3161.

If a federal prisoner is not indicted within the stipulated time the prosecution is dismissed. If the indictment is in time but the defendant is not brought to trial within the stipulated time he may move for a dismissal. If the prosecution is dismissed this may be either with prejudice or without prejudice depending upon the facts of the particular case. 18 U.S.C. § 3162.

In Barker v. Wingo, reported below, the Court made it clear that if the constitutional right to speedy trial should be implemented in the form of a time schedule, this could not be done by the Court but would require an Act of Congress. Congress carried out this sugges-

2. The Federal Speedy Trial Act, 18 U.S.C.A. § 1361 (1979) provides statutory standards within which a defendant must be brought to trial. The failure to meet the statutory time periods may result in the dismissal of the prosecution. The statutory time frame is generally more demanding than federal constitutional requirements. See Frase, The Speedy Trial Act of 1974, 43 U.Chi.L.Rev. 667 (1976); Misner, The 1979 Amendments to the Speedy Trial Act, 32 Hast.L.J. 635 (1981).

tion by enacting the Speedy Trial Act of 1974, which as amended, now appears as 18 U.S.C. Chapter 208—Speedy Trial. This specifies in detail the time limits for the various steps of the prosecution. If no indictment or information is filed within the time limit, the complaint shall be dismissed, with or without prejudice depending upon the circumstances. If the defendant is not brought to trial within the time limit, he may move that it be dismissed. Which also may be with or without prejudice. Failure to move for a dismissal constitutes a waiver of the right to dismiss. This statute applies only to federal prosecutions, but some states have their own provisions for speedy trial.[1]

BARKER v. WINGO

Supreme Court of the United States, 1972.
407 U.S. 514, 92 S.Ct. 2182.

MR. JUSTICE POWELL delivered the opinion of the Court.

Although a speedy trial is guaranteed the accused by the Sixth Amendment to the Constitution, this Court has dealt with that right on infrequent occasions. The Court's opinion in Klopfer v. North Carolina, 386 U.S. 213, 87 S.Ct. 988, 18 L.Ed.2d 1 (1967), established that the right to a speedy trial is "fundamental" and is imposed by the Due Process Clause of the Fourteenth Amendment on the States. As Mr. Justice Brennan pointed out in his concurring opinion in *Dickey,* in none of these cases have we attempted to set out the criteria by which the speedy trial right is to be judged. This case compels us to make such an attempt.

I

On July 20, 1958, in Christian County, Kentucky, an elderly couple was beaten to death by intruders wielding an iron tire tool. Two suspects, Silas Manning and Willie Barker, the petitioner, were arrested shortly thereafter. The grand jury indicted them on September 15. Counsel was appointed on September 17, and Barker's trial was set for October 21. The Commonwealth had a stronger case against Manning, and it believed that Barker could not be convicted unless Manning testified against him. Manning was naturally unwilling to incriminate himself. Accordingly, on October 23, the day Silas Manning was brought to trial, the Commonwealth sought and obtained the first of what was to be a series of 16 continuances of Barker's trial. Barker made no objection. By first convicting Manning, the Commonwealth would remove possible problems of self-incrimination and would be able to assure his testimony against Barker.

The Commonwealth encountered more than a few difficulties in its prosecution of Manning. The first trial ended in a hung jury. A sec-

1. See, e.g., Iowa Criminal Code § 812.2, Rule 27 (1978).

ond trial resulted in a conviction, but the Kentucky Court of Appeals reversed because of the admission of evidence obtained by an illegal search. At his third trial, Manning was again convicted, and the Court of Appeals again reversed because the trial court had not granted a change of venue. A fourth trial resulted in a hung jury. Finally, after five trials, Manning was convicted, in March 1962, of murdering one victim, and after a sixth trial, in December 1962, he was convicted of murdering the other.

The Christian County Circuit Court holds three terms each year—in February, June, and September. Barker's initial trial was to take place in the September term of 1958. The first continuance postponed it until the February 1959 term. The second continuance was granted for one month only. Every term thereafter for as long as the Manning prosecutions were in process, the Commonwealth routinely moved to continue Barker's case to the next term. When the case was continued from the June 1959 term until the following September, Barker, having spent 10 months in jail, obtained his release by posting a $5,000 bond. He thereafter remained free in the community until his trial. Barker made no objection, through his counsel, to the first 11 continuances.

When on February 12, 1962, the Commonwealth moved for the twelfth time to continue the case until the following term, Barker's counsel filed a motion to dismiss the indictment. The motion to dismiss was denied two weeks later, and the Commonwealth's motion for a continuance was granted. The Commonwealth was granted further continuances in June 1962 and September 1962, to which Barker did not object.

In February 1963, the first term of court following Manning's final conviction, the Commonwealth moved to set Barker's trial for March 19. But on the day scheduled for trial, it again moved for a continuance until the June term. It gave as its reason the illness of the ex-sheriff who was the chief investigating officer in the case. To this continuance, Barker objected unsuccessfully.

The witness was still unable to testify in June, and the trial, which had been set for June 19, was continued again until the September term over Barker's objection. This time the court announced that the case would be dismissed for lack of prosecution if it were not tried during the next term. The final trial date was set for October 9, 1963. On that date, Barker again moved to dismiss the indictment, and this time specified that his right to a speedy trial had been violated. The motion was denied; the trial commenced with Manning as the chief prosecution witness; Barker was convicted and given a life sentence.

Barker appealed his conviction to the Kentucky Court of Appeals, relying in part on his speedy trial claim. The court affirmed. In February 1970 Barker petitioned for habeas corpus in the United States District Court for the Western District of Kentucky. Although the District Court rejected the petition without holding a hearing, the court granted petitioner leave to appeal *in forma pauperis* and a certificate of probable cause to appeal. On appeal, the Court of Appeals for the Sixth Circuit affirmed. . . .

II

The right to a speedy trial is generically different from any of the other rights enshrined in the Constitution for the protection of the accused. In addition to the general concern that all accused persons be treated according to decent and fair procedures, there is a societal interest in providing a speedy trial which exists separate from, and at times in opposition to, the interests of the accused. . . .

A second difference between the right to speedy trial and the accused's other constitutional rights is that deprivation of the right may work to the accused's advantage. Delay is not an uncommon defense tactic. As the time between the commission of the crime and trial lengthens, witnesses may become unavailable or their memories may fade. If the witnesses support the prosecution, its case will be weakened, sometimes seriously so. . . .

Finally, and perhaps most importantly, the right to speedy trial is a more vague concept than other procedural rights. It is, for example, impossible to determine with precision when the right has been denied. We cannot definitely say how long is too long in a system where justice is supposed to be swift but deliberate.[15] As a consequence, there is no fixed point in the criminal process when the State can put the defendant to the choice of either exercising or waiving the right to a speedy trial. If, for example, the State moves for a 60-day continuance, granting that continuance is not a violation of the right to speedy trial unless the circumstances of the case are such that further delay would endanger the values the right protects. It is impossible to do more than generalize about when those circumstances exist. There is nothing comparable to the point in the process when a defendant exercises or waives his right to counsel or his right to a jury trial. . . .

The amorphous quality of the right also leads to the unsatisfactorily severe remedy of dismissal of the indictment when the right has been deprived. This is indeed a serious consequence because it means that a defendant who may be guilty of a serious crime will go free, without having been tried. Such a remedy is more serious than an exclusionary rule or a reversal for a new trial, but it is the only possible remedy.

15. "[I]n large measure because of the many procedural safeguards provided an accused, the ordinary procedures for criminal prosecution are designed to move at a deliberate pace. A requirement of unreasonable speed would have a deleterious effect both upon the rights of the accused and upon the ability of society to protect itself." United States v. Ewell, 383 U.S. 116, 120, 86 S.Ct. 773, 776, 15 L.Ed.2d 627 (1966).

III

Perhaps because the speedy trial right is so slippery, two rigid approaches are urged upon us as ways of eliminating some of the uncertainty which courts experience in protecting the right. The first suggestion is that we hold that the Constitution requires a criminal defendant to be offered a trial within a specified time period. The result of such a ruling would have the virtue of clarifying when the right is infringed and of simplifying courts' application of it. Recognizing this, some legislatures have enacted laws, and some courts have adopted procedural rules which more narrowly define the right.[17] The United States Court of Appeals for the Second Circuit has promulgated rules for the district courts in that Circuit establishing that the government must be ready for trial within six months of the date of arrest, except in unusual circumstances, or the charge will be dismissed.[18] This type of rule is also recommended by the American Bar Association.

But such a result would require this Court to engage in legislative or rulemaking activity, rather than in the adjudicative process to which we should confine our efforts. We do not establish procedural rules for the States, except when mandated by the Constitution. We find no constitutional basis for holding that the speedy trial right can be quantified into a specified number of days or months. The States, of course, are free to prescribe a reasonable period consistent with constitutional standards, but our approach must be less precise.

The second suggested alternative would restrict consideration of the right to those cases in which the accused has demanded a speedy trial. . . .

We reject, therefore, the rule that a defendant who fails to demand a speedy trial forever waives his right. This does not mean, however, that the defendant has no responsibility to assert his right. We think the better rule is that the defendant's assertion of or failure to assert his right to a speedy trial is one of the factors to be considered in an inquiry into the deprivation of the right. . . .

We, therefore, reject both of the inflexible approaches—the fixed-time period because it goes further than the Constitution requires; the demand-waiver rule because it is insensitive to a right which we have deemed fundamental. The approach we accept is a balancing test, in which the conduct of both the prosecution and the defendant are weighed.

17. For examples, see American Bar Association Project on Standards for Criminal Justice, Speedy Trial 14–16 (Approved Draft 1968); Note, The Right to a Speedy Criminal Trial, 57 Col.L.Rev. 846, 863 (1957).

18. Second Circuit Rules Regarding Prompt Disposition of Criminal Cases (1971).

IV

A balancing test necessarily compels courts to approach speedy trial cases on an *ad hoc* basis. We can do little more than identify some of the factors which courts should assess in determining whether a particular defendant has been deprived of his right. Though some might express them in different ways, we identify four such factors: Length of delay, the reason for the delay, the defendant's assertion of his right, and prejudice to the defendant.

The length of the delay is to some extent a triggering mechanism. Until there is some delay which is presumptively prejudicial, there is no necessity for inquiry into the other factors that go into the balance. Nevertheless, because of the imprecision of the right to speedy trial, the length of delay that will provoke such an inquiry is necessarily dependent upon the peculiar circumstances of the case. To take but one example, the delay that can be tolerated for an ordinary street crime is considerably less than for a serious, complex conspiracy charge.

Closely related to length of delay is the reason the government assigns to justify the delay. Here, too, different weights should be assigned to different reasons. A deliberate attempt to delay the trial in order to hamper the defense should be weighted heavily against the government.[32] A more neutral reason such as negligence or overcrowded courts should be weighted less heavily but nevertheless should be considered since the ultimate responsibility for such circumstances must rest with the government rather than with the defendant. Finally, a valid reason, such as a missing witness, should serve to justify appropriate delay.

We have already discussed the third factor, the defendant's responsibility to assert his right. Whether and how a defendant asserts his right is closely related to the other factors we have mentioned. The strength of his efforts will be affected by the length of the delay, to some extent by the reason for the delay, and most particularly by the personal prejudice, which is not always readily identifiable, that he experiences. The more serious the deprivation, the more likely a defendant is to complain. The defendant's assertion of his speedy trial right, then, is entitled to strong evidentiary weight in determining whether the defendant is being deprived of the right. We emphasize that failure to assert the right will make it difficult for a defendant to prove that he was denied a speedy trial.

A fourth factor is prejudice to the defendant. Prejudice, of course, should be assessed in the light of the interests of defendants

32. Note by the Court. We have indicated on previous occasions that it is improper for the prosecution intentionally to delay "to gain some tactical advantage over [defendants] or to harass them." United States v. Marion, 404 U.S. 307, 325, 92 S.Ct. 455, 466, 30 L.Ed.2d 468 (1971). See Pollard v. United States, 352 U.S. 354, 361, 77 S.Ct. 481, 485–486, 1 L.Ed.2d 393 (1957).

which the speedy trial right was designed to protect. This Court has identified three such interests: (i) to prevent oppressive pretrial incarceration; (ii) to minimize anxiety and concern of the accused; and (iii) to limit the possibility that the defense will be impaired. Of these, the most serious is the last, because the inability of a defendant adequately to prepare his case skews the fairness of the entire system. If witnesses die or disappear during a delay, the prejudice is obvious. There is also prejudice if defense witnesses are unable to recall accurately events of the distant past. Loss of memory, however, is not always reflected in the record because what has been forgotten can rarely be shown. . . .

. . . Finally, even if an accused is not incarcerated prior to trial, he is still disadvantaged by restraints on his liberty and by living under a cloud of anxiety, suspicion, and often hostility.

We regard none of the four factors identified above as either a necessary or sufficient condition to the finding of a deprivation of the right of speedy trial. Rather, they are related factors and must be considered together with such other circumstances as may be relevant. In sum, these factors have no talismanic qualities; courts must still engage in a difficult and sensitive balancing process. But, because we are dealing with a fundamental right of the accused, this process must be carried out with full recognition that the accused's interest in a speedy trial is specifically affirmed in the Constitution.

V

The difficulty of the task of balancing these factors is illustrated by this case, which we consider to be close. It is clear that the length of delay between arrest and trial—well over five years—was extraordinary. Only seven months of that period can be attributed to a strong excuse, the illness of the ex-sheriff who was in charge of the investigation. Perhaps some delay would have been permissible under ordinary circumstances, so that Manning could be utilized as a witness in Barker's trial, but more than four years was too long a period, particularly since a good part of that period was attributable to the Commonwealth's failure or inability to try Manning under circumstances that comported with due process.

Two counterbalancing factors, however, outweigh these deficiencies. The first is that prejudice was minimal. Of course, Barker was prejudiced to some extent by living for over four years under a cloud of suspicion and anxiety. Moreover, although he was released on bond for most of the period, he did spend 10 months in jail before trial. But there is no claim that any of Barker's witnesses died or otherwise became unavailable owing to the delay. The trial transcript indicates only two very minor lapses of memory—one on the part of a prosecution witness—which were in no way significant to the outcome.

More important than the absence of serious prejudice, is the fact that Barker did not want a speedy trial. . . .

We do not hold that there may never be a situation in which an indictment may be dismissed on speedy trial grounds where the defendant has failed to object to continuances. There may be a situation in which the defendant was represented by incompetent counsel, was severely prejudiced, or even cases in which the continuances were granted *ex parte*. But barring extraordinary circumstances, we would be reluctant indeed to rule that a defendant was denied this constitutional right on a record that strongly indicates, as does this one, that the defendant did not want a speedy trial. We hold, therefore, that Barker was not deprived of his due process right to a speedy trial.

The judgment of the Court of Appeals is affirmed.

Affirmed.[a]

SECTION 5. RIGHT TO BE PRESENT DURING TRIAL

In all criminal prosecutions the defendant has a right to be present in person during the proceeding from arraignment to sentence unless he has waived or forfeited it. A statute denying this right would be an unconstitutional violation of due process.

Many variations are found in the statute dealing with this subject. Most of them provide that the defendant must be "personally present" if the prosecution is for a felony. A number of them authorize the defendant to appear by counsel for arraignment in a misdemeanor case and provide that the trial may be had in his absence. A few provide that if the defendant escapes after any trial has commenced it may continue to verdict. Rule 43 of the Federal Rules of Criminal Procedure reads:

a. A state has some speedy-trial responsibility even as to a defendant currently incarcerated beyond its borders. Upon request, the other jurisdiction (state or federal) may make arrangements for the defendant to be present for trial. And the state has the duty to make such request whenever defendant has manifested a desire for a speedy trial. Smith v. Hooey, 393 U.S. 374, 89 S.Ct. 575 (1969).

Although delay prior to arrest or indictment may give rise to a due process claim under the Fifth Amendment, no Sixth Amendment right to a speedy trial arises until charges are pending. United States v. MacDonald, 456 U.S. 1, 102 S.Ct. 1497 (1982).

See Annotation, Accused's Right of Speedy Trial Under the Federal Constitution—Supreme Court Cases, 71 L.Ed.2d 983 (1983).

The Sixth Amendment right to a speedy trial does not apply until the arrest or charging of the defendant. United States v. Marion, 404 U.S. 307, 92 S.Ct. 455 (1971). However, preindictment delay may violate due process if the delay results in prejudice to the defendant and was for the purpose of gaining tactical advantage for the prosecution. United States v. Lovasco, 431 U.S. 783, 97 S.Ct. 2044 (1977).

Rule 43. Presence of the Defendant.

(a) Presence Required. The defendant shall be present at the arraignment, at the time of the plea, at every stage of the trial including the impaneling of the jury and the return of the verdict, and at the imposition of sentence, except as otherwise provided by this rule.

(b) Continued Presence Not Required. The further progress of the trial to and including the return of the verdict shall not be prevented and the defendant shall be considered to have waived his right to be present whenever a defendant, initially present,

(1) voluntarily absents himself after the trial has commenced (whether or not he has been informed by the court of his obligation to remain during the trial), or

(2) after being warned by the court that disruptive conduct will cause him to be removed from the courtroom, persists in conduct which is such as to justify his being removed from the courtroom.

(c) Presence Not Required. A defendant need not be present in the following situations:

(1) A corporation may appear by counsel for all purposes.

(2) In prosecutions for offenses punishable by fine or by imprisonment for not more than one year or both, the court, with the written consent of the defendant, may permit arraignment, plea, trial, and imposition of sentence in the defendant's absence.

(3) At a conference or argument upon a question of law.

(4) At a reduction of sentence under Rule 35.[1]

ILLINOIS v. ALLEN

Supreme Court of the United States, 1970.
397 U.S. 337, 90 S.Ct. 1057.

[Allen, on trial for armed robbery, engaged in speech and conduct so noisy, disorderly and disruptive that it was impossible to carry on the trial. After several warnings that he would be removed from the courtroom if such tactics were continued, he was removed and was not present during much of the trial. He was convicted and the conviction was affirmed by the Supreme Court of Illinois. He then filed a petition for a writ of habeas corpus in the federal district court. Finding no constitutional violation the district court refused to issue the writ. The Court of Appeals reversed and the case was taken to the Supreme Court.]

MR. JUSTICE BLACK delivered the opinion of the Court. . . .

1. For a summary of the statutes see American Law Institute, Code of Criminal Procedure 878–887 (official draft with commentaries, 1930).

The Confrontation Clause of the Sixth Amendment to the United States Constitution provides that "In all criminal prosecutions, the accused shall enjoy the right . . . to be confronted with the witnesses against him . . . ." We have held that the Fourteenth Amendment makes the guarantees of this clause obligatory upon the States. Pointer v. Texas, 380 U.S. 400, 85 S.Ct. 1065, 13 L.Ed.2d 923 (1965). One of the most basic of the rights guaranteed by the Confrontation Clause is the accused's right to be present in the courtroom at every stage of his trial. Lewis v. United States, 146 U.S. 370, 13 S.Ct. 136, 36 L.Ed. 1011 (1892). The question presented in this case is whether an accused can claim the benefit of this constitutional right to remain in the courtroom while at the same time he engages in speech and conduct which is so noisy, disorderly, and disruptive that it is exceedingly difficult or wholly impossible to carry on the trial. . . .

The Court of Appeals felt that the defendant's Sixth Amendment right to be present at his own trial was so "absolute" that, no matter how unruly or disruptive the defendant's conduct might be, he could never be held to have lost that right so long as he continued to insist upon it, as Allen clearly did. Therefore the Court of Appeals concluded that a trial judge could never expel a defendant from his own trial and that the judge's ultimate remedy when faced with an obstreperous defendant like Allen who determines to make his trial impossible is to bind and gag him.[1] We cannot agree that the Sixth Amendment, the cases upon which the Court of Appeals relied, or any other cases of this Court so handicap a trial judge in conducting a criminal trial. The broad dicta in Hopt v. Utah, supra, and Lewis v. United States, 146 U.S. 370, 13 S.Ct. 136, 36 L.Ed. 1011 (1892), that a trial can never continue in the defendant's absence has been expressly rejected. Diaz v. United States, 223 U.S. 442, 32 S.Ct. 250, 56 L.Ed. 500 (1912). We accept instead the statement of Mr. Justice Cardozo who, speaking for the Court in Snyder v. Massachusetts, 291 U.S. 97, 106, 54 S.Ct. 330, 332, 78 L.Ed. 674 (1938), said: "No doubt the privilege [of personally confronting witnesses] may be lost by consent or at times even by misconduct."[2] Although mindful that courts must indulge every reasonable presumption against the loss of constitutional rights, we explicitly hold today that a defendant can lose his right to be present at trial if, after he has been warned by the judge that he will be removed if he continues his disruptive behavior, he nevertheless insists on conducting himself in a manner so disorderly, disruptive, and disrespectful of the court that his trial cannot be carried on with him in the courtroom. Once lost, the right to be present can, of

1. In a footnote the Court of Appeals also referred to the trial judge's contempt power. This subject is discussed in Part II of this opinion. Infra, at 1061.

2. Rule 43 of the Federal Rules of Criminal Procedure provides that

"[i]n prosecutions for offenses not punishable by death, the defendant's voluntary absence after the trial has been commenced in his presence shall not prevent continuing the trial to and including the return of the verdict."

course, be reclaimed as soon as the defendant is willing to conduct himself consistently with the decorum and respect inherent in the concept of courts and judicial proceedings.

It is essential to the proper administration of criminal justice that dignity, order, and decorum be the hallmarks of all court proceedings in our country. The flagrant disregard in the courtroom of elementary standards of proper conduct should not and cannot be tolerated. We believe trial judges confronted with disruptive, contumacious, stubbornly defiant defendants must be given sufficient discretion to meet the circumstances of each case. No one formula for maintaining the appropriate courtroom atmosphere will be best in all situations. We think there are at least three constitutionally permissible ways for a trial judge to handle an obstreperous defendant like Allen: (1) bind and gag him, thereby keeping him present; (2) cite him for contempt; (3) take him out of the courtroom until he promises to conduct himself properly. . . .

The trial court in this case decided under the circumstances to remove the defendant from the courtroom and to continue his trial in his absence until and unless he promises to conduct himself in a manner befitting an American courtroom. As we said earlier, we find nothing unconstitutional about this procedure. Allen's behavior was clearly of such an extreme and aggravated nature as to justify either his removal from the courtroom or his total physical restraint. Prior to his removal he was repeatedly warned by the trial judge that he would be removed from the courtroom if he persisted in his unruly conduct, and, as Judge Hastings observed in his dissenting opinion, the record demonstrates that Allen would not have been at all dissuaded by the trial judge's use of his criminal contempt powers. Allen was constantly informed that he could return to the trial when he would agree to conduct himself in an orderly manner. Under these circumstances we hold that Allen lost his right guaranteed by the Sixth and Fourteenth Amendments to be present throughout his trial.

It is not pleasant to hold that the respondent Allen was properly banished from the court for a part of his own trial. But our courts, palladiums of liberty as they are, cannot be treated disrespectfully with impunity. Nor can the accused be permitted by his disruptive conduct indefinitely to avoid being tried on the charges brought against him. It would degrade our country and our judicial system to permit our courts to be bullied, insulted, and humiliated and their orderly progress thwarted and obstructed by defendants brought before them charged with crimes. As guardians of the public welfare, our state and federal judicial systems strive to administer equal justice to the rich and the poor, the good and the bad, the native and foreign born of every race, nationality and religion. Being manned by humans, the courts are not perfect and are bound to make some errors. But, if our courts are to remain what the Founders intended, the citadels of justice, their proceedings cannot and must not be infected with the sort of scurrilous, abusive language and conduct paraded before the Illinois trial judge in this case. The record shows that the Illinois judge at all times conducted himself with that dignity, decorum, and patience that befits a judge. Even in holding that the trial judge had erred, the Court of Appeals praised his "commendable patience under severe provocation."

We do not hold that removing this defendant from his own trial was the only way the Illinois judge could have constitutionally solved the problem he had. We do hold, however, that there is nothing whatever in this record to show that the judge did not act completely within his discretion. Deplorable as it is to remove a man from his own trial, even for a short time, we hold that the judge did not commit legal error in doing what he did.

The judgment of the Court of Appeals is reversed.[a]

Reversed.

MR. JUSTICE BRENNAN, concurring. . . .

I would add only that when a defendant is excluded from his trial, the court should make reasonable efforts to enable him to communicate with his attorney and, if possible, to keep apprised of the progress of his trial. Once the court has removed the contumacious defendant, it is not weakness to mitigate the disadvantages of his expulsion as far as technologically possible in the circumstances.

MR. JUSTICE DOUGLAS.

I agree with the Court that a criminal trial, in the constitutional sense, cannot take place where the courtroom is a bedlam and either the accused or the judge is hurling epithets at the other. A court-

a. [Added by the Compiler.] At adjournment of court, D was admonished to rise. He did not rise and when directed by the judge to approach the bench he refused. When the marshal took him by the arm and forcibly led him to the bench he went limp and lay prostrate on the floor as the court addressed him. A summary conviction of contempt of court was affirmed. Comstock v. United States, 419 F.2d 1128 (9th Cir.1970).

"If a prisoner so misconducts himself as to make it impossible to try him with decency, the Court, it seems, may order him to be removed and proceed in his absence." Stephens, Digest of the Law of Criminal Procedure, Art. 302 (1883).

"The right of a prisoner to be present at his trial does not include the right to prevent a trial by unseemly disturbance." United States v. Davis, 25 Fed.Cas. 773, 774 (No. 14,923) (C.C.S.D.N.Y.1869).

D waived his right to be present personally at his trial by voluntarily absenting himself during the trial. Warren v. State, 537 P.2d 443 (Okl.1975).

D, who was out on bond, did not reappear after a mid-trial recess. The trial was continued in his absence and he was found guilty. This was proper because by his voluntary absence he waived his right to be present. People v. Swan, 394 Mich. 451, 231 N.W.2d 651 (1975). The trial had been delayed several hours and then adjourned. It was after D had not reappeared four days later that the trial was continued in his absence.

To compel defendant to stand trial in prison clothing would violate the equal protection clause; but he may prefer this for sympathy purposes. Hence if he goes to trial in such attire without objection no constitutional violation is involved. Estelle v. Williams, 425 U.S. 1691, 96 S.Ct. 1691 (1976). The jailer had denied his request for civilian clothes but neither he nor his counsel had raised any objection to the prison attire.

room is a hallowed place where trials must proceed with dignity and not become occasions for entertainment by the participants, by extraneous persons, by modern mass media or otherwise.

My difficulty is not with the basic hypothesis of this decision, but with the use of this case to establish the appropriate guidelines for judicial control.

This is a state case, the trial having taken place nearly 13 years ago. That elapse of time is not necessarily a barrier to a challenge of the constitutionality of a criminal conviction. But in this case it should be. . . .

SECTION 6. RIGHT TO A PUBLIC TRIAL

One accused of crime has a common-law right to a public trial[1] which has been embodied in the federal constitution and in the constitutions of most states. This means that the defendant has a right to a trial that is open to the public. If the trial is so open, there is no requirement that it must stop merely because no one the defendant regards as a member of the public happens to be present. It had been assumed at times that a public trial was not necessary if expressly waived by him.[2] In any event it is clear that he has no general right to a secret trial.[3]

Neither the defendant nor anyone else has a right to require the judge to admit to the courtroom any unneeded person whose presence will interfere with the due and orderly conduct of the trial. Overcrowding will result in such interference. Hence if members of the general public are admitted until the seating capacity of the courtroom is exhausted, the exclusion of others is entirely proper. Furthermore, if all available space is taken by witnesses and other persons necessary to the trial or having some special and proper interest therein, the exclusion of disinterested members of the public is unavoidable.[4] Disorderly persons may be evicted, and if all who are not necessary to the trial are disorderly, all may be required to leave.[5] On the other hand it would be arbitrary and unreasonable if the

1. Radin, The Right to a Public Trial, 6 Temp.L.Q. 381 (1932).

For an exhaustive analysis of the leading cases on the subject of the right to public trial see State v. Lawrence, 167 N.W.2d 912 (Iowa 1969).

2. People v. Swafford, 65 Cal. 223, 3 P. 809 (1894). This case held, moreover, that failure to object constituted a waiver, but there is authority contra on this point. Wade v. State, 207 Ala. 1, 92 So. 101 (1921).

3. Gannett Co. v. DePasquale, 443 U.S. 368, 99 S.Ct. 2898 (1979).

4. Kugadt v. State, 38 Tex.Cr.R. 681, 44 S.W. 989 (1898).

5. Grimmett v. State, 22 Tex.App. 36, 2 S.W. 631 (1886).

It was held that the exclusion of the public except for members of the press and the bar was not unreasonable where it was apparent that D and his sympathizers were attempting to prevent an orderly presentation of the case. United States v. Fay, 350 F.2d 967 (2d Cir.1965).

Excluding spectators for a short time to prevent escape or violence did not infringe on right to public trial. State v. Harding, 635 P.2d 33 (Utah 1981).

judge, after having given such an order, should refuse to make any exceptions even upon a proper showing therefor. If the defendant's father, for example, or some other relative or friend whose presence was desired by him, should assure the judge that he had not participated in the disorder and would not in any way interfere with the due and orderly conduct of the trial, it would be prejudicial error to compel him to leave.

The chief controversy in this field has centered on the propriety of an order of exclusion based upon the salacious nature of the evidence to be introduced. An order excluding children from such a trial seems to have been free from question.[6] So also is an order temporarily removing those having no special and proper interest in being present, if this is necessary to get the testimony of a very young witness who is so emotionally disturbed by the embarrassing nature of what she is to reveal that she cannot give a coherent account of the facts without it.[7] It is equally clear, on the other side, that an order of exclusion is improper if it is so sweeping in its scope as unnecessarily to keep from the courtroom every relative or friend of the defendant, or if an order which was proper when made is arbitrarily continued after the emergency which induced it has passed entirely.

The real difficulty lies between such extremes. One type of exclusion order in cases in which the evidence was to be particularly salacious has been this in substance: That no persons not needed for the trial itself be admitted to the courtroom except members of the press and those whose presence is desired by the defendant. Such an order has been upheld by some courts but held by others to be reversible error.[8] It is difficult to conceive how the defendant could be prejudiced by an order which permits the presence of any person desired by him.

In a trial for compulsory prostitution, in which it was indicated that the evidence would disclose "obscene and sordid details", the trial judge gave an order excluding "the general public and the press . . . from the courtroom for the duration of the People's case." **D**, however, was permitted "to have present in the courtroom throughout the trial, any friends or relatives he deems necessary for the protection of his interests." The trial resulted in a conviction which was reversed because this order deprived **D** of his right to a public trial.[9] The court emphasized that the order was made "not to preserve order and decorum in the courtroom or to protect the rights

6. State v. Stafford, 213 Kan. 152, 515 P.2d 769 (1973), modified, rehearing denied 213 Kan. 585, 518 P.2d 136.

7. Moore v. State, 151 Ga. 648, 108 S.E. 47 (1921); State v. Callahan, 100 Minn. 63, 110 N.W. 342 (1907). Riley v. State, 83 Nev. 282, 429 P.2d 59 (1967).

8. The cases are cited in notes: 28 Tex.L.Rev. 265 (1949); 3 Vand.L.Rev. 125 (1949); 156 A.L.R. 265 (1945). See State v. Bowers, 58 Or.App. 1, 646 P.2d 1354 (1982).

9. People v. Jelke, 308 N.Y. 56, 123 N.E.2d 769 (1954).

D, on trial for rape, was denied his constitutional right to a public trial by the exclusion from the courtroom of all spectators except members of the press, court officials and near relatives of the prosecutrix and of **D**. Thompson v. Peo-

of the parties or witnesses at the trial, but in asserted deference to general considerations of public decency and morality." The court relied upon a statute which authorized the judge to exclude "all persons who are not directly interested therein, excepting jurors, witnesses, and officers of the court" from certain specified trials not including the one here involved.

The Supreme Court reversed a conviction because the trial had been telecast despite **D**'s motion to prevent it.[10] There was no opinion of the Court and the six opinions left doubt as to the exact significance. Several states experimented with television. Florida had a pilot program and in a case under it the Supreme Court held that with adequate safeguards a state may provide for television coverage of a criminal trial. Conviction in a televised trial was affirmed.[11]

An order "putting witnesses under the rule" [12] does not violate defendant's right to a public trial.[13]

RICHMOND NEWSPAPERS, INC. v. VIRGINIA

Supreme Court of the United States, 1980.
448 U.S. 555, 100 S.Ct. 2814.

Syllabus *

At the commencement of a fourth trial on a murder charge (the defendant's conviction after the first trial having been reversed on appeal, and two subsequent retrials having ended in mistrials), the Virginia trial court granted defense counsel's motion that the trial be closed to the public without any objections having been made by the prosecutor or by appellants, a newspaper and two of its reporters who were present in the courtroom, defense counsel having stated that he did not "want any information being shuffled back and forth when we have a recess as to . . . . who testified to what." Later that same day, however, the trial judge granted appellant's request for a hearing on a motion to vacate the closure order, and appellants' counsel contended that constitutional considerations mandated that before ordering closure the court should first decide that the defend-

ple, 156 Colo. 416, 399 P.2d 776 (1965). In this case the prosecutrix was nearly twenty-one and there was no showing that she was emotionally upset. The court's order expressly excluded friends of **D** who were not close relatives.

10. Estes v. Texas, 381 U.S. 532, 85 S.Ct. 1628 (1965).

11. Chandler v. Florida, 449 U.S. 560, 101 S.Ct. 802 (1981).

12. This order excludes all other witnesses from the courtroom while any one of them is on the witness stand.

13. State v. Worthen, 124 Iowa 408, 100 N.W. 330 (1904). Putting witnesses "under the rule" is within the discretion of the judge but it is error for the court to refuse to do so without exercising discretion under the theory that he has abandoned the practice. Charles v. United States, 215 F.2d 825 (9th Cir.1954).

* The syllabus constitutes no part of the opinion of the Court but has been prepared by the Reporter of Decisions for the convenience of the reader. See United States v. Detroit Lumber Co., 200 U.S. 321, 337, 26 S.Ct. 282, 287, 50 L.Ed. 499.

ant's rights could be protected in no other way. But the trial judge denied the motion, saying that if he felt that the defendant's rights were infringed in any way and others' rights were not overridden he was inclined to order closure, and ordered the trial to continue "with the press and public excluded." The next day, the court granted defendant's motion to strike the prosecution's evidence, excused the jury, and found the defendant not guilty. Thereafter, the court granted appellants' motion to intervene *nunc pro tunc* in the case, and the Virginia Supreme Court dismissed their mandamus and prohibition petitions and, finding no reversible error, denied their petition for appeal from the closure order.

Held: The judgment is reversed.

Reversed.

MR. CHIEF JUSTICE BURGER, joined by MR. JUSTICE WHITE and MR. JUSTICE STEVENS, concluded that the right of the public and press to attend criminal trials is guaranteed under the First and Fourteenth Amendments. Absent an overriding interest articulated in findings, the trial of a criminal case must be open to the public.

(a) The historical evidence of the evolution of the criminal trial in Anglo-American justice demonstrates conclusively that at the time this Nation's organic laws were adopted, criminal trials both here and in England had long been presumptively open, thus giving assurance that the proceedings were conducted fairly to all concerned and discouraging perjury, the misconduct of participants, or decisions based on secret bias or partiality. In addition, the significant community therapeutic value of public trials was recognized: when a shocking crime occurs, a community reaction of outrage and public protest often follows, and thereafter the open processes of justice serve an important prophylactic purpose, providing an outlet for community concern, hostility, and emotion. To work effectively, it is important that society's criminal process "satisfy the appearance of justice," which can best be provided by allowing people to observe such process. From this unbroken, uncontradicted history, supported by reasons as valid today as in centuries past, it must be concluded that a presumption of openness inheres in the very nature of a criminal trial under this Nation's system of justice.

(b) The freedoms of speech, press, and assembly, expressly guaranteed by the First Amendment, share a common core purpose of assuring freedom of communication on matters relating to the functioning of government. In guaranteeing freedoms such as those of speech and press, the First Amendment can be read as protecting the right of everyone to attend trials so as to give meaning to those explicit guarantees; the First Amendment right to receive information and ideas means, in the context of trials, that the guarantees of speech and press, standing alone, prohibit government from summarily closing courtroom doors which had long been open to the public at the time the First Amendment was adopted. Moreover, the right of assembly is also relevant, having been regarded not only as an independent right but also as a catalyst to augment the free exercise of the other First Amendment rights with which it was deliberately linked by the draftsmen. A trial courtroom is a public place where the people generally—and representatives of the media—have a right to be present, and where their presence historically has been thought to enhance the integrity and quality of what takes place. Pp. 2826–2828.

(c) Even though the Constitution contains no provision which by its terms guarantees to the public the right to attend criminal trials, various fundamental rights, not expressly guaranteed, have been recognized as indispensable to the enjoyment of enumerated rights. The right to attend criminal trials is implicit in the guarantees of the First Amendment; without the freedom to attend such trials, which people have exercised for centuries, important aspects of freedom of speech and of the press could be eviscerated. Pp. 2828–2829.

(d) With respect to the closure order in this case, despite the fact that this was the accused's fourth trial, the trial judge made no findings to support closure; no inquiry was made as to whether alternative solutions would have met the need to ensure fairness; there was no recognition of any right under the Constitution for the public or press to attend the trial; and there was no suggestion that any problems with witnesses could not have been dealt with by exclusion from the courtroom or sequestration during the trial, or that sequestration of the jurors would not have guarded against their being subjected to any improper information. Pp. 2829–2830.

MR. JUSTICE BRENNAN, joined by MR. JUSTICE MARSHALL, concluded that the First Amendment—of itself and as applied to the States through the Fourteenth Amendment—secures the public a right of access to trial proceedings, and that, without more, agreement of the trial judge and the parties cannot constitutionally close a trial to the public. Historically and functionally, open trials have been closely associated with the development of the fundamental procedure of trial by jury, and trial access assumes structural importance in this Nation's government of laws by assuring the public that procedural rights are respected and that justice is afforded equally, by serving as an effective restraint on possible abuse of judicial power, and by aiding the accuracy of the trial factfinding process. It was further concluded that it was not necessary to consider in this case what countervailing interests might be sufficiently compelling to reverse the presumption of openness of trials, since the Virginia statute involved—authorizing trial closures at the unfettered discretion of the judge and parties—violated the First and Fourteenth Amendments.

MR. JUSTICE STEWART concluded that the First and Fourteenth Amendments clearly give the press and the public a right of access to trials, civil as well as criminal; that such right is not absolute, since various considerations may sometimes justify limitations upon the unrestricted presence of spectators in the courtroom; but that in the present case the trial judge apparently gave no recognition to the right of representatives of the press and members of the public to be present at the trial.

MR. JUSTICE BLACKMUN, while being of the view that Gannett Co. v. DePasquale, supra, was in error, both in its interpretation of the Sixth Amendment generally, and in its application to the suppression hearing involved there, and that the right to a public trial is to be found in the Sixth Amendment, concluded, as a secondary position, that the First Amendment must provide some measure of protection for public access to the trial, and that here, by closing the trial, the trial judge abridged these First Amendment interests of the public.[1]

SECTION 7. RIGHT TO A TRIAL BY JURY

It has been said: "That the modern institution of trial by jury derives from Magna Carta is one of the most revered of legal fables." [1] "The 'judgment of his peers' there named is secured only to noblemen who are, by this provision, to be tried at the king's suit in the House of Lords." [2] But when we have shown that this protection was quite limited in its inception, and has since been broadened in its scope to include all people, we seem rather to have explained than to have contradicted the thought that this important benefit relates back to that great document. The right to trial by jury is still regarded by many as most important to liberty.

The usual common law classification of crimes recognizes three groups: (1) treason, (2) felony, and (3) misdemeanor. For certain important purposes of procedure, however, a different classification was employed. This emphasized the distinction between (1) indictable offenses and (2) petty offenses. Persons charged with very minor violations such as disorderly conduct, trivial breaches of the peace or infractions of municipal ordinances could be prosecuted without waiting for an indictment by the grand jury, and could be tried without the aid of a trial jury. Except for such petty offenses the common-law gives the defendant a right to a trial by jury in every prosecution for crime. This right is guaranteed by most of the constitutions. A

1. A Massachusetts law requiring trial judges, for sexual offenses where the victim was under age 18, to exclude the press and public from the courtroom during the testimony of the victim was held to violate the First Amendment. "We emphasize that our holding is a narrow one: that a rule of mandatory closure respecting the testimony of minor sex victims is constitutionally infirm. In individual cases, and under appropriate circumstances, the First Amendment does not necessarily stand as a bar to the exclusion from the courtroom of the press and general public during the testimony of minor sex-offense victims. But a mandatory rule, requiring no particularized determination in individual cases, is unconstitutional." Globe Newspaper Co. v. Superior Court, 457 U.S. 596, 102 S.Ct. 2613, 2622 (1982).

1. Frankfurter and Corcoran, Petty Federal Offenses and the Constitutional Guaranty of Trial by Jury, 39 Harv.L. Rev. 917, 922 (1926).

2. Beale, Criminal Pleading and Practice 253, note 1 (1899).

few of the provisions seem to extend the right even beyond its common-law scope.[3]

BALDWIN v. NEW YORK

Supreme Court of the United States, 1970.
399 U.S. 66, 90 S.Ct. 1886.

MR. JUSTICE WHITE announced the judgment of the Court and delivered an opinion in which MR. JUSTICE BRENNAN and MR. JUSTICE MARSHALL join.

Appellant was arrested and charged with "jostling"—a Class A misdemeanor in New York, punishable by a maximum term of imprisonment of one year.[1] He was brought to trial in the New York City Criminal Court. Section 40 of the New York City Criminal Court Act declares that all trials in that court shall be without a jury. Appellant's pretrial motion for jury trial was accordingly denied. He was convicted and sentenced to imprisonment for the maximum term. The New York Court of Appeals affirmed the conviction, rejecting appellant's argument that § 40 was unconstitutional insofar as it denied him an opportunity for jury trial. We noted probable jurisdiction. We reverse.

In Duncan v. Louisiana, 391 U.S. 145, 88 S.Ct. 1444, 20 L.Ed.2d 491 (1968), we held that the Sixth Amendment, as applied to the States through the Fourteenth, requires that defendants accused of serious crimes be afforded the right to trial by jury. We also reaffirmed the long-established view that so-called "petty offenses" may be tried without a jury. Thus the task before us in this case is the

3. The Sixth Amendment provides: "In all criminal prosecutions, the accused shall enjoy the right to a speedy and public trial, by an impartial jury. . . ." Some of the state constitutions are similarly worded. But the phrase "criminal prosecutions," in such a constitutional clause, has been interpreted to include only what Blackstone refers to as "regular" proceedings as distinguished from the summary trial of petty offenses. 4 Bl.Comm. 280. In other words it is construed to preserve the right of trial by jury as it existed prior to the constitution and not to extend it to a broader field. Frankfurter and Corcoran, Petty Federal Offenses and the Constitutional Guaranty of Trial by Jury, 39 Harv.L.Rev. 917, 969 (1926).

But an occasional provision has an added phrase, such as that "in all criminal prosecutions, and in cases involving the life or liberty of an individual, the accused shall have the right to a speedy and public trial by an impartial jury." Iowa Const. Art. I, sec. 10. Since any imprisonment involves the liberty of an individual, and some of the petty offenses were punished by imprisonment for a short period, such a clause extends the right of trial by jury.

1. "Jostling" is one of the ways in which legislatures have attempted to deal with pickpocketing. See Denzer & McQuillan, Practice Commentary, N.Y.Penal Law § 165.25 (McKinney 1967); Pickpocketing: A Survey of the Crime and its Control, 104 U.Pa.L.Rev. 408, 419 (1955). The New York law provides:

"A person is guilty of jostling when, in a public place, he intentionally and unnecessarily:

1. Places his hand in the proximity of a person's pocket or handbag; or
2. Jostles or crowds another person at a time when a third person's hand is in the proximity of such person's pocket or handbag." N.Y.Penal Law § 165.25 (McKinney's Consol. Laws, c. 40, 1967).

essential if not wholly satisfactory one, see *Duncan*, at 161, 88 S.Ct. at 1453, of determining the line between "petty" and "serious" for purposes of the Sixth Amendment right to jury trial.

Prior cases in this Court narrow our inquiry and furnish us with the standard to be used in resolving this issue. In deciding whether an offense is "petty," we have sought objective criteria reflecting the seriousness with which society regards the offense, District of Columbia v. Clawans, 300 U.S. 617, 628, 57 S.Ct. 660, 663, 81 L.Ed. 843 (1937), and we have found the most relevant such criteria in the severity of the maximum authorized penalty. Frank v. United States, 395 U.S. 147, 148, 89 S.Ct. 1503, 1505, 23 L.Ed.2d 162 (1969); Duncan v. Louisiana, supra, 391 U.S., at 159–161, 88 S.Ct., at 1452–1454; District of Columbia v. Clawans, supra, 300 U.S., at 628, 57 S.Ct., at 663. Applying these guidelines, we have held that a possible six-month penalty is short enough to permit classification of the offense as "petty," Dyke v. Taylor Implement Mfg. Co., 391 U.S. 216, 220, 88 S.Ct. 1472, 1475, 20 L.Ed.2d 538 (1968); Cheff v. Schnackenberg, 384 U.S. 373, 86 S.Ct. 1523, 16 L.Ed.2d 629 (1966), but that a two-year maximum is sufficiently "serious" to require an opportunity for jury trial, Duncan v. Louisiana, supra. The question in this case is whether the possibility of a one-year sentence is enough in itself to require the opportunity for a jury trial. We hold that it is. More specifically, we have concluded that no offense can be deemed "petty" for purposes of the right to trial by jury where imprisonment for more than six months is authorized.[6] . . .

Of necessity, the task of drawing a line "requires attaching different consequences to events which, when they lie near the line, actually differ very little." Duncan v. Louisiana, supra, at 161, 88 S.Ct., at 1453. One who is threatened with the possibility of imprisonment for six months may find little difference between the potential consequences which face him, and the consequences which faced appellant here. Indeed, the prospect of imprisonment for however short a time will seldom be viewed by the accused as a trivial or "petty" matter and may well result in quite serious repercussions affecting his career and his reputation. Where the accused cannot possibly face more than six months imprisonment, we have held that these disadvantages, onerous though they may be, may be outweighed by the benefits which result from speedy and inexpensive nonjury adjudications. We cannot, however, conclude that these administrative conveniences, in light of the practices which now exist in every one of the 50 States as well as in the federal courts, can similarly justify deny-

6. Decisions of this Court have looked to both the nature of the offense itself, District of Columbia v. Colts, 282 U.S. 63, 51 S.Ct. 52, 75 L.Ed. 177, as well as the maximum potential sentence, Duncan v. Louisiana, 391 U.S. 145, 88 S.Ct. 1444, 20 L.Ed.2d 491 (1968), in determining whether a particular offense was so serious as to require a jury trial. In this case, we decide only that a potential sentence in excess of six-months imprisonment is sufficiently severe by itself to take the offense out of the category of "petty." None of our decisions involving this issue have ever held such an offense "petty."

ing an accused the important right to trial by jury where the possible penalty exceeds six months' imprisonment. The conviction is

Reversed.[a]

MR. JUSTICE BLACKMUN took no part in the consideration or decision of this case.

BLACK and DOUGLAS, JJ. concurred in the judgment reversing the conviction because of a belief that the defendant in any criminal prosecution is entitled to a jury trial.

BURGER, C.J., and HARLAN and STEWART, JJ., dissented because they disagree with the "incorporation" theory and conclude that the trial of Baldwin did not deprive him of due process.

(A) WAIVER

At one time the jury trial of an indictable offense was considered by many to be a requirement rather than a mere right. As it was expressed by one author some years ago, "the weight of authority, as well as the better opinion, is, that in prosecutions for crime other than minor misdemeanors and petty offenses, the defendant cannot waive his right to a trial by jury, or consent to a trial by a less number than twelve." [13] A similar view was expressed by others; [14] and a

a. [Added by the Compiler.] At the same time that this case was decided the Court held that the jury clause of the Sixth Amendment does not require twelve jurors. A panel of six was held to satisfy the requirement. Williams v. Florida, 399 U.S. 78, 90 S.Ct. 1893 (1970).

The Louisiana constitution authorized criminal trials by juries of six, and authorized convictions on the vote of five jurors. B was on trial for exhibiting obscene motion pictures, an offense for which the punishment could be more than six months imprisonment. He was found guilty by a vote of five of the six jurors and sentenced to two consecutive 7-month terms that were suspended. It was held that conviction of a nonpetty offense by a vote of five of a six-person jury deprived B of his constitutional right of trial by jury. Burch v. Louisiana, 441 U.S. 130, 99 S.Ct. 1623 (1979). In another case the Court had invalidated a statute allowing conviction by a unanimous five-person jury in nonpetty criminal cases. Ballew v. Georgia, 435 U.S. 223, 98 S.Ct. 1029 (1978). Thus the Court has held that the constitution does not require a jury of twelve for the trial of nonpetty criminal cases. A jury of six is constitutionally permissible, but a jury of fewer than six is invalid for such trials. And the Court has held that the constitution does not require unanimous verdicts in such trial if the jury is large enough. But in no case may conviction of such an offense be based upon the verdict of fewer than six jurors.

Conviction by a nonunanimous jury did not violate the Fourteenth Amendment. Johnson v. Louisiana, 406 U.S. 356, 92 S.Ct. 1620 (1972) (9 of 12 jurors); Apodaca v. Oregon, 406 U.S. 404, 92 S.Ct. 1628 (1972) (10 of 12 jurors).

In a state in which there is no provision for a nonunanimous verdict, the jury sent word that it was hopelessly deadlocked at 11 to 1, with no indication which way. When defendant was told this he said he would accept the nonunanimous verdict. The verdict was received and it was 11 to 1 for conviction. The court held that a defendant has the power to waive his right to a unanimous verdict, but that this conviction must be reversed because the judge accepted the waiver without properly informing the defendant. People v. Miller, 121 Mich.App. 691, 329 N.W.2d 460 (1983).

13. Rapalje, Criminal Procedure § 151 (1889).

14. Hughes, Criminal Law and Procedure § 2979 (1901); Cooley, Constitutional Limitations 674–5 (8th ed. by Carrington, 1927).

number of convictions were reversed because the trial was without a full panel of twelve, although it was with the express consent of the defendant. The theory was that a common-law jury was essential to the jurisdiction of the court in criminal cases.

In *Patton* [15] the Supreme Court rejected this view, disposing of the jurisdiction theory as follows:

"In the absence of a valid consent, the District Court cannot proceed except with a jury, not because a jury is essential to its jurisdiction, but because the accused is entitled by the terms of the Constitution to that mode of trial".

And Rule 23 of the Federal Rules of Criminal Procedure expressly authorizes the waiver. On the other hand the defendant has no absolute right to demand a trial without a jury. The provision of the rule requiring the court and government to consent to the waiver of jury trial is valid, at least unless defendant can show some impelling reason in a particular case why he should be entitled to a trial by the judge alone.[16]

Today, the power of the judge to try a criminal case without a jury, when the jury has been waived, is accepted without question unless some state statute or constitution provides otherwise.

(B) ALTERNATE JURORS

While the verdict of a jury of thirteen will not support a judgment of conviction (in the absence of effective waiver by defendant), the mere presence of a thirteenth man on the panel is not necessarily fatal. It has been suggested, for example, that if the error is discovered before verdict the thirteenth member can be withdrawn and the trial proceed validly with the original twelve.[17] This suggested the possibility of one or more alternate jurors.

Now and then after the trial of a criminal case is well under way it becomes necessary to discontinue the proceedings and start all over again because a juror is unable to continue for some impelling reason such as illness. While not an everyday occurrence, a study of the records will disclose that this has happened time and again down through the years. It is particularly distressing to have this happen after the case has been in progress for many days, and perhaps weeks, whereas the longer the trial the greater is the likelihood of such a misfortune. The defendant can avoid the necessity of a fresh

15. Patton v. United States, 281 U.S. 276, 50 S.Ct. 253, 74 L.Ed. 854, 70 A.L.R. 263 (1930).

16. Singer v. United States, 380 U.S. 24, 85 S.Ct. 783, 13 L.Ed.2d 630 (1965).

California constitution, Article 1, Section 16, provides: ". . . A jury may be waived in a criminal case, by the consent of both parties, expressed in open court by the defendant and his counsel, . . . ". The consent of the trial judge is not necessary and he cannot overrule the decision of the parties. The consent of the prosecuting attorney is as essential as the consent of the defendant. People v. Terry, 2 Cal.3d 362, 85 Cal. Rptr. 409, 466 P.2d 961 (1970).

17. Bullard v. State, 38 Tex. 504 (1873).

start by waiving his right to a full panel. This, however, is not a satisfactory solution because it places entirely too much control in his hands. The court and the prosecution, normally inclined to support the defendant in any offer to waive the jury (in whole or in part), would be extremely hesitant to block his waiver under these circumstances. The defendant on the other hand will not waive the full panel if he thinks he can gain the slightest advantage by insisting upon his rights (as he is fully entitled to do).

In the effort to improve the procedure at this point there has been a trend in the direction of authorizing the selection of alternate jurors for cases likely to be protracted. Statutes to this effect have been passed in a number of states. The most recent provision reflecting the result of an exhaustive study on a nation-wide basis is found in Rule 24 of the Federal Rules of Criminal Procedure. This concludes with the following sub-division:

"(c) Alternate Jurors. The court may direct that not more than 6 jurors in addition to the regular jury be called and impanelled to sit as alternate jurors. Alternate jurors in the order in which they are called shall replace jurors who, prior to the time the jury retires to consider its verdict, become or are found to be unable or disqualified to perform their duties. Alternate jurors shall be drawn in the same manner, shall have the same qualifications, shall be subject to the same examination and challenges, shall take the same oath and shall have the same functions, powers, facilities and privileges as the regular jurors. An alternate juror who does not replace a regular juror shall be discharged after the jury retires to consider its verdict. Each side is entitled to 1 peremptory challenge in addition to those otherwise allowed by law if 1 or 2 alternate jurors are to be impanelled, 2 peremptory challenges if 3 or 4 alternate jurors are to be impanelled, and 3 peremptory challenges if 5 or 6 alternates are to be impanelled. The additional peremptory challenges may be used against an alternate juror only, and the other peremptory challenges allowed by these rules may not be used against an alternate juror." [18]

SECTION 8. RIGHT TO A FAIR AND IMPARTIAL TRIAL

The rather common constitutional clause guaranteeing the defendant a "trial by an impartial jury" does not exhaust the right to impartiality. The requirement of due process of law entitles the defendant to a fair and impartial trial in every respect.[1] The case in which a

18. Substitution of an alternate juror is constitutionally permissible after deliberations have begun where there is good cause for such action and where the jury is instructed to begin their deliberations anew. People v. Collins, 17 Cal.3d 687, 131 Cal.Rptr. 782, 552 P.2d 742 (1976).

1. "He is also entitled to a fair trial, which has been well defined, as 'a trial before an impartial judge, an honest jury, and in an atmosphere of judicial calm' ". State v. Leland, 190 Or. 598, 608, 227 P.2d 785, 790 (1951). Cf. Robedeaux v. State, 94 Okl.Cr. 171, 232 P.2d 642 (1951). See Holtzoff, Relation Between the Right to a Fair Trial and the Right of Freedom of the Press. 1 Syracuse L.Rev. 369 (1950).

"Inconsistency in a verdict is not a sufficient reason for setting it aside." In

violent mob moved into the courtroom and completely dominated the trial, intimidating witnesses, counsel, jurors and even the judge himself so that no one dared to do anything other than let the case proceed to a hasty conviction,[2] requires no discussion. Much less than this may be sufficient to deprive the defendant of a fair and impartial trial. The case of Tumey v. Ohio is illuminating.[3] The defendant was arrested and brought before a village mayor charged with unlawfully possessing intoxicating liquor. Ignoring a claim of disqualification, the mayor proceeded with a trial which resulted in a conviction. The judgment was reversed by the Court of Common Pleas on the ground that the mayor was disqualified as claimed, but this in turn was reversed by the Court of Appeals, and the State Supreme Court refused to disturb the conviction. The case was then taken to the Supreme Court of the United States upon a writ of error. The court discovered that under the relevant statutes and ordinances the mayor trying such a case was entitled to legal fees taxed in his favor in the event of a conviction but received nothing if an acquittal resulted. The court further found that the fees in this case amounted to $12.00 and that the mayor had been averaging about $100.00 a month from such fees in addition to his salary. In reversing the judgment the court said, speaking through Mr. Chief Justice Taft: "But it certainly violates the Fourteenth Amendment, and deprives a defendant in a criminal case of due process of law, to subject his liberty or property to the judgment of a court the judge of which has a direct, personal, substantial, pecuniary interest in reaching a conclusion against him in the case."

"As has often been stated, a defendant is entitled to a fair trial but not a perfect trial." [4]

SECTION 9. THE INTERPLAY OF RIGHTS AND PRIVILEGES

Methods employed by officers to "extract" confessions from reluctant suspects had long been a matter of increasing concern to the Supreme Court. The "third degree" had been supplanted, very largely by psychological torture—interminable questioning by relays of officers while the suspect received inadequate rest and refreshment. Even this was tending to give way to more subtle psychological techniques. Officers' manuals explained various tricks and devices that had proved useful in extracting confessions. And the Court wanted such practices brought to an end.

holding that this is not limited to jury trials but applies also to a bench trial the Court, without finding more than "apparent inconsistency" in the case at bench, added: "The Constitution does not prohibit judges from being excessively lenient." Harris v. Rivera, 454 U.S. 339, 102 S.Ct. 460, 464, 465 (1981).

2. Moore v. Dempsey, 261 U.S. 86, 43 S.Ct. 265 (1923).

3. 273 U.S. 510, 47 S.Ct. 437 (1926).

4. Moore v. United States, 375 F.2d 877, 882 (8th Cir.1967).

McNabb[1] was a case in which suspects had not been taken before a magistrate until several days after they were arrested. During that time they were questioned hour after hour until they finally confessed. Convictions based upon these confessions could have been reversed on the ground that the confessions were obtained by psychological torture and hence involuntary, but the Court seized upon this case to make new law. As this was a federal case the Court exercised its supervisory power over federal officers. The law requires that the person arrested shall be immediately taken before a committing officer. Since this was not done the officers obtained the confessions by violating the law, and confessions so obtained are excludable from evidence. In a later case, *Mallory*,[2] the lower courts felt that the delay in taking **D** before a magistrate was reasonable under the circumstances. In reversing the conviction the Court held that any delay "of a nature to give opportunity for the extraction of a confession" is unlawful, and any confession or admission so obtained is excludable. This came to be known as the McNabb-Mallory rule.[3]

Spano,[4] a state case, represented the next step in the Court's program of limiting the power of officers to interrogate suspects. **D**, who had been indicted for first-degree murder, was interrogated in the police station until he confessed, and this confession was introduced in evidence and resulted in a conviction. In holding that this conviction could not stand under the Fourteenth Amendment the court relied upon the totality of circumstances. But four concurring justices pointed out that the constitution required reversal upon the specific ground that the confession had been deliberately elicited by the police after **D** had been indicted and hence at a time when he was clearly entitled to a lawyer's help. While they emphasized the Sixth Amendment right to counsel it is clear that they considered that the violation of this right had resulted in a violation of the Fifth Amendment privilege against self-incrimination.

Massiah[5] carried the restrictive program a step further. **M**, who had been indicted for a violation of the federal narcotics laws, had retained counsel and been released on bail. Thereafter a federal agent arranged with **C**, who had been jointly indicted with **M**, for the installation in **C**'s car of a secret radio transmitter which would enable the agent in another car, parked out of sight, to listen to the conversation between **C** and **M**, during which **M** made several incriminating statements. Over timely objections the agent was permitted to testify to these statements in the trial in which **M** was convicted.

1. McNabb v. United States, 318 U.S. 322, 63 S.Ct. 608 (1943).

2. Mallory v. United States, 354 U.S. 449, 77 S.Ct. 1356 (1957).

3. The McNabb-Mallory rule has been modified by Congressional action. 18 U.S.C.A. § 3501(a), (c) (1969). See also Note, The Ill-Advised State Court Revival of the McNabb-Mallory Rule, 92 Jnl. CL & Crim. 204 (1981).

4. Spano v. New York, 360 U.S. 315, 79 S.Ct. 1202 (1959).

5. Massiah v. United States, 377 U.S. 201, 84 S.Ct. 1199 (1964).

In reversing this conviction the Court held that **M** was denied the Sixth Amendment protection of right to counsel "when there was used against him at his trial evidence of his own incriminating words, which federal agents had deliberately elicited from him after he had been indicted and in the absence of his counsel".

Next in this series was *Escobedo.*[6] **E,** a 22-year-old Mexican with no previous experience with the police, was arrested and interrogated about the fatal shooting of his brother-in-law. He retained a lawyer and was released on habeas corpus. Several days later, **D,** who was in police custody and was later indicted for the murder jointly with **E,** told the police that **E** had fired the fatal shots. **E** was again arrested and urged to confess but said he wanted to see his lawyer. For hours **E** asked to see his lawyer and his lawyer, who was in the station house, demanded to be permitted to see **E,** but the police did not permit the meeting until they had **E**'s statement. Ultimately, confronted by **D, E** said: "I didn't shoot Manuel, you did," thus admitting some knowledge of the crime. Later he further implicated himself and then gave a written statement. During this time no one advised him of his constitutional rights.

In this case also the conviction could have been reversed on the ground that the confession had been obtained by psychological torture, hence was involuntary and should not have been admitted in evidence against **E.** But the Court could not pass up the opportunity to make new law. It held that when the process of law enforcement "shifts from investigatory to accusatory—when its focus is on the accused and its purpose is to elicit a confession—our adversary system begins to operate, and, under the circumstances here, the accused must be permitted to consult with his lawyer."

The Court did not indicate whether a suspect is entitled to be told of his right to counsel, and other courts differed in their interpretation of the case in regard to this point.[7]

MIRANDA v. ARIZONA *

Supreme Court of the United States, 1966.
384 U.S. 436, 86 S.Ct. 1602.

MR. CHIEF JUSTICE WARREN delivered the opinion of the Court.

The cases before us raise questions which go to the roots of our concepts of American criminal jurisprudence: the restraints society

6. Escobedo v. Illinois, 378 U.S. 478, 84 S.Ct. 1758 (1964).

7. One view was that the police have no affirmative duty to warn an arrestee of his right to counsel and his right to remain silent and that a voluntary confession is not rendered inadmissible by the failure to give such warning. People v. Hartgraves, 31 Ill.2d 375, 202 N.E.2d 33 (1964); United States v. Childress, 347 F.2d 448 (7th Cir.1965). Contra, People v. Dorado, 62 Cal.2d 338, 42 Cal.Rptr. 169, 398 P.2d 361 (1965); State v. Neely, 239 Or. 487, 398 P.2d 482 (1965).

* The defendant was later killed in a barroom brawl. Miranda Slain; Main Figure in Landmark Suspects' Rights Case, N.Y. Times, Feb. 1, 1976, § 1, at 28, col. 4.

must observe consistent with the Federal Constitution in prosecuting individuals for crime. More specifically, we deal with the admissibility of statements obtained from an individual who is subjected to custodial police interrogation and the necessity for procedures which assure that the individual is accorded his privilege under the Fifth Amendment to the Constitution not to be compelled to incriminate himself. . . .

The constitutional issue we decide in each of these cases is the admissibility of statements obtained from a defendant questioned while in custody and deprived of his freedom of action. In each, the defendant was questioned by police officers, detectives, or a prosecuting attorney in a room in which he was cut off from the outside world. In none of these cases was the defendant given a full and effective warning of his rights at the outset of the interrogation process. In all the cases, the questioning elicited oral admissions, and in three of them, signed statements as well which were admitted at their trials. They all thus share salient features—incommunicado interrogation of individuals in a police-dominated atmosphere, resulting in self-incriminating statements without full warnings of constitutional rights. . . .

Our holding will be spelled out with some specificity in the pages which follow but briefly stated it is this: the prosecution may not use statements, whether exculpatory or inculpatory, stemming from custodial interrogation of the defendant unless it demonstrates the use of procedural safeguards effective to secure the privilege against self-incrimination. By custodial interrogation, we mean questioning initiated by law enforcement officers after a person has been taken into custody or otherwise deprived of his freedom of action in any significant way. . . .

The presence of an attorney, and the warnings delivered to the individual, enable the defendant under otherwise compelling circumstances to tell his story without fear, effectively, and in a way that eliminates the evils in the interrogation process. Without the protections flowing from adequate warning and the rights of counsel, "all the careful safeguards erected around the giving of testimony, whether by an accused or any other witness, would become empty formalities in a procedure where the most compelling possible evidence of guilt, a confession, would have already been obtained at the unsupervised pleasure of the police." . . .

In order fully to apprise a person interrogated of the extent of his rights under this system then, it is necessary to warn him not only that he has the right to consult with an attorney, but also that if he is indigent a lawyer will be appointed to represent him. Without this additional warning, the admonition of the right to consult with counsel would often be understood as meaning only that he can consult with a lawyer if he has one or has the funds to obtain one. The warning of a right to counsel would be hollow if not couched in terms that would convey to the indigent—the person most often subjected to interrogation—the knowledge that he too has a right to have counsel present.[42] As with the warnings of the right to remain silent and of the general right to counsel, only by effective and express explanation to the indigent of this right can there be assurance that he was truly in a position to exercise it.[43]

Once warnings have been given, the subsequent procedure is clear. If the individual indicates in any manner, at any time prior to or during questioning, that he wishes to remain silent, the interrogation must cease.[44] At this point he has shown that he intends to exercise his Fifth Amendment privilege; any statement taken after the person invokes his privilege cannot be other than the product of compulsion, subtle or otherwise. Without the right to cut off questioning, the setting of in-custody interrogation operates on the individual to overcome free choice in producing a statement after the privilege has been once invoked. If the individual states that he wants an attorney, the interrogation must cease until an attorney is present. At that time, the individual must have an opportunity to confer with the attorney and to have him present during any subsequent questioning. . . .

This does not mean, as some have suggested, that each police station must have a "station house lawyer" present at all times to advise prisoners. It does mean, however, that if police propose to interrogate a person they must make known to him that he is entitled to a lawyer and that if he cannot afford one, a lawyer will be provided for him prior to any interrogation. If authorities conclude that they will not provide counsel during a reasonable period of time in which investigation in the field is carried out, they may do so without violating the person's Fifth Amendment privilege so long as they do not question him during that time. . . .

In dealing with statements obtained through interrogation, we do not purport to find all confessions inadmissible. Confessions remain a proper element in law enforcement. Any statement given freely and voluntarily without any compelling influences is, of course, admissible in evidence. The fundamental import of the privilege while an individual is in custody is not whether he is allowed to talk to the

42. Cf. United States ex rel. Brown v. Fay, 242 F.Supp. 273, 277 (D.C.S.D.N.Y. 1965); People v. Witenski, 15 N.Y.2d 392, 259 N.Y.S.2d 413, 207 N.E.2d 358 (1965).

43. While a warning that the indigent may have counsel appointed need not be given to the person who is known to have an attorney or is known to have ample funds to secure one, the expedient of giving a warning is too simple and the rights involved too important to engage in *ex post facto* inquiries into financial ability when there is any doubt at all on that score.

44. If an individual indicates his desire to remain silent, but has an attorney present, there may be some circumstances in which further questioning would be permissible. In the absence of evidence of overbearing, statements then made in the presence of counsel might be free of the compelling influence of the interrogation process and might fairly be construed as a waiver of the privilege for purposes of these statements.

police without the benefit of warnings and counsel, but whether he can be interrogated. There is no requirement that police stop a person who enters a police station and states that he wishes to confess to a crime,[47] or a person who calls the police to offer a confession or any other statement he desires to make. Volunteered statements of any kind are not barred by the Fifth Amendment and their admissibility is not affected by our holding today.

To summarize, we hold that when an individual is taken into custody or otherwise deprived of his freedom by the authorities and is subjected to questioning, the privilege against self-incrimination is jeopardized. Procedural safeguards must be employed to protect the privilege, and unless other fully effective means are adopted to notify the person of his right of silence and to assure that the exercise of the right will be scrupulously honored, the following measures are required. He must be warned prior to any questioning that he has the right to remain silent, that anything he says can be used against him in a court of law, that he has the right to the presence of an attorney, and that if he cannot afford an attorney one will be appointed for him prior to any questioning if he so desires. Opportunity to exercise these rights must be afforded to him throughout the interrogation. After such warnings have been given, and such opportunity afforded him, the individual may knowingly and intelligently waive these rights and agree to answer questions or make a statement. But unless and until such warnings and waiver are demonstrated by the prosecution at trial, no evidence obtained as a result of interrogation can be used against him. . . .

If the individual desires to exercise his privilege, he has the right to do so. This is not for the authorities to decide. An attorney may advise his client not to talk to police until he has had an opportunity to investigate the case, or he may wish to be present with his client during any police questioning. In doing so an attorney is merely exercising the good professional judgment he has been taught. This is not cause for considering the attorney a menace to law enforcement. He is merely carrying out what he is sworn to do under his oath—to protect to the extent of his ability the rights of his client. In fulfilling this responsibility the attorney plays a vital role in the administration of criminal justice under our Constitution. . . .

Over the years the Federal Bureau of Investigation has compiled an exemplary record of effective law enforcement while advising any suspect or arrested person, at the outset of an interview, that he is not required to make a statement, that any statement may be used against him in court, that the individual may obtain the services of an attorney of his own choice and, more recently, that he has a right to free counsel if he is unable to pay. . . .

47. See People v. Dorado, 62 Cal.2d 338, 354, 42 Cal.Rptr. 169, 179, 398 P.2d 361, 371 (1965).

Because of the nature of the problem and because of its recurrent significance in numerous cases, we have to this point discussed the relationship of the Fifth Amendment privilege to police interrogation without specific concentration on the facts of the cases before us. We turn now to these facts to consider the application to these cases of the constitutional principles discussed above. In each instance, we have concluded that statements were obtained from the defendant under circumstances that did not meet constitutional standards for protection of the privilege.

No. 759. Miranda v. Arizona.

On March 13, 1963, petitioner, Ernesto Miranda, was arrested at his home and taken in custody to a Phoenix police station. He was there identified by the complaining witness. The police then took him to "Interrogation Room No. 2" of the detective bureau. There he was questioned by two police officers. The officers admitted at trial that Miranda was not advised that he had a right to have an attorney present. Two hours later, the officers emerged from the interrogation room with a written confession signed by Miranda. At the top of the statement was a typed paragraph stating that the confession was made voluntarily, without threats or promises of immunity and "with full knowledge of my legal rights, understanding any statement I make may be used against me."

At this trial before a jury, the written confession was admitted into evidence over the objection of defense counsel, and the officers testified to the prior oral confession made by Miranda during the interrogation. Miranda was found guilty of kidnapping and rape. He was sentenced to 20 to 30 years' imprisonment on each count, the sentences to run concurrently. On appeal, the Supreme Court of Arizona held that Miranda's constitutional rights were not violated in obtaining the confession and affirmed the conviction. In reaching its decision, the court emphasized heavily the fact that Miranda did not specifically request counsel.

We reverse. From the testimony of the officers and by the admission of respondent, it is clear that Miranda was not in any way apprised of his right to consult with an attorney and to have one present during the interrogation, nor was his right not to be compelled to incriminate himself effectively protected in any other manner. Without these warnings the statements were inadmissible. The mere fact that he signed a statement which contained a typed-in clause stating that he had "full knowledge" of his "legal rights" does not approach the knowing and intelligent waiver required to relinquish constitutional rights. . . . [a]

[CLARK, HARLAN, STEWART and WHITE, JJ., dissented.]

a. [Compiler's note.] Miranda applies to all suspects when they are deprived of their freedom in any way, even if not at the station house. **D** should have been given the warning even though he was in bed in his own home.

After the state had announced its determination to seek the death penalty against S, who had been indicted for murder, the judge or-

Under the facts he was "in custody". Orozco v. Texas, 394 U.S. 342, 89 S.Ct. 1095 (1969).

Reversal of a conviction is not required by the admission of an inadmissible confession which was merely a repetition of earlier confessions made (1) to private persons and (2) to officers in what was a "clearly investigatory stage". People v. Jacobson, 63 Cal.2d 319, 46 Cal.Rptr. 515, 405 P.2d 555 (1965). The sequence of the confessions was emphasized.

The use of a "truth serum" or its equivalent will not result in a voluntary confession. Townsend v. Sain, 372 U.S. 293, 83 S.Ct. 745, 9 L.Ed.2d 770 (1963).

Where a police officer requested defendant to contact him, a meeting was arranged at the police station, and defendant told he was not under arrest the interrogation of the defendant did not require a Miranda warning. Oregon v. Mathiason, 429 U.S. 492, 97 S.Ct. 711 (1977). Accord California v. Beheler, ___ U.S. ___, 103 S.Ct. 3517 (1983).

"As we have noted the statement made by defendant to the reporter was in no way the result of police interrogation but was wholly voluntary, and hence no reason appears for excluding it". People v. Price, 63 Cal.2d 370, 46 Cal.Rptr. 775, 781, 406 P.2d 55, 61 (1965).

"So long as the methods used comply with due process standards it is in the public interest for the police to encourage confessions and admissions during interrogation". People v. Garner, 57 Cal.2d 135, 164, 18 Cal.Rptr. 40, 57, 367 P.2d 680, 697 (1961). Quoted with approval in People v. Dorado, 62 Cal.2d 338, 42 Cal.Rptr. 169, 179, 398 P.2d 361, 371 (1965); People v. Price, 63 Cal.2d 370, 46 Cal.Rptr. 775, 780, 406 P.2d 55, 60 (1965).

The shield provided by *Miranda* cannot be perverted into a license to use perjury by way of defense, free from the risk of confrontation with prior inconsistent utterances. Hence a confession which would be inadmissible in evidence, in making the state's case in chief, may be used for impeachment purposes, if it meets the standards of trustworthiness and if the defendant takes the stand and gives testimony which is inconsistent with his pre-trial confession. The failure to give the warning required by *Miranda* does not preclude the use of the resulting confession for all purposes. Harris v. New York, 401 U.S. 222, 91 S.Ct. 643 (1971).

On his way to the station, Hass, who had been arrested for burglary, said he wanted to telephone a lawyer. The police continued to question him and he made statements that were admitted in evidence to impeach his veracity. He was convicted. This conviction was reversed by the Oregon Court of Appeals on the ground that statements made after he stated he wanted a lawyer were inadmissible. The Supreme Court of Oregon affirmed, but the Supreme Court reversed, following *Harris*. The fact that *Miranda* would not admit such statements in the prosecution's case in chief does not mean that they may not be admitted for impeachment purposes. Oregon v. Hass, 420 U.S. 714, 95 S.Ct. 1215 (1975).

To use a statement obtained from D in violation of the Miranda rule, even for the purpose of impeachment, violates the California constitution, and hence is reversible error in this state. People v. Disbrow, 16 Cal.3d 101, 127 Cal.Rptr. 360, 545 P.2d 272 (1976).

D, arrested in connection with certain robberies, and given the customary Miranda warnings, stated that he did not wish to discuss the robberies. Thereupon the officer ceased the interrogation. Two hours later another officer, after again giving the Miranda warnings, questioned D about an unrelated offense, and D made an inculpatory statement which was used in a trial that resulted in conviction. It was held that the use of this statement did not violate Miranda principles. D's right to cut off questioning was scrupulously honored. This does not mean that questioning could never be resumed under any circumstances. Michigan v. Mosley, 423 U.S. 96, 96 S.Ct. 321 (1975).

Where after Miranda warnings are given a suspect he requests that an attorney be present the suspect is not subject to further interrogation thereafter until counsel has been made available to him, unless the suspect himself initiates further communication. Edwards v. Arizona, 451 U.S. 477, 101 S.Ct. 1880 (1981). See also Fletcher v. Weir, 445 U.S. 603, 102 S.Ct. 1309 (1982), holding that impeachment by post-arrest silence where no Miranda warning was given was proper.

dered a pre-trial examination to determine S's competency to stand trial. The examination was held with no advance notice to S's counsel, and with no warning to S that he had a right to remain silent and that anything he said might be used against him. In the penalty trial (after S had been found guilty) the psychiatrist, basing his testimony on S's statements during that examination, testified that S would be a continuing threat to society, and the result of the penalty trial was that S was sentenced to death. The death sentence was vacated because the use of the doctor's testimony had violated S's Fifth Amendment privilege against self-incrimination, and his Sixth Amendment right to counsel. The Court carefully avoided saying that S had a right to have counsel present during the psychiatric examination, but held he had a right to have the advice of counsel as to whether to submit to the examination, and to what end the psychiatrist's findings could be employed.[1] The conviction stands and the state may conduct another penalty trial without the use of the psychiatrist's testimony.

If an accused, during custodial interrogation, asks for counsel, there can be no further questioning until his counsel is available un-

Where the suspect initiates a conversation after his request for counsel has resulted in termination of interrogation and he thereafter waives his rights under Miranda a resulting statement is admissible. Oregon v. Bradshaw, ___ U.S. ___, 103 S.Ct. 2830 (1983).

D, arrested for murder, was given his Miranda warnings and said he wanted to talk with a lawyer. Officers assigned to drive him to the police station were instructed not to interrogate him. On the way as two officers were conversing with one another, one mentioned that the area where a search for the murder-weapon was being conducted was near a school for handicapped children and said; "God forbid one of them might find a weapon with shells and might hurt themselves." The other agreed that it would be too bad if a little girl "would pick up the gun, maybe kill herself." D interrupted the officers and directed them to where the gun was concealed. It was held that Miranda was not violated since there was nothing to indicate that the officers had any reason to believe their conversation would cause such a response by D. Rhode Island v. Innis, 446 U.S. 291, 100 S.Ct. 1682 (1980).

B was arrested without a warrant and without probable cause. After being warned of his *Miranda* rights he made incriminating statements, which were used in evidence in a trial that resulted in a conviction of murder. This conviction was reversed on the ground that the giving of the *Miranda* warnings was not enough to make admissible the inculpatory statements of one who had been arrested unlawfully. Powell, joined by Rehnquist concurred in the result, but would distinguish between an arrest which was a flagrantly abusive violation of the Fourth Amendment, and one which was only a "technical" violation. Brown v. Illinois, 422 U.S. 590, 95 S.Ct. 2254 (1975). See also Taylor v. Alabama, 457 U.S. 687, 102 S.Ct. 2664 (1982).

D's privilege against self-incrimination was not violated when he was ordered by the court to put on a hat found at the scene of the crime. State v. Williams, 307 Minn. 191, 239 N.W.2d 222 (1976).

Defendants, who were given Miranda warnings at the time of arrest, did not complain to the arresting officers that they had been framed but gave their exculpatory story for the first time on the witness stand. Since the warning at time of arrest included a statement of the right to remain silent, it was held to be reversible error to cross-examine them as to why they did not speak up at that time. Doyle v. Ohio, 426 U.S. 610, 96 S.Ct. 2240 (1976). Pre-arrest silence may be used as evidence. Jenkins v. Anderson, 447 U.S. 231, 100 S.Ct. 2124 (1980).

1. Estelle v. Smith, 451 U.S. 454, 101 S.Ct. 1866 (1981).

less it is initiated by him. The fact that he later consents to answer questions is not enough.[2]

WYRICK v. FIELDS

Supreme Court of the United States, 1982.
___ U.S. ___, 103 S.Ct. 394.

PER CURIAM. In this case, the United States Court of Appeals for the Eighth Circuit, over a dissent by Judge Ross, directed that respondent Edward Fields' petition for a writ of habeas corpus be granted; it did so on the ground that Fields had been convicted with evidence obtained in violation of his Fifth Amendment right to have counsel present at an interrogation. We have concluded that the Court of Appeals' majority misconstrued this Court's recent decision in Edwards v. Arizona, 451 U.S. 477, 101 S.Ct. 1880, 68 L.Ed.2d 378 (1981), and imposed a new and unjustified limit on police questioning of a suspect who voluntarily, knowingly, and intelligently waives his right to have counsel present.

I

Respondent, a soldier then stationed at Fort Leonard Wood, Mo., was charged with raping an 81 year old woman on September 21, 1974. After his arrest on September 25, Fields was released on his own recognizance. He retained private defense counsel. After discussing the matter with his counsel and with a military attorney provided him by the Army, Fields requested a polygraph examination. This request was granted and the examination was conducted on December 4 by an agent of the Army's Criminal Investigation Division (CID) at the Fort.

Prior to undergoing the polygraph examination, Fields was given a written consent document, which he signed, informing him of his rights, as required by Miranda v. Arizona, 384 U.S. 436, 86 S.Ct. 1602, 16 L.Ed.2d 694 (1966), and of his rights under the Uniform Code of Military Justice and the Eighth Amendment. In addition, the CID agent read to Fields the following detailed statement:

> "Before I ask you any questions, you must understand your rights. You do not have to answer my questions or say anything. Anything you say or do can be used against you in a criminal trial. You have a right to talk to a lawyer before questioning or have a lawyer present with you during the questioning. This lawyer can be a civilian lawyer of your own choice, or a military lawyer, detailed for you at no expense to you. Also, you may ask for a military lawyer of your choice by name and he will be detailed for you if superiors determine he's reasonably available. *If you are now going to discuss the offense under investigation, which is rape,*

2. Edwards v. Arizona, 451 U.S. 477, 101 S.Ct. 1880 (1981). See also Oregon v. Bradshaw, ___ U.S. ___, 103 S.Ct. 2830 (1983).

with or without a lawyer present, you have a right to stop answering questions at any time or speak to a lawyer before answering further, even if you sign a waiver certificate. Do you want a lawyer at this time?"

Fields answered: "No."

At the conclusion of the polygraph examination, which took less than two hours, the CID agent told Fields that there had been some deceit, and asked him if he could explain why his answers were bothering him. Fields then admitted having intercourse with the victim on September 21, but said that she had instigated and consented to it. The agent asked Fields if he wished to discuss the matter further with another CID agent and with the Waynesville, Mo., Chief of Police. Fields said that he did. Then, in his turn, the police chief read Fields his *Miranda* warnings once again before questioning him. Fields repeated that he had had sexual contact with the victim, but that it had been consensual.

Respondent was tried before a jury in Circuit Court, Pulaski County, Mo. He sought to suppress the testimony of the two CID agents and the police chief regarding his "confessions" to voluntary intercourse. The trial court denied the motion, ruling that Fields had waived his rights. The testimony was admitted. Fields was convicted, and was sentenced to 25 years in prison. The Missouri Court of Appeals affirmed the judgment on the ground that Fields "had been repeatedly and amply advised of his rights and . . . voluntarily, knowingly and intelligently waived his rights."

Eventually, Fields sought a writ of habeas corpus in the United States District Court for the Eastern District of Missouri. The District Court, agreeing with the Missouri Court of Appeals that Fields had voluntarily, knowingly, and intelligently waived his right to counsel, denied respondent's petition. On appeal, however, the Eighth Circuit reversed and remanded the case with directions to order the State either to release Fields or to afford him a new trial.

II

The Court of Appeals found that the police conduct in question contravened the "clear import" of this Court's decision in Edwards v. Arizona: "a defendant's right to have counsel present at custodial interrogations must be zealously guarded." In *Edwards,* this Court had held that once a suspect invokes his right to counsel, he may not be subjected to further interrogation until counsel is provided unless the suspect himself initiates dialogue with the authorities. The Eighth Circuit recognized that what it called the "per se rule" of *Edwards* "does not resolve the issue present here." Fields and his counsel had agreed that Fields should take the polygraph examination, and Fields appeared voluntarily and stated that he did not want counsel present during the interrogation. Thus, the Court of Appeals conceded that "Fields thereby 'initiated' further dialogue with the authorities after his right to counsel had been invoked."

When the suspect has initiated the dialogue, *Edwards* makes clear that the right to have a lawyer present can be waived:

> "If, as frequently would occur in the course of a meeting initiated by the accused, the conversation is not wholly one-sided, it is likely that the officers will say or do something that clearly would be 'interrogation.' In that event, the question would be whether a valid waiver of the right to counsel and the right to silence had occurred, that is, whether the purported waiver was knowing and intelligent and found to be so under the totality of the circumstances, including the necessary fact that the accused, not the police, reopened the dialogue with the authorities."

Citing this language, the Eighth Circuit acknowledged—as it had to—that "[t]here is no question that Fields waived his right to have counsel present while the [polygraph] examination itself was being conducted." Yet that court found that the State had failed to satisfy its burden of proving that "Fields knowingly and intelligently waived his right to have counsel present at the post-test interrogation." The court suggested that had the CID agent merely "paus[ed] to remind the defendant" of his rights, thus providing "*meaningfully timed Miranda* warnings" (emphasis in original), there would have been no violation.

III

In reaching this result, the Court of Appeals did not examine the "totality of the circumstances," as *Edwards* requires. Fields did not merely initiate a "meeting." By requesting a polygraph examination, he initiated interrogation. That is, Fields waived not only his right to be free of contact with the authorities in the absence of an attorney, but also his right to be free of interrogation about the crime of which he was suspected. Fields validly waived his right to have counsel present at "post-test" questioning, unless the circumstances changed so seriously that his answers no longer were voluntary, or unless he no longer was making a "knowing and intelligent relinquishment or abandonment" of his rights.

The Court of Appeals relied on two facts indicating the need for a new set of warnings: the polygraph examination had been discontinued, and Fields was asked if he could explain the test's unfavorable results. To require new warnings because of these two facts is unreasonable. Disconnecting the polygraph equipment effectuated no significant change in the character of the interrogation. The CID agent could have informed Fields during the examination that his answers indicated deceit; asking Fields, after the equipment was disconnected, why the answers were bothering him was not any more coercive. The Court of Appeals stated that there was no indication that Fields or his lawyer anticipated that Fields would be asked questions after the examination. But it would have been unreasonable for Fields and his attorneys to assume that Fields would not be informed of the polygraph readings and asked to explain any unfavorable result. Moreover, Fields had been informed that he could stop the questioning at any time, and could request at any time that his lawyer join him. Merely disconnecting the polygraph equipment could not remove this knowledge from Fields' mind.*

The only plausible explanation for the court's holding is that, encouraged by what it regarded as a *per se* rule established in *Edwards,* it fashioned another rule of its own: that, notwithstanding a voluntary, knowing, and intelligent waiver of the right to have counsel present at a polygraph examination, and notwithstanding clear evidence that the suspect understood that right and was aware of his power to stop questioning at any time or to speak to an attorney at any time, the police again must advise the suspect of his rights before questioning him at the same interrogation about the results of the polygraph. The court indicated that this rule was needed because it thought that the use of polygraph "results" in questioning, although it does not necessarily render a response involuntary, is inherently coercive. But Courts of Appeals, including a different panel of the Eighth Circuit itself, and state courts, have rejected such a rule. The Eighth Circuit's rule certainly finds no support in *Edwards,* which emphasizes that the totality of the circumstances, including the fact that the suspect initiated the questioning, is controlling. Nor is the rule logical; the questions put to Fields after the examination would not have caused him to forget the rights of which he had been advised and which he had understood moments before. The rule is simply an unjustifiable restriction on reasonable police questioning. . . .

Because the Court of Appeals misapplied *Edwards* and created an unjustified *per se* rule, the petition for a writ of certiorari is granted and that court's judgment is reversed and the case is remanded.

It is so ordered.[a]

* The dissent suggests that, because the results of polygraph examinations are inadmissible in Missouri, Fields might reasonably have expected that he would not be subjected "to additional questioning that can produce admissible evidence." Although the results of the polygraph examination might not have been admissible evidence, the statements Fields made in response to questioning during the course of the polygraph examination surely would have been.

a. The Miranda warning need not follow any precise formulation as long as the elements of the warning are covered. California v. Prysock, 453 U.S. 355, 101 S.Ct. 2806 (1981).

Request by a juvenile suspect to talk to his probation officer is not to be treated the same as a request to consult with an attorney. Fare v. Michael C., 442 U.S. 707, 99 S.Ct. 2560 (1979).

The waiver of Miranda rights cannot be found from a suspect's silence. Tague v. Louisiana, 444 U.S. 469, 100 S.Ct. 652 (1980). However, an express oral or written waiver is not necessary if the circumstances establish a waiver. North Carolina v. Butler, 441 U.S. 369, 99 S.Ct. 1755 (1979).

JUSTICE MARSHALL, dissenting.

A summary reversal is an exceptional disposition. It should be reserved for situations in which the applicable law is settled and stable, the facts are not disputed, and the decision below is clearly in error. Because I do not believe that this is such a case, I dissent. . . .

UNITED STATES v. HENRY

Supreme Court of the United States, 1980.
447 U.S. 264, 100 S.Ct. 2183.

MR. CHIEF JUSTICE BURGER delivered the opinion of the Court.

We granted certiorari to consider whether rspondent's Sixth Amendment right to the assistance of counsel was violated by the admission at trial of incriminating statements made by respondent to his cellmate, an undisclosed Government informant, after indictment and while in custody.

I

The Janaf Branch of the United Virginia Bank/Seaboard National in Norfolk, Va., was robbed in August, 1972. . . . Henry was arrested in Atlanta, Ga., in November 1972. [Henry] was indicted for armed robbery under 18 U.S.C. §§ 2113(a) and (d). He was held pending trial in the Norfolk city jail. Counsel was appointed on November 27.

On November 21, 1972, shortly after Henry was incarcerated, Government agents working on the Janaf robbery contacted one Nichols, an inmate at the Norfolk city jail, who for some time prior to this meeting had been engaged to provide confidential information to the Federal Bureau of Investigation as a paid informant. Nichols was then serving a sentence on local forgery charges. The record does not disclose whether the agent contacted Nichols specifically to acquire information about Henry or the Janaf robbery.

Nichols informed the agent that he was housed in the same cellblock with several federal prisoners awaiting trial, including Henry. The agent told him to be alert to any statements made by the federal prisoners, but not to initiate any conversation with or question Henry regarding the bank robbery. In early December, after Nichols had been released from jail, the agent again contacted Nichols, who reported that he and Henry had engaged in conversation and that Henry had told him about the robbery of the Janaf bank. Nichols was paid for furnishing the information. . . .

Nichols testified at trial that he had "an opportunity to have some conversations with Mr. Henry while he was in the jail," and that Henry told him that on several occasions he had gone to the Janaf Branch to see which employees opened the vault. Nichols also testified that

Henry described to him the details of the robbery and stated that the only evidence connecting him to the robbery was the rental receipt. The jury was not informed that Nichols was a paid Government informant.

On the basis of this testimony, Henry was convicted of bank robbery and sentenced to a term of imprisonment of 25 years. . . .

On August 28, 1975, Henry moved to vacate his sentence pursuant to 28 U.S.C. § 2255. At this stage, he stated that he had just learned that Nichols was a paid Government informant and alleged that he had been intentionally placed in the same cell with Nichols so that Nichols could secure information about the robbery. Thus, Henry contended that the introduction of Nichols' testimony violated his Sixth Amendment right to the assistance of counsel. . . .

II

This Court has scrutinized postindictment confrontations between Government agents and the accused to determine whether they are "critical stages" of the prosecution at which the Sixth Amendment right to the assistance of counsel attaches. See, e.g., United States v. Ash, 413 U.S. 300, 93 S.Ct. 2568, 37 L.Ed.2d 619 (1973); United States v. Wade, 388 U.S. 218, 87 S.Ct. 1926, 18 L.Ed.2d 1149 (1967). The present case involves incriminating statements made by the accused to an undisclosed and undercover Government informant while in custody and after indictment. The Government characterizes Henry's incriminating statements as voluntary and not the result of any affirmative conduct on the part of Government agents to elicit evidence. From this, the Government argues that Henry's rights were not violated, even assuming the Sixth Amendment applies to such surreptitious confrontations; in short, it is contended that the Government has not interfered with Henry's right to counsel.

This Court first applied the Sixth Amendment to postindictment communications between the accused and agents of the Government in Massiah v. United States, [377 U.S. 201]. There, after the accused had been charged, he made incriminating statements to his codefendant, who was acting as an agent of the Government. In reversing the conviction, the Court held that the accused was denied "the basic protections of [the Sixth Amendment] when there was used against him at his trial evidence of his own incriminating words, which federal agents had deliberately elicited from him." Id., at 206, 84 S.Ct., at 1203. The *Massiah* holding rests squarely on interference with his right to counsel.

The question here is whether under the facts of this case, a Government agent "deliberately elicited" incriminating statements from Henry within the meaning of *Massiah*. Three factors are important. First, Nichols was acting under instructions as a paid informant for the Government; second, Nichols was ostensibly no more than a fellow inmate of Henry; and third, Henry was in custody and under indictment at the time he was engaged in conversation by Nichols.

. . . This combination of circumstances is sufficient to support the Court of Appeals' determination. Even if the agent's statement that he did not intend that Nichols would take affirmative steps to secure incriminating information is accepted, he must have known that such propinquity likely would lead to that result.

The Government argues that the federal agents instructed Nichols not to question Henry about the robbery.[8] Yet according to his own testimony, Nichols was not a passive listener; rather, he had "some conversations with Mr. Henry" while he was in jail and Henry's incriminatory statements were "the product of this conversation." While affirmative interrogation, absent waiver, would certainly satisfy *Massiah,* we are not persuaded, as the Government contends, that Brewer v. Williams, 430 U.S. 387, 97 S.Ct. 1232, 51 L.Ed.2d 424 (1977), modified *Massiah's* "deliberately elicited" test. In *Massiah,* no inquiry was made as to whether Massiah or his codefendant first raised the subject of the crime under investigation. . . .

It is undisputed that Henry was unaware of Nichols' role as a Government informant. The Government argues that this Court should apply a less rigorous standard under the Sixth Amendment where the accused is prompted by an undisclosed undercover informant than where the accused is speaking in the hearing of persons he knows to be Government officers. That line of argument, however, seeks to infuse Fifth Amendment concerns against compelled self-incrimination into the Sixth Amendment protection of the right to the assistance of counsel. An accused speaking to a known Government agent is typically aware that his statements may be used against him. The adversary positions at that stage are well established; the parties are then "arm's-length" adversaries.

When the accused is in the company of a fellow inmate who is acting by prearrangement as a Government agent, the same cannot be said. Conversation stimulated in such circumstances may elicit information that an accused would not intentionally reveal to persons known to be Government agents. Indeed, the *Massiah* Court noted that if the Sixth Amendment "is to have any efficacy it must apply to indirect and surreptitious interrogations as well as those conducted in the jailhouse." The Court pointedly observed that Massiah was more

8. Two aspects of the agent's affidavit are particularly significant. First, it is clear that the agent in his discussions with Nichols singled out Henry as the inmate in whom the agent had a special interest. Thus, the affidavit relates that "I specifically recall telling Nichols that he was not to question *Henry* or these individuals" and "I recall telling Nichols not to initiate any conversations *with Henry* regarding the bank robbery charges," but to "pay attention to the information furnished *by Henry.*" (Emphasis added.) Second, the agent only instructed Nichols not to question Henry or to initiate conversations regarding the bank robbery charges. Under these instructions, Nichols remained free to discharge his task of eliciting the statements in myriad less direct ways.

seriously imposed upon because he did not know that his codefendant was a Government agent.

Moreover, the concept of a knowing and voluntary waiver of Sixth Amendment rights does not apply in the context of communications with an undisclosed undercover informant acting for the Government. In that setting, Henry, being unaware that Nichols was a Government agent expressly commissioned to secure evidence, cannot be held to have waived his right to the assistance of counsel.

Finally, Henry's incarceration at the time he was engaged in conversation by Nichols is also a relevant factor.[11] As a ground for imposing the prophylactic requirements in Miranda v. Arizona, 384 U.S. 436, 467, 86 S.Ct. 1602, 1624, 16 L.Ed.2d 694 (1966), this Court noted the powerful psychological inducements to reach for aid when a person is in confinement. While the concern in *Miranda* was limited to custodial police interrogation, the mere fact of custody imposes pressures on the accused; confinement may bring into play subtle influences that will make him particularly susceptible to the ploys of undercover Government agents. The Court of Appeals determined that on this record the incriminating conversations between Henry and Nichols were facilitated by Nichols' conduct and apparent status as a person sharing a common plight. That Nichols had managed to gain the confidence of Henry, as the Court of Appeals determined, is confirmed by Henry's request that Nichols assist him in his escape plans when Nichols was released from confinement.

Under the strictures of the Court's holdings on the exclusion of evidence, we conclude that the Court of Appeals did not err in holding that Henry's statements to Nichols should not have been admitted at trial. By intentionally creating a situation likely to induce Henry to make incriminating statements without the assistance of counsel, the Government violated Henry's Sixth Amendment right to counsel. This is not a case where, in Justice Cardozo's words, "the constable . . . blundered,"; rather, it is one where the "constable" planned an impermissible interference with the right to the assistance of counsel.

The judgment of the Court of Appeals for the Fourth Circuit is Affirmed.

PEOPLE v. PACK

District Court of Appeals, Second District, Division 2, California, 1962.
199 Cal.App.2d 857, 19 Cal.Rptr. 186.

[A collision between two cars travelling in opposite directions resulted in the hospitalization of all the occupants. When officers ar-

11. This is not to read a "custody" requirement, which is a prerequisite to the attachment of *Miranda* rights, into this branch of the Sixth Amendment. Massiah was in no sense in custody at the time of his conversation with his codefendant. Rather, we believe the fact of custody bears on whether the Government "deliberately elicited" the incriminating statements from Henry.

rived the injured persons had been removed and no witnesses to the accident were found. From the position of the cars, which had not been moved, and from other evidence the officers concluded that one car, a Lincoln, had been travelling on the wrong side of the highway. On the floor of the Lincoln was found a "partially filled quart bottle of beer". One of the officers went to the hospital where he found defendant unconscious. At his request a blood sample was taken and tested and the result indicated that defendant had been intoxicated while driving. Based largely upon this evidence (People's Exhibit 5), admitted over timely objection, defendant was convicted of "felony drunk driving"—causing bodily injury as a result of driving while under the influence of liquor.]

FOX, PRESIDING JUSTICE. . . . The second aspect of defendant's contention is that People's Exhibit 5 was obtained and admitted in violation of his constitutional rights. Pertinent to defendant's position is the statement of the court in People v. Duroncelay, 48 Cal.2d 766, 770–771, 312 P.2d 690, 693: "It is settled by our decision in People v. Haeussler, 41 Cal.2d 252, 257, 260 P.2d 8, that the admission of the evidence did not violate defendant's privilege against self-incrimination because the privilege relates only to testimonial compulsion and not to real evidence.[1] We also held in the Haeussler case that the taking of the defendant's blood for an alcohol test in a medically approved manner did not constitute brutality or shock the conscience and that, therefore, the defendant had not been denied due process of law under the rule applied in Rochin v. People of California, 342 U.S. 165, 72 S.Ct. 205, 96 L.Ed. 183 [25 A.L.R.2d 1396]. This holding is in accord with the recent decision of the United States Supreme Court in Breithaupt v. Abram, 352 U.S. 432, 77 S.Ct. 408, 411, 1 L.Ed.2d 448, where blood for an alcohol test was taken by a doctor while the defendant was unconscious. The court pointed out that blood tests had become routine in everyday life and concluded that 'a blood test taken by a skilled technician is not such "conduct that shocks the con-

1. Accord: State v. Ayres, 70 Idaho 18, 211 P.2d 142 (1949); State v. Sturtevant, 96 N.H. 99, 70 A.2d 909 (1950); State v. Cash, 219 N.C. 818, 15 S.E.2d 277 (1941); State v. Kroening, 274 Wis. 266, 79 N.W.2d 810 (1957); S. Wigmore, Evidence, sec. 2263 (3d ed. 1940). The privilege against self-incrimination is not violated by requiring D to uncover his face so that a witness can identify him. People v. Clark, 18 Cal.2d 449, 116 P.2d 56 (1941). Or by the compulsory taking of his fingerprints. United States v. Kelly, 55 F.2d 67, 83 A.L.R. 122 (2d Cir. 1932); Shannon v. State, 207 Ark. 658, 182 S.W.2d 384 (1944); McGovern v. Van Ripper, 137 N.J.Eq. 548, 45 A.2d 842 (1946); McGarry v. State, 82 Tex.Cr.R. 597, 200 S.W. 527 (1918).

The Oklahoma Bill of Rights provides that "No person shall be compelled to give evidence which will tend to incriminate him. . . . " It was held that evidence of blood tests taken involuntarily violates this provision. Cox v. State, 395 P.2d 954 (Okl.Cr.1964); Lorenz v. State, 406 P.2d 278 (Okl.Cr.1965).

One who has been arrested on a charge of intoxication has a right to have an opportunity to call his physician for the purpose of a blood-alcohol test and a denial of this right is a denial of due process which will prevent a conviction of the offense charged. In re Newbern, 175 Cal.App.2d 862, 1 Cal.Rptr. 80, 79 A.L.R.2d 901 (1959). Cited with approval, In re Newbern, 55 Cal.2d 500, 506, 11 Cal.Rptr. 547, 550, 360 P.2d 43, 46 (1961).

science," [2] Rochin, supra, 342 U.S. at page 172, 72 S.Ct. at page 209, nor such a method of obtaining evidence that it offends a "sense of justice," Brown v. State of Mississippi, 297 U.S. 278, 285, 286 [56 S.Ct. 461, 464–465, 80 L.Ed. 682].' There is no claim in the present case that the blood sample was not withdrawn in a medically approved manner. The blood was extracted by a registered nurse, and her testimony shows that she sterilized defendant's arm and used sterilized instruments.

"The question remains as to whether the taking of defendant's blood constituted an unreasonable search and seizure in violation of his constitutional rights." The court went on to answer this question in the negative. At page 772, 312 P.2d at page 694 it was stated: "The incidence of death and serious injury on the highways has undeniably assumed tragic dimensions and has been due in a significant degree to the effects of alcohol upon drivers. See National Safety Council Accident Facts—1955, pp. 43–71. So long as the measures adopted do not amount to a substantial invasion of individual rights, society must not be prevented from seeking to combat this hazard to the safety of the public. The extraction of blood for testing purposes is, of course, an experience which, every day, many undergo without hardship or ill effects. When this fact, together with the scientific reliability of blood alcohol tests in establishing guilt or innocence, is considered in the light of the imperative public interest involved, the taking of a sample for such a test without consent cannot be regarded as an unreasonable search and seizure where, as here, the extrac-

2. In *Rochin* officers choked D in the effort to prevent him from swallowing the evidence, and after this failed they extracted it by means of a stomach-pump applied apparently with brutality.

In another case, which may be useful by way of analogy, it was held that a search of the person, following a lawful arrest by federal officers, and a seizure of narcotics concealed in arrestee's rectum, the examination having been conducted by physicians under sanitary conditions with the use of medically approved procedures, was not unreasonable. Blackford v. United States, 247 F.2d 745 (9th Cir.1957), certiorari denied 356 U.S. 914, 78 S.Ct. 672, 2 L.Ed.2d 586 (1958). See note, 106 U. of Pa.L.R. 1165 (1958).

In a lighter vein it may be mentioned that Melvin Belli (Bell eye) commented facetiously that the lawfulness of extracting evidence from the alimentary canal depends upon which end is approached.

Confronted with the question that it had left open in *Schmerber*, the Court held that the admission into evidence of a defendant's refusal to submit to a blood alcohol test does not offend the right against self-incrimination. South Dakota v. Neville, ___ U.S. ___, 103 S.Ct. 916 (1983). The Court added that it would not be a violation of due process to use defendant's refusal to take the test as evidence of guilt, even if the police had not warned him that his refusal could be used against him at the trial. See also People v. Sudduth, 65 Cal.2d 543, 55 Cal. Rptr. 393, 421 P.2d 401 (1966).

"We . . . here reject the contention of petitioner Willie Andrews that his rights under U.S.Const. Amend. V and Maryland Declaration of Rights, Art. 22 were infringed when a trial judge ordered him 'to refrain from shaving his head and facial hair' " until after the trial. Andrews v. State, 291 Md. 622, 436 A.2d 1315 (1981). The evidence indicated that, immediately after the crime, he had changed his appearance in order to make identification difficult. And the purpose of the order was so that his appearance at the trial would be more nearly as it was at the time of the crime.

tion is made in a medically approved manner and is incident to the lawful arrest of one who is reasonably believed to have violated section 501 [now 23101] of the Vehicle Code."

Defendant attempts to distinguish this case by reference to the fact that the blood was taken "incident to a lawful arrest" (although the arrest followed the taking of the sample), while here there was no arrest at all. The distinction is not sound. Our courts have repeatedly stated that: "A search or seizure may be justified even though it is in no way related to an arrest." "The real criterion as to the reasonableness of a search is whether or not . . . under the facts, the police officer has reasonable grounds to believe that defendant may have committed a felony."[3]

Here Officers Carlson and Ellis arrived at the scene of a collision between a Lincoln and an Oldsmobile on the evening of August 1, 1960. The Lincoln was on the wrong side of the highway; there were no skid marks. The officers found a partially filled quart bottle of beer on the front floor of the Lincoln. They checked with the Ventura police and learned that persons had been injured in the accident and taken to the Woodland Park Community Hospital. Investigation revealed that the Lincoln was registered in the name of defendant. Officer Ellis had previous experience in investigating automobile accidents. The position of the two cars indicated that the Lincoln was traveling east and the Oldsmobile in a westerly direction. He found marks on the highway and debris indicating the point of impact of the two cars. From this factual picture the officers had reasonable grounds to believe that the driver of the Lincoln went to the wrong side of the highway thereby causing the collision, and that the driver was under the influence of alcohol at the time. Therefore there was probable cause to believe that a felony had been committed. Hence the obtaining of a blood sample from defendant was not an unlawful search. Therefore the sample (Exhibit 5) together with its analysis was properly admitted in evidence.

It was important to get the sample as soon as possible in order that the analysis might the more accurately reflect the alcoholic content since such content became lower with the passage of time. It should also be pointed out that such tests are generally regarded as highly reliable and of substantial assistance in determining the issue

3. In the early morning hours officers came upon the scene of a traffic accident. The position of the vehicles made it clear that H's car had been travelling on the wrong side of the street. As there was a strong odor of liquor on H's breath and the driver of the other car had been injured this gave the officers strong reason to believe that H was guilty of felony drunk driving. Although H was unconscious a sample of his blood was taken under medically accepted conditions, and a test of this blood showed that he had in fact been intoxicated. The court recognized that the value of a blood test for alcohol depends upon the promptness with which the sample is taken. Hence it was held that there was such an emergency here that the search and seizure were lawful although there was no warrant, consent or arrest. People v. Huber, 232 Cal.App.2d 663, 43 Cal.Rptr. 65 (1965).

of intoxication, and that a test of this kind may serve to exonerate as well as to convict.

Affirmed.[4]

4. "It appears to be the consensus of the medical profession that when the blood alcohol concentrate of the driver of an automobile is 0.15% (by weight) such fact is conclusive evidence that the driver is under the influence of alcohol. (Committee on Tests for Intoxication of the National Safety Council, Chemical Tests for Intoxication (1938) p. 5; . . .)" Footnote in Lawrence v. City of Los Angeles, 53 Cal.App.2d 6, 9, 127 P.2d 931, 932 (1942).

Some persons have more tolerance for alcohol than is possessed by others. An amount which might impair the driving ability of one might not affect such ability of another. The interpretation of chemical tests for blood alcohol, based upon exhaustive study and research, makes due allowance for this difference. The analysis itself determines the per cent of alcohol in the blood by weight. If this percentage does not exceed 0.05 the presumption is that the person was not under the influence of intoxicating liquor. If the percentage amounts to 0.15, 0.10 or 0.08, depending on the jurisdiction the presumption is that he was under the influence. Between these limits the amount of alcohol in the blood gives rise to no presumption either way but is merely a fact to be considered with other available evidence. This is the recommendation of various national organizations interested in traffic safety. It has been adopted by statute in several states and is the guide to the expert's opinion even where not so adopted.

In some states an offense has been defined as driving a motor vehicle with a specified blood alcohol level. No proof of actual impairment need be shown. Greaves v. State, 528 P.2d 805 (Utah 1974). See West's Cal.Veh.Code §§ 23152–23153 (1982).

See Note, Under the Influence of California's New Drunk Driving Law: Is the Drunk Driver's Presumption of Innocence on the Rocks? 10 Pepperdine L.Rev. 91 (1982).

The validity of chemical tests to determine impairment of the faculties is now widely accepted, but there are many hurdles to be cleared in a particular case. In the first place the expert must be prepared to prove that the sample to be tested was properly taken,—and particularly that the technique used precluded the possibility of the addition of any alcohol to the sample. The skin of the area from which a blood sample is to be taken should not be sterilized with an alcohol-containing antiseptic. And no such antiseptic should be used on instruments or containers. Next the expert must be prepared to establish the "chain of possession" of the sample used. He must be able to prove that the test was made of the sample taken from the defendant on trial with no possibility of substitution or tampering. And needless to say he must be prepared to establish his qualifications as an expert in this field and fully to explain the test made and its interpretation.

For a thorough examination of these problems see Donigan, Chemical Test Case Law (1950); Ladd and Gibson, The Medico-Legal Aspects of the Blood Test to Determine Intoxication, 24 Iowa Law Review 191 (1939); Monroe, The Drinking Driver—Problems of Enforcement, 8 Quarterly Journal of Studies on Alcohol 385 (1947); Inbau & Moenssens, Scientific Evidence in Criminal Cases, 2d ed. pp. 71–95 (1978).

D, who drove on a federal parkway within Virginia while allegedly intoxicated, was prosecuted in the federal district court under the Virginia drunken driving statute made applicable by the Assimilative Crimes Act. It was held that the admission of a certificate showing that the alcoholic content of a sample of his blood had been determined by chemical analysis to be 0.15 per cent did not deprive him of his right of confrontation by witnesses, and that he was not deprived of any constitutional right by the jury's consideration of the statutory presumptions from such an alcoholic content. Kay v. United States, 255 F.2d 476 (4th Cir. 1958).

In reversing a conviction in which "voiceprint" evidence had played a major role, the court said: "Although the present record is insufficient to justify the admissibility of voiceprint evidence, the future proponent of such evidence may well be able to demonstrate in a satisfactory manner that the voiceprint technique has achieved that required general acceptance in the scientific community." People v. Kelly, 17 Cal.3d 24, 41, 130 Cal. Rptr. 144, 155, 549 P.2d 1240, 1251 (1976).

ASHBURN and HERNDON, JJ., concur.

Hearing denied; SCHAUER and PETERS, JJ., dissenting.

POINTER v. TEXAS

Supreme Court of the United States, 1965.
380 U.S. 400, 85 S.Ct. 1065.

[Pointer and Dillard were arrested in Texas on a charge of robbery and taken before a state judge for a preliminary hearing. Phillips, the chief witness, gave his version of the alleged robbery in detail, identifying Pointer as the man who had robbed him at gunpoint. The accused were both laymen and neither had a lawyer. Pointer did not attempt to cross-examine Phillips. Prior to the trial Phillips had moved to California and at the trial the state offered the transcript of Phillips' testimony given at the preliminary hearing as evidence. At the trial Pointer had counsel who objected that the use of this evidence would be "a denial of the confrontment of the witnesses against the Defendant". The objection was overruled and the trial resulted in a conviction which was affirmed by the highest state court to which the case could be taken. The Supreme Court granted certiorari.]

MR. JUSTICE BLACK delivered the opinion of the Court.

The Sixth Amendment provides in part that:

"In all criminal prosecutions, the accused shall enjoy the right . . . to be confronted with the witnesses against him . . . and to have the Assistance of Counsel for his defence."

Two years ago in Gideon v. Wainwright, 372 U.S. 335, 83 S.Ct. 792, 9 L.Ed.2d 799, we held that the Fourteenth Amendment makes the Sixth Amendment's guarantee of right to counsel obligatory upon the States. The question we find necessary to decide in this case is whether the Amendment's guarantee of a defendant's right "to be confronted with the witnesses against him," which has been held to include the right to cross-examine those witnesses, is also made applicable to the States by the Fourteenth Amendment. . . .

In this Court we do not find it necessary to decide one aspect of the question petitioner raises, that is, whether failure to appoint counsel to represent him at the preliminary hearing unconstitutionally denied him the assistance of counsel within the meaning of Gideon v. Wainwright, supra. In making that argument petitioner relies mainly on White v. State of Maryland, 373 U.S. 59, 83 S.Ct. 1050, 10 L.Ed.2d 193, in which this Court reversed a conviction based in part upon evidence that the defendant had pleaded guilty to the crime at a preliminary hearing where he was without counsel. Since the preliminary hearing there as in Hamilton v. State of Alabama, 368 U.S. 52, 82 S.Ct. 157, 7 L.Ed.2d 114, was one in which pleas to the charge could be made, we held in White as in Hamilton that a preliminary proceeding of that nature was so critical a stage in the prosecution that a defendant at that point was entitled to counsel. But the State informs us that at a Texas preliminary hearing such as is involved here, pleas of guilty or not guilty are not accepted and that the judge decides only whether the accused should be bound over to the grand jury and if so whether he should be admitted to bail. Because of these significant differences in the procedures of the respective States, we cannot say that the White case is necessarily controlling as to the right to counsel. Whether there might be other circumstances making this Texas preliminary hearing so critical to the defendant as to call for appointment of counsel at that stage we need not decide on this record and that question we reserve. In this case the objections and arguments in the trial court as well as the arguments in the Court of Criminal Appeals and before us make it clear that petitioner's objection is based not so much on the fact that he had no lawyer when Phillips made his statement at the preliminary hearing, as on the fact that use of the transcript of that statement at the trial denied petitioner any opportunity to have the benefit of counsel's cross-examination of the principal witness against him. It is that latter question which we decide here.

The Sixth Amendment is a part of what is called our Bill of Rights. In Gideon v. Wainwright, supra, in which this Court held that the Sixth Amendment's right to the assistance of counsel is obligatory upon the States, we did so on the ground that "a provision of the Bill of Rights which is 'fundamental and essential to a fair trial' is made obligatory upon the States by the Fourteenth Amendment." 372 U.S., at 342, 83 S.Ct., at 795. And last Term in Malloy v. Hogan, 378 U.S. 1, 84 S.Ct. 1489, 12 L.Ed.2d 653, in holding that the Fifth Amendment's guarantee against self-incrimination was made applicable to the States by the Fourteenth, we reiterated the holding of Gideon that the Sixth Amendment's right-to-counsel guarantee is " 'a fundamental right, essential to a fair trial,' " and "thus was made obligatory on the States by the Fourteenth Amendment." We hold today that the Sixth Amendment's right of an accused to confront the witnesses against him is likewise a fundamental right and is made obligatory on the States by the Fourteenth Amendment. . . .

There are few subjects, perhaps, upon which this Court and other courts have been more nearly unanimous than in their expressions of belief that the right of confrontation and cross-examination is an essential and fundamental requirement for the kind of fair trial which is this country's constitutional goal. Indeed, we have expressly declared that to deprive an accused of the right to cross-examine the witnesses against him is a denial of the Fourteenth Amendment's guarantee of due process of law. . . .

Under this Court's prior decisions, the Sixth Amendment's guarantee of confrontation and cross-examination was unquestionably denied petitioner in this case. As has been pointed out, a major reason underlying the constitutional confrontation rule is to give a defendant charged with crime an opportunity to cross-examine the witnesses against him. This Court has recognized the admissibility against an accused of dying declarations, and of testimony of a deceased witness who has testified at a former trial. Nothing we hold here is to the contrary. The case before us would be quite a different one had Phillips' statement been taken at a full-fledged hearing at which petitioner had been represented by counsel who had been given a complete and adequate opportunity to cross-examine. Compare Motes v. United States, supra, 178 U.S., at 474, 20 S.Ct., at 999. There are other analogous situations which might not fall within the scope of the constitutional rule requiring confrontation of witnesses. The case before us, however, does not present any situation like those mentioned above or others analogous to them. Because the transcript of Phillips' statement offered against petitioner at his trial had not been taken at a time and under circumstances affording petitioner through counsel an adequate opportunity to cross-examine Phillips, its introduction in a federal court in a criminal case against Pointer would have amounted to denial of the privilege of confrontation guaranteed by the Sixth Amendment. Since we hold that the right of an accused to be confronted with the witnesses against him must be determined by the same standards whether the right is denied in a federal or state proceeding, it follows that use of the transcript to convict petitioner denied him a constitutional right, and that his conviction must be reversed.[1]

Reversed and remanded.

MR. JUSTICE HARLAN, concurring in the result. . . .

For me this state judgment must be reversed because a right of confrontation is "implicit in the concept of ordered liberty," reflected in the Due Process Clause of the Fourteenth Amendment independently of the Sixth. . . .

It is too often forgotten in these times that the American federal system is itself constitutionally ordained, that it embodies values profoundly making for lasting liberties in this country, and that its legitimate requirements demand continuing solid recognition in all phases of the work of this Court. The "incorporation" doctrines, whether full blown or selective, are both historically and constitutionally un-

1. Where the chief evidence against D at a trial in Oklahoma was the reading of a transcript of the evidence of a witness who at the time of trial was a federal prisoner in Texas, the witness not being present at the trial but Oklahoma having made no effort to secure his presence, D was deprived of his Sixth and Fourteenth Amendments' right to be confronted with the witness against him. Barber v. Page, 390 U.S. 719, 88 S.Ct. 1318 (1968).

Testimony of a witness unavailable at trial given at a prior preliminary hearing on direct examination by defense counsel was admissible at the defendant's trial when offered by the prosecution. Defense counsel had a fair opportunity to and did develop the absent witnesses testimony at preliminary hearing. Such practice does not violate the right to confrontation. Ohio v. Roberts, 448 U.S. 56, 100 S.Ct. 2531 (1980).

sound and incompatible with the maintenance of our federal system on even course.

MR. JUSTICE STEWART, concurring.

I join in the judgment reversing this conviction, for the reason that the petitioner was denied the opportunity to cross-examine, through counsel, the chief witness for the prosecution. But I do not join in the Court's pronouncement which makes "the Sixth Amendment's right of an accused to confront the witnesses against him . . . obligatory on the States." That questionable *tour de force* seems to me entirely unnecessary to the decision of this case, which I think is directly controlled by the Fourteenth Amendment's guarantee that no State "shall . . . deprive any person of life, liberty, or property, without due process of law." . . .

MR. JUSTICE GOLDBERG, concurring.

I agree with the holding of the Court that "the Sixth Amendment's right of an accused to confront the witnesses against him is . . . a fundamental right and is made obligatory on the States by the Fourteenth Amendment." . . .

INDEX

References are to Pages

†